VILLAGE
LONDON

Titles available from The Village Press are:-

The London Library:

Hardback
Village London Volume I
Village London Volume II
London Recollected Volume I
London Recollected Volume II
London Recollected Volume III
London Recollected Volume IV
London Recollected Volume V
London Recollected Volume VI
Village London Atlas
Besant's History of London - The Tudors
Besant's History of London - The Stuarts

Paperback
Village London Pt. 1 West and North
Village London Pt. 2 North and East
Village London Pt. 3 South-East
Village London Pt. 4 South-West
Village London Atlas
Old Fleet Street
Cheapside and St. Paul's
The Tower and East End
Shoreditch to Smithfield
Charterhouse to Holborn
Strand to Soho
Covent Garden and the Thames to Whitehall
Westminster to St, James's
Haymarket to Mayfair
Hyde Park to Bloomsbury
Belgravia, Chelsea and Kensington
Paddington Green to Seven Sisters
Highgate & Hampstead to the Lea
(The above thirteen titles are extracts from the hardback edition of London Recollected.)

Other titles published are:

The Village Atlas - Birmingham and The West Midlands
The Village Atlas - Manchester, Lancashire & North Cheshire

VILLAGE LONDON

THE STORY OF GREATER LONDON

by

EDWARD WALFORD, M.A.

VOLUME I

THE ALDERMAN PRESS

First published 1883/4 by Cassell & Co. Ltd.,
under the title *Greater London.*

British Library Cataloguing in Publication Data.
Walford, Edward
      Village London: the story of Greater London.
      Vol. 1.
      1. London — History
      1. Title
      942.1   DA677
      ISBN 0-946619-05-0

Published by The Village Press Ltd
7d, Keats Parade, Church Street, Edmonton, N9 9DP

Published November 1983
First reprint January 1984
Second reprint August 1984
Third reprint March 1990

Printed and Bound in Great Britain by
Bookcraft (Bath) Ltd.
Midsomer Norton, Avon.

CONTENTS.

— ❖ —

INTRODUCTORY.

CHAPTER I.

CHISWICK, TURNHAM GREEN, ACTON, STRAND-ON-THE-GREEN.

PAGE

Gradual Extension of London—Horticultural Fêtes at Chiswick—Eminent Residents at Chiswick—Royal Visits—Corney House—Fairfax House—Grove Park—Sutton Court—Turnham Green—Bedford Park—Acton Green—Professor Lindley—Acton—Its Early History—Berrymead Priory—Lady Dudley's Bequest—Acton a Stronghold of the Puritan Party—The Rev. Philip Nye—Richard Baxter and Sir Matthew Hale—Other Distinguished Residents—An Anecdote of Sir Walter Raleigh—Ancient Manors and Houses—Lord Ferrers' Coach—Clergy Orphan Schools—The Village of Acton—The Parish Church—The Registers—Charitable Bequests—A Centenarian—The Steyne—Skippon, the Parliamentary General—South Acton—Acton Wells—Acton Races—Friar's Place Farm—The Goldsmiths' Alms-houses—Strand-on-the-Green 5

CHAPTER II.

GUNNERSBURY, EALING, AND HANWELL.

Gunnersbury—Descent of the Manor—The Princess Amelia a Resident here—Horace Walpole a frequent Guest—The Property bought by the Rothschilds—The Gardens and Grounds—Gunnersbury House—Ealing—Extent and Nature of the Soil—The Manor—The Parish Church—Sir John Maynard—John Horne Tooke—John Oldmixon—Christ Church—St. John's Church—Seats and Mansions—Dr. John Owen—Dr. William King and other Eminent Residents—Ford Hall—Castle Bar Hill—Princess Helena College—The Old Cross House—The Town Hall—Ealing Great School—Ealing Common—Mrs. Lawrence's Gardens—Fordhook House, and Henry Fielding the Novelist—The "Old Hat" Tavern—Hanwell—The Grand Junction Canal—The Parish Church—Jonas Hanway—The Town of Han-well—The Central London District Schools—Charitable Institutions—Hanwell Lunatic Asylum—The Cemeteries—Electric Telegraphy in its Infancy 17

CHAPTER III.

BRENTFORD.

Traffic through Brentford in the old Coaching Days—Government of the Parish—Old Bridge of the Brent—The Priory of the Holy Angels—Inundations—Fondness of George III. for Brentford—The Dangers of the Road—Early History of Brentford—The Soil and the Pleistocene Deposits—Murder of King Edmund—The Battle of Brentford—Visit of the Grand Duke of Tuscany—The "Two Kings of Brentford"—The Dirt and Squalor of Brentford—How the Duke of Wellington nearly came to grief here—Ancient Hostelries—Old (East) Brentford Church—New (West) Brentford Church—St. Paul's Church—The Town-hall and Market-house—Manufactories and Grand Junction Waterworks—Grand Junction Canal—Drinking Fountain—Bear Baitings—The Old Market-place—The Elections for Middlesex—"Wilkes and Liberty!"—A Brentford Elector—The Manor of Bordeston—Boston House—Sion House Academy—Wyke Farm—"Old Gang Aboot"—The Pitt Diamond—Mrs. Trimmer—Extracts from the Parish Register 29

CHAPTER IV.

HESTON, ISLEWORTH, AND SION HOUSE.

Osterley Park—Sir Thomas Gresham visited by Queen Elizabeth—Lord Desmond—The Manor of Heston—Heston Church—The Soil—Sir Joseph Banks and Anthony Collins residents here—Isleworth—Its Etymology—The River Cran—Sion House—Vicissitudes of the Nuns of St. Bridget—The Rule of the Order of St. Bridget—Early History of the Monastery—The Wardrobes of the Nuns—The Duties of the Abbess, Cellaress, &c.—Dissolution of the Monastery—Touching History of the Sisterhood—Remains of the Monastery—Katherine Howard a Prisoner here—Funeral of Henry VIII.—Building of Sion House—The Family of Percy, Dukes of Northumberland—The

PAGE

Princess of Denmark at Sion House—Description of the Building—The Gardens and Grounds—The Parish of Isleworth—Descent of the Manor—The Parish Church—Charitable Institutions—Church of St. John the Baptist—Brentford Union—Gumley House—Kendal House—Lacy House—Royal Naval Female School—Silver Hall—Gordon House—Sir Clipesby Crewe—Worton Hall—Syon Hill—Honnor's Home—London International College—Spring Grove 41

CHAPTER V.

HOUNSLOW AND HANWORTH.

Situation of Hounslow—A Priory founded here—Martyrdom of Archbishop Scrope—Markets and Fairs—Remains of the Conventual Buildings—Holy Trinity Church—The Manor House—Hounslow in the Old Coaching Days—Present Condition of the Town—The Churches of St. Stephen and St. Paul—Salvation Army Barracks—Hounslow Heath—Military Encampments—Knights of the Road—Site of the Gibbets—A Bishop Counterfeiting the Highwayman—The Gallant Highwayman—The Highwayman Outwitted—Horse-racing, &c.--Gunpowder Mills—Cavalry Barracks—Whitton Park – Hanworth Park—Hanworth House—The Parish Church . . . 60

CHAPTER VI.

TWICKENHAM.

Derivation of the Name of Twickenham—Situation and Extent of the Parish—Early History of the Manor—The Manor House—Arragon Tower—Eel-pie Island—The Parish Church—Holy Trinity Church—St. Stephen's Church—Charitable Institutions—Curious Easter Custom—The Metropolitan and City of London Police Orphanage—Fortescue House—Royal Naval Female School—The Town Hall—Perryn House—Economic Museum—"Bull Land."—Extracts from the Parish Register—An Amusing Anecdote of Sir James Delaval . 70

CHAPTER VII.

TWICKENHAM (continued).

Twickenham Park—The Naval School—Cambridge House—Richard Owen Cambridge—Mr. Bishop's Observatory—Marble Hill—The Witty Bishop Corbett—Ragman's Castle—Orleans House—Mr. Secretary Johnstone—Sir George Pococke—The Duke of Orleans—The Duc d'Aumale—The Orleans Club—York House—The Hon. Mrs. Damer—Sir Alexander Johnson—A Learned Brahmin—The Comte de Paris—The Grove—The Duke of Wharton— Lady Mary Wortley Montagu—Twickenham House—Earl Ferrers—Fielding—Other Noted Residents—Twickenham Common—Whitton—Kneller Hall—The Normal Training School 80

CHAPTER VIII.

TWICKENHAM (continued)—POPE'S VILLA.

Parentage and Birth of Alexander Pope—His Education—His Early Admiration for Dryden—His first Essays Poetic Effusions—Is introduced to Sir W. Trumbull and Wycherley—His Friendship with the Misses Blount—Translates the "Iliad"–Takes up his Residence at Chiswick—Publication of the "Odyssey"—Pope's Narrow Escape from Drowning—Publication of the "Miscellanies," "The Essay on Man," and other Poems—Death and Burial of Pope—Pope's Skull—Character and Temperament of Pope—His Personal Appearance—His Popularity—His Visitors—His Fondness for Animals—His Love of Economy—His Rank as a Poet—His Will—An Account of Pope's Villa and Grotto—Sale of the Villa to Sir William Stanhope—Its subsequent History 95

CHAPTER IX.

TWICKENHAM (continued)—STRAWBERRY HILL.

"Strawberry Hill Shot"—Colley Cibber a Resident there—Other Tenants—Lease of the House by Mrs. Chenevix—The Property purchased by Horace Walpole—His Description of the Place in 1747—Enlargement of the House by Walpole—Description of the Building, and particulars of some of its Principal Contents—The "Chapel" in the Gardens—The Earl of Bath's Panegyric—Biographical Notice of Horace Walpole—Macaulay's Estimate of his Character—Strawberry Hill Bequeathed to Marshal Conway—The Hon. Mrs. Damer—The Waldegrave Family—Sale of the Contents of Strawberry Hill in 1842—Subsequent History of the Building—Little Strawberry Hill and Mrs. Clive—The Misses Berry—Alderman Matthew Wood—"The Bachelors" 111

CHAPTER X.

TEDDINGTON AND BUSHEY PARK.

Situation and General Appearance of Teddington—Rise and Progress of the Village—Upper Teddington—Etymology of Teddington—Early History, and Descent of the Manor—"Queen Elizabeth's Hunting-Box"—The Manor House—The Parish Church—Dr. Stephen Hales—"Peg" Woffington—Extracts from the Parish Register—The Church of St. Peter and St. Paul—Recent Improvements in Teddington—The River Thames—"Swan-upping"—Bushey Park—The Ranger's Lodge—A Village Patriot 123

CHAPTER XI.

HAMPTON.

PAGE

Situation and Boundaries of the Parish—Early History of the Manor—It passes into the hands of Cardinal Wolsey—The Parish Church—The School of Industry—The Grammar School—Princess Frederica's Convalescent Home—Lady Bourchier's Convalescent Home—Noted Hostelries—Hampton Racecourse—Boxing Matches—Hampton Bridge—Thames Angling—Southwark and Vauxhall, and the Lambeth Water Companies—David Garrick and his Villa—Sir Christopher Wren's Residence at Hampton Court Green—Holland the Actor— Lord Sandwich—Sir Andrew Halliday—Sir Richard Steele—Hampton Wick—Abbs Court 132

CHAPTER XII.

HAMPTON COURT PALACE.

Wolsey Lord of the Manor—Terms of the Lease—Reconstruction of the House—Biographical Sketch of Wolsey—Hampton Court Presented to Henry VIII.—Grand Doings in Wolsey's Time—Henry's Wives at Hampton—The Fair Geraldine—A Woman's Promise—Queen Elizabeth at Hampton—The Maids of Honour—The Hampton Court Conference—Oliver Cromwell—Dutch William—His Alterations to the Building—The Georges at Hampton Court—Miss Chudleigh—An Application from Dr. Johnson—Later Inmates 142

CHAPTER XIII.

HAMPTON COURT PALACE (continued).

Early Reminiscences of Hampton Court Palace—Description of the Building—The Principal Entrance—Wolsey's Courts—The Clock Tower Court—A Curious Timepiece—The Great Hall—Theatrical Entertainments given here—The Withdrawing Room—The Kitchen Court— The Fountain Court—Sir Christopher Wren's Alterations and Additions to the Palace—The Chapel—The State Apartments—The " Beauty " Room—The Tapestry Gallery—The Cartoons of Raffaelle—The Gardens—The Wilderness and Maze—The Home Park— The Royal Stud House—A Narrow Escape of the Palace 158

CHAPTER XIV.

FELTHAM, SUNBURY, AND HALLIFORD.

Situation, Etymology, and General Appearance of Feltham—Population, &c.—Notice of the Parish in Domesday Book—Descent of the Manor —The Parish Church—Death of Miss Frances Kelly, the Actress—Middlesex Industrial School—The Convalescent Home—Sunbury— Its Etymology—History of the Manor—Col. Kenyngton, otherwise Kempton—A Royal Palace—Kempton House—Kempton Park Race- course—Sunbury Common—Sunbury Parish Church—Roman Catholic Chapel—The Village of Sunbury—Sunbury Place—The Pumping Stations of the London Waterworks Companies—Thames Angling Preservation Society—The Manor of Charlton—Halliford . . . 172

CHAPTER XV.

SHEPPERTON, AND THE VALLEY OF THE THAMES.

Situation and General Appearance of Shepperton—The River Exe—The Village and its Surroundings—Population—Early History and Descent of the Manor—The Manor-house—The Parish Church—The Rectory—Waterside Taverns—Thames Angling—House-boats on the Thames—River Scenery—Shepperton Green and the Railway Station—A Singular Story—Lower Halliford—Discovery of an Ancient Canoe and other Antiquities—The Valley of the Thames—The Wall Closes—Coway Stakes—Littleton 177

CHAPTER XVI.

LALEHAM, ASHFORD, AND STAINES.

Situation and General Description of Laleham—Remains of a Roman Castrametation on Greenfield Common—Mention of Laleham in Domesday Book—Descent of the Manor—The Parish Church—Laleham House—Dr. Thomas Arnold and his Residence here—The Village of Laleham—Population—The River Thames at Chertsey Bridge—Chertsey Meadows—Laleham Burway—Ashford—Descent of the Manor—The Village of Ashford—The Common—Population—The Parish Church—The Parish Registers—The Welsh Charity School— The West London District Schools—The Town of Staines—The Roman Road and Roman Antiquities—The Boundary Stone of the Thames Conservancy—The Ancient Forest of Middlesex—The Notice of Staines in Domesday Book—A Benedictine Abbey—The Parish Church—An Ancient Guild—The Town of Staines—Markets and Fairs—Population—Inns and Taverns—The Thames and the Water Supply—The Bridge—Duncroft House—Staines Moor—Yeoveney—Runnymede—Magna Charta Island—Ankerwyke—Egham—Cooper's Hill and Sir John Denham 182

CHAPTER XVII.

STANWELL, BEDFONT, AND CRANFORD.

PAGE

Situation and General Aspect of Stanwell—Stanwell Heath formerly a Rendezvous for Middlesex Elections—The Domesday Book Notice of Stanwell—The Forced Exchange of the Manor, *temp.* Henry VIII.—Subsequent Descent of the Manor—The Village of Stanwell—The Old School-house—Population—The Parish Church—Staines Moor, Stanwell Moor, and Poyle Park—West Bedfont—East Bedfont—The Parish Church—The " Peacocks"—Discoveries of Antiquities—Descent of the Manor of Bedfont—Spelthorne Sanatorium—Middlesex Industrial School for Girls—The " Black Dog"—Population of Bedfont—Cranford—Census Returns—The Village—Descent of the Manor—The Park—Cranford House—Cranford le Mote—The Parish Church—The Vicarage 192

CHAPTER XVIII.

HARLINGTON AND HARMONDSWORTH.

Situation of Harlington—The Village and Population—The Manor—The Parish Church—Dr. Trapp—The Yew Tree in the Churchyard—The Local Charities—The Earldom of Arlington—Dawley Court—Lord Bolingbroke—Harmondsworth, Situation and Nature of the Soil— Its Etymology—Harmondsworth Priory—The Manor—An Ancient Barn—The Parish Church—The Village—Census Returns, &c.— Heath Row—A Roman Encampment—Sipson—Longford—Colnbrook 198

CHAPTER XIX.

WEST DRAYTON AND HAYES.

Situation and Boundaries of West Drayton—Its Vegetable Products, Fishing, &c.—Its Etymology—Descent of the Manor—The Old Manor-house—Burroughs, formerly the Seat of General Arabin—The Parish Church—The Burial-ground—The Village of West Drayton— Population—The Catholic Church of St. Catharine—Thorney Broad—The Race-course—Yiewsley—Hayes—The Grand Junction Canal— Census Returns—Boundaries of the Parish—Its Nomenclature—Condition of the Parish in Tudor Times—Acreage of the Parish—Descent of the Manor—The Village of Hayes—Yeading Manor—Botwell—Cotman's Town—Wood End Green—The Parish Church—The Rectory—Distinguished Rectors—Schools and Charities—Extracts from the Parish Registers 205

CHAPTER XX.

NORWOOD, SOUTHALL, ETC.

The " Precinct" of Norwood—Situation and Boundaries of the Parish—Census Returns—Early History of the Manor—The Village—The Parish Church—Schools, &c.—Southall—The Church and Vicarage—The Manor House—The Grand Junction Canal and the Paddington Canal —The Metropolitan Workhouse School—Dorman's Well—Southall Park—Southall Market—Northolt, or Northall—General Description of the Locality—The Parish Church—Greenford—Its Etymology—The Soil, and Census Returns—The Parish Church—The Rectory and Advowson—Distinguished Rectors—Chemical Works at Greenford Green—Horsington Hill and Wood—Perivale—Extent and Population —Descent of the Manor—The Parish Church—West Twyford—Descent of the Manor—Twyford Abbey—The Chapel—Willesden Junction Station—Boundaries and Extent of the Parish of Willesden—Railway Communication—The River Brent—Sub-division of the Manor of Willesden—The Parish Church—Church End—Willesden Green—The " White Hart " and " Spotted Dog " Taverns—Brondesbury—The Jewish Cemetery—Warwick Dairy Farm—Harlesden—Cricklewood—Neasdon—The Metropolitan Railway Carriage Depôt—Sherrick Green and Dollis Hill—Stonebridge Park 215

CHAPTER XXI.

COWLEY AND HILLINGDON.

Situation and Boundaries of Cowley—Cowley Peachey—Cowley Church—Graves of Dr. Dodd and the Rev. John Lightfoot—Barton Booth, the Actor—Census Returns—Cowley House—Cowley Grove—Hillingdon—The Cedar House—Etymology of Hillingdon—Hillingdon Heath —Dawley Court—The Manor of Colham—The Church of St. John the Baptist—Tomb of John Rich, the Actor—The Church Library— The Parish Registers—An Old Engraving—Charities—The Village of Hillingdon—The Cemetery—Census Returns—The " Red Lion " Inn—Flight of Charles I. from Oxford 226

CHAPTER XXII.

UXBRIDGE.

Etymology of Uxbridge—Meeting of the Royalists and Roundheads—Public Reception of the Treaty—The Treaty House—The " Crown " Inn —The Colne and the Grand Junction Canal—The Bridge—The " Swan and Bottle "—Early Fortifications—Roman Roads and Anti-quities—Chief Streets of Uxbridge—Census Returns—The " Chequers"—Trade and Commerce—Fairs and Markets—Condition of the Roads—The Parish Church—The Curfew Bell—Parish Registers—The Rev. John Lightfoot—The Lecturer's House—St. Andrew's Church—St. John's Church—Nonconformists' Meeting-houses—Charities—Recreation Ground—Hillingdon House—Hillingdon Court— Martyrs for Conscience' Sake—Anecdotes—Milton's Favourite Stream—Denham 230

CHAPTER XXIII.

ICKENHAM, RUISLIP, AND HAREFIELD.

PAGE

"The Chestnuts"—Ickenham—Census Returns—The Village Green and Pump—The Parish Church—Descent of the Manor—Swakeleys—Visit of Samuel Pepys—A Curious Baptismal Register—Crab, the English Hermit—Ruislip—Boundaries and Population—Outlying Hamlets—Agricultural Produce, &c.—Extract from the Domesday Survey—Ruislip Priory—The Manor Farm—The Vicarage—The Parish Church—Charities, &c.—The Parish Records—Primitive Condition of the Inhabitants of Ruislip—Schools—The Grand Junction Canal Company's Reservoir—Ruislip Park—Eastcott—Northwood—How Theodore Hook obtained a Dinner without paying for it—Harefield, its Situation and Extent—Its early History—Descent of the Manor—Visit of Queen Elizabeth to Harefield—Lord Keeper Egerton, and the Countess of Derby—The Newdigate Family—The Parish Church—Moor Hall—Breakspears 238

CHAPTER XXIV.

PINNER AND HARROW.

Situation of Harrow, and Nature of the Soil—The Village of Pinner—Population—The River Pin—Miss Howard's Charity—Market and Fairs—The Parish Church—Centenarians—A Curious Custom—Schools and Cemetery—Pinner Hill House—Pinner Wood—Pinner Place—Pinner Grove—Pinner Park—Pinner Green, and Wood Hall—Woodrisings—Death of Mrs. Horatia Ward—The School of the Commercial Travellers' Society—Headstone, or Manor Farm—Etymology of Harrow—Domesday Book Record of the Parish—The Manor—Flambards—A Loyal Lady—Extent and Boundaries of Harrow—The Parish Church—Prior Bolton takes Refuge at Harrow—"Byron's Tomb"—The View from Harrow Hill—The Town and Public Institutions of Harrow 249

CHAPTER XXV.

HARROW (continued)—THE SCHOOL, ETC.

The Distinction between Harrow and Eton as a Public School—The Foundation of Harrow School—"Orders, Statutes, and Rules of the Government of the School"—Extract from the Founder's Will—Directions as to Children to be Educated—Terms of Admission—Government of the School—Forms and Divisions—Number of Scholars—Cost of Board and Education—Prizes and Scholarships—Description of the School Buildings—Athletic Sports and Recreations—Lines in Honour of John Lyon, the Founder—The Practice of Archery—Shooting for the Silver Arrow—Head Masters and Eminent Harrovians 259

CHAPTER XXVI.

HARROW WEALD, KINGSBURY, ETC.

Rural Aspect of the Locality—The Hamlet of Greenhill—Harrow Weald—Remnants of the Great Forest of Middlesex—Grime's Dyke—All Saints' Church—Weald Park—Daniel Dancer, the Miser—Roxeth—Sudbury—St. John's Church—The Girl's Home, &c.—Wembley—Descent of the Manor—The "Green Man," Wembley Hill—Kingsbury: its Rural Character, Boundaries, &c.—Kingsbury Reservoir—The "Welsh Harp"—Kingsbury Races—The Parish Church—A Supposed Roman Encampment—Fryern Farm and Kingsbury Green—Oliver Goldsmith's Residence—The Hamlet of the Hyde—Kenton 269

CHAPTER XXVII.

HENDON.

Extent and Boundaries of the Parish—The Brent River and Silk Stream—The Old Watling Street—Etymology of Hendon—Mention of the Parish in "Domesday Book"—Descent of the Manor—A Singular Immunity from Tolls—The Manor House—Hendon Place—The Parish Church—Almshouses—Brent Street, Golder's Green—Mill Hill—The Grammar School—Roman Catholic Missionary College—St. Mary's Franciscan Nunnery—St. Margaret's Industrial School—Littleberries—Highwood House—Sir Stamford Raffles—Visit of Baron Bunsen—William Wilberforce the Philanthropist 277

CHAPTER XXVIII.

EDGWARE AND LITTLE STANMORE.

Situation and Boundaries of Edgware—General Appearance of the Town—The "Chandos Arms" Inn—The "Harmonious Blacksmith"—Etymology of Edgware—The Descent of the Manor—The Manor of Edgware Bois—Edgware Market—Curious Local Customs—Death of Cosway the Artist—The Parish Church—Almshouses—Population, &c.—Edgware Races—Little Stanmore or Whitchurch—Acreage and Population—Early History of the Manor—Canons—The Family of the Lakes—James Brydges, afterwards Duke of Chandos—He Rebuilds the Mansion of Canons in a magnificent and costly manner—The Parish Church—Handel as Organist here—The "Harmonious Blacksmith" 284

CHAPTER XXIX.

GREAT STANMORE AND ELSTREE.

PAGE

Great Stanmore—Brockley Hill, the supposed Site of Sulloniacæ—Discovery of Roman Antiquities—The Great Forest of Middlesex—The Domesday Notice of Stanmore—Descent of the Manor—The Village—Population—The Bernays Memorial Institute—The Church—Stanmore Park—Bentley Priory—The Property purchased by Lord Abercorn—Queen Adelaide—Sir John Kelk—Elstree—Situation and General Appearance of the Village—The Manor—Parish Church—Burial Places of Martha Ray and William Weare—Female Orphans' Home—Elstree Hill House—Elstree Reservoir—Watercourses—Pudding-stones 297

CHAPTER XXX.

BUSHEY, ALDENHAM, AND RADLETT.

Bushey Heath—The Scenery described—Bushey Manor—The Parish Church—St. Peter's Church—Bushey Hall—Hartsbourne Manor House —Census Returns—Oxhey—Watford—Almshouses of the Salters' Company—Aldenham—Acreage and Population—Descent of the Manor—Kemp Row—Tibhurst Manor—Kendall Manor—Pickets, or Newberry—Aldenham House—Penn's Place—The Parish Church— The Grammar School—Discovery of Roman Remains—Radlett—Christ Church—Gill's Hill—The Murder of William Weare—Medburn —Village Schools and Improved Dwellings 305

CHAPTER XXXI.

SHENLEY, COLNEY, RIDGE, AND SOUTH MIMMS.

Extent and Population of Shenley—Descent of the Manor—Shenley Hall, or Salisbury—Newberries—Old Organ Hall—Porters—Holmes, otherwise High Canons—The Village of Shenley—The Chapel-of-Ease—The Parish Church—Colney House—London Colney— Tittenhanger—Colney Heath—Ridge—The Parish Church—South Mimms—Census Returns—General Appearance of the Village—The Old North Road—The Manor of South Mimms—The Church—Almshouses—Potter's Bar—Dyrham Park—Wrotham Park—Destruction of the Mansion by Fire—Hadley Common—Christ Church 312

CHAPTER XXXII.

HIGH BARNET.

Situation and Extent of Barnet—Its Etymology—The Manor—General Appearance of the Town—Census Returns—Markets and Fairs— The Parish Church—The Grammar School—The old "Crown Inn"—Jesus Hospital—Almshouses and Charitable Institutions—The Town Hall—Barracks—Chapels and Meeting-houses—Ravenscroft Park—The "Physic Well"—Historical Associations—Inns and Taverns—The Battle of Barnet—The Obelisk 319

CHAPTER XXXIII.

HADLEY, EAST BARNET, AND TOTTERIDGE.

Etymology of Monken Hadley—Descent of the Manor—Hadley Green—The Village and Common—Hadley Wood—Gladsmore Heath, or Monken Mead—Dead Man's Bottom—Hadley Church—Two Historic Trees—Almshouses—Noted Residents—Population—East Barnet —Lyonsdown—Census Returns—The Parish Church—The Boys' Farm Home—The Clock House—Cat's Hill—Oak Hill Park— Belmont—Totteridge—Its Etymology—Descent of the Manor—Census Returns—Condition of the Roads—The Church—Yew-trees in Churchyard—The Priory—Pointer's Grove—Copped Hall—Totteridge Park—Wykeham Rise 327

CHAPTER XXXIV.

WHETSTONE, FRIERN BARNET, AND FINCHLEY.

Situation of Whetstone—The Parish Church—Census Returns—Oakleigh Park—George Morland and the Chimney-sweep—General Appearance of the Village—The Manor of Friern Barnet—The Church—Almshouses—Finchley—Situation and Extent—Descent of the Manor— The Old Manor-house—Noted Residents—Church End—Census Returns—Races—The Parish Church—Christ's College—National Schools—East End—The Church, &c.—The "Dirt House"—Cemeteries for Marylebone and St. Pancras and Islington Parishes—North End—Christ Church—The Congregational Chapel—Finchley Common—Encampments and Reviews—Highwaymen—Turpin's Oak— The "Green Man" Tavern—Capture of Jack Sheppard—The Life of a Highwayman 335

CHAPTER XXXV.

COLNEY HATCH AND SOUTHGATE.

PAGE

Rapid Extension of Colney Hatch, or New Southgate—Its Situation and Etymology—Middlesex County Lunatic Asylum—St. Paul's Church—The Pumping Station of the New River Waterworks—Wood Green—The Drinking Fountain—Nightingale Hall—St. Michael's Church—The Printers' Almshouses—Fishmongers' and Poulterers' Asylum—Fullers' Almshouses—Royal Masonic Institution for Boys—Clock and Watchmakers' Asylum- -The Great Northern Cemetery—Southgate—The Village Green and "Cherry-tree" Inn—The Church—Arnold's Court, now Arno's Grove—Minchenden House—Bromefield Park—Bowes Manor—Bowes Park—St. Michael's Church—Culland's Grove—Grovelands—Palmer's Green—Southgate Village Hall—Winchmore Hill—The Church, &c.—Bush Hill Park—Sir Hugh Myddelton and the New River 342

CHAPTER XXXVI.

ENFIELD.

General Description of the Parish—Situation and Boundaries—Parochial Divisions—The Town and Principal Streets—Enfield Court—The New River—Railway Stations—Census Returns—Historical Reminiscences—The Barony of Enfield—Descent of the Manor—Fairs and Markets—Site of the Old Manor House—Camlet Moat—Oldbury—Edward VI. at Enfield—The Palace—Dr. Uvedale—The Market-place—The Parish Church—The Free Grammar School—Schools of Industry—John Keats's Schooldays—Charitable Institutions—Old Park—Chase Park—Chase Side House—Enfield Green—Little Park—Beycullah Park—Enfield Races—Churches and Chapels—The Cemetery—Forty Hall—Elsynge Hall—Sir Walter Raleigh and Queen Elizabeth—Anne Countess of Pembroke—Myddelton House—Gough Park—Distinguished Residents—Beautiful Women of Enfield 347

CHAPTER XXXVII.

ENFIELD CHASE.

General Description of a Chase—Form and Extent of Enfield Chase—Its Early History—The Last of the Staffords, Dukes of Buckingham—Drayton's Description of Enfield Chase—Its Present Condition—The Princess Elizabeth as a Hunter—James I. at Enfield Chase—A Portion of the Chase added to Theobalds—Seizure of the Chase by the Commonwealth—Sale of Different Portions of it—Macaulay's Account of Enfield Chase—Evelyn pays it a Visit—The Chase Re-stocked with Deer by Charles II.—The Chase used as a Sheep-walk—Punishment for Cutting Down and Destroying Trees in the Chase—Its Final Enclosure—Officers belonging to the Chase—Camlet Moat, the supposed Site of the Chief Forester's Lodge—Trent Park—Beech Hill Park—East Lodge—Chase Lodge—Hill Lodge, Claysmore—The Roman Road—Cock Fosters—Dangers of the Roads in Former Times—White Webbs House—The Gunpowder Plot—"The King and the Tinkler" 363

CHAPTER XXXVIII.

ENFIELD HIGHWAY, PONDER'S END, AND THE RIVER LEA.

Position and Extent of Enfield Highway—Population, &c.—The Lower North Road—Mr. Spencer and his Bride—Matthew Prior and John Morley—St. James's Church—Ponder's End—St. Matthew's Church—Lincoln House—Durants—The Manor of Suffolks—Enfield Wash—The Story of Elizabeth Canning, "Mother Wells," and the Gipsy Squires—Roselands—The Manor of Elsynge—The River Lea—Bull's Cross—Capels 371

CHAPTER XXXIX.

THEOBALDS.

Situation of Theobalds, and History of the Manor—The Estate Purchased by Sir William Cecil, afterwards Lord Burleigh—James I. at Theobalds—Entertainment to Christopher IV., King of Denmark—Narrow Escape of King James—His Death—Description of the Palace and Gardens—Demolition of the Palace—Present Condition of the Estate 376

CHAPTER XL.

CHESHUNT.

Situation and General Appearance of the Parish—Its Etymology—Supposed Site of a Roman Station or Camp—Discovery of Roman Coins, &c.—The Mound at Bury Green—A Curious Manorial Custom—Census Returns—The River Lea—A Disputed Landmark—Early History and Descent of the Manor of Cheshunt—The Manor of Moteland, or St. Andrew's le Mote—The Great House—The Parish Church—The Cemetery, &c.—Cheshunt College—Pengelly House—Cheshunt Park—The Cromwell Family—Other Notable Residents and Seats—Waltham Cross—"The Four Swans" Inn—The Spital Houses—Holy Trinity Church—The Benedictine Convent—Goff's Oak—St. James's Church 384

CHAPTER XLI.

NORTHAW

PAGE

Etymology of Northaw—Condition of the District at the Time of the Conquest—Disputed Ownership—Nynn House, and Manor—The Hook—Northaw Place—Acreage and Population—The Village and Parish Church—A Chalybeate Spring 394

CHAPTER XLII.

ENFIELD SMALL-ARMS FACTORY AND WALTHAM POWDER-MILLS.

The History of the Rifle—Situation of the Royal Small-arms Factory—Particulars of its Establishment—Extent of the Buildings, &c.—Perfection of the Machinery and Plant—The Government Powder Mills—Situation of the Buildings—Description of the Works—The Composition of Gunpowder—Quantities produced 395

CHAPTER XLIII.

WALTHAM ABBEY.

Situation of the Town—Its Etymology—Foundation of the Abbey by Jovi—Its Re-foundation by Harold—The Legend of the Holy Cross—Gifts bestowed on the Abbey—Harold's Tomb—The Church despoiled by William the Conqueror—Its Recovery under subsequent Sovereigns—Disputes between the Abbot and Townspeople—Henry III. and the Abbot's Dinner—An Incident touching the Reformation—Income of the Abbey at the Dissolution—Fuller, the Historian—The Conventual Estate passes into Secular Hands—Description of the Abbey Church—Sale of the Church Bells—Present Condition of the Remains of the Abbey—Rome-Land—The Abbey Gateway and Bridge 404

CHAPTER XLIV.

WALTHAM (*continued*) AND EPPING.

Extent of Waltham Abbey Parish—Census Returns—Rural Appearance of the Locality—Principal Seats and Mansions—Warlies—Copped Hall—Ambresbury Banks—The Story of Queen Boadicea's Conflict with the Romans—Obelisks in the Neighbourhood—Highwaymen and Footpads—The Village of Epping—Epping Church 416

CHAPTER XLV.

EPPING FOREST.

Primeval Condition of the Forest, as the Great Forest of Essex—Gradual Diminution of the Forest—Forest Charters of King John and Henry III.—Laws for the Regulation of the Forest—A Quaint Oath—Lord Warden, Steward, and other Officers of the Forest—The Swainmote Court and Court of Justice Seat—Extent of the Forest in the Middle Ages—Present Form of the Forest—Disposal of the Crown Rights in the Forest—Encroachments by Lords of Manors—The Battle of the Commoners with the Lords of Manors—Parliamentary Scheme for the Preservation of the Forest—The Matter taken up by the Corporation of London—The Case Settled by Arbitration—Dedication of Epping Forest to the "Free Use" of the People—The Science of Forestry—The Deer of the Forest—The Present Condition and General Appearance of the Forest 423

CHAPTER XLVI.

EPPING FOREST (*continued*)—SEWARDSTONE, HIGH BEECH, AND CHINGFORD.

Preliminary Remarks—Situation and Boundaries of Sewardstone—Seats and Mansions—High Beech Green—St. Paul's Church—Fairmead Lodge—Sotheby and Tennyson—Residents at High Beech—Fairmead House—John Clare—High Beech Hill—The "Robin-Hood" and "King's Oak"—"Harold's Oak"—Queen Victoria's Wood—Lappitt's Hill—Bury Wood and Hawk Wood—Situation and Etymology of Chingford—Its Extent and Boundaries—The Manor of Chingford St. Paul—The Manor of Chingford Earls—Friday Hill—Buckrills—A Singular Tenure—Census Returns—Chingford Old Church—The Ordnance Survey Obelisk—Queen Elizabeth's Lodge—The Royal Forest Hotel—Connaught Water 435

CHAPTER XLVII.

EPPING FOREST (*continued*)—BUCKHURST HILL, LOUGHTON, AND THEYDON BOIS.

Recent Improvements in Epping Forest—Connaught Water and other Lakes—Buckhurst Hill—Its Etymology—Census Returns—The Railway Station—St. John's Church—Congregational Church—Langford Place—The Essex Naturalists' and Field Club—The

PAGE

Epping Hunt—The "Bald-faced Stag"—The "Roebuck"—Situation of Loughton—Census Returns—Descent of the Manor— The Hall—The Old Parish Church—A Memorial Church—St. John's Church—General Appearance of the Village—Staple Hill— The "Lopping" Process—Loughton Camp—Debden Hall—Theydon Bois. 441

CHAPTER XLVIII.

CHIGWELL.

General Appearance of the Village of Chigwell—Its Etymology—Census Returns—Descent of the Manor—Rolls Park—Woolstons— Lexborough—The Warren—Belmont—The Parish Church—Archbishop Harsnett—Local Charities—Club-room—The Grammar School— The "King's Head" Tavern—Charles Dickens's "Maypole" Inn—Chigwell Row—Woodlands—Bowls—Gainsborough's Picture of "The Woodman"—The Mineral Waters 449

CHAPTER XLIX.

WOODFORD AND WALTHAMSTOW.

Boundaries of Woodford—Its Etymology—Its Subdivision—Descent of the Manor—The Manorial Custom of "Borough English"— Woodford Hall—Census Returns—Woodford Bridge—The Church—Claybury Hall—Ray House—Church End, Woodford—The Parish Church—Woodford Hall—Mrs. Gladstone's Convalescent Home—A Pauper's Legacy—Woodford Green—Congregational Church —The Union Church—Art and Industrial Society, and Social Institutions—Harts—Monkhams—The Firs—Prospect Hall—Woodford Wells—"The Horse and Well"—Knighton House—The Manor House—Noted Residents—Walthamstow—Its Area and General Appearance—Walthamstow Slip—Census Returns—Etymology of Walthamstow—Descent of the Manor—Highams—Salisbury Hall —Chapel End—Bellevue House—The Parish Church—Almshouses—Walthamstow House—Benjamin Disraeli's School-days—Noted Residents of Walthamstow—The Town Hall, and other Public Institutions—Hoe Street—Hale End—Marsh Street—St. James's—The Reservoirs of the East London Waterworks Company—Geological Discoveries—An Old Bridge—St. Stephen's Church—Whip's Cross— St. Peter's Church, Forest Side—Forest Grammar School 458

CHAPTER L.

SNARESBROOK AND WANSTEAD.

General Appearance of the Locality—Snaresbrook—The "Rights" of Commoners—The "Eagle" at Snaresbrook and the Eagle Pond— The Infant Orphan Asylum—Merchant Seamen's Orphan Asylum—Christ Church—Almshouses of the Weavers' Company—Area and Population of Wanstead—Its Boundaries, &c.—Etymology—Traces of Roman Occupation—Descent of the Manor—The Earl of Leicester and Queen Elizabeth—A "Spa" at Wanstead—Pepys' Opinion of Wanstead House—Visit of John Evelyn—Wanstead House Rebuilt by Sir Richard Child, afterwards Earl Tylney—Description of the House and Grounds—The Great Telescope—The Maypole from the Strand—Death of Lord Tylney—Subsequent History of Wanstead House—Its Demolition—Wanstead Park secured for the People by the Corporation of London—The Park, Gardens, and Grotto—Lake House, the Residence of Thomas Hood— Cann Hall—The Parish Church—The Village of Wanstead—The George Inn—An Expensive Pie—Park Gate—Wanstead Flats— The Princess Louise Home and National Society for the Protection of Young Girls—Dr. James Pound—The Maypole from the Strand—James Bradley the Astronomer—Admiral Sir William Penn—William Penn, the Founder of Pennsylvania 472

CHAPTER LI.

LEYTON AND LEYTONSTONE.

Extent and Boundaries of Leyton Parish—Walthamstow Slip—Census Returns—Discovery of Roman Remains and other Antiquities— Ancient Earthworks—General Appearance of the Village of Leyton—Railway Stations—Park House—Ruckholt House—The Manor House—Leyton House—Etloe House—The Parish Church—John Strype—The Vicarage—All Saints' Church—Schools and Charitable Institutions—Lea Bridge, and the East London Waterworks—Temple Mills—Eminent Residents of Leyton—Leytonstone—Census Returns—The Church of St. John the Baptist—Holy Trinity Church—Congregational Church—Union Workhouse—Children's Home . 483

CHAPTER LII.

HAINAULT FOREST AND ALDBOROUGH HATCH.

Situation, Boundaries, and Extent of Hainault Forest—Its Etymology—Its Ownership by the Abbey of Barking—It passes to the Crown— Subsequent Disposal—Is Disafforested—The Hamlet of Barking Side—Census Returns—The Church—Dr. Barnardo's Homes for Friendless Children—The "Maypole" Public-house—Fairlop Oak and Fairlop Fair—Aldborough Hatch 489

CHAPTER LIII.

ILFORD.

Chadwell Heath—Chadwell Street—The Old Coach Road—Will Kemp's Dance from London to Norwich—Great Ilford—Census Returns —Etymology—The River Roding—Ilford Church—Public Reading-Room and Library, &c.—Ilford Hospital—Cranbrook House— Valentines—Discovery of an Ancient Stone Coffin—Elephants in Essex 495

CHAPTER LIV.

LITTLE ILFORD, WEST HAM, ETC.

PAGE

Boundaries and Extent of Little Ilford—Census Returns—The Parish Church — Mr. Lethieullier's House at Aldersbrook—Ilford Gaol—
The "Three Rabbits"—West Ham—Its Division into Wards—Population—Market and Fairs—Chemical Works and Factories—The
Parish Church—A Curious Fresco—Upton Park—Forest Gate—Taverns and "Tea-Gardens"—Emmanuel Church—St. James's Church
—Extent and Population of Forest Gate—Pawnbrokers' Almshouses—Legg's Almshouses—Former Condition of Stratford—The Abbey of
Stratford-Langthorne—Pumping Station of the Metropolitan Drainage Works—St. John's Church—Christ Church—St. Paul's—St. Francis
of Assisi Congregational Church—Town Hall—Stratford New Town—Vegetable Market—Old Ford—Bow Bridge—Roman Roads   . 501

CHAPTER LV.

PLAISTOW AND EAST HAM.

Flat and unattractive Appearance of Plaistow—Its Sedate Aspect in Former Times—Its Sources of Wealth—The Destitute Children's Home—
The Metropolitan Main Drainage Works—Census Returns—Silver Town, Canning Town, and Hall Ville—Plaistow Church—St.
Andrew's Church—Congregational Church—East London Cemetery—Poplar Small-pox and Fever Hospital—Chemical Works and other
Manufactories—The Royal Victoria and Albert Docks—North Woolwich—St. Mark's Church—St. John's Church—North Woolwich
Gardens—Distinguished Residents at Plaistow—Descent of the Manor of East Ham—St. Nicholas's Roman Catholic School—A Curious
Manorial Custom—Situation and Extent of the Parish—The Parish Church—Emmanuel Church—St. John the Baptist—Plashet
House—Greenstreet House—Anne Boleyn's Tower—St. Edward's Reformatory—The High Level Sewer—Beckton Gas and Coke Works 509

CHAPTER LVI.

BARKING.

Situation and Extent of the Parish—Census Returns—Etymology—Early History and Foundation of Barking Abbey—The Abbey Burnt by
the Danes—Rebuilt by King Edgar—William the Conqueror takes up his Abode there—The Importance of the Abbey in Saxon Times
—The Convent Damaged by an Overflow of the Thames—Curious Entries of the Revenues of the Abbey—Dissolution of the Abbey—
The Abbey Gateway—Extent of the Original Buildings—Noted Abbesses—Manorial Estates of the Abbey—The Parish Church—The
Rural Deanery of Barking—The Manor of Barking—The Story of Osborne's Leap—The Manor of Clayhall—Malmains—Bifrons—
Eastbury House—The Road to Tilbury—Barking Town—Barking Creek—The Outfall of the Main Drainage Works—Powder
Magazine, &c.—The Roman Entrenchment at Uphall   516

CHAPTER LVII.

DAGENHAM.

Ripple Side, Barking—Ripple Castle—Extent and Boundaries of Dagenham—Census Returns—The Village—Church—Parslowes—Valence—
Dagenham Breach—Discovery of a "Moorlog"—The River Walls of the Thames—Dagenham Lake—Its Proposed Conversion into a
Dock—Failure of the Scheme—Origin of the Ministerial Fish Dinner   527

CHAPTER LVIII.

MILLWALL, LIMEHOUSE, AND POPLAR.

Situation and Boundaries of Millwall—Origin of the Name of the Isle of Dogs—The Chapel House—Blackwall—Millwall—Acreage of the
Isle of Dogs—Fertility of the Soil—Geology—A Submerged Forest—The Manor of Pomfret—Inundations of the Marsh—How Samuel
Pepys attended a Wedding Party—Ferries, and the Ferry House—Condition of the Isle of Dogs in the Last Century—Manufactories
and Shipbuilding Yards—Roman Cement and Terra-Cotta—The *Great Eastern* Steam Ship—Cubitt Town—St. Luke's Church—Limehouse—Poplar   533

CHAPTER LIX.

THE EAST AND WEST INDIA AND MILLWALL DOCKS.

The Vastness of Trade and Commerce—Arrival of Coal-ships and other Vessels in the Port of London—Number of Barges and other Craft
required for Traffic in 1792—Plunder carried on in the Lighters on the River—Institution of the Thames Police—Proposals for the Establishment of Docks—Foundation of the West India Docks—The Opening Ceremony—Description of the Docks—A Curious Museum—
New Dry Docks—The Wood Wharf—The Rum Quay—The South West India Dock—The Wool Warehouses—The East India Docks—
Millwall Dock—Insecurity of Merchandise before the Establishment of Docks or Institution of the Thames Police   549

CONTENTS.

CHAPTER LX.

THE RIVER LEA.

PAGE

Etymology of the River Lea—Its Source—Luton—Brocket Hall—Hertford—Ware—Amwell and its Quaker Poet—Haileybury College—The Rye House—Stanstead Abbots—Hoddesdon—Broxbourne—Cook's Ferry—Bleak Hall—The East London Waterworks—Lea Bridge—Fishing on the Lea—Hackney Marshes and Temple Mills—The Navigation of the Lea—Conservancy of the River.   559

CHAPTER LXI.

THE RIVER THAMES.

The Thames as a Political Boundary, and as a Boundary of Counties—Tributary Rivers—Breadth of the River—Its General Aspect and Character of Scenery—The Embankments—Shoals and Floods—Tides—The Thames as the Common Highway of London—Anecdote of Cardinal Wolsey—Sir Walter Raleigh and Queen Elizabeth—Abdication of James II.—Funeral of Lord Nelson—Water Traffic in the Time of Richard II.—The Conservancy of the Thames—Boating on the Thames   568

LIST OF ILLUSTRATIONS.

WALTHAM ABBEY.—*Frontispiece.*

	PAGE
Coronation Stone, Kingston	1
Manor House, High Beech	1
Harrow Church	1
Bedford Park: Houses in South Parade; a Porch; the Church; the "Tabard"; Gable of the School of Art; Houses in Bath Road	6
Sir Matthew Hale	7
Richard Baxter	7
Acton Church and Acton Town at the end of last Century	10
High Street, Acton	12
The Church, from the Rectory	12
Berrymead Priory	13
Gunnersbury House	18
Ealing Churches: St. John's; St. Mary's (the Parish Church); Christ Church	19
Ealing Green	24
The "Old Hat" in the Uxbridge Road	25
Brentford, from the River	30
The Stables of the "Three Pigeons," Brentford	31
Boston House	36
Mrs. Trimmer	37
Osterley Park	42
Heston	43
The Old Stables at Sion House	48
Sion House, from the South	49
Sion Abbey, from the South-West	54
Isleworth Church	55
The Powder Mills, Hounslow: Pellet House; the Storehouses and Mill Head; The Sluice and Mixing House	61
High Street, Hounslow	63
Whitton Park	66
Old Hanworth Church	67
Twickenham	72
Eel-Pie Island	72
A Plan of Twickenham, 1784	73
Sir Godfrey Kneller	78

	PAGE
Twickenham Park House	79
Mr. Pitt's House at Twickenham	84
Marble Hill	85
Philip, Duke of Wharton	90
Lady Suffolk	90
The Gardens of Orleans House, 1882	91
Kneller Hall	94
Pope	97
Pope's House	102
Lady Howe's Villa and Pope's Grotto	103
The Obelisk to Pope's Mother	108
"Pope's Villa"	109
Strawberry Hill in Walpole's Time	114
Strawberry Hill, 1882	115
Horace Walpole	120
Little Strawberry Hill in 1813	121
The Queen's Barge	126
The Anglery, Teddington Ferry	127
Hampton, from the River	133
Garrick	138
Hampton House	139
Hampton Court Bridge	144
Cardinal Wolsey	145
Hampton Court, as finished by King Henry VIII.	150
Old Hampton Court	150
Approach to Hampton Court	151
Hampton Court, from the River	156
Miss Chudleigh	157
Hampton Court: The Chapel; Interior of the Great Hall	162
Hampton Court: the First Court; Fountain Court	163
Hampton Court: Anne Boleyn's Gateway	168
Hampton Court	169
Hampton Court: Plan of the Maze	171
Halliford	174
Sunbury Church	175
Shepperton, from the River	180
Shepperton Rectory	180

	PAGE		PAGE
Laleham Church	186	Hadley Green (Site of the Battle of Barnet)	325
Street in Staines	187	Hadley Church	330
The City Boundary Stone	187	Copped Hall	331
Bedfont Church	192	Lord Lytton	331
Stanwell Village Green	193	Alms Houses, Friern Barnet	336
Harlington Church	198	Finchley Manor House and Turpin's Oak	337
"Bits" from Harlington Church: the Easter Sepulchre;		Colney Hatch	342
the Norman Door	199	Arno's Grove, Southgate	343
The Old Barn at Harmondsworth	204	Enfield Church	348
The Gatehouse, West Drayton	205	Beach Hill circ. 1796	349
West Drayton	210	Myddelton House circ. 1821	349
Font in West Drayton Church	210	Queen Elizabeth's Palace, Enfield, 1568	354
Hayes: Hayes Church; Hayes Village through the		The Palace, from the North	354
Lych Gate	211	The Old Market House, Enfield	355
Southall Manor House	216	Forty Hall and the Old Gateway	360
Interior of Perivale Church	217	Gough Park	361
Perivale Church, Exterior	219	View in Trent Park	366
Twyford Abbey	222	In Beech Hill Park	367
Willesden Church	223	Ponder's End	372
Hillingdon Church about 1740	228	Room in Mother Wells' Cottage	373
The Treaty House, Uxbridge	231	Old Theobalds Palace	378
Market House, Uxbridge	234	The Maze at Theobalds	379
St. Margaret's, Uxbridge; the Font	235	Cheshunt Church	385
Swakeleys	240	Richard Cromwell	389
Ruislip	241	The Old Manor House, Cheshunt	390
Harefield Place	246	Waltham Cross	391
Lady Derby's Tomb	247	Enfield Small Arms Factory	396
Pinner, in 1828	252	The Powder Mills, Waltham	397
Pinner Church, in 1800	253	The Cattle Market, Waltham	402
Harrow Church, Interior	258	On the Lea	403
Harrow	259	Waltham Abbey—Interior: Nave, Crypt, Lady Chapel	408
The Fourth Form Room	264	Gateway and Bridge, Waltham Abbey	409
Shooting for the Arrow	265	Copped Hall, near Epping	414
Arms of Harrow School	266	Ambresbury Banks	415
Byron's Name, from the Fourth Form Room	268	Map of Epping Forest	421
Distant View of Harrow	270	Views in Epping Forest: Connaught Water, Ching-	
The Welsh Harp and Reservoir	271	ford; A Glade at Theydon Bois; On the way to	
High House Farm	276	Copped Hall from Loughton; High Beech	427
Hendon Village	277	Royal Forest Hotel, Chingford	432
Littleberries	282	Flowers from Epping Forest	433
Sir Stamford Raffles	283	Chingford Church	438
Village of Edgware	288	Queen Elizabeth's Lodge	439
The Duke of Chandos	289	The "Roebuck"	444
Canons: Elevation of the Original South Front	291	The "Bald-Faced Stag"	444
Canons	294	Theydon Bois	445
Whitchurch Church: the East End	295	Chigwell Grammar School	450
Bentley Priory	300	William Penn	450
Queen Adelaide	301	Chigwell Church	451
Bushey Church	306	The "King's Head," Chigwell	456
Aldenham House	307	Churches at Woodford: The Old Parish Church; All	
Shenley Church and Village	312	Saints, Woodford Wells	459
Tittenhanger	313	Monkhams	462
Sir T. Pope	313	The "Horse and Well," Woodford Wells	463
Wrotham Park	318	Grammar Schools and Almshouses, Walthamstow	
High Street, High Barnet	319	Churchyard	468
Vews in Barnet: the Schools; the "Red Lion" Inn	324	Forest Grammar School	469

	PAGE		PAGE
The "Eagle," Snaresbrook	474	Eastbury House	522
Wanstead House	475	Market House, Barking	523
Monument to Sir J. Child, Wanstead Church	480	Dagenham Marshes, looking East	528
Park Gate	481	Walls of the Thames	529
Monuments in Leyton Church	486	The Thames from Ratcliffe to Woolwich, in 1588	534
Leyton Vicarage	487	Dagenham	535
Portrait of Strype	487	Millwall Docks	540
Dr. Barnardo's Homes	492	Millwall, from the River	541
Fairlop Oak, 1800	493	Launch of the *Great Eastern*	546
Valentines, near Ilford	498	Limehouse Church	547
Ilford Hospital	499	West India Docks	553
West Ham Church	504	Vaults at the Docks	555
West Ham Park	505	Entrance to the East India Docks	558
Royal Albert Docks : Looking East ; Looking West	510	Cook's Ferry	564
Anne Boleyn's Castle	511	At Lea Bridge	565
Ancient Bell Tower, Barking Abbey	516	The Thames, Barking Reach	570
Barking Creek	517	The Thames, Woolwich Reach	571

CORONATION STONE KINGSTON

MANOR HOUSE HIGHBEECH

HARROW CHURCH

GREATER LONDON.

INTRODUCTORY.

"GREATER LONDON!" What a vague and ill-defined term! We all know London proper, comprising the City and Westminster, and making up one metropolis. But "Greater London!" What can the words mean? What and where are its limits? and how far afield will it carry us? Do you mean the area ruled over by the Metropolitan Board of Works, or by the authorities of the Census Department, or by the Metropolitan Police, or that which the Postmaster-General takes as the limits of his suburban deliveries of letters?

The question is not very easily answered offhand, for we are free to own that there are several "Greater Londons," and that these are far from being coincident. The district ruled over by our Board of Works, though large, covers very little ground that has not been already travelled by us in "Old and New London," except in a single direction—that of the estuary of the Thames, the very district in which we have stopped the shortest. Again, the postal suburban limits are subject to frequent changes; and the Census authorities have fixed on somewhat ill-defined and arbitrary bounds, as to which it is impossible to say on what principle they have been settled. It remains, therefore, that we select, as open to the fewest objections, the circle of the Metropolitan Police jurisdiction, which extends, in every direction, about fifteen miles on an average from the centre of modern London, namely, Charing Cross. This embraces the whole of Middlesex and a part of Surrey, together with most of the suburban districts of Essex and Kent, reaching from Dagenham in the east to Uxbridge in the west, and from Colney and Cheshunt in the north to Epsom and Warlingham in the south—an almost perfect circle, some twenty-eight miles in diameter.

Greater London! "The spread of material London," it has been observed—"the London of bricks and mortar and stucco—is becoming a gigantic—one might almost say an appalling—factor in our national existence. Every day it becomes more difficult to say where the limits of the capital have been reached, and at what point the cockney may fairly be said to begin his long-sought 'day in the country.' Every week new building speculations absorb the green fields and hedgerows, and the quiet little village station becomes a suburban junction. To introduce some guiding principle into this labyrinth, Sir Brydges Henniker, our Registrar-General, has, in his returns, divided London into two portions—an inner and an outer zone. The inner zone comprises the fixed and permanent city, spreading in a continuous mass from Hampstead on the north to Norwood on the south, and from Bromley on the east to Hammersmith on the west. This area comprises, in round figures, about 78,000 acres, and, with the exception of parks and open spaces which have been saved by Parliament from the ruthless grasp of the builder, is already fully utilised for building purposes. . . . . It must not be forgotten that whilst there has been very considerable growth in districts within the central area, but approaching the outer zone, a process has been constantly at work in all the most central parts of London tending to drive further outwards the resident population. We may instance the construction of the new terminus of the Great Eastern Railway in Liverpool Street, and the lines of railway converging at that point; the construction of new thoroughfares by the various public bodies, all of which have passed through densely-populated districts; and the vast number of dwelling-houses which

have been swept away from the heart of London, upon the site of which now stand tall piles of warehouses and offices."

But in truth, when we speak of "London," we do not mean so much a city as a collection or gathering together of cities. Not only is our metropolis many-handed, like Briareus, and many-headed, like Cerberus: it is manifold. It is no longer singular, but plural; it consists no longer of one city, but of many. It has engulfed gradually many cities, towns, villages, and separate jurisdictions. Its present surface, as already intimated, includes large portions of four commonwealths, or kingdoms, those of the Middle Saxons, of the East Saxons, of the "South Rie" (Surrey) folk, and of the men of Kent. Taken in its widest acceptation, as above shown, London—or rather, the district which is under the rule of the Metropolitan Police—now embraces, not only the entire cities of London and Westminster, but the entire county of Middlesex, all the boroughs of Southwark and Greenwich, the towns of Woolwich and Wandsworth, the watering-places of Hampstead, Highgate, Islington, Acton, and Kilburn, the fishing-town of Barking, the once secluded and ancient villages of Hanwell, Cheshunt, Harrow, Croydon, Finchley, Twickenham, Teddington, Chigwell, Sutton, Addington, and many others. It will be seen, therefore, that there is some truth in the witty definition which has been given of London, namely—"That world of stucco which is bounded by Barnet on the north and Croydon on the south; which touches Woolwich in the far east, and Richmond and Twickenham in the far west."

"The growth of a great city," observes John Timbs, "must be an interesting study to a larger number of persons than we may at first imagine; its claims upon their attention are world-wide when that city is London. It may seem like national partiality when we speak thus; but it is only philosophic reasoning when we remember that no city of equal size and importance exists in the world, or ever did exist. Babylon 'the Great' was not so large, and imperial Rome was smaller in its palmiest days; even when mistress of the world it by no means rivalled modern London."

Of late years, the removal of dwellings in "London proper" for commercial purposes, and the consequent erection of others in the suburbs and outlying villages, has been rapid in the extreme. Streets, terraces, and villas, of all shapes and sizes, are springing up in all directions, and quite altering the hitherto rural aspect of the spots encroached upon. That this growth of London has not been one of a sudden and impulsive nature, consequent on some great panic or mania for building that may have seized on the commercial world—after the fashion of the "railway mania" of forty years ago —may be inferred when we state that Horace Walpole thus writes to his friend Sir Horace Mann, under date 1791 :—"There will soon be one street from London to Brentford ; aye, and from London to every village ten miles round !" The era of which he prophesied has long since arrived ; and not only Brentford, but Hounslow, is now connected with the metropolis by an almost unbroken row of bricks and mortar, in the shape of cottages, shops, and villas.

The elder D'Israeli, in "The Curiosities of Literature," mentions some remarkable features of the dread which our countrymen entertained of an overgrown metropolis :—"Proclamations warned and exhorted ; but the very interference of a royal prohibition seemed to render the metropolis more charming ;" though for all this, from Elizabeth to Charles II., proclamations continually issued against new erections. James I. notices "those swarms of gentry who, through the instigation of their wives, did neglect their country hospitality, and cumber the city : a general nuisance to the kingdom." He once said—"Gentlemen resident on their estates are like ships in port, their value and magnitude are felt and acknowledged ; but when at a distance, as their size seemed insignificant, so their worth and importance were not duly estimated." The England even of the present century is changed out of all possible knowledge ; indeed, those are yet living who can look back with a smile at the solemn county balls, which were almost as difficult of access, and as jealously guarded, as a Court presentation of these days.

Nor were good reasons wanted for eschewing London. Only two centuries ago a Sussex squire, Mr. Palmer, was fined in the sum of £1,000 for residing in London rather than on his own estate in the country, and that even in face of the fact that his country mansion had been burned within the two years before his trial took place ! We are told that this sentence struck terror into the London sojourners ; and it was followed by a proclamation for them to leave the city, with their "wives and families, and also widows." And now we have no difficulty in understanding why there are so many large mansions in small country towns. The habit of making the best of a hard lot influenced the gentry even long after it would have been safe to have followed Mr. Palmer's example ; and so we find, up to the Hanoverian period, large old-fashioned houses in some small country towns, that look, as Dickens says, as if they had lost

their way in infancy, and grown to their present proportions. The tendency of families to migrate to the county town instead of London in the "season," was partly owing to the difficulty of the roads (for nothing now in England can give an idea of the undertaking of a journey of 200 miles to London), but partly, also, to a singular law, which forbade, as far as possible, any country gentleman who was not in Parliament from residing in London. Railways, of course, have rapidly and completely changed the scene. The old moralist in Thackeray laments the change of times, when a man of quality used to enter London, or return to his country-house, in a coach and pair, with outriders, and now his son "slinks" from the station in a brougham.

Whether or not the architectural aspect of the streets of London is being improved by the wholesale demolition of its ancient buildings, and the erection on their sites of huge warehouses and commercial edifices, is not for us to say ; but a great advance has certainly been made of late years in the architectural appearance of the better class of suburban residences. It is true that there are many excellent specimens of house architecture even of Queen Anne's reign in remote villages within twenty miles of London. Many of these houses are now turned into boarding-schools or village tenements, having been shouldered out of the way as ugly and old-fashioned. But a reaction has at last set in against the massive and tasteless style so long characteristic of town and suburban buildings, and houses of the Queen Anne type are being erected in the suburbs on every side of London.

With all this, there are happily many places round London still unbuilt upon, within the limits of our present work, to which the cockney holiday-maker may take a day's excursion, where he will find the fields still green, the hedgerows fresh, and the forest-trees in summer-time in full leaf, and waving bravely in the breeze. That portion of the county of Surrey which will fall within the scope of our peregrinations has, to a very large extent, up to the present time, kept clear of the man of bricks and mortar. Indeed, it is not a little remarkable that a county so near to the metropolis should still contain so large an amount of waste lands. At the beginning of the present century it was reckoned that a sixth of its whole acreage was in a wild and uncultivated state ; but this condition of things has been greatly altered by enclosures. Still, however, near London there are Wimbledon Common and Putney Heath, Wandsworth and Clapham Commons, Streatham, Tooting, and Kennington Commons—in all, nearly 2,000 acres.   Farther afield are Bagshot Heath, Epsom, Leatherhead, Ashtead, Weybridge, Epping Forest, and other open spots, of many of which we shall have occasion to speak.

This area, almost every nook and corner of which—thanks to our railway system—may be visited on the Saturday afternoon holidays in summer, and most of them even in winter, contains, as we need hardly add, much that may interest the ordinary visitor, should he care for quiet and peaceful rural scenery, or the artist who may be in search of choice "bits." It does not include in its sphere a single cathedral, or castle, or abbey, at all events with extensive buildings above ground; but there are breezy heights commanding extensive views, mansions, and other buildings possessing historical associations; and we have only to mention a few names of places and persons who have been connected with it as residents, or by the accident of birth or death, in order to satisfy the reader that these five hundred and odd square miles are not devoid of interest. There are, for instance, Waltham Cross and Abbey, the latter traditionally the grave of the unhappy Harold; there is Chislehurst, with its memories of the antiquary Camden and the emperor Louis Napoleon; there are Hayes and Keston, the favourite haunts of Pitt and Wilberforce; there is Isleworth, with its monastery of Sion; Harrow, with its school and its memories of Byron's youth.   At Hounslow we shall find camps and footpads; the latter also at Finchley; at Merton we shall come upon Lord Nelson and Lady Hamilton; at Stanmore we shall visit the grave of Lord Aberdeen; at Mortlake we shall find Dr. Dee; at Elstree we shall rub shoulders with Thurtell and Hare; at "princely" Canons we shall be introduced to George Handel, and to his patron, the Duke of Chandos; at Wanstead we shall see the magnificent mansion of the Tylneys, brought to ruin, alas! by a Wellesley; at Gunnersbury, at Kew, at Brentford, at Kingsbury, at Nonsuch, at Enfield, and in Hainault Forest, royal memories will meet us; and we shall be overwhelmed by them when we come to Richmond and Sheen; Pope and Horace Walpole, Kitty Clive, Gay, Thomson, and a host of children of the Muses, will surround us at Twickenham; at Barnet we shall view the battle-field which crushed the hopes of the house of Lancaster; at Bexley we shall encounter the cavalcade of Chaucer's "Canterbury Pilgrims," whom we left at the *Tabard* in Southwark; at Barking we shall walk over the site of perhaps the earliest convent for ladies in England, full of sacred memories; at Theobalds we shall find King James, with all his wit and pedantry; at Edmonton we shall shake hands with Charles Lamb; at Croydon we shall have much to talk about in the long roll of primates who occupied the palace there till Addington became their home; at Epsom we shall see "the quality" drinking the waters, and Lord Derby and his friends inaugurating those races whose name is not only national, but world-wide; at Beddington we shall find the Carews and Sir Walter Raleigh; at Kew and Brentford we shall run up against "Farmer George" taking his morning rides; and at Kingston-on-Thames and at Hampton Court we shall reconnoitre the spots on which our Saxon kings were crowned, and our Tudor sovereigns and their courtiers walked and talked.   In each and all of these places, and a score of others, we shall try to bring our readers face to face with the great men and women who have added a light to the pages of English history, and, we doubt not, greatly to the advantage of the former, without doing harm to the latter, or calling them up from their silent graves.   In this way we shall hope to render the history of our land more full of enjoyment than heretofore, investing its heroes and heroines with the interest which attaches to personages who live and move amongst us, and have been animated by like passions with ourselves.   Our notices of them, as a rule, cannot be more than brief, but that is the necessary result of our plan, which may, indeed, be thought open to the charge of being desultory, though we hope that it will be acquitted of dulness and of malice.

With these few remarks by way of introduction or preface, we once more beg the reader to take in hand his pilgrim's staff, and to accompany us on our pleasant pilgrimage.

We ended our sketches of "Old and New London" near Chiswick Church and Turnham Green, and therefore it would seem but natural to begin again where we left off.   Accordingly, while the Scotchman—if we may believe Dr. Johnson—always travels south, and never looks behind him, we shall trudge along in a westerly direction for some days, and pursue our way leisurely up the valley of the Thames, which, at all events, will have much more to detain us now than it had in those unreckoned ages when it was an estuary of the silent sea.

CHAPTER I.

CHISWICK, TURNHAM GREEN, ACTON, STRAND-ON-THE-GREEN.

"Rus in urbe, urbs in rure."

Gradual Extension of London—Horticultural Fêtes at Chiswick—Eminent Residents at Chiswick—Royal Visits—Corney House—Fairfax House—Grove Park—Sutton Court—Turnham Green—Bedford Park—Acton Green—Professor Lindley—Acton—Its Early History—Berrymead Priory—Lady Dudley's Bequest—Acton a Stronghold of the Puritan Party—The Rev. Philip Nye—Richard Baxter and Sir Matthew Hale—Other Distinguished Residents—An Anecdote of Sir Walter Raleigh—Ancient Manors and Houses—Lord Ferrers' Coach—Clergy Orphan Schools—The Village of Acton—The Parish Church—The Registers—Charitable Bequests—A Centenarian—The Steyne—Skippon, the Parliamentary General—South Acton—Acton Wells—Acton Races—Friar's Place Farm—The Goldsmiths' Almshouses—Strand-on-the-Green.

THE gradual extension of London is sweeping away, bit by bit, much of the rural aspect of its surroundings. We have already seen in various chapters of "Old and New London" how it has affected Paddington and Bayswater, Stoke Newington and Hackney, Clapham and Camberwell. Although Chiswick still retains many of its suburban charms, still, the handiwork of the builder of recent times has already made a perceptible difference in the look of the smiling village which stood here half a century ago, before a part of the gardens of Chiswick House first became the head-quarters of the Horticultural Society, and the place began to wear a fashionable appearance during the London "season." Up to that time—for it must be remembered that there was no such a thing as railway conveyance in those days, and steamboats to Chiswick and Kew had scarcely come into existence—very few of the ordinary inhabitants of London even thought of visiting the place; but when the horticultural fêtes* were held here Chiswick achieved great popularity with the "upper ten thousand," and soon rose to be a place of popular resort.

The village, it is true, even as far back as the last century, contained many good houses, and could then, as now, boast of its "Mall" overlooking the river; and it has numbered among its residents many men whose names have become famous, such as Sir Stephen Fox, the friend of Evelyn, who occupied the Manor House; Pope, who lived for a time in Mawson's Buildings; Lord Heathfield, the defender of Gibraltar; Hogarth, Zoffany, and Loutherbourg, the painters; and Barbara, Duchess of Cleveland, who spent the last few years of her life here. The open-air entertainments given in the grounds of Chiswick House by the Duke of Devonshire formed a great attraction for the upper circles during the London "season" in days gone by. The place, too, has even had the advantage of visits from royalty, for in 1814 the Emperor Alexander I. of Russia, and the other allied sovereigns, honoured the Duke of Devonshire with their presence here, and in 1842 Her Majesty and the late Prince Consort visited His Grace at Chiswick. Two years later the duke gave here a magnificent entertainment to the Emperor (Nicholas) of Russia, the King of Saxony, and a large number of the nobility. Several of the finest trees in the grounds of Chiswick House were planted by royal hands, to commemorate the visits of the Emperor Nicholas, Queen Victoria, and other illustrious personages. More recently, the house has been tenanted by the Prince of Wales, as a nursery for his children; and, later, by Lord Bute.

As stated in the foregoing remarks, we now set out on our perambulation from the point where we parted company in our narrative of Chiswick in "Old and New London," namely, the grounds of Chiswick House and Corney House, leaving on our left the steam launch and torpedo manufactory of Messrs. Thorneycroft, which covers part of what once formed the grounds of Corney House, the residence of Lord Macartney, and where several scores of busy hands now find daily employment. At Chiswick Church we turn sharp to the right, past an old mansion, called Fairfax House, because at one time it was tenanted by that general. Here are preserved the kitchen clock and one or two other relics of Hogarth, removed from his house. On our right is the lofty stone wall which shuts out from view the duke's villa; on our left are broad and level meadows, reaching down to the silver Thames, which here makes a southward sweep. The meadows are as green as ever; no history attaches to them, and as yet they are not built upon. Of late years the sewage of Chiswick has been precipitated here, and utilised for the neighbouring market-gardens. Chiswick, evidently, is in advance of the rest of the metropolis. A little further to the north-west stands Grove House, a mansion once inhabited by titled families; it still

---

* The Horticultural Gardens here were first opened in 1818-19, for the purpose of advancing the science of gardening in this country.

BEDFORD PARK.

1. Houses in South Parade.
2. A Porch.
3. The Church.
4. The "Tabard."
5. Gable of the School of Art.
6. Houses in Bath Road.

has a fine portico, but has been docked of a storey in height, the late Duke of Devonshire not wishing to have any "grand" neighbour. The estate belongs to the duke, who has laid out Grove Park for villa residences. A church, St. Paul's, has

SIR MATTHEW HALE.

been built, and a district formed out of Grove Park and Strand-on-the-Green, of which latter place we shall have more to say presently. The edifice consists of chancel, nave, and aisles, and is in the Early Decorated style of architecture; it was erected chiefly at the expense of the ducal owner of the estate, and at a cost of about £5,000. The Grove Park estate adjoins the Chiswick station of the South-Western Railway. A road from Grove Park, called Sutton Lane, to Turnham Green, passes Sutton Court, once the residence of the lord of the manor, but now a school. Its grounds adjoin those of the Duke of Devonshire. Sutton Court was at one time the seat of the Earl of Fauconberg; the grounds attached to it had in them, two centuries ago, a very pretty maze or wilderness, somewhat after the fashion of that at Hampton Court.

A few minutes' walk brings us on to Turnham Green, which is here separated by a branch of the Metropolitan District Railway from another grassy plot to the west, called Acton Green, which leads on towards Gunnersbury.

According to Stukeley—whose word, however, must always be taken with some little reserve—the road from London to Regnum—possibly Ringwood, or Chichester—went through Turnham Green and Brentford. Of Turnham Green, and of the skirmish

of the Royalists with the Parliamentary army at the "Battle of Brentford," we have already spoken at some length;* but we may be pardoned for adding, on the authority of Whitlocke's "Memoirs," that when the Parliamentary army was here, such was the popular enthusiasm that the ladies of London sent them all sorts of supplies in the way of wine and good cheer, and even helped in throwing up the trenches. John Evelyn tells us in his "Diary" that he "came in with his horse and armes just at the retreate," but adds no further details.

Sir John Chardine's gardens, at Turnham Green, are mentioned more than once by John Evelyn as being very fine, and full of exquisite fruit. Sir John Chardine was a learned man and a great traveller, and having returned from the East with a good fortune, was made Paymaster of the Forces under Charles II.

A few years ago Turnham Green was a lonely and unlovely common, flat and dreary, and earlier still a favourite resort for footpads and highwaymen; but now it has grown more civilised, and the entire neighbourhood is putting on a more artistic look. On the west of Stamford Brook Green there has lately sprung into existence a veritable village, or rather, a little town, of "Queen Anne's" houses. These are built in small groups, or isolated, and stand in tiny patches of ground, with gardens attached, in which sun-flowers, holly-

RICHARD BAXTER.

hocks, and other old-fashioned flowers predominate. The land all around is level, and the houses

---

* See "Old and New London," Vol. VI., pp. 560–61.

suit the surroundings. The resident ladies, and even the very nursemaids and children as they stroll about, seem to have an old-fashioned cut about their dress which equally suits the houses. The church—dedicated to St. Michael, though it does not stand on an eminence—is also " pure Queen Anne," and externally, therefore, most ugly, for that style of architecture is secular, and not ecclesiastical. There are " Queen Anne " stores opposite, and a " Queen Anne " post-office, and the inn at the corner of the Common, in exactly the same style, rejoices in the sign of the *Tabard*. Why, however, it is impossible to say, as the place has no connection whatever with Chaucer or his pilgrims, and "tabards," as articles of clothing, are certainly of an older date than our last Stuart queen. Two minutes' walk from the " Tabard " is the " Club," where dramatic entertainments, balls, debates, &c., constantly take place. The architect is Mr. Norman Shaw, R.A., who also designed the church and several of the houses on the estate. The district is called Bedford Park, as having formed part of the estate of the Earls of Bedford.*

Acton Green, or Acton Back, adjoining Turnham Green and Bedford Park to the west and north-west, is said to have been the scene of the skirmish between the Royal and Parliamentarian armies (the latter under the Earl of Essex) in November, 1642. Here, in 1865, died Professor Lindley, F.R.S., the eminent botanist, for many years editor of the *Gardener's Chronicle*. Dr. Lindley was a native of Catton, in Norfolk, and was born at the end of the last century. After leaving school, he devoted himself to botanical science, and at the age of twenty published a translation of Richards's "Analyse du Fruit," which was followed closely after by another work, entitled, " Monographia Rosarum," in which he described several new species of roses. About the same time he contributed to the " Transactions of the Linnæan Society " various papers on botanical subjects. Some time afterwards he was appointed Assistant Secretary to the Horticultural Society, and was engaged by Mr. Loudoun to write the descriptive portion of his " Encyclopædia of Plants." In 1829 he was appointed Professor of Botany at the London University. Shortly after was published his " Introduction to Systematic and Physiological Botany, and a Synopsis of the British Flora," which was followed by " The Natural System of Botany " and "The Vegetable Kingdom." Dr. Lindley was most diligently employed as a practical botanist in describing new species, on which he wrote a large number of papers, contributed to botanical publica-

tions. In 1841 he became editor of the *Gardener's Chronicle*, which he conducted with great ability. In 1860 he was appointed examiner in his favourite studies in the University of London. He received the medal of the Royal Society as a reward for his services to botanical science.

Passing a little to the north-east, we arrive at Acton, a large parish, which is bounded by Hammersmith and Chiswick on the south and south-east, by Shepherd's Bush on the east, by Ealing on the west, and by Willesden on the north. As we learn from Kelly's " Post Office Directory," it is in the Kensington division of Ossulston Hundred ; it is five miles from London on the road to Uxbridge, and it has a population of about 12,000 souls. In 1871 it numbered 8,360 residents, which was nearly double of what it had contained ten years previously. In the beginning of the century we are told (in the " Beauties of England and Wales ") that the parish comprised about 2,000 acres of land, "chiefly used for farming purposes." The soil is a stiff clay to the north, and towards the south a rich loam.

The name of Acton is but slightly altered from " Oak-town," though it would seem now rather to have deserved the name of " Elm-town," for the trees which formed part of the Weald have mostly disappeared, except at Old-Oak Common, the name of which itself suggests such a change, and tells its own tale. In other parts the oak takes its turn in the hedgerows with the ash and elm. The name, however, is still appropriate enough to its northern parts, as will be seen by a walk across the fields towards Twyford Abbey, of which we shall have more to say hereafter. There is no doubt that in the Saxon times Acton was part of a large oak forest, a portion of the "weald" which stretched across Middlesex, north of London. One of the first notices of the parish is to the effect that the Bishop of London, who lived at Fulham, regarded it as pannage, or feeding for his pigs, which doubtless throve on its acorns. The Briton, the original tenant of the soil, had been driven out by the sword of the Saxon invader, and had carried with him into the far west not only his Druid worship, but such Christianity and civilisation as he had learnt from the Romans. One thing, at all events, remains to prove the reality of the Roman occupation in this part, and that is the great road which led this way to the West of England.

The Saxons were worshippers of Thor and of Woden, and their worship was chiefly carried on in the forests. Consequently, it is easy to imagine Ac-ton, the Oak Town, with its open-air temple, surrounded by low wooden huts, occupied by the priests and their attendants. Hither, perhaps, day by day came from the then distant Londinium many worshippers to offer their sacrifices in the village of the oak groves, to receive at the hands of the priests the sprinkling of the victim's blood, to feast on the pans of simmering horse-flesh, and to drink from twisted horn-cups draughts of mead or ale.

Scarcely, however, had the Saxons been weaned from this heathen worship by the great St. Augustine, when, as they had driven out the Britons, they were themselves attacked by the Danish sea rovers, and possibly the little Christian church had to witness a revival of Pagan rites. Be this as it may, the annals of Acton are a blank till after the Norman conquest, when, possibly, a Norman castle was built on its rising ground, to keep the Saxon serfs in awe and subjection. The district now known as Acton, along with Ealing,. became part of the great manor of Fulham, and was granted, or probably re-granted, to the see of London. In the parish were several lesser manors. " Peter, the son of Aluph," runs the old chronicle, " in the year 1220, gave to Geoffrey de Lucy, Dean of St. Paul's, in the City of London, his manor of twenty acres at Acton. Moreover, the dean bought three acres more from Walter de Acton, and then with the whole twenty-three acres founded a chantry in the said church of St. Paul's, for the good of his soul," the rent being, doubtless, applied to the payment of a priest to sing or say mass for him daily. The Almoner of St. Paul's has still a claim on some lands at Acton, and probably the claim has its origin in this bequest.

We next find that Henry III. (A.D. 1216-72) had here a mansion or palace, to which he often retired from the strife of tongues and from the Court, and from his turbulent nobles arrayed against him under Simon de Montfort. From this date Acton is without a history until the first inscription on a brass in the church—" Here lyeth Henry Gosse, and Alice, his wyff, 1485."

That the Reformation did not at once take full effect at Acton is clear from an inscription in the church in 1542, in which John Boid, priest, parson of Acton, begs the prayers of the faithful for the repose of his soul. Two years later a large part of Acton changed its owners, for Henry VIII. seized on one of its manors, and gave it to John, Lord Russell. It is probable that this manor consisted of the lands which had belonged to Berrymead Priory, and to another religious house which must have existed at Friar's Place. From Lord Russell these lands passed, probably by purchase, into the hands of Herbert, Earl of Worcester.

From the rolls of the reign of Edward VI., it appears that Acton contained 158 " houselyng folk," i.e., heads of families who communicated at Easter, a number which does not appear to have increased very rapidly, for in 1670 there were only 88 houses " assessed tow^{ds} the relief of maimed soldiers." In the Record Office is a return, dated August, 1552, of the church plate and other treasures, including pyxes, censers, bells, chrismatories, paxes, and painted cloths for the (Easter) sepulchre.

After the break-up of the existing state of things by Henry VIII., the village of Acton, being a pleasant suburb, became the residence of many families of the upper class. Thus we read that Lord Conway, afterwards Secretary of State to James I., had a mansion here : his widow's benefaction to the education of the poor still remains to perpetuate the name.

Berrymead Priory, on the south side of the high road at the entrance of Acton from London, was formerly the seat of the Marquis of Halifax (who died here in 1700), and afterwards of the Duke of Kingston, in whose time George II. was a frequent visitor at the house. The Priory, which is still standing, is a picturesque Gothic edifice of the Strawberry Hill type, and occupies the centre of several acres of ground, which are planted with fine trees and evergreens.

In 1640 Lady Dudley gave a carpet and some communion plate to the church of Acton ; this is still in use, and the flagon is of fine workmanship, but scarcely of ecclesiastical design. The bills for expenses incurred in bringing the plate from Lady Dudley's house are to be seen in the parish accounts. The carpet has long disappeared.

In the reign of Charles I. Acton became a busy place. It appears to have been a great stronghold of the Puritan party, and was made one of the head-quarters of Lords Essex and Warwick, at the head of the Roundhead Parliamentarian army. Accordingly, their cropped hair, high-crowned hats, and broad collars, appeared in every street and almost every house in the village. They turned out the rector, Dr. Featley, in order to accommodate Colonel Urry, one of the colleagues of Hampden and Holles, who encountered the king's troops near Brentford. Hearing that the Doctor was a " malignant," that is, a supporter of the king and of the Book of Common Prayer (styled by them " pottage "), they forced their way into the church, and tore up and burnt the rails of the communion table in order to prove their piety ; they also set fire to the rector's barn and stables. The Doctor escaped to Lambeth, but he died before the Restoration. In the register there are several entries of the burials of poor soldiers and troopers killed in various skirmishes between Acton, Brentford, and Turnham Green.

The Rev. Philip Nye, the next rector appointed by the Puritans, was a man of quite a different stamp from Dr. Featley. He was a rigid and austere Puritan, and was sent as a commissioner to the king when a prisoner in Carisbrooke Castle. He was very haughty and imperious, and wore a long beard, of which he was very proud. Hence the oft-quoted allusion in Butler's "Hudibras"—

> " With greater art and cunning reared
>   Than Philip Nye's thanksgiving beard.''

Nye did not vouchsafe to live among his own

Hampton Court. The Recorder also addressed him in terms of high compliment, and he was conducted with great pomp along the road to London. Nye had his reward, for in 1653 he was appointed one of the committee of "Triers," *i.e.*, those who tested every clergyman on his appointment as to whether he was for Calvinism, the Parliament, &c., and would follow the new "Directory" of public worship. In this post he seems to have behaved

ACTON CHURCH AND ACTON TOWN AT THE END OF LAST CENTURY.
(*From old Prints in possession of the Rector of Acton.*)

people, but kept a house in town. If we may trust a pamphlet entitled, "The Levites' Scourge," "he rode to London every Lord's day in triumph, in a coach drawn by four horses, to exercise them." It is clear, therefore, that he had no mean opinion of himself, and had not adopted the modern Sabbatarian notions.

This Nye was rector when Cromwell, after his "crowning mercy" at Worcester, was met at Acton on his way back to London, by the Mayor and Aldermen of London and a host of his Puritan admirers, and a train of more than 300 coaches. Nye doubtless delivered an address of welcome to the Lord Protector before he turned aside to

neither better nor worse than many of his colleagues.

At the Restoration in 1660 the intruder had to give place to a Royalist and loyalist. Nye was, naturally enough, ejected, and exempted from the general pardon. He spent his latter days in obscurity and retirement, nursing and displaying the beard of which he was so proud. His successor was Dr. Bruno Ryves, chaplain to the king, and Dean of Chichester. In his loyalty he erased from the registers and other parish books the titles, such as "right honourable," bestowed on Cromwell's lords and their "ladies," under-scoring their names with the words "traytor" and "knave." The tomb and monument of Philippa, wife of Rous, Provost of Eton College, and one of Cromwell's lords, may be seen thus defaced on the wall of the church; and in the register the same is done to the entry of a marriage, in April, 1655, between a Mr. Richard Meredith and Susannah, daughter of the "Right Honourable" Major-General Skippon, which was performed by a layman—"Sir" John Thorogood—Mr. Nye enlivening the occasion by a discourse, to which it is to be hoped the young people paid due attention.

But Puritanism still lived on at Acton in spirit. The snake was only "scotched," not killed. Hence, apparently, Richard Baxter came to live here on refusing to subscribe to the Act of Uniformity in 1664. His first house was opposite the old church door. Here he wrote his "Saint's Rest." Here, whilst preaching in his house, he narrowly escaped being shot by a stray Cavalier's bullet, and being denounced by a female spy, who had found her way into his conventicle as a "godly" person. During the Great Plague he left Acton, and went down into Buckinghamshire, but found his family all safe on his return. Baxter tells us that the Fire of London was a very grand and terrific sight as seen at Acton, and that the east wind carried large flakes of burning books as far afield, and farther.

We get some pleasant reminiscences of Sir Matthew Hale and Richard Baxter, as neighbours at Acton, in the Rev. R. B. Hone's "Life" of the former. He writes:—"In the year 1667 Sir Matthew Hale took up his residence at Acton, near London, and there commenced an acquaintance with Mr. Baxter, who resided in the same place, which proved agreeable to both parties, and ripened into warm friendship." Baxter himself, writing to another friend, gives us a few details of the origin of the acquaintance between the neighbours :—"We sat next each other at church many weeks, but neither did he ever speak to me, nor I to him. At last my extraordinary friend (to whom I was more beholden than I must here express), Serjeant Fountain, asked me why I did not visit the Lord Chief Baron? I told him, because I had no reason for it, being a stranger to him, and some against it, viz., that a judge, whose reputation was necessary to the ends of his office, should not be brought under Court suspicion or disgrace by his familiarity with a person whom the interest and diligence of some prelates had rendered so odious (as I knew myself to be with such), I durst not be so injurious to him. The serjeant answered—'It is not meet for him to come first to you; I know why I speak it; let me intreat you to go first to

him.' In obedience to which request, I did it, and we entered into neighbourly familiarity. I lived then in a small house, but it had a pleasant garden and back side, which the honest landlord had a desire to sell. The judge had a mind to the house, but he would not meddle with it till he got a stranger to me to come and inquire of me whether I was willing to leave it. I told him I was not only willing, but desirous ; not for my own ends, but for my landlord's sake, who must needs sell it ; and so he bought it, and lived in that poor house till his mortal sickness sent him to the place of his interment."

Baxter says elsewhere that "the house was well situated, but very small, and so far below the ordinary dwellings of men of his rank, as that divers farmers thereabouts had better; but it pleased him." The purchase was made in 1670.

Baxter did not leave Acton, but removed to another house, the Chief Baron maintaining much friendly intercourse with him, and finding his taste for metaphysical subjects of study and conversation in accordance with his own. "I will tell you" (writes Baxter to Sir Matthew's friend, a Mr. Stephens) "the matter and manner of our converse. We were oft together ; and almost all our discourse was philosophical, and especially about the nature of spirits and superior regions, and the nature, operations, and immortality of man's soul. And our dispositions and courses of thought were, in such things, so like, that I did not much cross the bent of his conference."

Baxter tells us what books Sir Matthew chiefly read :—"All new or old books on philosophy," to which he gave himself up "as eagerly as if he had been a boy at the university ;" and he defends him at needless length from the charge of being guilty of "idle speculations." The judge was slow of speech, and an excellent listener to Baxter's remarks. They talked but little on controversies, or on the then all-prevailing question of Conformity. "Once," writes Mr. Hone, "when Baxter advanced objections to the wealth and distinction assigned to the bishops, he gave no answer. He seems to have thought silence the wisest course in those heated times, and so to have trimmed his sails as not to fall out with either the king or the Parliament. He used, however, to express his regret at the spiritual neglect into which the country parishes were allowed to fall, and his wish that both Baxter and Calamy would accept bishoprics, or some high positions in the Establishment, if ever an altered state of things should come about. So far from being a High Churchman of the school of Laud, it is remarked by Baxter as singular that Sir Matthew did not bow in church at the name of Jesus, and that he would stand during the reading of the lessons. It appears, however, from Baxter's own testimony, that in essentials the two friends and neighbours were one at heart, though the former, for a time, sus-

attended the church both morning and evening. Sir Matthew Hale, it appears, approved of this proceeding. "The judge told me," says Baxter, "that he thought my course did the church much service, and would carry it so respectfully at my door that all the people might perceive his approbation."

But it is not to be wondered at that the rector regarded the plan as tending rather to schism than love; and perhaps, as he had been persecuted and plundered by the Presbyterians, he may on that account have looked with

1. HIGH STREET, ACTON.
2. THE CHURCH, FROM THE RECTORY.

pected Hale of being too much given to philosophy and doctrine, neglecting the more practical parts of Christianity. In the end, however, Baxter was fully satisfied that 'he plied practicals and contemplations in their season.'"

The house into which Baxter moved when he quitted that which Sir Matthew Hale had purchased was commodious in size, and, like the former, near to the parish church. Here he commenced a practice of assembling in it on Sundays some of the inhabitants of Acton, and of preaching to them between the services, always taking care, however, that they

a less favourable eye on Baxter's doings. Be that as it may, he procured the issuing of a warrant for Baxter's apprehension, and the judge gave him no "counsel," though he showed his sorrow by tears— "the only time," adds Baxter, "that I saw him weep." Baxter was committed to prison for six months; but, by the advice of his friend Serjeant Fountain, he moved for his release, and then "I found," he says, "that the character which Judge

Hale had given of me stood me in some stead, and every one of the four judges did not only acquit me, but said more for me than my counsel." But this imprisonment, he afterwards relates, " brought me the great loss of converse with Judge Hale, for the Parliament in the next Act against conventicles put into it divers clauses suited to my case, by which I was obliged to go dwell in another county, and to forsake both London and my former habitation, and yet the justices of another county were partly enabled to pursue me." With this ends the

physician to Charles II.; and Charles Fox, who gave a house and ground on the Steyne, on the north of the church, as a site for the almshouses still existing there.

Besides those already noticed, Acton can show a good list of names of people more or less celebrated in their day. Philip Thicknesse, the eccentric author of "Memoirs and Anecdotes," "The New Prose Bath Guide," &c. who died in 1792, lived here. The Countess of Derwentwater was living in the large house

BERRYMEAD PRIORY. (*See p.* 9.)

connection of Baxter with Acton and Sir Matthew Hale.

From this time the local history of Acton is little more than a list of distinguished persons who have been resident within its bounds. Notably, Lord Chief-Justice Vaughan, who died here in 1673; and, soon afterwards, Lloyd, Bishop of St. Asaph, one of the seven bishops who were tried in Westminster Hall for refusing to accept King James's "Indulgence in Matters of Religion"; Sir Charles Scarborough,

opposite the church at the time of her husband's execution for his share in the abortive Scottish rising in 1715. It is said that the iron gates at the end of the garden have never been opened since the day when her lord last passed through them on his way to the Tower. Alderman and Lord Mayor Gascoigne lived at Acton; so did Mrs. Barry, an actress under Sir William Davenant at the theatre in Lincoln's Inn Fields, who gained some celebrity in her day as excelling in the part of *Roxana*. Her last appearance was in "Love for Love," performed for Betterton's benefit, when she spoke the epilogue (1709). She died in 1713. In 1700 William, Marquis of Halifax, died at the Priory, which then passed into the hands of the Duke of Kingston, whose crest is still to be seen in one of the rooms. He was often visited here by George II. and his Court. Quite in our own day, the Priory was tenanted by Sir Edward Bulwer Lytton, who wrote within it one at least of his many works. Whether the notorious Judge Jeffreys ever lived at Acton is not quite certain; but at all events, Pennant tells us that he saw at Acton House an original portrait of that Judge, taken in 1690, when he was 82 years of age.

Acton may be said to have been in some way connected with Sir Walter Raleigh and tobacco. Aubrey implies that on its first introduction tobacco was regarded as a forbidden thing. He writes:— "Sir Walter Raleigh, standing in a stand at Sir R. Poyntz's park at Acton, took a pipe of tobacco, which made the ladies quit it till he had done." "Within these few years," he adds, "it was scandalous for a divine to take tobacco."

It is stated in the MS. additions to Norden's "Speculum Britanniæ" that King Henry III. had a mansion-house, and lay often at Acton. But no traces of its site are known, and the tradition is not confirmed. Still, Acton in its time has possessed a good many old mansions, though these are gradually passing away. Mr. Brewer tells us, in the "Beauties of England and Wales," that at the beginning of the present century there were "vestiges of several moated houses" here; but some have disappeared. Lysons writes in 1795:—"About half a mile to the north, in a field still called the 'Moated Meadow,' is a deep trench, enclosing a parallelogram about 100 yards in length and 40 in breadth, supposed by some to have been a Roman camp, but the name of the meadow seems to imply no greater antiquity than that of a moated farm-house or grange."

Near the Great Western Railway Station is an old moated house, with part of the moat remaining, called Friar's Place Farm. Another house, hard by, is said to have once had Oliver Cromwell for its occupant for a time, but the tradition cannot be verified.

In the parish of Acton there are two manors, one of which has belonged from time immemorial (as already stated) to the see of London, the other once belonged to the Dean and Chapter of St. Paul's, but was seized upon by Henry VIII., who alienated it. It has passed through various families: the Russells, Somersets, Lethuelliers, Fetherstonhaughs, &c.

One day in 1760 Acton was astonished by the arrival of a coach and six—it was the same in which Lord Ferrers had driven to be executed at Tyburn, and he had ordered it to be sent onward. The carriage was kept in a shed at Acton till it literally fell to pieces.

In 1749 the new Clergy Orphan Schools, since removed to St. John's Wood, were erected here.

The High Street, nearly half a mile in length, is quaint and irregular, large and small houses being strangely intermixed. Many of the old red tiles remain on the roofs. New streets have sprung up between the railway station and the town; these are irregularly built, and in many of them trees are planted. Altogether, from the quiet, out-of-the-way village of half a century ago, Acton has now become a very populous place, owing to the building of villas, consequent on the opening of the railways. It now possesses two or three churches; it has Congregational, Baptist, Wesleyan, and other chapels, a lecture hall, and also its Local Board of Health, public library, and reading-room.

"At the entrance of the village from London," writes Mr. Brewer in 1815, "is a public conduit, built by Thomas Thorney in 1612, and maintained by a small endowment left by him for repairs. Its use having been perverted, the right to its use was recovered in the last century by a lawsuit, and it has been superseded by a modern pump, erected by a Mr. Antrobus in 1819." The pump is now chained up and walled in, a notice being added that "the water is not fit for drinking purposes," probably in consequence of the opening of a new cemetery in its rear. Why does no charitable person revive the Acton pump, in the shape of a metropolitan drinking fountain, obtaining a supply from a fresh source?

The parish church, dedicated to St. Mary, as usual marks the centre of the original village, for cottages always sprang up round the manor-house and the house of prayer which was its adjunct. Brewer describes it in his day as of little interest—rebuilt of brick in a homely manner. The present edifice is built of red brick, with stone dressings. In 1766 the church tower was re-cased with brick; the oldest of the bells has the date 1583, the last was hung in 1810. In 1837 the church was enlarged, and became, in the opinion of Bishop Blomfield, the ugliest in the diocese. In 1865 the nave, chancel, &c., were pulled down, and a handsome Decorated building erected in its place, the old tower, which had been "new cased with brick" in 1766, being suffered to remain. This, however, was pulled down in 1877, and an elegant new tower erected in its place, as a memorial to two members of the Ouvry family. The bells were re-cast at the same time. It will be seen, therefore, that there have been three churches in succession since Her Majesty's accession; for the very plain structure of the last century was pulled down in 1838, and rebuilt in a still more hideous style, and that was pulled down in 1865, when the present handsome structure was built. It consists of a nave, chancel, and aisles, and many of its windows are already filled with stained glass.

The registers commence in 1539. Skippon's titles have been scratched out in the register, and over the name of Sir John Thorogood, who officiated at the marriage of Skippon's daughter, is written the word "knave," the word "traytor" being also twice written over the Major-General's name. Cromwell created Skippon a peer, but it is only fair to add that he refused to sit as one of the king's judges. The Protectorate titles, too, have been obliterated from the registers of "Lord" and "Lady" Rous. The former was buried at Eton College. In spite of being an author, Rous is mentioned by Lord Clarendon as "a person of very mean understanding"; and A'Wood tells us, in his "Athenæ Oxoniensis," that he was called "the illiterate Jew of Eton." His foundation of three fellowships at Pembroke College, Oxford, is perhaps his best memorial. Rous's house was styled in 1795 "The Bank House."

Bruno Ryves, who was appointed vicar by Charles II., was a contributor to our national history. He deserves to be remembered as the author of the "Mercurius Rusticus," a narrative of the sufferings of the Royalists in different parts of England.

Lady Dudley, whom we have mentioned in our account of St. Giles's-in-the-Fields* was a great benefactor to the parish and church, to which she gave (as stated above) a carpet and the communion plate.

The ancient font is now all that remains of the original church. All the ancient monuments have been carefully preserved, though those in the interior of the building have been mostly removed to the west end and to the entrance under the tower. Among them is one to Anne, Lady Southwell. On each side of this monument hangs a wooden tablet inscribed with panegyric verses, in the quaint and conceited style of the period (1636) :—

"The *South* wind blew upon a springing *well*,
Whose waters flowed, and the sweet stream did swell
To such a height of goodness, that," &c.

There are also monuments to Catharine, Lady Conway, who was a great benefactor to the parish; to Mrs. Elizabeth Barry, the actress already mentioned in connection with Betterton and Lincoln's Inn Theatre; and to Mr. Robert Adair, inspector-general of hospitals, and his wife, Lady Caroline Adair, daughter of the Earl of Albemarle. Inside the communion rails was a

* See "Old and New London," Vol. III., p. 198.

small brass commemorating John Byrde, who died in 1542, having been fifty-three years vicar of Acton.

Among the charitable bequests is that of a Mr. Edward Dickinson, who left a third part of the interest of £5,000 to be distributed annually among three poor and industrious couples who had been married at Acton in the preceding year. It is satisfactory to the statistician to learn that this charity has never lapsed for want of claimants.

Lady Conway's dole of bread, and loaves left by other charitable persons, are still disbursed on Sundays after service, at the west end of the nave, where they are set out in a row, between two gilt figures of wheatsheaves.

It is to be presumed that Acton is a healthy parish; at all events, it can boast it had at least one "veritable centenarian" among its residents. In the churchyard is buried William Aldridge, wheelwright, who died in 1698, in the 115th year of his age. A portrait of him when aged 112 may be seen in Lysons' "Environs," and a copy of it hangs in the vestry. Other centenarians' names appear in the register.

The living is a good one in point of emolument, and is still in the gift of the Bishop of London. The rectory house, a solid and substantial building north of the church, was built about 1725. The then rector, Mr. Hall, died soon after, and his successor, the witty Dr. Cobden, recorded the fact in some Latin lines, which he scratched with a diamond on a window-pane.

To the north of the church is a nearly square piece of ground, about two or three acres, called the Steyne. It appears as if it had been a village green, and to have been dug out for gravel, or, if that is not so, then terraces have been raised round two sides of it. It is covered with modern cottages, and fringed with some almshouses and schools.

Near the churchyard stood a house built by Sir Henry Garway in 1638, and which was, for a time, the residence of Skippon, the Parliamentary general mentioned above. It was afterwards used as a convent by the ladies of a religious order, who fled from the Continent during the first French Revolution. It was pulled down early in the present century. Its successor is now called Derwentwater House; it is probable that Sir Matthew Hale was tenant here.

South Acton has been cut off, and formed into a new ecclesiastical district, and a new church, of florid Gothic style, and built of red brick, was consecrated in 1872. It is dedicated to All Saints, and consists of chancel, nave, aisles, tower, and a lofty spire. One part of South Acton, having been largely occupied by artisans' dwellings, is now known as Mill Hill, after a windmill which once stood on it; it has its own church, chapel, and schools, and bids fair ere long to become a separate ecclesiastical district.

We must now make a slight detour of a mile eastwards to visit Acton Wells, before we take up our pilgrim's staff *en route* for Ealing. We are, however, rudely woke up from any dreams of the beauty and fashion of the reign of the Georges by finding ourselves within a "measurable distance" of the new military prison erected on Wormwood Scrubs, and soon after reach the line of the Great Western Railway. A "spa" which was discovered here in the early part of the last century became very fashionable as a place of resort about the year 1750, and its waters are mentioned along with those of Hampstead, Cheltenham, Bath, &c., as "on sale at Mr. Owen's original mineral water warehouse in Fleet Street." There were, in fact, three wells of mineral water here, which once possessed a fashionable name, and attracted to the neighbourhood many of the sick and gay. In Lysons' "Environs" we find a minute description of the waters, which were saline, and "supposed to be more strongly cathartic than any other in the kingdom of the same quality, except those of Cheltenham."

We have already seen at Hampstead * the transitory nature of the celebrity obtained by medicinal springs. "Acton," writes Mr. Brewer, "had its share in the day of fashion. An assembly-room was built, and for a few years East Acton and Friar's Place, a small adjacent hamlet, were thronged with valetudinarian and idle inmates, allured by the hope of remedy or tempted by the love of dissipation. Both classes have long " (he writes in 1815) "abandoned the spot; and the assembly-room has for many years been converted into a private dwelling." Dr. Macpherson says that these wells were popular from the year 1750 down to about 1790, and that races were run for the amusement of the company. The discovery of these medicinal waters, and the consequent resort of people to drink them, caused many pleasant houses with gardens to spring up around Friar's, or Prior's, Place, so called from having once belonged to the Prior of St. Bartholomew at Smithfield. The "season" here was in the summer. The wells went to decay before the end of the last century, but their site is still to be made out in the kitchen garden of a farmhouse near the Great Western Railway, and close to "Old Oak Common." How few of those who travel by the Great Western Railway at this point are aware that they are passing

over one of the fashionable resorts of the reign of George III. No print of the wells here is known to exist, and the place seems to have escaped notice in the comedies and satires of the day. Here is now a stud-farm, close to the old place where fashionable dames disported themselves. Not far off here, the "People's Garden," a place of Sunday amusement for the middle classes, was opened under German auspices in 1870. It is said to have the largest dancing platform in the country, but it never attracted any of the upper classes.

Between West and East Acton, on the north side of the London Road, are the Goldsmiths' Alms-houses for ten poor men and ten poor women, who receive each a pension and an allowance for coals. They were founded in 1656–7 by John Perryn, of East Acton, and the houses were rebuilt in 1811 or 1812, at the cost of £12,000. They form three sides of a quadrangle. In 1878 a church and parsonage-house were built by the Goldsmiths' Company on their estate in the rear of their almshouses.

In spite of its chalybeate attractions, East Acton is described in the "Beauties of England and Wales" (1815) simply as "a small hamlet or assemblage of houses to the north of the London road."

Leaving Acton, and retracing our steps for a mile southwards across Acton Green to Grove Park, already mentioned, we find ourselves at a quaint little old-fashioned waterside settlement, known as Strand-on-the-Green. It is almost wholly inhabited by fishermen, but partly occupied by malt-houses and hostelries. The place is as little changed as any spot within ten miles of London. Its low small mansions and red-bricked river-side cottages form a picturesque scene.

Down to the early part of the last century the hamlet of Strand-on-the-Green was inhabited almost wholly by fishermen, or by men whose daily avocations were carried on by the river-side. On the springing up of some better class of houses, however, the place for a time became more popular, and numbered among its residents one or two individuals whose names have become famous. Here, for instance, dwelt David Mallet, the poet; his first wife, who died in 1742, is buried in the churchyard of Chiswick. Here, too, lived for many years the facetious Joe Miller, whose tombstone is in King's College Hospital. He died here in August, 1738. Zoffany, the painter, lived at Strand-on-the-Green, and several of his fishermen neighbours sat as models for his pictures; he died here on the 11th of November, 1810, and his remains were interred in the neighbouring churchyard of Kew, on the

---

* See "Old and New London,' Vol. V., p. 468.

other side of the Thames. The house which Zoffany inhabited is still shown. It faced the river, in about the middle of the little terrace. We shall hear of him again at Brentford.

Some almshouses were built at Strand-on-the-Green in 1725, but they have been demolished.

The Kensington branch of the South-Western Railway here crosses the Thames by a handsome latticed iron bridge, which was built in 1869.

Opposite Strand-on-the-Green is an ait, or eyot, used by the Thames Conservancy Board for manufacturing and repairing purposes, and this forms a pleasing foreground to the river-side view of Kew Bridge from the east.

CHAPTER II.

GUNNERSBURY, EALING, AND HANWELL.

"Regumque palatia villis
Interfusa nitent."

Gunnersbury—Descent of the Manor—The Princess Amelia a Resident here—Horace Walpole a frequent Guest—The Property bought by the Rothschilds—The Gardens and Grounds—Gunnersbury House—Ealing—Extent and Nature of the Soil—The Manor—The Parish Church—Sir John Maynard—John Horne Tooke—John Oldmixon—Christ Church—St. John's Church—Seats and Mansions—Dr. John Owen—-Dr William King and other Eminent Residents—Ford Hall—Castle Bar Hill—Princess Helena College—The Old Cross House—The Town Hall—Ealing Great School—Ealing Common—Mrs. Lawrence's Gardens—Fordhook House, and Henry Fielding the Novelist—The "Old Hat" Tavern—Hanwell—The Grand Junction Canal—The Parish Church—Jonas Hanway—The Town of Hanwell—The Central London District Schools—Charitable Institutions—Hanwell Lunatic Asylum—The Cemeteries—Electric Telegraphy in its Infancy.

HAVING arrived at the foot of Kew Bridge, where the loop-line of the South Western Railway converges with that of the North London, we will step aside from our westward path, and retracing our way for a few yards towards West Acton, we will pass up a lane to the left, which takes us to Gunnersbury Park, in the parish of Ealing, though on the borders of Turnham Green. A century ago it was the residence of the Princess Amelia, daughter of George II., and aunt to George III. Here, while the young king lived at Kew, she gave fashionable parties to the be-wigged gentlemen and be-hooped ladies of "quality," and, indeed, kept up a sort of rival Court. She seems to have entertained very generously and hospitably, and to have been very popular with her friends, and at one time to have exercised some personal influence with members of the Cabinet. But sometimes her good-nature led her to do foolish things. For instance, Lord Brougham tells us, in his "Lives of Statesmen," that when Lord Bute had fallen from the favour of the king, the princess invited him and her nephew, the king, on the same afternoon, and caused them—quite accidentally, of course—to meet in one of the shady walks of her garden. Her stratagem, however, did not succeed; and the king was so offended and angry at the liberty which she had taken, that he desired such a trick might never be played on him again. "His word was law," even with his aunt; and the ruse was never repeated. It is dangerous to trifle with kings.

Gunnersbury stands on ground which may be called high in comparison with the flat market gardens which lie between it and the Bath road. The name of Gunnersbury is probably derived from Gunilda, or Gunylda, the niece of King Canute, who resided here. It was a manor in the parish of Ealing, but its manorial rights have largely fallen into neglect and disuse. Little is known of its descent; but in the fifteenth century it belonged to Sir Thomas Frowick, an Alderman of London, and father of Sir Thomas Frowick, Lord Chief Justice of the Common Pleas. The property was afterwards held by the knightly family of the Spelmans, and in the middle of the seventeenth century it passed by purchase into the hands of Sir John Maynard, who was an eminent lawyer under the Stuart kings, and who died here in 1690. Gunnersbury remained for many years in the occupation of his widow, who married Henry, Earl of Suffolk. On the death of the Countess Dowager, in 1721, the estate became the property of Sir John (afterwards Lord) Hobart, by whom it was ultimately sold to a Mr. Furnese. The place figures constantly in Bubb Dodington's "Diary," 1749-50.

On the accession of George III., in 1760, the estate was purchased for the Princess Amelia. Horace Walpole was one of the most frequent guests at her parties. He writes to his friend, Sir Horace Mann, in 1761, saying that he has been there once or twice a week ever since the late king's death; and a month later again he writes to Mr. Conway:—

"I was sent for again to dine at Gunnersbury on Friday, and was forced to send to town for a dress coat and a sword. There were the Prince

GUNNERSBURY HOUSE.
(From a Water-colour Drawing by Chatelain).

of Wales, the Prince of Mecklenburgh, the Duke of Portland, Lord Clanbrassill, Lord and Lady Clermont, Lord and Lady Southampton, Lord Pelham, and Mrs. Howe. The Prince of Mecklenburgh went back to Windsor after coffee, and the Prince and Lord and Lady Clermont to town after tea, to hear some new French plays at Lady William Gordon's. The Princess, Lady Barrymore, and the rest of us, played three posts at commerce till ten. I am afraid that I was tired, and gaped. While we were at the Dairy, the Princess insisted on my making some verses on Gunnersbury. I pleaded being superannuated, but she would not excuse me. I promised she should have an ode on her next birthday, which diverted the Prince; but all would not do."

The verses here referred to are printed in H. Walpole's "Letters," Vol. IX., p. 55, but they are scarcely worth repeating here.

In the last century Gunnersbury was a sort of rival of Strawberry Hill, as may be inferred from the song—

> "Some cry up Gunnersbury,
>   For Syon some declare;
> Some say with Chiswick's Villa
>   None other can compare."

The Princess Amelia died in 1786, and soon after that the mansion was pulled down, and the land sold. A Mr. Copland, who bought the lion's share, built a new house on the higher part of the grounds, and this still stands as a puny rival of the present mansion, which is in the Italian style.

It was bought about the middle of the present century by the Rothschilds, and is now owned by Sir Nathaniel Rothschild. It contains several fine paintings and statues, and a fine collection of china. The pictures in the principal rooms are chiefly portraits of the family and their friends. In the billiard-room there is one painting of historic interest—the introduction of the late Baron Lionel Rothschild into the House of Commons, on his first being allowed to take his seat for London, in 1858. He is walking up the centre of the House between his sponsors, Lord John Russell and Captain Bernal Osborne; and among the occupants of the front benches on either side are Lord Palmerston, Mr. Disraeli, Mr. Gladstone, Sir G. Cornewall Lewis, Lord Stanley, and other celebrities of the time.

The gardens and grounds are laid out with great taste; the latter extend to nearly a hundred acres,

EALING CHURCHES.

1. ST. JOHN S.   2. ST. MARY'S (THE PARISH CHURCH).   3. CHRIST CHURCH.

But the house is scarcely visible from any spot outside, owing to a lofty stone wall which surrounds the estate.

Of the house, as it was when occupied by the Princess Amelia, there is a scarce print by Evans, published in 1787. It was built by Webb, a son-in-law of Inigo Jones, and would seem to have been a plain, square, solid edifice, in the Classical or Italian style, of three storeys, and without wings. It is represented as embosomed in trees, and having a small lake or pond in front.

The windows in the centre of the first floor are different in shape, but the house is substantially the same as it was a century ago. The straight piece of water or canal is now altered into a serpentine form, and is called the Horseshoe Pond. There are other pieces of water in the grounds, which are made to curve in such a manner as to give an idea of greater extent than they possess. The cedars and other evergreens are very fine. Some of the summer-houses in the grounds, especially one called the Temple, bear the marks of Inigo Jones's design.

The vineries, hothouses, &c., are very extensive and most productive, and admirably arranged; and in the fernery are two gigantic trees of the fern kind, which were brought from Tasmania by Sir Charles Du Cane, and sent hither as a present.

Ealing—or, as it was sometimes written, Zealing, Yealing, and Yeling—lies on the high road to Uxbridge, and is about six and a half miles from the Marble Arch by road, and five and a half from Paddington by railway. It has two stations on the Great Western Railway, one in the "Broadway," and the other at Ealing Dean—known as Castle Hill. Ealing is also the terminus of the Metropolitan District Extension Railway, and the parish will soon be connected with other parts of London by a branch of the South Western line. The parish is bounded by New Brentford, Acton, and Chiswick on the south and east, by Greenford, Perivale, and Twyford on the north, and by Hanwell on the west. It extends from the river Brent in the valley north of Castlebar Hill almost to the Thames. Old Brentford is part of the ancient parish of Ealing; but now, with New Brentford (originally part of Hanwell), it forms a distinct township, and will accordingly be more conveniently dealt with hereafter.

The name of Ealing does not occur in the Domesday Book, so that apparently it had not become strictly parochial at that date. According to Lysons, it contains about 3,100 acres, about half of which in his time were grass lands, and about 1,220 arable, the rest being occupied by market gardens or left waste. The manor of Ealing has belonged to the see of London from the earliest times, and its history before the sixteenth century is a blank.

At the end of the reign of Henry VIII., or at the beginning of that of Edward VI., Bishop Bonner leased the Manor of Ealing-Bury to the Protector Duke of Somerset, after whose attainder, however, the lands passed to the Crown. The Manor, having passed through several intermediate hands, came into the hands of the Penruddockes, and in the eighteenth century to the Longs. In a survey taken about the time of the Restoration, it is described as "ruinated and lying open since the plundering thereof in the beginning of the last troubles," but the precise date and the extent of this "ruination" are unknown.

The chief manor still belongs to the see of London. It contains three subordinate manors, those of Gunnersbury, Coldhawe, and Pitshanger, the descents of which, though recorded by Lysons, have nothing of interest for our readers.

The parish church is dedicated to St. Mary. Robert, Bishop of London in the reign of Henry I., gave the tithes of Ealing to augment the salary of an officer of the church of St. Paul's, called the "Master of the Schools," and a part of them was subsequently settled on the Chancellor of St. Paul's, and on the Dean and Chapter, for the repairs of the cathedral. The living is now in the gift of the Bishop of London.

Robert Cooper, vicar in the reign of Charles I., was ejected by the Puritans during their ascendency, but reinstated at the Restoration, which, however, he survived only a few months. His successor was the learned Dr. William Beveridge, afterwards Bishop of St. Asaph. His portrait is in the vestry room.

The old church having begun to sink in 1729, a new one was built under an Act of Parliament, aided by a "brief," but it was not completed for ten years. It was almost entirely rebuilt, and considerably enlarged, between the years 1866 and 1872. The building is constructed of brick, and consists of a nave and chancel, organ chamber, ambulatories, and a square tower. The style of architecture is Romanesque, and the reredos is a striking feature of the interior.

The church is basilican in appearance, both outside and within; and its fine roof and handsome, new-painted windows are much admired. A baptistery stands where one would naturally look for a south transept. The monuments from the walls of the former structure are mostly collected in recesses at the west end.

At the entrance to the chancel is a mural tablet to "John Bowman, Batchelour of Divinitie and Chancellour of St. Pawle's, parson of this parish," with the date 1629. Another tablet in the chancel of "Jacobean" workmanship, and adorned with a grim death's head and cross-bones over an hour-glass, records a Mr. Richard Taverner, who died in 1638. On the north wall of the chancel, near the vestry door, is a rather fine brass to the memory of Richard Agmondesham (who is described as "Merchant of the Stapel of Calais"), his wife and children, of the date of Henry VII.

Here, too, lies buried Sir John Maynard, the eminent lawyer, who took the leading part in the prosecution of Strafford and Laud. He died at Gunnersbury not long after the Restoration of 1690. King William, noticing his great age when he came to court, observed that he must have out-lived nearly all the men of the law who had been his contemporaries; he wittily replied, "Yes, sir; and if your highness had not come over here, I should have survived even the law itself."

Here, in 1812, was buried John Horne Tooke, who died at Wimbledon, and desired to be interred there, but his wish was not carried out. Sir Francis Burdett and other politicians of the "advanced" school followed him to the grave. His tomb is a railed slab just in front of the south porch. It bears simply his name and the dates of his birth and death, 1736—1812, with the brief addition, "contented and grateful." There are many monuments to persons connected with the parish: one of them commemorates the wife of Mr. Serjeant Maynard, mentioned above.

In the old churchyard is buried John Oldmixon, the political writer of the last century, and the author of a "History of England" and of "The British Empire in America." He died in the year 1742. He is thus satirised by Pope in the "Dunciad," Book ii. :—

> "In naked majesty Oldmixon stands,
> And, Milo-like, surveys his arms and hands."

The old churchyard has long been closed for interments, and a parish burial-ground between Ealing and Brentford has been in use for many years. Sir William Lawrence, the eminent surgeon, who died in 1867, is also interred here.

Whereas half a century ago there was one church in Ealing, there are now four permanent churches, besides two iron chapels, which hereafter will doubtless blossom into churches.

Christ Church, which is situated in the Broadway, on the Uxbridge Road, was built in the year 1852, at a cost of about £10,000. It is in the "Geometrical Decorated" style of architecture, and was erected from the designs of the late Sir Gilbert Scott. Some of the windows are filled with stained glass.

St. John's Church, in Ealing Dean, was built in 1876. It is a brick structure, relieved with stone and terra-cotta dressings, and in the Early English style of architecture. St. Stephen's Church, near Castle Hill, is a stone building of Gothic architecture, and was erected in 1875.

There is a Wesleyan chapel at Ealing, with a somewhat striking pointed spire; and there are also chapels for the Congregationalists, Baptists, and Primitive Methodists. There is also a Presbyterian church.

The parish of Ealing in former days contained some fine gentlemen's seats, some of which are still standing. Among them may be mentioned Ealing House, once the abode of Sir James Montagu, Baron of the Exchequer, and afterwards of Nathaniel Oldham, the *virtuoso* and collector of paintings, of William Melmoth, the author of "A Religious Life" and the translator of Cicero and Pliny, and of Alderman Slingsby Bethell, Lord Mayor of London; and Ealing Grove, the seat successively of the Earl of Rochford and the Dukes of Marlborough and Argyll. At Place House, in Little Ealing, lived Sir Francis Dashwood, Sir Richard Littleton, Lord Brooke, and Lord Robert Manners. General Dumouriez also lived at Little Ealing, an outlying cluster of houses between Great Ealing and Brentford.

Amongst other residents of Ealing was Dr. John Owen, whom Lysons styles "the most voluminous and temperate among the Dissenters of the seventeenth century." Though a divine, he was returned as M.P. by the University of Oxford, and was both Dean of Christ Church and Vice Chancellor during Cromwell's usurpation. He died at Ealing in 1683. Wood mentions him in his "Athenæ Oxonienses" as affecting the layman, in spite of his high position at Oxford. "Instead of being a grave example, he scorned all formality, undervalued his office by going in *querpo* like a young scholar, with powdered hair, snake-bone bandstrings with very large tassels, lawn band, a large set of ribands pointed at his knees, and Spanish leather boots with lawn tops, and his hat mostly cocked."

Another resident of Ealing was Dr. William King, author of "Recollections," and editor of South's Sermons.

Zachary Pearce, Bishop of Rochester, was brought up at Ealing. Charles Dibdin wrote many of his best sea songs at his house in Hanger Lane.

Ford Hall, in this parish, was formerly the seat

of Sir Alexander Denton, a judge of the Common Pleas.

At his residence at Hanger Vale, in this parish, died at an advanced age, in October, 1863, Mr. John Bowyer Nichols, F.S.A., well known as an antiquary and a printer, and as the editor and proprietor of *The Gentleman's Magazine*. Mr. Nichols was the last surviving son of Mr. John Nichols, F.S.A., the historian of Leicestershire, and literary biographer of the eighteenth century, the disciple and successor of William Bowyer, the learned printer, and one of the friends of Samuel Johnson in his last days   The Duke of Kent lived many years at Castle Bar Park. The House was pulled down shortly after his death, which took place in 1820.

The great Lord Heathfield, the hero of Gibraltar, lived on Castle Bar Hill as General Eliott. At Castle Bar Hill is the College of the Society for Training Teachers of the Deaf, and for the diffusion of the " German " system in the United Kingdom. The students of the institution here are taught the art of teaching the deaf.

The Princess Helena College at Ealing was originally located near the Regent's Park, but in 1881–2 the new building here was erected and opened. It was founded for the purpose of a training school for governesses, and for educating the orphan daughters of officers of the Army and Navy, and of members of the Civil Service and clergymen. The work of this institution, which was formerly known as the Adult Orphan Institution, has been carried on in a quiet and unostentatious way ; but the good results which it has achieved have been extensive and lasting. It has throughout its history been specially patronised by the royal family. It was founded in memory of Princess Charlotte, was warmly encouraged by Queen Charlotte, and for many years Princess Augusta was its president. Since about 1876 her Royal Highness the Princess Helena (Princess Christian), whose name the institution now bears, has held the office of president, and has taken a strong personal interest in its welfare. It has been the aim of this institution not only to impart to the pupils at the college a sound education, but also to develop the mental and moral character which is so essential in a teacher ; and to this laudable object the comparatively small size to which the institution has been confined has materially contributed. The college provides instruction for about thirty foundationers or scholars, with about the same number of paying boarders ; and the college is so designed that the class-rooms, &c., can be enlarged as the demand for greater accommodation may

arise. In connection with it is a high school for girls.

The oldest part of the village is grouped quaintly and pleasingly round the church, in a most irregular fashion. On the north side the street opens out very broad, and here probably once stood a village cross. At all events, a tablet at the entrance of the churchyard informs us that the vestry hall (since re-constructed) was " built in 1840 out of the proceeds of the sale of the old Cross House."

This Cross House stood on the west side of the street, facing the tower of the parish church, adjoining the old workhouse and other parochial tenements. The house may have taken its name from a village cross in the street adjoining, or from standing near the place where four cross-roads met ; and it may possibly once have been the residence of the parson.

There was no Town Hall when Lysons wrote his History in 1790, but a large building was erected in 1877 for the use of the Local Board for Ealing, and comprises the requisite offices for such a body.

In the main street, on the west side, is a large private school, often called Ealing Great School, which enjoyed in the last generation a high reputation under Dr. Nicholas. It is now modernised into a large and lofty Italian villa. Not many private educational establishments can show a longer or more worthy roll of scholars than could its former master, Dr. Nicholas, who here educated as boys Sir Henry Lawrence and his brother Lord Lawrence, Bishop Selwyn, Charles Knight, Sir Henry Rawlinson, William Makepeace Thackeray (before he was sent to the Charterhouse), and last, not least, Cardinal Newman, who mentions it in his " Apologia." Charles Knight, in the first chapter of his " Passages of a Working Life," speaks tenderly and lovingly of this school :— " My school-life was a real happiness. My nature bourgeoned under kindness, and I received unusual favours from one of the masters, Mr. Joseph Heath, of St. John's College, Oxford." He gratefully records the fact that this gentleman introduced him to Mr. (afterwards Sir) Henry Ellis, of the British Museum, from whom he derived his earliest antiquarian and historical tastes. It is stated that Dr. Nicholas's school was the largest private school in England ; if so, it probably owed some of its numbers to the attack made by Cowper on our public schools in his " Tirocinium." The unfortunate Dr. Dodd also kept a school at the Manor House, since called Goodenough House. He was taken prisoner here, and carried off hence to Newgate to be tried for forgery. Here, too, a school was established by the late Lady Byron in 1833.

Ealing is well off, if not for parks, at all events for open spaces. Besides the green and the commons, there are what are called the "Lammas lands," part of which were bought in 1881 to be devoted to the purposes of recreation for the inhabitants of the village.

Ealing Common lies to the east of the village, between Ealing and Acton. It is now being planted round the edges and made level, in order to fit it for a recreation-ground. The house with walled grounds at the south-west corner of the Common, formerly the residence of the Right Hon. Spencer Perceval, is now a Lunatic Asylum for Indian soldiers. It was at one time called Hickes-on-the-Heath, and afterwards Elm Grove, and was successively inhabited by Sir William Trumbull, the friend of Pope, and by Dr. Egerton, Bishop of Durham.

Some meadow land in the vicinity of the village has also been, since 1865, occasionally used as a race-course; but the races which have taken place here have never achieved the celebrity of those at Hampton or Sandown, and other suburban spots where such sports and pastimes have become popular; indeed, they have been generally voted more of a nuisance than otherwise by the inhabitants of this parish.

Near this part of the village was a small nursery of the Horticultural Society of London, before they obtained a lease of the grounds at Chiswick, as already described by us.*

Much of the land in the neighbourhood of Ealing is cultivated as market gardens. Mrs. Lawrence's gardens at Ealing Park have in past times enjoyed such a world-wide reputation, that we must not omit to make mention of them here. They were constantly frequented during the summer season by all the rank and fashion of the metropolis, and formed a counter attraction to Chiswick.

One of the most interesting houses in the parish of Ealing is a building in the Uxbridge Road, standing in its own grounds, and embowered in trees; it is called Fordhook House, and is now the residence of Captain Tyrrell. It was once the residence of Henry Fielding, the novelist, who here wrote "Tom Jones" and "Amelia;" but has largely grown in size since it was the small cottage inhabited by Fielding, who has told us with what regret he left it when he went abroad—to die at Lisbon. The opening passage in the journal of his journey has often been quoted, but it is too pathetic not to bear repetition. Under date of

Wednesday, June 26, 1754, he writes :—"On this day, the most melancholy sun I had ever beheld arose, and found me awake at my house at Fordhook. By the light of this sun I was, in my own opinion, last to behold and take leave of some of those creatures on whom I doated with a mother-like fondness, guided by nature and passion, and uncured and unhardened by all the doctrine of that philosophical school where I had learned to bear pains and to despise death. In this situation, as I could not conquer nature, I submitted entirely to her, and she made as great a fool of me as she had ever done of any woman whatsoever; under pretence of giving me leave to enjoy, she drew me in to suffer the company of my little ones during eight hours; and I doubt not whether, in that time, I did not undergo more than in all my distemper. At twelve precisely my coach was at the door, which was no sooner told me than I kiss'd my children round, and went into it with some little resolution. My wife—who behaved more like a heroine and philosopher, though at the same time the tenderest mother in the world—and my eldest daughter followed me; some friends went with us, and others here took their leave; and I heard my behaviour applauded, with many murmurs and praises, to which I knew I had no title: as all other such philosophers may, if they have any modesty, confess on like occasions." Fielding died on the 8th of October following.

Fordhook was afterwards tenanted by Lady Byron; and in 1835 the poet's daughter, "Ada, sole daughter of my house and heart," was married in its drawing-room, by special licence, to Lord King, now Earl of Lovelace.

On the road towards Hanwell is a wayside inn, "The Old Hat," the sign-board of which claims for it three centuries of existence as a house of call and entertainment. If this assertion be true—and there is no reason for doubting it—what tales could its bar and snug parlour not tell! If neat and modernised in its outside, "The Old Hat" is old-fashioned enough in its interior arrangements. This ancient tavern is apparently not mentioned in Larwood's "History of Sign-boards," the author of which work suggests that "The Hat" "was the usual hatter's sign, although it may also be found before taverns and public-houses; in which case, however, it is probable that it was the previous sign of the house, which the publican on entering left unaltered; or it may have been used to suggest a 'house of call' to the trade."

The parish of Hanwell adjoins Ealing on the west, and is bounded on the south by Norwood and Heston, on the west by Southall, and on the

---

* See *ante*, p. 5.

north by Greenford. Although it figures in the Domesday Survey of William the Conqueror, under the name of Hanewelle, where it is stated that the manor " answers for two hides," and that " there was a mill of two shillings and twopence, pannage for fifty hogs," &c. ; and although it is on record that the manse was given at a very early period to Westminster Abbey, Hanwell seems to be one of those fortunate places whose history is a blank ; indeed, there is no allusion to it in any of

Catholics, the Congregationalists, Baptists, Wesleyans, &c., while the Established Church is represented by two edifices.

The parish church stands far away from the village, in the fields towards Greenford, on a knoll almost surrounded by the Brent, which here winds its way, almost choked with water-lilies, rushes, and reeds, its banks being lined with alders, the grass lands sloping pleasantly down to the banks of the stream. The present church is a poor

EALING GREEN.

Horace Walpole's " Letters," nor in any of the other gossiping chronicles of bygone days, so far as we can trace.

Hanwell lies on the Uxbridge Road, and partly occupies a broad valley through which the Brent river winds its course. The neighbourhood consists mostly of pasture land, pleasantly undulated, and affords much diversified and picturesque scenery. Near the centre of the parish the valley of the Brent is crossed by a lofty viaduct, nearly 700 feet in length, over which passes the Great Western Railway, which has a station here. The Grand Junction Canal also passes the village on its western side, on its way to join the Thames at Brentford. In the town there are churches and chapels, of more or less merit, for the Roman

specimen of modern Gothic, with large galleries and no chancel. It is a modern erection, having been built in 1841, in the place of an older structure, which had become too small for the increasing population. It was designed by Messrs. Scott and Moffatt, and is in the Early English style of architecture. It is constructed of dark flint and brick, with stone dressings, and consists of nave, aisles, and transept, with a tower and spire at the western end. Its predecessor was a mean and uninteresting brick building, dating from 1782, when it was erected on the site of a much more ancient edifice. Its form or plan was an oblong square, and its western end was adorned with a turret and cupola. The old church was devoid of monuments, with the exception, perhaps, of a single flat stone recording the decease of Sir John Clerke, Bart., in 1727, and his mother, Dame Catherine Clerke, who died in 1741. Its church-yard covers part of the slope to the bank of the river on the north, but it contains no tombs or memorials of interest. In the old graveyard was buried Jonas Hanway, whose name was almost as widely known as that of Captain Coram in the middle of the last century as the joint-founder of the Magdalen Hospital, and on account of many

the style of the period, and his face is strongly marked with benevolence and good sense. The early agenda books of the institution are religiously kept, and in them are to be seen the autographs of Hanway, of Mr. Benjamin D'Israeli (Lord Beacons-field's grandfather), and other celebrities of the reign of George II.'s day. The latter part of Hanway's life was employed in supporting, by his pen and personal exertions, a variety of charitable and philanthropic schemes; and he gained so high

The Old Hat in the Uxbridge Road.

other schemes of benevolence, and to whom we are mainly indebted for that very useful article of daily need, in our variable climate at least—the umbrella.* Hanway was also a social reformer, for it was mainly through his intercession that a Bill was introduced into Parliament for the regu-lation of the infant poor of several parishes in the metropolis. In the office of the Marine Society in Bishopsgate Street may be seen a very fine full-length portrait of this worthy philanthropist; the painter was no mean limner, but his name is not recorded. Hanway is represented as seated at a table, dressed in a blue suit, with ruffles, &c., in

and honourable a name, that a deputation of the chief merchants of London made it their request to Government that some substantial mark of public favour should be conferred on him. He was in consequence made a commissioner of the navy. Hanway was one of the great promoters of schools for the poor.

An account of this good man and philanthropist will be found in Dr. Smiles's "Self-Help." The son of a storekeeper in the dockyard at Portsmouth, he was brought up to a mercantile career, and made a fortune by trading in Russia. That fortune he spent in works of public utility and benevolence. He improved the highways of the metropolis; he organised a volunteer body of marines; he founded

---

* See "Old and New London," Vol. IV., p. 471.

the Marine Society (which is still one of the largest and most important of London charities) ; he largely re-modelled the Foundling Hospital ; he was one of the founders of the Magdalen ; like Howard, he explored the fever-dens of the poorer classes of London, and forced on the parochial authorities a system of registration, in order to protect infant life ; he got an Act passed for the protection of climbing boys employed by chimney-sweeps ; and, strange to say, was rewarded by the Government for his philanthropic efforts by being made a member of the Victualling Board. " His moral courage," writes Dr. Smiles, " was of the first order. It may be regarded as a trivial matter to mention that he was the first who ventured to walk the streets of London with an umbrella over his head. But let any modern London merchant venture to walk along Cornhill in a peaked Chinese hat, and he will find that it takes some moral courage to persevere in it. After carrying an umbrella for some thirty years, Mr. Hanway saw the article at length come into general use." Jonas Hanway died childless, and he left his fortune to those whom he had befriended in his lifetime.

Hanway was buried here, pursuant to his own request, in the month of September, 1786. Lysons, in his " Environs of London," thus writes of him : —"This valuable man, whose whole life was a continued scene of active benevolence, was the first promoter of various schemes of public utility, which he lived to see realised and established as permanent institutions. That useful charity the Marine Society, in particular, may be said to have owed its existence to him. His writings were very numerous, and all bore the marks of the most benevolent intentions, whether his object was to secure the health, or improve the morals and religion of his fellow-creatures, to abolish evil customs, or recommend the most deserving objects of charity. Besides the numerous treatises on these subjects, he published an account of a journey from Kingston to Portsmouth, and his travels through Russia, Persia, &c." Mr. Hanway was a commissioner in the Victualling Office from 1762 till 1783, and he frequently visited his friend and relation, Dr. Henry Glasse, at the rectory here. Dr. Glasse translated Mason's " Caractacus " and Milton's " Samson Agonistes " into Greek, and was also the author of " Contemplations from Sacred History." There is no monument in the church to the memory of Hanway, but one was erected in Westminster Abbey.

The village of Hanwell mainly consists of a long and wide High Street, which carries on the line of houses from Ealing, and ends at a bridge at the west end of the village, beyond which is the County Lunatic Asylum. The houses and shops are most irregularly built, and yet they are far from being tasty or elegant. In fact, a duller and plainer street is not to be found, even in Middlesex.

The Central London District Schools are an extensive range of buildings on Cuckoo Farm, about a mile northward of the railway station.

Among the charitable institutions of Hanwell is one founded by William Hobbayne, or Hobbyns, in 1484, for the benefit of the poor, and for twenty-four boys of the parish to be educated and provided with a suit of clothes free of charge, in the parochial school of Greenford Magna. There is also a Catholic Convalescent Home for women and children.

Standing on an eminence opposite to the church, but actually within the parish of Norwood, is the Hanwell Lunatic Asylum—one of the two lunatic asylums for the county of Middlesex. This asylum, since its first erection in 1829-31, has been repeatedly enlarged and greatly improved, and now affords accommodation for nearly 2,000 inmates. It is a conspicuous object for a long distance round, covering as it does a large space of ground, and occupying an elevated site. The general plan of the building is that of the letter E, or, in other words, a centre, in which is the principal entrance, with projecting wings at either end, the wards set apart for male patients being on the left of the entrance, and those for females on the right. Architecturally, the building is a model of simple plainness. There are extensive airing-grounds and gardens in the front and rear of the premises, laid out with shrubberies, gravel-walks, &c. ; and besides the wards of the asylum, there are kitchens, sculleries, larder, dairy, wash-houses, and laundries, bakehouse, brewhouse, and general store-room. The wards are provided with day-rooms, in which the patients take their meals, and where they spend the greater part of their time. The wards have not less than two attendants in each, in some there are three ; and on an average about fifty convalescent patients are under the care of two attendants, but in the refractory wards two attendants have the charge of about twenty-five patients. The attendants have to pay strict attention to the directions of the medical officers as regards the treatment, employment, amusement, and exercise of the patients, and in every instance they are required to treat them with the greatest kindness.

This institution owes its origin to an Act of

Parliament passed in the reign of George III., enabling the justices of the several counties to erect asylums for the reception and maintenance of the insane and lunatic poor, and to improve and ameliorate the condition of lunatics, by rescuing them from the neglect and inattention of the workhouse, or the cupidity, ignorance, and cruelty too often practised by those who farmed them in private asylums.

Nothing can more strongly mark the progress which society has made since the latter end of the last century than the different aspect under which the insane have been viewed, and the different way in which they have been treated. Formerly there was but little difference in the treatment of the criminal and the insane. In 1792, an intelligent and noble-hearted Frenchman, named Pinel, in the midst of surrounding horrors, brought commiseration and kindness within the walls of a lunatic asylum, and it is to his courage and humanity that we owe the many beneficial changes which have been brought about in this country in the treatment of the insane. The change of treatment, however, in this country was of slow growth; for long after the example which Pinel had set, though there were isolated attempts to introduce a humane system of management into the asylums, they were the exceptions only. Cruelties of the most revolting kind continued to be practised by sordid, unprincipled men. Mr. John Weale, in his "London Exhibited in 1851," observes that "almost the first, and certainly the greatest, benefit conferred upon the insane pauper was the Act of the 9th George IV., cap. 40, which was intended to facilitate the erection of county lunatic asylums for the poor, and to improve the condition of lunatics. Thenceforth, in those counties that wisely took advantage of the Act, the friends of the insane pauper could be assured of that which the laws of society are bound to afford —protection against cruelty and security against neglect."

On the completion of Hanwell Asylum, the committee appointed Dr. William Ellis and Mrs. Ellis to be the superintendent and matron, and from their united efforts the institution derived great benefit. Among the useful suggestions for which the asylum was indebted to Dr. and Mrs. Ellis was the extensive employment of the patients. In his very first report, Dr. Ellis mentions that considerable amelioration had taken place in the condition of the insane poor of the country, and adds :—" But with even the greatest solicitude for their comfort, the want of sufficient air and exercise, which can only be obtained in a large building with ample grounds, presents the most formidable obstacle to their cure." In December, 1832, Dr. Ellis writes that the system of employing the patients has been pursued most perseveringly in every variety of work adapted to their respective qualifications; and concludes by stating that "not a single accident had occurred from the patients having been trusted with the tools used in their different occupations." These, among other less formidable weapons, were spades, bill-hooks, and scythes. The same earnest endeavours to employ the patients in useful handicraft labour continued to engage the mind of Dr. Ellis during the remainder of his career as superintendent at Hanwell. During all this time the non-restraint system was gradually making its way, by the exertions of intelligent men, in two or three other public establishments in the kingdom, and was to some extent adopted in a few amongst the best conducted private establishments. Long experience had taught Dr. Ellis that the sufferings of the insane were often frightfully augmented by undue coercion, needless restraint, and the want of employment, and that their malady by these means was increased rather than alleviated. Well he knew that the cries of poverty and sickness can make themselves heard, while the voice of the mentally diseased does not reach the ear. Thus was he stimulated to try gentleness, employment, liberty (as far as was prudent), and social intercourse. His perfect success induced him to labour for the establishment of such a system for the wealthy classes of the insane, calling public attention to the subject by a work which he published on "Insanity," and taking every opportunity of influencing in private those who might assist in furthering his scheme. Dr. Ellis was knighted by William IV. soon after his nomination to the governorship of Hanwell Asylum. He resigned his appointment here in 1838, and died two years afterwards.

In their choice of a successor to Dr. Ellis, the committee of visiting justices, with whom the government of the asylum was placed, were not fortunate, for in less than a twelvemonth it became necessary to appoint another physician in his place. The choice fell upon Dr. John Conolly, the author of numerous works on insanity, and on the "Construction and Government of Lunatic Asylums," &c. To this gentleman the asylum is mainly indebted for the full establishment of the humane and rational system of non-restraint which had been introduced by Dr. Ellis. In one of his reports to the visiting justices, Dr. Conolly observes : "The great and only real substitute for restraint is invariable kindness. This feeling must animate every person employed in every duty to be performed. Constant superintendence and care, constant forbearance and command of temper, and a never-failing attention to the comfort of the patients, to their clothing, their food, their personal cleanliness, their occupations, their recreations—these are but so many different ways in which kindness shows itself, and these will be found to produce results beyond the general expectation of those who persevere in their application." Caroline Fox in her "Journals," June 22, 1842, writes : "Met Colonel Gurney at Paddington, and reached Hanwell in a few minutes. Were most kindly received by Dr. Conolly ; he has had the superintendence for two years, and at once introduced the system of non-coercion in its fullest sense, though feeling that it was a very bold experiment, and required intense watching ; but he dared it all for the sake of a deeply suffering portion of humanity, with the most blessed result. All the assistants seem influenced by his spirit, and it is a most delightful and heartcheering spectacle to see madness for once not treated as a crime."

The average number of patients at Hanwell Asylum is close upon 2,000, of whom by far the larger portion are females. The management of the patients, as regards their classification, employment, and treatment, is under the direction of two resident medical officers, one for the male, and the other for the female department. There is a bazaar upon the premises, for the sale of fancy and other needlework, &c., the produce of the female patients during the daytime who are desirous of amusing themselves by the production of such articles. The bazaar is under the care of a superintendent ; and the profit arising from the sale of such work to visitors is expended in little extra indulgences for the patients. There is a school for the male patients, and the schoolmaster occasionally gives lectures in the evening on some amusing subject. The amusements for the patients, in fact, are varied.

In the wards a good supply of books, bagatelle-boards, cards, &c., is kept up ; and in some of the wards there are also pianofortes, which have been presented by visitors for the use of those patients who are musically inclined. The male patients, and such of the female patients as may be fit for manual labour, may be seen from time to time labouring in the gardens and fields which lie round the asylum, and so contributing to the good of the institution, whilst harmlessly and healthfully employed.

The previous chapels having proved insufficient, a new chapel, in the Early English Gothic style, was added to the asylum in 1880. The architect was Mr. H. Martin, and it will seat about a thousand worshippers. It is of brick, and has a lofty tower and spire. Standing in front of the main entrance, it forms a conspicuous and central object in the general view of the place.

There are at Hanwell two cemeteries, one belonging to the parish of St. Mary Abbots, Kensington, and the other to St. George's, Hanover Square.

In these days of electric telegraphy, when a message can be sent from London to the uttermost corner of the globe in almost less time than it would take to be carried by hand from one end of the metropolis to the other, it is somewhat interesting to read such a scrap of intelligence as the following, which we cull from *The Mirror* of December, 1839 :—

" ELECTRO-MAGNETIC TELEGRAPH OF THE GREAT WESTERN RAILWAY.—This telegraph, which is the invention of Mr. Cook and Prof. Wheatstone, of King's College, has been, during two months, constantly worked at the passing of every train between Drayton, Hanwell, and Paddington. At the former station it, for the present, terminates. As soon as the whole line is completed, the telegraph will extend from the Paddington terminus to Bristol ; and it is contemplated that then information of any nature may be conveyed to Bristol, and an answer received in twenty minutes."

CHAPTER III.

BRENTFORD.

"We will turn our course
To Brainford, westward, if thou says't the word."—*Ben Jonson.*

Traffic through Brentford in the old Coaching Days—Government of the Parish—Old Bridge of the Brent—The Priory of the Holy Angels Inundations—Fondness of George III. for Brentford—The Dangers of the Road—Early History of Brentford—The Soil and the Pleistocene Deposits—Murder of King Edmund—The Battle of Brentford—Visit of the Grand Duke of Tuscany—The "Two Kings of Brentford"—The Dirt and Squalor of Brentford—How the Duke of Wellington nearly came to grief here—Ancient Hostelries—Old (East) Brentford Church—New (West) Brentford Church—St. Paul's Church—The Town-hall and Market-house—Manufactories and Grand Junction Waterworks—Grand Junction Canal—Drinking Fountain—Bear Baitings—The Old Market-place—The Elections for Middlesex—"Wilkes and Liberty!"—A Brentford Elector—The Manor of Bordeston—Boston House—Sion House Academy—Wyke Farm—"Old Gang Aboot"—The Pitt Diamond—Mrs. Trimmer—Extracts from the Parish Register.

WE now make our way in a south-westerly direction, skirting the hamlet of Little Ealing, and shortly find ourselves at Brentford, a long straggling village or town on the Hammersmith and Hounslow road, and extending about a mile and a quarter west from Kew Bridge, almost parallel with the Thames. The chief road to the west and south-west of England passed through Brentford in the days of coaching and posting. Some idea of the traffic along this road from London at the end of the reign of William IV. may be formed from the fact that the tolls of the Hammersmith Turnpike Trust were let in 1836 for £19,000 per annum, and that 247 coaches and public conveyances, and seven mails, passed through and returned to town on this road daily. Nearly all this traffic must have gone through Brentford. The road, at one time bordered by hedgerows, and passing through cultivated fields and market gardens, has been within the last half-century considerably altered in its appearance by the "demon of bricks and mortar;" indeed, Sir Horace Mann, writing under date of 1791, observes that "there will soon be one street from London to Brentford," and the era of which he prophesied, as we have already remarked in our opening chapter,* has long since arrived. Brentford is not included in any parliamentary borough, nor is it a corporate town ; but it is governed by a Local Board of Health. It is really a township in the parishes of Hanwell and Ealing : West, or New Brentford, being in the former parish, and East, or Old Brentford, being in the latter. The west, however, is really the older part of the town.

At the west end is a bridge of one arch over the Brent, superseding that mentioned by Leland in his "Itinerary." In his time it had three arches, and close to it stood a hospital of brick ; but we are not informed as to its character.

In the *Gentleman's Magazine* for 1802 is an engraving of the seal of "The Priory of the Holy Angels in the Marshlands, near Brentford." This is called by Bishop Tanner in his "Notitia Monastica," after Weever and Newcourt, a friary, hospital, or fraternity of the nine holy orders of angels, consisting of a master and several brethren in a chapel at the west end of Brentford, or, according to Stow, "by the bridge." Lysons mentions it, and places it "in Isleworth, at Brentford End." All Christian passengers were free of toll on passing this bridge, but Jews and Jewesses were forced to pay a halfpenny if on foot, or a penny if on horseback. Many centuries later, if we may trust Spence's "Anecdotes," the Jews offered to Lord Godolphin to purchase the town, with all its rights and privileges of trade, but that statesman declined the offer.

Its name explains itself*—the ford over the Brent, a small tributary of the Thames, which rises in Hendon, between the Hampstead and Stanmore hills, and, flowing in a south-westerly course for about eighteen miles, falls into the Thames at this point. Its situation on the banks of the Thames and the Brent being low and flat has been at times one of great inconvenience, owing to inundations. In 1682 we read of a great flood here, when "boats rowed up and down the streets, and the water got into the pews of the church."

In January, 1841, great damage was occasioned here by the rise of the waters of the Brent and the Grand Junction Canal, owing to an unusually rapid thaw and the bursting of a reservoir at Hendon. Numbers of boats, barges, and lighters were torn from their moorings and driven through the bridge towards the Thames, several barges being sunk, and many of the houses inundated.

"All the land to the south of the road passing from Brentford through Hounslow to Staines is so nearly level as to have no more than a proper drainage ; and much the greater part is less than ten feet above the surface of the river at Staines Bridge, and not more than from three to five feet above the level of the rivulets flowing through this district. From Staines, through Ashford and

---

* See *ante*, p. 3.

* See however, below, p. 31.

BRENTFORD, FROM THE RIVER.

Hanworth Common, to Twickenham, a distance of seven miles and a half, it is a perfect level, generally from ten to twenty feet above the surface of the Thames."*

King George II.—like his successor—it is well known, preferred Kew to Windsor, and loved the dead level of the neighbourhood. On the same principle he was very fond of Brentford, because its long low street reminded him of some of the towns in his kingdom of Hanover. For this reason he always ordered his coach to be driven slowly through it, in order that he might enjoy the scene.

The road connecting this town with the metropolis was, in the last century, much on a par with the other great thoroughfares radiating from London, so far as the dangers from highwaymen and footpads were concerned. We read in the *Gentleman's Magazine* for 1776, that in the September of that year the then Lord Mayor of London was stopped at Turnham Green, a mile east of Brentford, in his chaise and four, in the sight of all his retinue, and robbed by a single highwayman, who swore that he would shoot the first person that offered any resistance.

Cyrus Redding, in his "Fifty Years' Recollections," tells a strange story in connection with this place :—

"I had a relative, who, not long before railways were established, on stating his intention to come up to town, was solicited to accept as a fellow-traveller a man of property, a neighbour, who had never been thirty miles from home in his life. They travelled by coach. All went on well until they reached Brentford. The countryman supposed he was nearly come to his journey's end. On seeing the lamps mile after mile, he expressed more and more impatience. 'Are we not yet in London, and so many miles of lamps?' At length, on reaching Hyde Park Corner, he was told they had arrived. His impatience increased from thence to Lad Lane. He became overwhelmed with astonishment. They entered the inn ; and my relative bade his companion remain in the coffee-room until he returned, having gone to a bed-room for ablution. On returning, he found the bird flown ; and for six long weeks there were no tidings of him. At length it was discovered he was in the custody of the constables at Sherborne, in Dorsetshire, his mind alienated. He was conveyed home, came partially to his reason for a short time, and died. It was gathered from him that he had become confused more and more at the lights, and long distances he was carried among them ; it seemed as if they could have no end. The idea that he could never be extricated from such a labyrinth superseded every other. He could not bear the thought. He went into the street, inquired his way to the westward, and seemed, from his statement, to have got into Hyde Park, and then out again into the Great Western Road, walking until he could walk no longer. He could relate nothing more that occurred until he was secured. Neither his watch nor money had been taken from him."

It is time now for us to speak of Brentford itself.

* Middleton, "View of the Agriculture of Middlesex," p. 23.

In spite of the general opinion that Julius Cæsar, in his second invasion of England, crossed the Thames, at the Coway Stakes, near Shepperton (as we shall presently see), there are not wanting those who consider that it is more probable that the scene of that passage was much nearer to London, and the Rev. Henry Jenkins, in the "Journal of the British Archæological Association" for June, 1860, maintains at some length his belief that it was at Old Brentford that the emperor crossed his army. We learn from Gibson's edition of Camden's

since it allowed the Britons more space to fortify them with stakes, and, at the same time, afforded the Romans a fairer opportunity of plying their engines over the heads of their own men as they entered the river, and of striking the enemy posted on the topmost verge of the opposite side. Thus, whilst the cavalry, sent in advance to cross higher up the stream, were threatening the flank, the main body of the legions pressing forward in front, and sheltered, as it were, by the military engines, made good the passage of the river. Cæsar's words are

THE STABLES OF THE "THREE PIGEONS," BRENTFORD. (See p. 34.)
(From an Etching by W. N. Wilkins, 1848.)

"Britannia," that at Old Brentford the Thames was annually fordable with great ease, and was so still in Bishop Gibson's time, as now, there being at low ebb not above three feet of water in the bed of the river. "Here," writes Mr. Jenkins, "on many accounts, I am inclined to place the passage of Cæsar. Its British name, Brentford—i.e., Breninford—the king's road or way,* favours this supposition; for the name, even if it should not apply personally to Cæsar, establishes the fact that this part of the Thames was known to, and used by, the Britons as a ford. The height of the banks also at this place is an important consideration,

præmisso equitatu. By this I understand that the cavalry were sent in advance to attempt passage higher up the stream, at Kingston, Walton, or elsewhere, in order to distract the enemy's attention, and to draw off a part of his forces, whilst the infantry pressed forward to the ford directly in their front. The cavalry and infantry did not cross the stream together and at the same place. Such a plan would have caused inextricable confusion."

So far Mr. Jenkins, who considers that as soon as the emperor had brought together all his forces on the north side of the river at Old Brentford, he marched straight east. "His first and chief object, after he had crossed the Thames, must have been to have led his army into Essex, and form a junction with the Trinobantes;" and this he did, keeping between the river on his right and the forest on his

* This derivation entirely sets aside the derivation given above, which makes Brentford to have been so called from the ford across the Brent. It is not usual for towns, which, of course, are after-growths, to give names to rivers; the converse is almost always the case.

left. In this case he would have passed across what is now the north of London, passed the Lea at Old Ford, and so on to Ilford and Barking, on his way to head-quarters at Cæsaromagus, which Mr. Jenkins fixes at Billericay, near Brentwood.

A long, narrow strip of waste land, some two acres in extent, forming an island in the Thames, and known as " Brentford Eyot," adds not a little to the beauty of the river scenery at this point. It is overgrown with trees, and a suggestion has been raised by the Commissioners of Woods and Forests to sell it for the sake of the timber; but the idea has been strongly resented by the inhabitants.

The soil of Brentford is, or has been, very rich in remains of extinct species of animals; and in digging out brick-earth and excavating for other works, many of their bones have been found. In 1740 the skeleton of a "large beast of the bull kind" was found here. Professor Phillips, in his "Geology of Oxford and the Valley of the Thames," says—"At Brentford the pleistocene deposits above the London clay have been successfully examined, long since by Mr. Trimmer, and subsequently by Morris. The paper of Mr. Trimmer, referred to by Professor Phillips, was printed in the *Philosophical Transactions for the Year* 1813. In it an account is given of many interesting discoveries of bones of animals about ten feet below the present surface of the ground. There were found teeth and bones of both the African and Asiatic elephant, of the hippopotamus, and of several species of deer. The remains of hippopotami were so abundant that, in turning over an area of 120 yards, parts of six tusks of that animal were found, besides a tooth and part of the horn of a deer, parts of a tusk and a grinder of an elephant, and the horns, with a small portion of the skull of an ox." Many of these fossils are now in the possession of Thomas Layton, F.S.A.

" Since the period referred to by Professor Phillips and Mr. Trimmer," observes the Rev. T. E. Platten in his " Memorials of Old Brentford," " various excavations have been made for railway purposes at Kew Bridge and near the present Gunnersbury station. At Kew Bridge were found bones of several species of deer, horns of reindeer and red-deer, tusks of hippopotami, and remains of bisons." At Gunnersbury, where the London clay was reached, were discovered the remains of sharks, a fossil crab and fossil resin (amber), fine specimens of nautili, and other marine shells.

" If we could have looked on the place in those days," continues Mr. Platten, "a strange scene would have been presented to our eyes. The Thames then probably spread its waters from the Richmond hills on the south to the Harrow heights on the north. In its shallow pools, and amid the high thick rushes which lined its banks, the hippopotamus made his lair and bathed his unwieldy limbs. Here the elephant slaked his thirst at night, and the huge Irish elk, the largest of the deer species and now long extinct, took refuge from his ferocious enemies, and stood at bay in the waters of the friendly stream. It was a wilderness of waters —an arm of the sea rather than a river. The beasts held the land for their own, and reigned with undisputed sway, revelling in the warmth and rich luxurious vegetation of a tropical clime. Such is the scene of the distant past which these discoveries suggest.

" The next period, the records of which have been preserved by the river, is the stone age, carrying us back to a time when men did yet not know how to work the metals. In many parts of the Thames between Sion House and Strand-on-the Green during dredging operations interesting discoveries have been made of various stone implements, known as celts—*i.e.*, chisels and hammers of stone, some of which have been found let into bone or wooden handles. The stones are in many instances carefully shaped to suit the purposes for which they were required, but at the best they could not be very efficient implements to work with. To the stone succeeded the bronze age, and that again was followed by the iron. Of the bronze and iron ages, also, many relics have been found. There have come to light a great many specimens of bronze weapons, such as swords, spear-heads, wedges, axes, and part of the boss of a shield. Britons, Romans, and Saxons, from time to time, must have fought many battles in this neighbourhood, and these relics were probably the arms of soldiers who perished in trying to cross the Thames for attack or in flight. It seems probable," Mr. Platten adds, "that for a considerable time the river formed a boundary separating Britons from Romans, for as a rule ancient British remains are found along the left bank, while the Roman are mostly confined to the south side of the Thames."

Brentford has figured in history on at least two occasions : in the Saxon times, and again under the Stuarts. It was here that Edmund Ironside defeated the Danes in 1016, when many of the English were drowned in the Thames. A few days later King Edmund was himself treacherously slain at Brentford. Local tradition fixes the Red Lion Inn yard as the scene of the murder. Here, in 1642, Prince Rupert routed two regiments of the army of the Parliament, under Colonel Hollis, driving them out with considerable loss. The importance of this engagement, and the number of the slain, both in the encounter and in the skirmishing of the following day about Turnham Green, are probably much exaggerated. We are told in Clarendon's "History of England," that the common soldiers taken prisoners by the king's "army at Brentford were discharged on their simple promise not to take up arms again; but that the Puritan camp chaplains declared that they were not bound by such an oath, and absolved them from the necessity of keeping it!" We learn also that after the battle great damage was done in the neighbourhood by the Royalist soldiers, and liberal collections in aid of the sufferers were made. The Puritan John Lilburne was one of the prisoners taken in the encounter; and Charles I. rewarded the Scottish Earl of Forth for his share in the engagement by creating him Earl of Brentford. The earldom was renewed by William III. as the second title of his favourite officer, the Duke of Schomberg; but it became extinct a second time in 1719. On the news of this repulse, the Parliament at once ordered fortifications to be thrown up, in order to prevent the king from pressing on to London, and next day they sent out the Trainbands, under the Earl of Essex, who encamped on Turnham Green; and after a day of irresolution the king drew back to Kingston-on-Thames. On this occasion, as we learn from Whitelock's "Memoirs," "the good wives and others, mindful of their husbands and friends, sent many cart-loads of provisions, and wines, and good things to Turnham Green, with which the soldiers were refreshed and made merry, and the more when they heard that the king's army was retreated." Brentford must have seen Oliver Cromwell pass in a sort of triumphal procession through the town.

Samuel Pepys would seem to have been a frequent visitor here; at all events, several notices of the place occur in his Diary between the years 1665 and 1669. A Mr. Povy, who resided here at that time, was one of his friends. He was evidently a rich man, inasmuch as his stud of horses was, according to Pepys' notion, "the best confessedly in England, the king having none such." In August, 1665, Mr. Pepys found that "the plague was very bad round about here;" and in the following month, one of his watermen (he seems generally to have gone by water between London and Brentford) "fell sick as soon as he landed me in London, when I had been all night upon the water, and I believe he did get his infection that day at Brentford, and is now dead of the plague." A spot now known as "Dead Men's Graves," near the north end of Green Dragon Lane, is said to be the place of interment of those who died of the plague. In

no suburb of the metropolis were the deaths from this cause heavier than here.

Charles II. stayed a night here at an old house which was taken to form the approach to St. Paul's church, from the High Street. Nell Gwynne lived for a time at Brent House, in the Butts.

Brentford figures also in the blacker pages of English history, six persons having been burnt here in 1558 for advocating the "new" opinions.

Cosmo III., Grand Duke of Tuscany, who was travelling in England in 1669, passed through Brentford on his way to London. In the account of his travels which he afterwards wrote, he calls the place "a very large village," and adds that he "dined there in company with all the gentlemen who had been to wait upon him." His visit no doubt caused a general commotion in the neighbourhood, for he further remarks that "a very great number of people—men, women, and whoever were curious enough to come—were allowed to enter the dining-room."

Brentford was the capital of the kingdom of the "Middle Saxons," whose name survives in Middlesex. The "two kings of Brentford" have passed into a proverb. As to the precise date when they reigned history is silent, but it must have been, if ever, in the Saxon times. The Duke of Buckingham's Play, "The Rehearsal," was written as a satire upon Dryden and the playwrights of his time, who often made reference to two kings fighting for a throne. "The Rehearsal" contains no regular plot, but some of the scenes are amusing. The scene of the play is Brentford. There are "two kings" and "two usurpers," and the two kings are represented as being very fond of each other. They come on the stage hand-in-hand, and are generally seen smelling at one rose or nosegay. Hearing the bystanders whisper, they imagine that they are being plotted against, and one says to the other :—

"Then, spite of Fate, we'll thus combinèd stand,
   And, like true brothers, still walk hand-in-hand."

They are driven from the throne by the usurpers; but towards the end of the play "the two right kings of Brentford descend in the clouds, singing, in white garments; and three fiddlers sitting before them in green;" upon which one of the usurpers says to the other :—

"Then, brother Phys, 'tis time we should be gone."

The usurpers having disappeared, the first right king thus expresses his sentiments :—

"So firmly resolved is a true Brentford king
   To save the distressed and help to 'em bring,
   That ere a full-pot of good ale you can swallow,
   He's here with a whoop, and gone with a holla."

A dance is then performed before them, which is said to be "an ancient dance of right belonging to the kings of Brentford, but since derived, with a little alteration, to the Inns of Court."

Cowper, in his "Task" (Book 1), alludes to this dual sovereignty, comparing it to a "settee," or "sofa."

> "United, yet divided, twain at once:
> So sit two kings of Brentford on one throne."

There is also an old ballad by an anonymous writer, commencing :—

> "The noble king of Brentford
>   Was old and very sick ;
> He summoned his physicians
>   To wait upon him quick.
> They stepped into their coaches,
>   And brought their best physic."

Again, in Prior's "Alma," we read :—

> "So Brentford kings, discreet and wise,
> After long thought and grave advice,
> Into Lardella's coffin peeping,
> Saw nought to cause their mirth or weeping."

The reference here would be obscure and unintelligible were it not for the light thrown upon it by the play of "The Rehearsal," above.

Brentford, however, has gained notoriety in other ways than through its "two kings." In the "Merry Wives of Windsor," Falstaff is disguised as "the fat woman of Brentford;" and the town is referred to by Thomson, Gay, Goldsmith, and others, chiefly on account of its dirt. "With its long, narrow High Street, back slums, factories, and rough river-side and labouring population," writes Mr. J. Thorne, "Brentford has always borne an unenviable reputation for dirt and ill odours." He also quotes the following story from Boswell :— "When Dr. Adam Smith was expatiating on the beauty of Glasgow, Johnson cut him short by saying, Pray, sir, have you ever seen Brentford?' This, Boswell took the liberty of telling him, was shocking. 'Why then, sir,' he replied, ' *You* have never seen Brentford." No doubt he meant that dirty as parts of Glasgow may be, Brentford is worse.

Gay speaks of

> "—— Brentford, tedious town,
> For dirty streets and white-legged chickens known."

Thomson, who lived at Richmond, as our readers will remember, was a keen observer of nature, and thus alludes to Brentford at the end of his "Castle of Indolence" :—

> "Ee'n so through Brentford town, a town of mud,
>   A herd of bristly swine is preeked along ;
> The filthy beasts, that never chew the cud,
>   Still grunt and squeak, and sing their troublous song.
>   And oft they plunge themselves the mire among,
> But aye the ruthless driver goads them on."

The readers of Oliver Goldsmith will not forget the mention of this place in the "Citizen of the World," where he describes a race "run on the road from London to a village called Brentford, between a turnip-cart, a dust-cart, and a dung-cart." It was through Brentford, too, as readers of Charles Dickens will remember, that little Oliver Twist was made to tramp by Bill Sikes on his way to the burglary at Shepperton, which had such an effect on his subsequent career.

The long dreary High Street of Brentford is not only dirty, but dull and monotonous, and quite devoid of interest. Almost the only incident connected with it worth narrating respecting it is that the Duke of Wellington, returning to London from Windsor Castle late at night in 1814, met with an accident to his carriage, which might have proved fatal to the future conqueror of Waterloo. Lord William Lennox, who was with him as his aide-de-camp, tells us that the townspeople, on hearing who was the occupier of the chariot, wanted to fasten ropes to it, and to drag it on to town.

The inhabitants of this place seem to have been regarded as vulgar, for Shenstone writes :—"There are no persons more solicitous about the preservation of rank than those who have no rank at all. Observe the humours of a country christening ; and you will find no court in Christendom so ceremonious as 'the quality' of Brentford."

Lying on the direct road to the west of England, Brentford has long been famous for its hostelries. Near to the old market house was an ancient timbered inn, "The Three Pigeons," mentioned by Ben Jonson—"We'll tickle it at the Pigeons "—and the scene of some of the "Merry Jests" of George Poole, the early dramatist. It is known that many of Shakespeare's friends were visitors here ; and it is probable that the immortal poet himself may have been within its walls. The house was taken down several years ago, and its low carved and panelled chambers disappeared. Mr. Thorne says that "at the *Lion* Inn, Henry VI., in 1445, assembled a large party, and after supper created Alonzo D'Almada Duke of Avranches, and next morning held a Chapter of the Garter (the only instance of a Chapter being held at an inn), at which he created two knights." He gives, however, no authority for the statement.

The "Wagon and Horses," near Kew Bridge, probably occupies the site of a certain "inn that goes down by the water-side," where the genial old gossiper Samuel Pepys tells us that he was entertained, and returned by water to London, having attended service at Brentford Church,

"where a dull sermon and many Londoners."—
(Aug. 20, 1665.)

Another noted hostelry here was the "Tumble-
down Dick," a sign, by the way, which has given
rise to some little speculation as to its meaning.
"Tumble-down Dick," says the *Advertiser*, No. 9,
1752, "is a fine moral on the instability of greatness and the consequences of ambition." As such,
it was set up in derision of Richard Cromwell, the
allusion to his fall from power, or "tumble down,"
being very common in the satires published after
the Restoration; and amongst others, *Hudibras*,
thus, Part III., canto ii., 231 :—

> " Next him, his son and heir apparent
> Succeeded, though a lame vicegerent,
> Who first laid by the Parliament,
> The only crutch on which he leant,
> And then sunk underneath the State
> That rode him above horseman's weight."

The same idea, and almost the identical words,
occur again in his "Remains," in the tale of the
Cobbler and the Vicar of Bray :—

> "What's worse, old Noll is marching off,
> And Dick, his heir apparent,
> Succeeds him in the Government,
> A very lame vice-regent.
>
> He'll reign but little time, poor tool,
> But sinks beneath the State,
> That will not fail to ride the fool
> 'Bove common horseman's weight."

We meet with it also in the ballad, " Old England
is now a brave Barbary "—*i.e.*, horse—from a " Collection of Loyal Songs " reprinted in 1731, Vol. II.,
p. 321 :—

> " But *Noll*, a rank rider, gets first in the saddle,
> And made her show tricks, and curvate, and rebound ;
> She quickly perceived he rode widdle-waddle,
> And like his coach-horses,* threw his highness to ground.
>
> "Then Dick, being lame, rode holding the pummel,
> Not having the wit to get hold of the rein ;
> But the jade did so snort at the sight of a Cromwell,
> That poor *Dick* and his kindred turned footmen again."

"Tumble-down Dick" furnished the theme of
many an old song, and it was also the name given
to a dance in the last century.

In 1718, as we learn by a report in the *Original
Weekly Journal*, a most brutal murder was committed at the above inn.

Old (East) Brentford Church, dedicated to St.
George, is perhaps the ugliest of all the ugly
churches which were built in the darkest period
of architectural science, the first decade of George
III. It is literally a square box of bricks pierced
with apertures for windows, and nothing more.
It is be-pewed and be-galleried to the utmost
possible extent. Its only redeeming feature is a
painting over the communion-table, representing
the Last Supper. It was painted for this church
by Zoffany, who lived (as we have already stated)
at Strand on-the-Green. It is said that the faces
of the apostles were all taken from local fishermen, except that of St. Peter, which is a portrait
of Zoffany himself ; his own black slave is also
introduced. Zoffany, it may be added, was a
native of Frankfort-on-the-Maine, and was born in
1735. Early in life he went to Italy, where he
studied painting for some years. After his return
to Germany, he practised for a few years as an
historical and portrait painter at Coblentz on the
Rhine, from which place he came to England a few
years before the foundation of the Royal Academy,
as he was elected one of its first members in 1768.
In England Sir Joshua Reynolds and Garrick became valuable patrons to him, and he painted
the latter in several of his characters. He also
painted portraits of George III. and other members of the royal family. About 1781 Zoffany
went to India, and lived for some time at Luck-
now, where he met with the greatest success, and
painted many large pictures of Indian life. He
returned to London about the year 1796 with a
large fortune, and afterwards settled at Strand-on-
the-Green.

New (West) Brentford Church, at the other end
of the town, is not quite so monstrous a building,
though its body dates from about the same period.
The old tower still stands. It is dedicated to St.
Lawrence, whose festival was the day of Brentford
Fair. This church was built originally on account
of the springing up of a large river-side population,
who could not go two miles to "hear masse" at
their own parish church. The edifice was rebuilt
in 1762. John Horne Tooke was minister* here
before he threw up his orders and entered Parliament.

In the tower of this church is an ancient bell,
supposed to be one of the earliest cast in England.
The register, which dates from 1570, contains the
names of two centenarians, one of them a surgeon
in practice in the town. Apparently he took good
care of his own health. In the year of the Great
Plague the burials here were 103, the annual average being about 36.

This church contains some fine monuments in

---

* In allusion to Cromwell's accident in Hyde Park in October, 1654,
when his coach-horses ran away, and his highness, who was driving, fell
from the box between the traces, and was dragged along a considerable
distance.—See "Old and New London," Vol. IV., p. 382.

* " Brentford, the Bishopric of Parson Horne."—*Mason.*

stone and alabaster, including one in the chancel to Noy, the Attorney-General of Charles I., whose name figures in history in connection with the question of "ship-money." Noy's house, with its quaint barge-board roof, still stands close by the vicarage.

Among other persons buried here were Luke Sparks, a comedian of Covent Garden, and a friend of Quin—he spent his last years here, and died in 1768; Henry Giffard, and his wife Anna Mascella, who died in 1772 and 1777. He

1867–8, and is in the Early Decorated style of architecture, consisting of chancel, nave, aisles, tower, and a lofty spire.

The town-hall and market-house is a commodious building, and was erected in 1850.

Brentford is well stocked with works of various kinds, giving employment to a large number of hands. Here, for instance, are the gas-works, some extensive breweries and malt works, a large soap manufactory, a pottery, the Great Western Railway docks, spacious timber-yards and saw-mills.

BOSTON HOUSE. (See page 39.)
(From an old Print of 1799.)

was proprietor of the theatre in Goodman's Fields when Garrick first appeared as one of his company.

Weever, in his "Funeral Monuments," mentions here the tombs of William Clavet, who died in 1496; Christopher Caril, Norry king-at-arms (1510); Richard Parker, "servant in the butlery to Henry VIII.," and his wife Margaret, "servant to the Lady Mary's Grace." There are also monuments to the Clitherows and Spencers.

Maurice de Berkeley was a great benefactor to this parish, and the arms of Berkeley are preserved in stone on the walls of the church. Brentford, in fact, is well endowed with charities, schools, &c.

St. Paul's Church, in Old Brentford, was built in

At the entrance to the town from Ealing is a tall chimney, erected for the Grand Junction Waterworks; its height is nearly 200 feet, and it forms a conspicuous object from whichever side it is seen. There are six engines, by whose united power 12,000,000 gallons of water are propelled daily thence to the main reservoir at Paddington. Both the town and the neighbourhood are supplied from these works. The Grand Junction Canal is here brought into contact with the Thames; it passes the grounds of Osterley Park, and runs through a rich corn district near Hanwell, Norwood, Harlington, West Drayton, Cowley, and Uxbridge, to Harefield, not far from Rickmansworth, where it leaves the county. Its rise of level from Brentford to

Harefield is a little over a hundred feet. This canal was established by Act of Parliament, passed in 1793; it incorporates the Brent, rendering it navigable for upwards of a miie before it joins the Thames. The canal connects the metropolis with Warwickshire, Staffordshire, and Lancashire.

Opposite Kew Bridge is a handsome drinking-fountain, opened by the Duchess of Teck in 1879.

Brentford in former times was among the places celebrated for its "bear-baitings." It is to this knight relates the chapter of accidents which there befel him :—

> "And though you overcame the bear,
>   The dogs beat you at Brentford fair,
>   Where sturdy butchers broke your noddle."

In the second part of the same poem is told, in doggrel verse, the story of Hudibras and a French mountebank at "Brentford Fair."

Down to little more than a quarter of a century ago Brentford had a quaint old wooden market-

MRS. TRIMMER.   (*See page* 40.)
(*From a Portrait in the possession of the Family.*)

place, probably, that Butler alludes in his "Hudibras," Part I., cant. 1, 677 :—

> "In western clime there is a town,
>   To those that dwell therein well known.
>
> *   *   *   *   *
>
>   To this town people did repair
>   On days of market or of fair,
>   And to crackt fiddle and hoarse tabor
>   In merriment did trudge and labour.
>   But now a sport more formidable
>   Had raked together village rabble :
>   'Twas an odd way of recreating,
>   Which learned butchers call bear-baiting."

At all events it is probable that Brentford, to the "west" of London, is meant, especially when we remember the lines in Part II., cant. 3, where the

place, with a clock-tower and a roof of high pitch, like those with which we meet in the West of England. Edward I. granted a weekly market and an annual fair on St. Lawrence's Day. After the Reformation, the profits of the market and fair were held under the Crown, but they subsequently passed into private hands. The market-place stood in the Butts, which was also the scene of the elections for Middlesex. The market-day is now on Tuesday, and fairs are held three days in May, and also three in September. The elections for Middlesex were held on Hampstead Heath till the year 1701, when they were transferred hither. They appear generally to have been conducted in a very riotous fashion, one of the most disorderly being that of 1768, when Mr. John Glynn and Sir W. B. Proctor were the candidates. " The remembrance of the famous contests of 1768 and 1769, when party feeling ran so high in favour of the popular candidate, is still kept up," writes Lysons, " by the sign of Wilkes's Head and No. 45."

Brentford is still conventionally regarded as the chief town of Middlesex for election purposes, a fact which strongly attests our innate conservatism. The nominations of the county members have taken place here " from time immemorial," and all sorts of good stories and jokes are extant respecting these elections.

Bubb Dodington writes, under date March 8th, 1749 :—" The election for the county of Middlesex. Sir Francis Dashwood, Messrs. Furnese, Breton, and I, went in Sir Francis's coach at eight o'clock to Mr. Cooke's in Lincoln's Inn Fields. A great meeting there. We set out with him about nine —my coach following—and went through Knightsbridge, Kensington, by the Gravel Pits, to Acton, and from thence to Stanwell Heath, which was the general rendezvous. From thence to Brentford Butts, which was the place of poll. It began about one. I polled early, and got to my coach, which was so wedged in that, after much delay, I found it impossible to make use of it, so that Mr. Breton and I were forced to take two of my servants' horses, with livery housings, and ride without boots ten miles to Lord Middlesex's at Walton, to meet their Royal Highnesses at dinner. . . . My coach did not arrive till nine. . . . Poll for Mr. Cooke, 1617 ; for Mr. Honywood, 1201. We carried it by 416."

Paul Whitehead thus refers to the election at Brentford :—

" Now, nearer town, and all agog,
    They know dear London by its fog ;
Bridges they cross, through lanes they wind,
Leave Hounslow's dangerous heath behind ;
Through Brentford win a passage free
By shouting ' Wilkes and Liberty !'"

The cry of "Wilkes and Liberty !" held its ground for many a long day. Was it in order to furnish an example of the meaning of this cry that, in the election riots of 1769, when Wilkes was a candidate, the mob destroyed the poll-books, and killed one person at the hustings ?

Colonel Luttrell and Wilkes were standing together on the hustings at Brentford, when Wilkes asked his adversary, privately, " whether he thought there were more fools or knaves among the large crowds of Wilkites below ? " " I'll tell them what you say, and so put an end to you at once," said the colonel. Wilkes was unmoved ; and on Luttrell asking him why he felt no fear at such a threat, he

replied quietly, " Because I should tell them that it was a fabrication, and they would put an end to *you*, and not to me."

Mr. J. T. Smith, in his " Book for a Rainy Day," prints the following letter from Lord North to Sir Eardley Wilmot, under date of 1st April, 1769, having reference to the candidature of Colonel Luttrell and Wilkes :—

" My friend Colonel Luttrell having informed me that many persons depending upon the Court of Common Pleas are freeholders of Middlesex, &c., not having the honour of being acquainted with you himself, desires me to apply to you for your interest with your friends in his behalf. It is manifest how much it is for the honour of Parliament, and the quiet of this country in future times, that Mr. Wilkes should have an antagonist at the next Brentford election, and that his antagonist should meet with a respectable support. The state of the country has been examined, and there is the greatest reason to believe that the Colonel will have a very considerable show of legal votes, nay, even a majority, if his friends are not deterred from appearing at the poll. It is the game of Mr. Wilkes and his friends to increase those alarms, but they cannot frighten the *candidate* from his purpose ; and I am very confident that the voters will run no risk. I hope, therefore, you will excuse this application. There is nothing, I imagine, that every true friend of this country must wish more than to see Mr. Wilkes disappointed in his projects ; and nothing, I am convinced, will defeat them more effectually than to fill up the vacant seat for Middlesex, especially if it can be done for a fair majority of legal votes. I am, Sir, with the greatest truth and respect, your most faithful, humble servant,

" NORTH."

The judge, in his answer, dated on the following day, observed, " It would be highly improper for me to interfere in any shape in that election."*

The author of the work above quoted mentions several humorous ballads on this subject, particularly " The Renowned History and Rare Achievements of John Wilkes." The chorus ran thus :—

" John Wilkes he was for Middlesex,
    They chose him knight of the shire ;
And he made a fool of Alderman Bull,
    And called Parson Horne a liar." †

The popularity of Wilkes was carried to so great an extent, that his friends in all classes displayed some article on which his effigy was portrayed, such as salad or punch bowls, ale or milk jugs, plates, dishes, and even heads of canes. The squib engravings of him, published from the commencement of his notoriety to his silent state when Chamberlain of London, would extend to several volumes. Hogarth's portrait of him, which by the collectors was considered a caricature, is recom-

* See the Wilmot Letters, in the British Museum.
† " Parson Horne," of course, is Mr. Horne Tooke

mended as the best likeness by those who knew him personally.

In his personal appearance Wilkes was exceedingly ill-favoured, as a glance at his portrait will show ;* and the peculiar squint which he unfortunately possessed gave rise to the epigram in " Wine and Walnuts," beginning—

"The d——l at Lincoln climbed upon the steeple,
As Wilkes did at Brentford to squint at the people."

Macfarlane, the author of the " History of George III.," was killed by the pole of a coach during one of the election processions of Sir Francis Burdett, at the entrance of the town. In fact, as the *Annual Register* of 1802 informs us, to such a state of turbulence had the inhabitants of Brentford arrived on these occasions that " it is impossible for any but those who have witnessed a Middlesex election to conceive the picture it exhibited : it was a continued scene of riot, disorder, and tumult."

A good story is told of one of the inhabitants of Brentford in the last century. Happening to be travelling in Germany, where " Electors " are, or were, not uncommon, he was called on, as he entered the gates of a town, to describe himself, after the usual manner of strangers. " I am an elector of Middlesex," he replied. The German officials, knowing that an Elector was inferior only to a king or a prince, but knowing nothing of the meaning of the term in England, immediately ordered the guards to be called out, and received him with military honours.

The only manor in this parish, according to Lysons, is that of Bordeston, or Burston, commonly called Boston, which formed part of the possessions of the convent of St. Helen's, Bishopsgate. Edward VI. granted it to the Duke of Somerset, on whose attainder it reverted to the Crown. Queen Elizabeth granted it to Robert, Earl of Leicester, who sold it in the same year to Sir Thomas Gresham. Having passed through several intermediate hands, it was bought in 1670 by James Clitherow, Esq., a merchant of London, of which he was Lord Mayor and a representative in Parliament, and in whose family it still remains. Boston House stands on gently rising ground, a little less than a mile north-west of the town. It was built partly by Lady Reade, and partly by Mr. Clitherow. About half a mile to the north a large oak-tree, called Gospel Oak, divides Brentford from Hanwell.

Sion House Academy, near Brentford, was the first school to which the poet Shelley was sent as preparatory for Eton. Even here he showed that he was something of a philosopher, and that he had his own views on most subjects upon which boys are generally disposed to accept the opinions of others.

Wyke Farm, between Brentford and Osterley Park, was the residence of John Robinson, who rose by the favour of Lord Lonsdale from the position of a foot-boy at Lowther Castle to be M.P. for Appleby and for other places, and ultimately Secretary to the Treasury under Lord North's administration. A good story about this place is told by Mr. Serjeant Atkinson :—" King George III., in returning from the chase to Kew Palace, was obliged to ride across Wyke Farm. One day, on riding up to one of the gates, he found it locked. The king hailed a man who happened to be close by to open the gate, but the fellow was too lazy or too stupid to go out of his way to oblige a stranger. ' Come, come,' said the king, ' open the gate, my man !' ' Nae, ye maun gang aboot,' was the reply. ' Gang aboot, indeed !' said His Majesty. ' Open the gate at once ; I'm the king !' ' Why, may be,' said the chap, ' ye may be the king, but ye maun gang aboot for all that.' And sure enough His Majesty was obliged to ride round nearly the whole enclosure of Osterley Park. In the afternoon Mr. Robinson, who had been away in London, returned home, and heard of the king's disappointment. He at once ordered his carriage, and drove over post haste to Kew to offer his apologies. He was admitted without ceremony, as usual, and the king, in answer to his apologies, merely replied, ' Ah ! I wish I had such fine honest fellows in my pay as your old " gang aboot." Tell him from me that I like his honesty, and shall be glad to see him here some day.' Mr. Robinson was at once put at his ease ; and as for the man, he soon found out a more direct way than all round Osterley Park to Kew, where he was kindly received by the good-natured king. It is said that His Majesty never saw Robinson afterwards without making tender inquiries after ' Old Gang Aboot.' "

Among the former residents of Brentford was Mr. Pitt, the grandfather of the first Earl of Chatham. He is said to have been the son of a tradesman in a small way here, and his son's name is handed down to us by Pope in connection with what was known as the " Pitt diamond."

Pope is supposed to allude, in a well-known passage in the third epistle on his "Moral Essays," to this diamond, a gem brought to this country by Thomas Pitt, Governor of Madras, about 1700. Mr. Pitt purchased this celebrated diamond, which goes by his name, for £20,400, and sold it to the King of France for more than five times the sum.

---

* See " Old and New London," Vol. I., p. 420.

It was then reckoned the largest jewel in Europe, and weighed 127 carats. When polished it was as big as a pullet's egg; the cuttings amounted in value to eight or ten thousand pounds. It was placed among the crown jewels of France, and afterwards adorned the sword of state of Napoleon. The report that Mr. Pitt had obtained this diamond by dishonourable means was very general; and he was at last induced to publish a narrative of the circumstances connected with its purchase. The affair of the Pitt diamond may have suggested the incident of the stolen gem to Pope; but the whole episode appears fanciful, and the history of Sir Balaam and his family is highly improbable.

At Brentford lived for many years Mrs. Trimmer, so well known by her writings for young persons in the time of our parents and grandparents. She helped largely the thread of education here. This lady was the daughter of a Mr. Joshua Kirby, of Ipswich, and was born in 1741. Her father was a clever draughtsman, and held for some time the appointment of "tutor in perspective" to the Prince of Wales, afterwards George III. Miss Kirby was married at the age of twenty-one to Mr. Trimmer. Her literary labours commenced about the year 1780, the first of her published works being a small volume entitled "An Easy Introduction to the Knowledge of Nature." She died in 1810, very suddenly, in the arm-chair which she used generally to occupy in her study in the house in Windmill Lane, where she had resided for many years.

The parish rates of Brentford, it is said, in former times, were mainly supported by the profits of public sports and diversions, especially at Whitsuntide. If this story be true, the good people of Brentford, in spite of the dull situation of their town, must have been a jolly set of good fellows. Among the sports here referred to were such amusements as "hocking" and "pigeon-holes." These are constantly mentioned among the entries in the "chapel-wardens'" account books of the seventeenth century. At a vestry meeting held here in 1621, several articles were agreed upon with regard to the management of the "parish stock" by the chapel-wardens. The preamble, which is quoted by Lysons, states that "the inhabitants had for many years been accustomed to have meetings at Whitsuntide, in their church-house and other places there, in friendly manner, to eat and drink together, and liberally to spend their monies, to the end neighbourly society might be maintained; and also a common stock raised for the repairs of the church, maintaining of orphans, placing poor children in service, and

defraying other charges;" which stock not having been properly applied, it was ordered that a particular account should be given from year to year of their gains at those times, and the manner of the expenditure. In the "accoumpts for the Whitson-tide ale, 1624," the "gains" are thus set forth :—

Imprimis, cleared by the pigeon-holes	.	£4	19	0
,,	,, by hocking	. . .	7	3	7
,,	,, by riffeling	. . .	2	0	0
,,	,, by victualling	. .	8	0	2

£22   2   9

The "riffeling" here mentioned is synonymous with "raffling." The hocking occurs almost every year till 1640, when it appears to have dropped. It was collected at Whitsuntide.

1618 Gained with hocking at Whitsuntide . £16 12 3

Other curious entries in the account books, evidently bearing upon the public sports and pastimes of Brentford, are as follows :—

1620 Paid for 6 boules	. . . .	£0	0	8
,, for 6 tynn tokens	. . .	0	0	6
,, for a pair of pigeon-holes	. .	0	1	6
1621 Paid to her that was Lady at Whitsontide by consent	. . . .	0	5	0
,, to Goodwife Ansell for the pigeon-holes	0	1	6
,, for the games .	. . . .	1	1	0
1623 Received for the maypole	. .	1	4	0
1628 Paid for a drumbe, stickes, and case	.	0	16	0
,, for 2 heads for the drumbe	. .	0	2	8
1629 Received of Robert Bicklye for the use of our games	. . . .	0	2	0
,, of the said R. B. for a silver bar which was lost at Elyng	. . .	0	3	6
1634 Paid for the silver games	. .	0	11	8
1643 Paid to Thomas Powell for pigeon-holes		0	2	0

Among other articles of church furniture in the hands of the chapel-wardens in 1653 was "one little collar, a bell, one little bowl, and a pin of silver."

There are other singular entries in the account-books, as follows :—

1621 Paid for a beast for the parish use .	.	£2	6	8
,, Given to the French chapel by consent .		1	0	0
1625 For a coffin to draw the infected corpses .		0	8	8
1633 Given to a Knts. son in Devonshire, being out of meanes	. . . .	0	0	6
,, Paid for a book of sporting allowed on Sundaies	. . . . .	0	0	6
1634 Paid Robt. Warden, the constable, which he disbursed for conveying away the witches	. . . . .	0	11	0
1688 Paid for a "Declaration of Liberty of Conscience"	. . . .	0	1	0
,, For a form of prayer for the Dutch not landing	. . . . .	0	1	0
,, For a thanksgiving for deliverance from Popery	. . . . .	0	1	0

The two last entries immediately follow each other.

CHAPTER IV.

HESTON, ISLEWORTH, AND SION HOUSE.

Osterley Park—Sir Thomas Gresham visited by Queen Elizabeth—Lord Desmond—The Manor of Heston—Heston Church—The Soil—Sir Joseph Banks and Anthony Collins residents here—Isleworth—Its Etymology—The River Cran—Sion House—Vicissitudes of the Nuns of St. Bridget—The Rule of the Order of St. Bridget—Early History of the Monastery—The Wardrobes of the Nuns—The Duties of the Abbess, Cellaress, &c.—Dissolution of the Monastery—Touching History of the Sisterhood—Remains of the Monastery—Katherine Howard a Prisoner here—Funeral of Henry VIII.—Building of Sion House—The Family of Percy, Dukes of Northumberland—The Princess of Denmark at Sion House—Description of the Building—The Gardens and Grounds—The Parish of Isleworth—Descent of the Manor—The Parish Church—Charitable Institutions—Church of St. John the Baptist—Brentford Union—Gumley House—Kendal House—Lacy House—Royal Naval Female School—Silver Hall—Gordon House—Sir Clipesby Crewe—Worton Hall—Syon Hill—Honnor's Home—London International College—Spring Grove.

A LITTLE to the north-west of Brentford, in the parish of Heston, lies Osterley Park. The estate, which now belongs to the Earl of Jersey, was formerly the property of Sir Thomas Gresham, the great merchant of Elizabeth's reign, and founder of the Royal Exchange. He began to re-build the manor-house about the year 1570, when the estate was granted to him by the Crown. Norden, who published his "Survey of Middlesex" in 1596, says, in the quaint language of the period :—"Osterley, the house nowe of the Lady Gresham, a faire and stately building of bricke, erected by Sir Thomas Gresham, knight, citizen, and marchant adventurer of London, and finished about anno 1577. It standeth in a parke by him also impaled, well wooded, and garnished with manie faire ponds, which affordeth not only fish and fowle, as swanes and other water-fowle, but also a great rise for milles, as paper milles, oyle milles, and corn milles, all which are now decayed, a corn mille only excepted. In the same parke was a faire heronrie, for the increase and preservation whereof sundry allurements were devised and set up, fallen all to ruin."

Gresham had no fewer than four or five stately mansions in Norfolk ; but of these his favourite and chief residence was Intwood House, or, as he always called it, his "poor house at Intwood." Besides these, he had in his latter years this estate of Osterley, a magnificent old place (Mayfield) in Sussex, and apparently one or two houses in other parts of the kingdom, in which he occasionally resided.

In 1578 Queen Elizabeth visited Sir Thomas Gresham at Osterley Park, and was there entertained in a very sumptuous manner. "The Devises of Warre, and a Play at Awsterley, her Highness being at Sir Thomas Gresham's," is the title of a pamphlet mentioned by Lysons as having been published by Churchyard ; Lysons adding that it is "not known to be now (1795) extant." Fuller tells the following story of Queen Elizabeth's visit to Osterley :—"Her Majesty having given it as her opinion that the court before the house would look better divided with a wall, Sir Thomas Gresham in the night sent for workmen to London, who so speedily and so silently performed their task, that before morning the wall was finished, to the great surprise of the queen and her courtiers, one of whom, however, observed that it was no wonder that he who could build a Change should so soon change a building ; whilst others (reflecting on some known differences in this knight's family) affirmed that any house is easier divided than united."

From certain minutes in the Privy Council books of the period, it appears that some of Gresham's park-paling at Osterley was burned while the queen was there ; that Her Majesty being very much offended, commanded that the offenders should be searched out and punished ; and that shortly after four individuals were committed to the Marshalsea prison, charged with the offence. The same industrious investigator has further discovered that Gresham's great enclosure at Osterley was very unpopular, and that complaints were laid against him by sundry poor men for having enclosed certain common ground, to the prejudice of the poor.

The author of the "Life of Sir Thomas Gresham," in Knight's "Weekly Volumes for all Readers," observes that "it is not wealth that always makes the best temple for the household gods, and neither wealth nor caution could keep sorrow and sickness and fears out of this splendid mansion. In the year 1570 one of Gresham's servants fell sick of the plague in Osterley House, upon which the knight and his family fled in great dismay into Sussex."

In most of his places Gresham would seem to have sought, with more success than most persons, how to unite his profit and his pleasure. At Osterley he had within the circuit of his park both oil-mills and corn-mills, and also a paper-mill—the latter, it is said, being his own device of the first mill of that kind set up in this country. And besides this, he made himself useful to his royal mistress in a variety of ways, acting occasionally as one of Her Majesty's gaolers, or keepers of State prisoners ; for as money was saved by such an arrangement, it became a common practice with

Elizabeth thus to quarter her State prisoners, or those whom she wished to keep under her own control, upon her nobles and the richer gentry, making them personally answerable in case of their cage-birds escaping. Thus it appears that the Lady Mary Grey, the sister of Lady Jane, was for some time an inmate of Osterley Park. Upon one occasion, the knight and his wife would fain know what they are to do with my Lady Mary, "trusting that now Her Majesty would be so good as to remove her"—that is, send her to some other gentleman. But all was in vain; the queen seems to have thought that her captive could not be in safer or better keeping, and—sometimes in the London

herself in her captivity and grief with reading. As some of her books were French, and one or two Italian, it may be presumed that she knew those languages, and that, like her eldest sister, the Lady Jane Grey, she was an accomplished person.

Sir Thomas Gresham died in the following year (1579), and on the decease of his wife, to whom it had been left, the property was inherited by Sir William Read, her son by a former marriage. Soon after Lady Gresham's death, Lord Chief Justice Coke (then Attorney-General) appears to have been a resident at Osterley. One of his children was christened in the chapel there on the 3rd of January, 1597. George, Earl of Desmond, and his Countess

OSTERLEY PARK.

house, and sometimes at Osterley Park—the Lady Mary continued to reside with the Greshams from the month of June, 1569, to the end of 1572.

It should be explained that, alarmed at her sister's sufferings for having contracted a match with one of the highest nobles in the land, the Lady Mary had privately married a plebeian youth, named Keys; and that for this offence, and for this only, the unfortunate lady was detained in custody by the jealous queen, who apparently would allow of no marriages, whether high or low, among her kinsfolk and acquaintance. The poor woman died in 1578, in the parish of St. Botolph, Aldersgate, having outlived her husband only seven years. In Osterley she enjoyed a splendid residence, at once a palace and a prison; but she finished her days in poverty, leaving little behind her, except a few trinkets and a score or two of books. She appears to have been very fond of her books, and to have solaced

(who was one of the co-heirs to the estate) resided at Osterley for several years. Lysons, in his "Environs of London," tells a very remarkable story of this couple, on the authority of the "Strafford Letters:"—"Young Desmond (says Mr. Garrard, writing to Lord Wentworth), who married one of the co-heirs of Sir Michael Stanhope, came one morning to York House, where his wife had long lived with the duchess during his two years' absence beyond the seas, and hurried her away, half-undressed, much against her will, into a coach, and so carried her away into Leicestershire. At Brickhill he lodged, where she, in the night, put herself into milkmaid's clothes, and had likely to make her escape, but was discovered. Madam Christian, whom your lordship knows, said that my Lord of Desmond was the first that ever she heard of that ran away with his own wife. Modern times, however, have furnished a parallel. Lady Desmond's adventure was in 1635. It was about four years afterwards that she and the earl came to Osterley, where she bore him a numerous family."

After a few more changes of ownership, the manor was sold about the year 1655 to the famous Parliamentary General, Sir William Waller, who was resident at Osterley in the year 1657, and who died in 1668. Later on, the property belonged to Mr. Francis Child, the banker of Fleet Street, who rebuilt Osterley House, with the exception of the old turrets, and from whom it passed to his

The staircase of the house, as left by Mr. Child, was ornamented with a fine painting, by Rubens, of the Apotheosis of William III., Prince of Orange, brought from Holland by Sir Francis Child. The picture-gallery is forty yards in length, and contains some choice works. The mansion formerly contained a large and valuable collection of books, Mr. Child having purchased the whole library of Mr. Brian Fairfax, and a printed catalogue of the same was drawn up by Dr. Morell in 1771. In 1879 the

HESTON.

brother Robert, who completed the work, and fitted up the interior with great taste and magnificence. Mr. Robert Child's granddaughter, Lady Sarah Sophia Fane, daughter of the tenth Earl of Westmoreland, conveyed the estate in marriage to the fifth Earl of Jersey, grandfather of the present earl, who does not, however, reside here.

Osterley House is a large, square, red-brick building, and stands in an extensive park, in which is a lake covering several acres. Lady Ducie, a former occupant of the mansion, established in the garden a menagerie, containing a large collection of rare birds, which was, however, dispersed on the death of her ladyship. At the end of the last century an artist at Southall published in monthly numbers a series of coloured prints of the rare and curious birds from this menagerie.

building was greatly damaged by an outbreak of fire.

The village of Heston, about half a mile westward from Osterley Park, is situated on the cross-road between the main roads leading from London to Uxbridge and Staines. It was in ancient times annexed to the manor of Isleworth; and it appears by an inquisition taken after the death of Edmund, Earl of Cornwall, in the year 1300, that he died seised of that manor. The parish church, dedicated to St. Leonard, is a modern edifice, having been built in 1866. It is a stone structure, consisting of nave, aisles, and chancel, and was erected in the place of an ancient edifice, the tower of which alone was left standing, and which, although very old, is in a fair state of preservation. The old church, which was built principally of flints, comprised a nave and two aisles, and a double chancel. There were in it a few ancient monuments, but none of any public interest.

The church of Heston was given at a very early period to the monks of St. Valerie, in Picardy, to whom it was confirmed by Henry II. In 1391 the Prior of St. Valerie granted the rectory and advowson to the Warden and Fellows of Winchester College, whose successors surrendered it to the Crown in 1544. Queen Elizabeth, however, granted them to Bishop Grindall and his successors in the see of London. The parish registers date back to 1560, but during the last century they were very imperfectly kept up. From the entries of burials in 1665, it appears that the effects of the Great Plague of London were felt as far westward as Heston, for no less than thirteen persons are said to have died of the plague in this parish during that year.

The soil of this parish is, in general, a strong loam, and is noted for producing wheat of a very fine quality—the finest, at all events, in Middlesex. Camden speaks of it as having, long before his time, furnished the royal table with bread; and Norden, who bears the same testimony to its superior quality, says it was reported that Queen Elizabeth had "the manchets for her highness's own diet" from Heston.

Among the persons of eminence who have lived at Heston may be mentioned the learned and accomplished philosopher, and founder of the Linnæan Society, Sir Joseph Banks, of whom a biographical sketch will be found in the pages of OLD AND NEW LONDON.* He lived for some time at Smallbury Green, in this parish, probably in order to be near Kew, Chiswick, and Ealing. Anthony Collins, a deistical writer of some note in the seventeenth century, was born at Heston in 1676.

Isleworth adjoins Heston on the south; the boundary line between the two parishes, however, has not always been clearly defined, possibly from the bounds not having been beaten as regularly as they might have been; at all events, Lysons, in his "Environs," gives an account of a fray and dispute, which arose between the parishioners of Isleworth and of Heston in "beating the bounds" on a Rogation Day. Heston and Isleworth now, for educational and drainage purposes, together form a Local Board district, which includes the town of Hounslow. Isleworth is a large parish on the banks of the Thames, immediately westward of Brentford. It is a place of great antiquity, being mentioned in Domesday Book as "Ghistelworde." The name was afterwards spelt in various ways, as

Yhistelworth, Istelworth, and Thistleworth, the last-mentioned spelling being in vogue in Queen Elizabeth's time, and even used by Pope; but for the last two centuries it has been usually spelt Isleworth.

Lysons suggests that Skinner's derivation of the etymology of Islington, from *Gisel*, a hostage, and *tun*, a town, might more justly, with the alteration of *tun* for *worth*, a village, be applied to this place; for it does not appear that Islington in any ancient record is called Giselton, or Gistelton, but Isendune. "The most general idea of its derivation," he adds, "has been suggested by the modern name *Isleworth*; but I think that the constant usage of Istelworth for so many centuries leads one to seek for some other etymology, though perhaps it might be difficult to find one which would be entirely satisfactory." Might not its derivation be found in *Ise*, or *Isis*, which was a common Celtic name for a river, and *worth*, which in Anglo-Saxon is said to denote a nook of land between two rivers? Gibson, however, regards *worth* as signifying a farmhouse. When scholars disagree, who is to decide?

It was by Saxon husbandry and labour that Isleworth, Twickenham, &c., were reclaimed, enclosed, and improved. Before the reign of Henry III., the site now covered by Isleworth and its adjacent towns was part of the forest, or warren, of Staines. It extended from the river Brent to Staines, and even to the banks of the Coln, a little further west. It was disafforested in 1227. Very slight mention of this village is made in English history. It is, however, recorded that in 1263 Simon de Montfort and the other refractory barons pitched their tents in Isleworth Park; and that four centuries later—namely, in August, 1647—General Fairfax fixed his head-quarters here at the head of the Parliamentary army.

The river Cran, or Crane, which rises in the neighbourhood of Harrow, falls into the Thames at this place, having been augmented by an artificial cut from the Colne, made in bygone times by the abbess and convent of the monastery of Sion, for the convenience of their water-mills.

Sion, or Syon House, the seat of the Duke of Northumberland, occupies the site of the above-mentioned monastery, and is situated at the south-eastern angle of the parish. The monastery—the original site of which appears to have been in the adjoining parish of Twickenham—was founded by King Henry V. in 1415, for the accommodation of sixty sisters and twenty-five brothers belonging to the order of St. Bridget, a modified branch of the order of St. Augustine. This religious house, together with its twin monastery at Sheen—for such

---

* See Vol. III., p. 191.

it really was—is the subject of an allusion by Shakespeare in his play of *Henry V.*, where the king says:—

"Five hundred poor have I in yearly pay,
    Who twice a day their withered hands hold up
    Towards heaven to pardon blood ; and I have built
    Two chantries, where the sad and solemn priests
    Sing still for Richard's soul."

The dedication stone was laid by the king in February, 1416. The dimensions of the premises on which the convent stood are thus stated in an ancient record, quoted by Lysons :—The length, towards the river, 2,820 feet; towards Twickenham Field, 1,938 feet ; the breadth on one side was 980 feet, and on the other 960 feet. The building itself would appear to have been very small, and insufficient for the accommodation of the inmates ; for within eighteen years of the foundation of the monastery—namely, in 1431—permission was granted to the abbess and the holy community to remove to a more spacious edifice, which they had built upon their demesnes within the parish of Isleworth.

The Rev. J. H. Blunt, in his Introduction to "The Myroure of oure Ladye," formerly belonging to the ladies of this convent, and written specially for its use, states that Sion was the most important monastery founded in England during the 180 years preceding the Reformation. Be this, however, as it may, there can be no doubt that it stood at the head of convents for females, both in respect of its wealth, its learning, and its piety, and that for at all events a century and a quarter it enjoyed an "exceedingly prosperous" existence. When it was suppressed by Henry VIII. its net annual income was assessed at a sum equivalent to about £20,000 of our money, an income exceeded by only Westminster, Glastonbury, Clerkenwell, St. Alban's, Gloucester, Croyland, and Pershore, and larger than that of the great Benedictine monasteries of Canterbury, Durham, or Winchester. Cobbett, in his "History of the Reformation," gives the value of this house, at the Dissolution, as £1,944, and reckons that in the middle of the present century it would have been worth £38,891.

It was the custom with our sovereigns, soon after their accession, to found one or more religious houses for the benefit of the souls of their predecessors—and their own at the same time. In pursuance of this custom, Henry V. gave up part of his manors of Sheen (Richmond) and Isleworth for the foundation of a house of Carthusian monks at the former place, and of a house of nuns of the order of St. Bridget at the latter. The order of St. Bridget, according to Mr. Blunt, was founded

by that Swedish princess and saint at Watstein, in the diocese of Lincopen, about the year 1344, and it owed its introduction into England to the marriage of Eric XIII. of Sweden with Philippa, daughter of our Henry IV., some of the Swedish sisters having been sent over for that purpose in 1415. In the March of the following year a charter in their favour was signed by the king, defining their duties: "to celebrate Divine service for ever, for our healthful estate while we live, and for our soul when we shall have departed this life, and for the souls of our most dear lord and father, Henry, late King of England, and Mary, his late wife, our most dear mother ; also for the souls of John, late Duke of Lancaster, our grandfather, and Blanche, his late wife, our grandmother, and of other our progenitors, and of all the faithful departed." It was also decreed that the house should be called "the Monastery of St. Saviour and St. Bridget of Syon," but the name of St. Mary was commonly inserted subsequently between those of the Saviour and St. Bridget. "The buildings there and then commenced," we are told, "were situate near Twickenham, occupying a site which stretched for about half a mile along the river's bank, and about a third of that distance into the meadows."

The "Monastery," as stated above, was to consist of eighty-five persons : sixty sisters—of whom one was to preside as abbess—and twenty-five professed brothers. Of the latter, thirteen were to be priests, four deacons, and eight lay brothers, employed as sextons, gardeners, &c. The priests were to say and sing mass daily in the chapel for the nuns, and were to take turns with them also in saying the "offices," each seven times daily, so that the voice of praise and prayer was hardly ever silent within its walls. The choirs of the chapel were double, the two aisles being screened off from each other by a thick screen, or parclose, and there was no access from the one to the other, except only for the priests on their way to say mass at the altars. The monks and the sisters each also occupied a separate court.

"This double community," writes Mr. Blunt, "was in reality a combination, for purposes of Divine service, of two separate bodies, each of which had its own conventual buildings separately enclosed. Their two chapels were under the same roof, being, in fact, a double chancel, each with its separate stalls, and opening into each other by a 'grate,' or 'grille,' the gate of which was unlocked only for the entrance and departure of the clergy when they said mass at the altar of the sisters' chapel. The only other door of communication was one used at the profession of novices, which was in the sisters' cloister.   To this there were two keys, differing from each other, one kept in a chest on the brothers' side, and the other in a similar chest on the sisters' side.   To each of these chests there were three keys, none of the keys being alike, and these were kept by the abbess and two 'sistres that have drede of God on the one side, and by the Confessor-general and two brothers on the other, that so al occasion of sclaunder be vtterly take away both outwarde and inwarde' by means of such precaution."

The rule of St. Bridget was, as above stated, a modified form of the Augustinian rule, to which that saint gave the name of the Saviour, in the belief that it had been communicated to her by our Lord Himself.   We have fortunately this rule in existence, a translation of it into English by Richard Whitford, who styles himself in all humility "The Witch of Syon," having been printed by Wynkyn de Worde in 1525.   It will be found *in extenso* in Aungier's "History of Isleworth."   It is the most valuable record of monasticism that has come down to us, and it shows us the inner working of cloistered life.   Additions to the rules of the monastery of Sion are preserved in the library of St. Paul's Cathedral.   They were found some few years ago by the Rev. R. H. Barham, the well-known author of the "Ingoldsby Legends."   The copy in the British Museum is imperfect.

We find an interesting sketch of Sion in Professor Burrows's "Worthies of All Souls."   From this book we learn that it was founded by Henry V., by the advice of Archbishop Chicheley, afterwards the founder of All Souls College at Oxford.   At its opening Chicheley officiated, as archbishop. The convent was endowed, like All Souls, by the Crown, out of the estates of suppressed alien priories, and as it was one of the latest mediæval foundations, so also it was one of the most aristocratic.   Its monastic life under the rule of St. Austin (as then lately reformed by St. Bridget, Queen of Spain), its royal patronage, its great wealth, its beautiful position on the Thames at Isleworth, as well as its vast staff of eighty-five " religious," in honour of the thirteen apostles and the seventy-two disciples, made it a natural ally of the favoured college at Oxford so munificently dedicated by Chicheley to the memory of the princes of the House of Lancaster.   " No doubt scholars of the one became chaplains of the other, and no doubt many a nun of Sion was to be found as a pilgrim making her offerings at the glittering shrine of All Souls. . . .   But now, under Henry VIII., the crash came.   While the college was spared, the nunnery of Sion found its way into the hands of the Dukes of Northumberland, with whom it has ever since remained, and the nuns set forth on their toilsome wanderings abroad. The stout English spirit in their gentle blood forbade them to give way without a struggle, and their struggle was one of the most gallant and prolonged on record.   It lasted three hundred years. After the failure of their fond attempts to settle near their own land in the Low Countries and in France, they eventually found a home at Lisbon, still keeping their English nationality through all vicissitudes.   In the seventeenth century their convent was destroyed by fire, but that did not daunt them.   They diligently begged for alms, and re-built their nest.   Again their new abode was levelled to the ground in the famous earthquake of the seventeenth century, and again it was re-built. But what fire and earthquake had failed to effect was brought about by the Peninsular War.   When Lisbon became the head-quarters of our army, the convent became the English hospital, and the forlorn relic of the sisterhood, consisting of nine English ladies, made their way back to their own land once more in 1810."   We learn from Bandinel's edition of Dugdale that in 1825 two or three of them were still alive in the vicinity of the Stafford-shire Potteries.

But to return to the early history of the house. The royal charter having been supplanted by a papal bull from Martin V. in A.D. 1418, the first profession of novices took place in the new building before Archbishop Chicheley, on April 21st, 1420. It would seem that some of the first sisters, and also of the brethren, were very naturally Swedes. Shortly before his death, in 1422, their royal founder conveyed to his favourite convent the whole of his manor of Isleworth, which had previously belonged to the Duchy of Cornwall; and his successor enriched them with broad lands in half the counties of England, chiefly from the spoils of the alien priories.   Thus enriched, the community began to find their original quarters too narrow, and therefore obtained from the Crown a licence to erect new buildings a little further to the east on their demesne, the site, as already shown, being that of the present palace of the Duke of Northumberland.   Here their new chapel was begun in 1426, the first stone being laid by the Regent John, Duke of Bedford, who gave a "cramp-ring" to each sister, and a handsome set of office-books for the use of the new chapel.

Five years later, in 1431, the sisters received from Henry VI. letters patent, giving them full licence to remove to their new abode without hindrance to their original rights and privileges.

They made their removal on November 11th, the feast of St. Martin, when their new chapel was consecrated, in the presence of Humphrey, Duke of Gloucester.

"From this time forward," writes Mr. Blunt, "the 'Daughters of Syon' appear to have remained in tranquil possession of their beautiful river-side home and of their lands, which were distributed over the country, from St. Michael's Mount to Windermere." He adds that if their income reached a sum representing the present value of £20,000 a year, this would give £250 for each member of the community. "How this large income was expended there is no evidence to show," he continues; "but the character of the Sion community suggests that it would neither be wasted nor spent in self-indulgence; but one longs for the discovery of their account-books."

The abbess, as the superioress was styled, was a dignified female ecclesiastic, and was called in her house the "Reverend Mother." She was elected by the sisters alone; and if they were unanimous, the election was said to be by the Holy Ghost. The choice was, however—whether divinely sanctioned or not—subject to the confirmation of the Bishop of London. The title of "sovereign," given to the abbess in the formal rule of the house, shows that, although elective, her power was somewhat absolute; and it is on record that she administered a variety of punishments to her novices and to the professed sisters, in case of rebellion or wilful contempt of the regulations of the house. A list of the abbesses from the foundation of the convent down to its dissolution and its final dispersion will be seen in Mr. Blunt's book. Agnes Jordan, who was the last but one, is commemorated on a brass in Denham Church, near Uxbridge, where she lies buried. Catherine Palmer, the last, who held the office under Mary, lived till 1576. Figures of these brasses are given in Aungier's "History," already quoted.

Next to the abbess was the prioress, and under her, again, the treasuress and under-treasuress, who had charge of the "temporal goods." On this subject a writer observes:—"They had a great chest, with two different locks and keys, each one keeping a key, so that nothing could be put into the chest or taken therefrom without the knowledge and consent of both. This was 'to put away all affection of covetousness and all occasion of suspicion of evil.' Another of their duties, in the absence of the abbess, was to attend to all such business as involved interviews with strangers, farmers, and others. We can well imagine what important personages these two sisters would become in the estimation of the rest of the community. Separated from the outer world, but not without some interest in it—for had they not fathers and brothers?—the treasuress would be the means of communication between them and what was passing in England during the stormy years of Henry VI., Edward IV., and onward to the end. The estates of the monastery were scattered over the country, from St. Michael's Mount to Windermere. Its annual income amounted to over twenty thousand pounds of our money, so that the 'farmers and other persons' who had business to transact with the recluses of Isleworth would come from all parts, and would bring details of the sanguinary encounters at Barnet or Towton, or Wakefield or Bosworth; while others, nearer home, would no doubt convey whispers of dark deeds said to have been committed in the Tower and elsewhere during the terrible War of the Roses. And then, when Henry VIII. began to be worried by 'domestic troubles,' we can easily understand how these good sisters, in their hours of recreation, would sit round and chat about Queen Catherine, Queen Anne, and the rest of the queens of that generation, and how some would sympathise with one, and some with another. Happy sisters! they were spared all the active sorrows of that troublous time, but were, no doubt, vexed with other, if minor, cares."

The chamberess had duties peculiarly of a feminine nature, having charge of the "clothes, lynin, laces, poyntes, nedelles, threde, and the sewing and repairing of them, and keeping of them from wormes."

From an ancient record, quoted by Mr. Blunt we obtain a curious insight into the wardrobes of the "Daughters of Syon." It is confirmed by another document, preserved in the Record Office, namely, the "Account of Dame Bridget Belgrave," who was chamberess in 1536-7, and who appears not only to have provided all articles of apparel for the sisters, but to have bought no less than twenty-three pairs of spectacles—doubtless for the use of those whose eyesight was not as perfect as it once was—besides large supplies of "pynnes of dyuerse sortes" and "tagging of poyntes," and to have paid for the grinding of razors for the brethren. Among the articles mentioned in her account are "russettes, kerseys, soope (soap), holand and other lynen cloth, bristelles, nedilles, thymbilles, cappes, shethes, coverlettes," &c. Another important personage in the monastic community was the cellaress, whose duty it was to provide the sisters with such inward comforts as they might require, "the meat and drink for sick and whole, and for the servants who lived in the house, as well as for those who lived outside, and for the strangers who not unfrequently stayed as guests at the monastery." It is pleasant to note that in all their arrangements, both of kitchen, cellar, and treasury, there was a desire to live sensibly and soberly, neither despising the good things of this life nor yet abusing them : and in all these were the care and refinement suitable to those who

list of the live-stock belonging to the sisterhood. The list includes the following " catall "—2 bulles, 20 keen (kine), 6 oxen, 4 heyfers, 5 wayners, 122 shepe, wedders (wethers), ewes, 5 lambes. The swyne were as follows—6 boores, 12 sowes, 25 hogges, and 21 wayners. The cellaress, it appears, was authorised to charge for " expences at London," "rewardes to the servantes at Cristemas with their aprons," " sede " for the garden.

THE OLD STABLES AT SION HOUSE.   (See p. 50.)
(From Aungier's " History of Isleworth.")

did not cease to be English ladies when they became "Daughters of Syon," as they were usually designated.

The duties of the cellaress, however, would appear not to have been limited to the cellar of the house. She acted as purveyor-general, and not only bought and purveyed very many of the stores necessary for her fifty-nine sisters, but sold much of the produce of the estate. In the " accompte " of Dame Agnes Merett, cellaress in the year before the Dissolution, occur entries of " calve-skynnes " and " felles solde," besides " woode "—which seems to have fetched a good price. This account, which may still be seen in the Public Record Office, is interesting as giving a

" cover-lettes," sack-cloth, " cord," and " candill rushes."

The general superintendence of the sisters was in the hands of the prioress and four assistants, called " serchers," who are ordered to " have a good eye about " the house, and to see that order and silence are kept. The sisters of Syon, like those of most other religious orders, used to administer the discipline, not only to offenders against the rules of the house, but to each other at stated times, for their spiritual good. " Such exercises of those who live a cloistered life," remarks Mr. Blunt, " must not be criticised too closely by those whose life moves in a less narrow circle."

" The arrangement of the sisters' meals was that

SION HOUSE, FROM THE SOUTH.

of a high table and side tables, such as were then and long after common in the halls of bishops and great houses in the country, and such as may still be observed in colleges and public schools and inns of court. They were waited on by lay-sisters, or servitors, and there was a care and refinement about the arrangement of meals, such as befitted those who had not ceased to be ladies when they became nuns." The viands consisted of soups or "potages," sundry "metes, of flesche and of fysche, one fresche, another powdred boyled, or rosted, or otherwise dyghte after her discrecion, and after the day, tyme and nede requyreth, as the market and purse wyll stretche." Their drink was on some days water, on others ale, and the dinner was garnished with "two maner of froytes (fruits) at leste, yf it may be, that is to say, apples, peres, or nuttes, plummes, chiryes, benes, peson, or any such other." Some few trifling luxuries were allowed to those in weak health; and the Rules of the Saviour and of St. Austin were read aloud during meals by one of the sisters who acted as legister. It was the practice of the house—though its inmates were women—to keep silence, except at specified times, in every part of it.

A munificent endowment was provided for the monastery of Sion, the king, its founder, granting for its sustentation a thousand marks out of the revenues of the Exchequer, until other revenues should be provided; and at the dissolution the income of Sion amounted to the then considerable sum of £1,731 per annum.

Thomas Stanley, the second Earl of Derby, was buried within its precincts in 1521, a few years before its dissolution, which happened in 1532. Sion was one of the first of the larger monasteries that was suppressed, the convent having been accused of harbouring the king's enemies, and of being in collusion with Elizabeth Barton, the "Holy Maid of Kent." Henry VIII., indeed, is said to have selected this convent as an object of especial vengeance, as it was accused of affording an asylum to his "enemies." It was through the confessor of the convent at Sion that the monks of the Charterhouse in London were led to subscribe to the supremacy of Henry VIII., many of them having for a time refused to subscribe to the King's supremacy. Be this as it may, however, one of the monks of Sion, and also the Vicar of Isleworth, suffered at Tyburn along with Houghton, the prior of the Charterhouse.

After the dissolution the lands of the Sion sisterhood were sold or granted away by the Crown, but the house and its immediate domain were retained as the property of the sovereign.

The subsequent history of the sisterhood is touching and sad. They retired at first to a Bridgetine convent at Dermond, in Flanders. For two short years, at the end of Queen Mary's reign, they returned to their ancient home; but on the accession of Elizabeth, their sufferings recommenced. They again had to fly for refuge abroad, and found again a home with their Flemish sisters. After many changes of residence, and after undergoing great poverty, they were at last established in a new Sion, on the banks of the Tagus, at Lisbon, in the year 1594. Here they still remain after the lapse of nearly three centuries, restricting their membership entirely to English sisters, and still retaining the keys of their old home in the hope, never yet abandoned by them, of eventually returning to it. It is said that some half century or more ago, when they were visited at Lisbon by the then Duke of Northumberland, they told his Grace the story of having carried their keys with them through all their changes of fortune and abode, and that they were still in hopes of seeing their English home again. "But," quietly remarked his Grace, "the locks have been altered since those keys were in use." A full account of the wanderings of the sisters from Flanders to Rouen, and from thence to Lisbon, and their subsequent history, will be found in Aungier's "History and Antiquities of Isleworth."

It may be said, however, that though several ineffectual attempts have been made to revive the life of the Bridgetines in England—as at Peckham, in Surrey; at Newcastle, in Staffordshire; and at Spettisbury, in Dorsetshire—the "Sion" of Lisbon remains the real and legitimate representation of the "Sion" of Isleworth.

The nuns reckoned among their most remarkable treasures the original Martyrologium of Sion; the Deed of Restoration, signed by Queen Mary in 1557, and endorsed by Cardinal Pole; some curious seals and a silver bell; and a manuscript account of their wanderings in Flanders and Portugal.

No general view and but very few details of the original monastic buildings of "Sion" have been handed down to us; nor has its successor—the immediate predecessor of the present Sion House —fared much better. That it was a large and imposing structure there can be no doubt, considering the date of its erection. A doorway, of the Perpendicular period, highly ornamented, figures on the title-page of Aungier's work above quoted. The old stables, probably as old as the early Tudors, were mostly taken down about 1790. There is a view of them in Aungier's book (p. 136); where will be also seen a map of the domain.

The convent was probably renowned not only for its buildings, but for its furniture and fittings, and even for the vestments of its priests. In 1861 there was exhibited, under the auspices of the Archæological Institute, a magnificent cope from Sion, probably of the second half of the thirteenth century, which had been carried abroad by the sisters at the dissolution, and was presented by their successors to the Earl of Shrewsbury, who had given them a home in Staffordshire. It is described as "quite a storied vestment." On the higher part of the back is the Assumption and Crowning of the Virgin Mary; beneath is the Crucifixion; lower down is the Archangel Michael overcoming the dragon; high up on the right are the death of the Virgin, the doubting of St. Thomas, St. James the Less holding a club, another apostle with book and spear, St. Paul, St. James the Greater, the burial of the Virgin Mary, St. Mary Magdalen and our Lord, St. Philip, St. Bartholomew, St. Andrew, ten cherubim winged, and figures of religious persons holding scrolls. The hood, which was hung by three loops, is lost; the orphreys are two broad bands, bearing shields charged with the armorial bearings of several noble English houses; and the whole is surrounded by a narrower rim or fringe of shields, of somewhat later date than the rest. The dimensions of the cope are ten feet by four feet eight inches. The heraldic portions, about sixty in number, are probably woven, but the figures are all worked by the needle.

Another article of great value exhibited was a Mariola, or wax image of the Virgin Mary with the Saviour in her arms, probably the work of an English artist towards the close of the thirteenth century. This, too, was one of the Lares and Penates which the sisters carried with them abroad, and was also presented to John, Earl of Shrewsbury. Both of these in all probability were gifts to the convent at its first foundation. Another article exhibited at the rooms of the Archæological Institute in 1862 was a fine pectoral cross of solid gold of the sixteenth century, very probably a gift to the convent on its re-establishment by Queen Mary; and also a manuscript "Processionale ad usum Ecclesiæ de Syon," differing considerably from that in use at Salisbury. This was inscribed with the name of a sister named Slight, one of the inmates scattered by King Henry VIII., and brought back again by Queen Mary.

From the following extract from a letter of Thomas Bedyll, one of the "visitors" of the monasteries at the time of the dissolution, to Secretary Cromwell, under date of July 28th, 1534, it will be seen how the nuns of Sion were forced to acknowledge the king's supremacy. Bedyll writes:—"I have also been at Syon sith your departing with my lord of London, where we have found the lady abbas and susters as conformable in everything as myght be devised. And as towching the father confessor and father Cursone (whiche be the saddest men ther and best learned), they shewed thaimselfes like honest men; and I think the confessor wol now on Sunday next in his sermon make due mension of the kinges title of supreme hed, acording as he is commaunded. What towardnes or intowardnes we have seen in som other of the brethern there, I wol informe you at youre retorne to Londone, and omitte it now bicause I have som hope that by the wisdome of the father confessor and father Cursone the residue shal shortly be brought to good conformite. And if not, there be two of the brethern must be weded out, whiche be somewhat sediciose, and have labored busily to infect thair felowes with obstinacy against the kinges said title."

Later on, under date of 17th December, Bedyll thus writes to Cromwell, touching a visitation to Sion:—"As for the brethern, they stand stif in thair obstinacy as you left thaim. Here wer on Tuesday Doctor Buttes and the quenys amner to convert Wytford and Litell; and on Wensday here wer Doctor Aldrigge, Doctour Curven, Doctor Bawghe, and Doctor Morgan, sent by the kinges grace for that purpose, but they nothing proficted. I handled Whitford after that in the garden, bothe with faire wordes and with foule, and shewed him that throughe his obstinacy he shuld be brought to the greate shame of the world for his irreligious life, and for his using of badd wordes to diverse ladys at the tymes of thair confession, whereby (I seyed) he myght be the occasion that shrift shalbe layed downe throughe England. But he hath a brasyn forehed, whiche shameth at nothing. One Mathew, a lay brother, upon hope of liberte, is reformed. We wolde fanye know your advise what we shal do with Whitford and Litell, and a lay brother, one Turnyngton, whiche is very sturdy against the kinges title. We have sequesterd Whitford and Litell from hering of the ladys confessions, and we think it best that the place wher thes frires have been wont to hire uttward confessions of al commers at certen tymes of the yere be walled up, and that use to be fordoen for ever, ffor that hering of utward confessions hath been the cause of muche evyl, and of muche treson whiche hath been sowed abrode in this mater of the kinges title, and also in the kinges graces mater of his succession and mariage. On Wensday my Lord Wyndesore came hither, sent for by Maister Leighton and me, and labored muche that day for the converting of his suster and som other of his kynneswomen here ; and yesterday we had my Lord of London here in the chapter house of women, and the confessor also, whiche bothe toke it upon thair consciences and upon the perill of thair soulys that the ladys owght by Gode's law to consent to the kinges title, wherewith they wer muche comforted ; and when we wylled al suche as consented to the kinges title to syt styll, and al suche as wold not consent therunto to depart out of the chapter house, there was found none emong thaim whiche departed. Albeit I was informed this nyght that one Agnes Smyth, a sturdy dame and a wylful, hath labored diverse of her susters to stop that we shuld not have thair convent seal ; but we trust we shal have it this mornyng, with the subscription of thabbes for her self and al her susters, whiche is the best fassion that we can bring it to. The persone whiche ye spak with at the grate, covyteth very muche to speke with you, seyng she hath suche thinges whiche she wold utter to no man but to you, and what they be I cannot conject. We purpose this after none, or els to-morow mornyng, to awaite on the king grace, to know his pleasir in everything, and specially towching the muring up of the howses of utter-ward confessions. Maister Leyghton hath wreten certen compertes unto you, and therefor I forber to speke anything therof. The ladys of Sion besecheth you to be good maister unto thaim, and to thair house, as thair special trust is in you, and that they all run not into obloquy and slander for the mysbehavor of one person. A greate number of the ladys desired me to speke unto you that Bisshope and Parkere myght be discharged from the house of Sion, and Bisshope and Parker desire the same. I mervaile that they desire not like-wise to be discharged of the person with whom ye talked at the grate, seing Bisshope's caus and that is one." *

After the suppression of this religious house the conventual buildings were retained in the posses-sion of the Crown during the remainder of the reign of Henry VIII., and in 1541 its gloomy walls were selected as the prison-house of the ill-fated Katharine Howard, while the sentence was being prepared which was to consign her to the

scaffold. Seven years later the body of the king himself rested here for a night on its way towards Windsor Castle. The story was long current that the swollen corpse burst and bled profusely, and that the dogs licked up the blood of the wicked monarch here, as other dogs in their day had licked up the blood of Ahab in Samaria.

In the first year of the reign of Edward VI., the monastery of Sion was granted to the Lord Pro-tector, Edward Seymour, Duke of Somerset, who had already rented some premises at Isleworth under the Abbess and convent ; and it was this nobleman who founded, on the ruins of the monastic building, the magnificent edifice which ultimately became the seat of the Northumberland family, and the shell of which, though in part considerably altered, still remains. The works carried out here by the Duke of Somerset were very extensive, and executed at great cost, and the grounds appear to have been laid out in a manner rather superior to the fashion which then usually prevailed. Here he had a botanical garden, formed under the superintendence of Dr. Turner, who has been often spoken of as "the father of British botany ;" and here were planted some of the earliest, if not the very earliest, mulberry trees introduced into England, many of which are still green and flourishing. Here the Duke of Somerset was living when Allen, the conjuror and astro-loger, was brought before him, charged with prac-tising his art to the injury of the king, and was committed to the Tower.

On the attainder of the Duke of Somerset for high treason, the mansion reverted to the Crown, and was shortly afterwards granted to John Dudley, Duke of Northumberland, but became the residence of Lord Guilford Dudley, the son of that nobleman, who married Lady Jane Grey. It was from this house that Lady Jane went forth on her way to the Tower, to claim the throne of England, on the death of Edward VI.

The estate was again forfeited to the Crown by the attainder of the Duke of Northumberland, and Queen Mary retained it in her possession till 1557, when, as stated above, she was prevailed upon to restore the convent of Sion. She endowed it with the manor and demesnes of Isleworth, and with sundry other lands ; but its restoration was but short-lived, for on the accession of Elizabeth this monastery was again dissolved, and the queen held the estate of Sion House in her own hands until 1604, when it was granted, together with the manor of Isleworth, to Henry Percy, ninth Earl of North-umberland. This nobleman expended large sums in the repairs and improvement of the mansion, the

---

* "Letters Relating to the Suppression of Monasteries." Edited by T. Wright, Esq., for the Camden Society.

occupation of which he enjoyed but for a short time; for, having been convicted by the Star Chamber of complicity in the gunpowder plot, he was stripped of all his offices, sentenced to pay a fine of £30,000, and to be imprisoned for life in the Tower of London. To liquidate the fine he petitioned the king to accept of Sion House, as being the only property that he could part with, the rest being entailed.

"The great house of Percy," observes a writer in *The Quarterly Review*, "was strikingly unfortunate during the reign of the Tudors, and indeed long before. Their ancestor, Josceline de Lovaine, a younger son of the ancient princes of Brabant, and brother of Adelicia, second consort of our Henry I., married in 1122 Agnes de Percy, the heiress of a great northern baron seated at Topcliffe and Spofford, county of York, on condition that the male posterity should bear the name of Percy. Their son Henry was great-grandfather of Henry Lord Percy, summoned to Parliament in 1299, whose great-grandson Henry, fourth Lord Percy, was created Earl of Northumberland in 1377, at the coronation of Richard II. He was slain at Bramham Moor in 1408. His son Henry Lord Percy (Hotspur) had already fallen at Shrewsbury in 1403. Henry, second Earl, the son of Hotspur, was slain at the battle of St. Albans in 1455. His son, Henry, third Earl, was slain at the battle of Towton in 1461. His son, Henry, fourth Earl, was murdered by an insurrectionary mob at Thirske, in Yorkshire, in 1480. Henry, fifth Earl, died a natural death in 1527, but his second son, Sir Thomas Percy, was executed in 1537, for his concern in Ask's rebellion. Henry, sixth Earl, the first lover of Queen Anne Boleyn, died in 1537, issueless, and the honours were suspended for twenty years by the attainder of his brother, Sir Thomas Percy, in 1537, during which time the family had the mortification to see the dukedom of Northumberland conferred on John Dudley, Earl of Warwick. But this nobleman being attainted in 1553, the Earldom was restored to Thomas Percy, the son of the attainted Sir Thomas, who became seventh Earl of Northumberland. He was eventually beheaded in August, 1572. His brother, Henry Percy, was allowed, in right of the new entail, to succeed as eighth Earl of Northumberland. In 1585 this Earl, still blind to his family sufferings, entered into the intrigues in favour of Mary Queen of Scots, and, being committed to the Tower, committed suicide 21st June." His son, Henry, ninth Earl, is the nobleman to whom we have just referred as being charged with complicity in the gunpowder plot.

By Algernon Percy, son of the above nobleman, and tenth Earl of Northumberland, the buildings of Sion were thoroughly repaired, under the direction, it is believed, of Inigo Jones himself. In 1646 the House of Commons deputed to this earl the care of the offspring of Charles I.—so soon to pass on to the scaffold; and it was from Sion House that the young children were conveyed to St. James's Palace, to take a last farewell of their unhappy father—an affecting scene, which has often been seized upon for pictorial representation. From that time to the present the lords of Sion House have continued to be the chiefs of the illustrious house of Percy.

During the fatal year of the plague of London, the business of the State appears to have been at times transacted here; at all events, we read in John Evelyn's Diary, under date of July 7, 1665, the following entry:—

"To London, and so to Sion, where his Majesty sat at Council during the contagion (Great Plague). When business was over, I viewed that seate, belonging to the Earle of Northumberland, built out of an old Nunnerie, of stone, and faire enough, but more celebrated for its garden than it deserves; yet there is excellent wall fruite, and a pretty fountaine; nothing else extraordinary."

In 1692 the mansion became the temporary residence of the Princess of Denmark (afterwards Queen Anne), during the misunderstanding which existed between her Highness and the Queen, occasioned by the influence of the Duchess of Marlborough. And Sion House has since, at various times, been graced by the presence of royalty. William IV. paid a visit to it on July 31, 1832, and again he and Queen Adelaide were entertained here in June, 1833.

We will say a few words concerning the building itself, the general outline of which appears to remain much the same as it was left by the Protector Somerset. The house, it is stated, stands on the spot where the church belonging to the monastery formerly stood, and is a very large, sombre, and majestic edifice. It is faced with Bath stone, and built in a quadrangular form, the centre being occupied by a flower-garden about eighty feet square. The house is three storeys high; and although each of the four fronts is without ornament, the general character of the edifice is rendered impressive by the dignity of its proportions and the massive solidity of its several parts. The parapets are embattled, and at each angle of the building is a square embattled turret. The entrance to the house, from the principal fronts, is by flights of stone steps. The house is fronted by a lawn of some extent, terminated by two stone lodges embattled in the same manner as the house. Towards the Thames the lawn is bounded by a lake, and a meadow which is cut down into a gentle slope, so that the surface of the water may be seen from all the principal apartments of the mansion, which are situated on the ground floor.

The entrance to the mansion from the great western road is through an elegant gateway built after a design by Robert Adam. It consists of a central arch, surmounted by the lion passant, the crest of the ducal House of Northumberland, and

representing the "Raising of Lazarus," is especially curious.

In 1874 the famous lion which had for many years surmounted the front of Northumberland House was removed hither on the demolition of that building, and now occupies a conspicuous place on the top of the mansion facing the river. "The head of the lion is placed towards London, and the animal has been raised on a pedestal of masonry sufficiently high to be seen from the roadway through the park at the back of the house, as well as from the river." As already stated by us in OLD AND NEW LONDON, there is an apocryphal

SION ABBEY, FROM THE SOUTH-WEST. (*See p. 50.*)
(*From a Print by H. Buck, 1737.*)

is connected by colonnades with two lodges. The principal doorway of the house is protected by a *porte-cochère*, from which a flight of steps leads to the great hall.

The great hall is paved with black and white marble, and the ceiling richly ornamented with stucco; and it contains some antique statues, &c. Adjoining the hall is the vestibule leading to the dining-room and other state apartments, some of which are of large dimensions, and fitted up in a most luxurious and costly manner. Among other objects of interest in the vestibule is a large vase, which was brought from Northumberland House, at Charing Cross. In original pictures Sion House is anything but rich; but there are some good historical portraits by Vandyke, Lely, and Kneller; and there are also a number of Dutch and Flemish paintings by Van Eyck and others: one of these,

legend in connection with this noble brute, that when he was at first deposited on Northumberland House, his head was placed looking in the direction of Carlton House and St. James's Palace, but that afterwards, on the occasion of some slight received by one of the Dukes of Northumberland, the animal was turned round with its face towards the Corporation of London, —a position, therefore, which he has been allowed to retain in his new quarters.

In Dugdale's "Monasticon" (edit. 1830), it is stated that only a few scanty fragments in some walls are remaining of the old conventual buildings here. Some very ancient mulberry trees on the lawn, their branches braced with irons, are believed not only to have been planted, but to have been in bearing growth, before the dissolution of the monastery. One of them has upon it the date 1546.

Beyond are the out-offices, with their remains of the monastic house, already mentioned. In Aungier's "History of Isleworth and Sion" it is stated that "during some recent improvements in the hall, two very rich and elaborate doorways of Gothic workmanship were discovered; they remain in a very perfect condition, having been preserved by a covering of plaster."

"The grounds of Syon," observes a writer in the *Illustrated London News* of about twenty years ago,

worth Ferry, with the once notable gardens, had received little attention since the early days of Capability Brown, when the late Duke of Northumberland caused designs to be prepared for remodelling the whole of the grounds, seventy-five acres in extent. All the most interesting botanical introductions since Brown completed the gardens were then added to the collections of hardy trees and shrubs; whilst the most valuable ancient trees were preserved prominently in the new plan.

ISLEWORTH CHURCH. (*See p.* 57.)

"are beautifully diversified with rare shrubby and half-shrubby plants, and a double avenue of limes. Near the side of the water are admirable groups of deciduous cypress; and in other parts of the park, the old thorns have become trees. Picturesque groups of the common acacia exist on the westerly side of the park; and there are some extremely beautiful low-spreading horse-chestnuts and noble hop-hornbeams between the bridge and the entrance lodge. In going towards the mansion is a majestic cedar, one of the most venerable tenants of this truly fine old place. The extensive pleasure grounds skirting the Thames, from the middle of Brentford to Isle-

"Passing over the artificial rockery constructed for alpine plants, the grand feature of the improvements is the range of plant-houses, with the substitution of metallic framework for the wood-framed roofs and sides of the old school of hothouse manufactures.

"The range of plant-houses, four hundred feet in length, designed by Mr. Richard Forrest, consists of nine divisions, so contrived that each can be kept at its own independent temperature, suitable to the health and beauty of its plants; yet the doors can, upon any special occasion, be thrown open, giving the various climates of the world with their various inhabitants. These plant-houses take the form of a crescent; the centre rising into a dome sixty-five feet high; the two end houses being broader and higher than the intermediate part. The framework of the entire roof is formed of light iron bars; and the ends and centre have stone pillars and cornices. The whole range is filled with plate-glass. The metallic roofing was manufactured by Messrs. Jones and Co., of Birmingham; it has stood some twenty years without shrinking, and was the first metallic horticultural structure of any importance. The steam warming apparatus was fitted by Tredgold, the eminent engineer; the cast-iron pipes being laid beneath the pathways, and provided with valves for the admission, when required, of vapour, so conducive to the health of tropical plants; the whole being heated by one fire, three hundred feet from the building. The contractors for the heating apparatus were Messrs. Bailey of Holborn. Several things have, we believe, fruited here which have not borne fruit anywhere else in Britain; and many plants, which here fruit profusely, are scarcely ever to be seen in general collections. The houses stand upon a raised stone basement, adorned with elegant stone vases, sculptured with fruit and foliage, attributed to Gibbons. The end portions of the building are used as conservatories for orange-trees, camellias, &c., with a few showy flowers.

"In front of this range of plant-houses is a flower-garden, with a basin and fountain; and lines of standard roses by the side of the walks. The entire garden establishment is supplied with water from an artesian well four hundred and sixty-five feet deep.

"The kitchen-garden covers between three and four acres; and the forcing-houses have the roofs, fronts, and ends mainly of iron, the bars of the sashes being of copper. These, also, are the work of Messrs. Jones. The principal range, for early fruits, is four hundred feet long."

The late Dowager Duchess of Northumberland, who resided at Sion, was a distinguished botanist, and sometime *gouvernante* to our gracious Queen, who, during her minority, occasionally occupied, with the Duchess of Kent, the state apartments at Sion. The Queen's observation of the horticultural improvements here doubtless led to their originator, Mr. Forrest, being subsequently employed in the improvements at Frogmore, where he completed one of the most extensive ranges of metal-framed forcing-houses in the world, designed after that at Sion.

It may be added that the gardens and grounds of Sion have long occupied a foremost place in the horticultural world; and for private gardens may be said to be no mean rival to Kew.

Isleworth lies on the road from London to Sunbury and Shepperton, as we know from Charles Dickens, who makes Bill Sykes and little Oliver Twist travel through it in a market-cart, on their way to commit the burglary which ended so happily for the fortunes of the latter. The parish extends for about three miles along the north bank of the Thames, between Brentford and Twickenham, about a mile at the eastern end being taken up by the grounds of Sion House. The village itself almost surrounds the grounds of Sion, and with its red-brick houses, its sheds for boat-building, and its ivy-clad church tower, forms a pleasing break in the landscape, as seen from the opposite bank of the river at Kew. A considerable portion of land in the parish, which extends back from the river-side for about two miles, is cultivated as market-gardens and nurseries. There are also extensive brick-fields and cement-works here. Norden, writing at the commencement of the seventeenth century, mentions some copper and brass mills at Isleworth, where "workmen make plates both of copper and brasse of all syces, both little and great, thick and thyn, for all purposes; they make also kyttles." Lysons, in his "Environs" (1795), says that "these copper-mills still exist;" they have, however, long since been done away with, as also has another branch of industry, of more recent introduction, the manufacture of pottery and porcelain.

Isleworth, it may be here remarked, must have been a more important place than it is now in the days when the Thames was the great "silent highway." In a "Voyage up the Thames," published in 1738, for instance, there is an account of a public-house at Isleworth which was kept open all night for the express accommodation of parties travelling by the Thames, and the parties who frequented it were often of a most diverting character. A few years later we learn casually from Griffith's "Essay on the Jurisdiction of the Thames," that the fare from London hither was 3s. 6d., for a wherry that contained eight passengers. From the same source we learn that the Windsor carriers called here twice a week in the course of their voyage up the river from Queenhithe. At that time, too, doubtless, nearly all the produce of the market gardens about this locality was sent by water to the London market.

In the reign of Henry III., the manor of Isleworth, being vested in the Crown, was granted to the king's brother, Richard, Earl of Cornwall, and King of the Romans. The site of the ancient palace, or manor-house, is uncertain. Lysons says it seems probable that it was "a spot of ground behind the Phœnix Yard, called in old writings the 'Moted Place.'" Mr. Aungier, in his "History and Antiquities of Syon," places it near Isleworth House. It is on record that in 1264 Sir Hugh Spencer, "with a great multitude of the citizens of London, went to Isleworth, where they spoiled the manor-place of the King of the Romans, and destroyed his water-mylnes and other commodities that he there had." From the description of this manor in "Domesday Book," it will be seen that it includes Heston and Twickenham; and these two latter places are mentioned in an inquisition taken after the Earl of Cornwall's death as hamlets within the manor of Isleworth. Lysons states that in the parish chest at Twickenham is a small illuminated deed of the abbey and convent of Sion, with their seal annexed, and bearing date 22 Henry VI., whereby they discharge their tenants in the manor of Isleworth of a certain annual tribute, or payment of £20. In 1656 certain articles relating to the customs and privileges of the manor of Isleworth were agreed on between Algernon, Earl of Northumberland, and the principal copyholders. They were printed in the following year in the form of a pamphlet, entitled "Isleworth—Sion's Peace." Lands in this manor, observes Lysons, descend according to the strict custom of "Borough-English."

The parish church of Isleworth, dedicated to All Saints, is an attractive object from the river-side. It consists of a chancel, with nave and aisles, and the tower at its western end is profusely covered with ivy. Here, as is so often the case along the valley of the Thames between London and Windsor, the tower is the only old part of the church that is standing.

The body of the church, which was rebuilt in 1705, partly from the designs of Sir Christopher Wren—whose plans were first of all laid aside as too expensive to be carried out, but are said to have been at last brought out and used, subject to such modification and "improvement" as the churchwardens thought fit to make—is a poor structure, but since 1865 it has been considerably improved by the alterations of windows, &c. The materials of the old church were used in erecting at the west end of the churchyard a substantial mansion, the rent of which belongs to the poor.

A new chancel, of a correct ecclesiastical type, laid down with encaustic tiles, was added in 1866. The reredos represents the "Last Supper." The windows have been filled with painted glass, the roof heightened, and the old-fashioned pews made to give place to open benches.

Here are several monuments of more than ordinary interest; among them, one to Sir Orlando Gee, Registrar of the Admiralty, who died in 1705, in which the knight is represented by a marble bust to the waist, with peruke and long flowing cravat; another to Helena Magdalen, Countess de Randwick, a refugee from Holland, who died in 1797; another (a mural tablet) to Sir Richard Downton, Colonel of the Middlesex Militia under Charles II., who died in 1711; another to a poor woman who suddenly became enriched by a freak of fortune, and died equally suddenly. The person here commemorated was a Mrs. Anne Dash, better known by the name of Tolson. She was a great benefactress to the parish; and her history, as recorded in her epitaph, is very singular. She was the daughter of Mr. George Newton, of Duffield, Derbyshire, and having been twice married, first to one Henry Sisson, and afterwards to a Mr. John Tolson, was in her second widowhood reduced to very narrow circumstances, and obliged to set up a boarding-school as a means of procuring a livelihood; but blindness having rendered her unfit for that employment, she became an object of charity. In the meantime, Dr. Caleb Cotesworth, a physician, who had married a relation of Mrs. Tolson, died in 1741, having amassed in the course of his practice the sum of £150,000, the greater part of which—namely, upwards of £120,000—he left to his wife, who, surviving him only a few hours, died intestate, and her large fortune was divided between Mrs. Tolson and two others, as the nearest of kin. With a due sense of this signal deliverance, and unexpected change from a state of want to riches and affluence, she appropriated by a deed of gift the sum of £5,000, to be expended after her decease in building and endowing an almshouse at Isleworth for six poor men and six women. This lady died in the year 1750, aged 89, having married, subsequent to this deed of gift, a third husband, Mr. Joseph Dash, merchant.

In this church is a brass to Margaret Dely, one of the sisters of Sion in Mary's time; and a palimpsest brass, with a Flemish inscription, was to be seen some years since in the vestry.

The parish register, which dates from the middle of the sixteenth century, contains a few interesting entries. Among others there is recorded the baptism, in October, 1617, of Waller's "Sacharissa"—Dorothy, daughter of Sir Robert and Lady Dorothy Sidney. It appears by this entry that she was born at Sion House whilst her grandfather was a prisoner in the Tower. From the following extract from the parish accounts, it is clear that she resided at Isleworth in her widowhood:—"1655. Received of the Countess of Sunderland, for her rate for the poor for half a year, 15s." "Dorothy, the Lady and Countess of Northumberland, buried Aug. 14, 1619." She was "Sacharissa's" grandmother, wife of Henry, Earl of Northumberland, and daughter of Walter Devereux, Earl of Essex. By this date of her burial, it appears that she did not live to see her husband released from his confinement. The register also records the marriage, on the 27th March, 1679, of Henry Cavendish, Earl of Ogle, son and heir of Henry, Duke of Newcastle, to Lady Elizabeth Percy, daughter and heiress of Josceline, eleventh and last Earl of Northumberland. It also records the marriage of Lord Algernon Percy, afterwards second Lord Lovaine, with Isabella Susannah, sister of Peter, first Lord Gwydir; the ceremony was performed at Sion House by Dr. Thomas Percy, afterwards Bishop of Dromore.

Among the minutes of the vestry is entered a licence, bearing date April 28, 1661, given by William Grant, Vicar of Isleworth, to Richard Downton, Esq., and Thomasine, his wife, to eat flesh in Lent "for the recovery of their health, they being enforced by age, notorious sickness, and weakness to abstain from fish." These licences were by no means uncommon at an earlier date. After the Restoration, the keeping of Lent, which had been neglected by the Puritans, who entirely set aside the observing of seasons, was enforced by a proclamation from the king, and an office for granting licences to eat flesh in any part of England was set up in St. Paul's Churchyard, and advertised in the public papers, in 1663.

Nicholas Byfield, Vicar of Isleworth, 1615—20, was a laborious or "painful" preacher of the Puritan school; he was the father of Adoniram Byfield, one of the few persons stigmatised by name by Butler in his "Hudibras," and grandfather of Dr. Byfield, the "salvolatile" doctor, who is said in his epitaph to be "Diu volatilis, tandem fixus."

Dr. Cave, the learned author of the "Lives of the Fathers," "Primitive Christianity," &c., was Vicar of Isleworth from 1690 till his death in 1713. He is buried at Islington.

Aungier records the singular fact that Dr. Turner, the herbalist and physician to Edward, Duke of Somerset and Lord Protector, held the Deanery of Wells, though only a layman, and had a licence to preach at Isleworth against the errors of Pelagius. He is mentioned in Wood's "Athenæ Oxonienses." His lecture on this subject was answered in print, and his reply, dedicated to Bishop Latimer in 1551, was also published. The churchyard is spacious and well laid out. In the centre of it are three yew trees curiously linked together by a lych-gate, which forms a rustic arbour.

Isleworth was not neglected by the charitably-disposed in bygone times. Sir Thomas Ingram, in 1664, founded an almshouse here for six poor women, housekeepers of the parish; and the late Mr. John Farnell built and endowed a range of almshouses for six poor men and six women. In 1750 came the foundation of Mrs. Anne Tolson's almshouses, already mentioned; these houses have lately been rebuilt. Other almshouses have also been founded here by Mrs. Mary Bell and Mrs. Sermon.

The church of St. John the Baptist, in St. John's Road, was built in 1857, on a site given by the late Duke of Northumberland. It consists of chancel, nave, and aisles, and is in the Early English style of architecture. The are several meeting-houses and chapels for the various religious denominations in the village, besides schools and other public buildings. The Brentford Union is situated on the Twickenham Road, in the parish of Isleworth.

Among the residents of Isleworth, in the days of Queen Anne, was a large glass manufacturer named Gumley, whose only child and heiress carried his wealth into the Pulteney family by marrying the Earl of Bath. She is mentioned by Pope in his "Miscellanies," with a compliment at the expense of her husband—

"But charming Gumley's lost in Pulteney's wife."

Gumley House was built towards the end of the seventeenth century; and after the death of Mr. Gumley it became the residence of the Earl of Bath. The mansion subsequently became the property of General Lord Lake. It is now a Roman Catholic convent school for young ladies.

Shrewsbury Place—so named from having been formerly the residence of Charles Talbot, Duke of Shrewsbury, Secretary of State to William III. and Queen Mary—shared a similar fate to Gumley House, and became devoted to religious purposes. It is now a Roman Catholic school.

Not far from Gumley House, on the side of the road from Twickenham to London, stood another noted mansion, Kendal House, so called from the Duchess of Kendal, the favourite mistress of King George I., who resided there. The following story is related of her in the "Good Fellow's Calendar:"—"This gracious sovereign once, while *doing the tender* with the Duchess of Kendal, promised her that if she survived him, and if departed souls were so permitted, he would pay her a visit. The superstitious Duchess on his death so much expected the fulfilment of that engagement, that a large raven, or some black fowl, flying into one of the windows of her villa at Isleworth, she was fully persuaded it was the soul of her departed monarch so accoutred, and received and treated it with all the respect and tenderness of duty, till the royal bird or herself took *the last flight.*"

After the death of the Duchess (or the "Maypole," as she was irreverently called by the people) the mansion was sold, and opened as a place of public entertainment, and was frequently advertised as such in the years 1750 and 1751.

The *Daily Advertiser* of April the 4th, 1750, contains the following announcement :—" For certain, Kendal House, Isleworth, near Brentford, Middlesex, eight miles from London, will open for breakfasting on Monday, the 16th inst. The long room for dancing is upwards of sixty feet long, and wide in proportion ; all the other rooms are elegantly fitted up. The orchestra on the water is allowed, by all that have seen it, to be in the genteelest taste, being built an octagon in the Corinthian order, above fifty feet diameter, having an upper and lower gallery, where gentlemen and ladies may divert themselves with fishing, the canal being well stocked with tench, carp, and all sorts of fish in great plenty ; near which are two wildernesses, with delightful rural walks ; and through the garden runs a rapid river, shaded with a pleasant grove of trees, with various walks, so designed by nature, that in the hottest day of summer you are screened from the heat of the sun. The small but just account of the place falls greatly short of its real beauties. Great care will be taken to keep out all disorderly people. There is a man cook, and a good larder ; all things as cheap or cheaper than at any place of the kind."

The Princesses Amelia and Caroline, daughters of George II., who, in 1733, brought the well at Islington Spa, then called the New Tunbridge Wells, into fashion, by going thither to drink the waters, were, doubtless, occasional visitors here. At all events, this place appears to have enjoyed an equal share of popularity with its Islington rival, for, in a song called "Modern Diversions," published in the *Universal Magazine* in 1753, the following lines occur :—

> " To operas, assemblies,
>   Or else to masquerade,
>   New Tunbridge, or to Kendal House ;
>   And this shall be the trade.
>   We'll sally out to breakfast,
>   And hear the fiddlers play ;
>   And there we'll revel, feast, and dance,
>   And make a merry day.
>   For a roving we will go, will go,
>   For a roving we will go."

When the taste for amusements of this kind

died out, Kendal House was pulled down, and its site devoted to building purposes.

In the British Museum may be seen a perspective view of Kendal House, drawn by Chatelain in 1756 ; it represents probably one of the grand breakfast days for which the place was so celebrated. A large orchestra, filled with musicians, is "discoursing sweet music," while a number of ladies and gentlemen, the former dressed in hoops of monstrous size, are walking about, and some are amusing themselves by fishing.

The rivulet which runs through the grounds of Kendal House, rises on Norwood Common, and at Osterley it is formed into a canal of fish-ponds. Next it passes to Hounslow, whence it crosses the road and finds its way hither.

Kendal House, however, was not the earliest place of amusement in Isleworth ; for the *General Evening Post* of May, 1734, contains an advertisement of the "Isleworth Assembly" held in that and the previous year at "Dunton House"—a house which it is now impossible to identify.

A large house, formerly standing near the riverside, and known as Lacy House, was built by Mr. James Lacy, one of the patentees of Drury Lane Theatre. It was at one time the residence of Sir Robert Walpole, and of his daughter, Mrs. Keppel, widow of Dr. Keppel, Bishop of Exeter ; it was also some time in the occupation of the Earl of Warwick, and of Richard Brinsley Sheridan.

At St. Margaret's, towards the south-west end of the village, is the Royal Naval Female School, an institution founded "for the maintenance and education of the daughters of naval and marine officers." The house was built for the Earl of Kilmorey, but never occupied by him ; it was purchased in 1856, and converted to its present uses. The Marquis of Ailsa had a seat in this part of Isleworth many years back, but that mansion has long been demolished and the park built over. George Calvert, Lord Baltimore, one of Horace Walpole's "Noble Authors," likewise had a country seat here. His lordship was Secretary of State to James I., and the original grantee and founder, in 1729, of the city of Baltimore, the commercial metropolis of Maryland, in the United States.

Silver Hall, which formerly stood on the south side of the Twickenham Road, was built in the seventeenth century by John Smith, Esq., who was created a baronet in 1694, and whose arms were over the piers of the gate. The old building, which was ultimately used as a school, was pulled down some time ago, and a new mansion, called Silver

Hall, now the residence of Mr. Francis H. N. Glossop, erected on a different site.

Gordon House, in the Richmond Road, the seat of the Earl of Kilmorey, is a modern mansion. Isleworth House, close by, the residence of Mrs. McAndrew, is a fine building, and is celebrated for the beauty of its grounds and the views it affords of the river and surrounding scenery. The house was once the residence of Lady Cooper, who was here visited by William IV., by whose command, as Mr. Thorne tells us, in his " Environs of London," "the Syon vista in Kew Gardens was cut in order to open a view of pagoda and observatory to the front of the house."

Sir Clipesby Crewe was a resident of Isleworth in the seventeenth century, as we learn from the following entry in " Evelyn's Diary," under date of February, 1648 :—" I went with my noble friend, Sir William Ducy (afterwards Lord Downe), to Thistleworth, where we dined with Sir Clipesby Crewe, and afterwards to see the rare miniatures of Peter Oliver, and rounds of plaster, and then the curious flowers of Mr. Barill's gardens, who has some good medails and pictures. Sir Clipesby has fine Indian hangings, and a very good chimney-piece of water-colours by Breugel, which I bought for him."

Here, too, at one time, lived in a small house, retired from business, George Field, a metaphysician of the German school, and the author of some practical works on Chromatics, having made his money by preparing colours for painters. The exact site of his residence is now unknown.

Worton Hall, in Worton Road, midway between Isleworth and Hounslow, is a modern mansion, and perpetuates the manor of Worton, once a royal manor, which was granted by Henry VI. to the Monastery of Sion. In some records it is called the " Manor of Eystons "—thus perpetuating the name of a family which for three generations in the fourteenth century resided here, before they inherited Hendred, in Berkshire, where they are still located. The property now belongs to the Duke of Northumberland.

Syon Hill, a little to the south-east, a mansion built by the Earl of Holdernesse, who died in 1778, was at the close of the last century the residence of the Duke of Marlborough. The duke had a small observatory in the grounds, and, as Lysons observes, he " cultivated with much success the science of astronomy." The house has been taken down, and the park in part built upon.

At Spring Grove, in the north-eastern part of the parish, are some almshouses, recently erected, called " Honnor's Home." They were founded by a Mr. Honnor, a member of the Saddlers' Company, who are the patrons of the charity, and are for the benefit of decayed freemen, freewomen, and widows of freemen.

The London International College, founded under the auspices of the late Mr. Richard Cobden, is situated at Spring Grove. The institution was inaugurated by the Prince of Wales in 1867, and the college was established for the teaching of English, French, and German, side by side with mathematics, classics, and natural science.

Spring Grove was formed into a separate ecclesiastical district in 1856, out of the parishes of Heston and Isleworth. The church, dedicated to St. Mary, is a handsome building, consisting of a chancel, nave, aisles, and tower with a lofty spire, and stands on rising ground between the western high road and Osterley Park.

Before continuing our journey westward along the valley of the Thames, it will be as well to make a short *détour* to the north, in order to explore the classic regions of Hounslow, a portion of which lies really within the parish of Isleworth.

CHAPTER V.

HOUNSLOW AND HANWORTH.

" Formidare malos fures."—*Horace.* I., Sat. i. 77.

Situation of Hounslow—A Priory founded here—Martyrdom of Archbishop Scrope—Markets and Fairs—Remains of the Conventual Buildings—Holy Trinity Church—The Manor House—Hounslow in the Old Coaching Days—Present Condition of the Town—The Churches of St. Stephen and St. Paul—Salvation Army Barracks—Hounslow Heath—Military Encampments—Knights of the Road—Site of the Gibbets—A Bishop Counterfeiting the Highwayman—The Gallant Highwayman—The Highwayman Outwitted—Horse-racing, &c.—Gunpowder Mills—Cavalry Barracks—Whitton Park—Hanworth Park—Hanworth House—The Parish Church.

THE district which will form the subject of this chapter lies to the west of Isleworth, and is one which, considering its size and present condition, is perhaps better known than any other in England for the scenes of historical interest which it has witnessed, and for the notoriety which it gained at the hands of those "knights of the road" by whom it was infested during the seventeenth and eighteenth centuries.

The village, or town, of Hounslow, as stated in the preceding chapter, is situated partly in the parish of Isleworth; it is also partly in that of Heston. The place was called in "Domesday

came a certain man of his household to the house of the Holy Trinity at Hundeslaw for refreshment, who confessed that he was "one of three men who threw the corpse [of the king] into the river between Barking and Gravesend," whilst it was being conveyed from Westminster towards Canterbury for interment; and adds, "but the chest, covered with cloth of gold, in which the body had lain, we carried with great honour into Canterbury, and buried it." Nevertheless, in 1832, the royal tomb was opened in the presence of the Bishop of Oxford and others, and the remains of the

A Gunpowder Mill. (Pellet House No 24)

The Storehouses and Mill Head.

The Sluice. & Mixing House No 26

THE POWDER-MILLS, HOUNSLOW. *(See p. 68.)*

Book" Honeslowe, and later on it was spelt Hundeslawe and Hundeslowe. In the thirteenth century a priory, dedicated to the Holy Trinity, was founded here, the peculiar office of the brethren being to solicit alms for the redemption of captives. It is spoken of by Cobbett, in his "History of the Reformation," as "a friary."

One Clement Maydestone, a friar of this house, wrote a history of the martyrdom of Richard Scrope, Archbishop of York, to whom he had been a retainer, in which it is stated that within thirty days after the death of Henry IV., there

king were found in his coffin. This at once, of course, disposed of the story told by Maydestone.

In 1296 a weekly market was granted to the brethren of this priory, to be held on Wednesday, and an annual fair on the eve and feast of the Holy Trinity, and to last a week. The market has long been discontinued, but fairs are still held on Trinity Monday, and on the Monday after Michaelmas Day. At the dissolution the revenues of this priory were valued at £78 8s. 6d. In Cooke's "Topography of Middlesex," published early in the present century, it is stated that "the only remaining part of the conventual buildings is the chapel, which exhibits evident traces of the architecture of the thirteenth century. In the south wall of the chancel are three ancient stone stalls, and a double piscina, with narrow pointed arches, divided by a column. The chapel consists of a chancel, nave, and south aisle. In the nave is a small monument, with the effigies of a man in armour and his wife, kneeling; on the floor is a brass plate to the memory of Thomas Lupton, who died in 1512, and his wife Alice. In the windows of the south aisle there is some painted glass, representing the figure of St. Katharine and some other subjects." Mr. Brewer, in the "Beauties of England" (1816), says that "on one face of the exterior is a mutilated escutcheon, with the arms and quarterings of the Windsor family, who have been supposed, but, as it would appear, erroneously, to have been the founders of the priory."

This ancient chapel has now entirely disappeared, and in its place—although perhaps not quite on the same site—has arisen another church, dedicated to the Holy Trinity. This was built in the upper part of the main street about the year 1834; it is constructed of white brick, and is a plain and ugly edifice in the Italian style, of little or no architectural interest. It consists of a chancel, nave, aisles, porch, and bell-turret, and is surmounted with stone cupolas twelve in number. The building was enlarged by the addition of a chancel in 1856.

In the "Beauties of England" it is stated that the manor and the site of the priory were annexed by Henry VIII. to the honour of Hampton Court, but were both leased in 1539 to Richard Awnsham, Esq. The property was for some time vested in the Windsor family, long seated in the neighbouring parish of Stanwell. In 1705 it was purchased by Whitlocke Bulstrode, Esq., the author of a "Treatise on Transmigration" and of other publications, who enlarged the manor-house, an ancient brick structure facing the heath, at the western extremity of Hounslow, and also repaired the chapel which contains his monument.

The town consists mainly of a long, uninteresting, and monotonous street, with scarcely one picturesque or redeeming object on either side. As far back as about 1650 it was noted for its numerous inns and ale-houses, and later on it became a great place for posting-houses. In the "Beauties of England," it is stated that "the chief dependence of the place is on the immense tide of road traffic, which rolls to and from the metropolis with surprising vehemence and bustle. As this

hamlet is only one short stage from London, the principal business of the inns consists in providing relays of post-horses, and exchanges of horses for the numerous coaches travelling the road. All here wears the face of impatience and expedition. The whole population seems on the wing of removal; and assuredly the main street of Hounslow is a place from which the examiner would wish to remove with all the celerity familiar to the spot." At the accession of Queen Victoria there were as many as five hundred stage-coaches and one thousand five hundred horses daily employed in transit through the town. The "George Inn" was particularly noted as a great posting-house. Its several posting-houses were, in fact, very busy and prosperous till the traffic was diverted by the opening of the railways to Southampton and Bath.

For a long time after the coaching traffic of the high road had ceased, Hounslow remained in a very depressed condition; but business in the locality has, to a certain extent, revived, and the place has of late years acquired a fair local trade, whilst many of the new shops, public buildings, and new schools, all attest the progress which the town is now making.

In 1857 a Town Hall was erected. Here the ordinary public business of the town is transacted, and there is also a well-furnished reading-room within its walls, with a library containing upwards of a thousand volumes, for the use of the inhabitants.

St. Stephen's Church, situate in Hanworth Road, close to the London and South Western Railway Station, was built in 1875-6, and is in the Early English style of architecture. The ecclesiastical district to which it belongs was formed out of the parishes of Isleworth and Heston by an Order in Council, passed in 1877.

St. Paul's Church, which is in the Bath Road, near the heath, was built in 1873-4, the ecclesiastical district to which it is attached having been formed out of the parish of Heston. The building, like the one just mentioned, is in the Early English style, and its spire, standing one hundred and thirty feet high, is conspicuous for some distance round.

Among the latest additions to the town has been the extension of the Metropolitan District Railway hither, and the erection of a Salvation Army barracks, bearing the strange and ominous superscription—"Blood and Fire."

The celebrated Hounslow Heath adjoins the town on the west, and extends into the parishes and hamlets of Hounslow, Heston, Isleworth,

Brentford, Twickenham, Feltham, Harlington, Cranford, Harmondsworth, Stanwell, Bedfont, Hampton, and Teddington. According to a survey made in 1546, it contained at that time four thousand two hundred and ninety-two acres; but other accounts made its area much greater, Rocque's map setting it down as six thousand six hundred and fifty-eight acres. It was estimated by Messrs. Britton and Brayley, in 1810, to comprise about five thousand acres. The soil was then thought "very improvable," and accordingly, since then,

once it has been the rendezvous of the principal military force of this kingdom.

In 1267 the Earl of Gloucester, leading the Londoners against King Henry III., assembled them on Hounslow Heath in order to give battle to the king. The army of Charles I. is said to have been entrenched here the day after the battle of Brentford, in 1642; and in November of the same year the army under the command of the Earl of Essex was mustered here. Five years later the heath witnessed a general rendezvous of the

HIGH STREET, HOUNSLOW.

much of it has been brought into profitable cultivation under several Acts of Parliament, which have been passed for enclosing different parts, but it still remains one of the most unproductive parts of the county of Middlesex.

Cobbett, in his "Rural Rides," writes as follows with regard to the general aspect of the land in this locality:—"A much more ugly county than that between Egham and Kensington would with difficulty be found in England. Flat as a pancake, until you come to Hammersmith, the soil is a nasty, stony dirt upon a bed of gravel. Hounslow Heath, which is only a little worse than the general run, is a sample of all that is bad in soil and villanous in look. Yet all this is now enclosed, and what they call 'cultivated.'"

As above stated, Hounslow has long enjoyed a celebrity, in its way, in the annals of England. Vestiges of camps—either British or Roman—were visible on its surface down to a comparatively recent date. It has been the scene of military and other assemblies at different periods, and more than

Parliamentary forces under General Sir Thomas Fairfax, when there appeared 20,000 foot and horse, with a great train of artillery. The *Perfect Diurnal*, August, 1647, gives the following account of this rendezvous:—"There were present the Earls of Northumberland, Salisbury, and Kent, Lord Grey of Wark, Lords Howard of Escrick, Wharton, Say and Sele, Mulgrave, and others, the Speaker of the House of Commons, and above 100 of the members. The whole army was drawn up in battalions, near a mile and a half in length. The general, accompanied with the said lords and commons, rode along the army from regiment to regiment, and were received with great acclamation. Having viewed the army, they took leave of the general, and some went to the Earl of Northumberland's at Sion, and others to the Lord Say and Sele's at Stanwell. Soon after the Palgrave came into the field, who, with the general and many gentlemen, viewed the army." The encampment was attended by Algernon Sidney and several other members, and the leader was everywhere hailed with great enthusiasm.

In 1678 the army of Charles II. was encamped on the Heath, a fact which is thus duly recorded by John Evelyn, in his "Diary," under date June 29th of that year:—"Returned with my son by

Hounslow Heath, where we saw the newly-rais'd army encamp'd, design'd against France, in pretence at least, but which gave umbrage to the Parliament. His Majesty and a world of company were in the field, and the whole army in battalia: a very glorious sight. Now were brought into service a new sort of soldiers called Granadiers, who were dextrous in flinging hand granados, every one having a pouch-full; they had furr'd caps with coped crowns, like Janizanis, which made them look very fierce, and some had long hoods hanging down behind, as we picture fools: their clothing being likewise pybald yellow and red."

In 1686 James II., resolving not to yield in his struggle with his subjects, formed a camp of some thirteen thousand men on Hounslow Heath. The Londoners looked on it with terror, which, however, was soon diminished by familiarity. The camp was visited, as was only natural, by the beaux and belles of the West End, who flocked to it in such overwhelming crowds that, to use Macaulay's words, "a visit to Hounslow became their favourite amusement on holydays, and the camp presented the appearance of a vast fair. In truth," he adds, "the place was merely a gay suburb of the capital." The king had hoped that his army—or rather, the sight of it—would overawe London; but the result was quite different, for the army instead took its cue from London. Various tracts and pamphlets sprang up out of the camp, and a hot controversy ensued, which helped to bring about the events of 1688.

Under date of June 2, 1686, Evelyn again mentions the camp being located at Hounslow, but being "forced to retire to quarters from sickness and other inconveniences of the weather." Four days later he writes:—"The camp was now againe pitch'd at Hounslow, the commanders profusely vying in the expence and magnificence of tents."

During the time of the encampment in 1687, there was in use here a curious tabernacle, or chapel on wheels, which had been built by command of King James, to accompany him in his royal " progresses," in order that mass might be celebrated in his presence by his chaplain. As soon as the abdication of the king was known to be a fact, this chapel was brought by road up to London, and placed upon the site long occupied by its successor, Trinity Chapel, on the south side of Conduit Street, Regent Street. At the request of Dr. Tenison—afterwards Archbishop of Canterbury, but at that time Rector of St. Martin's-in-the-

Fields—this wooden structure was subsequently used as a temporary chapel of ease, for the use of the outlying portion of the inhabitants of his then wide and scattered parish.

Every reader of English history, even Macaulay's " schoolboy," is aware that James II. was with his army here when the news of the acquittal of the seven bishops was signalled from London. "Nowhere," writes Macaulay, "had the acquittal been received with more clamorous delight than at Hounslow Heath. In truth, the great force which the king had assembled for the purpose of overawing his mutinous capital had become more mutinous than the capital itself, and was more dreaded by the Court than by the citizens. Early in August. therefore, the camp was broken up, and the troops were sent to quarters in different parts of the country."

In the library of the Corporation of London, at Guildhall, may be seen three different views of the camp of James II. One is a woodcut, entitled " An exact Prospect of the King's Forces encamped on Hounslow Heath, 1686;" another woodcut is of the same date, but has a letterpress inscription; the third is a copper-plate, engraved by Harris, of about the same date. In the first volume of " Poems on Affairs of State," about the same date, is a very severe attack on King James in connection with this camp and heath; but this is not mentioned by Mr. Wilkes in his poem above on " Hounslow Heath."

Three years later, namely, in 1690, Queen Mary reviewed her troops here in the presence of the Duke of Marlborough. On the alarm of a French invasion in aid of the Stuart cause, the whole nation was stirred with a martial spirit, and, according to Macaulay, "two and twenty troops of cavalry, furnished by Suffolk, Essex, Hertfordshire, and Buckinghamshire, were reviewed by Mary at Hounslow, and were complimented by Marlborough on their martial appearance."

King George III. more than once held reviews here, the troops inspected being furnished from the ranks of both the regulars and volunteers.

The camp here seems to have been conducted very much as our summer volunteer camp at Wimbledon, the crowds of visitors including many ladies of quality, and the hospitality of the officers being so profuse as to add very seriously to their expenses. It was constantly visited by royalty; and in 1740 the list of distinguished personages here included the " Butcher" Duke of Cumberland, the Duke of Marlborough, the Earl of Dunmore, and several other officers of the highest rank. The Duke of Cumberland stayed here a week on this occasion, and gave more than one grand entertainment under canvas.

The camp at Hounslow Heath was always popular with the Londoners; and, in 1744 (as we learn from the *Daily Advertiser* of March 13) it formed the subject of a popular exhibition, at the bottom of Hay Hill, Dover Street. It was patronised by the Prince and Princess of Wales, and the admission was a shilling. The following is a copy of the bill: "To be seen, the whole Prospect of the (late) Camp at Hounslow, representing in proper order, both Horse and Foot, every officer in his proper post, with the nicest distinction of both their liveries and colours; in proportion and magnitude representing life nearer than anything of the kind hitherto invented. The train of Artillery in its proper decorum."

Hounslow Heath is the chief rival to Finchley Common in the "Lives of the Highwaymen," and is one of the "happy hunting-grounds" of the "Newgate Calendar." It was in the seventeenth century that the locality acquired its celebrity as the haunt of highwaymen. The reason will be obvious to readers of Macaulay, who writes in his "History of England":—"The peace (1698) had all over Europe, and nowhere more than in England, turned soldiers into marauders. . . . On Hounslow Heath a company of horsemen, with masks on their faces . . . succeeded in stopping thirty or forty coaches (of the nobility), and rode off with a great booty in guineas, watches, and jewellery."

Here General Fairfax was robbed by "Moll Cut-purse," the noted highway-woman, who was committed to Newgate for the offence, but managed to escape from the gallows.

Here, in 1774, on his way to Cranford, Lord Berkeley shot a footpad who wanted his money, and who would have shot his lordship if he had not been anticipated. An amusing, though possibly somewhat poetical, account of the affair will be found in Mr. Grantley Berkeley's "Life and Recollections," and in the seventieth chapter of Lord Mahon's (Stanhope's) "History of England." His lordship, in relating it, adds some remarks which tend to show the audacity of highwaymen, and the terror which they inspired as late as the reigns of our Hanoverian line. He writes in 1836:—"Much less than a century ago the great thoroughfares near London, and above all, the open heaths, as Bagshot and Hounslow, were infested by robbers on horseback, who bore the name of highwaymen. Booty these men were determined by some means or other to obtain. In the reign of George the First they stuck up hand-

bills at the gates of many known rich men in London, forbidding any one of them, on pain of death, to travel from home without a watch, or with less than ten guineas of money.[*] Private carriages and public conveyances were alike the objects of attack. Thus, Mr. Nuthall, the solicitor and friend of Lord Chatham, returning from Bath in his carriage . . . . was stopped and fired at near Hounslow, and died of the fright. . . . These outrages appear to have increased in frequency towards the close of the American War. . . . It is strange," he adds, "that so highly civilised a people should have endured these highway robberies so long . . . but stranger still, perhaps, to find some of the best writers of the last century treat them as subjects of jest, and almost of praise. From such productions as the 'Tom Clinch' of Swift or the 'Beggar's Opera' of Gay we may collect that it was the tone in certain circles to depict the highwaymen as daring and generous spirits, who 'took to the road,' as it was termed, under some momentary difficulties: the gentlefolk, as it were, of the profession, and far above the common run of thieves."

Mr. John Mellish, M.P. for Great Grimsby, was shot by highwaymen on Hounslow Heath as he was returning from hunting with the king's hounds, in April, 1798. His daughter lived down to 1880.

Charles Knight, in the commencement of his "Passages of a Working Life,"[†] tells us that he well remembered as a child the murder of Mr. Mellish by a footpad near the "Magpies," and the hanging of these knights of the road on the common, the scene of their misdeeds. "Between the two roads, near a clump of firs, was a gibbet, on which two bodies hung in chains. The chains rattled; the iron plates scarcely held the gibbet together; the rags of the highwaymen displayed their horrible skeletons within."

Hounslow Heath was still a favourite haunt of highwaymen even so late as the present century. A Mr. Steele was murdered here in 1806. This murder is remembered from the fact that at the execution of the assassin thirty persons were crushed to death in the crowd before the gallows.

Cyrus Redding writes thus of this spot in the above-mentioned year:—"It was a cold night when I crossed Hounslow Heath, about midnight, after eighteen hours' travelling. All the coaches had guards, and our's prepared his pistols and blunderbuses soon after we left Reading: a paradoxical

---

[*] "Lettres d'un Français en Angleterre," 1745, Vol. III., p. 211.
[†] Vol. I., p. 40.

mark that we were approaching the more civilised part of the kingdom. An officer had been shot at in his carriage by a highwayman while crossing the heath a few days before."

The gibbets seem, from Rocque's map of Middlesex, to have stood on the point of land formed by the junction of the Bath and Staines roads. Not far from them was Albemarle House, an "Academy" for youths, who seem to have had this humanising spectacle constantly before their eyes.

removed on account of the constant passing and re-passing of the royal family along this road on their journeys between London and Windsor.

Crabb Robinson mentions in his "Diary" in 1819 crossing Hounslow Heath on a stage-coach, and being told by one of his fellow-passengers that forty years previously the road was "literally lined with gibbets, on which were in irons the carcases of malefactors blackening in the sun." He might safely have written "twenty" for "forty."

WHITTON PARK. (*See p.* 69.)
(*From a Print by W. Woollett, about* 1800.)

There is a print of this school in the British Museum; it shows the boys exercising as volunteers, doubtless in expectation of the invasion of the great Napoleon in 1804. In the "Asylum for Fugitive Pieces," 1785, are the following coarse and vulgar lines, addressed to the young gentlemen of the Hounslow Academy :—

> "Take notice, roguelings, I prohibit
> Your walking underneath this gibbet;
> Have you not heard, my little ones,
> Of Raw Head and of Bloody Bones?
> How do you know but that there fellow
> May step down quick and up you swallow?"

The gibbets could never have been a very agreeable or edifying sight; and accordingly they were

The dangers of the road, in fact, were not at an end till many years of the present century had passed away; and, indeed, lasted very nearly down to the introduction of railways, which gave the "knights of the road" their final *congé*.

That the life of the "dashing" highwayman was invested with a sort of sensational romance there can be little doubt. "In the last half of the seventeenth century," writes Mr. James Thorne, in his "Environs of London," "it was no uncommon thing for the gay young cavalier to take to the road as the readiest mode of mending his fortune by lightening the purses of the well-to-do round-head citizens he held in supreme contempt; but even a century later stories were credited of other than vulgar footpads resorting at times to Hounslow Heath. It is gravely related, for example, that Twysden, Bishop of Raphoe, playing the highwayman there in 1752, was shot through the body, and died from the wound at a friend's house, his death being announced as from inflammation of the bowels." This story is related on the authority of the Hon. Grantley Berkeley, who tells it in his "Life and Recollections."

The readers of the "Beggar's Opera" will learn

No less a writer than De Quincey has endeavoured not merely to whitewash, but to throw a *couleur de rose* over the ideal highwayman. He followed "a liberal profession, one which required more accomplishments than either the bar or the pulpit, since from the beginning it presumed a most bountiful endowment of qualifications—strength, health, agility, and excellent horsemanship, intrepidity of the first order, presence of mind, courtesy, and a general ambidexterity of powers for facing all accidents,

OLD HANWORTH CHURCH. (*See p. 70.*)
(*From a Print published 1795.*)

from Captain Macheath how rapidly the information was circulated as to the wealth of intending travellers along the great western road. That the highwayman could at times be the "very essence of politeness" is not to be wondered at if they were made of such gentlemanly stuff. Claud Duval, as Macaulay tells us, "took to the road, and became captain of a formidable gang;" he adds that "it is related how, at the head of his troop, he stopped a lady's coach, in which there was a booty of four hundred pounds; how he took only one hundred, and suffered the fair owner to ransom the rest by dancing a coranto with him on the heath." This celebrated exploit has been made the subject of a painting by Mr. Frith, and has been engraved.

and for turning to a good account all unlooked-for contingencies." He considers that, beyond a doubt, the finest men in England, physically speaking, throughout the last century, the very noblest specimens of man, considered as an animal, were the mounted robbers, who cultivated their profession on the great leading roads. For the forger, and such as he, De Quincey has no sympathy; but he maintains that the special talents which led to distinction on the road had often no other career open to them. When every traveller carried fire-arms, the mounted robber lived in an element of danger and adventurous gallantry, so that admiration for the thief sometimes was extorted from the person robbed. "If to courage, address, promptitude of decision (writes Dutton Cook) he added courtesy and a spirit of forbearing generosity, he seemed to be almost a man who merited public encouragement." For it might be urged plausibly that if his profession was sure to exist, and that if he were removed, a successor might arise who would carry on the business in a less liberal spirit. Indeed, De Quincey seems to think that a shade of disgrace had fallen upon England in a previous generation, inasmuch as the championship of the road had passed for a time into the hands of a Frenchman like Claud Duval.

Notwithstanding the bold front which the highwayman was in the habit of assuming, he was occasionally outwitted. "Stand and deliver!" were the words addressed to a tailor travelling on foot by a highwayman, whose brace of pistols looked rather dangerous than otherwise. "I'll do that with pleasure," was the reply, at the same time handing over to the outstretched hands of the robber a purse apparently pretty well stocked; "but," continued he, "suppose you do me a favour in return. My friends would laugh at me were I to go home and tell them I was robbed with as much patience as a lamb; s'pose you fire your two bull-dogs right through the crown of my hat : it will look something like a show of resistance." His request was acceded to; but hardly had the smoke from the discharge of the weapons passed away, when the tailor pulled out a rusty old horse-pistol, and in his turn politely requested the thunder-struck highwayman to give up everything about him of value, his pistols not omitted.

The locality of Hounslow and its Heath is at best anything but a haunt of the Muses; but still it has inspired at all events one poem, for the Rev. Wetenhall Wilkes, who was minister of the Chapelry in the reign of George the Second, dedicated to the Duke of Argyll a poetical epistle, in verse, after the style of Pope, entitled "Hounslow Heath." The lines are turgid and bombastical enough, but they give us some particulars which would else have escaped notice. And a modern reprint of the poem, by Mr. W. Pinkerton, F.S.A., contains some interesting notes, on which we have drawn considerably. For instance, we learn that a century and a half ago the Heath was a frequent meet for the royal stag-hounds and fox-hounds, and that the King, the Prince of Wales, and the Princess Amelia were frequently seen here pursuing the pleasures of the chase. In the early part of the last century, horse-racing of a more plebeian character was here indulged in; to use the bombastic phrase of Mr. Wilkes in his poem,

"Near to the town behold a spacious course,
The scene of trial for the sportive horse."

The site of Hounslow Racecourse is laid down on Rocque's Map (1754). It was on the left of the road to Staines, a short distance from the Bell public-house. Many notices of these races are to be found in the newspapers of the time; for instance, in the *Evening Post* of July 20 and 23, 1734, when seven horses started, and one broke its leg in the last heat. The names of the horses and of the owners are given; but they evidently were not of the same stamp as those of which we read as figuring at Newmarket.

"Houses and inhabitants," writes the Honourable Miss Amelia Murray, "now occupy that part of Hounslow Heath where the grim gallows once stood within my recollection;" and Mason thus celebrates the place—

"Hounslow, whose heath sublimer terror fills,
Shall with her gibbets lend her powder-mills."

Large gunpowder-mills stand on the banks of a small stream about two miles to the south of the village. The powder-mills here, like those at Faversham, in Kent, and at other places, have been subject to accidental explosions at different times. One of the most serious which has occurred here took place on the 6th of January, 1772, when damage to a very great extent was done, the effects of the explosion being felt for many miles round. In November, 1874, another explosion occurred here, when five lives were lost. Every precaution is now taken, by the separation of the buildings, &c., to localise the effects of such accidents as far as possible, should any occur. It is said that the first gunpowder manufactured in England was probably manufactured on Hounslow Heath; and at a very early date indeed; for we are told that one William of Staines was employed by Edward III. in 1346 to make the gunpowder which enabled him to gain the victory of Crecy, the first battle in which powder was used. We shall have more to say on the subject of gunpowder manufactories when we reach Waltham Abbey.

In 1793 extensive cavalry barracks, capable of accommodating above four hundred men, were erected by the Government on that part of the Heath which is in Heston parish. There is an exercising-ground, about three hundred acres in extent, which is used for reviewing troops. The 4th, or Royal South Middlesex Militia, has its head-quarters here, and there is also an arsenal.

Mr. Wilkes celebrates in his poem the song-birds of Hounslow, and also the game which was to be found in the neighbourhood. His "Philomele" may still be heard here in summer nights; but it is to be feared that his "Moorcocks," his

"Curlieus," his "Teal and Widgeon," his "Easter-lings," and "Snipes," if they had any existence beyond the poetical imagination of the writer, have long since "flown to another retreat" upon the Surrey Hills, further out of the way of Cockney sportsmen.

Mr. Wilkes writes in his poem already quoted:—

"Four large patrician elms behind the town,
　True as a beacon to the traveller known,
　Their lofty boughs with ancient pride display,
　And to fair Whitton point the cheerful way."

According to Rocque's Map (1754), these elms stood a few yards down the Bell Lane, on the Whitton Road. Two of them still remain.

Whitton Park, on the edge of Hounslow Heath, the seat of Colonel Gostling-Murray, was, in the last century, the residence of the Duke of Argyll, formerly known as Lord Islay. The gardens were especially well laid out, planted and cultivated, and adorned with statuary. Among other ornaments was a celebrated group in marble by Gabriel Cibber: the figure of a Highland piper and his dog. It represents the piper described by De Foe in his "History of the Plague" as taken up for dead and carried off to his burial in the dead-cart, but awakening from his trance just as he was about to be thrown into the pit, sitting up in the cart, and playing on his pipes, after which it is said that he recovered. This is certainly wonderful; it would be more wonderful, however, to find that, being a Highland piper, and immortalised by the Duke of Argyll, he was anything but a Campbell. The group was afterwards to be seen in the flower-gardens at Stowe. The gardens of Whitton Park gave rise to the following epigram:—

"Old Islay, to show his fine delicate taste
　In improving his gardens purloined from the waste,
　One day bade his gardener to open his views
　By cutting a couple of grand avenues;
　No particular prospect his lordship intended,
　But left it to chance how his walks should be ended.
　With transport and joy he beheld his first view end
　In a favourite prospect—a church that was ruined.
　But, alas! what a sight did the next cut exhibit!
　At the end of the walk hung a rogue on a gibbet!
　He beheld it and wept, for it caused him to muse on
　Full many a Campbell who died with his shoes on.
　All amazed and aghast at the ominous scene,
　He ordered it quick to be closed up again
　With a lump of Scotch firs that would serve as a screen."

Again, Mr. Wilkes writes grandiloquently—

"To sing those scenes where peace and grandeur dwell,
　Whitton demands her verse; the Nine conspire
　To swell my numbers with poetic fire.
　There nature's genial powers impregn the ground,
　And all her fragrant sweets are spread around."

* "Walpole's Letters," Vol. I.

Although the Duke of Argyll was contemptuously called a "tree-monger" by Horace Walpole, the country is indebted to him for introducing many foreign trees and shrubs which, by the beauty of their forms and colours, have greatly contributed to the pleasing effect of the English landscape. Almost every tree at Whitton was raised from seed planted by the duke in 1724. The grounds were all laid out with careful precision, and included fish-ponds, a bowling-green, orange walk, a Gothic tower, a Chinese summer-house, aviary, &c. After the sale of the property to Mr. Gostling, shortly after the duke's death, the conservatory was converted into the elegant villa now known as Whitton House, upon the pediment of which is a bas-relief after the antique, representing the destruction of the Titans by Jupiter. There is a well-known print of the gardens at Whitton, as they appeared, filled with the "quality," in the time of the Duke of Argyll.

The southern portion of Hounslow, including the neighbourhood of Whitton Park, has lately been made into a separate parish under the name of Whitton, with a new church on a pleasant village green.

The mansion at one time occupied by Sir Godfrey Kneller stands near this, but in the parish of Twickenham, and consequently will be dealt with in a subsequent chapter.

Three miles south-west from Hounslow lies the village of Hanworth, the site of which was formerly a royal hunting seat. Hanworth Park was at one time a favourite resort of Henry VIII. One part of the gardens still remains just as it was laid out under the eye of Queen Elizabeth.

This was one of the jointure houses of the Queen Dowager, Katharine Parr, widow of Henry VIII., and here Elizabeth resided, both before and after the union of that lady with Lord Seymour of Sudley, whose loose conduct towards the young princess—apparently encouraged, or at least connived at, by his wife—was scandalous enough to deserve being mentioned in the histories of the time. If the "Burleigh Papers" are to be trusted, "on one occasion the queen held the hands of the young princess whilst the Lord Admiral amused himself with cutting her gown into shreds; and on another she introduced him into the chamber of Elizabeth before she had left her bed, when a violent romping scene took place (writes Lucy Aikin), which was afterwards repeated in the presence of the queen." It is clear, then, that whatever merits Catharine Parr may have possessed, the morals of this widow did not render her a fit duenna to the future queen of England. Happily, however, her stay at Hanworth did not last long after this, for a violent scene took place between the royal stepmother and stepdaughter, which ended, fortunately for the peace and honour of Elizabeth, in an immediate and final separation.

About the middle of the sixteenth century the manor of Hanworth was granted to Anne, Duchess of Somerset, the widow of the Protector, and mother of the Earl of Hertford. In 1578 Queen Elizabeth was here on a visit to the duchess ; the queen was here again in 1600, when she "hunted in the park." The mansion was at that time leased to William Killigrew, whose son, of the same name, the friend and servant of Charles I. and II., and a dramatic author of some note, was born here in 1605.

In 1627 Hanworth became the property of Sir Francis Cottington, who in the following year was created Baron Cottington of Hanworth. His lordship in 1635 here entertained Queen Henrietta Maria and her Court. On the fall of Charles I. Hanworth was confiscated, and given to President Bradshaw. Hanworth was, however, recovered by Lord Cottington's cousin and heir at the Restoration ; but in 1670 it was sold to Sir Thomas Chamber, whose granddaughter conveyed it in marriage to Lord Vere Beauclerk, who in 1750 was created Baron Vere of Hanworth—a title now absorbed in the ducal house of St. Albans.

Gossiping Horace Walpole thus writes to his friend, Sir Horace Mann, under date 1791:—"The Duke of St. Albans has cut down all the brave old trees at Hanworth, and consequently reduced his park to what it issued from—Hounslow Heath ; nay, he has hired a meadow next to mine for the benefit of embarkation, and there lie all the good old corpses of oaks, ashes, and chestnuts, directly before *your* windows, and blocking up one of my views of the river ! But, so impetuous is the rage for building, that His Grace's timber will, I trust, not annoy us long."

Old Hanworth House was destroyed by fire in March, 1797, but the moat and a few vestiges of the house may still be seen close by the western end of Hanworth Church. The grounds known as Queen Elizabeth's Gardens have retained to this day much of their old-fashioned character, being studded with fine specimens of pine and old yews, and other trees.

The present Hanworth House stands on higher ground than its predecessor, and is a well-built mansion of the ordinary type. It was long the property of Mr. Perkins, whose fine library, which was extremely rich in MSS., was dispersed under the hammer of Messrs. Gadsden, Ellis, and Co., in the year 1873. The collector of these treasures was Mr. Henry Perkins (of the firm of Messrs. Barclay and Perkins, of Southwark), who bequeathed them to his son, the late Mr. Algernon Perkins, who died in 1873. Under the tuition of the celebrated Dr. Parr, Mr. Henry Perkins acquired his love for books, and the bulk of the library was obtained between the years 1820 and 1830, from the great English and Continental sales. Among the treasures disposed of on that occasion were several curious MSS. of the thirteenth and fourteenth centuries ; two copies of the noted Mazarine Bible, and a large number of ancient Bibles, Evangelaries, Missals, Books of Hours, Pontificals, &c. ; there were also many very choice works of legend and romance, including Lydgate's "Siege of Troy," the "Romance of the Rose," &c. The house passed by sale into the hands of Mr. Lafone, a merchant of London.

Hanworth Church, dedicated to St. George, is a modern erection, having been built in 1865, on the site of the former parish church.

At Hatton, between this and Hounslow, Sir Frederick Pollock, many years Chief Baron of the Exchequer, spent the last twenty years of his life.

CHAPTER VI.

TWICKENHAM.

"Meadows trim, with daisies pied,
Shallow brooks, and rivers wide."—*Milton.*

Derivation of the Name of Twickenham—Situation and Extent of the Parish—Early History of the Manor—The Manor House—Arragon Tower—Eel-pie Island—The Parish Church—Holy Trinity Church—St. Stephen's Church—Charitable Institutions—Curious Easter Custom—The Metropolitan and City of London Police Orphanage—Fortescue House—Royal Naval Female School—The Town Hall—Perryn House—Economic Museum—"Bull Land"—Extracts from the Parish Register—An Amusing Anecdote of Sir James Delaval.

TWICKENHAM lies on the road between Isleworth and Teddington and Hampton Court, in a valley between the higher ground of Strawberry Hill on the north and Richmond Hill on the south, from which latter it is separated by the river Thames and some pleasant fertile meadows. It has long been a favourite locality for the residence of a large number of the aristocracy; indeed, in the last century it acquired much celebrity in the fashionable world as the favourite haunt of Horace Walpole, and in the literary world as the home of Alexander Pope. Many of its noted houses, it is true, have disappeared, but the halo shed over the spot by their former inhabitants still remains. Although the village and its surroundings have lost much of their rural seclusion of late years by the formation of a railway through its very centre, and the rapid increase of modern dwelling-houses in all directions, much of its sylvan beauties are still visible, and its river-side aspect is as attractive as of old. Indeed, the locality is a particularly favoured one by the followers of the "gentle craft" which Izaak Walton did so much to popularise. Hofman, in his "British Angler's Manual" (1848), writes thus of the place :—

"The neighbourhood of Twickenham is not only singularly beautiful and rich in its adornments of elegant villas and noble mansions, but it abounds in memorials interesting to the historian, the antiquarian, and the lover of literature and art. The manor-house was, for a long period, the jointure-house of the queens of England. Katharine of Arragon and Henrietta of France have here bewailed, in their day, a cruel and a martyred husband. Queen Anne was born here, in York House, and lost her promising son whilst inhabiting the mansion now, or lately, the property of Sir George Pocock, Bart., which was for some years inhabited by the present King of France, when Duke of Orleans. Strawberry Hill, the seat of the celebrated Horace Walpole (Lord Orford), the house where Lady Mary Wortley resided, that of Earl Howe, and several others of great interest, are all in view; and within a little distance is Marble Hill, immortalised by Swift and Gay; Ham House, the splendid seat of Lord Dysart; Twickenham Meadows House, once the property of the celebrated Richard Owen Cambridge : these met the admiring eye of the angler as he made his way to the *deep*, where he now rests, and from which he gazes, untired, on that spot of ground which presents the most remarkable objects and associations, endeared by time and taste. *Here*, Pope wrote 'The deathless satire, the immortal song,' which neither time, fashion, nor envy can obliterate; *here*, he entertained the most highly-gifted men of his own, or, perhaps, any other time, the most noble, influential, and amiable. The grotto which he formèd, and where he loved to sit with his friends, is before us, as well as the garden he planted; but which was much enlarged in dimensions, as well as beauty, by his first successor, as an inscription informs us :—

" 'The humble roof, the garden's scanty line,
    Ill suit the genius of the bard divine ;
    But fancy now displays a fairer scope,
    And Stanhope's plans unfold the soul of Pope.' "

The name of the parish, formerly spelt Twicknam, is said to be derived from its situation between two brooks which run into the Thames, one at each end of the parish. An alms-dish in the parish church, however, has upon it an inscription which runs thus :—"For the parish of Twitnaham." This alms-dish bears no date, but on a paten, dated 1674, the name is spelt exactly after the modern fashion. Norden says that "in several very ancient records antecedent to the Conquest, the name is written Twitnam, or Twittanham, or Twicanham." Twittenham, or Twitnam, survived as the common pronunciation of the name down almost to the present generation; in the last century it was a customary form of pronunciation, even among the best educated. Horace Walpole, who did so much to make Twickenham classic ground, invariably wrote the name Twit'nam, at least in his earlier works. In some verses of his, called "The Parish Register of Twickenham," the name is constantly written in that form :—

" Where silver Thames round Twit'nam meads
    His winding current sweetly leads :
    Twit'nam, the Muses' fav'rite seat,
    Twit'nam, the Graces' lov'd retreat ;
    There polished Essex went to sport,
    The pride and victim of a court ;
    There Bacon tuned the grateful lyre
    To soothe Eliza's haughty ire."

Pope, whose name is as closely associated with the memories of the parish as that of Walpole, spells the name "Twitenham" in most of his writings; and many other poets and men of letters of the last century wrote it in a similar manner. Thus, in Dodsley's collection of poems by various hands, we read :—

" I saw the sable barge along his Thames,
    Beating in slow solemnity the tide,
    Convey his sacred dust. Its swans expired ;
    Withered in Twitnam bowers the laurel bough.
    Silent, the Muses broke their idle lyres,
    Th' attendant Graces checked the sprightly dance,
    Their arms unlocked, and caught the starting tear,
    And virtue for her lost defender mourned."

Thomson also, in his poem on "Richmond Hill," writes :—

" Here let us trace the matchless vale of Thames,
    Far winding up to where the Muses haunt,
    To Twitnam's bowers."

And again, the Rev. T. Maurice, in a poem on the same subject, dated 1807, writes :—

"Twitnam ! so dearly loved, so often sung,
Theme of each raptured heart and glowing tongue."

The town is situated along the northern bank of the Thames, and to the natural beauties and advantages with which it is surrounded it owes a great proportion of the renown which it has possessed for the last three centuries, during which period it has numbered among its residents those who have occupied positions of eminence and influence, owing either to their exalted station in life, or to their literary, artistic, or political abilities.

ing date 1301, "Twykenham is entered as a hamlet appendant to the manor of Isleworth." Another record, dated 1390, says that the manor and hundred of Isleworth had always been deemed of the same extent. Lysons observes that this did not imply any jurisdiction over the lands of religious houses, which exercised manorial rights upon their own estates. "The Brethren of the Holy Trinity at Hounslow," he continues, "had a small manor within the hundred, independent of that of Isleworth. The monks of Christ Church had another in this parish from very ancient times, as will appear by the following account. Offa, King of the Mercians, between the years 791 and 794, gave to

TWICKENHAM.
(*From a Print published* 1749.)

EEL-PIE ISLAND.

The extent of the parish is about three and a half miles in length, by one and a half in breadth. It contains, according to the Ordnance Survey, rather more than 2,415 acres ; in the Isleworth Survey, taken in 1635, by order of Algernon, Duke of Northumberland, the number of acres is estimated at about 1,850.

The climate has always been celebrated for its pure and healthy influences, and in its vegetation it is the same as that of most parts of the course of the River Thames. Twickenham, in fact, with the country adjacent to it, has always been distinguished for the fertility of its gardens, which still send large supplies of vegetables and fruit, especially strawberries, to the London markets.

The parish is situated in the hundred of Isleworth, and for the most part within the ancient manor of Sion, of which the Duke of Northumberland is lord. The name of the place is not mentioned in "Domesday Book," for the simple reason, no doubt, that it was included in the parish of Isleworth. Lysons states that in a record, bear-

Athelard, Archbishop of Canterbury, among other benefactions, thirty tributaries of land on the north side of the river Thames, at a place called Twittanham, for the purpose of providing vestments for the priests who officiated in the church of St. Saviour in Canterbury. Warherdus, a priest, by his will, bearing date 830, gave to the church of Canterbury eight hides of land, with the manor of Twitnam, in Middlesex, which had been granted him by Ceolnothus, Dean of Canterbury (the same, it is probable, who was a few years afterwards Archbishop). In 941 Edmund the king, and Eldred his brother,

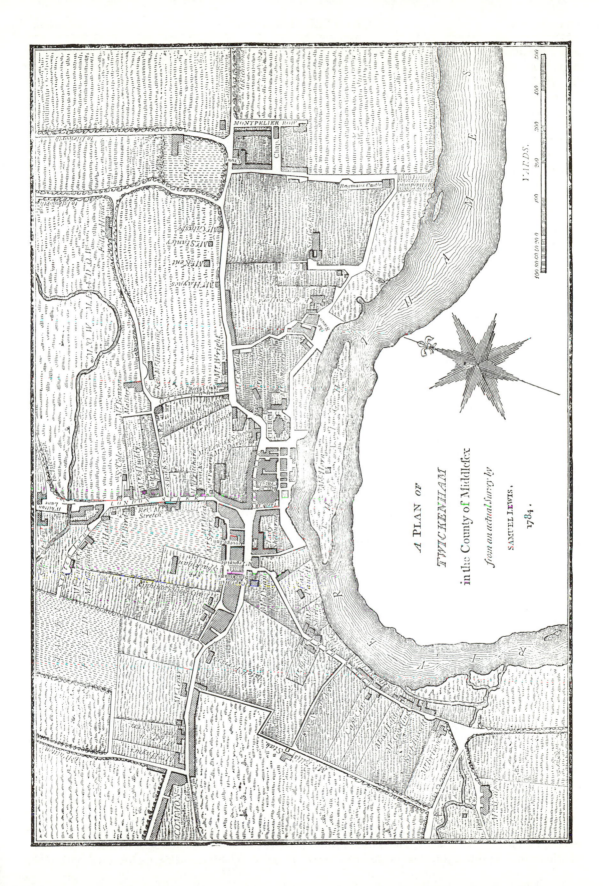

A PLAN OF
TWICKENHAM
in the County of Middlesex
from an actual Survey by
SAMUEL LEWIS,
1784.

and Edmund, the son of Edmund, restored to the monks of Christ Church, in Canterbury, all the lands which they had unjustly taken away from them. Among these was the manor of Twittanham. This restitution seems not to have been very effectual, for it appears that King Eldred, by his charter, bearing date 948, gave to the said monks, as a small offering, for the love of God and the benefit of his soul, the manor of Twiccanham, in the county of Middlesex, situated upon the river Thames, with all its appurtenances, exempting it from all secular burdens, taxes, and tolls, excepting contributions towards the building of bridges and fortifications, and the king's expedition; his charter concludes with the following bitter anathema against any persons who should venture to infringe it— 'Whatever be their sex, order, or rank, may their memory be blotted out of the book of life, may their strength continually waste away, and be there no restorative to repair it.' I suppose this manor to have been the same which, being then vested in the Crown, was annexed by King Henry VIII. in 1539 to the honour of Hampton Court, between 1539 and 1541, granted to Edward, Earl of Hertford, and in the latter year surrendered by him to the king. It remained in the immediate occupation of the Crown till the reign of Charles I., by whom it was settled, with other estates, as a jointure, on his queen, Henrietta Maria. When the Crown lands were put up to sale during the usurpation, this manor was purchased (anno 1650) by John Hemsdell, merchant, on behalf of himself and other creditors of the State. . . After the Restoration the queen-mother resumed possession of her jointure, and held it till her death. In 1670 this manor was settled for life on Katharine, consort of Charles II.; and in 1675 the king granted a reversionary lease for 41 years, commencing after the queen's death, or from the date of such leases as the queen might have granted, to John, Earl of Rochester. William Genew, Esq., in 1688, had a lease of the manor for twelve years, to commence in 1707. Lord Rochester's lease, which commenced at the expiration of Genew's, becoming afterwards vested in Lord Bolingbroke, it was forfeited to the Crown upon his attainder in 1715." The lease of the manor subsequently passed by sale into the hands of different capitalists, whose names would be of no interest to the general reader. "The manor of Twickenham," as the Rev. R. S. Cobbett informs us, in his "Memorials of Twickenham," "extends through the parishes of Twickenham, Isleworth, and Heston. The customs are primogeniture, and fines arbitrary. The other manors are those of Isleworth Syon and Isleworth Rectory,

the former belonging to the Duke of Northumberland, and the latter now to the Ecclesiastical Commissioners, but formerly to the dean and canons of Windsor."

The Manor House, a large red-brick building, stood opposite the north side of the church. It was for some time called Arragon House, from a supposition that Katharine of Arragon retired hither after her divorce from Henry VIII. This, however, is but a doubtful tradition. Katharine of Braganza, queen of Charles II., is said to have inhabited the mansion for a time; and it is supposed also to have been part of the jointure of Queen Katharine Parr, who may have used it during her residence at Hanworth or Hampton Court. In the early part of the seventeenth century the house was in the occupation of Lady Walter, widow of Sir John Walter, Lord Chief Baron of the Exchequer, who, it is probable, had resided in it also, for at his death in 1630 he left a benefaction to the poor of Twickenham. In a survey of the house and park which was taken in 1650, mention is made of "two round rooms in a brick turret," and also "a fair hall wainscoted," in which was a screen of excellent workmanship. Mr. Samuel Scott, an artist who acquired some celebrity in his day as a painter of river scenery, occupied the house for some time prior to his death, in the year 1772, after which it became the residence of his pupil, Mr. William Marlow, F.S.A., who also became distinguished as an artist.

The greater part of the Manor House was taken down some few years ago, but a portion still remains, and is called Arragon Tower. Mr. Cobbett, in his work above quoted, states that the house was large, but possessed no features of peculiar interest. "It was evidently a Tudor structure (a mantelpiece in it indisputably belonged to that period), renovated in the time of William and Mary. In an apartment which was used as a cellar was a carved door of considerable antiquity, and several vacant niches with an ecclesiastical look about them, similar to those existing in the vicarage. A large garden adjoined the house, in which was a magnificent walnut-tree, which, when cut down, was sold for about £80. The royal arms of England were placed within, in the hall or over the entrance door."

Of the village—or, perhaps, more properly speaking, the town—of Twickenham there is but little to be said. At the western end, near the river-side, stands the parish church. In the river, nearly opposite the church, is an "ait," or eyot (island), containing about eight acres, chiefly laid out as pleasure-grounds, and known as Eel-pie Island. The Eel-pie House has been a noted place of resort for two centuries for fishermen and for pleasure parties. The old house was taken down in 1830. Church Street, a somewhat narrow, old-fashioned thoroughfare, runs westward from the church into King Street, the principal street of the town. Some of the river-side approaches here corresponded till quite lately to Pope's description in his own days :—

" In ev'ry town where Thamis rolls his tide,
  A narrow pass there is, with houses low ;
  Where ever and anon the stream is ey'd,
  And many a boat, soft sliding to and fro.
  There oft are heard the notes of infant woe,
  The short thick sob, loud scream, and shriller squall.
  How can ye, mothers, vex your children so ?

        *   *   *   *   *

        *   *   *   *   *

" And on the broken pavement, here and there,
  Doth many a stinking sprat and herring lie ;
  A brandy and tobacco shop is near,
  And hens, and dogs, and hogs are feeding by ;
  And here a sailor's jacket hangs to dry.
  At every door are sun-burnt matrons seen,
  Mending old nets to catch the scaly fry,
  Now singing shrill, and scolding oft between ;
  Scolds answer foul-mouthed scolds ; bad neighbourhood,
      I ween.

" Such place hath Deptford, navy-building town,
  Woolwich and Wapping, smelling strong of pitch ;
  Such Lambeth, envy of each band and gown,
  And Twick'nham such, which fairer scenes enrich,
  Grots, statues, urns, and J——n's dog and bitch.
  Ne village is without, on either side,
  All up the silver Thames, or all adown,
  Ne Richmond's self, from whose tall front are ey'd
  Vales, spires, meand'ring streams, and Windsor's tow'ry
      pride."

In 1882, however, the Thames front here was ornamentally embanked.

At the eastern end of the parish, where it joins on to Isleworth, a new district of villas has sprung up, known respectively as Cambridge and Twickenham Parks ; while westward, in the neighbourhood of the Common, the Heath, and Strawberry Vale, building has been going on largely of late years.

The parish church, as stated above, stands near the river-side, and is dedicated to St. Mary the Virgin. With the exception of the tower, it is a modern red-brick building, of the nondescript order of architecture, and of little or no interest, apart from the monuments which it contains. It stands on the site of the original edifice, the body of which fell to the ground on the night of the 9th of April, 1713. The church of Twickenham was of old appropriated to the Abbey of St. Valery (or Walerie), in Picardy. The date of its foundation

is unknown; but "the style of the building, as exemplified by the tower," Mr. Cobbett observes, in his " Memorials of Twickenham," " must have belonged to the age of William of Wykeham; and as the vicarages of Twickenham and Isleworth were given to the Crown by that prelate, we may conclude that the parish church was rebuilt under his superintendence. Its date, in that case, would be about the middle of the fourteenth century. The ground plan of the church comprised at that period a nave (with or without aisles), and the still existing western tower. As far as can be ascertained," Mr. Cobbett adds, " no old view or engraving of it exists; the best notion of what it must have been like is supplied by the modern church of St. John's, Isleworth."

At the time of the fall of the church, Sir Godfrey Kneller was one of the churchwardens, and under his auspices the present building was erected. Mr. John James, who designed the church of St. George, Hanover Square, was the architect. " As a specimen of brick-work," writes Mr. Cobbett, "it is confessedly inimitable; a repetition of the accident which had deprived Twickenham of one church was at least amply provided against for the future. The walls are of prodigious thickness ; every detail is carried out conscientiously and thoroughly, and in such respects it puts to shame many more pretentious modern structures." What historic interest the interior of the church may have possessed—from its association with the time of Walpole, Pope, and their friends—was wholly swept away between the years 1859 and 1871, during which period the old galleries were lowered and rearranged, and the high cumbersome pews were made to give place to open benches. In lieu of a chancel, a *chorus cantorum* was formed at the east end ; a new vestry was erected on the south side of the church, and the restoration of the tower was effected. These alterations in the church provided additional sittings for about 400 adults, and a large increase of those for the school children. The wooden bell-turret which formerly crowned the tower, and is familiar to us in all old prints of the place, was taken down when the church was restored in 1859.

Apart from the parish registers, of which we shall speak presently, the monuments and their epitaphs are the only objects of interest to a casual visitor which Twickenham Church now possesses. Among these, the oldest is a stone slab placed upright against the south wall by the vestry door, and having upon it a brass plate in memory of Richard Burton, " chief cook to the king," and dated 1443. The monument erected by Bishop

Warburton to the memory of Pope is upon the north wall, and has upon it a medallion portrait of the poet, together with the line from the pen of Pope himself : " For one who would not be buried in Westminster Abbey," and the verse—

> " Heroes and kings, your distance keep ;
> In peace let one poor poet sleep,
> Who never flatter'd folks like you :
> Let Horace blush and Virgil too."

Why, however, Horace and Virgil should "blush" any more than the bard of Twickenham is not clear ; for were not all three courtier poets ?

On the east wall is a marble monument, erected by Pope to the memory of his parents and "to himself." In his "last will and testament" Pope gave the following instructions concerning his interment :—" As to my body, my will is that it be buried near the monument of my dear parents at Twickenham, with the addition, after the words *filius fecit*, of these only : ' *et sibi : Qui obiit anno* 17—*ætatis*—;' and that it be carried to the grave by six of the poorest men of the parish, to each of whom I order a suit of grey coarse cloth as mourning." The blanks left for the insertion of the date of the poet's death, and his age, have never been filled up, as they should have been.

Below the above-mentioned monument is a tablet inscribed to the memory of Mr. Richard Owen Cambridge, of whom we shall have more to say presently. Among the other monuments in the church are those to Sir William Humble and Sir Joseph Ashe ; to Lady Frances Whitmore, with an epitaph by Dryden ; to John, Lord Berkeley, of Stratton, who died in 1678 ; to Admiral Sir Chaloner Ogle, Sir Thomas Lawley, Sir Richard Perryn, and Louisa, Viscountess Clifden. Sir Godfrey Kneller lies buried here ; but, singularly enough, his monument is not here, but in Westminster Abbey, where his epitaph may be read. It is from the pen of Pope.

In the churchyard are a large number of tombs, of which may be mentioned those of Lieutenant-General William Tryon, sometime Governor of the Province of New York, who died in 1788, and Selina Countess Ferrers, who died in 1762. Admiral Byron, the author of the " Narrative of the Loss of the *Wager*," who died in 1786, was buried here, but there is no monument to his memory ; and the searcher after quaint inscriptions may also look in vain for the following, which in most books on epitaphs is stated to be in Twickenham churchyard, but is probably apocryphal :—

> " Here lie I,
> Killed by a sky-
> Rocket in the eye."

There is, however, one epitaph on the chancel wall which will rivet attention ; it is that to the memory of Mrs. Catherine Clive—"Kitty Clive"— who died in 1758. It has a long poetical inscription, written by Miss Jane Pope, an actress, and commencing :—

> " Clive's blameless life this tablet shall proclaim,
> Her moral virtues, and her well-earn'd fame."

Dr. Charles Morton, F.R.S., sometime the principal librarian of the British Museum, who died in 1799, and Mr. Edward Ironside, the historian of Twickenham, who died in 1803, lie in the new burial-ground ; and in the graveyard in Royal Oak Lane are monuments to Field Marshal Sir Edward Blakeney, Governor of Chelsea Hospital, who died in 1868, to the Rev. Charles Proby, Vicar of Twickenham, who died in 1859, and many others of the principal inhabitants of the parish.

Dr. Terrick, afterwards Bishop of London, was Vicar of Twickenham in Horace Walpole's time. He was succeeded in the vicarage by the "learned" Rev. George Costard, who was also an astronomer of some note in his time. He died in 1782, and was buried in Twickenham churchyard, but no memorial marks the place of his interment.

Holy Trinity Church, on Twickenham Common, erected in 1840, is a poor specimen of architecture, built of brick with stone dressings; transepts and an apsidal chancel were added in 1863. Some of the windows are filled with stained glass, and there are tablets to the memory of Sir William Clay, M.P., and Lady Clay, late of Fulwell Lodge, on the road to Hanworth. Attached to this church are some schools, generally known as "Archdeacon Cambridge's Schools." They were built by subscription as a memorial of Archdeacon Cambridge, "and in grateful remembrance of his liberal contributions towards the erection and endowment of the church."

St. Stephen's Church, East Twickenham, was built in 1876, in place of Montpelier Episcopal Chapel, which, never having been consecrated, is now made to serve the purposes of a public hall. The old building had been used for the service of the Church of England for about 150 years. St. Stephen's Church is a Gothic building, and is constructed of Kentish rag and Bath stone.

Among the charities and institutions of Twickenham are almshouses founded in 1704 by a Mr. Mathew Harvie, and in 1721 the Hon. Sarah Greville bequeathed £200 towards the expense of erecting six additional almshouses. Bequests of land have been made at different times by the charitably disposed for the benefit of the poor, some of which are distributed in money and some in bread, and so forth.

It is said by Lysons that there was here "an ancient custom of dividing two great cakes in the church on Easter Day among the young people;" but that, being looked upon as a "superstitious relic," it was ordered by the Parliament in 1645 that the parishioners should "forbear that custom," and instead of it should "buy loaves of bread for the poor of the parish with the money that should have bought the cakes." It adds, "it appears that the sum of £1 per annum is still charged upon the vicarage for the purpose of buying penny loaves for poor children on the Thursday after Easter."

Wellesley House, a large mansion in the Hampton Road, is now the Metropolitan and City of London Police Orphanage, an institution founded in 1870 for the purpose of maintaining, clothing, and educating destitute orphan children of the police forces, and of "placing them out in situations where the prospect of an honest livelihood shall be secured." The orphanage is supported almost entirely by the members of the force, aided by occasional subscriptions from the outside world. The buildings will hold about 200 children.

Fortescue House, a somewhat heavy-looking mansion near the centre of the town, has been long devoted to charitable purposes. The house was at one time the residence of a former Lord Fortescue, who possessed in it a valuable collection of paintings by the old masters. It was for many years used as a ladies' boarding-school and for other educational purposes, and served for some time as the orphanage of the police before its transfer to Wellesley House. It is now a Home for destitute boys.

The Royal Naval Female School at St. Margaret's was founded in 1840, mainly through the bequest of Admiral Sir Thomas Williams, G.C.B., who gave £1,000 to be invested in trust as the basis of an endowment fund. In 1856 the present building was purchased, and the school removed hither from Richmond. The object of the institution is "to provide at the lowest possible cost a good education for the orphan and other daughters of officers of Her Majesty's Army and of the Royal Marines." The number of pupils is limited to ninety, of which number twenty-six are received at the annual payment of £50; fifty-six are boarded and educated at the entire cost to the parents or guardians of £12 per annum; and five, whose fathers died during the Crimean campaign, are nominees of the Patriotic Fund, the establishment defraying the larger amount of actual cost through the means of voluntary contributions.

Among the most recent additions to the public buildings of Twickenham is a Town Hall, erected at the expense of Sir Charles Freake. It is a handsome building of red brick, with stone dressings; it contains a large assembly-room, which is used for concerts, meetings, &c.

North of the railway station, at the junction of the roads leading to Whitton and Isleworth, stands Perryn House, so called from having been formerly the residence of Sir Richard Perryn, a Baron of the Exchequer, who died in 1803. About the year 1835 the property was sold to Mr. Thomas Twining, a resident of the neighbourhood: his son, of the same name, commenced in 1856 the formation of a permanent Educational Exhibition of things appertaining to domestic and sanitary economy, which, from its having been devoted to the furtherance of what may be called economic knowledge, took the name of the "Economic Museum." In a certain sense, however, the idea first took shape and form in one of the departments of the Universal Exposition at Paris in 1855. It was a collection of every possible description of household treasures: in short, of all material things needful to man. It included "marvels of cheapness," ingenious devices for the economy of space, and specimens of food and clothing. Visitors called it "the exhibition of cheapness," yet it was something more than that—it was an exhibition of prudence, of forethought, of cleanliness, and of sanitary arrangement, which together form the foundation of domestic economy. The building stood in the grounds of Perryn House. Its contents included models or specimens of building designs, intended as a guide to persons desirous of improving the dwellings of the working classes; building materials, pictures, furniture, and household utensils; textile materials, fabrics, and costumes; food, fuel, and household stores; sanitary appliances, &c. Attached to the museum was a valuable and comprehensive library of books, pamphlets, and documents, both British and foreign, selected and arranged for convenience of reference in matters of domestic, sanitary, educational, and social economy and practical benevolence. The usefulness of the museum, and of the lectures explanatory of the subjects of which it contained examples, compiled by Mr. Twining, and delivered by his agents in various parts of London and the suburbs, gradually became felt and acknowledged by many persons whose opinion was of great weight and value. The museum and all its valuable contents, including the library, however, were totally consumed by fire in 1871. It was calculated that £10,000 would not replace the loss.

Before proceeding to describe other houses in the parish, and to mention the many eminent inhabitants whose residence here has gone far towards making Twickenham one of the most popular suburbs of London, it will, perhaps, be best to close this chapter with a few extracts from the parish register, and to deal with one or two other matters which have affected the rise and progress of the town. The minutes of the vestry and the churchwardens' accounts are, for the most part, in good preservation, and date respectively from 1618 and 1606. In the latter, "Strawberry Hill" and the "Bull Lands" are mentioned for the first time. Of Strawberry Hill we shall have occasion to speak at some length presently. With regard to the entry concerning the "Bull Land," it may be stated that from a copy of the Court Roll of the Manor of Isleworth Sion, dated December 20th, 1675, it appears that one Thomas Cole surrendered four acres one rood of land, lying in several places in the fields of Twickenham, called the parish land, anciently belonging to the inhabitants of Twickenham, "in trust for the keeping and maintaining a sufficient bull for the common use of the said inhabitants."

Amongst the receipts for 1631, and other years, are sums, usually about six shillings and sixpence, paid by other parishes, among which Teddington and Cranford are named, "for the loan of the parish pewter," as the sacramental plate was described. In 1652 the churchwardens made an inventory of the parish goods, which they handed over to their successors in office. It is as follows :—"A greater silver and guilt cupp, with the cover, given by Mr. Hollingsworth. A lesser silver cupp with a cover. Two pewter flaggons. A greene velvett cushion for the pulpitt. Greene carpett for the comunion table. Blacke cloth for the ffunerals. One joyned chest. Two joyned stooles. One little chest with two locks. One diaper table-cloth for the communion table." That the "free" and open seat movement was not thought of or dreamed about in the seventeenth century may be easily inferred from the following entry in the minutes of the vestry, under date of May 2, 1659 :—"That

SIR GODFREY KNELLER. (*See p. 75.*)
(*From the Painting by Himself*).

the little seat, on the back side of the one where Gooddy Raynor sittes now in, and one on the south side of the seate where Gooddy Barker now sitteth in, shall be hereafter belonging to the house which Mr. Peirce now hath by the water-side, in lue of the seate which did formerly belong to the said house." And again, under date of May 9, 1667 :— "Ed. Gray having complained that ye Erle of Clarendon's pew for his servants in the gallery had been taken away from him by the churchwardens," it was ordered "that noe person should sitt in ye said pew but by leave of my Lord Clarendon or his servants." On September 20th, 1674, it was ordered that bells were not to be rung "but according to a declaration, under my Lord Chief Justice's hand, how he sayes they may be legally ringed."

On April 17th, 1676, a parish officer was appointed "to secure the town against vagabones, beggars, and other persons harbouring in barnes or out-houses, also to prevent 'theefing' and robbing houses and grounds." That this precautionary measure did not have altogether the desired effect is pretty clear ; at all events, there were highwaymen busily plying their work here a century later, for Mrs. Kitty Clive writes to Garrick, under date June 10th, 1776 : —"Have you not heard of the adventures of your poor friend? I have been rob'd (*sic*) and murder'd coming from Kingston. Jimey and I in a post-chey (*sic*) at half past nine, just by Teddington Church, was stoppt. I only lost a little silver and my senses, for one of them come into the carriage with a great horse pistol to sarch (*sic*) me for my watch, but I had it not with me."

In 1686 the parish authorities were ordered by the deputy-lieutenancy of the county " to provide coats, hatts, and belts for sixteene maimed souldiers." A box was made to keep the articles so contributed.

Two curious entries occur in the accounts for 1688. The first is as follows :—"Item : Paid to the relief of a sick man brought naked out of the camp, and passing him away, 11s. 3d." James II., as we have already shown (see *ante*, page 64), had his camp at this time on Hounslow Heath. The other entry is as follows :—"Item : To Mr. Guisbey, for curing Doll Bannister's nose, 3s."

On May 11th, 1696, it was ordered that the beadle should have 20s. per annum and the Cross-house rent free, "for to ward within and about this parish, and to keep out all Beggars and Vagabonds that shall lye, abide, or lurk about the towne, and to give correction to such that shall anyways stand in Opposition contrary to the Statutes in that case made and provided." In the accounts of 1698 is this entry :—"Item : Paid old Tomlins for fetching home the Church-gates, being thrown into yᵉ Thames in the night by Drunkards, 2s. 6d."

In December, 1701, the parish allowed the Earl of Bedford, with the consent of His Grace the Duke

But Twickenham had not only its "rogues in grain," but its saints. At all events, at the end of the last century several of the leading inhabitants of the parish were staunch followers of the Wesleyan connection ; and it is recorded in the "Life of Wesley" that he dined with one of them here less than a fortnight before his death.

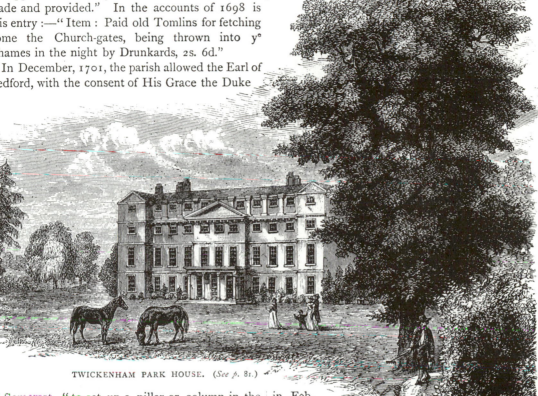

TWICKENHAM PARK HOUSE. (*See p. 81.*)

of Somerset, "to set up a pillar or column in the middle of Twickenham, as his lordship should see fit."

On December 5th, 1726, so many larcenies having been committed in the neighbourhood, and the sufferers being unwilling to prosecute, on account of expense, the vestry ordered that whenever any larceny, felony, or burglary was committed, Mr. James Taylor, of New Brentford, should be empowered to manage the prosecution of the same, and for his pains should be paid by a rate.

The churchwardens here, as in other country villages, were in the habit of paying for the destruction of vermin. In their accounts for the years 1773 and 1774, for instance, are these items : "Paid for 54 Hedgehogs, 18s. ;" and "Paid for 4 Pole-cats, 1s. 4d." Similar entries occur in large numbers down to quite recent times. On the 4th of October, 1790, it was ordered "that a whipping-post be put up at the workhouse *immediately*."

in February, 1791. It was probably the last occasion of his leaving home.

Still there was nothing specially austere in the customs of the inhabitants. It is stated in the *Mirror* for 1840 that "at the recent petty sessions here the magistrates granted the request of some of the inhabitants to enjoy the ancient right of playing at football on Shrove Tuesday—a custom observed in the principal suburban parishes of Middlesex and Surrey from time immemorial."

Since the formation of a Local Board, the duties of the parishioners, "in vestry assembled," have been much lessened and curtailed. All the responsibilities attaching to the lighting of the parish, the care of its roads and highways, and especially the urgent question of drainage, devolve upon the Board, and are now no longer managed by special committees, elected for such purposes, as was the case previous to the year 1868.

The roads in Twickenham and its immediate neighbourhood were in former times mostly very narrow and ill-kept, which sometimes made travelling along them in coaches or other vehicles anything but easy or pleasant, and occasionally led to awkward blocks, from vehicles coming in opposite directions. An instance of this occurred on one occasion to the carriages containing Sir James Delaval and the Duke of Somerset. The latter, who is known to historians as the "proud" Duke of Somerset, was an inordinately arrogant nobleman, who seemed in his conduct as if vested with regal honours. His servants obeyed him by signs, and were not allowed to speak, and scarcely to appear, in his presence. His children obeyed his mandates with profound and servile respect. The story goes that the pleasant Sir James Delaval laid a wager of £1,000 that he would make the duke give him precedency; but that was judged impossible, as his Grace was all eyes and ears on such occasions. Delaval, however, having one day obtained information of the precise time when the duke was to pass a narrow part of the road on his way to town, stationed himself there in a coach, emblazoned for the day with the arms, and surrounded by many servants in the livery of the head of the house of Howard, who called out, when Somerset appeared, "The Duke of Norfolk!" The former, fearful of committing a breach of etiquette, hurried his postilion under a hedge, where he was no sooner safely fixed than Delaval passed, who, leaning out of the carriage, bowed with a familiar air, and wished his Grace a good morning. He indignantly exclaimed, "Is it you, Sir James? I thought it had been the Duke of Norfolk!" The wager thus won was paid, and the town made merry with the stratagem used by Sir James to gain it.

A map of Twickenham as it was in 1784, which we give on page 73, shows the distribution of property as it stood a century ago. At the extreme south-west is shown Strawberry Hill, marked simply "Mr. Walpole." Between it and the main street of the village are, on the river side of the road, the seats of Lord Sefton, Mr. Ellis (Pope's villa), Miss and Mr. Shirley, and Lord Poulett; on the other side, the grounds of Mr. Briscoe, Sir F. Bassett, Mr. Gostling, Miss Holden, and Mr. Blake. On the south side of the road leading to Twickenham Common stands the mansion of the late Lord Ferrers (the same who not long before had been executed at Tyburn). Fortescue House, at the north of the village, appears as "the late Lord Fortescue's." Around it lie the properties of several nobodies; and, curiously enough, the spot now occupied by the South Western Railway Station is marked "Staten" Field. To the east of the parish church we note the mansions of Mr. Shakerly, Mr. Whitchurch, and Mr. Condell, some of whom doubtless knew Alexander Pope in the flesh. Between the centre of the main street and the river stands the mansion of Lady Shelburne, enclosed apparently within walls, adjoining Water Street, which probably then was an important thoroughfare as leading down to "the silent highway" of the river. To the east of the map is Sir George Pococke's mansion, and beyond it Ragman's Castle and Montpelier Row and Chapel, with Mr. Hardinge's house by the river-side facing a small eyot. Between "Mow" Meadow, on the north, and the extreme north-east of the map are two bridle roads to Isleworth, on the one of which stands Mr. Nettleship's, and on the other "Folly House." Across the brook at the north, where Pope probably narrowly escaped drowning, as we shall see later, are the grounds of Mr. Cole, whose family was connected with Twickenham for some two or three generations.

CHAPTER VII.

TWICKENHAM (continued).

"To Twitnam's mead the muse repairs."

Twickenham Park—The Naval School—Cambridge House—Richard Owen Cambridge—Mr. Bishop's Observatory—Marble Hill—The Witty Bishop Corbett—Ragman's Castle—Orleans House—Mr. Secretary Johnstone—Sir George Pococke—The Duke of Orleans—The Duc d'Aumale—The Orleans Club—York House—The Hon. Mrs. Damer—Sir Alexander Johnson—A Learned Brahmin—The Comte de Paris—The Grove—The Duke of Wharton—Lady Mary Wortley Montagu—Twickenham House—Earl Ferrers—Fielding—Other Noted Residents—Twickenham Common—Whitton—Kneller Hall—The Normal Training School.

THERE are few, if any, places within "a measurable distance" of the metropolis where there have resided such a host of distinguished persons as Twickenham. Among its former inhabitants have been statesmen, poets, philosophers, painters, authors, ecclesiastics, military and naval men, as well as many women of eminence in the worlds of society and of letters. Its classic bowers, in fact, gained for it from Horace Walpole the name of "The Baiæ of Great Britain." In the lapse of years it would be difficult, perhaps, in every instance, to point out exactly the residences and characteristics of all these Twickenham worthies; but still, enough remains upon record, or lives in local tradition, to identify a goodly list, with their respective homes. First and foremost stand the names of Pope and Horace Walpole; but of each of these there is sufficient to form a separate chapter.

In 1722, De Foe wrote, in his "Tour through England and Scotland":—"Twittenham, a village remarkable for abundance of curious seats, of which that of Boucher, the famous gamester, would pass in Italy for a delicate palace. The Earl of Marr, the Earl of Strafford, the Earl of Bradford, the Lord Brook, the Lord Sunderland, the Lady Falkland, have each their pretty villas in this parish; but I think that of Secretary Johnstone, for the elegancy and largeness of the gardens, his terrace on the river, and the situation of his house, makes much the brightest figure here." Horace Walpole, in his letter to Bentley, about thirty years later, writes of the place in much the same strain. He observes that "Nothing is equal to the fashion of this place: Mr. Muntz says we have more coaches here than there are in half France. Mrs. Pritchard has bought Ragman's Castle, for which my Lord Lichfield could not agree. We shall be as celebrated as Baiæ or Tivoli; and if we have not such sonorous names as they boast, we have very famous people: Clive and Pritchard, actresses; Scott and Hodson, painters; my Lady Suffolk, famous in her time; Mr. H——,* the impudent lawyer, that Tom Harvey wrote against; Whitehead, the poet; and Cambridge the everything." In dealing with the annals of this parish, we have, fortunately, the "Memorials of Twickenham," by the Rev. R. S. Cobbett, to draw upon, and from this work we shall have occasion to quote largely in this and one or two succeeding chapters.

Commencing our survey of the houses at the north-east corner of the parish, near the banks of the river, and at the junction of the parish with Isleworth, we shall commence with Twickenham Park, a spot which lays claim to being the oldest among the Twickenham demesnes. It was originally called Isleworth Park, and also the New Park of Richmond. Honest John Stow, in his "Annals," tells us that in 1263, during the disturbances in the reign of Henry III., "Simon de

Mountfort, with the barons, pitched their tents in Isleworth or Thistleworth Parke." The site of the encampment is in the parish of Twickenham. In this park there stood from 1414 to 1431, as stated in a previous chapter,* the ancient monastery of Sion. The Rev. Mr. Cobbett, in his "Memorials of Twickenham," says that in the parish chest of Twickenham are two deeds: one of them, dated 1444, is "a release from Matilda, abbess of the monastery, to their tenants of Istelworthe, of a certain yearly tallage of £20, which they were held to pay to the said abbess and convent;" and the other, bearing the same date, is a deed confirming the grant of sundry manors to the abbess and convent. One of these deeds had been lost sight of for many years, and came to light again only on the restoration of the parish church in 1859.

Robert Boucher was appointed keeper of Twickenham Park in 1547; but the park, as such, seems to have been soon after broken up; for Norden, in the manuscript additions to his "Speculum Britanniæ," made towards the end of the sixteenth century, remarks that "Twyckenham Parke is now disparked." In 1574 the estate was demised to Edward Bacon, third son of Sir Nicholas Bacon, the celebrated Lord Keeper. In 1581 it was leased to one Edward Fitzgarret. Sir Francis Bacon, whom Voltaire calls "the father of experimental philosophy," spent much of his time here during the earlier period of his studious life; and in 1592 he somewhat suddenly took refuge here with several friends, owing to "a pestilential distemper which broke out in London, and dispersed the members of Gray's Inn—a community to which Bacon then belonged." At the end of that year he was honoured by a visit from Queen Elizabeth, "at his lodging in Twickenham Park," when he presented her Majesty with a sonnet in praise of her favourite, the Earl of Essex. Among the MSS. in the British Museum is a paper entitled "Instructions from the Lord Chancellor Bacon to his servant, Thomas Bushell," in which is set forth a scheme which he entertained for the purpose of exploring abandoned mineral works. On the supposition that such a project would meet with due encouragement, he says, "Let Twitnam Park, which I sold in my younger days, be purchased, if possible, for a residence for such deserving persons to study in, since I experimentally found the situation of that place much convenient for the trial of my philosophical conclusions, expressed in a paper sealed to the trust, which I myself had just in practice, and settled the same by Act of Parlia-

---

* "This was Joseph Hickey, the 'most blunt honest creature' of Goldsmith's 'Retaliation,' whose 'one only fault,' in Oliver's estimation —though 'that was a thumper'—was that he was a special attorney."— Thorne's "Environs of London"

* See page 44, ante.

ment, if the vicissitudes of fortune had not intervened, and prevented me."

In the seventeenth century the ownership or lesseeship of Twickenham Park frequently changed hands. In 1608 it was held by Lucy, Countess of Bedford, whose memory has been preserved to posterity by the verses of Dr. Donne, Dean of St. Paul's, and by Ben Jonson, who wrote at her request an epigram or two. In 1618 the estate passed to Sir William Harrington, who, a few years later, sold it to Mary, Countess of Home. In 1668 it was alienated to John, Lord Berkeley of Stratton, who died here in 1678, and lies buried in Twickenham church. The estate was afterwards held by the Earl of Cardigan, who in 1698 sold it to the Earl of Albemarle; and about four years later we find it in the hands of Thomas Vernon, who had been secretary to the Duke of Monmouth. The property was purchased of his heirs in 1743 by Algernon, Earl of Mountrath, whose widow, Diana, daughter of the Earl of Bradford, bequeathed it by her will, dated 1766, in a somewhat curious manner, "to the Duchess of Montrose during the joint lives of the Duke and Duchess of Newcastle; but if the Duchess of Newcastle should survive the duke, the Duchess of Montrose to quit possession to her; and if she should survive her, to enjoy it again during *her* life. After the death of the Duchess of Montrose, to remain (revert) to Lord Frederick Cavendish and his issue; on failure of which, after his death, to Lord John Cavendish and his issue, with remainder to Sir William Abdy, Bart., and his heirs in fee." It is remarkable that, except in the instance of Lord John not surviving Lord Frederick Cavendish, everything happened for which the countess thus singularly provided. Lord Frederick Cavendish was owner of Twickenham Park House when Angus published his view of that place, in 1795. From this it appears to have been a large and roomy edifice of red brick with stone dressings, and to have consisted of three storeys above the ground floor, with eleven windows in each, the centre having a portico and pediment, and that and the wings slightly projecting. In Angus's work the building is described as "containing several handsome apartments, with a noble staircase, painted in a similar manner to that at Windsor Castle." Ironside, in his "History of Twickenham," gives the following minute particulars concerning this building:—"The house stands in the two parishes of Twickenham and Isleworth. In the hall, fronting to the south-west, is laid in the mosaic pavement of black and white marble a small iron cross, which divides the two parishes, and in their perambulation of the bounds,

the parishioners of Twickenham direct a man to enter a window at the north-west end of the house, who proceeds to the centre, comes down-stairs, and joins the company in the hall, where they sing the hundredth psalm. He then goes up-stairs, and proceeds to a south-west window, and comes down a ladder on the outside, joins the company again, and thus the ceremony ends."

Early in the present century the greater part of Twickenham Park was sold in lots for building purposes. In 1817 the old mansion was advertised for sale, and was eventually demolished; on its site sprang up a row of "neat villas," which has now culminated in almost a new town.

A large portion of the Twickenham Park estate was purchased by Mr. F. Gostling, whose seat in the parish of Isleworth adjoined it. The Earl of Cassillis (afterwards Marquis of Ailsa) subsequently built a house on part of the property. This, however, was taken down by Lord Kilmorey, when he lived in the large house which is now the Naval School.

Between Twickenham Park and Richmond Bridge, pleasantly situated in Twickenham Meadows, stands a house, called, after its most celebrated occupant, Cambridge House. It was built in the early part of the seventeenth century by Sir Humphry Lynd, whom Anthony à Wood describes as a "zealous Puritan." After his death it became the residence of Joyce, Countess of Totness, who died there in 1636. Later on the property was sold to Sir Joseph Ashe, whose son, Sir Windham Ashe, built the west front and greatly enlarged the mansion. In the middle of the last century it was bought by Richard Owen Cambridge, the well-known author of the mock-heroic poem of the "Scribleriad," and who may be said to have here realised the poetical delineation of Thomson, for in the society of a few choice spirits, he was here blessed with

> "An elegant sufficiency, content,
> Retirement, rural quiet, friendship, books,
> Ease, and alternate labour."

Mr. Cambridge must be well known to the readers of Boswell's "Life of Johnson" as a man of high literary attainments. Besides the "Scribleriad" mentioned above, he was the author of some poems in the sixth volume of Dodsley's collection, and one of the ablest contributors to the periodical work called *The World*. He also wrote an "Account of the War in India between the English and French, on the Coast of Coromandel, from the Year 1750 to 1760," &c. Mr. Cambridge was born in London in 1717, and received his education at Eton and St. John's

College, Oxford. He was for some time a member of Lincoln's Inn, but ultimately determined to abandon the legal profession. He was living at Twickenham when Pope first went to reside in that neighbourhood, and he was on an intimate footing with him, as well as with the most distinguished characters in this country. Mr. Cambridge possessed great powers of conversation, and abounded in choice anecdotes, which he always told with peculiar neatness and point. His connection with *The World* gave rise to a *bon mot*, which is related by his son, Archdeacon Cambridge, who writes :—"A note from Mr. Moore requesting *an essay* was put into my father's hands on a Sunday morning as he was going to church. My mother, observing him rather inattentive during the sermon, whispered, 'What are you thinking of?' He replied, 'Of the *next world*, my dear.'" Mr. Cambridge wrote two epilogues, which were spoken by Miss Pope and by a daughter of Mrs. Pritchard at their respective "benefits." He died in September, 1802, at the age of eighty-five. In an obituary notice of him in *The Gentleman's Magazine*, it is remarked that he "enjoyed an advantage very rarely possessed by the poetical tribe, for he had the 'elegant sufficiency' which Thomson represents as a *desideratum* in human happiness, and was therefore enabled to follow the bent of his genius, and only obey the inspirations of the muse when she chose to be propitious. One of his last literary amusements was a very pleasant versification of the historian Gibbon's account of his own life, with which Mr. Cambridge used to entertain his friends in company, but would not commit to paper."

In the year after his death the literary works of Mr. Cambridge were collected and published in a quarto volume, with a memoir prefixed from the pen of his son, who speaks of him as "an elegant rather than a profound scholar. The liveliness of his parts," he continues, "was more adapted to quick discernment than deep thinking; he had, therefore, but little inclination for abstruse studies and those researches which demand laborious investigation. . . His fondness for books served to increase rather than diminish his study of human nature. His insight into men was correct, judicious, and acute; he viewed with the eye of a philosopher the influence of the passions, not only in the great and leading points of human conduct, but in the trifling incident of human life. The follies of mankind excited his mirth rather than his spleen; but his vein of comic humour was ever regulated by that native benevolence which would not allow him voluntarily to inflict the slightest pain. . .

In his political as well as all other opinions, he manifested that candour which arose from knowledge as well as temper. His life and principles were alike free from corruption; his purity and independence equally untainted." Among his intimate and valued friends may be mentioned Lords Bathurst, Hardwicke, and Mendip, Sir Richard Lyttelton, Horace Walpole, Lord North, Garrick, Sir Joshua Reynolds, Dr. Johnson, Bishop Porteus, Lord Hyde, and Admiral Boscawen. His residence at Twickenham, in fact, became a favourite resort of the most distinguished among his contemporaries. Thus we find Boswell referring with unusual warmth to Mr. Cambridge's "extensive circle of friends and acquaintances, distinguished by rank, fashion, and genius."

After the death of Mr. Cambridge, his villa devolved on his son, the archdeacon, who, however, subsequently removed to a smaller house, which he built at a short distance southward. Cambridge House then became the residence of Lord Mount-Edgcumbe. About the year 1840 it became the seat of Mr. Henry Bevan, and afterwards of his daughter, Lady John Chichester.

Meadowbank, which is the name of the house mentioned above as being built for Archdeacon Cambridge, was for many years the residence of Mr. George Bishop, who had here fitted up an observatory, which has acquired a world-wide reputation from the observations and discoveries made in it under its distinguished superintendent, Mr. John Russell Hind, F.R.S., who resides close by, in Cambridge Park Gardens.

At a short distance westward from Meadowbank, and near the river-side, is Marble Hill—or, as it seems usually to have been called in former times, Marble Hall. The house was built at the expense of George II. for Mrs. Henrietta Howard, who was then a bed-chamber woman, but afterwards Countess of Suffolk, and Groom of the Stole to the queen. The building was designed by the Earl of Pembroke; and, as Swift writes, "Mr. Pope was the contriver of the gardens . . . and the Dean of St. Patrick's (Swift himself) chief butler and keeper of the ice-house." "The intention of the architect," observes Mr. Cobbett, in his "Memorials of Twickenham," "was evidently to make the rooms on the first floor of most imposing proportions, and to effect this, the height of the lower and upper storeys has been somewhat unduly sacrificed. The staircase is made entirely of finely-carved mahogany, and some of the floors are of the same wood. . . The interior of the house is plain in the extreme." Mrs. Howard, in a letter to Gay, dated July, 1723, begs him not to mention the

MR. PITT'S HOUSE AT TWICKENHAM.

(From a Print published by Boydell, 1753.)

plan which he found in her room, as it was necessary to keep the affair secret, although, as she ventures to tell him, "the house was almost entirely furnished to her satisfaction." The reason of secrecy thus enjoined on Gay was probably the fact that the king had extensively contributed to its cost.

Born a Hobart, the Countess of Suffolk—Pope's "Chloe"—had for her first husband the Hon. Charles Howard, and was appointed a Lady of the Howard was looked upon as a very pattern of propriety." Lord Hervey tells us that Mrs. Howard had £2,000 a year from the prince, and £3,200 a year after he became king, besides several little 'dabs' of money, both before and after. The final 'dab' was £12,000 towards building Marble Hill. The house was designed by Lords Burlington and Pembroke; the garden was laid out by Lord Bathurst and Pope; whilst Gay, Swift, and Arbuthnot, constituted themselves superintendents of the house-

MARBLE HILL.   (*See p.* 83.)
(*From a Drawing by P. De Wint*, 1819.)

Bed-chamber to the Princess, afterwards Queen, Caroline. She was noted for her sweetness of temper and pleasant manners; and Pope writes of her—

"Yet Chloe sure was formed without a spot."

Separated from her husband, she became mistress to the prince, afterwards George II. All the wits and poets of the day paid their court to her; poor Gay, for instance, was always trusting to her influence for some appointment which would make him happy, but it never came. "It is scarcely possible," writes an annotator on Pope's works, "to conceive anything more gross than the morals of the English Court under the two first Georges, as related by Walpole and Lord Hervey. Every department was affected; and among the maids of honour, just as among the wits and divines, Mrs. hold at large. The lady's husband lived long enough to become Earl of Suffolk, and dying opportunely, left her, at the age of a little over forty-five, in a position to marry the Hon. George Berkeley. They lived together very happily for eleven years. After Mr. Berkeley's decease, in 1746, she survived twenty-one years, gratifying her neighbour, Horace Walpole, with Court anecdotes long after all the actors in them had passed away." "Lady Suffolk," says Walpole, "was of a just height, well made, extremely fair, with the finest light brown hair, was remarkably genteel, and always well dressed with taste and simplicity. Those were her personal charms, for her face was regular and agreeable rather than beautiful; and those charms she retained, with little diminution, to her death."

It was from Lady Suffolk that Pope picked up much of the Court scandal of the day. Warton tells us that the poet being one day at dinner with her, heard her give an order to her footman to put her in mind to send to know how Mrs. Blount, who was ill, had passed the night. This incident, insignificant enough perhaps in its way, gave rise to the following couplet in Pope's "Moral Essays" :—

"Would Chloe know if you 're alive or dead?
She bids her footman put it in her head."

Contemporary writers are unanimous in declaring that Lady Suffolk was gentle and engaging in her manners, and much beloved by all who knew her. Horace Walpole, who lived on terms of the greatest intimacy with her in her later years, and whose testimony to her personal charms we have already quoted, says that "her mental qualifications were by no means shining—her eyes and countenance showed her character, which was grave and mild. Her strict love of truth and her accurate memory were always in unison. She was discreet without being reserved, and having no bad qualities, and being constant in her connections, she preserved no common respect to the end of her life, and from the propriety and decency of her behaviour, was always treated as if her virtue had never been questioned." Her letters to and from her correspondents, which have been published, prove how much she was respected and beloved. Lady Suffolk died at Marble Hill in 1767, in her eightieth year. She was sister of John, first Earl of Buckinghamshire, who resided at Marble Hill for some time after the death of the countess. Later on, the house was occupied by Mrs. Fitzherbert, who had been privately married to the Prince of Wales, afterwards George IV., and subsequently it became the residence of Lady Bath.

Marble Hill afterwards was the residence of the Marquis Wellesley, brother of the Duke of Wellington; and on his quitting it, about the year 1824, it became the property and seat of the late General Peel, whose widow, Lady Alicia Peel, youngest daughter of the first Marquis of Ailsa, now resides there.

Readers of Swift will not forget his witty "Pastoral Dialogue between Marble Hill and Richmond Lodge," across the river, on hearing the news of the death of George I.

Marble Hill wittily complains that henceforth its lady owner, Lady Suffolk—

"—— will not have a shilling
To raise the stairs, or build the ceiling,
For all the courtly madams round
Now pay four shillings in the pound."

The poor mansion goes on to prophesy :—

"No more the Dean,* that grave divine,
Shall keep the key of my no—wine,
My ice-house rob as heretofore,
And steal my artichokes no more ;
Poor Patty Blount no more be seen
Bedaggled in my walks so green.
Plump Johnny Gay will now elopè,
And here no more will dangle Pope.

* * * * *

Some South Sea broker from the City
Will purchase me, the more 's the pity ;
Lay all my fine plantations waste
To get them to his vulgar taste.
Changed for the worse in every part,
My master, Pope, will break his heart."

In the upper part of Twickenham, towards Isleworth, lived the witty and poetical Dr. Corbett, Bishop of Norwich, whose house was a rendezvous for poets and men of letters. His house stood alone on a small common, and was a most secluded retreat from the noisy world. Here he was visited frequently by Daniel, the poet, and by Michael Drayton, author of the "Polyolbion," and by other choice spirits.

Another ancient house close by was in 1797 the residence of the Duke of Montrose.

In this parish, in 1742, died, in poverty and of a broken heart, Nicholas Amhurst, the author of the once-celebrated satire on Oxford, "Terræ Filius," and editor of the *Craftsman*, the most effective of all the publications aimed at Sir Robert Walpole.

Mr. H. G. Bohn, the publisher, has lived for many years at North End House, in the Richmond Road, where he formed a valuable collection of antiquities, rare books, china, and pictures.

Opposite the lane leading from Orleans Road down to the river formerly stood a small house, called "Ragman's Castle," at one time the residence of Mrs. Pritchard, the actress, who "enlarged and much improved the house, at a considerable expense." The house in the later stages of its existence was known as "Lawn Cottage." Its original appellation has been variously accounted for : some attribute it to the fact of its having been built by an individual who had amassed a fortune in the marine store, or "rag" and bone business, and others say that on its site formerly stood an alehouse, which was a favourite resort of bargemen, ragmen, beggars, &c. However this may be, on the death of Mrs. Pritchard, in 1758, the house became the residence of the Earl of Cholmondeley, and subsequently of Sir Charles Warwick Bampfylde. About 1783, Mr. George Hardinge, who had been

* Swift.

Attorney-General to Queen Charlotte, and afterwards a Welsh judge, took up his abode here. Judge Hardinge was "a man of learning, a good lawyer, and of infinite pleasantry and wit." He was the father of that brave Captain Hardinge who lost his life and his ship in fighting an American frigate of far superior force. Mr. Justice Hardinge died in 1816, and his speeches at the Bar and in the House of Commons, with his miscellaneous works, including a series of letters to Burke on the impeachment of Hastings, have been collected and published. "Ragman's Castle" was taken down by Lord Kilmorey during his occupation of Orleans House, near to which it stood.

Orleans House, so called from the late King of the French, Louis Philippe, having lived in it when Duke of Orleans, was built in the reign of Queen Anne by Mr. Secretary Johnstone, a man whom Pope satirised most bitterly. In one of these attacks, already quoted on page 75 *ante*, Pope refers with considerable spite to Johnson's "dog and bitch." No commentator on Pope's works," writes Mr. Edward Jesse, in *Once a Week* (Vol. III., p.110), " has ever been able to discover what was meant by a reference to these animals. I have, however, been the means of making the discovery. On each side of the lawn of Orleans House there are walls covered with ivy. In the centre of each wall the ivy appeared much raised above the rest. A friend residing near, at my request, examined these portions of the walls, and concealed in the raised ivy he discovered on one wall a dog carved in stone, and on the other a stone bitch."

Mr. Jesse narrates an anecdote of the poet concerning one of the old watermen who was employed for many years in rowing Pope on the Thames. Pope was in the habit of having his sedan-chair lifted into the punt. If the weather was fine, he let down the glasses; if cold, he pulled them up. He would sometimes say to the waterman (this is his own account), " John, I am going to repeat some verses to you; take care and remember them the next time I go out." When that time came, Pope would say, " John, where are the verses I told you of?" " I have forgotten them, sir." " John, you are a blockhead—I must write them down for you." John said that no one thought of saying, when speaking of him, " Mr. Pope," but that he was always called " Mr. Alexander." " It is certain," adds Mr. Jesse, " that when John punted the poet up and down the river he could readily see the anmals above referred to, and hence his satire."

Mr. Johnstone was very self-sufficient, and proud of his post as Scottish Secretary of State. He lived to a great age, in the enjoyment of a pension, to which Pope alludes :—

> " Strike off his pension by the setting sun,
>   And Britain, if not Europe, is undone."

There was a house on this spot before Mr. Johnstone bought the property. In the Parliamentary Survey which was taken in 1650, it is described as a "pleasant and delightful tenement, about twenty poles from the river, built partly with brick and partly with timber, and Flemish walls, with comely chambers; the gardens not only rare for pleasure, but exceedingly profitable, being planted with cabbages, turnips, and carrots, and many other such-like creatures." In that ancient house the Princess of Denmark (afterwards Queen Anne) resided for some time before her accession to the throne, for the benefit of the air for her youthful son, Prince William Henry, Duke of Gloucester, who brought with him his regiment of boys, which he used to exercise on the ayot opposite the house.

The ancient structure was removed by Mr. Johnstone, who built the present house after the model of country seats in Lombardy. At one end of the house he constructed a large octagon room, especially for the reception and entertainment of Queen Caroline, consort of George II., who visited him here. The queen, during her residence at Hampton Court, was in the habit of coming down the river early in the morning to visit Lady Catherine Johnstone, and to breakfast in the beautiful gardens, in which Mackay (in his "Tour through England," which was published in 1720) says that " Secretary Johnstone had the best collection of most gentlemen in England; that he had slopes for his vines, from which he made some hogsheads of wine a year; and that Dr. Bradley, in his 'Treatise on Gardening,' ranked him among the first gardeners in the kingdom."

After the death of Mr. Johnstone, the property was purchased by Mr. George Morton Pitt.* It afterwards passed, through the marriage of that gentleman's daughter, to the Lord Brownlow Bertie, brother of the Duke of Ancaster. Shortly after the death of Lady Bertie, the estate was purchased by Sir George Pococke, K.B., who had married a granddaughter of Mr. Pitt.

The Duke of Orleans took up his residence here in 1800, on his arrival in England from New York, and it was whilst living here, in 1807, that he had the misfortune to lose his brother, the

---

* Ironside and other writers have stated that this gentleman was known as "Diamond Pitt," confusing him with Thomas Pitt, Governor of Madras, and grandfather of the Earl of Chatham.

Duke of Montpensier, whose epitaph on his tomb in Westminster Abbey was the joint composition of the Duke of Orleans and General Dumouriez. The following anecdote concerning Louis Philippe —when in after years, subsequent to his banishment from his kingdom, he was living again in England—is still remembered by some of the inhabitants of Twickenham. The ex-king was staying at the "Star and Garter" at Richmond, and walked one day by himself to Twickenham, for the purpose, as he said, of seeing some of the old tradesmen who had served him when he resided there. As he passed along that place, a man met him, pulled off his hat, and hoped his Royal Highness was well. "What's your name?" inquired the ex-king. He was told it. "I do not recollect it," said his Majesty. "What were you when I lived here?" "Please your Royal Highness," replied the man, "*I kept the 'Crown'*" (an alehouse close to the entrance of Orleans House). "Did you?" said Louis Philippe. "Why, my good fellow, you were lucky; you did what I was unable to do."

Among other good stories told here about Louis Philippe is the following:—His Highness was walking many years ago in a nursery-ground in the neighbourhood, and was directing the attention of a companion to a luxuriantly-loaded apricot-tree, when the head gardener came up, and offered the duke some remarkably fine Orleans plums. "I thank you, sir," replied the duke; "I have already had a taste of that bitter fruit, and no longer relish it."

In 1827 Orleans House was sold to Mr. Alexander Murray, of Broughton, M.P. for the county of Kirkcudbright; in 1846 it was purchased by Lord Kilmorey, from whom it was again bought by the Duc d'Aumale, who considerably altered and improved the building by the erection of a large picture-gallery and a commodious library. The Duc d'Aumale ceased to reside here when the fall of the French Empire rendered possible his return to France, and the house was subsequently for a short time occupied by another royal exile, Don Carlos. It was somewhat remarkable that the Orleanist should be succeeded by the Carlist. Don Carlos would, no doubt, have found more sympathy from the Comte de Chambord than he would receive from the Comte de Paris.

In 1876-7 Orleans House was offered for sale, and having been purchased by a company, has been converted into a club, called the Orleans Club, and as such, combines in itself all the advantages of a country house with the ordinary social intercourse and facilities of a club.

The house, a very fine one, overlooks the river,

and the grounds, which are about forty acres in extent, come down to the water's edge. They are one of the prettiest sights on the river Thames during "the season." An ornamental wall has been built as a kind of embankment, which is crowned with vases, wherein the duke used to plant the loveliest flowers. A writer in the *Gentleman's Magazine*, in 1802, thus describes the house as it existed at the commencement of the present century:—"It is a handsome building of brick; but the front has been spoiled by removing the entrance, and throwing out a bow from the bottom to the upper storey. Before this alteration, there was a handsome door-case of Portland stone, with a window over it suitably ornamented. The present way into the house is in the centre of a wing added to it, or a passage to an elegant octagon room at the end, which was built on purpose for the reception and entertainment of her late Majesty Queen Caroline. These additional buildings make one very long wing, which has an awkward appearance, for want of somewhat to answer it on the other side for the sake of uniformity. This passage to the octagon is made use of as a music-room, in which is a handsome organ." A roadway intersects the lawn of the house from the river meadow, but there are tunnels, rustic bridges, and happily-contrived devices designed to obviate any objection which might be raised to this pretty place calling itself a river-side estate. The house was erected by a sensible architect, and the gardens laid out with a loving respect for nature. The deep shady recesses, the broad thick sashes dividing the panes, the deep wide fire-places, the marble halls, the conservatory corridors thickly planted with camellias, the cosy bed-rooms looking out over Richmond Hill, across the river, or back over the park to Twickenham, the libraries, the billiard-rooms, and the boudoirs, all are distinguished for their substantial comfort; whilst the gardens, lawns, and meadows, are so designed as to combine the ease of retirement with the sense of variety.

The Orleans Club is not a man's club alone, a mere dining place, a dim solemnity, an excuse for extravagance and play, but a social rendezvous, where ladies can adorn the lawn, preside over the drawing-room, and repose under umbrella tents, whilst the men play lawn tennis, or devote themselves to whatever form of violent exercise may please them. With this object the Orleans Club was started. There is a "bachelor wing," and also a "married wing," with luxuriously-appointed bedrooms. There are card-rooms and billiard-rooms for the men; there are drawing-rooms, pianos, and boudoirs for the ladies; and, above all, there is that lovely garden, common to all. Here, under the beautiful trees or reclining on the indolent lawn, it will be possible to breathe the fresh air, and to forget the ball-room, the opera, and the perpetual park. It is not so much a question what to do at the Orleans Club as what cannot be done. There are lawn games in abundance; there are flower gardens and conservatories; there are boats and steam launches, ready at a moment's notice for a row to Moulsey or a long day to Windsor; there are stalls enough, too, in the stables to accommodate the Four-in-Hand and Coaching Clubs whenever they drive down from town; and every arrangement has been made for giving as capital a dinner as can be eaten at the close of the summer holiday.

Near Twickenham Church, and on the banks of the Thames, stands the building historically known as York House, the reputed residence of James II. when Duke of York, and for some time in the occupation of the Comte de Paris. The house was for many years the property of Sir Alexander Johnstone, and it is associated with the name of Lord Clarendon.

The mansion, with other valuable presents, appears to have been given by Charles II. to Lord Clarendon, on the public announcement of the marriage of his daughter with James II., then Duke of York. The Chancellor was accustomed to pass here the summer months; and when he attended the king at Hampton Court he was in the habit of coming home every night "to his own house at Twickenham." From the reply of Lord Clarendon (as given by his biographer) to the courtiers commissioned by King Charles II. to inform him of the clandestine marriage of his daughter Anne with the Duke of York (afterwards James II.), it has been concluded that his lordship was either a very unnatural father or a very great hypocrite. From his well-known affection for his accomplished child, it is highly improbable that he ever did officially advise her committal to the Tower; and from the tradition that "he actually presented his Royal Highness with his favourite villa, York House, observing that it was already named after him," it is probable he was aware of the duke's affection for his daughter, but feared to discover any knowledge or participation in an act which he knew would be displeasing to the king. Here the royal duke and his much-loved bride passed some years in uninterrupted happiness; here several of their children were born, and amongst them the Princesses Mary and Anne, successively Queens of England. The state-chamber,

which still bears the name of Queen Anne's Room, presents the same appearance which it wore when that monarch first saw the light, in February, 1665, saving those changes which time—merciless time—has inflicted on the perishable materials with which it was adorned. Tradition also says that the great Chancellor wrote some of his essays in the garden walks.

There is little difficulty in retracing the descent of this interesting property from the date of its original demise to T. Jermyn, in 1566, down to the present proprietor. In 1661, York Farm, a parcel of the manor, was granted to Lord Clarendon; at his lordship's death, in 1674, it passed to his second son, Lawrence Hyde, Earl of Rochester. In 1740 it was sold to J. Whitchurch, Esq., and by his representatives to Lieut.-Col. J. Webber, who disposed of the freehold to Prince Stahremberg, Envoy Extraordinary and Minister Plenipotentiary from the Court of Vienna. His Excellency retained possession of York Villa during the whole term of his ambassadorial attendance at St. James's, and the cheerfulness and hospitality of his disposition rendered it the scene of continued gaiety. Having fitted up one of the wings as a private theatre, dramatic representations were frequently exhibited there, when the prince and princess, their daughters, and several foreigners of distinction, displayed their talents in the histrionic art. The plays most frequently performed were the little French pieces which were then so popular in this country; and the lists of the *dramatis personæ*, published at the time, establish this fact, and disclose the titles of the eminent foreigners, who by their talents and accomplishments excited so much interest, and afforded so much intellectual amusement to the many families of distinction then residing in the vicinity.

York House subsequently became the residence of Dr. Cleaver, Archbishop of Dublin, who, from mental disease, was unable to discharge the duties of his see. In 1817 the house was purchased by the Hon. Mrs. Damer, of whom we shall have more to say when we reach Strawberry Hill. Mrs. Damer had acquired great reputation as a sculptress, and on taking up her residence here, she fitted up one wing of the house as a studio and gallery of art. It was here that many of those able performances which have conferred upon her an abiding celebrity were designed and executed. Mrs. Damer's attention was first called to this pursuit, so unusual amongst ladies, by that celebrated philosopher, David Hume, whilst he was private secretary to her father, Field-Marshal Conway. Having observed the precocious ability of the young sculptor, he exhorted her to cultivate it with her best energies; and it was by his advice, and at his pressing instance, that Mrs. Damer devoted her talents so entirely to the statuary art. Mrs. Damer towards the close of her life espoused the cause of the unfortunate Queen Caroline, whom she frequently entertained here. She lived to a great age, respected and admired by the most eminent of her contemporaries, and at her death in 1828 the estate of York House passed by bequest to her

two Brahmins standing on the terrace at York House, near the banks of the Thames, on the relative merits of the religion, customs, and manners of the Hindoos, and the religion, customs, and manners of the English. His design was to show how much superior the latter were to the former, by the wonderful progress which the English had made in a knowledge of government, arts, and sciences, while the Hindoos had remained stationary for ages; and to conclude by the pros-

PHILIP, DUKE OF WHARTON.
(See p. 91.)

LADY SUFFOLK.
(See p. 85.)

cousin, Lady Johnston, only daughter of Lord William Campbell, son of the fourth Duke of Argyle, on whose premature decease she had been placed under the guardianship of her uncle, the late Duke of Argyle. Afterwards, when she married, the estate became vested in her ladyship's husband, the Right Hon. Sir Alexander Johnston.

A frequent visitor to York House during its occupancy by Sir Alexander Johnston was the celebrated Brahmin and Oriental philosopher, Ramohun Roy, who drew up a sketch of a work while here, which, had he lived, he meant to have published, upon the plan of the "Tusculan Questions" by Cicero, and the "Minute Philosopher" by Berkeley,* professing to be a dialogue between

pects which are now held out, by the discovery of steam navigation, and the constant use of the route from England to India through Egypt, that the Hindoos (from being brought by these circumstances so much nearer to England than they were before) would soon become equal to the English in their knowledge of government, and in all the different arts and sciences which must raise their moral, intellectual, and political character.

Among the subsequent occupiers of York House were the Dowager Duchess of Roxburgh and Lord Lonsdale, the latter of whom died here in 1844. A few years afterwards the mansion was sold to the Duc d'Aumale for his nephew, the Comte de Paris, eldest son of the late Duc d'Orleans, and grandson of Louis Philippe, late King of the

---

* See the collected works of Berkley, Bishop of Cloyne, 1843.

French. The Comte de Paris vacated the house about 1871, and some two years later the house and grounds were submitted for sale by public auction.

The mansion, which occupies a pleasant position on an elevated plateau overlooking the river Thames, is built in what is now known as the "Queen Anne" style of architecture, and consists of a centre and wings, and the apartments are both numerous and spacious. A grand staircase of oak with carved

"Wharton, the scorn and wonder of our days,
Whose ruling passion was the lust of praise;
Born with whate'er could win it from the wise,
Women and fools must like him, or he dies.
Though wondering senates hung on all he spoke,
The club must hail him master of the joke.
Shall parts so various aim at nothing new?
He'll shine a Tully and a Wilmot too.
Thus, with each gift of nature and of art,
And wanting nothing but an honest heart;
Grown all to all, from no one vice exempt,
And most contemptible to show contempt;

THE GARDENS OF ORLEANS HOUSE, 1882.

balustrade, &c., gives access from the hall to the principal chambers in the upper storeys. From the drawing-rooms and library windows open upon a broad terrace walk, which extends the whole length of the river front. The gardens and grounds, about nine acres in extent, are admirably laid out, and include a wilderness, fernery, flower-garden, lawns, &c.

In a house, called The Grove, long since swept away, but which stood in or near what is now King Street, in the western part of the town, lived for some time the witty and clever, but disreputable, Duke of Wharton, whose character is summed up by Pope in one of his "Moral Essays" in the following often quoted lines :—

His passion still to covet general praise,
His life, to forfeit it a thousand ways;
A constant bounty, which no friend has made;
An angel tongue, which no man can persuade;
A fool, with more of wit than half mankind;
Too rash for thought, for action too refined;
A tyrant to the wife his heart approves,
A rebel to the very king he loves.
He dies, sad outcast of each church and state,
And, harder still, flagitious, yet not great.
Ask you why Wharton broke through every rule?
'Twas all for fear the knaves should call him fool."

"It is difficult," remarks Horace Walpole, in the "Royal and Noble Authors," "to give an account of the works of so mercurial a man, whose library was a tavern, and women of pleasure his muses. A thousand sallies of his imagination may have been lost, for he wrote for fame no more than he acted for it." Perhaps Horace Walpole on this occasion, as on many others, "hit the right nail on the head." The duke must have been indeed "mercurial." "Like Buckingham and Rochester, Philip Duke of Wharton comforted all the grave and dull," says Horace Walpole, "by throwing away the brightest profusion of parts on witty fooleries, debaucheries, and scrapes, which may mix graces with a great character, but can never make one." Mr. Seward observes that the character of Lovelace in "Clarissa" has always been supposed to be that of this noble-man; and the supposition is rendered the more probable as Richardson printed the *True Briton*, in which the duke wrote constantly.

Well and wittily is it remarked by Bolton, in his "Extinct Peerage," that Philip, Duke of Wharton, "succeeded his father, Thomas, in all his titles and abilities, but in none of his virtues." And it is indeed strange that the man who could give £2,000 as a present to a poet, and administer a witty rebuff to an officious ambassador, could be guilty of such a silly and unmeaning trick as knocking up his guardian in the middle of the night, in order to borrow a pin; or at another time, in France, serenad-ing respectable persons at their country châteaux, one of whom very nearly killed him by a stray shot, mistaking him for a robber.

Some interesting facts about the Duke are to be found in a scarce work, entitled "Memoirs of the Life of his Grace Philip, late Duke of Wharton, by an Impartial Hand." It is prefixed to two octavo volumes, published in 1732, entitled "The Life and Writings of Philip, late Duke of Wharton," but which contain only the seventy-four numbers of the *True Briton*, and the speech on the bill of pains and penalties against Atterbury, the paging of which is a continuation of that of the *True Briton*, although it has a title-page of its own dated 1724. There is another publication, in two volumes octavo, without date, entitled "The Poeti-cal Works of Philip, late Duke of Wharton, and others of the Wharton Family, and of the Duke's Intimate Acquaintance, particularly Lord Boling-broke, Dean Swift, Lady Wharton, Doctor Delany, Lord Dorset, Major Pack, the Hon. Mrs. Wharton, &c." These two volumes, however, appear to have been all printed in 1727 (before the duke's death), with the exception only of this general title-page and a life of the duke, which is substantially the same with that noticed above, and is here stated to be "communicated by a person of quality, and one of his grace's intimate friends." The first volume contains very little that is even attributed to the duke; but in the second are some letters in prose, addressed to Lady Wharton, his father's first wife, and her poetical paraphrase of the "Lamentations of Jeremiah."

The duke died at Tarragona, in Spain, in 1731, and a vindication of his character is to be found in a volume of scarce broadsides in the British Museum. It bears no printer's name, but only the date 1728; it was probably printed in Dublin.

During Pope's time the Grove was the residence of his friend, the younger James Craggs, who succeeded Addison in the post of Secretary of State in 1718, and who, like his father, was ruined by the South Sea scheme. Craggs was the friend of Steele and Tickell, and the opponent of Sir Robert Walpole in Parliament. The Grove, which was pulled down many years ago, is said to have been originally built by Inigo Jones for the Earl of Rochester. Its site is marked by a solitary cedar, with a pond near it.

At Twickenham the Duke of Wharton was the neighbour and acquaintance of Lady Mary Wortley Montagu, who wrote an epilogue for a tragedy which he began on "Mary Queen of Scots." This poem was never finished, and all of it that remains is a brace of couplets preserved in a "Miscellany," like "flies in amber." They run as follows:—

> "Sure were I free, and Norfolk were a pris'ner,
> I'd fly with more impatience to his arms
> Than the poor Israelite on the serpent gaz'd,
> When life was the reward of every look."

Lady Mary Wortley Montagu lived at Saville House, close by the Grove. She came to reside there mainly through the persuasion of Pope, with whom at one time she lived on terms of great inti-macy and friendship; but they quarrelled, and hated each other cordially for the remainder of their lives. Lady Mary died in 1762, and her successor here was Lady Saville, from whom the house derived its name; she was the mother of Sir George Saville, who, among many others, is said to have been the original of Richardson's "Sir Charles Grandi-son."

Twickenham House, a fine old building, standing on the south side of the main road, near the rail-way bridge, has a little history of its own, as having been the residence of Sir John Hawkins, who enjoyed the distinction, according to the poet, of being buried "in his shoes and stawkings," and who was described by the Earl of Rochford (then one of the Secretaries of State) as "the best magistrate in the kingdom." Sir John was a devoted fisher-man—a pastime in which his residence on the banks of the Thames enabled him freely to indulge.

He brought out, with notes, an edition of "Izaak Walton's Complete Angler," and also "The History of Music" and a "Life of Dr. Johnson." Hawkins was one of the original members of the Literary Club, and in the gardens of Twickenham House, as we learn from Mr. Cobbett's "Memorials," there is a building which was used for the meetings of the club. Attached to the house is a circular room with a domed roof, now used as a drawing-room; this, Mr. Cobbett tells us, was originally Sir John's concert-room. The grounds contain a curious relic, consisting of a garden-fence, curiously wrought with sword-blades brought from the field of Culloden. Twickenham House has been long the residence of Dr. Hugh Diamond.

Nearer the town of Twickenham, on the site of what is now Heath Lane Lodge, stood in former times a house which was the seat of more than one Earl Ferrers. Mr. Cobbett, in his work above mentioned, states that "tradition asserts that Laurence, the 'mad' Earl Ferrers, who shot Mr. Johnson, his steward, was taken from this house to execution." This statement, however, is very doubtful. There was in the original house a portrait of one of Lord Ferrers' daughters—the lovely Lady Frances Shirley, who was one of Pope's personal friends, and who was sung by Chesterfield as "Fanny, blooming fair."

It will not be forgotten that Pope commemorates the residence of Fielding in this place in his "Parish Register of Twickenham":—

> "When Feilding met his bunter muse,
> And as they quaffed the fiery juice,
> Droll Nature stamped each lucky hit
> With unimaginable wit."

The aristocratic owner of Strawberry Hill has not failed, as Scott observes in his "Lives of the Novelists," to stigmatise the lowness of Fielding's habits, and of the society which he kept.

Fielding, though sprung from a collateral branch of the Feildings, Earls of Denbigh, did not care to follow the latter mode of spelling his name. On being asked why his father had departed from the accepted orthography, he replied, somewhat cynically, that "he supposed it was because he was the first of his race who knew how to spell."

Another resident here was Paul Whitehead, notorious as a venal politician and a second-rate satirist. Dr. Doran, in his "Habits and Men," speaks of him as "one of the fine gentlemen of his day, who associated only with the finest of that class. At Twickenham he had not only his country house, but a coruscant circle of wits around him, whose brilliancy was not considered as tarnished by the most mouldy blasphemy."

Dr. Donne, the poet, was also an inhabitant of this place. He died in 1631, and has been immortalised by Isaac Walton. Here, too, lived Mrs. Margaret Godolphin, perhaps the only virtuous lady of the vicious Court of Charles II., the story of whose "saintly life" has been told so well by her friend and correspondent, John Evelyn.

Robert Boyle, the celebrated philosopher, at one period of his life lived at Twickenham. His name occurs in the parish register, but the exact locality where he resided is unknown. He was the fifth son of the great Earl of Cork, and died in 1691. Mr. Boyle founded the lectures which bear his name.

Edward Stillingfleet, D.D., Dean of St. Paul's, and afterwards Bishop of Worcester, may also be numbered among the former residents of Twickenham; and so was the Rev. Dr. Waterland, the author of many learned works, and sometime vicar of the parish, who died in 1748. Another celebrated vicar was the Rev. George Costard, who wrote and published several works on astronomy, and contributed to the "Transactions of the Royal Society," of which he was a member.

Andrew Stone, at one time preceptor to George III., lived here in style, occupying a large old-fashioned brick house near the river-side. He was a brother of the founder of the bank of Martin, Stone, and Co., at the sign of the "Grasshopper," Lombard Street. He was a friend of Horace Walpole, who mentions him in one of his works. He is buried in the north aisle of the nave of Westminster Abbey.

Twickenham Common was till recent times an open space, doubtless available as a playground for the children of the poor, and as pasturage for their donkeys and geese.

> "But times are altered, trade's unfeeling train
> Usurp the land, and dispossess the swain."

Here may be seen the house formerly occupied by General Gunning, brother to those celebrated beauties the Duchesses of Hamilton and Argyll and Lady Coventry. The Marchioness of Tweeddale resided in it before General Gunning.

In Ailsa Park Villas lived Lord Beaconsfield's sister Sarah. She was betrothed to a Mr. Meredith, a gentleman of wealth, and of literary repute as the patron of Thomas Taylor, the translator of Aristotle. She died in December, 1859, and is buried in the Willesden Cemetery.

Coming down to more recent times, we find that here "Boz," in the first flush of prosperity caused by the success of "Pickwick," took a cottage for part of the summer of 1838. Here Talfourd, Thackeray, Jerrold, Maclise, Landseer, Stanfield, Cattermole, and Harrison Ainsworth, were among his visitors, as narrated by Forster, in his "Life of Dickens;" and here he indulged to the full in "the grand enjoyment of idleness," abandoning himself to what must at that time have been an inexperienced delight—the luxury of laziness.

Montpelier Row was the last residence of Mr. Augustus Mayhew, one of the "Brothers Mayhew," the author of "Paved with Gold," "The Greatest Plague of Life," &c., who died at the close of 1875.

its builder and first occupant, Sir Godfrey Kneller, who called it in his lifetime "Whitton House." It was built in 1710. The hall and staircase were painted by La Guerre, under the direction and with the occasional assistance of Sir Godfrey. The house was made the artist's summer residence.

Sir Godfrey Kneller lives in the verses of half the poets of his age; few, however, paid him a higher compliment than Matt Prior:—

KNELLER HALL.   (*See p.* 94.)

We must not omit to mention amongst the celebrated persons who have resided at Twickenham the Lady Augusta Murray, the unhappy wife of the late Duke of Sussex, and the mother of his two accomplished children.

Mr. W. Andrews, in his "Book of Oddities," records a curious devise of property here as lately as 1862, when Mr. Henry Budd left an estate, called Pepper Park, to his son, on condition of his not wearing a moustache; in event of his doing so, the property to pass to a brother.

On the north-eastern side of the parish, and just within the boundary of the hamlet of Whitton, stands a building of some interest and importance, namely, Kneller Hall, so called after

" When Kneller's works of various grace
    Were to fair Venus shown,
  The goddess spied in every face
    Some features of her own.

" But viewing Myra placed apart,
    ' I fear,' says she, ' I fear,
  Apelles, that Sir Godfrey's art
    Has far surpassed thine here.' "

Again, Dryden thus sings the praises of Sir Godfrey:—

" At least thy pictures look a voice; and we
  Imagine sounds, deceiv'd to that degree,
  We think 'tis somewhat more than just to see."

Sir Godfrey Kneller was a native of Lubeck, in

Germany, and was born in 1648. Having evinced at an early age talents of no mean order, he became a pupil of Ferdinand Bol and of Rembrandt. He subsequently visited Italy, studied at Rome under Carlo Maratti, and came to England in 1674. He was shortly after commissioned by the Duke of Monmouth to paint a portrait of the king, and his success as a portrait painter was at once established. Sir Godfrey received the appointment of portrait painter successively to Charles II., James II., William and Mary, Anne, and George I. It was not only royalty, however, that sat to Kneller; indeed, there was hardly a person of note or distinction in his day whom he had not painted. Bishop Burnet, John Evelyn, the "Court beauties" of his day, the Admirals at Hampton Court, and the members of the Kit-Cat Club, are amongst Sir Godfrey's most noted works. He was knighted by King William, and created a baronet by George I.

Among the anecdotes told of Sir Godfrey Kneller is one to the effect that he painted so fine a full-length picture of Lady Kneller, that, leaving the door of his studio open, Lady Kneller's favourite spaniel got access to it, and seeing, as he thought, his beloved mistress, he jumped up at her likeness and injured the picture, which had been taken from the easel and placed against the wall.

Sir Godfrey's vanity displayed itself in his last moments. Pope, who came over to visit him two days before his death, observes that he had never seen in his life such a scene. He was sitting up in bed, and contemplating the plans which he was making for his own monument!

Sir Godfrey died in 1723, and is said, but falsely, to have been buried in the garden of Kneller Hall, but of the place of his interment there is no trace there, for he lies in Twickenham church. There is a monument to his memory, with an inscription by Pope, in Westminster Abbey.

Some time after the death of Sir Godfrey Kneller the mansion became the residence of Sir Samuel Prime; and in 1847 it was purchased by the Committee of the Council of Education, to be used as a normal training school, and Dr. Temple, now Bishop of Exeter, received the appointment of Principal. In 1856 the establishment passed into the hands of the War Department, and in the following year a school of military music was opened here. What with alterations and enlargements at different periods, the house may be said to have been almost entirely rebuilt since Kneller's time.

CHAPTER VIII.

TWICKENHAM (*continued*).—POPE'S VILLA.

"Pope, to whose reed beneath the beechen shade,
The nymphs of Thames a pleased attention paid."—LORD LYTTELTON, "*The Progress of Love.*"

Parentage and Birth of Alexander Pope—His Education—His Early Admiration for Dryden—His first Essays Poetic Effusions—Is introduced to Sir W. Trumbull and Wycherley—His Friendship with the Misses Blount—Translates the "Iliad"—Takes up his Residence at Chiswick—Publication of the "Odyssey"—Pope's Narrow Escape from Drowning—Publication of the "Miscellanies," "The Essay on Man," and other Poems—Death and Burial of Pope—Pope's Skull—Character and Temperament of Pope—His Personal Appearance—His Popularity—His Visitors—His Fondness for Animals—His Love of Economy—His Rank as a Poet—His Will—An Account of Pope's Villa and Grotto—Sale of the Villa to Sir William Stanhope—Its subsequent History.

APART from the name of Horace Walpole, there is none that is more closely associated with Twickenham than that of Alexander Pope; and it is mainly owing to the memory of these two men that Twickenham has been so long "the favourite retreat of scholars, poets, and statesmen."

Alexander Pope was born in London in the month of May, 1688. His parents were members of the Roman Catholic Church; his father, according to the poet's own account, was "of a noble family;" but according to some of his biographers, he kept a linendraper's shop in the city; others state that he was a mechanic, a hatter, and even a farmer. In a foot-note in his "Moral Essays," it is stated that Mr. Pope's father was of "a gentle man's family in Oxfordshire, the head of which was the Earl of Downe, whose sole heiress married the Earl of Lindsey." His mother was the daughter of William Turner, Esq., of York. She had three brothers, one of whom was killed; another died in the service of King Charles; the eldest, following his fortunes, and becoming a general officer in Spain, left her what estate remained after the sequestrations and forfeitures of her family. Be this, however, true or not, Pope's father left London during the childhood of his son, and retired first to Kensington, and then to Binfield, on the borders of Windsor Forest, and there, in his twelfth year, the youthful poet joined him. Young as he was, Pope here formed his first plans of study, and in the seclusion of the country set himself vigorously to read, and occasionally to write. He had received the rudiments of his education in Latin and Greek from the family priest, and he was for a short time at a Roman Catholic school at Twyford, and also at a school near Hyde Park Corner, in London. His poetic abilities displayed themselves even at that early age, for he is credited with having written a play, based on certain events in the "Iliad," and made up of the speeches in Ogilby's translation, which was acted by the elder boys in the school, the part of Ajax being sustained by the master's gardener. Whilst he was living at Binfield Dryden became the subject of his greatest admiration; and it was to Wills' Coffee-house, in Russell Street, Covent Garden, that Pope, when a mere child, induced his friends to carry him, in order that he might gaze on the great poet whose mantle he was destined in after life so worthily to wear.* "Who does not wish," writes Dr. Johnson, "that Dryden could have known the value of the homage that was paid him, and foreseen the greatness of his young admirer?" In later years Pope became a constant frequenter of "Wills'," though not till after the illustrious Dryden's death. "Pope had now," again writes Dr. Johnson, "declared himself a poet, and thinking himself entitled to poetical conversation, began at seventeen to frequent 'Wills'' . . where the wits of that time used to assemble, and where Dryden had, when he lived, been accustomed to preside."

At the age of twelve Pope wrote his "Ode to Solitude," which was followed soon after by a translation of the first book of the "Thebais" of Statius, and Ovid's "Epistle of Sappho to Phaon." Whilst living at Binfield young Pope formed the acquaintanceship of Sir William Trumbull, by whom he was introduced to Wycherley the dramatist; but his friendship with the latter was but of short duration, owing, it is said, to Pope's somewhat too free strictures on a volume of poems which Wycherley was preparing for publication, and had submitted to Pope for his revision. It was about this time that the intimacy sprang up between Pope and Mr. and the Misses Blount, who were living at Mapledurham, near Reading. Pope was strongly suspected by some of his friends in after life—among others by Lepel, Lady Hervey—of being privately married to his friend and correspondent, Miss Martha Blount, the elder of the two sisters.

"There can be little doubt," observed a writer in the *Gentleman's Magazine*, "that one of the most faithful friendships of Pope's life was that

with the fair-haired Martha Blount. It was an early friendship, with a dash of sentiment about it, that might, under happier circumstances, have ripened into love. And it was a perfectly intelligible friendship. There may be, as Mrs. Oliphant has well said, a love between man and woman which does not point to matrimony, and there seems no ground for the scandal that assailed the life-long intimacy of Martha and the poet. . .

In his early days Pope seems to have felt an equal affection for Teresa, the elder sister; but at a later period, from some doubtful cause, there was a complete estrangement between them. . . Both sisters, by the way, were considered beautiful in their youth, but neither of them married. . . . Martha Blount returned Swift's affection, and was, as Pope told the dean, 'as constant to old friendships as any man'; and in another letter Swift is told that she speaks of him constantly, and 'is one of the most considerate and mindful of women in the world towards others, the least so in regard to herself.'"

At the age of sixteen Pope composed his "Pastorals," but they were not printed till some five years later (1709), when they appeared in "Tonson's Miscellany." He next wrote his "Essay on Criticism," which was followed shortly after by "The Rape of the Lock" and the "Temple of Fame"; "Windsor Forest" and "The Ode on St. Cecilia's Day" were published in 1713. In a letter to Addison, written in this year, Pope speaks of his passion for the art of painting, which he had studied under Jervas, but the pursuit of which he was prevented from following up by the weakness of his eyesight.

The want of money led Pope about this time to issue proposals for a subscription to a translation of the "Iliad." The whole work was completed between his twenty-fifth and thirtieth year. Concerning the writing of this work, an amusing story is told by Pope himself in his correspondence. He writes:—"When I had finished the first two or three books of my translation of the 'Iliad,' Lord Halifax desired to have the pleasure of hearing them read at his house. Addison, Congreve, and Garth, were there at the read. In four or five places his lordship stopped me very civilly, and with a speech each time, much of the same kind. 'I beg your pardon, Mr. Pope; but there is something in that passage that does not quite please me. Be so good as to mark the place, and consider it a little at your leisure. I'm sure you can give it a little turn.' I returned from Lord Halifax's (continues Pope) with Dr. Garth, in his chariot; and as we were going along, was saying to the doctor that my

---

* See "Old and New London," Vol. III., p. 276.

lord had laid me under a good deal of difficulty by such loose and general observations; that I had been thinking over the passages ever since, and could not guess at what it was that offended his lordship in either of them. Garth laughed heartily at my embarrassment, and said I had not been long enough acquainted with Lord Halifax to know his way yet; that I need not puzzle myself about looking those places over and over when I got home. 'All you need do,' says he, 'is to leave them just as they are; call on Lord Halifax two or three months hence, thank him for his kind observations on those passages, and then read them to him *as altered*. I have known him much longer than you have, and will be answerable for the event.' I followed his advice; waited on Lord Halifax some time after; said, I hoped he would find his objections to those passages removed; read them to him *exactly as they were at first*, and his lordship was extremely pleased with them, and cried out, 'Ay, now they are perfectly right; nothing can be better!'"

By the subscription list for his translation of Homer Pope's circumstances were so materially improved that he persuaded his father to remove from Binfield, and take up his residence nearer London; and, accordingly, we soon after find the family settled in Mawson's Buildings, Chiswick.* Here Pope continued the "Iliad," and wrote the "Epistle from Eloisa to Abelard." Pope subsequently took a long lease of a house and five acres of ground at Twickenham, and at once set about the work of improvement, as we shall presently see.

From this time may be dated the most important portion of the poet's career. "He was," writes Mr. Cobbett, in his "Memorials of Twickenham," "one of the very few literary men who in his own or any previous time acquired a competence through their dealings with the booksellers." Happily he escaped from the meshes of the Curlls and Stocks

POPE. (*From a Contemporary Portrait.*)

of his day. In 1726 Pope published a translation of the "Odyssey," in which he had the assistance of Broome and Fenton. Pope translated twelve books, Broome eight, and Fenton four.

About this time an incident occurred—trifling, perhaps, as it happened, but which might have ended Pope's earthly career. It is recorded by Carruthers, in his "Life of Pope," as follows:— "The poet had been dining with Bolingbroke at Dawley, and late at night the peer sent his friend home in a stately fashion in a coach and six. A small bridge about a mile from Pope's residence was broken down, and the postillion taking the water, the coach came in contact with the trunk of a tree, and was overturned. Before the coachman could get to Pope's assistance the water had reached the knots of his periwig. The glass was broken, and he was rescued, but not until he had received a severe wound in his right hand, which for some time disqualified him from writing. Voltaire, who was on a visit to Dawley, sent his condolences in an *English* epistle, stating that the water into which Pope fell was 'not Hippocrene's water, otherwise it would have respected him.' 'Is it possible,' he added, 'that those fingers which have written the "Rape of the Lock" and the "Criticism," which have dressed Homer so becomingly in an *English coat*, should have been so barbarously treated?'"

The accident here referred to probably occurred either at the north end of the village, near where is the railway station now, or else in the little river Cran, which sweeps round to the east near the Hounslow powder-mills, and runs parallel with the road from Twickenham to Hanworth. In one place on the road to Hanworth it is dammed up so as to form a broad lake.

In 1827 were published two volumes of "Miscellanies" by Pope and Swift, to which Gay and Arbuthnot contributed, and in these "Miscellanies" was printed the piece of satire entitled "Martinus Scriblerus"; this was followed up in 1729 by the publication of the first three books of the "Dunciad,"

---

* See *ante*, p. 5.

in which he took summary vengeance upon certain exasperating scribblers who were, or thought they were, ridiculed in the " Miscellanies." In 1733 Pope published the " Essay on Man," and in the following year appeared his " Characters of Men ; or, Moral Essays." These were preceded and followed by imitations of Horace ; and in 1742 the list of Pope's poems is concluded with an additional book of the " Dunciad." In the next year Pope's health began to decline, and on the 30th of May, 1744, he died here of asthma and decay of nature.

Pope was buried, as he directed, in Twickenham Church, " in a vault in the middle aisle, under the second pew from the east end." A stone inscribed with the letter " P " marks the spot, which is now hidden by the flooring of the seats.

By some of Pope's biographers it is asserted that the head of the poet was abstracted from his coffin during some repairs of the church. On this subject Mr. Howitt, in his " Homes and Haunts of the British Poets," writes as follows :—" By one of those acts which neither science nor curiosity can excuse, the skull of Pope is now in the private collection of a phrenologist. The manner in which it was obtained is said to have been this :—On some occasion of alteration in the church, or burial of some one in the same spot, the coffin of Pope was disinterred, and opened, to see the state of the remains. By a bribe to the sexton of the time, possession of the skull was obtained for the night, and *another* skull returned instead of it. I have heard that fifty pounds were paid to manage and carry through this transaction. Be that as it may, the undoubted skull of Pope now figures in the phrenological collection of Mr. Holm, of Highgate, and was frequently exhibited by him in his lectures, as demonstrating, by its not large but well-balanced proportions, its affinity to the intellectual character of the poet."

" Such statements," observes Mr. Cobbett, in his work already quoted, " are hard to be disproved, more especially when motives of interest support them. It is fair, however, to the Rev. Charles Proby (the vicar during whose time the alleged theft was committed), and to the then officials of the church, to give, as he communicated it to Mr. Powell, his churchwarden, his unqualified denial of each and every part of the story. Mr. Proby had seen Mr. Howitt's paragraph, and desired, as he was too old to enter into a paper war, that the real facts which gave rise to the report should be published, if a new history of Twickenham were ever written. Mr. Proby's statement is as follows :— ' Upon opening a vault some years ago in the middle aisle of the church, adjoining Pope's, the latter fell in, the coffin was broken, and disclosed the skeleton, which was very short, with a large skull. I was immediately informed of it, when I directed my curate, Mr. Fletcher, to remain in the church, and not to leave until the whole was restored and built up. *A cast of the skull was taken, with my permission,* by the mason employed, who well knew how to accomplish it. I am quite sure that Mr. Fletcher rigidly carried out my instructions. No such abstraction could have been made.' "

Pope throughout his whole life never enjoyed good health. A sickly child, of mild temper, with a sweet voice which earned him the sobriquet of " the little nightingale," his physical weakness determined the bent of his tastes and the nature of his pursuits. In the churchyard at Twickenham there is a stone raised by Pope himself in " gratitude " to his " faithful servant," Mary Beach, who nursed him in his infancy, and constantly attended him for thirty-eight years. It is worthy of remark that the peculiar make and conformation of Pope rendered a faithful servant of inestimable value. Johnson assures us that " he was so weak as to stand in perpetual need of *female* attendance, and was so extremely sensible of cold, that he wore a kind of fur doublet under a shirt of very coarse warm linen, with fine sleeves. When he rose he was invested in stays made of stiff canvas, being scarce able to hold himself erect till they were laced, and he then put on a flannel waistcoat. One side was contracted. His legs were so slender that he enlarged their bulk with three pairs of stockings, which were drawn on and off by the maid : for he was not able to dress or undress himself, and neither went to bed or rose without help. His weakness made it very difficult for him to be clean. His hair had fallen almost all away, and he used to dine with Lord Oxford privately in a velvet cap. His dress of ceremony was black, with a tye wig and a little sword. The indulgence and accommodation which his sickness required had taught him all the unpleasing and unsocial qualities of a valetudinarian. He expected that everything should give way to his ease or humour, as a child, whose parents will not hear it cry, has an unresisted dominion in the nursery.

'C'est que l'enfant toujours est homme
C'est que l'homme est toujours enfant !'

When he wanted to sleep he nodded in company, and once slumbered at his own table while the Prince of Wales was talking of poetry."

In spite of living so much in the world of fashion and of letters, Pope was, if not averse to society, yet at all events fond of solitude; and this he gained in his garden and grotto at Twickenham. "As much company as I have kept, and much as I like it, I love reading better, and I would rather be employed in reading than in the most agreeable conversation."

Pope became the subject of unnumbered epigrams, odes, references, and allusions, amongst the literary circle of which he was the centre. One complimentary epigram will suffice as an example:—

"On erecting a Monument to Shakespeare, under the direction of Mr. Pope, Lord Burlington, &c.

"To mark her Shakespeare's worth and Britain's love,
Let Pope design, and Burlington approve:
Superfluous care! When distant time shall view
This tomb grown old, his works shall still be new."

Throughout his life his health was bad, and he perhaps imagined it worse than it was. His faults —if such they may be called—were in a great measure consequent on this fact; he was peevish, capricious, and fretful, and demanded incessant attention. His character, indeed, has been very diversely represented by foes and by friends; some, as we have seen, called him "the nightingale," whilst his enemies called him "the wasp" of Twickenham; and Lady Mary Wortley Montagu went so far as to style him "the wicked asp." But every man, it would seem, has his good points; for Lord Bolingbroke, on the contrary, says that he "never knew a man that had so tender a heart for his particular friends, or a more general friendship for mankind." But possibly, Lord Bolingbroke, the "my St. John" of the poet, was not an impartial witness.

Sir Joshua Reynolds thus describes Pope from personal acquaintance:—"He was about four feet six inches high, very hump-backed and deformed. He wore a black coat, and, according to the fashion of the time, had on a little sword. He had a large and very fine eye, and a long handsome nose; his mouth had those peculiar marks which are always found in the mouths of crooked persons; and the muscles which ran across the cheek were so strongly marked that they seemed like small cords."

Pope's diminutive and misshapen person was a standing joke with his enemies, who caricatured him as a monkey in a library or with books. Macaulay, in his "Essays," speaks of him severely as "the little man of Twickenham"—a softened phrase, which means much in the way of disparagement. The following anecdote which has been told respecting his personal appearance will bear repeating:—"A gentleman and his little child were walking with a friend through Twickenham, when Pope met them. The child was alarmed at his figure, and drew back. The friend told them it was the great Mr. Pope. He wore an old soiled suit of black stained with snuff, cocked hat, and looked poor and mean."

Pope frequently assumed the *nom de plume* of "Martinus Scribblerus" in writing his attacks on those who criticised him adversely. One of his numerous enemies founded on this the title of the "Martiniad," a sort of answer, or counterblast to his "Dunciad," giving the following portrait of Pope's person, cruelly exposing its deformity:—

"At Twickenham, chronicles remark,
There dwelt a little parish clerk,
A peevish wight, full fond of fame,
And 'Martin Scribbler' was his name:
Meagre and wan, and steeple-crown'd,
His visage long and shoulders round;
His crippled corse two spindle-pegs
Support, instead of human legs;
His shrivelled skin's of dusky grain,
A cricket's voice and monkey's brains."

And another lampooner in verse compared the "Dunciad," in terms equally savage and cutting, to the progeny of the fabulous "Pope Joan."

It is stated that Pope seldom or never laughed; that his sole passion was to acquire fame, his most conspicuous weakness "inordinate self-conceit." "He delighted in artifice, and attempted to gain all his ends by indirect methods. 'He hardly drank tea without a stratagem.' Lady Bolingbroke said that 'he played the politician about cabbages and turnips.'" He was somewhat too much inclined to indulge his appetite; fond of highly-seasoned dishes, conserves, and drams. So fond was he of lampreys, that, if we may trust a statement made in the "Life of Nollekens," he would leave off in the midst of writing in order to cook them in a silver saucepan on his own fire.

Like most invalids, even in his own house he was irritable and fussy to a degree, and on account of his temper constantly got into sad trouble with the literary men of his day. For example, not long after the publication of the "Dunciad," in 1728, there appeared in the newspapers a fictitious account—afterwards known to have been written by Lady Mary Wortley Montagu—of a horsewhipping which the poet had received from two gentlemen at Ham. His sensitive nature was so touched that he condescended to insert in the *Daily Post* of June 14th, in that year, the following advertisement:—

"Whereas there has been a scandalous paper cried about the streets, under the title of 'A Popp upon Pope,' insinuating that I was whipped in Ham Walks on Thursday last; this is to give notice that I did not stir out of my house at

Twickenham all that day, and the same is a malicious and ill-grounded remark.—A. Pope."

Pope, as we have already stated, had in former years been on terms of the greatest friendship with Lady Mary Wortley Montagu. So intimate, indeed, was he at one time with her, that it is difficult to distinguish some of her writings from those of Pope, to such an extent were they intermixed. For instance, "Roxana, or the Drawing-Room," and the "Basset Table," though printed among Pope's "Miscellanies," seem really to belong to Lady Mary, and form part of her "Town Eclogues." And yet these once friends lived to become, as we have seen, the bitterest of enemies.

Notwithstanding Pope's fondness for repose and quietude, he had many friends, and probably his vanity was gratified by great people coming and making him an oracle. According to Thackeray, "Pope withdrew in a great measure from this boisterous London company"—that of club-house life—"and being put into an independence by the gallant exertions of Swift and his private friends, and by the enthusiastic admiration which justly rewarded his great achievement of the ' Iliad,' purchased that famous villa at Twickenham which his song and his life celebrated, duteously bringing his old parents to live and die there, entertaining his friends within its walls, and making occasional visits to London in his little chariot, in which Atterbury compared him to ' Homer in a Nutshell.' " In explanation of the above remark, it should be stated that Swift was most active and generous in promoting the subscription for Pope's "Iliad," and that it was he who introduced its author to both Harley and Bolingbroke ; and that it was out of the profits of this literary venture, about £5,000, that he purchased his celebrated villa.

Swift, too, who rarely had a kind word to say of any one, commemorates Pope as one—

"—— whose filial piety excels
Whatever Grecian story tells."

Yet even here, with his garden and his grotto, purchased with the proceeds of his pen though they were, Pope was not happy. He thus comments on his loneliness to Gay, who had congratulated him on finishing his house and gardens :—

" Ah, friend ! 'tis true—this truth you lovers know—
In vain my structures rise, my gardens grow ;
In vain fair Thames reflects the double scenes
Of hanging mountains and of sloping greens :
Joy lives not here,—to happier seats it flies,
And only dwells where Wortley* casts her eyes.
What are the gay parterre, the chequer'd shade,
The morning bower, the evening colonnade,

———————
* Lady Mary Wortley Montagu.

But soft recesses of uneasy minds,
To sigh unheard into the passing winds ?
So the struck deer in some sequester'd part
Lies down to die, the arrow at his heart ;
He, stretch'd unseen in coverts hid from day,
Bleeds drop by drop, and pants his life away."

Though not sweet-tempered, Pope was so witty and well-informed that he enjoyed a sort of popularity, and became the centre of a host of friends ; but to this end, no doubt, his independence largely helped. He has the merit of having been as constant in his friendships as he was bitter in his enmities. And notwithstanding the fact that he had been brought up in the Roman Catholic faith, his three most intimate friends were Bishop Atterbury, a high churchman, Bishop Warburton, a low churchman, and Lord Bolingbroke, an avowed unbeliever.

Pope took under his patronage Gay, who had been one of the household of the celebrated Duchess of Monmouth, and "taught him the art of rhiming." Gay is said to have written at Twickenham his very successful play called " The Beggar's Opera." "Pope," it has been observed by a writer in the *Gentleman's Magazine,* "soon learnt to feel his own superiority to his early patrons, and in the case of Wycherley expressed it too bluntly. His genius, indeed, matured so rapidly that a short time sufficed to place him on a level with men who are still the greatest ornaments of a great literary age—with Addison and Steele, with Swift and Congreve, with Arbuthnot and Bolingbroke. . . It may be doubted, however," he continues, "that Pope was a very genial host, for Swift has a gentle sneer at him for stinginess about wine, and observes that he was a silent, inattentive companion. He said himself that, though he loved company, he loved reading better than talk. Moreever, he never laughed heartily ; and the man who cannot laugh is not likely to enliven conversation."

Swift lived very constantly with Pope at Twickenham ; and here Pope was visited by Voltaire, who, being invited to dine with the poet, talked at table with so much indecency, especially with regard to religion, that the poet's mother was obliged to retire in disgust. Nevertheless, Voltaire was invited to Twickenham more than once subsequently. On one occasion, walking in the garden, Pope confidentially told Voltaire that he was himself the author of a certain "occasional letter," which had really been written by Lord Bolingbroke—such was his vanity.

Pope numbered among his visitors even Frederick, Prince of Wales, who in many ways showed much deference to his taste and judgment. To his visits

Pope alludes with natural pride, when, after enumerating other great and illustrious persons who had honoured him with their regard and friendship, he continued—

> " And if yet higher the proud list should end,
> Still let me add no Follower, but a Friend."

On one occasion, when the Prince of Wales was on a visit here, Pope, after expressing the most dutiful professions of attachment, gave his Royal Highness an opportunity of observing very shrewdly that his (the poet's) love for princes was inconsistent with his dislike of kings, since princes may in time become kings. Said his Royal Highness : " Mr. Pope, I hear you don't like princes." " Sir, I beg your pardon." " Well, then, you do not like kings." " Sir, I must own that I like the lion best before his claws are grown." No reply could well have been happier.

Warburton and Pope met for the first time in Lord Radnor's garden at Twickenham, and Dodsley, the bookseller, who was present, told Dr. Warton that he was astonished at the high compliments paid by Pope to Warburton. The acquaintanceship soon ripened into the most intimate friendship, and not long afterwards we find Warburton writing :—

" I passed about a week at Twickenham in a most agreeable manner. Mr. Pope is as good a companion as a poet, and, what is more, appears to be as good a man." That his friendship with Pope turned out to his own advantage will be easily seen, when it is stated that through Pope's introduction to Mr. Allen of Bath—humble Ralph Allen, who " did good by stealth, and blushed to find it fame "—Warburton gained a wealthy wife, and ultimately the Bishopric of Gloucester. Pope, when he died, left this fortunate prelate the property of his works, which was estimated at four thousand pounds ! Whatever might have been the motive of Warburton in thus officiously advocating a man whom he once so much undervalued, certain it is that he met with an ample reward.

Spence, like Warburton, won the friendship of Pope by praising his poetry ; and his " Anecdotes" of the poet are full of interest for all lovers of literature.

In Pope's translation of Homer beauty of sentiment predominates, and this is particularly the case in his description of the " Dog of Ulysses," taken from the " Odyssey." This is communicated by Pope in a letter to a friend, with an introduction and conclusion which illustrate his happy talent for epistolary composition, and which is quoted here

to show his fondness for animals. " Now I talk of my dog," he writes, " that I may not treat of a worse subject, which my spleen tempts me to. I will give you some account of him (a thing not wholly unprecedented, since Montaigne, to whom I am but a dog in comparison, has done the same thing of his cat). *Dic mihi quid melius desidiosus agam?* You are to know, then, that as it is likeness that begets affection, so *my favourite dog* is a little one, a lean one, and none of the finest shaped. He is not much of a spaniel in his fawning, but has (what might be worth any man's while to imitate him) a dumb, surly sort of kindness, that rather shows itself when he thinks me ill-used by others than when we walk quietly and peaceably by ourselves. If it be the chief point of friendship to comply with a friend's motions and inclinations, he possesses this in an eminent degree ; he lies down when I sit, and walks when I walk, which is more than many good friends can pretend to : witness our walk a year ago in St. James's Park. Histories are more full of examples of the fidelity of *dogs* than of friends, but I will not insist upon many of them, because it is possible some may be almost as fabulous as those of Pylades and Orestes, &c. Homer's account of Ulysses' dog *Argus* is the most pathetic imaginable, all the circumstances considered, and an excellent proof of the old bard's good-nature. Ulysses had left him at Ithaca when he embarked for Troy, and found him at his return, after twenty years ; you shall have it in verse :—

> " When WISE ULYSSES from his native coast
> Long kept by wars, and long by tempests tost,
> Arrived at last, poor, old, disguis'd, alone,
> To all his friends and e'en his *Queen* unknown ;
> Changed as he was, with age and toils and cares,
> Furrow'd his reverend face and white his hairs,
> In his own palace forc'd to ask his bread,
> Scorn'd by those slaves his former bounty fed,
> Forgot of all his own domestic crew—
> The FAITHFUL DOG alone his rightful master knew !
> Unfed, unhous'd, neglected, on the clay,
> Like an old servant now cashier'd, he lay,
> Touch'd with resentment of ungrateful Man,
> And longing to behold his ancient lord again !
> *Him* when he saw, he rose, and crawl'd to meet
> ('Twas all he could), and fawn'd, and kiss'd his feet,
> Seiz'd with dumb joy—then, falling by his side,
> Own'd his returning lord, look'd up, and DIED !

" Plutarch, relating how the Athenians were obliged to abandon Athens in the time of Themistocles, steps back again out of the way of his history purely to describe the lamentable cries and howlings of the poor dogs they left behind ! He makes mention of one that followed his master across the sea to Salamis, where he died, and was honoured with a tomb by the Athenians, who gave the name of The Dog's Grave to that part of the island where he was buried. This respect to a dog in the most polite people of the world is very observable. A modern instance of gratitude to a dog (though we have but few such) is, that the chief Order of Denmark (now injuriously called the Order of the Elephant) was instituted in memory of the fidelity of a dog, named Wildbrat, to one of their kings, who had been deserted by his subjects. He gave his Order this motto, or to this effect, 'Wildbrat was faithful.'

love of economy, that he wrote most of his verses on scraps of paper, and particularly on the backs of letters.

Swift styles him " paper-sparing Pope ;" but he nevertheless apostrophises his friend in terms of somewhat exaggerated praise :—

" Hail ! happy Pope ! whose generous mind
Detesting all the statesmen kind,
Contemning courts, at courts unseen,
Refus'd the visits of a queen.
A soul with every virtue fraught
By sages, priests, or poets taught,
Whose filial piety excels

POPE'S HOUSE. (*From a Print dated* 1785.)

" Sir William Trumbull has told me a story, which he heard from one that was present. King Charles the First being with some of his Court during his troubles, a discourse arose what sort of dogs deserved the pre-eminence ; and it being on all hands agreed to belong either to the spaniel or greyhound, the king gave his opinion on the part of the greyhound, because (he said) it has all the good-nature of the other, without fawning ! A good piece of satire upon his courtiers, with which I will conclude my discourse on dogs. Call me a cynic, or what you please, in revenge for all this impertinence, I will be contented, provided you will but believe me when I say a bold word for a Christian, that, of all dogs, you will find none more faithful than,—Yours, &c., A. P."

It has been mentioned, as a proof of the poet's

Whatever Grecian story tells :
A genius for all stations fit,
Whose meanest talent is his wit ;
His heart too great, though fortune little,
To lick a rascal statesman's spittle :
Appealing to the nation's taste
Above the reach of want is placed;
By Homer dead was taught to thrive,—
Which Homer never could alive ;
And sits aloft on Pindus' head
Despising slaves that cringe for bread."

A supplementary volume of the poet's works was published, containing pieces of poetry not inserted in the earlier editions, and also a collection of sentiments, selected from his correspondence, arranged under the title of " Thoughts on Various Subjects," which have often been quoted, showing that Pope was—as a poet should be—

deeply versed in the hidden springs of human nature.

Pope's rank as a poet has been variously estimated, and doubtless there will always be great difference of opinion; in the judgment of some he stands almost without a rival, others would deny him the title of poet altogether, but his popularity has always been great. In contrasting Pope's earlier with his later poems, it has been well remarked that his early gaiety of spirits must have been heightened by the "voluntary vein" of the "Rape of the Lock," which established his reputation, and by the success of his "Homer," which

the first playful effort of satire without ill-nature, at once gay, elegant, and delightful :

'Belinda smiles, and all the world is gay.'

"The man of severer thought now appears in the 'Essay on Man.' The same vein shows itself in the 'Moral Essays,' but the investigation is directed to individual failings, and mingled with spleen and anger. In the later satires we witness the language of acrimony and bitterness. The 'Dunciad' closes the prospect, and we there behold the aged bard among a swarm of enemies, who began his career all innocence, happiness, and smiles."

LADY HOWE'S VILLA AND POPE'S GROTTO. (*From a Drawing by G. Banet*, 1882.)

rendered him independent in his circumstances. Mr. Bowles has an interesting note, comparing the succession of Pope's original productions with the progress of his mind and character :—"In his earliest effusion—the 'Ode on Solitude'—all is rural quiet, innocence, content, &c. We next see, in his 'Pastorals,' the golden age of happiness, while the—

' Shepherd lad leads forth his flock
Beside the silver Thame.'

"His next step, 'Windsor Forest,' exhibits the same rural turn, but with views more diversified and extended, and approaching more to the real history and concerns of life. The warm passions of youth succeed, and we are interested in the fate of the tender Sappho or the ardent and unfortunate Eloise. As the world opens, local manners are displayed. In the 'Rape of the Lock' we see

Dr. Johnson, in his "Life of Pope," writes as follows with reference to the respective excellences of Pope and his model and predecessor, Dryden. "Dryden," he says, "knew more of man in his general nature, and Pope in his local manners; the notions of Dryden were formed by comprehensive speculation, those of Pope by minute attention. There is more dignity in the knowledge of Dryden, more certainty in that of Pope. Dryden is sometimes vehement, Pope always smooth; Dryden's page is a natural field, Pope's a velvet lawn. If the flights of Dryden are higher, Pope continues longer on the wing. If of Dryden's fire the blaze is brighter, of Pope's the heat is more regular and constant. Dryden often surpasses expectation, and Pope never falls below it. Dryden is read with frequent astonishment, and Pope with perpetual delight."

Thackeray says of the concluding verses of the

"Dunciad" that "no poet's verse ever mounted higher." "In these astonishing lines," he writes, "Pope reaches, I think, to the very greatest height which his sublime art has attained, and shows himself the equal of all poets of all times. It is the brightest ardour, the loftiest assertion of truth, the most generous wisdom, illustrated by the noblest poetic figure, and spoken in words the aptest, grandest, and most harmonious. It is heroic courage speaking : splendid declaration of righteous wrath and war. It is the gage flung down, and the silver trumpet ringing defiance to falsehood, tyranny, deceit, dulness, and superstition. It is Truth, the champion, shining and intrepid, and fronting the great world-tyrant with armies of slaves at his back. It is a wonderful and victorious single combat in that great battle which has always been waging since the world began. . . In considering Pope's admirable career, I am forced into similitudes drawn from other courage and greatness, and into comparing him with those who achieved triumphs in actual war. I think of the works of young Pope as I do of the actions of young Bonaparte or young Nelson. In their common life you will find frailties and meannesses as great as the vices and follies of the meanest men ; but in the presence of the great occasion the great soul flashes out, and conquers transcendent. In thinking of the splendour of Pope's young victories, of his merit, unequalled as his renown, I hail and salute the achieving genius, and do homage to the pen of a hero."*

"Although now regarded as by far the greatest poet of the day," writes the Rev. T. Thomson, in the "Comprehensive History of England," "neither place nor pension rewarded his (Pope's) labours ; for being a Papist in religion and a Tory in politics, every avenue of Court patronage was closed against him. He was thus obliged to depend for recompense upon the patronage of the reading public, as yet not numerous enough for a poet's wishes and wants ; and therefore, at the age of twenty-five, he commenced in earnest to write for money, by undertaking a translation of the works of Homer, which had long been a desideratum in the literary world, and was so successful that he was enabled, when not more than thirty years old, to purchase his classical villa at Twickenham, on the Thames, where he spent the rest of his life in study, combined with gardening. . . In poetry, Pope was a follower of Dryden, who was the founder of what has been called the 'poetry of artificial life.' But he polished and perfected what the other had

founded, and thus became the leader of the school, in preference to Dryden. And here the comparison which Johnson has drawn between the pair may be alluded to, as the best estimate which has yet been formed of their respective merits. To Dryden, indeed, belonged a strength, majesty, and fervour, which his successor never attained ; but, on the other hand, Pope exhibited a delicacy and tenderness of feeling, and a sustained, well-balanced dignity of thought and style, of which Dryden was incapable. This distinction can be easily felt by a comparison of 'Alexander's Feast' and the 'Elegy on Mrs. Anne Killigrew,' Dryden's best productions, with Pope's 'Epistle of Eloisa to Abelard,' his 'Elegy on the Death of an Unfortunate Lady,' and the 'Rape of the Lock.' In the same manner, as satirists, both were equally terrible, the one in 'Mac Flecno' and 'Absalom and Achitophel,' the other in the 'Dunciad' and his 'Epistles' ; but if Dryden's satire was an iron mace, that shattered and crushed while it killed, Pope's was the keen-edged scimitar of the Eastern sultan, that with a silent wave bereaved the shoulders of their head or the body of a limb. While both were thus poets of the highest order, the superior polish and epigrammatic point, as well as better sustained and even dignity of the poetry of Pope, have caused it to be more universally quoted, and given it a greater influence than the more energetic, but unequal, productions of the other. Indeed, with the exception of Shakespeare, no writer throughout the whole range of English poetry has ever been the source of such frequent reference as the bard of Twickenham."

In speaking of the illness and death of Pope, Mr. Cobbett, in his "Memorials of Twickenham," says :—"Among his latest acts was one of kindness to the talented and unprincipled poet, Savage. In his illness he was patient and placid, viewing the approach of death with magnanimity and resignation. The infidel Bolingbroke is said to have been disgusted at the firmness of Pope's Christian hope. During a lucid interval in the course of a temporary aberration of reason with which he was attacked, he was found busily engaged early one morning on an essay on the 'Immortality of the Soul.' Shortly before his death he observed, 'I am so certain of the soul's being immortal, that I seem to feel it within me.' On the third day before his death he desired to be brought to the table where his friends were at dinner. All present noticed that he was dying. Miss Anne Arbuthnot exclaimed involuntarily, 'Lord have mercy upon us ! this is quite an Egyptian feast !' Next day he sat for three hours in a sedan-chair in his garden, taking his last look at scenes so dear to him, then in their early summer beauty. To this occasion Dr. Johnson's incredible statement about Martha Blount appears to belong. He says that one day, as Pope was sitting in the air with Lord Bolingbroke and Lord Marchmont, he saw his favourite, Martha Blount, at the bottom of the terrace, and asked Lord Bolingbroke to go and hand her up. Bolingbroke, not liking the errand, crossed his legs and sat still; but Lord Marchmont, who was younger and less captious, waited on the lady, who, when he came to her, asked, 'What, is he not dead yet?' She is said, continues the Doctor, 'to have neglected him with shameful unkindness in the latter time of his decay.' The improbability of the question," continues Mr. Cobbett, "is seen on the face of it. Could Martha Blount be possibly ignorant whether Pope were alive or dead? Or, if the question were really put, it need not necessarily be construed harshly—nay, it may have been so uttered as to imply pity and tenderness for the lingering agonies of the sufferer."

In the "Imitations of Horace," Pope has these curious lines respecting himself:—

" Weak tho' I am of limb, and short of sight,
　Far from a lynx, and not a giant quite;
　I'll do what Mead and Cheselden advise,
　To keep these limbs and to preserve these eyes;
　Not to go back is somewhat to advance,
　As those move easiest who have learned to dance."

Speaking of his obligations to these great physicians and to others of the faculty, he says, about a month before his death, in a letter to Mr. Allen, "There is no end to my kind treatment from the faculty; they are in general the most amiable companions and the best friends, as well as the most learned men I know."

If we may believe Mallet, when Pope was in a dying state Mallet went to see him. As he sat by the bedside, the poet, in a delirium, said that he felt his head open and Apollo come out of it, and enter that of Mallet. For this story, however, we have no authority except that of the person whom, if true, it compliments so highly.

The will of Pope is so illustrative of his character and connections, that we may be pardoned for quoting it in part:—

"The last will and testament of Alexander Pope, of Twickenham, Esq., In the name of God, Amen. I, Alexander Pope, of Twickenham, in the county of Middlesex, make this my last will and testament. I resign my soul to its Creator, in all humble hope of its future happiness, as in the disposal of a being infinitely good. As to my body, my will is that it be buried near the monument of my dear parents

at Twickenham, with the addition, after the words *Filius fecit*, of these only—*et sibi, qut obiit anno* 17—, *ætatis*——, and that it be carried to the grave by six of the poorest men of the parish, to each of whom I order a suit of grey coarse cloth as mourning. If I happen to die at any inconvenient distance, let the same be done in any other parish, and the inscription be added on the monument at Twickenham. I hereby make and appoint my particular friends, Allen, Lord Bathurst, Hugh, Earl of Marchmont, the Hon. William Murray, his Majesty's Solicitor-General, and George Arbuthnot, of the Court of Exchequer, Esq.—the survivors or survivor of them—executors of this my last will and testament."

He leaves his MSS. to his "noble friend" Lord Bolingbroke, or, in event of his death, to Lord Marchmont. And then, after bequeathing individual books, busts, statues, and pictures, to different friends, as Lord Mansfield, Lord Bathurst, and Mr. G. Arbuthnot, he leaves his library to Ralph Allen and Dr. (Bishop) Warburton; other bequests, in the way of money, to buy mourning-rings and family pictures, he leaves to his sister-in-law and sundry friends; £100 to his servant John Searl, £20 to the poor of Twickenham. He leaves £1,000 and the furniture of his grotto, the urns in his garden, his plate, household goods, chattels, &c., to his friend Martha Blount, with a reversion to his sister-in-law, Mrs. Magdalen Rackett. This will, which is dated December 12th, 1743, is witnessed by his neighbour Lord Radnor, the Rev. S. Hales, minister of Teddington, and Dr. Joseph Spence, Professor of History in the University of Oxford.

From speaking of the man we will now pass on to an account of the house which he made so famous. When Pope took the lease of the premises here, consisting of a cottage and five acres of ground, he at once set about the work of improvement. The house itself, except by its being freed from contiguity with ten still smaller structures, was not much altered.

The author of "Verses occasioned by Warburton's New Edition of Pope's Works" (1751) gives us some information on the localities of Pope's Villa:—

" Close to the grotto of the Twickenham bard,
　Too close, adjoins a tanner's yard.
　So verse and prose are to each other tied,
　So Warburton and Pope allied."

The allusion is thus explained by Mr. J. B. Nichols, in the *Gentleman's Magazine* for 1836:—"Pope's Villa in his time was, we believe, in the neighbourhood of small mean houses; a tallow-chandler's was close to him, and we here find a tanner's yard joining the grotto. The house itself was old and in bad repair; the grounds included about half the present garden that fronts the Thames."

Mrs. Vernon, from whom the poet held his lease for life, died about a year before Pope. He had then some idea of purchasing the property (valued at about £1,000), if any of his "particular friends" wished to have it as a residence. No such arrangement was made, and after the poet's death, the house, as we shall presently see, was bought by Sir William Stanhope. The name of Mrs. Vernon is immortalised by the poet in his "Imitations of Horace" :—

> " Well, if the use be mine, can it concern one
>   Whether the name belong to Pope or Vernon ? "

In his "Imitations of Spenser," Pope speaks of the place to which his long residence here had so much attached him as a town "which fairer scenes enrich." And such would seem to have been the case; for these five acres of land, Horace Walpole tells us in one of his letters, Pope twisted, and twirled, and rhymed, and harmonised, till they appeared "two or three sweet little lawns opening and showing beyond one another, and the whole surrounded with thick impenetrable woods."

The house, or "villa"—a "villakin" Swift called it—when it was occupied by Pope, consisted of "a small body with a small hall, paved with stone, and two small parlours on each side, the upper storey being disposed on the same plan." Pope added somewhat to the building; but his chief delight was in laying out the gardens and grounds, and in the formation of the grotto which is so familiar to every reader of Pope's life. The grounds were laid out on the principle of landscape gardening (for he had ridiculed some years before, in a humorous paper in the *Guardian*, the barbarous practice of cutting trees into fantastic shapes, and designing the walks after the stiff and formal rules imported from the Continent), and in adorning his grotto, Pope used his utmost ingenuity in producing a variety.

> "To build, to plant, whatever you intend,
>   To rear the column, or the arch to bend,
>   To swell the terrace, or to sink the grot,
>   In all let Nature never be forgot :
>   Still follow sense, of every art the soul,
>   Parts answering parts shall slide into a whole."

Pope acted on the principles laid down by him in these lines, and in his little grounds steered clear of the Italian and Dutch styles of gardening. In fact, in laying out his garden, Pope carried out the precepts of his pen :—

> " First follow Nature, and your judgment frame
>   By her just standard, which is still the same.
>   *   *   *   *
>   Those rules of old discovered, not devised,
>   Are Nature still, but Nature methodised.
>   Nature, like Liberty, is but restrained
>   By the same laws which first herself ordained."

A writer in the *Gentleman's Magazine*, in 1801, observes that "the far-famed willow came from Spain, enclosing a present to the late Lady Suffolk, who came over with George II., and was a favourite of the king. Mr. Pope was in company when the covering was taken off the present. He observed that the pieces of sticks appeared as if there were some vegetation in them, and added, ' Perhaps they may produce something we have not in England.' Under this idea he planted it in his garden, and it produced the willow-tree that has given birth to so many others."

The famous willow died in 1801. Cuttings of it had been sent to St. Petersburg, at the request of the Empress of Russia, in 1789. A correspondent of the *Gentleman's Magazine* writes, under date of July 8, 1801 :—" Last month I went with a friend to Twickenham for the amusement of angling. My first care, however, was to visit the sacred willow planted by the hand of Pope ; and to my bitter grief, only two or three feet of the trunk remain, the upper part having been cut away." What was left of the trunk, it is said, was converted into " Popeian relics " by an eminent jeweller, who worked it up into trinkets and ornaments of all kinds, which had an extensive sale.

In order that the view from his own garden might not be hindered or obstructed, three walnut-trees were, at Pope's request, cut down in the garden of his neighbour. The fact is mentioned in one of Pope's poems, where it is stated that they belonged to a "lord." Warton says the peer alluded to was Lord Radnor. The Countess of Hertford, in her correspondence with the Countess of Pomfret, says that the trees belonged to Lady Ferrers, " whom he makes a lord."

No sooner was the poet settled in his new abode than, like one of the clients of the Muse, one of that

> " Genus ignavum, somno quod gaudet et umbrâ,"

he set to work upon the erection of the above-mentioned "grotto."

The grotto was (and is) a subterranean passage constructed under the roadway, which separates the two portions of the grounds, which lie on either side of the high road from Twickenham to Strawberry Hill and Teddington. The house stands between this road and the river. The garden beyond the road and the lawn sloping down to the banks of the Thames contain many large trees, under which Pope doubtless used to sit, including some of the finest and earliest planted cedars of Lebanon in the neighbourhood of London. The grotto was formed to obviate the necessity of crossing the high road every time the best part of the gardens had to be reached. On either side of it is a chamber, and these, together with the intervening passage, richly lined with felspar and Devonshire and Cornish marbles, mostly the gifts of the poet's friends, preserve the grotto to us much as it was a century and a half ago, when he described its beauties in his letters. Among the contributors of natural specimens in the formation of this grotto were Sir Hans Sloane, and Dr. Borlase the historian of Cornwall. Some of the letters which Pope addressed the latter gentleman are still preserved at Castle Horneck, near Penzance, the seat of Mr. John Borlase.

Addison suggests in his *Spectator* (No. 632) that the making of grottoes* is a work on which the ladies might well employ their hands. "There is a very particular kind of work which of late several ladies in our kingdom are very fond of, and which seems very well adapted to a poetical genius. It is the making of grottoes. I know a lady who has a very beautiful one, composed by herself, nor is there one shell in it that is not stuck up by her own hands." And he apostrophises the fair designer in the following lines, half in jest, half serious :—

 "To Mrs. ———— on her *Grotto*.
" A *grotto* so compleat, with such design,
What hands, *Calypso*, cou'd have form'd but thine?
Each chequer'd pebble, and each shining shell,
So well proportion'd, and dispos'd so well,
Surprising lustre from thy thought receive,
Assuming beauties more than Nature gave.
To her their various shapes and glossy hue,
Their curious symmetry they owe to you.
Not fam'd *Amphion's* lute, whose powerful call
Made willing stones dance to the *Theban* wall,
In more harmonious ranks cou'd make them fall.
Not ev'ning cloud a brighter arch can show,
Not richer colours paint the heav'nly bow.

" Where can unpolish'd Nature boast a piece
In all her mossy cells exact as this?
At the gay parti-colour'd scene we start,
For chance too regular, too rude for art.
Charm'd with the sight, my ravish'd breast is fir'd
With hints like those which ancient bards inspir'd ;
All the feign'd tales by superstition told,
All the bright train of fabled nymphs of old,
The enthusiastic muse believes are true,
Thinks the spot sacred, and its genius you."

* A similar grotto, at Amwell, in Hertfordshire, stands recorded as having been visited by Dr. Johnson.

"A grotto," remarks Dr. Johnson, "is not often the wish or pleasure of an Englishman, who had more frequent need to solicit than exclude the sun, but Pope's excavation was requisite as an entrance to his garden ; and, as some men try to be proud of their defects, he extracted an ornament from an inconvenience, and vanity produced a grotto where necessity enforced a passage."

The best description of Pope's grotto, and of the poet's satisfaction and pleasure in it, is contained in an often-quoted letter of the poet to his friend Edward Blount, dated June 2, 1725 :—

" I have put the last hand to my works of this kind, in happily finishing the subterraneous way and grotto. I there found a spring of the clearest water, which falls in a perpetual rill, that echoes through the cavern day and night. From the river Thames you see through my arch up a walk of the wilderness, to a kind of open temple, wholly composed of shells in the rustic manner ; and from that distance under the temple you look down through a sloping arcade of trees, and see the sails on the river passing suddenly, and vanishing as through a perspective glass. When you shut the doors of this grotto, it becomes on the instant, from a luminous room, a camera-obscura, on the walls of which all objects of the river, hills, woods, and boats are forming a moving picture in their visible radiations ; and when you have a mind to light it up it affords you a very different scene. It is finished with shells, interspersed with pieces of looking-glass in angular forms ; and in the ceiling is a star of the same material, at which, when a lamp (of an orbicular figure of thin alabaster) is hung in the middle, a thousand pointed rays glitter, and are reflected over the place.

" There are connected to this grotto by a narrower passage two porches : one towards the river, of smooth stones, full of light, and open ; the other toward the garden, shadowed with trees, rough with shells, flints, and iron ore. The bottom is paved with simple pebble, as is also the adjoining walk up the wilderness to the temple, in the natural taste agreeing not ill with the little dripping murmur and the aquatic idea of the whole place. It wants nothing to complete it but a good statue, with an inscription, like that beautiful one which you know I am so fond of :—

" ' Hujus Nympha loci, sacri custodia fontis,
    Dormio dum blandæ sentio murmur aquæ.
  Parce meum, quisquis tangis cava marmora, somnum
    Rumpere ; sive bibas, sive lavere, tace.'

" ' Nymph of the grot, these sacred springs I keep,
    And to the murmur of these waters sleep ;
  Ah ! spare my slumbers, gently tread the cave !
    And drink in silence, or in silence lave.'

" You'll think I have been very poetical in this description, but it is pretty near the truth. I wish you were here to bear testimony how little it owes to art, either the place itself or the image I give of it."

At the entrance to the grotto was a stone, inscribed with the following line from Horace :—

" Secretum iter et fallentis semita vitæ."

In Pope's " Miscellanies," the following lines are addressed as an apostrophe to the pilgrim visitor :—

" Thou who shalt stop where Thames' translucent wave
Shines a broad mirror through the shadowy cave,
Where lingering drops from mineral roofs distil,
And pointed crystals break the sparkling rill,
Unpolish'd gems no ray on pride bestow,
And latent metals innocently glow;
Approach. Great Nature studiously behold !
And eye the mine without a wish for gold.
Approach : but awful ! lo ! the Ægerian grot,
Where, nobly pensive, St. John* sat and thought ;
Where British sighs from dying Wyndham stole,
And the bright flame was shot through Marchmont's soul.
Let such, such only, tread this sacred floor,
Who dare to love their country, and be poor ! "

On another occasion we find him writing :—

" Know, all the distant din that world can keep
Rolls o'er my grotto, and but soothes my sleep.
There, my retreat the best companions grace,
Chiefs out of war, and statesmen out of place.
There St. John mingles with my friendly bowl
The feast of reason and the flow of soul :
And he, whose lightning pierced the Iberian lines,
Now forms my quincunx, and now ranks my vines,
Or tames the genius of the stubborn plain
Almost as quickly as he conquer'd Spain." †

Pope's fondness for and pride in his Twickenham villa—my " Tusculum," as he called it—is expressed by him in letters and poems continually. In a letter to his friend Mr. Digby, he writes :—
" No ideas you could form in the winter can

make you imagine what Twickenham is in the summer season. Our river glitters beneath an unclouded sun, at the same time that its banks retain the verdure of showers ; our gardens are offering their first nosegays ; our trees, like new acquaintances brought happily together, are stretching their arms to meet each other, and growing nearer and nearer every hour; the birds are paying their thanksgiving songs for the new habitations I have made them ; my building rises high enough to attract the eye and curiosity of the passenger from the river, when beholding a mixture of beauty and ruin, he inquires what house is falling or what church is rising ; so little taste have our common Tritons of Vitruvius, whatever delight the poetical god of the river may take in reflecting on their streams my Tuscan porticos or Ionic pilasters."

In some verses, entitled "The Cave of Pope : a Prophecy," to be seen in the third volume of " Dodsley's Collection of Poems," the curiosity of future visitors and their pilfering of gems as relics is duly prophesied as follows :—

" When dark oblivion in her sable cloak
Shall wrap the names of heroes and of kings,
And their high deeds, submitting to the stroke
Of time, shall fall amongst forgotten things.

' Then, for the muse that distant day can see,
On Thames' fair bank the stranger shall arrive
With curious wish thy sacred grot to see ;
Thy sacred grot shall with thy name survive.

" Grateful posterity from age to age
With pious hand the ruin shall repair ;
Some good old man, to each inquiring sage,
Pointing the place, shall cry, ' The Bard lived there.'

" Whose song was music to the listening ear,
Yet taught audacious vice and folly shame.
Easy his manners, but his life severe,
His word alone gave infamy or fame.

" Sequestered from the fool and coxcomb wit
Beneath this silent roof, the muse he found ;
'Twas here he slept inspired, or sat and writ ;
Here with his friends the social glass went round.

THE OBELISK TO POPE'S MOTHER.

" With awful veneration shall they trace
    The steps which thou so long before hast trod,
With reverend wonder view the solemn place
    From whence thy genius soar'd to Nature's God.
" Then some small gem, or moss, or shining ore,
    Departing each shall pilfer, in fond hope
To please their friends on ev'ry distant shore,
    Boasting a relic from the cave of Pope."

It need scarcely be remarked that the above prophetic lines have been amply fulfilled.

It is said that the original mansion, as left by

Horace Walpole, however, viewed the alterations and enlargements made by Sir William Stanhope in a very different light, and criticised them somewhat severely in a letter which he wrote to his friend Sir Horace Mann, in 1760.

On the death of Sir William Stanhope, the property passed to his son-in-law, the Right Hon. Welbore Ellis (afterwards created Lord Mendip), who seems to have had a special veneration for the poet's memory, and to have guarded with reverence

" POPE'S VILLA."   (See p. 110.)

Pope, was humble and confined, and that " veneration for his memory enlarged its dimensions." Upon his decease the estate was sold to Sir William Stanhope, brother of the Earl of Chesterfield. By him the house was enlarged by the addition of wings, and the gardens were also extended by the addition of a piece of ground on the opposite side of the lane, connected with the premises by a second subterraneous passage, over the entrance to which were placed the following lines, from the pen of Lord Clare :—

" The humble roof, the garden's scanty line,
    Ill suit the genius of the bard divine ;
But fancy now displays a fairer scope,
    And Stanhope's plans unfold the soul of Pope."

every memorial, and preserved the house, as far as possible, in its original condition.

Lord Mendip was a worshipper of the muses, and also well known in the political world ; and during his occupancy of Pope's Villa the place became celebrated for its fine statuary, marbles, and Oriental vases.

A view of Pope's house (still so called) is given in the *Gentleman's Magazine* for 1807. It is a tall and spacious mansion, and very different to the humble dwelling of the poet ; and the dwelling represents the building as consisting of a centre and wings, whilst a large double flight of stone steps leads up to the centre of the river front. The willow which was planted by Pope figures in the foreground.

After the death of Lord Mendip the estate was sold to Sir John Briscoe, and on the decease of that gentleman, in 1807, it passed by sale into the hands of the Baroness Howe. Her ladyship's connection with Pope's residence is soon told. She rased the house to the ground, and with complete indifference to its associations, as far as possible, blotted out every memorial of the poet.

Miss Berry, in her "Journal," under the date of November 21st, 1807, writes :—"We went into Pope's back garden, and saw the devastation going on upon his 'quincunx' by its now possessor, Baroness Howe. The anger and ill-humour expressed against her for pulling down his abode and destroying his grounds are much greater than one would have imagined."

Lady Howe built for herself a new mansion, not on the site of Pope's house, but about a hundred yards to the north of it. It was formed partly out of a dwelling which had been erected by Hudson the painter, Sir Joshua Reynolds's master. Lady Howe was the daughter of the celebrated Admiral Lord Howe, the "hero of the glorious 1st of June." She was twice married—firstly to the Hon. Penn Assheton Curzon, by whom she had a son, afterwards created Earl Howe ; and secondly to Sir Jonathan Wathen Waller, Bart. The baroness and Sir Jonathan were long remembered in the neighbourhood for their hospitality. The garden parties, which were frequently attended by members of the royal family, were held almost weekly during the summer months, and the "1st of June" was always a red-letter day with them, being celebrated by a rowing-match on the Thames, when a silver cup was competed for. Mr. Brewer, in the "Beauties of England and Wales," suggests that Lady Howe may have been tempted by the chance of selling the building materials of the old house, which were worth, he estimates, about forty or fifty pounds ; and adds, "If the baroness had been desirous of constructing a more commodious residence than that inhabited by Lord Mendip, she might, without any great blot to the grounds or injury to the prospect, have suffered the central part of the structure to remain, the portion once inhabited by Pope, and so highly reverenced and carefully preserved by Lord Mendip." But this hint, alas ! was given too late. Probably Lady Howe did not want to be the proprietor of a public exhibition ; she knew nothing of Pope, and perhaps cared less ; and she was, no doubt, annoyed by his admirers coming to view the house and grounds which the poet had rendered famous. Pope's house is stated to have stood exactly over the entrance to the grotto, which formed as it were a part of the basement.

The author of a "Tour of a Foreigner in England," published in 1825, writes as follows with reference to a pilgrimage which he made to Pope's residence :—"I reached Twickenham by an agreeable walk along the banks of the Thames, where at every step the eye is greeted by a succession of varied prospects and elegant structures. So many splendid buildings may perhaps be displeasing to the lovers of the wild or purely rural scenery ; but one is soon reminded that among these villas once arose the residence of Pope, the poet of civilisation. There he modernised the sublime muse of Homer, for whose simple dignity he indeed occasionally substitutes the meretricious graces of a coquette. There, too, Pope applied the language of poetry to philosophy, and composed satires and epistles such as Horace would have written had he lived at the Court of Queen Anne. In 1807, Baroness Howe pulled down Pope's Villa, and built in its stead a residence better suited to a lady of rank, and, no doubt, infinitely more comfortable. How many do the English sacrifice for that favourite adjective ! The famous grotto, which Pope himself adorned with shells and minerals, has been almost entirely stripped by the 'pilgrims of his genius.' The weeping willow which the poet planted with his own hands is dead, and another bends its branches over the remains of the withered trunk. Farther on, in a more retired part of the grounds, is the obelisk which Pope erected to the memory of his mother. The best work he ever wrote could not have afforded me so much pleasure as the sight of this monument of filial affection. Happy the son who can deposit a wreath of laurel on the grave of the parent whom he has rendered proud and happy by his well-earned fame !"

In January, 1840, "Pope's Villa," as the new structure was wrongly called, was advertised for sale, and the building materials of the same shortly after. In the end, the Baroness Howe's house was partly taken down, its outside wings being demolished, and the central portion cut up into two tenements.

Subsequently a scheme was set on foot for building a new house, "exactly like Pope's," and for restoring, as far as possible, the grotto to its original condition ; but this idea was ultimately abandoned. A new house, however, was built shortly after by a Mr. Thomas Young, a tea merchant, who gave to it the name of "Pope's Villa." It does not stand on the site of the original residence of Pope, but is nearer to it than was Lady Howe's. The building is a "combination of an Elizabethan half-timber house and a Stuart renaissance, with the addition of Dutch and Swiss, Italian and Chinese features." Such is the description of it given by the author of "Rambles by Rivers," who adds that it was probably designed when its architect was fresh from a diligent study of the paintings in Lord Kingsborough's work on "Mexican Antiquities." Some people, however, have suggested more simply that its design was, in the main, copied by the tea merchant who built it from one of those elaborate Chinese ornamentations which are to be seen on tea-chests.

In 1876 "Pope's Villa" and the grounds adjoining were again advertised for sale by public auction, and later on it became for a time the residence of Mr. Labouchere, M.P. Whatever may be the ultimate fate of that building is of no national importance. Suffice it to say that, beyond his tomb in Twickenham Church, the only memorials of the poet now visible here are the gardens and the famous grove in which he took such great delight, and also the grotto—or rather, the tunnel, for it has been despoiled of most of its rare marbles, spars, and ores, and is now a mere damp subway.

CHAPTER IX.

TWICKENHAM (*continued*)—STRAWBERRY HILL.

"Some cry up Gunnersbury,
  For Syon some declare,
And some say that with Chiswick House
  No villa can compare.
But ask the beaux of Middlesex,
  Who know the country well,
If Strawb'ry Hill, if Strawb'ry Hill,
  Don't bear away the bell."

William Pulteney, Earl of Bath.

"Strawberry Hill Shot"—Colley Cibber a Resident there—Other Tenants—Lease of the House by Mrs. Chenevix—The Property purchased by Horace Walpole—His Description of the Place in 1747—Enlargement of the House by Walpole—Description of the Building, and particulars of some of its Principal Contents—The "Chapel" in the Gardens—The Earl of Bath's Panegyric—Biographical Notice of Horace Walpole—Macaulay's Estimate of his Character—Strawberry Hill Bequeathed to Marshal Conway—The Hon. Mrs. Damer—The Waldegrave Family—Sale of the Contents of Strawberry Hill in 1842—Subsequent History of the Building—Little Strawberry Hill and Mrs. Clive—The Misses Berry—Alderman Matthew Wood—"The Bachelors."

NOT far from Pope's Villa, at the corner of the Upper Road, leading to Teddington, is Strawberry Hill, the celebrated villa of Horace Walpole (afterwards Earl of Orford). Everybody has heard of Strawberry Hill, with its brick and mortar turrets, its Gothic windows, and its lath-and-plaster walls. It has been much, and perhaps deservedly, ridiculed; but, although the mansion has been considerably altered and enlarged since Walpole's time, its interior is not only fitted up with much good taste, and even splendour, but contains many articles of great historical interest.

The house stands on a piece of ground called in old documents "Strawberry Hill Shot." It was originally a small tenement, built towards the end of the seventeenth century by the Earl of Bradford's coachman, and let as a lodging-house. This cottage, says Mr. Cobbett, in his "Memorials of Twickenham," was called by the common people Chopped-straw Hall, as "they supposed that by feeding his lord's horses with chopped straw he had saved money enough to build his house."

Colley Cibber, we are told, was one of the first tenants of the above-mentioned cottage, when he was in attendance for acting at Hampton Court, and one at least of his plays was written here, namely, "The Refusal; or, the Lady's Philosophy." In consequence of its pleasant and healthy situation, the cottage became at different times the summer residence of many great personages, among others, of Dr. Talbot, Bishop of Durham, and of Henry Bridges, Marquis of Carnarvon, son of James, Duke of Chandos. It was afterwards hired by Mrs. Chenevix, a noted toy-shop keeper of Regent Street. After her husband's death, this good lady sub-let the house to Lord John Sackville, second son of Lionel, Duke of Dorset, who resided in it for about two years.

In May, 1747, Horace Walpole took over the remainder of Mrs. Chenevix's lease, and in the following year purchased the fee-simple of the property by Act of Parliament, it being then in the hands of three minors of the name of Mortimer. Walpole, in a letter to Field-Marshal Conway, gives the following particulars of the place shortly after first taking possession of it. They have been often quoted, but will bear repetition :—

"TWICKENHAM, June 8, 1747.

"You perceive by my date that I am got into a new camp, and have left my tub at Windsor. It is a little plaything house that I got out of Mrs. Chenevix's shop, and is the prettiest bauble you ever saw. It is set in enamelled meadows, with phillagree hedges.

A small Euphrates through the place is rolled,
And little fishes wave their wings in gold.

Two delightful roads, that you would call dusty, supply me continually with coaches and chaises ; barges as solemn as Barons of the Exchequer move under my window. Richmond Hill and Ham Walks bound my prospects ; but, thank God, the Thames is between me and the Duchess of Queensberry. Dowagers as plenty as flounders inhabit all around, and Pope's ghost is just now skimming under my window by a most poetical moonlight. The Chenevixes had tricked the cottage up for themselves. Up two pairs of stairs is what they call Mr. Chenevix's library, furnished with three maps, one shelf, a bust of Sir Isaac Newton, and a lunar telescope without any glasses. Lord John Sackville *predecessed* me here, and instituted certain games called *cricketalia*, which have been celebrated this very evening in honour of him in a neighbouring meadow."

At the time it passed into the hands of Walpole the property consisted of the cottage and some five acres only, but this was subsequently extended by the purchase of outlying lands. Walpole soon conceived the idea of enlarging the cottage, and at once determined to adopt the Gothic style of architecture, in order, as he informs us, to prove, if he could, its adaptability to domestic buildings and their decorations. "Walpole's experiments in Gothic architecture" (writes Eliot Warburton), " as exemplified in his various plans and improvements at Strawberry Hill, showed that he was learning the art of building while he was practising it. In the game of putting up and pulling down, which he carried on for so many years, he was like a tyro at chess, who knows only the names of the pieces and their appropriate positions. . . . . He never became a first-rate architect. Nevertheless, he contrived to put together a structure which will outlast in interest buildings erected on more correct principles, and constructed with materials much more durable and solid."

"The Castle," as Walpole chose to call it, " was not entirely built from the ground, but formed at different times, by alterations of and additions to the old small house. The library and refectory, or great parlour, were entirely new built in 1753 ; the gallery, round tower, great cloister, and cabinet, in 1760 and 1761 ; the great north bed-chamber in 1770."

In spite of all his social pleasures, in September, 1774, Walpole bitterly complains of want of occupation. "What can I do ? " he asks his cousin Conway. "I see nothing, know nothing, do nothing. My castle is finished ; I have nothing new to read ; I am tired of writing ; I have no new or old bits for my printers ; I have only backwoods around me." This idleness, however, was partly affected ; for in general Walpole complained of having too much, not too little, on his hands. "He had

always," writes Eliot Warburton, " something to do ; as a correspondent, as an author, as a connoisseur, as a patron, as a politician, as a fine gentleman, there was always plenty for him to employ his thoughts upon."

That he still went on with the enlargement of his " castle " is clear from the fact that in 1776 the " Beauclerk tower " and " hexagon closet " were added ; continual additions, in fact, were made to the building, according as Walpole's stock of articles of *vertu*—" knick-knacks," as they have been vulgarly called—increased. What the results of Walpole's efforts as an architect were has been variously estimated. To some critics the work has appeared as possessing " the genuine appearance of former times, without the decay ; " some have approved, together with its possessor, of "the choice selection of the best specimens of what is called Gothic architecture ; " whilst others have not hesitated to stigmatise it as " the most trumpery piece of gingerbread Gothic ever constructed : as a whole, monstrous ; in detail, incorrect ; " or to sum it up as " a rickety, miserable, oyster-grotto-like profanation."

The designs for different parts of the edifice were collected from all quarters—at home and abroad. The embattled wall by the road-side was copied from a print of Aston House, Warwickshire, in Dugdale's history of that county, whilst portions of the ornamentations of tombs of bishops and princes in various cathedrals were made to do duty in the component parts of fire-places, doorways, and windows. Most of the windows were filled with painted glass. The general effect of the whole has been poetically summed up in the following lines by Maurice :—

" At every step we take fresh raptures move,
    Charm in the house and ravish in the grove.
    Within, the richest silks of China glow,
    Without, the flow'rs of both the tropics blow ;
    What matchless colours in the solar beam,
    Warm, vivid, varied, thro' the casements stream !
    Here the deep ruby seems to blush in blood,
    There the bright topaz pours a golden flood ;
    With Heav'n's blue vault the beaming sapphire vies,
    And emeralds glow with ocean's azure dyes ;
    While thro' those casements to th' astonish'd sight,
    O'er hills and valleys ranging with delight,
    A brighter, richer landscape shines display'd
    Than ever Poussin sketch'd or Claude pourtray'd ! "

The entrance to the house has been considerably altered. Originally, after entering by the north gate into the grounds, the first noticeable object was an " oratory," wherein were " vessels for holy water, and an enshrined saint." An iron screen, copied from the tomb of Roger Niger, Bishop of London, in Old St. Paul's, parted off the "abbot's garden" on the right. On the left, before the entrance to the house was reached, a small cloister had to be passed, in which were two objects of interest. The first was a bas-relief in marble of the Princess Leonora D'Este—"Dia Helionora"—with whom Tasso was in love. This was sent to Horace Walpole from Italy by Sir William Hamilton, minister at Naples. The second was the blue-and-white china tub in which Walpole's favourite cat was drowned. To the pedestal on which it stood was affixed the first stanza of Gray's well-known ode on the occasion :—

> "'Twas on this lofty vase's side,
> Where China's gayest art has dy'd
> The azure flow'rs that blow ;
> Demurest of the tabby kind,
> The pensive Selima reclin'd,
> Gaz'd on the lake below ! "

The hall, in its original condition, was small and gloomy, being lighted only by two narrow windows of painted glass. It was connected with the stair-case, in the well of which depended a Gothic lantern. This latter, and also the balustrade, at each corner of which is an antelope (one of Lord Orford's supporters) holding a shield, were designed by Mr. Richard Bentley, the son of the learned Dr. Bentley, Master of Trinity College, Cambridge.

On the left of the hall, approached through a small passage, over the entrance to which is an ancient carving in wood of the arms of Queen Elizabeth, is the refectory or great parlour, "hung," says Walpole himself in his description of the build-ing, "with paper *in imitation of stucco !* " This apartment contained several portraits of members of the family, most of which are still at Strawberry Hill, although differently placed. Amongst them may be mentioned Sir Robert Walpole, his two wives and three sons ; an early production of Sir Joshua Reynolds's, called "A Conversation," repre-senting George Selwyn, Lord Edgcombe, and G. I. Williams, all intimate friends of Walpole's ; and the three beauties, the Ladies Laura, Maria, and Horatia Waldegrave, by the same eminent master.

In the waiting-room was a bust of Colley Cibber, formerly the property of Mrs. Clive the celebrated actress, and after her death presented by her brother, Mr. Rastor, to Lord Orford. There was also a bust of Dryden, who was great-uncle to Catharine Shorter, Horace Walpole's mother ; and a curious emblematic picture of a man standing (small whole length), with a bust of Charles II., seemingly previous to his restoration.

The contents of the china-room adjoining were much prized by the owner, and fill no less than thirteen pages of his list. Among them were "two Saxon tankards, the one ornamented with Chinese figures, and the other with European." " These tankards," wrote Horace Walpole, "are extremely remarkable. Sir Robert Walpole drank ale : the Duchess of Kendal, mistress of King George I., gave him the former ; a dozen or more years after-wards, the Countess of Yarmouth, mistress of King George II., without having seen the other, gave him the second ; and they match exactly in form and size." The floor of this apartment has some ancient tiles with armorial bearings from Gloucester cathedral. The upper part of the chimney was copied from the window of an ancient farm-house, formerly called Bradfield Hall, belonging to Lord Grimston, in Essex ; and the lower part from a chimney at Hurstmonceaux, in Sussex ; it was adorned with the arms of Talbot, Bridges, Sackville, and Walpole, the principal persons who have in-habited Strawberry Hill.

The chimney-piece in the Little Parlour is re-markable as having been taken from the tomb of Thomas Ruthall, Bishop of Durham, in Westmin-ster Abbey. In this room, amongst other things, was the original model in terra-cotta, by Mrs. Damer, of two sleeping dogs, which she after-wards executed in marble for the Duke of Rich-mond.

On the first landing of the staircase is a boudoir formerly known as the Blue Breakfast Room, which contained several portraits of the Digby family and others. In this room was preserved the watch given to General Fairfax by the Parliament, after the battle of Naseby ; also a curious picture of Rose, the royal gardener, presenting to Charles II. the first pine-apple raised in England. This pic-ture was bequeathed by the grandson of Loudon, the nurseryman, to the Rev. Mr. Pennicott, of Ditton, who gave it to Walpole.

On the staircase was a suit of steel armour which had belonged to Francis I. It was pur-chased in 1772 from the Crozat collection, on the death of the Baron de Thiers, and realised £320 5s. at the Strawberry Hill sale in 1842. Amongst other articles here were an ancient curfew, or cover-fire, and the top of a warming-pan which had be-longed to Charles II., with his arms and the motto "Sarve God and live for ever."

The library contained a valuable collection of about 15,000 volumes, chiefly of antiquarian and historical subjects. The book-cases were modelled from the choir of Old St. Paul's, as represented by Dugdale, and the chimney-piece was copied partly from the tomb of John Eltham, Earl of Cornwall, in Westminster Abbey, and partly from that of

Thomas, Duke of Clarence, at Canterbury. The most remarkable objects in the library were an old painting representing the marriage of Edward VI.; a silver-gilt clock, richly chased, presented by Henry VIII. to Anne Boleyn, on their marriage; a screen of the first tapestry made in England, and the osprey eagle modelled life-size in terra-cotta by Mrs. Damer.

In the Star Chamber, so called from the adornment of its ceiling with golden stars in mosaic,

actor, for twenty guineas. Among the treasures of the library are Bentley's set of original designs in illustration of Gray's poems. They are immortalised by the latter in his "Stanzas to Mr. Bentley" :—

"In silent gaze the tuneful choir among,
    Half pleas'd, half blushing, let the Muse admire,
While Bentley leads the sister art along,
    And bids the pencil answer to the lyre."

Though Bentley had been very useful to Horace

STRAWBERRY HILL IN WALPOLE'S TIME.
(*From Contemporary Drawings by Paul Sandby.*)

stood the famous bust of Henry VII., designed for his tomb by Torregiano. The chimney-piece in the Holbein Room was designed chiefly from the tomb of Archbishop Warham, at Canterbury. A part of the room is divided off by a screen, the pierced arches of which were copied from the gates of the choir of Rouen cathedral. Two highly interesting relics were preserved in this room, among them being "a very ancient chair of oak, which came out of Glastonbury Abbey;" and "the red hat of Cardinal Wolsey, found in the great wardrobe by Bishop Burnet, when clerk of the closet. From his son, the judge, it came to the Dowager Countess of Albemarle, who gave it to Mr. Walpole." This red hat was bought by Mr. Charles Kean, the

Walpole in putting Strawberry Hill together, yet he did not retain the great man's friendship for long, for, as was the case with Walpole and Lady Mary Wortley Montagu, the Misses Blount, and others, a quarrel arose between him and the lord of Strawberry Hill, which put an end to their friendship.

The gallery, nearly sixty feet in length, was the largest and most attractive apartment in the house. "The ceiling is taken from one of the side aisles in Henry VII.'s Chapel. The great door is copied from the north door at St. Albans, and the two smaller are parts of the same design. The side recesses, which are finished with a gold network over looking-glass, is taken from the tomb of Archbishop Bourchier at Canterbury."

STRAWBERRY HILL, 1882.

Leaving the gallery by its great door, we reach the new boudoir, drawing-room, and other rooms added to the house by its present owner. This new wing was built about 1860, and though erected to harmonise with the general edifice, is, it is almost needless to add, as solid and substantial as the latter is fragile. The drawing-room contains a large number of family portraits of the Waldegraves and Walpoles, and also Magni's celebrated piece of sculpture, "The Reading Girl," exhibited at the London International Exhibition of 1862. In the adjoining boudoir are a Madonna by Sasso Ferrato, and a few other pictures. A wide staircase leads from this room into the garden. The new dining-room is enriched by a large number of pictures, mostly from the old collection.

Returning to the original part of the building, we pass from the further extremity of the gallery into the Round Drawing-room. The design of the chimney-piece of this room was copied from the tomb of Edward the Confessor, and executed in white marble inlaid with scagliola. The ceiling was taken from a round window in Old St. Paul's.

The "Tribune" is "a square room, with a semi-circular recess in the middle of each side, with windows and niches, the latter taken from those on the sides of the north door of the great church at St. Albans. The roof, which is copied from the chapter-house at York, is terminated by a square of yellow glass." In this room was formerly preserved the large collection of miniatures by Petitot and other masters, and also a vast number of antiquarian objects. Among the latter was one of the seven mourning rings given at the burial of Charles I.; the dagger of Henry VIII., which was purchased by Mr. Charles Kean for £54 12s.; a pendant golden heart-shaped ornament, richly jewelled and enamelled, made in memory of the Earl of Lennox, Regent of Scotland, who was murdered in 1572. This jewel was purchased by the Queen at the sale in 1842. Here, too, was a curious silver bell, made for Pope Clement VII. by Benvenuto Cellini, "with which to curse the caterpillars." The bell came out of the collection of Leonati at Parma, and was bought by the Marquis of Rockingham. Walpole, who prized it very highly, exchanged for it all his collection of Roman coins. It was purchased by Lord Waldegrave, at the sale in 1842, for the sum of £252.

The fireplace of the "Great North Bedroom" was designed by Walpole from the tomb of Bishop Dudley in Westminster Abbey; the room itself was originally hung with crimson damask, and contained several interesting pictures, the most noticeable of which were those of Henry VIII.

and his children, and the original sketch of "The Beggar's Opera," with portraits of Walker as Macheath, Miss Lavinia Fenton (afterwards Duchess of Bolton) as Polly, Hippesley as Peach'em, and Hall as Lockit. Among the curiosities preserved in this room was the "speculum of cannel coal" used by the famous impostor Dr. Dee in the reign of Queen Elizabeth.

The "Beauclerk Closet," originally hung with blue damask, is an hexagon in shape, and was built in 1776 on purpose to receive seven drawings by Lady Diana Beauclerk, in illustration of Walpole's tragedy of "The Mysterious Mother." A portrait of Lady Diana, by Powell, after Sir Joshua Reynolds, which formerly hung in this room, has been removed to the billiard-room; as also has a portrait of Mrs. Clive, by Davison, which formerly adorned the library over the Round Drawing-room, now a bedroom.

So multifarious was the collection of Strawberry Hill, that no less than 113 quarto pages are devoted to the details of it in the second volume of Walpole's printed works; and in order that no visitor might be deceived as to its precise nature and definite complexion, Walpole remarked, in a letter to a friend :—" The chief boast of my collection is the portraits of eminent and remarkable persons, particularly the miniatures and enamels, which, so far as I can discover, are superior to any other collection whatever. The works I possess of Isaac and Peter Oliver are the best extant; and those I bought in Wales for three hundred guineas, are as well preserved as when they came from the pencil !"

Walpole never allowed large parties to go over Strawberry Hill; he made an exception, however, in favour of great people, as shown by the following letter to the celebrated actress, Mrs. Abington :—

"MADAM,

"You may certainly always command me and my house. My common custom is to give a ticket for only four persons at a time ; but it would be very insolent in me, when all laws are set at nought, to pretend to prescribe rules. At such times there is a shadow of authority in setting the laws aside by the legislature itself; and though I have no army to supply their place, I declare Mrs. Abington may march through all my dominions at the head of as large a troop as she pleases ;—I do not say, as she can muster and command, for then I am sure my house would not hold them. The day, too, is at her own choice ; and the master is her very obedient humble servant,

"HOR. WALPOLE.

" Strawberry Hill, June 11th, 1780."

In the gardens Walpole in 1771 erected a sham chapel, but this has been demolished and removed. It was built of brick, with a front of Portland stone, copied from the tomb of Bishop Audley in Salisbury Cathedral. Fronting the door stood a " shrine " of mosaic work, three storeys in height, having on one side, in a recess, a figure of an ancient king of France, and on the other side a figure of the Virgin Mary in bronze. On a tablet over the doorway of the chapel the following particulars were given :—

"The shrine in front was brought in the year 1768 from the Church of Santa Maria Maggiore, in Rome, when the new pavement was laid there. The shrine was erected in the year 1256, over the bodies of the holy martyrs, Simplicissa, Faustina, and Beatrix, by John James Capoccio and his wife, and was the work of Peter Cavalini, who made the tomb of Edward the Confessor in Westminster Abbey. The window was brought from the church of Bexhill, in Sussex. The two principal figures are King Henry III. and Eleanor of Provence, his queen, the only portraits of them extant. King Henry died in 1272 ; and we know of no painted glass more ancient than the reign of his father, King John, of Magna Charta memory."

At the end of the winding walk in the garden was placed a large seat in the form of a shell, carved in an oak, which had a very pretty appearance.

That Strawberry Hill and its varied contents— its pictures, and statuary, and curiosities—should have been made the subject of verse by the aspirants for poetic fame at the end of the last century is scarcely to be wondered at. Maurice thus writes :—

> " Hail to the Gothic roofs, the classic bow'rs,
> Where, laurell'd Damer ! glide thy tranquil hours ;
> Where the rude block, from Parian quarries brought,
> Bursts into life, and breathes the glow of thought ;
> While all the cherish'd Arts and Muses mourn
> Round polish'd Walpole's venerated urn—
> In one lov'd spot their blended charms combine,
> And in their full meridian glory shine !—
> Of rarities, from many a clime convey'd,
> O'er many an ocean, to this hallow'd shade :
> How bright ! the rich assemblage charms my eyes,
> What prodigies of daring Art surprise !
> In pictures, vases, gems of various hue,
> And bring all Greece and Latium to my view !
> While Albion's chiefs, of more sublime renown,
> And ermin'd senators, in marble, frown,
> Bright polish'd helms heroic times recall,
> And gleaming corslets hang the storied wall ! "

The Earl of Bath's panegyric on his son's residence is well known. The humorous composition was completed by Walpole himself. The first stanza is given as the motto to this chapter ; of the remainder, as here given, Lord Bath wrote only the second stanza :—

> " Some love to roll down Greenwich Hill,
> For this thing and for that,
> And some prefer sweet Marble Hill,
> Though sure 'tis somewhat flat ;
> Yet Marble Hill and Greenwich Hill,
> If Kitty Clive* can tell,
> From Strawb'ry Hill, from Strawb'ry Hill,
> Will never bear the bell !
>
> " Though Surrey boasts its Oatlands
> And Clermont kept so jim,
> And some prefer sweet Southcote's,†
> 'Tis but a dainty whim ;
> For ask the gallant Bristow,‡
> Who does in taste excel,
> If Strawb'ry Hill, if Strawb'ry Hill,
> Don't bear away the bell ?
>
> " Since Denham sung of Cooper's,
> There's scarce a hill around
> But what in song or ditty
> Is turn'd to fairy ground—
> Ah, peace be with their mem'ries !
> I wish them wondrous well ;
> But Strawb'ry Hill, but Strawb'ry Hill,
> Must bear away the bell !
>
> " Great William ‖ dwells at Windsor,
> As Edward did of old ;
> And many a Gaul, and many a Scot,
> Have found him full as bold :
> On lofty hills like Windsor
> Such heroes ought to dwell ;
> Yet little folks like Strawb'ry Hill,
> Like Strawb'ry Hill as well ! "

In January 1772 the mansion of Strawberry Hill suffered considerably from the effects of an explosion at the powder-mills at Hounslow. Walpole thus amusingly makes mention of it in a letter to the Hon. H. S. Conway :—" The north side of the castle looks as if it had stood a siege. The two saints in the hall have suffered martyrdom. They have their bodies cut off, and nothing remains but their heads."

The career of Horace Walpole may be briefly summed up thus :—Born in 1717, he was the third son of Sir Robert Walpole, by his marriage with the daughter of a Mr. John Shorter, who had been " appointed Lord Mayor of London by the special favour of King James II." Mr. Walpole was educated at Eton (where he commenced his friendship with Gray), and whence he proceeded to King's College, Cambridge. In 1738 he was appointed to a Government post, which he shortly after exchanged

---

* Mrs. Clive, the celebrated actress, lived near Strawberry Hill, in a house which Walpole bought, and gave to her, and of which we shall have more to say hereafter.

† Woburn Park, near Chertsey, the seat of Mr. Philip Southcote.

‡ William Bristow, Esq., brother of the Countess of Buckingham, friend of Lord Bath, and a great pretender to taste.

‖ William, Duke of Cumberland, who defeated the rebels at Culloden in 1746.

for the sinecure office of Usher of the Exchequer, at a salary of £3,000 per annum. Other posts followed in quick succession, mainly through the influence of his father, which brought the sum total up to about £17,000 per annum. In 1739 he travelled abroad, in company with Gray, visiting Florence, Venice, &c. On their return, Walpole was elected M.P. for Callington, in Cornwall. He afterwards sat for Castle Rising and for King's Lynn in Norfolk. In Parliament he evinced his filial piety by a spirited speech against a motion made by Lord Limerick for an inquiry into his father's conduct. But he was not fond of public life, and in 1767 he communicated to the Mayor of Lynn his intention of abandoning his seat in Parliament. Not long before his death he declared that "he was *once*, forty years ago, at the late Duke of Newcastle's levee, the only minister's levee, except that of his father's, at which he was ever present."

He soon turned his attention to the fine arts and literature. In 1753 he became one of the fashionable contributors to the periodical paper entitled *The World*; and in 1757 he set up a printing-press at Strawberry Hill; and between that date and 1784, when he printed his "Description of Strawberry Hill," a large number of works were produced, including Walpole's "Royal and Noble Authors," his "Anecdotes of Painting in England," and "The Castle of Otranto." Walpole, although an author himself, held the profession of an author in contempt; for in one of his letters to Hume he remarks:—"You know, in England (speaking of writers) we read their works, but seldom or never take any notice of authors. We think them sufficiently paid if their books sell, and of course leave them to their colleges and obscurity, by which means we are not troubled with their vanity and impertinence."

Walpole's fame as an author rests mainly upon his "Letters." "He loved letter-writing," says Lord Macaulay, who ranks his "Letters" above all his other works, "and had evidently studied it as an art. It was, in truth, the very kind of writing for such a man: for a man very ambitious to rank among wits, yet nervously afraid that while obtaining the reputation of a wit he might lose caste as a gentleman."

It cannot be said that Walpole was a patron of men of letters. He has been much blamed in regard to his conduct towards the unfortunate Chatterton, who, having left a provincial attorney's office, came to London to starve, and ultimately to die by his own hand. He appealed in his penury to Walpole, who is said to have turned a deaf ear to his case. Walpole is stated to have gone to Paris with the young poet's compositions—which had been sent to him with Chatterton's request for help—in his possession, to have neglected his request for their return, and to have repudiated his complaint of such conduct as an insolent piece of presumption. On Walpole's return he found a very resentful letter from Chatterton, peremptorily requiring the papers, and telling Walpole that "he would not have dared to use him so had he not been acquainted with the narrowness of his circumstances." The following are the poor boy Chatterton's verses to Horace Walpole :—

" Walpole ! I thought not I should ever see
So mean a heart as thine has proved to be :
Thou, nursed in luxury's lap, behold'st with scorn
The boy who, friendless, fatherless, forlorn,
Asks thy high favour. Thou mayst call me cheat—
Say, Didst thou never practise such deceit ?
Who wrote Otranto ? But I will not chide ;
Scorn I'll repay with scorn, and pride with pride.
Still, Walpole, still, thy prosy chapters write,
And flimsy letters to some fair indite ;
Laud all above thee ; fawn and cringe to those
Who for thy fame were better friends than foes ;
Still spurn the incautious fool who dares to plead,
And crave thy service in the hour of need.

.   .   .   .

Had I the gifts of wealth and luxury shared,
Not poor and mean—Walpole ! thou had'st not dared
Thus to insult. But I shall live, and stand
By Rowley's side when thou art dead and damned ! "

Of the struggles of poor Chatterton, from the time of his arrival in London until his tragic end by poison in a garret in Brooke Street, Holborn, we have already spoken at some length in the pages of OLD AND NEW LONDON.*

Walpole gathered around him at Twickenham a select social circle, which included Garrick, Mrs. Pritchard, Kitty Clive, Paul Whitehead, the two Misses Berry, General Conway, the Ladies Suffolk and Diana Beauclerk, George Selwyn, Richard Bentley, Gray, Lord Edgecombe and Strafford, and Sir Horace Mann. The friendship of Walpole for Hannah More did not commence till 1784, when he was sixty-seven years of age; and that with the two Miss Berrys dates only from 1788, when he met them with their father at the house of Lady Herries. At the age of seventy and more his heart warmed towards them as it had never warmed towards any woman before, and he never was happy except when they were with him or when they were corresponding with him. They both outlived him some sixty years! When they went to Italy, the doting old beau wrote to them regularly once a week; and when, on their return, they

---

anchored at the neighbouring villa—which, by the way, they called Little Strawberry Hill, in his honour —then and then only does he seem to be contented. His friendship for these two young ladies reminds us in some of its details of that of Pope for Martha and Teresa Blount.

Still, although he steered clear of the meshes of matrimony, there was nothing that Walpole liked better than acting as squire or cicerone to fine ladies, and especially in a pleasant row on the river Thames. But twice at least his gallantry nearly cost him his life: on one occasion, in returning with Lady Browne from Lady Blandford's in the ferry-boat, when the boat was carried down the stream to Isleworth, and forced against the piers of the new bridge ; and again, in 1778, when in a boat with his two nieces, Miss Keppel and Lady Bridget Tollemache, to see the Goldsmiths' Company returning in their barges from a dinner *al fresco* close to Pope's Villa, when their boat was run down by some half-drunken cits, and the party were much alarmed, though not actually upset. On this Walpole remarks in one of his letters, that " Neptune never would have had so beautiful a prize as the four girls !"

In 1791, in his seventy-third year, Walpole succeeded to the Earldom of Orford, on the death of his nephew, an event which he himself commemorated in a few lines, called an " Epitaphium vivi Auctoris," as follows :—

" An estate and an earldom at seventy-four !
  Had I sought them or wished them, 'twould add one fear
        more—
  That of making a countess when almost four-score.
  But Fortune, who scatters her gifts out of season,
  Though unkind to my limbs, has still left me my reason ;
  And whether she lowers or lifts me, I'll try
  In the plain simple style I have lived in to die :
  For ambition too humble, for meanness too high."

Carrying out these principles in action, Horace Walpole would never assume the earldom, and seldom even signed his name as " Orford." He amused himself to the last with adding to the treasures and decorations of Strawberry Hill, where he was, in 1795, honoured by a visit from the queen and royal family. He never even took his seat in the House of Peers, but ended his days amidst his books and art treasures, surrounded by his friends. He died at his house in Berkeley Square on the 2nd of March, 1797, and with him died the last survivor of the family of Sir Robert Walpole.

Of Walpole's personal appearance we have the following particulars, written by Miss Hawkins in 1772 :—" His figure was not merely tall, but more properly long, and slender to excess; his complexion, and particularly his hands, of a most unhealthy paleness. . . His eyes were remarkably bright and penetrating, very dark and lively ; his voice was not strong, but his tones were extremely pleasant, and, if I may say so, highly gentlemanly. I do not remember his common gait, he always entered a room in that style of affected delicacy which fashion had made almost natural : *chapeau bras* between his hands, as if he wished to compress it under his arm, knees bent, and feet on tiptoe, as if afraid of a wet floor ! His dress in visiting was most usually, in summer, when I most saw him, a lavender suit, the waistcoat embroidered with a little silver, or of white silk worked in the tambour, partridge silk stockings and gold buckles, ruffles and frill, generally lace. I remember when a child thinking him very much undressed if at any time, except in mourning, he wore hemmed cambric. In summer no powder, but his wig combed straight, and showing his very smooth pale forehead, and queued behind ; in winter powder."

" In everything in which Walpole busied himself," writes Lord Macaulay, " in the fine arts, in literature, in public affairs, he was drawn by some strange attraction from the great to the little, and from the useful to the odd. The politics in which he took the keenest interest were politics scarcely deserving of the name. The growlings of George the Second, the flirtations of Princess Emily with the Duke of Grafton, the amours of Prince Frederick and Lady Middlesex, the squabbles between Gold Stick-in-waiting and the Master of the Buckhounds, the disagreements between the tutors of Prince George — these matters engaged almost all the attention which Walpole could spare from matters more important still : from bidding for Zinckes and Petitots, from cheapening fragments of tapestry and handles of old lances, from joining bits of painted glass, and from setting up memorials of departed cats and dogs. While he was fetching and carrying the gossip of Kensington Palace and Carlton House he fancied that he was engaged in politics, and when he recorded that gossip he fancied that he was writing history."

Burke, indeed, was not unjustly severe when he characterised Walpole as an " elegant trifler," and Strawberry Hill as a " Gothic toy." Dr. Aikin has drawn his character in these words :—" Horace Walpole, though forming his plan of life chiefly upon a system of personal enjoyment, possessed kind and social affections, and was capable of very generous actions to his friends. He had seen too much of the world to give easy credit to professions and appearances ; but he respected virtue, and had warm feelings for the rights and interests of mankind. As an author, if he does not merit a place in the higher ranks, he has done enough to preserve his name from oblivion."

Crabbe, in his "Tales of the Hall," sums up Walpole's taste for castle-building, as exemplified in his work at Strawberry Hill, in the following mock-heroic lines :—

> " He built his castles wondrous rich and rare,
> Few castle-builders could with him compare ;
> The hall, the palace, rose at his command,
> And these he filled with objects great and grand."

Walpole bequeathed Strawberry Hill and its contents, in the first instance, to his cousin, Marshal Conway, and to the Countess of Ailesbury during their lives ; then to their daughter, the Hon. Mrs. Damer, the sculptress, for her life ; and after her, to Lord Waldegrave.

Marshal Conway, who was for many years a Member of Parliament, seems to have been one of those many mediocrities who found their way into high official position under the good old patronage system which prevailed through the first twenty years of the reign of George III.

Mrs. Damer made Strawberry Hill her abode for several years, most of her time being occupied in her favourite pursuit of sculpture. At a somewhat early period of her progress Mrs. Damer attained almost to perfection in the art, and acquired a celebrity not only in her own country, but on the Continent of Europe, her title to which will be readily acknowledged when the number and excellence of her works are called to mind. They include the following figures, statues, and designs :—

1. The Dog, for which she was so highly honoured by the Academy of Florence.

2. An Osprey, formerly belonging to Horace Walpole, and exhibited in his collection at Strawberry Hill, but afterwards the property of Sir Alexander Johnston.

3. Charles James Fox, which she presented to the Emperor Napoleon at Paris, on his return from Elba.

4. The colossal bust of Nelson, executed by her in marble, shortly after he returned from the battle of the Nile, and sat to her for it, and which she presented to the City of London, whose officers placed it in the Council Chamber at Guildhall, where it now stands.

5. A bust of Nelson, executed in bronze by her for the King of Tanjore, and presented by her to His Highness.

6. A similar bust, presented by her to King William IV. when Lord High Admiral, which is now at Windsor.

7. Heads of Thames and Isis, for the keystones of the bridge over the Thames at Henley ; presented by her to the Town of Henley, near which stood her father's country-house, called " Park Place."

8. Two Dogs, executed in marble, and presented by her to her sister, the Duchess of Richmond ; now at Goodwood.

9. Several pieces for Boydell's Shakespeare.

10. A bust of herself, presented by her to Payne Knight.

11. Her mother, the Countess of Ailesbury.

12. Miss Farren (the late Lady Derby).

HORACE WALPOLE.
(From a Portrait by Sir Joshua Reynolds.)

13. Miss Berry, editor of Horace Walpole's works.

14. Prince Labomirthy.

15. Peniston Lamb, the eldest son of the late Lord Melbourne.

16. The second Lord Melbourne, when a child.

17. Sir Humphrey Davy.

18. Queen Caroline, consort of George IV.

Finding, however, the situation of Strawberry Hill lonely when her mother died, Mrs. Damer gave up the house and property, together with the £2,000 per annum left to her by its founder for its maintenance, to Lord Waldegrave, in whom the fee was vested under the will, and removed to a mansion of Lady Buckinghamshire, at East Sheen.

Strawberry Hill has since continued in the possession of the Waldegrave family, though they did not care to reside there. In 1842 the contents of the house were sold by public auction. The sale lasted from April 25th to May 21st, and realised the sum of £33,468. It was conducted by Mr. George Robins in a large temporary building erected on the lawn for the purpose.

"The fate of Strawberry Hill," writes Eliot Warburton, " was lamentable. For four-and-twenty days the apartments sacred to Horatian pleasantries echoed with the hammer of the auctioneer. Circumstances that need not be more particularly alluded to rendered this degradation unavoidable, and it was only with difficulty that the most sacred of the family possessions could be preserved from the relentless ordeal of a public sale." The shrine which had been visited with so much interest and veneration was now overrun by a well-dressed mob, who glanced at its treasures, and at the copious catalogue in which they were enumerated, with a like indifference. But doubtless, at the actual sale this indifference changed to the most anxious desire to obtain possession of some relic of the man whose name was invested with so many pleasant associations; and the more interesting portion of the thousand trifles created a degree of excitement for the library. But above all, I should like to have a little drawing or two by a certain amateur artist, and trust, at all events, that they will not be allowed to go into the hands of mere strangers. Altogether, I suppose, they will bring a good deal of money; and so passes the glory of this world! Vanity of vanities!"

The treasures of Strawberry Hill made their way into royal and private hands, and some found a

LITTLE STRAWBERRY HILL IN 1813. (*From a Contemporary Sketch.*)

which would almost have reconciled their former owner to such a distribution."

Lord Jeffrey, in a letter to Miss Berry, written at the time of the sale, gives his own "private opinion" of the value of the collection in the following words: "I have been amusing myself lately," writes his lordship, "by looking over the catalogue of the 'Strawberry Hill' collections, and, as you may suppose, have had you often enough in my mind as I went through names and little anecdotes which must be pregnant to you with so many touching recollections. I should like, if I were rich enough, to have some twelve or twenty of the pictures and miniatures, but would really give nothing for the china, furniture, and *bijouterie*, and not a great deal

refuge in other collections, which they still swell and probably will continue to swell, until some ducal, or at least noble, family is in difficulties, when they will put in an appearance at the rooms of Messrs. Christie and Manson.

The house remained from the above date dismantled and neglected, and in a most forlorn and desolate condition for some time, until it became the property of its late possessor, Frances, Countess of Waldegrave, who, having thoroughly renovated and much improved and enlarged the building, made it, from the sumptuousness of its interior adornment, inferior to few of the mansions of the nobility in the kingdom; and under her rule Strawberry Hill became famous for its *réunions* and garden-parties, at which royalty was often present.

Lady Waldegrave, the widow of the seventh Earl, carried it in marriage to her second husband, Mr. Chichester Fortescue, now Lord Carlingford. She was the daughter of Braham the singer, and was celebrated as one of the leaders of society in London.

After the death of the countess, Strawberry Hill became once more unoccupied as the residence of the Waldegrave family, and in 1881 it was again offered for sale. The property still (Dec. 1882) remains in the market; it is rumoured that it is about to be turned into an American hotel, but as yet, happily, this is not true.

At the end of a verdant meadow bordering upon the lower road to Teddington, and just on the confines of Twickenham parish, Walpole purchased a comparatively small house, in which the celebrated Kitty Clive, the actress, resided, and which is still known as Little Strawberry Hill. He would constantly trip across that field, accompanied by his pet spaniel, in order to enjoy the society of that fascinating woman.

Born in 1711, Mrs. Clive made her first appearance in boy's clothes, in the character of Ismenes, the page of Ziphores, in the play of "Mithridates," at Drury Lane Theatre. In 1732 she married a gentleman of the law, a brother of Lord Clive; but the union was soon dissolved, being unproductive of happiness to either party. During the year 1769 she quitted the stage, though to the last she was admirable and unrivalled. Retiring to this spot, she lived in ease and independence, and died here, beloved by her friends, and respected by the world. No individual ever took a more extensive walk in comedy—the chambermaid in every varied shape which art or nature could lend her—characters of whim and affectation, from the high-bred Lady Fanciful to the vulgar Mrs. Heidelberg—country girls, romps, hoydens, dowdies, superannuated beauties, viragos, and humourists—engaged her versatile talents with an inimitable felicity. It was a saying that "no man could be grave when Clive was inclined to be merry." At the same time her character throughout life was exemplary. Not only Horace Walpole, but many other persons of rank and eminence, courted her society, attracted by her wit and drollery; besides which, as old Pepys would have said, "a mighty pretty woman she was too." Mrs. Clive retired from the stage to this pleasant retreat very soon after speaking her farewell epilogue, written by Walpole, on her benefit night, April 24th. "Kitty," in spite of all her attractiveness, must have been a formidable person in her way.

The following anecdote rests on Horace Walpole's authority:—"When some persons in the neighbourhood wanted to stop up a foot-road, the opponents were very numerous, but they wanted a leader; some one then suggested that Mrs. Clive should be applied to; and on the morning of the meeting, Kitty—not 'the beautiful and young,' but the old and red-faced—appeared on the scene, with so determined an aspect that the assailants laid down their arms."

The "elegant trifler" wrote the following inscription for an urn to the memory of Mrs. Clive, which is placed in the garden:—

> "Ye smiles and jests still hover round;
> This is mirth's consecrated ground:
> Here liv'd the laughter-loving dame,
> A matchless actress, Clive her name.
> The comic muse with her retired,
> And shed a tear when she expired."

Mrs. Clive died suddenly on the 7th of September, 1785, at the age of seventy-five, and was buried at Twickenham. A marble tablet on the outside of the east end of the church bears an inscription to her memory, by Miss Pope.

Miss Mary and Miss Agnes Berry afterwards occupied the cottage, which was bequeathed to them for life by Walpole. The Misses Berry first took up their residence here after their return from Florence in 1791, and the cottage continued to be their residence for many years. "In the person of these ladies," observes Mr. Cobbett, "the memories of those who well recollect them are united to the older and more celebrated days of Twickenham. The elder of the two, born in the third year after King George the Third's accession, lived to be in her old age privately presented to Queen Victoria."

In 1813 Little Strawberry Hill was taken on lease by Mr. Matthew Wood, M.P., Alderman of London; during his occupancy the cottage enjoyed a fair share of popularity. The author of "Excursions through England," in describing Little Strawberry Hill, says:—"Hither have the citizens of London made delightful aquatic excursions during the summer season of the year. Indeed, it is usual for the members of the Corporation to indulge in these excursions under every mayoralty. These sons of pleasure generally travel by land to Kew, where they embark, and proceed to Hampton, the accustomed spot of destination. Some, indeed, have gone up as far as Oxford; and a few have had courage to penetrate the fountain-head, near Cheltenham, in Gloucestershire! The members of the Corporation are accompanied by their wives, and allowed to take a friend. These excursions in the City barge are not unfrequent, and when the heavens smile, impart no inconsiderable gratification. The entertainment provided is liberal, the company disposed to please and to be pleased; whilst a band of music, whose tones are reverberated from the opposite banks, soothes the senses, delights the imagination, and exhilarates the heart." The City State barge, which was often to be seen during the summer months on the reaches of the river about Twickenham, was named the *Maria Wood* after Alderman Wood's beautiful daughter.

One at least of the Miss Berrys must have been a woman of taste, for she was the designer, and apparently the engraver, of Mrs. Damer's bookplate. Both the Misses Berry died in 1852, Agnes in January, and her elder sister in November, at the age of ninety, and both lie buried in Petersham churchyard, where an epitaph from the pen of the Earl of Carlisle is inscribed to their memory.

However charming and attractive Strawberry Hill may have been in the last century, in consequence of the literary and social circles of which it formed the central point, the neighbourhood was not without its drawbacks. For instance, owing probably to the large extent of open and unenclosed lands about Twickenham, the highwaymen and footpads would try their skill on noble and gentle travellers in their carriages. Horace Walpole, writing in 1782, complains that, "having lived there in tolerable quiet for thirty years, he cannot now stir a mile from his own house after sunset without one or two servants armed with blunderbusses."

Though Strawberry Hill still stands, and though its grounds are as yet intact, yet probably they are both doomed to destruction. "Coming events," they say, "cast their shadows before them;" and therefore it may be worth while to add that on the opposite side of the road a large tract of land, extending up to the Strawberry Hill railway station, has been taken in hand by a firm of London builders, who are rapidly covering the green fields with villas.

In Strawberry Vale, almost opposite to Little Strawberry Hill, on the margin of the river, is a row of suburban villas, the last of which, called "The Bachelors," is a landmark familiar to rowing-men; this, too, is the last house in the parish of Twickenham on the confines of Teddington.

CHAPTER X.

TEDDINGTON AND BUSHEY PARK.

" Hæ latebræ dulces, etiam si credis, amœnæ."— *Horace.*

Situation and General Appearance of Teddington—Rise and Progress of the Village—Upper Teddington—Etymology of Teddington—Early History, and Descent of the Manor—"Queen Elizabeth's Hunting-Box "—The Manor House—The Parish Church—Dr. Stephen Hales—" Peg " Woffington—Extracts from the Parish Register—The Church of St. Peter and St. Paul—Recent Improvements in Teddington—The River Thames—" Swan-upping "—Bushey Park—The Ranger's Lodge—A Village Patriot.

PURSUING our pilgrim way in a south-westerly direction, a road, skirting on the one side the grounds of Strawberry Hill, and on the other the greenest of Thames-side meadows and eyots, conducts us to the lower end of pleasant Teddington, a place familiar to all anglers and boating-men, as marking the first lock and weir upon the Thames, and consequently, the ending of the tidal way—though as a matter of fact the effects of the tide are scarcely felt at all above Richmond and Twickenham. From this point, however, the mud banks which more or less mark every tidal estuary disappear, and we see Father Thames flowing along all the more full and brimming, but not the less picturesque, because of the artificial means by which his course is regulated.

But a few years ago—long since the accession of Queen Victoria—Teddington was a quiet rural village, with its two or three squires, its "Grove," its "Manor," its little waterside church, and its broad expanse of open meadows. Now all is changed: rows of spruce villas and "neat" terraces have sprung up along the roads to Twickenham and to Hampton Wick, and all over the upper end of the village, which now must soon call itself a town, with its grand "hotels" and magnificent "stores," which have fairly driven out the keepers of its hostelries, and threaten to swallow up the "small trader" class. This growth of Teddington is in a great measure owing to the introduction of the railway.

The district which is called Upper Teddington is provided with a church, schools, a large hotel, and shops of a more attractive and showy nature than those in the older part of the village. A large portion of the parish is still cultivated as market-gardens.

Teddington is situated on the left bank of the

Thames, and adjoins the southern end of Twickenham. The main road from Richmond Bridge to Bushey Park and Hampton Court passes through the older part of the village, which possesses a few good shops and public buildings. There is here a station on the Kingston extension line, in connection with the South-Western Railway. The village has long been a favourite spot for the disciples of Izaak Walton, and three of its principal inns—the "King's Head," the "Royal Oak," and "The Anglers"—are largely patronised by the fishing fraternity. The river about Teddington and Twickenham abounds in barbel, roach, and dace, in such quantities as to induce many who delight in angling to fix upon this spot for their summer "outing." Readers of Pope will not have forgotten the following lines, descriptive of fishing in the Thames :—

> "In genial spring, beneath the quiv'ring shade,
> Where cooling vapours breathe along the mead,
> The patient fisher takes his silent stand
> Intent, his angle trembling in his hand—
> With looks unmov'd he marks the scaly breed,
> And eyes the dancing cork and bending reed.
> Our plenteous streams a various race supply—
> The bright ey'd perch, with fins of Tyrian dye,
> The silver eel in shining volumes roll'd,
> The yellow carp in scales bedropp'd with gold,
> Swift trouts diversified with crimson stains,
> And pikes, the tyrants of the wat'ry plains !"

The Queen's state barge, though no longer used on public occasions, is kept high and dry at Teddington. We have already mentioned this barge in OLD AND NEW LONDON. (See Vol. III. p. 309.) It is of antique shape, with lofty bows, and is said to date from 1600. Its form is familiar to all who remember the engraving of Charles I. feeding the swans on the river at Hampton Court. It has not been used since 1849.

The parish of Teddington extends from the river on the one hand—close by which stands the parish church and the main portion of the mother village—towards Twickenham on the other, and stretches also westward in a very irregular manner to the gates of Bushey Park.

Fortunately, in treating of the early history of this parish, we are largely assisted by a most careful series of papers which appeared in the local "Parish Magazine" in 1875-76, from the pen of the ex-vicar, the Rev. D. Trinder.

Teddington has been thought by casual and superficial scholars to have been so named as being the place at which the Thames ceases to be a tidal river—"Tide-end-town"; but in all probability that mode of spelling its name is not two centuries old : at all events, there is no proof of its use before the year 1700. Previously it was known as "Todyngton," "Tuddington," or "Totyngton."

If it be true, as suggested by Mr. Trinder, that "tot" means a small grove, and "ing" a meadow or pasture, then the name of Totyngton was not inappropriate to the place, but very descriptive of it, being "derived from the beautiful meadow, as older inhabitants remember it, sloping from the manor-house down to the river-side, with 'The Grove' in the background—an attractive and pretty spot, the choice of which does justice to the good taste of our British and Saxon ancestors." But we have our doubts as to the meaning above assigned to the word "tot," which appears in such names as Tothill, Tottenham, Totham, Totteridge, Tooting, &c., and which is generally believed to point to a lofty beacon.*

There is no record as to the founder of Teddington, whether he was a Briton, a Roman, or a Saxon. No Roman remains have been found *in situ;* and probably the place grew gradually into existence as a fishing station long before it obtained its Saxon name of "Tuddyngton," or "Todyngton." As far as appears from history and tradition, there was no ford here, nor indeed any need of a ferry, because there was little or no intercourse between the "Mid Saxons" and the men of the "South Rey," or Surrey. "Remote from thoroughfares, and lying in the midst of an extensive forest, to which Bushey and Richmond Parks originally belonged, the place was reached only by the river—that silent highway. But when reached, it presented good fishing ground and fair pasturage, and these were just the advantages that the Briton of old times valued. Accordingly, it is scarcely unhistorical to assume that the forerunner of our water-side population was some ancient Briton, who paddled his cranky canoe on the flood-tide to the first fall of the river, and rejoicing to find there plenty of fish and meadows sloping to the river, built his clay and straw-thatched hut somewhere between the old church and the river, fenced round the meadow for his cows, and set up his idols in the neighbouring grove for the chance of some Druid passing that way."

"Centuries of quiet rolled over this retired fishing station. The lordly Roman doubtless bought the fish, revelling in the costly dish of lampreys ; and perhaps in his hunting expeditions drank a bowl of milk at the poor Briton's river-side hut, but took no further notice of it, and passed on his way."

Teddington was in the Saxon times a "tithing" in the Hundred of Spelthorne. As a tithing, it must even then have been the abode of ten

---

families of freemen, for it was part and parcel of the Anglo-Saxon constitution that every freeman should belong to a *tithing*, a *hundred*, and a *shire,* the members of each tithing being security for the good behaviour of each other. Thus a mutual dependence of each man upon his neighbour was established, and also along with it the principle of self-government. The chief officer in the county was the sheriff, or shire-reeve, who was assisted in his judicial functions by the alderman (elder), who was the supreme judge of the county court. The court of the Hundred took cognisance of matters too important for the *tithing* to decide; and as an alderman was chosen by each Hundred, so a tithing man was appointed by each Tithing to collect the king's dues and fines, and to preserve the peace. In some places this right would seem to have belonged to the manor court; and it is only within the last few years that the inhabitants of Teddington have ceased to assemble in vestry at Easter to appoint a head-borough or tithing-man, as their Saxon ancestors did before them ten centuries ago.

In the times before the Conquest there was doubtless here the usual complement of slaves and ceorls, or churls, dependent on some Thane or noble Saxon, whose flag they followed, and whose leadership they acknowledged under the king. The Thane would naturally erect near his manor-house a chapel, or "bell-house;" and this was done here. The little "Bell House" probably was dedicated from the first to St. Mary. The monks of the Order of St. Benedict at Staines had the charge of the parochial duties here before the Conquest; but in all probability Teddington was annexed by gift of Edward the Confessor to the more important Abbey of Westminster.

Mr. Trinder writes in the magazine above mentioned:—"It was not until the Saxon pirate, blue-eyed, fair-haired, and keen as his own long sword, swarmed upon the coast, explored the rivers, and gave his name to the land of the South Saxons (Sussex), those of the west (Wessex), those of the east (Essex), and to that which lay below them (Middlesex), that our name was heard. The place took the fancy of the plunderer, and a Saxon village with a Saxon name arose. Hence we have certain wide limits between which the historical origin of Teddington lies; for the Kingdom of Middlesex was founded A.D. 527, and in A.D. 838 a General Council of the United Saxon Kingdom was held by Egbert at the neighbouring town of Kingston-on-Thames—an event which shows the importance of the place, and the unlikelihood that any available places in its neighbourhood, especially on the banks of the river, had remained unoccupied."

Though no mention of the place occurs in Doomsday Book, yet authentic records show that even before the Conquest Teddington was closely connected with Staines, and that the Manor of Teddington was held by the abbot and convent of Westminster, King Edgar having granted to that body "the monastery which is called Staines, and all that belongeth to it, viz., Teddington, Halliford, Feltham, and Ashford." Again, we find that early in the thirteenth century the Manors of Teddington and Sunbury were assigned for the support of one Robert Papillon, who had been deposed from the abbotship of Westminster. In 1223, some disputes having arisen as to the question of patronage, it was agreed that the Abbot of Westminster should nominate and appoint the chaplain of Teddington.

In 1371, and again in 1427, "Todyngton" was taxed at nine marks, equal to about £6, as its rateable value, and was called upon to contribute 6s. 8d. to the service of the king. As the whole Hundred of Spelthorne produced the sum of £21, the population of it would not probably exceed 1,300 adults. What proportion of this belonged to Teddington may be inferred from the fact that in the year of the battle of Agincourt, when Henry V. required large supplies for his glorious, but fruitless, campaign in France, the Hundred of Spelthorne raised a tenth and a fifteenth, amounting to nearly £52, out of which Todyngton supplied 37s. 5½d. Somewhat later—namely, in 1435—this charge of a tenth and a fifteenth was found to be in excess of what this part of the country could bear, owing to its having been "desolated, laid waste, destroyed, or excessively impoverished;" the parish received a remission of 8s., along with Sunbury and Staines, whilst Feltham and Bedfont received each nearly double of that amount.

In 1539, Abbot Boston, of St. Peter's, Westminster, surrendered into the hands of his royal master the manor and advowson of Teddington. The manor then became part of a larger demesne, "the honour of Hampton," which the king formed into a royal hunting chase. Thenceforward the chaplain of Teddington was appointed by the lord of the manor, who was bound to provide a stipend of £6 4s., a charge which has been continued to the present day, though, owing to the change which has taken place in the value of money since then, it ought to be nearly £50.

In 1603, James I. granted the reversion of the manor to John Hill, whose son appears also in connection with it a few years later as Mr. Auditor Hill; he was probably, therefore, a nominee of Lord Buckhurst, formerly Lord Treasurer. It would seem that among the inhabitants of Teddington were several official personages, for the two monuments in the church belonging to the Stuart era commemorate an "Escheator" for the county of Somerset, and a "yeoman in ordinary" to Queen Elizabeth.

About the year 1670 the manor came by purchase into the hands of Sir Orlando Bridgman, who succeeded, on the fall of Clarendon, as Lord Keeper of the Great Seal. On his ceasing to hold this

The Royal Barge. built about 1600 In the custody of J. A. Messenger. Her Majesty's Bargemaster.

THE QUEEN'S BARGE.

office, in 1672, he retired to Teddington, where he relieved many of the clergy who had suffered during the reign of the Puritan faction. He was buried here two years later. In 1833, when the church was altered, his coffin was found open, but his remains, having been embalmed, were almost perfect, even to his pointed beard. It was this Lord Keeper, an ancestor of the present Earl of Bradford, who settled on the church the slender endowment which it has enjoyed down to the present time.

It was only about the year 1850 that the "court-leet" of the Manor of Teddington was last held. The bailiff (a Norman official, who displaced the old

Saxon beadle, or rather, bedel) used to summon all the tenants of the manor, whether copyholders or freeholders; but this has now disappeared, the manor having been sold, and the copyholders' lands having been enfranchised.

The manor probably grew out of the first settlement in Saxon times, the proprietorship of the Thane under the later Saxon kings having been little different, save in name, from the seignoralty of the Norman lord, and having gradually been merged in it. It is probable that the residence of the feudal lord stood on or near the site of the present Manor House, but it is not mentioned in "Domesday"—nor, indeed, as already stated, is the "vill" of Teddington itself.

The "Old House" has been from time immemorial styled "Queen Elizabeth's Hunting-box," and there is no doubt that the tradition is genuine; for the royal chase which Henry VIII. had formed stretched in every direction around Hampton Court, and could not have stopped short of the present boundary-wall of Bushey Park, and probably it extended even further. Outside of it lay a large tract of unenclosed waste, the common land of the parish, leaving but a small portion for private domains and farms. On the other side of the river was Richmond Park, running up to and almost touching the old Deer Park, near which stood the palace of Sheene. Now, between these palaces and scenes of royal sport no halfway house could be more conveniently situated for a halting place, where the virgin queen could rest from the labours of the chase; and "the Old House, in strict Elizabethan style, with its simple construction and triple gables, bespeaks the purport of its erection, and justifies the tradition." In all probability it was built early in Elizabeth's reign, when the queen was young and devoted to the pastime of the chase; and Leicester dates a letter from Teddington in 1570.

There was, indeed, in the parish another Elizabethan residence, namely, the Manor House; but there is no proof that this was ever in the hands of the queen or of members of her Court, except that its reversion was granted in 1582 to Sir Amias Paulet; neither is there any proof that he ever lived there, and the fact that the arms of Lord Buckhurst were found carved in one of its apartments would seem to point to the conclusion that the house dates its erection from the early part of the seventeenth century. In the last century the old mansion was for many years the residence of Viscount Dudley rebuilt the house. Queen Elizabeth's hunting-seat was pulled down recently to make room for a new road.

The parish church, dedicated to St. Mary, is a brick-built structure, of little or no architectural pretensions, though prettily situated in the meadows,

The Anglers Teddington Ferry

and Ward, who made great alterations in the house and remodelled the grounds. Walpole, in a letter to the Earl of Strafford, dated 28th July, 1787, says that Lord Dudley here constructed "an obelisk below a hedge, a canal at right angles with the Thames, and a sham bridge, no wider than that of a violin." All these things, however, were done away with by a Captain Smith, who came into possession of the property through marrying his lordship's widow, and who also to a great extent near the river. The south aisle doubtless formed part of an earlier building, though patched and coated over, and much altered in outward appearance. In the church still survives the original chapel of the hamlet, but probably more than once renewed and rebuilt.

On the south wall is a brass, asking the prayers of the faithful for John Goodyere and Thomasyne, his wife. The north aisle was built about the middle of the last century, mainly at the expense of the then minister of the parish, Dr. Stephen Hales, who also built the tower in the following year. The chancel is a recent addition, and is constructed of brick in the Decorated style of architecture.

At the east end of the chancel is a mural monument to Henry Flitcroft, the eminent architect patronised by Lord Burlington. The oldest monument is dated 1674, and commemorates Sir Orlando Bridgman, who was commissioner for Charles I. at the treaty of Uxbridge, and after the Restoration held successively the posts of Chief Baron of the Exchequer, Chief Justice of the Common Pleas, and Lord Keeper of the Great Seal: from this last-named office, however, he was dismissed in 1672, for refusing to sign the Declaration of Indulgence.

Paul Whitehead, the poet, who died in Henrietta Street, Covent Garden, was buried in Teddington churchyard in December, 1774; but his heart was deposited in the mausoleum of his patron, Lord Le Despencer, at High Wycombe, whence it was stolen in 1839. Here, too, lies Richard Bentley, the sometime friend of Horace Walpole, and his adviser and draughtsman in the erection and decoration of Strawberry Hill. There is also a tablet here to the memory of Mr. John Walter, the founder and principal proprietor of the *Times*. He had a residence at Teddington, where he died in 1812.

This church contains also the remains of Dr. Stephen Hales, Clerk of the Closet to the Princess of Wales (mother of George III.), and for upwards of half a century incumbent of Teddington. Dr. Hales was one of the most active Fellows of the Royal Society, and a frequent contributor to its "Transactions." He was the author of "Hæmostatics," a treatise on the circulation of the blood, and of a similar treatise on the "Sap in Vegetables." To his practical turn the country was indebted for some improvements in the ventilation of prisons, hospitals, and ships of war, and these very largely reduced the deaths by "gaol fever" in Newgate.

"Plain Parson Hale" (whose name has been deprived of a letter by Pope by the inexorable laws of rhyme) was this same Dr. Stephen Hales, who was also one of the witnesses to Pope's will. Dr. Hales seems to have been a simple, benevolent man, delighting in his quiet village and pastoral duties. He rebuilt the tower of Teddington church, as stated above, and at a ripe old age he was interred beside it, dying in 1761, in his eighty-fourth year. Pope had a sincere regard for his amiable and scientific neighbour; but, according to Spence, he

looked with horror on some of his experiments. "I shall be very glad to see Dr. Hales, and always love to see him, he is so worthy and good a man. Yes, he is a very good man; only I'm sorry he has his hands so much imbrued in blood. What! he cuts up rats? Ay, and dogs too! Indeed, he commits most of those barbarities with the thought of being of use to man! But how do we know that we have a right to kill creatures that we are so little above as dogs, for our curiosity, or even for some use to us? I used to carry it too far; I thought they had reason as well as we. So they have, to be sure: all our disputes about that are only disputes about words. Man has reason enough only to know what is necessary for him to know, and dogs have just that too. 'But then they must have souls, too, as unperishable as ours!' And what harm would that be to us?"

Here, in 1760, was buried the once popular and charming actress, Margaret—or, as she was commonly called, "Peg"—Woffington. She is said to have been a native of Dublin, and, according to the inscription on her tomb, was born in 1720. Her histrionic talent appears to have been displayed even in childhood; as in 1728, being one of Madame Violante's Liliputian company, she obtained great applause by enacting the part of Polly in the *Beggar's Opera*. Her first speaking character on the Dublin stage was Ophelia, which she performed on February 12th, 1737; and on November 6th, 1740, she made her *début* in London, at Covent Garden Theatre, in the part of Sylvia, in Farquhar's comedy of *The Recruiting Officer*. In the following season she performed at Drury Lane Theatre, and was pre-eminently distinguished in the higher walks of comedy; in some characters, particularly in that of Mrs. Loveit, she surpassed Mrs. Oldfield. In tragedy she had also considerable merit, but had not the power of touching the passions equal to Mrs. Cibber or Mrs. Pritchard. Among her best characters were "Cleopatra," "Roxana," and the "Distressed Mother." Having in her youth been taught by Madame Violante all that a dancer of first-rate reputation could teach her, she had accustomed herself to French society; and upon a visit to Paris, Dumesnil willingly imparted to her all the manner she professed of the dignified passion of the French drama, and this infected Mrs. Woffington with the prevailing pompous mode of elocution which preceded Garrick's style, and in which she was confirmed by Cibber, who at seventy was delighted to fancy himself her gallant. She maintained a decided preference to male society, and is said to have more than once presided at the meetings of the Beef-Steak Club. Her act ing in male attire, in which she was fond of displaying herself, was unequalled; and Sir Harry Wildair was one of her most admired characters. In 1757, being then engaged at Covent Garden, she rendered her last acknowledgments to her friends in the character of Lothario, for her benefit, and took her farewell leave of the public on May 17th as Rosalind, one of her most favourite parts, in male attire, in which she at the close resumed the female costume, just to "make curtesy and bid farewell." While speaking the epilogue, she was seized with an indisposition from which she never recovered, though she retained the unrivalled beauties of her face and person to the last. She died March 28th, 1760.

Her monument, on the east wall of the north aisle, near the pulpit, is of marble, and bears the following inscription :—"Near this monument lies the body of Margaret Woffington, spinster, born October 18th, 1720, who departed this life March 28th, 1760, aged thirty-nine years." The arms on the monument are, *Or, three leopards' faces, gules.* On the lower compartment is another inscription, as follows :—" In the same grave lies the body of Master Horace Cholmondely, son of the Honourable Robert Cholmondely and of Mary Cholmondely, sister of the said Margaret Woffington, aged six months." A reference to Sir Egerton Brydges' "Peerage of England" shows "Master Horace" to have been born February 18th, 1753, and baptised March 16th following at St. George's, Hanover Square. The date of this sepulture, therefore, was August, 1753.

The parish registers commence in Elizabeth's reign, the first baptism and burial recorded being dated 1558, and the first marriage three years later.

In 1635, one Matthew Rendall, curate of Teddington, as mentioned in Neal's "History of the Puritans," was denounced by an aggrieved parishioner, and suspended by the bishop under the High Commission for preaching long sermons ! Possibly many congregations would be glad if such a penalty could be inflicted now for the same offence.

At the Reformation several acres of land which had been left to the church for the maintenance of services then voted superstitious were surrendered to the king, who gave them out among his courtiers or devoted them to the payment of his personal debts. At this time there were seventy-two "houseling people," that is, Easter communicants, and "but one priest found to serve the cure": words which would seem to imply that the parish had not gained by the recent changes in religion.

John Cosens, DD., the author of "The Tears of Twickenham," "Œconomics of Beauty," and other poems, was Dr. Hales' successor in the incumbency of Teddington.

The church of St. Peter and St. Paul, in Upper Teddington, was partly erected in 1866, and completed (with the exception of the tower and spire) in 1873, under the incumbency of the Rev. Daniel Trinder. The edifice is constructed of yellow brick, with dressings of red brick; it is in the Early English style of architecture, and was built from the designs of the late Mr. G. E. Street, R.A. Close by is a commodious school-house, of similar architecture, which was built in 1874. In 1875 a new school chapel was erected at Teddington Wick.

Lewis, in his "Topographical Dictionary" (1835,) mentions here large bleaching-grounds and manufactories of candles and of spermaceti; but these no longer exist.

That rapid strides have been made of late years in the growth of Teddington and the number of its inhabitants will be easily seen when it is stated that in 1835 the population was given as 895, whilst between the years 1861 and 1871 it had increased from 1,183 to 4,063. The town—for such it is—has now grown sufficiently large to have its Mutual Instruction Society, which is well supported, and also a working-man's club and horticultural and building societies; and will shortly have its town hall.

Among the "eminent inhabitants" of Teddington whose names have not already been mentioned above was William Penn, the celebrated Quaker, and founder of the colony of Pennsylvania. The son of Admiral Sir William Penn, he was born in London in 1644, and studied at Christ Church, Oxford, but was expelled from the University in consequence of the enthusiasm which he displayed in the new doctrine of Quakerism, which had its rise about that time. It was from Teddington, in 1688, that Penn dated the letter in which he rebutted the charge of being a Papist which had been brought against him. Francis Manning, the author of a translation from the French of a "Life of Theodosius the Great," lived here for many years; and, according to an entry in Sir Joshua Reynolds's pocket-book, quoted in Leslie and Taylor's "Life of Reynolds," John Wilkes—of whom we have already spoken at some length in our account of Brentford (see page 38, *ante*)—occupied for a short time "an out-of-the-way lodging in the second turning past Teddington Church" whilst still an outlaw, and during a surreptitious visit to England.

In Walpole's time there lived here a gentleman named Prescott, who used to beat his wife so unmercifully that she ran away, aided by a groom, and shortly afterwards "swore the peace" against her husband. The case came before Lord Mansfield, who asked the groom if he had not helped his mistress to escape. "Yes, my lord; and my master has never yet thanked me for it!" was the cool reply. "Why should he thank you, my lad?" asked his lordship. "Because, my lord, if I had not done so, he would have murdered his wife, and then he would have been hanged for it." Lord Mansfield and the Court were so amused that they acquitted the witty lad of all blame for his share in the transaction.

The river Thames at Teddington, as we have already observed, is a familiar friend to the "brethren of the angle," who have long regarded the neighbourhood and the "weir" as among the pleasantest of all their river memories. "These memories," writes Mr. S. Carter Hall, in his "Book of the Thames," "are in truth very pleasant, for, although it has 'fallen from its high estate,' and is by no means as productive of sport as it used to be, there is still plenty to be had in several 'pitches,' where abound all the various denizens of the populous river, while enjoyment is ever enhanced by associations of the past," which are suggested at every spot of ground beside which the punt is pushed or moored. The venerable and picturesque lock of Teddington—the first, by the way, to be met with in the voyage up the river, and one which has often been made the subject of an artist's sketch—has given way before the "march of improvement" to a new and more substantial structure of masonry. In bygone times, before the construction of bridges, locks, and other obstructions, the tide, in all probability, ascended much higher than Teddington. At the present time it flows but feebly some way below this parish, and high water here is nearly an hour and a half later than at London Bridge, a distance of nineteen and a half miles.

It may be interesting to know that the "intake" of all the London Water Companies, as authorised by the Metropolis Water Act of 1852, must be above Teddington Lock. A Government Commission, consisting of Professors Graham, Miller, and Hoffman, in 1852-4, reported that enormous supplies of spring water were to be obtained at a very small cost from the chalk strata surrounding London; but the companies, evidently led on through a feeling of self-interest, persisted in still having recourse to the Thames, though they were forced to have their "intake" above Teddington

Lock, which still contains many particles of impurity, and therefore seeds of disease, brought down from the towns higher up the river.

In the pages of OLD AND NEW LONDON* we have spoken of the interesting ceremony called "Swan-upping" on the Thames, a custom which has been observed for upwards of four centuries. As the duties of the "swan-upper," or marker, however, are confined principally to that portion of the river which lies above Teddington Lock, we may be pardoned for again reverting to the subject. From Teddington to Oxford, over the whole hundred and odd miles of which old Father Thames winds his silvery course, there is perhaps no prettier sight than a herd of swans. The royal bird, "floating double, swan and shadow," sails up and down the long reaches, and in and out among the eyots, a thing of wonderful beauty and grace—a noble ornament to a noble river. Poets of all ages and all countries, from the mythical Orpheus of Thrace down to our own poet laureate, have claimed the creature as their own. Apart altogether from his exquisite beauty and majesty, and the conscious grace with which, "with arched neck between his white wings mantling," he "proudly rows his state with oared feet," tradition claims for the bird of Apollo the divine gift of song, and tells us how, when the swan seeks the waste, to die there unseen and alone, "her awful jubilant voice, with a music strange and manifold, flows forth on a carol free and bold, as when a mighty people rejoice with shawms, and cymbals, and harps of gold." Nor is it poets alone who delight to honour the noble bird, and to claim in him a special property. Ever since the lion-hearted Richard brought back to England from the fair island of Cyprus the first "cobs" and "pens" that ever floated on the Thames, the swan has remained a royal bird, guarded jealously by special statutes, and with a royal swanherd deputed to watch over him. The subject can only keep swans by special licence, along with which he has also granted to him a swan mark, or device, to be cut with a sharp knife in the upper bill. But our swanholders have sadly fallen off since the days of "good Queen Bess," when "close upon a thousand corporations and individuals" were privileged to keep "a game of swans." A swannery is now as rare a sight as even a heronry itself. Our old customs and institutions are dying out, and swans, being fowl, must go the way of all flesh. The Corporation of Oxford has a swannery by prescription, although no swans

---

* See Vol. III., p. 302.

are now reared, and it is doubtful whether the privilege has not long since abated. The noble Abbotsbury "game" is still kept up by the Earls of Ilchester, in Dorset. And upon the Thames, the Crown, conjointly with the Worshipful Companies of Vintners and Dyers, still sends out on each 1st of August an organised expedition of "swan-uppers" to catch and "nick" the young birds. But even thus, the numbers of our "games" are sadly decreasing. Some century and a half ago the Vintners' Company had no less than 500 cobs between London Bridge and Staines. There are now little more than 500 birds, cobs, pens, cygnets, and grey birds, all told, between London Bridge and Cricklade Weir. Of these, the Queen owns 397, the Vintners' Company 55, and the Dyers' Company 67.

Turning once more inland, we will now make our way towards the historic region of Hampton and Hampton Court.

At the extreme south-western end of Teddington are the entrance-gates and lodge of Bushey Park. The park is upwards of a thousand acres in extent, and with its noble avenue of horse-chestnut trees, more than a mile in length, forms a stately approach to Hampton Court Palace.

Bushey Park, lying as it does on the confines of both Teddington and Hampton, is actually in the former parish, and forms a good connecting link between them and the avenues, which were planted by William III. in true Dutch fashion. The principal avenue has four others on each side of it. The breadth of these nine avenues is upwards of 560 feet, and they cover nearly seventy acres. These avenues are perhaps unequalled for extent and beauty in Europe. At nearly the farther extremity of the avenue is a circular piece of water, called the Diana Water, from a fine bronze fountain of that goddess, seven feet in height, placed in the centre of it. It stands on a block of statuary marble, and is surrounded by small figures, also of bronze.

Immediately to the right of the entrance to Bushey Park stands the house formerly occupied by William IV. He lived here for thirty-six years like a country gentleman, superintending his farm and entertaining his neighbours with great hospitality. His Majesty, whilst residing here, like a true sailor, had a part of the foremast of the *Victory*, against which Nelson was standing when he received his fatal wound, deposited in a small temple in the grounds, from which it was removed to the upper end of the dining-room, where it supported a bust of Nelson. Mr. Jesse tells us in his delightful "Gleanings" that a large shot had

passed completely through this part of the mast, and that while it stood in the temple a pair of robins had built their nest in the shot-hole, and had reared a brood of young robins, to which the king and Queen Adelaide were much attached.

The original lodge was inhabited by Bradshaw the regicide, in the time of Oliver Cromwell. Charles II., it is on record, gave it to a keeper who rejoiced in the name of Podger, and who had shown his loyalty during the troubles of the Commonwealth; and he afterwards partook of an entertainment from him at the lodge. On taking down the old church at Hampton a few years ago, Podger's tomb was discovered under the reading-desk; it is now put up in the new church. The present building is a square, substantial brick edifice; it was erected by Lord Halifax in the reign of George II.

Lord North lived here while premier, and used to gather around his hospitable and jovial table at Bushey Park the distinguished men of all countries; and here he would spend his Saturdays and Sundays among his children, throwing aside all the cares of official life.

The great feature of Bushey Park is its splendid avenue of chestnut-trees, already mentioned, which forms a great attraction to Londoners and others during the early summer months, when their branches are heavily laden with the spiry flowers, and the leaves are of their brightest colour. With the exception of its avenue, Bushey Park is somewhat scantily supplied with trees, though in the open space behind the lodge there are some fine oaks and thorns, survivors of the forest of Middlesex. There are still several hundred head of deer in Bushey Park. Norden, who wrote an account of Hampton Court in the reign of Queen Elizabeth, describes the parks belonging to the palace, and says that they were surrounded with brick walls, except on the north side, which was protected by the river. One park was a place for "deare," and the other for "hares"—a distinction which is worth noticing. Other writers have spoken of the "Old Park," the "New Park," the "Middle" or "North Park," and the "Hare Warren"; at present, however, the royal demesne is known only by the special names of the "Home Park" and "Bushey Park." As there is most wood in the former, it is probable that to it was originally applied the name of the "Deer Park," and that Bushey Park—which, no doubt, took its name from being dotted over with *bushes*, and on that account made a capital retreat for hares and rabbits—was known as the "Hare Warren."

"Among the records preserved by the steward of the manor of Hampton," observes Mr. Jesse, in his "Gleanings in Natural History," "is a strong remonstrance from the inhabitants of that place to Oliver Cromwell, complaining of his having encroached upon their rights by adding a part of their common to Bushey Park. This remonstrance seems to have had its effect, as a grant of some land in the neighbourhood was made over to them in lieu of what had been taken from them. The ancient boundaries of Bushey Park are found in several places."

There is a right-of-way, in the shape of a footpath, through Bushey Park, which had been closed for many years during part of the reign of George II. This right-of-way, however, was re-established by the energy and determination of an inhabitant of the former place, one Timothy Bennet, who carried on the humble avocation of a shoemaker, and who was "unwilling," as was his favourite expression, "to leave the world worse than he found it." Brewer, in his "Account of Middlesex," suspiciously intimates that this "village patriot" must have been backed by some persons of wealth or influence, else he would not have carried his point. The story is that Timothy Bennet consulted an attorney upon the practicability of recovering this road for the public good, and the probable expense of a legal process for that purpose. "I do not mean to cobble the job," said Timothy, "for I have seven hundred pounds, and I should be willing to give the awl, that great folks might not keep the upper-leather wrongfully." The lawyer informed him that no such sum would be necessary to try the right; "then," said the worthy shoe-maker, "as sure as soles are soles, I'll stick to them to the last." And Lord Halifax, the then Ranger of Bushey Park, was immediately served with the regular notice of action; upon which his lordship sent for Timothy, and on his entering the lodge, his lordship said with some warmth, "And who are you, that have the assurance to meddle in this affair?" "My name, my lord, is Timothy Bennet, shoemaker, of Hampton Wick. I remember, an't please your lordship, to have seen, when I was a young man, sitting at work, the people cheerfully pass my shop to Kingston market; but now, my lord, they are forced to go round about, through a hot sandy road, ready to faint beneath their burthens, and I am unwilling to leave the world worse than I found it. This, my lord, I humbly represent, is the reason why I have taken this work in hand." "Begone," replied his lordship, "you are an impertinent fellow." However, upon mature reflection, we are told, his lordship, convinced of the equity of the claim, beginning to compute the shame of a defeat by a shoemaker, desisted from his opposition, notwithstanding the opinion of the Crown lawyers, and re-opened the road, which is enjoyed by the public without molestation to this day. Honest Timothy died about two years after, in the 77th year of his age, and was followed to the grave by all the populace of his native village; and such was the estimation in which he was held that a mezzotint portrait of him was published, bearing an inscription which sets forth that this man succeeded in putting the law of the land into operation, to the furtherance of British liberty, because "he was unwilling to leave the world worse than he found it."

CHAPTER XI.

HAMPTON.

" Whose turf, whose shade, whose flowers among
Wanders the hoary Thames along
His silver-winding way."
GRAY.

Situation and Boundaries of the Parish—Early History of the Manor—It passes into the hands of Cardinal Wolsey—The Parish Church—The School of Industry—The Grammar School--Princess Frederica's Convalescent Home—Lady Bourchier's Convalescent Home—Noted Hostelries—Hampton Racecourse—Boxing Matches—Hampton Bridge—Thames Angling—Southwark and Vauxhall, and the Lambeth Water Companies—David Garrick and his Villa—Sir Christopher Wren's Residence at Hampton Court Green—Holland the Actor—Lord Sandwich—Sir Andrew Halliday—Sir Richard Steele—Hampton Wick—Abbs Court.

THE village of Hampton is somewhat irregular in shape, having grown up as a sort of fringe round the edge of Bushey Park. 'It occupies the outer curve of a long reach of the Thames, and extends from Hampton Wick on the east to Sunbury on the west, including within its bounds the whole of

Hampton Court Palace and a portion of Bushey Park.

The place is mentioned in Domesday Book by the name of Hamntone, and it is stated that the manor in the reign of Edward the Confessor, belonged to Earl Algar; it is added that the sum of "three shillings was payable as dues for fishing and laying nets in the Thames;" and that "the whole value of the manor was but forty shillings." In 1211, Lady Joan Grey, of Hampton, left her manor and manor-house there, with several thousand acres of land, to the Knights Hospitallers of St. John

Innworth, Esher, Oatlands, together with the manors within the limits of Hampton Court Chase, and also the manors of Hampton, Hanworth, Feltham, and Teddington, and even Hounslow Heath.

The parish church, dedicated to St. Mary, at the entrance of the village, is a plain, commonplace edifice, dating its erection from 1830, when it was built in the place of the old church, which had become dilapidated. The old building was constructed chiefly of brick, and, according to the author of the "Beauties of England and Wales," "was evidently composed at various periods." The

HAMPTON, FROM THE RIVER.

of Jerusalem. "In the year 1180 there was at Hampton a 'Preceptory,' in which resided a sister of the Order of St. John. She was removed, with other sisters of the same order, from Preceptories in various places, to a convent at Buckland, in Somerset.*

Of this estate Cardinal Wolsey obtained a lease for ninety-nine years from Sir Thomas Docwra, the last prior. On the suppression of the Order of St. John, the Crown annexed it, and in 1540 the Parliament created Hampton Court a separate "honour." Some idea of the vast extent of the manor may be formed when it is stated that it comprised within its bounds the lesser manors of Walton-upon-Thames, Walton Legh, Byflete, Weybridge, East and West Moulsey, Sandon, Weston,

chancel bore marks of considerable antiquity, and was partly formed of stone and flint. A somewhat rough and coarse picture of the old church, painted about a century ago by a local artist, shows a red brick building of the conventional type, so common along the Middlesex shore of the Thames, with a heavy square tower, but no marks which would help us to assign it to any particular era. In front is a heavy-looking gate, from which stone steps lead down to the river-side. The new church is constructed of white brick, in the Perpendicular style of architecture, and it consists of a nave and aisles, and a square pinnacled tower at the western end. The church contains several interesting monuments, preserved from the old church. At the entrance is one under a canopy, supported by Corinthian columns, to Mrs. Sibel Penn, nurse to Edward VI.: it comprises a tomb, with her effigy, arms, and a

---

* "Dugdale's Monasticon," vol. ii. p 554.

long rhyming epitaph. Mrs. Penn died in 1652, and the inscription on her monument, close to the entrance, tells us that—

" To Court she called was to foster up a king
    Whose helping hand long lingering sutes to spedie end did bring."

Here is buried Richard Tickell, a political writer, grandson of Tickell the poet. "He distinguished himself," says Mr. John Fisher, in his "Environs of London," "by publishing a political pamphlet, called 'Anticipation,' in which the debate on the king's speech at the opening of Parliament was so successfully anticipated that some of the members who had not seen the pamphlet are said to have made use of almost the very words put into their mouths." Tickell committed suicide in 1793. According to a letter from Walpole to Miss Berry, he "threw himself from one of the uppermost windows of the palace at Hampton Court, an immense height." Here, too, was buried Edward Podger, whom we have mentioned in our account of Bushey Park.* He was Page of Honour to Charles I., Groom of the Bedchamber to Charles II., and died in 1714, according to Le Neve, "at the age of 96, of the anguish of cutting teeth, he having cut four new teeth, and had several ready to cut, which so inflamed his gums that he died." There is a memorial of David Garrick, nephew to the great actor, with an inscription from the pen of Mrs. Hannah Moore ; and another to the memory of Richard, son of George Cumberland, the celebrated dramatic writer. John Beard, a famous singer, who died in 1791, lies buried here. He left the stage on his marriage, half a century previously, with Lady Henrietta Herbert, daughter of James, Earl of Waldegrave, and widow of Lord Edward Herbert; some years later, however, he returned to the stage, and acquired great popularity. In 1759 he married, as his second wife, a daughter of John Rich, the patentee of Covent Garden Theatre, to the management of which he succeeded on the death of his father-in-law.

The churchyard is old, and is full of most aristocratic corpses. Here lie Lord Charles Fitzroy, Lady Emily Ponsonby, Lady Roberts, Lord and Lady Munster, Lady Guillamore, and innumerable Pagets, &c., who died at the palace, and whose bodies were brought hither for interment.

Amongst the celebrities buried here are Thomas Rosoman,† the well-known owner of Sadler's Wells Theatre (1782), and his wife (1776), the latter with a poetical inscription ; the Rev. Dr. Mortimer,

late head master of the City of London School ; Huntington Shaw, the artist (1710), who wrought the fine iron gates at the entrance of Hampton Court palace ; Dr. Smethurst (who was tried for poisoning a lady), and also his first wife ; Thomas Ripley, architect, who designed the Admiralty.

In a nameless grave near the public path, at the north-east corner of the churchyard, lie the remains of a woman who enjoys the unenviable reputation of having stirred up mischief between Lord Byron and his wife, and so having caused their separation. How she did so must for ever remain a mystery. Her name, be it here recorded, was Mary Anne Clermont. The mischievous old maid is described in the register as " of Hampton Wick." She died May 11th, 1850, at the age of 77. It is said that before living at Hampton Wick she resided at Walton-on-Thames. Our readers will remember the scathing lines beginning—

" Born in a garret, in a kitchen bred."

In the street leading away from the river and the church towards New Hampton is a School of Industry, which bears on its front the date 1804. The street consists of private houses in good and large grounds, with here and there a shop between them.

The Grammar School, founded in the middle of the sixteenth century, is well endowed, and has a branch school at Hampton Wick. At one time the village abounded in private schools ; at one of these Lord Dufferin and Sir Frederick Roberts were brought up.

As might be expected from the number of wealthy families who have lived within its borders, Hampton is fairly well off for parochial charities ; one of the most useful of these is the Princess Frederica's Convalescent Home for Married Women after Childbirth. Lady Bourchier has a Convalescent Home here, at Hope Cottage, for four or five cases ; it was established in 1868, and is intended " for female servants, needlewomen, &c., on payment of a small weekly fee." At Tangley Park, in the immediate neighbourhood, is a Female Orphan Home, which was instituted in 1855, and has done much good work in the support and education of destitute orphan girls.

Hampton is within fifteen miles of London, and has its railway-station on a branch of the London and South-Western Railway, and also a station on the Thames Valley Railway. It can boast of several good inns and places of refreshment for visitors, notably the " Red Lion," the " Greyhound," and the " Bell," the last-mentioned house being much frequented by anglers.

---

* See *ante*, p. 131.
† His name is perpetuated in Rosoman Street, Clerkenwell.

Here is another inn, bearing for its sign "The Widow's Struggle," a sign which, as Mr. Larwood says, in his "History of Signboards," "may possibly be the romance of a life. Who knows?"

Mr. Larwood tells us that the "Toy" Inn, at Hampton—a name probably dating from the frivolous age of the second Charles—used to be a favourite resort with Londoners till 1857, when it was pulled down in order to make room for the erection of private houses. Tokens of this house in the seventeenth century are in existence. Lysons also tells us that "in the survey of 1653, in the Augmentation Office, mention is made of a piece of pasture-ground near the river, called the Toying Place, the site probably of a well-known inn near the bridge now called the Toy." The "Toy" is said to have been built by Oliver Cromwell, as a dormitory for his Roundhead soldiers, of whom he was very fond—but at a distance, for he did not like admitting them into the palace.

What is called the Hampton Racecourse is on the opposite side of the river, on an open common, known as Moulsey Hurst (in Surrey), and is approached by a ferry across the Thames. The summer and autumn races here bring down a large and motley assemblage of low betting-men from London.

This spot in former times was famous—or rather, infamous—for "boxing matches," and at such times was the resort of large numbers of the votaries of "fisticuffs" and patrons of the "noble art of self-defence." That the pugilists themselves thought much of their performance on those occasions may be inferred from the following notice, which was printed in May, 1817:— "Thomas Oliver begs leave to inform his friends and the public that he regrets the disappointment of his combat with Painter, not only as regards himself, but that the amateurs should be disappointed. Oliver having been taken by the authority of a warrant, he is held in sureties to keep the peace. In justice to himself and regard for his friends, he begs leave to state that he is in good training, and is ready to depart either for Calais or Waterloo, the field of English glory!!!"

A bridge over the Thames connects Hampton Court and East Moulsey. The first bridge here was erected in pursuance of an Act of Parliament, passed in 1750, in favour of one James Clarke, the then lessee of the ferry under the Crown. It was a light wooden structure, of eleven arches, or spans; the present structure is an iron girder bridge of five spans, and was built in 1865.

"Many years since," says the "Book of the Court," "a man named Feltham rented Hampton Court Bridge, where he made several alterations. As he was anxious to thrive by his tolls, he kept the gate locked when nothing was passing. One morning the royal hunt came across Hounslow Heath to the bridge, where the stag had taken water and swum across. The hounds passed the gate without ceremony, followed by a large party, crying 'The King!' Feltham opened his gate, which he closed again after they had rushed through without paying; when a more numerous and showy party came up, vociferating more loudly, 'The King!' He stood with the gate in his hand, though menaced with horsewhips. 'I'll tell you what,' said he, 'hang me if I open my gate again till I see your money. I pay £400 a year for this bridge, and I laid out £1,000 upon it. I've let King George through, God bless him: I know of no other king in England. If you have brought the King of France, hang me if I let him through without the blunt!' Suddenly the king himself appeared among his attendants; Feltham made his reverence, opened his gate again, and the whole company went over to Moulsey Hurst, where the hounds were at fault. The king, chagrined for the moment, sent back Lord Sandwich to know the reason of the interruption. The man explained the mistake, and added that when royal hunts passed over this bridge a guinea had been always paid, which franked all, and that this was 'his first good turn.' Lord Sandwich returned to the king, but his Majesty hastily desired him to pay for all his attendants, who amounted to less than forty of the whole party. The matter was eventually satisfactorily explained to the king, who, crossing the bridge some time afterwards, on a visit to the Stadtholder, then resident at Hampton Court, pulled down the carriage window, and laughing heartily, said to old Feltham, 'No fear of the King of France coming to-day.'"

Hampton is a favourite place for pleasure-parties on the water, and on fine afternoons in summer quite a fleet of small yachts may be seen with their white sails spread upon its long and open reach. But it is even more famed as the head-quarters of the disciples of Izaak Walton.

"Hampton," writes Mr. Thorne, in his "Handbook of the Environs of London," "may be considered the head-quarters of the Thames Angling Preservation Society; and here and a little higher up on the Surrey side are the ponds and streamlets made by the Thames Conservancy, and maintained by the Society, for hatching and rearing fish ova—chiefly salmon, grayling, and trout. The young fish are kept in the streams for eight or nine months, when, being considered able to take care of themselves, they are turned into the river. About 50,000 fish are annually sent into the Thames from these ponds; and anglers acknowledge a decided improvement in the fishing. The river here is strictly preserved along what is known as Hampton Deep, which extends from the lawn of Garrick Villa to Tumbling Bay, 960 yards. From 20 lbs. to 30 lbs. of roach or perch are accounted a good day's fishing."

The Southwark and Vauxhall and the Lambeth Water Companies derive their supplies from the Thames above Hampton; but year by year the drainage-ground or watershed of the Thames is being more densely populated, and consequently a larger quantity of pollution finds its way into the river. So bad is the condition of the Thames water, though artificially filtered, that the Commissioners appointed to inquire into the domestic water supply of Great Britain recommended, in their report to her Majesty in 1874, "that the Thames should, as early as possible, be abandoned as a source of water for domestic uses, and that the sanction of the Government should be in future withheld from all schemes involving the expenditure of more capital for the supply of Thames water to London;" and the press and many members of both Houses of Parliament have strongly urged the necessity of acting on this recommendation.

A large male otter, measuring forty-seven inches from snout to tail, was shot in the Thames here in January, 1880.

The western part of Hampton is called Thames Street, because it extends along the river in the direction of Sunbury. Its pleasant rural aspect is much spoiled by the three gigantic reservoirs of as many water companies—the West Middlesex, the Grand Junction, and the Southwark and Vauxhall. It is said that they take from the river upwards of 100,000,000 gallons of water daily; but this can hardly be the case, as they do not supply anything like the whole area of the metropolis. Their tall shafts are anything rather than an ornament. Beyond them is the new Grammar School, a building of the domestic Tudor style.

At the northern extremity of the parish a considerable village, called New Hampton, has sprung into existence within the last few years. The district was made into a separate ecclesiastical parish in 1864. The church, dedicated to St. James, consists of a chancel, nave, and north aisle, and is a red brick building in the Early English style.

When we have said that the present church is built of brick in the Gothic style of George IV., we have really described it. It has no chancel, but spacious galleries, and pointed windows without mullions or bracery. In fact, it is simply an edifice of the churchwarden style of art. The monuments removed from the former structure adorn its walls, but many of these are so "skied" as to be unreadable from the floor. On either side of the communion-table are the Moses and Aaron of the last century, and also two oak chairs elaborately carved by the hands of Dr. Merewether, late Dean of Hereford, a former curate of Hampton.

Among the vicars of Hampton was Dr. Samuel Croxall, Chancellor and Canon of Hereford, and Archdeacon of Salop. This gentleman was the author of an edition of "Æsop's Fables," a dramatic piece called *The Fair Circassian*, and several political pamphlets in the Whig interest, written during the reign of Queen Anne.

Hampton appears to have been classic ground as far back as the reign of Elizabeth; at all events, Ben Jonson, in his "Epigrams," speaks of his own retirement—

"'Mongst Hampton's shades and Phœbus' grove of bays."

At a short distance eastward from the church, and close by the river-side, is a spot which has long been held sacred by lovers of the Thespian art—namely, "Garrick's Villa." The house, although separated from the river by a lawn and the roadway, forms a prominent feature in the landscape on approaching Hampton by water, its tall central portico and pediment standing out boldly amid the foliage of the surrounding trees.

Garrick purchased the house and grounds in the middle of the last century, and made many alterations and improvements in them. To the house, which was originally distinguished as Hampton House, considerable additions were made from the designs of Adam; and several purchases having been made by Garrick for the purpose of extending his premises, the gardens were laid out with much taste, and under his own direction.

Hampton House was thus described by a local writer of Garrick's time :—" It stands in the town of Hampton, but is quite concealed by a high wall. Nothing can be neater or fitted up with more decent elegance than this little box; every room shows the true taste and genius of the owner; the whole is like a fine miniature picture, perfectly well finished, though exceedingly small. The drawing-room is, however, of a handsome size, and may be called a large room; 'tis hung with canvas painted in all greens in the most beautiful colours imaginable, and decorated with carvings of the same colour. The garden is laid out in the modern taste, with a passage cut under the road to a lawn, where, close by the water-side, stands the Temple of Shakespeare. This is a brick building in the form of a dome, with a handsome porch, supported by fine pillars. Opposite to the entrance, in a niche, stands a statue of the poet by Roubilliac, as large as life, at his desk in the attitude of thought. The figure is bold and striking ; the drapery finished in the most elegant manner." The statue of Shakespeare was bequeathed by Garrick to the British Museum, and now stands in the hall of that institution. Walpole proposed to adorn the outside of the Temple with a motto from Horace—

"Quod spiro et placeo, si placeo, tuum est,"

along with the following English version, spun out, as will be seen, into four lines :—

"That I spirit have and nature,
That sense breathes in every feature ;
That I please, if please I do,
Shakespeare, all I owe to you."

At Garrick's villa, Henry Angelo, when a boy at Eton, spent one at least of his summer holidays. He describes the house as "standing by the roadside, and having (like Pope's villa at Twickenham) a short tunnel under the road, connecting the grounds with the classic summer-house by the river-side which enshrined the bust of Shakespeare."

"A garden on a flat, it is said, ought to be highly and variously ornamented, in order to occupy the mind, and prevent its regretting the insipidity of an uniform plan. The effect of such a walk is admirably exemplified in Mr. Garrick's polished ground at Hampton ; but surely it would have been time enough to have represented Shakespeare there in stone or marble when the very genius of Shakespeare no longer presided."— Cradock's "Memoirs."

Garrick first saw the light of day on the 20th of February, 1716, at the Angel Inn, Hereford, at which city his father, Captain Peter Garrick, of the Old Buffs, was then on a recruiting expedition. His mother, whose maiden name was Arabella Clough, was the daughter of one of the vicars of Lichfield Cathedral. David received his early tuition under the care of Mr. Hunter, master of the Grammar School of Lichfield, and in 1735 he became a pupil of Dr. (then plain Mr.) Samuel Johnson, with whom, in March, 1736, he set out for the metropolis. Shortly after his arrival in London he entered himself on the rolls of the Society of Lincoln's Inn, with the view of following the profession of the law. On the death of his father, however, he commenced business as a wine merchant, in partnership with his elder brother, Peter Garrick. This partnership was soon dissolved, and in 1741 David Garrick finally resolved to adopt the profession of the stage, and, under the assumed name of Lyddal, made his first appearance at Ipswich as Aboan, in the play of *Oroonoko*. So great was his success in that character, that he was induced by the manager of the Ipswich Theatre to make his *début* in London, at the theatre in Goodman's Fields, of which he was also the proprietor. Here, in the character of Richard III., Garrick at once established his reputation as an actor.

His fame, indeed, was such, that Drury Lane and Covent Garden were soon deserted. Quin was jealous of his success, remarking, in his queer way, that "Garrick was a new religion ; Whitfield was followed for a time, but they would all come to Church again !" Garrick, who had a happy talent in pointing an epigram, gave this reply :—

"Pope Quin, who damns all churches but his own,
Complains that *Heresy* corrupts the town ;
Schism, he cries, has turn'd the nation's brain,
But eyes will open, and to Church again !
Thou great Infallible, forbear to roar,
Thy bulls and errors are rever'd no more ;
When doctrines meet with general approbation,
It is not *Heresy*, but—*Reformation !*"

At the close of the season, in May, 1742, Garrick played for three nights at Drury Lane Theatre, and then set off for Dublin, accompanied by Mrs. Woffington. In Ireland he sustained his reputation, and so great was the crowd at the theatre that, in conjunction with the heat of the weather, an epidemic ensued which was called "the Garrick fever." In the following October Garrick returned to London, and commenced an engagement at Drury Lane in Otway's tragedy of *The Orphan*. In 1745 he was for a short time joint manager, with Mr. Sheridan, of a theatre in Dublin, but in 1746 he again returned to London, and was engaged by Mr. Rich, the patentee of Covent Garden Theatre. On the close of that engagement, he purchased, in conjunction with Mr. Lacy, the Theatre Royal Drury Lane, which he opened in September, 1747, with the play of *The Merchant of Venice*, Dr. Johnson writing a prologue for the occasion.

In 1749 Garrick married Eva Maria Violette, the daughter of a respectable citizen of Vienna. She had been educated as a dancer, and had made her first appearance at Drury Lane some three years previously. Her real family name was Veigel, but she assumed the name of Violette by command of the Empress Maria Theresa,

Mrs. Garrick was said to be "the most agreeable woman in England." Sterne, who saw her among the beauties of Paris in the Tuileries Gardens, declared " she could annihilate them all in a single turn." Even Horace Walpole could forsake his cynicism, and say of her that her " behaviour is all sense and all sweetness." "During the twenty-eight years of their married life," observes a writer in *Chambers's Journal*, "David was not so much the husband as the lover ; and his affection was rewarded with a love as true and as constant as his own. Mrs. Garrick survived her husband more than forty years, and for at least thirty of these she would not allow the room in which David died to be opened. Buried, at her own re-quest, in her wedding sheets, she occupies the same grave with her hus-band at the base of Shakespeare's statue, "un-til the day dawn and the shadows flee away. Doubt-less a helpmate so at-tractive, and so congenial and pure, greatly aided the actor in striving to attain his ideal."

In September, 1769, Garrick put into execu-tion his favourite scheme of the jubilee in honour of Shakespeare, at Strat-ford-on-Avon, and pro-duced a pageant on the subject at Drury Lane in the following month. In June, 1776, having been manager of Drury Lane Theatre for nearly thirty years, Garrick took his leave of the stage in the character of Don Felix in *The Wonder*.

Garrick died at his house in the Adelphi on the 20th of January, 1779, in the sixty-fifth year of his age, his disorder gradually increasing, and admit-ting of no remedy. His physicians knew not how to designate his illness. Observing many of them, the day before his death, in his apartment, he asked who they were ; being told they were physicians, he shook his head, and repeated these lines of Horatio, in the *Fair Penitent* : —

    " Another and another still succeeds,
      And the last *Fool* is welcome as the former ! "

Few men have been the subjects of more epi-grams, repartees, and *bon mots* than David Garrick, and few men living in the society of the witty and the learned have had more poetry addressed to them. Dr. Barnard, Dean of Derry, Johnson's friend, for instance, thus apostrophises him :—

    " The art of pleasing teach me, Garrick,
      Thou who reversest odes Pindaric,
        A second time read o'er ;
    Oh, could we read thee backward too,
    Last thirty years thou should'st review
      And charm us thirty more !"

From the *Gentleman's Magazine* for 1761 we cull the following :—

    " Says *Garrick*, amongst other sociable chat,
    What could I without *Shakespeare* do ? tell me that."

It was replied—

    " Great connexions you have with each other,'tis true :
    But, *now* — what can Shakespeare do, sir, without you ?"

The following colloquial epigram appeared about the same time :—

    " *Wilmot*.

    " You should call at his house, or should send him a card,
    Can Garrick alone be so cold ?

    " *Garrick*.

    " Shall I, a poor player, and still poorer bard,
    Shall folly with Camden make bold ?
    What joy can I give him, dear Wilmot, declare :
    Promotion no honours can bring ;
    To him the Great Seals are but labour and care.
    Wish joy to your country and king."

GARRICK.

Wishing Sir Joshua Reynolds to make one of a party to dine with him at Hampton, and finding some difficulty in persuading him to come so far from Leicester Fields, Garrick said to him, "Well, only come, and you shall choose your dinner, though that is a favour I would not grant to everybody with such an insatiable *palette* as yours."

"David would indulge some few friends "—says Charles Dibdin—" but it was very rare—with what he used to call his *rounds*. This he did by standing behind a chair, and converging into his face every possible kind of passion, blending one into the other, and, as it were, shadowing them with a pro-digious number of gradations. At one moment you laughed, at another you cried; now he terrified you, and presently you conceived yourself something horrible, he seemed so terrified *at* you. Afterwards he drew his features into the appearance of such dignified wisdom that Minerva might have been proud of the portrait; and then—degrading, yet admirable, transition—he became a driveller. In short, his face was what he obliged you to fancy it—age, youth, plenty, poverty, everything it assumed."

The following lines were written by Garrick to a conversation with him said, "Dear sir, I wish you were a little *taller;*" to which he replied, "My dear madam, how happy should I be, did I stand *higher* in your estimation."

"Will your figures be as large as life, Mr. Foote?" asked a titled lady, when he was about to bring out at the Haymarket his comedy of *The Primitive Puppet Show.* "No, my lady," replied Foote, "they will be hardly larger than Garrick."

Garrick having a green-room wrangle with Mrs.

HAMPTON HOUSE.
(*From a Print published in* 1787.)

nobleman who asked him if he did not intend being in Parliament :—

> "More than content with what my labours gain,
> Of *public favour* tho' a little vain,
> Yet not so vain my mind, so madly bent,
> To wish to *play* the *fool* in parliament;
> In each dramatic unity to err,
> Mistaking *time* and *place*, and *character!*
> Were it my fate to quit the mimic art,
> I'd ' strut and fret ' no more in any part;
> No more in *public scenes* would I engage,
> Or wear the *cap* and *mask* of any stage." *

Garrick's stature was slightly under the middle size, but manliness, elasticity, ease, and grace, characterised his deportment. A lady one day in

Clive, after listening to all she had to say, replied, "I have heard of tartar and brimstone, and know the effects of both; but you are the *cream* of one and the *flower* of the other."

Garrick once gave at his lodgings a dinner to Harry Fielding, Macklin, Havard, Mrs. Cibber, &c., and fees to servants being then much the fashion, Macklin, and most of the company, gave Garrick's man (David, a Welshman) something at parting—some a shilling, some half-a-crown, &c., whilst Fielding, very formally, slipped a piece of paper in his hand, with something folded in the inside. When the company were all gone, David seeming to be in high glee, Garrick asked him how much he got. "I can't tell you yet, sir," said Davy, "here is half-a-crown from Mrs. Cibber, Got pless

* *Gentleman's Magazine,* 1761.

hur—here is a shilling from Mr. Macklin—here is two from Mr. Havard, &c.—and here is something more from the poet, Got pless his merry heart." By this time David had unfolded the paper, when, to his great astonishment, he saw it contained no more than one penny! Garrick felt nettled at this, and next day spoke to Fielding about the impropriety of jesting with a servant. "Jesting!" said Fielding, with a seeming surprise, "so far from it, that I meant to do the fellow a real piece of service; for had I given him a shilling or half-a-crown, I knew you would have taken it from him; but by giving him only a penny, he had a chance of calling it his own."

A gentleman asked a friend who had seen Garrick perform his first and last character if he thought him as good an actor when he took his leave of the stage at old Drury as when he first played at Goodman's Fields, he gave for an answer the following *extempore*:—

> "I saw him rising in the East
> In all his energetic glows;
> I saw him setting in the West
> In greater splendour than he rose."

By the same, on his being told Wilson was thought to be a better actor than Ned Shuter:—

> "I've very often heard it said,
> Nine tailors make a man;
> But can nine Wilsons make a Ned?
> No, bless me if they can."

It is related by a friend of Garrick that, in walking up the stage with him, until the burst of applause which followed one of his displays in *Lear* should subside, the great actor thrust his tongue in his cheek, and said in a chuckle, "Joe, this is stage feeling."

We have seen how that Garrick and Johnson came up to London with the view of starting in the "race for wealth." While the career of the former was one long-continued success, that of Johnson was anything but prosperous, the great lexicographer being at times almost on the verge of starvation. "Sudden prosperity had turned Garrick's head," writes Lord Macaulay; "continued adversity had soured Johnson's temper. Johnson saw with more envy than became so great a man the villa, the plate, the china, the Brussels carpet, which the little mimic had got by repeating what wiser men had written, and the exquisitely sensitive vanity of Garrick was galled by the thought that whilst all the rest of the world was applauding him, he could obtain from one morose cynic, whose opinion it was impossible to despise, scarcely any compliment not acidulated with scorn."

Mr. Cradock writes in his "Literary Memoirs":— "The strongest likenesses of Garrick are best preserved by Sir George Beaumont, who was intimately acquainted with him; the two drawings of Garrick, in "Richard," and "Abel Drugger," are superior, in point of resemblance, to either of the celebrated pictures, from which they are chiefly taken; the prints from them are just published by Mr. Colnaghi."

Garrick's widow continued to occupy the villa long after her husband's death, and she entertained her friends here nearly to the last. She died in the Adelphi, in the year 1822, at the age of nearly 100.

Old anglers who have fished in the Thames about here will remember at the bottom of the lawn two willows, rendered sacred by adjoining the temple erected to Shakespeare. They were planted by Garrick's own hand. In the midst of a violent storm, which proved fatal to one of them, Mrs. Garrick was seen running about, like Niobe, all tears, exclaiming, "Oh, my Garrick! my Garrick!"

A fonder pair never lived than David Garrick and his wife; when alive they might easily have claimed the Dunmow flitch of bacon.

Garrick's villa is still kept, so far as modern taste will allow, in the same state in which it was when occupied by its illustrious owner. The paintings and the sculptures on the wall are still there; their colours have been slightly renewed where necessary, and the modern furniture has been dressed in Chinese patterned chintz to correspond. The classical medallions, designed by Bentley or Wedgwood, still run round the walls below the cornices, and the marble mantelpieces, with their slight and slender carvings, remain in *statu quo*. The eastern wing and the central portion of the house are unaltered, or almost unaltered; but the old dining-room on the west of the entrance-hall is now made to do duty as a billiard-room, a new dining-room of lofty proportions having been added to the western end. In order to add this room to the house, it was found necessary to sacrifice four fine trees, under which Garrick doubtless had often sat. The lower room in the eastern wing is low, the height so gained being thrown into the upper room, which was evidently designed for music, and is still used as the chief drawing-room. Garrick's bed-room, on the first floor, has a northern aspect, and it remains but little changed.

The original statue of Shakespeare in the octagonal temple in the garden was of marble; a duplicate of it, worked in less ambitious stone, still occupies the same post of honour. The walls of the temple are adorned with stuffed fish, trophies of the rod, caught in the river adjoining. It forms a large and pleasant summer-house. It is overshadowed by a noble group of cedars, Scotch firs, and lime-trees, and the land slopes deliciously down to the river.

The villa was owned by Mrs. Garrick till her death, in the year 1822 (as above stated), when it was bought by a gentleman named Carr. He sold it to a Mr. Philips, from whom it was purchased, about 1864, by Mr. Edward Grove, whose widow still occupies it, and feels a most praiseworthy pride in the preservation of the fabric and all its associations.

The greater part of the village of Hampton forms the margin of an extensive "green," on one side of which is a broad roadway, and also a foot-path overshadowed by trees, known as the " Maids of Honour Walk."

At the end of his long and active career, Sir Christopher Wren retired in peace to his home at Hampton Court Green, his spirit not embittered by the ungrateful treatment which he had received, and simply saying that henceforth he desired to spend his days in tranquil study. Cheerful in his solitude, and as well content to die in the shade as in the blaze of his noontide fame, his son observes of him, in his " Parentalia," that " the vigour of his mind continued with a vivacity rarely found in persons of his age till within a short period of his death, and not till then could he quit the great aim of his life—to be a benefactor to mankind." The five last years of his life were spent here in complete repose, returning to London occasionally to superintend the repairs of Westminster Abbey, his only remaining employment, and filling up his leisure hours with mathematical and astronomical studies. Time, though it enfeebled his limbs, left his faculties unclouded to the last. His great delight, to the very close of life, was to be carried into the heart of the huge city to see his great work, " the beginning and completion of which," says Horace Walpole, " was an event which one cannot wonder left such an impression of content on the mind of the good old man, that it seemed to recall a memory almost deadened to every other use." Wren's death was as calm and tranquil as the tenor of his existence had been. On the 25th of February, 1723, his servant, conceiving that he slept after his dinner longer than usual, entered his room, and found him dead in his chair.

Holland, the actor, who was buried at Chiswick, was the son of a baker in this village. On the stage he was an imitator of Garrick, who so much valued him that he played the Ghost in *Hamlet* to aid his benefit. Foote, who attended his funeral, re-garded him in another light, as may be gathered from the fact that, after the interment was over, a friend accosting him with, " So, Foote, you have just come from my dear friend Holland's funeral," he replied, sarcastically and heartlessly, " Yes; we have just put the little baker into his oven."

Lord Sandwich (writes Cradock in his "Memoirs"), as First Lord of the Admiralty, in 1771-2, occupied " a retired mansion belonging to Lord Halifax, on the edge of Hampton Green."

Here, too, lived Sir Andrew Halliday, the eminent physician, to whom we owe the first general move-ment in favour of the lunatic poor. When a poor and unknown student at the University of Edinburgh, he addressed a pamphlet on the subject to Lord Henry Petty, afterwards Marquis of Lansdowne, then Chancellor of the Exchequer. A Parliamentary inquiry was appointed, which led to the passing of an Act in 1808 for the establishment of county asylums.

Not content with the town house in Bury Street already mentioned,* Sir Richard Steele, on his marriage with Mistress Scurlock in 1707, took for his wife a country house here, which he called " The Hovel," and to which he soon added a chariot and pair, enjoying also the luxury of a horse for his own riding, and going abroad like a dandy of the time, in a laced coat and a large black buckled periwig, which, Thackeray reckons, must have cost somebody fifty guineas. He was at this time a well-to-do gentleman, with the pro-ceeds of an estate in Barbadoes, and his twofold office of gentleman-waiter on H.R.H. Prince George and one of the writers of the *Gazette*. " But," adds Thackeray, " it is melancholy to relate that with these houses, and chariots and horses, and income, Captain Steele was constantly in want of money, for which his beloved bride was asking as constantly. In the course of a few pages we find the shoemaker calling for money, and some directions from the captain, who has not thirty pounds to spare. He sends his wife—'the beautifullest object in the world,' as he calls her— . . . now a guinea, then half a guinea, then a couple of guineas, then half a pound of tea; and again no money and no tea at all, but a promise that his ' darling Prue' shall have some in a day or two; with a request, perhaps, that she will send over his nightgown and shaving plate to the tem-porary lodgings where the nomadic captain is lying hidden from the bailiffs. To think that the pink and pride of chivalry should turn pale before

---

* See "Old and New London," Vol. IV., p. 202.

a writ! Addison sold the house and furniture at Hampton, and after deducting the sums which his incorrigible friend was indebted to him, handed over the residue of the proceeds of the sale to poor Dick, who was not in the least angry at Addison's summary proceedings, and, I dare say, was very glad of any sale or execution the result of which was to give him a little ready money."

Hampton Wick is that portion of the parish abutting upon the Thames at the foot of Kingston Bridge. It was made into a separate parish for ecclesiastical purposes, and the chapel of St. John the Baptist, which was built in 1830, has become the parish church of the district. It consists almost entirely of detached villas, inhabited by wealthy Londoners. In a map of 1823, a park on the west side of the village of Hampton, away from the river, appears as belonging to the late Sir C. Edmonstone, Bart.

Near Hampton Court was a pleasant seat, "Abbs Court," which belonged in Pope's days to Edward Wortley Montagu, the husband of Lady Mary Wortley Montagu, whose general avarice and habit of selling his game is satirised (under the name of Wordley) by Pope in his "Imitations of Horace":—

> "Delightful Abbs Court, if its fields afford
> Their fruits to you, confesses you its lord.
> All Wordly's hens, nay, partridges, sold to town,
> His venison too, a guinea makes your own."

CHAPTER XII.

HAMPTON COURT PALACE.

> ' Let any wight (if such a wight there be),
>   To whom thy lofty towers unknown remain,
>   Direct his steps, fair Hampton Court, to thee,
>   And view thy splendid halls : then turn again
>   To visit each proud dome by science praised,
>   ' For kings the rest ' (he'd say), ' but thou for gods wert raised.' "
>
> J. P. ANDREWS, *after* GROTIUS.

Wolsey Lord of the Manor—Terms of the Lease—Reconstruction of the House—Biographical Sketch of Wolsey—Hampton Court Presented to Henry VIII.—Grand Doings in Wolsey's Time—Henry's Wives at Hampton—The Fair Geraldine—A Woman's Promise—Queen Elizabeth at Hampton—The Maids of Honour—The Hampton Court Conference—Oliver Cromwell—Dutch William—His Alterations to the Building—The Georges at Hampton Court—Miss Chudleigh—An Application from Dr. Johnson—Later Inmates.

IN the preceding chapter we have seen how, early in the reign of Henry VIII., Cardinal Wolsey acquired a lease of the manor of Hampton from the prior of the Order of St. John of Jerusalem, or Knights Hospitallers. He had been induced to fix upon this spot as the site of his residence by certain physicians, whom he had asked to choose for him the most healthy and pleasant site within an easy distance of London, the springs of Coombe Wood, in the immediate neighbourhood of Hampton, affording water best suited to the requirements of the cardinal, who was at that time suffering from some internal complaint. In the *Gentleman's Magazine* for January, 1834, is printed a copy of the lease of the manor and manor-house, extracted from the Cottonian Manuscripts as follows:—

"This Indenture made between Sir Thomas Docwra, Priour of the Hospitall of Seynt John Jerusalem, in England, and his bredren knights of the same hospitall, upon that oone partie, and the most reverend fader in god Thomas Wulcy, Archebisshop of Yorke and primate of England upon that other partie, Witnessith that the said priour and his bredren with theire hole assent and auctorite of their Chapitur, have graunted and letten to fferme to the said Archebusshop, their manor of Hampton Courte, in the countie of Midd., with all landes and tenements, medowes, leanes, and pastures, rentes, and services, vewe of ffranciplegis, perquesites of courts, ffishing and ffishing weres, and with the waren of conys, and with all manner proufites and commodites, and other things what so ever they be in any manner of wise to the forseid manor belonging or apperteigning. To have and to holde the foreseid manor with the appurtenaunces to the foreseid most Reverend ffader in god Thomas Wulcy, Archebisshop of Yorke, and to his assignes ffro the ffest of the Nativite of Seynt John Baptist last past before the date hereof unto thend and terme of lxxxxix yeres than next following, and fully to be ended, yielding and paying therefor yerely to the seid priour and his successors in the tresoury of there hous of Seynt John's of Clarkenwell beside London, fifty poundes sterling at the ffestes of the purification of our Lady and of Seynt Barnabe thappostle, by even porcions. And also payeing and supporting all manner of charges ordinary and extraordinary due and goying oute of the seid manor, with the appurtenances during the seid terme. And the seid Archebusshop and his assignes yerely during the seid terme shal have allowance of the seid priour and his successors in the paymentes of the rent and ferme of fifty poundes aforesaid iiij$^{li.}$ xiij$^{s.}$ iiij$^{d.}$ sterling, at the ffestes aforeseid, by even porcions, towards and for the exhibition of a preste for to mynister divine service within the Chapell of the seid manor. And the seid priour and his brethren for them and their successors graunten the seid Archebusshop and his assignes yerely during the seid terme shal have and take at their libertie foure loades of woode and tymber able for pyles for the reparacion and sustentacion of the were called Hampton were, the same woodes and tymber to be felled and conveyed at the costes of the seid Archebusshop, and his assignes at their libertie at all tymes during the seid terme shall take down, alter, transpose, chaunge, make, and new byeld at theire propre costes any howses, walles, mootes, diches, warkis, or other things within or aboute the seid manour of hamptoncourte, with the appurtenaunces, without empeche-ment of wast and without any payne or punysshment to be or ensue to the seid Archebusshop and his assignes during the seid terme. And the seid Archebusshop and his assignes shall bere all manner of reparacions of the seid manour with the appurtenaunces during the seid terme, and in thend of the seid terme all the same shall leve to the seid priour and bredren and to theire successours sufficiently re-pared. Ffurthermore, the seid Archebusshop and his assignes shall leve the seid priour and his successours m$^{l.}$ couple of conys in the waren of the seid manour, or elles for every couple that shall want iiij^{d} And moreover the seid priour and his bredren graunted that the seid Archebusshop and his assignes shall have and occupie during the seid terme all suche parcells as be conteyned upon the bak of this enden-ture, and in thend of the same terme all the same shall leve and delyver to the seid priour and his successours, or the value of the same. And if it happen the seid yerely fferme or rent of v$^{li.}$ during the seid terme of lxxxxix yeres, to be behynde and not pade in part or in the hole after eny terme of payment befor specified which it ought to be paid by the space of two hole yeres, that then it shalbe lawful to the seid priour and his successours to re-enter into the same manour and othre the premisses dismised, and theym to have ayen as in their first and pristinat estate, this endenture or eny therin conteigned notwithstandyng. And the seid priour and his bredren promitte and graunte for theym and theire successours, and theym bynde by thies presentes to the seid Archebisshop, that when so ever the said Archebisshop or his assignes at any oone tyme within the terme of this present leas shall come to the seid priour and his bredren, or to their suc-cessours, and demaunde to have a newe graunte and lesse of the saide manour of hamptoncourte with the appurtenaunces to theym to be graunted under their commen seale of the seid hospitall for the terme of other lxxxxix yeres next ensuying this present terme, that then the seid priour and his bredren nowe being or their successours than for tyme beyng for that oone tyme shall graunte and make a newe leesse of the seid manour of hamptoncourte with the appurtenaunces to the seid Arche-bisshop and to his assignes under the common seale of the seid hospitall for the terme of othre lxxxxix yeres after the forme, tenour, and effecte of the seid covenauntes and agre-mentes conteyned in this present endenture, the substaunce thereof in nowise chaunged nor mynyshed. And at the delyverie of the same new endenture this endenture to be cancelled if it shall than rest and be in the keping of the seid Archebisshop or his assignes. And if the seid endenture fortune to be lost, and be not in the keping of the seid Archebisshop or his assignes, nor in the kepyng of any per-son or their uses, then the seid Archebisshop or his assignes, before the seid newe graunte or lesse to be made, shall surrender and so promytte by thies presentes to surrender all suche title and interest as they or any of theym have or may have, by reason of this formar lease at all tymes after suche surrendre and newe lesse made utterly to be voide and of no effecte. In witnesse whereof to the oone part of theis presente endenturs towardes the seid Archebusshop re-maynyng, the said priour and his bredren have put their common seale. And to that othre part of the same enden-turs towardes the seid priour and his bredren remaynyng the seid Archebusshop hath put his seale. Yeven in our Chapitur holden in oure house of Seynt John's of Clarkenwell beside London, the xj day of Januarie, in the yere of our lord god a thousand fyve hundreth and fourteene, the sixt yere of the reigne of our soveraigne lord king Henry the Eight.

"*In the Chapel*, First, a chalesse of silver, a pix of copur for the sacrament, ij alter clothes, a corporaxe, ij candle-stikes of laton, a massebook, a porteux, a pewter botil for wyne, a crewet of pewter, a crosse of tynne, a paxbrede of tree, an alter clothe of whyte and blue lyke unto armyn, an ymage of our lord of tree, an ymage of our lady of tree, an ymage of seynt John, an ymage of seynt Nicholas, an ymage of the crosse paynted on a borde, ij alte clothes, ij pewes with a chest of wynscott, an holy waterstok of laton with a stryngel of laton, ij bells in the towre, one of them broken.—Of *bedsteddis* in all xx$^{ti.}$, ii towrned chyars.—*In the parlour*, a table of Estriche bourde with ij tristells.—*In the haule*, ij tables dormant, and oon long table with ij tristells, a close cupbourde, iiij fourmes, iiij barres of yron about the harthe.—*In the kechen*, a pot of bras cont. **v** galons, a cadron sett in the fournace cont. xx.galons, a spyt of yron, ij awndyrons, a trevet, ij morters of marbil, a cawdron of iij galons, di. a stomer of laton, a flesshehoke, a frying pan, ij pailes, a barre of yron in the kechen to hange on pottes, a grete salting troughe, a steping fatte, an heire of the kyln of xxiij yerdes, ij grate byunes in the kechen, a byune in the buttry, a knedyng troghe.—*In the stable*, a pitchfork, a dongfork.—A presse in the *towre-chambre*, a great coffar in oon of the towre chambres; a parclose in the towre, a parclose in the parloure."

Wolsey had no sooner taken possession of the manor than he set about rebuilding the manor-house in a style of grandeur that was, perhaps, unsur-passed at that time by few mansions in England, and upon a scale of unparalleled magnificence. Of that building, however, there is now but little or any portion left standing; for after the cardinal's "fall," Henry VIII., with a view, no doubt, to remove from the palace some portion of its founder's *prestige*, demolished the great hall and chapel, and replaced them with erections of his own. The popular belief which attributes to the cardinal the erection of the present hall is therefore incorrect. The present hall was the work of Henry, and was in all probability in no way superior, but rather the contrary, to that of the cardinal, whose taste and architectural skill were notorious. The design of Wolsey's building appears to have comprehended five distinct courts, the whole composed of brick, and highly ornamented; and the interior was so capacious that it is said to have been provided with two hundred and eighty beds for visitors of superior rank. Only two of the courts of Wolsey's palace now remain, so that but little idea can be formed of the extent of the building as he left it. Mr. Jesse, in his work on Hampton Court, observes that Wolsey "had evidently meant to construct at Hampton such a splendid specimen of Grecian correctness as might give a new bias to the architecture of this island. It is probable that he was unable to contend with the still lingering relics of prejudice, and therefore we have to regret that the Gothic and Grecian styles were blended in the cardinal's magnificent building with equal bad taste and impropriety."

These ancient buildings—or, at least, such of them as remain—are extremely interesting. Their

The clerk of the works received 8d. *per diem*, and his writing clerks 6d. each.

In 1838, whilst removing one of the old towers built by Wolsey, the workmen came upon a number of glass bottles which lay among the foundation. They were of a curious shape; and it has been suggested that they were buried to denote the date of the building.

Here Wolsey lived in more than regal splendour; and when it is considered that he had nearly one thousand persons in his suite, we shall be less surprised at the vastness of his palace.

Before proceeding with a more detailed account of the building, it will be best to give a

HAMPTON COURT BRIDGE. (*From an Engraving by J. C. Allen, after P. Debouit*)

structure is of red brick, interlaced with dark-coloured bricks in diagonal lines, the windows, cornices, and dressings being of stone. Wolsey appears to have employed the Warden and certain members of the Freemasons as his architects in building his palace, as he did also at Christ Church, Oxford, originally called Cardinal's College. In an article in the *Edinburgh Review*, by Sir F. Palgrave, on the "Architecture of the Middle Ages," are given some curious accounts of the expenses of the fabric of Hampton Court Palace, extant amongst the public records of London. The following items are extracted from the entries of the works performed between the 26th February, 27 Henry VIII., to March 25th, then next ensuing :—

Freemasons.

Master, at 12d. the day, John Molton, 6s.

Warden, at 5s. the week, William Reynolds, 20s.

Setters, at 3s. 8d. the week, Nicholas Seyworth (and for three others), 13s. 8d.

Lodgemen, at 3s. 4d. the week, Richard Watchet (and twenty-eight others), 13s. 4d.

short biographical sketch of Wolsey, and to deal with the history of the palace since Wolsey's time.

Thomas Wolsey, afterwards "Archbishop of York, Chancellor of England, Cardinal Priest of Cicily, and Legate a latere," was born at Ipswich, in Suffolk, in 1471. He was descended, according to some of our best historians, from poor but honest parents, and of good reputation; the common tradition is that he was the son of a butcher. Feeling a stronger inclination for the disputations of the schools than for the business of his father, he acquired the rudiments of grammar, and received a learned education; and entering the University of Oxford at a very early age, he took the degree of Bachelor of Arts when he was fourteen years old, and in consequence was commonly called the "Boy Bachelor." He was soon after elected a Fellow of Magdalen College. His next step was to have the care of the school adjoining that college committed to him, and to receive as pupils three of the sons of the Marquis of Dorset, who, in reward for the progress which they made under his tuition, presented him to the rectory of Limington, in Somerset, which happened to be vacant at that time, and was in his lordship's patronage. During his residence in that locality a piece of ill-luck appears to have befallen " Mr."

was presented. In the early part of the reign of Henry VIII., Fox, Bishop of Winchester resolved to introduce Wolsey to royal favour, and in a very little time he obtained such a footing in Henry's good graces that he was appointed to the most trusty and confidential posts. Notwithstanding his sacred calling, we are told that Wolsey participated

CARDINAL WOLSEY. (*After Holbein.*)

Wolsey. He was put in the stocks, as some say, on a charge of drunkenness, by Sir Amias Paulet, an affront which he is reported to have resented somewhat unmercifully in after life, when Sir Amias happening to come within his clutches, he sentenced him to keep within the bounds of the Temple for five or six years.

Wolsey was next appointed chaplain to Henry VII., who employed him in a secret negotiation for his proposed marriage with Margaret of Savoy. His reward for the talent he displayed in that business was the Deanery of Lincoln, to which he

in the dissipations of the youthful Henry, which afforded him numerous opportunities " to introduce business and State affairs, to insinuate those political maxims and that line of conduct he wished his monarch to adopt." In due course Wolsey became a member of the Council, and subsequently sole and absolute minister. He was now made almoner to the king, and other honours flowed thick and fast upon him. In 1513 he obtained the Bishopric of Tournay, in Flanders, and before the end of the year succeeded to that of Lincoln.

In 1515 he reached the height of his ambition, being created a cardinal, by the title of "Cardinal of St. Cecilia beyond the Tiber." He was also Chancellor of England.

" And now," writes his biographer, "the splendour of retinue and magnificence of living he so loved began to distinguish his establishment, which might be said to have been almost more than royal; his train consisted of eight hundred servants, many of whom were knights and gentlemen; some even of the nobility put their children into his family as a place of education, and, in order to ingratiate them with their patron, allowed them to bear offices as his servants."

Of the pomp and state of the cardinal at this time the following account is given by Mr. G. Howard, in his " Wolsey and his Times " :—" The cardinal rose early, and as soon as he came out of his bedchamber he generally heard two masses, either in his ante-chamber or chapel. Returning to his private apartments, he made various necessary arrangements for the day; and about eight o'clock left his privy chamber ready dressed, in the red robes of a cardinal, his upper garment being of scarlet, or else of fine crimson taffeta or crimson satin, with a black velvet tippet of sables about his neck, and holding in his hand an orange, deprived of its internal substance, and filled with a piece of sponge, wetted with vinegar 'and other confections against pestilent airs, the which he most commonly held to his nose when he came to the presses, or when he was pestered with many suitors.' This may account for so many of his portraits being painted with an orange in the hand. The Great Seal of England and the cardinal's hat were both borne before him 'by some lord, or some gentleman of worship right solemnly;' and as soon as he entered the presence-chamber, the two tall priests, with the two tall crosses, were ready to attend upon him, with gentlemen ushers going before him bare-headed, and crying, 'On masters before, and make room for my lord.' The crowd thus called on consisted not only of common suitors, or the individuals of his own family, but often of peers of the realm, who chose, or were perhaps obliged, thus to crouch to an upstart—a character not in very great repute in those days. In this state the proud cardinal proceeded down his hall, with a sergeant-at-arms before him, carrying a large silver mace, and two gentlemen, each bearing a large plate of silver. On his arrival at the gate, or hall door, he found his mule ready, covered with crimson velvet trappings. When mounted, his attendants consisted of his two cross-bearers and his two pillar-bearers, dressed in fine ... mounted on great horses capa-

risoned in like colour, of four men on foot, with each a pole-axe in his hand, and a long train of gentry, who came to swell his triumph as he proceeded to the Court of Chancery, where he generally sat until eleven o'clock to hear suits and to determine causes. With all this state he seems to have affected some degree of familiarity; for, previous to taking his seat in the court, he generally stopped at a bar made for him below the chancery, conversing with the other judges, and sometimes with individuals of less apparent consequence. As soon as his chancery business was over, he commonly proceeded to the Star-chamber, where, as has been—we hope truly—reported of him, ' hee neither spared high nor low, but did judge every one according to right.'"

Dr. Johnson has drawn the character of the cardinal in the following energetic lines :—

" In full-blown dignity see Wolsey stand,
Law in his voice and fortune in his hand;
To him the church, the realm, their powers consign,
Through him the rays of regal bounty shine;
Turn'd by his nod, the stream of honour flows,
His smile alone security bestows !
Still to new heights his restless wishes soar,
Claim leads to claim, and pow'r advances pow'r;
Till conquest unresisted ceas'd to please,
And right submitted left him none to seize !
At length his sovereign frowns, the train of state
Mark the keen glance and watch the sign to hate;
Where'er he turns he meets the stranger's eye,
His suppliants scorn him and his followers fly;
Now drops at once the pride of awful state,
The golden canopy, the glittering plate,
The regal palace, the luxurious board,
The livery'd army, and the menial lord !
With age, with cares, with maladies oppress'd,
He seeks the refuge of monastic rest;
Grief aids disease, remember'd folly stings,
And his last sighs reproach the *faith* of kings ! "

Among the younger scions of the nobility who were placed under the guidance of Wolsey was the youthful Lord Percy, who, accompanying the cardinal to court, had frequent opportunities of seeing and conversing with the beautiful and unfortunate Anne Boleyn, whose affections he gained, and whom he privately agreed to marry. This coming to the ears of the king, the cardinal was forthwith charged to summon his pupil's father to the presence of his royal master, and the contract was formally broken. The Lady Anne, as readers of English history know, was soon after dismissed the Court, and sent to one of her father's estates in the country, the contract being dissolved by the cardinal, as having been made "without the king's or the young lord's father's knowledge," Earl Percy soon after marrying a daughter of the Earl of Shrewsbury.

"It has been conjectured, not without reason," writes Mr. J. F. Murray, in his "Environs of London," "that upon this apparently unimportant incident depended the future of the cardinal's power, Anne never having forgiven him for depriving her of Percy, though, to augment her rising influence with the king, it was necessary that she should dissemble, and she accordingly, with womanly dissimulation, appeared to treat Wolsey with the greatest external respect.

"The determination of Henry to repudiate Katharine, his queen—the first fatal declension from his position as king and father of his people to that of a brutal and wanton tyrant—and the honest opposition of Wolsey to that iniquitous procedure, hastened the hour of his downfall. Anne Boleyn, now recalled to Court, industriously fostered the dislike to the cardinal which had grown up in the mind of Henry, and the crisis of Wolsey's fate had arrived."

Long before this, however—namely, in 1526—Wolsey had thought it expedient to "present" Hampton Court Palace to the king; but it was a gift not of love, but of despair.

It has been suggested that it was in a vault of this palace that the incident occurred which opened Henry's eyes to the wealth acquired by his favourite cardinal. As the story goes, the king's fool was paying a visit to the cardinal's fool, and the jocose couple went down into the wine vaults. For fun, one of them stuck a dagger or some other pointed instrument into the top of a cask, and, to his surprise, touched something that chinked like metal. The meddlesome pair upon this set to work, and pushed off the head of the cask, discovering that it was full of gold pieces. Other casks, by their sounds, gave indications that they held wine, and not gold. The king's fool stored up this secret, and one day, when Henry VIII. was boasting about his wine, the fool said, satirically, "You have not such wine, sire, as my Lord Cardinal, for he hath casks in his cellar worth a thousand broad pieces each;" and then he told what he had detected. Whether this be true or not, it is certain that Wolsey was so far awake to the fact that he was so suspected by the monarch as to deem it prudent to present him with Hampton Court.

There was one memorable circumstance connected with Wolsey's palace, namely, that it did not present to the beholder a moat, a drawbridge, or loopholes, without which, up to that time, no nobleman thought of erecting a mansion. What Wolsey spent on Hampton Court can only be guessed at. After the great lord cardinal died Henry set himself to the carrying out of various

improvements; and in return for the "present" of his palace, Henry VIII. bestowed upon Wolsey the manor-house of Richmond, an old and favourite residence of his predecessor, Henry VII., and also of Henry VIII. himself in the early part of his reign; or, as Stow quaintly puts it, "in recompense thereof, the king licensed him to lie in his manor of Richmond at his pleasure, and so he lay there at certain times."

Although the cardinal thus relinquished the right of possession, he occasionally lived at Hampton Court Palace at a subsequent period. In 1527, in obedience to the desires of King Henry, Wolsey here feasted the ambassadors of the Court of France. An account of this entertainment is given in Cavendish's "Life of Wolsey," which, as it is well calculated to convey an idea of the magnificence with which this palace was furnished on State occasions, and is such an interesting feature in the history of the building, we may be pardoned for quoting it in these pages:—

"Then there was made great preparation of all things for this great assembly at Hampton Court; the Cardinall called before him his principal officers —as steward, treasurer, controller, and clerk of his kitchen—to whom he declared his mind touching the entertainment of the Frenchmen at Hampton Court, commanding them neither to spare for any cost, expense, or travayle, to make such a triumphant banquet, as they might not only wonder at it here, but also make a glorious report of it in their country, to the great honour of the king and his realm. To accomplish his commandment, they sent out caters, purveiors, and divers other persons, my lord's friends, to make preparation; also they sent for all the expert cookes and cunnyng persons in the art of cookerie which were within London or elsewhere, that might be gotten to beautify this noble feast. The purveiors provided, and my lord's friends sent in such provision as one would wonder to have seen. The cookes wrought both day and night with suttleties and many craftie devices, where lacked neither gold, silver, nor other costly thing meet for their purpose; the yeomen and groomes of the wardrobe were busied in hanging of the chambers, and furnishing the same with beds of silk and other furniture in every degree; then my Lord Cardinall sent me (Mr. Cavendish), being his gentleman usher, with two other of my fellows, thither, to foresee all thing touching our rooms to be nobly garnyshed: accordingly our pains were not small nor light, but daily travelling up and down from chamber to chambers. Then wrought the carpenters, joiners, masons, and all other artificers necessary to be had to glorify this noble feast. There was carriage and re-carriage of plate, stuff, and other rich implements, so that there was nothing lacking that could be imagined or devised for the purpose. There was also provided two hundred and eighty beds, furnished with all manner of furniture to them belonging, too long particularly to be rehearsed; but all wise men do sufficiently know what belongeth to the furniture thereof, and that is sufficient at this time to be said.

"The day was come to the Frenchmen assigned, and they ready assembled before the hour of their appointment, whereof the officers caused them to ride to Hanworth, a place and parke of the Kinge's, within three miles, there to hunt and spend the day untill night, at which time they returned againe to Hampton Court, and every one of them was conveyed to their severall chambers, having in them great fires, and wine to their comfort and relief, remaining there untill their supper was ready. The chambers where they supped and banquetted were ordered in this sort: first the great wayting chamber was hanged with rich arras, as all other were, and furnished with tall yeomen to serve. There were set tables round about the chamber, banquetwise covered; a cupboord was there garnished with white plate, having also in the same chamber, to give the more light, four great plates of silver set with great lights, and a great fire of wood and coales. The next chamber, being the chamber of presence, was hanged with very rich arras, and a sumptuous cloth of estate furnished with many goodly gentlemen to serve the tables, ordered in manner as the other chamber was, saving that the high table was removed beneath the cloth of estate toward the middest of the chamber covered. Then there was a cupboord being as long as the chamber was in breadth, with six deskes of height, garnyshed with guilt plate, and the nethermost desk was garnyshed all with gold plate, having with lights one paire of candlestickes of silver and guilt, being curiously wrought, which cost three hundred markes, and standing upon the same, two lights of waxe burning as bigge as torches to set it forth. This cupboord was barred round about, that no man could come nigh it, for there was none of all this plate touched in this banquet, for there was sufficient besides. The plates that did hang on the walls to give light were of silver and guilt, having in them great pearchers of waxe burning, a great fire burning in the chimney, and all other things necessary for the furniture of so noble a feast.

"Now was all things in readiness, and supper tyme at hand; the principal officers caused the trumpetters to blow to warne to supper; the officers discreetly went and conducted these noblemen from their chambers into the chambers where they should suppe, and caused them there to sit downe, and that done, their service came up in such abundance, both costly and full of suttleties, and with such a pleasant noyse of instruments of musicke, that the Frenchmen (as it seemed) were rapt into a heavenly paradise. You must understand that my Lord Cardinall was not yet comen thither, but they were merry and pleasant with their fare and devised suttleties. Before the second course my lord came in, booted and spurred, all sodainely amongst them, and bade them *preface*,* at whose coming there was great joy, with rising every man from his place, whom my lord caused to sit still and keep their roomes, and being in his apparell as he rode, called for a chayre, and sat down in the middest of the high paradise, laughing and being as merry as ever I saw hym in all my lyff. Anone came up the second course, with so many dishes, suttleties, and devices, above a hundred in number, which were of so goodly proportion and so costlie, that I thinke the Frenchmen never saw the like. The wonder was no less than it was worthie indeed. There were castles, with images the same as in St. Paul's Church for the quantity, as well counterfeited as the painter should have painted it on a cloth or wall. There were beasts, birds, and personages, most lively-made and counterfeited, some fighting with swords, some with guns and cross-bowes, some vaulting and leaping, some dauncing with ladies, some on horses in complete harnesse, jousting with long and sharp speares, with many more devices. Among all, one I noted was a chesseboord, made of spiced plate, with men thereof the same; and for the good proportion, and because the Frenchmen be verie cunning and expert in that play, my Lord Cardinall gave the same to a gentleman of France, commanding there should be made a goodlie case for the preservation thereof in all haste, that he might convey the same safe into his country. Then took my lord a boule of gold filled with ippocrass, and putting off his cappe, said, 'I drink to the king, my soveraigne lord, and next unto the king, your master,' and therewith drank a good draught. And when he had done, he desired the *graund maistre* to pledge him, cup and all, the which was well worth 500 markes, and so caused all the boordes to pledge these two Royal Princes; then went the cups so merrily about, that many of the

---

* An obsolete French term of salutation, abridged from *Bon prou voux face: i.e.,* "Much good may it do you."

Frenchmen were faine to be led to their beds. Then rose up my lord, and went into his privy chamber to pull off his bootes, and to shift him, and then went he to supper, and making a very short supper, or rather, a repast, returned into the chamber of presence to the Frenchmen, using them so lovingly and familiarly, that they could not commend him too much; and whilest they were in communication, and other pastimes, all their liveries were served to their chambers; every chamber had a bason and an ewer of silver, a great liverey pot of silver, and some guilt; yea, and some chambers had two liverey pots, with wine and beere, a boule, a goblet, and a pot of sylver to drink in, both for their wine and beere; a silver candlesticke both white and plaine, having in it two sizes, and a staff torche of waxe, a fine manchet, and a cheat loaf. Thus was every chamber furnished through the house; and yet the cupboords in the two banquetting chambers were not touched. Thus when it was more than time convenient, they were conveyed to their lodgings, where they rested that night. In the morning, after they had heard mass, they dined with the Cardinall, and so departed to Windsor."

Such were the merry and grand doings at Hampton Court Palace in the days of Wolsey's prosperity. "It would have been out of nature, on entering Hampton Court," observes Mr. Howitt, in his "Visits to Remarkable Places," "not to pause and contemplate for a while the singular story and fate of the great man who raised it. These ancient towers and courts are full of the memory of that strange fortune, and will be for many a long generation yet; and now that the great mass of the people is at once admitted to education and to this place, the history of Wolsey—at one time said to be a butcher's son, at another stretching his lordly hand over this realm, making foreign princes tremble at it, and reaching it out even to the papal tiara, and then again a poor and sinking suppliant, exclaiming—

"'O father abbot,
An old man broken with the storms of state
Is come to lay his weary bones among ye;
Give him a little earth for charity!'

—will be more widely known and wondered at. But many have been the sad and singular passages which have occurred to royal and ambitious heads in these chambers since then."

In 1538, Henry, as stated above, made Hampton the scene of his sylvan sports. He extended his chase through fifteen parishes, and enclosed the whole as hunting-grounds, which he kept strictly preserved for his own use. After his death the wooden paling was removed, and his chase thrown open. In 1537 Jane Seymour died here, after giving birth to Edward VI. On this occasion Henry VIII., contrary to his usual habit (for he married that queen within twenty-four hours after the execution of Anne Boleyn), went into mourning, and compelled all his Court to do so. Whether it was that he was really attached to her, or whether he had not had time to get tired of her—she only having been married for seventeen months—historians do not pretend to decide. Suffice it to say he had her body removed to Windsor, and interred there with great pomp, and he remained a widower for some years, when he espoused Anne of Cleves. In 1540 the ill-fated Catharine Howard was openly shown as queen at this palace, with much splendour and many joyous celebrations. Here, too, after Catharine Howard had met her fate upon the scaffold, Henry married his last wife, Lady Catharine Parr, who fortunately survived him. Henry's last festival at Hampton Court occurred in the year 1545.

The palace was chosen by the guardians of Edward VI. as his residence, and he was residing here when the Council rose against the authority of the Protector Somerset, and the young king was removed by him hence to Windsor Castle, lest the Council should obtain possession of his person. Two of his servants having died of the "black death" in 1550, King Edward and his attendants removed from London hither in hot haste, and remained till the alarm had passed away.

About this time the garden of Hampton Court was the frequent scene of interviews between the youthful and accomplished poet the Earl of Surrey, and the "fair-haired, blue-eyed Geraldine," the most interesting particulars of whose personal and family history have been handed down to us compressed within the compass of a sonnet by her gallant lover himself. The "fair Geraldine," who proves to have been the Lady Elizabeth Fitzgerald, afterwards the wife of a certain Earl of Lincoln—of whom little is known, save that he married the woman whom Surrey had loved—was half-sister of "Silken Thomas," and daughter of Gerald, ninth Earl of Kildare, an ancestor of the Duke of Leinster. Her mother was the Lady Elizabeth Grey, her father's second countess, whose grandmother, Elizabeth Woodville, became queen of Edward IV. The Fitzgeralds, as Surrey tells us in the sonnet above alluded to, derive their origin from the Geraldi of Tuscany; hence—

"From Tuscan came my ladye's worthy race,
Fair Florence was sometime their ancient seat."

"Fair Geraldine" was born and nurtured in Ireland. As above stated, her father was Earl of Kildare, her mother allied to the blood royal:

"Her sire an Earl, her dame of Prince's blood."

fourteen or fifteen, as it appears from contemporary dates; and Surrey says very clearly,

"She wanted years to understand
The grief that I did feel."

HAMPTON COURT, AS FINISHED BY KING HENRY VIII.
(*From a Drawing by Hollar, Engraved by J. Pye, and published by the Society of Antiquaries.*)

She was brought up (through motives of compassion after the misfortunes of her family) at Hunsdon, in Hertfordshire, with the Princesses Mary and Elizabeth, where Surrey, who frequently

But even then her budding charms made him confess, as he beautifully expresses it,

"How soon a look may print a thought,
That never may remove!"

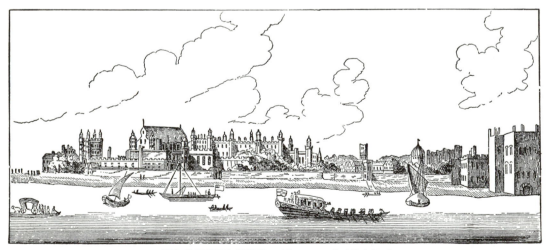

OLD HAMPTON COURT.   (*From an ancient Painting.*)

visited them in company with the young Duke of Richmond,* first beheld her:

"Hunsdon did first present her to mine eyes."

She was then extremely young, not more than

---

* Natural brother of the Princesses; he was the son of Henry VIII., by Lady Talbot.

The garden here has also been generally credited with being the scene of the following story:—"Henry Carey, cousin to Queen Elizabeth, after having enjoyed her Majesty's favour for many years, lost it in the following manner:—As he was walking one day, lost in thought, in the palace garden, under the queen's window, the latter perceived him, and asked him in a joking way what he was thinking about, and added, 'What does a man think of when he is thinking of nothing?' 'Of a woman's promise,' answered Carey. 'Well done, cousin,' said Elizabeth. She retired, but she did not forget Carey's answer; for some time afterwards he solicited the honour of a peerage, and reminded the queen that she had promised it to him. 'True,' said she; 'but you will remember, cousin, that it was *only a woman's promise!*' Seeing that Carey looked disappointed and vexed, the queen added, 'Well, Sir Henry, I must not confute you: anger makes dull men witty, but it keeps them poor.'"

Here Queen Mary and her husband, Philip of Spain, passed their honeymoon in great retirement;

contemporary chronicle, still preserved in the British Museum, affords several particulars of her entertainment on this occasion. "On Christmas Eve, the great hall of the palace being illuminated with a thousand lamps artificially disposed," writes Lucy Aikin, "the king (Philip) and queen supped in it, and the princess was seated at the same table with them, next to the cloth of estate. After supper she was served with a perfumed napkin and a plate of 'comfects' by Lord Paget, but retired to her ladies before the revels, masking, and disguising began. On St. Stephen's Day she heard matins (? mass) in the queen's closet adjoining the chapel, where she was attired in a robe of white

APPROACH TO HAMPTON COURT.

satin strung all over with large pearls; and on the 29th December she sat with their Majesties and the nobility at a grand spectacle of jousting, when two hundred spears were broken by combatants, of whom half were accoutred in the Almaine and half in the Spanish fashion."

About the end of the following April the princess was again admitted to visit her royal sister, who was expecting her confinement; but she was as much a prisoner as a guest, and the intercourse of the two sisters would seem to have been mutually repulsive. At all events, after a few weeks spent at one or two of the seats of royalty in the neighbourhood of London, she was allowed to establish herself permanently at Hatfield House, in Hertfordshire, which thenceforth was her home till she succeeded to the crown.

and here, after her imprisonment at Woodstock, the queen's sister—the Princess Elizabeth—was invited to spend some time with the royal pair, when she was entertained with "banquets, masqueings, and all sorts of revelries."

Hither again the Princess was sent as a sort of State prisoner on March 15, 1554, on reaching London from Ashridge, in obedience to her sister's commands.

At Christmas following the Princess Elizabeth was once more invited by her sister as a guest, probably on account of the presence of the Duke of Savoy, whose suit the queen thought that her sister would be more likely to accept if she met him personally and saw his attractive qualities. A

From Hampton Court, Queen Mary, when stricken with her last and fatal sickness, in the autumn of 1558, was carried to Westminster to die. After her accession to the throne, Elizabeth made Hampton Court one of her favourite residences, and here she continued occasionally to assemble her brilliant Court, and to "keep Christmas" in right royal fashion, as Mary, Edward, and her father had done before.

In the "pleasances" of Hampton Court Palace, as one of the ambassadors to her Court tells us, Queen Elizabeth delighted to "go a walking" with her ladies and a gay train of attendants, especially on cold frosty mornings. Did space permit, much interesting gossip could be related touching those fair attendants upon royalty, called "Maids of Honour," from Queen Elizabeth's time to the present day; but we must be content with a few general remarks concerning them. Pope in describing prudery (to a maid of honour) as

> "A beldam,
> Seen with youth and beauty seldom,"

plainly proves, by adding,

> "'Tis an ugly, envious shrew,
> Who rails at dear Lepel and you,"

that the "dear Lepel"—"youth's youngest daughter"—the fairest of the maids of honour of the time when Lady Suffolk was lady of the bedchamber both to the king and queen—had been made a mark for the ill-nature of the Court. Yet Pope's was an era when there were wars and rumours of wars to occupy the whispers of Kensington and Hampton Court—when there was a king to squabble with his ministers, and afford public news to keep in movement the private echoes of Windsor Castle. Had "sweet Lepel" been railed at during a period of petticoat government, when the back-stairs, instead of being haunted by Herveys, Walpoles, and Chesterfields, had been the resort of mantua-makers and milliners, "black, white, and grey, with all their trumpery," Pope would have known that the "*railing*" was an inevitable concomitant of the "*post*" of—Maid of Honour. He would have rather addressed the future Lady Hervey with "Be thou as chaste as ice, as pure as snow, thou shalt not escape calumny!"

Grammont has recorded the recreations of the high-born maidens of his time, who, disguised as orange-girls, escaped from the purlieus of the palace of Whitehall to frequent those of the theatres; and St. Simon acquaints us on what grounds the Duchess de Noailles, mother of the maids of honour of Anne of Austria and her royal successor, was forced to have double iron bars affixed to their chamber windows. The Queen of Scots had her Maries; and she who recorded in song that

> "There was Mary Seyton, and Mary Betoun,
> And Mary Carmichael, and me,"

hath also bequeathed to posterity the confession of her fault. Queen Elizabeth was forced, by the incontinence of *her* fair attendants, to find them occasional lodgings in the Tower of London, even when so great a man as the gallant Raleigh was the avowed author of the mischief; and Pope and Lady Mary Wortley have told remarkable tales of the honourable maidenhood of Queen Caroline's Court.

"In the furniture of the palaces," writes Bohun, in his "Character of Queen Elizabeth," "her Majesty ever affected magnificence and an extraordinary splendour. She adorned the galleries with pictures by the best artists; the walls she covered with rich tapestries. She was a true lover of jewels, pearls, all sorts of precious stones, gold and silver plate, rich beds, fine coaches and chariots, Persian and Indian carpets, statues, medals, &c., which she would purchase at great prices. Hampton Court was the most richly furnished of all her palaces; and here she caused her naval victories over the Spaniards to be worked in fine tapestries, and laid up among the richest pieces of her wardrobe. . . . When she made here any public feasts, her tables were magnificently served, and many side-tables adorned with rich plate. At these times many of her nobility waited on her at table. She made the greatest displays of her regal magnificence when foreign ambassadors were present. At these times she would also have vocal and instrumental music during dinner, and after dinner, dancing."

The joyful tidings of the defeat of the Spanish Armada arrived on Michaelmas Day, and, as the story goes, was communicated to Queen Elizabeth whilst at dinner here, partaking of a *goose*. Hence the origin of eating that savoury dish on Michaelmas Day.

Here, James I., immediately after his accession, assured his Roman Catholic subjects of his intention to grant them "toleration"—a promise which he never fulfilled. Here, too, a few weeks afterwards, he held a conference between the divines of the Established Church and the Nonconformist body, over which he presided, and which resulted in the victory of the former. It was settled at this conference that there should be certain amendments in the Prayer Book, and that "care should be taken that one uniform translation of the Bible should be provided and read in the Church, and that without notes." The king forthwith appointed a commission of fifty-four, and took exceeding interest in the work, calling it "our translation." The king in 1604 wrote a letter to the Bishop of London, urging that provision should be made for some of the translators by prebendal stalls and livings. The Bishop of London accordingly issued letters. The translation, delayed by the death of one of the translators, came out in 1611. The king's printers printed it, and asserted on the title-page, "Appointed to be read in churches." Notwithstanding that Lord Selborne tells us that a fire at Whitehall destroyed the rolls and patents of the period, a catena of evidence, beginning with 1612 up to 1640, is supplied by the Visitation Articles, showing how this version of 1611 was deemed lawful and authorised, and enforced by episcopal and archidiaconal authority.

In 1606 the king and queen gave here a splendid series of entertainments, extending over a fortnight, to Francis, Prince of Vaudemois, son of the Duke of Lorraine, and to a large company of noblemen and gentlemen. Here, in 1618, died the queen of James, Anne of Denmark.

Charles I. resided at Hampton Court both in his happiest and most melancholy days. Like Philip and Mary, his Majesty and his queen, Henrietta Maria, daughter of Henry IV. of France, came here in 1625 to spend their honeymoon. On summer evenings he and the queen and the rest of the court, would "take barge" on the Thames and amuse their leisure hours by feeding the swans.

Laud was appointed Dean of the Chapel of Hampton Court in 1626, soon after his translation to Bath and Wells; but his memory is associated less with Hampton than with Lambeth Palace.

In 1641 King Charles took refuge at Hampton Court during the troubles in London. It is related that "one day whilst his Majesty was standing at one of the windows of the palace, surrounded by his children, a gipsy or beggar-woman came up to it, and asked for charity. Her appearance excited ridicule and probably threats, which so enraged the gipsy that she took out of her basket a looking-glass, and presented it to the king; he saw in it his own head decollated. Probably with a natural wish to conciliate so prophetical a beggar, or for some other reason, money was given to her. She then said that the death of a dog in a room the king was then in would precede the restoration to his family of the kingdom which the king was then about to lose. It is said that Oliver Cromwell afterwards slept in the room referred to. He was constantly attended by a faithful dog, who guarded his bed-room door. On awakening one morning, he found the dog dead, on which he exclaimed, in allusion to the gipsy's prophecy, which he had previously heard, 'The kingdom is departed from me.' Cromwell died soon after, and the subsequent events are sufficiently known."

In 1647 the ill-fated Charles was brought hither by the army from Holmby, in Northamptonshire. Whilst here he was treated with respect, and even kindness, being allowed also the melancholy satisfaction of often seeing his children, through the favour of the Earl of Northumberland. His Majesty was kept here, not actually in imprisonment, but under restraint, by the Parliament and the army from the 24th of August down to the 11th of November, when he escaped. Great had been the change in his circumstances during those few months—the generals, who had been hopeful that they might come to an arrangement with the king, found that he was only playing with them to gain time, and carry his own schemes. The Scotch Commissioners could do nothing with him; and, alarmed by rumours that in the ranks of the soldiery were men who would not scruple to assassinate him, Charles departed, to put himself in a worse condition in the Isle of Wight.

We find in the "Diary" of John Evelyn, under date of October 10th, 1647, the following entry:—"I came to Hampton Court, where I had the honour to kisse his Majesty's hand, he being now in the power of those execrable villains who not long after murder'd him."

In 1651 the Parliament sold the whole of the estate of Hampton Court to a Mr. John Phelpe, a member of the Lower House, for the sum of £10,765 19s. 6d.; but in 1656, Oliver Cromwell, enriched by the wreck of the State, again acquired possession of the palace, for which he appears to have had a special liking, and made it one of his principal places of residence. The marriage ceremony of his daughter Elizabeth, who espoused Lord Falconberg, was here celebrated in 1657; and in the following year the Lord Protector's favourite daughter, Mrs. Claypole (who is said to have severely remonstrated with him, in her last hours, on the subject of his dangerous ambition), here breathed her last. Hither Oliver Cromwell would repair, when Lord Protector of the Realm, to dine with his officers. Mr. Secretary Thurloe thus records the fact in sundry minutes in his pocket-book, given by John Milton to his nephew, Mr. John Philips:—"Sometimes, as the fit takes him, to divert the melancholy, he dines with the officers of his army at Hampton Court, and shows a hundred antic tricks, as throwing cushions at them, and putting hot coals into their pockets and boots! At others, before he has half dined, he gives orders for a drum to beat and call in his foot-guards, like a kennel of hounds, to snatch off the meat from his table and tear it in pieces, with many other unaccountable whimsies; immediately after this, fear and astonishment sit in his countenance, and not a nobleman approaches him but he fells him! Now he calls for his guards, with whom he rides out, encompassed behind and before, for the preservation of his Highness, and at his return at night, shifts from bed to bed for fear of surprise." Once, we read, he narrowly escaped assassination while riding through the narrow part of Hammersmith, on his way to this pleasant London suburb. George Fox, the Quaker, in his "Chronicles," relates how he went out on a day in 1658 to protest to Cromwell against the severities inflicted on the eccentric members of his persuasion, and meeting the Protector riding in Hampton Park at the head of his life-guard, Fox said what he believed he was inspired to say, and withdrawing, felt a "waft of death" go out against the Protector. Nor was it many days afterwards that, on the advice of his physicians, Cromwell left Hampton Court for Whitehall, the place of his decease on September 3rd, 1658.

In an article in the *Gentleman's Magazine* for 1877, entitled "Oliver Cromwell at Hampton Court," are published some details of an "Inventory of Goods and Servants at Hampton Court," taken by order of the House of Commons, in June, 1659. This interesting document is preserved in the State Paper Office, among the uncalendared papers of that period. The reason for taking the inventory is set forth in a kind of preamble, "so as there be not embezzlement of" the goods. "In looking over the inventory," observes the writer of the article in question, "it is curious to note that only four looking-glasses are mentioned. This could not have arisen from any scarcity of that article at the period, because in the celebrated inventories of the palaces of Henry VIII. there are fourteen mentioned and fully described. The first mentioned in Hampton Court was in the 'rich bed-chamber,' and is thus described: 'one large looking-glass in an ebony frame.' Then 'in the lower wardrobe' were 'two small looking-glasses, one of them being broke.' The fourth hung in a room which, in the time of Charles I., was occupied by the Bishop of Canterbury, and during Cromwell's Protectorate was used by his daughter, Mrs. Claypole, as a nursery. The description is as follows: 'One large looking-glass in an ebony frame, with a string of silk and gold.' The absence of any

further reference to looking-glasses is rather suggestive. Perhaps Oliver Cromwell objected to them on principle, as leading to vanity; or possibly such as were in use were regarded as personal property, and the owners carried them away when they left the place. Hampton Court has been greatly altered since Cromwell's time, and there is not one chamber which is now associated with his memory. The Great Hall, of course, remains, in which were two organs—the larger one a gift from Cromwell's friend, Dr. Goodwin, President of Magdalen College, Oxford; but the hall is more closely associated with the grand entertainments given by Wolsey, and the revels of Henry VIII., than with Cromwell. In like manner the chapel is only in a general way associated with his memory. More interesting reminiscences will occur in the 'Mantegna Gallery,' as it is called, after the painter of a series of pictures now hung in it. In Cromwell's time this was called the 'Long Gallery.' The pictures, nine in number, and of gigantic size, formed at one time part of a collection belonging to the Marquis of Mantua, the whole of which Charles I. purchased, at a cost of £80,000. They represent the triumphs of Julius Cæsar, and were painted by Andrea Mantegna. . . . Cromwell must have looked upon these grand pictures every time he strode along the gallery. They seem now to identify themselves with his spirit, and to depict the ideal triumphs that he would fain have won for England."

After the death of Cromwell it was thought undesirable to allow the palace to be stripped, in anticipation of the arrival of Charles II. Charles, apparently forgetful of his royal parent's misery, often enjoyed the song and dance of revelry in this palace.

At Hampton Court he spent a large part of his time both before and after his marriage with Catharine of Braganza. For a king to aspire to "happiness" is a pretension beyond his condition of life. It suited Lady Castlemaine as little that Charles should be "well acquainted" with his youthful bride as it suited the courtiers that he should think himself happy in wedlock. Before the royal party arrived at Hampton Court for the enjoyment of the honeymoon, mischief had been at work; and though the month was May (a season that seems expressly created by nature for honeymoons) breezes were blowing more boisterous than the turbulent equinox. Still, strangely enough, Hampton Court, in the hours of her after life, was a spot ever dear to Catharine of Braganza, on account of its memory of the transient dream of happiness connected with her honeymoon.

A small summer drawing-room in the suite of apartments overlooking the river was the favourite chamber selected by the unhappy queen for receiving such persons as she admitted to private audience. Nothing could be simpler than the furniture of this unadorned chamber; the mouldings and wainscotings were of pure white, and the hangings of pale sea-green damask; a chair and footstool, somewhat richer than the rest, alone served to mark the seat of the queen herself, whose pale and sallow complexion was not shown off to advantage thereby. Here, however, "the blazing and audacious beauty of Lady Castlemaine often 'paled' its ineffectual fires before the mild lustre of the queen's girlish and almost saintly meekness."

Here, deserted by the servile tribe of flatterers, an object of pity to some, of contempt perhaps to more, Catharine was obliged to look on tamely, and see the homage of the courtiers paid before her face to other " stars," while she was abandoned and desolate in a foreign country; her only chance of winning even decent courtesy of her profligate husband depended on the degree of patience which she could exhibit.

James II. occasionally visited Hampton Court palace, and at times held his councils there. A good story is told about the poet Waller and King James. His Majesty treated Waller with great familiarity, and one day took him into the royal closet, and asked him how he liked one of the pictures, at the same time pointing to a lady's portrait. " My eyes, sir, are dim," answered Waller, " and I cannot distinguish it." " It is the Princess of Orange," said the king. " She is like the greatest woman in the world, sir," answered Waller; and on the king asking whom he meant, he answered again, " Queen Elizabeth." " I wonder," said his Majesty, " that you should think so; but I must confess she had a wise council." " And, sir," asked Waller in return, " did you ever know a fool choose a wise council?"

William III. and his queen appear to have preferred this palace to all their other residences. Specimens of the beautiful embroidery of her Majesty and her female attendants might at one time be seen here.

Many persons were angry because " Dutch William " tried to improve upon a structure which had been good enough for the many royal personages who had preceded him; but it was not his habit to study public opinion. Sir Christopher Wren pulled down various portions of the old palace, leaving untouched, however, the entrance court, and only so far altering the middle quadrangle as to introduce, with bad taste, an Ionic

colonnade amongst Wolsey's antique turrets. The third quadrangle, or Fountain Court, is almost entirely Wren's work, as are also the grand eastern and southern fronts. It is from the Fountain Court that the State Apartments are reached by a staircase, which was painted by Verrio, a man who regarded William as an usurper, which led Lord Orford to make the satirical remark that this artist painted the staircase as badly as if he had spoilt it out of principle.

Mr. J. T. Smith, in his work above quoted, observes :—" King William III., who took every opportunity of rendering these apartments as pleasing to him as those he had left in 'the house in the Wood,' introduced nothing by way of porcelain, beyond that of delf, and on that ware, in many instances, his Majesty had 'W.R.,' surmounted by the crown of England, painted on the fronts. Of the various specimens of this clumsy blue-and-white delf, displayed in the numerous rooms of this once magnificent palace, the pride of Wolsey and splendour of Henry VIII., the eight large pots for the reception of King William III.'s orange-tree, now standing in her Majesty's gallery, certainly have claims to future protection. As for the old and ragged bed-furniture, it is so disgraceful to a palace, that, antiquarian as I in some degree consider myself, I most heartily wish it in Petticoat Lane."

John Evelyn was again at Hampton Court shortly after William III. ascended the throne, for under date of July 16th, 1689, he writes in his " Diary":—" I went to Hampton Court about buisinesse, the Council being there. A greate apartment and spacious garden with fountaines was beginning in the park, at the head of the canal."

It was in the park that the king met with the accident that caused his death. Macaulay writes :— " On the 20th of February, 1702, William was ambling on a favourite horse, named Sorrel, through the park of Hampton Court. He urged his horse to strike into a gallop just at the spot where a mole had been at work. Sorrel stumbled on the mole-hill, and went down on his knees. The king fell off and broke his collar-bone. The bone was set, and he returned to Kensington in his coach, but the jolting of the rough roads of that time made it necessary to reduce the fracture again." It is not to be wondered at that William never recovered this double shock to his system, and that fever supervening, he died a few days subsequently.

The sister of Queen Mary, then Princess of Denmark, and afterwards Queen Anne, here gave birth on the 24th of July, 1689, to the Duke of Gloucester, who died at eleven years of age, and thus made room for the house of Brunswick. His royal mother occasionally resided here after her accession to the throne.

It is to this place that Pope alludes when he thus apostrophises Queen Anne, the first English sovereign by whom we know for certain that "Bohea," the new and fashionable beverage of that day, was patronised :—

"Oh ! had I rather unadmired remained
In some lone isle or distant northern land,
Where the gilt chariot never marks the way,
Where none learn Ombre, none e'er taste Bohea !"

The sovereigns of the house of Brunswick have not shown any great partiality for Hampton Court Palace as a royal abode. George I. sometimes visited the palace, as did his successor on the

HAMPTON COURT, FROM THE RIVER.

"Here thou, great Anna, whom these realms obey,
Dost sometimes counsel take, and sometimes tea."

Tea, it must be remembered, was a rare article in those days. It had not then been many years introduced into England, for in Pepys's "Diary," under date of September 25th, 1660, we find this entry :—"I did send for a cup of tee (a China drink), of which I had never drank before."

In the "Rape of the Lock" Belinda is made to exclaim :—

"Happy ! ah, ten times happy had I been,
If Hampton Court these eyes had never seen !
Yet am I not the first mistaken maid
By love of courts to numerous ills betrayed.

throne, who was the last monarch who made it his residence. The two first Georges, however, were devoid of taste, and illiterate, and that may account for the fact. "It is curious that not one solitary epistle in the handwriting of George II. is known to exist. This circumstance is more remarkable if we refer to his gallantries and intrigues, so severely commented upon and recorded by Walpole and others." Such is the statement of a writer in the columns of the *Times*.

Miss Chudleigh may be regarded as the ideal and type of the set of pert, or even malapert, young ladies who acted as maids of honour in the courts of the first two Georges. A good story is told by Charles Knight in his "London," which, whether it be true or false, is at all events characteristic of her transcendent impudence :—Apartments in Hampton Court palace having been allotted to her mother, the king good-naturedly asked Miss Chudleigh one day how the old lady felt in her new abode. "Oh, very well, if the poor woman had only a bed to lie upon !" "That oversight must be repaired," said the king. On this hint, the maid of honour (who continued a maid of honour for twenty years after her clandestine marriage with the Hon. Mr. Hervey, afterwards Earl of Bristol) acted, and in due time there appeared among the royal household accounts, "To a bed and furniture for the apartments of the Hon. Mrs. Chudleigh, £4,000." The king, who, though decidedly fond of money, was a man of his word, paid the bill, but remarked that if Mrs. Chudleigh found the bed as hard as he did, she would never sleep in it.

For the last century or more apartments in Hampton Court Palace have generally been bestowed on the poorer female members of noble families, or on widows of distinguished generals and admirals who have died in the service of their country. It is not generally known that once at least in his life Dr. Johnson cast a longing eye upon this privileged place. At all events, the following letter was published a few years ago in the *Athenæum* :— "The following interesting letter of Dr. Samuel Johnson has never been in print :—'My Lord, —Being wholly unknown to your lordship, I have only this apology to make for presuming to trouble you with a request—that a stranger's petition, if it cannot be easily granted, can be easily refused. Some of the apartments are now vacant, in which I am encouraged to hope that, by application to your lordship, I may obtain a residence. Such a grant would be considered by me as a great favour ; and I hope, to a man who has had the honour of vindicating his Majesty's government, a retreat in one of his houses may be not improperly or unworthily allowed. I therefore

MISS CHUDLEIGH.

request that your lordship will be pleased to grant such rooms in Hampton Court as shall seem proper to, my lord, your lordship's most obedient and most humble servant, SAM. JOHNSON, Bolt Court, Fleet Street, April 11, 1776.' Endorsed, 'Mr. Samuel Johnson to the Earl of Hertford, requesting apartments at Hampton Court, 11 May, 1776.'— The answer : 'Lord C. presents his compliments to Mr. Johnson, and is sorry that he cannot obey his commands, having already on his hands many engagements unsatisfied.' "

In 1795, William, Prince of Orange, Hereditary Stadtholder of Holland, driven from Holland by the advanced wave of the French Revolution, found here a hospitable asylum ; "and here," writes gossiping Sir Nathaniel William Wraxall, "the princes of our royal family and the nation at large vied in demonstrations of respect, compassion, and attention towards him." It was his son who was at one time designed to be the husband of our Princess Charlotte, but Providence decreed otherwise.

In 1810, after being deposed from the Swedish throne by the great Napoleon, Gustavus IV. came to England, and occupied a set of apartments here. He died in February, 1837.

The favoured inmates of Hampton Court palace during Her Majesty's reign have consisted largely of members of the following families, all of whom are more or less nearly connected with the Peerage :—Paget, Grey, Byng, Capel, Talbot, Ponsonby, Murray, Cathcart, Ward, Swinburne, Crofton, &c. In many cases these persons have been the widows of distinguished officers of the army and navy who have fallen in battle in the service of their country.

Since the year 1839 those parts of the palace which are not occupied by private residents, and the gardens, have been thrown open to the public, and during the summer months the whole place forms daily a great attraction to hundreds of sightseers, both English and foreign, who come to it by road or rail or river.

CHAPTER XIII.

HAMPTON COURT PALACE *(continued)*.

"A place which Nature's choicest gifts adorn,
Where Thames' kind streams in gentle currents turn,
The name ot Hampton hath for ages borne ;
Here such a palace shows great Henry's care,
As Sol ne'er views in his exalted sphere,
In all his tedious stage !"—CAMDEN.

Early Reminiscences of Hampton Court Palace—Description of the Building—The Principal Entrance—Wolsey's Courts—The Clock Tower Court
—A Curious Timepiece—The Great Hall—Theatrical Entertainments given here—The Withdrawing Room—The Kitchen Court—The
Fountain Court—Sir Christopher Wren's Alterations and Additions to the Palace—The Chapel—The State Apartments- The " Beauty"
Room—The Tapestry Gallery—The Cartoons of Raffaelle—The Gardens—The Wilderness and Maze—The Home Park—The Royal Stud
House—A Narrow Escape of the Palace.

IT is remarked in OLD AND NEW LONDON *
that although Windsor Castle is unequalled as a
royal residence of the type of a mediæval stronghold, yet Hampton Court is, after all, but a poor
substitute for the Château of Versailles. Nevertheless, few places possess more attractions than
Hampton Court. Its interest is not that of old
feudal associations : it was never half-palace, half-
fortress. It was never surrounded by a moat, nor
could it ever boast of a drawbridge or frowning
battlements and watch-towers ; all these things had
been banished by "society" when Hampton Court
palace was founded. The better portion of it, as
we have shown in the preceding chapter, was the
creation of that princely-minded churchman—the
last of that race of English dignitaries who combined in themselves the powers and attributes of
the priest and the noble. Founded by a cardinal,
continued by one king, completed by another, and
since inhabited by many of royal blood and station,
and containing within its walls some of the finest
efforts of the painter, and the most elaborate productions of the obsolete but beautiful skill of the
workers of tapestry, Hampton Court palace is a
building that well repays the visitor. Nor are these
attractions confined to the palace itself : its parks
and gardens, extending to many hundreds of acres,
are equally attractive, and afford plenty of scope
for the most reflective mind to ruminate upon, or
for the most frivolous to carry out the best of his
enjoyment in his own peculiar way.

The Rev. A. C. Cox, in his " Impressions of
England," writes :—" In the grounds of the palace,
and in Bushey Park, I found a formal grandeur, so
entirely becoming a past age, and so unusual in this,
that it impressed me with a feeling of melancholy
the most profound. Those avenues of chestnuts
and thorns, those massive colonnades and dreamy
vistas, wear a desolate and dreary aspect of by-

gone glory, in view of which my spirits could not
rise. They seemed only a fit haunt for airy echoes,
repeating an eternal *Where?* Nothing later than
the days of Queen Anne seems to belong to the
spot. You pass from scenes in which you cannot
but imagine Pope conceiving, for the first time, his
'Rape of the Lock,' into a more trim and formal
spot, where William of Orange seems likely to
appear before you, with Bishop Burnet buzzing
about him, and a Dutch guard following in the
rear. Then, again, James the Second, with the
Pope's nuncio at his elbow, and a coarse mistress
flaunting at his side, might seem to promise an
immediate apparition ; when once more the scene
changes, and the brutal Cromwell is the only
character who can be imagined in the forlorn area,
with a file of musketeers in the background,
descried through a shadowy archway. Here is a
lordly chamber, where the meditative Charles may
be conceived as startled by the echo of their tread ;
and here another, where he embraces for the last
time his beloved children. There, at last, is
Wolsey's hall, and here one seems to behold old
Bluebeard leading forth Anne Boleyn to a dance.
It still retains its ancient appearance, and is hung
with mouldering tapestry and faded banners, although its gilding and colours have been lately
renewed. The ancient devices of the Tudors are
seen here and there in windows and tracery, and
the cardinal's hat of the proud churchman who
projected the splendours of the place still survives
in glass, whose brittle beauty has thus proved less
perishable than his worldly glory.

"Yet let no one suppose the magnificence of
Hampton Court to consist in its architecture. One-
half is the mere copy of St. James's, and the other
is the stupid novelty of Dutch William. The
whole together, with its parks and with its history,
is what one feels and admires. I am not sure but
Royal Jamie, with his bishops and his Puritans on
either side, was as often before me when traversing

* See Vol IV., p. 122.

the pile, as anything else : and for him and his conference the place seems fit enough, having something of Holyrood about it, and something scholastic or collegiate also. Queen Victoria should give it to the Church, as a college for the poor, and so add dignity to her benevolence, which has already turned it into a show for her darling 'lower classes.' I honour the queen for this condescension to the people ; and yet, as I followed troops of John Gilpins through the old apartments, and observed their inanimate stare and booby admiration, it did strike me that a nobler and a larger benefit might be conferred upon them in a less incongruous way. Perhaps the happiest thought would be to make it for the clergy just what Chelsea is to the army and Greenwich to the naval service."

As we pass round the open courts and issue from under the low archways, we almost expect a robed and chained official of "the cardinal's" splendid household admonishing a "clerk of the kitchen," or conversing with a "gentleman of the chamber ;" nor would it startle the ear of fancy to hear the silence broken by the hearty, but coarse, laugh of "bluff King Hal" himself, sauntering familiarly with the cardinal, during one of those visits when the monarch came to Hampton to enjoy the hospitality—and, alas ! to envy the splendour—of his host. We wander into the blooming, though rather formally-disposed gardens ; and as we saunter up a shady avenue we can almost hear the rustle of the silks and brocades of a group of lords and ladies attending the royal Anne.

In imagination it is easy to picture to oneself the Watteau-like group formed by the Belindas and Sir Plumes of the age when Pope wrote his "Rape of the Lock"; when French glitter was spread over Dutch uniformity, as they loiter by the side of the canal, the beaux elaborately complimentary, and the belles condescendingly attentive, yet with a dash of something that keeps familiarity at fan's length. But it is time now to pass from these fanciful themes to a description of the reality.

Skirting the picturesque green, or common, of Hampton, the visitor enters the palace through an archway in the western quadrangle—that portion of the edifice appropriated, for the most part, to families who have obtained small Government pensions, with apartments in the palace. The west front exhibits, to some disadvantage, the monastic style of architecture, with all its stateliness and gloom. The pillars of the principal gateway are surmounted by a large lion and unicorn, as supporters of the royal arms, and each of the side gates by a military trophy. Along the left side of

the area of the outer court are barracks and such-like offices ; the greater part of the right side is open towards the river. In front are two other gateways—that to the left leading to the "kitchen court," the other conducting to the first quadrangle. This chief gateway is in excellent keeping with the older parts of the building. It is flanked with octagon towers, pierced with a fine pointed arch, over which are cut, in high relief, the royal arms, and above them projects a large and handsome bay window, framed of stone.

Through this archway is entered the first of Wolsey's courts remaining. There were originally five courts, the three first of which were pulled down to make way for William III.'s great square mass of brickwork. The writers who saw the palace in its glory describe it in entirety as the most splendid palace in Europe. Grotius says :— "Other palaces are residences of kings ; but this is of the gods." Hentzner, who saw it in Elizabeth's time, speaks of it with astonishment, and says :— "The rooms, being very numerous, are adorned with tapestry of gold, silver, and velvet, in some of which were woven history pieces ; in others Turkish and Armenian dresses, all extremely natural. In one chamber are several excessively rich tapestries, which are hung up when the queen gives audience to foreign ambassadors. All the walls of the palace shine with gold and silver. Here is likewise a certain cabinet, called 'Paradise,' where, besides that everything glitters so with silver, gold, and jewels, as to dazzle one's eyes, there is a musical instrument made all of glass, except the strings."

The two courts which remain are said to have consisted only of offices ; and, indeed, in old views of the palace the first court is represented much lower than the next, which did not itself nearly equal the stateliness of the rest. Mr. Howitt, in his "Visits to Remarkable Places," observes that "the old dark red brick walls, with still darker lines of bricks in diamond shapes running along them—the mixture of Gothic archways and square mullioned windows—the battlemented roofs, turrets, and cupolas, and tall twisted and cross-banded chimneys, all are deeply interesting, as belonging to the unquestionable period of Wolsey—belonging altogether to that Tudor or transition style when castles were fast turning into peaceful mansions, and the beauties of ecclesiastical architecture were called in to aid in giving ornament where before strength had only been required."

Of late years attempts have been made here and there at a restoration in the original style of such portions of the original structure as required repair; and quite recently the fine oak gates, which had been laid aside as lumber for many years, have been re-hung, after careful repair, at the entrance gateway; they are of massive dimensions, are ornamented with the usual linen-fold pattern, and are evidently of Wolsey's time. The outer face of the gates is pierced with shot and bullet-holes, which may have been occasioned during skirmishes in the civil wars, when fighting was going on outside the palace between the Cavaliers and Roundheads; or, as has been suggested, the holes may have been made through the gates having been set up as targets for the villagers of Hampton.

The work of restoration has included the vaulting and flanking turrets of the gateway, and also the vaulting to the gateway of the second, or Clock-tower Court, which we now enter. This court, called also the "middle quadrangle," is somewhat smaller than the former, measuring 133 feet from north to south, and about 100 from east to west. It received the name of the Clock Court from an astronomical clock which adorns the gateway on the east side. This curious and antique timepiece was removed some years ago, but in 1880 the dial was replaced, and now, with new works by Messrs. Gillett and Bland, again shows not only the hours of the day and night, but also, among other things, the day of the month, the motion of the sun and moon, the age of the moon, the phases and quarters of the moon, and other interesting matters connected with the lunar movements. The dial is composed of three separate copper discs of different sizes, with a common centre, but revolving at various rates. The smallest of these is 3ft. 3½in. in diameter, and in the middle of this is a slighly projected globe, painted to represent the earth. The quarters marked on the centre disc by thick lines are numbered with large figures, and round the edge this disc is divided into twenty-four parts, a red arrow painted on the second disc pointing to these figures, and showing at once the quarter in which the moon is and the time of "southing." Next to the figure of the earth in this centre disc, a circular hole, 10in. in diameter, allows a smaller disc travelling behind to show the phases of the moon. On the second disc, 4ft. 1½in. in diameter, but of which only the outer rim is seen, are twenty-nine divisions, and a triangular pointer, projecting from behind the central disc, shows the moon's age in days. The largest of the three discs is 7ft. 10in. in diameter. There are many circles painted on so much of the rim of this as is seen, the inner, or—following the order above observed, and proceeding from the centre—the first circle, giving the names of the months, the second the days of the

month (only twenty-eight for February), the third the signs of the zodiac, and on the rim, with 30 degrees for each space filled by a sign, a circle divided into 360 parts. A long pointer, with a gilded figure of the sun attached, projecting from behind the second disc, shows on this third or outermost disc of the dial the day of the month and the position of the sun in the ecliptic. This pointer performs another duty, acting like the hour-hand of an ordinary clock, and showing the time of day or night as it passes the twenty-four figures—two sets of twelve—painted on the stonework within which the dial revolves. The diameter of this outer immovable circle on the stone is 9ft. 8in., and the figures of the hours, Roman numerals, are 9in. in length. About the original clock very little is known, and even the name of the maker is not to be found in any of the works in which information on a matter of so much interest would be looked for. The date of its construction is known, and but little more. On a bar of the wrought-iron framework to which the dial is fixed is to be found, deeply cut and distinctly engraved, "N.O., 1540." One other evidence of its antiquity is derived from an entry, mentioned by Mr. E. J. Wood, in his "Curiosities of Clocks and Watches," of a payment made in 1575 to one George Gaver, "serjeant painter, for painting the great dial at Hampton Court Palace, containing hours of the day and night, the course of the sun and moon," and so on, though the author has not given a reference to the record in which he found this fact set down. Since Master Gaver exercised his art in decorating the dial-face, many clockmakers, it seems probable, from time to time repaired and altered the works; for Dr. Derham, describing the condition of the clock in 1711, when it had been recently repaired by Mr. Lang Bradley, of Fenchurch Street, said it had been found that the original pricked wheel and pinion had been removed, by some ignorant workman, as he supposed. Judging from the numbers given by Dr. Derham of the toothing of the wheels, the clock, it appears, even with the changes made by Mr. Bradley, could not have performed its functions accurately. It is not unlikely that the astronomical clock had long been useless, for as early as the year 1649 another clock-face had been placed on the other side of this gate-tower, over the entrance to the Great Hall, and a striking part had been added to the works of the clock.

In 1835 the works of the old clock were removed, but what became of them is not known. On the works of the clock removed in 1880 was found the following inscription:—"This clock, originally made for the Queen's Palace in St. James's Palace, and for many years in use there, was, A.D. 1835, by command of His Majesty King William IV., altered and adapted to suit Hampton Court Palace by B. L. Vulliamy, clock-maker to the King;" and on another plate on the clock—"Vulliamy, London, No. 352, A.D. 1799." The motive-power of this clock had evidently not been sufficient to drive in addition the astronomical dial, and the useless dial had been taken down and stowed away in a workshop at the palace, the gap left being filled by a painted board. When Mr. Bland, of the firm of Gillett and Bland, who had been commissioned by the Office of Works to make a new clock, examined the wheels by which the dials were to be moved, he found by the number of teeth in some of the wheels that the astronomical clock could not possibly have served its purpose. New wheels were therefore cut. The new works drive both the astronomical dial and the hands of the ordinary clock-face on the opposite or western side of the tower. In the mechanism many ingenious contrivances have been employed, and the clock is guaranteed not to vary more than five seconds a week. The bells are in the little hybrid classical cupola of painted wood which disfigures the nobly-proportioned Tudor tower of Cardinal Wolsey's palace. That on which the hours are struck weighs about 18 cwt., and two smaller bells chime the quarters. The large bell has plainly at some time been hung for ringing, and was probably fixed for striking when the two small bells, which were brought from another tower of the palace, were placed with it. In size, the clock—i.e., the mechanism within the clock-chamber—is, giving over all measurements, 7ft. 6in. long, 3ft. 6in. wide, and 3ft. 6in. deep, the main wheels being 14, 16, and 16 inches respectively in diameter. The clock face, of slate, on the west side of the tower, is 5ft. 8in. in diameter. It may interest the visitor to know that the small circular space, 3ft. in diameter, above the square clock front, now filled with a slab of slate, on which is cut the monogram of William IV., was, as the form of the brickwork behind shows, filled at an earlier period (probably until Vulliamy's clock was put up) by a clock dial, perhaps the one spoken of in a description of the palace in 1649 quoted by Mr. Wood. It is said that in the "clock-case upon the Great Hall there is one large bell and a clock under it, very useful for the whole house, having a fair dial or finger, upon the end of the said Great Hall, facing in the Great Court."

The south side of the Clock Court is partly concealed and disfigured by a colonnade, supported by pillars of the Ionic order, the design of Sir Christopher Wren. The oriel windows above each of the gateways of this court are adorned with the arms of Henry VIII., whilst on the face of the octagonal turrets on either side of the archway are busts of the Cæsars in terra-cotta. These, with other medallions in the adjoining court, were the gifts of Pope Leo X. to Cardinal Wolsey. Over the archway leading into the Clock Court are the arms of Wolsey, together with his motto— "Dominus mihi adjutor"—"God is my helper."

The south of the Clock Court is occupied by the Great Hall. This splendid apartment was built— or at all events completed—by Henry VIII., whose arms and cognisances enrich the ceiling, after the death of Wolsey. The archway forming the entrance to the hall has a rich fan-traceried roof. This handsome groined ceiling, having become ruinous and in danger of falling, was restored in 1880, the greatest care being taken to preserve and reproduce the exact form and details of the original. The apartment is reached by a short flight of stone steps. The following details of the hall are quoted from Mr. Jesse's able description of the building, in his "Summer's Day at Hampton Court:"— "The dimensions of this very noble room are —in length 106 feet, in breadth 40 feet, and in height 60 feet. The roof is very elaborately timbered, and richly decorated with carvings of several of the royal badges and with pendent ornaments, executed in a style which shows that the Italian taste had already made considerable advances in this country.

"Seven capacious windows on one side, and six on the other side, with a large window at each end, all placed considerably above the floor, throw a fulness of light throughout the apartment. A bay window on the daïs, extending from the upper part of the wall nearly to the floor, contributes very essentially to the cheerfulness of the general effect. This window has been enriched by Mr. Willement with compartments of stained glass, containing the arms, initials, and badges of King Henry VIII., the arms and motto of Queen Jane Seymour, 'Bown'd to obey and serve,' and the full insignia and motto of Wolsey, 'Dominus mihi adjutor.' On the lower part is seen the following inscription—'The lorde Thomas Wulsey, Cardinal, legat de latere, Archbishop of Yorke, and Chancellor of Englande.' The whole of the stained glass in the hall and in the presence-chamber is modern, and of Mr. Willement's fashioning and framing.

"It was, if we may trust tradition, upon one of the panes of glass of this window that Henry Howard, Earl of Surrey, so famous for the tenderness and elegance of his poetry and for his martial nature, wrote some lines with a diamond on the "fair Geraldine"; and it is told, with what certainty we know not, that the first play acted in this hall was that of 'Henry VIII., or the Fall of Wolsey.' Shakespeare is said to have been one of the actors in this play.

"Above the entrance-door, leading into the presence-chamber, or withdrawing-room, has been inserted a richly-carved stone bracket, inscribed 'Seynt George for merrie Englande,' on which, in full panoply, stands our patron saint, surrounded by a halo of ramrods, transfixing with his spear his antagonist, the dragon. On each side of this stands a smaller bracket, bearing figures clothed in bright plate armour. These figures were placed here by permission of the Board of Ordnance from the stores in the Tower. He has also arranged a fine group of armour under the east window.

"Between each of the side windows there is a noble pair of the horns of deer, with finely-carved heads of the animal, and carved wreaths round each of them. These horns, which form a part of a large collection, were probably placed in the hall in the reign of Henry VIII., when it was called the Hall of Horns. They have been preserved in the palace, and the

tioned. From the under part of the side windows to within a few inches of the pavement, the walls are covered with tapestry of such excellent design, and such costliness of material, that it may be

THE CHAPEL.

safely asserted that its parallel does not exist in Europe at this time. Three pieces hang on each side of the hall, and two others at the daïs end.

"'For round about the walls yclothed were
    With goodly arras of great majesty,
Woven with gold and silke so close and nere,
That the rich metal lurked privily,
As feigning to be hidd from envious eye;
Yet here, and there, and everywhere, unwares
It shewed itselfe and shone unwillingly;
Like a discoloured snake, whose hidden snares
Through the green grass his long bright-burnished back
    declares.'"   SPENSER.

INTERIOR OF THE GREAT HALL.

original colours have been restored as nearly as it was possible to do so. Over the horns are banners, having the devices of Henry VIII. and the arms of Wolsey, and of his several benefices, painted on them. The stringcourse above the tapestries has also been enriched with the rose, portcullis, &c., in colours. The most interesting, however, of the decorations to be seen in this truly regal apartment have yet to be men-

This noble apartment is commonly spoken of as "Wolsey's Hall," but it was probably only designed by him. Mr. Brewer, in the "Beauties of England and Wales," says that "it has been supposed that as this room is not described in the account by Cavendish of Cardinal Wolsey's entertainment of the French ambassadors, it was entirely a part of the additional buildings raised by King Henry. But it formed so important a feature in the design of the mansion, that we may safely ascribe the exterior walls and embellishments to the magnificent Wolsey, though we shall speedily show that

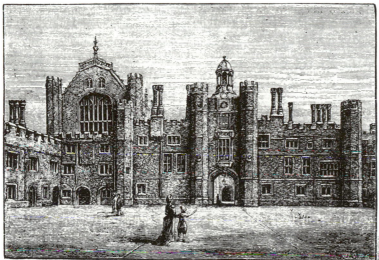

THE FIRST COURT.

the interior was not completed till 1536, or the succeeding year." At a meeting of the British Archæological Association here in 1882, Mr. Hubert Hall stated that from the accounts kept at the Record Office, and the papers in the British Museum, it was clear that " this hall was not finished when Wolsey was compelled to 'give' the palace to Henry VIII., and that it was completed by the king." Till about 1770, when it was restored, it had a large open fireplace in the centre, and the roof above was pierced by a lantern, which added picturesqueness to the external sky-line.

The subjects of the arras tapestry—eight in number—ranged round the hall illustrate the history of Abraham, and are as follows :—(1) God appearing to Abraham, and blessing him. (2) The birth and circumcision of Isaac, and the expulsion of Hagar and Ishmael. (3) Abraham sending his servant to seek a wife for his son Isaac. (4) The Egyptians sending away Abraham and Sarah with gifts. (5) Abraham entertaining three angels. (6) Abraham purchasing the Cave of Machpelah for a

burying-place. (7) Abraham and Lot parting. (8) Abraham offering up Isaac. The tapestries are mentioned by Evelyn in his " Diary." Of them he says :—"I believe the world can show nothing nobler of the kind than the stories of Abraham and Tobit." They are supposed to have been executed by Bernard Van Orlay, a pupil of Raffaelle. They were bought by Oliver Cromwell, and valued in the inventory at £8,260. At the entrance to the hall are some smaller pieces of similar tapestry, but of earlier date.

At the west end of the hall is the " Minstrels' Gallery," above which is arranged a group of armour, halberts, pikes, and banners.

This hall (as stated above) was occasionally used as a theatre for plays and masques in the merry days of Queen Elizabeth. It was again used for a similar purpose as late

FOUNTAIN COURT.

as the reign of George I., when, however, not more than seven plays were performed. It is significant that one of these dramas, acted on the 1st of October, 1718, was *Henry VIII.* Sir R. Steele, being asked by a grave nobleman—after Shakespeare's *Henry VIII.* had been performed here—how it pleased the king, replied—"So terribly well, that I was afraid, my lord, I should have lost all my actors ; for I was not sure the king would not keep them to fill the posts about the Court, for that he saw them so fit for the play."

On the 16th of October, 1731, the hall was

again used for a theatrical performance for the entertainment of the Duke of Lorraine, afterwards Emperor of Germany. Not until towards the close of the last century were the disfigurements to this hall removed. In 1829, during the rebuilding of Hampton church, the hall was fitted up for the purposes of divine service, and was used as the parish church for about two years.

After an interval of 150 years, the great hall, in 1880, was once again the scene of a theatrical entertainment. This was an amateur dramatic performance, given by special permission of Her Majesty the Queen, in aid of Princess Frederica's Home at Hampton. A stage was erected above the daïs at the east end of the hall, the large withdrawing-room forming a splendid "green room" for the performers. The plays performed were *Yellow Roses*, a dramatic sketch by Sir Charles Young, which was enacted by the author and Lady Monckton, and *Tears*, an amusing trifle, in which also Sir Charles Young and Lady Monckton assumed the principal characters.

"The circumstances of regal banqueting connected with the hall," writes Mr. Brewer, in the "Beauties of England and Wales," "are equally numerous and interesting. The unfortunate Catharine Howard was here first openly shown as queen, as also was Catharine Parr, her more prosperous successor. Henry VIII. often kept wassail within these walls; and here, during the Christmas of 1543, he entertained Francis Gonzaga, the Viceroy of Sicily. Edward VI. likewise presided, in puerile magnificence, over the table in the high place in the hall. Philip and Mary kept their Christmas at Hampton Court in 1554."

The withdrawing-room is entered by a doorway from the centre of the daïs in the hall, and is a noble apartment, sixty-two feet in length by twenty-nine feet in width, and the same in height. The ceiling is beautifully enriched with pendent ornaments, interspersed with the cognizances of the rose, portcullis, and other badges, and with coats-of-arms. The walls of this chamber are hung with tapestry in seven compartments, supposed to be of an early period of the French school. The subjects are as follows:—"Fame," "The Triumph of Virtue," "The Influence of Destiny," "The Death of Hercules," "Peace and War," &c. Above the tapestry are seven large cartoons, painted by Carlo Cignani, the subjects of which are as follows:— "Cupid riding on an Eagle," "The Triumph of Venus," "Cupid with a Torch," "Apollo and Daphne," "Jupiter and Europa," "The Triumph of Bacchus, Venus, and Ariadne," and "Cupid and a Satyr." These cartoons were designed for frescoes painted in the ducal palace at Parma, about the year 1660.

A passage on the north side of the great hall leads to Tennis Court Lane, whence a good view is obtained of the older parts of the palace, of which the Kitchen Court, with its curious circular erection, is not the least interesting.

The Fountain Court, or Eastern Quadrangle, as it is now called, was built, as we have already noted, by Sir Christopher Wren, in 1690. It is encircled by a colonnade of the Ionic order, with duplicated columns. Wren was appointed to the office of Surveyor-General of his Majesty's Works in 1668, and was employed by William III. to pull down part of the old palace, and to build in its place the quadrangle now under notice. The alterations and additions made here by Sir Christopher are far from being favourable specimens of his art. The studies made by him from the buildings of Louis XIV. had but too visible an effect on his palaces and private buildings; so that, as Horace Walpole remarks, "it may be considered fortunate that the French built only palaces, and not churches, and therefore St. Paul's escaped, though Hampton Court was sacrificed to the god of false taste." Wren's failure at Hampton Court palace, however, may be largely attributed to his having worked there under the directions of King William, one of whose favourite residences it was, and whose taste in architecture was of the lowest grade; indeed, when the arrangement of the low cloisters was criticised, the king took the whole blame on himself, acknowledging that they had been constructed by his own particular orders.

The Fountain Court is nearly a square, more than a hundred feet each way. In the area is a grass-plat railed in, with a circular basin in the centre, and a small fountain playing. This court occupies the site of the chief or grand court, which was described by Hentzner, in the reign of Elizabeth, as "paved with square stone, and having in its centre a fountain which throws up water, covered with a gilt crown, on the top of which is a statue of Justice, supported by columns of black and white marble."

The chapel is situated on the north side of the Fountain Court. The edifice having undergone alterations in successive reigns, its architecture can scarcely be assigned to any particular period. On the outer wall, on either side of the door, are the arms of Henry VIII. impaling those of Seymour, and the initials "H. J." united by a true lover's knot. From these indications it appears probable that the chapel was a part of the additional buildings constructed by King

Henry, and finished during the short-lived felicity arising from his marriage with Jane Seymour. Mr. Lysons, in his notice of Hampton Court, gives the following particulars concerning the chapel:— "Before the civil war this chapel was ornamented with stained glass and pictures, which were demolished in 1645, as appears by the following paragraph, taken from a weekly paper of that date: 'Sir Robert Harlow gave order (according to the ordinance of Parliament) for the pulling down and demolishing of the Popish and superstitious pictures in Hampton Court, where this day the altar was taken down, and the table brought into the body of the church, the rails pulled down and the steps levelled, and the Popish pictures and superstitious images that were in the glass windows were also demolished, and order given for the new glazing them with plain glass; and among the rest there was pulled down the picture of "Christ nailed to the Cross," which was placed right over the altar, and the picture of Mary Magdalen and others weeping by the foot of the cross, and some other idolatrous pictures, were pulled down and demolished.' The chapel was fitted up in its present state by Queen Anne; it is pewed with black and white marble, and fitted with Norway oak. The carving is by Gibbons. The original roof remains—a plain Gothic pattern, with pendent ornaments. Hentzner, who visited England in Queen Elizabeth's reign, speaks of the chapel as most splendid; and says that the queen's closet was transparent, with windows of crystal."

The State apartments are approached from the Fountain Court by means of the grand staircase, the walls and ceiling of which were painted by Verrio with mythological subjects, supposed to be allusions to the marriage of the Thames and Isis. Upon the ceiling are represented Jupiter and Juno seated upon a rich throne, with Ganymede riding upon Jupiter's eagle, and presenting to him the cup. Juno's peacock is in the front, and one of the fatal sisters is waiting, with her scissors in her hand, ready to cut the thread of life, should Jove give her orders. Verrio—the propriety of whose taste may be estimated by the fact of his having introduced himself and Sir Godfrey Kneller in one of his pictures in long periwigs, as spectators of our Saviour healing the sick—was paid for the whole palaces of Windsor and Hampton Court ceilings, sides, and back stairs at the rate of 8s. a foot, exclusive of gilding, and had wine daily allowed him, and lodgings in the palaces, and, when his eyesight failed, a pension of £200 per annum and an allowance of wine for life. He was devoted, from religious and political feelings, to the government of James II., and it seems that he was prevailed on with much difficulty even to *paint* for the successor of his former master.

The first room entered is the Guard Chamber, the walls of which are partly covered with arms and military trophies, in the shape of halberts, muskets, swords, &c., fancifully disposed in various ornamental forms. On the lower panels of this apartment are a few pictures, mostly portraits of admirals and military subjects; and including a spirited battle-piece, by Giulio Romano, and Canaletti's "Ruins of the Colosseum." It will be impossible in the space at our disposal to mention anything near a tithe of the pictures and objects of interest that meet the eye of the visitor whilst passing through the long suite of rooms, nearly thirty in number. Most of the chambers are hung with tapestry, and have painted ceilings. In one he will be attracted by the picture of "St. William," painted by Giorgione; in another by the portrait of Bandinelli the sculptor, by Correggio, which has always been considered a picture of great delicacy; nor will the paintings by Velasquez fail to arrest his attention. In the Audience Chamber, pictures by Ricci, Giulio Romano, Rubens, and Sebastian del Piombo, will meet his gaze; whilst in the King's Drawing-room he may compare the "Agony of our Saviour in the Garden," by Nicholas Poussin, with a military picture by the late Sir William Beechey, in which George III. is represented as reviewing the 10th Hussars. In the bed-room of William III. he may feast his eyes on the counterfeit presentments of the "beauties" of the Court of Charles II. In this chamber is the State bed of Queen Charlotte, the hangings of which were worked for her Majesty by the orphan daughters of clergymen. The ceiling of this room, which is in good preservation, was painted by Verrio, and is intended to represent "Night" and "Morning." The clock in this room was made by Daniel Quare, and requires winding-up only once in twelve months. The portraits round the room are as follows:—Anne, Duchess of York; Lady Byron; Princess Mary, as Diana; Queen Catharine; Mrs. Knott; Duchess of Portsmouth; Duchess of Richmond; Nell Gwynne; Countess of Rochester; Duchess of Somerset; Mrs. Lawson; Countess of Northumberland; Lady Denham; Countess of Sunderland; Lady Middleton; Lady Whitmore; Countess of Ossory; Duchess of Cleveland; and the Countess de Grammont. Of the above portraits, those of the Duchess of Somerset, Mrs. Knott, and Mrs. Lawson, were painted by Verelot, the Duchess of Portsmouth by Gasker, and the remainder by Sir Peter Lely. There are thirteen other portraits of ladies, whose names are unknown.

Another apartment, formerly known as the "Beauty Room," contains the portraits of Queen Mary, consort of William III., and the following eight distinguished ladies of her court:— The Duchess of St. Albans; Isabella, Duchess of Grafton; Carey, Countess of Peterborough; the Countess of Ranelagh; Mary, Countess of Essex; Mary, Countess of Dorset; Lady Middleton; and Mrs. Scrope. These "beauties" were painted by Sir Godfrey Kneller. "The thought," says Lord Orford, "was the queen's, during one of the king's absences, and contributed much to make her unpopular; as I have heard from the authority of the old Countess of Carlisle (daughter of Arthur, Earl of Essex), and who died within these few years, and remembered the event. She added that the famous Lady Dorchester advised the queen against it, saying—'Madam, if the king was to ask for the portraits of all the wits in the court, would not the rest think he called them fools?'"

It is on record that among the visitors one day, in the middle of the last century, were "those goddesses, the Gunnings"—the two fair sisters who turned the heads of half London, and became respectively Lady Coventry and Duchess of Hamilton. As they were going into the "Beauty Room" another batch of visitors arrived. The housekeeper said: "This way, ladies; here are the beauties." The fair Gunnings flew, or pretended to fly, into a passion, and asked her "what she meant by her words; for they had come to see the palace, and not to be made a show themselves."

The Queen's Gallery—or, as it is sometimes called, the Tapestry Gallery, from seven pieces of tapestry, taken from the history of Alexander the Great, from paintings by Le Brun—is eighty feet long and twenty-five feet wide. The tapestries have now given place to an interesting and well-arranged collection of pictures, among which the Elizabethan group is well worth the attention of the visitor; among them are two large pictures, representing the embarkation of Henry VIII. at Dover, and the meeting of that king and Francis I. of France in the field called the Cloth of Gold, near Calais.

"These pictures are not only historically very interesting, but," says Mr. Jesse, "a curious fact is connected with one of them. After the death of Charles I., the Commonwealth were in treaty with a French agent, who had expressed his desire of purchasing these pictures for the King of France. Philip, Earl of Pembroke, who was a great admirer and an excellent judge of painting, and considered these valuable pictures an honour to an English palace, came privately into the royal apartments, cut out that part of the picture where King Henry's head was painted, and, putting it into his pocket-book, retired unnoticed. The French agent, finding the picture mutilated, declined purchasing it. After the Restoration, the then Earl of Pembroke delivered the mutilated piece to Charles II., who ordered it to be replaced. On looking at the picture in a side light, the insertion of the head is very visible. It may fairly be doubted whether Holbein painted these pictures, they are too coarse; besides, he did not arrive in England till six years after the interview depicted, and therefore could not have taken the many excellent English portraits which are introduced into the pictures at that time. It is, however, immaterial, as their intrinsic merit and historical interest will always demand attention."

Throughout the whole of the State apartments there is much to gratify the taste of those who love to revel in "Pictureland," particularly if their taste or curiosity leads them to penetrate the semblances of those who lived in "the good old times," whether they be by Rembrandt, Titian, the Claudes, the Guidos, Caravaggio, Spagnoletto, Mantegna, or Holbein.

Among the paintings which enrich the principal apartments there now remain but comparatively few of those which were brought together with so judicious a hand by Charles I. The most noble purchase made by that king—the seven great cartoons of Raffaelle, which found here for many years their appropriate home—have been removed to the South Kensington Museum, as more easily accessible to the student as well as the London sight-seer. They had previously been on view at Windsor Castle, and before that occupied an octagonal apartment at Buckingham Palace.* These cartoons were executed by Raffaelle while engaged in the chambers of the Vatican, under the auspices of Popes Julius II. and Leo X. As soon as they were finished they were sent to Flanders to be copied in tapestry, for adorning the Pontifical apartments; but the tapestries were not conveyed to Rome till after the decease of Raffaelle, and probably not before the dreadful sack of that city in 1527, under the pontificate of Clement VII.; when Raffaelle's scholars having fled from thence, none were left to inquire after the original cartoons, which lay neglected in the store-rooms of the manufactory, the money for the tapestry having never

---

* See "Old and New London," Vol. IV., p. 64.

been paid. The revolution that happened soon after in the Low Countries prevented their being noticed during a period in which works of art were wholly neglected. They were purchased by Charles I., at the recommendation of Rubens, but had been much injured by the weavers. At the sale of the royal pictures in 1653 these cartoons were purchased for £300 by Oliver Cromwell, against whom no one would presume to bid. The Protector pawned them to the Dutch Court for upwards of £50,000, and after the revolution King William brought them over again to England, and built a gallery for their reception in Hampton Court. Originally there were twelve of these cartoons, but four of them have been destroyed by damps and neglect. The subjects were "The Adoration of the Magi," "The Conversion of St. Paul," "The Martyrdom of St. Stephen," and "St. Paul before Felix and Agrippa." Two of these were in the possession of the King of Sardinia, and two of Louis XIV. of France, who is said to have offered 100,000 louis d'ors for the seven, which are justly represented as "the glory of England, and the envy of all other polite nations." The twelfth, the subject of which was "The Murder of the Innocents," belonged to a private gentleman in England, who pledged it for a sum of money; but when the person who had taken this valuable deposit found it was to be redeemed, he greatly damaged the drawing, for which the gentleman brought an action against him.

In spite of the additions made to the collection of pictures here by Charles I., Mr. J. T. Smith, in his "Book for a Rainy Day," somewhat sneeringly endeavours to give the chief praise to Henry VIII. as the greatest promoter of the taste for the fine arts in England. "It is curious to observe," remarks Mr. Smith, "how fond Horace Walpole, and indeed all his followers, have been of attributing the earliest encouragement of the fine arts in England to King Charles I. That is not the fact; nor is that monarch entitled, munificent as he was, to that degree of praise which biographers have thought proper to attribute to him as a liberal patron; and this I shall immediately prove. King Henry VIII. was the first English sovereign who encouraged painting, in consequence of Erasmus introducing Hans Holbein to Sir Thomas More, who showed his Majesty specimens of that artist's rare productions. Upon this, the king most liberally invited him to Whitehall, where he gave him extensive employment, not only in decorating the panels and walls of that palace with portraits of the Tudors as large as life, but with easel pictures of the various branches of his family and courtiers, to be placed over doors and other spaces of the State chambers. Holbein may be recorded as the earliest painter of portraits in miniature, which were mostly circular, and all those which I have seen were relieved by blue backgrounds. He was also the designer and draughtsman of numerous subjects for the use of the Court jewellers, as may be seen in a most curious volume preserved in the print-room of the British Museum, many of the drawings in which are beautifully coloured."

Mr. William Howitt, in his "Visits to Remarkable Places," thus concludes his notice of the pictures at Hampton Court:—"Here we must quit the presence of these noblest of the conceptions of the divine Raffaelle—rejoicing, however, that they are now free to our contemplation as the very landscape around them, and that we can, at our pleasure, walk into this fine old palace, linger before these sacred creations at our will, and return to them again and again.

"Quitting them, we shall now hastily quit the Palace of Hampton Court; for though there is a small room adjoining, containing Casanova's drawing of Raffaelle's celebrated picture of 'The Transfiguration,' and several other interesting paintings, and yet another long Portrait Gallery, filled from end to end with the forms and faces of celebrated persons by celebrated artists, we can but gaze and pass on; and yet, who would not delight to have that one room to himself, to haunt day after day, and to ponder over the features and costumes of Locke, Newton, Sheridan, Boyle, Charles XII. of Sweden, Caroline, the Queen of George II., made interesting to all the world by the author of 'Waverley,' in the interview of Jeanie Deans? Who would not pause a moment before even the little Geoffrey Hudson, and think of all that diminutive knight's wrath, his duel, and his adventure in the pie? Lord Falkland's fine and characteristic face is a sight worth a long hour's walk on a winter's morning; and the Earl of Surrey, flaming in his scarlet dress, scarlet from head to foot—who would not stop and pay homage to the memory of his bravery, his poetry, and his Geraldine? But there are Rosamond Clifford and Jane Shore. Lely had not brought the Graces into England in their day, and therefore, instead of those wondrous beauties which we expect them, we find them— ghosts.

"Here, too, is another portrait of Queen Elizabeth, a full-length by Zucchero, where 'stout Queen Bess' is not in one of her masculine moods of laconic command—when she looked 'every inch a queen' —but in a most melancholy and romantic one indeed. She is clad in a sort of Armenian dress—a loose figured robe, without shape, without sleeves, and trimmed with fur—a sort of high cap, and Eastern slippers. She is represented in a wood, with a stag near her; and on a tree are cut, one below the other, after the fashion of the old romances, the following sentences:— INJUSTI JUSTA QUERELA. — MEA SIC MIHI. — DOLOR EST MEDICINA DOLORI. And at the foot of the tree, on a scroll, these verses, supposed to be of the royal manufacture :—

" 'The restless swallow fits
　　my restless minde,
　In still revivinge,
　　still renewinge
　　wrongs ;
　Her just complaints of
　　cruelty unkinde
　Are all the musique
　　that my life pro-
　　longes
　With pensive thoughtes
　　my weepinge stags
　　I crowne,
　Whose melancholy
　　teares my cares ex-
　　presse ;
　Hes teares in sylence,
　　and my sighes un-
　　knowne,
　Are all the physicke
　　that my harmes
　　redresse.
　My onely hopes was in
　　this goodly tree,
　Which I did plant in
　　love, bringe up in
　　care,
　But all in vaine, for
　　now too late I see
　The shales be mine,
　　the kernel others
　　are.
　My musique may be plaintes, my physique teares,
　　If this be all the fruite my love-tree beares.'

"We step through the door on which Jane Shore's spectral visage is hung, and lo! we are on the Queen's Staircase, and descend once more to the courts of Wolsey. Long as we have lingered in this old palace, we have had but a glimpse of it. Its antiquities, its pleasantness, and its host of paintings, cannot be comprehended in a visit: they require a volume; and a most delicious volume that would be which should take us leisurely through the whole, giving us the spirit and the history, in a hearty and congenial tone, of its towers and gardens, and all the renowned persons who have figured in its courts, or whose limned shapes now figure on its walls."

ANNE BOLEYN'S GATEWAY.
(*From Lysons.*)

The gardens of Hampton Court are about forty-four acres in extent. They were originally laid out by Cardinal Wolsey, and greatly improved by Queen Elizabeth and Charles II. It is said that the gardens were closed against the public in the time of George I., who, being unaware of the circumstance, inquired of the gardener one morning why the gates were shut against the people. "Because, your Majesty," replied the man in office, "they *steal* the flowers." "What," returned the good-natured monarch, "are my English subjects so fond of flowers? Plant more, then!" This story, however, is told also of Kensington. George III. also took great pride and pleasure in them, and often drove over from Kew to visit them.

The public gardens are separated by an iron fence from what is called the Home Park. The gardens and park were put into their present form by Messrs. Loudoun and Wise, gardeners to their Majesties William and Mary. The gardens themselves are perfectly flat, and are laid out in the Dutch style—stiff and formal, with long-drawn avenues and opening glades, after the fashion of the Low Countries. The east front of the palace is open to the gardens, and is here seen to the best advantage. It is constructed of bright red brick, with stone dressings, and in the centre four fluted three-quarter columns, of the Corinthian order, sustain an angular pediment, on which are sculptured in bas-relief the triumphs of Hercules over Envy. Along this front of the building there is a broad gravel walk, leading, on the one hand, down to the banks of the Thames, and on the other to a gate, called the Flowerpot Gate, which opens on the Kingston Road. At the southern end of the east front is the entrance to the private garden, which contains a few rare plants, the remains of Queen Mary's botanical garden. Here, too, is a large

HAMPTON COURT.
(From a Print published about 1770.)

lean-to house, containing the famous grape-vine. The inside dimensions of this house are seventy-two feet in length by thirty feet in breadth. The vine is planted inside the house, and the roof is almost entirely covered with branches, some of which are over a hundred feet in length. The average yearly produce of this vine is said to amount to about 1,200 pounds, and the grapes are sent to supply her Majesty's table. The tree is believed to have been planted in 1768 by Lancelot Brown, who was once chief gardener here, and who afterwards became so much noted as one of the first practitioners of the English style of landscape gardening. On approaching the vine we pass two large greenhouses, which contain some orange-trees and other plants. Amongst them is an orange-myrtle, said to have been brought to this country by William III.

In the reign of Charles II., the large semicircle on the east side of the palace was planted ; but it was not till the reign of William III. that the grounds were brought to anything like perfection. At this period the art of clipping yew and other trees into regular figures and fantastic shapes reached its highest point, being greatly favoured by the king. Four urns, said to be the first that were used in the gardens, were also planted by William III. in front of the palace. Walpole says that the walls were once covered with rosemary, and that the trees were remarkable specimens of the "topiary" art, as the fashion of clipping trees into stiff unnatural forms was then called.

On the northern side of the palace is a large space of ground, called "the Wilderness," which was planted and laid out by William III. In this part of the grounds is a labyrinth, or maze, which affords much amusement to visitors. Near the labyrinth is an entrance known as the "Lion Gates," which are particularly handsome, being designed in a bold and elegant style. The large stone piers of the gates are richly decorated, their cornices supported by fluted columns, and surmounted by two colossal lions *couchant*.

Hampton Court Palace is supplied with water from some springs in Coombe Wood, whence it is conducted through pipes which were laid down by Cardinal Wolsey at a very great outlay. The distance is about two miles, in the most direct line, and the leaden pipes which convey the water are carried across the bottom of the River Thames. There are two pipes from each conduit, making altogether eight miles of leaden pipes.

Hampton Court (or the Home) Park immediately adjoins the palace gardens, and is about five miles in circumference. It extends from the borders of the gardens to Hampton Wick, and is bounded on the south by the River Thames, and on the north by the high road to Kingston. This park is well stocked with deer. It is watered by a canal about half a mile in length, having a fine avenue of lime-trees on each side of it. Another canal to correspond was partly excavated by William III., and near it the spot is still pointed out where the accident happened which cost him his life. The avenues in this park were planted by William III. Near the upper deer-pen is a fine old oak-tree about forty feet in circumference; and there is also near the stud-house an elm known by the name of "King Charles's Swing," which is peculiarly curious in shape. A building, called the Pavilion, which was erected by Sir Christopher Wren in the reign of William III., was the occasional residence of the late Duke of Kent, in his official capacity as "ranger" of this park.

In the park may still be seen some lines of fortifications, which were originally constructed for the purpose of teaching the art of war to William, Duke of Cumberland, when a boy—the same duke who became so celebrated afterwards in the Scottish rising of 1745.

The Stud-house, in the centre of the Home Park, was founded by the Stuarts ; but George IV. was its great supporter and maintainer, for both as prince regent and as king he was devoted to racing, and began breeding race-horses here systematically and on an extensive scale.

The cream-coloured horses used on State occasions by the sovereign are kept here. They are descended from those brought over from Hanover by the princes of the Brunswick line, being a special product of those countries. The breed is kept up here most religiously, and the animals are the last representatives of the Flemish horses, once so fashionable. They are slow and pompous in their action, and many of them are upwards of twenty years old. They look small in comparison with the great lumbering state coach ; but most of them are sixteen, or at least fifteen, hands high. The State harness and trappings of each horse do not weigh less than two hundred-weight.

Here are kept the Arabs and other Eastern horses presented to her Majesty. It is not etiquette to give any of them away, much less to sell them ; nor are they put to any use, nor killed when they get old. They have a happy enjoyment of life, till death calls them away.

"Nimrod," writing in *The Turf* in 1834, observes that "great regard has always been paid here to what is known in sporting circles as 'stout blood'—namely, horses of sinew and strength, rather than of speed." He adds a list of the sires and mares kept here, and also states that " from prudential motives the royal stud at Hampton Court was broken up, only one or two sires and mares being kept."

Sir Richard Steele was, for a time, surveyor of the royal stables here ; and the Earl of Albemarle, Groom of the Stole, lived for some years at the " Stud-house," which is still the official residence of the Master of the Horse, though not generally occupied as such.

In December, 1882, the entire palace had a narrow escape from being destroyed, a large portion of the upper rooms in the east wing, overlooking the gardens and the fountain court, and which were in the occupation of private families, having been accidentally burnt.

In a leading article, congratulating the country on the fact that the galleries have been spared, the *Times* made the following remarks, which may most appropriately close this chapter :—" Hampton Court is pre-eminently the palace of the ordinary Londoner's predilection.

PLAN OF THE MAZE.

neither very intelligent nor very keen, find their way throughout the summer to Hampton Court, and return much the better for their outing, even if their knowledge of history remains as vague as ever, and their feeling for art as cold. For this reason alone—because of the simple and wholesome pleasures it affords in one way or another to every visitor—the destruction of Hampton Court would have been regarded as an irreparable calamity. Apart from its suroundings, moreover, which we suspect attract more visitors than its contents, the palace itself is a building which the country could ill afford to spare. It is a record of pomp of Wolsey and of the genius of Wren, and its history includes associations as diverse as the theological lucubrations of James I. and the revels of his scapegrace grandson, the gloomy broodings of Cromwell in his hours of dejection, and the busy statecraft of William III. Of the treasures of its picture gallery it is unnecessary to speak at length. The collection, as a whole, is rather copious than select. Some few pictures are undoubtedly of priceless value ; the art

This is not, perhaps, because of its historical interest as a relic of Wolsey's magnificence, or as the home of the Stuarts and the elder Georges, nor even exclusively because of the interest attaching to its gallery of pictures. Its place in the heart of Londoners is largely due to more homely associations. It is easily and quickly reached from London, and its surroundings are rich in everything that the country-going Londoner has learnt to love. Its stately and rich-toned buildings, its well-kept gardens, its spacious parks with their matchless trees, and its unrivalled situation on the banks of the placid Thames, all give it an attraction which for variety of charm can hardly be matched in England. To this must be added the fact that the palace contains the only national collection of pictures which is open to the public on Sundays, and this, perhaps, accounts as much as anything else for the pre-eminent popularity which Hampton Court enjoys. Thousands to whom the historical associations of the place are rather vague, thousands more whose enjoyment of a gallery or pictures is

of the world would be palpably the poorer for their destruction. Others, again, are interesting as specimens of painters whose works are rare, or as commemorating events of moment in English history. But these are only a small percentage of the whole. The remainder are interesting rather because they have long hung on the walls of Hampton Court, and seem to partake of the character of the place, than because they can claim any very eminent merit of their own. There is some royal furniture also of ancient date in several of the public rooms of the palace, and a portion of this is reported to have been damaged by the floods of water employed to extinguish the fire. Such things have a certain popular interest, no doubt, but if anything was to be destroyed, it is safe to rejoice that a capricious fate has spared the pictures and only taken the upholstery. If by an irreparable stroke of fortune the Holbeins, the Mantegnas, or any other of the real treasures of the gallery had been destroyed, it would have been a poor consolation to learn that Queen Anne's bed had been preserved, or even that her portmanteau was safe."

CHAPTER XIV.

FELTHAM, SUNBURY, AND HALLIFORD.

"Est et honor campis."—*Ovid.*

Situation, Etymology, and General Appearance of Feltham—Population, &c.—Notice of the Parish in Domesday Book—Descent of the Manor
—The Parish Church—Death of Miss Frances Kelly, the Actress—Middlesex Industrial School—The Convalescent Home—Sunbury—
Its Etymology—History of the Manor—Col Kenyngton, otherwise Kempton—A Royal Palace—Kempton House—Kempton Park Race-
course—Sunbury Common—Sunbury Parish Church—Roman Catholic Chapel—The Village of Sunbury—Sunbury Place—The Pumping
Stations of the London Water-works Companies—Thames Angling Preservation Society—The Manor of Charlton—Halliford.

THE parish of Feltham lies to the south-west of Hampton, and is particularly flat and uninteresting. It is bounded on the east by the parish of Hanworth, which we have already dealt with in a previous chapter (see pages 69, 70). The name, according to Mr. Brewer, in the "Beauties of England," is supposed to be a corruption of *Feldham*, signifying the "Field Village, or Village in a Field."

The country all about here, and indeed as far west as Staines, is covered with market gardens, or fields devoted to vegetable produce, which is sent up to market at Covent Garden. The village of Feltham is long and straggling; it is chiefly of a rural and humble character, and contains a few old-fashioned houses and shops; but in the immediate neighbourhood, particularly to the north and west of the village, and at Feltham Hill, about a mile to the south, are several better-class villas and residences of a more ornamental description. There is also here a station on the Windsor branch of the South-Western Railway. In 1871 the number of houses in the parish was 387, whilst the population numbered 2,748 souls, but this estimate included upwards of 900 persons in the Middlesex Industrial School. This number has somewhat decreased since that period, being, according to the returns for 1881, only 2,709.

The manor of Feltham is thus noticed in "Domesday Book":—"Earl Moreton (Mortain in Normandy) holds the manor of Feltham, taxed at twelve hides. The arable land is twelve carucates. There are six hides in demesne, on which is one plough; three more might be employed. The villanes have eight ploughs. There are fourteen villanes, who hold a virgate each; five others have each a virgate each, and two slaves, or bondmen. There is meadow-land equal to ten carucates, and pasture for the cattle of the village. The total value is £6 per annum; when it came into the Earl's possession it was only £4, but in the reign of King Edward it was £8. Two thanes were then seised of this manor: one of them, a vassal of the king, held five hides as a separate manor; the other, a vassal of Earl Harold, had seven hides as

a separate manor also, and could alien to whom he pleased."

From the above extract it will be seen that this parish was devoted to agriculture as far back as eight centuries ago.

The two manors above referred to were united under the Earl of Mortain, and became subsequently the property of Hawise, Countess of Rumaze, who gave the conjoined estate to the Hospital of St. Giles' Without-the-Bars, near Holborn, in whose possession it remained till the dissolution in 1537, when it was surrendered to the king, Henry VIII. Early in the seventeenth century the manor was granted in fee to trustees for Lord Cottington, and it was subsequently sold, together with the advowson, to Sir Thomas Chamber. Since then, the property has changed hands many times. "The manor of Feltham," observes Mr. Brewer, in his "Beauties of England and Wales," "is only nominal, and exercises no manorial rights, the whole of this parish being subject to the jurisdiction of the adjacent manor of Kennington"— now Kempton.

The greater part of this Thames valley would seem to have been anything rather than a haunt to the Muses, who doubtless thought it dull and tame. It has, in fact, no literary history.

The parish church, which stands on the road to Sunbury, is a plain brick-built edifice, dating from the beginning of the present century, when the taste for ecclesiastical architecture was at a very low ebb. It is dedicated to St. Dunstan, and replaced the former parish church, which had become ruinous and dilapidated. The old church is described in Lysons' "Middlesex" as "a small structure, consisting of a chancel, nave, and a north aisle. It is built of flint and stone, chiefly the *lapis compositus*, commonly called the 'plum-pudding' stone. At the west end is a wooden tower and spire, almost covered with ivy, issuing from a single stem, eighteen inches in girth." That building was taken down in 1802, and the present church erected in its place. This latter edifice was enlarged by the addition of aisles in 1856. At the west end is a tower with an embattled parapet, surmounted by a spire. The edifice contains a few monuments preserved from the old church, but none of general interest.

It appears from a survey made by order of Parliament in 1650, that Job Iggleton, the then incumbent, was presented by President Bradshaw, who possessed the estates of Lord Cottington which were confiscated for his attachment to the royal cause.

In the churchyard is the grave of William Wynne Ryland, an eminent line engraver of the last century, who was executed in 1793 for forgery on the East India Company.

Another church of greater pretensions has of late sprung up near the railway station, to meet the wants of an increasing population.

At Feltham, in December, 1882, died "a nonagenarian and something more," Miss Frances Maria Kelly, an actress of some note in her time. Born in the year 1790, she was one of the last survivors of a great school of actors, her first appearance on the stage dating as far back as 1807. In the following year she was a member of Mr. Colman's company at the Haymarket, and she enjoyed a high reputation at Drury Lane, Covent Garden, and the English Opera House. Among her contemporaries were Mrs. Siddons, John Kemble, Edmund Kean, and Mrs. Jordan. In 1840, as recorded in OLD AND NEW LONDON,* Miss Kelly founded a school for acting in Dean Street, Soho, which afterwards blossomed into a theatre, and is now known as the Royalty.

In the fields to the west of the village stands the Middlesex Industrial School or Reformatory for boys convicted of crime. It was opened in 1859, and is under the charge and control of the magistrates for the county of Middlesex. The building, which, since its foundation, has been greatly enlarged, is capable of accommodating about 1,000 boys, who are sentenced to detention here for periods varying from one to three years, the ages of the boys ranging from seven to fourteen years. It is constructed of red brick with stone dressings, and consists of a large principal building, a chapel, infirmary, workshops, farms, sewage works, &c.; in the grounds is the model of a ship, for the purpose of enabling the boys to practise seamanship, or at all events to learn the rudiments of nautical tactics. Nearly 150 acres of land are kept under cultivation by the inmates, so as to supply the wants of the establishment.

At Feltham a convalescent home has been established in connection with Mrs. Hilton's

Crèche, Orphan Home, and Infant Infirmary, at Stepney. There is also a "Nunnery" here, under the superintendence of "Father Ignatius."

Passing southward by Feltham Hill and Meadhurst Park, we now make our way towards Sunbury, a pleasant river-side village a mile and a half above Hampton Court, in the Hundred of Spelthorne, and a spot which has long been a favourite resort of anglers. The name of this place is often written, in ancient records, "Sunnabyri," or "Sunneberie," the derivation of which is from two Saxon words : "sunna," the sun, and "byri," a town. In "Domesday Book" the manor is entered under the name of "Suneberie," and is there described as parcel of "the ancient demesnes of the church of St. Peter," otherwise Westminster Abbey, to which it was given in the time of Edward the Confessor. In 1223 it was assigned to the Bishop of London, and the vicarage to the Dean and Chapter of St. Paul's. The latter arrangement holds good to the present day. James I. conveyed the manor to the Stratfords, and in 1693 it was possessed by Sir John Tyrwhit, son-in-law of Francis Phelips, who had become possessed of the property in 1676. Early in the last century it was sold to John Crosse, and having subsequently changed hands several times, finally passed into the hands of the Mitchisons, by whose family the manor is still possessed. The manor-house, now the seat of Mr. William Anthony Mitchison, is a large red-brick building, on the western side of the parish.

Besides the principal manor of Sunbury, and a manor formerly styled "Cerdentone," but now Charlton, there is a manorial district, mentioned in "Domesday Book" under the name of Chenetone. "This manor," observes Mr. Brewer, in the "Beauties of England," "was afterwards termed *Col Kenyngton*, or *Cold Kennington*, and is now known by the name of Kempton. Robert, Earl of Cornwall and Mortain, was succeeded in his title and estates by his son William, who rebelled against Henry I., and his estates were seized by that king in the year 1104. The manor thus becoming vested in the Crown, the manor-house was constituted a royal dwelling, and it so remained until the reign of King Edward III." Lysons, in his "Middlesex Parishes," makes the following observations respecting this manor :—"It is probable, from the name of this manor, that the manor-house had been a royal palace during the reign of the Saxon kings. It must be observed that where Kennington occurs in the date of royal charters, it has hitherto, I believe, been always understood of Kennington, near Lambeth, where also was

* See Vol. III., p. 194.

a palace ; for I cannot find that even tradition has preserved the memory of the palace which once stood in Kempton Park, but, on the contrary, supposes the traces of ancient buildings which occur there to have been the remains of a religious house, of whose existence there are no proofs either from history or record."

The manor-house, or palace of Col Kenyngton is mentioned in a survey made by order of Edward III. in 1331, for the purpose of inquiring into the state of the palace and park at that time. The original

calculated at 30s. The house called the *Aumerye* is so ruinous that it threatens to fall down. There is wanting in the larder a door with proper fastenings, which may be made for 2 shillings. The repairs of the chamber beyond the gate, with the steps leading to it, are estimated at 100 shillings. The dresser in the great kitchen and hall is quite broken down. The repairs of the farm-house and the gate next to the granary are estimated at 40s. The repair of the park-wall is estimated at 13s. 4d., and that of the walls round the manor at 10s."

HALLIFORD.   (*See page* 176.)

of this document is preserved among the public records, and it describes the palace as having fallen, through neglect, into a state of dangerous dilapidation. A translation of this document is given by Lysons in his account of the parishes of Middlesex, in which the following particulars occur :—" There are dilapidations in the great hall, and in the pantry and buttery at the east end, the expense of repairing which is estimated at £4 6s. 8d. The great chamber, with the chapel and wardrobe adjoining, are much out of repair, as are the Queen's chamber, with the chapel and wardrobe adjoining. The repairs of the cellar under the Queen's chamber are estimated at 13 shillings. The repair of the chamber called the *Aleye*, which must have new beams, are

The custody of the ancient manor of Col Kenyngton was granted by the reigning sovereign to different persons, either for a certain term of years or for life, on condition of their paying yearly a valuable consideration, until 1631, when it was granted in fee to Sir Robert Killigrew. The manor-house is mentioned in the diary of the first Lord Shaftesbury as the seat of his relative, Mr. Carew Raleigh, whom he occasionally visited there. Later on, the manor was inherited by Sir John Chardin Musgrave, who sold it to a Mr. Edward Hill. By this gentleman many noble and venerable forest-trees, by which the park was thickly adorned, were cut down, and the demesne despoiled of much of its picturesque beauty. Kempton Park, however, has still some fine pollard-oaks dotted up and down it. It is about 300 acres in extent, and is bounded on the east and north by a little stream, or rivulet, a tributary of the Thames, which rises near Bedfont and Feltham. The Thames Valley branch of the South Western Railway also skirts the north side of the park. In a map of Middlesex published in 1823, Kempton House figures as the property of F. Manners, Esq., but it has since several times changed hands.

entered by a pointed and embattled gateway. The interior of the mansion is not yet finished, but many of the rooms have an air of comfort, and are of agreeable proportions." The author adds in a foot-note :—"Since the above account of Kempton House was written, the 'Gothic greenhouse,' forcing-houses, &c., have been sold by public auction. At the same time, some painted glass in the windows and doors was exposed to sale in a similar manner. It would thus appear that it is not intended to complete the mansion ; but

SUNBURY CHURCH. (*See page 176.*)

Kempton House, at the beginning of the present century, appears to have been a sort of rival to "Strawberry Hill." Writing in 1816, Mr. Brewer thus describes the mansion in the "Beauties of England" :—"The present mansion of Kempton is an imitation of the Gothic style, different parts of which were executed under the direction of both the last-named gentlemen (Mr. Hill and Mr. Fish). Indeed, it is evident that the whole was constructed in attention to a single design. The building is extensive, but has, on the exterior, all the gloom of the ancient English style, without any of those fascinating graces which were sometimes produced by genius while revelling in entire disdain of rule. Yet ample use is made of what is termed the Gothic ; even the stables and greenhouse have embattled parapets, and the garden is

we have suffered our article to remain as previously written, from a consideration that it may be the only descriptive notice extant of a costly building that will probably soon be levelled with the ground."

The present house is a good substantial mansion of the ordinary type. There are no traces visible of the ancient palace. About 400 acres of Kempton Park are enclosed within a ring fence, and set apart as a race-course. It is close by the Sunbury Station, on the Thames Valley Railway, and is much such another place as "Sandown," near Esher, in Surrey. Here steeplechases and coursing races take place, and its spring and autumn meetings are largely patronised.

Sunbury Common is a large tract of not very good or profitable land, occupying the northern part of the parish, towards Ashford. It has been largely enclosed during the past half century.

The parish church of Sunbury, dedicated to St. Mary, was built in the middle of the last century, on the site of an older church which had been taken down. It was erected by Mr. Wright, who was some time Clerk of the Works at Hampton Court, and was long an unsightly brick structure, of little or no architectural pretensions. Its appearance, however, has been immensely improved of late years by the insertion of new windows and the carrying out of other structural arrangements, including a porch at the western end, enriched with arcades at the sides and decorative carvings, and a semi-circular chancel. The church is, in fact, one of the cleverest transformations of a "Church-warden" structure into a Byzantine church to be seen in the kingdom. The tower, which is a conspicuous object as seen from the river, is surmounted by a parapet and a singular-looking cupola. On the south wall of the church is a monument to Lady Jane, sister of Philip, Duke of Wharton, and the last of her noble family. Her ladyship was the wife of Mr. Robert Coke, of Longford, in Derbyshire, and died in 1761. The churchyard is tolerably crowded with tomb-stones, but there are none calling for particular mention.

Besides one or two places of worship for Dissenters of different denominations, there is in the village of Sunbury a Roman Catholic chapel of some little architectural pretensions. It was consecrated by Archbishop (now Cardinal) Manning in 1869, and is built of Kentish rag and Bath stone, in the Early English style. The altar, which is enriched with precious stones and mosaic work, was the gift of Mr. Richard Lamb, of River Meades.

The village of Sunbury lies principally along the left bank of the River Thames, and contains several good old-fashioned brick-built dwelling-houses and shops. In Lewis's "Topography" (1835) the population is given as 1,863, a number which had increased in 1871 to 3,368 (when the houses are recorded in the census returns as 663), and ten years later to 3,500.

Sunbury appears to have been formerly a favourite locality for the residence of gentry, its "sunny" situation on the north bank of the Thames, with its pleasantly-situated villas, rendering the spot one of the most attractive in the immediate neighbourhood of London. Among the residents here at the end of the last century was the celebrated Admiral Lord Hawke.

At the eastern end of the village is Sunbury Place, which, at the commencement of the present century, was the occasional residence of the Hon. Percy Wyndham. The mansion is described in the "Beauties of England" at that time as showing four fronts, and as having an ornamental pavilion at each corner.

The opposite, or Surrey, shore is here flat, and of no very interesting character; but the river scenery in the neighbourhood, with its eyots and weirs and swans, is pleasant and attractive to water-parties and fishermen. Both here and on the opposite shore are the pumping-works and filtering reservoirs of two or three London Water-works Companies. At Sunbury are the rearing ponds of the Thames Angling Preservation Society, and the broad reach of the river at this point affords good fishing for jack and barbel, and occasionally trout. Nearly 700 yards of the river, extending from the weir eastward to the break-water, are known as "Sunbury Deeps," and are maintained by the Thames Conservancy.

Passing from the regions of fact to those of fancy, we may remark that through Sunbury passed Oliver Twist, under the charge of Bill Sykes, on his way to commit the burglary at Shepperton. "As they passed Sunbury church," writes Charles Dickens, "the clock struck seven. There was a light in the ferry-house opposite, which streamed across the road, and threw into more sombre shadow a dark yew-tree, with graves beneath it. There was a dull sound of water not far off, and the leaves of the old tree stirred gently in the night wind. It seemed like quiet music for the repose of the dead."

The manor of Charlton mentioned above was given in far-off ages to the Abbey of Merton, in Surrey, by which it was held till the Reformation, after which it passed into the hands of Sir John Mason. Since the beginning of the seventeenth century the manor has been several times alienated. The hamlet of Charlton lies about two miles to the north-west of the village of Sunbury.

Halliford, called in old maps (as late as 1790) Harleyford, extends westward from Sunbury along the river bank. It consists of two divisions, Upper and Lower, the former being a hamlet of Sunbury, and the latter a hamlet in the parish of Shepperton. It is a favourite haunt of anglers, the reaches of the river here abounding in perch and chub. We shall describe it in the next chapter.

CHAPTER XV.

SHEPPERTON, AND THE VALLEY OF THE THAMES.

"While Thames
Among his willows from thy view retires."
AKENSIDE.

Situation and General Appearance of Shepperton—The River Exe—The Village and its Surroundings—Population—Early History and Descent of the Manor—The Manor-house—The Parish Church—The Rectory - Waterside Taverns—Thames Angling—House-boats on the Thames—River Scenery—Shepperton Green and the Railway Station—A Singular Story—Lower Halliford—Discovery of an Ancient Canoe and other Antiquities—The Valley of the Thames—The Wall Closes—Coway Stakes—Littleton.

WHERE the country is a dead flat, and the scenery as unromantic as that of Holland : where the parish churches have been robbed of all antiquity and of more than half their interest : where there are no feudal castles and few old manor-houses : and where the literary associations of the place are a blank—it is scarcely possible to find materials for a chapter which shall satisfy the intelligent reader.

The parish of Shepperton, or Sheperton, is situated to the west of Sunbury, and lies so low that it is often flooded in the winter, and the meadows present the appearance of an inland sea, reaching for miles in either direction, and quite obscuring the banks of the river. There are, too, plenty of pollard-willows, marking the lines of brooks which abound.

The eastern portion of the parish of Shepperton, extending for upwards of a mile down the river towards Sunbury, is known as Lower Halliford, and is so called from a ford over the Thames, a little to the east, by which Julius Cæsar is supposed to have crossed into Middlesex, and of which we shall have more to say presently.

A small river, called the Exe, which rises near Staines, and runs through the park of Littleton, finds its way into the Thames between Upper and Lower Halliford.

Lower Halliford consists for the most part of a small collection of humble, old-fashioned habitations, the gardens of which slope pleasantly down to the water-side. There are, however, one or two dwellings of a better kind, including some pretty villas. The Thames, which here makes an abrupt bend, is crossed at this point by an iron bridge, which connects Lower Halliford with Walton, in Surrey.

Shepperton is a quaint, old-fashioned village, with no one principal street, but built irregularly along several roads, which cross each other. Some of the cottages are very substantial and old-fashioned, their doorways and timbers carrying us back to the days of the Tudors. The village itself is situated on the banks of the Thames, and is of small extent ; but there are a few good and substantial dwelling-houses scattered about in the neighbourhood. In 1871 the number of houses in the parish amounted to only 241, the population numbering 1,126 souls, which has since increased to nearly 1,300.

In the "Domesday Book" the name of this parish is written *Scepertone*, and in other ancient records it is entered as *Scepertune*. *Sceapheardton*, it may be stated, is the Saxon term for the habitation of shepherds. In the "Domesday Record" the manor is said to be held by the Abbot of St. Peter (Westminster Abbey), to whom it was either given or confirmed by Edward the Confessor. The condition of the locality at that distant period may be judged from the fact that "there was land to seven ploughs, and meadow equal to the same. Pasture for the cattle of the village, and one 'wear,' valued at six shillings and eightpence. A priest had fifteen acres."

The manor was alienated, among several others belonging to the Abbey of St. Peter, by Gervase, the abbot, a natural son of King Stephen. It has since passed through various hands, and remained for nearly a century with the Beauchamp family. In the fifteenth century it was possessed by John Tiptoft, Earl of Worcester, who was executed in 1471. At a subsequent period it was vested in the family of Spiller ; and at the beginning of the present century it was the property of the Dugdales, of Merevale Hall in Warwickshire.

The manor-house was purchased by the late Mr. William S. Lindsay, M.P., one of the most successful shipowners of our time. He died in 1877, and it is now occupied by his widow. The park lies low, and is frequently flooded. It contains some fine elms.

In most of the parish churches along the Thames Valley the towers alone survive from the pre-Reformation times, the bodies having been pulled down and rebuilt at various dates. But the reverse is the case at Shepperton, where there is a cruciform building, substantially of the Decorated or Edwardian period, though sadly "beautified "—or rather, mutilated—while a most puny and meagre modern brick tower, of the true Churchwarden type, with an embattled parapet, has been added to the west end. The tower, with its parapet, was built in 1710, at the expense of the then rector, the Rev. Lewis Atterbury, a brother of the celebrated Dr. Atterbury, Bishop of Rochester.

From the mention of a priest in the Norman survey, it would appear that there was a church at Shepperton at a very early period, but no marks of such remote antiquity are observable in the present structure.

William Grocyn, who was instituted to this rectory in 1504, is supposed by Newcourt, the author of the " Repertorium," to have been the celebrated friend of Erasmus, and who was largely instrumental in rendering the Greek language a general object of study.

The old rectory, a most substantial red brick building, with projecting beams and a picturesque roof, adjoins the north side of the churchyard. Before it is a small square, now gravelled, but which once, doubtless, was a village green. One side of it is occupied by a hostelry, much frequented by the angling fraternity, " The Anchor." There are other smaller inns, all of them in the same line of business. In fact, the river at Shepperton, and from thence to Chertsey up stream, and to Halliford down, is " piscosissimus." During the summer months the disciples of Izaak Walton flock hither in large numbers, and some good sport is obtained, the river at this point being particularly plentiful in roach, barbel, perch, and jack. " 'Tis observed by Gesner," writes honest Izaak Walton, in his " Angler," " that there is none bigger salmon than in England, and none better than in Thames." Salmon have been caught in Shepperton Deep many years back, but they are no longer taken here. Recently much antagonism has existed, respecting the right of fishing in the Thames, between the anglers and the " riparian " owners of land abutting upon the river; and the question has been taken up by a society called the Thames Rights Defence Association.

Of late years a fashion has grown up of spending a part of the summer in a house-boat on the river. These house-boats are much affected by the artist tribe : we see signs of the craft in the easel, the palette, and the paint-box left outside, and on the pictures which adorn the walls of the dwelling-room. These human water-houses, moored to the banks, are simply caravans set on a substantial boat instead of on wheels.

The Thames at this point has many pleasant reaches, and across the river we see Oatlands Park and the fir-woods about Walton and Weybridge. Oatlands was the favourite residence of the Duke

and Duchess of York. It is now an hotel for resident families.

In our account of Teddington (see page 130, *ante*) we have spoken at some length of the swans on the Thames. They are to be met with here in plenty during the bright days of summer, and add not a little to the beauty of the river scenery—

"The gentle swan, with graceful pride,
  Her glossy plumage laves,
And sailing down the silver tide,
  Divides the whispering waves."

What a charming description of the long reaches about Shepperton, Twickenham, Teddington, and Richmond !

The present Shepperton Green—a long, narrow strip of land, pleasantly fringed with stately elms and chestnut-trees—lies between the village and the railway-station, which is about half a mile distant to the northward, and where is the terminus of the Thames Valley branch of the South-Western Railway.

Shepperton is one of those fortunate places which possesses no " history " worth recording, and, consequently, we may be pardoned for quoting a singular item of information concerning it which appears in " Social Gleanings." The writer remarks :—

" Either the late Mr. Fisher, or Mr. Elwes, of Kempton Park, Sunbury, Middlesex, was in the habit of paying an annual visit to the Rev. Mr. Hubbard, the rector of Shepperton—that well-known rendezvous on the banks of the Thames for the disciples of Izaak Walton. The rector's son, who told me the story, described a peculiarity in regard to this annual visit worth recording. The visitor was stone blind, both his carriage horses were stone blind, and his coachman was a Cyclops, having only one eye."

Here, at the commencement of the present century, lived Mr. Josiah Boydell, a gentleman of some little antiquarian taste. Among the objects which he possessed was a canoe, which would appear to have been constructed in a very remote and rude age. This interesting vestige of antiquity was discovered in September, 1812, and was presented to Mr. Boydell, who furnished the following particulars of it to Mr. Brewer, the author of the " Beauties of England " :—" The canoe is obviously hewn out of one solid block of oak, and when perfect the dimensions must have been as follows : the entire length 12 feet, the depth of the sides 20 inches, the width across the top 3 feet 6 inches in the middle. The sides are 1½ inches thick, the keel or bottom is, in the middle, 15 inches wide and 2 inches thick, but grows narrower as it approaches the ends.

Throughout the whole there is not any appearance of a peg or nail having been used. At one end was a piece hewn out of the solid wood, and left across the boat, apparently to hold the sides together; and it is supposed that there was a similar piece at the other end; but one end and one side of this curious relic were unfortunately broken before it was inspected by Mr. Boydell. This canoe was found about twenty yards within the brook, in the part nearest to Shepperton town, and was lying in a shelving position, buried in a bed of gravel, within two inches of a layer of peat. Above was a mass of gravel 3 feet 6 inches in depth, and over that were 4 feet of mud. Within a few yards of the canoe, and beneath an equal mass of gravel, mud, &c., was found a stag's horn, the stem and one of the sharp antlers being perfect. . . . Near the above was found a boar's tusk, supposed to be of the wild black breed, and perfect, with the exception of the extreme point, where half an inch appears to have been broken off."

All sorts of antique articles of manufacture, of British, Roman, Saxon, and more recent periods, have been found from time to time in the bed of the Thames. Some idea of their number and variety may be formed if we state that the list of them, including celts, urns, and other pottery, swords, spear-heads, bosses, shields, daggers, seals, pilgrims' tokens, pyxes, axe-heads, coins, &c., occupies a column in the index volume of the Royal Archæological Institute.

The whole valley of the Thames is considered by geologists to be quite "an after-thought" of Nature, having come into being, as shown by Professor Ramsay, after the close of the Miocene age. The vegetation preserved in the London clay is of a tropical and even Indo-Australian character, being composed of palms, cypresses, &c., not unlike those of Tasmania and the Philippine Islands.

"In some small fields, to the north-east of the village, termed the Wall Closes," writes Mr Brewer, in the "Beauties of England" (1816), "are several artificial inequalities of surface, which Gale and Dr. Stukeley conjecture to be the remains of a Roman camp. Mr. Lysons, in his 'Middlesex Parishes,' supposes these to be merely the vestiges of buildings on the site of the old manor-house; and, according to the tradition of the neighbourhood, an ancient mansion assuredly appears to have occupied a portion of the Wall Closes. But these earthworks, though much levelled within the last twenty years, would still seem more extensive than the probable site of a manorial dwelling, even allowing it to have possessed the ornamental circumstances of terrace walks. The adjacency of remains, confidently supposed to be Roman, induces us to believe that there may be foundation for the conjecture of Dr. Stukeley in regard to these inequalities of surface; but it certainly appears difficult to pursue them through any traces bearing resemblance to the form of a regular encampment."

At a short distance eastward from Lower Halliford is the site of the celebrated Coway Stakes, which are by tradition said to have been placed across the Thames to oppose the passage of Julius Cæsar over this river, when in pursuit of Cassivelaunus, and many antiquaries have agreed as to the probable connection with fact of such a traditionary assertion.

We read in the account of the second expedition of Julius Cæsar (B.C. 54), that, having landed at Pevensey, he marched further inland, and came upon the Thames at a distance of about eighty miles from the sea. He found the river fordable at only one point; here the natives were drawn up in array to oppose his passage, and the river was fortified with sharp stakes. He, however, effected his passage, though only with great difficulty, and pursued his way into the territory of Cassivelaunus —probably Hertfordshire, the ancient home of the Cassii. The British chief submitted, and Cæsar returned to Rome, carrying off some of the natives as hostages.

The exact spot where Cæsar crossed the Thames has been for centuries a matter of dispute amongst antiquaries, many of whom have claimed Wallingford, and others Kingston, as the place. But it is recorded, on the most undoubted authority, that stakes sheathed with lead or iron were to be seen at this spot under water down to the seventeenth, and even the eighteenth, century.

Camden and Hearne, two of the very highest authorities on this matter, strongly incline to the belief that Coway Stakes mark the spot, following the testimony of the Venerable Bede, who makes this statement on the authority of a London priest, Nothelin, afterwards Archbishop of Canterbury; and he adds that the remains of the stakes were visible in his own time. Mr. T. Wright, however, in his "Celt, Roman, and Saxon," whilst agreeing in the main in this view, suggests that these stakes, though of Roman workmanship, were of later date, and perhaps connected with the navigation or fishery of the Thames in a way which we cannot now explain.

Camden was the first in recent times to point out Coway Stakes as the ford which the Britons defended. "It is impossible," he observes, "I should be mistaken in the place, because here the river is scarce six feet deep ; and the place at this day, from those stakes, is called Coway Stakes ; to which we may add that Cæsar makes the bounds of Cassivelan, where he fixes this his passage, to be about eight miles distant from that sea which washes the east part of Kent, where he landed ;

and that the tide probably ran up as high as this spot.

Of the stakes themselves, Gale, the antiquary, says :—" The wood of these stakes proves its own antiquity, being by its long duration under the water so consolidated as to resemble ebony, and will admit of a polish, and is not in the least rotted.

SHEPPERTON, FROM THE RIVER.

SHEPPERTON RECTORY. (See page 178.)

now this ford we speak of is at the same distance from the sea ; and I am the first, that I know of, who has mentioned and settled it in its proper place." *

The position of these stakes is described in the *Archæologia* by the Hon. Daines Barrington, who inspected the spot in 1740, and it is said that one of them is preserved in the British Museum, having been obtained here in 1777. It must be remembered that in early times there were no weirs or dams so near to the mouth of the river,

It is evident, from the exterior grain of the wood, that the stakes were the entire bodies of young oak-trees, there not being the least appearance of any mark of any tool to be seen upon the whole circumference ; and if we allow in our calculation for the gradual increase of growth towards its end, where fixed in the bed of the river, the stakes, I think, will exactly answer the thickness of a man's thigh, as described by Bede ; but whether they were covered with lead at the ends fixed in the bottom of the river, is a particular I could not learn." None of the stakes remain now, the last having been removed about the year 1840. They are said to have been capped with metal for convenience of driving, but whether it was with brass, iron, or lead, is very uncertain, as the different accounts vary.

Both Daines Barrington and Dr. Owen, it may be observed, doubt whether Cæsar ever did pass the Thames at all. They allege that stakes intended to oppose the landing of an enemy would have been so placed as to line the friendly shore with their armed points inclining to the adverse bank; whereas Coway Stakes range directly *across* the river, and therefore could not have obstructed troops attempting to pass the ford. Those who are thus minded suppose that *the Stakes of Coway were merely intended for a fishing weir!* And yet some still say that the stakes were too massive and armed for a mere fishery. These are the opinions of the learned, and such is the glorious uncertainty of antiquity.

In the *Archæological Journal* for September, 1866, will be found a full account of the campaign of A. Plautius, by the late Dr. E. Guest, with a plan of the fortified ford at Halliford and the Coway Stakes. Dr. Guest thinks that the stakes mentioned as protecting the ford were there many years before the arrival of the Romans.

Mr. Brewer, in his work above quoted, writes :— " We confess that the position of the stakes appears an insuperable objection to believing that they were meant to oppose the landing of an enemy intent on passing from the Surrey to the Middlesex shore; but their massive and armed character would appear to be the result of too much labour and cost to allow of our supposing that they are no more than the remains of a weir for fishing." In the same work it is observed that " Mr. Bray (a writer not likely to be misled by careless and futile assertion) 'was informed by a fisherman who has lived at Walton, and known the river all his life, that at this place he has weighed up several stakes of the size of his thigh, about six feet long, *shod with iron;* the wood very black, and so hard as to turn an axe.' On St. George's Hill, at a short distance from the Thames, on the Surrey shore, is a camp, called Cæsar's Camp, appearing to be Roman, which comprehends in its area more than thirteen acres, and which probably communicated with a much larger castrametation at Oatlands. We have already observed that Stukeley supposed he had discovered the remains of Roman works at Shepperton; on Greenfield Common he also notices an encampment; and on Hounslow Heath, in the parish of Harmondsworth, nearly in a line with the presumed march of Cæsar when pursuing Cassibelan, were, until lately, the perfect remains of a camp appearing to be formed by the Romans." In a foot-note the above writer remarks :—" We cannot avoid observing that, in a meadow immediately bordering upon Coway Stakes, on the Middlesex side of the river, there are vestiges of a broad raised road, which would appear to have led from a spot near the present bridge of Walton towards Halliford. The road terminates about 100 yards on the Halliford side of the river, but the cessation may be accounted for by observing that a mill, with large enclosures, occupied, within memory, the space now level."

About midway between Sunbury, Shepperton, and Laleham, is Littleton, where formerly stood a magnificent mansion, the seat of the Wood family. It stood in a pleasant but level park, but was burnt down a few years ago, and has not been rebuilt. The house was rather of the Dutch type, reminding one of Kensington Palace. It contained some fine pictures, which perished in the flames, including Hogarth's celebrated painting of " Actors Dressing." It is not intended to rebuild the mansion. The late General Thomas Wood, of Littleton, was for ten years M.P. for Middlesex, and colonel of the 84th Regiment, and his father, Colonel Thomas Wood, was for upwards of half a century M.P. for Brecon, and colonel of the East Middlesex Militia. General Wood died in 1872, when the property passed to his son, Mr. Thomas Wood, the present owner.

Littleton would seem to be one of the smallest parishes in Middlesex; at all events, according to the census of 1881 it had only about twenty inhabited houses, and a population of 126 souls. The church, dedicated to St. Mary Magdalen, is an ancient structure, of Early English architecture, but of no particular interest. The chancel, which contains several brasses and memorials of the Wood family, was restored a few years ago.

CHAPTER XVI.

LALEHAM, ASHFORD, AND STAINES.

"Such tattle often entertains
My lord and me as far as Staines,
As once a week we travel down
To Windsor, and again to town."—POPE's *Satires*.

Situation and General Description of Laleham—Remains of a Roman Castrametation on Greenfield Common—Mention of Laleham in Domesday Book—Descent of the Manor—The Parish Church—Laleham House—Dr. Thomas Arnold and his Residence here—The Village of Laleham—Population—The River Thames at Chertsey Bridge—Chertsey Meadows—Laleham Burway—Ashford—Descent of the Manor—The Village of Ashford—The Common—Population—The Parish Church—The Parish Registers—The Welsh Charity School—The West London District Schools—The Town of Staines—The Roman Road and Roman Antiquities—The Boundary Stone of the Thames Conservancy—The Ancient Forest of Middlesex—The Notice of Staines in Domesday Book—A Benedictine Abbey—The Parish Church—An Ancient Guild—The Town of Staines—Markets and Fairs—Population—Inns and Taverns—The Thames and the Water Supply—The Bridge—Duncroft House—Staines Moor—Yeoveney—Runnymede—Magna Charta Island—Ankerwyke—Egham—Cooper's Hill and Sir John Denham.

PURSUING our course along the left bank of the Thames, we soon reach the south-western limit of the county of Middlesex, and, at the same time, the most westerly point of the jurisdiction of the Thames Conservancy at Staines. Laleham, the first village through which we pass, possesses nothing attractive in the way of scenery, but is simply a continuation of the dead level which pervades the district which we have just left behind us. The village is situated about midway between the towns of Chertsey on the south and Staines on the north. It has but few historical associations, but it is stated in *The Gentleman's Magazine* that Queen Anne had a fishing-box on the river side here, though no proof of the fact is given, and no allusions to it occur in the diaries and personal biographies of her reign.

Dr. Stukeley notices the remains of a Roman castrametation on Greenfield Common, in the parish of Laleham, which he supposes to have been the camp in which Julius Cæsar halted after passing the Thames. But Stukeley is not always to be trusted. Indeed, the statement is considered by the inhabitants to be altogether a myth; but traces of a camp in the Ferry Field are still very evident, as also are others on the top of St. Ann's Hill, on the opposite side of the Thames.

Mr. Brewer, in the "Beauties of England and Wales," observes that "Dr. Stukeley pursues his supposition to a great extent, and raises several hypotheses on grounds entirely conjectural. If Cæsar crossed the Thames at Coway Stakes, it is quite possible, and perhaps probable, that he might then form an encampment here on his march toward Hertfordshire. But every appropriation of the relics to a particular passage of history must needs proceed from an unsatisfactory ingenuity of surmise." Mr. Lysons, having carefully examined and measured these remains about the year 1800, says:—"There are two camps; the fosses, being very

discernible, as measured with a line, are nearly as follows:—North side of the outward camp, about 400 feet; south side, about 390; east side, about 420; west side, nearly 500. North side of the inner camp, about 245 feet; south side, about 230; east side, about 285; west side, about 290."*

Between Ashford and Bedfont Roman coins and other objects have been dug up, in quantities sufficient to make it probable that these level plains were the site of a camp or station during the occupation of the Imperial Eagles.

Laleham is recorded in "Domesday Book" under the name of *Leleham*, and it is stated that "the Earl of Moreton (Mortain, in Normandy) holds in Leleham two hides, which are held under him by the Abbot of Fescamp in Normandy." Robert Blount is also described as holding eight hides of the king in this parish, which were held under him by "one Estrild, a nun."

In the thirteenth century the manor of Laleham formed part of the possessions of Westminster Abbey, and early in the seventeenth century it was annexed, together with the smaller manor of Billets, in this parish, to the Honour of Hampton Court, and subsequently granted in fee to the trustees of Sir Henry Spiller, by whose daughter it was afterwards conveyed in marriage to Sir Thomas Reynell.

About the middle of the last century, Laleham House, together with the lordship of the manor, was bought by Sir James Lowther, who, having for several years represented the counties of Cumberland and Westmoreland in Parliament, was elevated to the peerage in 1784 by Mr. Pitt as Earl of Lonsdale. His lordship, having no issue, obtained a new patent in 1797, creating him Baron and Viscount Lowther, with remainder to the heirs male of his cousin, the Rev. Sir William Lowther, Bart., of Swillington, in whose favour the

---

* "Middlesex Parishes," p. 197.

earldom was revived. Laleham, however, in 1803, passed, by purchase, into the hands of the Earl of Lucan.

The quaint old parish church, dedicated to All Saints, stands near the river-side, and consists of a nave with north aisle and chancel, with chancel-aisle. Here Dr. Arnold used frequently to officiate when residing here with his pupils, 1820—28. The edifice is a low, irregular structure, built at different periods, the more modern parts, including the tower at the west end, being constructed of brick. The nave and side-aisle are separated by circular arches with round pillars, which have Norman capitals. The interior of the edifice has lately been restored and renovated, the old-fashioned " pews " giving way to open benches. Over the communion-table is a large picture representing the miracle of Christ walking on the sea, painted by Mr. George Henry Harlow, and presented in 1811 by Mr. George Hartwell of this parish. The monumental inscriptions in this church do not contain anything remarkable. Among them is one to the Rev. Dr. Downes, who died in 1798, and who is there said to have been one of " his *Magestie's* chaplains in ordinary ;" and one, dated 1780, to the memory of Sir George Perrott, Baron of the Exchequer. The chancel-aisle mentioned above belongs to the family of the Earl of Lucan, who is at once a gallant field-officer and a great practical agriculturist. His seat, Laleham House, stands in a park of considerable extent on the southern side of the village. It was the residence of Donna Maria, Queen of Portugal, when in England. Lord Lucan was in command of a division of cavalry in the Crimean War, 1854, and was wounded at Balaclava. His lordship is not forgetful of his duties as a landowner, for in 1864 he erected in the village some schools, with a residence for the masters. Laleham House—or, " the great house," as it is called by the natives— is now the residence of Lord Bingham, the eldest son of the Earl of Lucan.

At the lower end of the village stood the house formerly occupied by Dr. Thomas Arnold, the distinguished scholar and schoolmaster. It was a large and substantial old-fashioned brick building, with a large garden attached. ' Arnold settled," writes Dean Stanley, " in 1819 at Laleham, near Staines, with his mother, aunt, and sister, where he remained for the next nine years, taking seven or eight young men as private pupils for the Universities, for a short time in a joint establishment with his brother-in-law, Mr. Buckland, and afterwards independently by himself." In the following year he married Miss Mary Penrose, youngest daughter of the Rev. J. Penrose, Rector of Fledborough, Nottinghamshire.

Here, it is remarked by Arnold's biographer, a great and decisive change came over his character. " The indolence and restlessness by which his early years had been marked entirely disappeared, and he acquired those settled, serious, earnest views of the nature and purpose of life which actuated him ever after. It was this ' intense earnestness ' which gave him so much power over his pupils, and which roused every one who came within the sphere of his influence to the consciousness that they had powers to cultivate, duties to discharge, and a mission to accomplish."

" His situation," writes Dean Stanley, " supplied him exactly with that union of retirement and work which, more than any other condition, suited his natural inclinations. . . . Without undertaking any directly parochial charge, he was in the habit of rendering constant assistance to the Rev. Mr. Hearn, the curate of the place, both in the parish church and workhouse, thus uniting with his ordinary occupation a familiar intercourse with his poorer neighbours. Bound as he was to Laleham by all these ties, he long loved to look upon it as his final home ; and the first reception of the tidings of his election at Rugby was overclouded with deep sorrow at leaving the scene of so much happiness. Years after he had left it he still retained his early affection for it, and till he had purchased his house in Westmoreland, he entertained a lingering hope that he might return to it in his old age, when he should have retired from Rugby. Often he would re-visit it, and he delighted in renewing his acquaintance with the families of the poor whom he had known during his residence ; in showing to his children his former haunts ; in looking once again on his favourite views of the great plain of Middlesex, the lonely gravel walks along the banks of the Thames, the retired garden, with its ' Campus Martius ' and its ' wilderness of trees,' which lay behind his house, and which had been the scenes of so many sportive games and serious conversations ; the churchyard of Laleham, then doubly dear to him, as containing the graves of his infant child, and of his mother, aunt, and his sister Susannah, who had long formed part of his domestic circle."

The cedars which graced the garden alone remain to mark the spot. The greater part of the garden, and the " Campus Martius," have been converted into an arable field.

Arnold's life at Laleham was on a smaller scale the precursor of his subsequent life at Rugby. He would keep no pupil whom he could not " sophronise," to use his favourite Oxford term : none whose presence would be likely to infect his companions. One of his pupils, in after life, declared that the most remarkable thing which used to strike him was the wonderful heartiness of tone and feeling which prevailed in the little house at Laleham. He "gave such an earnestness to life;" every pupil was made to feel that there was a work for him to do, and that his happiness as well as his duty lay in doing that work well. This created a respect for the tutor which re-acted on his disciples, and set them to toil in earnest to prepare themselves for their commencing career as a step towards after life.

Whilst at Laleham, Arnold's own studies were chiefly philology and history, and here he commenced, in the shape of a lexicon, his work on Thucydides, which afterwards gave him such credit as a scholar. Here, too, he began to write a short history of Greece, which was never finished ; and contributed to the *Encyclopædia Metropolitana* several important articles on the history of Rome from the times of the Gracchi to that of Trajan. Whilst here, also, he made himself a German scholar, and made practical acquaintance with Niebuhr and Bunsen. The sermons contained in the first volume he published were preached in Laleham church, where also most of his children were baptised. At Laleham, his eldest son, Mr. Matthew Arnold, so well known as poet, essayist, and scholar, was born, in 1822.

Arnold's life at Laleham must be regarded as a preliminary and probational existence, during which he was working out mentally, and testing by partial and limited experiment, those school reforms which he afterwards carried out into practice at Rugby, thereby justifying the prophecy of Dr. Hawkins, the late Provost of Oriel College, Oxford, that "he would change the face of education all through the public schools of England." As the place where this great movement was first conceived, Laleham must always be a place of interest to all persons who take an interest in the progress of English public-school education.

To Laleham, and its pleasant mixture of hard work and fresh and youthful interests, Dr. Arnold constantly recurs in his correspondence with his friends at Rugby and at Fox How ; and he never mentions the place without some tender and touching word, which shows how truly he loved its recollections to the very last. Arnold died suddenly at Rugby in 1842, shortly after having been appointed Professor of Modern History at Oxford. His successor at Rugby was Archbishop **Tait**. His house at Laleham was pulled down

about the year 1864, and the materials were used in the construction of a National School.

The village of Laleham possesses a few old-fashioned houses of a humble kind. Most of the inhabitants belong to the agricultural class, but the village is much frequented during the summer months, like its more popular neighbours, Hampton and Sunbury, by the lovers of the gentle craft of angling. In 1871 the number of inhabited houses in the parish amounted to 110, the population amounting to 567 souls, a number which was somewhat diminished in the course of the next ten years, when the sum-total, as recorded in the census returns, was 544.

The Thames here becomes somewhat contracted in width, and being very shallow, runs with considerable strength south-east in a tolerably straight line for nearly two miles, the view in that direction being closed by Chertsey Bridge, which spans the Thames. It is of stone, and has seven arches, and was built in 1780—85, from the designs of Mr. James Payne, at a cost of about £13,000. Across the river and meadows, and at some little distance from the bridge, we see the tower of Chertsey Church, and further westward is St. Anne's Hill, the seat of Lady Holland, and at one time the favourite residence of Charles James Fox. Many interesting recollections cling to the neighbourhood of Chertsey, for—

"Here the last accents flow'd from Cowley's tongue,"

as may be seen from the inscription inserted in the walls of his house, by his friend and brother angler, Mr. Clark. Shakespeare, too, has given the village of Chertsey immortality in his *Richard III.* In the Chertsey meadow, across the ferry, on the Surrey side, are to be seen the remains of an encampment of undoubted Roman character, probably an outlying portion of the station *Ad Pontes*, which modern antiquarians have usually identified with Staines.

A meadow, called Laleham Burway, belongs to the parish of Laleham, though on the opposite side of the river. There is a tradition that it was given by an abbot of Chertsey to the Laleham fishermen as an acknowledgment of their having supplied the Abbey with fish during a time of pestilence and dearth. The meadow was used as a common ground by the inhabitants of Laleham, and their cattle used to cross the Thames every morning to pasture on it, but Laleham Burway, like so many other commons, is now "enclosed and divided."

But we must not longer linger over the view, and so, turning our steps northward, we will at once make our way to Ashford.

The general surroundings of this village, as of those which we have lately been describing, are a dead flat all away to Feltham in one direction, and to Staines in another; but the country around is nevertheless well-cultivated ground and woodland. It is sufficiently diversified, at all events, to have pleased the eye of Arnold. Scattered about in the fields are plenty of pollard oaks, marking the site of what once was part of the great forest of Middlesex.

This parish is noticed in the "Domesday Survey" by the name of *Exeforde*, and in ancient records of a subsequent period by those of *Echeleford* and *Eckleford*, from the ford over the little river Exe, or Echel, which, however, runs at some little distance west of the village.

King Edgar is said to have granted the manor of Staines, with land at Ecclesford, to the abbey and convent of Westminster. On the surrender of that monastery, this manor (together with Staines) was annexed to the honour of Hampton Court. The manor of Ashford was granted by Queen Elizabeth, in 1601, to Guy Godolphin and John Smythe, and it has since then been held by different families. It is now (January, 1883) the subject of litigation.

Ashford, which is a very scattered parish, was, till recently, a chapelry annexed to Staines, but with regard to its civil jurisdiction it has long been a separate parish. The village is situated nearly a mile to the south of the great western road, and about fourteen miles from London. Twenty years ago the neighbourhood was very aristocratic; and even at the present time there are many wealthy residents. The village consists for the most part of substantial houses occupied by gentry. Ashford Common extended south-east almost as far as Sunbury Common. Here George III. formerly held frequent reviews of cavalry, but the display of military pomp many years ago yielded to the humbler labours of the plough. The Common has long been enclosed. The old village of Ashford lies half a mile eastward of the station on the Windsor branch of the South-Western Railway; a new village is now rapidly springing up in the direction of Sunbury. In 1871 the number of inhabited houses in the parish was 181, and the population amounted to 1,019 souls, a number which has now swelled up to 2,281; but this is inclusive of the inmates of two public institutions in the parish.

The parish church, which stands near the entrance to the village, is a modern erection, dating back only from the year 1858. It is dedicated to St. Matthew, and is in the Gothic style of architecture. The edifice comprises a chancel, nave, aisles, south transept, and a tower and dwarf spire at the south-west angle. It was built by subscription. Mr. Butterfield was the architect of the present church, which is the third that has stood near the same site within the last century. The previous church was dedicated to St. Michael.

The original church stood in the same churchyard, but further east, near a tall fine yew-tree. It was an ancient building of brick and stone, the south door exhibiting evidences of Norman or Saxon workmanship in its zig-zag mouldings. The edifice which succeeded it, and was erected in 1796, was a plain brick building, with a tower surmounted by a tall spire. That church was built chiefly by a voluntary subscription among the inhabitants, but the chancel was rebuilt at the expense of the lord of the manor.

The church of Ashford was formerly served by a curate appointed by the vicar of Staines, and is said by Newcourt, in the "Repertorium," to be endowed with "a house, twenty-eight acres and a half, and two yards of glebe." Among the tombs in the churchyard is one to the memory of the Rev. John Jebb, D.D., Dean of Cashel, father to the celebrated Bishop Jebb. In the floor of the nave, near the font, is inserted a brass, removed from the old church; it has upon it the effigies of Edward Woode and his wife, six sons, and two daughters, and is dated 1525.

The registers of Ashford are very imperfect, none of them going back further than 1699. They are in existence from that date to 1708, afterwards there is a gap down to 1760; and their absence is accounted for by a fire in which they perished along with the original church plate. New plate of a very handsome type was purchased, and this, too, was for some time lost to the parish, having found its way into private hands, from which it has only lately been recovered. The church books contain some curious entries. Amongst others, very many of sums paid for killing "vermin" and sparrows. Among the charitable bequests is one, now producing about £7 yearly, and divided between three old men and three old women; it was left by a Mrs. Anne Webb to her dog, for life, with reversion to the poor as above. She left other charities to poor chimney-sweep boys in London, in the place of a treat which she used to give them in her lifetime; and also a duplicate of her canine legacy to the parish of Merton, in Surrey.

There are several charitable institutions in this parish. Near the railway-station, on the road to Stanwell, is the Welsh Charity School. The institution belongs to the Honourable and Loyal Society of Ancient Britons. It was originally intended for poor Welsh orphans of either sex, but is now a middle-class school for Welsh girls; and it was founded in 1714–15. The present school was erected in 1857, and is a large stone-fronted building of Elizabethan architecture, and holds 200 children.

The West London District Schools are situated to the west of the station, about midway between Ashford and Staines. The inmates are pauper children, mainly from the parishes of Fulham, caused this town, contrary to what is generally the case, to expand in an easterly direction. It consists mainly of one long street, which runs from east to west, and terminates at Staines Bridge, which joins the town to Egham, in Surrey.

The Roman road from London to Silchester is supposed to have crossed the Thames in this neighbourhood, but the exact spot where it crossed is not known with any certainty, though Egham is generally identified with the Roman Bibracte. As

LALEHAM CHURCH. (*See page* 188.)

Paddington, and St. George's, Hanover Square. The edifice, which is constructed of brick with stone dressings, covers a large space of ground, and is capable of containing nearly 800 children. It was built in 1872.

The town of Staines, which we have now reached, lies about two miles westward from Ashford, and at the extreme west of the Thames Valley, in Middlesex, being situated at the mouth of the Colne, which, rising in Hertfordshire, and passing by Harefield, Uxbridge, and Colnbrook, debouches here into the Thames in several channels. The meadows along the banks of the Colne being low and flat, whilst its waters are "brimming" both in summer and winter, have

Staines was the Roman station *Ad Pontes*, it is scarcely a matter of wonder that its neighbourhood is rich in Roman remains. For instance, in a pit near Savery's Weir, on the Thames, between Staines and Laleham, a large brass coin of the Emperor Trajan was dug up in 1858. It was found at the depth of six feet from the surface, and was much defaced. The coin is described minutely in the *Journal of the Archæological Institute*.[*]

Within the last few years very many strong confirmations of the Roman origin of Staines have been found in a variety of antique objects that have been dug up in its vicinity—Roman bricks, tiles, vases, and swords, one of the last being found by dredging in the Thames. Pins, tweezers, and strigils, from a Roman bath, have also been disinterred. A very fine collection of these has been made by Mr. Ernest Ashby, a resident in the town, who has formed out of them the nucleus of a private museum. Axe-heads made of flint and other rude materials, probably of an earlier period, and stags' horns of very large size, have been unearthed in the vicinity.

tion refers to the boundary-stone by the side of the river, which is said to bear date A.D. 1280, together with the words, "God preserve the City of London." This stone was repaired and raised on a pedestal in 1781, during the mayoralty of Sir Watkin Lewes. The stone—be it Roman, Saxon, or Norman, in its origin—still stands on the north bank, a little above the bridge, near the church, on the Lammas lands. It is adorned with the City arms and motto, and the names of sundry Lord Mayors who have visited

THE CITY BOUNDARY STONE.

STREET IN STAINES.

Antiquaries are not agreed as to whether this town derives its name from a Roman milestone, or milliarum, placed here, or from the stone on the banks of the Thames which marks the limits of the jurisdiction of the Lord Mayor of London over the western portion of the river. Dr. Stukeley endeavours to support the former theory by asserting that near Staines Bridge there are traces of an old Roman road.

It is generally said, however—and we suppose that the statement may be accepted—the derivation of the name of the town is usually given as from "Stane," or "Stana," the Saxon term for stone; and it is supposed by Camden, and by various subsequent writers, as stated above, that the appella-

It officially for the purposes of enforcing their jurisdiction, or on swan-upping expeditions. On its base it bears engraved the words "Conservators of the River Thames," who, it may here be mentioned, regard the river above this point as the Upper Thames; whilst from here down to Yanlet Creek, at the mouth of the Medway, it is called the Lower Thames.

The Court of Conservancy of the Thames, over which the Lord Mayor presides, holds eight sittings every year, within the counties of Middlesex, Surrey, Kent, and Essex. It is in this capacity that the Lord Mayor of London is comically apostrophised by Tom Hood as—

" Conservator of Thames from mead to mead,
　Great guardian of small sprites that swim the flood,
　Warder of London stone."

When Alderman Venables, as Lord Mayor, went by barge to Oxford, in 1826, it was part of the programme that the City banners should be waved over the stone. It may be added that several attempts were made in former times to extend the Lord Mayor's jurisdiction over the Thames as far as Oxford; but in this the City did not succeed, and ancient custom has determined the limit as already mentioned.

The citizens of London, we know, had the right of "free warren": that is, they were at liberty to hunt in certain limits around their city; and this circuit included the "warren" of Staines. A forest anciently extended from this place to Hounslow eastwards, but it was disafforested and diswarrened early in the thirteenth century, and the district has since been gradually enclosed.

It is said that the town was once surrounded by a moat or ditch; but if this ever was the case, very scanty traces of it remain, except in what is known as Penton Ditch.

Staines figures only once in pre-Norman history, namely, in A.D. 1009, when the Danes, hearing that an army was marching from London to oppose them, are said to have crossed the river here on their way to their ships from Oxford, which they had burnt.

The next period which furnishes materials for a historical notice of Staines occurs subsequent to the Norman conquest. In the survey made by order of William I., the circumstances of property in this place are described in the following manner:—"The Abbot of St. Peter holds *Stanes* for nineteen hides. There is land to twenty-four ploughs. Eleven hides belong to the demesne, and there are thirteen ploughs therein. The villanes have eleven ploughs. There are three villanes of half a hide each; and four villanes of one hide; and eight villanes of half a virgate each; and thirty-six bordars of three hides; and one villane of one virgate, and four bordars of forty acres; and ten bordars of five acres each; and five cottages of four acres each; and eight bordars of one virgate; and three cottagers of nine acres; and twelve bondmen; and forty-six burgesses, who pay forty shillings a year. There are six mills of sixty-four shillings; and one wear (guort) of six shillings and eight pence, and one wear which pays nothing. Pasture for the cattle of the village. Meadow for twenty-four ploughs, and twenty shillings over and above. Pannage for thirty hogs; and two arpents of vineyards. Four berewicks belong to this manor, and they belonged to it in King Edward's time. Its whole value is thirty-five pounds; the same when received in King Edward's time forty pounds. This manor laid and lies in the demesne of the Church of St. Peter [at Westminster]."

Here, in the Saxon days, is said to have stood a Benedictine abbey, the monks of which would seem to have served the adjoining parishes. Both Speed, in his "Catalogue of Religious Houses," and Weever, in his "Funeral Monuments," confirm this assertion, and add that the abbey, or priory, was founded by Ralph, Lord Stafford; but Newcourt shows that the Priory of Staines alluded to by those writers is really situated at Stone in Staffordshire, which place, like Stone, near Dartford in Kent, was often termed *Stane* in ancient records.

The distance from Staines Bridge to London Bridge is twenty miles by land, and, in consequence of the circuitous course of the Thames, more than double that distance by water. Staines is in Spelthorne Hundred, and in the rural deanery of Hampton. It is a vicarage to which the chapelries of Ashford and Laleham were formerly annexed, but these have been separated, and formed into distinct parishes. The *Penny Cyclopædia* of 1839 speaks of all three as *one*. Sundry disputes having arisen on the subject of patronage between the Bishop of London and the Abbey of Westminster, it was agreed that the vicarage of Staines should be devoted to the use of wayfaring and sick folk at Westminster Abbey, and that the vicar of Staines should appoint chaplains for Laleham and Ashford. The vicar of Staines held under the great abbey by a curious tenure—namely, that of supplying two large wax candles for the altar of St. Peter's church, to be burnt on the eve of Epiphany.

It is certain that the Norman church was not the earliest here. We learn on the authority of Leland,[*] that, in the Saxon times, Ermengildis, daughter of King Wulfhere, before the year 700, built a small chapel in the forest here; and also that its successor, erected by the first Christian King of Mercia, was built "ex lapidibus" and "venustiori modo" than its predecessor.

From this statement it appears probable that the earliest Christian church here was of wood, very small and simple in plan. At all events, we learn that as far back as the ninth century a building of that description was standing here, and that the rude tenements of the Saxon town clustered round "God's Acre." This little oratory, in due course of time, was probably superseded by a church of stone.

The present church, dedicated to St. Mary, is a modern structure, ugly and plain, and stands in the midst of meadows on the banks of an arm of the Colne. Its Norman predecessor having become dilapidated, the nave was rebuilt in the last century; but one corner of it fell down about the year 1828, and the present structure

---

* See Parker's "Glossary of Architecture," iii , 9.

erected on the same site, the lower part of the tower being made to do duty. It was built in the dark ages of church architecture, the reign of George IV., and tells its own tale—an imitation Gothic structure of the poorest type. Its square embattled brick tower is said to have been erected by Inigo Jones in 1631, but it is scarcely one of the best specimens of his artistic design. The church was erected under an Act of Parliament which conferred freehold rights in pews to the contributors of certain sums to the building fund. The architect was a man named Watson, who is said to have been chosen by competition, securing his election to the job by sundry presents of barrels of oysters and cods' heads and shoulders to the sapient committee to whom the choice of an architect was entrusted ! In Walpole's " Anecdotes of Painting," it is stated that Inigo Jones lived for some time at Staines; but it does not appear that any notice of his residence here is to be found in the parish books.

In a small apartment under the staircase leading to the gallery at the west end of the old church were for many years preserved two unburied coffins, containing human remains. They were placed beside each other on trestles, and bore respectively the following inscriptions :—" Jessie Aspasia, the most excellent and truly beloved wife of Fred. W. Campbell, Esq., of Barbreck, N.B., and of Woodlands, in Surrey. Died in her 28th year, July 11th, 1812." " Henry E. A. Caulfield, Esq., died Sept. 8th, 1808, aged 29 years." As it was naturally supposed that coffins thus open to inspection would excite much curiosity, a card was preserved at the sexton's house, which stated, in addition to the intelligence conveyed by the above inscriptions, that the deceased lady was the daughter of W. T. Caulfeild, Esq., of Raheenduff, in Ireland, by Jessie, daughter of James, third Lord Ruthven, and that she bore with tranquil and exemplary patience a fatal disorder, produced by grief on the death of her brother. These coffins were buried on the erection of the new church.

The church and churchyard are singularly deficient in interesting tombs and monuments. Dame Letitia Lade, who lies buried between the church and the road, was a cast-off mistress of the Prince Regent, who married her to his coachman, one Mr. John Lade, whom he knighted as a reward for his pliancy in the matter, or for his skill in handling the ribbons. It is said that Sir John Lade also is buried here, but his name is not recorded on the tombstone.

The church has a peal of eight bells, remarkably sweet in their tone, and said to be the finest belonging to any of the churches in the Middlesex valley of the Thames, excepting Fulham.

The church books contain some curious entries : lists of books, plate, and moneys in the hands of the churchwardens, entries of sums paid to " distressed gentlewomen," " poore schollers," " poore ministers " and their wives; to a " poore gentlewoman to ransom her husband " (sixpence); and sixpence to a " poore merchant's wife." In 1657 sixpence is paid for an " houre glass." Two years later about £20 is spent on the re-casting, &c., of a bell; and in 1660 £3 for painting the king's arms. There are other disbursements for " prosecuting ye Quakers;" for going to London by water, (sixpence); "given to a poore Mayde, 2s."; for "excommunicating Pritt," 17s. ; for ferrying to church, 1s. ; and sundry collections in answer to briefs.

It is perhaps worth notice that the Rev. Gerald Wellesley, brother of the great Duke of Wellington, was at one time vicar of Staines, and largely improved the vicarage.

A guild, in honour of God and the Virgin Mary, was founded in 1456, by John Lord Berners, Sir John Wenlock, and several other persons, over the chapel of the Holy Cross in the church of Staines. This guild consisted of two wardens and a certain number of brethren and sisters. The lands appertaining to it were valued, in 1548, at £11 17s. 6d. per annum, including 6s. 8d. for a chamber, called the chantry-priests' chamber.

The town consists mainly of one long straggling street, irregularly built. The High Street, towards the west end of the town, forks off, and is continued to the north-west by Church Street, which leads to the parish church. The main street of the town is upwards of a mile in length, and contains a fair sprinkling of commodious shops and good old-fashioned houses ; whilst in the immediate neighbourhood are extensive mills, and linoleum and other manufactories. In Church Street is a large brewery, belonging to the Messrs. Ashby ; another brewery in the town belongs to Mr. Harris. At the west end of the High Street stands a handsome new Town Hall, which has been built in the place of a smaller one in a miserable and low thoroughfare known as Blackboy Lane.

Staines was a great place for the "Society of Friends," whose meeting-house is a specimen of the architecture of years long gone by. There are also chapels for different denominations of Dissenters. A large new town, with a mission chapel destined to blossom into a church, has of late years sprung up about the railway-station, which here forms a junction of the Windsor and the Wokingham lines. The internal polity of the town was formerly regulated by two constables and four "head-boroughs." The government is now vested in a Local Board; whilst the welfare of the town is further enhanced by the advantages gained from a Literary and Scientific Institute, and also a Mechanics' Institute.

There was a weekly market held on Friday, but it has long been discontinued; two fairs, however, are still held annually. One of these fairs was granted by Henry III., in the year 1228, to the abbot and convent of Westminster. The fairs are held on the 11th of May for horses and cattle, and on the 19th of September for toys, &c.

The *Penny Cyclopædia* gives the population of Staines in 1839 as 2,486. From the census returns in 1871, we learn that the parish contained 722 inhabited houses, and that the population then numbered 3,659 souls, a number that is by this time nearly doubled.

Lying as it did, in the good old coaching days, on the high road to Salisbury and the south-western counties, just one stage west of Hounslow, Staines was a large posting-town, and its inns were very numerous. Many of these since the days of railways have been turned into private houses, and such hostelries as remain depend mainly for support on boating parties and on the disciples of Izaak Walton.

If not literally the "half-way house," Staines was at all events one of the resting places, and a halt for changing horses, in the coaching and sporting days, on the "royal road" to Windsor. Hence the town was a favourite with good old George III. and Queen Charlotte and their family; and hence probably it came to pass that royalty took part in the ceremony of opening the new bridge across the Thames.

The Vine Inn, "at the bridge foot," is often mentioned by the first Lord Shaftesbury in his "Diary" as an inn where he slept a night on his way between Dorsetshire and London. The tavern, however, has long passed away. Readers of Swift will not forget how the prude Phillis, having run off with her father's groom, John, the couple settle down to lead a cat-and-dog life as landlord and hostess of the Blue Boar, which still exists and flourishes :

"They keep at Staines the old Blue Boar."

To one at least of these inns an anecdote attaches, which may be worth recording here :—

A lady of fashion in the last century is said to have cut with a diamond on a pane of glass the following inscription, "Dear Lord D—— has the softest lips of any man in England." Foote,

coming into the room soon after, scored underneath the following couplet :—

"Then as like as two chips
Are D——'s head and his lips."

While on the subject of inns and taverns—of which, by the way, Staines possesses a fair share—it may not be out of place to note the fact that at the Staines and Egham races the landlord of the "Cricketers," near Chelsea Bridge, used to display a signboard which had been painted by George Morland, and which travelled about with him.

The water supply of Staines has of late years been largely augmented by the Sunningdale District Water Company, which has been formed for the purpose of supplying the several parishes of Staines, Egham, and Old Windsor.

The river Thames in the neighbourhood of Staines is highly favourable for boating and fishing parties, and as a natural result the town is much frequented by visitors during the summer months.

Staines Bridge was for many a century the only one above London Bridge leading to the west of England; hence the importance of it to the sovereign, especially as it helped to connect both Windsor and Portsmouth with the metropolis; and hence, probably, it happened that the barons assembled at Runnymede while enforcing King John to sign the Magna Charta; and hence, in 1262, we read of three large oak-trees being granted by the Crown out of Windsor forest for the repair of this edifice. Numerous grants of *pontage*, or a temporary toll to defray the charge of repairs, were made at different times previous to the year 1600.

In 1791 an Act of Parliament was obtained for the erecting of a new bridge, and under enactment, certain tolls were allowed to be taken, on which the sum expended in raising the structure was charged. In pursuance of this Act a stone bridge of three arches was begun in August, 1792, and was opened in March, 1797. But the work had been executed with so little skill that one of the piers shortly gave way, and the bridge was necessarily taken down. A similar fate befel its successor—an iron bridge of one single arch, which, through some structural defect, had to be supported and propped up with wooden piles and framework. This bridge in the end was considered altogether unsafe, and the present stone bridge was built in 1832, and opened by William IV. and Queen Adelaide, the approach to it, at the same time, being altered and improved. Some remains of the approaches of the former bridge may still be seen, especially on the Surrey side of the river.

Quite close to the vicarage and church is Duncroft House, at one time the property and occasional residence of Lord Cranstoun. It is said that King John slept here the night after signing Magna Charta at Runnymede, but the tradition may be doubted. The house is a late Elizabethan or early Jacobean structure, resembling in its details portions of the Charter House in London. The room said to be King John's has a fine oak chimney-piece, curiously inlaid; and the timbers of the upper part of the house are massive and strong. An earlier structure may possibly have occupied the spot, but no traces of it exist.

Staines Moor, extending upwards to Stanwell, consists of common-lands, over which the poor of Staines have certain rights of turbary, &c.

Yeoveney, a hamlet consisting of a farm-house and a few cottages, about a mile to the north of the town, was an ancient chapelry attached to the mother-church of Staines. Its chapel has long since disappeared; and even its site is not known for certain, though an oak door, said to have formed a part of it, is still preserved in the neighbouring farm-house.

Within sight of Staines, though on the other side of the river, is Egham, between which and the river-side is the meadow of Runnymede, on which Egham races are annually held, and on which it is said that Magna Charta was signed. The roadway between Staines Bridge and Egham was built by the monks of Chertsey. Akenside, the author of "The Pleasures of Imagination," wrote the following spirited lines as an inscription for a column to be erected here :—

"Thou who the verdant plain dost traverse here,
  While Thames among his willows from thy view
  Retires ; O stranger, stay thee, and the scene
  Around contemplate well. This is the place
  Where England's ancient Barons, clad in arms
  And strong with conquest, from their tyrant king
  (Then rendered tame) did challenge and secure
  The charter of thy freedom. Pass not on
  Till thou hast blest their memory, and paid
  Those thanks which God appointed the reward
  Of public virtue. And if chance thy home
  Salute thee with a father's honoured name,
  Go, call thy sons, instruct them what a debt
  They owe their ancestors, and make them swear
  To pay it, by transmitting down entire
  Those sacred rights to which themselves were born."

A small eyot a little higher up the river, opposite Egham and Ankerwyke, still bears the name of Magna Charta Island. In it is kept and shown a table bearing the names of the proud Barons who forced the King to sign the Charter. Here are some of the finest trees in the kingdom, the park having once been a religious house ; but these are beyond our limits. A walnut tree at Ankerwyke, which still stands and thrives, is said to have been vigorous when it witnessed the signing of Magna Charta.

"A small island opposite Runnymede, now covered with willows, was the temporary fortified residence of the barons, where, in 1215, they retired from the pressure of the surrounding army, personally to receive the signature of the king to the great *palladium* of English liberty."

At Egham resided the great and good Judge Doddridge, who lies buried in Exeter Cathedral ; but the place is chiefly memorable on account of Cooper's Hill, an eminence near the London Road, the beauties of which are celebrated in a poem written in 1640 by Sir John Denham, and which acquired for him from Dr. Johnson the just and merited rank of an "original author." The following four lines of "Cooper's Hill," having reference to the Thames, which is now before us, have been often quoted, but will bear repetition :—

"Oh ! could I flow like *thee*, and make thy stream
  My great *example*, as it is my theme ;
  Though deep, yet clear, tho' gentle, yet not dull,
  Strong without rage, without o'erflowing full."

A good story is told of Sir John Denham. There was in the Puritan army a poetaster named Withers, some of whose lands at Egham Sir J. Denham had got into his clutches. When Withers was taken prisoner by the Cavaliers, Denham interceded with King Charles for his life, because as long as he lived he (Sir John) would not be reckoned the worst poet in England.

On the west side of Cooper's Hill stands the Indian Civil Engineering College, founded by Government in 1871 for the scientific training of young men as civil engineers for service in India. The college is built upon an estate formerly called Ankerwyke Purnish, which was given to the nuns of Ankerwyke, on the opposite side of the Thames, by Hugh, Abbot of Chertsey, in the reign of King Stephen.

The father of the poet Denham, who was also a Sir John Denham, lived for some time at Egham, in the house now the vicarage. He was for some time Chief Baron of the Exchequer in Ireland. Pope sang his praises in the following lines :—

"On Cooper's Hill eternal wreaths shall grow
  While lasts the mountain or while Thames shall flow ;
  I seem through consecrated walks to rove,
  I hear *soft music* die along the grove ;
  Led by the sound, I rove from shade to shade,
  By godlike poets venerable made.
  Here his first lays majestic Denham sung,
  There the last numbers flow'd from *Cowley's* tongue !"

BEDFONT CHURCH.   (*From an old Print. See page* 195.)

CHAPTER XVII.

STANWELL, BEDFONT, AND CRANFORD.

"Ecce horti campique nitent."—OVID.

Situation and General Aspect of Stanwell—Stanwell Heath formerly a rendezvous for Middlesex Elections—The Domesday Book Notice of Stanwell—The Forced Exchange of the Manor, *temp.* Henry VIII.—Subsequent Descent of the Manor—The Village of Stanwell—The Old School-house—Population—The Parish Church—Staines Moor, Stanwell Moor, and Poyle Park—West Bedfont—East Bedfont—The Parish Church—The "Peacocks"—Discoveries of Antiquities—Descent of the Manor of Bedfont—Spelthorne Sanatorium—Middlesex Industrial School for Girls—The "Black Dog"—Population of Bedfont—Cranford—Census Returns—The Village—Descent of the Manor—The Park—Cranford House—Cranford le Mote—The Parish Church—The Vicarage.

THE parish of Stanwell stands high in comparison with the flat country all around it, and its church spire forms a conspicuous landmark.   The village lies about two miles nearly due north from Staines. The parish is separated from Buckinghamshire by a branch of the river Colne, and in other directions is bounded by Bedfont, Staines, and Harmondsworth.   Down to the end of the last or beginning of the present century, upwards of 500 acres of land in the parish were an open waste, of which some 350 acres formed a portion, or continuation, of Hounslow Heath.   This state of things, however, is now all altered, and what was once barren and profitless has been turned into green pastures and smiling cornfields.

It would appear from "Bubb Dodington's Diary" that in the reign of George II. Stanwell Heath

was the great rendezvous of the electors of Middlesex, before they rushed off to the poll at Brentford Butts, as already recorded by us.*

In the "Domesday Survey," *Stanwelle* is stated to be held of the king by Walter Fitzother. "There were four mills, yielding seventy shillings, and four hundred eels, save twenty-five; and three wears, which produced one thousand eels, meadow for twelve ploughs (or each to twelve carucates). Pasture for the cattle of the village ; and pannage for one hundred hogs.   Its whole value was fourteen pounds ; when received six pounds."

William, the eldest son of the above-mentioned Walter Fitzother, held the post of Warden of Windsor Castle, and in consequence of this

* See *ante*, p. 38.

appointment he assumed the name of Windsor. His descendants possessed the manor of Stanwell until the year 1541, when it passed from them to the Crown by a very singular and unjustifiable method, if the story generally received be indeed correct.

Sir William Dugdale, who heartily disliked the memory of Henry VIII., on account of his dissolution of the monastic houses, and who had the account from the lips of Thomas, Lord Windsor,

king, with a stern countenance, replied that it *must* be, commanding him, *on his allegiance*, to repair to the Attorney-General, and settle the business without delay. The Attorney-General showed him a conveyance, ready prepared, of Bordesley Abbey, in the county of Worcester, with all its lands and appurtenances, in exchange for the manor of Stanwell. Being constrained, through dread of the king's displeasure, to accept of the exchange, he conveyed this manor to his Majesty,

STANWELL VILLAGE GREEN. (*See page 194.*)

relates in the following manner the story of the forced exchange of this manor by the then lord, in consequence of an "*invitation*" of the king :—

"The manor of Stanwell continued in the Windsor family till the year 1543, when King Henry the Eighth, having been advised to dispose of the monastic lands by gifts or exchange to the principal nobility and gentry, thought fit to make an exchange of this sort with Andrews, Lord Windsor. To this purpose he sent a message that he would dine with him at Stanwell, where a magnificent entertainment was accordingly provided. The king then informed the owner *that he liked his place so well that he was determined to have it*, though not without a beneficial exchange. Lord Windsor made answer that he hoped his Highness was not in earnest, since Stanwell had been the seat of his ancestors for so many generations. The

being commanded to quit Stanwell immediately, though he had laid in his Christmas provision for keeping his wonted hospitality there, saying that they should not find it *bare Stanwell*."

According to the above-mentioned story, Lord Windsor conveyed the manor to the king *before* Christmas ; but the deed of exchange, which is preserved in the Public Record Office, bears date the 14th of March, 33rd of Henry VIII. (1543), or more than three months subsequent to that season.

The title of Windsor would seem to have been happily chosen, for the original occupants of the manor-house here could see, across the well-watered meadows of the Colne, the towers of that royal castle and town from which they took their title.

In the year 1603, the manor and the demesne

lands were granted by James I. to Sir Thomas, afterwards Lord, Knyvet. The Princess Mary, daughter of King James, was placed under the care of this nobleman at Stanwell, and died there in 1607. The estate was subsequently vested in the family of the Carys, Lords Falkland, and in 1720 it was sold by John, Earl of Dunmore. A few years later it was purchased by Sir John Gibbons, Bart., K.B., and it is now the property of his descendant, Sir John Gibbons, Bart. The manor-house, called Stanwell Place, is a spacious modern mansion, standing in a small park.

The village of Stanwell is somewhat secluded, lying as it does off the main roads, and the ordinary beaten track of commerce. It is situated on the east side of the park, and the cottages and other buildings are scattered round a small, but picturesque, village green, which has about it sufficient evidences of rural life to render it a charming "bit" for the pencil of an artist. The ancient school-house on the London Road, which was built and endowed for the charitable instruction of poor children, in accordance with the will of Thomas, Lord Knyvet, has remained down to the present time as a monument of his care for the requirements of future generations.

According to the census returns for 1871, the number of inhabited houses in the parish was 364, the population amounting to 1,955 souls; but this number included upwards of 300 in the district of St. Thomas, Colnbrook, and nearly 250 in Staines Union Workhouse, which is situated to the south of the village, and abuts upon the Bedfont Road. In 1881 the population had increased to 2,155, inclusive of the inmates of the workhouse, but exclusive of Colnbrook.

The parish church of Stanwell, dedicated to St. Mary, is an ancient building, composed of stone interspersed with flint, and is a mixture of the Early English, Decorated, and Perpendicular styles of architecture. Unlike most of the churches of the Thames Valley, it consists of a nave, with clerestory, a double chancel, aisles, a picturesque wooden porch with tiled roof on the north side, and a low square tower at the western end. The church was thoroughly restored in 1863, at which time the north aisle was rebuilt and the porch added. The tower is constructed of flint and stone, in chequer work, and from it rises a lofty octagonal shingled spire, somewhat out of the perpendicular. The interior is spacious, well lighted, and much superior to the generality of the village churches in this county. Its nave and aisles are divided by Pointed arches, which spring from massive pillars, some being octagonal, and others

circular. Some of the windows are filled with stained glass. On the south wall of the chancel are two stone stalls and the remains of a piscina, beyond which, towards the nave, extends an arcade of eight niches, or seats, probably intended for the accommodation of the brethren of Chertsey Abbey, to whom the rectory of Stanwell was appropriated by Richard de Windsor about the year 1415.

There was in this church an "Easter Sepulchre," formed, as will be seen, out of one of the tombs.* "On the north side of the chancel," writes Mr. Bloxam, in his "Gothic Architecture," "is a high tomb, over which is a canopy with an obtuse arch, ornamented with quatrefoils. Beneath this arch were placed upright in the wall brass plates, with the effigies of the deceased and his wife, all long ago removed. This is the monument of Thomas Windsor, who died A.D. 1486. By his will, made in 1479, after directing that his body should be buried on the north side of the 'quier' of the church of our Lady of Stanwell, "afor the ymage of our Lady wher the sepulture [sic] of our Lord stondith;" he adds, 'I will that there be made a playne tombe of marble, of a competent hyght, to th' entent that yt may ber [bear] the blessed body of our Lord, and the sepulture at the tyme of Estre to stand upon the same.'"

The above Thomas Windsor was the father of Andrews, first Lord Windsor, the nobleman who, as stated above, was "despoiled" by the king of the manor of Stanwell.

On the same wall as the above tomb is one of a more stately character to the memory of Thomas, Lord Knyvet, and Elizabeth, his wife, which rises nearly to the roof of the chancel. This monument is of veined marble, with columns of the Corinthian order, and, as stated in "Walpole's Anecdotes of Paintings," was the work of Nicholas Stone, who received for executing it the sum of £215. The effigies of Lord and Lady Knyvet are represented life-size, in a kneeling attitude. On a tablet is an inscription in Latin, setting forth at considerable length the descent and virtues of the deceased, both of whom appear, from an inscription on the floor, to have died in the year 1622.

This church appears in former times to have been particularly rich in monumental brasses, but these have mostly disappeared, either by theft, or in that most dangerous of processes, "restoration."

The rectory of Stanwell was formerly a sinecure in the patronage of the Windsor family. In 1415

---

* The same is the case with Harlington Church, as will be seen presently.

Richard de Windsor exchanged the rectory and advowson for the manor of West Bedfont, with the Abbot and Convent of Chertsey. At about the same time a vicarage was endowed, to which the Abbots of Chertsey presented until the Dissolution, since which period the patronage of the vicarage has remained with the Crown, through the Lord Chancellor.

The celebrated Dr. Bruno Ryves, author of the "Mercurius Rusticus, or an Account of the Sufferings of the Royalists," was vicar of this parish. He was deprived during the Civil War, but recovered his preferment on .the Restoration. We have already had occasion to mention him in our account of Acton.*

To the west of the village are Staines Moor and Stanwell Moor, broad expanses of land bordering upon the River Colne, the latter being partly covered with houses ; and also Poyle Park, a small seat in the neighbourhood of Colnbrook, a part of which village, as shown above, belongs to the parish of Stanwell.

West Bedfont, a hamlet about half a mile east of Stanwell, on the road to East Bedfont, was in former times an independent manor, but it now forms part and parcel of the manor of Stanwell.

The roadway by which we now make our way to Bedfont follows the course of the "Queen's River," which ripples merrily along through the meadows on our left ; whilst at a short distance further northward flows the "Duke of Northumberland's River," on its way to unite its waters with the River Crane, in the neighbourhood of Hounslow.

Bedfont, formerly called East Bedfont, in order to distinguish it from West Bedfont, lies on the high road, about equidistant from Hounslow and Staines. With its long village green and pond, both fringed with fine elms and other trees, and its irregular string of houses and cottages retreating so gracefully behind their gardens on either side of the road, it has a quaint and primitive air, which would hardly lead one to believe that he is within thirteen miles of the great metropolis. The quaintness of its appearance is increased by its little Norman church, with its wooden tower and dwarf steeple, and its pair of trim and formal yew-trees, cut out into the shapes of peacocks, with the date 1704, and the initials of the churchwardens of that time, still legible in the cropped foliage. The local tradition is that they represent satirically two sisters who lived at Bedfont, and who were so very haughty that they both refused the hand of

some local magnate, who thus immortalised them, being "as proud as peacocks." This, however, is a legend only. These are some of the grotesque shapes with which a stiff, formal, and unnatural age loved to decorate its gardens, lawns, and alleys ; and they are only a "survival" of what once was a common fashion.

If the peacocks have rendered the two maiden ladies above mentioned immortal, they have in their turn been immortalised by Thomas Hood, who makes them the subject of one of the most serious of his early "serious" poems :—

"Where erst two haughty maidens used to be,
    In pride of plume, where plumy Death hath trod,
  Trailing their gorgeous velvet wantonly,
    Most unmeet pall, over the holy sod :
  There, gentle stranger, thou may'st only see
    Two sombre peacocks. Age, with sapient nod
  Marking the spot, still tarries to declare
  How once they lived and wherefore they are there.

"Alas ! that breathing vanity should go
    Where pride is buried ; like its very ghost
  Unrisen from the naked bones below,
    In novel flesh, clad in the silent boast
  Of gaudy silk, that flutters to and fro,
    Shedding its chilling superstition most
  On young and ignorant natures—as is wont
  To haunt the peaceful churchyard of Bedfont."

Pope, who must often have seen these quaint artificial ornaments, satirised them in No. 173 of the *Guardian* :—"How contrary to simplicity is the modern practice of gardening ! We seem to make it our study to recede from nature not only in the various tonsure of greens into the most regular and formal shapes, but even into monstrous attempts beyond the reach of the art itself; we run into sculpture, and are yet better pleased to have our trees in the most awkward figures of men and animals than in the most regular of their own. . . . A citizen is no sooner proprietor of a couple of yews, but he entertains thoughts of erecting them into giants, like those of Guildhall. I know an eminent cook who beautified his country seat with the coronation-dinner in greens (evergreens), where you see the champion flourishing on horseback at one end of the table, and the queen in perpetual youth at the other." And he adds a list of some fifteen or sixteen subjects cut in evergreens, from Adam and Eve and Noah's Ark down to Queen Elizabeth, which are to be disposed of by an "eminent town gardner," of his acquaintance. In spite of all Pope's quiet satire, those at Bedfont still hold their place; but at Harlington, as we shall presently see, the yew-tree has been allowed of late to grow at its own sweet will.

The church itself is Norman, as shown by its

* See ante, p. 15.

ornamental and round-headed south doorway and a similar chancel arch, and a small round-headed window in the north wall of the chancel. At the north-east angle of the nave, near the chancel arch, is a double recess, which looks as if it had once formed an aumbry or the reredos of an altar. On the plaster being recently stripped off the wall, two fresco paintings were revealed, the one representing the Crucifixion, and the other the Last Judgment. The great Judge is seated, in His human nature, with the five wounds conspicuous, and over His right eye is a daub of dark paint, as if pointing to a passage in the Book of Ecclesiastes, where God is said to "wink at the sins of men." Both paintings, it may be added, though they can still be deciphered, have suffered severely from iconoclasts or friendly plasterers. On the wall of the chancel is a small brass of Jacobean date, as shown by the ruff and frill. In the south wall of the nave, close to the chancel arch, is a recess with a small window, which may have contained the steps to a rood-loft, or possibly have been a place for lepers, &c., to hear mass. The frescoes are of the twelfth or thirteenth century, and have been attributed to the reign of Stephen.

Behind the church on the north is an ugly excrescence, forming a huge transept, of modern date, and of the "Churchwarden" style. This church was restored "upon the old lines" in the year 1866.

It is probable that Bedfont was at one time a Roman station, for in a field between the village and Feltham have been dug up considerable quantities of Roman coins, mixed with urns, bones, &c., and the vestiges of some barrows of uncertain date.

The name of this parish is Bedefunt and Bedefunde, in the "Domesday Record," and the principal manor is there said to be held by Richard of Walter, the son of *Other*. Another manor at Bedfont, noticed in the same record, is described as lying within the manor of Feltham, and was held by the Earl of Moreton, half-brother of the Conqueror. The principal manor of Bedfont and the manor of Hatton, included within the same parochial district, are described in the "Beauties of England and Wales" as the property of the Duke of Northumberland. On the Sion House stream, at the eastern extremity of the parish, are some powder-mills.

In 1878 an institution known as the Spelthorne Sanitorium was opened here, as a refuge for women "who have fallen into habits of intemperance." It affords accommodation for about twenty "patients," who are employed in laundry and needlework.

Adjoining, and under the same management, is the Middlesex Industrial School for Girls.

The village of Bedfont, beyond the church and its famous yews, and the institutions just referred to, contains nothing of interest to detain the visitor, excepting, perhaps, he may feel inclined to make a call at the "Black Dog," whose former landlord is commemorated in Colman's "Random Recollections" in the following lines :—

> "Harvey, whose inn commands a view
> Of Bedfont's church and churchyard too,
> Where yew-trees into peacocks shorn,
> In vegetable torture mourn."

The inhabitants of the village, as may be inferred from its surroundings, are almost wholly employed in agriculture. In the year 1871 the population, including that of the hamlet of Hatton, amounted to only 1,288 souls, whilst the inhabited houses were set down in the census returns at 279. In the year 1881 the population had increased to 1,452.

Making our way in a north-easterly direction, and passing through the hamlet of Hatton, we soon arrive at Cranford, a spot which, from the sylvan beauty of its park, forms quite an "oasis in the desert," the greater part of the country around being level and uninviting arable land, or in parts cultivated as wheat-fields and orchards. Cranford Bridge, which has taken the place of the *Ford* over the Crane, or *Cran*, from which the parish took its name, lies two miles west of Hounslow, along the old Bath road. That part of it which was open heath half a century ago is now enclosed, and covered with houses and market-gardens.

It is a straggling village, with a population of some 500 souls, which is a diminution of about 50 from the number recorded in the census returns for 1871. The place possesses no regular "street," and seems to have grown up at haphazard round the outside circuit of Cranford Park, for the last two centuries and a half one of the residences of the Earls of Berkeley, and now belonging to Lord Fitzhardinge. There is nothing to remark about it, except that at the lower end of the village there is, as above stated, a bridge of three arches over the River Crane. The park is small, containing about 140 acres, and is very strictly preserved. The manor-house, which stands near the centre of it, is a dull, heavy-looking structure of any and every age, not built upon any regular plan. The stabling is fine and good, and evidently in former days formed a most important part of the mansion. It is rarely inhabited by the family, owing to the superior attractions of Berkeley Castle as a residence.

About the time of the Conquest the manor of Cranford, or Craneforde, as it is termed in "Domesday Book," was divided, and the separate manorial districts were distinguished by the names of Cranford St. John and Cranford le Mote. The first of these was for some time possessed by the Knights Templars, and after the abolition of that order, was vested in the Knights Hospitallers of St. John of Jerusalem. The manor of Cranford le Mote was long the property of the Abbot and Convent of Thame, in Oxfordshire. On the dissolution of the religious houses, both these manors were granted by Henry VIII. to Henry, Lord Windsor, and after several intermediate transfers, were purchased, in the year 1618, of the co-heirs of Sir Roger Aston, gentleman of the bedchamber to James I., by Elizabeth, Lady Berkeley, for the sum of £7,000.

Inside the park, the Crane is artificially dammed up so as to form a lake ; but it is as straight as an arrow, thus showing that it was planned in the old artificial days of gardening—not unlike the straight "canal"* in St. James's Park. It abounds with fish and wild fowl, and the game all over the property is very strictly preserved.

For a long time Cranford House has been for most of the year untenanted, except by a caretaker, and it has somehow gained the reputation of being haunted. The Hon. Grantley Berkeley, in his "Life and Recollections," has given a detailed account of these nocturnal visitants. The house contains, besides a few family portraits, others of Dr. Harvey, Dean Swift, Fuller the historian, Sir William Temple, &c. The residence of the Berkeley family here is thus celebrated by Mr. W. Wilkes, in his ambitious and rather prosaic poem of "Hounslow Heath" :—

> "Two miles from Hounslow towards the west is plac'd,
> With all the beauties of retirement grac'd,
> A grand and rural seat in Berkeley fam'd,
> Gay Crantford's castle by the Muses nam'd ;
> Where health's preserved in unpolluted air,
> Where smiling peace extirpates every care ;
> Where Amalthea holds her golden horn,
> And brisk diversions wake with every morn."

The Hon. Thomas Moreton Fitzhardinge-Berkeley, son of the fifth Earl of Berkeley, lived for many years at Cranford Cottage, in the immediate outskirts of the park. He died in August, 1882, never having assumed the title, although by a decision of the House of Lords, in 1811, he was virtually declared entitled to it.

The manor-house of Cranford le Mote occupied

a moated site, at a short distance from the church on the north-east. The ancient building on this spot, which was the residence of Sir William Fleetwood, Receiver of the Court of Wards about the commencement of the seventeenth century, was taken down about the year 1780.

The church, dedicated to St. Dunstan, adjoins the manor-house, and having no aisles, remains in its original tiny proportions. As is so frequently the case along the Middlesex valley of the Thames, the tower is the only original part of the building which still stands. The nave and chancel have been modernised, the latter with heavy, but substantial, mahogany and oak.

On the walls are some fine Jacobean and more recent monuments to members of the Berkeley family, but these are not in a good state of repair. In the chancel there is a fine Jacobean monument to Sir Roger Aston, whose kneeling figure and those of his two wives and daughters, exhibit the fanciful ruffs, frills, &c., of the period. At his foot is a small bambino, representing a son who died in infancy. The marriages of the daughters are recorded, with some pride, upon the panel below, whilst the armorial bearings of Aston, with several impalements, are introduced in several parts of the monument together with a narrative inscription of considerable length. Close by the above is a mural tablet of black marble set in a frame of alabaster, to the memory of the celebrated Dr. Thomas Fuller, author of the "Church History of Britain," the "Worthies of England," and many other learned works. Dr. Fuller was warmly patronised by George, Lord Berkeley, in whose family he was chaplain, and by whom he was presented to the rectory of Cranford in 1658. Fuller died at his lodgings in Covent Garden in August, 1661, his body was brought from London and buried in the chancel of Cranford church, 200 clergy following him to the grave, and his funeral was conducted under the immediate direction of Lord Berkeley, who defrayed all the expenses incident to the solemnity. The successor of Dr. Fuller as rector of Cranford was the eminent divine John Wilkins, afterwards Bishop of Chester.

Under the chancel repose several members of the Berkeley family. Mr. Henry Berkeley, formerly for many years M.P. for Bristol, and the great advocate of the ballot, lies under a plain tomb-stone beneath the east window of the chancel. In the churchyard are some fine yews and other evergreens, which, if the truth must be told, make the edifice dark and damp. The rectory, an old structure modernised, stands just within the park gates.

---

* See "Old and New London," Vol. IV., p. 54.

HARLINGTON CHURCH.   (*See page* 199.)
(*From an Engraving dated* 1803.)

CHAPTER XVIII.

HARLINGTON AND HARMONDSWORTH.

Situation of Harlington—The Village and Population—The Manor—The Parish Church—Dr. Trapp—The Yew Tree in the Churchyard—The Local Charities—The Earldom of Arlington—Dawley Court—Lord Bolingbroke—Harmondsworth, Situation, and Nature of the Soil—Its Etymology—Harmondsworth Priory—The Manor—An Ancient Barn—The Parish Church—The Village—Census Returns, &c.—Heath Row—A Roman Encampment—Sipson—Longford—Colnbrook.

HARLINGTON is a small straggling village, about a mile and a half north-west of Cranford, and nearer to Southall and Hayes, and also some three miles south of Uxbridge. It is in the Hundred of Elthorne and Union of Staines. The village contains several very old cottages, probably of the sixteenth century; much of the parish is still devoted to market gardens, and especially to cherry orchards, which impart to the lanes in the locality a green and shady aspect.

Good brick earth is obtained on the surface, especially in the northern part, though gravel predominates below, and the result is that much brick-making is carried on in the neighbourhood. In 1871 this parish contained inhabited houses to the number of 254, whilst the population amounted to 1,296 souls. According to the census returns for 1881 the number of the inhabitants had increased to 1,538. The acreage of the parish is set down at 1,464, and the rateable value at £11,433.

The name of Harlington appears to have been originally spelt Herdington, or Herdyngton. Under the former name it is mentioned in "Domesday Book" as a manor answering for ten hides, and having "land for six ploughs," and held under Earl Roger by Alured and Olaf. It speaks of a priest as owning half a hide of land there, and of twelve *villani*, holding half a virgate each; mention is made also of eight cottagers and one bondsman. Its whole value is given as one hundred shillings. "It is taxed," writes the author of the *Antiquarian Cabinet*, "in the ancient valors at nine marks yearly. In the

King's Books it is valued at £24. The Inquisition taken in 1650, by order of the Parliament, states the parsonage to be worth £140 a year, exclusive of 36 acres of glebe. Some of these acres, however, are now lost to the living, though its money value is largely increased."

The chief manor appears to have been divided at an early period into two, both of which now belong to the Berkeley family. The manor of Hardington, Harlington, or "Lovells," having been in the hands of the Harpendens, the Lovells, and the great Lord Bolingbroke, passed to the Earl of Uxbridge, who sold it to the late Earl of Berkeley. The other manor of Harlington-cum-Sheperton came to the same family by the marriage of George, Lord Berkeley, with a daughter of Sir Michael Stanhope.

There is in this parish a third reputed manor, of small extent, which is noticed in the "Norman Survey" under the name of "Dalleger." It answered in "Doomsday" for three hides. It was afterwards called Dalley, or Danley; and under the more recent name of Dawley it belonged to Lord Bolingbroke, and now to Count Fane de Salis.

The church, dedicated to St. Peter and St. Paul, stands near the north end of the village, and consists of nave, chancel, and a square embattled tower. A north aisle was added at the restoration of the building in 1881. The edifice is chiefly built of flint, with stone facings, and the chancel is higher than the nave. There is a fine Norman font, and also a Norman south doorway, with zig-zag mouldings. One singular and interesting feature in the ornamentation of this doorway is that the outer member of the arch comprises a series of cats' heads, the tongues being fancifully

carved, and turned over a moulding corded and beaded. The pillars which support the arch are of modern brick, but the capitals are Norman, and are dissimilar and much embellished.

The Easter Sepulchre.

The Norman Door, Harlington.

"BITS" FROM HARLINGTON CHURCH.

The mouldings have been formerly cut away to admit the addition of a wooden porch of much more recent date, finely carved. This, however, has been raised, and the defects of the noble doorway have been repaired. This doorway is altogether a very handsome specimen of late and elaborate Norman work, its ornamentation being equal to the well-known examples of Iffley, Barfreston, and Patrixbourne, near Canterbury.

This church, which has been carefully restored upon the old lines, affords examples of nearly every style of architecture. There are two early Norman, or possibly Saxon, windows north and south of the nave; the Decorated windows on the sides of the chancel are very fine in their tracery;

and the east window, of post-Reformation Gothic, cannot fail to remind visitors of Oriel and Wadham Colleges at Oxford. The church altogether is, perhaps, the best specimen of a mediæval country church in all the Middlesex valley of the Thames. It is rendered all the more picturesque by a fine yew-tree—said to be 700 years old—on the south side of the churchyard, and a noble cedar in the vicarage garden adjoining it on the north.

In the church are brasses to members of the Lovell family, and one, half-length, to John Yarmouth, a former rector, who is duly robed in the Eucharistic vestments. On the north wall of the chancel is the monument of Dr. Joseph Trapp, rector of this parish in 1732—47, and some time Professor of Poetry in the University of Oxford. He died in 1747. His monument bears the following lines :—

" Death, judgment, heaven, and hell ! think, Christian, think,
  You stand on vast eternity's dread brink ;
  Faith and repentance, piety and prayer,
  Despise this world, the next be all your care.
  Thus, while my tomb the solemn silence breaks,
  And to the eye this cold dumb marble speaks,
  Tho' dead I preach : if e'er with ill success,
  Living, I strove th' important truth to press,
  Your precious, your immortal souls to save ;
  Hear me, at least, oh, hear me from my grave."

Dr. Trapp's want of poetical ability, as exemplified in his attempts to translate Virgil and Milton, is recorded in some severe epigrams. There is a portrait of him in the Bodleian Library.

The Bennets, Lords Tankerville, are still buried here, though the family have long lived in Northumberland. On the floor is a memorial to Charles, Earl of Tankerville, who died in 1767 ; and the last earl, who died in 1859, has also a memorial here. There are also monuments to various members of the family of Lord De Tabley, his first wife having been a De Salis.

There are some fine modern tombs and two painted windows erected in memory of members of the family of De Salis of Dawley Court, whose fortunes were founded in this country by one Peter de Salis, sent hither as envoy in 1709 from the Emperor Joseph I.

A fresco painting on the south wall of the nave was discovered on removing the monument of Sir John Bennet, Lord Ossulston, who died in the year 1695. The monument, which has been replaced, has upon it busts of Lord Ossulston and his two wives.

Affixed to the south wall of the nave is a carved hour-glass of oak, thought by some to be of the thirteenth or fourteenth century. The Easter sepulchre—a handsome piece of stone carving on the north side of the chancel—is thought by some antiquarians to be the reredos of an altar. The registers, which commence in 1540, are in fairly good condition ; they are curious as containing the names of many "travellers"—one result of the parish being situated just one day's tramp on the great road to the west from London.

Among former rectors was a John of Tewkesbury, who was the author of some learned books ; and also John Kyte, who resigned the living in 1510 ; he was probably the same person who was sent as ambassador to Spain, and died in 1537 Bishop of Carlisle. He was a native of London, and is buried at Stepney.

The magnificent old yew-tree in the churchyard above referred to grows now in a healthy and natural fashion ; but, as shown in our illustration taken early in the present century, it used to be clipped and cut into artificial shape. From some verses by the parish clerk, John Saxy, affixed to a large copper-plate engraving, it would seem that in 1729 this yew-tree was upwards of fifty feet high. It was surrounded at the base by a circular seat, over which hung a large canopy, formed by the dark boughs of the tree, in the words of this rural poet—

" So thick, so fine, so full, so wide,
  A troop of Guards might under 't ride."

Some ten feet higher up again was another smaller canopy, above which the tree towered up solid, till its topmost leaves formed a sort of nest in the shape of a globe, with a cock or hen seated above it.

" A weather-cock, who gapes to crow it,
  ' The globe is mine and all below it,' "

writes the rhymer, who adds his deliberate opinion of the tree, that—

" It yields to Harlington a fame
  Much louder than its Earldom's name."

Without going quite so far as the worthy clerk, we may state that the tree, until it ceased to be clipped, some half century ago, was the great curiosity of the place, and was visited by scores of persons. It is thought to be as old as the Conquest, and it is still one of the largest yew-trees in the home counties : its branches formerly reached to the church porch, and are said to have covered a space of 150 feet. The clipping and clearing of the tree was a village holiday, as important in its way and in its place as the scouring of the White Horse on the Berkshire Downs. The last occasion on which it was clipped was in 1825.

In our view of the church the old yew does not appear to be so high as when sung of by the parish clerk. It figures also in Loudon's "Arboretum Britannicum," but in that work its dimensions are exaggerated.

The fantastic idea of thus clipping the yew-tree was a survival of the old formal style of gardening which prevailed under our Tudor and Stuart sovereigns.

The charities in this parish are considerable. One rector, named Cooper, left an annual sum to the clerk for repairing his tomb; but this reverend gentleman's body has been removed from his grave to another part of the churchyard; the benefaction, however, remains. Some land was left to the bell-ringers to provide them a leg of pork for dinner on Guy Fawkes' Day, and this is called the Pork Half-Acre. The land has since been sold for £100, and the proceeds invested for their benefit; and about fourteen acres were set apart for the poor at the last enclosure, in lieu of their ancient right to cut turf.

Dawley Court, in this parish, once the residence of the great Lord Bolingbroke, is no longer standing, except the steward's apartments, or what is said to have been the laundry, consisting of two fine rooms. This for many years has been the only building on the estate, the remainder of the land having been cut up into prosaic brick-fields.

The mansion itself was pulled down about the year 1776.

The manor-house at Dawley must have been a spacious structure; it was the residence of the Lovells and of the Bennets before it came into the hands of Lord Bolingbroke. Its succeeding owner, Lord Uxbridge, is said to have built round it a wall nearly a mile long, to keep out the small-pox.

Dawley became the property of the Bennets early in the sixteenth century. Sir John Bennet, who appears to have been the first of that name residing here, was a distinguished member of Parliament in the reign of Queen Elizabeth, and was judge of the Prerogative Court of Canterbury in the reign of James I. In 1617 he was sent as ambassador to Brussels, to interrogate the archduke on behalf of his royal master, the King of Great Britain, concerning a libel written and published, as it was supposed, by Erycius Puteanus, in his Imperial Highness's dominions. His eldest son and successor, Sir John Bennet, of Dawley, ancestor of the Earls of Tankerville, received the honour of knighthood in the lifetime of his father at Theobalds, in 1616. He was the father of Henry Bennet, who

will be remembered as a member of the "Cabal Ministry," and who was raised to the peerage in 1663 as Viscount Thetford and Earl of Arlington. His lordship meant to choose this place as that from which he should derive his title; but the scribes of the Herald's College, or some other officials, were not as attentive to their "H's" as they should have been, and so, when the patent reached his hands, or when he read his new dignity in the *Gazette*, he found that he had been created Earl, not of Harlington, but of "Arlington." It was too late for any alteration to have been made, for "the proof had been worked off," so Arlington he remained; and the street which runs out of Piccadilly towards St. James's Palace is Arlington also.

The Arlington coronet is now merged in the ducal title of Grafton, through the marriage of the first duke with Lady Isabella Bennet, only daughter of the above-mentioned earl; consequently, the Duke of Grafton reckons among his inferior titles the barony of "Arlington, of Harlington, county of Middlesex."

From the Bennets Dawley Court passed to the celebrated Lord Bolingbroke, and became his favourite country house, or, as he liked to style it, his "farm." He lived here during a memorable period of his eventful life, the time of his estrangement from public affairs, and from the gay world as well. To use his own figurative language, he was now "in a hermitage, where no man came but for the sake of the hermit; for here he found that the insects which used to hum and buzz about him in the sunshine fled to men of more prosperous fortune, and forsook him when in the shade." Here he was often visited by "Glorious John Dryden."

Lord Bolingbroke adorned his house with paintings of rustic subjects, "trophies of rakes, spades, prongs," &c. (as Pope tells us in a letter addressed by him from hence to Swift), and over the door he placed an inscription, slightly altered from Horace:—

"Satis beatus ruris honoribus."

Living as he did within some six or seven miles of Dawley, Pope was a constant visitor here; and so was Voltaire occasionally, whilst staying in London.

It is said that some of the same wild oxen which are now to be seen at Lord Tankerville's park in Northumberland were kept here in the time of the Bennets; but this is probably an error.

A poem, entitled "Dawley's Farm," in the first

volume of the *Gentleman's Magazine*, gives us some glimpses of the place as it appeared in 1731 :—

> " See, emblem of himself, his villa stand,
>   Politely finish'd, elegantly grand !
> Frugal of ornament, but that the best,
> And with all curious negligence express'd.
> No gaudy colours deck the rural hall,
> Blank light and shade discriminate the wall ;
> Where through the whole we see his lov'd design,
> To please with mildness, without glaring shine,
> Himself neglects what must all others charm,
> And what he built a palace calls a farm.
>
> Here the proud trophies and the spoils of war
> Yield to the scythe, the harrow, and the car,
> To whate'er implement the rustic wields,
> Whate'er manures the gardens or the fields.
>
> *   *   *   *   *   *
>
> Here noble St. John, in his sweet recess,
> Sees on the figured wall the stacks of corn
> With beauty more than theirs the room adorn ;
> Young winged Cupids smiling guide the plow,
> And peasants elegantly reap and sow.
>
> *   *   *   *   *   *
>
> O, Britain ! but 'tis past.   O lost to fame,
> The wondrous man, thy glory and thy shame,
> Conversing with the mighty minds of old—
> Names like his own in time's bright lists enroll'd,
> Here splendidly obscure, delighted lives,
> And only for his wretched country grieves."

Lady Luxborough, Lord Bolingbroke's sister, mentions the place in one of her letters in terms which fully justify these not very poetical lines. She writes :—" When my brother Bolingbroke built Dawley, which he chose to call a 'Farm,' he had his hall painted in stone colour, with all the implements of husbandry placed in the manner one sees, or might see, arms and trophies in some general's hall; and it had an effect that pleased everybody."

Voltaire occasionally came here whilst staying in London ; and Pope, who lived within some six or seven miles of Dawley, was a constant visitor. In a letter written from hence by Pope to Dean Swift, we find the following :—" I now hold the pen of my Lord Bolingbroke, who is reading your letter between two hay-cocks ; but his attention is somewhat diverted by casting his eyes on the clouds—not in admiration of what you say, but for fear of a shower. He is pleased with your placing him in the triumvirate between yourself and me ; though he says that he doubts he shall fare like Lepidus, while one of us runs away with all the power, like Augustus, and another with all the pleasures, like Anthony. It is upon a foresight of this that he has fitted up his farm. Now his lordship is run after his cart, I

have a moment left to myself to tell you that I overheard him yesterday agree with a painter for £200 to paint his country hall with trophies of rakes, spades, prongs, &c., and other ornaments, merely to countenance his calling his place a farm."

His lordship, we are told, was happy in possessing "a mind formed for the world at large, and not dependent on the contingencies of court favour "; though it is to be regretted that the poetical warmth of his imagination often led him, in his retired as well as in his busy hours, to flights of dangerous mental indulgence. A temper so ardent could never find a semblance of repose but in extremes.

"In the earlier days of his character," writes Mr. Disraeli, "Lord Bolingbroke meditated over the formation of a new party—that dream of youthful ambition in a perplexed and discordant age, but destined in English politics to be never more substantial than a vision. More experienced in political life," he continues, "Lord Bolingbroke became aware that he had only to choose between the Whigs and the Tories, and his sagacious intellect, not satisfied with the superficial character of these . . . divisions, penetrated their interior and essential qualities, and discovered, in spite of all the affectation of popular sympathy on the one side, and of admiration of arbitrary power on the other, that his choice was, in fact, a choice between oligarchy and democracy. From the moment that Lord Bolingbroke, in becoming a Tory, embraced the national cause, he devoted himself absolutely to his party ; all the energies of his Protean mind were lavished in their service ; and although . . . restrained from advocating the cause of the nation in the Senate, his inspiring pen made Walpole tremble in the recesses of the Treasury ; and in a series of writings, unequalled in our literature for their spirited patriotism, their just and profound views, and the golden eloquence in which they are expressed, eradicated from Toryism all those absurd and odious doctrines which Toryism had adventitiously adopted, clearly developed its essential and permanent character, discarded the *jus divinum*, demolished passive obedience, threw to the winds the doctrine of non-resistance, placed the abdication of James and the accession of George on their right basis, and in the complete reorganisation of the public mind laid the foundation for the future accession of the Tory party to power." But a man of fashion, and fond of society and of politics, Lord Bolingbroke soon found that the country was wearisome, and resolved to part with his beloved Dawley. He sold it in 1739, when the house was nearly all pulled down again. One wing alone was left, and this was made into a steward's residence. The lands were bought by the Pagets, then Earls of Uxbridge, and living at Harmondsworth, from whom again they passed into the hands of the family of De Salis. The once beautiful grounds where Boling-broke read Pope's letter as he reclined on a hay-cock are now turned into brick-fields, through which pass a canal and the Great Western Railway— a mournful commentary on the short-lived pleasures of great men.

It is said that on grand occasions in Lord Bolingbroke's or Lord Uxbridge's days the road from Dawley to West Drayton used to be hung with artificial lamps, to guide his aristocratic visitors on their way home at night; and one of the fields which it crosses is still called "The Lanterns."

It might be said of "Dawley Farm" as truly as of Canons itself (of which we shall speak here-after):—

> " Another age shall see the golden ear,
> Imbrown the slope and nod on the parterre;
> Deep harvests bury all his pride has plann'd,
> And laughing Ceres re-assume the land."

But here the transformation is almost more com-plete, for Ceres herself has had to give way in her turn to the goddess, if there be one, who presides over brick-fields and brick-makers.

Opposite the Dawley Manor Farm, and near the church, are to be traced the remains of a moated grange, in a meadow still known as "The Moats"; but nothing is known of its history.

The parish of Harmondsworth adjoins Harling-ton on the west, and is separated from Bucking-hamshire by a branch of the River Colne. The whole district is flat and uninteresting, but the soil is fertile, and productive of good crops of corn and vegetables, whilst much fruit finds its way from this locality to the London markets. The land hereabouts is intersected by several small rivulets, or streams, which creep in dull obscurity, without imparting to any portion of the parish the elements of the picturesque.

The name of the parish is familiarly pronounced "Harmsworth" by the "natives." In the "Domes-day Book" it is written *Hermondesworde*, and it is stated in that record that the Abbot of the Holy Trinity at Rouen held the principal manor of the king. Tanner says that there was here a priory of the Benedictine order, which was a cell to the above-mentioned abbey of the Holy Trinity, but no traces of such a priory have been discovered in recent times.

Cobbett mentions, in his list of religious houses confiscated by Henry VIII., an alien priory here, which was granted in the first year of Edward VI. to one of the Tudor courtiers, Sir William Paget. He gives, however, no particulars as to its name, its site, or its value. Perhaps it was the same as the above.

"This manor," observes the author of "The Beauties of England and Wales," "shared the fate of many other possessions of the alien priories, and was seized by King Edward III. in the year 1340. The arable land belonging to the demesne was then valued at 4d. an acre, the meadow at 8d., and the pasture at 2d. There were two water-mills: one for corn, let at 18s. per annum; the other for malt, at 8s. The manor was afterwards conveyed to William of Wykeham, who settled it upon the collegiate establishment of his founda-tion; but it was again obtained by the Crown, in exchange for other possessions, in the reign of Henry VIII. By Edward VI. it was granted to Sir William Paget, from whom it descended to the present noble possessor, the Marquis of Angle-sey. As a manorial custom, of a character not very frequent, it may be observed that tenants have a right of fishery in all the rivers and common waters within the manor on Wednesdays, Fridays, and Saturdays. It is probable that the ancient manor-house occupied the site of a farm-dwelling near the church, which claims notice, as there is in the attached yard a barn of remarkably large dimensions, it being 191 feet in length and 38 feet in breadth."

The fine old barn above mentioned is perhaps the most interesting object of antiquity in this neighbourhood. The walls are built of con-glomerate, commonly called "pudding-stone," and found in this locality. The body of the barn is divided into a nave and aisles by two rows of massive pillars. There are three floors, and the roof is of open timber-work, in good preservation. In former times the building was much larger, having an angular projecting wing, or transept, at the north end, which was pulled down about the year 1775, at the same time as the old manor-house, near which it stood. This portion of the old barn was re-built—or rather, the roof of it was re-erected on walls of modern brick-work and sup-ported by the original oak columns—at Heath Row, about a mile and a half distant. The building, of which we have given an engraving on the next page, is commonly called "the Gothic barn," because its interior is so like the nave of a cathedral.

The manor was sold by the Pagets, and is now

the property of Mr. George Harmond. Although the mansion has disappeared, the gardens and stables still remain. Some subordinate manors in the parish, lying in the hamlets of Longford, Sipson, and other parts, formerly belonging to the Pagets, have passed into the the hands of the Earl of Strafford and other owners.

The parish church, dedicated to the Virgin Mary, notwithstanding that it was restored in 1863, bears the marks of considerable antiquity, portions of it dating as far back as the Norman times. It is a tolerably fine building, rather like those of West Drayton and Harlington.

The village of Harmondsworth consists chiefly of scattered rural dwellings, many of which are in that ancient and simple mode of construction— half timber and plaster, projecting upper storeys, and thatched roofs—so favourable to the picturesque. There are also one or two old mansions, with cedars in the grounds. But to the parish, as a whole, no historical interest whatever is attached. According to the census returns for the year 1871 the parish contained 326 inhabited houses, the number of the population being 1,584, which had increased to 1,800 in the course of the next ten years.

THE OLD BARN AT HARMONDSWORTH.   (*See page* 203.)

The body of the structure is composed of stone and flint, and is of the Perpendicular style of architecture. It consists of a nave with aisles, chancel with north aisle, and a square brick tower of modern erection at the south-west corner. The tower, however, is poor, and cased with plaster. The south doorway is of Norman workmanship, but not a richly-worked specimen of that style of architecture; the chief feature of it, however, is a range of birds' heads, the beaks being thrown over a torus-band moulding. In the south side of the chancel are three stalls, or seats, together with a piscina and credence table. In digging a grave of unusual depth in the churchyard in the year 1870, some silver coins, twenty-five in number, belonging to the Tudor and Stuart periods, were discovered.

Heath Row, mentioned above, lies in the eastern part of the parish, to the south of the great western road, and it takes its name from its situation on the margin of Hounslow Heath. Close by this spot are slight traces of the Roman encampment which Stukeley, as already stated in our account of Coway Stakes, believed to have been formed by Cæsar after he had crossed the Thames, and during his progress towards Hertfordshire. This camp, of which a view is given in the " Itinerarium Curiosum," is considered to have measured about 300 feet square, and to have been defended by a single ditch. The hamlet of Sipson—or Shepiston, as it was sometimes called —is situated in this neighbourhood.

Longford is a hamlet in this parish, on the road to Slough. It takes its name from its situation on a branch of the River Colne, which supplies Hampton Court with water, and which is crossed by a bridge, erected in 1834, called the Queen's Bridge. The district hereabout lies low, and is subject to inundation from the overflowing of the stream above mentioned.

Colnbrook, which lies about two miles west of Longford, is the utmost limit of our perambulation in this direction, being just on the borders of the jurisdiction of the Metropolitan Police. The town is located on four channels of the River Colne, over each of which there is a bridge. The greater part of the town, Colnbrook proper, is in Buckinghamshire; but the eastern part, forming part of the parish of Stanwell, is in the county of Middlesex. The town contains many old houses and hostelries, in one of which Queen Elizabeth is said to have been in the habit of resting for the night on her way to Windsor Castle. It is a long straggling town, and stands in two counties and in four parishes, and, like Uxbridge and Maidenhead, it has only lately been made parochial.

THE GATEHOUSE, WEST DRAYTON. (*See page* 207.)

CHAPTER XIX.

WEST DRAYTON AND HAYES.

Satis beatus ruris honoribus.' —*Paraphrased from Horace by Lord Bolingbroke.*

Situation and Boundaries of West Drayton—Its Vegetable Products, Fishing, &c.—Its Etymology—Descent of the Manor—The Old Manorhouse—Burroughs, formerly the Seat of General Arabin—The Parish Church—The Burial-ground—The Village of West Drayton—Population—The Catholic Church of St. Catharine—Thorney Broad—The Race-course—Yiewsley—Hayes—The Grand Junction Canal—Census Returns—Boundaries of the Parish—Its Nomenclature—Condition of the Parish in Tudor Times—Acreage of the Parish—Descent of the Manor—The Village of Hayes—Yeading Manor—Botwell—Cotman's Town—Wood End Green—The Parish Church—The Rectory - Distinguished Rectors—Schools and Charities—Extracts from the Parish Registers.

TAKING a fresh start north from Harmondsworth, a journey of a couple of miles brings us to Drayton—or, as it is commonly called, West Drayton, probably to distinguish it from Drayton Green, close by Castle Hill, Ealing, some four miles eastward. Drayton is a large, irregular village, on the western border of Middlesex. The parish is separated on its western side from Buckinghamshire by the river Colne, which meanders peacefully along through meadows and corn-fields, and having here and there upon its banks a mill or a farmyard, which imparts a certain amount of life

and animation to a landscape which might otherwise, perhaps, be considered dull and monotonous.
It is bounded in other directions by the parishes of
Hillingdon, Harlington, and Harmondsworth. A
considerable quantity of fruit is grown in this
neighbourhood, which in due course mostly finds
its way into the London markets. The Grand
Junction Canal passes by the village, a little to the
north of the railway station. The name points to
its sylvan and rural origin. It is the town or
village of "dreys," as the squirrels' nests are still
termed in the rural districts of Hampshire and
Berkshire.

Beyond describing the descent of the manor,
there is almost nothing historical to record in
connection with the parish of Drayton. Out of the
way of turmoil and strife, the place has apparently
enjoyed from the earliest period of its existence
one of peaceful retirement and seclusion. We find
in the "Domesday Book" the name of the parish
written *Draitone*, and it is there stated that it belonged to the canons of St. Paul's, to whom it had
been given by King Athelstan. It is also recorded
in the above-mentioned survey that "it answered
for ten hides, that there was a mill rented at thirteen shillings and fivepence, pasture for the cattle
of the village, and a stream rented at thirty-two
pence." According to Bawdwen's "Translation of
Domesday for Middlesex," "its whole annual value
is said to be six pounds; the same when received;
in King Edward's time eight pounds." In a survey,
bearing date 1181, it is stated that "the manor of
Drayton was taxed in the time of Henry I. and
William the Dean at ten hides, as it still is. It
paid then 5 shillings to the sheriff, but since the
war, 10 shillings, besides which, it pays 11 shillings
for the right of frank-pledge."

The manor of Drayton remained in the possession of the Dean and Chapter of St. Paul's until
about the middle of the sixteenth century, when
Henry VIII. obtained it in exchange for other
lands, and shortly afterwards granted it to Sir
William Paget, who, during the latter years of
Henry's reign, had been actively and confidentially
employed, often as a diplomatist upon secret and
important missions, and who at one time filled the
office of Secretary of State. Besides the manor of
Drayton, Sir William Paget received a legacy of
£300 from the king, who constituted him one of
his executors, and of the council to Edward VI.
Sir William Paget subsequently formed a close
alliance with the Protector Somerset, and was thus
retained to do good service for the State. In 1552
he was summoned to Parliament as Baron Paget
of Beaudesert, in the county of Stafford; but

having taken a prominent part in the Government
of the Protector, and shared in the downfall of his
patron, he was committed to the Tower, fined
£6,000 by the Star Chamber, and divested of the
insignia of the Garter. Within a short time, however, he obtained his liberty, with a general pardon
for all offences, and a remission of the debt due to
the Crown. On the death of Edward, he espoused
the cause of Mary, and after her accession to the
throne was sworn a member of the Privy Council.
He had also a restoration of the Garter, and obtained several important grants from her Majesty.
On the accession of Elizabeth, in 1558, Lord Paget
retired from public life, at his own request; and
Camden informs us that her Majesty "retained an
affection and value for him, though he was a strict
zealot of the Romish Church."

On the attainder of Thomas, third Lord Paget,
in 1587, on suspicion of favouring Mary, Queen of
Scots, his property was confiscated to the Crown,
the manor of Drayton being afterwards granted to
Sir Christopher Hatton for life. It was subsequently leased to George Carey, afterwards Lord
Hunsdon; but after the death of Lord Paget the
reversion was granted (in 1597) to William, the
son of that nobleman, who was restored by Act of
Parliament, at the commencement of the reign of
James I., to his rank and honours, and to a grant
also of the remainder of his father's estate. From
William, Lord Paget, the manor of Drayton
descended to the grandson of Henry, seventh
lord—Henry, Earl of Uxbridge—who had been
advanced to that earldom in 1714. On the death
of the earl without issue, in 1769, this manor
devolved, in conjunction with the barony of Paget,
to Henry Bailey, Esq., his heir-at-law, who assumed
the name of Paget, and was created Earl of
Uxbridge in 1784. The second earl is better
known to history as Field-Marshal the Marquis of
Anglesey, one of the Duke of Wellington's com-
panions-in-arms in the Peninsula and at Waterloo.
Lord Uxbridge sold this manor in 1786 to Mr.
Fyshe De Burgh, and it has since continued in the
possession of his descendants.

The Manor House, which was erected by the
Paget family, has long since been demolished,
having been pulled down by the Earl of Uxbridge
about the middle of the last century. It was a
spacious red brick mansion, standing to the south
of the church, and was approached by stately
avenues of trees. Its gardens surrounded the
churchyard. Some of the walls which enclosed
the gardens are still standing, together with a
large part of the out-offices and stables, the upper
chambers of which were formerly occupied by

the servants and retainers, and the principal entrance to the courtyard. This gate-house is of red brick, not unlike some of the details of Hampton Court, and commands a view down the street to the entrance of the Hall. Though low, it is massive, and a fine specimen of the Tudor style. It consists of a Pointed arch, flanked on either side by large octangular turrets; it is in very good preservation, and still inhabited as a separate dwelling-house. The original oak doors remain. The site of the old mansion is now occupied, with some attached ground, by a market gardener. The manor-house and the church here stood close together, in accordance with the old Christian theory of the sacred edifice being built originally as the chapel or oratory for the dwellers in "the great house" and their dependents. The present residence of the De Burghs, lords of the manor, called Drayton Hall, is a commodious dwelling, at a short distance from the church, and was formerly the property of Lord Boston.

An old and spacious mansion in this village was formerly the residence of General Arabin, and was sometimes called Burroughs, or Buroughs, from the circumstance of a house on this spot having in bygone times belonged to Sir Thomas Burgh, who was esquire of the body to King Edward IV. "This," observes the author of the "Beauties of England and Wales," "is the site of a small manor belonging to the Bishop of London, which was granted in the year 1462 to the above-mentioned Thomas Burgh, by whom it was aliened in 1476. This manor was given by King Edward VI. to the Bishop of Westminster; and on being surrendered again to the Crown in 1550, was granted to the see of London. This small manorial district is now united with the manor of Colham Garden, in the parish of Hillingdon, which is also the property of the Bishop of London." The mansion was bought, on a sale of the property in lots, by Robert, sixth Earl Ferrers, of whose family it was purchased by the above-mentioned General Arabin. The writer of the notice in the "Beauties of England" concludes as follows:—"This is a residence of the dull, secluded character, favourable to traditional story. Many a marvellous tale is accordingly told respecting its hall, its chambers, and the pensive shaded walks of the grounds. Among these stories, it may be mentioned as the most remarkable that not a few rustic neighbours believe the mansion of Burroughs to have been an occasional residence of Oliver Cromwell, and that the body of the Protector was privately conveyed to this place when threatened with disgraceful exposure, and was re-buried beneath the paving of the hall."

The parish church of Drayton, which lies at the east end of the village, bears a "strong family likeness" to those of the neighbouring parishes of Harlington and Harmondsworth, being a handsome Gothic structure of the Perpendicular style. It is built of stone and flint. It is dedicated to St. Martin, and comprises a chancel, a clerestoried nave, side aisle, with an open porch, formed of wood, projecting a considerable distance from the south wall, and a massive western tower profusely overgrown with ivy, and surmounted by a small wooden turret. Some of the windows are filled with stained glass, and the church is in good repair, having been thoroughly restored in 1850, at which time the old-fashioned pews were superseded by open benches. The font is octangular and very curious, being elaborately ornamented. In the upper part, which is divided into panels, are represented the "Crucifixion of Our Lord," a sculptor at work on some foliage, and "Our Lady of Pity;" the remaining panels being filled with angels holding shields. The chancel contains several monuments, chiefly to the families of the De Burghs and Pagets. The helmets and banners which adorned them are gone. In the floor are brasses to the memory of Richard Roos, citizen of London (1406); Robert Machell, gentleman, a retainer to the Lord Paget (1557); and John Goode, an eminent physician (1581).

Besides the churchyard, there is here another burial-ground, at some distance from the church, and not far from the present hall. This singular arrangement was brought about by the wish of Sir William Paget, who, in the year 1550, procured an Act of Parliament enabling him to give an acre of ground, forming the present parochial cemetery, in exchange for the ancient place of burial, which he enclosed within his garden wall. This ground is now laid out as a flower-garden.

The village of West Drayton is about fourteen miles from London, and there is a station about half a mile to the north, on the Great Western Railway.

West Drayton proper has a population of a little over a thousand. This is a slight increase over the number recorded in the census of 1871, when there were 984 souls, the inhabited houses at that time being given as 192. In the centre of the village, and facing a broad open green, is the Roman Catholic Church of St. Catharine, the first stone of which was laid by Archbishop (now Cardinal) Manning in 1868. In the district of West Drayton there is a large straggling population of Roman Catholics of very humble means, and previous to the establishment of the mission their religious welfare was much neglected, those who had the in-clination to attend Divine service having to travel a distance of six miles to the church at North Hyde. Services were first introduced in a barn at West Drayton, and it was in that humble sanctuary that the Archbishop first administered the rite of confirmation to the hitherto poor, neglected children.

Thorney Broad, about three-quarters of a mile south of the railway station, is a favourite spot for trout-fishing. Indeed, the disciples of Izaak Walton find much to occupy their attention during the fishing season, in the rivers and streams here-abouts. Trout have been turned into the Colne, but not yet with great success. A race-course was established at West Drayton about the year 1865, in a large river-side meadow, on the south of the railway. The periodical gatherings which take place there were a great nuisance to the neigh-bourhod, the sports being among the most fre-quented of those suburban races which are patro-nised by the lowest classes of sporting " roughs."

Near the station is a small cluster of houses, with the " Railway Inn." This spot is known as Yiewsley—the lee or meadow adorned with yews, which form so marked a feature in the villages of West Middlesex; but it is a hamlet actually belonging to the parish of Hillingdon. St. Matthew's Church, in this district, was built from the designs of Sir Gilbert Scott in 1869.

The first stone of the new schools at Yiewsley was laid by Bishop Claughton in August, 1871. The schools will hold about 300 children.

From the hamlet of Yiewsley we turn our steps once more eastward, following, for the most part, the courses of the Grand Junction Canal and the Great Western Railway, and leaving Cowley, Ux-bridge, and Hillingdon, away on our left, to be dealt with on our return journey.

After our long perambulations through the flat and level districts which are called the Valley of the Thames, but which scarcely form a valley—for the lack of hills, at all events on the Middlesex side—it is pleasant to find ourselves once more on a slight " upland," at the ancient village of Hayes, crowned with its historic church. It stands about a mile to the north of the Great Western Railway, which has a small station near the meeting of the parishes of Hayes and Harlington, and named after the former. The district all round the railway station in every direction is covered with brick-fields, which sadly mar its appearance; but these are rather decreasing in number, the supply of clay being not inexhaustible. The Grand Junction Canal—which conveys goods, and once conveyed

passengers also, below Uxbridge and London —runs here almost parallel with the railway; and the cottages are all inhabited by an indus-trial population, who find their occupation in either brick-making or barge-driving. In 1871 the num-ber of inhabited houses in the parish amounted to 524, with a population of 2,654 souls. This latter number was gradually increased during the ten following years, for, according to the census returns for 1882, Hayes numbered a population of 2,891.

The village of Hayes is very extensive, and, unlike its neighbours, it has a history. It is bounded on the south by Heston, Harlington, and Cranford, and on the west by Hillingdon; and northwards it extends to Northolt and Ickenham, while eastwards it originally stretched as far as Hanwell, for Southall and Norwood were once portions of it. The fact is that Hayes was, in Anglo-Saxon times, a country residence of the Archbishop of Canterbury, who held the manor and the rectory of Hayes. Consequently, though most of the paro-chial duties were discharged by a vicar, who held the " cure of souls," the rector of Hayes was always a great Church dignitary, whose ecclesiastical rank invested the place with an honour and a sanctity peculiar to itself.

It is very remarkable that whilst in some counties nearly every name mentioned in " Dooms-day Book " has disappeared, in Middlesex the names of well-nigh every parish and hundred remain almost unchanged, after the lapse of eight cen-turies. Thus, in that ancient record this place figures as *Hesa*—probably then pronounced as Haisa—in the Hundred of Osulvestane, or Ossul-ston.* After a description of the king's land, the book tells us that " Archbishop Lanfranc holds Hesa for forty-nine hides; there is land for forty ploughs. To the demesne pertain twelve hides; and there are two ploughs there. Among the free-men and the villanes there are twenty-six ploughs, and there could be twelve more."

Lysons tells us that the name is probably derived from the Saxon word " Haeg," a hedge (in French " Haye "), which comes very near to its present appellation. From Hesa it became Hease, Heyse, Hays, Heesse, Hesse, and Hese, at different times.

The old road from London to Oxford passes though the whole length of the parish, nearly bisecting it. In the days of the Tudors the western part of the parish was an open heath, adjoining that of Hillingdon; and it would seem,

---

* It is now in the Hundred of Elthorne.

from the map of John Norden (about 1625), that the road ran in a somewhat different direction, turning to the north, along what is now called Mellow Lane, the fine old trees of which point backwards to the distant past, and look like the features of an ancient highway; and this is confirmed by local tradition. The course of the road was doubtless altered as enclosures were gradually made.

The manor and parish of Hayes apparently have differed greatly in extent at different times. In the Saxon era it is said to have comprised thirty-two hides, or about 3,840 acres. In "Doomsday," the hides in the hands of Lanfranc are given as fifty-nine, which would give about 7,080 acres, if we reckon 120 acres to the hide. According to the Ordnance Survey of the year 1865, the exact acreage is 5,772, of which nearly 1,520 acres are arable, nearly 1,250 pasture-land, while 300 are occupied as brick-fields, woods, osier-beds, orchards, &c., &c. (This includes the "precinct" of Norwood.) "Little care, however," writes Mr. Mills, in an unpublished "History of Hayes," "has been taken of the boundaries of the parish. The custom of 'beating the bounds' has not been performed for a great number of years, and few boundary stones or other marks exist, and such as are in existence have been mostly defaced." The fact is, that a divided rule never answers. The rector left the vicar, and the vicar left the rector, to see to this duty on "Rogation Days," and between the two, that useful ceremony was neglected.

The earliest mention of Hayes is in A.D. 830, when a priest—Warherdus, or Walherdus—bequeathed the manor of Hayes, which he styles his own patrimony, to the church of Canterbury. And if it be true that manors were so called from *manere*, it is probable that he lived here, and exercised the "cure of souls" as well as the rights of a "squire" over his tenants. The next owner of the manor who is mentioned by name is Stigand, the last Saxon archbishop, who crowned King Harold. Lanfranc we have already mentioned. He died in 1089, and was succeeded, after a four years' interval, by the saintly Anselm, who was not only the owner of the manor, but occasionally resident here, as well as at Harrow and Mortlake. One Whitsuntide, we are told, the king summoned Anselm to his neighbourhood at Windsor. On this occasion he stayed at Hayes, where he was visited by nearly all his suffragan bishops, who in vain persuaded him to make up his quarrel with William. In the long run the worthy ecclesiastics prevailed, and here or at Windsor the king handed to him the pall which had been sent from Rome by Pope Urban, as the sign of his metropolitan jurisdiction. It is pleasant to think that so sweet and pious a character as Anselm must have walked along the roads and trod the fields about Hayes. As a writer, a philosopher, and a leader of men, he was one of the foremost characters of his own age, and is regarded by all parties as one of the brightest ornaments of the English Church.

The early history and patronage of this church and of the manor are coincident down to the reign of Henry VIII. Hayes was a "Peculiar" of Canterbury—that is, although situate in Middlesex, which is in the diocese of London, it was directly under the spiritual control of the Archbishop of Canterbury—like Harrow-on-the-Hill. This arrangement lasted into the present century; but through the abolition of all such "peculiar" jurisdictions by Act of Parliament, it is now subject to the see of London, and the present rector attends the visitations of the Bishop of London and the Archdeacon of Middlesex.

To mention the several owners of this manor and rectory from Anselm to the Reformation would be to give a list of the Archbishops of Canterbury. But amongst them should be mentioned the names of Thomas à Becket, Langton, Islip, Langham, Simon de Sudbury, Fitz-Alan, Morton, and Warham, all of whom must have been occasional visitors at least at the Rectory House, which still has something quite palatial about it.

Archbishop Cranmer is said to have presented in 1543 the manor, with the advowsons of both the rectory and the vicarage, to Henry VIII., in exchange for other preferments. Five years later we find the king bestowing them on Sir Edward North, afterwards Lord North, one of the greatest possessors of Church lands. In the year 1613 Lord North sold both the manor and the advowsons, which have passed into the hands of several private families in succession—as Millet, Franklyn, Jenyns, Cooke, Ayscough, Blencowe, and Villiers, many of whom lie buried in the church. The manor now belongs to Sir Charles Mills, of Hillingdon; and the rector's family hold the consolidated advowson of both rectory and vicarage.

There were formerly several handsome mansions in this parish, and a few still remain, but none are worthy of individual description, or to which literary and other recollections are attached. The aspect of the village, in spite of brick-fields, railways, and canals, is still rural and peaceful. Mr. Mills writes, in his "History of Hayes":—"In a perambulation of the village for the purpose of discovering and describing antiquities, I was charmed to find within twelve miles of the bustle, din, and smoke of London the real country, with its wide, rich pastures and waving corn, its trees, hedgerows, wild flowers, and gardens; and, to complete the picture, I should have been happy to have added, interspersed with timber-built houses with overhanging storeys, gables, and dormers; but truth compels me to admit that such is no longer the case. Here and there may still be seen the thatched one-storey cottage, with low bulged walls and other details, which would delight the painter and the poet. Some chimney-stacks at Yeading,

family, and now by Mr. Thomas Salt, of Weeping Cross, Staffordshire. "Yealding" is really Saxon for "Eald," or old, and "ing," a meadow; the property belonged five centuries ago to the Bishops of Lichfield and Coventry, who had a charter of free-warren within its limits. A little more than a century ago the Court Rolls of the manor mention that John Turner, a copyholder, was permitted to plant a grove of elm-trees across "the waste of Yealding Green;" the trees that Mr. Turner planted can still be identified, but the "waste"

WEST DRAYTON.

FONT IN WEST DRAYTON CHURCH.

built with thin kiln - burnt bricks, and affording the large chimney-corners of a former age, a gable next the churchyard, and some cottages near Botwell Cross, are all the objects that can claim the attention of the antiquary, and these only in a very moderate degree."

Within the parish there would appear to have been several manors: not only those of Norwood and Southall, now erected into separate and distinct parochial districts, but also those of Yealding, or Yeading, Botwell, and Hayes-with-Park-Hall. The last two, however, have long disappeared as manors proper, though they exist as hamlets; Yeading remains: it was owned by the Petit

and the "green" they were to adorn are both gone. So true are Goldsmith's lines—

> "Trade's unfeeling train
> Usurp the land and dispossess the swain."

Lysons tells us, in his "History of Middlesex," that the principal hamlets in Hayes are Botwell, Yeading, Hayes End, and Wood End; to these he might have added Cotman's Town, all of which still retain their ancient names. Botwell and Yeading are distinct places, and form the centres of two localities devoted to brick-making. Cotman's Town is the cluster of houses to the east of the church, beyond which lies a district called Cold Harbour. Wood End Green lies between the west end of the church and Hillingdon.

The parish church is dedicated to St. Mary the Virgin, to whom Mr. Mills thinks that it was dedicated by Anselm himself. If so, however, nothing of that structure remains, except a stone in the north face of the tower, some ten feet square, and carved with triangles arranged in the form of crosses. The font is a fine specimen of the transitional

Norman style, of English marble, and has a solid base, supporting a central pillar, with detached shafts, carrying a massive bowl, which is externally sculptured with foliage. Doubtless, however, there remain at the west end of the church, where they fence off the lower part of the tower from the nave.

The axes of the nave and chancel have not the same orientation—as is the case at St. Mary's,

HAYES.

was a smaller and plainer church here in the old Saxon times, one which was probably constructed of wood, as at Staines and elsewhere.

The chancel, which is of the Early English style, was probably erected about the year 1220. The nave is mostly of the Decorated, or Edwardian period; and the north and south side aisles followed as necessity arose. At the east end of each aisle was a chantry chapel, with an altar, and a separate endowment for a chantry priest. These chapels were marked off by screens, parts of which still

Oxford, and other well-known instances. The chancel deflects considerably to the north-east. It is thought by some persons that in such cases the true east point had not been chosen by the builders of the earlier portion, whether nave or chancel, and that the builders of the latter portion intended to correct their blunder; while another theory has been maintained which attaches to it a symbolical meaning—namely, that it was intended to represent the Saviour on the cross, whose sacred head inclined at a slight angle to the right or the left. It is more probable that it was an ingenious device of the architect to give an appearance of greater length to the interior.

The walls of the church are mostly of flint and chalk, the latter probably imported from the Buckinghamshire or Hertfordshire hills; the facing, for the most part, is of rough-hammered flint. The walls are solid and substantial, and have worked into them several fragments of wrought stone, portions of an earlier structure. The external buttresses are simple; those at the angles of the chancel have niches for the statues of saints—probably the patron saints of the church. The windows are of various dates, ranging from 1220 down to 1600, examples of almost every style being shown—and their details are well worth study. The great east window is of Elizabethan date and workmanship, and has recently been filled with painted glass, commemorating an event in the life of a son of the present rector.

The north and south doorways are under Pointed arches, the latter having in front of it a handsome wooden porch. At the west end is a fine specimen of Perpendicular architecture, the door and window being under one main arch, a sill-window separating the door from the three-light window above. The tower is of three storeys, but looks bare and unadorned, being devoid of buttresses. It contains a peal of six bells.

The nave has a lofty pitch, and a plain waggon-headed roof, divided into compartments, and lit by some very late and ugly-shaped dormer windows. The carved crosses at the intersections of the panels are curious, and the seamless côat, the nails, the spear-head, and the wounded hands and feet, and the other emblems of the Passion, appear on nearly all of them. Mixed with them are fleur-de-lys and Tudor roses, marking the late period of its construction. Fine roofs of oak, and of a more artistic style, cover the chancel and side aisles. In the chancel are an ancient aumbry, a piscina in a very perfect state, and sedilia—all of elegant proportions. In the flooring are some good old encaustic tiles. The walls, previous to the recent restoration of the church, were covered with hatchments, and several flags, coats of armour, and helmets hung on them; but these were all decayed, and, as too often is the case, disappeared on that occasion. Over the communion-table there formerly hung a painting of the "Adoration of the Magi," given by the lord of the manor, Mr. Jenyns, in 1726; but it now stands on the ground near the vestry, at the east end of the south aisle. On the wall of the north aisle, near the door, is a roughly-executed life-sized fresco of St. Christopher, representing that saint as carrying on his shoulder the Divine Child as he strides through the water. Below can be seen the crab, the eel, the flat-fish, and a mermaid with her comb in her hand. Above is a figure fishing. Such an ornament is frequent on the walls of churches in Norfolk and Suffolk, but very rare in Middlesex.

The pulpit, of deal, was made to stride across the entrance to the chancel, with a desk on either side for the curate and parish clerk, thus blocking up the view of the east end altogethei Happily this monstrosity—the production of some tasteless churchwarden or lord of the manor—is a thing of the past, and a decent, and even handsome, pulpit has been set up elsewhere in its stead.

In the church is a parish muniment chest of curious structure, more than three centuries old; it is of oak, and the top is made out of one solid block of timber. It is bound with iron, and has very substantial bands, hinges, and locks. At the entrance of the churchyard is an old and picturesque lych gate, in a very fair state of preservation.

In the chancel is a fine monument to Sir E. Fenner, a judge of the King's Bench, who died in 1611; and there is another Jacobean monument, the inscription on which has been long stolen. Sir Edward Fenner's monument is of alabaster and choice marbles, and represents the worthy judge in a recumbent position. In the north aisle is a Purbeck marble slab, with brass, commemorating Walter Grene, who died in the fifteenth century, but the exact date is lost. At the east end of the south aisle is an altar-tomb to Thomas Higate, part of the brass on which has disappeared. Here, cut in brass, in the attitude of prayer, may be seen the worthy squire and his dame, with their nine children, with inscriptions in Latin and English verse—neither very good. Of the remaining monuments little need be said, except that they seem to imply that the dead are uniformly virtuous, and to suggest, therefore, that we must look among the living for the vicious and wicked. The inscription over one of the rectors of the parish, the Rev. Mr. Samuel Spence, 1730, should not be omitted here, as suggestive of the happy *via media* between Romanism and Dissent, of which we have heard so much:—

" Just underneath there lays (lies) a priest interred,
  Not led by error into faction's herd ;
  No Sectaries encouraging at home :
  Proof against those as well as those of Rome."

Under the east window of the chancel, on the outside, is a monument to William Walker, lecturer on astronomy, 1816, inventor of the Eidouranion, &c. Four persons are recorded in the churchyard as having died upwards of ninety years old, and the parish has produced at least one centenarian.

The registers do not commence till the first year of Elizabeth. In them are some quaint manuscript notes and apothegms from Cicero, &c. They note the usual number of "burials in woollen"—burials of foreign women; and in 1748-9 they record the fact that both John and Charles Wesley preached in the church. The registers from 1762-68 have been stolen.

No doubt the rectory, a little to the east of the church, stands on the site of the archbishop's former country-house, and possibly on the manse of the priest Warherdus. The rectory is perhaps the largest and best in the entire county, and probably there are few better rectory-houses in England. It is large, lofty, solid, and substantial, built very largely of solid oak; and its possession has always been sold along with the advowson. Two rooms in the house are still pointed out as having been occupied by Cranmer: one on the ground floor formed part of the great dining-hall, but is now divided into two storeys; the other, on the first floor, at the back of the house, now cut up into bed-rooms, is traditionally said to have been his library. In the former is a lofty carved oak chimney-piece, thought by some to be as old as the Reformation, and the panelling of the walls is probably coeval with it. On the ground floor there is a set of wainscot oaken architraves, finely moulded. The remainder of the house was largely altered and modernised in 1862.

The rectory garden is extensive, and its paths must have been often trodden by the archbishops of the Norman and Plantagenet eras. In one part there are a few traces of an ancient moat, in which, as the local tradition runs, was once found a flagon, which was deposited in the British Museum. No record, however, of such an article is to be found, either at Hayes or at Bloomsbury. Beyond the garden to the east is a fine avenue of shapely lime-trees. Here, again, local radition connects the trees with Eugene Aram, who is said to have frequently walked beneath their shade: but there is not a shadow of proof for the story. Equally shadowy is another tradition that Queen Elizabeth once attended service in the parish church, whilst staying at "Pinkwell." No such place is known to exist or to have existed near Hayes, and there is no record of the queen's visit in the books of the parish.

The rectory is a valuable one, and was once even more so than it is now. In 1793 it is given as worth £1,038 a year, with a small deduction for the payment of the "curates" of Norwood and Southall. It is now stated officially as worth £700 a year and a house.

Two or three of the rectors and vicars of Hayes have some interest attaching to their names. Henry Gold, who became vicar in 1520, was implicated in the doings of Elizabeth Barton, "the Holy Maid of Kent." The maid was a servant at Allington, in Kent, where, having been subject to hysterical fits, her mind became disordered, and she pretended that she saw visions which God had revealed to her from heaven, to the effect that in case the king should divorce his lawful wife, Catharine of Arragon, and take another spouse, his royalty would not last a month. The "Maid" and her accomplices, or dupes, were examined by the Star Chamber, conveyed to the Tower of London, convicted of high treason, attainted, and executed at Tyburn, April 20, 1534. On this occasion Gold was one of the number. The "Maid" at the last confessed her imposture. Amongst her lying wonders, one has been thus set forth by a writer of the period :—

> "That candles were alighted without fire:
> 　The candle ment is even hir tender hart,
> 　Which Edward Bocking set on flaming fire,
> 　For he must play the ghostly father's part,
> And shrift was such as they did both desire.
> The place was apt, they toke their times by night ;
> I think I have resolved this riddle right."

In the beginning of the seventeenth century the rectory was held by the Rev. Robert Wright, who was nominated first Warden of Wadham College, Oxford, but resigned that post because the foundress, Dorothy Wadham, would not suffer her Warden to marry. He afterwards became Bishop of Lichfield and Coventry, and was one of the twelve bishops accused of high treason, and committed to the Tower in 1642, "for preferring a petition, and making a protestation to the subverting of the fundamental laws of Parliament." He escaped, however, from the scaffold.

Another rector, Patrick Young, ejected in 1640, is worthy of note, as being a man who, "though he sided with the Presbyterians, could not be loved by them, as he had too much learning to comply with their eclesiastical mould, and too much honesty to digest their politicks." He was stripped of his preferments by either the Presbyterians or Independents—it is not certain by which—and retired to Broomfield, in Essex, where he died in retirement and melancholy.

The parish is educationally better off than most. There are national schools at Wood End Green, which were opened in 1836. In 1860-3 were built some larger schools, out of the benefaction of a Dr. Triplett, who left a large sum for that purpose at his death, in 1670, for the benefit of Hayes, Petersham, and Richmond. The learned doctor was a Prebendary of Westminster and York, and he lies in Poets' Corner. The poor parishioners of Hayes also benefit by Lady Dacre's charity of Emmanuel Hospital at Westminster. Among the other benefactors to the parish is Robert Cromwell, whose family are mentioned in the registers in 1596-8, and who gave some lands, the proceeds of which were to be laid down in "six gowns of strong blue cloth for as many poor widows, or other women, of Hayes." These benefactions are all administered by a board of trustees of the amalgamated charities.

The Tithes Commutation Act, passed in 1836, put an end to the annual payment of tithes throughout the kingdom; but this measure was anticipated, so far as Hayes was concerned, in 1809, when the Act was obtained for enclosing the common and extinguishing the tithes.

We will conclude this chapter with the following remarks of Mr. Mills on the Hayes Registers :— "Here we may read of the baptisms of children bearing their fathers', and of children bearing only their mothers' names, and many of children marked as bastards and baseborn ; of marriages completed, and of one begun, and not completed ; of burials of rich and poor, lords of the manor, esquires, knights, ladies, coachmen, &c., and of that of Elias Dupree, said to have been hunted to death in the parish, and to whose memory a slab is said to be affixed in Gloucester Cathedral; and of many 'strange women.' Also many singular entries arising out of and illustrating the laws relating to burial in woollen : how John Hart, a farmer, to escape a certain part of the due on a baptism (20s.), declares that he is not worth £50 per annum in real estate, or £600 personal ; then of Roger Jenyns, 'Esquire,' in haste, possibly finding himself excluded from or not sufficiently appreciated in John Jenyns' will, hurries off to James Clitherow, the magistrate, gives sworn information that John Jenyns had

been that day buried in a coffin fitted with velvet —in which case there would be a fine, and Roger, as the informant, would be entitled to one-half. Again, Rachel Lee (honest London woman) desires to be buried in linen ; she pays the £50 fine, and has her desire. Again, we read of taxes and fines, or penalties, on births, deaths, and marriages ; there are payments under the two first heads, but I find no mention of single men or of widowers remaining unmarried, and paying the fines or penalties. We read of 'Plague Years,' of a time when the year ended in March instead of in December, and of numerous instances of longevity. We find these registers signed by vicars, and sometimes—when they could write—by churchwardens, and when they could not, then marked by them with a cross. We read of two of the Wesleys preaching here. We read of an early attempt at a popular week-day service, which met with great success at its introduction.

"As to education, we may gather from the marriage register that, whereas in 1763, out of every 100 persons married only 37 could write their names, in 1872 the percentage of those who could do so had risen to 69. Finally, we may read in these registers that peace has not always been the rule. The clergy have turned their backs on each other in the church ; some parishioners have smoked their pipes, drank their beer, made noises, and rung the church bells during service, while others have not refrained from cock-fighting and digging graves in the churchyard, in defiance of authority.

"There is much, then, in these old registers that we must regret to lose. These books allowed the man of taste and education to make his remarks, and to enter them in the language that he liked best. Did he wish to quote Cicero, or to protect a book by a malediction, to state where he dined on Sunday, to express his opinion on taxes and other matters, he did so freely in these registers. But now that the hard and fast forms prevail, printed in columns, with certain ink to be used, and certain exact particulars only to be stated, no room is left for taste ; and while science and statistics may be advanced, the individuality of man and the interest of the ancient record must alike disappear."

CHAPTER XX.

NORWOOD, SOUTHALL, ETC.

"Pagos et compita circum."—VIRG. *Georg.*, ii. 328.

The "Precinct" of Norwood—Situation and Boundaries of the Parish—Census Returns—Early History of the Manor—The Village—The Parish Church—Schools, &c.—Southall—The Church and Vicarage—The Manor House—The Grand Junction Canal and the Paddington Canal—The Metropolitan Workhouse School—Dorman's Well—Southall Park—Southall Market—Northolt, or Northall—General Description of the Locality—The Parish Church—Greenford—Its Etymology—The Soil, and Census Returns—The Parish Church—The Rectory and Advowson—Distinguished Rectors—Chemical Works at Greenford Green—Horsington Hill and Wood—Perivale—Extent and Population—Descent of the Manor—The Parish Church—West Twyford—Descent of the Manor—Twyford Abbey—The Chapel—Willesden Junction Station—Boundaries and Extent of the Parish of Willesden—Railway Communication—The River Brent—Sub-division of the Manor of Willesden—The Parish Church—Church End—Willesden Green—The "White Hart" and "Spotted Dog" Taverns—Brondesbury—The Jewish Cemetery—Warwick Dairy Farm—Harlesden—Cricklewood—Neasdon—The Metropolitan Railway Carriage Depôt—Sherrick Green and Dollis Hill—Stonebridge Park.

THE village of Norwood is officially and legally described as a "precinct" in the civil parish of Hayes. The "precinct" is a term which savours of a cathedral city, and no doubt it was given to this hamlet on account of the connection of Hayes with the see of Canterbury in ancient times.

Norwood—the "north wood"—doubtless was so called with reference to the Thames and its "riparian" dwellers, just as Norwood, in Surrey, derived its name from its relative situation to the great town of Croydon. The village lies on the edge of Osterley Park, between Heston and Southall, and the country around, although somewhat level, is nevertheless well-wooded and pleasant. The Grand Junction Canal skirts the village on its northern side. Like the district which we have just left, much of the land hereabouts is well adapted for brick-making, a branch of industry which is still largely carried on here, though somewhat on the decline; whilst in the immediate outskirts of the village are market gardens and orchards, with an occasional farm. Many of the inhabitants are engaged as bargemen on the canal.

No literary interest attaches to the parish, which is very small, and shows but little signs of increasing in population, lying in a retired spot, far away from a railway station. In 1871 the population of the entire "precinct," which includes the inmates of Hanwell Lunatic Asylum, and also those of Marylebone Workhouse Schools on Southall Green, was given in the census returns as 5,882, and in 1881 the number was returned as 6,688.

The first mention of Norwood as a manor occurs in the will of Warherdus, A.D. 830, who left it to the church of Canterbury. It then contained 120 acres. No mention of it is made in "Domesday," when it probably was joined to that of Hayes. At the time of the Reformation it belonged to the Cheesemans, who held it under the archbishop, to whom a knight's fee (£5) was payable at every death or alienation. It afterwards was in the hands of Fynes, Lord Dacre, and his widow, the worthy founder of sundry almshouses in Westminster,[*] on whose death, in 1595, the manor was sold. It was afterwards in the hands of the Childs, of Osterley Park, and later on it belonged to the Earls of Jersey, from whom it passed to Sir Charles Mills, Bart. The Earl of Jersey is, however, the chief landowner.

Norwood consists of several handsome and substantial houses, surrounding a triangular village-green of some twenty acres, adorned with fine elms. The cedars, yews, and evergreens in the various gentlemen's gardens help to give the village a leafy and well-wooded appearance, even in the winter.

At the north corner of the green, nearly opposite to the vicarage, stands the church, which modern restoration, by the importation of colour both inside and outside, has rather succeeded in disguising, so that it looks like a new erection of the Cambridge Camden, or the Oxford Architectural Society. It is small, with a dwarf wooden tower and spire, and a fine wooded porch on the south side. One of the arches dividing the nave from the north aisle is Norman.

The restoration of the church was carried out in 1864, down to which period there were several helmets and coats of armour hanging upon the walls; but these have all disappeared, except one helmet, which is kept loose on a canopied altar-tomb on the north side of the chancel, within the altar rails; and even from this some stray visitor, with light fingers, but without a conscience, has managed to carry away part of the vizor.

Some of the windows contain fragments of old painted glass; but the east window is filled with modern coloured glass, which was inserted on the restoration of the church. In the chancel is a brass to the memory of Francis Awsiter, dated 1624, and in the nave one to Matthew Huntley, dated 1628. There are a few interest-

---

* See "Old and New London," Vol. IV., p. 23.

ing monuments and tablets, notably the altar-tomb mentioned above, which is to the memory of Edward Cheeseman, who was Cofferer to Henry VII., and who died in 1547. Another monument, consisting of a sarcophagus bearing upon it a life-sized semi-recumbent effigy of the deceased, commemorates John Merick, Esq., of Norcut, who died in 1749. The font, which is large, and designed for entire immersion, is of an octangular form, and ornamented with quatrefoils. A fine yew-tree stands in the churchyard, as in most of the Middlesex parishes.

forced into a separate district. In 1838 a small chapel was erected on a waste spot of land then called Southall Green; but it is of no interest whatever, and serves only as a specimen of the very worst and poorest attempts at modern Gothic art before its revival by the elder Pugin and Sir Gilbert Scott.

Opposite the church is a small and modest vicarage, with a good garden in the rear. Adjoining it is Elmfield Lodge, a handsome villa of the suburban type, with a magnificent cedar-tree on its lawn. Here was born Mrs. Challice, the

SOUTHALL MANOR HOUSE.

In the early part of the last century a small portion of land and some cottages were bequeathed by one Francis Courtney for the purpose of charitably educating poor children in the parish "till the world's end." In 1772 Elisha Biscoe bequeathed a large sum of money for the purpose of educating and clothing thirty boys and ten girls belonging to the parishes of Norwood, Heston, and Hayes. The school-house of Norwood was erected in 1767.

Southall is quite a new parish, having really been called into existence by the construction of the Great Western Railway. It is the centre of a very flat and dreary district. As Norwood was cut off from the mother church of Hayes, so has Southall in its turn been cut off from Norwood and

accomplished authoress of "Memories of French Palaces," "Distinguished Women of France," and of several novels, a lady whose premature death was deeply regretted.

Between the green and the railway-station stands a fine old manor house, of the Jacobean type, with plain mullioned windows. In its hall is a finely-carved oak mantel-piece, not unlike those which we have seen in the Charter House, London,* and at Duncroft House, Staines.† The entrance-hall is fine, and retains its Elizabethan windows and Jacobean fire-place, and many of the other rooms still remain in their original state. It was formerly

---

* See "Old and New London," Vol. II., p. 3c3.
† See page 191, *ante*.

the seat of a family named Awsiter, who left their mark on history, having been merchants, aldermen, or lawyers in the City of London.

The grounds in the rear are laid out in the trim fashion of the reign of William III., so prevalent

family of Shoredyke, and afterwards by those of Cheeseman, and of Fynes, Lord Dacre. It has since passed, along with that of Norwood, to the Childs and Villierses.

The Grand Junction Canal, which, as we have

INTERIOR OF PERIVALE CHURCH. (*See page* 221.)
(*From an Etching by W. L. Wilkins,* 1848.)

about this neighbourhood, the yews being carefully clipped and rounded off into artificial shapes.

Northall and Northolt are but variations of the same name, as we shall presently see; so it is probable that Southall is only another form of Southolt—the Southern Holt, or wood. The manor of Southall was held in the Plantagenet times under the Archbishop of Canterbury by the

already stated, separates the two villages of Norwood and Southall, receives the waters of the Paddington Canal at Bull Bridge, a short distance westward from the green, where there is commodious wharfage. Close by the railway-station stands the Metropolitan Workhouse School, a large building, which will hold between 500 and 600 children, who are here lodged, educated, and taught various branches of industry. Dorman's or Domer's Well, a farm-house about half a mile north-east of Southall Street, was formerly the seat of Lord Dacre whilst he held the lordship of the manor. Southall Park, a large red-brick mansion facing the Great Western Railway, formerly the seat of Sir William Ellis, stands in some pleasant grounds, and is now a private lunatic asylum.

The village of Southall doubtless once derived great benefits from its weekly market, the charter for which was granted in 1698 by William III. "A lease of this charter," we are told in the "Beauties of England," "was purchased by Mr. William Welch in the year 1805, at which time there were weekly markets of some consequence for the show of cattle at Beaconsfield, Hayes, Hounslow, and Knightsbridge. Mr. Welch, immediately on ac-quiring possession of his lease, constructed a market-place at Southall peculiarly well-adapted for showing cattle and accommodating the dealers. He has also, in other respects, acted with so much spirit and judgment that the neighbouring markets are now almost discontinued, while this at Southall is become inferior only to Smithfield in regard to the sale of fat cattle in Middlesex."

From Southall Station, a walk of about three miles brings us to Northolt, or, as it is sometimes written, Northall, which, as stated above, is simply another form of this word. The name of the village is generally spelt Northall in ancient documents; but Norden terms the place Northolt, and derives the latter syllable from the "German *holt*, signi-fying a wood." The mode of spelling used by Norden has been followed to this day.

The route thither, after crossing the great western road, lies along narrow lanes and cross-roads, and for the most part over what in summer-time would be green and smiling meadows, but which in winter, or during a prevalence of wet weather, are little better than a huge morass. The village of Northolt—the name of which in the "Domesday" Survey appears as *Northala*—is quiet and retiring, the few humble dwellings which it contains being mostly inhabited by farm labourers and brick-makers, the land in the neighbourhood being chiefly under grass, dotted over here and there with a busy homestead, its barns and hay-ricks affording an agreeable relief to the surround-ing trees. At the brick-fields hereabouts large quantities of bricks are made, and carried up to London by the barges on the Paddington Canal, which skirts the eastern side of the parish. The village green is intersected by the roadway running north-east to Sudbury and Harrow-on-the-Hill; and the church, dedicated to St. Mary, stands on the

summit of a small hillock, on the east side of the green. The architecture is a mixture of the Deco-rated and Perpendicular. It is built chiefly of flint and rubble, almost hidden by a thick coating of cement, and whitewashed over; it consists of a nave and narrow chancel, with a wooden belfry turret, surmounted by a short octagonal spire, which rises from the western end of the tiled roof. The windows of the chancel are filled with stained glass, that over the communion-table being a modern imitation of the Decorated period; the window at the south-east corner of the nave is also of painted glass, the work of Mr. George Harris, F.S.A., of Islip Manor, the "squire" of the parish, and was inserted in 1871. The font is octagonal, of the Perpendicular style, but the lid bears date 1624. A gravestone in the floor of the chancel, within the altar rails, commemorates Samuel Lisle, Bishop of St. Asaph, who died in 1749; there is also a similar memorial to Thomas Arundell, dated 1697; brasses to Henry Rowdell (1452), Susan, wife of John Gyfforde (1560), and to Isaiah Bures, vicar of this parish (1610). On the south wall of the chancel is a tablet to the memory of Lancelot Shadwell, Esq., who died in 1861, son of the Vice-Chancellor Sir Lancelot Shadwell, who was lord of the manor of Northolt, and with whose family it has still continued. In the church-yard is buried Dr. Stephen Demainbray, who died in 1782, having been some time Astronomer to the Royal Observatory at Richmond.

The extensive valley to the north-west of this parish was the scene of several skirmishes during both the Wars of the Roses and the Civil War in the time of Charles I.

From Northolt the road winds somewhat circuitously in a south-easterly direction to Green-ford, a small and retired village, situate on the road towards Sudbury and Harrow, and about nine miles from Hyde Park Corner. There is, in summer-time, a pleasant walk thither from the churchyard of Northolt, across the meadows, stretching away eastward, through which the Pad-dington Canal winds its course, and which are also watered by numerous streams and bournes. The village of Greenford consists of about twenty or thirty cottages and small shops, together with a commodious school-house, and other buildings.

In legal documents the name of this parish is usually written Greenford Magna, or Great Green-ford, to distinguish it from Greenford Parva, or Perivale, which lies about two miles eastward, on the road towards Twyford Abbey. Greenford pro-bably took its name from a ford over the River Brent, which meanders pleasantly through the meadows on the south-east. The parish is said by Northcourt, in his "Repertorium," to have been called in ancient documents *Grenefeld*, and also Gernford; in the confirmation of Edward I., and also in "Domesday Book," however, it is written *Greneforde*, so that the name may be said to have undergone but little or no alteration since the time of the Conquest.

The soil hereabouts is a fertile clay, and the parish is almost wholly agricultural. In 1871 the

this day. A modern brick-built mansion near the church is termed the manse house.

The parish church, dedicated to the Holy Cross, on the west side of the village street, is a small building, apparently of the fourteenth century, being of the Early Perpendicular style. The edifice is peculiar in having no constructional west end, the space being occupied by a timbered turret, carrying a low shingle spire, painted white. With the exception of this turret and spire, which are devoid of all

PERIVALE CHURCH, EXTERIOR. (*See p.* 221.)

number of houses in the entire parish was 116, with a population of 578, a number which had somewhat diminished in the next decennial period.

The manor of Greenford Magna was given to Westminster Abbey by King Etheldred. In the "Norman Survey" it is said that "the Abbot of St. Peter holds Greneforde for eleven hides and a half." There was "pannage for three hundred hogs, and pasture for the cattle of the village." Upon the dissolution of religious houses, this property was made part of the revenues of the short-lived Bishopric of Westminster; but was surrendered to the Crown in 1550 by Thomas Thirlby, the only bishop of that see. The manor, however, was in the same year granted to the Bishop of London and his successors, with whom it has continued to

dignity, the church consists of a nave and a narrow chancel, which are separated by a Pointed arch. The original chancel-arch, of rude Early English work, was re-constructed upon a larger scale in 1871, since which time the whole fabric has been restored in a most thorough manner, the work consisting of a new nave roof of open timber and a fresh seating of varnished pitch-pine; the floor of the chancel being raised, fresh windows opened, and the walls of the chancel, which were rough-cast, being re-faced with flint-work and stone dressings. The windows of the chancel contain many fragments of stained glass, chiefly dating from the middle of the fifteenth century, collected and re-arranged by the Rev. Edward Betham, a former rector. They include a number of examples of the arms of King's College, Cambridge, the patrons of the living, some heads of angels, foliage, and crowns, and some curious quarries, probably Flemish, representing windmills. There are also several brasses—notably, a half-length figure of a priest in eucharistic vestments, that of Richard Thornton, who died in 1544; close by is a second priest's brass, that of Thomas Symons, dated 1508; a third brass is an effigy of a lady wearing a butter-fly head-dress. At the south-east end of the nave is a mural monument to Bridget, wife of Simon Caston, dated 1637. The effigy of the deceased is kneeling before a desk, on which is an open book; before her kneel her five children, whilst in a niche in the upper compartment is the three-quarter effigy of a man in mourning attitude and garb. On the north wall of the chancel is a mural tablet, with two kneeling figures, commemorating Michael Gardner, a former rector of this parish, who died in 1630, and Margaret, his wife. There are also several inscriptions to the Castell family. The pedestal of the font bears the name of Francis Coston, and the date 1638.

The rectory and advowson of Greenford, in con-junction with the manor, were possessed at an early period by the Abbey of St. Peter, West-minster. John de Feckenham, the last abbot of Westminster, held the rectory of Greenford in the middle of the sixteenth century. On the subsequent grant of the manor to the see of London, the advowson became the property of Sir Thomas Wroth, of Durance. On the last alienation of the rectory and advowson, they were purchased, in 1725, by the Provost and Scholars of King's College, Cambridge.

Edward Terry, who was appointed to the rectory of Greenford in 1629, was a man of some note in his day. He had a few years previously accom-panied some merchants to the East Indies. On his arrival there, he was sent for by Sir Thomas Roe, then ambassador to the Great Mogul, with whom he resided as chaplain for more than two years at the court of that emperor. He is said by Anthony Wood to have been "an ingenious and polite man, of a pious and exemplary conversation, and much respected in the neighbourhood where he lived." During his residence at Greenford—the benefice of which parish he enjoyed for more than thirty years—he published several works, among which was "A Character of King Charles II.," printed in 1660. He died in that same year, and was buried in the chancel of his church.

The Rev. Edward Betham, whose name is mentioned above, and who was rector towards the close of the last century, built at his own cost a school-house, and provided an endowment for the salary of a master and mistress, and for gifts to the poor of the parish.

The hamlet of Greenford Green, which lies away about a mile to the north of the village, is chiefly noticeable for the chemical works of Messrs. Perkin and Sons, which give employment to a large number of hands. The building covers a large space of ground, and its tall chimney-shafts are a landmark all around.

Between this place and Harrow are Horsington Hill and Wood, which command a fine view across the meadows to Harrow and Pinner, the church-spire of Harrow crowning the hill, and forming a pleasing object in the landscape.

Perivale, formerly known as Greenford Parva, lies about two miles eastward from Greenford Magna, and about the same distance to the north of Ealing Station, on the Great Western Railway. It has borne its present name, which Lysons regards as a corruption of Parva, only since the sixteenth century. Norden supposes that the term Perivale has reference to the salubrity of the vale in which the village is situated, and calls it "Pery-vale, more truly Purevale." The village is located in the valley of the Brent; and what with its old-fashioned look and its extreme seclusion—which is almost as perfect as if it were a hundred miles from London—it is not to be wondered that its growth is very slow; indeed, but little progress appears to have been made during the last century, for in 1816 Mr. Brewer described it, in the "Beauties of England," as containing five dwellings only, whilst according to the census returns for 1881 the number of inhabited houses is seven, whilst the population is set down as 34 souls. The Rev. C. J. Hughes, the rector of Perivale, in a letter to the Times (1882), writes:—"A parish in Wales with only 21 inhabitants and 620 acres in extent . . . . is hardly so peculiar as a parish seven miles from the Marble Arch, with only 34 inhabitants and 626 acres in extent. The parish of Perivale, adjoining Ealing parish, and less than two miles from Ealing Station, fulfils these con-ditions (there are in all five houses), being the smallest parish in the diocese of London, and one of the smallest in England."

It need scarcely be stated that such a retired spot as Perivale should be devoid of "historic interest." In "Domesday Book," however, it is recorded that "Gulbert held in Greneford three hides of Geoffry (de Mandeville). There was land to one plough and a half; but land for one plough only was used. Pannage for forty hogs. The value of the land was stated at twenty shillings;

when received, ten shillings; in King Edward's time, forty shillings. Two Sokemen held this land; one was a canon of St. Paul's, the other was a vassal of Asgar's, the master of the horse. In the same village Ansgot held half a hide of Geoffry de Mandeville; and Ælveve, the wife of Wateman, held half a hide of the king." The subsequent history of this little district, until the reign of the second Edward, appears to be a blank. At that time the manor of Greenford Parva—then called Cornhull, or Cornhill—together with the advowson of the church, was surrendered to the Crown, in exchange for the churches of Cestreton and Worsfield, in Warwickshire, by Walter de Langton, Bishop of Coventry and Lichfield. The king granted it shortly afterwards to Henry de Beaumont, by whose descendants it was alienated, in 1387, to Thomas Charleton. After this period it successively became the property of various families, and was purchased about the middle of the last century by Richard Lateward, Esq. On the death of Mr. Lateward, the manor passed by bequest to John Schreiber, Esq., who afterwards took the name of Lateward.

The parish church, as may be imagined for so small a district, is very diminutive. The building bears marks of age, apparently of the fourteenth century, and on its north side stands the vicarage, an interesting half-timbered building, of semi-Gothic architecture. Like most of the parish churches which we have lately described, that of Perivale is constructed chiefly of flint and stone, and consists of a nave and narrow chancel, with a square wooden tower and a short spire at the western end, and a south porch. The interior was restored, and the east wall rebuilt, in 1875. The nave is separated from the chancel by a dwarf screen, apparently of seventeenth century workmanship, and in some of the windows are fragments of stained glass, among them being representations of St. John the Baptist and St. Matthew. In the south-west corner is a small hagioscope. The font-cover bears the date 1665, though the font itself is undoubtedly much earlier. On the floor of the chancel is a brass to the memory of Henry Myllet, who is represented in effigy, together with his two wives and fifteen children; it is dated 1500. There are a few monuments to former lords of the manor of Greenford Parva—including the families of Lane, Harrison, Myllet, and Lateward—but none of them are of sufficient public interest to merit description. Here, in 1765, was buried Philip Fletcher, Dean of Kildare, brother of Dr. Fletcher, Bishop of Kildare, and author of a poem in Dodsley's collec-

tion called "Nature and Fortune," and of another entitled "Truth at Court," which acquired some little popularity at the time of its publication, but which is now well-nigh forgotten.

Passing in an easterly direction for about a mile, we come to another parish almost as small as Perivale—namely, Twyford, or West Twyford, so called to distinguish it from the hamlet of East Twyford, in the adjoining parish of Willesden. This parish—if it may be called one—comprises only about 200 acres, and but eight houses, with a population of seventy-five. Twyford is described by Lewis, in his "Topographical Dictionary," in 1835 as being "in the Kensington division of the Hundred of Ossulston," and as containing a population of forty-three souls.

It is not a little singular that within a mile and a half of the great railway junction at Willesden, and within six or seven miles of Hyde Park Corner, there should have been, down to a comparatively recent date, an extra-parochial liberty, whose inhabitants own no ecclesiastical allegiance to the Bishop of London. But so it is. The land, having belonged to one of the smaller religious houses, Twyford Abbey was forgotten to be included in the general survey.

The whole "parish" of Twyford contains less than 300 acres, and but one important house— Twyford Abbey and its dependent farm-buildings. It does not appear that this district ever possessed a resident population. Mr. Brewer, in the "Beauties of England," states, on the authority of the records of St. Paul's, that "there were six tenements in Twyford in the earlier part of the fifteenth century, one of which formed the residence of the minister, and the rents of the others assisted in supporting him. These tenements were situated near the church." In the year 1251, according to Lysons' "Environs of London," there were ten inhabited houses in the parish, in addition to the manorial seat. Only one of these, the manor-house, was remaining in the reign of Queen Elizabeth, and the parish continued in the same depopulated state until the beginning of the present century.

In the "Domesday Survey" the manor of Twyford is dealt with under the name of "Tveverde," and it is there stated that Gueri, a canon of St. Paul's, holds two hides of land; the record proceeding:— "There is land to one plough and a half. There is a plough in the demesne, and a half may be made. There are two villanes of one virgate, and one bordar of six acres, and three cottagers. Pannage for fifty hogs," &c.

Early in the twelfth century the manor was

leased to Walter de Cranford and his wife, "with all the tithes of corn, sheep, and goats," by the Dean and Chapter of St. Paul's. It afterwards passed through various changes of ownership, and towards the end of the fifteenth century it was procured by a citizen of London, one John Philpot, with whose family it remained through many generations. In the last century it was conveyed, by the marriage of an heiress, to the Cholmeley family, of whom it was purchased in 1806 by "Thomas Willan, Esq., of Marybone Park." This

is probable that the place took its name of Twyford.

On the lawn, close to the house, is a small chapel. It is built of plain brick, covered with stucco, and an attempt was made early in this century to give it a Gothic character by the addition of a porch and some other minor details. The chapel is much improved in appearance by a luxuriant growth of ivy, the effect of which is heightened by the various elms and cedars that stud the lawn. The building contains a few monuments of interest.

TWYFORD ABBEY.

gentleman pulled down the old manor-house, which was at that time occupied as a farm. The building was surrounded by a moat, and approached by a drawbridge. The building having been demolished, the moat was filled up. Mr. Willan shortly after commenced the erection of a new manor-house on a fresh site hard by, from the designs of Mr. Atkinson. It is a handsome residence in the "Strawberry Hill" Gothic style of architecture ; the principal front is advanced and embattled, with octagonal turrets at either end. The surrounding grounds are pleasantly wooded, and of an ornamental character. The River Brent, which forms the northern margin of the parish, winds through the grounds. Besides this, another brook runs near it. Both these streams are, or were, fordable at a certain point, and from this circumstance it

One of these is to Robert Moyle, Esq., Prothonotary of the Common Pleas, who died in 1638, and who is represented by a bust habited in a black cap and gown. Another monument, with a bust, commemorates Walter Moyle, Esq., who died at Twyford in 1660. On the north wall is a tablet to the memory of Henry Bold, the author of some humorous poems, who died in 1683.

About two miles due east from Twyford Abbey lies what was once the village of Willesden, or Wilsdon, but which is now a rapidly-increasing suburb of London. The western side of the parish is skirted by the London and North-Western Railway, which has a station at Harlesden, about a mile from Willesden proper, called the Willesden Junction Station, which serves also for the North London line. There is here almost as great a network of railways as at Clapham Junction,* the lines radiating hence to almost all parts of London, both north and south of the Thames ; and the arrangement of the station is, if possible, more consummately bewildering to the unhappy traveller who has to "change."

The parish of Willesden is bounded on the east by the Edgware Road, and stretches away north to Wembly and Neasdon, west to Twyford, and southward to Acton and Shepherd's Bush. It comprises in all between 4,000 and 5,000 acres, the greater part of which was meadow and pasture-land, intersected by pleasant lanes and hedge-rows. At the beginning of this century the houses were comparatively few and widely scattered. Even as

London Line ; Harrow Road, on the Midland ; at Neasdon, on the Metropolitan Extension, and also on the Midland Railway ; and at Willesden Green, on the Metropolitan. All the above stations are situated within the boundaries of the parish. There is also a station at Dudding Hill, on the Midland Railway, a short distance north-eastward of Willesden Church ; that at Harrow Road meeting the requirements of the new district called Stonebridge Park.

The River Brent waters the north and west sides of the parish, but this stream is subject to floods, which are very injurious to the land on its immediate borders.

The name of this place is written "Wellesdone"

WILLESDEN CHURCH.   (*See p.* 224.)
(*From a Print in the "Gentleman's Magazine,"* xci.)

recently as 1861 the population did not amount to 4,000 ; but in the course of the next ten years, so rapid had been the increase of buildings in the neighbourhood, the number amounted to almost 16,000. According to the census returns for 1881, the population has now swelled up to over 27,000. Such has been the rapidity with which the builder has invested this once rural and retired district, that the green fields are now fast disappearing in all directions, to give place to streets and rows of villa residences. One great cause for all this rapid extension of the metropolis is undoubtedly the facility which is afforded by the railways for communication with the City and other parts of London ; for, apart from Willesden Junction, mentioned above, there are stations at Brondesbury, on the North-Western, North-London, and Metropolitan Railways ; at Kensal Green, on the North

in the "Norman Survey," and the manor is there stated to belong to the Canons of St. Paul's, to whom it had either been given or confirmed by King Athelstan. The manorial district was afterwards sub-divided, so that there are now in Willesden eight distinct manors, "seven of which," says Mr. Brewer, in his "Beauties of England," "are held by the same number of prebends (prebendaries) in St. Paul's Cathedral, or by their lessees." The manor of Twyford is in lay hands.

The parish church, dedicated to St. Mary, dates probably from the early part of the fourteenth century, a few fragments being of even an earlier period. Most of the marks of its antiquity were removed on the restoration of the building, about 1850, down to which time the church consisted of a nave and chancel, a south aisle and porch, and a square embattled tower at the western end of the aisle. The exterior at that time appeared rugged with age, and an interesting air of antiquity pre-

* See "Old and New London," Vol. VI., p. 483.

vailed over the whole structure, except that the large east window had been contracted, and a mean framework of wood substituted for the stone mullions. The walls were partly covered with stucco; but the church had a picturesque appearance, and was often a subject for the artist's pencil. In 1851 it was carefully repaired and enlarged; and again, in 1872, a further and more complete restoration was made, a north aisle, porch, and transept being added, the interior of the tower being at the same time opened out to the body of the church. During these restorations, fragments of Norman work, in the shape of the round arches of two narrow windows, were discovered on removing the north wall. In the north wall of the chancel is an Easter sepulchre; and another is in the south wall of a chantry which is formed of the eastern bay of the south aisle, and which opens into the aisle and chancel by arches. The font is probably late Norman. The old-fashioned pews were replaced by open benches, and new sedilia, reredos, and pavement of encaustic tiles, were placed in the chancel in 1872. Most of the windows are filled with painted glass, the subject of that over the altar being the crucifixion of Our Lord. The pulpit, of carved oak, was erected in 1877, in memory of members of the Wood family.

Scattered about are four or five ancient brasses, the earliest of which, dated 1492, commemorates Bartholomew de Willesden; and there are also several ancient monuments, one of which, with kneeling figures, is in memory of Richard Paine, who was "gentleman pensioner to five princes," and who died in 1606. Sir John Franklyn, who died in 1647, is also commemorated here; as also is General Charles Otway, "an officer of great bravery in the reigns of Anne and George I."

In the description of this edifice in the "Beauties of England" (1816), it is stated that "the whole furniture of the church is of a rustic and humble description; yet devotees from various parts were formerly attracted to this spot by an image of Our Lady, renowned for dispensing benefits among those who visited it in pilgrimage." An inventory of the goods and ornaments belonging to this church, taken about the middle of the thirteenth century, makes mention of "a scarlet banner, with the figures of the Virgin Mary of cloth of gold," the gift of the vicar, and "also two large images of the Virgin;" and in another inventory, taken about 1547, mention is made of two "Masers" that were "appointed to remayne in the church, for to drink yn at brideales," but these have long since disappeared, along with the jovial custom referred to. With

reference to this entry, Mr. Brewer, in the "Beauties of England," remarks:—"It will be recollected that wine, in which sops, or pieces of cake, or wafer, were immersed, was first blessed by the priest at marriages, and then drunk by the bride, the bridegroom, and their company. The allusions to this custom are numerous in our old dramatists."

It is doubtful whether "pilgrimages to Our Lady of Wilsdon" ever became so popular with Londoners as those to the holy martyr of Canterbury and to "Our Lady of Walsingham," both of which were suppressed, and the images destroyed, about the same time, in 1548.

Francis Close, some time Dean of Carlisle, who died in 1882, was in early life a curate here. Having held for a short time the curacy of Church-Lawford, near Rugby, he was transferred hither in 1822. Two years later, however, he was appointed to a curacy at Cheltenham, of which parish he became rector in 1856. He held that appointment, exercising an almost absolute sway over the Evangelical circles of that fashionable watering-place, till 1856, when he was nominated to the Deanery of Carlisle, a post which he resigned about a twelvemonth before his death. He was almost the last of the followers of Simeon, Venn, Thomson, and Wilberforce, and the rest of the "Clapham sect."

In the *Gentleman's Magazine* is given a spirited little engraving of Willesden church as it appeared a little more than half a century ago. It shows the western end of the building, with its tall tower backed by trees. In the churchyard, and to the right of the view, several cottages are represented.

The churchyard in former times was encumbered with some old buildings; but these have all been pulled down, and the grave-yard extended, laid out with ornamental walks, and planted.

Mr. Harrison Ainsworth selected Willesden as the scene of some of the exploits of the romantic Jack Sheppard, whom he declares to have been buried in Willesden churchyard; but the interment does not appear to be recorded in the parish register, which, it may be added, dates from the middle of the sixteenth century. Mr. Harrison Ainsworth himself lived for some time at Kensal House, in this parish; and hence, probably, his association of this locality with the name of Jack Sheppard.

Church End is the name given to the cluster of houses in the immediate neighbourhood of the parish church. A short distance to the north is Queen's Town, a district which, although quite of modern growth, can boast of its Working Men's Institute, its Workman's Hall, &c. About half a mile further northward is Willesden Green. In

1880 a new ecclesiastical district, St. Andrew's, was formed here. A school for the new district, constructed of red brick, with stone dressings, and which also serves the purposes of a church, stands at the junction of Villiers and Chaplin Roads.

Willesden Green was formerly one of the most rustic spots in the neighbourhood of London, and the tea-gardens of its roadside tavern, the "Spotted Dog," used to be a favourite resort for Londoners. Its rural character, however, is now altogether changed, for in the place of picturesque old cottages, long rows of streets are fast springing up in all directions, and the humble and cosy tavern just mentioned has blossomed into a large "hotel," fitted up after the modern style. The "White Hart Inn" and pleasure-grounds at Church End, and the "Old Spotted Dog" at Neasdon, are also favourite summer haunts for Londoners.

The outlying hamlets of Willesden are Brondesbury, Harlesden, Neasdon, Dollis Hill, Sherrick Green, and Stonebridge Park.

Brondesbury is of great antiquity, and gives its name to a prebendal stall in St. Paul's Cathedral, the lands comprised in the hamlet having been for many centuries attached to that office. It lies in the eastern part of the parish, near the Edgware Road and Kilburn Wells, and is now being rapidly covered with houses. It was formed into a separate ecclesiastical district in 1866. Christ Church, which stands at the corner of Willesden Lane, is a large building in the Early English style, cruciform in plan, with a lofty tower and spire. Several of the windows are filled with stained glass.

The Jewish Cemetery, in Willesden Lane, comprising about twelve acres, was consecrated in 1863, and is prettily laid out and planted with shrubs and evergreens, and has a rabbi's house and mortuary chapel, built of Kentish rag-stone. Here, in 1874, was buried Baron Meyer de Rothschild, of Mentmore, Bucks, M.P. for Hythe; and in 1876 Baron Anthony de Rothschild was interred here.

A short distance southward of Brondesbury, near the Elgin Road, Maida Vale, is a large establishment known as the Warwick Farm Dairy, recently erected for Messrs. Welford and Sons, at a cost of upwards of £20,000. The buildings cover about two acres of ground.

Harlesden is another rapidly-increasing district, about one mile south-west from Willesden church. Willesden Junction station, as mentioned above, is in this neighbourhood. The ecclesiastical dis-

trict of All Souls was formed here in 1875. The church, of Early English design, was consecrated in 1879. The Presbyterian church, built in 1876, is a Gothic structure, of cruciform shape; and the Wesleyan chapel, erected in 1882, is a large red brick building, also of Gothic design, with a tall spire. Harlesden House is a large mansion here, the grounds of which have become famous for their floricultural displays. Much of the land in Harlesden, comprising portions of the Manor Park Estate, has been sold of late years for building purposes.

Cricklewood, a hamlet of Willesden, lying on the Edgware Road, to the north-west of Brondesbury, and closely bordering upon Hampstead, still retains much of its rural character, notwithstanding that it contains a railway-station on the Midland line.

Neasdon, a short distance further westward, is also intersected by the Midland and South-Western Junction Railways, which have a station here at Dudding Hill. The reservoir of the Regent's Park Canal, which extends to this hamlet, covers upwards of 360 acres of ground. There are also extensive works here in connection with the Metropolitan Railway, as a depôt for the carriages, engines, and rolling stock generally, belonging to that company, and for the repair of the same. The works have been constructed upon a plan similar to those belonging to the Great Eastern Railway Company at Stratford,[*] and gives employment to about 500 hands.

Sherrick Green and Dollis Hill are both pretty little hamlets. The former lies in a secluded valley, watered by one of the feeders of the river Brent; and the latter in an upland, well-wooded district. Dollis Hill House, which occupies a commanding site here, is the residence of the Earl of Aberdeen.

Stonebridge Park, about a mile to the southwest of Willesden church, on the main road to Harrow, comprises a large number of villas, occupied chiefly by City men, who prefer the quiet retirement of the country to the noise and bustle of the town. It has a large hotel and a station on the Midland Railway.

We must now beg the reader to accompany us, in imagination, on a railway trip as far as West Drayton, which we have already visited and described,[†] in order to start afresh in our explorations in that neighbourhood.

---

[*] See "Old and New London," Vol V., p. 573.
[†] See *ante*, pp. 205-8.

CHAPTER XXI.

COWLEY AND HILLINGDON.

"Ruris amatorem . . . . . . salvere jubemus."—HORACE.

Situation and Boundaries of Cowley—Cowley Peachey—Cowley Church—Graves of Dr. Dodd and the Rev. John Lightfoot—Barton Booth, the Actor—Census Returns—Cowley House—Cowley Grove—Hillingdon—The Cedar House—Etymology of Hillingdon—Hillingdon Heath—Dawley Court—The Manor of Colham—The Church of St. John the Baptist—Tomb of John Rich, the Actor—The Church Library—The Parish Registers—An Old Engraving—Charities—The Village of Hillingdon—The Cemetery—Census Returns—The "Red Lion" Inn—Flight of Charles I. from Oxford.

A WALK of a mile and a half northwards from West Drayton, through Yiewsley, we arrive at Cowley, a singularly scattered parish geographically, consisting of isolated patches of land, mixed up with Hillingdon in such a way as defies description, and must puzzle the authorities when they come to "beat the bounds." It is bounded on the west by the Colne, more than one of whose branches run through it; and it is also intersected by another rivulet, the Blackwater, or Cowley Brook, which runs from Hillingdon, and finds its way into the Colne. It is a small parish of between 300 and 400 acres, scattered about on the cross-road between West Drayton and Uxbridge. Its name is said by Lysons to be derived from the Anglo-Saxon *Co'l leag*, the cold meadow. Mr. Thorne, however, inclines to a simpler derivation—that of "Cow" and "ley," or lea, the Cow's Meadow; but in the "Domesday Book" it figures as "Cove lei." The manor, formerly in the hands of the Abbey of Westminster, passed many centuries ago into the hands of the Peacheys, whence a part of the parish is still called "Cowley Peachey."

The chief part of the population is gathered into Cowley Street, along the road to Uxbridge, from which town Cowley is about a mile distant. The neighbourhood is mostly agricultural, and the meadows and lanes are pleasant and open.

The quaint little church, dedicated to St. Lawrence, stands adjoining the rectory, a little to the east of the village, on the Hillingdon Road. It consists of a small nave and chancel, but the latter is not cut off, as usual, by a chancel-arch, and it has a roof of red tiles, which, being of lofty pitch, while the tower is low, gives a high-shouldered appearance to the structure. The tower and spire belong to the last century.

The church, in spite of some partial restorations, remains very much in the same state as in the last century, the royal arms being there, and tiers of galleries towering to the ceiling at the west end. Where the chancel-arch would naturally be looked for is a solid beam of oak, which supports the Creed, the Lord's Prayer, and the Ten Commandments. Before the Reformation it probably was the rood-beam. The east window consists of an Early English triplet of lancets; and there are one or two other good windows of the Decorated period, some of them filled with modern painted glass. The monuments in the church are numerous, but of no general interest; the most ancient is one to the memory of Walter Pope, yeoman, who died in 1502. In the churchyard, in an angle formed by the western tower, lies in a nameless grave the body of the unfortunate Dr. Dodd, who was executed for forgery in the year 1777.[*] Here, too, lies the body of the Rev. John Lightfoot, the learned botanist and naturalist, and some time Lecturer of Uxbridge, where we shall meet him again, who died in 1788.

The parish, small and remote as it is, has its dramatic associations. Barton Booth, the actor, of Drury Lane celebrity, and also his widow, lie buried here. The latter, who died in 1773, erected a monument to the memory of her husband in Westminster Abbey, which is ornamented with his bust in medallion, and bears a somewhat fulsome inscription.[†] Booth, it appears from Davies's "Life of Garrick," was the owner of a small estate in this parish.

Altogether, this parish is almost the least changed of any in Western Middlesex, for whilst it figures in the census of 1871 as having only ninety-two inhabited houses, with a population of 491 souls, the number had not amounted to 500 when the returns for 1881 were taken. Still, it contains several good houses, the largest and most important being Cowley House, the seat of Mr. William Hilliard, who is lord of the manor and patron of the rectory. This mansion contains a fine collection of family pictures, including two by Gainsborough, which were exhibited at South Kensington in 1862.

Cowley Grove, the residence of General Van Cortlandt, C.B., is a conspicuous house at the entrance of the village on the Uxbridge side, and is memorable as having been, as it is believed, the residence of Booth the actor above-mentioned. Booth became famous as a tragedian; he was the

---

* See "Old and New London," Vol. V., p. 190.
† See "Old and New London," Vol. III., p. 223.

great hero of the stage between the reigns of Betterton and Quin, and was the first representative of the part of Cato in Addison's fine tragic poem. The house was afterwards occupied for many years by John Rich the actor and some time patentee of Covent Garden Theatre.

It is quite pleasant, after our long tour amongst the flattest of meadows and arable lands, to find oneself again on breezy uplands, and few parishes in Middlesex can exhibit a more delightful variation of scenery than Hillingdon, which we enter from Cowley. It is diversified by, at all events, two large parks—belonging respectively to Sir Charles Mills and Mr. Cox—and by several smaller houses, standing in extensive grounds. Among them is the "Cedar House," a fine red brick Elizabethan mansion, to the north of the church; and a still larger house some little distance to the south, the successor of an earlier mansion given or sold by the Bishop of London, in the seventeenth century, to the Bishop of Worcester, who needed a resting or halting place in his progresses to and from London. The latter building was used as the rectory previous to the erection of a new house on the opposite side of the road. The reason assigned, in the endowment of the vicarage of Hillingdon, for the appropriation of that church to the see of Worcester was, "that the Bishop of Worcester, being often sent for by the Archbishop and by the king to London, had not, in his way, any inn in this neighbourhood where, upon unavoidable and pressing occasions, he might sleep and lodge as he ought."

Lysons says that the Cedar House was so called from a fine cedar on the front lawn, which tradition assigns to Mr. Samuel Reynardson as its planter. He lived here from 1678 to 1721, but the house was known by its present name some years previously. Gilpin, in his "Forest Trees," published in 1791, mentions this tree as the finest cedar that he had seen, and considers that it was between 130 and 140 years old. Loudon, however, shows that Mr. Gilpin's estimate is an exaggeration, and mentions especially the cedars at Wilton House, near Salisbury, as far larger and finer.

Mr. Reynardson, of Cedar House, was a man of great learning, especially in botany. His garden was full of rarities. Like Solomon, he "spoke of trees, from the cedar that is in Lebanon, unto the hyssop which springeth out of the wall." It was, therefore, natural for the next generation, who knew him only at second-hand, to credit him with having planted the cedar which gave its name to his house. After the death of Mr. Richardson, the house was occupied by General Richard Russell.

Norden, in the MS. additions to his "Speculum Britanniæ," supposes that Hillingdon derives its name from "its situation on a hill, or downe." "Hillingdon Heath, a considerable tract of land to the south-east of the village," observes Mr. Brewer, in the "Beauties of England," "affords a sanction to this mode of derivation, as its comparative eminence is sufficiently proved by the extent of prospect which it commands at many points." To the south of the heath is Dawley Court, the property of the Count de Salis, which we have already noticed.* The house, which is in the parish of Hillingdon, stands on an estate formerly called Coomes, *alias* Little London, and was sometimes called Hillingdon Place.

It would appear that in the Saxon times the parish of Hillingdon comprised concurrently two manors, named respectively Colham and Uxbridge, or Woxbridge; but how far they were identical or independent is not quite certain. In "Domesday" the only mention is that of the Manor of Colham, which was taxed at eight hides, and was held by the Earl of Arundel. "The land is seven carucates; there are six hides in demesne, on which are three ploughs; and the villains have three ploughs. There are six villains, who hold a virgate each, and four others who hold two virgates jointly. The priest had one hide. There are ten bordars, each of whom has five acres; there are four cottars and eight slaves. There are two mills, meadow pasture for the cattle of the manor, pannage for 400 hogs, and one acre of vineyard." It appears from the same document that it was then valued at £8 yearly, having stood at only £6 when it came into the earl's possession, though under Edward the Confessor it was held from the king at £10 rent. In very early times the Manor of Colham formed part of the Honour of Wallingford, and belonged in part to the Abbot of Evesham before it was seized by the Conqueror. In Henry II.'s time it was in the hands of the Bassets, and in 1246 it belonged to William de Lang Espée, Earl of Salisbury. It then devolved on the Earls of Leicester, and from them on the Le Stranges, from whom it came by marriage into the hands of the Stanleys; and Thomas Earl of Derby died at his manor-house of Colham in 1521. After the death of Ferdinand Earl of Derby in 1594, it passed to his widow, Alice, of whom we shall hear more presently, when we reach Harefield. We will only mention here the fact that when the burgesses of Uxbridge disputed her ladyship's claim, in right of her manor, to a toll on the markets and fairs of the

---

* See *ante*, p. 201.

town, she maintained her right at law, and by threatening them with a prosecution before the Star Chamber, forced the good people within it to recognise her rights and to sue for her pardon. This done, she forgave them, and even sent them some venison for a civic feast. The lordship of the manor passed from her to the Lords Chandos, and from them to the Pitts; and having passed through two or three intermediate families, was purchased in 1782 by the De Burghs of West Drayton.

According to Leland, the manor-house of Colham were part of the original structure. The embattled tower at the western end, which was built early in the seventeenth century, remains nearly in its original condition. The roofing of the church is new throughout, and some of the windows, the tracery of which has been renewed, are filled with painted glass. The Perpendicular font is curious, and there are on the walls of the church many monuments and inscriptions to local worthies.

On the north wall of the chancel is a costly monument of marble to the memory of Henry

HILLINGDON CHURCH ABOUT 1740.
(*From an old print at the Vicarage*).

was an ancient building, situate about a mile above Uxbridge, between Longford and Colnbrook. It was taken down many years ago. Colham Green, about a mile to the south, is a hamlet of Hillingdon.

The old church, dedicated to St. John the Baptist, stands between the village green and the common. The former is a quaint and irregular open space of about an acre and a half, adorned with two or three elm-trees many centuries old, and reminds one of the Green at Stanwell.

The church stands on a slight elevation. It is of the Decorated or Edwardian period, and consists of spacious nave, chancel, side aisles, and transepts. The latter were added by Sir Gilbert Scott when he restored the church, in 1848, but look as if they

Paget, Earl of Uxbridge, who died at the family seat at Drayton in 1743. The deceased is represented by a semi-recumbent effigy, habited in Roman costume. On the monument is a lengthy inscription, commemorating his social qualities, &c. His lordship had been created Baron Burton in 1712, during his father's lifetime, and he was advanced to the Earldom of Uxbridge in 1714. The title, however, became extinct on the death of the grandson of that nobleman, in 1769, but was revived in 1784 in the person of Henry Bailey, ninth Lord Paget, whose son and successor was created Marquis of Anglesey, in consequence of his gallant military achievements on the Continent. On the opposite side of the chancel is the monument of Sir Edward Carr, who died in 1635. The effigies of the deceased and of his lady (Jane, daughter of Sir Edward Onslow) are represented kneeling before books. Sir Edward is attired in rich armour; and at the foot of the monument, on a projecting pedestal, are the effigies of his two daughters. In the floor of the chancel is the brass of two figures, under a double Gothic canopy. They represent a knight and his lady: the former in armour and bare-headed, and the latter habited in a mantle and kirtle, with a veiled head-dress. The inscription is gone, but the brass is supposed to cover the tomb of John, Lord le Strange, and Jane, his wife, who was the daughter of Richard Woodville, Earl Rivers, and sister of Elizabeth, queen of Edward IV. This Lord Strange died in 1476. Mr. Brewer, in his work already quoted, says that "it is known that a tomb was placed for Lord le Strange and his lady in this church, and the Latin inscription to their memory is preserved in Weever, and has been reprinted in Gough's 'Sepulchral Monuments,' in the 'Environs of London,' and in 'Ecclesiastical Antiquities.'"

The most important tomb in the churchyard is that containing the remains of John Rich the actor, mentioned above. Rich was the first and most famous of English harlequins, a character which he performed under the assumed name of "Lun." His "matchless art and whim" in the representation of this mute hero are recorded by Garrick. He died in the year 1761, having been for many years the lessee of Covent Garden Theatre.* Among other tombs in the churchyard is that of Major-General Richard Russell, son of Sir John Russell, and grandson of Oliver Cromwell. He died in 1793, having been for many years a resident of the Cedar House, in this village.

In the vestry at the west end of the south aisle is a church library. It was left by Mr. Reynardson, of the Cedar House, in 1721. It contains a large number of works on divinity, natural history, and medicine, together with some voyages and travels, and numerous historical and poetical publications, and a first edition of the "Eikon Basilike." The books are, on the whole, in a fair condition.

The registers commence in the year 1559, the second year of Elizabeth. As usual, the records are absent during the troubled years of Parliamentarian rule, 1644-49; from this latter date to 1653 they are confused and imperfect.

With the restoration of Charles II. came a new vicar, one Thomas Boston, who seems to have been both a scholar and a wag. At all events, his entries are comical, and full of sarcastic allusions to the "sectaries," whose sway was just over. He calls base-born children "terræ filii," and he records all sorts of incidents, including the murder of one of his parishioners: but newspapers, it must be remembered, were then in their first infancy. He chronicles the fact of children baptised at home, though not in weak health, and of the contempt of the law by their parents in omitting to bring them afterwards to the church. He notes also, in terms of harsh censure, the invasion of his rights by the neighbouring clergy, who dared to baptise and to bury those whom he claimed as his parishioners. It is probable, judging from the entries in the register, that the population of Hillingdon under Charles II. could scarcely have been a third of what it is now. Among the burials are recorded those of many Londoners, showing that even two centuries ago the neighbourhood was attractive to strangers on account of its healthiness. In spite of the two towns—for so they are called—of Hillingdon and Uxbridge having been a stronghold of Nonconformity, there are many proofs in the register that Hillingdon was greatly used as a halting-place between London and the quarters of the Court at Oxford in the reign of Charles I.

In 1665 the burial list is increased by several entries of deaths, probably of strangers and wayfarers, who died of the plague.

In 1663, the hearse of the Archbishop of Canterbury, Dr. Juxon, on its way from London to Oxford, appears to have been met at the church gate by the vicar in surplice and hood, "the great bell solemnly tolling all the while"—probably as a loyal mark of respect to the prelate who had stood by the side of King Charles on the scaffold at Whitehall.

Mr. Boston died in 1677, and the registers of succeeding vicars scarcely call for remark.

In the vicarage is a copy of a curious engraving of the church in its former condition, probably about 1740 or a little later. The tower is much the same as now, but the southern aisle is a monstrous high-shouldered erection, with "churchwarden" windows. To the south of the churchyard stands a lofty yew, clipped, as at Bedfont, into a fantastic shape; and there is a row of four smaller yew-trees along the west front, by the side of a lych-gate, below which again are the parish stocks, the terror of small boys. There is still living an old parishioner who can remember as a boy climbing these yew-trees. The engraving is very scarce, and the vicar's copy has been made by him a heir-loom for his successors.

* See "Old and New London," Vol. III., p. 228.

Up to 1871 a considerable amount of bread was given away in doles for several charities ; but owing to abuses and scandals, these gifts, with the sanction of the Charity Commissioners, were commuted for a money payment towards providing clothing for poor school children and help for necessitous parishioners.

The village of Hillingdon is situated on the main road between London and Oxford, and is fourteen miles from Hyde Park Corner, and rather more than a mile from Uxbridge Station, on a branch of the Great Western Railway. The Grand Junction Canal passes through the parish ; and at the western end of the village, fronting the Uxbridge Road, is the cemetery, which was consecrated in 1867. It comprises an area of about six acres, and contains two mortuary chapels. These buildings, which are constructed of Kentish rag-stone with Bath stone dressings, and have tiled roofs, are in the Decorated style of architecture, from the designs of the late Mr. Benjamin Ferrey, F.S.A.

Hillingdon, in 1871, appears by the census to have had 1,615 inhabited houses, with a population of 8,237, a number which was increased by upwards of fifteen hundred in the course of the next ten years.

One of the principal hostelries in the village, the "Red Lion," directly opposite the church, has been a noted house in its day. Here Charles I. rested after his escape from Oxford, with his chaplain, Dr. Hudson, and Ashburnham, his groom of the chamber, when besieged by Fairfax, in April, 1646, and hence he made his way by cross roads towards Hertfordshire.

The following extract from the evidence of "Dr. Michael Hudson's Examination before the Committee of Parliament touching the King's Escape from Oxford to the Scots at Southwell," as printed in Peck's "Desiderata Curiosa," is of interest :—
"After we had passed Uxbridge, at one Mr. Teasdale's house a taverne in Hillingdon, we alighted and stayed to refresh ourselves, betwixt 10 and 11 of the clocke [Monday morning, April 27], and there stayed two or three hours, where the king was much perplexed what course to resolve upon, London or Northward. The consideration of the former vote, and the apparent danger of being discovered at London, moved him to resolve at last to go Northward and through Norfolke, where he was least knowne. . . . About 2 of the clocke we took a guide towards Barnet."

In order to meet the requirements of the increasing population of this parish, a new church was erected in 1865 at Hillingdon End, near to Uxbridge, but of this we shall have more to say presently.

CHAPTER XXII.

UXBRIDGE.

Etymology of Uxbridge—Meeting of the Royalists and Roundheads—Public Reception of the Treaty—The Treaty House—The "Crown" Inn—The Colne and the Grand Junction Canal—The Bridge—The "Swan and Bottle"—Early Fortifications—Roman Roads and Antiquities—Chief Streets of Uxbridge—Census Returns—The "Chequers"—Trade and Commerce—Fairs and Markets—Condition of the Roads—The Parish Church—The Curfew Bell—Parish Registers—The Rev. John Lightfoot—The Lecturer's House—St. Andrew's Church—St John's Church—Nonconformists' Meeting-houses—Charities—Recreation Ground—Hillingdon House—Hillingdon Court—Martyrs for Conscience' Sake—Anecdotes—Milton's Favourite Stream—Denham.

THE town of Uxbridge, to which we next come, though spoken of in legal documents as a "borough and manor," is really neither the one nor the other, in the full acceptation of those terms. It is, in its origin, a hamlet of the parish of Hillingdon, and probably grew up gradually and naturally at the ford over the Colne. Its origin, no doubt, is to be sought in the Saxon times; and Messrs. Redford and Riches, in their "History of Uxbridge," state that "there are reasons which render it probable that it was one of the regular, though possibly smaller, boroughs established by King Alfred, or by some of his immediate successors." Its name does not occur in "Domesday," but as early as the year 1139 it is mentioned in a curious deed by one Brian Fitz-Count, under the name of Oxebridge ; and it is constantly mentioned in later times under this name, and as Woxbridge. Skinner, half as much in jest as in earnest, says in his "Lexicon" that its right name is Waxbridge, and defends the name as appropriate, on account of the waxy and tenacious nature of the clay which composes its surface soil.

That Uxbridge was reckoned a borough is clear from an ancient (Henry II.) grant from Gilbert Basset, in which its inhabitants are spoken of as burgesses, and from several manuscripts and legal records, in which the "borough ditch" is mentioned.

Though we now generally restrict the term borough to towns which return members to Parliament, we are not justified in doing so, for a borough is originally nothing but a burgh, or town, with a certain amount of local government and local privileges.

It is supposed by some that, like Oxford, the town derived its name from the number of oxen* continually passing through it from Buckinghamshire and the western counties on their way up to London; but probably the last syllable of the name is a variation of Bruge, an equivalent to Burgh, for the Colne appears to

town of Uxbridge is of a date long subsequent to the Plantagenet or even the Tudor era. It was just before the beginning of the war between King Charles and his Parliament, in 1644, that Uxbridge was chosen as the place where certain royal commissioners should meet those of the

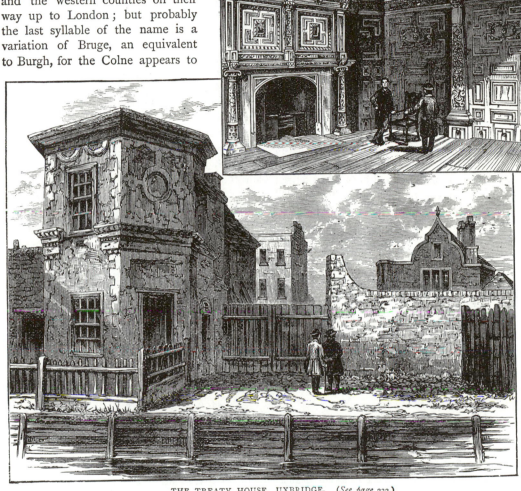

THE TREATY HOUSE, UXBRIDGE. (See page 232.)
(From the "History of Uxbridge," 1818.)

have been crossed here by a ford, and not by a bridge, down to a comparatively recent era. The ditch by which the town was surrounded in old times enclosed about eighty-five acres, and a portion of the ditch was visible in 1818, when the "History of Uxbridge" was published.

The chief historic event connected with the

rebel party, in the vain hope of bringing the differences between them to an amicable issue. The hope was vain, for religion and politics were both engaged in the conflict, the king being resolved to stand by Episcopacy, while the Roundheads were equally anxious to get rid of everything that looked in the Popish direction. On the king's part, the commission was headed by the Duke of Richmond, the Earls of Southampton, Hertford, Kingston, and Chichester, and Sir Edward Hyde, afterwards Lord Clarendon. The Presbyterians

* A writer in the *Cornhill Magazine* (1882) argues that the first syllable in Oxford and Uxbridge is the same, but has nothing to do with "oxen." It is simply the Celtic *uisg*=water, as in Usk. The suggestion is well worthy of consideration.

were represented by the Duke of Northumberland, Lords Pembroke, Denbigh, and Salisbury, Sir Harry Vane, and Bulstrode Whitelock; whilst the Scotch sent Lord Loudoun, then Lord Chancellor, Lord Argyll, and other great persons from the north of the Tweed, as their spokesmen.

Lord Clarendon gives, in an often-quoted passage of his "History of the Great Rebellion," an interesting account of their session, from which it appears that one side of the town was assigned to the king's commissioners, and the other to those of the opposite party. "There was a good house at the end of the town, which was provided for the treaty, where was a fair room in the middle of the house, handsomely dressed up, for the commissioners to sit in, a large square table being placed in the middle, with seats for the commissioners, one side being sufficient for those of either party, and a rail for others who should be thought necessary to be present, which went round. There were many other rooms on either side of this great room, for the commissioners on either side to retire to when they thought fit to consult by themselves, and to return again to the public debate; and there being good stairs at either end of the house, they never went through each other's quarters, nor met but in the great room."

And then Clarendon goes on to record the ceremonious civilities practised on either side, and the professions of intense wishes for peace from those who had bitter war in their hearts all the while. He tells us also how the king's commissioners would gladly have attended the services in the parish church, but that the Book of Common Prayer had been superseded by the Parliament, so that they were obliged to have the Church prayers read in the great room of the inn.

The debates at the conference lasted about three weeks, when the commissioners on either side agreed to separate and return to their masters. The king was resolute in his demands for the establishment of Episcopacy; the Parliamentarians were equally resolved to have none of it. The king's friends went back to Oxford, and the others to London, leaving the state of matters, if anything, rather worse than they had found it.

The conference gave rise to no little dissension and bitterness throughout the country; and one famous Presbyterian, Christopher Lover, preached against the intended treaty, saying that "no good could come of it, for that the king's emissaries had come from Oxford with blood-stained hands." This warlike gentleman afterwards lost his head under Cromwell.

The mansion which was the scene of the con-ference is described in the "Perfect Occurrences," a journal of the time, as "a very fair house at the farther end of the town, in which house were [was] appointed to them a very spacious room, well-hanged, and fitted with seats for the commissioners."

The great room, mentioned by Clarendon, is still standing in its original state, as is also the presence chamber, so called, adjoining. It is a fine large apartment, wainscoted with dark oak.

The house was then much larger than now, and it stood in a large garden, with an ornamental "Lodge" entrance; the high road now passes through a part of its grounds. It had been previously the seat of the Bennets, who afterwards became Earls of Arlington and of Tankerville; and at the time of the treaty it was called "Mr. Carr's house."

The Earl of Northumberland was the only commissioner on the opposite side who was accommodated here; Lord Pembroke lodged in another "fair house," now a brew-house or beer-house.

Each party had its place of rendezvous, and the best houses of the inhabitants were put into requisition for the accommodation of the commissioners and their attendants. Each party took a principal inn for its head-quarters, like the Oxford and Cambridge crews at Putney before the annual boat-race. It may be interesting to note that the king's commissioners chose the "Crown," and the Parliamentarians the "George"—both near the market-place, and on opposite sides of the way. In the year 1818 the "Crown" stood opposite to the "White Horse," and its grounds reached from the High Street down to the Colne. The name has long since been transferred to the "Treaty House" itself, which is now an inn, and bears the name of the "Crown and Treaty," or, as it is locally styled, "The Crown and treat ye." At the above date the "George Inn" remained, though partly converted into a private dwelling-house.

The Treaty House was visited more than once by Edmund Burke on his way between Beaconsfield and London, while his horses were feeding, and was found by him to be "most amusing and interesting."

In the rear of the Treaty House is an octagonal building, said to have been formerly used as a "round-house"; and the garden front is enriched by excellent brick-work, especially in fine hexagonal stacks of chimneys.

The town of Uxbridge lies at the foot of one of the ranges of small hills which occupy the north-western corner of Middlesex, by which flow the clear waters of the twin rivers, formed by the union of the Colne, Gade, Verum, Chess, and Misbourne. The larger of these streams, the Colne, is crossed by a substantial bridge of five arches. The smaller of the two, the Frayswater, flows through the lower part of the town, and turns the town mills, after which it separates the borough and the suburb of Chiltern View from the more populous district of St. John's.

The Grand Junction Canal also runs through Uxbridge, connecting the chief towns of the midland counties with the Thames at Brentford, and with London at Paddington. At one time the canal boats carried passengers between Uxbridge and London; but the business did not answer, and has long since been abandoned.

The bridge across the Colne, at the west end of the town, is still called the High Bridge: it consists of two parts, the central portion standing on an island. A bridge is mentioned as existing here as early as the reign of Richard II., when it was in a very ruinous condition; but it would seem that it was adapted only for horses, not for carts or waggons. This improvement dates only from the time of Henry VIII., when Lord Loughborough and Sir Edward Peckham, the one resident in Buckinghamshire and the other in Middlesex, enlarged and widened it, "out of charitie." It is probable that in this case charity began "at home." It was repaired in 1600, at the cost of Lady Derby, the lady of the manor, being then of wood. The present bridge is of brick, and dates from about 1770, the high road being slightly diverted at the time. At the foot of the bridge, on the Buckinghamshire side, is a river-side inn, with the quaint sign of the "Swan and Bottle." It is a favourite haunt of anglers. Leland, in his "Itinerary," mentions two wooden bridges here. That which he describes as the more western is the High Bridge, mentioned above; and he tells us that it crosses "the great arme of Colne river," while "the lesser arme goeth under the other bridge, and each of them serve a great mill." We have a proof of Leland's accuracy in the fact that the two mills and the two bridges are still there, though the latter are now built of more solid materials than wood.

From its position on the great western highway and on the Colne, there is no doubt that Uxbridge was fortified at a very early date; indeed, we already know that it had its town ditch. From documents in existence, it is clear, however, that it had also—at all events at times—a garrison. At the outbreak of the great rebellion it was under the command of a Captain Lampton, or Lambton, and the troops under him are styled "the garrison," and the register of burials records the deaths of more than one soldier "from the garrison." In 1647, when the western parts of Middlesex were held by the Parliamentarians, their head-quarters were fixed for some time at Uxbridge; and Lysons tells us in whose houses Cromwell, Fairfax, Ireton, Fleetwood, &c., were quartered. Even as late as 1688–9, the accounts of the chapel-wardens and overseers contain entries for the repairs of the "guard-house;" but under the tranquil reigns of our Brunswick line, the need of garrisons and guard-houses here has ceased to exist.

It is said that a Roman road ran from High Wycombe towards Beaconsfield and Uxbridge, but if so, its course cannot now be traced. To the north of the town, near Breakspears and Harefield, sufficient remains of Roman burials have been found to justify the supposition that the road to Verulam or to London passed not far from Uxbridge.

The chief streets of Uxbridge are the High Street, extending the whole length of the town from south-east to north-west; Windsor Street, formerly called the Lynch, running south-west from the market-house and church; and Vine Street, bounding it on the south-east, and probably marking the site of an ancient vineyard. The eastern part of High Street is legally styled Hillingdon End, and, in fact, is situated in Hillingdon parish.

Uxbridge disputes with Brentford the claim to being the chief or county town of Middlesex. In 1871 the parish contained 659 houses, and a population of 3,364 souls—a number which has somewhat diminished since that time, seeing that according to the census returns for 1881 the sum total of the inhabitants was only 3,346.

The "Chequers" is the oldest inn in the place, and may date back to the sixteenth, or even as remote as the fifteenth, century. It has some fine and substantial timbers in its roof and staircases, but much of the inside, as well as of the outside, is modernised. In former times the inns and taverns were numerous, compared with the size of the town, being nearly three times as many as there are at present.

The corn and flour trade is the staple business of Uxbridge, but there are also a few manufactories, breweries, an iron foundry, and saw and planing mills; whilst in the neighbourhood, on the south and south-west, are extensive brickfields.

The fairs at Uxbridge are now four in number. They are principally cattle fairs, and are held on Lady Day, on July 31st, on September 29th, and October 11th. The two last are used as statute fairs. In olden days the town must have worn a gay and festive appearance on these annual gatherings, when the steward of the Countess of Derby and the bailiffs of the town clothed in her ladyship's livery, and preceded by bands of music, used to march in solemn state to open the proceedings.

The market-house was built in 1788. It stands partly on the site of an older and smaller structure, which projected into the High Street. The present building, however, might well be removed, as it sadly obstructs the view of the parish church. It

reminding one of the description which Macaulay gives us of the leading high roads of the kingdom in the days of the Stuarts.

It is only since 1856 that Uxbridge has reached the honour of a separate ecclesiastical parish, having previously, since 1842, ranked only as a " district chapelry." It was originally a mere hamlet of Hillingdon ; and though the parish church was built as far back as the reign of Henry VI., yet until the present reign it was only a chapel-of-ease,

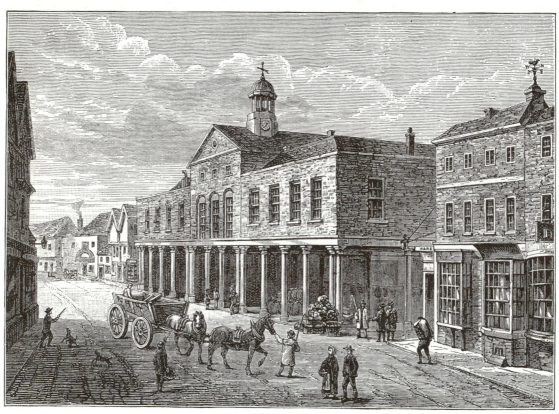

MARKET HOUSE, UXBRIDGE.
(*From the "History of Uxbridge,"* 1818.)

is open below. On the upper floor are spacious rooms, used for educational and other purposes, and also a large granary for storing corn from one week to another. Weekly markets are held on Thursdays and Saturdays ; at the former a good deal of corn is sold, whilst the latter is for cattle, pigs, and articles of domestic use. The market on Thursdays is the result of a charter, or grant, from Gilbert Basset, who probably held this manor and the Honour of Wallingford, as a reward for his fidelity to King Henry II. and his mother, Matilda, in their struggle against Stephen.

Though the great Oxford road passes through Uxbridge, yet even as late as 1797–8 the highways about here were almost impassable from mud,

or curacy, annexed to that rectory. In 1869, by an Order in Council, Uxbridge was made a Vicarage ; it was, however, called a Vicarage as far back as 1548.

The church is dedicated to St. Margaret. It is supposed that an older chapel stood on this site as far back as 1281 ; and that it had attached to it a religious house, which was suppressed by Henry VIII. No particulars, however, of its existence are known for certain.

The present church was terribly " beautified " by amateur architects during the last century. In 1872 the fabric was restored to something like its normal condition by the removal of galleries and a thorough renovation of its walls, under the superintendence of Sir Gilbert Scott. It consists of a nave and one side aisle, with a short chancel, and a tower at the north-west corner, in which is a peal of six bells. There is a very fine oak roof to the south aisle. The font is of Perpendicular workmanship, and handsome of its kind. On the north side of the chancel is a handsome monument, in the Jacobean style, to Leonora, Lady Bennet, who is represented in a reclining posture, in her every-day dress, a charnel-house being seen beneath her.

Among the burials in 1755 is that of a widow aged 104. During the Great Rebellion the banns of marriage appear to have been published not in the church, but in the open market-place, and the ceremony was performed by a civil magistrate.

The Rev. John Lightfoot, F.R.S., one of the chief founders of the Linnæan Society, was " Lecturer " of Uxbridge in the middle of the last century. He died in 1788, and lies buried at Cowley, as mentioned above.

THE FONT.   ST. MARGARET'S, UXBRIDGE.
(*From the " History of Uxbridge," 1818.*)

The curfew was rung regularly here during the winter months at eight p.m. until thirty or forty years back, when it was discontinued owing to the economy of the local authorities.

The registers of Uxbridge are in fair condition. They commence in 1538; but the marriage registers cease with 1694, from which date all weddings were ordered to be solemnised only in the mother church of Hillingdon. They contain the usual amount of curious entries. One young woman brings her illegitimate child to be christened, but she has to purchase the baptismal rite dearly, for she is forced to do public penance in the church on the same day. On another page are recorded the baptisms of four children, all born at one birth.

The lecturership and the vicarage are now accidentally held by one and the same person. His parsonage, which adjoins the railway-station, is the house built for the lecturer on land purchased for that minister, and is not, therefore, correctly termed the vicarage.

The lecturer's house is of the Queen Anne type and old-fashioned, oak-panelled within, and with a lofty roof. It is built of red brick; and a handsome modern drawing-room was added early in this century. The story runs that one day the Duchess of Portland, being at Bulstrode Park, said to the then lecturer that she hoped soon to call on him and his wife. "Madam," he replied, "I am sorry to say that I have no room fit to receive your Grace in." "Then," said the duchess, "I will build you one;" and in a few weeks she was as good as her word.

We have already stated that all the eastern part of the town of Uxbridge lies in the parish of Hillingdon. The church being small, it was accordingly felt that the accommodation for the increase in the population was inadequate, and so about the year 1860 a subscription was commenced for building a new church at the entrance of the town, on the Hillingdon Road. In the event, Sir Gilbert Scott was engaged as the architect; and the result was that in 1865 a handsome and spacious Gothic church, of the Decorated style, was completed and dedicated to St. Andrew. It consists of a lofty nave, chancel, and side aisles, and its tower is surmounted by a shingled spire, 170 feet high. A vicarage house close by was purchased, and good schools were built. A considerable part of the northern suburbs of Uxbridge lies in St. Andrew's district. Though officially styled St. Andrew's, Hillingdon, it so thoroughly belongs to the town of Uxbridge that it is better to deal with it here.

A small church, St. John's, of very unpretending character, was built about 1835 to the west of the town, on Uxbridge Moor, to meet the wants of a large population at the west end of the town, including the families of many boatmen.

Uxbridge has always been a stronghold of Nonconformity. The Quakers (who have been largely engaged in trade) have a meeting-house, which dates from 1693; and a letter from George Fox, one of the founders of that sect, addressed to the townsfolk of Uxbridge in no measured terms of reproach, is printed *in extenso* in the "History of Uxbridge," already referred to. The annals of the Presbyterian chapel here go back at least as far, and the Independent chapel was built in 1796. There are also meeting-houses for the various denominations of Wesleyans, Congregationalists, &c.

The various sects of Nonconformists made a sad display of their variations when they met at the Treaty of Uxbridge. As Butler says, in his "Hudibras," Part I., cant. ii. :—

> " For when we sware to carry on
> The present reformation,
> According to the present mode
> Of churches best reformed abroad,
> What did we else but make a vow
> To do we know not what, nor how?
> For no three of us will agree
> Where or what churches these should be."

Uxbridge is well off for literary societies and for educational and charitable endowments.

On the north-east of the town the ground rises gradually, and on its breezy heights is a public recreation-ground—all that remains of an extensive common, which was enclosed early in the present century. From this spot an extensive view is gained of the Thames Valley and of the level country reaching eastwards to Harrow and Hampstead. It is, perhaps, worthy of note that the old common contained a large rabbit-warren—said to be the only one in Middlesex.

There is also a race-course in the neighbourhood, but the races have taken place only occasionally since 1865, the meetings, like those at Acton and other metropolitan suburbs, having been voted a great nuisance by the majority of the inhabitants.

At a short distance from the town, on the London road, stands Hillingdon House, a large mansion, which was built in 1717 by the last Duke of Schomberg, who had lived for several years in an ancient house on the estate. The property afterwards passed into the hands of the noble family of Chetwynd, and towards the end of the last century it was purchased by the Marchioness of Rockingham. It has since changed hands on several occasions, its owner at the beginning of the present century being Mr. Richard Henry Cox, the well-known army agent. A rivulet, a tributary of the Colne, passes through the grounds, where it has been expanded into a lake. Beyond it, to the north, is Hillingdon Court, the seat of Sir Charles Mills, Bart.

On the edge of what was once Uxbridge Common, and in the immediate vicinity of the town, Mr. Thomas Harris, the joint patentee of Covent Garden Theatre, had a residence at the beginning of the present century. The house, a large brick building, was probably built about a century earlier. The gardens were originally laid out in straight lines and formal parterres, after the fashion of those times. Mr. Harris added considerably to the adornment of the grounds, of which the following description is quoted from the "Beauties of England:"—" A mimic hermitage, fancifully bedecked with vestiges of marble sculpture, spars, stained glass, and with apposite mottoes, opens to an apartment of handsome proportions, hung throughout with pictures, which the admirers of the histrionic art cannot fail to hold in very precious esteem. Here is preserved a large and valuable collection of original portraits of the principal theatrical performers from the date of Garrick, when all the stage was nature, to the present period, at which a monotonous, half-singing style of recitation is so often employed as a substitute for simplicity and truth. In addition to this interesting series of portraits, there are, in the same garden-saloon, pictures representing Melpomene and Thalia, and two fine paintings by Northcote from scenes in Shakespeare's tragedy of 'Richard III.' The house is still standing, but has been somewhat modernised, and in the gardens are some fine cedars."

In the troublous times of the Reformation, Uxbridge witnessed the horrors of seeing several persons who ventured to reject the dominant creed burnt at the stake. Fox has recorded their names; they appear to have been three at the least. Tradition says that the scene of their suffering was the Lynch Green, near Windsor Street, a little to the west of the burial-ground. This was in August, 1555.

A singular story, which refers to this town, is told by Mr. H. Fynes Clinton respecting his great-great-grandfather, one Norreys Fynes, alias Clinton. He was in the Royalist army under Charles I., and was taken prisoner at Northampton; but Prince Rupert having captured a man of importance, a Mr. Wright, of Uxbridge, an exchange of prisoners was arranged, and the trumpeter announcing this exchange arrived in the market-place at Uxbridge just as the rope had been put round and the last psalm or hymn was being sung, at the end of which he was to be turned off. Thus the existence of a large collateral branch of the ducal family of Newcastle for some minutes depended on the length to which a psalm was drawled out.

We may perhaps be pardoned for here introducing an amusing anecdote concerning a former Lord Mayor of London, whose early life was connected with this town, namely, Sir William Staines, who was London's chief magistrate in 1801. He started in life as a bricklayer's labourer, and at City banquets, with great glee, he used to introduce the following anecdote:—When he was a youngster, he was employed in repairing the parsonage house at Uxbridge. One day, going up the ladder with his hod of mortar, he was accosted by the parson's wife, who told him that she had had a very extraordinary dream. She told him that she had dreamed he would one day become Lord Mayor of London. Astonished at such a prophecy, Staines could only scratch his head, and thank her for such a vast promotion. He said he had neither money nor friends. The parson's wife, however, was not so easily to be turned from her prognostication, and this dream had evidently left a great impression. Her mind was bent on young Staines, and Lord Mayor he should be. The same dream occurred again, and the same communication was repeated to him that he was to be Lord Mayor. The matter passed off, and young Staines left the parsonage house at Uxbridge with no other impression than the kindness which had been shown and the notice that had been taken of him. It was not until he became sheriff that this dream came to be talked about, though there is little doubt that the dream made a lasting impression upon his own mind, and was an incentive to laudable industry through life. The Uxbridge parson had by this time become old, but he lived long enough to be chaplain to Staines when sheriff, and he died during his shrievalty.

On the north and west sides of the town, the Colne (or, as it was formerly called, Colney) pursues its course in two branches, each "brimming and very fishful," through the meadows and on either side of Uxbridge Moor, the principal arm going on to Colnbrook, and dividing the counties of Middlesex and Buckinghamshire. The clearness and purity of its stream have long been celebrated. Milton, who must often have walked by its banks when living at Horton, on his way to Harefield, in his "Epitaphium Damonis," also has immortalised its waters in Latin verse, thus translated by Cowper:—

"What ho! my friend—come, lay thy task aside;
　Haste, let us forth together, and beguile
　The heat beneath yon whisp'ring shades a while,
　Or on the margin stray of Colne's clear flood,
　Or where Cassibelan's grey turrets stood.
　There shalt thou cull me simples, and shalt teach
　Thy friend the name and healing powers of each,
　From the tall bluebell to the dwarfish weed,
　What the dry land and what the marshes breed;
　For all their kinds alike to thee are known,
　And the whole art of Galen is thine own."

The Colne has its sources among the chalk hills of Hertfordshire. The rights of fishing in the river still belong to the town-folk of Uxbridge, and form, indeed, almost the only rights left to them since the enclosure of their common.

Just above Uxbridge, on the opposite side of the river, at the junction of the roads leading to the Chalfonts and to Rickmansworth, is the pretty and retired village of Denham, a place haunted by the followers of Izaak Walton and the gentle craft. Sir Humphry Davy, the genius of angling in the nineteenth century, who often used to invite his London friends to join him for a day at the Fishery, writes:—"A light carriage, with good horses, will carry us to the ground. . . . The river is most strictly preserved; not a fish has been killed here since last August."

Denham was, under the Stuarts, one of the resorts of the proscribed Roman Catholics; and frequent mention is made in "Troubles of our Catholic Forefathers" of Sir George Peckham's house in this parish, as having sheltered priests from the bloodhounds of the law.

CHAPTER XXIII.

ICKENHAM, RUISLIP, AND HAREFIELD.

"The Chestnuts"—Ickenham—Census Returns—The Village Green and Pump—The Parish Church—Descent of the Manor—Swakeleys—Visit of Samuel Pepys—A Curious Baptismal Register—Crab, the English Hermit—Ruislip—Boundaries and Population—Outlying Hamlets—Agricultural Produce, &c.—Extract from the Domesday Survey—Ruislip Priory—The Manor Farm—The Vicarage—The Parish Church—Charities, &c.—The Parish Records—Primitive Condition of the Inhabitants of Ruislip—Schools—The Grand Junction Canal Company's Reservoir—Ruislip Park—Eastcott—Northwood—How Theodore Hook obtained a Dinner without paying for it—Harefield, its Situation and Extent—Its early History—Descent of the Manor—Visit of Queen Elizabeth to Harefield—Lord Keeper Egerton, and the Countess of Derby—The Newdigate Family—The Parish Church—Moor Hall—Breakspears.

CONTINUING our pilgrimage northward from Uxbridge, by way of the Recreation Grounds, we pass "The Chestnuts," a small mansion built under the Stuarts, on the road towards Ickenham, and now the residence of Sir William Stephenson. It is interesting as having once been occupied by William Wilberforce the philanthropist, and before him by Bishop Horne, the commentator on the Psalms.

Turning eastward, shortly after passing the "Warren House," a walk of between two and three miles brings us to the village of Ickenham, the houses of which place, few in number, are located round the village green, or scattered about in picturesque confusion in the surrounding lanes. The entire area of the parish is under 1,500 acres, and the population in 1881 numbered only 376 souls, being a slight diminution upon the census returns in 1871.

The main roads running north and south from Hillingdon to Ruislip, and that from the eastern side of Ickenham to Harefield in the north-west, cross on the Green, in the centre of which stands the village pump. This structure was erected about 1860. It has a tall conical roof, and is surrounded with seats. On the north side of the Green, in an angle formed by the two cross-roads, stands the village church. This building, almost hidden from sight by tall trees, is small and ancient, apparently dating as far back as the fourteenth century, the architecture showing examples of the Decorated and Early Perpendicular styles. It consists of a nave, north aisle—or rather, a double transept—and chancel, with a wooden belfry surmounted by a dwarf spire—similar to that of Norwood, Northolt, and other places which we have visited—rising from the western end of the nave. The bells, three in number, bear the date of 1582. The walls of the body of the church are composed of flint and stone, mostly encased with plaster. On the south side of the nave is a wooden porch, and the red tiles form a pleasant contrast. The chancel arch is modern, having been added when the church was restored a few years ago. In the chancel there is a brass commemorating William Say,

gent., who died in 1582, "registrar to the Queen's Majesty in causes ecclesiastical," with effigies of himself, his wife, and sixteen children; also one with figures of the deceased and his wife, to the memory of Henry Edmund, who died in 1584. There are also several other monuments to the family of Shordiche, formerly lords of the manor; and also to the Turners, Clarkes, and Dixons, families which have been at one time or another connected with this parish, either as landowners or as residents. A mural tablet on the west wall, executed by Banks, to the memory of Mr. John George Clarke, a barrister-at-law, who died in 1800, is curious: it bears upon it a figure typical of Religion, which is represented with a book in one hand, the other resting on a coffin partially hidden by a pall.

In the churchyard there is a very fine yew-tree; and at the west end of the church there is an unsightly charnel-house belonging to the family of the Clarkes, of Swakeleys.

This parish—which figures in ancient documents, under the respective names of Ticheham and Tykenham—is noticed in the Domesday survey, where it is recorded that "three knights and one Englishman held the manor, under Earl Roger. It answered for nine hides and a half. Land for six ploughs; pasture for the cattle of the village; pannage for two hundred hogs;" &c.

"The manor of Ickenham," observes Mr. Brewer in the "Beauties of England," "has been the subject of less frequent family alienations than is usual with property near the metropolis. It was conveyed in 1348 to John de Charlton, citizen and mercer, for life, with remainder to Nicholas Shordiche, Ivetta his wife, and their heirs." The manor remained in the hands of the Shordiche family for many generations, down to the end of the last century, when it passed to the present family of Clarke, of Swakeleys.

The most interesting feature of this parish is Swakeleys, a fine old substantial square red-brick mansion of Tudor architecture, standing in an extensive park, just outside the village, on the Hillingdon Road, and surrounded on all sides by broad green meadows and pasture-lands. The mansion consists of a centre with two slightly projecting wings, the latter terminating in large bay windows, and in the upper storey is a range of scroll-work pediments and gables, above which rise clusters of ornamented chimney stacks. The entrance is through a porch in a central turret, which opens into a hall paved with black and white stone. At the lower end of the hall is a handsome carved oak screen, painted white, and adorned with busts of Charles I. and others. This screen was probably designed for a loftier room, as it reaches nearly to the ceiling. The entrance hall is likewise remarkable for its fine massive Jacobean chimney-piece, on which are busts of Milton and Harrington.

The staircase, also of oak, has the walls and ceiling painted with several classical subjects, the principal one being the " Death of Dido," from Virgil's " Æneid." The long gallery is now cut up into three apartments, the centre forming a ball-room or drawing-room.

The grounds belonging to the house are somewhat flat, but well wooded, and are intersected by a little rivulet, which is dammed up into a miniature lake. The estate is strictly preserved, and the rabbits and pheasants walk and run about almost tame by the road-side, as we drive through the park.

Though very much smaller than either the one or the other, Swakeleys has about it many points of resemblance to Knole and Holland House; indeed, next to Holland House, this is the most interesting Jacobean mansion in the whole county of Middlesex. The gardens are quaint and trim, laid out in something of the old-fashioned style, and a long avenue of elms adorns the front of the house to the south.

This estate probably derives its name from Robert Swalclyve, who owned it four centuries ago. About the middle of the fourteenth century the estate passed to John de Charlton, who, as above stated, was the owner of the manor of Ickenham. On the attainder of Sir Richard de Charlton, in 1486, his property was forfeited to the Crown, but was shortly afterwards granted to Sir Thomas Bourchier, whose descendant, Henry Bourchier, Marquis of Exeter, sold Swakeleys, about 1550, to one Robert Pexall. The property later on was divided, one portion falling into the hands of Oliver Becket, and the other passing to the family of Brocas. Norden, writing of Swakeleys in 1596, in his " Speculum Britanniæ," mentions it as " some time a house of the Brockeyes, now of Sir Thomas Sherleye's." In 1629 the manor became the property of Edmund Wright, afterwards Sir Edmund Wright,

an alderman of London, by whom the present mansion was erected about ten years later, as appears from the date, 1638, with the initials E.W., to be seen in different parts of the building. Sir Edmund was chosen Lord Mayor of London in 1641, after the removal from that office, by Act of Parliament, of Sir William Acton. The mansion subsequently became the property and residence of Sir William Harrington, one of the judges who sat on the trial of King Charles I., and who, on the Restoration, escaped the fate of his associates by flight. It afterwards passed to Sir Robert Vyner, Lord Mayor of London, whose familiar and facetious conduct on the entertainment of Charles II. at Guildhall * were long remembered. Pepys, in his Diary under date of September 7, 1665, gives us the following insight into Sir Robert Vyner's mansion of Swakeleys shortly after he purchased it :—" To Branford [Brentford]. . . There a coach of Mr. Povy's stood ready for me, and he at his house ready to come in, and so we together merrily to Swakeley, to R. Vyner's ; a very pleasant place, bought by him of Sir James Harrington's lady. He took us up and down with great respect, and showed us all his house and grounds, and it is a place not very moderne in the garden nor house, but the most uniforme in all that ever I saw ; and some things to excess. Pretty to see over the screene of the hall, put up by Sir J. Harrington, a Long Parliament man, the King's head and my Lord of Essex on one side, and Fairfax on the other ; and upon the other side of the screene, the parson of the parish and the lord of the manor and his sisters. The window-cases, door-cases, and chimneys of all the house, are marble. He showed us a black boy that he had, that died of a consumption ; and, being dead, he caused him to be dried in an oven, and lies there entire in a box. By and by to dinner, where his lady I find yet handsome, but hath been a very handsome woman ; now is old. Hath brought him over £100,000, and now he lives, no man in England in greater plenty, and commands both king and council with his credit he gives them. After dinner Sir Robert led us up to his long gallery, very fine, above stairs ; and better, or such, furniture I never did see."

After one or two changes of ownership, Swakeleys passed by sale in 1750 to the family of the Clarkes, and is now the seat of Mr. Thomas Truesdale Clarke. The patronage of the rectory of Ickenham had been annexed to the manor time out of mind, until it was purchased by Mr. Thomas Clarke, in 1743.

---

* See "Old and New London," Vol. I., p. 405.

"A branch of the noble family of Hastings," observes the author of the "Beauties of England," "formerly resided in this parish, and it appears that here 'Katharine, the dowgter of the Lord Hastyngs and the Lady his wyff, was borne, the Saterday before our Lady-day the Assumption, being the 11 day of August, and was christened the 20 of August, the Godmother Quene Kateryn, by her *debite*, beyng her syster, one Mr. Harberd's wiff; the other Godmother the Lady Margaret Dugles, the Kyng's nece, and the Godfather the

of Ickenham, we again find ourselves in a remote and straggling village, four miles from every railway station, and therefore most primitive. Out of its entire population of some fifteen hundred souls, only a hundred or so live round the original village green, now an open roadway, on the eastern side of which stands the finest and handsomest village church in all Middlesex, Harrow only excepted. The churchyard has been raised in its level by the burials of the inhabitants for centuries, and at its south-west and north-west

SWAKELEYS.

angles are some picturesque church-houses, which show by their projecting timbers that they have stood there for centuries.

Ruislip, which is always pronounced as Ricelip, has had its name spelt in an almost endless variety of ways, as Riselepe, Rouslip, Rueslyppe, Ruslip, and Rislepe. It is bordered on the north by the hills of Hertfordshire; whilst Northolt and Ickenham touch it on the south. On the west and north-west it is bounded by Harefield. It is said to be the largest parish in Middlesex, with the single exception of Edmonton; its area being about 6,350 acres, with a population in 1871 of 1,482. Of these, however, no less than 500 belong to Eastcot, while 500 live on Ruislip Common; about 250 also live in the ecclesiastical district of Northwood. In 1881, as in many rural parishes, the number of the inhabitants had somewhat diminished.

Lord Russell, beyng the Lorde Prive Seale, by hys *debite*, Master Francis Russell, hys son and heyre, 1542.' This daughter of Francis Lord Hastings, afterwards Earl of Huntingdon, whose baptism is thus curiously recorded, was married to Henry Clinton, Earl of Lincoln. Anne Parr, daughter of the Marquis of Northampton, and wife of William Herbert, afterwards Earl of Pembroke, is the personage described as 'one Mr. Harberd's wiff.'"

Roger Crab, a singular fanatic, of whom a very curious account was published in a pamphlet entitled "The English Hermit, or the Wonder of the Age; 1655," resided for many years in this parish. We shall have more to say regarding this worthy when we visit his tomb at Stepney.

At Ruislip, about a mile and a half to the north

It comprises several hamlets, which were doubtless manors in former times, and East-cote,

Southcote, and West-cote, still remain as local names. A moated manor-house at Southcote has been pulled down only within the memory of the present generation.

Owing to its remote situation Ruislip has undergone but little change for many generations. At the end of the last century more than half the land in the parish was open and unenclosed, or "common fields." The north-west side of Ruislip is described in 1810 as consisting chiefly of woodland copses.

The demand for hay in the metropolis has slowly but surely brought about the extinction of arable which is taxed at 30 hides. The land is 20 carucates; there are 11 hides in demesne, on which are 3 ploughs. The freeman and villans have 12 ploughs between them, and five more might be employed. The priest has half a hide. Two villans hold a hide jointly. There are 17 villans who have a virgate each, 10 who have half a virgate each, and 7 bordars who have each 4 acres. There are 8 cottars and 4 slaves. Four foreigners hold 3 hides and a virgate. There is pasture for the cattle of the manor, and a park for beasts of the forest. Pannage there is for 1,500 hogs,

RUISLIP.

land in this locality, and so only a few acres remain under cultivation. This would have been a sad misfortune to the poorer inhabitants, but it is compensated by a new industry which has sprung up, that of sorting and cutting up firewood, of which the supply is inexhaustible. This occupies the women and children as well as the cottars.

The poor, in compensation of their ancient common lands, have the right of turning their cattle out to graze on certain meadows at Ruislip and Eastcote.

In "Domesday Book" the manor and rectory were held by the same person, the lord of the former receiving both the rents and the tithes, and paying the clergy. The following is an extract :— "Ernulph de Hesding holds the manor of Rislepe, and twenty pence rents. The total value is £20 per annum. When entered on by its present owner it was £12; in King Edward's time it was £30. It was then the property of Wilward the King's Thane."

The Ernulf here mentioned gave the manor to a monastery in France, and it is uncertain whether the monks built a priory here or found one in existence, at the time of the transfer; but in 1259 it appears that there was at Ruislip a religious house with a prior, dependent on the abbey of Bec in Normandy. Before the end of the same century, it would seem to have been annexed to the priory of Okeburn, or Ogborne, in Wiltshire. The latter, however, was confiscated by Henry IV., and soon afterwards we find the manor of Ruislip in the hands of John, Duke of Bedford (the king's third son), who bestowed the manor on the Dean and Canons of Windsor, who still are its owners and patrons. According to Cobbett's " History of the Reformation " the annual value of the above-mentioned priory at the Dissolution, was £18. On the death of the Duke the manor was given (1442) to the University of Cambridge, but subsequently to the Provost and Fellows of King's College, Cambridge, who still own the manor farm— a moated house a little north-west of the church, and probably standing on the site of the former priory.

Little is known of the other manors in Ruislip, except that in the year 1378 that of Southcote was held by Alice Perrers, under the priors of Harmondsworth and Okeburn. It now belongs to the Sheppard family.

In 1650 the vicarage of Ruislip was valued at £60, including 29 acres of glebe; but this value has been largely augmented by the enclosure of the common fields.

The prior of Okeburn would seem to have first appointed a vicar to discharge the spiritual duties of the parish; and the list of vicars is pretty complete from 1300 to the present time.

The parish church is dedicated to St. Martin: its details are described at length in "Church Walks in Middlesex" (1845). At that time the beauty of the fabric was spoiled by a huge west gallery, and other monstrosities of the "Church-wardian" era. It consists of a nave, chancel, and side aisles, separated from the nave by circular and octagonal pillars placed alternately, with Pointed arches. The south aisle is four feet higher than the north, and has at its western extremity a lofty tower. It is probably the oldest part of the church, and may have been, indeed, the original edifice.

The ancient font is square, supported by four circular pillars rising out of a stone base. It is probably Late Norman or Early English. The nave is separated from the chancel by two low and ancient carved doors, and a Pointed arch, beneath which in former times was the rood-loft.

The roofs of the side-aisles are very handsome, and are in their original condition; the corbels that support the roof timbers are still uncarved. The latter are of oak or walnut, and the carvings of the bosses are fine.

As might be expected in a church belonging to a religious house, there are traces of several altars having formerly existed here; and most of the walls, even those above the arches of the nave, were covered with frescoes, which have been gradually brought to light by the removal of the plaster with which the interior was long disfigured. Those in the nave are said to illustrate the parables of the New Testament; at the east end of the north aisle is a fine fresco of an angel weighing a soul in a balance, the Virgin Mary standing by and lightening the scale by the touch of her finger.

In the chancel is a long series of memorials of the Hawtrey family, whose seat was at Eastcote in this parish. The most ancient of these is to John Hawtrey, Esq., who died in 1593, and contains the effigies, in brass, of the deceased and his wife. Another stone commemorates John Hawtrey, "who made the royal oratory at Cambridge his grave and monument;" he died in 1674. On the south side of the chancel is a marble monument to another of the Hawtreys, Mary, Lady Bankes, who so gallantly defended Corfe Castle, Dorsetshire, against the Parliamentary forces in the Civil War, as did Lady Blanche Arundell at Wardour, and Lady Derby at Lathom House. She was the widow of the Hon. Sir John Bankes, Lord Chief Justice of the Court of Common Pleas, and died within a year of the day on which she saw the restoration of the monarchy.

In the north-west corner of the church is a memorial to the Rev. Thomas Bright, vicar, who left, in 1697, a weekly dole of bread to be distributed to the poor of this parish. The shelves on which the bread is put out are kept bright and clean under the tower.

Ruislip is well off for charities; some were founded by the Hawtreys, and Lady Franklin in 1737 left £100 to be distributed in clothing to poor widows; there are also other charities of later date.

The church has a fair share of new painted windows, but none are deserving of any special notice. The building was well restored about the year 1870 by Mr. Christian and Sir Gilbert Scott, the former undertaking the chancel, and the latter the nave, aisles, and tower. Many of the old open benches remain, and the rest of the church is "free and open" also. There was once here a fine peal of ten bells, but these sadly need renewal.

The registers are fairly kept. They date from the last decade of the 17th century, but contain nothing of special interest, except the record of the deaths of six centenarians between the years 1700 and 1838, a fact which speaks well for the healthiness of the parish.

In the vestry are two fine large oak chests, with ancient bands and locks of iron. In one of these is kept a copy of Jewell's " Apology," with other tracts and sermons by the same prelate; it is in its original covering of board, and has part of the chain by which it was once fastened to a desk in the nave; but it is much torn and defaced.

As a proof of the primitive condition of the inhabitants of this village, it used to be said that "one half of the population of Ruislip would be found to answer to one of four surnames." Remote from other places, the inhabitants never went abroad for their wives.

School-houses were built by King's College, Cambridge, about 1870. Mr. Thomas Clarke, of Swakeleys, established some schools here at the beginning of the present century for the gratuitous education of fifty poor children; and with the aid of subscriptions from other wealthy individuals, the children of the poorer inhabitants are partly clothed.

The reservoir on Ruislip Common extends from Cannon's Bridge for nearly a mile towards Rickmansworth. It covers an area of 80 acres, and belongs to the Grand Junction Canal Company, who use it to supply the deficiency caused by the waste of water in working their canal. The reservoir is much frequented by anglers.

Ruislip Park, which bounds the village on the east, is the seat of Frederick Tompson-Delmar, Esq. It covers upwards of forty acres of land, and is charmingly laid out with picturesque drives, and ornamented by rare old timber. It is a famous fox-hunting meet.

The hamlet of Eastcote, often called Ascot, lies about a mile eastward from the village of Ruislip, on the road towards Pinner, in the midst of a rich agricultural country. Eastcote House, the residence of Sir Samuel Morton Peto, was formerly the seat of the Hawtrey family, who were once of great note in this parish, and for many years lessees of the rectory, and of whom, as stated above, Ruislip church contains so many memorials. The mansion belongs to Mr. Francis H. Deane. On coming into the possession of his family it was considerably altered and modernised.

High Grove, another mansion in this locality, is the seat of Sir Hugh H. Campbell, Bart. The house stands on a commanding site, and the grounds, about fifty acres in extent, are prettily laid out.

Sir Thomas Franklyn resided at Eastcote in the early part of the last century. His house, which occupies a low site, was afterwards the seat of the Woodroffe family.

Northwood, a long straggling hamlet in the parish of Ruislip, on the road towards Rickmansworth, was in 1854 formed into an ecclesiastical district, which includes within its bounds portions of the parishes of Watford and Rickmansworth, in Hertfordshire. The church, dedicated to the Holy Trinity, is a handsome structure of flint and stone, in the Early English style, and many of the windows are filled with painted glass.

Northwood Hall, the seat of Mr. Daniel Norton, is the principal residence in this locality, most of the poorer inhabitants of which are occupied in agricultural pursuits or employed in the preparation of firewood.

Before we quit Ruislip it may not be out of place to mention a story having reference to the place, which has been related by the Rev. Mr. Barham, and which has Theodore Hook for its hero. Hook and a friend having borrowed a horse and gig, took a drive in the country, and had reached this village when they bethought them of dining. "Of course, you have money with you?" said Hook. "Not a sixpence; not a *sou*," was the reply. Theodore was in the same predicament—the last turnpike having exhausted his supply. "Stay," said Hook, reining up; "do you see that pretty little villa? Suppose we dine there." The suggestion was capital. "You know the owner, then?" inquired he. "Not the least in the world," was the reply. "I never saw him in all my life; but that's of no consequence. I know his name: it's E——w, the celebrated chronometer-maker; the man who got the £10,000 premium from Government, and then wound up his affairs and his watches, and retired from business. He will be delighted to see us." So saying, up he drove to the door. "Is Mr. E——w at home?" Answer: "Yes." In they went. The old gentleman appeared, and after a little staring at each other, Hook began: "Mr. E——w, happening to pass through your neighbourhood, I could not deny myself the pleasure and honour of paying my respects to you. I am conscious that it may seem impertinent, but your ability overcame me in regard for the common forms of society, and I and my friend here were resolved, come what might, to have it in our power to say that we had seen you, and enjoyed, for a few minutes, the company of an individual famous throughout the civilised world."

The old gentleman was caught. Shaking of hands and a few more compliments followed, and presently the remark, "But, gentlemen, you are far from town; it's getting late; pray do me the honour of staying and dining, quite, as we say, in the family way—now, pray, gentlemen, do stay."

The two visitors consulted gravely. It was impossible. They must return to town, Hook adding a little more compliment, which elicited a still more pressing invitation from the chronometer-maker. At length they agreed to stay and dine, and join in a bottle of "Barnes's best." The dinner despatched, the bottle was multiplied by six. The host was as happy as a king, and would not allow his new friends to depart without a pledge to repeat their visit.

Harefield, to which place we now direct our steps, adjoins Uxbridge on the north, and occupies a wide extent of country lying to the north-west of Ruislip. It is a long and scattered village, and, like Ruislip, extends to the extreme north of the county, where it is bordered by the parish of Rickmansworth. It consists mostly of pleasant upland scenery, from which a good view of the long broad meadows on either side of the river Colne is obtained.

The Colne and the Grand Junction Canal, which unites the Thames at Brentford with Staffordshire and the North, serve as a boundary on the left as you walk from Uxbridge to Harefield, and cut off the wayfarer from the pleasant groves and fisheries of Denham. In fact, the Colne bounds the parish on the west for nearly five miles. This river and its surroundings are evidently alluded to by Milton in the following lines in " L'Allegro " :—

> " Meadows trim, with daisies pied,
> Shallow brooks and rivers wide."

Harefield is more rich in historical associations perhaps than any rural village within the county of Middlesex. When Milton was resident at Horton the old manor house was the residence of Lord Keeper Egerton and his wife, the Countess Dowager of Derby, whom Queen Elizabeth had once honoured by a visit of three days in one of her royal progresses. The courtly knight and his lady survived the costly visit. But we are anticipating the order of events.

Of the early history of Harefield Lysons tells us that in the time of Edward the Confessor the place belonged to the Countess Goda, and that at the Domesday survey it was held by Richard, the son of Gilbert, Earl of Briou. It afterwards passed into the hands of the Bacheworths, and from them by marriage to the Swanlands, and from them in the same manner to the Newdigates ; but was alienated by them to the Andersons, by whom the property was sold at the commencement of the 17th century to the Egertons, from whom it passed in marriage to Grey, Lord Chandos. In 1655 Lord Chandos bequeathed Harefield to his widow, who re-married, first with Sir William Sedley, Bart., and secondly, on the decease of Sir William, with Mr. George Pitt. By this latter husband (in whom and his heirs she had vested all her estates) the manors of Harefield and More Hall—of which latter we shall speak presently— were sold to Sir Richard Newdigate, Bart., Serjeant-at-law, and grandson of Mr. John Newdigate, who had exchanged the estate with Sir Edmund Anderson, and so came back to a squire whose ancestors have held it, with only a temporary interval, for

nearly 600 years—a fact without parallel in Middlesex.

But the greatest event in the history of Harefield was the three days' visit of Queen Elizabeth to Sir Thomas Egerton, to which we have already alluded. It took place in July—August, 1602, and is fully described, from the Newdigate MSS., in J. G. Nichols's " Progresses of Queen Elizabeth," vol. iii., pp. 586—93, and also in the " Pictorial Shakespeare," from which we quote the following particulars :—" The Queen came to Harefield on the 31st of July, and remained there during the 1st and 2nd of August. In those days Harefield Place was a 'fair house, standing on the edge of the hill, the river Coln passing near the same through the pleasant meadows and sweet pastures, yielding both delight and profit. . . .' The weather, we learn from a copy of verses presented to the Queen on the occasion, was unpropitious :—

> " ' Only poor St. Swithin now
> Doth hear you blame his cloudy brow.'

Some great poet was certainly at work on this occasion, but not Shakespeare. It was enough for them to present the sad story of

> " ' The gentle lady married to the Moor.'

Another was to come within some thirty years, who should sing of Harefield with the power of rare fancy working upon classical models, and who thus makes the genius of the wood address a noble audience in that sylvan scene :—

> " ' Yet know, by lot from Jove, I am the power
> Of this fair wood, and like in oaken bower
> To nurse the sapling tall, and curl the grove
> With ringlets quaint, and wanton windings weave ;
> And all my plants I save from nightly ill
> Of noisome winds and blasting vapours chill ;
> And from the boughs brush off the evil dew,
> And heal the harms of thwarting thunder blue ;
> Or what the cross dire-looking planet smites,
> Or hurtful worm with canker'd venom bites.
> When evening grey doth rise, I fetch my round
> Over the mount and all this hallowed ground ;
> And early, ere the odorous breath of morn
> Awake the slumbering leaves, or tassel'd horn
> Shakes the highth thicket, haste I all about,
> Number my ranks, and visit every sprout
> With puissant words, and murmurs made to bless.'

Doubly-honoured Harefield ! Though the mansion has perished, yet are thy groves still beautiful. Still thy summit looks out upon a fertile valley, where the gentle river wanders in silent beauty. But thy woods and lawns have a charm which are wholly their own. Here possibly the *Othello* of Will Shakespeare was acted by his own company ; here is the scene of the 'Arcades' of John Milton."

The visit of the virgin queen to Harefield was

within a year or two of her death, and when she was upwards of seventy. In the Newdigate MSS. above referred to the curious reader will find how her Majesty was met near the dairy-house by a dairy-maid and a bailiff, who celebrated her praises in alternate verse, whilst the royal personage herself sat on her horse beneath a tree on account of the rain. In another part of the grounds her Majesty was entertained by a "dialogue of welcome" between some fanciful characters, called "Place" and "Time;" and again on the next morning she was serenaded as—

> "Beauty's rose and virtue's book,
> Angel's mind and angel's look."

It should be added that the queen was addressed in the same style of fanciful and fulsome flattery at her departure.

"It has been said," observes Mr. Thorne, in his Handbook of the Environs of London, "that the Lord Chamberlain's company was brought down to Harefield to play *Othello* before her, Shakespeare himself being present probably to direct the performance." But this statement he sees reason to distrust, both on other grounds and on account of the silence of the Newdigate MSS. on the subject. Still, the Egerton Papers, published by the Camden Society, under date August 6th, 1602, give us the following entry among the steward's expenses during Elizabeth's visit to Harefield: "Rewards to the Vaulters, Players, and Dancers, £64 18s. 10d.;" and it is known that Shakespeare was one of the company so indicated. One would like to be certain, however, that the eyes of Shakespeare as well as those of Milton, once looked on these scenes.

We gather from the Life of Milton that during the five years of his early manhood, which he spent mainly at his father's house at Horton, he was a frequent visitor at Harefield; and the heading of his "Arcades" tells us that it formed "part of an entertainment presented to the Countess Dowager of Derby at that place by some noble persons of her family." As her ladyship was then advanced in years, it is more than probable that these "noble persons of her family" were her little youthful grandchildren, the issue of the Earl of Bridgewater (son of the Lord Keeper Egerton), who had married Lady Frances Stanley, the second daughter of the Countess. One would like to have been there to witness their graceful appearance on the scene "in pastoral habit, and moving toward the seat of state," whereon sat the Countess as a "Rural Queen," as they sang the first stanza of "Arcades," probably alluding to Queen Elizabeth's previous visit—

> "Look, nymphs and shepherds, look,
> What sudden blaze of Majesty
> Is that which we from hence descry?
> Too divine to be mistook.
>   This, this is she
> To whom our vows and wishes bend
> Here our solemn search hath end."

Another stanza sung by the youthful band ran as follows :—

> "Mark, what radiant state she spreads,
>   In circle round her shining throne,
> Shooting her beams like silver threads;
>   This, this is she alone,
> Sitting like a goddess bright,
> In the centre of her light."

It is probable that Milton was thinking of the festivities at Harefield when he wrote in "L'Allegro":—

> "There let Hymen oft appear
> In saffron robe with taper clear,
> And pomp, and feast, and revelry,
> With masque and antique pageantry;
> Such sights as youthful poets dream
> On summer eve by haunted stream."

Harefield Place was burnt to the ground in 1660, the fire being traditionally referred to the carelessness of the witty and accomplished Sir Charles Sedley, the profligate companion of Charles II., who is said to have been reading in bed.

"This tradition," observes the author of "The Beauties of England," "is not altogether destitute of an air of probability, for although Sir William Sedley died in 1656, and his widow had in the meantime taken a third husband, George Pitt, Esq., yet it is by no means unlikely that the gay and careless Sir Charles might, in 1660, be at Harefield, on a visit to his sister-in-law."

The mansion was rebuilt by Sir Richard Newdigate, who had re-purchased the property of Mr. Pitt, in 1675, but not quite on the same site as the old house.

Sir Roger Newdigate was residing at Harefield Place, in 1743, when he was elected M.P. for Middlesex. Sir Roger was the founder of the prize for English Verse which bears his name at Oxford, and causes him to be commemorated among the benefactors of the University. Having fixed his principal residence at Arbury, in Warwickshire, Sir Roger sold Harefield Place, disjoined from the manor, to John Truesdale, Esq., from whose executors it was purchased, in 1780, by William Baynes, Esq., whose son, Christopher, was created a baronet, by the title of Sir Christopher Baynes, of Harefield Place.

Mr. Charles Newdigate Newdegate, who inherited the Middlesex estates of Sir Roger, re-purchased

Harefield Place from Sir Christopher Baynes, and having chosen for his residence a seat near at hand, called Harefield Lodge, he pulled down Harefield Place towards the end of the last century.

The avenue of elms through which Queen Eliza-

in the last century may be seen in the *Gentleman's Magazine* for January, 1815. The old manor-house must have been well off for the accessories of shady trees in Milton's time, if he wrote of it, as doubtless he did, without exaggeration—

HAREFIELD PLACE. (*From a Print in the Gentleman's Magazine, 1815.*)

beth rode from Dew's Farm to the house is gone, though several of the trees were still standing in the time when Lysons wrote, and one or two even as late as 1814-15, if we may believe "Sylvanus Urban;" but, alas! they are now no more, though vigorous successors have taken their place. The house, too, as above stated, is gone, but its site can still be plainly seen in the rear of the church, where the old garden walls and fine level terraces still attest its former grandeur. A view of it as it was

" O'er the smooth enamell'd green,
　Where no print of step hath been,
　　Follow me, as I sing,
　　And touch the warbled string,
　Under the shady roof
　Of branching elm star proof,
　　　Follow me ;
　I will bring you where she sits,
　Clad in splendour, as befits
　　　Her deity.
　Such a rural queen
　All Arcadia hath not seen. "

And the whole demesne must have had beauties and charms, which have disappeared with the old mansion, if he could write with truth—

> Nymphs and shepherds, dance no more
>   By sandy Ladon's lilied banks ;
> On old Lycæus, or Cyllene hoar,
>   Trip no more in twilight ranks ;
> Though Erymanth your loss deplore,
>   A better soil shall give ye thanks.
> From the stony Mænalus
> Bring your flocks and live with us ;
> Here ye shall have greater grace,
> To serve the lady of this place."

The "Arcades" was performed here, as we learn from Milton's Life, in 1635, and the worthy " lady of this place" did not long survive. Her fine marble monument in the chancel of the church bears the date of her death, 1637.

What would one not have given to have seen with his own eyes the poet brushing the morning dew, as he sauntered through the meadows along the bank of his favourite river, the Colne, with its " brimming waves," or quietly trudging along the road through Uxbridge, on his way from Horton to Harefield Place, which doubtless then was, in his own words—

> "Bosom'd high in tufted trees."

The elms and beeches and evergreens behind the site of the house are still fine, but few, except one stately cedar, would seem to be able to recall the look of the poet.

About a furlong south-west of the site of the old manor-house, abutting on the edge of the meadows of the Colne, opposite the " Fishery" at Denham, and standing a little from the road, is an old farm-house, some parts of the interior of which retain the ancient panelling and large fire-places, suggesting that in the olden time large logs were burnt here in the winter, and profuse hospitality was exercised. The house is now cut up into three labourers' cottages. It is still called the Moor Hall, and is the most ancient manor-house in the parish. The greater part of the old hall was pulled down towards the end of the last century.

Lysons tells us that the manor of Moor Hall was the property of the Knights Hospitallers, to whom it was given by Alice, daughter of Baldwin de Clare. Close by it, indeed almost adjoining it, is an Early English chapel, with lancet windows, externally almost perfect, though quite " gutted" in its interior of every vestige of its once sacred uses. The timber roof stands sound and good, just as it did in the days of the Tudors and Plantagenets. This chapel was probably a cell subject to the Priory of St. John at Clerkenwell. Some persons

consider that the building was not a chapel, but a refectory, but for this there are no grounds. The building and cottages are rich in red and grey tints, and they have been often sketched by artists.

A short walk across some upland grass fields leads from Moor Hall to the church, which is situated, as was so often the case, in the middle of the squire's park, some three or four hundred yards from the road.

The church, so far as can be ascertained through the veil thrown over it by a poor modern " restora-

LADY DERBY'S TOMB.   (See page 248.)

tion," seems to be of the " Decorated" period, but perhaps a somewhat late specimen. It consists of nave and chancel, with aisles on either side. Probably no country church is so rich in mural monuments, mostly of the Tudor and Jacobean eras. The Egertons, Ashbys, and Newdigates innumerable here mix their aristocratic dust with that of their poorer brethren. A really fine collection of helmets, casques, gloves, and other funeral armour, once belonging to the Bacheworths and Swanlands and Egertons, but now taken down from the walls, lies heaped together, dusty and uncared for, on the sedilia to the south of the communion-table. The Brackenbury chapel, which forms the south aisle, is constructed of alternate dice-work, or diversified compartments of flint and stone. The chancel is elevated above the nave, and is reached by an ascent of six steps. On the east wall of the Brackenbury chapel is a monument, bearing a long Latin inscription, to the memory of Sir Richard Newdigate, Bart., who died in 1678. Sir Roger Newdigate, the last baronet of his family, who died in 1806, is also commemorated by a tablet, as also are many other members of that ancient house. The monument of Milton's friend above mentioned, Alice, Countess Dowager of Derby, who died in 1637, occupies the south-east corner of the chancel. It is an elaborate work of art, after the fashion of the above period, being gorgeously decorated with drapery and heraldic ornaments. The effigy of the countess, in her state dress, reposes beneath a lofty canopy, while the lower compartment, which is level with the floor of the chancel, contains the kneeling effigies of her three daughters, Lady Chandos and the Countesses of Bridgewater and Huntingdon. The countess, as stated above, became the wife of Lord Keeper Egerton, who, as the inscription on this monument states, had, by his first wife, an only daughter, who was mother of Juliana, Lady Newdigate. The monuments of various members of the Newdigate family might be said to "adorn" the walls of the church, if it were not that such cumbrous and costly structures sadly detract from the beauty of the sacred edifice itself, and tell rather of human pride and vain-glory than of humility and repentance. Among others is a kneeling effigy of Lady Newdigate, formerly one of the maids of honour to Queen Elizabeth. When Mr. Newdigate, as lord of the manor and squire, "restored" the church, he ordered the monuments to be repaired, and their inscriptions and heraldic bearings repainted.

On the north side of the chancel is a parclose, screening off the chantry and burial-place of the family of Ashby of Brakespeare. A mural tablet on the north wall, bearing the effigy of a man in armour, kneeling at a faldstool beneath a canopy, commemorates Sir Robert Ashby, who died in 1617; and close by is another mural tablet, to the memory of Sir Francis Ashby, who died in 1623. Between this aisle and the nave is a monument to the memory of John Pritchett, Bishop of Gloucester, who died in 1680. He was promoted to the see of Gloucester in 1672, after having been curate of this parish for nearly thirty years.

On the outside of the north wall of the chancel is a most curious monument and epitaph. It consists of a medallion, with a portrait, in rather slight relief, of a gamekeeper with his dog and gun, passing through a background of trees. Beneath it is the following inscription, which I believe has never been printed in any collection of epitaphs, though its quaintness well merits such an honour:

"William Ashby of Brakespeare, Esquire, erected this to the memory of his faithful servant, Robert Mossenden, who departed this life Feby. 5th, 1744, aged 60 years.

"In frost and snow, through hail and rain,
He scour'd the woods and trudg'd the plain;
The steady pointer leads the way,
Stands at the scent, then springs the prey;
The timorous birds from stubble rise,
With pinions stretch'd divide the skys;
The scatter'd lead pursues the sight,
And death in thunder stops their flight.
This spaniel, of true English kind,
Who's gratitude inflam'd his mind:
This servant in an honest way,
In all his actions copy'd Tray."

The village of Harefield stretches away along the roadside for a considerable distance through a quiet valley, having on the north and east well-wooded uplands, dotted over with lordly domains, and on the south-west broad green meadows, bordering the canal and River Colne. Harefield numbered altogether in 1881 between 300 and 400 houses, with a population of 1,500, being a slight diminution upon the census returns for 1871. The village, with its Lecture Hall and Working Men's Club, possesses a quiet and flourishing appearance, and the name of one of its principal local worthies of bygone times is perpetuated in the "Brakespeare Arms," the sign given to a quiet roadside hostelry.

It may be added, that, lying as it does so far out of the beaten tracks, this parish is perhaps richer than any other within Middlesex in country seats. Towards the northern end are Harefield Park, the seat of Colonel Vernon, and Harefield House, of Sir John Byles. Brakespeare, formerly the seat of the Ashbys, now the seat of Mrs. Drake, is nearer to the church, and towards the centre of the parish. It is said to have got its name from having once belonged to the family which gave Pope Adrian IV. to the Western Church. The house is old-fashioned, and stands on high ground in a pleasantly-wooded park.

Nearer to Uxbridge stands the modern Harefield Place, lately sold by Mr. Newdegate, and now the property and residence of Colonel Cox. All the game hereabouts is strictly preserved; and in consequence, as you walk along the shady lanes leading to the "Brakespeare Arms" from the church, you may see partridges and pheasants strutting about to their heart's content, and secure from harm.

CHAPTER XXIV.

PINNER AND HARROW.

"Again I behold where for hours I have ponder'd,
  As reclining at eve on yon tombstone I lay ;
  Or round the steep brow of the churchyard I wander'd,
  To catch the last gleam of the sun's setting ray."
                                                    BYRON.

Situation of Harrow, and Nature of the Soil—The Village of Pinner—Population—The River Pin—Miss Howard's Charity—Market and Fairs—The Parish Church—Centenarians—A Curious Custom—Schools and Cemetery—Pinner Hill House—Pinner Wood—Pinner Place—Pinner Grove—Pinner Park—Pinner Green, and Wood Hall—Woodrisings—Death of Mrs. Horatia Ward—The School of the Commercial Travellers' Society—Headstone, or Manor Farm—Etymology of Harrow—Domesday Book Record of the Parish—The Manor—Flambards—A Loyal Lady—Extent and Boundaries of Harrow—The Parish Church—Prior Bolton takes Refuge at Harrow—"Byron's Tomb"—The View from Harrow Hill—The Town and Public Institutions of Harrow.

IT is refreshing, after the many miles of dead level river-side scenery through which we have travelled, to " break ground " afresh, and to come at once upon new country. We have left the grassy vale which stretches across the west of the county from Uxbridge and Hayes, and find ourselves, after some four or five miles' walk, at the foot of the only steep ascent which Middlesex can produce, except the "northern heights" of Hampstead and Highgate. The soil is a deep stiff clay ; and we shall find that Harrow differs from those other links of the hilly chain of which it once formed part in having no deposit of gravel and sand on its summit.

The broad vale of Harrow, which stretches from the foot of the hill to Edgware and Stanmore in the north-east, and to Uxbridge and Hayes in the south-west, has really no history, and is quite a modern Bœotia. The roads are muddy and miry in winter, and till the beginning of the present century it took a waggoner and his team the best part of a day to carry a load of hay up to London ; and even then he often had to lay down a faggot of sticks in the ruts in order to enable him to get along at all. The district, however, smiles sweetly in early June, and has its attractions for the hunter in the depth of winter.

Norden, writing in the reign of Elizabeth, gives the following account of this parish :—"It may be noted how nature hath exalted that high *Harrow-on-the-Hill*, as it were in the way of ostentation to shew it selfe to all passengers to and from London, who beholding the same may saye it is the centre (as it were) of the pure vale ; for Harrow standeth invironed with a great contrye of moste pure grounds, from which hill, towardes the time of harveste, a man maye beholde the feyldes rounde about, so sweetly to address themselves to the sicle and syth, with such comfortable haboundance of all kinde of grayne, that it maketh the inhabitants to clappe theyre handes for joye to see theyr

valleys so to laugh and singe. Yet this fruiteful and pleasant country yeldeth little comforte unto the wayfaringe man in the winter season, by reason of the clayish nature of the soyle, which after it hath tasteth the autombe showers it beginneth to mix deep and tirtye, yeldinge unsavory passage to horse and man. Yet the countrye swayne holdeth it a sweet and pleasant garden, and with his whippe and whysell, can make himself melodye, and dance knee deepe in dirte, the whole daye not holdinge it any disgrace unto his person, Such is the force of hope of future proffitt.

  The deepe and dirdiest lothsome soyle
  Yeldes golden grayne to carefull toyle.

And that is the cause that the industrious and painful husbandman will refuse a pallace, to droyle in theys golden puddles."

Pinner, through which we must pass before reaching Harrow, is situated on the main road running north-westward to Rickmansworth and Amersham, about equi-distant from Ruislip and Harrow-on-the-Hill, being about three miles from each of those places, a mile and a half south-west from Pinner Station on the North-Western Railway, and about thirteen miles from London. It is a busy and thriving village, the main street being broad, well paved, and lighted with gas, and containing several respectable shops and private houses of modern growth, interspersed with many of a more picturesque and antiquated appearance, of the lath-and-plaster style of building, with projecting storeys and gabled roofs. Not the least interesting among these houses is the "Queen's Head," an old-fashioned roadside tavern on the north side of the street, dating its erection from early in the last century, as the date 1705, painted upon its front, bears witness.

In 1871 the number of inhabited houses in Pinner was set down in the census returns as 396, the population amounting to 2,332, of whom about 250 were inmates of the Commercial Travellers'

Schools, of which we shall speak presently. The number of the inhabitants had increased during the succeeding ten years to a little over 2,500.

The village is pleasantly located on the rising ground which forms the north-western side of the vale of Harrow, and from this elevated spot flows one of the feeders of the River Colne, a little rivulet, called the Pin, which is crossed at the bottom of the main street by an antiquated bridge of one arch. Near the bridge stand three dwellings for widows of officers, founded by Miss Maria Charlotte Howard, of York Place, about half a century ago. Miss Howard, it appears, left the sum of £45,000 in money and land to found a charity, to erect twenty-one houses on her property here. They were to have been built in the form of a crescent : the centre house for the trustees, and the remainder to be appropriated to twenty widows, who were to live in them rent and tax free, and to receive each a stipend of £50 a year. The widows of naval men were to have the preference, after them the widows of military men, and afterwards the widows of clergymen. This munificent bequest, however, was never fully carried out, for, owing to some family feud, the estate got into Chancery, with the result that only three of the houses have as yet been built. They are good, substantial brick-built residences, and, in accordance with the stipulation of the bequest, are in the occupation of the widows of officers.

Pinner was simply a hamlet and chapelry of Harrow, and part of the same demesne, but was made into a separate parish about a quarter of a century ago. The village, nevertheless, formerly possessed a weekly market, which was granted by Edward III. in 1336 to the Archbishop of Canterbury, who was at that time lord of the manor. Two yearly fairs were also granted at the same time, of which, however, only one survives. This has degenerated into an insignificant pleasure-fair, which is held annually on Whit Monday.

At the eastern or upper end of the main street stands the parish church, the picturesque effect of which, as seen on approaching it, is heightened by the almost leafless trunk of an aged elm-tree. The church, dedicated to St. John the Baptist, is of ample dimensions, consisting of chancel, with a side aisle or chapel, appropriated to the use of the children of the Commercial Travellers' Schools, transepts, a clerestoried nave of five bays, aisles, south porch, and an embattled tower at the west end. The tower has a pyramidal tiled roof, surmounted by a tall wooden cross, and at the north-west corner a bold turret rises high above the battlements. The interior of the tower is open to the nave, and the bells bear the date of 1772. The building is constructed mainly of flint and stone ; and although its erection was completed in 1321, the lancet-shaped windows of the transepts and south aisle would appear to have belonged to a building of much earlier date. The church has been considerably altered and enlarged at various periods, the chancel aisle having been added as recently as 1879, at which time the edifice was thoroughly restored. The nave is separated from the aisles by Pointed arches, springing from octangular pillars. In the south transept are the remains of a piscina of the Perpendicular period. The font is large and of about the same above-mentioned date ; the exterior of the basin forms an octagon, the different compartments of which are ornamented with devices of roses, &c., in quatrefoils, the basin itself resting upon an octangular pillar. Several of the windows contain painted glass, that of one of the lancets being of ancient date. The east window, of Perpendicular design, is modern, a reproduction of its predecessor, but is now filled with stained glass. It is of five lights, and was inserted in memory of the Rev. Edward Thomas Burrow, incumbent, who died in 1861. The reredos, which is very handsome, was erected in 1871 by Mr. John Weall, of this parish, in memory of his wife and two daughters. This church contains but few monuments, and even those are but of little interest. Among them is a mural tablet, of black marble, to the memory of John Day, minister of Pinner, who died in 1662. On this tablet is represented the effigy of the deceased in profile, kneeling before a desk ; and it has also upon it an inscription, commencing—

" This portraiture presents him to thy sight
    Who was a burning and a shining light."

The families of Clitherow, Page, and Hastings, are also commemorated by monumental inscriptions in the church. In the vestry is preserved a small brass, originally in the chancel, to the memory of a "chrysom child," the daughter of Eustace Bedingfeld, dated 1580.

In the churchyard, close by the south porch, is the gravestone of Sir Bartholomew Shower, of Pinner Hill, who died in 1701, and who, if an entry in the parish register is to be believed, was "buried in sheep's wool only." If we may judge from the ages recorded on many of the head-stones here, Pinner would appear to be a healthy place to live in, or at all events one favourable to longevity. Several may be noticed buried here whose ages have exceeded the allotted "three score years and ten." In 1851, Ann, widow of James Winfield, died at the age of 100; in 1553, Betty, the widow of William Evans, passed away at the age of 102; and William Skenelsby, who died in 1775, appears to have reached the extraordinary age of 118.

It is recorded that the barbarous custom of throwing at cocks as a Shrovetide festivity was formerly practised at Pinner with much public ardour, and the money collected at this disagreeable celebration was applied to the aid of the poor's rates. The custom was discontinued about the year 1680.

National schools, capable of holding 300 children, were established in this village in 1866. A new cemetery has been laid out on the east side of the village, it comprises about two acres, and contains two mortuary chapels.

In the neighbourhood of Pinner are several good seats and family residences. Pinner Hill, which lies away on the high ground to the north-west, is the seat of Mr. William Arthur Tooke, at whose cost the church has been principally restored. The house stands in ornamental park grounds, and commands extensive views. It was formerly the residence of Sir Christopher Clitherow, and afterwards of Sir Bartholomew Shower, whose name we have mentioned above. Sir Bartholomew was an eminent lawyer in his day, and was the author of some legal works and political pamphlets. Sir Albert Pell, some time a Judge of the Court of Bankruptcy, lived here half a century ago.

Pinner Wood House, near the above, the residence of Mr. R. H. Silversides, was for some time in the occupation of Lord Lytton, who here wrote his " Eugene Aram."

Pinner Place, the seat of Mr. James Garrard, was formerly the residence of Mr. John Zephaniah Holwell, some time Governor of Bengal, and author of a narrative of the sufferings of himself and fellow-prisoners in the " Black Hole " of Calcutta. Mr. Holwell was also the author of an historical work relating to Hindostan.

Pinner Grove, northward of the village, is approached through a fine avenue of elms, and stands in ornamental park-like grounds. It was formerly the residence of Sir Michael Foster, one of the Justices of the King's Bench in the last century, and afterwards of Sir Francis Milman, Bart., M.D.

Pinner Park appears to have been formerly a district of some importance, as Nicholas, Abbot of Westminster, was appointed its keeper in 1383. The estate, however, has long been broken up and converted to agricultural puposes. In the reign of Henry VIII. it was granted, together with the manor of Harrow, to Sir Edward (afterwards Lord)

North; and in 1630 the property was alienated by Dudley, Lord North, to the Hutchinson family. The estate ultimately passed into the possession of St. Thomas's Hospital, having been purchased in the year 1731 by the governors of that institution, by whom it is now held.

About half a mile north of the village is Pinner Green, and near at hand is an estate, known as Wood Hall. Woodriding is a hamlet further to the north-east; it boasts of some good villa residences and a chapel-of-ease. Here, in March of the year 1881, died, at the age of eighty, Mrs. Horatia Nelson Ward, widow of the Rev. Philip Ward, Vicar of Tenterden, Kent. She was the " little Horatia," the adopted daughter of Emma, Lady Hamilton, whom her father, Lord Nelson, with his dying breath, commended to the care of his ungrateful country.

Close by the Pinner railway station stand the schools belonging to the Commercial Travellers' Society, which were founded in 1845. The building, a large and roomy structure of red brick, with stone dressings, of Gothic design, was opened in 1855, the ceremony being presided over by the Prince Consort. The plan of the building consists mainly of a large central hall, the upper floor of which forms the principal school-room, having beneath it the dining-hall. At each end of the hall are the dormitories, and the residences of the masters and mistresses. In 1868 wings were added to the original building, rendering it capable of holding between 300 and 400 children. A cloister-like arcade, extending along the principal front, on either side of the hall, serves as a covered playground for the children. In 1876–77 the building was extended by means of a subscription amounting to £17,000, raised in a single year by Mr. James Hughes; and in 1878 an infirmary and baths were added, through the bequest of Mr. George Moore, the philanthropist.

The design of this institution is "the clothing, maintenance, and education of the destitute orphans of deceased and the children of necessitous commercial travellers." The institution is carried on by means of donations and subscriptions given for that purpose, and the government of the affairs of the schools is vested in a general court and a board of management. On the walls of the entrance-lobby are several ornamental tablets commemorative of munificent bequests to the institution, and in the board-room are several full-length portraits of governors and others connected with the schools. The institution, it may be added, seems admirably conducted. The boys receive a superior education, and leave the schools at the age of fifteen.

At a short distance from Pinner, towards the south-east, is a farm, termed "Headstone," or, more generally, the "Manor Farm." The dwelling-house is large and of some antiquity, and is surrounded by a moat. The name was formerly written Heggeton, or Hegeston; and a mansion on the site was the occasional residence of the Archbishops of Canterbury in times long gone by. This manor is mentioned in records of the fourteenth century, at which time it was held by the see of Canterbury. When an inquisition was taken of the estates of Archbishop Arundel, who was banished ages, as stated above, one of the residences of the Archbishops of Canterbury. The most memorable event relating to the visits of these powerful manorial lords occurs in the year 1170. The famous Thomas à Becket, then Archbishop, while travelling towards Woodstock for the professed purpose of paying respect to Prince Henry, who had been recently allowed to participate in the government of the kingdom, was denied access to the Court, and commanded to repair immediately to his own diocese. It is recorded that he passed some days, on his return, at his manor of Harrow,

PINNER, IN 1828. (*From an Etching by Cook.*)

for high treason in the year 1398, it was found that he was possessed, together with other property, " of the manor of Southbury [now Sudbury], in Harrow, consisting principally of 500 acres of land, then valued at 3d. per acre ! The manor of Woodhall (a member of the former) chiefly consisted of 120 acres of land, valued at 6d. an acre ! The manor of ' Heggeton' (likewise a member of Southbury), comprising a well-built house and 201 acres of land, valued at 6d. an acre, besides meadow."

Mr. Brewer, in the "Beauties of England," says it is to be regretted that the site of the ancient manor-house of Harrow is not known, as the spot would acquire a fair share of interest from its connection with long past scenes of sacerdotal splendour. But this manor-house is most probably the place in question, as it was for many in the exercise of much dignified hospitality, and during his stay exchanged many acts of kindness with the Abbot of St. Albans. This was only a short time previous to the assassination of Becket, and the spirit of animosity which prevailed very generally in regard to this high-minded Churchman was evinced in a conspicuous manner by the resident clergy of the place. Nigellus de Sackville, rector of Harrow, and Robert de Broc, the vicar, treated him with boisterous disrespect, and are said to have maimed with their own hands one of the horses bearing his provisions, for which offence they were both excommunicated at Canterbury on the ensuing Christmas. It is a tradition in this neighbourhood that it was in the building that occupied the site of the present farm-house of Headstone that Becket sojourned at the period above mentioned; and some even go as far as to assert that he slept here on the night before his assassination. But this tradition has little to support it.

Archbishop Boniface held a visitation at Harrow in 1250, and Archbishop Winchelsye dates from Harrow in the year 1300. It may be added that Cardinal Wolsey, who, among his other preferments, held the rectory of Harrow, is said to have occasionally resided at the old manor-house. King Charles, in his flight from Oxford, came to Harrow;

usually written Herges,* the derivation of which, observes Mr. Brewer, in the "Beauties of England," probably is "from the Saxon *Hearge, Hergh,* or *Herige,* which is usually supposed to signify a concourse of armed men, but which is also translated a *church.* If," he continues, "we accept the latter reading, we may suppose that a sacred structure on the lofty hill of Harrow formed a conspicuous feature in this part of the county as early as the beginning of the ninth century, at which

PINNER CHURCH IN 1800. (*From an old Print. See page 250.*)

and had he not half-heartedly turned aside towards Newark, it is more than probable that there might never have been fought a battle of Worcester.

The present manor-house of "Heggeton," or Headstone, is a good, substantial, modern-looking residence, containing in its structural arrangements portions of an older house. The moat, square in form, and partaking somewhat of the character of those so well known at Ightham and Hever, in Kent, is crossed by a brick bridge, and encloses the house and gardens, &c., the farm buildings, including a barn of great length, being situated in front of the bridge. Some of the outbuildings are ancient and picturesque.

In ancient records the name of Harrow is

time a notice of the place first occurs on record." Lysons supposes the derivation of the name to be from the Anglo-Saxon *Hearge,* which, he says, is "sometimes translated a troop of soldiers, and sometimes a church," and adds his inclination to adopt the latter derivation, which is the same as that given above. Mr. Thorne, in his "Environs of London," observes that "*Herige* was a legion or division of an army; and as, from its commanding position, Harrow would certainly be made a military station by the Romans, it is probable that the name was given to it as the camp or station of a

* Hence Harrow School is often spoken of as Schola *Hergensis*, as well as *Harroviensis*.

legion." The syllable *Har*, it may be added, signified in the olden times *high*, or the high ground.

As we have already observed, Harrow was a place of some consideration for two or three centuries immediately succeeding the Norman Conquest, from its being the occasional residence of the Archbishops of Canterbury. Newcourt, in his "Repertorium," states, on the authority of Somner's "Antiquities of Canterbury," &c., that in the year 822 "Wilfred, Archbishop of Canterbury, recovered this place of *Herges*, together with several other lands which had been taken from the Church of Canterbury by Kenulf, King of the Mercians." If this be true, the connection of Harrow with the Church was of very early date.

"Among the MSS. formerly belonging to Bishop Tanner, now deposited in the Bodleian Library, is a bond executed by Margetta, Prioress of Kilburn, in which the name is written *Hareways*." *

In the "Domesday Survey" it is stated that the manor of *Herges* was held by Archbishop Lanfranc. "It answered (as in the time of King Edward the Confessor) for one hundred hides. There was land for seventy ploughs. Thirty hides belonged to the demesne, on which were four ploughs, and a fifth might be added. A priest had one hide, and three knights held six hides. There was pasture for the cattle of the village, and pannage for two thousand hogs," &c.

This manor of Harrow was given by Archbishop Cranmer, in exchange for other estates, to Henry VIII., and shortly after, it was granted to Sir Edward North, subsequently created Lord North. Concerning this grant, a story to the following effect is related in Collins's "Peerage." The king having taken offence at some part of Sir Edward's conduct, ordered him to his presence, and, after regarding him a while with every indication of anger, said, "We are informed you have cheated us of certain lands in Middlesex!" To this unexpected accusation the knight answered with a humble negative. "How was it, then," resumed Henry, "did we *give* those lands to you?" "Your Majesty was indeed pleased so to do," replied Sir Edward.

It appears that the question was not urged further, and the estates remained in the possession of the North family until the year 1630, when they passed by sale to the families of Philips and Pytts. By the marriage of Alice, daughter of Edmund Pytts, the manor passed to James Rushout, who in 1661 was created a baronet, and the manorial rights have ever since continued in the family.

This Sir James Rushout purchased an estate at Northwick, in Worcestershire, and he was for many years M.P. for Evesham. His son, Sir John, took an active part in public affairs, and was a distinguished opponent of the administration of Sir Robert Walpole. He married Lady Anne Crompton, daughter of the fourth Earl of Northampton, and was succeeded by his son—likewise Sir John—who, after having represented Evesham in several Parliaments, was created Lord Northwick in 1797.

The manor-house of Flambards, formerly the seat of Lord Northwick, and one of the principal residences in the town, derived its name from a former possessor, Sir John Flambard, who lived in the reign of Edward III. The property was subsequently vested in the family of Gerard, from whom, after an intermediate transmission, it passed to that of Page. The last of that name, Mr. Richard Page, commenced re-building the house, which, on his death, was sold to and completed by Lord Northwick. Harrow Park covers part of old Flambards. The name is perpetuated in that of a modern house on the site, occupied by Mr. William Winkley, F.S.A., who owns the picture of Elizabeth the heiress of Sir Charles Gerard and grandmother of the first Lord Lake, a descendant of Henry VII. and Elizabeth of York.

Another manor-house in Harrow parish, called Uxendon, or Oxinden, was the house of a widow named Bellamy, a pious lady, who secreted there several missionary priests—including Anthony Babington, and Father Southwell the poet—when they were being hunted down by Walsingham, under Queen Elizabeth. Mrs. Bellamy perished in the Tower of London.

The old parish of Harrow is not less than forty-five miles in circumference. It meets Hertfordshire on the north, in the neighbourhood of Watford and Bushey; westward it is bounded by Ickenham and Ruislip; southward by Perivale, Twyford, and Willesden; and eastward by Kingsbury and Hendon. At the beginning of the present century, when the whole parish was enclosed under the operation of an Act of Parliament, it contained about 13,600 acres of land, and comprised within its bounds the hamlets of Pinner, Roxey (or Roxeth), Wembley, Harrow Weald, Apperton, Kenton, and Preston, where part of John Lyon's buildings are still standing. Pinner, as we have already seen, is now made into a separate parish for civil purposes.

Harrow was one of the pleasant suburbs occasionally visited by Charles Lamb, and is frequently mentioned in his charming correspondence; but

---

* Park's "History of Hampstead," p. 187.

apart from such occasional visits, and the fact that Byron passed some of his school-boy days within its bounds, there are but few or no literary or artistic reminiscences to be gleaned here, such as we find along the banks of the Thames, and as we have already dwelt upon in dealing with the sister hills of Hampstead and Highgate.*

The parish church of Harrow, from its situation on the summit of a hill, some 300 ft. above the surrounding "plain," and insulated, as it were, in the midst of a country by no means remarkable for the boldness of its hillocks, is an object unusually conspicuous, and cannot fail to attract the notice of all who travel along the North Western Railway. It is recorded that when some divines were disputing with King Charles II. about the *visible Church*, his Majesty said that he "knew not where it was to be found, except, indeed, at Harrow." The church is large and spacious, comprising a chancel, with chancel chapel, a clerestoried nave, aisles and transept, and a square embattled tower at the west end, surmounted by a lofty spire. It appears to have been originally built by Archbishop Lanfranc, in the time of the Conqueror, though not to have been consecrated till the time of Archbishop Anselm, his successor in the see of Canterbury.

Mr. Rule writes, in his "Life and Times of St. Anselm":—"The venerable western doorway of the parish church of Harrow recalls to the historian the last grief-stricken days of Archbishop Lanfranc, who, though he outlived the completion of the sacred fabric, died ere he could cause it to be consecrated. It also recalls the pensive opening of Anselm's primacy and his first *dedicatio ecclesiæ;* for it was beneath the curiously-carved and boldly-sculptured lintel of that venerable western doorway that, on a cold January morning in A.D. 1094, the new Archbishop, arrayed in his pontifical insignia, stood, and making the sacred sign, sang aloud—

'Ecce Crucis signum, fugiant phantasmata cuncta.'

Whereupon the doors unfolded, and entering, he proceeded to perform the more solemn rites of consecration."

But Anselm was not allowed to perform this solemn act without interruption, for it appears that the Bishop of London sent two of his canons to beg him to desist, and to confer with the bishop about their mutual rights. Mr. Rule tells us that, by way of enforcing the bishop's claim, the cathedral dignitaries stole, or ran off with, the holy oil, and so broke off the ceremony. Eadmer, the

historian, tells us that the dispute respecting the consecration of this church was referred to Wulstan, Bishop of Worcester, "the only one of the Saxon prelates then remaining," and that his decision, as most consonant to the customs of the Church, was in favour of the Archbishop; and down to the present day the Archbishop of Canterbury has special rights in Harrow, and is *ex-officio* Visitor of the school; but the patronage of the living has long since passed into private hands.

Lysons, writing in 1795, asserted that "some parts of Lanfranc's building still remain—namely, the circular columns which divide the aisles from the nave, and part of the tower at the west end, where is a Saxon arch of singular form." In a paper read by Mr. Hartshorne at a meeting of the St. Paul's Ecclesiological Society, in 1882, it was stated that the circular columns were of a period long after that of Lanfranc, and that the western arch was evidently not Saxon. It was the fashion in Lysons' time to call all Norman work "Saxon," but it was probable that not one stone of Lanfranc's work now remained. "In all likelihood," continued Mr. Hartshorne, "his work consisted of buildings at the east end only, the church being carried on gradually towards the west, the tower being finally undertaken about the middle of the twelfth century. The date of 1150 would agree very well with the character of the western doorway. It was probable that this tower did not originally come much above the nave, and that it was capped with a pyramidal roof. From inside it could still be seen that the tower was once lighted by windows on the north and south, of which the inner arches remained." The most striking features of the tower are its gigantic buttresses, which are of several types. It is surmised that originally the northern tower had shallow buttresses, but that when the church was rebuilt in the early part of the fourteenth century the tower was raised from what was now the first break in the clasping buttresses. As time went on, the tower failed under the additional weight. "It was the old story of works in the Middle Ages," observed Mr. Hartshorne—"bad foundations and want of cohesion in the walls. The ruptures were remedied by casting the Late Norman pilasters—a work resulting in the formation of the ponderous clasping buttresses, probably in the early part of the fifteenth century. Fully half a century later the men of Harrow, undeterred by the failures of their forefathers, added the present wooden and leaden spire. It was a bold stroke, but it made Harrow Church, in the words of Charles the Second, ' *The* Visible Church.' . . . The isolated spire of Harrow had, perhaps, left a

---

more vivid impression upon a multitude of culti-vated minds than any other erection of the same sort throughout the kingdom. Its unique and commanding position had contributed much to this renown ; but, probably, few had realised upon what a bolstered-up sub-structure this spire was raised. Strictly speaking, it was but a wooden skeleton, craftily enough put together, but exhibiting no lines of beauty, such as might be seen in the delicate entasis of the stone spire at Leighton Buz-zard, that fitting crown of a noble cross church. Harrow spire was, in short, a surprising, and not really artistic, result of the vaulting ambition of eager, but unpractical, builders. But what boldness, what belief in their powers to surpass their prede-cessors, did it not show ! Untrammelled by the exigencies of Revivals, the Harrow men were no mere vulgar copyists : they honestly did their work in the church which they delighted to honour, and we might truly rejoice to-day that the spire still lives to tell the story of their faith."

On a fine clear day, it is said that you can see no less than thirteen counties from the top of the church-tower, almost at the foot of which, a little to the south-west, is "Byron's tomb"—not his grave, but the tombstone on which, when a boy at the school, he would lie at full length on summer afternoons and evenings, and watch the setting sun.

This tomb is an altar-shaped monument, near the south-west corner of the church. It is mentioned in the lines quoted as the motto of this chapter, from the poet's verses "On a Distant View of the Village and School of Harrow-on-the-Hill;" and it is also thus referred to by Lord Byron in a letter to Mr. Murray, dated May 26, 1822 :—"There is a spot in the churchyard, near the footpath, on the brow of the hill, looking towards Windsor, and a tomb under a large tree (bearing the name of Peachie, or Peachey), where I used to sit for hours and hours when a boy. This was my favourite spot." The tomb was re-paired by Mr. John Murray and other admirers of the poet a few years ago.

The whole body of the church, from the tower eastward, was apparently rebuilt in the first quarter of the fourteenth century, and the circular columns mentioned above belonged rather to that period than to Lanfranc's time, as Lysons supposed.

The walls of the church as they now stand are almost wholly modern, externally at least, the building having been "thoroughly restored" by Sir Gilbert Scott in 1840. "Forty years ago," remarked Mr. Hartshorne, in his lecture above quoted, "the stones of this building were alive to tell their own story, for each successive generation

of builders had left its mark upon the church in its own style. The story was, perhaps, not always a pleasing one : for instance, the works of the Georgian period did not always commend them-selves to our judgment ; but where was any part of that story now ? One would have liked to have found on the outside as well as inside some original evidence of the genius of the workmen of the four-teenth and fifteenth centuries—some fragment at least of the ancient Perpendicular, some vestige of old flint work. Not a scrap of any of those things remained. The human interest of an old building was not comprised solely in its date, its early or incidental work or repairs ; we could not choose the one period and reject the other any more than we could pin our historic faith upon the strifes of the Roses and ignore the nobler struggles of the Civil Wars. The whole fabric of an old church was a sermon in stone, easily read, and showing in its successive changes the poverty, wealth, earnestness, and faith of the community in which it was set down ; it was a chapter in the history of a country ; it was in one sense the story of a district. But it was cheering to believe that a restoration of the kind which this church underwent would be nearly impossible at the present day. We had learned much in the last forty years, but the teaching had involved the loss of much that was very precious—much that, properly understood, was of the deepest historical interest, for it was impossible in the case of an old church to divorce history from architecture."

At the time of the restoration of the church in 1840, the chancel was lengthened, and a north aisle added to it ; and the noble open timber roof, of the Perpendicular period, with upright figures of angels playing on musical instruments on the corbels, was exposed. The east window is filled with painted glass, in memory of the Rev. John W. Cunningham, who died in 1861, having been for half a century vicar of this parish. Apart from the tower, the roofing, and the very fine chancel arch, there is now but little of antiquarian interest in the walls of this church, excepting the north and south doorways, both of which are of the Decorated period, that on the south side having a priest's chamber, or parvise, over it. The font, a large circular marble basin, rudely carved, and resting upon a thick cable pedestal, is probably a remnant of Lanfranc's church ; or, at all events, the bowl would appear to date back to the eleventh century ; the rim and base, however, are modern. This font had for about half a century done duty as a water-trough in the vicarage garden, but was restored to the church a few years ago, and now stands near the south entrance.

The tombs and monumental inscriptions in the church are both numerous and interesting. A brass, now fixed on the chancel arch, commemorates John Lyon, the founder of Harrow School. The inscription runs as follows :—"Heare lyeth buried the bodye of John Lyon, late of Preston, in this parish, yeoman, died the 11th day of Octr., in the yeare of our Lord 1592, who hath founded a free grammer schoole in this p'she, to have continuance for ever ; and for maintenance thereof, and for releyffe of the poore, and of some poore schollers in the universityes, repairinge of highwayes, and other good and charitable uses, hath made conveyance of lands of good value to a corporation granted for that purpose. Prayers be to the Author of all goodness, Who make us myndful to follow his good example."

Another brass, representing a knight in armour beneath a canopy, has an inscription in memory of Sir John Flambard, who, in the reign of Edward III., held one of the manors in Harrow. The inscription which Weever records for John Byrkhed, rector of Harrow, who died in 1480, is gone, although the headless figure, canopy, and arms, in brass, are still remaining. There is also the headless brass of another priest, Simon Marchford, who died in 1442.

Among the monuments is one to Dr. Sumner, Head Master of Harrow School, who died in 1771 ; it bears a Latin inscription from the pen of Dr. Parr. Dr. Samuel Garth, an eminent physician in his day and author of "The Dispensary," was buried in the chancel in 1719. In Hay's "Religio Philosophi" it is stated that Garth ordered a vault to be made for himself and his lady in this church, in consequence of an "accidental whim."

Lysons, in his "Environs of London" (1795), says that this church "is in the peculiar jurisdiction of the Archbishop of Canterbury, being reckoned among the parishes belonging to the Deanery of Croydon in Surrey." Peculiars, however, are now abolished, and Harrow is included in the diocese of London.

"Formerly," says Newcourt in the "Repertorium," "there was at Harrow both a rectory and a vicarage ; the rectory was a sinecure, to which the Archbishop collated a rector, who thereupon became patron of the vicarage."

A chantry appears to have been founded in this church by William de Bosco, one of the rectors, in the year 1524.

Among the old rectors, Cuthbert Tunstall, Bishop of Durham from the year 1511 to 1522, was the most remarkable. He was succeeded by William Bolton, the last prior but one of St. Bartholomew's,

in Smithfield. Concerning this last-mentioned worthy a singular story is told. He is reported to have made Harrow-on-the-Hill a "city of refuge" to which he and his brethren retreated at the end of January, 1524, on account of a prophecy which a credulous public had believed, that London would be washed away by a rising of the waters of the Thames, on the 1st of February. Camden says that Prior Bolton "built a house here, for fear of an inundation after a great conjunction of planets in the watery triplicity." He is said to have remained here for two months. Dr. Mackay, in his "Memoirs of Popular Delusions," after telling us how most of the upper classes withdrew on this occasion to Hampstead, Highgate, and the Surrey Hills, adds the following narrative, which does not raise the prior in our estimation :—

"Bolton, the Prior of St. Bartholomew's, was so alarmed, that he erected, at very great expense, a sort of fortress at Harrow-on-the-Hill, which he stocked with provisions for two months. On the 24th of January, a week before the awful day which was to see the destruction of London, he removed thither, with the brethren and officers of the Priory and all his household. A number of boats were conveyed in waggons to his fortress, furnished abundantly with expert rowers, in case the flood, reaching so high as Harrow should force them to go further for a resting-place. Many wealthy citizens prayed to share his retreat ; but the Prior, with a prudent forethought, admitted only his personal friends, and those who brought stores of eatables for the blockade.

"At last the morn, big with the fate of London, appeared in the east. The wondering crowds were astir at an early hour to watch the rising of the waters. The inundation, it was predicted, would be gradual, not sudden ; so that they expected to have plenty of time to escape, as soon as they saw the bosom of old Thames heave beyond the usual mark. But the majority were too much alarmed to trust to this, and thought themselves safer ten or twenty miles off. The Thames, unmindful of the foolish crowds upon its banks, flowed on quietly as of yore. The tide ebbed at its usual hour, flowed to its usual height, and then ebbed again, just as if twenty astrologers had not pledged their words to the contrary. Blank were their faces as evening approached, and as blank grew the faces of the citizens to think that they had made such fools of themselves. At last night set in, and the obstinate river would not lift its waters to sweep away even one house out of the ten thousand. Still, however, the people were afraid to go to sleep. Many hundreds remained up till dawn of the next day, lest the deluge should come upon them like a thief in the night.

"On the morrow it was seriously discussed whether it would not be advisable to duck the false prophets in the river. Luckily for them, they thought of an expedient which allayed the popular fury. They asserted that, by an error (a very slight one) of a little figure, they had fixed the date of this awful inundation a whole century too early. The stars were right, after all, and they,

privileges were obtained for the inhabitants through the intercession of the Archbishops of Canterbury. The market, which was granted in 1262, appears to have fallen into disuse before the reign of Elizabeth. Norden, writing at that period, observes that "Harrow-on-the-Hill was a market-towne in the time of Doct. Borde's peregrination, as appeareth by a little Treatise of his in writing." Although no longer possessed of the benefits arising from a regular mart, Harrow is still but

HARROW CHURCH, INTERIOR. (*See page 256.*)

erring mortals, were wrong. The present generation of cockneys were safe, and London would be washed away, not in 1524, but in 1624. At this announcement Bolton, the Prior, dismantled his fortress, and the weary emigrants came back."

Great doubts, however, it is only fair to add, hang over this entire story.

Outside the churchyard, on the western slope of the hill, a terrace has been formed, with seats for visitors. The view from this spot is very extensive, embracing as it does the green and level expanse of western Middlesex, and commanding a view of Windsor Castle and the Oxfordshire hills.

The town of Harrow could once boast of its weekly market and its annual fair, both of which

little inferior in size and population to some market-towns; what it lacks in that respect being, in all probability, made up to it by its famous school. In 1871 the number of inhabited houses was 1,503, the population numbering some 8,500 souls; but such has been the additional advantage offered of late years by railway communication with the metropolis—for there are now two railway-stations here, one on the North-Western and the other on the Metropolitan line—that nearly 5,000 more have been since added to the number of the inhabitants. The town, too, possesses its Fire Brigade, its Literary Institution and Young Men's Society, and a Workman's Hall. The Public Hall is a large building of "Elizabethan" design, capable of holding upwards of 600 persons; it was erected in 1877 by a limited liability company. There is also a Cottage Hospital, which was erected in 1872, in the Roxeth Road, on land given by Mr. Charles Leaf, who also bore the principal part of the expense of the building; the institution is supported by voluntary contributions. Harrow has also its Local Board of Health, its gas and water works, and its weekly *Gazette.* Some races were held here between the years 1864 and 1869, but they have since been abandoned.

In 1873 a Catholic chapel was erected in the Roxborough Road. It is dedicated to Our Lady and St. Thomas of Canterbury, being named after Thomas à Becket, who, as stated above, spent

the hill, and possesses altogether an air of quiet respectability, its shops, most small and unassuming, being largely mixed up with private houses and schools, most of which in the architecture are in keeping with the larger institution to which Harrow at this day owes its fame, and of which we shall speak in the following chapter.

As we have already intimated, Harrow cannot boast of having numbered among its inhabitants, apart from the school, any men whose names have become famous in history; but it may be worth stating that early in the present century, at the foot of the hill, lived Mr. Benjamin Rotch, some time M.P. for Knaresborough. Though a magistrate for Middlesex and Chairman of the

HARROW. (*From a Pencil Sketch taken in 1817.*)

much of his time at Harrow and Pinner. There are also meeting-houses for different denominations of Dissenters, and many schools for children.

The principal street of the town is at the top of

Commissioners of the Peace, he sent a challenge to the Lord Mayor of London, Alderman Winchester; but the latter retaliated by a criminal information.

CHAPTER XXV.

HARROW (*continued*).—THE SCHOOL, ETC.

" Again I re-visit the hills where we sported,
The streams where we swam and the fields where we fought,
The school where, loud warn'd by the bell, we resorted,
To pore o'er the precepts by pedagogues taught."—BYRON.

The Distinction between Harrow and Eton as a Public School—The Foundation of Harrow School—" Orders, Statutes, and Rules of the Government of the School"—Extract from the Founder's Will—Directions as to Children to be Educated—Terms of Admission—Government of the School—Forms and Divisions—Number of Scholars—Cost of Board and Education—Prizes and Scholarships—Description of the School Buildings—Athletic Sports and Recreations—Lines in Honour of John Lyon, the Founder—The Practice of Archery—Shooting for the Silver Arrow—Head Masters and Eminent Harrovians.

THE chief interest of Harrow in the present day is centred in its school, which, in spite of the absence of a regular collegiate foundation, stands second

only to Eton among those nurseries of great and distinguished men—the "public schools" of the kingdom. Though resembling it in its aristocratic connection, and in some of its other features, Harrow differs radically and distinctly from Eton. It never was an ecclesiastical foundation, nor even an adjunct to one. At Harrow, therefore, there is no venerable Provost or body of Fellows to act as a check upon the head-master.

The founder of Harrow, as shown in the preceding chapter, was a plain yeoman, John Lyon, who lived in the hamlet of Preston, within the bounds of the parish to which he proved himself so great a benefactor. Even in his middle life he set apart "twenty marks" yearly for the instruction of poor children; and in the thirteenth year of Elizabeth's reign (1571) he obtained letters patent and a charter from the queen, empowering him to found a "Free Grammar School" at Harrow, and to draw up statutes for its regulation and government.

It was nearly twenty years after the issue of the above-mentioned charter, and only two years before his death, which took place in October, 1592, that John Lyon drew up and promulgated the document, entitled his "Orders, Statutes, and Rules for the Government of the School," containing full instructions for the disposal of the property which he intended to devote to that purpose. The sum of £300 was to be expended on the building of a school, with houses for the master and usher, who were to be elected by the governors : the former "to be on no account below the degree of Master of Arts," nor the latter "under that of Bachelor of Arts."

The founder expressly particularises the estates with which, after the death of himself and his wife, Johan, he intends to endow his establishment. At this period a house for the reception of the scholars had not been provided, and the founder thus expresses his intentions on that head :—" And I, the said John Lyon, doe purpose, by ye Grace of God, to build wth some pte of my lands lying within the towne of Harrow uppon ye Hill meete and convenient Roomes for the said Schoole Master and Usher to inhabite and dwell in ; as alsoe a large and convenient Schoole house, with a chimney in it. And, alsoe, a celler under the said Roomes or Schoole house, to lay in wood and coales, which said Celler shall be divided into three several Roomes, ye one for ye Mr, the second for the Usher, and ye third for ye schollers."

The property left by John Lyon for the support of his school, and for the repairing of the road between London and Harrow, consists of lands which now bring in, it is said, an income of £4,000 a year; but it so happens that the lands in Marylebone and Paddington, which now are by far the most valuable, were assigned to the latter of these two purposes, so that the school, though it seems to have been the principal object of Lyon's charity, reaps comparatively but little benefit therefrom.

The founder directs that a competent number of scholars, children of "inhabitants within the parish," shall be educated freely; but he allows the schoolmaster to "receive over and above . . so many 'foreigners' as that the whole number may be well taught, and as the place can conveniently contain, at the judgment and discretion of the governors. And of the 'foreigners' he may take such stipends and wages as he can get, except they be of the kindred of John Lyon, the founder, so that he take pains with all indifferently, as well of the parish as 'foreigners,' as well of poor as of rich ; but the discretion of the governors shall be looked to that he do."

No boy can be admitted into the school without passing an entrance examination, sufficient to show that he has mastered the chief difficulties of his Latin Grammar, and has made some progress in his Greek Grammar, and also in Arithmetic. No boy can be admitted after completing his fifteenth year, or in any case without a certificate of good conduct from his master or tutor ; nor can he remain in the school (without special permission) after sixteen, unless he has reached the Shell at least ; after seventeen, unless he has reached the "Upper Remove ; " or after eighteen, unless he is in the Sixth Form.

Every boy at Harrow, however high or low, be he a boarder or a day-boy (home-boarder), is expected to have a private tutor ; and some portion of the work taken up by the lower boys to the school must be previously gone over by him with his tutor in "Pupil-room." In this respect, the system of Harrow agrees in principle with Eton, though in the practice of the two schools there are many points of difference, which we have not space to explain here.

The school is under the control of a governing body, and is subject to the Archbishop of Canterbury and the Bishop of London as Visitors.

The school consists of fifteen "monitors ;" a Sixth Form, divided into two "Removes ; " a Fifth Form, divided into four "Removes :" "the Remove," in two "divisions ;" the "Upper Shell," in two "divisions ;" followed by a third and a fourth "Remove" of the same ; a Fourth Form in three "Removes ;" and, lastly, a Third Form, which contains only a few boys. The Second and First Forms no longer exist.

The numbers of the school, which in the last

century rarely rose above 100, have fluctuated during the present century from 300, under the late Dr. G. Butler and Dr. Longley, to between 70 and 80 under Dr. Wordsworth. Under Dr. Vaughan the numbers steadily rose to between 480 and 500 ; and under his successor, the present Dr. H. Montagu Butler, they have reached 580, which the Governors have now fixed as the limit beyond which it is not desirable that the school should increase.

Every boy at Harrow is obliged to learn French, as part of the system ; but after reaching a certain place in the school he learns either French or German. Of late years much greater prominence has been given to the teaching of modern languages than was the case in former times.

The cost for school-fees, board, and tuition, at Harrow, is about £135 in the larger houses, and in the smaller houses £180 a year. This represents the total of *necessary* expenses, exclusive of " extras " and tradesmen's accounts.

At Harrow there are plenty of motives for exertion, in the shape of prizes and scholarships, which are awarded by public competition. First and foremost stand the " Lyon," or " entrance scholarships " (six or seven in number), of an annual value of from £30 to £80, besides which there are annually given eleven other scholarships, called, after their founders, the Sayer, Spencer, Neeld, Gregory, Botfield, Leaf, Anderson, Baring, Roundell, Clayton Memorial, and Ponsonby, varying from £30 to £100 a year. There are also annual prizes of books, and of gold and silver medals, founded by Mr. A. Beresford-Hope, by the late Sir R. Peel, Isabella Gregory, the late Mr. Beriah Botfield, Lord Charles Russell, Viscount Ebrington, Mr. Oxenham, and Mr. Cyril Flower, for compositions in English, Latin, and Greek prose and verse, modern languages, &c. ; and the successful compositions are publicly recited on " Speech Day," the first Thursday in July. The late Mr. Joseph Neeld also founded an annual prize for mathematics—a gold medal, of the value of ten guineas ; the head master gives prizes for natural science and for English and Latin composition. There are also annual prizes for the knowledge of the Holy Scriptures, Shakespeare, modern history, reading, and English literature.

It is almost needless to add that the monitorial and fagging systems—both, if rightly understood and properly applied, the best guarantees against tyranny and bullying—are in full operation at Harrow.

The school is situated immediately to the south of the church, whilst the houses of the masters are scattered about the town. The school buildings form, as it were, the centre of attraction. These are mostly of red brick ; they stand between the head-master's house and the churchyard. The most interesting part of these buildings is the " Fourth Form Room ; " it is also the largest of all the school-rooms, though small in comparison of the Upper School at Eton. This was the original school-room of Lyon's foundation. It is a small, plain apartment, still containing the original fittings—a canopied master's seat at the further end, a lesser arm-chair and desk for the usher near the centre, and tiers of low benches and backless forms placed on either side of the room. It has an interest peculiar to itself; for on the dingy oak panelling which surrounds it are rudely carved the names and initials of some of the most illustrious sons of Harrow, cut by their own hands when boys : among the number are " Byron," " Robert Peel," " Robinson " (afterwards Earl of Ripon), " Aberdeen," " Temple " (afterwards Lord Palmerston), " Sir William Jones," " R. B. Sheridan," and " Normanby." The names of Harrovians of recent date are carved by a hired and experienced hand, and in a more regular way, so as to prove a record of most who leave the school. The opposite wing of the school buildings contains the old " Speech Room," erected about sixty years ago by subscription, under the auspices of the late Dr. Butler, then head-master, afterwards Dean of Peterborough. It is said to have cost £10,000. In it, as may be inferred from its name, the annual " speeches " were formerly held every summer. It was furnished with seats capable of accommodating about 500, and on " Speech Day " it was filled with all the rank and beauty of the land, even royalty itself not unfrequently being present. The room is now used for the purposes of school examinations. In stained glass in the windows are the armorial bearings of Queen Elizabeth and George III., and of sundry governors, head-masters, and benefactors. The " Fourth Form Room " is used for school prayers for some of the scholars, and on wet holidays and half-holidays instead of the school-yard, for calling over the " bill " of names, as the roll-call, or " absence " of Eton, is here termed.

In 1871, at a meeting of " Old Harrovians," it was decided to celebrate the tercentenary of the foundation of the school by the erection of a new " speech-room " and other buildings connected with different branches of education, including school-rooms, a museum, laboratory, gymnasium, lecture-rooms, &c. In order to carry out these various objects, a subscription was immediately set on foot; and the first stone of the new buildings was laid by the Duke of Abercorn on Speech-day, July 2nd, 1874. The new speech-room stands on the opposite side of the road to the old college chapel, and it was built from the designs of the late Mr. William Burges, at a cost, including the site, of nearly £20,000. It is a semi-circular building, the chord being occupied by a large platform stage, while the tiers of seats rise in rows against the opposite wall. In the floor of the orchestra, below the desk of the head-master, is the keyboard of an organ, trackers being carried under the platform to the pipes against the outer wall. The roof is vaulted in pitch-pine, carried on slender iron columns, and the entire effect is quite dissimilar from any other building of the kind.

The boys of Harrow School attended Divine service in the parish church down to about the year 1840, when, under the head-mastership of Dr. Wordsworth, a chapel was built for them at the north end of the High Street, which they attended for afternoon services. It was a brick building, erected in a style to harmonise with the other portions of the school, from the designs of Mr. C. R. Cockerell, R.A. In 1854 that chapel was pulled down, and a new and larger chapel built on its site. The new school chapel was designed by Sir G. Gilbert Scott, and built under Dr. Vaughan's head-mastership. It is a handsome Gothic structure, consisting of nave, chancel, and side aisles, one of which was erected in memory of the Harrovians who fell in the Crimean war. A few yards beyond the chapel is the Vaughan Library, erected in 1860 in memory of Dr. Vaughan, who was head-master from 1845 to that date. It was built from the designs of Sir Gilbert Scott, and is in the Decorated Gothic style. It is a large and spacious room, and contains not only a good and serviceable library for the use of the boys in the Upper School, together with cabinets of minerals, coins, bronzes, and china, but also some interesting relics of Harrow in the olden days, and a series of portraits of the head-masters from Thackeray downwards, and of sundry illustrious old Harrovians, among whom Lord Palmerston, the Marquis of Dalhousie, Lord Herbert, Lord Byron, and the late Earls of Aberdeen and Ripon, stand conspicuous.

Almost adjoining to the library is the house of the head-master; it is a plain substantial edifice of red brick, with mullioned windows, and, including a wing recently erected, can contain about sixty boys.

In 1864 a sanatorium, which bears the reputation of being well arranged and organised, was erected at a little distance from the school; and in 1874—5 further additions were made in the shape of a gymnasium, and laboratories, and Natural Science schools. All these new buildings have been erected out of the Lyon Memorial Fund of 1871.

There is a covered and other racket-courts just below the school buildings, on the slope of the hill, leading down towards the cricket-field. This is far inferior in beauty to the exquisite "playing fields" of Eton; but the Harrow boys have frequently shown at Lord's that they can produce far better "elevens" than their great rivals. The game of the winter months is football. Not only in cricket and football do the Harrow boys bear away the palm, but also in rifle practice they may be said to hold their ground among the public schools, having carried off the Ashburton Challenge Shield no less than nine times.

By his will John Lyon settled the salaries of the masters, and specified the numbers of the "forms" in the school; their books and their exercises; their school hours, recreations, and vacations; and he recognised as lawful and appropriate games "driving a top," "tossing a hand-ball," and "running and shooting." The latter diversion was even insisted on: for the parents were required to furnish their children with "bow-strings, shafts, and bracers, to exercise *shooting.*"

With such solicitude for the well-being of the scholars, not only during the school hours, but also in play-time, it is not to be wondered that the name of the founder of the school is held in high veneration by Harrovians. As it is written in "The Carthusian"—

"A Harrow man vows that there's οὐδὲν βέλτιον
To be met with on earth than his founder, John Lyon."

The following lines on "Lyon of Preston, Founder," were sung at the Tercentenary Festival of Harrow in 1871:—

"Lyon, of Preston, yeoman John,
    Full many a year ago,
Built, on the hill that I live on
    A school that you all may know;
Into the form, first day, 'tis said,
    Two boys came for to see:
One with a red ribbon, red, red, red,
    And one with a blue—like me!

"Lyon, of Preston, yeoman John,
    Lessons he bade them do;
Homer, and multiplica-ti-on,
    And spelling, and Cicero;
'Red Ribbon' never his letters knew,
    Stuck at the five times three;
But Blue Ribbon learnt the table through,
    And said it all off—like me!

" Lyon, of Preston, yeoman John,
　　Said to them both ' Go play.'
Up slunk ' Red Ribbon' all alone,
　　Limped from the field away;
' Blue Ribbon' played like a hero's son,
　　All by himself played he :
Five score runs did he quickly run,
　　And was still Not Out—like me

' Lyon, of Preston, yeoman John,
　　All in his anger sore,
Flogged the boy with the Red ribbón,
　　Set him the Georgics four ;
But the boy with the Blue Ribbon got, each week,
　　Holidays two and three,
And a prize for sums, and a prize for Greek,
　　And an Alphabet prize—like me !

" Lyon, of Preston, yeoman John,
　　Died many years ago,
All that is mortal of him is gone,
　　But he lives in a school I know.
All of them work at their cricket there,
　　And work at their five times three ;
And all of them, ever since that day, wear
　　A ribbon of blue—like me ! "

It is quite clear that the worthy Master Lyon considered archery a most necessáry part of what the old Greek philosophers styled the " gymnastic" part of education. At Harrow, at all events, the practice of archery was coeval with the school ; and here the " gentle art" would seem to have been kept alive down to a comparatively recent date by the observance of an annual custom.

To encourage archery Lyon instituted a prize of a " silver arrow," to be shot for annually on the 4th of August ; but the day was subsequently changed to the first Thursday in July. " In my time," says Bishop Latimer, writing in 1509, " my poor father was as diligent to teach me to shoot as to learn me any other thing, and so I think other men did their children ; he taught me how to draw, how to lay my body to the bow, and not to draw with strength of arms, as divers other nations do, but with strength of body. I had my bow bought me according to my age and strength ; as I increased in them, so my bows were made bigger and bigger ; for men shall never shoot well except they be brought up in it. It is a worthy game, a wholesome kind of exercise, and much commended in physic."

There were six, and in later times twelve, competitors for John Lyon's silver arrow ; and he who first shot twelve times nearest to the central mark was proclaimed the victor, and carried off the prize, a triumphal procession of boys attending him. The competitors were attired in fancy dresses of spangled satin, generally of white and green, with green silk sashes and silken caps.

The Butts were at the entrance, on the left of the London road, entering the village. They were backed by a lofty knoll, crowned with trees ; on the slope of this eminence were cut rows of grassy seats, gradually descending, and worthy, according to Dr. Parr, of a Roman amphitheatre.

We hear from the Harrow " School Lists" that the last contest for the silver arrow took place in July, 1771. In the following September, Dr. Sumner, the head-master, died, and was succeeded by Dr. Heath. The arrow prepared for the next year's contest (being the last ever made for this purpose, and, as the arrow-shooting was abolished in 1772, never shot for) became the property of the Rev. B. H. Drury, one of the assistant-masters, son of the Rev. Henry Drury (himself for many years an assistant, and for some time before his death under-master), to whom it had descended from his uncle, Dr. Heath. Mr. Drury presented it a few years since to the school library, where it is still religiously kept.

The abolition of the practice of arrow-shooting will ever be a source of deep regret to all Harrovians. Nevertheless, Dr. Heath, the head-master who suppressed it, must not on this account be too severely blamed. The reasons which induced him to abandon this ancient custom are stated to have been a serious accident which befel one of the competitors, the frequent exemptions from the regular business of the school which the shooters claimed *as a privilege not to be infringed upon !* as well as the band of disorderly persons whom this exhibition brought down to the village, in consequence of its vicinity to the metropolis. These encroachments and annoyances had at length become so injurious to discipline, as, after some vain attempts at the correction of the evil, to call for the total abolition of the usage.

About the year 1810, the charming spot called The Butts, where the shooting for the silver arrow took place, were denuded of wood, and the knoll itself has at length disappeared, its site being now entirely occupied by private dwelling-houses. The prefatory introduction to the School Lists says that " in the school there may now be seen a humble representation of ' The Butts' on the day of the annual contest." " In that frontispiece" (according to the testimony of the late Rev. H. Drury, in a letter of the 20th July, 1838) " the village barber is seen walking off like one of Homer's heroes, with an arrow in his eye, stooping forward, and evidently in great pain, with his hand applied to the wound. It is perfectly true that this Tom of Coventry was so punished ; and I have somewhere a ludicrous account of it in Dr.

Parr's all but illegible autograph." This testimony is confirmed by that of the late Lord Arden, an old Harrovian, in a letter of the 17th July, 1838:— "I remember a print representing the circumstance of one of the boys having shot so wide of the mark that his arrow struck a man, or boy, in the eye, that the stooping individual in the print represented Goding, the barber, " who," she said, " was shot *in the mouth*, and lost two or three of his teeth thereby." This is evidently another version of the above story, substituting only the gaping mouth as a various reading for the peeping eye.

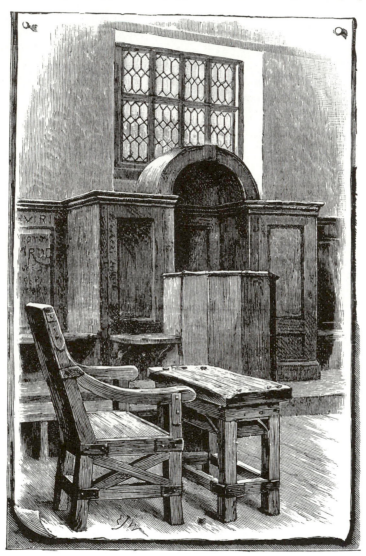

THE FOURTH FORM ROOM. (*See page 261.*)

which, I believe, was the occasion of the shooting for a silver arrow being discontinued." Whether Lord Arden's conjecture as to the cause of the suppression of the arrow-shooting be correct or not, his lordship's testimony, it has been well observed, is of considerable value, as showing the traditional opinion held in his day about the interpretation of the point. Moreover, a few years ago, a Mrs. Arnold, an octogenarian inhabitant of Harrow, with a clear memory of bygone times, fully believed

The names of many of the successful competitors for the " silver arrow " may be found in the earlier volumes of the *Gentleman's Magazine*, from which we take the following :—-

Vol. I. " Thursday, 5 August, 1731.—According to an ancient custom, a silver arrow, value £3, was shot for at ' The Butts,' at Harrow-on-the-Hill, by six youths of that free school, in archery habits, and won by Master Brown, son of Captain Brown, commander of an East-Indiaman." Vol. XXVII.,

p. 381. "Thursday, 4, August 1757.—The silver arrow shot for by the young gentlemen of Harrow School was won by Master Earle." Vol. XXXI., p. 329. "Thursday, 2 July, 1761.—The silver arrow was shot for (as usual) by twelve young gentlemen at Harrow-on-the-Hill, and was won by the Earl of Barrymore." Vol. XXXIV., p. 346. "Thursday, 5, July 1764.—The silver arrow annually shot for at Harrow was won by Master Mee."* Vol. XXXV., p. 344. "Thursday, 4

and bears this inscription (for which, it may be charitably presumed, the learned head-master did not hold himself responsible) : ' PretiumVictoriæ a Carolo Wager Allix potitum tertia Mensis Julii, 1766.' Several of the old people (Mother Bernard, Dick Martin, &c.) told me they remembered well my father's winning it, and that it was very warmly contested, one of the shooters being peculiarly desirous to gain it, inasmuch as three of his brothers in succession had previously been the

SHOOTING FOR THE ARROW.
(*From an Old Print*, 1769.)

July, 1765.—The silver arrow was shot for by twelve youths of Harrow School, and won by Master Davies. Some Indian warriors, at that time in England, were present to witness the exhibition." From a private letter :—"Thursday, 3 July, 1766.— The silver arrow was shot for as usual, and won by Master Charles Wager Allix." Respecting this last-mentioned arrow, Dr. Butler, the head-master, received from Mr. Charles Allix, of Willoughby Hall, Lincolnshire, son of the prizeman, a communication to the following effect :—" It is nearly," he writes, " of the size and shape of a real arrow,

victors. On this occasion, therefore, the boy's father and family were present, and most intense was their anxiety for his success. ' For ' (as Mother B. expressed it) ' the father had stuck up the *three* arrows already in the *three* corners of his drawing-room, and so especially wanted the *fourth* to fill up the other corner.' I have now the bow with which it was won ; and my father has told me that only a week before the day of shooting he discovered that by some one it had been maliciously broken. This discovery plunged him into the deepest despair ; however, he sent the bow immediately to London, for the chance of its being repaired. It was repaired, but considerably shortened. Still, to his inconceivable delight, he

* It would be interesting to know if this " Master Mee " was the grandfather of Lord Palmerston, who was an Harrovian, and whose mother, according to the Peerages, was the daughter of one Benjamin Mee, Esq.

found, upon trying it, that he could shoot with it even better than ever, and HE WON THE PRIZE."

With reference to the shooting in 1769, the following interesting anecdote was communicated to the Dean of Peterborough (Dr. Butler) upon the authority of the late Hon. Archibald Macdonald. On the day of the competition, two boys, Merry and Love, were equal, or nearly so, and both of them decidedly superior to the rest, when Love, having shot his last arrow into the bull's eye, was greeted by his school-fellows with a shout, "Omnia vincit Amor!" "Not so," said Merry, in an under voice; "Nos non cedamus Amori;" and carefully adjusting his shaft, shot it into the bull's eye a full inch nearer to the centre than his exulting competitor. So he gained the day. As the name of "Love" does not occur in the list of shooters for that year, it is clear that it must have been a nickname by which one of them was familiarly known.

The "arrow" still forms part of the armorial bear-

ARMS OF HARROW SCHOOL.

ings of the school; and in the Monitors' Library at Harrow is still to be seen one of the embroidered silk dresses which the boys wore at their annual archery festival. The "silver arrow," however, has not been shot for since the year 1771.

On the abolition of the archery contests, public "speeches" were adopted in their place on the first Thursdays in May, June, and July, and were numerously attended by old Harrovians and friends of the boys. The ten monitors used to speak on each of the three days, together with six of the Sixth Form, according to their seniority, of whom each six so chosen spoke on *one* of the three days only during that year. This custom continued till 1829, when the number of speech-days was reduced by Dr. Longley (then head-master) to two; and that number was subsequently reduced by his successor, Dr. Wordsworth, in his last year, 1844, to one. The subjects of the speeches used to be passages in prose and verse, selected from the best authors, Greek, Latin, and English. With these, in process of time, were combined original prize compositions, commencing with the year 1820, and increasing in number and variety of style as the kindness of the governors and the bounty of

sundry old Harrovians and others successively added to the list of prizes.

Since the foundation of the school the post of head-master has been held by clergymen of the highest eminence as scholars, and of the most distinguished ability and talents. In 1660 the Rev. W. Howe, Fellow of King's College, Cambridge, was elected to the office. Dr. Thackeray, chaplain to the Prince of Wales, who was head-master at the middle of the last century, was succeeded in 1760 by the Rev. Dr. Sumner, under whose superintendence the number of pupils in the school rose to 250. It is difficult to discover the proximate cause of the sudden rise in the numbers of the school during the head-masterships of Dr. Thackeray and Dr. Sumner (1740–71), except it is to be found in the fact that the former was a personal friend of the Prince of Wales, and a supporter of the side of Bishop Hoadley in the Bangorian controversy, and that possibly Eton was thought too "High Church" for those times, when everything that looked in the direction of the nonjuring communion was at a discount among the aristocracy. It is more than probable, though not at present provable, that such was the case.

On the death of Dr. Sumner, in 1771, Dr. Heath was elected to the office. Mr. (afterwards Dr.) Parr, the defeated candidate on that occasion, had been an assistant-master at Harrow under Dr. Sumner, and he seemed to be generally pointed out, by his learning and abilities, as the successor of the late head-master; indeed, his popularity with the boys was so great that when the election fell on Mr. Heath they endeavoured to avenge the cause of their favourite by overt acts of rebellion, the "senior form" considering it "an indignity to have an Eton assistant put over them, when they had in their own school a person of superior learning." Among the boys who took part in this rebellion was one Richard Wesley, or Wellesley, afterwards Marquis Wellesley, and elder brother of another Arthur Wesley, afterwards better known as Sir Arthur Wellesley. He was removed by his guardian, Archbishop Cornwallis, to Eton, whither he was soon afterwards followed by his younger brother, who was sent there "under his wing." Had this not been the case, possibly "the battle of Waterloo" would not have been "won on the playing fields at Eton," but on the slope of a hill-side in Middlesex.

But to return from this digression. Such was Dr. Parr's mortification at his failure that he threw up his situation as assistant-master, and retired to Stanmore, where he founded a school, and where we shall meet with him again presently.

That establishment, however, failed in the end, and Mr. Parr was appointed to the living of Hatton, in Warwickshire, and afterwards to a prebendal stall in St. Paul's. Dr. Heath's popularity was by no means enhanced by one of his earliest measures — the abolition of the time-honoured custom of shooting for the silver arrow, as already mentioned.* On Dr. Heath's resignation, Dr. Drury succeeded to the head-master's chair. Under his auspices the school attained a greater eminence than it had ever previously known. At one period the number of scholars exceeded 350, and the whole establishment was, in consequence, much enlarged. Among the pupils under Dr. Heath were two whose names will ever be regarded with the deepest veneration by Harrovians: namely, Lord Byron and Sir Robert Peel. On the retirement of Dr. Drury in 1805, Dr. Butler, afterwards Dean of Peterborough, was elected. The most flourishing condition of the school during Dr. Butler's head-mastership was in 1816, when the numbers amounted to 295. In 1829 Dr. Butler resigned, and was succeeded by Dr. Longley, whose period of office extended over the short space of only seven years, for he resigned in 1836, on being appointed to the bishopric of Ripon. Dr. Longley was translated to Durham in 1856, became Archbishop of York in 1860, was translated to the see of Canterbury in 1862, and died in 1868.

Dr. Longley's successor at Harrow was the Rev. Christopher Wordsworth. He was a Fellow of Trinity College, Cambridge, where his father, a man of eminent learning, was Master. He passed a brilliant career at the University, having won the Chancellor's English medal, and been Porson's prizeman, Browne's medallist, and Craven scholar. On leaving Harrow in 1844 he was appointed successively Canon and Archdeacon of Westminster, and in 1869 he was consecrated Bishop of Lincoln. Dr. Wordsworth's contributions to literature have been numerous and of great value. An edition of "Theocritus," "Athens and Attica," "Greece," a "Tour in Italy," a "Diary of France," the Greek Testament and other portions of the Holy Bible annotated, "Theophilus Anglicanus," and "Memoirs of William Wordsworth," are the best known among his works, which include several volumes of sermons on the passing topics of the day.

Dr. Charles John Vaughan held the head mastership from 1844 till 1859. He was Craven University Scholar and Porson's prizeman at Trinity College, Cambridge, in 1836 and 1837, and Chancellor's medallist in 1838. He was afterwards elected to a Fellowship of his college. He held the vicarage of St. Martin's, Leicester, from 1841 to his appointment to Harrow. From 1851 to 1879 he was Chaplain in Ordinary to the Queen. He was appointed Vicar of Doncaster in 1860, Master of the Temple in 1869, and Dean of Llandaff in 1879, and he has more than once refused a bishopric.

Dr. Henry Montagu Butler, the present headmaster, is the youngest son of a former head-master, the Rev. George Butler, D.D., who died in 1853. Dr. Butler was born in 1833, and was educated at Harrow School, whence he proceeded to Trinity College, Cambridge, where he closed a brilliant undergraduate career by graduating B.A. in 1855 as Senior Classic. In the same year he was elected Fellow of his college. In 1859, on the retirement of Dr. Vaughan, he was elected to the head-mastership of his old school, over which, as before shown, his father had so long presided.

Of the large number of "eminent men" which Harrow has contributed to the political and literary world, it will be impossible, in the limited space at our command, to do more than briefly notice a few of the most important. As the school was then only of local importance, few names of great note appear in the annals of Harrow previous to the commencement of the last century.

William Baxter, the author of several classical and antiquarian works, entered the school about the year 1668. He was a nephew of the celebrated Richard Baxter, the Nonconformist divine, and a native of Wales. Baxter will be best remembered by his well-known edition of Horace, and his "Glossarium Antiquitatum Britannicarum." He died in 1723.

James Bruce, the celebrated Scotch traveller, was here between 1742 and 1746. After traversing the greater part of Asia Minor, he set off in June, 1768, to discover the source of the Nile. An account of this journey was published in 1790. It is stated in the "Harrow Calendar" that Bruce's long residence abroad "produced no abatement in his attachment to the place of his education." He died in 1794.

Sir William Jones, the distinguished linguist and orientalist, entered the school in his seventh year, under Dr. Thackeray, and was so diligent in his studies that he became known as the "great scholar." In 1766 he became tutor to Lord Althorp, and he afterwards travelled in the East. He published a "Persian Grammar," the "Laws of Menu," &c. In 1783 he was appointed a Judge at Calcutta, where he founded an Asiatic Society.

---

* See *ante*, p. 263.

Dr. Samuel Parr, whose scholarship was the pride of Harrow School, was the son of a tradesman in the town, and was entered on the foundation in 1752. While a boy at the school he fought with Lord Mountstuart. He made such rapid progress with his learning that at the age of fourteen he was at the head of the school. Dr. Parr was a great scholar, but little more. The two dreams of his life were a four-in-hand, attained late in years, and a bishopric. In 1792 he published a " Letter from Irenopolis to the Inhabitants of Eleutheropolis " upon the Priestley controversy. As a schoolmaster, he belonged to the order of the " Flagellants," only his flogging was vicarious; he flogged others, not himself. As a critic, his want of acumen was shown by his signing a confession of faith as a guarantor of the Ireland Shakespeare forgeries. Dr. Parr died in 1825.

The gallant Admiral Lord Rodney, the hero of the 12th of April, 1782, was at school here before he went to sea.

In the present century Harrow can boast that four Prime Ministers of England, all living at the same time, had been its *alumni*—Lord Ripon, Lord Aberdeen, Sir R. Peel, and Lord Palmerston.

Richard Brinsley Sheridan,* the distinguished dramatist, wit, and politician, was a Harrovian. He died in 1816.

Theodore Hook, the eminent dramatist and novelist, whose feats of practical joking have often been mentioned in these pages, displayed his characteristic love for that particular species of wit in the early days of his schoolboy life. " The first night of his arrival here was signalised by a feat of throwing a stone at a window where an elderly lady was undressing. The window was broken, but the lady escaped unhurt. The act was perpetrated at the instigation of Byron." Hook's powers as an improvisatore gained for him a passport into " society." He was patronised by the Prince Regent, and in 1812 was appointed to a Government post in the Mauritius, but was recalled in 1818 in consequence of deficiencies and irregularities in his accounts. He afterwards devoted himself to journalism and literature, and his name will be long remembered in connection

BYRON'S NAME, FROM THE FOURTH FORM ROOM.
(See page 261).

with the publication of that witty Tory organ, *John Bull.*

Sir Robert Peel, Bart., the Conservative statesman, who conceded the Repeal of the Corn Laws, and was instrumental in bringing about the Catholic Emancipation, was a contemporary of Byron at Harrow. The story is told that one day when Peel was being severely thrashed, another little boy ran up to his tormentor, and coolly asked him how many blows he was going to give him. " What's that to you, you little rascal? " was the reply; " be off." "Because," answered the little fellow, " I would take half myself." That brave and generous little boy was Lord Byron. Peel was first elected to Parliament in 1809. In 1817 he was chosen representative of Oxford University, and in 1829 he was elected for Tamworth. Sir Robert Peel was successively Under Secretary for the Colonies, Chief Secretary for Ireland, Home Secretary, Chancellor of the Exchequer, and twice First Lord of the Treasury. He was accidentally killed by a fall from his horse in 1850.

Lord Byron was entered at Harrow, under Dr. Drury, in 1801, and left in 1805. " During his stay there," as we learn from the ' Harrow Calendar,' " he showed symptoms of that morbid melancholy which so unhappily distinguished him in after-life. He himself says that he was 'a most unpopular boy, but led lately.' He was particularly distinguished for the opposition he made to Dr. Butler's appointment after the retirement of Dr. Drury, to whom he had been singularly attached. A reconciliation, however, took place between him and the Doctor before his departure for Greece. He says in his Diary, ' I have retained many of my school friendships and all my dislikes— except to Dr. Butler, whom I treated rebelliously, and have been sorry ever since.' " The poems in which Byron refers to Harrow are the following :— " On a Change of Masters at a Great Public School," " To the Duke of Dorset," " On a Distant View of the Village and School of Harrow," " Lines to Edward Noel Long, Esq." (whom the poet elsewhere addresses as " Cleon "), " Lines written beneath an Elm in Harrow Churchyard," " Lines on Revisiting Harrow." Among his principal friends here were Curzon, Hunter, Long, and

---

* See " Old and New London," Vol. IV., p. 311.

Tattersall, whom he addresses as "Davus" in his "Hours of Idleness," and who is said to have saved the poet's life by arresting a blow made at him by a farmer, in a feud on the subject of the cricket-ground.

The Right Hon. Spencer Perceval, born in 1762, entered Parliament in 1801 as member for Northampton, and was successively Attorney-General, Chancellor of the Exchequer, and Chancellor of the Duchy of Lancaster, and, subsequently, in 1809, First Lord of the Treasury. He was shot by Bellingham in the lobby of the House of Commons in 1812.

Lord Elgin, the ambassador, and the celebrated collector of the Elgin marbles; the third Earl Spencer, better known as the Lord Althorp of the Reform Bill era; Lord Cottenham, some time Lord Chancellor; Lord Moira, afterwards Marquis of Hastings and Governor-General of India; Lord Clare, Governor of Bombay in 1832, addressed as "Lycus" in Byron's "Hours of Idleness;" Earl de la Warr, some time Lord Chamberlain, addressed as "Euryalus" in the same poem; the Marquis Wellesley (before he was sent to Eton); Lords Dalhousie and Herbert; Sir Henry L. Bulwer; the Earl of Shaftesbury; Mr. A. Beresford-Hope; Sir John B. Karslake; the late Viscount Strangford; Bishop Charles Wordsworth; Mr. Herman Merivale; Cardinal Manning; Archbishop Trench; Mr. William Spottiswoode, F.R.S.; the first Lord Rendlesham, author of the famous Thellusson will, which gave so much business to the lawyers; Dr. Douglas, master of Benett (Corpus Christi) College, Cambridge; and the poet Sotheby.

CHAPTER XXVI.

Rura per et valles. — Ovid.

HARROW WEALD, KINGSBURY, ETC.

Rural Aspect of the Locality—The Hamlet of Greenhill—Harrow Weald—Remnants of the Great Forest of Middlesex—Grime's Dyke—All Saints' Church—Weald Park—Daniel Dancer, the Miser—Roxeth– Sudbury—St. John's Church—The Girl's Home, &c.—Wembley—Descent of the Manor—The " Green Man," Wembley Hill—Kingsbury: its Rural Character, Boundaries, &c.—Kingsbury Reservoir—The " Welsh Harp "—Kingsbury Races—The Parish Church—A Supposed Roman Encampment—Fryern Farm and Kingsbury Green—Oliver Goldsmith's Residence—The Hamlet of the Hyde—Kenton.

NOTWITHSTANDING the gradual extension of London, and the speed with which most of the outlying villages and hamlets are being connected one with another in all directions, there are still left a few fields and hedgerows to which the cockney holiday-makers can betake themselves. Here, in the neighbourhood of Harrow and Kingsbury, the fields are still green, the hedgerows fresh, the forest trees put on their summer garb as of yore, and even the smaller streams, which here and there expand into broad lakes and ponds, are not yet forced to burrow underground. It has been observed that the inhabitants of our mighty metropolis are marvellously neglectful of their privileges. With the exception, perhaps, of Vienna, there is no capital in Europe with scenery so beautiful, and so easily accessible. Yet we see innumerable Londoners, even of intelligence and refinement, going on flying trips across the Channel in the briefest holiday-time, or gathering into some overcrowded watering-place, where the charges are outrageous and the accommodation is indifferent. It is certain, however, that if they did otherwise we should have no such sequestered and peaceful scenery anywhere within the borders of the metropolitan counties as is to be met with in the "green lanes" hereabout.

As we have shown in the preceding chapters, Harrow Hill rises abrupt and isolated. Seen from this the elevating country for miles around has the appearance of an almost level plain. This surrounding land is mostly under cultivation either for corn or grass; indeed, the land between Harrow and Heston, which lies away some six miles to the south, still bears an excellent reputation for its corn, as it did in the time of "good Queen Bess." *

In the immediate neighbourhood of Harrow, nestling, as it were, under the sheltering wing of the hill, lie several suburban ecclesiastical districts, some of them at one time being reckoned as hamlets of the mother parish. Between the town and the railway-station, at the foot of the hill to the north, is Greenhill, a small cluster of villas and houses of modern growth. A church for the district, dedicated to St John the Baptist, was built in 1866. It is a cruciform, brick-built edifice, small and unpretending.

---

* See ante p. 44.

Stretching away northward as far as the rising ground about Stanmore and Watford, and bounded on the west by Pinner and on the east by Hendon, is the broad level tract of country known as Harrow Weald, a district which retains in its name an allusion to its former umbrageous and rude character, the term *weald* signifying in the Saxon a wood. It was, in fact, a vast wild woodland, part of the great forest of Middlesex; and, although it has long been "enclosed" and cultivated, there is still much timber growing here. Britton tells us that much of the timber used for the construction

favoured with due antiquarian observation. This is locally termed Grime's Dyke, and consists of a ditch, or hollow way, lying to the west of the road leading from Harrow to Watford. This dyke is in some places nearly twenty feet wide, but is chiefly overgrown by furze or screened by aquatic weeds." The heights of the Weald, on the common, present some extensive and beautiful landscape scenery.

The hamlet of Harrow Weald lies about two miles north-east of Harrow Station on the North-Western Railway, and consists of a few farm resi-

DISTANT VIEW OF HARROW.

of the roof of Henry VII.'s Chapel at Westminster Abbey was obtained from the forest about Harrow.

"Near the northern extremity of this Weald," observes the author of the "Beauties of England," "is a spot of ground supposed to be the most lofty elevation in the parish of Harrow, and which is said to form a landmark to mariners approaching England from the German Ocean. The attention of the person examining this elevated neighbourhood may be directed to some contiguous trees, so ancient, yet so sturdy under the wear of centuries, that, with a moderate license of conjecture, they may be supposed to present memorials of the great Forest of Middlesex. He will likewise find, near at hand, a curious, but obscure, vestige of some very remote age, which has hitherto not been

dences and private houses. It was formed into an ecclesiastical district in 1845, at which time a church was erected. This is a small building in the Decorated style, and is dedicated to All Saints. A lych-gate at the entrance to the churchyard was erected to the memory of the Rev. Edward Monro, the author of "Sacred Allegories," and who was for upwards of twenty years vicar of this parish, and who founded and conducted here a school for training Church schoolmasters.

Weald Park and Bentley Priory are the principal seats in this neighbourhood; but, as the greater part of the latter estate lies in the parish of Stanmore, it will be best noticed in the chapter devoted to that place. The former, the seat of Mr. Alexander Sim, is a large castellated mansion on the left of the roadway leading to Bushey, and it stands on high ground, commanding a pleasant view for miles over the surrounding country. In the park is a mineral spring.

Harrow Weald, if it has produced no great and

century, the celebrated John Elwes, a member of Parliament, who possessed property in Marylebone* worth nearly half a million, was accustomed to push his horse across ploughed fields and dine upon hard eggs, to escape the ruinous

THE WELSH HARP AND RESERVOIR.　(*See page* 275.)

distinguished men whose names have been handed down to us in the pages of history, has, at all events, contributed one individual whose eccentricities made him famous in his day: namely, Daniel Dancer, commonly known as "the miser of Harrow Weald Common." Probably no class of men has ever exhibited such painful and ludicrous eccentricities as those unhappy people who have devoted themselves to the amassing of money as an end in itself. Towards the end of the last

expense incidental to turnpikes and taverns; and this same legislator, who would play a rubber at whist for a couple of hundred guineas, walked home on foot every night from the gaming house, to save a shilling for a hackney coach! Again, Scheven, a rich banker of Hamburgh, who lived also in the last century, is said to have denied himself not only the comforts, but even the neces-

* See "Old and New London," Vol. IV., p. 242.

saries, of life; and, among other instances of penuriousness, it is recorded that after a faithful service of seventeen years he called in the aid of a German tailor for the purpose of attempting to *turn his coat !*

Daniel Dancer, who was born in 1716, was descended from a respectable yeoman's family in the county of Hertford, and his grandfather appears to have been settled at Bushey, near Watford, where he followed the occupations of mealman and maltster. His father, who resided at Stone Causeway, on Harrow Weald Common, possessed considerable property in land, which he farmed himself; he had four children, and on his death, in 1736, his eldest son, Daniel, succeeded to the estate.

It was in the paternal mansion at Astmiss, at Causeway-gate, that Daniel was doomed by the fates to spend the whole of his life, which seems to have been one uninterrupted dreary blank. His wretched habitation was surrounded by about eighty acres of his own rich meadow land, with some of the finest oak timber in the kingdom upon it; and he possessed an adjoining farm, called Waldos, the whole of the annual value of about £250 per annum, if properly cultivated. But *cultivation* was expensive, and so Daniel permitted grass only to grow there; indeed, in so neglected a state was the place for many years, that the house was entirely surrounded by trees, the fields were choked with underwood, and the hedges of such an amazing height as wholly to exclude the prospect of mankind, and create a dreary gloom all around. A tree had actually pushed its top through the roof of his house, which he entered by means of a ladder, dragged in after him; for he had fastened the rotten door on the inside, for fear of burglars, and determined never to enter the house again through that aperture. Dancer appears to have led the life of a hermit during more than half a century, and to have been as much unacquainted with, and unknown to, the world, although residing within ten or eleven miles of the capital, as if he had been the inhabitant of a desert. His only dealing with mankind arose from the sale of his hay; and he was seldom accosted by anybody, except when he wandered about the common to pick up a stray lock of wool, collect the dung of sheep under the hedges, or trudged along the road in search of paper, old iron, or cast horse-shoes.

His wealth thus brought him no happiness, but, on the contrary, it seemed to carry a curse along with it to its wretched possessor, for he is reported to have been robbed frequently to a large amount. In order the more effectually to secure his wealth and riches, he actually dug a hole, or what military men term a

trou de loup, before the entrance, which he covered over with loose straw, in such a manner as to secure the *principal approach* towards his castle, and entrap any incautious assailant who might have the temerity to invade his darling property. After exhibiting this specimen of his talents as an engineer, the modern Midas seems to have slept in safety amidst his gold.

His sister, who lived along with him for many years, at length died, and left a considerable sum of money behind her, which went towards the increase of his wealth, and served rather to stimulate than diminish his avarice. About this time he commenced an acquaintance with the Tempest family, which, while it soothed his pride, alleviated the sufferings and sorrows of his declining age. The following particulars concerning the death and burial of Miss Dancer are gleaned from a biographical sketch of the miser published shortly after his death :—

" Lady Tempest, who happened to live in his neighbourhood, compassionating the situation of Miss Dancer, took her into her house during her last illness, and treated her with uncommon kindness. But the disease, which, dreadful to relate, is supposed to have proceeded originally from inanition, proved mortal, and rendered all the good old lady's care ineffectual.

" Although Daniel never evinced any affection for his sister, he determined to bury her in such a manner as should not *disgrace the family.* He accordingly contracted with an undertaker, who agreed to take timber in return for a coffin, as Mr. Dancer had no idea of using the precious metals as a vehicle of exchange; he, however, could not be prevailed upon to purchase proper mourning for himself; yet, in consequence of the entreaty of his neighbours, he unbound the haybands with which his legs were usually covered, and drew on a second-hand pair of black worsted stockings. His coat was of a whitish-brown colour; his waistcoat had been black about the middle of the last century, and the immediate covering to his head, which seemed to have been taken from Mr. Elwes' wiggery, and to have descended to Daniel as an heirloom, gave a grotesque appearance to the person of a chief mourner but too well calculated to provoke mirth. This, indeed, was increased by the slipping of his horse's girth at the place of burial, in consequence of which the rider—to the great diversion of some of the Harrow boys who attended—was precipitated into the grave !"

The old miser at length died, in September, 1794, at the age of 78, and was buried in Harrow churchyard.

"Notwithstanding the miserable aspect of the house and its inhabitants—both brother and sister (the former especially, who was nearly naked)—yet on Daniel's death, not only plate, table-linen, and twenty-four pairs of good sheets, but clothes of every description, were found locked up in chests. The female attire, of which there was a correct inventory in the brother's own handwriting, was valued at seventeen pounds. He also, among other apparel, had some excellent boots; but he preferred to encase his legs with the still warmer covering of hay-bands.

"Although he possessed two ancient but tolerably good bedsteads, with the proper furniture, originally belonging, as well as the house, to the Edlins, a family of some property, yet they were carefully secluded from the light of heaven, and both he and his sister slept on sacks stuffed with hay, and covered with a horse rug.

"During the last twenty years Daniel's house is said to have been entered at least fourteen times by thieves, and the amount of his losses is calculated at two thousand five hundred pounds. As the lower part was in such a ruinous state as to admit a person with ease, it was recommended to him to get it repaired; but he replied, 'that this would be only throwing away more money, for then they would get in at the windows.' In order to employ the attention of the marauders, until he should escape to his hiding-place, he was accustomed to strew the ground floor with farthings and sixpences wrapped up in paper.

"The whole of Dancer's property, on his decease, amounted to about ten thousand pounds —a sum which, by proper management, he might have doubled, and at the same time allowed himself all the comforts of life.

"In his miserable habitation were found some hundred-weight of waste-paper, the collection of half a century, and two or three tons of old iron, consisting of nails, horse-shoes, &c., which he had picked up. On the ground floor several pieces of foreign gold and silver were dug up, and some coins, among which were a crown and a shilling of the English Commonwealth."

Roxeth, which unites itself with Harrow on the south-west side, was formerly an outlying hamlet, but since 1863 has been a distinct ecclesiastical district, separated from the parish church. It is, however, a separate manor from that of Harrow, having been granted by the Archbishop of Canterbury in the fourteenth century to Sir William Brembre and his heirs. Prior to that time it appears to have been merely an estate within the manor of Harrow, belonging to William Roxeth,

who was outlawed for felony. Christ Church, which was built in 1862, to meet the requirements of this rapidly-increasing district, is built in the Early English style, of flint, with stone and brick dressings.

Winding round the base of the hill in an easterly direction, we come next to Sudbury, another hamlet of Harrow. "Originally," as we learn from Kelly's "Directory of Middlesex," "it was a large tract of land, extending from the spot on which now stands the railway-station to the foot of Harrow Hill, known as Sudbury Common: it was enclosed shortly after the passing of an Act of Parliament in 1803; for civil purposes it forms a part of the parish of Harrow, but for ecclesiastical purposes part of it is attached to, and forms part of, the ecclesiastical parish of St. John's, Wembley." Sudbury, as a hamlet, is evidently a place of quite recent growth, for it is not described, or even mentioned, by Lewis in his "Topographical Dictionary." The manor of Sudbury—or, as it was formerly called, Southbury (the South Bury)—however, dates from a very remote period, having at the end of the fourteenth century formed, as above stated, part of the possessions of Archbishop Arundel, who was banished for high treason, when an inquisition was taken of his estates.

The church of the united district of Sudbury, Wembley, Appleton, and Preston, dedicated to St. John the Baptist, is situated near the Sudbury railway-station. It was built in 1846, from designs by Sir Gilbert Scott, and is in the Decorated style. In the neighbourhood of the church rows of cottages and a large number of villas have sprung up; and to meet the wants of the inhabitants there have been erected a district school, a Cottage Hospital, Workman's Hall, and a Young Men's Institute. Here, too, is the Girls' Home, a branch refuge for homeless girls of the National Refuges Institution, whose training ship for homeless boys has long been a familiar object off Greenhithe to passengers up or down the Thames. The building, known as Sudbury Hall, will accommodate 100 destitute girls, who are trained for domestic service.

From Sudbury we pass by a pleasant pathway to Wembley, about half a mile to the north-east.

The manor of Wembley in old times belonged to the Priory at Kilburn, in whose possession it continued down to the time of the Dissolution. It was afterwards granted by Henry VIII. to certain persons, who in the same year (1543) conveyed it to one Richard Page. The family of Page long possessed very considerable property in the county of Middlesex; and this property remained vested in their hands until the beginning of the present century, when it was sold by another Richard Page to the family of the Grays, the present owners. The manor-house was rebuilt by Mr. Gray about the year 1810, and is now the seat of the Rev. John Edward Gray. Wembley Park, some 250 acres in extent, is agreeably undulated, abundantly wooded, and watered by a branch of the river Brent.

From Wembley Hill, a local eminence, good views are obtained of the surrounding country. The top of the hill is occupied by the "Green Man" tavern, with its adjacent "tea-gardens," which are largely patronised during the summer months by holiday folks and Londoners.

The seats in this neighbourhood are Wembley House (Mr. John Turton Woolley), Hill House (Mr. Thomas Nicoll), and Oakington Park (Colonel the Hon. Wellington Talbot).

Continuing our course, by a somewhat circuitous path in a north-easterly direction, by Wembley Green, and skirting the park, we arrive at length at Kingsbury, a spot which happily still retains its rural character, and which is also one of the most charming resorts in the whole county for wild fowl and other aquatic birds. The Brent meanders pleasantly through the parish, whilst the meadows on either hand are intersected with field-paths, lanes, and flowery hedgerows, all combining to render it one of the most attractive in the vicinity of the metropolis for the lovers of country scenery. Dotting the lanes leading to the village, a picturesque antiquated cottage may here and there be met with, adding not a little to the rustic beauty of the scene. Altogether it is a curious old-fashioned, out-of-the-way place, with a population numbering about 600. Although most of the houses and farms are of modern growth, there is still, at all events, one cottage, mostly of wood, which dates from the thirteenth, or, at latest, from the fourteenth century.

A writer in the *Hampstead Express* recently, in drawing attention to the closing of some of the field-paths about Kingsbury, observes:—" Ruin seems unnoticed here, as it adds to 'the beautiful and wild.' Our noble old Brent river is a flowery stream; Cæsar's mansion is gone, also another near it, and two deep recesses in the well-known 'Church-path' field adjoining the church mark the spots where, doubtless, the two old buildings tumbled down when they could stand no longer. Well, it is the same with Kingsbury Bridge in Neasdon Lane, which has fallen into the Brent stream on fragrant herbs and flowers, including wild rue, which is fragrance indeed. This adds to ruined grandeur here, and pilgrims come from all quarters. As history mentions Oliver Cromwell here, so we may imagine his friend Milton the

poet, was, for Milton wrote his 'Paradise Regained' a few miles 'farther west.' Then Lord Byron, when at Harrow School, loved the 'beautiful and wild' around it, so let us imagine him here also."

Kingsbury is bounded on the north by Whitchurch or Little Stanmore, on the east by Hendon, and on the south by Willesden. Westward, as shown above, lies the parish of Harrow, with its adjacent hamlets of Wembley, Sudbury, and Kenton. This parish is mentioned in the Domesday Book under the name of *Chingesberie*, from which circumstance it is conjectured by Mr. Brewer in his "Beauties of England," "it would appear to have formerly contained a royal residence. King Edward the Confessor," he adds, "gave to Westminster Abbey, at the time that he confirmed to that foundation the manor of Chelsea, a third of the fruit growing 'in his woods of Kyngesbyrig;'" and it is probable that a palace in this neighbourhood had appertained to some of the preceding Saxon monarchs." It may, however, be assumed that Kingsbury was merely a royal hunting-box in the weald of Middlesex when the kings of the Middle Saxons reigned at their traditional capital of Brentford.

At the time of the Domesday survey this district doubtless formed part of the Great Forest of Middlesex; at all events, it appears to have been thickly wooded, as it afforded "pannage for 1,200 hogs." At the beginning of the present century the whole parish was in the hands of the farmer; it comprised about 1,500 acres of land, of which about thirty were woodland, sixty were arable, and the remainder were under cultivation as grass land. A large portion of the parish at the present time is covered by the Kingsbury reservoir, a sheet of water some 350 acres in extent. This reservoir, which is sometimes called "Kingsbury Lake," is about two miles in length, and, in one part, about a half a mile in width, the margin of the entire reservoir extending to about eight miles. It was formed in 1838, on that part of the Brent running from near Kingsbury church eastward, beyond the Brent bridge on the Edgware Road and the Welsh Harp station on the Midland Railway; a branch of the reservoir extends northward on the Silk stream towards The Hyde and Hendon, crossing the Edgware Road at Silk Bridge. The reservoir was constructed for the purpose of supplying the locks of the Regent's Canal. It is well stocked with fish, and at different periods of the year it is still visited by almost all the known species of water-birds. A complete list of the various species of "waders" and of wild fowl that have been observed or shot here since the formation of the reservoir will be found in

"The Birds of Middlesex," by Mr. J. V. Harting, who lived for many years in this parish, and who has preserved a large number of specimens; as also have Mr. Mitford, of Hampstead, Captain Bond, of the Zoological Society's Gardens, and Mr. Warner, of the "Old Welsh Harp," at Kingsbury; these include all the known species of tern, whimbrels (or curlews), the several varieties of snipe, plovers, gulls, widgeons, and spoon-bills, and even such rare birds as the heron, the turnstone, the avocet, and the bar-tailed godwit. During the winter the wild duck and teal are frequent visitants. The fishing in the reservoir, which is rented by the worthy host of the "Welsh Harp," is strictly preserved. From the "Rules and Conditions of the Fishery," it appears that the period for jack and perch fishing extends from the 1st of June to the end of February, and that "bottom fishing" lasts all the year round; that the annual subscription is one guinea, and the charge for " daily fishing with live bait" is 2s. 6d., and for " daily bottom fishing," 1s. To many lovers of the rod and line these waters are comparatively unknown; most of its frequenters are members of recognised clubs, so that the "takes" are jealously weighed, and each finny specimen closely scrutinised. The kinds of fish taken here are jack, bream, perch, and carp, and the weights compare favourably with those of other spots where knights of the rod do mostly love to congregate.

In the rear of the "Welsh Harp," and abutting upon the lake, are some pleasantly-laid-out tea-gardens, which are much frequented during the summer, the boating on the lake serving as a special attraction.

In this parish, close to the " Welsh Harp," a race-course was laid out about twenty years ago, which enjoyed, not without good cause, the reputation of being a nuisance and a disgrace to the whole of our north-west suburbs. The race-meetings were low, vulgar, and commonplace to a degree, and were utterly ignored by the committees who arrange the details of Epsom and Ascot. Their name was un-known to the Jockey Club, and so they were under no sort of regulation which might operate as a guarantee of their being conducted honestly and respectably. They were started and maintained as a mere money speculation by the owners of neighbouring taverns, who netted large sums as "gate-money" as often as these occasions recurred. The bookmakers here were obliged in self-defence to take with them a body of prize-fighters, and the scenes which followed can be better imagined than described. So bad was their order, indeed, and so ineffectual proved all appeals to the law to put them down,

that in the end, about the year 1878, a Bill was introduced into Parliament to suppress all horse-races within ten or twelve miles of the metropolis; and this having been passed, Kingsbury races were abolished, and the racecourse has since been converted into the more creditable uses of a farm. That Kingsbury races were quite modern is proved by the fact that in Ruff's "Guide to the Turf" for 1863 not a single horse-race is mentioned as being run within twelve miles of London; whereas the names of the Alexandra Park, Brentwood, Bromley, Croydon, Ealing, Edgware, Eltham, En-field, Finchley, Harrow, Hendon, Kingsbury, Lillie Bridge, Streatham, Uxbridge, and West Drayton, figure, in 1873, amongst others, in the list of "Suburban Meetings." At Kingsbury these meetings were held on an average four times a year.

Kingsbury Church stands away by itself at some little distance from the village. It is dedicated to St. Andrew, and is a small building, consisting of nave and chancel, and a wooden tower sur-mounted by a short spire. The stonework of the windows is of the Perpendicular style, and there was once a wooden porch here of the Decorated period, its barge-boards cut into a handsome ogee arch, but it has been removed. The church, how-ever, is thought by Mr. M. H. Bloxam to be of Anglo-Saxon date, though its rude walls are covered over with coats of plaster and rough-cast, con-cealing the peculiar features of the structure. The building was restored about the year 1870, at which time the steeple was rebuilt. The churchyard is planted with evergreen shrubs which conceal and dampen the fabric itself.

Dr. Stukeley imagines that this church stands within the area of a Roman encampment, which was Cæsar's second station after his presumed passage of the Thames at Coway Stakes. * Gale, the antiquary, in reference to this opinion, observes that it certainly lies near the great Roman road which led from London to Sulloniacæ and thence to Verulamium (St. Albans). This church was visited by Gale in the summer of 1750, and is described by him as being built chiefly of Roman bricks, which Stukeley thought might have been taken from the ruins of Verulam, but which the former supposed to have "come from the *Kings-bury*, or *Villa Regia*, whence the parish appears to derive its name." "The alleged existence of a Roman castrametation on this spot," observes Mr. Brewer in the "Beauties of England," "may, possibly, be one of those chimerical speculations in which Dr. Stukeley was accustomed to indulge;

---

* See *ante*, p. 179.

but," he adds, "perhaps it may be worthy of notice that a field adjoining the churchyard exhibits evident marks of an artificial inequality of surface."

The church is old and weather-worn, and contains a few monuments of interest, notably one in the chancel, and enclosed by the altar-rails, to the memory of John Bul, who died in 1621. He was "Gentleman of the Poultry to Queen Elizabeth and King James;" and another dated 1626, to Thomas Scudamore, who was also a servant to those sovereigns for a period of 47 years. There is also

his "History of Animated Nature." Here Goldsmith was visited by Boswell, and Mickle, the translator of "The Lusiad." Boswell has inserted a notice of this visit in his "Life of Dr. Johnson." It appears that Goldsmith was not "at home;" "but having a curiosity," writes Boswell, "to see his apartments, we went in, and found curious scraps of descriptions of animals scrawled upon the walls with a black-lead pencil." It appears to have been in or about the year 1773 that Goldsmith joined a fellow-countryman and took up his

HIGH HOUSE FARM.

abode here, giving to the house the name of the "Shoemaker's Paradise," it having been built in a whimsical style by a knight of St. Crispin. Here, besides the works above named, he wrote his popular, but superficial, "History of England," which, on its first appearance, anonymously, passed for the production of Lord Lyttelton.

a brass to the memory of John Shephard and Ann and Matilda, his wives, with their eighteen children, and bears the date of 1520. William, third Earl of Mansfield, who died in 1840, is buried in a vault in the churchyard.

A pathway across the meadows northward of the churchyard leads to Fryern Farm and Kingsbury Green, a collection of cottages and villas somewhat larger than the village itself. From the Green a lane passes eastward to the Edgware Road, near the sixth milestone from London, and at a place called The Hyde. On the left of this lane is a farmhouse, called High House, or Hyde House, Farm, where Oliver Goldsmith was living when he wrote some portions of the "Vicar of Wakefield" and *She Stoops to Conquer*. He engaged this lodging chiefly "for the purpose of deep retirement," while preparing

The house is said to be between 200 and 300 years old, and is of brick, and of two floors. The front portion of the building, with the exception of some of the windows having been renewed and that the heavy beams of the ceiling have given place to flat stucco work, remains in much the same condition as when it was occupied by Goldmith more than a century ago. The rooms at the back, however, were rebuilt only a few years ago, at which time a small chamber, which had been used by Goldsmith as his study, was unfortunately demolished. This room, we understand, contained a small cupboard, which might have been used by him as a book-case, and bore unmistakable signs of having been occupied by the author of "Animated Nature."

The hamlet of The Hyde is a row of houses and small shops bordering the high road ; but, beyond a Congregational chapel of Gothic design, possesses nothing to attract the notice of the passing stranger. Here the Passionists, under Father Spencer, were located before they settled at Highgate.*

John Lyon, the founder of Harrow School, possessed property not only at Harrow, but in Kingsbury. In the statutes which he made for the regulation of his school he directs that the governor "shall see and provide that tenn loads of wood, that is to say, six good loads of lath bavines, and fower good loads of tall wood, shall be yearely brought into ye schoolehouse from his lands att Kingsbury, to and for ye comon use of ye schollers of ye said schoole."

Kenton is a small hamlet belonging to Harrow, about midway between that town and the Hyde. The district is extremely rural, comprising, as it does, besides the "great house," called Kenton Lodge, and another mansion known as Kenton Grange, merely two or three farmhouses, with their attendant farm-buildings and cottages.

HENDON.

CHAPTER XXVII.

HENDON.

"Flumina amem sylvasque inglorius."—LUCRETIUS

Extent and Boundaries of the Parish—The Brent River and Silk Stream—The Old Watling Street—Etymology of Hendon—Mention of the Parish in "Domesday Book"—Descent of the Manor—A Singular Immunity from Tolls—The Manor House—Hendon Place—The Parish Church—Almshouses—Brent Street, Golder's Green—Mill Hill—The Grammar School—Roman Catholic Missionary College—St. Mary's Franciscan Nunnery—St. Margaret's Industrial School—Littleberries—Highwood House—Sir Stamford Raffles—Visit of Baron Bunsen—William Wilberforce the Philanthropist.

CROSSING the Edgware Road, and making our way in a north-easterly direction past the Hendon station on the Midland Railway, after a walk of about a mile up a somewhat steep lane, we find ourselves at the village of Hendon. This is an extensive parish, being about seven miles from north to south, and from two to four miles in width. It is bounded on the east and south-east by Finchley and Highgate, on the south by Hampstead, and on the north by Edgware and Barnet.

The whole parish is pleasingly diversified by hills and valleys, the former commanding extensive and varied prospects, and the latter falling in gentle slopes, agreeably sprinkled with ornamental timber. The land is mostly laid out in meadows and pastures, intersected by pleasant field-paths and shady lanes and hedgerows ; and it is also well wooded, the trees yielding an abundance of timber. In the northern part of the parish the principal elevations are Highwood Hill, Mill Hill, and the rising ground occupied by Hendon village. In the south the little river Brent wanders through the meadows, its bulk being augmented by the numerous head-streams which take their rise in this parish. The Silk stream also flows through the valley westward of the village, and as stated in the preceding chapter, unites its waters with those of the Brent in the Kingsbury Reservoir.

According to Camden and Norden, a Roman road, supposed to be the Watling Street, passed along this neighbourhood, but no traces of it now remain, though the present Edgware Road is presumed to occupy its track. Norden was a resident at Hendon, and must therefore have possessed an accurate knowledge of the existing state of this parish in the time of James I. In his "Speculum Britanniæ" he describes this presumed Roman road as "an auncient high waie, leading to Edgeworth through an olde lane, called Hendon-wante.' The dedication to Norden's "Surveyor's Dialogue" (1607) is dated from his " poore house at Hendon." A lane leading through Colin Deep from Hendon to the Edgware Road is called in old surveys "Ancient Street."

The name of this parish is said to have been originally written *Heandune*, and is derived from two Saxon words which signify *High-down*, and which therefore apply very correctly to its elevated circumstances of situation. In " Domesday Book " the name of the place is written *Handone*, which Norden derives from *Highendune*, "which signifyeth Highwood, of the plenty of wood there growing on the hills." Taylor, in his " Words and Places," asserts that Hendon comes "from the Anglo-Saxon *hean*, poor." But to this Mr. James Thorne takes objection in his " Environs of London," where he says, "the soil is fertile rather than sterile, and it is to *héan*, high, rather than *hean*, poor, that we may look for the probable derivation."

At the time of the Domesday survey—and indeed for some time previously—the manor of Hendon belonged to the Abbots of Westminster. " There was land for sixteen ploughs," and "a priest had one virgate," which would of course imply that there was a church here at that early period. The survey adds that " there was meadow sufficient for two oxen, and pannage for 1,000 hogs," so that it would appear that the greater part of the land formed part of the forest of Middlesex.

The principal manor was alienated by Gervais de Blois, Abbot of Westminster, in the reign of King Stephen, and it continued in lay hands till early in the fourteenth century. During a part of this time it was held by the Le Rous family, who, according to Lysons, probably had a residence here, for, in the 50th year of Henry III., Geoffrey le Rous, Sheriff of the counties of Bedford and Bucks, "petitioned for a remuneration for the burning of his houses and corn, and for the loss of horses, arms, clothes, and other goods, of which he had been despoiled at his manor of Hendon, by John de Egville and other turbulent chiefs of that period, to whom he might officially have made himself obnoxious." In 1312 the manor was restored to the Abbey of Westminster, having been exchanged by the then holder, Richard le Rous, for that of Hodford, also in this parish, and it was afterwards made part of the endowment of the newly-created bishopric of Westminster. The name of Hodford is still given to some of the lands belonging to the Dean and Chapter of Westminster, at North End, bordering on Hampstead Heath. On the dissolution of the see of Westminster in 1550, this manor was granted by the Crown to Sir William Herbert, with whose descendants, the Earls of Powis, it remained till the middle of the last century, when it was purchased by the celebrated David Garrick. A nephew of his, the Rev. George Garrick, was vicar of Hendon for some time. In 1790, after Garrick's death, the manor was sold to a Mr. John Bond, and it has since changed hands several times.

This parish, observes Mr. Brewer, in his work already quoted, possesses a singular *immunity*, which was granted as early as the year 1066, and was confirmed by various subsequent charters. Divers lands in this parish had been granted by King Edward the Confessor to the church of St. Peter at Westminster, that monarch at the same time freeing the inhabitants from all *tolls*, both by land and water. Henry III. and Richard II., by charters, the former dated at Woodstock in the ninth year, and the latter at Westminster, in the seventeenth year, of their respective reigns, confirmed these immunities, which were further conceded and confirmed by the several charters of Henry VIII., Edward VI., and James I. Lastly, William and Mary, by letters patent dated at Westminster in the fifth year of their reign, granted and confirmed to Sir William Rawlinson, Serjeant-at-law, the charters of their predecessors, with all their privileges; and thereby "freed the inhabitants of Hendon from all tolls in all fairs and markets, and from all street tolls, and every other toll whatever, in every fair and every market, and every bridge, and every way and water, and also by sea, for themselves and their wares, for ever."

The manor-house stood near Church End, which is the name given to a cluster of houses built in the neighbourhood of the church, and on or near the site now occupied by Hendon Place. The original mansion was used, in the early part of the sixteenth century, as a country residence by the abbot of Westminster. It was here that Wolsey first rested, when travelling, in a state of disgrace, towards York. Stow, in his "Annals," says that the Cardinal "having sent to London for livery clothes for his servants that should ride with him, in the beginning of Passion week, before Easter, set forward and rode from Richmond to a place of the Abbot of Westminster at Hendon." Norden, writing in the time of Elizabeth, describes the manor-house as the property of Sir Edward Herbert, and the residence of Sir John Fortescue. The family of Nicoll appear to have resided here during the greater part of the seventeenth century. The house was purchased towards the middle of the last century by a Mr. Thomas Snow, who took down the ancient building, which is described as having contained "a spacious gallery," and erected the present house. Among the later occupants of the house have been the Earl of Northampton and Lord Chief Justice Tenterden.

Hendon Place is a well-proportioned and handsome mansion, comprising a body and two wings, and the grounds are rendered attractive by various picturesque undulations. The river Brent, which skirts the eastern side of the grounds, has been artificially widened so as to form a moderate lake, which, with the bridge by which it is crossed, adds not a little to the beauty of the landscape. There are several fine trees on this estate, and among them one or two flourishing cedars. In the *Gentleman's Magazine* for 1779 is a communication from Sir John Cullum, giving the dimensions of a large cedar which formerly stood on the north side of Hendon Place, but which was blown down by a high wind on the 1st of January in that year.

The parish church of Hendon occupies an elevated position on the brow of a hill immediately to the north of the main street. It is a plain-looking edifice, the walls, with the exception of the tower, being covered with plaster. It comprises a nave with clerestory and aisles, a chancel with side chapels, and a square stone tower, with embattled parapets, at the west end; this latter is evidently the most ancient part of the fabric. The greater portion of the church was probably erected late in the fifteenth century, but the windows are mostly modern: those of the clerestory and at the east end of the chancel are filled with painted glass. The font is Norman, square in form, and ornamented on each of the four sides with an arcade of round-headed interlaced arches. The arches of the nave spring from octagonal columns; the whole body and aisles of the church are encumbered with unsightly pews and deep galleries.

In the north chapel of the chancel is the tomb of Sir William Rawlinson, one of the Commissioners of the Great Seal, who died in 1703: the effigy of the deceased, by Rysbach, is represented in a semi-recumbent attitude, attired in legal robes and insignia. Close by is an elaborate monument of veined marble to Edward Fowler, Bishop of Gloucester, who died in 1714. At the west end of the north aisle is the burial-place of Sir Francis Whichcote and his family, over which is an apartment fitted up and used as a vestry-room, by permission of Sir Francis. On the south side of the chancel is a mural tablet to several of the family of Colmore, of Warwickshire. This monument is the work of Flaxman, and bears upon it the emblems of Faith and Hope. There is also a handsome monument to the memory of several branches of the Herbert family, many of whom are buried in this church; Sir Coutts Trotter, Bart., who died in 1838, is also commemorated by an elaborate mural monument. A brass in this church bears date 1564; there is another, very ancient, without date, embedded in a stone slab in front of the vestry door.

In the churchyard, among other tombs and monuments, are those of Sir Joseph Ayloffe, Bart., a distinguished antiquary, and Keeper of the State Papers, who died in 1781; Nathaniel Hone, R.A., who died in 1784; Abraham Raimbach, engraver, who died in 1843, and whose name will be remembered for his numerous works after Wilkie. James Parsons, M.D., "eminent as a physician, man of science, and antiquary," who died in 1770, is commemorated by a monument; and there are also the family vaults of the Earls of Mansfield, and many other local worthies, including Charles Johnson, a dramatist, dated 1748; Edward Longmore, the "Herefordshire Colossus," seven feet six inches high, who died in 1777; and Sarah Gundry, who died in 1807, and whose grave-stone is noticeable on account of its epitaph, which runs as follows :—

" Reader ! she wander'd all the desert through
    In search of happiness, nor found repose
  Till she had reach'd the borders of this waste.
  Full many a flower that blossom'd in her path
  She stoop'd to gather, and the fruit she pluck'd
  That hung from many a tempting bough—all but
    The rose of Sharon and the tree of life.
  This flung its fragrance to the gale, and spread
  Its blushing beauties : that its healing leaves
  Displayed, and fruit immortal, all in vain.
  She neither tasted nor admired—and found
  All that she chose and trusted fair, but false !
  The flowers no sooner gather'd than they faded ;
  The fruits enchanting, dust and bitterness ;
  And all the world a wilderness of care.
  Wearied, dispirited, and near the close
  Of this eventful course, she sought the plant
  That long her heedless haste o'erlook'd, and proved
  Its sovereign virtues ; underneath its shade
  Outstretch'd, drew from her wounded feet the thorns,
  Shed the last tear, breathed the last sigh, and here
  The aged pilgrim rests in trembling hope ! "

The churchyard is kept in very good condition, and from the entrance-gate to the south door of the church runs an avenue of clipped lime-trees, which has a very pretty effect, and there are also several yew-trees of moderate size ; whilst the view from the north side of the old churchyard embraces a large extent of country, including Stanmore, Edgware, Harrow, and the distant hills of Buckinghamshire and Hertfordshire, together with the hamlets of Highwood and Mill Hill, to which latter place a pleasant footpath leads across the intervening valley.

Hendon is a vicarage, but was anciently a rectory also, the latter being a sinecure. The rectors presented the vicars until late in the fifteenth century, when the church was appropriated to the abbot and convent of Westminster, with whom the right of presentation remained until the dissolution of monastic houses. Later on, the advowson was granted, with the manor, to the Herbert family, and it descended in conjunction with the manorial property until the year 1794, when it passed into separate hands.

At a short distance from the church, at the entrance to the main street, are almshouses for six poor men and four women, erected in 1729. They were founded in 1681 by Robert Daniel, who bequeathed the sum of £2,000 for the purpose of building " an almshouse within twelve miles of London." The almshouses, which are of red brick, were repaired in 1853.

At Burrows, a hamlet lying on the road between the village and the railway-station, is the Metro-politan Convalescent Institution, which affords a comfortable home for forty little girls.

Races have taken place here yearly since 1864, but they have proved to be a great nuisance to the inhabitants.

Brent Street is the name given to a hamlet of Finchley ; one of the houses here was formerly the seat of the Whichcotes, and afterwards of Sir William Rawlinson, whose monument has been already noticed in the church. Although it has been modernised, some parts of the house appear to be of considerable antiquity. A new chapel-of-ease, Christ Church, was built here in the year 1881, the " foundation stone " being laid by Lady Burdett-Coutts. The building is in the Early English style, and was erected from the designs of Mr. Salter. A spacious Congregational church, of Gothic design, has been erected in this locality ; and at the lower end of the street a bridge over the river Brent leads to Golder's Green, another hamlet of Hendon, which is pleasantly situated on the road to Hampstead.

Golder's Green consists of a few decent cottages and villa residences fringing the roadside, the larger part of the " green " proper being now enclosed. The " White Swan " tavern, with its tea-gardens, is a favourite resort of London holiday-makers in the summer-time, the various walks by rural lanes and field-paths in the immediate neighbourhood adding much to the charm of the locality. Of Golder's Hill, at North End, which was once the residence of Jeremiah Dyson, clerk to the House of Commons, and the friend of Mark Akenside the author of the " Pleasures of Imagination," an account will be found in OLD AND NEW LONDON, in the chapter on Hampstead.* Akenside was a frequent guest at his friend's house here, and often made it his home. In one of his poems, " An Ode on Recovery from a Fit of Sickness in the Country," written in 1758, Akenside thus apostrophises this lovely spot :—

" Thy verdant scenes, O Golder's Hill,
    Once more I seek, a languid guest ;
  With throbbing temples and with burden'd breast
  Once more I climb thy steep aërial way.
  O faithful cure of oft returning ill,
      Now call thy sprightly breezes round,
      Dissolve this rigid cough profound,
  And bid the springs of life with gentler movement play."

Page Street is the name of a small hamlet which lies in the valley between Hendon Church and Mill Hill. The most conspicuous object here is Copt Hall, the residence of the Nicoll family. The house was built early in the seventeenth century by Randall Nicoll, Esq., and is a fair example of the domestic architecture of that age.

Mill Hill surmounts a fine swell of ground, which rises by an easy progress to a considerable height, and the views afforded at different stages of the ascent are both extensive and varied, including, it is said, on clear days, the distant towers of Windsor Castle. Mill Hill has numbered among its inhabitants one or two individuals whose names have become famous. Peter Collinson, the naturalist, had a house here, and formed a curious botanical garden. Linnæus commemorated a visit to this garden by planting several trees. The premises were afterwards purchased by means of a subscription among the Independents for the purpose of a foundation grammar-school, and is now known as Mill Hill College. The school was till lately the only public school for Protestant Nonconformists. It is stated in the *Mirror* (August 8th, 1835) that the original school-house here could boast of having been once the " dwelling of Linnæus, and the occasional residence of architects."

The Nonconformists' Grammar School was established on the basis of a sectional, if not sectarian, limitation only, because all the old foundations were exclusive and sectarian in the opposite direction. Even as a Nonconformist's school, Mill Hill has had a history. It had not only educated many men well known to Evangelical Nonconformity, but some men of larger reputation had been among its alumni. The late Justice Talfourd, Mr. Challis (the astronomer), and Dr. Jacobson (the present Bishop of Chester) were all educated at Mill Hill in the old days. " As the more national foundations became less sectarian," observes a writer in the *Daily News*, " so the Dissenting schools have become less Dissenting. The old Nonconformists always declared that Dissent was forced upon them as an unwelcome necessity, and in the matter of education their descendants are giving proof of the statement. As a sign of the times, we note this change with unmixed satisfaction. It is one of the good results of rendering our middle-class education as far as possible unsectarian. A like policy applied to the highest education in the universities and to the lowest education in the primary schools will have a similar result."

The present building was erected by Sir William Tite in 1825. It is simple and bold, rather than grand, and forms a long Italian villa on a terrace. Its chief front looks away from the road, and commands a fine view of Harrow. It has a noble portico supported by six Italian pillars, and surmounted by a pediment. The dining-hall is near the centre ; the chapel at the north end is a poor, mean structure. The cost of the building was above £25,000.

The opening of the universities to Dissenters has helped to fill the school, as, happily, it is now worth the while of Nonconformists, with a view to the advantages held out by the older universities, to be at the expense of a classical education for their sons.

Mill Hill was once the residence of John Wilkes, the politician, and of the late Alderman Sir Charles Flower.

In the " Beauties of England " we read :—" There still remains (1816) on Mill Hill, though in an almost ruinous state, one of the ancient domestic structures of the neighbourhood. This building is in the best taste of the reign of Charles I. The walls of one of the apartments are curiously painted with the story of the Prodigal Son, and over the chimney are the initials of the Nicoll family. The house is now divided, and tenanted by the poor." This building, however, appears to be long since clean swept away ; at all events, nothing is now known of its existence at Mill Hill.

Hendon seems to have long been in high favour with Roman Catholics. The " Dames de Nazareth," founded in France by the Duchesse de la Rochefoucauld for the higher education of young ladies, have an establishment here, which is under the special patronage of the Cardinal Archbishop of Westminster ; and here they receive, in addition to their French pupils, a limited number of English young ladies.

St. Joseph's College of the Sacred Heart, for Foreign Missions, founded by Bishop Vaughan of Salford, is at Mill Hill. The first stone of this institution was laid by Archbishop (Cardinal) Manning in 1869, and a portion was completed and opened in 1871. The grounds of the college are about forty acres in extent, and the buildings, which are somewhat heavy and in the monastic style, were erected from the designs of Mr. G. Goldie. The architecture of the college is " Lombardo-Venetian," and it is built in the form of a quadrangle surrounded by cloisters, one side of which is occupied by the chapel, which has a lofty campanile tower, surmounted by a gilded statue of St. Joseph, which is seen for miles around. Students of every nationality are admitted, and bind themselves by solemn vows to leave Europe for life upon missionary labours.

Two other Roman Catholic institutions are located at Mill Hill: namely, the Franciscan convent of St. Mary and the St. Margaret's Industrial School.

The church for the ecclesiastical district of Mill Hill was built in 1832, by William Wilberforce. It is dedicated to St. Paul, and is in the Early English style. It is a poor structure. Six alms-houses near the church were erected in 1696, at the charge of Thomas Nicoll, of this parish, for the use of the poor.

Among the seats and mansions in this neigh-

Mr. Scharf gives the following interesting particulars concerning this old house, which stands on a slope near the public road :—

"The mansion is an ordinary square building of red brick, with irregular corners, that has been much added to at various times. The entrance door leads directly into the hall, which has a low flat ceiling, the floor being on a level with the carriage-drive in front. The rooms are irregular, but they enclose a central apartment, which appears

LITTLEBERRIES.

bourhood is Littleberries, a good old substantial residence of brick, which tradition says was built by Charles II. It is often said also that Nell Gwyn lived here ; but the assertion rests only on tradition. The house probably does date back to the days of Charles II., and in one room are medallion portraits, which tradition has assumed to be of that king and some of his mistresses, but which, in the opinion of Mr. George Scharf, the Secretary of the National Portrait Gallery, are representations of sovereigns of much more recent date. It has also been stated that the house was at one time tenanted by Louise de Quérouaille, Duchess of Portsmouth ; but this is very doubtful.

In *Notes and Queries* for January 21st, 1882,

to have belonged to a former and much more important residence. This central apartment is not large, but lofty ; it is floored with wood, and has only one actual door, opening into the staircase hall. It contains an amount of rich wood-carving and mural decoration; it is known as the Gilt Room. Broken pediments, Greek frets, guilloches, egg-and-tongue mouldings, shell patterns, festoons, female masks, and lions' heads are to be seen everywhere. The tone of this elaborate ornamentation is of the period of Queen Anne or the two first Georges."

The panels of the " Gilt Room " are painted with copies, full size, of pictures by Rubens, Van Dyck, and other artists, and of such subjects as " Venus and Cupid," "Hesperides Gathering Fruit," &c. One picture, however, is of a totally different character to the rest : it represents the full-length figure of a young lad, standing, and wearing the robes of the Garter. It is inscribed : "Charles Lennox, Duke of Richmond and Lennox, Born 29 July, 1672, Dyed 27 May, 1723." This picture, in the opinion of Mr. Scharf, seems to have been inserted in the panel in the place of something else. In the coved cornice of this apartment, over the centre of each wall, is a large circular medallion in white plaster of a crowned sovereign, the size of life, in alto-relievo. That above the fire-place, observes Mr. Scharf, in the article above quoted, contains a portrait of Caroline of Anspach, queen consort of George II., of whom there is a portrait on the opposite wall. On the side facing the door, and over the windows, the medallion exhibits a portrait of George I., whilst the remaining medallion, over the door, contains a portrait of William III. The chimney-piece of this room is elaborately carved in wood, the principal figures in the ornamentation being emblematic of "Justice" and "Peace."

SIR STAMFORD RAFFLES.
(*From the bust by Chantrey.*)

"Throughout the whole buildings," observes Mr. Scharf, in the article from which we have quoted above, "there is no indication, either by coronet, garter, or heraldic cognizance, that the place ever belonged to any person of rank or distinction. The only exception where heraldry appears is in the pediment of the summer-house at the end of the grounds. There the arms of the Pawsons of Shawdon, in Northumberland, are carved on a plain shield, and may be referred to a period when the front of the building was altered, and the spaces between the columns filled in with windows of coloured glass. The walls and domed ceiling of the summer-house are decorated with figures and ornaments in white plaster. They include portrait medallions of females, supported by sphinxes, mermaids, and tritons. These faces are all in profile, full of individuality, and probably

represented members of the family who then occupied the house. On the east wall is a curious circular medallion, containing a view in white plaster alto-relievo of the mansion as it formerly appeared from this spot, showing the different levels of ground, and reproducing the building in its original state, including the Gilt Room and steps leading up to it. We see by this that the central façade was flanked on each side by massive walls, large windows, and an elevated roof. In the sloping plane in front of the house there are no basins of water ; nor is any figure introduced so as to give indication by the costume of the exact period when the view was taken."

At Highwood Hill, at the distance of about a mile from Mill Hill, at one time—namely, from 1826 to 1831—lived the great philanthropist, William Wilberforce ; and here, too, dwelt Lord William Russell, previous to his arrest. Highwood House, early in the present century, was the residence of Sir Stamford Raffles, Governor of Java, and founder and first President of the Zoological Society. Wilberforce became Sir Stamford Raffles's "next-door neighbour" in June, 1826, only about a month before the death of the latter. Lady Raffles continued to reside here after the death of her husband, and was here visited on more than one occasion by Baron Bunsen. In the Baroness Bunsen's "Memoirs of Baron Bunsen" appears the following reference to the house and grounds, under the date of 1839 :—

"A visit to Highwood gave an opportunity for commenting upon the dignity, the order, the quiet activity, the calm cheerfulness with which Lady Raffles rules the house, the day, the conversation ; and the place and its neighbourhood were full of those memorials of the honoured dead which served to enhance the natural beauty of the prospect and the interest attaching itself to the residence of Sir Stamford Raffles. The ground of Highwood must have been trodden by the footsteps and hallowed by the life and sorrows of Rachel,

Lady Russell, even though no family recollection exists to mark the spot which she inhabited, when she dated some of her letters from Totteridge, a village lying near. But the beautiful portion of wood in which Lady Raffles' friends have enjoyed walking with her contains within its precincts a chalybeate spring, walled round, and marked by an inscription as having been enclosed by Mistress Rachel Russell, at a date when the eldest daughter of Lord and Lady Russell must have been under twelve years old ; yet is there nothing unreasonable in the supposition that the mother should have caused the work to be performed as a public benefit (the healing quality of the spring being in repute among the poor), and assigned to it the name of her daughter instead of her own. Moreover, in that wood there is a spot, evidently cleared of trees in a regular circle, from the centre of which it was remembered by the lower class of inhabitants, at the time when Sir Stamford Raffles made the purchase of the ground, that a previous proprietor, about the middle of the last century, had caused the loose stones to be removed, which formed a 'monument to the memory of the gentleman who was beheaded.' This piece of forest might have been a portion of Lady Russell's own large Southampton inheritance ; as an original Russell property it is gone out of remembrance."

Here, at Moat Mount, lived for some time the late Mr. Serjeant Cox, Recorder of Portsmouth, and latterly an assistant judge at the Middlesex Sessions. His name is well known as a man of science and a philanthropist, and as the establisher of the *Field*, *Queen*, and *Law Times* newspapers. He died suddenly in 1880. Mrs. Porter, an actress of some note in the last or beginning of the present century, was also a resident here for many years.

CHAPTER XXVIII.

EDGWARE AND LITTLE STANMORE.

" Lives of great men all remind us
We can make our lives sublime ;
And, departing, leave behind us
Footprints on the sands of time."—LONGFELLOW

Situation and Boundaries of Edgware—General Appearance of the Town—The "Chandos Arms" Inn—The "Harmonious Blacksmith "—Etymology of Edgware—The Descent of the Manor—The Manor of Edgware Bois—Edgware Market—Curious Local Customs—Death of Cosway the Artist—The Parish Church—Almshouses—Population, &c.—Edgware Races—Little Stanmore or Whitchurch—Acreage and Population—Early History of the Manor—Canons—The Family of the Lakes—James Brydges, afterwards Duke of Chandos—He Rebuilds the Mansion of Canons in a magnificent and costly manner—The Parish Church—Handel as Organist here—The "Harmonious Blacksmith."

THE town of Edgware, which we now reach by a cross-road westward from Mill Hill, Hendon, from which it is distant about two miles, together with the neighbouring estate of Canons, has been for the last century and a half associated with no less a name than that of Handel. On this account alone the spot would be worthy of a pilgrimage, notwithstanding that "princely Canons" is a thing of the past.

Edgware is eight miles from Hyde Park Corner, and extends for about a mile along the great high road to St. Albans (*Verulamium*), a thoroughfare which, as we have stated in the preceding chapter, is supposed by Camden, Norden, and other antiquaries, to occupy the track of the ancient Watling Street. The parish is bounded on the east and west by Hendon and Little Stanmore, and on the north and south by Elstree and Kingsbury. The town consists mainly of one wide and long street, made up of the usual class of buildings to be met with in a small country town, namely, shops mostly small and antiquated, humble cottages, mixed up with a few dwelling-houses of a better kind. There are also a few respectable taverns and hostelries, which, doubtless, in the "good old coaching days" were houses of some consequence. One of these, "The Chandos Arms," keeps in remembrance the associations of the neighbouring palace of Canons. In one of the rooms of this inn is an antiquated fireplace, which was brought from Canons, on the demolition of that mansion. The west side of the street belongs in reality to the parish of Little Stanmore, or Whitchurch. The visitor to Edgware will now look in vain for the blacksmith's shop, in which, according to tradition, Handel took shelter during a shower, and in which worked William Powell, the Edgware blacksmith—or, as he is commonly called, the "Harmonious Blacksmith"—whose performance on the anvil is said to have suggested to Handel the well-known melody named after him.

Of this worthy we shall have more to say on reaching Whitchurch, where he was buried, and where Handel was for many years organist.

Norden conjectures that the name of this parish was originally Edgworth, " signifying a fruitful place upon the edge, or utter part, of the shire ; " but such a mode of etymology, Mr. Brewer contends, in the " Beauties of England," appears to rest entirely on surmise. The Irish Edgworths, of Edgworthtown, whose name has been made so widely known by the writings of Miss Edgworth, came originally from this place, if we may believe their pedigree as set forth by Sir Bernard Burke. Lysons observes that in the most ancient record in which he has seen the name mentioned (dated in the reign of Henry II.) it is written "Eggeswere;" and that the same form of orthography prevailed until the age of Henry VIII., when the present mode of spelling was adopted, and has since been uniformly used in legal and in ordinary writings.

The name of Edgware, or even Eggeswere, does not appear in "Domesday Book." In the latter part of the twelfth century, according to Lysons, the principal manor belonged to Ella, Countess of Salisbury, wife of William Longespee, " who granted it to her son Nicholas and his espoused wife, to be held of her by the render of a sparrow-hawk." Towards the close of the succeeding century, Henry de Lacy, Earl of Lincoln, was the owner of this manor, in right of his wife, Margaret, Countess of Salisbury. The property was after-wards conveyed in marriage by the daughter and heiress of the last Earl of Lincoln, of the De Lacy family, to the Le Stranges, with whom it con-tinued down to the year 1431, when it passed to the Darells, by whom again it was sold shortly after to Thomas Chichele and other persons, as trustees for All Souls' College, Oxford. With that college the property still continues. An inferior manor within this parish, called Bois, or Edgware Bois, was formerly owned by the Priory of St. John of Jerusalem, and afterwards by the Dean and Chapter of Windsor. In the Chartulary of the Priory of St. John this manor is styled *Egelware Bois*, or *Eggesware*. Towards the end of the fifteenth century, this manor having passed by exchange or otherwise to the Dean and Chapter of Westminster, was surrendered by that body to the king. Henry VIII. granted it, in the year 1544, to Sir John Williams and Anthony Stringer, from whom it passed by sale to the Pages. It was afterwards owned by the Earl of Coventry, and subsequently sold to the Lees, by whose representative it is still held. A hamlet, now called Edgware-Bury, lies about a mile and a half northward from the town.

About two miles beyond the town, on the borders of the county, is an eminence called Brockley Hill, which by Camden and other antiquaries is supposed to be the site of the Roman station Sulloniacæ. Of the numerous Roman remains which have been discovered at different times both here and at places in the immediate neighbourhood, we shall have more to say in the next chapter.

Edgware had in former times a weekly market on Thursdays, but that had been "for some time discontinued" when Lysons wrote his "Environs of London" in 1795. Indeed, it is on record that as far back as 1668 the site of the market was con-veyed by Sir Lancelot Lake, of Canons, to certain trustees upon trust for a public school. In the year 1867 the Privy Council licensed the holding of a cattle market here on the last Thursday in every month.

The parish records contain some curious items, referring to customs which have long since become obsolete. From some of these, quoted by Lysons, it appears that in 1328 one hundred acres of land were held under the manor of Edgware by the render of a pair of gilt spurs, and fifty acres by the rent of a pound of "cummin." At the court held in 1551, two men were fined here for playing at "cards and tables." In the next year the inhabi-tants were "presented" for not having a "tum-brel and cucking-stool"—the latter, of course, as a terror to "scolds." In 1558 a man was fined for selling ale at an "exorbitant price," namely, one pint and a half for a penny !

Sir William Blackstone mentions a curious custom appertaining to the manor of Edgware, namely, that it was usual for the lord to provide a minstrel, or piper, for the amusement of the tenants while they were employed in his service—a custom which has been kept in remembrance by the name given to a small tract of land in this parish, called " Piper's Green."

It was on the road to Edgware that the artist Cosway, the favourite of the Prince of Wales, suddenly breathed his last, at the age of eighty, in 1821, whilst being taken out for an airing in the carriage of a friend.

The parish church of Edgware, dedicated to St. Margaret, stands about the middle of the town, on the east side of the roadway, and, with the exception of the tower, is modern and uninteresting. It consists of a chancel, nave, and transepts, and is built of brick, in imitation of the Perpendicular style. The tower, which is constructed of flint and stone, and has an embattled parapet and an octagonal angle turret, is part of a former church, which is supposed to have belonged to a religious house, or monastery, dedicated to St. John of Jerusalem. Kelly tells us, in his "Directory of Middlesex," that "amongst the Augmentation Records is preserved a certificate of the goods and plate of the church and monastery of Edgware at the time of the dissolution of religious houses." The body of the original church having become dilapidated, was rebuilt about the middle of the last century, and this again was renewed or rebuilt in 1845. The east window, of three lights, is filled with stained glass, as also are those of the transepts. The only monument in the church worthy of notice is one to Randulph Nicoll, who died in 1658. He was a native of this parish, and, if the Latin inscription on his monument may be trusted, a man of great learning and accomplishments. In the chancel is a brass representing an infant in swaddling clothes, inscribed "Anthonie, son of John Childe, goldsmith;" the said infant died in 1599, aged three weeks.

The Rev. Francis Coventry, the author of the romance entitled "The Life of Pompey the Little," and of the fifteenth number of the *World*, containing strictures on modern gardening, &c., held the incumbency of this church in the last century. The Rev. Thomas Martyn, Professor of Botany at Cambridge, also held the living for some years.

Close by the church was, in pre-Reformation times, a call, or station, belonging to the abbey of St. Albans, which served as a halting-place for the monks in their journeys to and from London.

In 1680, Samuel Atkinson, a native of Edgware, built and endowed almshouses here for four poor women. There are also in the town almshouses for twelve poor persons, endowed by the late Mr. Charles Day.

Edgware is one of the polling-places for the county of Middlesex, and at the present time the terminus of a branch line of the Great Northern Railway from their main line at Finsbury Park. The town is also within a mile and a half of the Mill Hill Station, on the Midland Railway. At the end of the last century the number of houses in the town, exclusive of almshouses, was 76. In 1871 they had increased to 137, or nearly doubled. The population at the last-mentioned date was 655, to which nearly two hundred more have since been added.

Races were held at Edgware in 1869 and 1873, but they did not acquire the popularity of those at Hampton, Sandown, and other suburban racecourses. They have now died a natural death.

Little Stanmore—or Whitchurch, as the village is more popularly called—lies about half a mile to the west of Edgware. The parish, with the exception of that portion forming one side of the main street of Edgware, is almost wholly agricultural. The entire area of the parish is rather over 1,500 acres, and the number of the inhabitants in 1881 amounted to 818. Much of the land in the parish bordering the main road northward of Edgware is taken up by the demesne of Canons, whilst the remainder is occupied by broad undulating meadows, intersected by shady lanes and avenues of stately trees.

The parishes of Little Stanmore and Edgware run parallel northward as far as Elstree, in Hertfordshire, the boundary of the two being in the middle of the road, in a similar manner to that in which Hendon and Kingsbury are separated. It is probable that at the time of the Domesday Survey both the parishes of Stanmore Magna (Great Stanmore) and Stanmore Parva (Little Stanmore) were united. In that record it is stated that "Roger de Rames held in Stanmere nine hides and a half;" and it is further set forth that "there was land for seven ploughs, pannage for eight hundred hogs, pasture for the cattle of the village," &c. The land held by Roger de Rames—or Reymes, as the name is sometimes written—had been, previous to the Conquest, in the hands of Algar, "a servant of Earl Harold." It was possibly a subordinate manor, and it continued for several generations in the possession of the family of Rames, who owned also much landed estate in the neighbouring county of Essex, which was constituted a barony. Lysons observes that this manor was "in Stanmore Parva, and appears to have been of equal extent with the Earl of Cornwall's manor in Great Stanmore." At the marriage of Isabel, sister of Henry III., with Frederick, Emperor of Germany, "half a knight's fee was paid by Henry Bocoynte for his lands in the parish of Stanmore Parva, held of the Barony of William de Raymes." The estate next passed into the hands of the Prior of St. Bartholomew, in Smithfield, from which circumstance it is conjectured that the property received the ecclesiastical name of "Canons;" for on the dissolution of religious houses, the estate was granted, under the name of the "manors of Canons and Wimborough, in Whitchurch," to Hugh Losse. The old house now known as the "Chandos Arms," on the Whitchurch side of Edgware Street, is supposed by Lysons to have been the mansion formerly occupied by the Losse family. Over the chimney-piece in one of the rooms were formerly to be seen the arms of Losse, with the initials R. L. (Robert Losse), and the date 1557. The next occupiers of Canons were the family of Franklyn, who were living there in the reign of

Elizabeth. John Franklyn, who died in 1596, was buried in the parish church. Early in the seventeenth century the estate was sold by Sir Hugh Losse to Sir Thomas Lake, who had been in early life the amanuensis of Sir Francis Walsingham, and who held the office of Clerk of the Signet to Queen Elizabeth, and also occupied the post of principal Secretary of State under James I.

In this latter capacity Sir Thomas appears to have conducted himself with equal integrity and talent. Fuller, in his " Worthies," says that his " dexterity of dispatch and his secrecy were incredible." But he had unhappily become involved by his wife in a quarrel with the Countess of Essex, and was in consequence dismissed from his office, and sent as a prisoner to the Tower, and fined in the sum of £15,000. In the " Sidney Papers " it is stated that the king advised him to " give up " his wife and daughter, who had been the chief instruments in the quarrel, on which he observed that he could bear ill-fortune with patience, but that he could " not cease to be a husband and a father." Sir Thomas Lake died at Canons in 1630, and was succeeded in the estates by his son, Sir Lancelot Lake, who appears to have taken great interest in the welfare of the parishioners, for he not only founded a boys' school, endowing it with land producing £58 per annum, but " restored to the church those great tythes which had been wrested from her, and of which he was the lay impropriator." The church, therefore (which before this restitution had a donative of only £40 a year), became re-possessed of the rectorial tithe, and from that time, says Lysons, " the incumbents have been styled rectors in the parish register." General Lake, who distinguished himself by his military services in India at the close of the last century, was a descendant of Sir Thomas Lake. The general was raised to the peerage in 1804 by the title of Baron Lake, and three years later was advanced to a viscountcy.

The manor of Canons continued to be held by the family of the Lakes down to about the year 1710, when it was conveyed in marriage by Mary, daughter and heiress of Sir Thomas Lake, and great-granddaughter of the above Sir Thomas Lake, to James Brydges, Esq., afterwards Duke of Chandos.

It would seem from Swift's poems that James Brydges had been one of his friends until he was raised to a dukedom. At all events, he is thus referred to in one of the Dean's bitterest epigrams:—

" James Brydges was the dean's familiar friend,
James grows a duke : their friendship here must end.
Surely the dean deserves a sore rebuke
For knowing James, to say he knows a duke. "

This nobleman was Paymaster of the Forces during the war in Queen Anne's reign, under Godolphin's administration, and amassed an immense fortune ; or, in other words, " appropriated " to his own use very large sums of the public money. The House of Commons, in 1711, instituted a committee of inquiry into the public expenditure, when it was found that a deficit existed in the accounts to the extent of thirty-five millions, or that a sum to that amount remained unaccounted for, and, further, that about one-half of that sum was connected with the accounts of Brydges. His answer to the charge was that the accounts had been regularly presented, but that " the mode of scrutinizing and passing them was tedious and complex, owing to a system pursued by the Duke of Newcastle." Great carelessness with regard to the public accounts is said to have existed at that period, and such was the low state of political morality that almost every public man in office was charged with peculation. Johnson, in his pamphlet on the Falkland Islands, sarcastically alludes to the compensation which the nation received at the close of a ten years' war, for the death of multitudes, and the expense of millions, by contemplating the sudden glories of paymasters, and agents, contractors. and commissaries, " whose equipages shine like meteors, and whose palaces rise like exhalations." Chandos gave rise for scandal by the large sums which he spent in building, and by the style of magnificence in which he lived. He had, it appears, determined on building two magnificent houses. He fixed the site of his London residence in Cavendish Square, and the building was commenced with much grandeur of preparation, but was never completed.* His country palace, however, was the favourite object of his attention, and the spot he first selected for its erection was a little to the north of the town of Brentford, on the spot afterwards occupied by the seat of the Earl of Holderness ;† but he shortly relinquished his idea of building his mansion in the neighbourhood of the stately and commanding Syon House, and accordingly removed his workmen to Canons, where he set about the erection of an edifice which was to be the wonder of the age for its splendour. In this great work the Duke is said to have spent no less a sum than £200,000. Its splendour, however, was but short-lived, for in an equal degree the edifice became the wonder of the succeeding age by its abrupt declension and premature ruin.

---

* See " Old and New London," Vol. IV., p. 443.
† See *ante*, p. 60.

Although the grandeur and magnificence of the mansion became the theme of poetic inspiration, and evoked the satirical remarks of a poetical writer whose verse is calculated to survive the finest building of stone, very little as to detail occurs concerning it in the prosaic pages of topography. Three architects appear to have been employed on the building, namely: Gibbs, James of Greenwich, and Sheppard, who designed the theatres in Goodman's Fields and Covent Garden; and Dr. Alexander Blackwell, the author of a "Treatise on Agriculture," superintended the laying out of the grounds and pleasure-grounds.

The house was commenced in 1715, when the north front was built by Strong, the mason who

expense of the building and furniture is said to have amounted to £200,000. Gough, in his "Additions to Camden," sets down the cost at a quarter of a million sterling.

It is somewhat strange that no painting of Canons, as it was in its glory, is known to exist; nor is there any engraving of it in the print-room of the British Museum, though there are two elevations of its principal front in the King's Library, dated in 1721 and 1730, engraved by Hulsberg. These display its chief features: eleven windows in three tiers above one another, divided by lofty columns, the cornice at the top being crowned with six or seven classical and symbolical statues, not unlike those to be seen in old

VILLAGE OF EDGWARE. (*From a Sketch made in* 1858.)

was employed on the building of St. Paul's Cathedral. "It stood," writes Lysons, in his "Environs of London," "at the end of a spacious avenue, being placed diagonally, so as to show two sides of the building, which at a distance gave the appearance of a front of prodigious extent. Vertue describes it as 'a noble square pile, all of stone; the four sides almost alike, with statues on the front; within was a small square of brick, not handsome; the outhouses of brick and stone, very convenient and well-disposed; the hall richly adorned with marble statues, busts, &c.; the ceiling of the staircase by Thornhill; the grand apartments finely adorned with paintings, sculpture, and furniture' (Strawberry Hill MSS.). The columns which supported the building were all of marble, as was the great staircase, each step of which was made of an entire block, above twenty feet in length. The whole

drawings of the "Queen's House," the predecessor of Buckingham Palace. The building also bore a strong family likeness to Wanstead House, Essex, of which we shall give a description later on in this volume.

In the "Gentleman's Tour through Great Britain," Canons is said to have been "one of the most magnificent palaces in England, built with a profusion of expense, and so well furnished within, that it had hardly its equal. The plastering and gilding were the work of the famous Pargotti, an Italian. The great *salon*, or hall, was painted by Paolucci. . . . The avenue was spacious and majestic; and as it gave you the view of two fronts joined, as it were, in one, the distance not admitting you to see the angle which was in the centre, so you were agreeably drawn in to think the front of the house almost twice as large as it was. And yet when you came nearer you were again surprised by seeing the winding passage opening, as it were, a new front to the eye of near one hundred and twenty feet wide, which you had not seen before ; so that you were lost awhile in looking near at hand for what you so plainly saw a great way off."

The building, which was in the Classical or Palladian style, appears to have been designed with the view of standing for ages, seeing that the walls were "twelve feet thick below, and nine feet above." The north front of the mansion was adorned with pilasters and columns of stone ; and above every window in each front was an antique head carved in stone, and at the top of each front were ranged statues as large as life. The locks and hinges to the doors of the state rooms were of gold or silver, and the fitting-up of the apartments matched this costliness. Altogether, Canons must have been exceedingly magnificent.

The park, several miles in extent, swarmed with deer, and avenues of elms led to each corner of the house from the surrounding roads. The principal avenue, nearly a mile long, was on the side towards Edgware, and the entrance to it was gained by iron gates enriched with the arms of Chandos, the stone pillars being crowned with the supporters. This avenue was broad enough to admit of three coaches going abreast, and had a large round basin of water in the middle. In an account of Canons, written before its demolition, are the following particulars concerning the adjacent grounds :—" The gardens are well designed in a vast variety, and the canals very large and noble. There is a spacious terrace that descends to a parterre, which has a row of gilded vases on each side down to the great canal ; and in the middle, fronting the canal, is a gilt gladiator. The gardens, being divided by iron balustrades, and not by walls, are seen all at one view from any part of them. In the kitchen-garden are curious bee-hives of glass ; and at the end of each of the chief avenues there are neat lodgings for eight old

THE DUKE OF CHANDOS.

sergeants of the army, whom the duke took out of Chelsea College to guard the whole, and perform the same duty at night as the watchmen do in London, and to attend his Grace to chapel on Sundays."

Few families have played a more conspicuous part in the history of England than that of Brydges, Lords Chandos of Sudeley, and afterwards Dukes of Chandos. Sir Bernard Burke traces them up to one Sir Simon de Bruge, or Brugge, a knight of large possessions in the county of Hereford in the reign of Henry III., whose immediate descendants for several generations represented both that county and also Gloucestershire in Parliament, whilst one of them fell fighting at Agincourt, and several married the heiresses of illustrious houses. One of their descendants, Sir John Bruges, held Boulogne as governor against the French king in the reign of Henry VIII., who afterwards constituted him Governor of the Tower, and gave him a grant of the manor and honour of Sudeley Castle, which his grandson gallantly held for King Charles against the Parliamentary Roundheads. Henry also created him Lord Chandos of Sudeley, in consideration not only of his nobility and loyalty, but of his quality, valour, and other virtues. Whilst his elder son continued the line of the Lords Chandos, his younger son became the father of a line of baronets, who adopted the orthography of Brydges, and were seated for some generations at Wilton Castle, in Herefordshire, a pleasant seat on the Wye. Sir James Brydges, the third baronet, by the failure and extinction of the elder line about 200 years ago, succeeded to the Barony of Chandos, and was summoned as such to the House of Peers, and sent as ambassador to Constantinople. He married the daughter and heiress of a rich Turkey merchant, who proved herself a " fruitful vine," as she brought him no less than twenty-two children, fifteen of whom lived to be christened, and seven grew up to manhood and womanhood.

James Brydges, the builder of Canons, was born

in 1673, and, in the lifetime of his father, was elected knight of the shire for Herefordshire in several successive Parliaments. In 1707 he was called to the Council of Prince George of Denmark in the affairs of the Admiralty, and was afterwards, as stated above, appointed Pay-master-General of the Forces on active service. With reference to the large sums of money which he secured to himself out of the above offices, Smollett, in his continuation of Hume's "History," writes:—"Mr. Brydges accounted for all the moneys that had passed through his hands excepting three millions;" and he adds that "all means had proved ineffectual to deter and punish those individuals who shamefully pillaged their country; the villany was so complicated, the vice so general, and the delinquents so powerfully screened by artifice and interest, as to elude all inquiry."

At the time of his marriage with the daughter and heiress of Sir Thomas Lake of Canons, he appears to have had a town house in Albemarle Street, for Dean Swift writes, March 3, 1711:— "Mr. Brydges' house in Albemarle Street was much damaged by a fire at Sir William Wyndham's, next door." Lord Chandos died in 1714, and was buried in the parish church of Whitchurch. On the accession of George I., his son and successor was created Viscount Wilton and Earl of Carnarvon, and in 1719 he was advanced to the Marquisate of Carnarvon and Dukedom of Chandos.

About this time a curious event is said to have happened to the duke. When travelling to or from Herefordshire, his Grace stopped at the "Castle Inn" at Marlborough, when, as he drove into the court-yard, his ears were deafened by piercing screams. The duke hastily alighted, and beheld a very lovely young woman, scarcely beyond girlhood, in the grasp of a powerful fellow, the ostler of the inn, who was striking her in a most ferocious manner with a heavy horse-whip. Blood was streaming from her face, neck, and arms; and a crowd stood round, filled with compassion, yet afraid to interfere between the ferocious brute and his victim. But the duke pressed through the group, and sternly ordered the ruffian to desist. The man, daunted by the look and manner of the nobleman, let his whip and victim both fall to the ground, and replied to his questions that the young woman was his wife, and that he had a right to do what he liked to her, offering, however, at the same time, to sell this right to his Grace for a sum of money. Really touched by the sufferings of the beautiful girl, the duke unhesitatingly closed with the offer: a sum of £20 was gleefully accepted by the brute of a husband, and the stricken young

wife became, according to an old English custom, the purchaser's own, to do with as he would. But the duke was a noble-minded gentleman; the cast-off wife was treated by him as his ward, and placed where she would be educated and moulded into a lady. The result of his care gave him complete satisfaction; and, some years later, when his second duchess died childless, in 1735, his Grace raised the whilom ostler's cast-off spouse to be his third wife. It is certain that the duke never repented of his bargain, for he says in his will:—"I owe the greatest comfort I have enjoyed in this life (since I have been blessed with her) to my duchess, Lydia Catherine;" and he orders that she shall be buried in the same depository as his own corpse, and that a marble figure of her should be set up in the monument room, but it was not to cost more than £200. A curious book in the British Museum, bound in some crimson velvet that remained over and above the quantity required for covering the coffin of this duchess, tells this story, and much more also, about Canons and its master.

On April 22, 1736, Mrs. Pendarves writes to her friend, Dean Swift:—"The Duke of Chandos's marriage has made a great noise, and the poor duchess is often reproached with her being bred up in Burr Street, Wapping." To this a note is attached, to the effect that "she was a Lady Davall, widow of Sir Thomas Davall, and had a fortune of £40,000." This is borne out by the inscription on her tomb; so that it would appear that the beautiful victim who had been rescued by the duke was married in the interval to a city knight as her second husband, and that she became a third time a wife herself when she married his Grace.

It would be scarcely possible to exaggerate the pomp and grandeur which marked even the every-day life of the owner of "Princely Canons." The author of "A Journey through England" says of the duke:—"When his Grace goes to church he is attended by his Swiss Guards, ranged as the Yeomen of the Guards at St. James's Palace; his music also plays when he is at table; he is served by gentlemen in the best order; and I must say that very few sovereign princes live with the same magnificence, grandeur, and good order."

Though most liberal, his Grace never was improvident or lavishly profuse. When he first arranged the plan of Canons, one of the ablest accountants in England was employed by him to make out a table of yearly, monthly, weekly, and even daily, expenditure. This scheme was engraved on a large copper-plate, and was an extraordinary specimen of economical wisdom. The duke sold all the garden fruit which was not required for his own table, and would say, " It is as much my property as the corn and hay and the produce of my fields." An aged man, who had been the duke's servant, and who appeared

" The sad historian of the pensive scene,"

informed the writer of an article on Canons, published some forty years ago in the *Chimney-Corner Companion*, that in his occasional bounties to his labourers the duke would never exceed sixpence each. " This," he would say, " may do you good ; more may make you idle and drunk."

" Epistle on False Taste," in the " Moral Essays," addressed by Pope to the Earl of Burlington, have been often quoted, and speak for themselves :—

At Timon's villa let us pass a day,
Where all cry out, ' What sums are thrown away !'
So proud, so grand, of that stupendous air,
Soft and agreeable come never there.
Greatness, with Timon, dwells in such a drought
As brings all Brobdignag before your thought.
To compass this, his building is a town,
His pond an ocean, his parterre a down ;
Who but must laugh, the master when he sees,
A puny insect, shivering at a breeze !
Lo ! what huge heaps of littleness around,

CANONS, ELEVATION OF THE ORIGINAL SOUTH FRONT.

In spite of great losses by his concerns in the African company, and by the Mississippi and South Sea speculations, the duke was ever a liberal patron of learning and merit, as the following story will show :—A clergyman whom he much esteemed was one day looking over the library at Canons, and was bidden by its noble owner to fix upon any book he liked, and it should be his. The gentleman very politely chose one of no great price, but afterwards found a bank bill of considerable value between its leaves. Greatly surprised, he brought the bill and the book back to Canons. The duke took back the bill, but only to exchange it for one of double the value, saying, " Accept that, sir, for your honesty."

It was always said that the Duke of Chandos was abused by Pope under the name of Timon, and probably because his Grace had passed by and forgotten the spiteful little poet in his liberalities to men of letters. The following lines, from the

The whole a labour'd quarry above ground ;
Two Cupids squirt before, a lake behind
Improves the keenness of the northern wind.
His gardens next your admiration call,
On every side you look, behold the wall !
No pleasing intricacies intervene,
No artful wildness to perplex the scene ;
Grove nods at grove, each alley has a brother,
And half the platform just reflects the other.
The suffering eye inverted Nature sees,
Trees cut to statues, statues thick as trees,
With here a fountain, never to be play'd,
And there a summer-house that knows no shade ;
Here Amphitrite sails through myrtle bowers,
There gladiators fight, or die in flowers ;
Unwater'd, see the drooping sea-horse mourn,
And swallows roost in Nilu's dusty urn.
My lord advances with majestic mien,
Smit with the mighty pleasure to be seen.
But soft, by regular approach—not yet—
First through the length of that hot terrace sweat ;
And when up ten steep slopes you've dragg'd your
    thighs,
Just at his study door he'll bless your eyes."

In his library the duke could boast of having a valuable collection of MS. records of Ireland before, during, and after the troubles of the Civil War, originally collected by Sir James Ware. When Lord Clarendon was Lord Lieutenant of Ireland (1686), he obtained these MSS. from the heir of Sir James, and brought them to England, and after his death they were bought by the Duke of Chandos. Dean Swift was very anxious that his Grace should present them to the public library at Dublin, but did not see his way to asking the favour. The following lines from the " Essay on Taste " are supposed to refer to the duke's library here :—

" His study ! with what authors is it stor'd ?
    In books, not authors, curious is my lord.
    To all their dated backs he turns you round :
    These Aldus printed, those Du Sneil has bound.
    Lo ! some are vellum, and the rest as good
    For all his lordship knows, but they are wood.
    For Locke or Milton 'tis in vain to look,
    These shelves admit not any modern book."

The duke's style of living was on a par with the splendour of his house. He dined in public, with flourishes of trumpets announcing each change of dishes. De Foe, in his " Tour through England " (1725), writes :—"Here are continually maintained, and that in the dearest part of England as to house expenses, not less than one hundred and twenty in family, and yet a face of plenty appears in every part of it ; nothing needful is withheld, nothing pleasant is restrained ; every servant in the house is made easy, and his life comfortable." Pope thus deals with the duke's style of living :—

" But hark ! the chiming clocks to dinner call :
    A hundred footsteps scrape the marble hall ;
    The rich buffet the well-colour'd serpents grace,
    And gaping Tritons spew to wash your face.
    Is this a dinner ? This a genial room ?
    No ; 'tis a temple and a hecatomb.
    A solemn sacrifice, perform'd in state,
    You drink to measure, and to minutes eat.
    So quick retires each flying course, you'd swear
    Sancho's dread doctor and his wand were there.
    Between each act the trembling salvers ring,
    From soup to sweet wine, and ' God bless the king !'
    In plenty starving, tantalised in state,
    And complaisantly help'd to all I hate,
    Treated, caress'd, and sir'd, I take my leave,
    Sick of his civil pride from morn to eve ;
    I curse such lavish cost and little skill,
    And swear no day was ever passed so ill.
    Yet hence the poor are cloth'd, the hungry fed ;
    Health to himself, and to his infants bread
    The labourer bears. What his hard heart denies
    His charitable vanity supplies."

The garden and terraces, the hall, the library, and even the chapel (which was no other than the parish church of Whitchurch), come under the lash of the poet :—

" And now the chapel's silver bell you hear,
    That summons you to all the pride of prayer ;
    Light quirks of music, broken and uneven,
    Make the soul dance upon a jig to Heaven.
    On painted ceilings you devoutly stare,
    Where sprawl the saints of Verrio or Laguerre,
    Or gilded clouds in fair expansion lie,
    And bring all Paradise before your eye.
    To rest the cushion and soft dean invite,
    Who never mentions Hell to ears polite."

" The graceless saints with which Laguerre disfigured the chapel walls of Canons," observes the author of the " Beauties of England," " probably identify the satire of Pope more unequivocally than any other circumstance of allusion in his essay ; but assuredly the poet should have omitted to censure the Duke of Chandos for a want of correct taste as to music." In Hawkins's " History of Music " it is remarked that " his Grace determined on having Divine service performed in his chapel with all the aid that could be derived from vocal and instrumental music. To this end he retained some of the most celebrated performers of both kinds, and engaged the greatest masters of the time to compose anthems and services with instrumental accompaniments, after the manner of those performed in the churches of Italy." It appears that Handel composed not less than twenty of his finest anthems for the use of this chapel.

Hogarth found a patron in the duke ; and when Pope disgraced his muse by unjust and sarcastic wit levelled at the owner of Canons, the painter punished the bard of Twickenham by representing him as standing on a scaffold whitewashing Burlington House, and bespattering the Duke of Chandos's carriage as it passes along Piccadilly.*

Pope, in a letter written by him to Aaron Hill, denied that there was any truth in the supposition that the character of " Timon ' in the essay above quoted was ever intended to apply to the Duke of Chandos ; and in the Prologue to the Satires he poetically mentions, as the most severe enemy of an honest muse, that fop—

" Who has the vanity to call you friend,
    Yet wants the honour, injur'd, to defend ;
    Who tells whate'er you think, whate'er you say,
    And, if he lie not, must at least betray ;
    Who to the dean and silver bell can swear,
    And sees at Canons what was never there."

The public, however, would not give credit to

either the prose or the poetry of Pope when his satire exceeded the bounds of fact; and as the duke was highly respected for genuine worth of heart, and was said to have presented the poet with the sum of one thousand pounds as a tribute to his literary merits, much indignation was excited by the presumed libel. In one of the many brochures published against Pope occur the lines—

> "Great Chandos' stream of bounty flow'd too high;
> Chandos' high soul forgets as he bestows."

Whether Pope's lines were or were not really intended to be applied to the Duke of Chandos, the glory of Canons was but of short duration; hence the concluding lines of the essay were, at all events, in a certain sense fulfilled. In a truly prophetic spirit Pope foretells the transformation of the proud and formal domain into pasture and farm-land :—

> "Another age shall see the golden ear
> Imbrown the slope and nod on the parterre;
> Deep harvest bury all his pride has plann'd,
> And laughing Ceres re-assume the land."

These lines were sadly verified in the very next generation, as we shall see. The duke's eldest surviving son, John, Marquis of Carnarvon, died in the lifetime of his father, leaving—by his marriage with Lady Catherine Tollemache, a daughter of the Earl of Dysart—one only daughter, also named Catherine. The duke himself died in 1744, and his widow followed him to the grave some six years later. Owing to disputes with the duke's younger son and successor, Henry, second Duke of Chandos, the duchess-dowager ordered that the provisions of her lord's will with regard to her interment should not be carried out, and she was accordingly buried elsewhere; but in the following year her remains were disinterred, and laid in the Chandos vault; no monument, however, representing the duke's best beloved wife was ever placed in the mortuary chapel. His Grace had experienced great losses from several public speculations in which he had embarked, the most important of which was the South Sea scheme, which had been productive of such a wide-spread ruin in the year 1720. He continued, however, to reside at Canons, though, as it would appear, with diminished splendour, till his death.

Under the second duke the estate became more sadly encumbered than ever; and on his death, his executors found it necessary to put Canons up for sale, a special Act of Parliament having been passed to enable them to do so. No purchaser, however, could be found for the mansion and estate as a whole; so at last the house was pulled to pieces, and the materials sold by auction in 1747, in separate lots, that which had cost half a million to build producing only £11,000. The costly furniture was also sold, crowds flocking to the scene— as a hundred years later crowds flocked to the Stowe and Strawberry Hill sales. The marble staircase was bought by Lord Chesterfield for his house in Mayfair; some of the pillars, too, at Chesterfield House originally belonged to Canons, and were termed by the witty earl "the *canonical* pillars of his house." The fine columns became a portico for Wanstead House, mentioned above, and which has since been also demolished. The equestrian statue of George I. (one of the many sculptures which adorned the grounds at Canons) was transferred to Leicester Square, where it was allowed to perish. The statue of George II. in Golden Square, too, was part of the Canons spoil. One of the marble fireplaces found a settlement at the "Chandos Arms" inn at Edgware; and a grand carving in wood, by Grinling Gibbons, which, as we find in Evelyn's "Diary," was purchased by the duke, was transferred to the great hall of Bush Hill Park, near Enfield.

The immediate cause, or, at all events, one cause, of the break-up and forced sale of Canons was the attempt of the second duke to buy up— at all sorts of fancy prices of course—the whole of the land which lay between his country seat and his town house near Cavendish Square—a house still immortalised by the name of Chandos Street. This he wished to do in order that he might drive his coach and six from the one place to the other without passing the bounds of his estate. Two of the large houses * standing on the north side of Cavendish Square were erected as residences for the duke's porters and other members of his household. In order to carry his idea into effect, the duke would have had to buy up half Marylebone, St. John's Wood, Hendon, and Kingsbury—purchases for which no ducal coffers could have sufficed.

The tourist who wishes to make a pilgrimage to Canons at the present time will find it very much like the play of "Hamlet," with the part of Hamlet left out. The park is still there; but, though for the most part under grass, it is cut up by hedges and railings into separate fields. A few of the fine elms which once formed the avenues still stand like solitary sentinels; the carp and tench still swim lazily about in the two large fishponds on either side of the carriage road which leads up to the present mansion from the town

---

* See "Old and New London," Vol. IV., p. 443.

of Edgware ; the shrubberies are still green with magnificent bays, laurels, cypresses, and other ornamental trees, interspersed with oaks, hazels, and chestnuts ; and beyond the west end of Whitchurch churchyard may be distinctly traced, though now grown over with turf—not with corn, as prophesied by Pope—the splendid road down which the duke and his duchess used to drive in their coach and six, and with their tall guards in front, on Sundays, to hear Handel's music in their velvet-

sion itself may be formed from the fact that the two porters' lodges, each having six rooms on the ground floor, being raised a storey higher by the new owner of Canons, were let to private gentlemen, one of them being a baronet, Sir Hugh Dalrymple.

Mr. Hallet's villa, built of stone, was a somewhat modest, but capacious, residence, and has been enlarged in recent times. The house stands on a gentle elevation, in the midst of a moderate-sized and well-timbered park. The property was sold by

CANONS. (*From a Print published in 1782.*)

lined gallery, or tribune, at the west end of the sacred edifice. But the old mansion itself is clean gone, though the vistas which it once commanded may be seen. The iron gates which once closed the southern entrance now span the centre of the gardens of New College, Oxford ; and it is said that the golden lamps which lighted the chief avenue to the house were for many years to be seen at Day and Martin's shop in Holborn. *Sic transit gloria.*

Mr. Hallet, a cabinet-maker in Long Acre, bought the greater part of the estate and a large quantity of building materials, with which he erected a villa on part of the site of the original house. Some idea of the magnificence of the man-

Mr. Hallet's grandson to Captain Dennis O'Kelly, whose name was well-known in the sporting world as the owner of a famous race-horse, "Eclipse," which in its old age is said to have been brought hither all the way from Epsom on a carriage made specially for him. This wonderful horse was bred by the Duke of Cumberland, and being foaled during the *great eclipse*, was so named by the duke in consequence. His royal owner did not survive to witness the very great performances he himself had predicted. When a yearling only, the horse was disposed of by auction, with the rest of his stud. At four or five years old Captain O'Kelly purchased half of him for 250 guineas, and in a short time after gave 750 for the remainder. The following curious mock epistle in a book of sporting anecdotes, printed at the end of last century, may be of interest to sporting readers even in the present day :—

"AN EPISTLE FROM ECLIPSE TO KING FERGUS.

"DEAR SON,—I set out last week from Epsom, and am safe arrived in my new stables at this place. My situation may serve as a lesson to man: I was once the fleetest horse in the world, the rest of my progeny, will do honour to the name of their grandsire,   ECLIPSE.

"*Canons, Middlesex.*

"P.S. Myself, Dungannon, Volunteer, and Vertumnus, are all here.—Compliments to the Yorkshire horses."

This noble animal, who performed the feat of galloping a mile in a minute, is said to have been stuffed and kept in the hall. One of his hoofs, set in

WHITCHURCH CHURCH : THE EAST END.

but old age has come upon me, and wonder not, King Fergus, when I tell thee I was drawn in a carriage from Epsom to Canons, being unable to walk even so short a journey. Every horse, as well as every dog, has his day; and I have had mine. I have outlived two worthy masters: the late Duke of Cumberland, that bred me, and the Colonel with whom I have spent my best days, but I must not repine; I am now caressed, not so much for what I can do, but for what I have done, and with the satisfaction of knowing that my present master will never abandon me to the fate of the *high-mettled racer !*

"I am glad to hear, my grandson, Honest Tom, performs so well in Ireland, and trust that he, and

gold, is the property of the Jockey Club, and constitutes a prize annually contended for at Ascot Races, the owner of the winning horse retaining the relic in his possession for a year. The remains of the above famous racehorse are interred in the park of Canons.

The estate was subsequently sold by the nephew of Captain O'Kelly to Sir Thomas Plumer, who was some time Vice-Chancellor of England, and afterwards Master of the Rolls ; and the property, after the death of Sir Thomas, remained in the possession of Lady Plumer till her decease. It was next held by Mr. Thomas Hall Plumer, the eldest son of Sir Thomas, and more recently by Mr. David Begg, M.D., since whose death, in 1868, Canons has been owned by his widow.

The parish church of Whitchurch, close by the southern entrance to the park of Canons, and almost hidden from sight by the trees which surround it, is a small building, dedicated to St. Lawrence, and, with the exception of the tower, which is ancient, was built about the year 1715, at the expense of the Duke of Chandos, as the "chapel" of Canons. The internal decorations, which are in a style very rarely to be seen in country churches, were not completed till five years later. In the words of Pope, quoted above—

"Here sprawl the saints of Verrio and Laguerre."

At all events, the latter artist is said to have painted the ceiling and the walls. On each side of the Communion Table is "The Nativity" and "The Dead Christ," by Bellucci; behind it, instead of a reredos, is a recess for the organ supported by Corinthian columns. The organ was rebuilt and enlarged in 1878. In the background are paintings of "Moses Receiving the Tables of the Law" and of "The Saviour Preaching." Handel, who resided at Canons for three years as chapel-master to the duke, is said to have composed his sacred drama of *Esther* for the consecration of this church. During his stay here he produced also the two "Chandos" *Te Deums*, the twelve "Chandos" Anthems, and *Acis and Galatea*.

In September, 1790, some thirty years after his death, a grand miscellaneous concert of sacred music, selected from the works of Handel, was performed in his honour and memory in this church.

The large chamber, or mortuary chapel, on the north side of the chancel, built by the Duke of Chandos, and containing one or two monuments to members of his family, reminds the visitor in some degree of the tombs of the Russells at Chenies, in Buckinghamshire. The chamber, which is constructed over the family vault, is reached by a flight of steps. The ceiling and sides are painted, and the floor is paved with black and white marble. Within is a statue of the duke, in Roman costume, as large as life, standing between the statues of Mary, his first wife, and his first duchess, Cassandra, sister of Thomas Willoughby, Lord Middleton, whom the duke married in 1713, just one year after the death of the heiress of Canons. The two last-named effigies kneel on either side of that of the duke, in mourning attitudes. The inscription records the interment of the duke's third wife, "Lydia Catherine, daughter of John Vanhattem, Esq., and widow of Sir Thomas Davall, M.P., who died in the year 1714." This monument was restored by the Duke of Buckingham and Chandos in 1865. At the western end of the church is the "Chandos gallery," containing a spacious semicircular recess, with seats for the owner of Canons. The ceiling of this gallery is painted with a copy of Raphael's "Ascension," by Bellucci.

At the south-eastern corner of the churchyard is a grave-stone to the memory of William Powell, the "harmonious blacksmith." The stone, which bears, in a sunk medallion, a hammer, anvil, laurel wreath, and a bar of music, records his name, and date of death, "February 27th, 1780, aged 78," and adds that "he was parish clerk during the time the immortal Handel was organist of this church." The stone was raised by subscription in 1868, in place of a wooden rail, which formerly bore a similar inscription. This is the blacksmith in whose forge, one afternoon in 1721, Handel is said to have taken refuge during a storm, when he found Powell standing at his work, and singing a beautiful melody, that chimed in exactly with the tone emitted by his anvil, as blow after blow fell upon it. Powell informed his delighted visitor that he had heard the tune, and caught it up, but did not know the name of the composer. So Handel, as the story goes, carried the melody in his head back to Canons, and elaborated the theme into the well-known "Harmonious Blacksmith." The original MS. air, in the treble only, may be still seen in an old book in the British Museum. A lady who endowed some almshouses at Whitchurch has left it on record that Powell was a fine-looking man, nearly six feet high, and that he always wore a clean shirt, with the collar thrown back on his shoulders, and a red cap on his head, and she adds that he sang constantly as he worked. His anvil still exists, and its tone, when struck, is really in the same key as the "Harmonious Blacksmith." Both the anvil and hammer, having been long kept as sacred relics, were sold among the Snoxell collection of curiosities by Messrs. Puttick and Simpson, in June, 1879.

On the north side of the churchyard are some heavy-looking and substantial almshouses, which were founded about 1640 by Lady Lake, the widow of Sir Thomas Lake of Canons, for seven poor persons. The recipients of this charity were to be appointed by Sir Thomas Lake's descendants, as long as they should be possessed of Canons, and afterwards by the minister and churchwardens. The endowment at the present time supports only four persons. The charity had an income of £44 per annum, which has been recently augmented by a bequest of £1,000 by Miss Hurst. The almshouses are built of red brick, of one floor, and form three sides of a quadrangle.

CHAPTER XXIX.

GREAT STANMORE AND ELSTREE.

Per fines et aprica rura.—HORACE.

Great Stanmore—Brockley Hill, the supposed Site of Sulloniacæ—Discovery of Roman Antiquities—The Great Forest of Middlesex—The Domesday Notice of Stanmore—Descent of the Manor—The Village—Population—The Bernays Memorial Institute—The Church—Stanmore Park—Bentley Priory—The Property purchased by Lord Abercorn—Queen Adelaide—Sir John Kelk—Elstree—Situation and General Appearance of the Village—The Manor—Parish Church—Burial-places of Martha Ray and William Weare—Female Orphans' Home—Elstree Hill House—Elstree Reservoir—Watercourses—Pudding-stones.

GREAT STANMORE, which we have now reached, lies on the border-line of Middlesex and Hertford-shire. The name of the parish, which appears as *Stanmere*, or *Stanmera*, in "Domesday Book," signifies a boundary-mark or stone. In legal documents it is written Stanmore Magna (or Great Stanmore), to distinguish it from the adjoining parish of Stanmore Parva (Little Stanmore), or Whitchurch, which we have just left. Both districts would appear to have formed one parish only at the time of the Norman survey, though the period at which they were divided has not been ascertained.

At the time of the Roman invasion, and probably for a long time afterwards, this locality was thickly wooded, and formed part of that dreary tract which was known in more recent times as the forest of Middlesex. Many interesting evidences of the Roman occupation have been discovered in this neighbourhood, particularly in the north-eastern division of the parish, close by the high ground known as Brockley Hill, about midway between Edgware and Elstree, a spot which Camden, Stukeley, and other writers, have fixed upon as the site of the ancient city of Sulloniacæ. Reynolds, in his edition of the "Itinerary of Antoninus," unhesitatingly ascribes the site of that city to Brockley Hill; and after mentioning the numerous vestiges of Roman habitation which have been discovered there, observes that "no evidence is wanting on the subject, but to show that the distance is agreeable to the numerals." The distance between the presumed site of this city and Verulamium (St. Albans) is estimated, according to Mr. Reynolds, at nine miles and a quarter, which comes very near to the truth.

Roman antiquities, consisting chiefly of coins, urns, rings, fibulæ, and other articles, are said to have been found in large quantities from the site of Bentley Priory, which lies to the north-west of the village of Stanmore, eastward as far as Brockley Hill. These discoveries, says Lysons, gave rise to the following local couplet :—

" No heart can think, nor tongue can tell,
What lies 'twixt Brockley Hill and Pennywell."

Pennywell, however, lies at some little distance to the north-east of Brockley Hill, and nearer to Elstree than Stanmore. Norden asserts that Watling Street, which we have mentioned in a previous chapter as having followed the track of the present Edgware Road, crossed over Brockley Hill, passing in its course through a wild and dangerous range of woodland. Matthew Paris, in his "Life of the Twelfth Abbot of St. Albans," describes these woods as "almost of an impenetrable character, and so much infested by outlaws and beasts of prey, that the numerous pilgrims who travelled along the Roman road for the purpose of devotion at the shrine of Albanus were exposed to very imminent danger." Fitz-Stephen, whose "Survey of London" was written between the years 1170 and 1182, says that "beyond the suburbs of the city, which afford corn-fields, pastures, and delightful meadows, an immense forest extends itself, beautiful with woods and groves, and full of the lairs and coverts of beasts and game—stags, bucks, boars, and wild bulls." In this forest the citizens of London enjoyed the right of free chase—a privilege which was confirmed to them by several royal charters. The forest of Middlesex was "disafforested" early in the thirteenth century, but considerable tracts of the ancient wood remained down to much later ages. At the time of the Conquest, although there was probably a preponderance of woodland—from the large and frequent mention of "pannage"—it would appear that much even of this portion of the country was under the plough, and a fair proportion used as meadow-land, or for the purpose of pasturage. The entry in "Domesday Book" respecting this parish is as follows :—-" Stanmere is held by the Earl of Moreton. It answered for nine hides and a half. There is land for seven ploughs. In the demesne are six hides and a half, and there are two ploughs therein, and another may be made. The villanes have one plough and a half; and two ploughs and a half might be made. A priest has half a hide there ; and there are four villanes of one virgate each, and other two of one virgate ; and three cottagers of ten acres, and other three of one acre. Pasture for the cattle of the village; pannage for twelve hundred hogs, and for herbage twelve pence." *

In the reign of Henry I. the manor was wrested from the Earl of Moreton's successor, and it continued in the hands of the Crown till 1220, when it was given to the monks of St. Albans, under whom it was held till the middle of the fourteenth century by the family of Francis. It next passed, subject to an annual rent to that abbey, to the priory and convent of St. Bartholomew, in Smithfield. After the dissolution of religious houses the manor passed through the possession of various persons, among whom was Sir Peter Gambo, a Spaniard, who was murdered near St. Sepulchre's Church, London, in 1550, by a Fleming named Gavaro. In the reign of James I. the estate was granted to Sir Thomas Lake, of whom we have spoken in our account of Little Stanmore and Canons; and it subsequently underwent various changes, and towards the close of the last century the manor passed, by the marriage of the daughter and sole heiress of James Brydges, third and last Duke of Chandos, to Richard, Duke of Buckingham and Chandos. His Grace, who died in 1839, was the grandfather of the present duke. The ownership of the manor has since passed into the hands of Sir John Kelk, Bart., of Bentley Priory.

The village of Great Stanmore is about a mile in length; it is built on the slope of a hill, and lies on the road to Watford, about two miles north-west from the Edgware Station of the Great Northern Railway. It is quiet and secluded, and the houses generally have a neat and respectable appearance. Both in the village and in the immediate neighbourhood are several good old-fashioned residences, and close by are some large and well-wooded parks and lordly domains.

On Stanmore Hill, a gentle elevation on the north side of the village, the celebrated Dr. Parr opened a school on quitting Harrow,† in 1771; here he received a large number of pupils, many of whom became distinguished in after life. The school was pulled down many years ago, and the site afterwards built upon.

In 1871 the number of houses in the parish was 265, the population at the same time amounting to 1,355. In 1881 it had slightly risen.

A conspicuous building in the village is the Memorial Institute, which was erected by subscription in memory of Mr. Ernest Bernays, a son of the Rev. Leopold John Bernays, many years

rector of this parish, who was accidentally drowned in 1870. The building, which is of Gothic design, is used for concerts, lectures, and similar entertainments.

The church, dedicated to St. John the Evangelist, stands at the western end of the village, and was built, from the designs of Mr. Henry Clutton, in the Decorated style. The foundation-stone was laid by the Earl of Aberdeen (whose son, the Hon. and Rev. Douglas Gordon, was the vicar), in the presence of the Dowager Queen Adelaide, who then appeared for the last time in public. She did not live to see it opened. The building is constructed of stone, and consists of a nave, having north and south aisles, a chancel, with spacious south aisle, and a lofty tower at the north-west corner of the nave, in which is a peal of six bells, removed from Little Stanmore Church in 1720. The east window, by Willement, was erected by subscription as a memorial of Queen Adelaide. There are in the church several other stained glass windows, presented by the rector and others, among them being one presented by the Earl of Wicklow in memory of his two daughters, the Ladies Harriet and Isabella Howard. The font, of Caen stone, was the gift of the Queen-Dowager shortly before her death.

This is the third church in succession that the parish has had within little more than two centuries. The original structure stood at a considerable distance, and its exact site is preserved only by tradition and a single tombstone. The second structure was built about 1632, and was consecrated by Archbishop Laud. It was of brick, in the worst style of ecclesiastical architecture, and was built at the expense of Sir John Wolstenholme, who is said by Newcourt to have been "nursed at this parish." Its consecration by Archbishop Laud constituted one of the accusations afterwards brought against that prelate with fatal success. The extending of the ceremony of consecration to *chapels* was made one of the charges against the archbishop, and this structure was perversely termed a "chapel" by the accuser. In reply, Laud admitted the consecration, but observed that the edifice was "a *parish church*, erected by Sir John *Worstenham*, in the place where he was born, and in the diocese of himself." The remains of this church, roofless, and seemingly held together by the thick clusters of ivy which cover them, are still standing a few yards distant from the western end of the new church. They are built of red brick, square in form, and with an embattled tower at the west end. The porch was designed by Nicholas Stone, who re-

* Bawdwen's "Translation of Domesday for Middlesex."
† See *ante*, p. 266.

ceived £30 for work done at this part of the building.* For a monument of Sir John Wolstenholme, the founder of this church, Stone received the sum of £200. This monument, which was on the north side of the communion-table, represents the deceased as lying upon a mattress. There are other monuments and inscriptions to different members of the Wolstenholme family. A large tablet of white marble, with a long inscription, commemorates Catherine, Marchioness of Abercorn, wife of John, first marquis, and daughter of Sir Joseph Copley, Bart., of Sprotborough, Yorkshire. The floor of the old church is carpeted with turf, and in the centre is an elaborate mausoleum, of Gothic design, for the family of the Hollonds, of Stanmore Hall. Lord Henry Beauclerk, who died in 1761, was buried in this church, as also was Mr. John Drummond, M.P., who died in 1774, and other members of the families of Beauclerk and Drummond. Charles Hart, a celebrated tragedian of the seventeenth century, "the Roscius of his age," lies buried in the churchyard. According to Lysons, Hart had a "country house" at Stanmore, where he was enrolled a copyholder in 1679. Close by the entrance to the churchyard is a handsome cottage, erected as a memorial of the late Mr. R. Hollond, M.P., of Stanmore Hall, the aëronaut, who died in 1876.

Almost abutting upon the south-west angle of the churchyard, and stretching away for some distance towards Harrow, is Stanmore Park, the seat of Lord Wolverton. Early in the last century the estate, then known as Belmont, was purchased by Mr. Andrew Drummond, the founder of the great banking-house bearing his name at Charing Cross. Mr. George H. Drummond, who subsequently possessed the property, preserved here a large and valuable collection of original portraits, which were bequeathed to the Hon. Mrs. Drummond by the Duke of St. Albans. The mansion was for a short time occupied by Lord Castlereagh, and later on, early in the present century, it was the residence of the Countess of Aylesford. In 1840 the estate was purchased by the Marquis of Abercorn, and the collection of portraits above mentioned, which comprised among their number several by Kneller and Lely, was shortly after sold by auction. The mansion and estate next passed by sale to Mr. George Carr Glyn, who was in 1869 raised to the peerage, with the title of Lord Wolverton. His lordship died in 1873, and was succeeded by his son, the Hon. George Grenfell Glyn, the present Lord Wolverton.

The mansion is a good modern building, consisting of a centre, with two slightly-projecting wings. The park is extensive and well wooded, and is rendered attractive by fine undulations of surface and a handsome lake. At the southern extremity of the park is a hill, termed Belmont, thrown up by the Duke of Chandos, whence the estate derived its original name. It is approached by a fine avenue, and on its summit is a summer-house, which is a conspicuous object from several neighbouring points.

Bentley Priory, the seat of Sir John Kelk, Bart., lies to the north-west of the village, and though far nearer to Stanmore than to Harrow-on-the-Hill, actually stands in the latter parish. The estate comprises upwards of 460 acres. The mansion is approached from the high roads, which almost surround the estate, by carriage-drives, with six ornamental entrance-lodges ; it is placed on the southern slope of the hill, well sheltered by its own woods from the north, and commanding most charming and panoramic views of its own beautiful terraces, gardens, lawns, and undulating deer-park, adorned with oaks, beeches, and other grand forest trees.

The eastern entrance to the estate is at the top of Stanmore Hill, near the junction of the roads leading on the right to Elstree, and on the left to Bushey Heath and Watford. From the Harrow station of the London and North-Western Railway, a long winding walk, up-hill and "against the collar," through the pretty district of Harrow Weald, leads us past several handsome residences in pretty grounds nearly to Stanmore Common. Turning sharply to the east at Bamford's Corner, and leaving the estates of the Hermitage and Woodlands on the left, and, further off, Lord Wolverton's seat, Stanmore Park, on the right, at the end of about three miles the tall trees which surround Bentley Priory are seen on the left. The house is not visible from the road, as the mansion lies about a mile and a half from the park gates at this point. The Watford road, from Harrow Station, skirts the grounds of the Priory on the north-west. Proceeding to the mansion by this road, the visitor will pass, on his left, the pretty little lodge-house of Harrow Weald Park,* and, as he ascends the hill, obtain a good view of its castellated mansion, the seat of Mr. Alexander Sim. He will find an entrance to the Bentley Priory estate at the top of the hill, near the "Hare" hostelry. The house is called a Priory for as good a reason as that for which the ducal residence of

---

* Walpole's "Anecdotes of Painting."　　　　　* See *ante*, p. 270.

Woburn is called Woburn Abbey; for in the far-off middle ages there stood here a priory, but to what order the monks belonged the local historian makes no mention. The good brethren would seem to have lived the "hidden life" to perfection—

"Far from the madding crowd's ignoble strife."

At all events, very little is known of the history of the house. The Priory did not come to an

The next that we hear of Bentley Manor and Priory Farm is in 1706, when it appears to have belonged to the family of Coghill, who, early in the previous century, had settled in the neighbouring parish of Aldenham. In 1734 it was bequeathed by Thomas Coghill to his nephew, Thomas Whittewronge, who left it in 1761 to a certain Mr. John Bennet. In the following year it passed by sale to Mr. William Waller, who about 1766 alienated it to a Mr. Duberly.

BENTLEY PRIORY. (*From a View taken in* 1849.)

end until the reign of Henry VIII., when it was seized among the lesser monasteries, and suppressed, its revenues being assigned, not to the king, but to the monks of Canterbury. In A.D. 1543 we are told that Cranmer gave to the king, in exchange for other lands, the late Priory of Bentley, with all lands, tenements, &c., thereunto belonging in Harrow and Stanmore, "being parcel of the possessions of St. Gregory's Priory, at Canterbury."

No sooner, however, did the royal tyrant get possession of Bentley than he granted it—doubtless not without good consideration—to Henry Needham and William Sacheverel, who sold the property in the same year to Elizabeth Colte.

It is stated in the additions made to Camden's "Britannia," by Gough, that the house of Bentley Priory was taken down and rebuilt by Mr. Duberly, and it is observed in the same work that a chapel, then appertaining to the structure, but long since demolished, "stood detached on the common."

From Mr. Duberly, Bentley Priory was bought in 1788 by the first Marquis of Abercorn, who made great additions to the original house, converting it into a noble mansion, "in which," says Lysons, in his "Environs of London," "convenience is united with magnificence in a manner rarely to be met with."

Under Lord Abercorn, whose reign here extended over thirty years, Bentley Priory was one of the most celebrated houses in the kingdom for its fashionable and intellectual gatherings. Amongst those who frequented it were Sir William and Lady Hamilton (Nelson's Emma), the "Heaven-born Minister" Pitt, Addington, George Canning, Lord Liverpool, the Duke of Wellington, Sir Walter Scott, and "Athenian" Aberdeen, afterwards our Premier during the Crimean war. Samuel Rogers also was an occasional visitor, in spite of his undisguised preference for Holland House. In fact, during the latter half of the reign of George III., and through a part of the Regency, Bentley Priory was one chief rendezvous of the Tory party, and as such is frequently mentioned in the personal reminiscences of many of our statesmen. Mr. Thorne, in his "Handbook of the Environs of London," tells us that "the Prince Regent (afterwards George IV.) came here with the King of Prussia to meet Louis XVIII. when he left Hartwell to return to France;" this was on the conclusion of the war with the great Napoleon. He also asserts that "in April, 1807, Sir Walter Scott, when on a visit here, corrected the revises of his 'Marmion,' and at the suggestion of Lord Abercorn added the complimentary verses on Fox:

QUEEN ADELAIDE.

"'For talents mourn, untimely lost,
When best employ'd and wanted most.'"

Indeed, Lockhart tells us, in his "Life of Sir Walter Scott," that they "came from the marquis's own pen;" but this may mean only that he had a hand in them.

On the death of the first marquis, in 1818, Bentley Priory came into the ownership of his grandson, the second Marquis (and now Duke) of Abercorn, who, however, did not enter into actual possession of it till he attained his majority. He was sent to school at Harrow, and used to spend his holidays here with his guardian and stepfather, Lord Aberdeen.

The duke resided partly here from 1832 to about 1840; and it was here that Sir Edward Landseer painted one of his most attractive pictures,

in which the younger members of the Abercorn family are introduced.

In April, 1848, Bentley Priory was taken on lease by the Dowager Queen Adelaide, the widow of William IV., who made it her home for the last year and a half of her life. Queen Adelaide, notwithstanding her increasing infirmities, was enabled to take frequent carriage airings in the neighbourhood. She breathed her last here on the 2nd of December, 1849, and by her death the poor of Stanmore and its neighbourhood felt that they had lost a real friend, for her sojourn among them had been distinguished by that active kindness and liberality which always characterised her. Her last public act, as we have already stated, was to assist at the laying of the first stone of the new parish church at Stanmore.

After her death the priory was scarcely used or occupied till 1852, when the estate was bought from the Marquis of Abercorn by Mr. (now Sir) John Kelk, the eminent railway engineer, who represented Harwich in Parliament from 1865 to 1868, and was created a baronet in 1874. He has since purchased the estate of Tedworth, near Andover, in Hampshire, from the Assheton-Smiths, and taken up his residence there, resolving to sell Bentley Priory, which he had largely improved both internally and externally, adding large and well-placed conservatories, several hundred yards in length, which were built at a cost of about £9,000.

The mansion is entered, on the north side, by an ivy-covered *porte-cochère*, with double folding-doors, opening into a spacious entrance-hall, with groined ceiling, supported by fluted classic columns. The grand staircase, on one side of the hall, is of Portland stone, with a carved oak balustrade; the ceiling is enriched, and the walls panelled.

From the inner hall is a corridor, also with groined ceiling, having panelled walls ornamented with medallions, leading to the noble suite of reception-rooms. These are all about twenty feet in height, most artistically decorated. Passing by the boudoir, with its walls ot embossed green silk, and the lofty and spacious dining-room, we enter the drawing-room. This is fifty feet by thirty feet; it is highly enriched with painting and gilding, and has two carved statuary marble mantelpieces, surmounted by paintings on panel. The windows of this room open on to a broad portico, from which two flights of stone steps lead to the terraces and Italian gardens. The only other rooms on the ground floor that need be mentioned are the picture-gallery and billiard-room, the library, the smoking-room, the morning-room, or study, and an apartment called "the queen's room," probably from its having been the favourite room of Queen Adelaide. At the western end of the house is the conservatory, whence a corridor leads to a lawn-tennis court or skating-rink. Another important feature of the mansion at this end is a lofty clock-tower.

Immediately in front of the mansion, on the south side, is the Italian garden, intersected by broad terrace walks, and divided into lawns and parterres, adorned with vases on pedestals for flowers. The lawn, studded with oak, beech, plane, and other trees, slopes gently down to the deer-park, which is enclosed by iron fencing, well screened by belts of plantations, and adorned with wide-spreading forest trees. A gravel walk through a shrubbery skirting the deer-park leads to the ornamental "lake," which comprises about four and a quarter acres, a portion of which is covered with water-lilies.

On the margin of the lake is a summer-house, commanding a view of the park and mansion, and it is believed that it was in the quiet seclusion of this charming spot that Scott revised the proof-sheets of his "Marmion." In an adjoining alcove Rogers is said to have written some of his "Pleasures of Memory."

On the north side of the mansion, and approached from the carriage-drive, is a cedar garden and orangery. It is laid out in lawns and flower-beds, and ornamented with cedars, yews, and other evergreen trees. It contains a circular rosary, and in the centre of the garden is the orangery.

Close by is another rosary, and thence a walk leads to a romantic fernery, constructed of rock-work overshadowed by trees. Approached by two shady avenues of lime-trees is a rustic summer-house, containing two rooms; it is situated in the most secluded part of the gardens, and is said to have been the favourite resort of Queen Adelaide.

The plantations and shrubberies adjoining the cedar gardens, and skirting the park, contain many fine specimens of the cedar and fir tribe, cypresses,

junipers, &c., with a profusion of laurels and rhododendrons, and other choice flowering shrubs and trees, interspersed with ground covered with brake and ferns, forming a pleasing contrast to the dressed grounds. They are intersected by some miles of winding green walks and drives, which combine a variety of scenery with entire seclusion.

Besides the seats above described, there are a few good residences in the parish, especially in the neighbourhood of the Heath: among them may be mentioned Stanmore Hall, the residence of Mrs. Hollond, an elegant stone-built mansion at the top of the hill; and Broomfield, the seat of the Greigs, a large house of Gothic design, whence, from its lofty situation, extensive views are obtained over the surrounding country. Near the above house, at the edge of the Heath, is The Grove, the residence of Mr. Brightwen. Towards the end of the last century this house was occupied by one Aaron Capadoce, a Jew, who is said to have died here at the age of 105 years. His successor in the occupancy of the Grove House was a German, named Fierville, whose admiration of Rousseau led him to erect a tomb and to form an island on these premises, "in imitation of the tomb and the *Isle des Peupliers* at *Ermenonville*."

A plot of ground between the Grove estate and the high road is known as the Bowling Green. The great Duke of Chandos erected a building close by this spot as a pavilion, or banqueting-house, attached to a bowling-green, which he formed here, in preference to having it near his house at Canons.

We now wend our steps by the cross road running north-east from Stanmore Hill, and, turning northward on regaining the high road at Brockley Hill, soon find ourselves at Elstree. This village, which is pleasantly situated on the brow of a hill, consists mainly of one long street on the St. Albans road. Most of the houses are built of red brick, and have a neat and trim appearance; it is of small extent, for the population does not much exceed 500. It is situated at the intersection of the road from London to St. Albans (the ancient Watling Street) with that from Bushey to Barnet. The latter road separates Middlesex from Herts, and the four parts cut off by these roads are in four different parishes and two dioceses. The north-eastern portion, with the church, is Elstree proper; the north-west is in Aldenham parish, both belonging to Hertfordshire; while the south-east part is in Edgware, and the south-west in Little Stanmore, both in the county of Middlesex. The village is about a mile and a half distant from the Elstree and

Boreham Wood Station, on the Midland Railway. The latter part of the name of Elstree is doubtless "Street," the village being so called from lying on the old Watling Street. In ancient deeds its name figures as Idelstree, Ilstrye, Idelestree, and Eaglestree. The name of Idelstree, or Eaglestree, is still recognised locally.

According to Norden's "Historicall and Chorographicall Description of Hertfordshire," Elstree is "derived from Eaglestree: that is, *Nemus aquilinum*, a place where it may be thought that eagles bred in times past." Lysons, however, contends that the name is rather a corruption of *Eald Street*, or the old road; in other words, the ancient Watling Street, upon which it is situated.

The manor was granted by Offa to St. Albans Abbey, after the dissolution of which Henry VIII. gave it to Anthony Denny, whose grandson sold part of the estate to the Briscoes, by whom it was possessed down to the middle of the last century, when it passed by sale into other hands; and it has again changed hands on several occasions, finally passing to the Byngs, now represented by the Earl of Strafford.

The manor-house of Elstree Hall, more than three centuries old, was pulled down in 1880–1. It had in it some fine quaint carved chimney-pieces, each of which was adorned with four full-length figures, said by Miss Phillimore, in her "Twelve Churches," to be "exact representations of the fetishes or gods worshipped in Africa and the West Indies." The wood-work was transferred by Mr. H. H. Gibbs to Aldenham House.

The church, dedicated to St. Nicholas, stands on the east side of the street, and its tall spire is conspicuous for miles round. It is a modern Gothic structure, built of brick, and faced with dark flint, with stone dressings, and it consists of nave, aisles, and chancel, with a tower and shingled spire at the south-west corner. Some of the windows are filled with stained glass; that at the east end of the chancel, a large five-light window, in memory of the Rev. John Morris, D.D., was inserted by his pupils. This edifice was erected about thirty years ago, in the place of the old church, a mean and dilapidated structure, consisting of a nave, chancel, and south aisle, separated by octagonal columns and Pointed arches. The building was one of primitive rudeness and hoary antiquity, and was composed of a number of little patches and compartments, which appeared to have been built at different times. Part of the walls was of rubble-work and of great thickness, and some portion was even composed of timber. The font, which is preserved in the new church, is of antique workmanship, and was perhaps the only interesting feature in the old building. Another feature of the old church which has been retained is the stonework (late Perpendicular) of the doorway known as the "Pilgrims' door."

The monuments are few in number, and of little or no importance. In the church and church-yard are buried two individuals—Martha Ray, and William Weare of Lyons Inn—whose murders may be numbered among the most notorious in the annals of crime; but their graves are without monuments. The former, who was buried on the 14th of April, 1779, was the mistress of the Earl of Sandwich, and mother of Basil Montagu, the editor of Bacon's Works.[*] She was shot in the piazza of Covent Garden by the Rev. James Hackman, who had conceived a too ardent passion for her, and who fired at her while she was getting into her carriage after leaving the theatre, on the evening of the 7th of the same month. Her frantic murderer, who had made an unsuccessful attempt to destroy himself at the same instant, was tried within a few days at the Old Bailey, and was executed at Tyburn on the 19th of April. Hackman's behaviour after his condemnation, we are told, "evinced most perfect resignation to his fate, united with the settled composure of a man that felt he had survived everything that was dear to him." Hackman's execution became, according to the custom, the subject of some of the most ludicrous verses by the ballad-mongers of the day, of which Mr. Thorne, in his "Handbook," quotes the following as an example:—

> "O clergyman! O wicked one!
> In Covent Garden shot her;
> No time to cry upon her God,
> It's hoped He's not forgot her!"

Miss Ray was the daughter of a labourer living at Elstree, and hence it was that she was buried here. Weare was a well-known betting-man of his day, and was murdered in 1823 by Thurtell and Probert, two of his associates, near the residence of the latter at Gill's Hill, Radlett, where we shall have again to refer to the subject. The body of Weare was interred at midnight, in the presence of a large number of spectators. The contemporary newspapers rivalled each other in sensational accounts of the ghastly ceremony.

Close by the church was established, about a quarter of a century ago, an institution which in its time has done much good work—namely, the Female Orphans' Home, a charity which has since been transferred to Tangley Park, near Hampton

---

[*] See "Old and New London," Vol. III., p. 100.

Court. This "Home" had a very humble origin. Towards the close of the year 1855, a private gentleman, not rich in broad acres nor in stores of gold and silver, but pursuing his business as an accountant in the City, resolved to open a "home for destitute orphan girls." He was living with his mother in this pleasant London suburb, when a little girl was left wholly destitute, her father and mother having perished by the cholera. They resolved to adopt the helpless little one, and to make it the "nest-egg" of an orphanage. They were not rich; they had no friends or relatives to "back them up," as the world speaks; they had no funds in hand; but a few pounds were soon subscribed by Christian friends, in coppers, in silver, and in gold, and the newly-adopted stranger was not allowed to be a heavy burden to her foster-parents. Soon another helpless and shipwrecked child was cast at these hospitable doors, borne thither by "the waves of this troublesome world," and landed happily within reach of friendly aid and succour. Then came another, and then another; and the good work was mentioned privately among friends, and subscriptions came in, apparently just as they were needed. A few years ago the founder of the home issued a small pamphlet, or prospectus, in which he tells us that "not only has this particular effort been blessed, but the manager has reason to believe that it has been the means of leading many people to feel, and to act upon, their responsibility in this matter—a responsibility which has been constantly urged upon them from time to time in the reports which have been circulated to some extent. Many similar homes have been opened in London and in the country; and it is hoped that the time will arrive when every *destitute* orphan child will be brought under home influences and sympathies, and thus saved from the cold and withering blight of the union, where, from its very nature, these influences would seem to be impossible."

Elstree is not very rich in literary memories, but we may mention that here Macready had a country house; it was here that he first met Robert Browning, and introduced the author of "Paracelsus" to John Forster and other friends.

At the entrance to the village from Brockley Hill, on the right-hand side of the road, is a large, old-fashioned red-brick mansion, called Elstree Hill House, which has been converted into a collegiate school; and in the corner of a meadow on the opposite side of the road is a handsome brick-built church, of Gothic design. The meadow is fringed with stately elms, and its farther side shelves down to the Elstree Reservoir, a large sheet of water, which adds considerably to the beauty of the landscape. This reservoir is about three-quarters of a mile in length, and a quarter of a mile across at its widest part. It was formed for the supply of the Grand Junction Canal, and, like the reservoir at Kingsbury,* has become a favourite haunt for wild fowl and "waders." Mr. Harting, in his "Birds of Middlesex," says that when the water has been drawn off for the supply of the canal, or "when it has been much reduced by evaporation and want of rain, the herons are here in all their glory. They are then enabled to wade out to some distance, and regale themselves among the roach and eels with which the reservoir abounds." The reservoir is well known to London ornithologists and anglers. It is a beautiful lake, nearly one hundred acres in extent, embosomed in grassy hills, secluded with aquatic trees, and consequently the great attraction of the place.

On our way to Elstree, just before reaching the border of Middlesex and Herts, we cross a watershed. This watershed runs from Stanmore Heath, on the west, to Brockley Hill and Deacon's Hill on the east, and it divides the botanical district of the Upper Colne, in Hertfordshire, from that of the Upper Brent, in Middlesex. Several small streams originate on the north side of Brockley Hill and on the east of Stanmore Heath, and flow into Elstree Reservoir. The water of this reservoir flows north as a small stream, which is by some writers considered the true Colne, and joins the Colne at Colney Street, in Hertfordshire.

The neighbourhood of Elstree has, indeed, many attractions too for the geologist, the peculiar kind of Hertfordshire stone known as "pudding-stone" being here met with. Mr. Walker, the author of "Rambles round London: Rural and Geological," says:—"The name of pudding-stone is aptly chosen. These blocks are masses of conglomerate. The matrix is sandstone; it is as thickly studded with pebbles as the popular Christmas pudding is with plums. . . Pudding-stones with flat faces were used as mill-stones in ruder times, the unequal wearing away of the harder pebbles and softer matrix well fitting them for that purpose. Hand-mills of Roman and Saxon times, made of this pudding-stone, are among the antiquities of our museums." In some of the gardens of the villagers at Elstree the pudding-stone may be seen doing duty as clinkers in miniature rockeries, and a "quern," made out of this peculiar stone, is in the Geological Museum, Jermyn Street.

* See *ante*, p. 274.

CHAPTER XXX.

BUSHEY, ALDENHAM, AND RADLETT.

"Straight mine eye hath caught new pleasures,
While the landscape round it measures;
Russet lawns, and fallows grey,
Where the nibbling flocks do stray."—MILTON.

Bushey Heath—The Scenery described—Bushey Manor—The Parish Church—St. Peter's Church—Bushey Hall—Hartsbourne Manor House—Census Returns—Oxhey—Watford—Almshouses of the Salters' Company—Aldenham—Acreage and Population—Descent of the Manor—Kemp Row—Tibhurst Manor—Kendall Manor—Pickets, or Newberry—Aldenham House—Penn's Place—The Parish Church—The Grammar School—Discovery of Roman Remains—Radlett—Christ Church—Gill's Hill—The Murder of William Weare—Medburn—Village Schools and Improved Dwellings.

AFTER crossing the Elstree reservoir, and pursuing a westerly course, by Caldecott Hill, a walk of about two miles brings us to Bushey Heath, a breezy spot which, although now greatly curtailed by enclosures, or by the handiwork of the builder, still retains fragments of its former beauty, in the shape of broad open patches of green sward, which in summer time are lighted up with banks of golden gorse and wild flowers. The heath is remarkable for its lofty situation, and the view from it embraces a wide range of scenery on all sides. The towers of Westminster Abbey, Hampton Court, Windsor Castle, and the Surrey hills, are visible on the south side, looking towards Bentley Priory and Stanmore Common; northward, the prospect extends for miles into Hertfordshire, the most prominent object visible in the distance being the lofty tower of St. Albans Abbey. On the northeast, Hill Field Lodge stands out prominently in the middle distance; whilst on the north-west the town of Watford occupies the foreground, the tall clock-tower of the London Orphan Asylum rising conspicuously from amid the surrounding greenery, and further westward the rising smoke marks the situation of the town of Rickmansworth.

Bushey, called *Bissei* in the Domesday survey, was granted by the Conqueror to Geoffrey de Magnaville, or Mandeville, and on the failure of male issue of his family, it reverted to the crown in the reign of King John. Henry III. bestowed it on David de Jarpenvil, who, in the reign of Edward I., obtained, among other privileges, the liberty of free warren and the grant of a weekly market for this manor. Having again reverted to the crown, it was granted by Edward II. to his brother, Edmond of Woodstock, Earl of Kent, who was beheaded through the machinations of Queen Isabella and her paramour, Mortimer, in the fourth year of Edward III. From this period the manor descended through a long line of ill-fated princes. These included Thomas de Holland, Duke of Surrey (grandson of John Plantagenet), who was beheaded at Cirencester, in the rebellion against Henry IV., and Thomas de Montacute, Earl of Salisbury, who, after obtaining the highest honours in the campaigns in France with Henry V., was killed by the splinter of a window-frame driven into his face by a cannon ball at the siege of Orleans. Richard, the stout Earl of Warwick, another possessor, was killed at the battle of Barnet. George, Duke of Clarence, was murdered in the Tower, and was succeeded in the possession of this manor by Richard Duke of Gloucester (afterwards Richard III.), whose fate at Bosworth Field is well known. The venerable Lady Margaret de la Pole, Countess of Salisbury, another in the long list of unfortunate owners of Bushey, was cruelly beheaded, at the age of seventy-two, in the reign of Henry VIII., seemingly in revenge for a supposed affront by her to her son, Cardinal Pole. Since the above period, the ownership of the manor has passed through various hands, and it is now held jointly by the Earl of Essex and Colonel Walker.

The parish church, dedicated to St. James, is of Early English date, but, having undergone a thorough restoration in 1871 at the hands of Sir Gilbert Scott, it has lost most of the marks of its antiquity. Down to the above date the fabric had remained for many years in a deplorable condition; its walls had been patched and mended at different times, in part covered with plaster and rough-cast, and propped up with large, heavy buttresses. On making some repairs or alterations a few years ago, an inscription of doubtful credit was discovered which stated it to have been "built in the year 1006." The inscription in question was transferred to an iron plate affixed to the wall of the western end of the church. On the restoration of the building at the date above mentioned, the plaster was removed, and a uniform surface given to the walls by facing them with flint and stone, and the church was at the same time enlarged by the addition of aisles to the nave, the interior restored and improved by the substitution of open benches for the high old-fashioned "pews" by which it was formerly encumbered; the open timber roof was repaired, most of the windows were filled with stained glass, and a fresh paving of ornamental tiles laid down. No portion of the present church would now appear to be of the age mentioned in the inscription referred to above. The oldest parts are the chancel and the base of the tower, which are Early English; the present east window, however, a triplet of lancets, was inserted at the restoration in 1871 in place of a

gested the inhuman act of disinterring and hanging the bodies of the Protector and certain of the regicides." On a slab in the church, to the memory of two Bakewells, one of whom died in 1643, is the following quaint epigram :—

"Here's two in one, and yet not two but one,
Two sonnes, one tomb, two heirs, one name alone."

In the churchyard is a tomb, embellished with a carved representation of a palette and brushes, to the memory of Henry Edridge, A.R.A., who

BUSHEY CHURCH.

Perpendicular window of five lights. The chancel is separated from the nave by a carved oak screen. The timber roof of the chancel is decorated with paint and gilding, and on the north side of the altar is an ancient ambry.

The monuments in the church are few and unimportant. In the floor of the chancel is a marble slab inscribed to the memory of Lady Barnard, wife of Gilbert, Lord Barnard; she died in 1728. In 1667 was buried in the chancel Colonel Silas Titus, a Presbyterian Royalist, who has the credit of having planned the escape of Carisbrooke Castle, and with having written the famous tract, entitled "Killing no Murder," with a view to procure the assassination of Cromwell, and who also has the discredit of having "sug-

died in 1821, and close by it is an upright slab commemorating Thomas Hearne, a once well-known artist and antiquary, author of the "Antiquities of Great Britain," who died in 1817. "Both these monuments," observes Mr. James Thorne, in his "Environs of London," "were erected by Dr. Munro, the physician, of the Adelphi, a generous friend to young artists, and the early patron of Turner, Girtin, and William Hunt. Dr. Munro had here a country residence, to which he used to invite his young students, that they might sketch in the vicinity. Turner and Girtin have left hundreds of these sketches." There are also in the churchyard some memorials of the Cappers, of Wiggen Hall, in this parish, one of whom purchased the manor of Bushey at the commencement of the last century; also a tomb of Mrs. Elizabeth Fuller, of Watford Place, who founded the Free School in Watford town, and who died in 1709. Mr. William Jerdan, the veteran editor of *The Literary Gazette*, also lies buried here.

St. Peter's Church, which stands in the hamlet of Bushey Heath, is a modern erection of the early English style; its walls are partly concealed in rich clusters of ivy.

From the churchyard, a narrow lane through shops and private houses, with here and there a pleasant shady lane. At the beginning of this century there were about 180 houses in this parish, with a population of about 850. According to the census returns for 1871 the population then reached a total of 4,543, which number in the course of the next ten years had increased to 4,786.

About a mile to the west of Bushey, but rather beyond our beat, lies the hamlet of Oxhey, nestling cosily on the banks of the Colne. The chapel,

ALDENHAM HOUSE. (*See page* 309.)

Little Bushey leads to Bushey Hall, which has been lately fitted up as a hydropathic establishment. The house is built in the Italian style, and has been fitted up in a most elaborate manner, some of the rooms being inlaid with cedar, at a cost of £200,000. There are several other good residences in the neighbourhood, notably Hartsbourne Manor House, the seat of the Sladens, which lies away to the north-west in a pleasant valley watered by the Harts Bourne rivulet, one of the numerous feeders of the river Colne, which it joins after flowing through Carpenders Park.

The main thoroughfare of Bushey stretches for nearly two miles northward on the Berkhampstead road, from Clay Hill, by Stanmore Heath, towards Watford. It is well sprinkled on either side with

which was built in 1612, and which is the only remaining relic of the Jacobean mansion of Oxhey Place, is now used as a chapel-of-ease for Watford.

Bushey has now become a kind of southern suburb of Watford, from which it is separated by the river Colne, which flows through the lower part of the town. As Watford lies just beyond our jurisdiction, we can do no more than express our regret that we are not able to carry our readers with us to Cassiobury, the seat of the Earl of Essex, with its pleasant park and fine family pictures. We must also, for the same reason, leave unvisited the new London Orphan Asylum, which was transferred hither in 1871 from Clapton. The almshouses of the Salters' Company, founded by Beamond and Nicholas, were lately removed hither from London. They are built of red brick with stone dressings, and comprise a centre and detached wings, and an embattled tower. Accommodation is afforded for six men and twelve women.

A walk of about two-and-a-half miles from Bushey Station, on the North-Western Railway, through pleasant rural lanes, by way of Bushey Grove and Berry Wood, brings us to Aldenham, a quiet and retired village, situated midway between the high road to Rickmansworth and that to St. Albans, and about two miles from Radlett Station, on the Midland Railway. The area of the parish is nearly 6,000 acres, and the population, according to the census of 1871, exclusive of the separated district of Radlett, amounted to 1,486. In 1881 they had risen to 1,833.

Long before the Conquest the manor of Aldenham—or Ealdenham, as it was then spelt—belonged to the Abbot of St. Albans, to whom it was given by Wulfsinus, or, as some historians have it, by Offa, King of the Mercians.

Soon after the Conquest the Abbot of Westminster obtained a grant of it for a period of twenty years, for an annual payment of twenty-one hundred shillings and four oxen at Easter, "on condition that he so kept the woods here that persons journeying from St. Albans to London might be safe from the robbers who infested the neighbourhood." The Abbot of Westminster appears to have fulfilled his part of the conditions under which he held the land, but would not give up possession of a wood near Aldenham, which claim the Abbot of St. Albans resisted until long after the expiration of the term.

"There can be little doubt," observes Mr. Cussans in his "History of Hertfordshire," "that the manor of Aldenham really belonged to the Abbey of St. Albans, and that they were unlawfully dispossessed of the greater portion. Constant feuds occurred between the abbots of the two houses of St. Albans and Westminster. At length the Abbot of Westminster brought a suit against his brother of St. Albans, for that the latter had, on Tuesday after Pentecost, in the year 1249, taken fifteen beasts from his manor of Aldenham, and driven them to the manor of Parkbury, in St. Albans; and again, on St. John's Day in the same year, had in like manner taken three other beasts (*haveros*). At the trial St. Albans asserted that the then king had confirmed to their abbey a proportion of the fines coming to the Crown on the circuits of the king's judges within the liberty of St. Albans, a privilege they had held from time immemorial; that certain men belonging to West-

minster, living in that portion of the manor of Aldenham, within the liberty, had been amerced at the last circuit in the sum of five marcs, six shillings and eightpence, whereupon the Abbot of St. Albans seized upon the said cattle. The Abbot of Westminster replied that the same king had granted to his monastery the amercements of all their own men, and the chattels of fugitives and persons condemned. Finally, in Hilary Term, 1256, it was agreed that the abbot and monks of St. Albans should have a View of Franc-pledge in Aldenham once a year, and that on that occasion, whether any fines were levied or not, Westminster should pay St. Albans four shillings, the remainder, if any, to be retained by the metropolitan abbey; that every villein of Aldenham, within the Hundred of Cashio, should render suit at the Hundred Court once in three years, and should attend on juries, &c., when summoned; and if any of the men of Aldenham were amerced (other than at the View of Franc-pledge) before the bailiffs of either the abbeys of Westminster or St. Albans, the said abbeys should equally share such amercement; and, lastly, that the gallows erected in a place called Keneprowe should be common to both abbots, on which to hang persons condemned to death in the Court of Aldenham." Keneprowe—now corrupted into Kemp Row, or Camp Row—is situated between the church and the railway-station at Radlett, and is now a farm. "A man suspended by the neck was supposed to be a wholesome moral lesson, to be taught to so many of his former associates as possible. The abbots, therefore," Mr. Cussans adds, "acted wisely in their selection of Keneprowe, for on its elevated site the result of unlawfully taking a fish from the abbatial waters could be plainly seen both by the men of Aldenham and of St. Albans."

This unsatisfactory state of things between the two abbots came effectually to an end at the dissolution of monasteries, for the manor then "reverted" to the Crown—if the seizure by Henry VIII. of the property of the Church can be called a reversion. It was, however, shortly afterwards granted to the Stepneys, by whom it was sold to Sir Edward Cary, Master of the Jewel Office to Queen Elizabeth and James I., whose son, Sir Henry Cary, was created Viscount Falkland, and subsequently held for some years the office of Lord Lieutenant of Ireland. In the reign of Charles II. the manor was in the hands of Lord Holles. After a few other changes of ownership, it passed, at the end of the last century, to the Thellussons, afterwards Lords Rendlesham, in whose hands it still remains. The advowson of the vicarage, however, was sold by Lord Rendlesham in 1877 to Mr. Henry Hucks Gibbs, of Aldenham House.

There are in the parish one or two manors of minor importance, notably Titeberst, or Tibhurst, and Kendall. The former of these lies on the south-eastern border of the parish, at Theobald's Street, and is owned by the Phillimores, but its history is of little or no importance. The manor of Kendall, the name of which is preserved in Kendall Lodge and Kendall Hall, which lie on either side of the St. Albans Road in the eastern part of the parish, was, in the reign of James I., granted, together with the manor of Tibhurst, to Robert, first Earl of Salisbury. It was afterwards held by the Jephsons, and about the middle of the last century it was bequeathed to Mr. William Phillimore, grandfather of the present owner.

In 1700 Chauncy writes, in his "Antiquities of Hertfordshire":—"Pickets, or Newberry, is another small manor, which William Briscoe, one of the Yeomen of the Guard, held in this vill. Upon his death it came to Edward Briscoe, who was his son and heir, and is the present owner thereof." This manor is now known as Piggots, and is situated near Letchmoor Heath. Although it still retains the name of a manor, the independent rights appertaining to it have long been merged into the manor paramount of Aldenham. As it appears from the above quotation from Chauncy, the manor of Newberry was formerly incorporated with that of Pickets, or Piggots; they are now, however, distinct estates. The manor of Newberry, now called New-berries, is near the railway-station at Radlett, and extends into the adjoining parish of Shenley.

Aldenham House, the seat of Mr. Henry Hucks Gibbs, is a spacious red brick building, standing in a park about 200 acres in extent. The mansion was formerly known as Wigbournes, which, in its turn, appears to have been the successor of a mansion called Penn's Place, or Aldenham Hall, but which, by the way, stood on a small farm now bearing the name, at a short distance from the present house. In dry weather, Mr. Cussans tells us, the foundations of a large building are plainly to be traced. The site, which occupies an acre of ground, is enclosed by an almost rectangular moat, or, rather, the traces of a moat, the eastern side of which, bordering Grub's Lane, has been filled up. The estate derived its name from the family of Penn, to whom it formerly belonged, and it was afterwards owned successively by the Cades, the Coningsbys, and the Coghills. Chauncy, in his "History" above quoted, speaks thus of Penn's Place:—"It is a small manor, situated upon the common where Henry Coghill, Esq., built a fair

house of brick." It is not quite clear from Chauncy whether the "fair house of brick" was the mansion known as Penn's Place and Aldenham Hall, or the house mentioned above as Wigbournes. In the will of Sarah Hucks, dated 1767, Penn's Place is spoken of as a then existing mansion; but in a subsequent deed, executed in 1815, it is described as a farm.

Under its former name of Wigbournes, Aldenham House passed, early in the seventeenth century, to the Coghills; and on the death of Thomas Coghill, in 1734, it passed to his niece, Sarah Hucks, who had already inherited Penn's Place. Her son, Robert Hucks the younger, made sundry additions to the house. After his death, in 1814, the house remained unoccupied for many years, and was allowed to fall into a dilapidated condition. In 1846 Mrs. Gibbs, the mother of the present owner, took up her residence here; but after her death, in 1850, it again remained unoccupied by the family for nearly twenty years, when Mr. Gibbs came again into residence. This gentleman has since thoroughly restored the old building, making many improvements, but in no way altering the character of the building. The family of the present owner was connected by marriage with the families of the Suttons, Hucks, and Coghills, former owners of the estate.

Aldenham is mentioned more than once in the diary of the first Lord Shaftesbury as the seat of Sir Job Harbye, with whom he was an occasional guest.

The parish church, dedicated to St. John the Baptist, stands near the centre of the village, and is an interesting building, chiefly of the Perpendicular period. It consists of a clerestoried nave, with aisles; also a chancel, with aisles, and a lofty embattled tower, surmounted by a shingled spire, at the west end. The nave and aisles are separated by three octagonal columns on each side, from which spring high Pointed arches. The nave-roof is of timber, the principal rafters being painted, and the wall-shafts resting on grotesquely-sculptured stone corbels. The church was restored by Sir Charles Barry in 1840, at which time a timber waggon-headed roof was added to the chancel, and a large five-light window of Decorated character inserted over the altar. This window, and several others in the church, are filled with stained glass. At the east end of the north aisle are faint traces of mural painting.

Among the monuments is one in the chancel, a large altar-tomb, to the memory of John Coghill of Berry, who died in 1714. On the south wall of the chancel, under flat-arched canopies, are the recumbent effigies of two females, whose names are unknown. They form a single monument, and, according to Chauncy's "Antiquities of Hertford-shire," are supposed by tradition " to represent two sisters here entombed, the founders of this church, and co-heirs to this lordship." "The costume of the figures," observes Mr. Cussans, " shows that the monument was erected towards the end of the reign of Edward II.—perhaps as late as the year 1400, but certainly not ten years later. The arrangement of the arms shows that the ladies were not the two wives of one man, nor were they sisters." Near the above is a monument, in the form of a sarcophagus, of coloured marble, em-bellished with a medallion of white marble, on which are carved in low-relief portraits of Robert Hucks, and Sarah his wife, to whom the monument was erected. In the floor of the chancel are four or five small brasses, but none of any importance.

The south aisles of the chancel and nave were formerly separated by a carved oak screen, which was swept away when the church was restored, in 1840 ; parts of it, however, remained in the village, and these scattered fragments have lately been collected by Mr. Gibbs, of Aldenham House, and replaced in their original position. A somewhat similar screen on the north side still remains.

In the vestry are preserved two helmets of ancient date. There is also in the church a curious muni-ment chest, nearly ten feet in length, carved out of a single block of oak, and firmly bound and clamped with iron. The font, in the centre of the nave, between the north and south entrances, has a square bowl of Purbeck marble, resting on a solid circular stem, with detached columns at the corners. It is ascribed to about 1250, the date of the present church, which, by the way, was built on the founda-tions of an earlier structure.

Aldenham Grammar School, a large red-brick building, of Elizabethan design, is situated on Boydon Hill, in the south-eastern part of the parish. It was founded and endowed, along with six almshouses, in 1599 by Richard Platt, a brewer of London, who entrusted the government of both institutions to the Brewers' Company. In 1875 a new scheme was sanctioned by the Queen in Council, under which the Grammar School was a strictly high-class school, and two lower schools were established out of the endowment, for the use of the parishioners. There are several scholar-ships, tenable in the school ; and there are also three exhibitions a year, tenable at any university.

In 1878, while excavations were being made for the purpose of forming a swimming-bath on the north side of the school, the workmen came upon a large quantity of broken Roman tiles and pottery,

at a uniform depth of four or five feet from the surface. It is supposed that there was a pottery factory close by, and that the fragments which were here so plentifully scattered about were broken in the course of manufacture.

Radlett, whither we now direct our steps, is an outlying hamlet of Aldenham, about two miles to the north-east. In 1863 a separate district was assigned to it for ecclesiastical purposes. It lies in a valley, through which runs a stream, called the Leat, or Lete, one of the feeders of the Colne. This stream, before the introduction of the present system of land-drainage, passed through a gravelly soil, and thereby became of a red colour, as it does now in wet weather ; and it is from this circum-stance that the place is presumed to have derived its name. Rad-lett, or Red-lett, would therefore signify the red mill-stream.

About a quarter of a mile south of Radlett station, on Cobden Hill, stands Christ Church, which was built in 1864 to meet the requirements of the newly-formed ecclesiastical district. It is a cruciform building, constructed of flint and stone, with bands of red brick, and is in the Early Decorated style. The mullions and dressings of the windows are of Bath stone, and the tower is surmounted by an octagonal spire of the same material. Most of the windows are filled with stained glass. The church stands near the site of a small chantry, belonging formerly to the Abbey of St. Albans. In old deeds the name of Cobden Hill is written Copdene Hill, signifying the "Hill at the Head of the Valley." The chantry is stated by Mr. Cussans to have been founded about the year 1510, by Sir Humphrey Coningsby, who endowed it with the following lands lying in the parishes of Aldenham and Elstree :—Paynes, Organ Hall, Tyttescroft, Hilles Stowe, Mole Hill Acre, Chalk Croft, and Woodwards. On the dissolution of religious houses these lands came to the Crown, and were granted by Henry VIII. to Thomas Strete, one of the grooms of his privy chamber. On the accession of Queen Mary, John White, the ejected incumbent of the chantry, was allowed a pension of £5 per annum.

The country round about Radlett is exceedingly rural, much of the land being used for agricultural purposes, the remainder being preserved as park-lands. The district is of too recent growth to have a " history ; " but early in the present century it acquired some celebrity from the murder of William Weare, of Lyons Inn, whose body, as already stated, lies buried in Elstree churchyard.* The murder took place in October, 1823, close by Gill's Hill cottage, which is reached by a narrow and crooked lane, running westward from Radlett Station towards Batler's Green. Weare was shot by one John Thurtell, his gambling associate, while driving with him in a gig to the house of one William Probert, in the above-mentioned lane. After the murder Weare's body was deposited in a pond behind the cottage, while the murderers divided the spoil, and it was afterwards dragged through a hedge into a field at a short distance from the house. Suspicion having been aroused, a search was made for the body, which was soon discovered. The murderers were forthwith arrested, and Thurtell and Hunt were tried at Hertford, and, being found guilty, the former was condemned and executed, and Hunt was sentenced to transportation for life. Probert, who turned "king's evidence," was discharged, but was afterwards apprehended, tried, and hanged, for horse-stealing.

The details of this old story have been often told; they caused great excitement at the time, and even now read more like fiction than fact. The careful plot, every detail of which fell out quite otherwise than it was planned; the body hidden and sunk, now here, now there; a brother's blood still crying for vengeance; the utter distrust of each other shown by Thurtell's confederates; and the supper on the fatal night, cheered or solaced, as the case might be, by the fitful minstrelsy of Joseph Hunt, an accomplice in the crime; Thurtell's family position, too—for his father was an alderman of Norwich—gave additional interest to the tragedy, which became a fruitful theme for itinerant theatres and peep-shows at country fairs; and " the actual roan horse and yellow gig in which Weare was carried were exhibited on the stage." Poetry came to the aid of the drama—if such doggerel as the following can be called poetry :—

> " They cut his throat from ear to ear,
>   His brains they battered in ;
> His name was Mr. William Weare,
>   He dwelt in Lyons Inn."

Carlyle more than once alludes to the incidents connected with the tragedy; and Sydney Smith pressed the unpromising subject into his service some three years after the event. It happened that in 1826 he was noticing in the *Edinburgh Review* Charles Waterton's " Wanderings in South America." He had to describe a certain Demerara " goatsucker," which, like other birds of its kind, makes night hideous with the most dreadful screeching. This he thought "a stranger would take for Weare being murdered by Thurtell !" Sir Walter Scott not only carefully read the account of the

murder at the time, but more than four years afterwards, when returning from London to the North, did not hesitate to go some two or three miles out of his way in order specially to visit the scene. The author of " Waverley," however, was not happy in his visit to Radlett. He writes in his diary, under date of May 28, 1828 :—

" Our elegant researches carried us out of the highroad and through a labyrinth of intricate lanes, which seem made on purpose to afford strangers the full benefit of a dark night and a drunken driver, in order to visit Gill's Hill, in Hertfordshire, famous for the murder of Mr. Weare. The place has the strongest title to the description of Wordsworth :—

> ' A merry spot, 'tis said, in days of yore,
>   But something ails it now—the place is curst.'

The principal part of the house is destroyed, and only the kitchen remains standing. The garden has been dismantled, though a few laurels and flowering shrubs, run wild, continue to mark the spot. The fatal pond is now only a green swamp, but so near the house that one cannot conceive how it was ever chosen as a place of temporary concealment for the murdered body." Scott's description, however, seems to be somewhat exaggerated. The cottage occupied by Probert, and where Thurtell and Hunt spent the night following the murder, is still standing : it is an ordinary one-storeyed house, with a high-pitched tiled roof. In the rear is the pond which Scott describes as a " green swamp."

Midway between Radlett and Elstree, in the hamlet of Medburn, is a substantial and commodious boys' school, with master's house, garden, and playground. It was built out of the funds of the bequest of Richard Platt, mentioned above, and serves for the boys of both villages. Near Radlett church stands a school for girls and infants, built, in the year 1878, from the designs of Mr. Blomfield, and is in the style commonly named after " Queen Anne." It is of flint, with red-brick dressings, and a tile roof. Since the erection of this latter building, a school at Batler's Green has been converted into cottages.

Mr. William B. Phillimore, of Kendalls Hall, is the chief owner of property at Radlett, and lord of the manor of Elstree and Theobald Street, and his family have been great benefactors to Radlett, by the improvement of the dwellings of the labouring classes. Newberries Park, the seat of Mr. Thomas Bagnall, is a large house in a pleasant park sloping down to the railway. It was purchased from the Phillimores about twenty years ago.

CHAPTER XXXI.

SHENLEY, COLNEY, RIDGE, AND SOUTH MIMMS.

"Per amica silentia campi."—LUCRETIUS.

Extent and Population of Shenley—Descent of the Manor—Shenley Hall, or Salisbury—Newberries—Old Organ Hall—Porters—Holmes, otherwise High Canons—The Village of Shenley—The Chapel-of-Ease—The Parish Church—Colney House—London Colney—Tittenhanger—Colney Heath—Ridge—The Parish Church—South Mimms—Census Returns—General Appearance of the Village—The Old North Road—The Manor of South Mimms—The Church—Almshouses—Potter's Bar—Dyrham Park—Wrotham Park—Destruction of the Mansion by Fire—Hadley Common—Christ Church.

THE village of Shenley lies about two miles east-north-east from Radlett Station on the Midland Railway; the road thither, tortuous, but pleasant,

gave "Scenlea" to the above-mentioned monastery, "in perpetual alms;" "but," as Mr. Cussans infers in his "History of Hertfordshire," "as in a charter

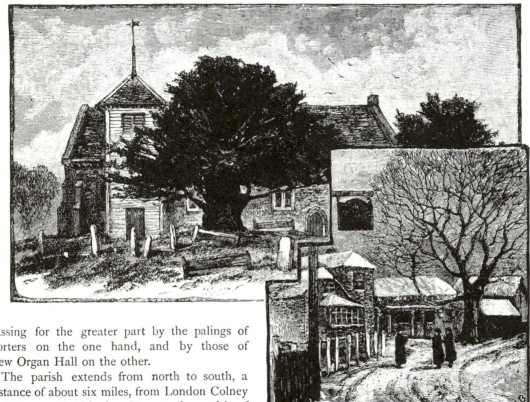

SHENLEY CHURCH AND VILLAGE.

passing for the greater part by the palings of Porters on the one hand, and by those of New Organ Hall on the other.

The parish extends from north to south, a distance of about six miles, from London Colney to Elstree and Chipping Barnet; the parish of Ridge forms its eastern boundary, and a long detached strip, belonging to the same parish, occupies the greater portion of its western side.

The number of houses in Shenley parish in 1871 was 301, the population at the same time amounting to 1,380. Of this number, 382 belonged to the ecclesiastical district of Colney St. Peter. During the next decade the number of the inhabitants had slightly diminished.

From an ancient Chartulary, formerly belonging to the Abbey of St. Albans, but now preserved in the British Museum, it appears that before the time of the Conquest one Thurefleda, a pious lady,

of Edward IV. to the abbey (in which the confirmations of grants by previous kings are all recited at length) there is no mention of Shenley, it is probable that the manor, which in Domesday Book is said to have belonged to St. Albans, was the same manor which was afterwards known as Ridge. This supposition is strengthened by the fact that Ridge is not mentioned in Domesday, and that the abbot's manor of Shenley is there described as being in Albaneston Hundred (the Hundred of Cashio), and the other two within the

Hundred of Danais, or Dacorum." About two hundred years after the Conquest the manor was in the possession of John Fitzacre, who, in 1267–8, granted it, together with the advowson of the church, and the chapel of Colney, to Adam de Stratton, and in the same year obtained from the king a grant to hold an annual fair and a weekly market within this manor. At the close of the thirteenth century the manor was forfeited to the Crown, and shortly afterwards it was granted by Edward III. to Sir John de Pulteney, or Poultney, who was five times Lord Mayor of London. The of Newberries was formerly known as Old Organ Hall, and appears to have been first called Newberries by its late owner, Mr. Phillimore, from whom it was purchased by Mr. Thomas Bagnall. The building now known as Old Organ Hall, which lies on the east side of the railway, near to Boreham Wood and Elstree Station, is a farmhouse on the estate.

The estate of Porters, mentioned above, covers a large portion of the parish, being no less than 1,300 acres in extent. The mansion, the seat of Mr. Myers, who is lord of the manor, occupies the

TITTENHANGER.

SIR T. POPE.

manor remained vested in the Poultneys for just three centuries, when it was carried, by the marriage of an heiress, to the Crewes, of Crewe Hall, Cheshire. It subsequently passed to the family of Lomax, in whose possession it remained down to 1850, when it was sold to Mr. William J. Myers, of Porters Park, in the parish, and with his descendant it still continues.

The manor of Shenley Hall, otherwise Salisbury, lies in the north-eastern part of the parish, near London Colney. It derived its name from the family of Montacute, Earls of Salisbury, who owned the property in the fourteenth century. The manor subsequently descended in the same way as that of Bushey, and seems to have reverted to the Crown in 1471, on the death of the Earl of Warwick, the "kingmaker," as we shall see presently, at the Battle of Barnet. It now belongs to the Phillimores, late of Newberries. The present mansion summit of a pleasant hill, commanding an extensive view towards the south-west. Chauncy, in his "Antiquities of Hertfordshire," describes Porters as "an old seat," and Sir Richard Coxe, who died in 1623, is described as "of Porters." From the Coxes, the estate passed by marriage to Sir Edmund Anderson, with whose family it continued for many years. Nicholas Hawksmoor, the architect, a pupil of Sir Christopher Wren, whom he assisted in rebuilding St. Paul's Cathedral, was living here at the time of his death, in 1736; he may, however, have been only a tenant, for in 1750 died Mr. John Mason, who was at that time lord of the manor of Weld, which had become amalgamated with this estate, and who, on his tomb in Shenley churchyard, is described as "of Porters."

The estate of Holmes, otherwise Canons, but

commonly called High Canons, is situated about a mile south-east of the village, on the left of the road towards Barnet. The property derives its name from the fact of its having formerly belonged to the Prior and Canons of St. Bartholomew, in Smithfield, in whose possession it remained till the dissolution of religious houses, when it passed to the Crown. In 1543 High Canons was sold to one Nicholas Bristow, and since that time it has undergone several changes of ownership. Mr. Thomas Fitzherbert, who purchased the estate at the end of the last century, expended a large sum of money in improving the grounds and mansion, which was shortly after again sold. In 1812 the property was purchased by Mr. Enoch Durant, with whose family it now remains.

The village of Shenley fringes the cross-roads at the south-eastern extremity of Porters. It consists of a few straggling cottages and general shops, and, from its lofty situation, possesses some charming views, particularly towards the north-west, where, at a distance of about five miles, the city of St. Albans, with its venerable abbey, is plainly discernible, cresting the opposite range of hills. In 1841, in consequence of the distance of the church from the bulk of the population, a plain brick-built chapel-of-ease was erected in the centre of the village. It consists of a chancel and nave, with a small belfry turret at the south-west angle. Here the afternoon and evening services are performed, the morning service being still continued in the old parish church, to which we will now direct our steps.

This edifice, dedicated to St. Botolph, lies about a mile north-west from the village, at the foot of the hill, and a little to the right of the road to St. Albans. The church originally consisted of chancel, nave, south aisle, and tower; but in 1753, the edifice having become dilapidated, the tower was demolished, the western end built up, the chancel and tower arches and the arcading of the nave pulled down, the open timber roof demolished, and baulks of timber laid from wall to wall, with the result that the structure has been converted into a good-sized rectangular chamber, with a flat plaster ceiling. On the site formerly occupied by the south porch is now a square wooden tower, painted white, with a tiled roof, and containing three bells. The walls of the body of the church are of chalk, faced with squared flints, and the buttresses between the windows have been partially repaired with brick. The windows are of the Perpendicular style throughout. The large four-light east and west windows, and also three or four others, are filled with memorial painted glass. The font is ancient, and stands at the west end of the church under the organ gallery; and in the exterior of the south wall is an old sun-dial. The pulpit and a carved oak reredos and altar-rails were erected by subscription in 1878.

In the churchyard are several fine yew-trees. The tomb of Nicholas Hawksmoor, the architect, mentioned above, is in the churchyard. It is an altar-tomb, the slab of which is broken, and the inscription barely legible. Hawksmoor was the architect of St. George's, Bloomsbury, St. Mary Woolnoth, Lombard Street, and other well-known City churches. Close by the belfry is the memorial of a former parish clerk; it consists of a board supported by two uprights, and bears the following lines :—

"Joseph Rogers, died August 17th, 1828, in the 77th year of his age, having been clerk of this parish a half century.

> " Silent in dust lies mould'ring here
> A Parish Clerk of voice most clear ;
> None Joseph Rogers could excel
> In laying bricks or singing well.
> Though snapp'd his line, laid by his rod,
> We build for him our hopes in God,
> The Saviour God, that He will raise
> Again that voice to sing His praise,
> In Temple blest, which always stands,
> The Church of God not made with hands."

Colney House, in the hamlet of Colney Chapel, about a mile northward from Shenley Church, and the same distance south-west from the village of London Colney, but belonging to the parish of Shenley, is a spacious stone mansion, built about a century ago by Governor Bouchier, at an expense of £53,000, including the charges for laying out the pleasure-grounds and making other improvements in the park, which is about 150 acres in extent. The house is a handsome and regular structure, with slightly projecting wings, and is double-fronted. The principal front, facing the roadway, has a semicircular portico at the entrance, surmounted by a half-dome. The west front, overlooking the park, has a bay-window on either side of the doorway. These bays rise to the level of the second floor, and are surmounted with balustrades. The park contains some fine oak and elm trees, and the pleasure-grounds are extensive. The estate was sold by Governor Bouchier to Margaret of Anspach, who resided here for three years, after which it was disposed of to the Earl of Kingston. Early in the present century it was sold to Mr. George Anderson, with whose family it remained for many years. It was subsequently owned by the Oddies; and in 1871 it was disposed of to Sir Andrew Lusk, Bart., who sold it some years later.

The above estate was formerly part of the extensive manor of the Weald, or Wild, and obtained the name of Colney Chapel, it is supposed, from a religious house which is thought to have stood on a small piece of land in the park, surrounded by a moat, though now planted and laid out in walks.

The river Colne skirts the north side of the park in its course towards Aldenham and Watford. It is crossed by a wooden foot-bridge in the line of the roadway at this point, but is fordable for vehicular traffic. Following the course of this stream in a north-easterly direction we soon find ourselves at London Colney.

London Colney, which is partly in the parishes of Shenley and Ridge, and partly in those of St. Peter and St. Stephen, in St. Albans, is a large village of some 850 inhabitants, and was formed into a separate ecclesiastical district in 1826. It stands on the great high road through Barnet and South Mimms to St. Albans, from which place it is distant about three miles and a half. The principal part of the village slopes upward from the north bank of the River Colne, from which the place derives its name, and which is here crossed by a brick bridge of seven arches. The church, dedicated to St. Peter, was built in 1825, by Philip, third Earl of Hardwicke. It is a plain rectangular brick building, with semicircular-headed windows; that at the east end, of three lights, is filled with stained glass, representing "The Ascension," and was designed by Louisa, Dowager-Marchioness of Waterford; it was erected in 1865 as a memorial to the founder of the church.

The hamlet of Tittenhanger lies to the east of London Colney; it forms part of the parish of Ridge, and consists of two or three humble cottages, nestling pleasantly near the winding Colne, and on the outskirts of Tittenhanger Park, the seat of the Countess of Caledon. The manor of Tittenhanger belonged, at the time of the Conquest, to the Abbots of St. Albans, who frequently resided here, though their manor is stated to have been but a "mean building." About the end of the fourteenth century, however, Abbot John de la Moote commenced the building of a new and stately mansion here, "where," according to Chauncy, "he and his successors might retire for their ease and pleasure, and recreate themselves with their friends and relations, but died before he could finish the same." This was afterwards completed, on a more extensive and elaborate scale, by his successor, Abbot John of Whethamsted, in the reign of Henry VI., and the property continued to belong to the abbots till they were despoiled of their possessions at the dissolution of monasteries. Thorne, in his "En-

virons of London," observes that "there is a tradition that Wolsey expended a large sum on it, intending to make it one of his residences." In 1528, Henry VIII. and Queen Katherine are stated to have taken up their residence at Tittenhanger during the continuance of the malady known as the "sweating sickness" in London. In 1547, the last year of his reign, Henry VIII. granted the manor and estate to Sir Hugh Paulet, from whose family it was conveyed by marriage to Sir Thomas Pope, the founder of Trinity College, Oxford. Sir Thomas, who had been the fortunate recipient of many grants of the lands of the dissolved monasteries, made Tittenhanger his principal residence, having greatly improved the house; and on his death, without issue, in 1559, it continued in the possession of his widow, Elizabeth, the daughter of Mr. William Blount, of Blount Hall, Staffordshire. This lady was succeeded by her nephew and heir, Mr. (afterwards Sir) Thomas Pope Blount; and from him the estate descended to Philip, third Earl of Hardwicke, in right of his mother, Catherine, first wife of the Hon. Charles Yorke, Lord Chancellor of Great Britain, she being the sole heiress of the ancient Hertfordshire families of Pope, Blount, and Freeman. These Blounts became extinct by the death of Sir Henry Pope Blount about the middle of the last century. On the death of the Countess of Hardwicke, in 1858, the property was inherited by her daughter, Catherine, Countess of Caledon.

The present mansion of Tittenhanger was built about the middle of the seventeenth century by the first Sir Henry Pope Blount, from the designs of Inigo Jones, and it is described by Chauncy as "a fair structure of brick, with fair walks and gardens." The house is of Tudor architecture, large and convenient, oblong in form, and has an inner court. It was originally surrounded by a moat, but this has been filled up; the gardens, too, were long ago destroyed, and much of the park has been broken up and converted into a farm. What there is left of the park is pleasant and well wooded, and is watered on its western side by the river Colne.

Colney Heath, the extreme northern limit of the metropolitan area, and consequently the utmost extent of our wanderings in this direction, abuts upon the north-east side of Tittenhanger Park. The district was formed into an ecclesiastical parish in 1846. The church, dedicated to St. Mark, is a brick building in the Byzantine style, consisting of an apsidal chancel, a nave, and a small bell-tower.

We must now make our way homewards once more, but by way of the high road, through South

Mimms to Barnet. The road for some three or four miles is as "straight as an arrow," and the land on either side pleasantly diversified by cultivation and woods. Ridge Hill, which we ascend about two miles from Colney, takes its name from the quaint little old-world village of Ridge, which lies some little distance away to the right of our road, and is approached through narrow winding lanes. The district is exceedingly rural, and has a population of about 450 souls. Apart from the dozen or more of humble cottages, a general shop, and an inn, forming the village, there are one or two houses of a better class, notably Ridge Hall, Rabley House, and Deeves Hall, with here and there a farm scattered about. The parish, which has really no literary history, probably derives its name from the "ridge" of high ground which runs along its border, and it is wonderfully unchanged among all the changes of time. The green lanes on every side wind between hedgerows of thorns and elders, very much as they must have done two centuries ago ; and the farm-houses have a sleepy and respectable appearance, which seems to indicate that their owners do not care much for " progress."

The parish church, dedicated to St. Margaret, is an ancient building, standing away by itself on the west side of the village. The edifice is small, built of flint and stone, and consists of a chancel in the Early Decorated style, and a Perpendicular nave. The west end is surmounted by a low wooden tower, crowned with a spire. It is as yet "unrestored," so that it still exhibits all the marks of the Georgian interior arrangements. There are high deep pews of deal on either side of the central passage up the nave, with hatchments in abundance, and the royal arms in a conspicuous position. Like Kingsbury, it is quite innocent of aisles, and the distinction between nave and chancel is of the very slightest kind. The structure is chiefly remarkable for the abundant coats of whitewash which have been inflicted on it by successive incumbents and churchwardens. It is also noticeable for the tombs and monuments of the family of the Blounts of Tittenhanger, who lie buried here. Of these, the best known are those of Sir Henry Pope Blount, the author of the "Voyage into the Levant," who died in 1682, and his sons, Sir Thomas Pope Blount, author of "De Re Poetica," &c., who died in 1697, and Charles Blount, the deistical writer, who died by his own hand in 1693, having been driven to frenzy by his unsuccessful endeavours to obtain a license to marry his deceased wife's sister, and her refusal to marry him without it. The event is thus recorded in the Cæsar Manuscripts, under date of August 31, 1693 :—" Mr. Charles Blount, of

Tittenhanger, in Hartfordshire, died in London, *felo de se*, five weeks after he had shot himself into the belly with a pistoll : for love of Mrs. Hobby (his wife's sister), who was a rich widow." Pope, too, commemorated Mr. Blount's death in the following line in his "Epistle to the Satires " :—

"If Blount despatch'd himself, he play'd the man."

Blount's books were reprinted in a collected form by Gildon, in 1695.

The parish of South Mimms is bounded on the west by Ridge, on the north by Northaw and North Mimms ; Monken Hadley and Enfield encompass it on the east, and it stretches away southward to High Barnet. It occupies the northern portion of the Hundred of Edmonton, and is the most extreme point northward of the county of Middlesex. The name of the parish has in times past been variously written as Mims, Mymes, and Mymmes. The additional term of "South" is evidently applied to the village to distinguish it from its neighbour in Hertfordshire, which has become famous as the home of Sir Thomas More, but which, by the way, lies just beyond the limits of our peregrinations. This parish, which includes the hamlet of Potter's Bar, about two miles eastward from the village (where there is a station on the Great Northern Railway), and also the ecclesiastical district of Christ Church, Barnet, has a population of nearly 4,000. In 1871 the number of the inhabitants of South Mimms proper was 775, and the census for 1881 shows very slight change.

The parish contains within its bounds about 5,400 acres of land, of which 1,097 were allotted by an Act of Parliament passed in 1777, on the enclosure of Enfield Chase. The old "Royal Chase" formed the southern boundary of South Mimms, as far as Potter's Bar.

The general outline of the parish is agreeably diversified with hill and dale, and the village itself, with the church in the midst—there is no regular street, in the ordinary sense of the term—is built upon undulating ground along the line of the old road—which is now a picturesque lane, winding up from its lower end to North Mimms, but in ancient times was the great highway northwards. This road is intersected by the present high road, which was formed early in the present century. The course of the old road was somewhat sinuous, but it contrasts pleasantly enough with the dull and monotonous uniformity of the more modern high road to St. Albans. On quitting Barnet, it traversed Hadley Green, and leaving the road by Potter's Bar to Hatfield on the right, was carried thence by Kitt's End under the fence of Wrotham Park to

Dancer's Hill. Here, bending abruptly to the right, along the wall of Dancer's Hill House, it passed over Mimms Wash, and crossing the present high road, reached South Mimms village. After traversing the entire length of this, it followed the present lane, but branched off sharply to the left shortly before reaching the lodge of North Mimms Park. The present high road, continuing in a straight line from Barnet, passes through the village to the east of the church and churchyard, and then almost bisecting the houses of the village, passes on again in an equally straight line to Colney and St. Albans.

The manor of South Mimms is not mentioned in the "Domesday Survey," and it probably then formed part of the royal chase of Enfield, which belonged at the time of the Conquest to Geoffrey de Mandeville, who owned much property in this part of Middlesex. Through several ages, previous to the year 1479, the manorial rights were vested in the Leuknore, or Lewkenor, family, but it afterwards became annexed to the Crown; and in 1484 it was granted by Richard III. to his zealous adherent, Richard Scrope. It was subsequently owned by the family of Windsor; and about the middle of the seventeenth century it passed to the family of the Marquis of Salisbury, with whom it still continues.

The church, dedicated to St. Giles, stands almost in the centre of the village, and, from its lofty situation, is visible for many miles round. It consists of a nave and chancel, separated from a north aisle, erected at a later period, by octagonal pillars and six obtuse arches. At the western end is an embattled tower, tall and massive, with a small staircase turret at the south-east angle. The main body of the church is in the Early Perpendicular style, and has the walls faced with flint; but the north aisle, looking prim and new from recent restoration, is of red brick, and of Tudor architecture, having been built in 1526. There is no chancel arch, but the chancel is slightly narrower than the nave. At the eastern end of the north aisle, and separated from it by a carved oak parclose, or screen, of Gothic design, is the Frowyke chantry, or chapel, now used as a vestry. The chancel was newly paved and decorated at the restoration of the church, by Mr. G. E. Street, in 1868. The font, of Early English character, consists of a plain square block of stone hollowed in the form of a circular basin, resting upon four small circular columns, and a square centre support, with shallow Perpendicular tracery. One or two of the benches are old, and contain some good examples of wood carving. The five windows of the north aisle

contain in their centres some fragments of ancient stained glass, forming a series, thought to have been part of the original decoration of the re-built aisle. In the south wall of the chancel is a trefoil-headed piscina, apparently of the thirteenth century. On the north side of the chancel is an altar-tomb, with an elaborately carved canopy, supported by four Renaissance columns. It is without arms or inscription; but the initials R. H. are worked into the rose and quatrefoil ornamentation of the tomb. It is very doubtful whom this handsome tomb commemorates. In the Frowyke chapel is an altar-tomb, belonging to the family of Frowyke. It bears the recumbent effigy of a knight in armour, under a rich open canopy. The tomb is without inscription or date. There are in the floor of the church two or three brasses to different members of the Frowkyes.

Close by the churchyard, and facing the street, is a row of almshouses for six widows. They were founded in the year 1687 by James Hickson, between Dancer's Hill and Hadley, but were moved hither in 1856 by the Brewers' Company, who are trustees of the charity.

Potter's Bar, which, as stated above, is an ecclesiastical district of South Mimms, lies about two miles eastward from the latter place. It is a long, straggling village, about a mile in length, with a population of rather more than 1,200 souls. The church, dedicated to St. John, stands towards the north end of the village. It was built in the year 1835, chiefly at the expense of the late Mr. George Byng, M.P., of Wrotham Park. It is constructed of white brick in the Norman style, and several of the windows are filled with memorial stained glass. Here the Byng family were formerly interred; but owing to some differences between them and the incumbent of the parish, Lord Strafford erected in Wrotham Park a mausoleum, which was consecrated by the Bishop of London, as their burial-place.

On the west side of the high road which leads towards Barnet is the estate of Dyrham (or Derham) Park, the seat of the Trotters. The entrance gate, which is approached from the St. Albans road, consists of a tall central arch between Tuscan columns, with entablature and scrolls, and surmounted by a large vase. It is said to have formed originally the triumphal arch which was erected in London by General Monk on the occasion of the public entry of Charles II. in 1660. The old mansion having been burnt down early in the present century, the present house was built by Mr. John Trotter, the then owner of the estate. It is a large and heavy square building in the Classical style, and is situated in the midst of a well-wooded and undulating park of about 170 acres in extent. The estate derived its name from the Derhams, by whom it was possessed in the latter part of the thirteenth century, when it was conveyed in marriage to the Frowykes. This latter family retained possession of the property through many generations, and late in the seventeenth century it became the property of the Austen family. In 1733 it was purchased from Sir John Austen, Bart., M.P. (who lies buried in the churchyard of South Mimms), by Anne, Countess of Albemarle; and at the end of the last

accidentally destroyed by fire in March, 1883, was a handsome edifice in the Classical Italian style, which was so fashionable in the reigns of the two first Georges. It was erected from the designs of Ware in 1754, its then owner being the unfortunate Admiral Byng, who was executed a few years afterwards, under circumstances well known to every reader of English history. The house bore a strong resemblance to Southill, in Bedfordshire, another seat of the Byngs in the last century. The principal front of the mansion looked to the west,

WROTHAM PARK.

century, having, in the meantime, once more changed hands, it was sold to Mr. John Trotter, the founder of the Soho Bazaar,* and with his family it still continues.

The "Butcher" Duke of Cumberland is said to have turned aside out of the Great North road, on his way back to London, after the victory of Culloden, in order to spend a night or two here before going on to join the king at Kew.

On the opposite side of the road, and occupying some 250 acres of ground in the fork of the two roads, passing northwards to St. Albans and to Hatfield and York, is Wrotham Park, the seat of the Earl of Strafford. The mansion, which was

commanding fine views across the park towards Elstree and Watford. It consisted of a spacious centre, with side colonnades, terminating in octagonal wings; it had a deeply-recessed tetrastyle portico, and a pediment extending along the second storey; and the whole was surmounted by a handsome balustrade. The name of the house was derived from Wrotham, near Sevenoaks, Kent, where was the ancient seat of the Byngs, Lords Torrington. The house contained a fine gallery of pictures and an excellent library.

It is somewhat singular that the mansion of Wrotham Park stood a narrow escape from destruction by fire shortly after its erection from the hands of an infuriated mob, during the riots which followed on Admiral Byng's trial and disgrace.

* See "Old and New London," Vol. III., p. 190

Admiral Byng was never married, and at his decease the estate came to his nephew, George Byng, Esq., whose eldest son, also George, was for upwards of half a century M.P. for Middlesex, and who died in 1847. Upon the death of his widow, Wrotham Park reverted to his brother John, a gallant Peninsular officer, who was in 1835 created Baron Strafford, and in 1847 advanced to an earldom; and from him it descended, in 1860, to his son, the present peer, who was well known in his day on the turf, and has held several Court and administrative appointments.

At the southern extremity of the park is Hadley Common, where we meet with the obelisk or pillar set up to commemorate the battle of Barnet; but of this we shall have more to say in the next chapter.

Christ Church, adjacent to the town of Barnet, but in the parish of South Mimms, was built in 1852, at the expense of the late Captain Trotter, of Dyrham Park, but has since been enlarged.

HIGH STREET, HIGH BARNET.

CHAPTER XXXII.

HIGH BARNET.

"I will away towards Barnet presently."—SHAKESPEARE, *Henry VI.*, III., Act V., Sc. 1.

Situation and Extent of Barnet—Its Etymology—The Manor—General Appearance of the Town—Census Returns—Markets and Fairs—The Parish Church—The Grammar School—The old "Crown Inn"—Jesus Hospital—Almshouses and Charitable Institutions—The Town Hall —Barracks—Chapels and Meeting-houses—Ravenscroft Park—The "Physic Well"—Historical Associations—Inns and Taverns—The Battle of Barnet—The Obelisk.

THE small busy town of High Barnet stands at a fork where the road to Elstree and Watford branches off from the Great Northern road, along which Dick Turpin used to ride; and the long High Street still shows marks of having been a street of inns and posting-houses, as being in the old coaching days the first stage out of London on the road both to York and Manchester, for those roads diverge just beyond the northern end of the town.

The town stands high and "wind-swept," extending along a ridge which commands distant views in every direction, and it is from this circumstance that it acquired the prefix of "High." Mr. Thorne, in his "Environs of London," says it is the belief of the older natives that "Barnet stands on the highest ground between London and York." But this, we fancy, can hardly be the case. The town is also called Chipping Barnet, from its market, "which Henry II. granted to the abbots of St. Albans to be kept in this town; it was famous for cattle, and was held on every Monday."

Barnet is considered to belong to Hertfordshire, but not all the town is in that county, nor does the town lie in a single parish. Middlesex and Hertfordshire interlace here, and so do the parishes of South Mimms, Hadley, and High Barnet, to an extent which makes it difficult to describe the place with accuracy. There is, in fact, great confusion, because there are two Barnets, two miles apart—East Barnet and *Chipping* Barnet, or, as it is commonly called, *High* Barnet; and to these must be added a third, "New" Barnet, which lies between them both, and is rapidly being covered by modern streets and villas, of the common suburban type. Lying as it does, for the most part, between two lines of railway—the Great Northern main line and the Finchley and High Barnet branch—this central district enjoys the advantage of very frequent communication with London, and therefore is a favourite abode of City men.

As to the origin of the name, Barnet is thought by some antiquaries to be probably at root the same word with Brent, the river which rises in the valley between the town and Totteridge. It is fair to state that it is here called the "Dollis brook"—*i.e.*, boundary, from an old Kentish word, dolestone, a landmark, a word which also occurs in the Homilies.* But according to Chauncy's "Antiquities of Hertfordshire," the name of the town appears in very early deeds as *Bergnet*, "from the high situation thereof; for the word Bergnet in the Saxon language signifies *monticulus*, a little hill."

In the far-off Saxon times the whole of this district, including East Barnet, formed part of an extensive forest, called Southaw, which belonged to the abbots of St. Albans. The manor continued in the hands of that monastery long after the Conquest; but after the dissolution it was granted by Queen Mary to Anthony Butler, whose descendants, in 1619, sold it to Sir John Weld. It has since passed through the hands of various families, and is now, according to Kelly's "Directory of Hertfordshire," the property of Mr. William Henry Richardson, of Southampton.

Though High Barnet is now commonly known as "Barnet," without any prefix, yet it must not be supposed that it is the original place of that name. East Barnet, which, as stated above, lies a mile and a half away, nearer to the borders of Essex, is shown, by its Norman church, to be the mother, though the

daughter has risen into greater note, from its situation on the Great North road which led to York and Scotland.

We must, however, mention the daughter first, both because it comes first geographically, and also on account of the extent to which it is mixed up with the adjacent village of Monken Hadley, which really forms its northern suburb.

The main street of the town is about a mile in length, broad and well paved, and bears a strong family likeness to that of Highgate; the sign-boards of its numerous inns and hostelries indicate the importance of the town before the invasion of the railway, and when upwards of one hundred and fifty stage-coaches passed through it daily. Of late years the town has greatly improved, not only in its general appearance, but also in growth, particularly on its western side, about the Common, or, as it is now called, "Arkley." This suburb of the town is situated on high ground, and commands extensive views towards Bedfordshire and Buckinghamshire on the north, while on the south may be discerned from it the high grounds of Hampstead, Highgate, and Muswell Hill. The neighbourhood is studded with villa residences, a branch railway giving easy access to the City.

According to the census returns for 1871 the number of houses in High Barnet was 601, the inhabitants at the same time numbering 3,375; this latter number, in the course of the next ten years, had swelled up to 4,283, or about four times what it was at the beginning of this century.

The market, which was granted to the town by Henry II., is still held, but on Wednesday instead of Monday. The horse and cattle fair held yearly, in September, has made the name of Barnet known not only throughout the kingdom, but even abroad. It is held in the fields surrounding the railway-station at High Barnet, and many thousand head of cattle from the Highlands change hands here. Even Cossacks from the neighbourhood of the Don, in Russia, have been known to attend the fair, clothed in the costume of their native country. The horse and cattle fair used formerly to be wound up with a pleasure fair and races, which became very popular with London roughs; but on the formation of a railway, in 1871, the racecourse was broken up, and the races were of necessity abandoned—an event on which the good people of Barnet may well be congratulated.

The parish church, which stands in the middle of the town, at the junction of the north road with that leading to Elstree and Watford, is dedicated to St. John the Baptist, and was originally erected about the middle of the thirteenth century. About

---

* See Homily for Rogation Week, Fourth Part, "Accursed be he, saith Almighty God by Moses, who removeth his neighbour's doles and marks."

a century later was built the tower, wholly disconnected from the body of the fabric. In 1400, John de la Moote, Abbot of St. Albans, rebuilt the body of the church, which consisted of a chancel, nave, and aisles, separated by Pointed arches rising from clustered columns, with a low embattled tower at the west end. In the chancel was a fine east window, with Perpendicular tracery. A vestry was added to the building in the reign of James I., by a great benefactor of the town, Thomas Ravenscroft, to whose memory there is in the church an altar-tomb, with Pointed arches, supported on Doric pillars, with a recumbent effigy of the deceased in veined marble. He died in 1620; several others of his family are also buried here. In 1839 the church was enlarged, and in 1875 it was thoroughly restored, and further enlarged by the addition of a nave, chancel, and tower, the original nave being converted into a north aisle, while the old north aisle remained beyond it. The old tower, too, was partly taken down, and added to the former nave, and a new tower of flint and stone, in squares, raised at the west end. The church, as it now stands, consists of chancel, south transept, with the mortuary chapel of Thomas Ravenscroft, nave, two north aisles, and tower. The re-building was carried out under the direction of Mr. Butterfield, at a cost of about £16,000, mainly at the cost of the endowments left by Mr. Ravenscroft to the Jesus Hospital, of which we shall speak presently.

The Grammar School is in Wood Street; it flourishes under the shadow of the parish church. It consists of one large and lofty hall, which is as old as the reign of Elizabeth, dating from 1573, and has much of the Tudor style of architecture, with a turret at either end. It is now used as a dining-hall, a new and lofty range of buildings, from the designs of Mr. White, having been erected in the rear. The dormitories above the large hall are almost coeval with the building itself, and the eastern end once contained rooms, in which more than one of the masters lived. These being now removed, the hall now extends to fifty-five feet in length.

The charter for the school (the original of which is extant) was granted " at the humble request of our well-beloved cousin and counsellour, Robert, Earle of Leicester, Knight of the most noble Order of the Garter, Master of our Horse."

Few records of the past history of the school exist; two of its early masters, however, rose to become bishops in Ireland; one of its governors, named Westfield, was Bishop of Bristol in the reign of Charles I.; and another, Sir Robert Berkeley, of East Barnet, suffered imprisonment in the Tower for having, as a judge, pronounced ship-money to be lawful. There is much that is inaccurate in the accounts of the foundation of the school, as given by Lysons, Clutterbuck, and Chauncy; and it seems probable that the fabric owes its erection to a Mr. E. Underne, Rector of Barnet, aided by funds from the Corporation of London, and from one Lonison, or Lannyson, a goldsmith and citizen. Among the earlier governors occur the names of Brockett, Briscoe, Coningsby, Weld, Blount, Berkeley, Lord Coleraine, and other persons of good families connected by ties of property with the neighbourhood.

It appears that from time to time the governors of the school put their hands in their pockets liberally with subventions towards repairs of the buildings and other purposes. By the authority of the Corporation of London collections were made from time to time in the City churches towards the erection and repair of the school buildings here.

The statutes compiled for regulating the school in 1634 ordain that "the master shall be a clergyman, approved by the Bishop of London, and that the scholars be male children, free from infectious disease; that the children of residents in the parish of Barnet shall pay twenty shillings a year, and no more, but that for others a charge may be made, as the parents and the master may agree. The boys are to be catechised on Saturdays, and to attend the parish church on Sundays, and that the daily work of the school be opened and closed with prayers. The employment of the senior boys as Monitors, or 'Præpositi,' is approved; and every scholar shall be taught the 'Qui mihi discipulus' in Lilly's Grammar. There are to be weekly 'Orations' and exercises in prose and verse; the Latin alone shall be spoken in the highest forms, and immoderate correction shall not be used." A further curious statute provides that if the Governors of Merchant Taylors' School, in London, shall choose to send any boy for health's sake to Barnet, he shall be " readily entertained " there; and that if any of the wardens, governors, or masters of Merchant Taylors' School " be pleased to looke into this schoole," the master is to provide a " gratulatorie oration in Latin or English, to be publicly delivered by one of his schollers for their entertainment and welcome."

The school contains over a hundred boys, and the course of studies is modern and practical rather than strictly classical, in the ancient sense of the term. Its pupils some twenty years ago had dwindled down to the most insignificant number; but a " new scheme " was proposed, and warmly seconded by the inhabitants, and in the end the new school was opened in 1875.

According to the new scheme, under the Endowed Schools Act of 1869, the Jesus Hospital was ordered to pay £5,000, and also a yearly sum of £400, towards the advancement of education in the school. The governing body was ordained to consist of twelve persons, mostly of local standing, three of whom were to be nominated by the Visitors of the hospital. These governors manage the financial affairs of the school, but wisely judge it the best course to leave the internal arrangements to the head-master whom they appointed, the Rev. J. R. Lee, of Exeter College, Oxford, formerly second master of the Grammar School at Bedford.

That this school, prior to the above mentioned date, had sunk to a very low ebb, may be inferred from the manner in which, under a thin guise, it was once referred to in a popular periodical.

In *Household Words*, No. 86, November 15, 1851, is given, under the title of "A Free (and easy) School," an account of Queen Elizabeth's "Royal Grammar School at Thistledown," under Dr. Laon Blosse, head-master, who, besides superintending the education of seven foundation or free boys, seeks private pupils of his own, who are to qualify themselves for admission by bringing with them silver forks and spoons. Under scarcely-veiled aliases, the writer describes the approach to "Thistledown" from the railway-station, the general grouping and arrangement of the little town, and the ivy-grown school-room, with its dull, heavy entrance-court, and its flanking round, or rather angular, turrets at either extremity. The writer is, of course, none other than Charles Dickens himself. In no indistinct phrases he informs his readers that the pretence of carrying out the original purposes of the foundation is simply a delusion and a snare, though he confesses to being somewhat affected at the notion of standing in a "school-room built in the old days of Queen Elizabeth, not at all large, but tolerably lofty."

Little is known of its schoolmasters during the sixteenth and seventeenth centuries. "It is to be regretted," writes Mr. Cass, "that that gossiping Samuel Pepys, on that cold August Sunday morning when he visited the Physicke Well, did not look in at the school on his way to or from it; and that Elias Ashmole never strolled thither by Enfield Chase and Hadley, or across the meadows between Mount Pleasant and the top of Barnet Hill, nor make a halt there when journeying to visit his friends Mr. and Mrs. Hutchinson, at Delrow, near Watford."

The old "Crown" Inn, adjoining the school-house,

was purchased quite recently from the governors of Harrow School, its site and the yard in the rear being added to the school grounds. The inn was a picturesque structure, with overhanging gables. It was at this house, in all probability, that the Lady Arabella Stuart stopped in making her escape from East Barnet to join her husband.*

Almost every town has its local hero or benefactor, and Barnet forms no exception to the rule. James Ravenscroft, a worthy citizen of High Holborn, London, who died in 1680, left a large property in Stepney in order to found a hospital, called Jesus Hospital, for "six poore antient women" in Wood Street, in this town. The recipients of this charity are to be "neither common beggars, common drunkards, backbiters, tale-bearers, common scolds, thieves, or other like persons of infamous life or evil name or repute; or vehemently suspected of sorcery, witchcraft, or charming; or guilty of perjury; nor any idiot or lunatic." The founder lies buried in the church of High Barnet, where, as already stated, a fine Jacobean tomb, with recumbent figures of himself and his wife, commemorates his good deeds. He also left money to support the Grammar School, which dates from just a century earlier, having been established by Queen Elizabeth in 1573. The funds left by Master Ravenscroft for the benefit of the above hospital were augmented by a bequest in 1737, of Miss Mary Barcock, a daughter of a former master of the Grammar School.

The endowments left by James Ravenscroft having largely increased, through the increased value of land at Stepney, have been utilised in various ways at Barnet. Amongst other objects the parish church has come in for a share, having been doubled in size, as stated above, out of the superfluous wealth of Jesus Hospital.

Barnet is tolerably well off for charitable institutions. Besides the above-mentioned almshouses, there are others in Wood Street, founded by John Garrett, in 1729, for six old spinsters or widows, each of whom receives a small dole of money weekly. Palmer's Almshouses (for men and women), beyond the new public gardens, which were part of Barnet Common, all now enclosed, were founded in 1823, from the proceeds of a bequest in 1558 by one Eleanor Palmer, a widow, of Kentish Town, London, for the support of six aged married couples, who receive eight shillings weekly. The Leathersellers' Almshouse, at the junction of Union Street and Wood Street, was erected in the year 1843 by Mr. Richard Thornton, for six poor freemen of the Leathersellers' Company,

* See 'Old and New London," Vol. V., p. 404.

and for six freemen's widows. The buildings, of Gothic architecture, are of white brick, and were enlarged in 1865 by the addition of eight new houses.

Barnet is under the control of a Local Board, which has been established with a district comprising Chipping Barnet and part of the parishes of Hadley and South Mimms. The Town Hall, which is situate in Union Street, is a brick building, of little or no architectural pretensions; and in the neighbourhood of the town are barracks for a detachment of the King's Rifle Corps.

There are chapels and meeting-houses in the town for the various denominations of dissenters, and there is also a Roman Catholic chapel in Union Street, dedicated to Saints Mary the Immaculate and Gregory the Great.

A large open space of land adjoining the west end of the town was utilised in 1880–81 by being drained, planted, and laid out as a recreation ground. It is surrounded by pleasant villas, and the district has taken the name of Ravenscroft Park, after the local worthy already named.

Beyond the spot which was till lately known as Barnet Common, in a field a mile and a half from the town, on the south of the road to Elstree, is a chalybeate spring of a mild purgative nature, that was discovered about the middle of the seventeenth century, and was formerly in much repute. It is mentioned and extolled in "The Perfect Diurnal" in 1652. In the year 1667 Alderman John Owen, a "citizen and fishmonger" of London left the sum of £1 yearly for keeping the "Physic Well" in repair. It would be surprising to find no mention of it in the diary of the gossiping Samuel Pepys. That worthy paid a visit to the spot in 1667, which is duly recorded under the date of Sunday, August 11, in that year :—

"To the wells at Barnett by seven o'clock, and there found many people a-drinking; but the morning was very cold, so we were very cold all the way in the coach. And so to Hatfield, to the inn next my Lord Salisbury's house, and there rested ourselves and drank, and bespoke dinner; and so to church."

A Dr. Trinder published, in 1812, a small treatise on the medical virtues of this water. But he could not revive or preserve its fame; yet it still exists, for a pound is paid annually for its preservation out of the funds of the Grammar School. It is, however, quite unused, and is a mere survival of past memories. Indeed, the farmer on whose ground it stands, if the truth must be told, does not appreciate the pump, and has

painted it green, so as not to attract the notice of passers-by.

The waters of Barnet and Northaw were not very powerful, but they were extremely popular in the reign of Charles II. The Northaw spring was in a bottom, half a mile east of the village. Fuller mentions these waters along with those of Epsom and Tunbridge. Dr. Wittie, in his account of Scarborough Spa in 1669, favours us with these doggrel lines :—

"Let Epsom, Tunbridge, Barnet, Knaresborough, be
In what request they will, Scarborough for me."

"The old well-house," observes Mr. Thorne, in his "Environs," "was pulled down, and a small farmhouse erected on the foundations in 1840. The well is now covered over, and the water is obtained from it by a small iron pump. To reach it, you go along Wood Street (by Barnet Church) for a quarter of a mile, and down the lane on the left, in front of the Union Workhouse, to where the lane is crossed by a light iron gate. Here turn through a small clap-gate on the left into a field-path, which presently passes through a gap in the hedge, on the right, into a field, in the midst of which the pump will be seen, and above it the well house. The well is quite open to every one, and is still occasionally resorted to by invalids. The visitor who is disposed to test the efficacy of the water will remember Pepys' experience."

Barnet is not without its literary and historic associations. The great conflict between the rival houses of York and Lancaster, commonly known as the "Battle of Barnet," took place really in the parish of Monken Hadley, on the outskirts of the town, as we shall presently see.

At Barnet William Hailes was put to death for heresy, under Queen Mary, in 1555. Here, too, James Thomson lived as tutor to Lord Binning's son, before he became celebrated as the author of "The Seasons;" and here, too—if we may be allowed to pass from fact to fiction—Tom Jones was met by the assumed highwayman on his way from St. Albans to London.*

Though the town of Barnet has no "maltings" and breweries, like Hertford and Ware, yet it is extremely rich in inns, the survivals of old posting-houses of repute in the olden days, when 150 coaches passed through it, either on the up or down journey, and, for the most part, changed horses there. The inns themselves, as is the case still in some other country towns, were patronised exclusively by the "Whig" and the "Tory" magnates; and many persons now living can re-

---

* See "Old and New London," Vol. II., p. 550.

member the day when old and chivalrous ladies refused to change horses when travelling post at any inn that did not bear the colours of their family. The "Green Man," at the junction of the great high road and the new road to St. Albans, formed the head-quarters of the Liberals, "Woolpack," and the "Salisbury"—the latter named, doubtless, after the Cecil family. The interior of it still bears marks of antiquity; and so did its inn-yard till recently. It is now the head-quarters of the neighbouring bicyclists.

There are in Barnet scarcely any side or back

VIEWS IN BARNET.
THE SCHOOLS.   THE "RED LION" INN.

while the Tories patronised exclusively the "Red Lion"—possibly as symbolising the British Constitution. Probably the reason why political differences were thus emphasised at Barnet is to be found in the fact that it was half-way to Hatfield, the seat of the Tory Cecils, and that the head of the Whig house of Byng, the lord of Wrotham, lived just outside the town.

Among the chief inns whose sign-boards still hang along the street are the "Red Lion," the

streets, and hence the town is remarkably free from "slums." Indeed, it has altogether a thriving and "respectable" appearance—in this respect a pleasing contrast to Staines, Uxbridge, Hounslow, and Brentford.

On the outskirts of the town, in the year 1471, was fought the famous battle between the rival houses of York and Lancaster, which terminated in the death of the Earl of Warwick, and established Edward IV. upon the throne.

The facts of the battle of Barnet, and those which led to it, are to be read in every history of England, and, with some embellishments, in the concluding chapter of Sir Edward Bulwer Lytton's work, the "Last of the Barons." It would be impossible to enter as fully into the latter subject as it deserves without almost writing a fresh history of the Wars of the Roses. It is enough here to refer the reader to other sources of information, and to say that in the early part of the year 1471 (the same year, by the way, in which William Caxton set up his printing-press at Bruges), Edward of York landed from the Continent on the shores of forming an irregular triangle, of which one side "impinges" on the village of Monken Hadley. Sir John Paston, who fought on that day on the Lancastrian side, fixes the scene of the battle precisely, in a letter written to his mother from London, only a few days after. He states it to have been about half a mile from Barnet; and this agrees with the words of one Edward Halle, judge in the Sheriff's Court, who probably conversed in his lifetime with several who were present:— "This toune (Barnet) standeth on a hill, on whose toppe is a faire plain for two armies to joyne together;" and on one part of this plain Warwick

HADLEY GREEN (SITE OF THE BATTLE OF BARNET).

Yorkshire, to encounter the deadly opposition of his former ally, Warwick, the "King Maker," who had now thrown in his lot with Henry of Lancaster and Margaret of Anjou. Edward rapidly advanced on London, and entered it in state, having the weak Henry VI. a prisoner in his hands. Warwick and his comrade Montagu hastened from their head-quarters at Coventry towards London to oppose him; but on reaching St. Albans they found that Edward had come out from London to Barnet, about half-way, in order to give them battle. The contest could not be declined; and it is clear that each party knew that on the issue of the battle depended the entire future of the throne and the kingdom.

The heath, to the north of the town, formerly called Gladsmore Common, is the spot which has been fixed upon by most historians as the scene of the encounter. It is still an open space, "pitched his fielde." Stow, the annalist, also fixes the spot as distant half a mile from Barnet; and the present Hadley Green, with the level ground adjoining it, exactly answers the description.

A very slight glance at the spot will satisfy the most ordinary observer that the spot was well chosen for the purposes of war. "A modern commander similarly circumstanced," writes the Rev. F. C. Cass, in his paper on the "Battle of Barnet," in the "Transactions of the London and Middlesex Archæological Society," "would doubt-less have occupied the town in force, entrenching himself along the high ground sloping towards the south-east, between the top of Barnet Hill and Hadley Church, and have placed his reserves somewhere to the west, on Barnet Common, to secure his right flank from being turned. With his artillery he would have swept the ascent of Barnet Hill, and would have taken care to line the edge of

Hadley Wood with riflemen." And he shows in detail how Warwick, on reaching Hadley Green, or Gladsmore Heath, being first in the field, and having the choice of ground, could hardly have made a different selection, at a time when a tolerably level space was necessary for the movements of heavy-armed horsemen, and horses almost as heavily armed themselves.

On the eve of the battle, which took place on Easter Day, in April, 1471, the king and his troops held the northern suburbs of the town, being quartered along the great northern road; while Warwick came up with his forces along the road from St. Albans. On the common they met face to face, the right wing of Lord Warwick being opposed to the king's left.

"In the profound darkness of the night and the thick fog," writes Bulwer Lytton, in the "Last of the Barons," "Edward had stationed his men at a venture on the heath at Gladsmoor, and hastily environed the camp with palisades and trenches. He had intended to have rested immediately in front of the foe, but in the darkness he mistook the extent of the hostile line, and his men were ranged opposite only to the left side of the earl's forces—towards Hadley—leaving the right unopposed. Most fortunate for Edward was this mistake, for Warwick's artillery, and the new and deadly bombards that he had constructed, were placed on the right of King Edward's army; and the provident earl, naturally supposing Edward's left was there opposed to him, ordered his gunners to cannonade all night. Edward, as the flashes of the guns illumined by fits the gloom of midnight, saw the advantage of his unintentional error; and to prevent Warwick from discovering it, reiterated his orders for the most profound silence. Thus even his very blunders favoured Edward more than the wisest precautions had served his fated foe."

If we may trust the graphic sketch drawn by the novelist's master-hand, the early morning of Easter Day was raw, cold, and dismal; but the signal for battle was given, and the deadly encounter began. On that battle of Barnet, though the numbers engaged in it were small according to modern ideas, depended the ruin or triumph of a dynasty, the fall of a warlike baronage, and the rise of a crafty, plotting, imperious despotism, which ultimately developed into the stern and vigorous rule of the house of Tudor. "The stake was high, the die was cast—the king won, and the Earl of Warwick lost. He proved the last of those powerful barons who, under the Plantagenets, had held **royalty in check.** The battle of Barnet secured the

crown of England to the House of York, and sent King Henry back a prisoner to the Tower." Lytton describes in detail, doubtless with some little exaggeration, the chief incidents of that hard-fought field, and the doughty deeds of the leaders of either army; but we may accept as true the particulars of the death of Warwick, who, even when he saw that all was lost, refused to fly and save his life. He was hewn down by the battle-axe of one of Edward's officers, and his body, having been placed in a hearse, was carried to London, to be exposed to the gaze of the public in St. Paul's, whence, a few days later, it was carried to its final resting-place in Bisham Abbey, near Marlow.

During the battle, if we may believe Lord Lytton, who follows in this respect the annalists, King Edward was kept in countenance by a sorcerer, one Friar Bungay, who took up his position a little to the east of the battle, near the spot where Monken Hadley Church now stands, the captive King Henry also standing by as a sort of hostage.

As for the "blood-stained" field of Barnet, various estimates are given of the numbers which fell that day; some writers fix them as low as 1,500, whilst others say that 20,000 were slain. Let us hope that the former figures are nearer the truth.

Although the accounts of the numbers engaged in the battle vary very much, and cannot be reconciled, yet as to the details of the engagement there is no doubt. The first shots fired in the early dawn of that Easter Sunday were fired at random, owing to the dense fog which covered the hills, and concealed the foes from each other; but as the morning waxed on to noon, the sun broke forth, and the combatants found themselves face to face. The king and the earl respectively rode along their ranks, each encouraging his followers. One wing of Edward's army was being driven back, when a mistake between the two rival congnizances of the star with five points and the sun with rays threw the hosts of Lord Warwick into confusion, of which Edward was not slow to take advantage, calling into action a reserved force, whilst Warwick's men were too exhausted to answer their leader's call. "The day," writes Mr. Cass, "was visibly lost, and nothing remained but for Warwick to sell his life dearly. By ten o'clock, or at noon according to some writers, victory rested with the Yorkists, and Warwick and Montagu were slain."

The Dukes of Somerset and Exeter and the Earl of Oxford escaped with their lives from the field, but only to die elsewhere. The common soldiers who fell in the engagement were buried on the field, but the exact spot of their interment is not known. The conqueror rode back to London immediately—the captive King Henry following in his train—and presented himself next day at St. Paul's to offer up his standard, and to return thanks to the God of battles.

As a proof that the battle of Barnet was of great practical importance in its results, it is reported that no subsequent Lancastrian rising troubled the reign of King Edward.

There is still on the edge of the common an old moated farm-house, or grange, which some of Lord Warwick's men are said to have occupied on the eve of the battle.

The place where Warwick made his last stand is marked by an obelisk, erected in the last century, and bearing a brief record of the fact and of the date of the battle. The exact spot where he fell is said by tradition to be marked by two trees

planted in the place of others which perished from age, about twenty yards north of the obelisk.

The obelisk on the field was erected in 1740 by Sir J. Sambrooke, of Gobions, an estate in North Mimms, more anciently called More Hall, the property of Sir Thomas More.

"Barnet," writes Mr. Cass, "has greatly changed from the little town through which Edward passed on his way to a battle on which his throne depended; but still, behind the plastered or brick-faced fronts of the buildings lining its modern street are perhaps hidden the timbers of dwellings from whose windows men and women and little children looked out upon the victor, as, early on that Easter afternoon, he rode past with Henry in his train." Is it not a satire on Christianity itself that, whilst the service of song and praise was being offered in the church which stood by the battle-field, Christians should have been spending their Sunday in cutting each other's throats and cleaving each other's skulls with battle-axes?

CHAPTER XXXIII.

HADLEY, EAST BARNET, AND TOTTERIDGE.

Etymology of Monken Hadley—Descent of the Manor—Hadley Green—The Village and Common—Hadley Wood—Gladsmore Heath, or Monken Mead—Dead Man's Bottom—Hadley Church—Two Historic Trees—Almshouses—Noted Residents—Population—East Barnet—Lyonsdown—Census Returns—The Parish Church—The Boys' Farm Home—The Clock House—Cat's Hill—Oak Hill Park—Belmont—Totteridge—Its Etymology—Descent of the Manor—Census Returns—Condition of the Roads—The Church—Yew-trees in Churchyard—The Priory—Pointer's Grove—Copped Hall—Totteridge Park—Wykeham Rise.

MONKEN HADLEY—or Hadley, as it is colloquially styled—as stated in the preceding chapter, adjoins on the north the town of High Barnet, of which it forms almost a suburb. The parish, which was formerly a part of Enfield Chase and a hamlet to Edmonton, is bounded on the north-east by the parish of Enfield, and comprises in its area nearly 600 acres, of which about 240 were allotted in lieu of its right of common, on the enclosure of the royal chase above mentioned. According to Lysons and other topographers, the village owes its name to its elevated situation, being "compounded of the Saxon words *Head-leagh*, signifying a high place. The "*ley*" in its designation, however, would seem to imply a meadow, or clear open space in the forest land, as in the case of Cow*ley*, already referred to.* The adjunct *Monken* occurs in many ancient documents, and is adopted in the description of this parish in the Act for enclosing Enfield Chase; and it is probable that it

was derived from the former connection of the place with the Abbey of Walden, to which it was given by Geoffrey de Mandeville, Earl of Essex, about the middle of the twelfth century, under the name of the "Hermitage of Hadley."

Hadley is not mentioned in the Domesday survey; but it appears at a very early period to have belonged to the Mandevilles, from whom it was alienated, as above stated, to the monks of Walden, the abbey of which place was founded by Geoffrey de Mandeville. After the dissolution of monasteries, the manor was granted to Thomas Lord Audley, who shortly afterwards surrendered it to the Crown. In 1557 it was granted by Queen Mary to Sir Thomas Pope. A few years later it was alienated to the Kymptons, but was soon after sold to the family of Hayes, in whose hands it remained for about a century. Towards the end of the last century it was purchased by Mr. Peter Moore, who rendered himself unpopular a few years later by asserting a right to enclose Hadley Green, including the whole of the waste, without

---

See *ante*, p. 226

the consent of the parishioners. This assumed right he defended in a court of law, but failed in his endeavour, as Sir Thomas Wilson failed at Hampstead,* and the immemorial privileges of the parish were fully established on appeal.

The village is situated on the east side of the Great North road, on the margin of Hadley Green, and round about the common—a broad open space which stretches away eastward from the church. The common, with its ponds and trees, much resembles Clapham Common, and is now said to be the only unenclosed portion of the ancient Chase of Enfield. It is a picturesque piece of undulating upland, sloping away rapidly towards the east, where it abuts upon Beech Hill Park. The lower or easternmost part of the common, where it is crossed by the railway, is generally called by the natives Hadley Wood; it is one of the most beautiful pieces of woodland scenery to be found within many miles of the metropolis. This narrow strip of forest scenery runs eastward as far as the hamlet of Cock Fosters.

The high ground towards the west and north-west of the common was sometimes called of old Gladsmore Heath, but more often styled Monkey (or Monken) Mead, and is the spot now generally accepted by antiquarians, as shown in the pre-ceding chapter, as that whereon was decided the great Battle of Barnet. The obelisk which has been set up to commemorate that event stands at the upper end of Hadley Green, in the fork of the two roads leading respectively to Hatfield and St. Albans. It bears the following inscription :— "Here was fought the famous battle between Edward IV. and the Earl of Warwick, April 14th, 1471, in which the Earl was defeated and slain."

The low ground adjoining Monken Mead is named on the early maps "Dead Man's Bottom," either from having been the chief scene of slaughter at the battle of Barnet, or else for being the burial-place of the slain.

Hadley Church, dedicated to St. Mary, stands on the very edge of the battle-field of Barnet. But it is not old enough to have witnessed that en-gagement, having been built in the year 1494. It stands not very far from the mound on which Lord Lytton, in his "Last of the Barons," represents Friar Bungay as carrying on those solemn incan-tations which were destined to clear away the fog and mist and to give the victory to the House of York. Close by it there is to the present day a gate across the road, marking the fringe of the Chase, and giving entrance to that royal demesne.

We shall have more to say about it presently. The church is a cruciform building in the Per-pendicular style, and consists of chancel, nave, aisles, transepts, and an ivy-covered tower at the west end. This church is finer than most parish churches, and bears a strong resemblance in its general features to those of High Barnet and South Mimms. The church is constructed of black flint and Bath stone disposed in alternate squares. On the top of a turret at the south-west angle of the tower is affixed an iron "cresset" fire-pan or pitch-pot, an almost unique survival of other days. It is supposed to have been placed there as a guide to wayfarers through the neighbouring forest. Mr. Bloxam tells us in his work on "Gothic Archi-tecture," that it was used and fired so late as the year 1745—probably at the time of the alarm caused near London by the Stuart rising in the North. It was also again used more recently at the marriage of the Prince of Wales.

The church was restored, and in part rebuilt, under the rectorship of Dr. Proctor, between the years 1848 and 1850, by Mr. G. E. Street, and the south aisle was added as a memorial of the late rector, Mr. Thackeray. Several new windows were inserted at the time of the above-mentioned restoration. Most of the windows are filled with painted glass ; the nave, of four bays, opens into the tower, and it is separated from the aisles by depressed arches resting on octagonal columns. Over the west doorway of the tower is the date 1494, having on one side the device of a wing and on the other that of a rose. Lysons, in his "Environs of London," says that they are probably "the cognizance either of the abbey, or one of the Abbots of Walden." Mr. Brewer, in the "Beauties of England," observes that the same devices occur in Enfield Church, which likewise belonged to the abbey founded by Geoffrey de Mandeville. "It is certain that these emblems," he adds, "had no reference to the arms of Walden Abbey ; but they were possibly meant as the cognizance of the abbot at that time, whose name was John Sabys-worth, or Sabrisfort." The south porch was erected in memory of Dr. Proctor's son, the Rev. G. H. Proctor, of Balliol College, Oxford, who died be-fore Sebastopol, where he was serving as an army chaplain. Dr. Proctor was a brother-in-law of Mr. John Payne Collier, the learned dramatic author ; and he was said to have been the original of the "Dr. Blimber" of Charles Dickens, in "Bleak House."

There are several monuments of the seventeenth century, the most remarkable being that in memory of Sir Roger Wilbraham, solicitor-general of Ire-land in the reign of Queen Elizabeth, and his lady, with marble busts of each by Nicholas Stone ; and there is a mural brass of the fifteenth century.

Among the fragments of ancient painted glass in the church, is a piece containing the rebus of the family of Goodere, who occupied an important position in this parish and neighbourhood in the fifteenth and sixteenth centuries. It consists of a partridge, with an ear of wheat in its bill, and having on an attached scroll the word " goode " in black letter. On the capital of one of the pillars are two partridges with ears of corn in their beak, an evident reproduction of the above punning device. The Gooderes are thought to have been considerable benefactors towards the rebuilding of the church. Weever, in his " Funeral Monuments," mentions a mutilated inscription to the memory of " John Goodyere, esquyre, and Jone, his wyff," with the date of 1504. This is no longer visible ; but a brass still commemorates Anne Walheden, " descended of the Goodere's auncyent race," who was buried in 1575.

In the churchyard, to the east of the chancel, lies under a plain flat slab Mrs. Hester Chapone, the once popular authoress of " Letters on the Improvement of the Mind," addressed to young ladies, and which had a great run in the last century. She died in the year 1801. Her maiden name was Mulso ; and among her friends were Mrs. Elizabeth Carter, Mrs. Montagu, and Dr. Johnson, who valued her highly, and condescended even to argue with her. In early life she was a frequent guest at the house of Richardson. Here also are buried Dr. John Monro, who acquired some celebrity as a physician and writer on insanity, at the end of the last century, and Dr. Proctor, the late rector, who died in 1882.

Nearly opposite the church, close by the gate that leads to the common, still stands the weather-beaten trunk of an aged oak, long ago divested of its bark, which is mentioned by Lord Lytton in his " Last of the Barons," when describing the closing events of the battle of Barnet, as the " gaunt and leafless tree " whereon the wizard Friar Bungay, mentioned above, hangs his hated rival, Adam Warner, whilst at its foot lay the life-less form of his daughter Sibyll, " and the shattered fragments of the mechanical ' eureka ' on which he had spent the labours of his life." The old trunk was upset a few years ago by some drunken volunteers, but it has been replaced in position, and railed in.

Not far distant is another tree which has become historic, called " Latimer's Elm," from a local tradition that Latimer once preached beneath its branches,

Near the church are the Priory, a modern Gothic edifice, with pleasant grounds and gardens, and also two rows of almshouses : the one was founded by Sir Roger Wilbraham, in 1616, for six " decayed housekeepers," each of whom receive a sum of £18 per annum ; the other, founded by Sir Justinian Paget, in the seventeenth century, for three poor men and a like number of women, was rebuilt about fifty years ago.

The mansions facing the east side of Hadley Common have had some celebrated tenants in their day. Mrs. Trollope, the novelist, lived in the house nearest to the Wilbraham Almshouses ; and it may be remembered that Anthony Trollope, in his novel, " The Bertrams," alludes to his sister being buried in the adjoining churchyard. The house at the southern end of the same row— called the Grange—was formerly occupied by the grandfather of William Makepeace Thackeray, of the same name, at the beginning of the present century. At The Mount House, on the north-west side of the common, lived for many years Professor Joseph Henry Green, F.R.S., the author of " Spiritual Philosophy, founded on the teachings of the late Samuel Taylor Coleridge." Professor Green died in 1863, about thirty years after the friend whose philosophy he had done so much to interpret and popularise.

In Fuller's " Worthies " it is stated that Sir William Starmford, or Stamford, an eminent lawyer of the sixteenth century, was a native of this place. He was the author of a legal work, entitled " The Pleas of the Crown," and is said by Fuller to have been born in 1509, and to have been buried at Hadley in 1558. Hadley was also the birthplace of Sir Robert Atkyns, the learned author of the " History of Gloucestershire." He was born in the year 1647, being a son of Sir Robert Atkyns, Lord Chief Baron of the Exchequer, who was himself the author of several political pamphlets.

In 1871 the number of houses in the parish of Hadley amounted to 200, the population at the same time numbering 978. In consequence of the increased railway facilities of late years, for communication with the metropolis, the number of the inhabitants has since increased to nearly 1,200.

East Barnet, whither we now direct our steps, lies in a pretty valley about a mile east of the great high road to the north, and some mile and a half south-eastward from Hadley. The parish is bounded on the east by Enfield, on the south by Friern Barnet and Southgate, and on the west by High Barnet and Elstree. The rural aspect of the neighbourhood has been somewhat curtailed since the formation of the Great Northern Railway, and the consequent growth of a town. This, however, is the mother or cradle of the other parishes bearing the name of Barnet, and it is called East Barnet to distinguish it from High (or Chipping) Barnet, and Friern Barnet immediately adjoining. Within the last few years, even, another ecclesiastical district, generally called New Barnet, but legally known as "Lyonsdown," has sprung up, having been formed out of the parishes of Chipping Barnet and East Barnet. A church of Gothic

been erected by an abbot of St. Albans as far back as early in the twelfth century. North Wall, with its small round-headed deep-splayed windows, still remains in its original state. The fabric seems to have remained in its tiny dimensions for centuries; for it was not till the middle of the seventeenth century that the chancel was built, the cost of its erection being defrayed by Sir Robert Bartlet, who was probably a native of the parish. The tower is modern, and poor in the extreme;

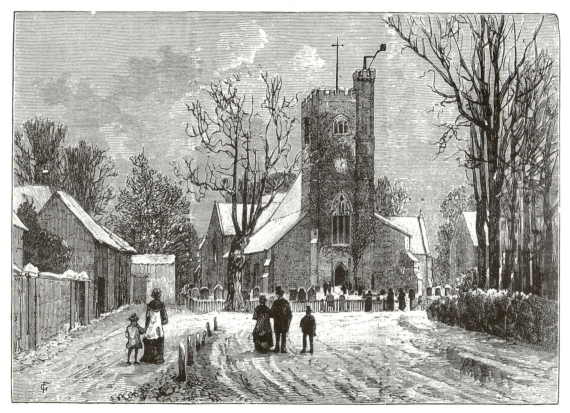

HADLEY CHURCH.   (See page 328.)

design, in the Decorated style, was built in 1865. It is constructed of coloured bricks, and has an apsidal chancel. In 1871 the number of houses in East Barnet (including the district of Lyonsdown) was 531, the inhabitants being nearly 3,000. According to the census returns for 1881 the population has now reached nearly 4,000.

The manor of East Barnet has been part and parcel of that of Chipping Barnet since the time of the Conquest.

The church, dedicated to St. Mary the Virgin, is the original and mother church of the district, and it is partly Norman. It consists of a nave, chancel, south aisle, with a brick-built tower at the west end. The nave is the oldest part of the building, having

the south aisle, which is constructed of Kentish ragstone, with Bath stone dressings, was added as recently as 1868, at which time the interior of the church was thoroughly restored and refitted.

In the churchyard is the tomb of General Augustus Prevost, a native of Geneva, who died in 1786. He served with distinction in the British army, taking part, in 1779, in the gallant defence of Savannah "against the combined armies of France and America, supported by a powerful fleet." In the corner of the churchyard is a tall Gothic structure, almost like a market cross, erected to the memory of Sir Simon Clarke, who lived at Oak Hill Park, in the parish.

Dr. Richard Bundy, a Prebendary of Westminster, the author of a voluminous Roman history, and of the "Apparatus Biblicus," was rector of this parish in the early part of the last century ; his predecessor was Gilbert Burnet, son of the celebrated Dr. Burnet, Bishop of Salisbury.

At Church Farm, near the church, is the "Boys' Farm Home," a branch of the "Boys' Home" in the Regent's Park Road, near Chalk Farm.* It lodges, boards, and trains for agricultural and industrial pursuits, above eighty poor orphan boys, "not convicted of crime."

the north end of the old village street, and opposite the parish fountain—now a pump—was formerly an inn : it has been said that Lord Macaulay's father lived here ; there is, however, no foundation for the statement.

Cat's Hill is the name given to the steep ascent leading from East Barnet up to Southgate, and is so called from the "Cat" inn which stands by the roadside at its foot. "The Cat," *pur et simple*, is not a very common sign ; though Larwood mentions one at Egremont in Cumberland yet he omits

COPPED HALL.   (*See page 334.*)

LORD LYTTON.   (*See page 334.*)

The grounds cover nearly fifty acres, and the farm is cultivated by the boys, who are admitted between the ages of six and sixteen years. The institution, with its dining-hall, carpenters' shops, &c., which is mainly supported by voluntary contributions, is well worth a visit.

The Clock House, at the foot of Cat's Hill, at

"the Cat" here. The sign is common enough, however, with an adjective, as the "Black Cat" at Lancaster, the "Red Cat" at Birkenhead and at the Hague ; and still more common in connection with some ludicrous appendage, such as the "Cat and Cage," the "Cat and Lion," the "Cat and Parrot," and the "Cat in the Basket." The last named was a favourite sign on the booths when the Thames was frozen over in 1739-40. "The sign," writes Mr. Larwood, "was a living one—a basket hanging outside the booth with a cat in it." In the illustrated "Pennant" in the British Museum is a print representing the Thames at Rotherhithe in the great frost of 1789 : there is a booth with a merry company inside, while the sign over the door, inscribed "The Original Cat in the Cage," represents poor Tabby in a basket. "The sign," writes Mr. Larwood, "doubtless originates from the cruel game, once practised by our ancestors, of shooting at a cat in a basket." It is possible, and even probable, that East Barnet was one of the

* See "Old and New London," Vol. V., p. 296.

places where this cruel "sport" was practised by the roughs of North London when out on a holiday.

There are a few good mansions and seats in the neighbourhood. Among them may be mentioned Oak Hill Park, the seat of Mr. Young, and formerly the residence of Sir Simon Clarke. The house occupies an elevated site in the midst of an extensive park, on the east side of the village. Another mansion, near to Oakleigh Park Station, called Belmont, but formerly known as Mount Pleasant, was at one time the home of Elias Ashmole, the founder of the Ashmolean Museum at Oxford.

Totteridge lies to the south-west of East Barnet, on the western side of the Great North road. It is really a "spur" of the long ridge of which Mill Hill forms the central and southern part; and it occupies the extreme south-eastern angle of Hertfordshire, between Highwood Hill and Whetstone, in Middlesex. As to its etymology, it is supposed to have been derived from its situation on the ridge of a hill. The first syllable of the name is derived probably from the Anglo-Saxon word "Tot," or "Toot," a beacon-hill, or from the Welsh word "Twt," a sloping or rising; and it may have been given to it—as in the case of *Tot*-hill, Westminster*—from a beacon placed here, as the highest spot in this district. Taylor, however, in his "Words and Places," thinks such places as Tot Hill and the like "may possibly have been seats of Celtic worship, the names coming from the Celtic deity, *Taith*, the Teutates of Lucan." The antiquary, Mr. Wykeham Archer, too, derives the name from Teut, the chief divinity of the Druids, and the equivalent of Thoth, the Egyptian Mercury, adding that the "Tot," "Teut," "Tut," or "Thoth"—often, by the way, styled "Tuttle" or "Tut-hill" was the spot on which solemn proclamations were made to the people. "Tot" or "Toot," also, in one of its varied forms, is not an uncommon prefix to the names of other places in different parts of England —as *Tot*nes, *Tot*ham, *Toot*ing, *Tot*tenham, *Tut*bury, &c. ; and, it may be added that all these places are considerably elevated, in comparison with the surrounding parts.

The manor of Totteridge in early ages formed part of the possessions of the monks of Ely, and afterwards of the bishops of that see, from one of whom, in the reign of Elizabeth, it was alienated to the Crown, together with Hatfield, in consideration of an annual sum of £1,500, to be paid to

him and his successors in the see of Ely. In 1590 the queen granted this manor to John Cage, from whom it passed in succession to the Peacocks and the Whichcotes. Sir Paul Whichcote, in the year 1720, sold the property to James Brydges, Duke of Chandos ; but it was again disposed of by the second duke to Sir William Lee, Lord Chief Justice of the King's Bench. The manor is now held by the representatives of the late John Lee, LL.D. The advowson of the living is still held, with that of Hatfield, by the Marquis of Salisbury, the annual value of the combined livings being £2,500.

Totteridge is neither a town nor a village, but a group of isolated villas and gentlemen's seats and small parks. The small cluster of houses and shops forming the street fringe the roadway to Mill Hill, at a short distance westward of the church. The village green extends at least a quarter of a mile south from the church, gradually widening out into a leg-of-mutton form, and fringed on either side with rows of elms and other trees of a dark foliage. It is very picturesque and rural.

Totteridge has lately been brought more near to the great metropolis by the opening of a new station in the low ground between it and Whetstone, on the High Barnet branch of the Great Northern Railway.

At the beginning of the present century Totteridge had 48 houses and a population of 280 souls. The census returns for 1871 showed that these had increased respectively to 91 and 474. In 1881 the number of the inhabitants was 656.

The roads about Totteridge are still anything but good in the winter, the soil being hereabouts a stiff clay ; but they are better now than a century or two ago, when the carriage folk would send fagots to be laid in the ruts on the road which they intended to travel, and put four horses to their carriages, not by way of display, but of necessity. We find Lord Montague writing to the Privy Council, in the reign of Charles II., to apologise for his absence from one of its meetings on the plea of the badness of the roads.

The church is generally said to be dedicated to St. Andrew, and Thorne, in his "Environs of London," repeats the blunder. Being attached to Bishop's Hatfield, and thereby connected with the see of Ely, it was dedicated to St. Etheldreda, who was generally known as St. Audrey, and the transition from "St. Audrey" to "St. Andrew" was easy.

The former church, having become rickety and unsafe. was pulled down in 1789, when the present

---

structure superseded it. It was then a plain square preaching room, with large deal pews of the regulation height, and square windows; in fact, as tasteless and common-looking an edifice as could well be conceived. About the year 1870 it was internally re-modelled, the seats being lowered and thrown open, and a small apsidal chancel being added of a more ecclesiastical pattern. An organ and some painted windows have since been added, and the western gallery pulled down. Rising from the roof at the western end of the church is a low, square embattled tower of wood, painted white, and containing two bells. The tower was formerly surmounted by a spire. One monument, now on the wall of the tower, remains to connect the present structure with its predecessor. Among the entries of burials here is one under date of March 2nd, 1802, to "Elizabeth King, widow, for forty-six years clerk of this parish."

In the churchyard is the family tomb of the Pepys family. It contains the bodies of Sir Lucas Pepys, and also of Sir William Weller Pepys, and his brother Lord Chancellor Cottenham who died in 1851. Lady Rothes and Lady Cottenham also lie buried here.

It is quite a popular error to suppose that Lord Mohun, the scampish duellist who fell in Hyde Park,* was buried here. He lies in the vaults under the church of St. Martin's-in-the-Fields.

At the west end of the churchyard is a fine old yew-tree, of great girth, and supposed to be seven centuries old. It does not denote, as would seem at first sight to appear, that a church stood on the spot in the Saxon-Norman times, but is simply the last survival of a yew forest.

It is of classical note, for it is made the subject of communications in the *Gentleman's Magazine,*† and is mentioned by Nichols in his "Literary Anecdotes." Sir John Cullum states that when he measured it, a century ago, it was about twenty-five feet in circumference; and its girth is unaltered now.

Generally, though not always, yews are found in close proximity to the church, where they look like symbols of eternity. But they were also planted for other lasting purposes, as, for example, to mark boundaries of properties, or the courses of primitive roads. It is said that the pilgrims' route from Silchester to Canterbury, across the Surrey hills, can be almost made out by the long line of yew-trees with which it was fringed. The yew, however, served even yet another purpose. In

the will of King Henry VI. is the following item :— "The space between the wall of the church and the wall of the cloyster shall conteyne 38 feyte, which is left for to sett in certaine trees and flowers, behovable and convenient for the service of the same church." Now, it has often been asked, and never satisfactorily answered, "For what purpose were yew-trees anciently planted in churchyards?" In times when it was considered as a matter of importance that the churches should, at certain seasons, be adorned with evergreens, and when to strew branches in the way, and to scatter herbs and flowers into the grave, were practised as religious rites, was it not "behovable and convenient for the service of the church" that every churchyard should contain at least one yew-tree? Several reasons may be assigned for giving this tree a preference to every other evergreen. It is very hardy, long-lived, and though in time it attains a considerable height, produces branches in abundance so low as to be always within reach of the hand, and at last affords a beautiful wood for furniture.

Near the church, at the corner of the Barnet Road, stands an old-fashioned house known as the Priory, and traditionally said to have been occupied by Lady Rachel Russell. But there is no proof of such occupation by Lady Rachel, beyond the statement of Lady Bunsen, on page 284, which may be an error; and it is very doubtful whether Totteridge ever boasted of a prior or prioress. The house, however, dates evidently back to the Tudor times.

Richard Baxter, to whom we have been already introduced at Acton,* lived here for some years in retirement, being probably led to take up his abode here in order to be near Mr. Charlton, whose wife was his sister. His name occurs once as a rate-payer in the village books here.

Totteridge has always been a favourite residence with the wealthier classes in London, and several legal and City knights lived here at one and the same time.

Pointer's Grove (or Poynter's), at the south-eastern extremity of the parish, facing the Green, has long been the abode of the Pugets, a family of French refugee extraction. The late Mr. Puget, M.P., built, in 1827, a small chapel and schools on the road to Whetstone. The estate of Pointers belonged, in the middle of the seventeenth century, to Lady Gurney, the widow of Sir Richard Gurney, who died a prisoner in the Tower, in 1647. Later

---

* See "Old and New London," Vol. IV., p. 398.
† See Vol. LXXV., Part II., pp. 1142, 1212.

* See *ante*, p. 11.

on the property was possessed successively by Sir John Aubrey, Sir Thomas Aleyne, Sir Peter Mayer, and Sir John Sheffield, from whom it passed to the Pugets, with whose family it still continues.

Copped Hall, which stands on the Green, facing the Church, was for some years the seat of Sir E. Bulwer Lytton. Whilst staying here he would constantly pay visits to the battle-field of Barnet, to which he has given such interest in his "Last of the Barons."* The estate is about a hundred acres, well timbered, and planted with avenues of limes and other trees. A fine dining-room and conservatory have been added by the present owner, Mr. Bolton.

Half a century ago the property was owned by Mr. William Manning, M.P., and Governor of the Bank of England, the father of Cardinal Manning, who was born here in 1809. The Cardinal was educated at Harrow, and Balliol College, Oxford, and was afterwards a Fellow of Weston College. He resigned his rectory of Graffham, Sussex, and the Archdeaconry of Chichester in 1851, when he became a Roman Catholic. In 1865 he was consecrated Archbishop of Westminster, and he was created a Cardinal in 1875. The Cardinal's elder brother, who died young, lies buried at the east end of the churchyard. Mr. Manning probably came to live at Totteridge on account of its proximity to Highwood, at Mill Hill, where Mr. William Wilberforce was then living, both being "pillars" of the "Evangelical" faith, as taught by Wesley and Simeon.

From the Mannings the estate of Copped Hall passed to the Scarletts, and from them to a building speculator, who sold it to Lord Lytton. His lordship, however, lived here only occasionally, his chief seat being in another part of the county, at Knebworth, near Stevenage. He added largely to this place, however, and re-faced the outside, which he made to resemble an Italian villa, with a terraced front, adorning the upper portion with classical heads, copied from genuine antiques. He hung the library with tapestry, painted the

* See *ante*, p. 326.

ceilings of the chief rooms in the Italian fashion, repeating in several compartments his own initials E. B. L., and adding over the mantelpiece the motto so accordant with his taste, "Absque Musis frigent Lares." He stayed here off and on between 1858 and 1875, during which time he wrote "Pelham," "Lucretia," and the "Last of the Barons." The terrace in the rear of the house commands extensive views, extending to Hampstead, Highgate, and Harrow, with peeps of the Surrey Hills beyond. The rivulet which divides the two counties, flows at the bottom of the park-like grounds, and is dammed up into a lake which covers four acres. Mr. Manning planted in the grounds a "spinney," or circular plantation, consisting of a variety of forest trees, to commemorate the jubilee of George III.

The mansion in Totteridge Park, at the western extremity of the village, on the right-hand side of the road leading to Hendon, occupies the site of the old manor house, and its successor, a small hunting-seat, which was purchased from Lord Bateman by Sir William Lee, the Lord Chief Justice mentioned above. He enlarged the mansion, and resided there for many years. The present house, which has been recently converted into a boarding-school for boys, is a large red brick edifice, consisting of a centre and wings, and crowned by an octagonal domed clock-turret. It stands in a finely-wooded park, about 100 acres in extent, and is approached through a broad avenue of elms. In the "Memoirs of Baron Bunsen" it is stated that the Baron lived here in 1848 and the following year, and that during that time he here entertained many distinguished visitors, and greatly enjoyed the grounds, with their "grand trees, those lofty firs, the pride of Totteridge, the fine terrace, the charming garden," and its general surroundings. "Oh, how thankful," he wrote, "I am for this Totteridge! Could I but describe the groups of fine trees, the turf, the terrace walks!"

Among other mansions at Totteridge is one standing in what is now called the Wykeham Rise Estate. It was formerly well known as the residence of the late Dr. Shuttleworth, Bishop of Chichester.

CHAPTER XXXIV.

WHETSTONE, FRIERN BARNET, AND FINCHLEY.

" Ut jugulent homines, surgunt de nocte latrones."—HORACE.

Situation of Whetstone—The Parish Church—Census Returns—Oakleigh Park—George Morland and the Chimney-sweep—General Appearance of the Village—The Manor of Friern Barnet—The Church—Almshouses—Finchley—Situation and Extent—Descent of the Manor—The Old Manor-house—Noted Residents—Church End—Census Returns—Races—The Parish Church—Christ's College—National Schools—East End—The Church, &c.—The "Dirt House"—Cemeteries for Marylebone and St. Pancras and Islington Parishes—North End—Christ Church—The Congregational Chapel—Finchley Common—Encampments and Reviews—Highwaymen—Turpin's Oak—The "Green Man" Tavern—Capture of Jack Sheppard—The Life of a Highwayman.

WHETSTONE lies to the east of Totteridge, from which village it is distant about a mile, the station of Totteridge and Whetstone, on the High Barnet branch of the Great Northern Railway, serving as a means of communication for both places. Till recently it was a portion of the parish of Friern Barnet, which lies to the east of it. It was, however, cut off from the mother parish, and made a separate ecclesiastical district in 1833, a portion of Finchley being at the same time embodied in it. The district round about it still retains some features of its once rural character, in spite of large building operations, and is situated at the north-eastern extremity of the hundred of Ossulston.

Whether the name of Whetstone has anything to do with that vicious locality called Whetstone Park, on the north side of Lincoln's Inn Fields, we know not. Neither Lysons nor the author of the "Beauties of England" offer any suggestion as to the derivation of the name; they simply state that it is the name given to "a manor in Friern Barnet." The local tradition that the place derived its name from a large stone which was there found, and on which the soldiers sharpened their swords and battle-axes preparatory to the Battle of Barnet, is almost too absurd to be mentioned seriously, and may be dismissed with a smile.

The church, dedicated to St. John, stands on the west side of the road at the south end of the village. It is a small brick structure, of the commonplace type of the time, and is shut in from the roadway by a high brick wall, partly overhung with ivy. A chapel is supposed to have been originally built here early in the fifteenth century, in the Perpendicular style. The present building, however, as may be guessed from the date of its erection, is but a poor attempt at Gothic architecture. Till 1879 it was an oblong chapel-like building, with small rectangular turrets or pinnacles at each of its four corners, and a small bell-turret in the centre of the west gable. In the above year, however, a chancel was added to the existing nave, a vaulted roof replaced the old flat ceiling, and Early-English windows were inserted. The window at the east end is of stained glass, and was inserted as a memorial of two members of the Baxendale family, whose residence is in the neighbourhood.

The village contains one or two chapels and schools, and since the opening of the railway the place has rapidly increased in growth and population. In 1871 the number of the inhabitants was over 2,300, and in the course of the next decade this has been considerably increased. A large district, called Oakleigh Park, has lately become in part built over with terraces and modest villas; these, however, have not materially altered the old-fashioned look of the main street, which, as of yore, still contains, for the size of the village, a large number of roadside inns, taverns, and ale-houses.

George Morland, the artist,* whose delight was to pass his time in village taverns, and then perchance to balance his "score" by painting a sign-board for the worthy host, met with a slight *contretemps* on one occasion when passing through this village. Allan Cunningham, in his "Life of Morland," tells the following anecdote about him. "He once (we are told) received an invitation to Barnet, and was hastening thither with two friends, when he was stopped at Whetstone turnpike by a lumber or jockey cart, driven by two persons, one of them a chimney-sweep, who were disputing with the toll-gatherer. Morland endeavoured to pass, when one of the wayfarers cried, 'What! Mr. Morland, won't you speak to a body!' The artist endeavoured to elude further greeting, but this was not to be; the other bawled out so lustily that Morland was obliged to recognise at last his companion and crony, Hooper, a tinman and pugilist. After a hearty shake of the hand, the boxer turned to his neighbour the chimney-sweep, and said, 'Why, Dick, don't you know this here gentleman? 'tis my friend, Mr. Morland.' The sooty charioteer, smiling a recognition, forced his unwelcome hand upon his brother of the brush; they then both whipt their horses and departed. This rencontre

---

* See "Old and New London," Vol. V., p. 222.

mortified Morland very sensibly; he declared that he knew nothing of the chimney-sweep, and that he was forced upon him by the impertinence of Hooper; but the artist's habits made the story be generally believed, and 'Sweeps, your honour,' was a joke which he was often obliged to hear."

The long main street, which lies along the high road from Barnet to Finchley, is singularly void of interest, being really little more than a succession of public-houses, small shops, and tasteless villas with tiny gardens in front of them, interspersed

Such being the case, and there being no river or attractive scenery, Whetstone would seem to have had no place among the favourite suburban residences of Londoners, and accordingly it has no literary history, its name being scarcely mentioned, except in connection with the heroes of the "Newgate Calendar."

The principal manor of Friern Barnet, under the name of Whetstone, or *Freren* Barnet, was in ancient times part of the extensive possessions of the Priory of St. John of Jerusalem. The word

ALMSHOUSES, FRIERN BARNET. (*See page* 322.)

with blacksmiths' forges, or sheds that have done duty as such in the good old days of stage-coaches.

But the good old coaching days, it must be remembered, were also the days of highwaymen and footpads, as we saw when dealing with the locality of Hounslow Heath, next to which the spot of which we now treat enjoyed the highest reputation of any place in Middlesex. Dick Turpin positively loved this highway and its associations, and his "Knights of the Road" followed his taste. So great was the terror which they inspired among the wealthier classes, that many Scotch lords and squires preferred to make the journey from their native hills to the Parliament at Westminster by sea, rather than encounter the terrors of the Great North road within ten or twelve miles of London.

Freren probably means belonging to the friars, *freres*, or brethren of the Order. The name of Barnet, as already remarked, is common to several parishes in England. Lysons says it was anciently written Bernette, or Bergnet, which, as Chauncy remarks in his "Hertfordshire," signifies "a little hill;" the addition of "Friern" or "Friarn" denotes that it was monastic property.

According to Lysons, Sir William Weston, the last of the Priors of St. John of Jerusalem, held a court here in 1539, and Henry VIII., after the dissolution, granted the manor to the Dean and Chapter of St. Paul's, in whose possession it has ever since continued. The manor house, near the church, is described by the above authority as a "very ancient structure." It has undergone many alterations, but a considerable part of the old building, namely, a long passage, or wooden cloister, with a carved ceiling, was remaining far into the present century. "The recluse situation of this manorial house," observes the author of the "Beauties of England," "would seem favourable to tradition and legendary story. Accordingly, it is supposed by some that this was a cell to the the Decorated and Early English types of architecture, and although in the main an ancient building of flint with stone dressings, wears, in consequence of recent restoration and enlargement, a somewhat new and modern appearance. It consists of a chancel, nave, and south aisles, separated by an arcade of four bays, with a square tower and spire at the west end. The south door,

FINCHLEY MANOR HOUSE AND TURPIN'S OAK.

Priory of St. John, and by others that it was an inn or resting-place for the knights in journeys between London and St. Albans. A gateway, which appears to have been formerly the chief place of entrance, is termed the 'Queen's Gate,' an appellation that probably refers to 'a visit of Queen Elizabeth to this house." Norden, writing concerning Friern Barnet in the reign of Elizabeth, says that "Sir John Popham, Knt., Lord Chiefe Justice of England, sometimes maketh this his abode."

The parish church, dedicated to St. James, is of protected by a light porch, is of Norman workmanship, round-headed, and of somewhat rude construction, ornamented only with a moulding of chevron work. On the east wall of the chancel aisle is a mural monument to sundry members of the Cleve family, dated 1726, and in the exterior wall is a small tablet bearing the date February 7th, 1638. The east window of stained glass is new; it was inserted in memory of George and Johanna Homan.

Near the church are schools for boys, girls, and infants, the site of which was given by Mr. John

Miles, of the Manor House. Close by the schools, by the side of the road leading from the church to Whetstone, and shaded by a noble row of elms, stands a row of almshouses, seven in number, and of a somewhat picturesque appearance. They were founded in 1612, by Laurence Campe, for twelve aged persons, and they were repaired and altered in 1843. The parish allows the inmates 2s. 6d. each per week. The long stone front of the houses, with the Tudor arched doorways and square-headed windows, give the buildings a some-what "collegiate" appearance. On the front are three shields, with the arms of London; of the family of the founder, namely, a chevron between three griffins' heads; and of the Drapers' Com-pany. There are also tablets with such moral and religious inscriptions as these—

> "Every morning before you feed,
> Come to this house, and prayers read;
> Then you about your work may go,
> So God may bless you and yours also."

Another tablet bears the following texts—

> "Exhort them that are rich in this world, that they be ready to give, and glad to distribute."—1 Tim. vi. 1.
> "He that hath pity upon the poor, lendeth unto the Lord."—Proverbs xv.

A new church, of Early English design, dedicated to All Saints, has lately been completed in this parish. It is of stone, and has at the west end a lofty tower and spire, which is conspicuous for miles round.

Mr. Thorne tells us in his "Environs of London" that "in olden times the Great North Road passed through Friern Barnet by way of Colney Hatch," but that, becoming inconvenient "by reason of the deepness and dirty passage in the winter season," the Bishop of London undertook to make a new and more direct road to Whetstone through his park at Highgate; and that to compensate the in-habitants of Friern Barnet for the loss of traffic on their road, he made them free of the tolls levied at the Bishop's Gate.*

Finchley, although a very large parish, and lying within eight miles of London, on the great high road to the north, is singularly void of historical interest, with the exception perhaps of two or three encampments on the Common. Its name, how-ever, like that of its neighbour, Whetstone, is somewhat largely mixed up with the annals of highwaymen and footpads, who infested these parts in the last century, and gave to them a reputation second only to that of Hounslow Heath. Finchley proper still retains a few vestiges of its

once rural character; but it is the same old story over again: its surrounding meadows and pastures are being rapidly covered by untasteful buildings. The parish itself extends about three miles north-wards from the district known as East End, to Whetstone, the greater part of which, as stated above, is included in Finchley parish. There are here two stations on the Great Northern branch line to Edgware, and one at Woodside Park, on the High Barnet branch. The river Brent flows along in the valley between the great North Road and Hendon towards the west.

The manor of Finchley, although it does not figure in Domesday Book, belonged from time im-memorial to the see of London. In the reign of King John, the bishop and his Finchley tenants obtained from the Crown a grant of freedom from toll, which grant was confirmed by Charles II. In the fifteenth and sixteenth centuries, a manor here, called Finchley Manor, was held by the Marches, Leyndons, and Comptons. In 1577 a license was granted to the Earl of Huntingdon, Anne, Coun-tess of Pembroke, and Henry Lord Compton, to alienate the manor to trustees, for the use of the countess for life, with remainder to Thomas, se-cond son of Lord Compton, and his heirs.

The old Manor House is still in existence, and retains many of its ancient features. It stands between the hamlet of East End and the parish church. The house is a large old-fashioned brick building, but has been much altered to suit modern requirements. It is still surrounded by the moat, which encloses a large oblong area through which passes the public roadway. The mansion is occu-pied by Mr. George Plucknett, F.S.A., a magistrate for the county, and in its ancient oak-panelled hall justice continues to be meted out to evil-doers, as in days of yore.

Finchley has in times long gone by had some noted residents. Here, for instance, lived Sir Thomas Frowick, the Lord Chief Justice of the Common Pleas under the Tudors. The Frowicks, as we have seen, were influential about South Mimms, Hadley, and the neighbourhood.*

The village locally known as Church End is a rambling and scattered collection of cottages and interspersed houses of a better class. Many of the principal residences are detached; but rows of houses, streets, and terraces, are daily springing up everywhere, and the green lanes are fast disappear-ing. In 1808 the number of houses in the parish was 250, the population at the same time amount-ing to 1,500. In 1871 the number of dwellings

---

had increased to over 1,250, and the inhabitants had reached a total of 7,150, which number, during the next decade, had swelled up to over 11,000.

Races were held here in the years 1869 and 1872, but they have apparently been abandoned as a public nuisance.

The church stands on an eminence in the centre of the village, about a mile from the great north road. It is, like many ancient parish churches, dedicated to St. Mary, and is in the Perpendicular style, from which it would appear to have been erected in the fifteenth century. It was restored in 1872, when the thick coating of plaster with which the stonework was covered up was removed, and the building enlarged by the addition of a north aisle, and an extension of the chancel, and a low embattled tower at the western end, containing a clock and six bells. On the smallest bell, which is dated 1770, is the following inscription :—

> " Good people all that hear us ring,
>   Be faithful to your God and king."

The roofs of the chancel and aisles are of open timber; that of the nave is flat, with ornamental panels of plaster set in wooden framework. Most of the windows are new. There are several monuments and brasses of the fifteenth century. On the south wall is a plain marble slab to the memory of William Seward, F.R.S. and F.S.A., who died in the year 1799. He was the author of "Anecdotes of Distinguished Persons," and "Biographiana." Alexander Kinge, who died in 1618, is commemorated by a monument containing two figures kneeling before open books. The oldest brass is that of Richard Pratt, and Johanna, his wife, it is engraved with effigies of the deceased, and is dated 1487. In the chancel is one to Simon Skudemore, gent., and his wife, bearing date 1609, and on the same stone a small plate commemorating Nicholas Luke, gent., and his wife, Elizabeth, daughter of the above-named Simon Skudemore. In the west wall of the church are visible a few traces of rude stonework supposed to be Norman, possibly "suggesting the existence of an earlier fabric." Nothing, however, is known for certainty of the existence of a church here dating as far back as that era. The register dates from the year 1560, and the records of the rectory go no further back than the fourteenth century.

Two of the rectors of Finchley have been elevated to the episcopal bench. Dr. Cotton, who held the living towards the close of the sixteenth century, was promoted to the bishopric of Exeter; and Dr. Bancroft, who was rector in 1608, was raised to the see of Oxford. Dr. John Barkham, Bishop Bancroft's successor in the rectory, was a noted antiquarian in his day, and largely assisted Speed in his " English History."

In the churchyard lies buried Major Cartwright, the once popular political reformer, whose statue now adorns Burton Crescent, St. Pancras, London. His grave is marked by an obelisk bearing the following inscription :—" In this place are deposited the remains of John Cartwright, the son of William and Anne Cartwright, Commander in the Royal Navy, and many years Major in the Nottingham Militia. He was the author of various works on legislation; the earliest, most strenuous, and disinterested Reformer of his time; the intrepid advocate of liberty, whose labours for the public good terminated only with his life, on the 23rd of September, 1824; aged eighty-four. Also the remains of his beloved wife, Anne Catherine Cartwright, who died on the 21st of December, 1834." Thomas Payne, the bookseller of the Mewsgate, " whose little shop," writes Mr. James Thorne, " was the daily haunt of scholars and book collectors," was buried here in February, 1799.

Adjoining the churchyard is Christ's College, which was instituted in 1857 by the late Rev. Thomas Reader White, rector of Finchley, " for the purpose of providing first-class education at a moderate cost." The school is divided between two buildings. The old mansion, which serves the purposes of the lower school, contains also the dining-hall of both schools; the new school is situated on the opposite side of the churchyard. Both buildings are constructed of red brick. The school has acquired a good position among the educational institutions of the country. It is conducted by the principal and resident assistant masters, and several scholarships are awarded annually to boys resident in the college. The average number of pupils in the college is about 200.

The National Schools for St. Mary's, in Ballard's Lane, near the church, were erected in 1852. They are built of brick, with stone dressing, in the Gothic Style, and consist of schools for boys, girls, and infants, with residences for the master and mistresses.

The hamlet of East End lies to the south-east of Finchley proper, and extends to the Barnet Road. It was formed into a separate parish for ecclesiastical purposes in 1846. The church, dedicated to the Holy Trinity, is a stone building, in the Early English style, comprising chancel, nave, and aisles. The Congregational Chapel at East End was built in 1875, in the place of an old chapel which had been burnt down. The building is of brick, in the

Early Decorated style of Gothic architecture, and consists of a nave, aisles, transept, and an apse for the use of the choir. At the north-east angle is a tower, surmounted by a lofty spire. Some of the windows are filled with stained glass.

The "Old White Lion" public-house, at East End, has been for many years locally known as the "Dirt House," a name which was bestowed upon it in consequence of its being the regular "house of call" of the men in charge of the carts and waggons, which, taking hay and other produce to London, usually returned to the country laden with soot, manure, and the like. Near the above inn is a wood, called in old maps "Dirt House Wood," which, it is conjectured, obtained its name from its proximity to the "Dirt House," and to distinguish it from the other small woods in the neighbourhood, all of which are remnants of the great forest of Middlesex.*

The cemetery for the parish of St. Mary, Marylebone, is situated near Church End, and comprises more than thirty acres, with the usual chapel and offices. On the east side of the Barnet Road is the joint cemetery for the parishes of St. Pancras and St. Mary, Islington. It comprises on the whole nearly ninety acres, and contains two mortuary chapels, lodges, and residences for the officers, &c. The grounds are tastefully laid out, and planted with evergreens, shrubs, and trees. Here, in 1855, was buried Sir Henry Bishop, the musical composer : a granite monument, bearing a bronze medallion, marks his grave. This cemetery was taken out of Finchley Common, on another part of which has lately sprung into existence the hamlet of North End, comprising several respectable shops and private residences. The church (Christ Church) was commenced in 1870, but has not yet been completed, the nave only having as yet been built : this is in the Decorated style. North End possesses also a Congregational chapel of the regulation ecclesiastical pattern—Decorated Gothic—with a tower and spire rising nearly one hundred feet in height. It was built in 1865.

Of Finchley Common very little is now left as an open space. At the beginning of the present century it was described as the largest tract of poor land in Middlesex, except Hounslow Heath. It was estimated in 1810, by Messrs. Britton, to contain about 1,500 acres of "somewhat inferior quality, but capable of great improvement under proper cultivation. On this common a large number of sheep and cattle," they add, "is fed in the spring." But this is no longer true.

Dr. Hunter, in his "History of London and its Environs" (1810), writes, "Finchley is chiefly known by being annexed to the extensive *Common*, a place formidable to travellers from the highway robberies of which it has been the scene." He estimates the common to contain 2,010 acres, and adds, "the waste and uncultivated state of which, so near the metropolis, is disgraceful to the economy of the country." The eastern side of the common, and the northern slopes of Hampstead and Highgate are reckoned by Messrs. Britton, in 1810, as mostly woodland copses.

The few historical events which relate to Finchley are connected with its former common. Here General Monk, in his march to London, previous to the restoration of Charles II., drew up his forces on the 3rd of February, 1660. When the young Chevalier, Charles Edward, was at Derby, during the Scottish rebellion of 1745, there was a great panic in London, and volunteers of all descriptions offered themselves to serve in the ranks. "The whole body of the law," observes the author of the "Comprehensive History of England," "formed themselves into a regiment, under the command of Lord Chief Justice Willes, and were to have done duty at St. James's, to guard the royal family, in case it had been necessary for the king to take the field with the army that lay encamped about Barnet and Finchley Common. Luckily that force was not required, and did little more than scare away the highwaymen from their usual beat. Weavers, and other London artisans, were probably not the best of troops, and it became the fashion to turn the Finchley camp and the march to Finchley into ridicule ; but there was, nevertheless, some good regular troops on that point, both horse and foot, with thirty-two pieces of artillery ; and the Life-Guards and Horse Grenadiers were ready to march out of London at a moment's notice." Hogarth's famous picture of the "March of the Guards to Finchley," which found a home at the Foundling Hospital,* is well known. Another memorable encampment on Finchley Common was that of the troops, comprising several regiments, hastily brought together here, in 1780, on account of the Gordon riots. This review was the subject of an engraving which was published at the time, and is now very scarce.

Finchley Common continued the favourite "hunting ground" of highwaymen down till near the close of the last century. Sir Gilbert Elliot, afterwards Earl of Minto, in a letter to his wife in 1790, wrote, when within a few stages of London,

---

* See *Notes and Queries*, June, 1881, pp. 471-2.

* See "Old and New London," Vol. V., p. 362.

that instead of pushing on that night, as he easily could, he should defer his arrival till the morning, for, he adds, " I shall not trust my throat on Finchley Common in the dark."*　At the London end of what was once the common, nearly opposite the " Green Man " Inn, at a place called " Brown's Wells," on the Barnet Road, and a little way north of the St. Pancras Cemetery, is an old oak, behind which it is traditionally stated that Dick Turpin used to take up his position.　The tree, which is still called " Turpin's Oak," is green and flourishing, though considerably shorn of its upper branches. Pistol-balls, it is stated, which are supposed to have been fired at the trunk to deter highwaymen, have been frequently extracted from the bark.　Mr. Larwood, in his " History of Signboards," tells us that the " Green Man " has the following verses under two pipes crossed over a pot of beer :—

> " Call softly, drink moderate ;
>   　Pay honourably, be good company ;
>   　Part friendly ; Go home quietly ;
>   Let these lines be no man's sorrow ;
>   　Pay to-day and trust to-morrow."

The notorious Jack Sheppard, who kept half London in terror, and who once, at least, effected his escape out of Newgate, was captured on Finchley Common in 1724.　He was disguised in a butcher's blue frock and a woollen apron.

As to the life of a highwayman, a writer in the *London Magazine* some years ago remarks :—

" An highwayman is a wild Arab, that lives by robbing of small caravans, and has no *way* o living but the king's *highway*.　Aristotle held him to be but a kind of huntsman ; but our sages of the law account him rather a beast of prey, and will not allow his game to be legal by the forest law.　His chief care is to be well mounted, and, when he is taken, the law takes care he should be still, while he lives.　His business is to break the law of the land, for which the hangman breaks his neck, and there's an end of the controversie. He fears nothing, under the gallows, more than his own face, and, therefore, when he does his work, conveys it out of sight, that it may not rise up in judgment, and give evidence against him at the sessions.　His trade is to take purses and evil courses, and when he is taken himself, the laws take as evil a course with him.　He takes place of all other thieves as the most heroical, and one that comes nearest to the old knights-errant, though he is really one of the basest, that never ventures but upon surprisal, and where he is sure

of the advantage.　He lives like a Tartar, always in motion ; and the inns upon the road are hordes, where he reposes for awhile, and spends his time and money, when he is out of action. . . . He is more destructive to the grazier than the murrain.　When he despatches his business between sun and sun he invades a whole county, and, like the Long Parliament, robs by representative.　He calls concealing what he takes from his comrades *sinking*, which they account a great want of integrity. After he has roved up and down too long, he is at last set himself and conveyed to the jail, the only place of his residence, where he is provided of a hole to put his head in, and gathered to his fathers in a faggot cart."

Mr. Harrison Ainsworth, in his " Rookwood," has turned the life and career of a highwayman to good account.　We quote from it the following

"CHAPTER OF HIGHWAYMEN.

> " Of every rascal of every kind,
>   　The most notorious to my mind
>   　　Was the royalist captain, gay Jemmy Hind !
>   　　　Which nobody can deny.

> " But the pleasantest coxcomb among them all
>   　For lute, coranto, or madrigal,
>   　　Was the galliard Frenchman Claude Du Val !
>   　　　Which nobody can deny.

> " Yet Tobygloak never a coach could rob,
>   　Could lighten a pocket or empty a fob,
>   　　With a neater hand than Old Mob, Old Mob !
>   　　　Which nobody can deny.

> " Nor did housebreaker ever deal harder knocks
>   　On the stubborn lid of a good strong box,
>   　　Than that prince of good fellows, Tom Cox, Tom Cox !
>   　　　Which nobody can deny.

> " And blither bellow on board highway
>   　Did never with oath bid traveller stay,
>   　　Than devil-may-care Will Holloway !
>   　　　Which nobody can deny.

> " Then in roguery naught could exceed the tricks
>   　Of Gettings and Grey, and the five or six
>   　　Who trod in the steps of bold Neddy Wicks !
>   　　　Which nobody can deny.

> " Nor could any so handily break a lock
>   　As Sheppard, who stood in the Newgate dock,
>   　　And nicknamed the gaolers around him " his flock!"
>   　　　Which nobody can deny.

> " Nor did highwayman ever before possess,
>   　For ease, for security, danger, distress,
>   　　Such a mare as Dick Turpin's Black Bess, Black Bess !
>   　　　Which nobody can deny."

Finchley Common was the scene of the depredations of most of the worthies whose names are introduced in the above piece of verse ; but a great change has taken place in it since their time. In fact it is now nearly entirely blotted out of the map, being either enclosed or built over.

---

* " Life and Letters of Gilbert Elliot, first Earl of Minto," Vol. I., p. 372.

CHAPTER XXXV.

COLNEY HATCH AND SOUTHGATE.

" Insanire juvat."—HORACE

Rapid Extension of Colney Hatch, or New Southgate—Its Situation and Etymology—Middlesex County Lunatic Asylum—St. Paul's Church—The Pumping Station of the New River Waterworks—Wood Green—The Drinking Fountain—Nightingale Hall—St. Michael's Church—The Printers' Almshouses—Fishmongers' and Poulterers' Asylum—Fullers' Almshouses—Royal Masonic Institution for Boys—Clock and Watchmakers' Asylum- -The Great Northern Cemetery—Southgate—The Village Green and "Cherry-tree" Inn—The Church—Arnold's Court, now Arno's Grove—Minchenden House—Bromefield Park—Bowes Manor—Bowes Park—St. Michael's Church—Culland's Grove—Grovelands—Palmer's Green—Southgate Village Hall--Winchmore Hill—The Church, &c.—Bush Hill Park—Sir Hugh Myddelton and the New River.

COLNEY HATCH—or New Southgate, as its inhabitants prefer to style it—comes next in our perambulation. Half a century ago, or less, this

Colney Hatch is in reality a hamlet of Friern Barnet, from which parish it has been cut off for ecclesiastical purposes, the new district having

COLNEY HATCH.

part was rural and retired; but the construction of the Great Northern Railway, with its modern station and the accessories of villas and shops, and that of the still more modern County Asylum for the Lunatics of Middlesex, have largely altered the appearance of the place—it is needless to add, scarcely for the better. As the Asylum is officered by a staff of some three hundred persons, a small village has sprung up, as if by magic, round its gates; and the population of Colney Hatch itself has been doubled in little more than a quarter of a century.

assigned to it the name of New Southgate; and it forms, as it were, a connecting link between Friern Barnet on the west, and Edmonton and the district once known as Enfield Chase on the east. The name of Colney—or Colne—Hatch is mentioned in a Court Roll of the reign of Henry VII.; and in a map published in the last century it is printed Coney Hatch. The term "Hatch" evidently has reference to a side gateway or entrance to the Royal Chase of Enfield. Numerous instances of the term occur in various parts of the country. The "Pilgrims' Hatch," near Brentwood.

is a name well known, as marking the south entrance to the once great forest of Waltham.

The Asylum, which stands close to the west side of the railway station, is a handsome Italian structure, though plain and to a great extent void of ornament. The late Prince Consort laid the first stone of it in 1849, and it was opened for the reception of patients two years later. It has since been considerably enlarged, and now holds a little over two thousand inmates, of whom, as we saw was the case also at Bedlam,* the majority are females.

for which their previous education or trade fits them—as, for instance, in gardening, baking, cooking, &c. In fact, steady kindness and constant employment are the chief machinery used in humanising these waifs and strays of humanity. Such work as painting and decorating the wards, and also the necessary repairs or alterations in the building, are mostly executed by the patients, of course under proper supervision. By this means the Asylum is partly self-supporting, or, at all events, the expenses are largely diminished.

ARNO'S GROVE, SOUTHGATE. (*See page* 346.)

The discipline exercised over them seems to be one of kindness, not of fear or of punishment; and the whips and strait-waistcoats of the days before Dr. Conolly and Dr. Elliotson are not called into requisition, though some cases require to be isolated in rooms with softly-padded walls. The patients enjoy as much liberty as is possible consistent with the maintenance of order; and the monotony of their lives is occasionally varied by dancing. Music they have in plenty, not only in the chapel, but in the larger rooms.

The patients are employed in various industries

It is stated that the cost of erecting the Asylum was a little over half a million, and that about £60,000 a year is devoted to its maintenance out of the rates of the metropolitan county.

The building, which is of brick with stone dressings, was erected from the designs of Mr. S. W. Daukes, and covers about four acres of ground. It occupies an elevated and healthy site, and its ventilating towers and central cupola are conspicuous objects for some distance round. The principal front of the building, nearly 2,000 feet in length, faces the north, and is the only part of the exterior upon which any attempt at architectural embellishment is visible; and even this is not very profuse.

* See "Old and New London," Vol VI., p. 359.

The grounds of the Asylum are enclosed by a brick wall of moderate height, which extends along the roadway from New Southgate westwards towards Finchley. In the centre, facing the principal entrance, are some iron gates and the gatekeeper's lodge. A carriage-drive extends from the gates to the main entrance, in the centre of the north front, having on either side a broad piece of greensward, with gravel-walks, shrubs, and evergreens.

The front part of the central block of building is flanked on either side by a slightly projecting ventilating tower, whilst from the roof rises an octagonal-domed cupola. Across the base of this building runs an open arcade, a doorway in the centre opening into a long corridor, which extends right and left to the wards and offices. In the wall opposite the door is the foundation-stone, bearing an inscription, to the effect that it was laid by the Prince Consort on the 8th of May, 1849. The stone is carved with an ornamental bordering, together with the arms of the county. The chapel, which occupies the centre of the north front, immediately at the back of the corridor mentioned above, is a large square, or rather oblong, room. It is lighted from the roof, and also by windows of tinted glass above the communion-table. It was originally fitted with galleries, the rows of seats rising gradually from one end of the building to the other; but in 1874 the galleries were removed and the seats levelled. The walls of the chapel are painted with a delicate blue tint, and enriched with stencilling and texts of Scripture. The chapel will seat 600, and the services are held twice every week-day and four times on Sundays. The Rev. Henry Hawkins, who has held the chaplaincy since 1867, was for some time chaplain of the Sussex Asylum, at Hayward's Heath. Under his wardenship is an "Association of Friends of the Infirm in Mind." It was instituted in 1871, and has for its object the "after care" of convalescents. The Asylum cemetery was consecrated by Bishop Blomfield in 1851.

The wards and infirmaries are light and airy, and fitted up with every attention to the comfort of the unfortunate inmates. The building includes residences for the principal officers connected with the institution, airing courts, laundry, and workshops, which, with the gardens and airing grounds, cover rather more than one hundred acres. In addition to this, there is a farm adjoining, which comprises another one hundred and fifty acres.

There are separate departments for the several classes of patients, and separate buildings for the two sexes, either wholly unattached, or connected only by the chapel and offices common to both. The accommodation for the female patients is fully one-third greater than that for the males. The ground-plan of the Asylum somewhat resembles the letter **E**, and it is so situated as to afford an uninterrupted view of the country, and to admit the free access of air and sun; whilst the several galleries and wards are so arranged that the medical officers and others may pass through all of them without retracing their steps. On the male side have lately been added two new infirmaries, fitted up after the most approved principles.

As the treatment administered here is in principle the same as that which has long prevailed in Bethlehem Hospital, or "Bedlam," our readers may consider that the remarks on that subject to be found in OLD AND NEW LONDON * may be repeated here—*mutatis mutandis*, of course. As the Colney Hatch Asylum has been in existence for so short a period it has few historical reminiscences, and fewer romantic stories attach to this institution than to its elder sister. This could hardly be otherwise.

A new church, dedicated to St. Paul, was erected in 1873 for this neighbourhood. It is of Gothic design, one of Sir Gilbert Scott's most successful imitations of the Early English period. Not far from it is a pumping-station of the New River Waterworks—a low and unsightly structure, with a lofty campanile in the semi-Italian style.

On the east and south-east sides of the Asylum the land slopes away gradually into a pleasant valley, on the opposite side of which are the rising grounds of Wood Green and Muswell Hill, the latter crowned by the Alexandra Palace and gardens. Twenty years ago, or even less, Wood Green was a retired country spot, hemmed in by green lanes and shady hedgerows, and having here and there a cosy tavern and "tea-garden," whither the ruralising cockney might betake himself—or herself, or both—in the summer-time. The transformation here, however, is almost as great as at Finchley, which we have lately visited. Since the establishment of the Alexandra Palace, and the formation of a railway through its centre, Wood Green has become quite a busy town, built round about the large open space which was once a green and fringing the Southgate road. In the centre of the Green is a drinking-fountain, surmounted by a tall granite obelisk; it is inscribed to the memory of Mrs. Catherine Smithies, of Earlham Grove, Wood Green, the founder of the "Band of Mercy" movement. Not far off is the pleasant seat of Nightingale Hall, standing in its own grounds, and showing by its name that it was once a rural and sequestered spot. St. Michael's Church, on the west side of the Green, is a large and handsome Gothic building, with a lofty spire. What will, perhaps, most attract the attention of visitors to this locality is the architectural beauty of the various asylums and institutions devised by charity and public spirit for the succour of the aged, and the education and protection of the young and helpless. Of these institutions, the Printers' Almshouses, a handsome Tudor range of buildings near the church, were erected in 1850.* Close by is the Asylum for Aged Fishmongers and Poulterers, a red brick building of Elizabethan architecture, also dating its erection from about 1850. Then there are the Fullers' Almshouses, in Nightingale Lane, and the Royal Masonic Institution for Boys, in Lordship Lane, both of which buildings were erected in 1865.

H. Crabb Robinson, in his "Diary," records a pleasant walk from Hampstead by way of Ken Wood to Finchley Common, and so by "a good turnpike road" to Colney Hatch. "On the heath," he adds, "I was amused by the novel sight of gipsies. The road from Colney Hatch to Southgate very pleasing indeed."

By the side of the pleasant green lane here referred to, and through which we make our way from Colney Hatch in a north-easterly direction towards Southgate, stands the Clock and Watch Makers' Asylum, another picturesque cluster of dwellings, twenty-one in number, that in the centre being occupied by the committee-room, &c. They are of red and black brick, and of Tudor design. This institution was founded in 1853, and is supported by voluntary contributions and by the members of the trades for which it was erected, the funds being largely augmented by the annual subscriptions of the Goldsmiths' and the Clockmakers' Companies.

Leaving on our left the roads to Whetstone and Friern Barnet, and also to the Great Northern Cemetery, which lies stretched out before us like a map on the slope of the opposite hill, we now follow the course of the winding roadway across the valley, and on reaching the summit of the next range of hills find ourselves in the village of Southgate.

Southgate, as its name implies, marks the chief southern entrance into the old Royal Chase of Enfield; and though now possessed of its own church and ecclesiastical district, it is historically but a hamlet of the parish of Edmonton. Though only eight miles from the metropolis, and near stations on two lines of railway, it still retains much of that pleasant rural character which it wore when it was the suburban seat of the Welds of Lulworth and of His Grace of Chandos.

The shops and villas which compose the village border the high road for some distance, or are tastefully grouped round a green, which once was fringed by tall and shady elms. A few of these monarchs of the forest remain, and the "Cherry Tree" is the name of the village inn, which for a century or more has faced the Green. Mr. Larwood, in his "History of Signboards," tells us that the "Cherry Tree" was not uncommon, and that down to the reign of William IV. it was the sign of a famous place of resort in Clerkenwell, with a bowling-green and alley; and doubtless it was not chosen without a like reason at Southgate, as one of the haunts of pleasure-seeking Londoners. The "Cherry Gardens" at Bermondsey* will be remembered by readers of Samuel Pepys † as a place of entertainment in the days of the Merry Monarch.

"Southgate," writes H. Crabb Robinson in the "Diary," "is a delightful village. No distant prospect from the Green; but there are fine trees admirably grouped, and neat and happy houses scattered in picturesque corners and lanes. The great houses, the Duchess of Chandos's, &c., have, I suppose, a distant view."

The church, a handsome edifice of the Early English style, built in 1862, from the designs of Sir Gilbert Scott, stands a little to the west of the village, and is said to occupy the site of the chapel attached to the old seat of the Welds, who have always been Roman Catholics. The old chapel was built in 1615 by Sir John Weld, of Arnold's Grove, in this parish. It was a plain brick building, and contained no monument worthy of mention, excepting perhaps that of the founder, who died in 1622. The church, which is built of stone, consists of a clerestoried nave, with north and south aisles, a chancel with aisles, and a tower surmounted by an octagonal spire. Several of the windows are enriched with painted glass, and the picturesque appearance of the exterior of the building is heightened by the thick cluster of ivy which has overgrown its walls. The churchyard is well kept, and prettily laid out with firs and evergreens.

The seat of the Welds stood in an extensive park on the south side of the church, and was called Arnold's Court, probably after a still earlier possessor; but it was demolished in the reign of George I., when the present mansion was built. Fifty years later it was enlarged by an Irish peer, Lord Newhaven, who had purchased the estate

---

* See "Old and New London," Vol. V., p. 562.

* See "Old and New London," Vol. VI., p. 130.
† See "Pepys' Diary," June 15, 1664.

from the Colebrookes. The house, of which an engraving was published by Watts of Chelsea a century ago, and which is also figured in the "Beauties of England," was erected for Sir George Colebrooke. The house is now styled Arno's Grove.

Close by the grounds of Arno's Grove, and adjoining the churchyard, formerly stood Minchenden House, which the Duke of Chandos occupied as a country seat in the last century, after the demolition of Canons.* The house was a large brick-built mansion, shut out from the roadway by a high brick wall and heavy-looking wooden gates. It was built by a Mr. John Nicoll, but was purchased by the Duke of Chandos, and it continued the occasional residence of the Duchess Dowager of Chandos until her death, in 1813, when it passed to the Marquis of Buckingham, in right of his wife, who, as already stated, was the daughter and heiress of the last Duke of Chandos. The old mansion was pulled down many years ago, but its name is kept in remembrance by Minchenden Lodge, a smaller house, which was built some thirty years ago a little further to the north. Mr. Ford tells us, in his "History of Enfield," that a pollard oak still standing in the grounds of old Minchenden House covers a larger extent of ground than any other tree in England. Ten years ago (1873) its spread was no less than 126 feet, and it is still growing.

Bromefield Park, formerly for many generations the seat of a family named Jackson, adjoins Arno's Grove, and is a handsome house of the late Tudor or Early Stuart times, remarkable for its finely preserved staircase of dark oak, richly carved, and for ceilings and walls painted by Sir James Thornhill. The house stands in a park of eighty acres, and has in front an avenue of elms.

Bowes Manor, on the road towards London, lately the seat of Mr. Alderman Sidney, is now destined to be pulled down and obliterated by the all-devouring builder. It is worthy of mention as having been for some years the country seat of Lord Chancellor Truro, who spent here the latter part of his life, and died here in 1855. He lies buried in the family mausoleum in the graveyard at St. Lawrence, near Ramsgate.

Bowes Park is the name given to a small ecclesiastical district, which was formed in 1874, in the neighbourhood of Bowes Manor. The church, dedicated to St. Michael, is in the Palmerston Road, and was built from the designs of Sir Gilbert Scott. It is in the Early English style, and consists of chancel, nave, aisles, transepts, and a bell turret. Bowes Park is a station on the Great Northern Railway.

Another mansion, to the east of the village, is Culland's Grove, which was, early in the present century, the seat of the eccentric Alderman Sir William Curtis, sometime Lord Mayor of and M.P. for London, the same who is said to have first advocated the general teaching of "the three Rs"—reading, 'riting, and 'rithmetic—as a panacea for the evils of society. The house is now called Grovelands. Mr. Harting tells us, in his "Birds of Middlesex," that the sheet of water in these grounds was frequented by some ospreys, which used to catch and eat the fish, and were shot at till they were driven away.

Palmer's Green, a hamlet of Southgate, is a small cluster of houses, with a railway-station, to the south-east of the village, on the road to Winchmore Hill, and is reached by a pleasant footpath to the left of the "Cherry Tree" inn.

Southgate contains a village-hall, a large roomy brick-built structure, of Gothic design, which has been erected by the side of the main street, and is used for concerts and other entertainments.

A walk of about two miles along a pleasant shady roadway skirting the park of Grovelands, and by a footpath through a wood to the left, brings us to Winchmore Hill, a large ecclesiastical district, crowning the eminence from which it takes its name. It contains between 400 and 500 houses, and has a population of some 2,000 souls. Sixty years ago there were only about fifty houses in the district. It is a straggling village; but the houses are mostly built round a large triangular-shaped green, the surface of which is relieved by a circular pond and a few trees. At one end of the green is a railway-station, on the Enfield branch of the Great Northern line, and also a Congregational chapel, built of brick, after the newest style of ecclesiastical Gothic architecture. The village was converted into an ecclesiastical district, out of the civil parish of Edmonton, in 1851. The church, dedicated to St. Paul, stands at the north end of the village, and dates from the close of the reign of George IV. It was consecrated by Bishop Howley in 1828, and partly burnt down in 1844, but subsequently repaired. It is built of white brick, with stone dressings in the Perpendicular style. Crocheted pinnacles rise at each of the four corners, and a bell-turret in the centre of the gable at the western end. The church consists of simply a nave and small recessed chancel. The east window represents, in twelve medallions, the principal scenes and events in the life of St. Paul. Sharon

---

* See *ante*, p. 293.

Turner the historian, and Thomas Hood the poet, resided here for some years. Part of the village, on the east side of the railway, extends over Bush Hill, on the road towards Edmonton.

On Bush Hill was formerly held a fair, called "Beggar's Bush Fair." It was granted by King James I., when he laid out a part of Enfield Chase into Theobalds Park, and is now held at Cathol Gate, on the road leading to Northall.

Of Bush Hill Park, the principal seat in this locality, an account will be found in OLD AND NEW LONDON.* It may, however, be stated here that the property has lately been sold, and is now being laid out for the erection of villa residences. One part of it is called Sambrooke Park. The old Clock-house itself, as the mansion is called, has been sadly spoilt by its new owners, who have destroyed its best features, whitewashing its fine red brick-work, and superseding its iron gates of scroll-work by a paltry wall of modern white brick. The fine summer-house, too, said to have been designed by Inigo Jones, has been pulled down, and the materials sold, and is now (April, 1883), in the course of re-erection in the grounds of Mr. E. Ford, at the Old Park, at Enfield.

At Red Ridge, on the side of Bush Hill nearest to Enfield, Sir Hugh Myddelton resided during the formation of the New River, for the purpose of superintending the works. Some parts of the old building were standing early in the present century, although great alterations and improvements had been effected in the house. The New River was carried across the dell in the grounds by means of a wooden trough or aqueduct, upwards of 650 feet in length. This aqueduct was regarded at the time as a triumph of engineering skill; but it was removed towards the end of the last century, and an embankment thrown up in its place.

Edmonton lies about two miles eastward from Bush Hill. The name of the parish has become famous throughout the length and breadth of the land by Cowper's humorous poem descriptive of "Johnny Gilpin's Ride;" by the residence and grave of Charles Lamb; by the "Merry Devil of Edmonton;" and by the "Witch of Edmonton"—all of which matters will be found fully dealt with in the pages of OLD AND NEW LONDON.* Mr. J. T. Smith, the author of "A Book for a Rainy Day," speaks in high terms of the salubrity of the air of Edmonton, and also of its aristocratic exclusiveness:—"The resident families would not quit their mansions, but kept themselves snugly within their King William iron gates and red brick crested piers, so that there was no longer any opening for new comers, nor would the landowners allow one inch of ground to the builders."

At the Firs, in this village, lived Sir James Winter Lake, Bart., the friend and patron of Mr. J. T. Smith, and to whom he dedicated one of his many works on London. "Sir James," writes Mr. Smith, "was a governor of the Hudson Bay Company—a situation, it is well known, he filled with credit to himself as well as the satisfaction of every one connected with that highly-respected body. Sir James most kindly invited me to take a house near him at Edmonton, where I had the honour, for the space of seven years, of enjoying the steady friendship of himself and family. Lady Lake, who then retained much of her youthful beauty, by her elegance of language and extreme affability charmed every one. Their family mansion was distant about a mile from the 'Angel,' and called the 'Firs.'"

CHAPTER XXXVI.
ENFIELD.

"The Enfield House, that 'longes unto our Queene,
They all behold, and with due reverence
Salute the same."—VALLENS' *Tale of Two Swannes.*

General Description of the Parish—Situation and Boundaries—Parochial Divisions—The Town and Principal Streets—Enfield Court—The New River—Railway Stations—Census Returns—Historical Reminiscences—The Barony of Enfield—Descent of the Manor—Fairs and Markets—Site of the Old Manor House—Camlet Moat—Oldbury—Edward VI. at Enfield—The Palace—Dr. Uvedale—The Market-place—The Parish Church—The Free Grammar School—Schools of Industry—John Keats's Schooldays—Charitable Institutions—Old Park—Chase Park—Chase Side House—Enfield Green—Little Park—Beycullah' Park—Enfield Races—Churches and Chapels—The Cemetery—Forty Hall—Elsynge Hall—Sir Walter Raleigh and Queen Elizabeth—Anne Countess of Pembroke—Myddelton House—Gough Park—Distinguished Residents—Beautiful Women of Enfield.

ENFIELD is one of the many suburban villages whose names are, or have been, associated with royalty, though not to the same extent as Hampton or Richmond. Built upon the fringe of a royal chase, Enfield is just what the old writers would have styled "a right pleasant and joyous place," though somewhat sleepy and quiet in its appearance. Especially in the central square, near the Church Grammar School, High Cross, and Palace, it is decidedly old-fashioned ; and its outlying mansions, for the most part, are such as to keep them company. Once inhabited by princes, and lords and fair ladies, it still wears a courtly look ; and it is not difficult to fancy the youthful princess Elizabeth riding along the pleasant roads which lead in the direction of that Chase which, alas ! is now a chase only in name.

the parishes which we have visited in our perambulations, for it has numbered among its residents, besides two at least of the sovereigns of England, for longer or shorter periods, such celebrities as Sir Walter Raleigh, Isaac Disraeli, Gough the antiquary, Dr. Abernethy, Charles Babbage, Captain Marryatt, and Charles Lamb ; and the annals of the neighbourhood are connected with many other important personages distinguished in the general history of the country.

The parish is nine miles distant from London,

ENFIELD CHURCH. (*From an old Print*, 1827.)

In many, though perhaps scarcely in most places, the "parish" and the "manor" were identical in their limits, but this could hardly be the case in such a widespread locality as Enfield, nearly twenty miles in circumference. On the contrary, it comprised, apparently, no less than eight separate manors, two of which, in old times, were appanages to royalty, viz., Enfield (proper), Durants, or Durants Harbour, Elsynge *alias* Norris or North Farm, Suffolks, Honylands, and Pentriches *alias* Capels, Goldbeaters, Worcesters, and the Rectory Manor. The two royal manors were those of Enfield and Worcesters, each of which had its own palace and park. Enfield is richer in historic and literary associations than many of

almost due north, and it is bounded on the east by a branch of the River Lea, called the Meereditch or Mardyke ; on the west by Hadley and South Mimms ; on the north by Northaw and Theobalds Park, in Hertfordshire ; and on the south by Edmonton and Southgate. From east to west its measurement is between eight and nine miles, and from north to south it is rather more than three miles by the main road, although in some parts it ranges from five to six miles. Norden describes Enfield as "a parish standing on the edge of the Chase, of such extent, that if it were measured by the ring it would be found at least twenty miles in extent, some time parcell of the Duke of Lancaster's lands, now Queene Elizabeth's. The

Chase, called Enfield Chase, taketh its name of this place."

"Few districts in the vicinity of London," writes Mr. Edward Ford in his "History of Enfield," "retain so much of rural and sequestered character, owing no doubt in part to its formerly tedious and circuitous means of access. Since the opening of two new lines of railway, however, this

BEACH HILL CIRC. 1796.

isolation cannot much longer continue. The beauty and variety of the scenery, the upland Chase, still so nobly timbered, the more cultivated lowlands, watered for many a mile by the windings of the New River and the Lea, and the long-sustained character of the parish for health and longevity (rating the second in England), are drawing the attention of the country-loving public to this picturesque and interesting neighbourhood. From the more elevated situations extensive prospects may be obtained in all directions over the adjoining counties—from Camlet Moat and from the Ridgeway Road across the broad expanse of the Chase; far down into Hertfordshire from the wood at Forty Hall; and away into the heart of Buckinghamshire from above Potter's Bar; and the

long range of Epping and Hainault forests from everywhere. The bridle-road across Hadley Common, perhaps the last remains of genuine forest scenery in Middlesex, leads to the highest ground in the parish, whence, looking south, distant gleams of the Thames and the white sails of its shipping may be seen in the far horizon."

The parish is separated into four quarters—namely, the Town Division, which comprises the central part of the parish and the eastern portion of Chase Side; Chase Division, which includes Windmill Hill, the west half of Chase Side, and the whole of Enfield Chase; Bull's Cross Division, embracing Forty Hill, Bull's Cross, and the north-eastern

MYDDELTON HOUSE CIRC. 1821.

section of the parish, stretching away to Enfield Wash; and Green Street Division, which includes Ponder's End, Green Street, and Enfield Highway.

Enfield, on the whole, it is scarcely necessary to state, is a widely-scattered place. It is more than a village, and something less than a town. True, it has its market-place and its square, at one corner of which are painted up in large letters the words "The Town;" but it has nothing that can be styled a High Street, being laid out on the most irregular of plans, if plan it can be called. It is a large cluster of gentlemen's seats and substantial houses of the Dutch and Queen Anne style, with high-browed doorways and heavy-sashed windows, standing for the most part near the road, and screened off from it by lofty red-brick walls and iron gates, some of which afford really handsome specimens of iron scroll-work. Mixed up with these larger houses, in most admired confusion, are small shops and modern villas, for the most part the abodes of industrious City clerks and retired tradesmen.

The central part of the parish, comprising the town, is situated on the cross-road leading from Enfield highway in the east to Barnet and Hadley in the west. The principal feature of the town is the broad central square above mentioned, containing a market-cross and the parish church.

Baker Street and Silver Street are the names of the thoroughfares running northwards from the market-place towards Forty Hill and Cheshunt. In Baker Street is the vicarage, heavy, solid, and substantial, close to the churchyard, and opening into it; Enfield Court, the seat of Colonel Somerset; the old rectory, and Fox Hall, both remarkable for their tall iron gates, surmounted by heraldic bearings; and a quaint little square of humble cottages, occupied by the industrious classes, and dating from the seventeenth century, rejoicing in the grand name of Carterhatch Square. One side of it, however, has been cut off to make room for an unsightly Independent chapel.

Enfield Court is the most important mansion in the neighbourhood. The estate, which contains about eighty acres, was formerly part of the manor of Worcesters. The original structure dates from the latter end of the seventeenth century, since which time it has received many successive additions. The southern wing was re-built in 1864, at which time great alterations were made in the gardens and grounds. The garden on the west side of the house still bears traces of having been originally laid out in the time of William III., with its broad terrace walk 400 feet in length, and its clipped yews and hollies of the Dutch style of gardening. At the bottom of this garden stands a quaint and picturesque summer-house, a small building, having an upper chamber and a pointed roof. There is also an oblong fish-pond, crossed by a bridge, the remains of a former "canal."*

The principal thoroughfares, running north and south, extend for about two miles, and are crossed

and re-crossed by the New River, which curves and meanders, "at its own sweet will," through the parish, as if loth to leave the woodland Chase through which Sir Hugh Myddelton carried it. Its course within the limits of Enfield cannot be much short of five miles; so that it seems to belong to Enfield more truly than to any other parish in Middlesex.

The New River enters the parish at Bull's Cross in the north, and leaves it at Bush Hill in the south; and it winds about with so many twists and twirls, that it seems to have started on its course with a deliberate intention of visiting every gentleman in Enfield in succession, for really there is scarcely one mansion which has not some part of its grounds washed by its clear waters. One of these seats (Myddelton House), that of Mr. Carrington Bowles, stands on the site of a building called Bowling Green House, once the abode of Sir Hugh Myddelton, to whom the New River may be said to owe its existence. Its history from the time when, in the reign of King James I., the above-mentioned worthy knight persuaded the Common Council of London to transfer to him the power granted by certain Acts then recently passed enabling them to convey a stream of water to London from any part of Middlesex, will be found fully described in OLD AND NEW LONDON.* Sir Hugh Myddelton, who, as we have seen in the preceding chapter, lived at Winchmore Hill whilst superintending the formation of this river, offered, in four years, at his own risk and charge, to bring the Chadwell and Amwell springs from Hertfordshire up to London, by a route more than thirty-eight miles long; and the work was completed in September, 1613. The "Third Report of the Historical MSS. Commission" gives a melancholy proof, if proof be needed, of the injustice with which this benefactor of London was treated by his fellow-citizens. The patriotic goldsmith, who spent his whole fortune in procuring a priceless boon for the Londoners, never received any recompense for his skill and labour; and Lysons tells us that within the memory of his own generation the last male descendant of Sir Hugh was allowed by them to become a pensioner on the bounty of the New River Company. Verily, virtue in this country is too often its own sole reward!

Enfield Highway, the most easterly division of the parish, stretches along the Hertford road from Ponder's End in the south-east, to Enfield Wash and Bullsmoor Lane in the north-east, and will be more fully dealt with in a subsequent chapter. It

---

* See "Old and New London," Vol. IV., p. 50.

* See Vol. II., p. 266, and Vol. V., pp. 430 and 538.

is connected with the town by numerous lanes and thoroughfares. The River Lea and the Lea and Stort Navigation both flow through the marsh land, a short distance to the east of Enfield Highway. Here, on the banks of the Lea, about a mile distant from the Wash, stands the Royal Small Arms Factory. This, too, we shall presently describe in detail.

Chase Side, as the western division is called, slopes up gradually from the town towards Trent Park (or Cock Fosters) and Beech Hill Park, and so on to Hadley.

Railway communication with the metropolis has of late years been the cause of a great extension of the town in almost all directions, particularly at Chase Side. Here, on Windmill Hill, the Great Northern Railway has the terminus of a short branch line; and close by the "Nag's Head" inn, near the centre of the town, is the terminus of a branch line of the Great Eastern Railway; whilst at Ponder's End, and at the Ordnance Factory, are stations on the main line itself, affording easy communication with Enfield Highway and the eastern parts of the parish.

The parish contains altogether 12,650 acres, inclusive of the Chase, 350 acres of which were enclosed by Act of Parliament in 1801. In 1871 the population was rather over 1,600, to which about 3,000 were added during the next ten years.

The general appearance of the main road running north and south through the town, with its numerous antiquated cottages and mansions, which have been inhabited by generations long since passed away, is quite in keeping with its historical associations, which are by no means small or unimportant.

Almost immediately on the accession of Mary, the jealous Queen sent for her sister Elizabeth, who was at Ashridge on the borders of Hertfordshire and Buckinghamshire, peremptorily ordering her attendance at Court. The Princess, being ill, was obliged to travel in the Queen's own litter, and the rate of progress was so slow that she took four days in making a little less than thirty miles. She was carried, by easy stages, by way of Enfield to Highgate, where she was met by a large number of her friends.

In 1603, when James VI. of Scotland made his triumphal entry into London as James I. of England, his route from Theobalds lay along the road through Forty Hill and the town. "All the road from Enfield to Stamford Hill was lined and thronged with people. I heard many greyheads speak it, that in all the meetings they had seen or heard of, they had never heard or seen the tenth mass of those that were to be seen that day betwixt Enfield and London. Every place in this space was so clogged with company, that His Highness could not pass without pausing, ofttimes willingly enforced, though more willing to have proceeded, if conveniently he could without peril to his beloved people." Such are the fulsome comments of Mr. John Savile on the King's first "progress."

The scenery all round the town is delightfully rural and pleasant, particularly towards the south, in those parts through which we have journeyed hither. H. Crabb Robinson writes in his "Diary":—"I followed a path to Winchmore Hill, and another to Enfield—the last through some of the richest verdure I ever saw. The hills exquisitely undulating, with very fine clumps of oak-trees. . . . Enfield town, the large white church, the serpentine New River, Mr. Mellish's house [Bush Hill Park], with its woody appendages, form a singularly beautiful picture. . . . . Before dinner we lounged round the Green, and saw the cedar of Lebanon which once belonged to Queen Elizabeth's palace, of which only a chimney remains." This last statement, we must add, is not quite accurate.

Enfield conferred the title of Baron on the Nassaus, Earls of Rochfort, the first of whom married a daughter of Sir Henry Wroth, of Durants, and was created Baron of Enfield by William III. in 1695. It now gives the title of Viscount to the Earl of Strafford, whose estates adjoin the Chase.

In Domesday Book the parish is called Enefelde, and the variation in spelling in subsequent records are very trifling—as Endfield, Enfeld, Enefield, Envild, and, lastly, Enfield. As to its etymology, Norden says, "It is called of some Enfen, and so recorded in regarde of the fenny scytuation of some parte thereof, upon the marshes or meerish ground, which, though now brought to be good meadow and profitable pasture, it hath in time past been fenny." "This statement," Mr. Ford observes, in his work above quoted, "is not supported by any authority. The termination 'field' is the past participle of the verb 'fællan,' to fell, and opposed to woodland, as land where the trees have been cleared."

It is stated in the "Domesday Survey" that in the time of Edward the Confessor the manor of 'Enefelde' was held by Asgar, master of the horse to the king, who was likewise lord of the neighbouring manor of Edmonton. At the time of this survey this manorial district was possessed by Geoffrey de Mandeville, from whose family it descended to Humphrey de Bohun, Earl of Hereford. Eleanor, Duchess of Gloucester, was the daughter and co-heiress of the last Earl of Hereford of the Bohun family; and on her death, in 1399, this manor was inherited by her sister Mary, wife of Henry, Duke of Lancaster, afterwards Henry IV. The principal manor of Enfield thus became vested in the Crown, and was shortly after annexed to the Duchy of Lancaster, of which it still continues to be parcel.

Early in the fourteenth century Edward I. granted a license to Humphrey de Bohun and his wife (Elizabeth, Countess of Holland, and the King's daughter), and their heirs, to hold a weekly market here on Mondays; and James I., in 1619, by writ of Privy Council, granted to certain persons therein named license to hold a weekly market here on Saturdays, and at the same time established a "Court of Pie Powder." The market, however, from various causes seems to have been discontinued many years ago; but several ineffectual attempts have been made to revive it, and the very name of "Pie Powder" has been long forgotten.

Two fairs were formerly held in the town annually, in August and November. The first, which, from some unknown cause, had latterly been held in September, and had long ceased to answer any legitimate purposes of trade, but had become a source of lawlessness and disorder, and having grown a nuisance to the inhabitants of the town, was abolished in 1869, on a petition from the leading residents. The other fair, held on St. Andrew's Day, was at one time celebrated as a cheese-fair, but is now chiefly frequented for the sale of horses and cattle.

Richard II. granted to the inhabitants an exemption from certain tolls for their goods and merchandise, and various other privileges, in " all fairs, markets, villages, and other places throughout England, out of the Duchy of Lancaster, in the county of Middlesex." It is stated, however, observes Mr. Ford, that this exemption has been resisted in Covent Garden and Whitechapel markets. The above grant was confirmed and extended by Henry IV. and Henry VI., and other sovereigns, down to George III. An exemption from toll at Ware Bridge was also granted to the inhabitants of Enfield by Queen Elizabeth, and subsequently confirmed by George III.

It is curious, observes Mr. Ford in a supplement to his " History of Enfield," to compare the valuation here given of the mansion and manor of Enfield in the reign of Edward III. with the appraisement, in the same reign, of Holland House and the manor of Kensington, and to note the much higher value of both land and houses in the then much more fashionable and aristocratic suburb of

Enfield, the former standing at 32s. 10d., whilst the latter is only 7s. The yearly value of the mansion and dove-house at Kensington is less than that of the Enfield dove-house alone, and the value of woodland per acre is only one-tenth of that of the old park at Enfield.

The site of the original manor house of Enfield has long been a subject of antiquarian research. Camden says that " almost in the middle of the Chase there are the ruins and rubbish of an ancient house, which the common people from tradition affirm to have belonged to the Mandevilles, Earls of Essex." At a short distance from the West Lodge, Trent Park, near the road which leads over the Chase towards Hadley, are still in existence traces of the site above alluded to; it is called Camlet Moat, and is a large quadrangular area, overgrown with briars and bushes. When measured, in 1773, the length of the moat was 150 feet. In describing these remains, Mr. Ford observes that " at the north-east corner is a deep well, paved at the bottom, in which it is pretended lies an iron chest full of treasure, which cannot be drawn up to the top, and that the last owner to whom the Chase belonged being attainted of treason, hid himself in a hollow tree, and falling into this well perished miserably. . . . . The tiles scattered over the area, the well, and the traces of the enclosures and avenues, would seem to be rather the works of the fifteenth or sixteenth centuries than of any earlier period." Here Sir Walter Scott brings some of the characters in " The Fortunes of Nigel," and the place has been, as a matter of course, invested with something of the glamour of his marvellous genius in consequence. It is now almost the only spot where any trace of the original wildness of Enfield Chase can be met with.

In Dugdale's " Baronage " it is stated that Humphrey de Bohun, Earl of Hereford, procured, in 1347, the king's license to fortify his manor house at Enfield. In a meadow to the east of the church, near to " Nag's Head " lane, there are traces of a moat and extensive embankments, with an artificial mount. Lysons and other topographers suppose that these are the remains of Humphrey de Bohun's castle, and that when the manorial residence was removed it acquired the name of " Oldbury," by which it is still known.

Early in the sixteenth century the site of the manor was leased to private individuals; but the lease appears to have reverted to the Crown towards the latter part of the reign of Henry VIII., at which time the house was retained as a royal residence. At that time the original manor house of the Bohuns had fallen into decay, and the royal children, Edward and Elizabeth, were brought up at Elsynge Hall (called also Enfield House), which belonged to the manor of Worcesters.

Here Edward VI. was living when prince, and here he was waited on by many of the Scottish nobility, who had been brought to London as prisoners after the defeat at Solway Firth, and tendered him their homage as destined by the arbitrary king, whose heir he was, to become in due time the husband of the infant Princess Mary of Scotland. But, though a Tudor proposes, God disposes.

At the death of Henry VIII., Prince Edward was living at Hertford, but was shortly after conducted to Enfield, where the Princess Elizabeth was then living, and it was not till then that he was made acquainted with the fact of his father's death, and consequently of his own accession to the throne. On the following Monday Edward was conducted to London. In the State Paper Office is a letter from the Earl of Hertford to the Council: "From Envild this Sunday night att xj. of the clok." He writes, "We intend the King's Matie shal be a horsbak to-morrow by xj. of the clok, so that by iij. we trust His Grace shal be att the Tower."

The following anecdote connected with the garden of the palace at this period is extracted from Tuft's "History of Enfield":—"There is one very remarkable feature connected with Enfield Palace that has come to light but recently. It was in the garden at Enfield that the Earl of Hertford took the opportunity of communicating to his companion, the master of the horse, *his intention to assume the office of Protector*, in contravention to the late King's will, which had designated eighteen executors, with equal powers.

"We are told that, 'after commoning in discourse of the state,' Sir Anthony 'gave his frank consent to the proposal;' upon which, as we learn from another letter, Hertford had previously 'devised' with Secretary Paget, who was now left at Court to arrange matters with the other counsellors.

"Edward was not again at Enfield Palace during his reign, but his sister, Elizabeth, continued to reside here; and there is mention also of the Queen Dowager (Katharine Parr) paying Enfield a visit."

William Wightman writes thus to Secretary Cecil:—"Myne old master, the master of th' orses, albeit, as is commonly known, he did much dissent from the proceedings in matters of religion, yet was I long sins by himself right well assured that he, commoning with my Lordes Grace *in the garden at Endfielde*, at the King's Majesties coom-

ing from Hartforde, gave his franke consent, after communication in discourse of the state, that His Grace should be Protector, thinking it (as indede it was) both the surest kynde of government, and most fyt for this commonwelth." [*]

And again, another courtier, Paget, writes to the Protector Somerset [†] :—"Remember what you promised me in the gallery at Westminster, before the breath was out of the body of the King that dead is. Remember what you promised immediately after, *devising with me concerning the place which you now occupy*, I trust in the end to good purpose, however things thwart now."

About the middle of the sixteenth century the manor of Enfield was settled by Edward on the Princess Elizabeth, at which time it is considered probable that he either built, or re-built, on the site of a former structure, the house known as the Palace, some portion of which is still standing on the south side of the High Street, opposite the church and market-place. This house was of red brick, with stone dressings. The principal front of the palace faced the north, and is described by Dr. Robinson, in his "History of Enfield," as consisting of a centre and two wings, with bay windows and high gables. The wings were decorated with the arms of England, crowned and supported by a lion and dragon, with the letters E. R. at the sides. The north-east side of the building, of which an engraving is given in Dr. Robinson's work, was of two storeys, and had a boldly-projecting bay in the centre, terminating in a tall gable, and stone-mullioned square-headed windows.

The greater part of the palace was demolished towards the close of the last century, and the materials were made use of for building purposes. A warrant was issued in 1608 for paying the expenses of taking down what was then called the King's House at Enfield. The materials were by the same order directed to be conveyed to Theobalds, in Cheshunt, there to be used in the intended buildings in course of erection. How any part came to be retained *in situ* is a fact not to be traced in the muniments or records of the period. Considerably later on a further demolition ensued; and alterations—certainly not improvements—were made, not only in the interior, but in the exterior. What still remains is almost obscured from public view by houses and shops built in front of it, and bears externally nothing to denote any semblance to the residence of royalty, so thorough and complete has been the change effected from the

* "Literary Remains of King Edward VI." (printed for the Roxburghe Club, 1558), p. ccxlvii.
† *Ibid*, p. lxxxvi.

mediæval aspect of the ancient dwelling. "Notwithstanding the great alterations which it has undergone, the interior still preserves some vestiges of its ancient magnificence, and a part of one of the large rooms on the ground floor remains nearly in its original state, with its fine fretted panels of oak, and its ornamental ceiling, with pendants of four spreading leaves, and enrichments of the crown, the rose, and the fleur-de-lis. The chimney-piece is of stone, beautifully cut, and supported by Ionic and Corinthian columns, decorated with foliage and birds, and the rose and portcullis, crowned with

the Princess Elizabeth to her brother, Edward VI. It is dated "Enfield, Feb. 14," the year, however, is not recorded. Could it have been sent as a valentine? Other letters by Elizabeth, dated from the same place, are preserved in the Bodleian Library at Oxford. When she became queen at the death of her sister Mary, Elizabeth did not forget her former residence, but frequently went there, holding her court, and enjoying the sport of hunting on the beautiful free and open Chase. That she was well acquainted with the condition of the forest trees growing in her demesne is

QUEEN ELIZABETH'S PALACE, ENFIELD, 1568.

THE PALACE, FROM THE NORTH.

the arms of England and France quarterly in a garter, and the royal supporters, a lion and a dragon. Below is the motto, 'Sola salus servire Deo; sunt cætera fraudes.' The letters E. R. are on this chimney-piece, and were formerly on each side of the wings of the principal building. The monogram is clearly that of Edward VI., as the same room contains part of another chimney-piece, which was removed from one of the upper apartments, with nearly the same ornaments, and the motto, 'Vt ros super herbam est benevolentia Regis,' alluding, no doubt, to the royal grant. Several of the ceilings in the upper rooms are decorated in a similar manner to those below." Among these, the principal are the drawing-room and some sleeping apartments, now used as the boys' bedrooms, for the building has for many years served the purposes of a school.

Among the collection of royal letters in the British Museum there is one * in Latin, written by

evidenced by a letter dated Dec. 30, 1570, wherein she authorises Sir Ralph Sadleir to deliver to Sir William Cecil certain oak timber trees, all to be taken out of the manor of Enfield. Queen Elizabeth was here from the 8th to the 22nd of September, 1561, and again from the 25th to the 30th of July, 1564. The court was here again in July, 1568. Some years later on the queen quitted the Manor House, and fixed her residence at Elsynge Hall.

In 1582 Enfield Palace was leased by Queen Elizabeth to a private gentleman, and did not again revert to the Crown during her reign. From

* Harl. MSS., No. 6986, p. 14.

1600 to 1623 it appears to have been held by Lord William Howard; and in 1629 it was granted by Charles I. to Edward Ditchfield and others, as trustees for the City of London, by whom it was afterwards conveyed to Sir Nicholas Raynton, who is commemorated by a handsome monument in the church. About the year 1660 the palace was let to Dr. Robert Uvedale, master of the Grammar School, who acquired great fame in his day for his knowledge of the science of botany, and had some distinguished pupils in his house as boarders.

An account of Dr. Uvedale's garden is given in the "Archæologia,"* and in Pulteney's "Anecdotes of Botany" mention is made of a plant called *Uvedalia*, out of compliment to him.

In Robinson's "History of Enfield" the following singular story is told relating to the above-mentioned pedagogue and botanist :—"Dr. Uvedale, in the great plague of 1665, as a preventive against its fatal effects, caused a brick to be put into the fire over night, and the next morning, when red hot, poured a quart of vinegar on it, and placed it in the middle of the hall floor, the steam of which was received by the whole family standing round. They then went to prayers, and afterwards, locking up the house, walked to Winchmore Hill, and on their return went to school. By this precaution not one of the family caught the infection."

A curious knife, found here, is figured and described in the *Gentleman's Magazine*, Vol. IX., page 595. Probably it may have belonged to some of Dr. Uvedale's aristocratic pupils.

In the garden stands a magnificent specimen of the cedar of Lebanon. It cannot claim to be of the time of Queen Elizabeth, having been planted by Dr. Uvedale soon after he took the premises. This worthy, being a scholar and a distinguished botanist, took much pride in his collection of flowers and plants of all kinds. In the year 1793, at three feet from the ground, it is stated to have measured twelve feet in girth, and since then has increased. It was greatly injured by a severe storm in 1794, and lost one of its best branches. It is certainly one of the largest specimens of the cedar known in this country; some say that it is the finest. It may be seen from many points round about Enfield.

The greater part of the palace was pulled down by Dr. Callaway, it having been struck by lightning; he is said to have designed cutting down the cedar also; but he desisted from his intention on account of the remonstrances of the inhabitants.

The market-place is a large open space in the centre of the town, and in the last century must have been highly picturesque. On the south side stood the palace above described, its gardens bordering the main street, which passes through the town westward at this point. On the east side of the square were in former times the open market and shambles, the south-east corner being occupied by a large hostelry called the "King's Head," with a quaintly-gabled front, and its signboard swinging from an elaborate iron standard. This building is no longer an inn, but is now used as offices by a firm of solicitors, and as the office of the Local Board; it also serves the magistrates as a house

THE OLD MARKET HOUSE, ENFIELD.
(*From Dr. Robinson's "Enfield."*)

for the local petty sessions. A new "King's Head" has sprung up in its place at the south-west corner of the churchyard. The "King's Head" is the most common of all loyal signs, and is most frequently to be met with where the footprints of "bluff King Hal" may be traced. Hence it could hardly fail to be the chief sign in Enfield. In spite of his savage cruelty, still his face and figure, the impersonation of jollity and good cheer, made the royal tyrant popular at all events on the confines of every royal chase.

The old market-house, of which a drawing is given in Dr. Robinson's "Enfield," was a wooden building of an octagonal form, supported by eight columns and a central pillar. There were also a portable pillory and stocks in the market-place, both of which were long ago removed. The stocks, however, found a permanent settlement close by the police-station. The present market-cross—a gingerbread example of the "Strawberry Hill" Gothic, a poor imitation of its neighbours at

Waltham and Tottenham—was built in 1826, at a cost of about £200, which was raised by a subscription among the inhabitants. The structure is built of brick, thickly coated with cement; it stands on an octagonal platform of steps, and is enclosed by iron railings; at the sides are inscriptions recording the date of its erection, and also the date of the several charters granting the market. The cross was restored in 1866, but is again in a somewhat dilapidated condition.

The parish church, dedicated to St. Andrew, stands within a spacious churchyard, on the north side of the market-place. It dates from the thirteenth century, and consists of a chancel, clerestoried nave, aisles, and towers at the west end containing a peal of eight bells. Some of the windows are filled with stained glass. The exterior of the church is somewhat poor and bare, having been "restored" in the very dawn of the Gothic revival, when it was plastered over neatly with cement. There are several engravings of the church in the last century and in the early part of this, showing it with the east window blocked up, and a quaint old parvise, or muniment-room, with a projecting gable, and a sun-dial surmounting the south porch. The fine yew-tree near the south chancel window was at that time cropped into a formal triangle, after the fashion of those which we have seen at Harlington and Bedfont. The embattled tower, built of flint and rubble, with stone quoins in three stages, gradually tapering and without buttresses, has lost much of its ancient appearance by the alteration of its windows in the two lower stages, and by its walls being cased in cement. Inside its proportions are fine, but they are marred by the intrusion of some unsightly galleries. Though the organ has been removed to the east end of the south aisle, yet its "case" still grins down upon the congregation from a gallery across the west end—a tribute to the prejudices of some of the more old-fashioned parishioners. The walls between the arches and the clerestory are coloured with a delicate tint, and stencilled with an effective pattern. These decorations are modern.

The chancel is separated from the nave by a lofty arch, and in the chancel are sedilia and piscina, erected in 1852, in the place of others discovered during some alterations in the building. A lancet-window and hagioscope in the south wall of the chancel were opened during a restoration of the church in 1866, at which time the church was new roofed throughout. Over the arches of the nave are placed alternately the devices of a rose and wing, which are also found on the tower of Hadley Church.* Lysons, in his "Environs of

London," supposes that these emblems had some connection with the Abbey of Walden; but Mr. Ford, in his history of the parish, says "there can be no doubt but that a rose and wing were borne as badges by Sir Thomas Lovell, K.G., who, on the death of Lord Roos, in 1508, without issue, succeeded to the Manor of Worcesters, in right of his wife Isabella, sister to Lord Roos." Pennant mentions in his "Itinerary" that in his time the same emblems, a rose and a wing, were to be seen on a wall which formerly belonged to Holiwell Nunnery, in Shoreditch, to which Sir Thomas Lovell was a great benefactor, and where he was buried in 1524, after his body had been laid in state in Enfield church, on the way from Elsynge Hall to London.

In the year 1777, when the chancel was undergoing alterations, a very curious allegorical picture was discovered, representing the Resurrection, in six compartments, painted on wood; this singular piece of Church antiquity was given to Mr. Gough the antiquarian, who was then residing at Enfield.

The oldest and most interesting monument in the church is that of Joyce, Lady Tiptoft, who died in 1446. She was mother of the learned Earl of Worcester, and wife of Sir John Tiptoft, nephew of Robert, the last Lord Tiptoft. The monument is a large altar-tomb under the easternmost arch on the north side of the chancel, and over it is a stone canopy of later date. The tomb is covered with a slab of grey Purbeck marble, inlaid with a very fine brass, in good preservation, representing the figure of the deceased richly attired in the fashion of the time. She wears an heraldic mantle, and over her head is a triple canopy, on the pillars of which are the arms of Tiptoft, Powes, Holland, and Charlton. Round the edge of the slab is a brass fillet, at the corners of which were the four evangelistic symbols, though only one— that of St. Matthew—now remains. In Dr. Robinson's work, published in 1823, three are represented. The words of the inscription are divided by representations of birds, beasts, fishes, &c. The canopy over the tomb is supposed to have been erected by Thomas, first Earl of Rutland, either as a memorial of Edmund, Lord Roos, or as a memorial of his sister Isabel, Lady Lovell. This monument is enriched with gold and colouring; it was restored a few years ago by the Duke of Rutland, who is a representative of the Roos family.

In the north chancel aisle is a large and richly-

---

* See *ante*, p. 328.

decorated monument of Sir Nicholas Raynton, of Forty Hall, sometime Lord Mayor of London, who died in 1646, and of his wife Rebecca, who died six years previously. Sir Nicholas is represented in armour, reclining under a canopy, supported by two columns of black marble, in his robes as Lord Mayor; and below him is an effigy of his wife in a similar posture, holding a book in her left hand. Below these again are the figures of his son and his son's wife and their four children. One of the fine Jacobean monuments is "skied" up into the south-west corner of the gallery.

John Abernethy, the eminent surgeon, who died at Enfield in 1831, is commemorated by a mural monument.

On the floor are brasses of William Smith and Jane, his wife, "who served King Henry VIII., Edward VI., Queen Marie, and now Queen Elizabeth." He died in 1592, leaving £4 out of his land "to be given to the godlie poore of Enfield."

There is a beautiful monument on the north chancel pier to the memory of Mrs. Martha Palmer, one of the Palmers of Dorney. It is mentioned by Horace Walpole as the handiwork of Nicholas Stone, sculptor and master-mason to James I., and greatly celebrated for his works. Vertue quotes from his pocket-book an entry of the cost of this monument: "Mrs. Palmer, at Enfield, £16."

Previous to the last restoration of the church, in 1866, there was a brass in the floor of the chancel, inscribed to the memory of Ann, daughter of Richard Gery, Esq., of Bushmead, Bedfordshire, with the following curious epitaph :—

> " Here lies interr'd
> One that scarce err'd ;
> A virgin modest, free from folly ;
> A virgin knowing, patient, holy ;
> A virgin blest with beauty here ;
> A virgin crown'd with glory there :
> Holy virgins, read, and say,
> We shall hither all one day.
>   Live well, ye must
>   Be turn'd to dust."

The vestry, at the north-east corner of the church, is supposed to have formerly constituted a chantry-chapel. Chantries were founded in this church by Baldwyn de Radyngton in 1398, and for the souls of Robert Blossom and Agnes, his wife, in the reign of Edward IV.

At the east end of the churchyard, near the entrance to the vicarage garden, is the tomb of Lord and Lady Napier of Merchistoun. On the grave-stone of John White, Surveyor to the New River Company, is the following quaint epitaph :—

> " Here lies John White, who, day by day,
> On river works did use much clay,
> Is now himself turning that way :
> If not to clay, yet dust will come,
> Which to preserve takes little room,
> Although enclos'd in this great tomb.
> I served the New River Company, as Surveyor, from Lady-day, 1691, to Midsummer, 1723."

The vicarage has numbered among its occupants but few, if any, whose names have become famous in history. We may, however, state that the Rev. Wm. Roberts was ejected from the living of Enfield by the Parliamentary Commissioners in 1642, and that Dr. Maclagan, now Bishop of Lichfield, was for some few years curate-in-charge of the parish, before becoming rector of Newington and vicar of Kensington. He had previously been an officer in the Indian army.

On the west side of the churchyard stands the Free Grammar School, which was founded in the sixteenth century. The school-house was rebuilt in the seventeenth century. It is a large, old-fashioned red-brick building, with dormer windows ; modern sash-windows have superseded the old stone-mullioned frames. The management of the school is in accordance with a scheme drawn up in 1873 by the Endowed Schools' Commissioners, and it is under a board of local gentlemen as governors.

The Established Church and the Dissenters at Enfield have each their "School of Industry," founded in 1806. The former stands in Silver Street, and the latter in Baker Street. A handsome new building for the Church school was opened in 1876, its foundation stone having been laid by Miss Somerset. The school, which had been carried on for seventy years in "The Old Coffee House," now accommodates one hundred children, who are taught washing, cooking, and housework, to fit them for domestic service.

At a school kept here by a Mr. Clarke, John Keats spent the greater part of his childhood and boyhood, from five to fifteen. Here, on half-holidays, when the rest of the boys were at cricket, he would remain indoors, translating his Virgil or his Fénelon. If his master forced him to go out and take exercise, he would walk up and down the garden, book in hand—Shakespeare, or Lempriére's "Dictionary," or Spence's *Polymetis*, or "Robinson Crusoe." He left this school in 1810 to be apprenticed to Mr. Hammond, a surgeon, at Edmonton. The story of the rest of his short life, spent at Hampstead,* in London, and in Italy, is known to most English readers.

This parish is well off for charitable institutions,

almshouses, &c. ; and there are also a large number of chapels for Nonconformists of different denominations.

On the south side of the town, near the Great Northern Railway station, is Old Park, so called to distinguish it from the Little Park, or New Park, on the northern side of the parish. The estate, as we learn from Mr. Ford's " Enfield," " was formerly the Home Park of the ancient manorial palace of Enfield, at which the Princess Elizabeth resided." From a survey of 1650, the house appears to have been then a ranger's lodge, and from the remains of massive foundations in every direction, must have been of considerable extent ; but the greater part of the original structure has long since been pulled down, and the remainder transformed into a comparatively modern residence of the early Hanoverian period. In the library still remain the original open chimney and hearth, with fire-dogs, and a "reredos," with figures of the time of James I. There are also several interesting curiosities, autographs of the queen, &c. ; and the original statuette of Oliver Goldsmith, the *chef-d'œuvre* of Foley, graces his library.

The park, about 200 acres in extent, is well wooded, and the lawn in front of the house is surrounded on three sides by a circular entrenchment, from which various interesting relics have at different times been obtained. It is mentioned by Camden as the site of an ancient Roman Oppidum.

A long lease of the Old Park was granted by the merry monarch, on his restoration, to Monk, Duke of Albemarle; but reverting to the Crown on the death of his successor's wife, the second duchess, it was bestowed by William III., in the first year of his reign, upon John, ninth Earl of Rutland. It afterwards passed through the hands of the Clayton and Lewis families; it is now the seat of Mr. Edward Ford, upon whose " History of Enfield" we have drawn so largely in this chapter.

Chase Park, the original house of which stood near the entrance lodge from Chase Green, was formerly part of the Old Park estate. The present mansion, which has been many years in the possession of the Adams family, was built in 1822, about which time the New River Company, under a mutual agreement, formed an ornamental sheet of water in front of the house.

The estate of Chase Side House, the seat of Mrs. Twells, widow of Mr. Philip Twells, M.P., was also originally part of the Old Park, which formerly extended as far as the town, and included the palace, with its gardens, &c. The part of the town in which this property lies was, in the seventeenth century, known as Enfield Green, the pre-

sent green being at that time a portion of the unenclosed Chase ; and, as Mr. Ford tells us, down to the present century several trees were still standing, marking the former boundary of the Old Park. In the middle of the seventeenth century Sir Robert Jason was living at Enfield Green, in a house probably occupying the site of the present Chase Side House.

The present green is a broad open space of turf, environed with a few trees, and skirted on the east side by the picturesque windings of the New River, which is here crossed by two or three bridges. It is a pleasant spot, and lies midway between the town and the Great Northern Railway station, on the gentle slope which begins to rise towards Windmill Hill and the Ridgeway. It has long been a favourite lounge. " I sunned myself," writes Henry Crabb Robinson in his " Diary," " on the beautiful Enfield Green."

Thomas Trevor, of Enfield Green, was created a baronet in 1641, and made a Knight of the Bath at the coronation of Charles II. He was the grandson of John Trevor of Trevallin, in Denbighshire, ancestor of the Viscounts Hampden, and son of Sir Thomas Trevor, Chief Baron of the Exchequer.

Little Park, lying between the church and the Chase Side, was built in 1750–60. It is the property of Mr. Cornelius Walford, the eminent authority on insurance matters and other social subjects. The old road from the church to the Chase is said to have passed between some fine dark pine-trees on the estate.

On the west of Enfield, on the hill leading up from the green towards the Ridgeway, and close to the Great Northern Railway station, is Beycullah Park—now being laid out for the erection of villas —where the Enfield races were held. They have, however, been lately given up, much to the satisfaction of the more respectable portion of the community. It is said that this was the first place in the kingdom at which horse-racing was established ; and the statement is probably true, on account of its vicinity to the court held by James I. at Theobalds, near Cheshunt. The races were then called " Bell-courses," because the prize was a silver bell, afterwards altered into a cup. Hence comes the phrase, " to bear the bell."

In this part of Enfield a new church (St. Mary Magdalene) has been erected, at the expense of Mrs. Twells, of Chase Side. It is built of stone, in the Perpendicular style, with a bright red-tiled roof. It consists of a clerestoried nave, aisles, transepts, and chancel, and has a tower with a tall spire, which forms a conspicuous object on all sides. Christchurch Congregational Chapel, at Chase

Side, was built in 1878. It is in the Early English style, and has a tower surmounted by a tall tapering spire. St. Michael's Church, at Chase Side, was consecrated in 1874, as a chapel-of-ease to the parish church. It is built of Kentish rag-stone, with Bath stone dressings, and consists of a chancel and nave, with aisles, and a tower at the western end.

The church of St. John the Baptist, at Clay Hill, is a small building in the Early English style, constructed of brick with stone dressings, and consisting of chancel, nave, and aisles, with a bell-turret at the west end. It was erected in 1857, from the designs of Mr. J. St. Aubyn. All the windows are filled with stained glass.

The cemetery, at Brigadier Hill, is pleasantly situated on a gentle slope, overlooking Clay Hill. It covers about nine acres, and was laid out in 1872, at a cost of about £9,000.

Jesus Church, Forty Hill, at the northern end of the town, on the road towards Cheshunt, was built in 1835, at the expense of Mr. Christian P. Meyer, of Forty Hall. It is a poor imitation of the Early English style. Several of the windows are filled with stained glass; that over the altar is in memory of the founder, and one at the west end is to the memory of Dr. Weir, who held the vicarage from 1863 till his death, in 1874.

On the left hand stands Forty Hall, the seat of Mr. James Meyer. It is the manor-house of the ancient royal manor of "Worcesters."* The house is a heavy but handsome structure, built of brick early in the seventeenth century, and was erected by Inigo Jones for Sir Nicholas Raynton, but was much altered by the Wolstenholmes about the year 1700. It has finely-clustered chimney-stacks, and a lofty tiled roof, reminding the travelled reader of the châteaux of Normandy. The principal rooms are large, and have the ceilings enriched with panelling and tracery. The mansion contains a good collection of pictures by the first masters, including Rubens, Teniers, Canaletti, Annibal Caracci, Raphael, and Bassano; also a portrait of Sir Nicholas Raynton in his civic robes (1643), supposed to be by Dobson, the pupil of Vandyck. The house stands in a park nearly 300 acres in extent, many of the trees of which were full grown in the days when royal Tudors hunted here, and probably formed part of the forest of Middlesex in Plantagenet and even Norman times. The grounds are studded with several fine cedars, limes, and chestnuts, and an ornamental sheet of water in front of the house adds much to its picturesque appearance. The fine old gateway of the stables, consisting of a semicircular arch, surmounted by a pediment, and a smaller arch on either side, embattled at the top, is still standing. It is said to be the work of Inigo Jones.

The manor of Worcesters belonged, in the reign of Edward II., to the knightly family named de Enefeld, and in 1413 it passed to Sir John Tiptoft, whose descendant was the learned and well-known Earl of Worcester, the Lord High Treasurer, who lost his head in 1471 for his attachment to the house of York. "O good, blessed Lord!" says Caxton of Tiptoft, Earl of Worcester, "what grete losse was it of that noble, vertuous, and well-disposed lord. The axe did then at one blow cut off more learning than was left in the heads of all the surviving nobility."* From this family the manor obtained the name of Worcesters. It was afterwards vested in Thomas, Lord Roos of Hamlake, and in Sir Thomas Lovell, some time Treasurer of the Household. Sir Thomas resided for many years at Enfield, where he was honoured, in 1516, with a visit from Margaret, Dowager Queen of Scotland, and sister of Henry VIII. Sir Thomas died at Enfield, and was buried with great pomp in a chapel which he had founded in the Priory of Holywell. The body lay for eleven days and nights in the chapel adjoining his mansion here. It was removed on the twelfth day to the parish church, and on the following day it was conveyed to the place of interment. On the decease of Sir Thomas Lovell, the manor descended to Thomas, Earl of Rutland, by whom it was given, in 1540, to Henry VIII., together with the manor-house called Elsynge Hall, sometimes also called Enfield House, of which mention has been made above as the residence of Edward VI. and Queen Elizabeth. One of the queen's visits hither is recorded in the memoirs of Carey, Earl of Monmouth, where it is observed that in 1596 "the queen came to dinner to Enfield House, and had toils set up in the park to shoot at bucks after dinner."

Later on the manor of Worcesters was devised by the Crown to Sir Robert Cecil, first Earl of Salisbury, and by the Cecils it was alienated to Sir Nicholas Raynton, Alderman, and sometime Lord Mayor of London. From the Raynton family it passed in marriage to the Wolstenholmes, and at the end of the last century it was purchased by the family of the present owner.

Lysons states that the site of Elsynge Hall is not known for certain, but he is inclined to believe that it stood about a quarter of a mile from Forty Hall, near the stream which runs down to Enfield

---

* See *ante*, p. 348.

* Horace Walpole to Mason, September 19th, 1772.

Wash, where tradition says that Queen Mary had a "palace." He notes some irregularities in the ground, and the outlines, apparently, of some fish-ponds, as still marking the spot. Dr. Robinson, who wrote in 1823, follows suit; but Mr. Ford, in his more recent "History," places the site of this palace further west, "towards the bottom of the avenue at Forty Hall, between the house and the Maidenbridge brook. Here," he writes, "in dry seasons, the outlines of an extensive fabric may be

from the parische-church." Weever ranks it among the princely mansions heritable by the Crown; and Vallens, in his tale of "Two Swannes," as quoted in the motto to this chapter, calls it "Enfield House y^t longs unto our Queene."

The scene of the incident in the life of Sir Walter Raleigh, where he is reported to have gained the favour of Queen Elizabeth by spreading his "new plush coat" on the ground for her Majesty

FORTY HALL AND THE OLD GATEWAY. (See p. 359).

traced on the ground by the withering of the grass; and here the remains of foundations have frequently been dug up."

There can be no doubt that it was at Elsynge Hall that Elizabeth resided, when at Enfield, after her accession to the throne. Norden distinctly states that the mansion was "builded by an Earle of Worcester;" and it is described by him as being a "Howse or Palace of Queen Eli." in his map of Middlesex (1593), where it is represented as surrounded by a park paling, enclosing the "New Park," and about a mile distant from the town; a similar enclosure is placed for the "Old Park," which adjoined the manor-house of Enfield. In the account of Sir Thomas Lovell's funeral, the house is stated to have been "a good myle distant

to step upon, in order not to soil her shoes, has been variously laid at Greenwich and at Kenil-worth. Mr. Ford, however, is inclined to fix upon the grounds of Elsynge Hall as the spot where this little act of gallantry was performed. It is supposed to have taken place shortly after Raleigh left college, and it is distinctly said to have been his *first introduction* to his sovereign. At that time the queen was holding her court at Elsynge Hall, and, as Mr. Ford observes, "every native of Enfield may be excused if, with the evidence before him, he should, with more likelihood, place the scene of action on an autumnal day in 1568, in one of the forest walks of Forty Hall (then Elsynge Hall), leading along the banks of the 'Maiden Bridge Brook.'" Tradition is silent, Mr. Ford adds, as to the origin of this name, but in the earliest survey of the Chase the stream has the less romantic appellation of "Old Pond Gutter." In one of the Forty Hall deeds (temp. James I.), the bridge which crosses it is called "Cole's Bridge, otherwise Maiden's Bridge."

"When the manor of Worcesters was granted to the Cecils," observes Mr. Ford, "Elsynge Hall was reserved to the Crown; but in 1641 it was sold by Charles I., along with the 'Little Park' and 'The

and the price low. Let them repair to the Coach and Horses, Drury-lane, where they shall have speedy passage every day. The coachman's name is Richard How."*

Myddelton House, mentioned above as occupying the site of the house where Sir Hugh Myddelton lived, stands at a short distance north-east from Forty Hall, and close by Maiden Bridge.

At the upper end of Baker Street, near Forty Hill, stands a good old-fashioned family residence,

GOUGH PARK.

Warren' adjoining (part of the Duchy of Lancaster), to Philip, Earl of Pembroke and Montgomery." It was the widow of this nobleman who wrote the oft-quoted letter to Sir J. Williamson, Secretary of State, who had "presumed" to propose a candidate for her borough of Appleby:—"I have been bullied by an usurper, I have been neglected by a court, but I will not be dictated to by a subject. Your man shan't stand.—ANNE, Dorset, Pembroke, and Montgomery."

The following advertisement, which was published a few years after the death of the Earl of Pembroke, must refer to this house:—"At Enfield House are several wholesome baths erected, wet and dry, cold and moist, for several diseases; the rates are easy,

once the abode of the celebrated antiquary, Richard Gough. His father, Mr. Harry Gough, sometime M.P. for Bramber, and a director of the East India Company, &c., in 1723, purchased the property, which was much improved by his son. Mr. J. T. Smith, in his "Book for a Rainy Day," mentions having been introduced to the antiquary Gough at Forty Hill. Mr. R. Gough became possessed of this property on the death of his mother, in 1774, and continued to reside here, with the interruption of the various journeys connected with his topographical pursuits, until the time of his decease, in 1809. His extensive library

* "Perfect Passages," Oct. 22, 1632.

of valuable books (with the exception of the department of British topography, which he bequeathed to the Bodleian Library at Oxford) was sold, in pursuance of his own directions, in 1810. Mr. Gough was elected a Fellow of the Society of Antiquaries in 1767, and nominated director in 1771; he was also for some years a Fellow of the Royal Society. He was a great admirer and collector of stained glass, of which a few good specimens, the contributions of friends, were preserved in the windows of his house.

Mr. Gough's residence, still known as Gough Park, is a good two-storeyed building, clearly not built at a more recent date than Queen Anne's reign. The New River winds through the grounds, and at the front and side of the house are two handsome gates of iron scroll work.

The father of John Howard, the philanthropist and prison reformer, was living at Enfield at the beginning of the last century, but he removed to Clapton about the time of the birth of his son, which occurred in 1727.* By some writers it has been doubted whether John Howard was really born here or at Clapton. His father was apparently in good circumstances, as he "paid the fine rather than serve the office of Sheriff of London."

Another distinguished resident at Enfield was Isaac D'Israeli, the father of Lord Beaconsfield. His house, afterwards used as the Eastern Counties railway-station, was a small mansion standing in its own grounds to the east of the town. It was of the Queen Anne period, and was remarkable for the beauty of the details of its brick-work. There is a view of it in Ford's "History of Enfield." The central part of it is now in the South Kensington Museum. "My father," writes the future Lord Beaconsfield, "who came up to town to read the newspapers at the St. James's Coffee House, found their columns filled with extracts from the fortunate effusion of the hour, conjectures as to its writer, and much gossip respecting Walcot and Harley. He returned to Enfield laden with the journals, and presenting them to his parents, broke to them the intelligence that at length he was not only an author, but a successful one."

Benjamin D'Israeli, Lord Beaconsfield's grandfather, appears to have been a man of considerable wealth; he was one of the founders of the "Stock Exchange" of London, and was regarded as a rival of the Rothschilds. Indeed, it is said that on one occasion, early in the present century, the Emperor of Russia, when he required to raise a loan, applied to him for help; and it was only on

his refusal that he placed the negotiation in the hands of the house of Rothschild. He was, as Lord Beaconsfield tells us, "a man of ardent character; sanguine, courageous, speculative, and fortunate; with a temper which no disappointment could disturb, and a brain, amid reverses, full of resource. He made his fortune in the midway of life, and settled at Enfield, where he formed an Italian garden, entertained his friends, played whist with Sir Horace Mann (who was his great acquaintance, and who had known his brother at Venice as a banker), ate maccaroni (which was dressed by the Venetian consul), sang canzonettas, and notwithstanding a wife who never pardoned him for his name, and a son who disappointed all his plans, and who to the last hour of his life was an enigma to him, lived until he was nearly ninety, and then died in 1817, in the full enjoyment of prolonged existence." The date here given, however, is evidently a mistake, for in the *Gentleman's Magazine* for December, 1816, occurs the following notice of Mr. D'Israeli's death: "On the 28th of November, at Stoke Newington, in his eighty-seventh year, Benjamin D'Israeli, Esq." It is remarkable that Lord Beaconsfield never had the curiosity to pay a visit to Enfield, to see his father's house, though he mentions it in the preface to the collected edition of his father's works, quoted above.

At Chase Side Charles Lamb and his sister were living at the close of the life of the former, in 1833. One day in that month (December 19th) he strolled into the "Crown and Horseshoes" inn, as usual, and having taken a drop too much, fell down on the ground on his way home. His face was injured, and a murder having taken place on that day at Enfield, he was for a moment suspected of complicity in it. He was charged, with others, before the magistrates; but the matter was soon explained, and he was set at liberty. He died in the following year.

Major Cartwright, the distinguished politician and writer of the last century, whose burial-place at Finchley we had occasion to notice,* was a native of Enfield. Charles Babbage, the inventor of the calculating machine, passed his early years here, at a school kept by the Rev. Stephen Freeman, in "a large brick house, at the upper end of Baker Street," and where he had as a schoolfellow Captain Marryat, the naval novelist. Frederick Joyce, the inventor of the percussion-cap, was likewise a pupil at this school. Sir William Grey, Lord Bramwell, and his brother Sir Frederick J. Bramwell, the distinguished civil engineer, were edu-

---

cated at the Palace School, under Dr. May. Sir Ralph Abercromby was educated here, by the same master as Isaac D'Israeli. Mrs. André, the mother of the unfortunate Major André, lived at Forty Hill, as also did Dr. Birkbeck.

The unfortunate Lady Cathcart, who was forcibly abducted from Tewin Water by her husband, Colonel Maguire, who imprisoned her in Ireland, was a native of Enfield, being a daughter of one Mr. Malyn, of the Chase, a partner in the brewery in Southwark which afterwards was Thrale's. It is said that Sir Richard Steele, meeting her, when quite young, on horseback in the Chase, was so struck with her beauty that he could never forget it, and that he always regarded her as the pattern of loveliness. She died in 1789. The story of her abduction is told in the "Tales of Great Families" (2nd series). She was met by her Tewin-bury tenants at Barnet on her return from Ireland; they drew her carriage all the way home; and when upwards of eighty she danced at the Hertford ball.

Lady Cathcart does not appear to have been the only beautiful woman in Enfield, for in the early part of the last century the town was remarkable for the number of handsome women among its inhabitants, a fact which is commemorated by a local poet, a Mr. H. Baker, in 1725, in a dull poem of 140 lines, full of quaint conceits, which is published *in extenso* at the end of Robinson's "History of Enfield," and from which we quote two couplets :—

> "But much superior in each heavenly grace
> Appear the fair ones of the Enfield race ;
> Born to command, supremely bright they shine,
> And with their eyes assert the right divine."

CHAPTER XXXVII.

ENFIELD CHASE.

> " Jove's oak, the warlike ash, veyn'd elm, the softer beech,
> Short hazell, maple plain, light aspe, the bending wych,
> Tough holly, and smooth birch, must altogether burn ;
> What should the builders serve, supplies the forgers' turn,
> When under public good base private gain takes hold,
> And we, poor wofull woods, to ruin lastly sold."   FULLER.

General Description of a Chase—Form and Extent of Enfield Chase—Its Early History—The Last of the Staffords, Dukes of Buckingham—Drayton's Description of Enfield Chase—Its Present Condition—The Princess Elizabeth as a Hunter—James I. at Enfield Chase—A Portion of the Chase added to Theobalds—Seizure of the Chase by the Commonwealth—Sale of Different Portions of it—Macaulay's Account of Enfield Chase—Evelyn pays it a Visit—The Chase Re-stocked with Deer by Charles II.—The Chase used as a Sheep-walk—Punishment for Cutting Down and Destroying Trees in the Chase—Its Final Enclosure—Officers belonging to the Chase—Camlet Moat, the supposed Site of the Chief Forester's Lodge—Trent Park—Beech Hill Park—East Lodge—Chase Lodge—Hill Lodge, Claysmore—The Roman Road—Cock Fosters—Dangers of the Roads in Former Times—White Webbs House—The Gunpowder Plot—" The King and the Tinkler."

BY a Chase is meant a large space of open or forest land, either natural or artificial, and set apart for the purposes of those field sports in which almost all kings and princes, from the days of Xenophon and Cyrus, and those of Herodotus and Xerxes, and even from the ages of Babylonian and Assyrian splendour, have so constantly indulged. The successors of Charlemagne, the French sovereigns of the House of Capet, kept up the tradition, which they handed on in their turn to William the Conqueror and the rest of our Norman kings, under whom the " New " Forest, in Hampshire, was made a royal " Chase," at the cost of sad cruelties, it is to be feared, to the luckless inhabitants. There were other royal chases in Sherwood, Whittlebury, and Needwood Forests, whose broad glades were kept alive during the winter season by the horn of royal hunters in the days of the Plantagenets and Tudors.

Drayton, in the " Polyolbion," describes Enfield Chase thus :—

> " A forrest for her pride, tho' titl'd but a Chace ;
> Her purlieus and her parks, her circuit full as large
> As some, perhaps, whose state requires a greater charge.
> Whose holts* that view the east, do wistly stand and look
> Upon the winding course of Lea's delightful brook."

Enfield Chase is—or was—an extensive tract of land, lying chiefly to the north-west of the town, and stretching into several neighbouring parishes. The name first occurs, it is believed, in a record of the reign of Edward II. " Its form," as we learn from Mr. Ford's " History of Enfield," " was very irregular ; its north and longest side was nearly straight, as was also its west side ; its south and east sides were full of angles. Its greatest length

---

* A term still in use in Hampshire and elsewhere to denote high woods.

was about four miles and a half from east to west—that is, from Parsonage Lane to Ganna Corner; from north to south—from Cattle Gate to Southgate—about four miles; its shortest length from east to west—that is, from Potter's Bar to Hadley Town—two miles and three-quarters. On the north side it abuts on Northaw Common, with which it communicates by Cattle Gate, Stock Gate, Cooper's Lane, and Potter's Bar. On the east it adjoins Enfield parish, its outlets to which are White Webbs, Clay Hill, Cocker or Crook Lane, New Lane, Parsonage Lane, and Enfield Green, or the Town. On this side also it extends into Edmonton parish, communicating with it by Winchmore Hill and Southgate."

In the notice of "Enfelde" in the "Domesday Survey," it is stated that there was "a park" here; but the term park, as used in that record, is of an indefinite character. At that period, and down to the time of its enclosure, the district is supposed by Lord Lyttelton to have formed part of the ancient forest of Middlesex. Previous to the reign of Edward II. it was called "Parcus Extrinsecus," the Outer Park, to distinguish it from the "Parcus Intrinsecus," the Home Park, or Great Park, as it was locally called—though, of course, far smaller than the Chase.

In very early times it formed part of the possessions of the Mandevilles, and afterwards of the Bohuns, their successors; but since the marriage of Henry IV. to the daughter and ultimate heiress of Humphrey de Bohun, it has belonged to the Duchy of Lancaster.

In 1483, the Chase, together with the manor of Enfield, is said to have been given by Richard III. to Stafford, Duke of Buckingham, as a reward for his services in raising him to the throne; but if so, it shortly after reverted to the Crown; for, having conspired with the Bishop of Ely to dethrone the king, and been betrayed by his servant, the duke was beheaded in the market-place at Salisbury, without going through the ceremony of a trial. Buckingham, it seems, had claimed the whole or the greater part of the immense inheritance of Humphrey de Bohun in right of descent, which Edward IV. had kept to himself.

The last holder of the dignity and estates of the great family of Bohun, Edward Stafford, Duke of Buckingham, executed on Tower Hill in 1521, was the wealthiest subject in England, the lineal representative of the Plantagenets, and the mortal enemy of Cardinal Wolsey, whom he had offended. On his way to the Tower from Westminster, he was led to his barge by Sir Thomas Lovel, of Forty Hall, who also treated him with respect, asking the

fallen nobleman to take his seat on the carpet and cushions that he had laid for him. But he declined the offer, saying, "When I came here, I was Lord High Constable and Duke of Buckingham, but now poor Edward Bohun, the poorest wretch alive." Holinshed calls him "a most wise and noble prince, and the mirror of all courtesy." With him became extinct the office of Lord High Constable of England, which had been hereditary in his family from the days of Magna Charta." On his attainder, his dukedom and earldom and estates were confiscated. His son Henry retained the title of Baron Stafford; but he was so impoverished that he was glad to borrow the loan of a sovereign in the year before his death, in 1588. His son was even more embarrassed; and in 1639 his grandson was deprived by Charles I. of his rank and honour, on account of his poverty and abject condition." Thus ended a noble line, who had flourished for one-fourth of the entire Christian era.

The Chase now consists of a series of farms, of more or less value, and of gentlemen's seats; but in former times—that is, from the period when it became the "happy hunting ground" of royalty down to the time when the district was "dischased," in 1779—it was full of trees, and herds of deer roamed in its wild glades.

Whilst residing at Hatfield, under the charge of Sir Thomas Pope, the Princess Elizabeth was gratified by her host with a display of romantic magnificence, which was exactly agreeable to the taste of the times and of herself. "She was invited," writes Lucy Aikin, "to repair to Enfield, there to take the amusement of hunting the hart. Twelve ladies in white satin attended her on their ambling palfreys, and twenty yeomen, all clad in green. At the entrance of the forest she was met by fifty archers in scarlet boots and yellow caps, armed with gilded bows, one of whom presented to her a silver-headed arrow winged with peacock's feathers. The splendid show concluded, according to the established laws of the chase, by the offering of the knife to the princess as first lady on the field, and her *taking say** of the buck with her own fair and royal hand."

Whilst staying with Sir Robert Cecil at Theobalds, on his way from Edinburgh to London, in 1603, King James spent a morning in Enfield Chase, whither he rode, "accompanied by many of the nobility; but his visit was cut short by the showers of rain. He rode," says an eye-witness, "the most part of the way from the Chase between two honourable persons of our land (England), the

---

* Cutting the throat.

Earl of Northumberland upon his Majesty's right hand, and the Earl of Nottingham upon his left hand." Such is the minuteness of the " special correspondents" of three centuries ago.

In 1606 Sir Robert Cecil again entertained King James, and also Frederick III. of Denmark, at Theobalds. About this time the extent of the Chase was considerably reduced, for, according to Clutterbuck's " Hertfordshire," " the king having become enamoured of this place, from its proximity to an extensive tract of open country favourable to the diversion of hunting (his favourite amusement), he prevailed upon his Minister to exchange it with him for his Palace of Hatfield, in the county of Herts. The king, having obtained possession of the manor, enlarged the park by taking in part of the adjoining Chase, and surrounded it with a wall of brick ten miles in circumference."

The Chase remained in the possession of the Crown till after the death of Charles I., when it was seized by the Commonwealth as public property, and, by an order of the House of Commons, was surveyed in 1650, when it was reported to contain 7,900 acres, its value being set down at rather more than £4,700 per annum. Shortly subsequent to that date the district had been divided into parcels and sold to different individuals. A considerable part was consequently enclosed, and several houses built. But the enclosure created great disturbances among those who claimed the right of common, and who were accustomed to obtain their fuel from this waste. In the Bodleian Library at Oxford is preserved an original survey of the Chase, a duplicate of which is in the possession of the vestry clerk of Enfield ; it is entitled " A Description of Enfield Chase, situate in the Parish of Enfield, and County of Middlesex, as the same is now divided between the Commonwealth and the Commons, by Edmund Rolfe and Nicholas Gunter, in the year 1658." In this survey the gate of the Chase at Winchmore Hill is called " Highmore, *alias* Winsmore." The Pest House mentioned in Ford's " Enfield " (p. 311) is distinctly marked, standing on the present Green.

In his account of the state of England in 1685, Macaulay observes that Enfield Chase, though hardly out of the sight of the smoke of the capital, was " a region twenty-five miles in circumference, in which the deer wandered by thousands, as free as in the American forests ; " still, there is no record of there ever having been more than 3,000 head of deer in Enfield Chase. The last wild boars which had been preserved, here and elsewhere, for the royal diversion, and had been, up to that time, allowed to ravage the cultivated lands with their tusks, were for the most part slaughtered by the exasperated rustics in the course of the Civil War. It is said that the last grey badger in Enfield Chase was not killed till ten or eleven years after the accession of Queen Victoria.

Evelyn makes the following entry in his "Diary" with reference to a visit which he paid to Enfield. On June 2nd, 1676, he writes :—" I went with my Lord Chamberlaine to see a garden at Enfield towne, thence to Mr. Sec. Coventry's Lodge in the Chase. It is a very pretty place, the house commodious, the gardens handsome, and our entertainment very free, there being none but my lord and myselfe. That which I most wondered at was, that in the compass of twenty-five miles, yet within fourteen of London, there is not a house, barne, church, or building, besides three lodges. To this lodge are three great ponds and some few inclosures, the rest a solitarie desert, yet stor'd with not less than 3,000 deere. There are pretty retreats for gentlemen, especially for those who are studious and lovers of privacy."

In a survey of the manor of Enfield, taken in 1686, it is stated that on a former perambulation the Chase had been found to contain 7,600 acres, of which 500 had been since enclosed in Theobalds Park. This enclosure, as stated above, was made by James I. while he resided at Theobalds. Though at that time the Chase was well stocked with deer, the Parliamentary Army during the Civil War destroyed the game, cut down the trees, and let out the ground into small farms. In this state it remained until the Restoration, when young trees were planted, and the Chase was again stocked with deer.

Another survey was taken in 1698, in order to a fall of timber, by which several new " ridings " were to be formed, and a square lawn of 300 acres laid out for the deer to feed in. The " ridings," marked out when the Chase was to be divided into farms at the time of the Commonwealth, and still distinguished by hedges and ditches, were Cock-Fosters, and the Ridgeway from the gravel-pits by East Lodge to Ganna Corner.

Mr. Ford, in his " History of Enfield," says :— " The Chase was formerly considered to have been a sheep-walk belonging to the family of Coningsby, of Wales, one of whom having a complaint lodged against him for having too many sheep, brought up a parcel of goats, which did great damage. This circumstance, it seems, gave rise to the right of sheep-walk on the Chase annexed to certain farms in this neighbourhood for a certain time of the year. Norden says, 'there ariseth a profit unto

VIEW IN TRENT PARK.

the poore inhabitants there by the use of the Chase, where they have common of pasture for all kinde of cattle, pannage, and wood;' but the parish, it seems, thought otherwise, finding itself overburthened by numerous and disorderly poor, who availed themselves of the privilege of the Chase to support dissolute lives of idleness and beggary. The deer were stolen and exposed for sale with the greatest audacity; venison could be purchased cheaper than mutton. The poachers were sometimes transported, but at the expiration of their time returned to their old habits." In 1762 it is recorded in the *Gentleman's Magazine* "that one John Batt, of Potter's Bar, was committed to Bridewell for cutting young beech-trees on the Chase, and carrying them away in a cart. He was sentenced to be publicly whipped in the market-place at Enfield once every month during his imprisonment." The *Public Ledger*, 1764, also records the fact of a woman, "an old offender," being "conveyed in a cart from Bridewell to Enfield, and publicly whipped at the cart's tail by the common hangman, for cutting down and destroying wood in Enfield Chase."

In 1777 an Act of Parliament was passed for the purpose of dividing the Chase, and assigning allotments to such parishes and individuals as claimed right of common; and in 1801 another Act was passed "for dividing and enclosing the open and common fields, common marshes, and lammas grounds, Chase allotments, and other commonable and waste lands within the parish;" and the same "have been divided and allotted accordingly, among the tithe owners, lords of manors, and proprietors of freehold and copyhold lands, and others entitled thereto."* At the present time nearly the whole of the Chase is enclosed, and but little of its original appearance remains, the wildest parts being at Hadley Common,† Trent Park, Winchmore Hill Wood,‡ and a portion of White Webbs Park. The deer, which, as shown above, were at one time very numerous, were taken to the estate of the Earl of Bute, at Luton Park, in Bedfordshire. The last red deer killed here was shot by Mr. William Mellish, M.P., of Bush Hill Park, and its horns are now in the possession of Mr. Edward Ford, of Old Park. Still, it is clear that all indications of a Chase have not clean died out, for a woodcock was shot at Old

* Ford's "Enfield," p. 52.   † See *ante*, p. 328.   ‡ See *ante*, p. 346.

Park in January, 1874, and a bittern was taken on the banks of the Lea, not far from Ponder's End, in 1847.

The officers belonging to the Chase were—besides the Chancellor, the Receiver General, and the Attorney General of the Duchy of Lancaster—a Master of the Game, a Forester, a Ranger, Keepers, a Woodward, a Steward, a Bailiff, and Verderers, who were annually chosen in the King's Court of the Manor of Enfield, a sort of Supervisor of the Wood. The name of Verderers is still kept up in connection with Epping Forest, as we shall see presently.

There were on the Chase four ancient lodges, called respectively the East, the West, the North, and the South Bailies. These lodges were the official residences of the persons who were connected with the government of the Duchy of Lancaster, some of whom were Chancellors of the Court. These lodges were also used as hunting-seats during the time of Queen Elizabeth, James I., and Charles I.

In the preceding chapter we have spoken of Camlet Moat, now within the bounds of Trent Park, and almost in the centre of the Chase, as having been the subject of much antiquarian speculation. Camden says:—"Almost in the middle of the Chase there are the ruins and rubbish of an ancient house, which the common people from tradition affirm to have belonged to the Mandevilles, Earls of Essex." Lysons, however, considered the tradition to be destitute of any foundation, and suggested that the spot was merely "the site of the principal lodge, and the residence of the chief forester."

Trent Park, the seat of Mr. Bevan, consists of upwards of a thousand acres, and is still covered with such an abundance of timber as to give some idea of what the Chase must have been in early ages. Its charming vistas and forest scenery have been thus graphically described by Sir Walter Scott in the "Fortunes of Nigel:"—"The sun was high upon the glades of Enfield Chase, and the deer with which it abounded were seen sporting in picturesque groups among the ancient oaks of the forest, when a cavalier and a lady sauntered slowly up one of the long alleys which were cut through the park for the convenience of the hunters. . . The place at which he stopped was at that time little more than a mound, partly surrounded by a ditch, from which it derived the name of Camlet Moat. A few hewn stones were there which had escaped the fate of many others that had been used in building different lodges in the forest for the

IN BEECH HILL PARK. (*See page* 368.)

royal keepers. These vestiges marked the ruins of the abode of a once illustrious, but long-forgotten, family—the Mandevilles, Earls of Essex, to whom Enfield Chase and the extensive domains adjacent had belonged in elder days. A wild woodland prospect led the eye at various points through broad and apparently interminable alleys, meeting at this point as from a common centre."

A lease of this property was granted by George III. to his favourite physician, Richard Jebb, on whom he conferred a baronetcy. Dr. Jebb afterwards purchased the freehold; and on his building a residence here, the king gave it the name of Trent Place, "in commemoration of the great skill by which the life of his brother had been preserved in his severe illness at Trent, in the South Tyrol." On the death of Sir Richard Jebb the estate was sold to Lord Cholmondeley, and later on it had among its possessors Sir Henry Lushington. The mansion is a spacious brick structure, stuccoed and whitened, and its situation on gently rising ground, overlooking a broad extent of the park, is very fine.

Beech Hill Park, which lies near the western extremity of the Chase, bordering upon Hadley Common, comprises nearly 700 acres, which was granted to Mr. Francis Russell, a Fellow of the Royal Society, who was some time Secretary of the Duchy Court of Lancaster, and through whose suggestion, it is said, the final enclosure of the Chase was brought about. The house is placed on the brow of a gentle eminence, and, like that of Trent Park, it has the advantage of a fine stream of water flowing through the grounds.

The East Lodge is described in the survey of 1650 as "a brick building, covered with tiles." It was occasionally used by Charles I. as a hunting-seat. Towards the end of the last century the lodge was occupied by Lord Chancellor Loughborough, afterwards created Earl of Rosslyn; later on it was pulled down, and the present house built on its site. West Lodge, which was that occupied by Mr. Secretary Coventry, mentioned above as visited by Evelyn, was rebuilt in 1832, the house having become ruinous, and in danger of falling. South Lodge stands about a mile and a half west of Enfield Town, on the Ridgeway. It was for some years the occasional residence of the Earl of Chatham, to whom it was bequeathed, together with a legacy of £10,000. Mr. Tuff, in his "Historical Notices of Enfield," tells the following amusing story concerning the earl :—" Lord Chatham desired the owner of a windmill, which stood on a post on the top of Windmill-hill, to paint the

whole body moving to the face of the wind, on that side next South Lodge, at his expense. The miller did so, but when his lordship looked out of the window and saw the windmill not painted, he sent for the miller, who declared it had been done agreeably to his lordship's direction. The earl pointed to the mill, when the miller informed him that the *wind had changed*, but that he was quite ready to paint that side also on the same terms! The mill in question was pulled down many years ago, and the present one erected on its site."

Chase Lodge, Hill Lodge, and Claysmore, are smaller estates which have been at different times allotted out of the Chase.

Of Potter's Bar, which formed the extreme north-western limits of the Chase, we have spoken in our account of South Mimms,* to which parish the hamlet belongs; and Southgate, which, as its name implies, was the southern limit of the royal demesne, has been also dealt with, together with its near neighbour, Winchmore Hill.†

The ancient Roman road, called Ermen, or Ermine, Street, lay through a part of the Chase in its passage to Hertford. From the Cripplegate or Moorgate of London, it passed through Newington, thence through several green lanes to the east of Hornsey, and having entered Enfield Chase, proceeded thence through Hatfield to Hertford. "This was the road (for the present north road was not then in existence) by which the Londoners marched, with King Alfred at their head, against the Danes, in the year 895, to a stronghold or fortification built by them at Hertford." ‡

Cock Fosters is a small village lying to the west of Trent Park, about four miles west from Enfield town, and two miles east from New Barnet railway-station. It was formed into an ecclesiastical parish in 1839. Christ Church, which was built in 1837, at the expense of Mr. Bevan, of Trent Park, is a small plain structure, with a tower and spire, and is profusely overgrown with ivy. The derivation of the name of Cock Fosters—or Forsters, as it is sometimes written—has been the subject of speculation among antiquarians. Mr. Thorne, in his "Environs of London," says, "there can be little doubt that Forsters is a corruption of *foresters* (in either the English or French form). The derivation of Cock is not so palpable. It has been suggested that it comes from *bicoque*, a small house, hut, or collection of huts. Cotgrave renders it *Bicoque*, a little paltry town; and if the huts of the Chase

* See *ante*, p. 317.   † See *ante*, p. 345.
‡ Tuff's "Historical Notices of Enfield."

foresters and woodmen were collected here, the place may have been called *Bicoque Forestière;* but a more obvious explanation is that here may have been the house of the chief forester, *Coq de Forestières."*

The roads round about here in times past were not the most inviting to travel in after midnight. Camlet Moat is said to have been the lurking-place of the notorious highwayman and robber, Dick Turpin, whose grandfather, one Nott, kept the "Rose and Crown," by the brook called "Bull Beggar's Hole," at Clay Hill. The moat is distant but a few miles from the scene of Turpin's exploits on Finchley Common, whence he could easily conceal himself in such a place in the then wild state of Enfield Chase.

As lately as December, 1832, in a lane near Enfield Chase, on the road between Enfield and Barnet, was committed a cruel murder on a Mr. B. C. Danby. For this a man named Johnson was executed. The spot where the murder was perpetrated was long marked by an inscription on the bark of a tree by the wayside.

Not only were the roads dangerous in consequence of the highwaymen and footpads who lurked about, but down to early in the present century they were in a very unfit condition for vehicular traffic. Mr. Ford relates that Lady Elizabeth Palk, who resided at Enfield Rectory, was accustomed, when she intended to call on Mrs. Elphinstone at East Lodge, to send out men two or three days in advance to fill the ruts with faggots, to enable her carriage to pass. "Within living memory," Mr. Ford adds, "it was possible to travel from Hadley Church through Enfield Chase, Epping and Hainault Forests, to Wanstead without ever leaving the green turf or losing sight of forest land."

It is singular that there should have been no "haunted house" in the parish of Enfield. "Formerly (says Bourne in his "Antiquities") almost every place had one. If a house was built in a melancholy situation, or in some old romantic manner, or if any particular accident had happened in it—a murder or a sudden death, or such like—to be sure that house had a mark set on it, and it was afterwards esteemed the habitation of a ghost." "The most diligent inquiry," observes Mr. Ford, in his work already quoted, "has been unsuccessful in tracing the vestige of one here, though the Chase was formerly notorious as the residence of witches. The Witch of Edmonton, in the fine drama of Ford and Dekker, was a true story; and the unfortunate old woman, who was condemned and executed for witchcraft in 1622, was a denizen of the Chase."

The estate of White Webbs, as stated above, lies at the north-eastern extremity of the Chase, and is of some historic interest, from its connection with the "Gunpowder Plot." Old White Webbs House stood on a portion of the grounds now belonging to Myddelton House,* which was of old known as Bowling Green House, and originally formed part of the manor of Worcesters and of Goldbeaters. In 1570 Queen Elizabeth granted White Webbs House to Robert Huicke, her physician. The house was, in the middle of the seventeenth century, the property of Dr. Brockenham; it afterwards came into the family of Garnault, and was pulled down about 1790. A tradition, which (says Lysons) is perhaps not much to be depended upon, states that White Webbs House was hired by the conspirators of the Gunpowder Plot for the purpose of watching the signal of their success. The tradition, however, observes Mr. Ford, "is fully substantiated by existing deeds, and by the following extracts from the documents of the State Paper Office, which also identify the locality beyond any doubt. In the confession of 'John Johnsonne (alias Guido Fawkes), he further saith that the Wednesday before his apprencon he went forthe of the towne to a house in Enfielde Chase, on this side of Theobalds, where he stayed till Sunday night following'" (9-10 November, 1665). The report to the Council of the search of White Webbs House says, "The search ended in the discovery of Popish books and relics, but no papers or munitions, and the house was found to be full of trap-doors and passages." In the examination of "James Johnson," it was stated by him that the house "had been taken of *Dr. Hewicke,* by his master, Mr. Meaze, of Berkshire (the Jesuit father Garnet), for his sister, Mrs. Perkins (*alias* Mrs. Ann Vaux); that Mrs. Vaux had spent a month there, and mass had been said by a priest, whose name deponent did not know."

The following paragraph, having reference to the connection of Old White Webbs House with the Gunpowder Plot, occurs in the "Works of that high and mighty Prince James I.," in the discourse on the Gunpowder Treason:—"Meanwhile Mr. Fawkes and myselfe alone (Winter's confession) brought some new powder, as suspecting the first to be *danke,* and conveyed it into the cellar, and set it in order, as we resolved it should stand. Then was the Parliament anew prorogued until the 5th of November, so as we all went down until some ten days before, when Mr. Catesby came up with Mr. Fawkes to an house by Enfield-chase, called

---

White Webbes, whither I came to them, and Mr. Catesby willed me to enquire whether the young Prince came to the Parliament : I tolde him I heard that His Grace thought not to be there. Then must wee have our horses, said Mr. Catesby, beyond the water, and provision of more company to surprise the Prince, and leave the Duke alone."

Mr. Ford mentions the fact that Mr. Bowles, the present owner of Myddelton House, has in his possession a deed, dated 1570, containing a grant of " all the vaultes and all the conduit and pipes of lead laid within the said Chase at the charges and expenses of our servant (Robert Huycke) for the leading and conveying water into the Newe Howse of our said servant, abuttinge in parte uppon the saide Chase, which mansion house is within the parish of Enfield, in our said co. of Midd.," and for supplying water to the mansion house, gardens, ponds, and orchards.

The site of old White Webbs extended across White Webbs Lane (formerly called Rome Road).

White Webbs House was pulled down towards the end of the last century, and the present mansion, bearing the same name, was built on another part of the estate, called White Webbs Farm, which had been purchased by Dr. Wilkinson, the grandfather of Mr. Henry Cox Wilkinson, the present owner. Of late years both the mansion and the park have been augmented ; the latter now comprises about 250 acres, 100 of which are woodland, and covered with old oaks and underwood, the remains of the original Chase, or forest.

In an open glade in the park stands a small brick building enclosing a circular tank, or well of pure water. This is the old " Conduit house," mentioned above as having been granted by Queen Elizabeth to her physician, Dr. Huicke, for the supply of his mansion-house at White Webbs.

An old ale-house, bearing the sign of " The King and the Tinker," in this lane probably retains some of the out-buildings. "With this little beer-shop," writes Mr. Ford, "is popularly identified the ballad of 'The King and the Tinker,' the incident of which is supposed to have occurred during the residence of James I. at Theobalds." Mr. Thorne, in his " Environs," however, says :—" The ballad of ' King James and the Tinkler' is eminently a border ballad, and is popular throughout the northern counties ; *tinkler* is the northern term for a tinker, but was never used, as far as we know, in the south ; and in the received version of the ballad (though not in that printed by Mr. Ford), the tinkler says—

'The King 's on the *border*, a chasing the deer.'

The ballad must, therefore, we fear, be disassoci-

ated from Enfield, notwithstanding the beer-house sign." The line above referred to in Mr. Ford's version reads—

" The King is a-hunting the fair fallow deer,"

which, adds Mr. Thorne, " has hardly the old ballad ring." The term *tinkler* is, in Scotland and the border towns and villages, applied not merely to a " mender of pots and kettles," who in England is generally called a " tinker," but it is also used to denote any person who picks up a livelihood by tramping about from place to place, doing odd jobs of any kind, as chance might throw in his way.

Nevertheless, here is the old ale-house called " The King and the Tinker ;" and as local tradition has fixed upon it as being the scene of the incident described in the ballad, we reprint it *in extenso* :—

"KING JAMES AND THE TINKLER.

" And now, to be brief, let's pass over the rest,
  Who seldom or never were given to jest,
  And come to King Jamie, the first of our throne—
A pleasanter monarch sure never was known.

" As he was a-hunting the swift fallow deer,
  He dropt all his nobles, and when he got clear,
  In hope of some pastime, away he did ride,
Till he came to an ale-house hard by a wood-side,

" And there with a Tinkler he happened to meet,
  And him in kind sort he so freely did greet:
' Now pray thee, good fellow, what hast in thy jug,
Which under thy arm thou dost lovingly hug ?'

" ' In truth,' said the Tinkler, ''tis nappy brown ale,
  And to drink to thy good health, faith, I will not fail—
For although thy jacket looks gallant and fine,
I hope that my two-pence is as good as thine.'

" ' Nay, by my soul, man, the truth shall be spoke ;'
  And straightway the monarch sat down for to joke ;
He called for his pitcher, the Tinkler another,
And so they went to it like brother and brother.

" While drinking, the King he was pleased to say,
  ' What news, honest fellow ? come tell me, I pray ;'
' There 's nothing of news, except that I hear
The King is a-hunting the fair fallow deer ;

" ' And truly I wish I so happy may be,
  That whilst they are hunting the King I may see ;
For though I have travelled the land many ways,
I never saw the King, sir, in all my old days.'

" The King, with a hearty brisk laugh, then replied,
  ' I tell thee, honest fellow, if thou canst but ride,
Thou shalt get up behind me, and thee I will bring
To the presence of Jamie, thy sovereign King.'

" ' Perhaps,' said the Tinkler, ' his Lord will be drest
  So fine that I shall not know him from the rest ;'
' I tell thee, honest fellow, when thou dost come there,
The King will be covered, the nobles all bare.'

" Then up got the Tinkler, and likewise his sack,
  His budget of leather and tools at his back ;
And when they came to the merry green wood,
The nobles came round him, and bareheaded stood.

" The Tinkler then seeing so many appear,
    Immediately whispered the King in the ear,
    Saying, ' Since they are all clothed so gallant and gay,
    Which is the King? come tell me, I pray.'

" The King to the Tinkler then made this reply—
    ' By my soul, man, it must be either you or I ;
    The rest are uncovered you see, all around.'
    This said, with the budget he fell to the ground

" Like one that was frightened quite out of his wits,
    Then up upon his knees he instantly gets,
    Beseeching for mercy—the King to him said,
    ' Thou art a good fellow, so be not afraid ;

" ' Come, tell me thy name.' ' It is John of the Vale,
    A mender of kettles, and a lover of good ale.'
    ' Then rise up, Sir John, I will honour thee here,
    And create thee a Knight of five hundred a year.'

" This was a good thing for the Tinkler indeed ;
    Then unto the Court he was sent with all speed,
    Where great store of pleasure and pastime was seen
    In the royal presence of both King and Queen."

The sign of " The King and the Tinker " is probably unique ; it is not mentioned by Larwood, but sign-boards of a similar character are found in other parts of the country. " The King and the Miller," for instance, at Mansfield, Notts, celebrates a like adventure of Henry II. and a merry rustic of that town. Similar stories are told of different sovereigns—such as King John and the miller of Charlton,* after whom Cuckold's Point is said to have been named ; of King Edward III. and the tanner of Drayton Basset ; of King Henry VIII. and the Abbot of Canterbury ; of James V. of Scotland (the " gude mon of Ballangeich ") ; of Henry IV. of France and the pig-merchant ; of Charles V. of Spain and the cobbler of Brussels ; of Joseph II. ; of Frederick the Great ; and even of Haroun-al-Raschid, who used to go about his dominions *incognito*, under the name of Il Bondocani.

There is an old proverb which says that—

" Cobblers and tinkers
    Are the best ale-drinkers ;"

and possibly this circumstance, be it real or not, may have something also to do with the sign.

CHAPTER XXXVIII.

ENFIELD HIGHWAY, PONDER'S END, AND THE RIVER LEA.

" The old Lea, that brags of Danish blood."—DRAYTON's *Polyolbion.*

Position and Extent of Enfield Highway—Population, &c.—The Lower North Road—Mr. Spencer and his Bride—Matthew Prior and John Morley—St. James's Church—Ponder's End—St. Matthew's Church—Lincoln House—Durants—The Manor of Suffolks—Enfield Wash—The Story of Elizabeth Canning, " Mother Wells," and the Gipsy Squires—Roselands—The Manor of Elsynge—The River Lea—Bull's Cross—Capels.

ENFIELD HIGHWAY—which, as we have stated in a previous chapter,* runs along the eastern division of this parish, from north to south—although of much more recent growth than Enfield Town, is in reality far out-numbering it in population—a state of things which may be accounted for by the fact of its having within its limits several large factories, and more especially the Royal Small Arms Factory, where, on the whole, upwards of 1,500 hands are employed, and of which we shall speak in a subsequent chapter. According to the census returns for 1881 this division alone contains a population of more than 9,000 inhabitants. The district comprises the hamlet of Ponder's End, Enfield Highway (proper), the Royal Small Arms Factory, and Frezywater. Several narrow lanes and thoroughfares radiate from the main road on either side, bearing such names as South Street, Nag's Head Lane, Green Street, Carterhatch Lane, Enfield Wash, Hoe Lane, Welch's Lane (now Ordnance Road, Turkey Street, and Bullsmore Lane. Enfield Highway is the name given to that portion of the Cheshunt and Hertford road which, after passing through Edmonton, enters the parish of Enfield at Ponder's End, and running in almost a direct line due north, parallel with the Great Eastern Railway (Cambridge line), and for a distance of about two miles, leaves it just beyond Bullsmore Lane. It is made up of the usual admixture of shops and private houses to be met with in villages that are located on main public roads—taverns and ale-houses, as a matter of course, somewhat predominating.

The thoroughfare occupies part of the track of the old Roman road called Ermine Street, described in the preceding chapter. It is still the modern highway to the north-east, and is now known by the name of the Lower North Road. It is needless to say that it presents marked differences to what it exhibited a century or so ago, although

---

* See *ante*, p. 350.

* See " Old and New London," Vol. VI., p. 233.

at that time it was the great northern road, and was the occasional scene of cavalcades and royal "progresses," such as might break the dull monotonous life of the inhabitants. For example, the villagers must have been astonished in December, 1755, at seeing Mr. (afterwards Lord) Spencer and his bride coming up to London from Althorpe, if Lady Hervey's letters are to be trusted, with three coaches-and-six and 200 horsemen. Lady Hervey adds that the country-folk armed

a memorial of his wife. All the windows are filled with stained glass, chiefly in memory of his family.

The hamlet of Ponder's End has lost much of its rural appearance since the formation of the Great Eastern line and the establishment of a railway-station in its vicinity. Besides gas and water works, and two or three large and tall factories, the place can boast of several inns and taverns, and, like most other suburban villages which have been invaded by the "railway king," villas and

PONDER'S END.

themselves with spades and pitchforks, fancying that it was either the Pretender or the King of France who had invaded them !

Along this road must have passed Matthew Prior and his friend John Morley, on their way to dine at the " Bull " Inn at " Hodsdon," *en route* to Down Hall, near Harlow, which had been presented to the poet by Harley, Earl of Oxford.

Enfield Highway was formed into a separate parish for ecclesiastical purposes in 1833. The church, dedicated to St. James, was built in 1831. It is in the Perpendicular style, and comprises a nave, with galleries, an apsidal sanctuary, and a chancel and transepts. The chancel and transepts, which are of Early English architecture, were added in 1864 by the late vicar, the Rev. John Harman, as

"genteel residences" are fast springing up in all directions. The church, dedicated to St. Matthew, erected in 1877, is a chapel-of-ease to St. James's, Enfield. It is built in the Early English style, and consists of a nave and north aisle.

On the southern side of Ponder's End, a little to the west of the high road, stands Lincoln House, which, according to Mr. Ford, is said to take its name from the Earls of Lincoln, of whom Henry and Thomas, the second and third earls, lived here at the beginning of the seventeenth century. In Gough's "Camden," it is stated that the house was the residence of the *Bishops* of Lincoln, "or of that other William of Wickham, bishop of that diocese, who was born here." Mr. Ford, however, says that William of Wickham was born in the manor-house of Honylands, or Pentriches, otherwise Capels, at the northern end of the parish, near Bull's Cross, and of which his father was lessee in the reign of Henry VIII. Lincoln House was a brick building, with heavy buttresses, and bore marks of antiquity. Under one of the windows, between two marble pillars, there was, in 1750, a tablet inscribed " R. L. 1520."

In the " Beauties of England and Wales " it is stated that " there was lately some painted glass remaining in the windows, containing, among other armorial bearings, the arms and quarterings of Howard, with a viscount's coronet, and the inscription ' Henry Howard, 1584.' The whole of this

whose daughter and heiress conveyed it in marriage to John Wrothe ; and the manor of Durants, to which that of Gartons was at an early period annexed, descended to their son, William Wrothe, who died in 1408, after which it continued in the hands of the Wrothe family for many generations. Fuller, in his " Worthies," says :—" Sir Thomas Wrothe was of the Bedchamber, and a favourite of King Edward the Sixth, who (as I am informed) at his death passed out of the armes of him, his faithfull servant, into the embraces of Christ, his dearest Saviour. Soon after Sir Thomas found a great change in the English Court, but no alteration, as many did (to their shame), in his own

ROOM IN MOTHER WELLS' COTTAGE.

glass is now (1816) removed, and the building has been newly fronted ; but the interior comprises several ancient decorated ceilings." From the above-mentioned arms the house appears to have belonged to Henry Howard, Viscount Bindon, the head of a branch of the ducal house of Norfolk. Other coats of arms in the windows were those of the Lord Keeper, Sir Thomas Coventry (1627), and of George Villiers, first Duke of Buckingham. Some of the rooms were wainscoted, apparently of the date of James I. Part of the house was burnt down a few years ago, but has been rebuilt.

Eastward of the high road, between Ponder's End and Green Street, stood the historic manor-house of Durants, or Durant's Harbour, which was burnt down at the end of the last century. In the reign of Edward I. the manor belonged to Richard de Plessitis ; but in default of heirs male, it subsequently devolved upon Thomas Durant,

conscience, in preservation of which he was fain to fly beyond the seas." It was observable, he adds, that the family of this man, who went away for " his own conscience," was the only family in Middlesex, out of all those mentioned by Norden, which was not extinct in his time (1660). A curious letter from his son, Sir Robert Wrothe, who died in 1605, is preserved among the Lansdowne MSS., and printed by Mr. Ford in his " History of Enfield." As this letter vividly depicts the state of the country round about London, and particularly those parts of which we shall have occasion hereafter to speak in these pages, we take the liberty of quoting it :—

" Sir Robert Wrothe to Mr. Michael Hickes. — Intelligence concerning robbers who frequented Layton Heath [? Loughton], in Essex.

(MS. Lansd. 87, Art. 60, *orig.*)

" My very good frende, Mr. Hickes,—I am informed that now, towardes these darke evenings, there are sertaine lewde fellowes—sumtimes horsemen, sumtimes footemen—disguis-ing themselves with beardes that they carry aboute them in their pockets, which doe frequente and use aboute Layton heath and at or about Snaresbrooke, in your brother Col-stone's walke. I have appoynted sum espiciall spyall of them to bewray them and to know them, either by theire horses apparell or otherwise, and I hope in time to have them discifared. Yet for better surety thereof, I pray you lett me intreate you to speake to your brother Colstone, that with some secresy he woulde take such order with sum of the discreatest keepers he hath, that towardes eaveninges they woulde have an eye upone the heath and about Snaresbrooke for such kinde of persons, and to discry them by their horses or otherwise, if they can. They come not above one or two in company untill they meete about the heath, and when they have obteyned that they come for, they sever themselves in the like manner; and sumtimes sum of them ride over by Temple Mill, where I pray you take likewise secret order with the miller that he woulde keepe his gate shute up in the nighte; besides sumtimes they ride over by Hackney; and yf they doe discry any of them, that I may have notice thereof, and I doubte not but to have them quickly appre-hended, for I have notice of sum of their hauntes. And so, with my commendations to your good wiffe, I will bid you farewell.　　　　　　　　　"Your assured frende,

　　　　　　　　　　　　　　　　"ROBERT WROTHE.

"Lucton, the 16th of October, 1599.

"One of them usethe to ride on a whit mare. Let them have a diligent care if they doe see any such man.—To my verie loving friend Mr. Michaell Hickes,* at his house at Duckett, or elsewhere."

The family of Wrothe became extinct in 1673, on the death of Sir Henry Wrothe, the grandson of Sir Thomas, to whose exile, in the reign of Queen Mary, Fuller again refers in his dedication to Sir Henry of part of his "Church History":—"Hence it is that I have seen in your ancient house at Durance the crest of your armes (viz., a lion's head erased), with the extraordinary addition of sable wings, somewhat alluding to those of bats, to denote your ancestour's dark and secret flight for his safety. However, God brought him home again on the silver wings of the dove, when peaceably restoring him in the dayes of Q. Elizabeth to his large possessions."

On the death of Sir Henry Wrothe, the manor was sold by his executors to Sir Thomas Stringer, whose son William bequeathed the property to his wife Margaret, daughter of the celebrated Judge Jeffreys, who was a frequent visitor here. It after wards underwent a few changes of ownership, either by purchase or otherwise; and at the end of the last century it passed into the hands of Newell Connop, Esq., in whose family it still remains.

The entrance to the old moated manor-house was by a bridge of two arches and a large gateway, with a postern, &c. From the description of the building in Dr. Robinson's "Enfield," the house seems to have formed a quadrangle, of which part of the north and west sides—standing in 1775—were built of brick; and at the south end stood a chapel, on the south and west sides of which were small Gothic windows with iron bars, and at the north end a square window, with round pillars in the middle and at the sides, and a square tower, with a spiral stone staircase. "On the east side," wrote Dr. Robinson in 1823, "there was an arch which was stopped up, with some Saxon (i.e., Nor-man) capitals much defaced; the whole was built of clunch, brick, and masses of pebbles, cemented together with mortar, and plastered over. Over this building was a room, then used as a pigeon-house. This chapel appeared to be the most ancient part of the house, the rest probably having been built about the latter end of the fifteenth or the beginning of the sixteenth century, and was pulled down about the year 1776 by Mr. Poe. At the south-west extremity of the moat, and without it, there was part of another square brick building, with an arched entrance, and a circular room with a fire-place. Behind the chapel there was a long square canal and the garden, which had been divided into two parts by a brick wall; there are also the remains of two square piers of a gate, on which were two eagles, with wings displayed, holding shields with three eagles' heads on the face. At right angles with this wall there were parts of others, or rather, two detached walls, near which were steps to the moat. These two walls were parallel with the north side of the house, which appeared to have formed the south side of the quadrangle, in the centre of which stood a dial on a square block of stone mounted on brick-work.

"On the west side of the moat there was a sum-mer-house, with a balcony and weathercock, sur-mounted by a flying-horse on a pyramid of ironwork, with Neptune, Bacchus, &c., painted on the west front of the building. From this summer-house there was an avenue to the road."

The manor of Suffolks, which was also situated near Ponder's End, was, in the fifteenth century, held under the Crown by Sir R. Parr, Comptroller of the Household. At the end of the last century it passed to Mr. Newell Connop, the then owner of the manor of Durants, with which it became merged.

Enfield Wash is the name now given to that portion of the main road which lies immediately beyond Enfield Highway. The Wash, observes Mr. Thorne, in his "Environs of London," "owes its name to the little stream which, rising in the Chase, here crossed the road, and spreading out, made the *wash*, through which horses and carriages had to flounder, but which is now carried under it,

---

* Mr. (afterwards Sir Michael) Hickes, was Burghley's secretary.

and turning to the south-east, falls into the Lea a little below the ordnance factory."

On the east side of the high road at Enfield Wash, at the corner of the lane leading to the ordnance factory railway-station, stands the cottage of " Mother " Wells, a gipsy, once so famous as the scene of Elizabeth Canning's real or fictitious imprisonment, which excited the kingdom for months in 1753–54, divided society into two parties, the " Egyptians " and the " Canningites," and called into existence a whole crop of ephemeral publications: in fact, quite a literature, nearly fifty pamphlets in all, and not far short of twenty portraits, views, etchings, and a plan and elevation of the cottage itself. A ground plan and interior view of the cottage appear in the *Gentleman's Magazine*, vol. xxiii., pp. 306–7, and also in Dr. Robinson's " History of Enfield." The cottage remains substantially the same as it was a century and a half ago. It is a plain wooden-fronted structure, of two storeys, and with a window on each side the door—just such a house as would be naturally the residence of a curate in a country village. The door or window from which Canning effected her escape into the lane is still there, and so is a part of the loft in which she was kept. It is understood that the house will soon be pulled down.

Horace Walpole writes, in a letter to the Countess of Ailesbury, Oct. 10, 1761 :—" I am in such a passion, I cannot tell you what I am angry about—why, about virtue and Mr. Pitt : two arrant cheats, gipsies. I believe he was a comrade of Elizabeth Canning when he lived at Enfield Wash."*

The story may be briefly summed up as follows :—Elizabeth Canning, a servant girl about eighteen years of age, went, with the consent of her master, to visit a relation on New Year's Day, 1753. She did not return, nor was anything heard concerning her for nearly a month, at the expiration of which time she went to her mother's house in an emaciated and wretched condition, and accounted for her long disappearance by declaring that she had been " violently assaulted in Moorfields by two men, who had robbed her of her money, and dragged her away into the country along the Hertfordshire road, and that at length they carried her to the house of one Mother Wells, at Enfield Wash, where she said one Mary Squires, a gipsy, and two girls were in the kitchen ; and where she had been confined till the day of her return." During the whole time of her confinement, she asserted that she had existed upon a few

crusts of bread and a pitcher of water, and that she had effected her escape by jumping out of a window. In stating the articles of which she had been robbed, she accused Squires of cutting away and taking her stays, and that a young woman named Virtue Hall stood by, and witnessed the act.

In consequence of these charges, Squires, Hall, and Wells, were apprehended, and taken before a magistrate. Hall solemnly denied all knowledge of any such transaction having happened since she had been in Wells' house, and she was discharged ; but Squires was committed to prison for the robbery, and Wells for aiding and abetting. They were tried at the Old Bailey, and the former was sentenced to be hanged. Many doubts, however, arose as to the veracity of Canning's depositions, and inquiries took place, which were laid before the king, who referred the case to the consideration of the Attorney and Solicitor General. In the result, the tables were turned : the gipsy received his Majesty's pardon, and Elizabeth Canning was tried and convicted of perjury ; but on quitting prison she returned to England, and inherited a legacy left to her by an old lady of Newington Green, who believed in her innocence. She also still commanded so much sympathy, if not credit, that a subscription was got up to enable her to emigrate to America, where she married a wealthy planter. She died about the year 1773.

Wells came back to Enfield, where she died a pauper, as appears from the register, in 1763. Mary Squires, the gipsy, died in 1762, and was buried at Farnham, Surrey, being followed to the grave by several " Egyptians " as mourners.

Roselands, on the south side of Turkey Street, is an estate some fifty acres in extent, with a goodly mansion, and has been in the possession of the family of the present owner for many years.

The manor of Elsynge, or Norris, according to Mr. Ford's " Enfield," appears to have no connection, beyond its name, with Elsynge Hall. It is said to have been situated in Ordnance Road, and in the middle of the sixteenth century was held under the Crown by a family named Wilforde.

The river Lea, as above stated, forms the eastern boundary of this division of the parish of Enfield. " It begynnethe (says Lambarde) near Whitchurche, and from thence passinge by Hert forde, Ware, and Waltham, openethe into the Thames at Ham, in Essex, whence this place is at this day called Lee-mouth. It hath of long tyme borne vessels from London twenty myles towards the head, for in the tyme of King Alfrede the Danes entered Leymouth, whence King Alfrede espied that the channell of the ryver might be in

---

* Mr. Pitt lived, however, as stated in the preceding chapter, at Enfield Chase.

such sorte weakened that they should want water to returne. He caused, therefore, the water to be abated by two greate trenches, and setting the Londonners upon them, he made their batteil wherein they lost four of their capitaines. Not long after they were so pressed that they forsoke all, and left their shippes as a prey to the Londonners, which breakyne some and burninge other, conveyed the rest to London."

The old and irregular course of the river is now of little use as a means of transit, having long ago been superseded by the Lea and Stort Navigation.

A curious celt was found some years ago in the Marsh at Enfield, twelve feet below the surface. It is figured in the *Gentleman's Magazine*, 1807.

The hamlet of Bull's Cross, which lies on the northern side of the parish, and in a bend of the New River, about half a mile westward of Enfield Highway, is said to have derived its name from an old cross which formerly stood there. In a deed of conveyance of land in this locality to one John Fforde (*temp*. Edward IV., 1483), it is called "Bedell's Cross." Chapel House, the residence of the Warrens, is situate at Bull's Cross, near the site of the old manor-house of Capels, *alias* Honeylands and Pentriches, which were formerly part of the possessions of Sir Giles Capel, who, in exchange for other lands, conveyed them to the Crown in 1547. The old mansion, together with the estate, was sold by Queen Elizabeth in 1562 to one William Horne, a merchant, and after passing through the hands of various successive purchasers, became, at the end of the last century, the property of the late Mr. Rawson H. Boddam, some time Governor of Bombay. Mr. Boddam pulled down the old manor-house, reserving little more than the stables, and transferred its name of Capel House to his own villa, which is said to occupy the site of the outbuildings of the palace of James I. at Theobalds. The old manor-house stood near a field, now called North Field, where are still the remains of an old garden, with some remarkable trees.

CHAPTER XXXIX.

THEOBALDS.

" You see these lifeless stumps of aspen wood :
Some say that they are beeches, others elms.
These were the Bower, and here a mansion stood,
The finest palace of a hundred realms !
The Arbour does its own condition tell :
You see the stones, the fountain, and the stream,
But as to the great Lodge, you might as well
Hunt half a day for a forgotten dream."—WORDSWORTH'S *Hart Leap Well*.

Situation of Theobalds, and History of the Manor—The Estate Purchased by Sir William Cecil, afterwards Lord Burleigh—James I. at Theobalds—Entertainment to Christopher IV., King of Denmark—Narrow Escape of King James—His Death Description of the Palace and Gardens—Demolition of the Palace—Present Condition of the Estate.

PASSING from Enfield in to the neighbouring parish of Cheshunt, we cross the border-line which separates the two counties of Middlesex and Herts. Before proceeding with a detailed account of that parish, however, it may be as well to bring before our mind's eye the regal domain of Theobalds, with its magnificent palace—once the favourite residence of the great Lord Burleigh, and afterwards of James I.

The estate—the name of which in ancient documents is variously written Theobals, Tibbolds, or Thebaudes (supposed to be the name of some previous owner)—immediately adjoined, and indeed included, part of Enfield Chase, and the manor of Capels at Bull's Cross, as mentioned at the end of the preceding chapter. The manor was formerly called *Cullynges*, and in the fourteenth century belonged to one William Attemore, of Cheshunt, who, being indebted to William de Tongge in the sum of £101, made over to him this manor, together with an estate named Le Mores, and from him it obtained the name of Tongge. It was afterwards named Thebaudes, and under that appellation was granted, in 1441, by the Crown to John Carpenter, Master of St. Anthony's Hospital, in London, and others, to hold "by the annual rental of a bow valued at 2s., and a barbed arrow, value 3d." The manor subsequently passed through various hands, until it was bought by Sir William Cecil (afterwards Lord Burleigh), from Robert Burbage of Theobalds, in the third year of Elizabeth. Robert Burbage was grandson of a William Burbage, who married Cicely, daughter and heiress of Sir Robert Green of Theobalds, whose mother was a daughter and co-heir of Sir John Cley, also of Theobalds, which would appear, as far back as 1450, to have had a character for feasting and revelry.

Sir William Cecil had been twice member of Parliament, Master of Requests, and Secretary of State to Edward IV. and Queen Elizabeth. In 1570 he increased the estate by the purchase of Cheshunt Park from Mr. Harrington, a fact which is duly entered in Sir William's Diary for the above year.

The original house at this time is supposed to have been placed on a small piece of rising ground, still visible. But in the summer of 1564, Queen Elizabeth having honoured him with a visit, and probably having expressed her intention of repeating it, he conceived the plan of enlarging the house, so as to entertain his royal mistress on subsequent occasions with becoming magnificence. He therefore erected a more spacious mansion, adorning it with beautiful gardens, and surrounding it with a moat filled with water, and wide enough for a pleasure-boat to ply between the "tall flag-flowers" and the turreted walls. The palace and grounds were completed by September, 1571, when the queen visited him again, and was presented with "a copy of verses" and a "portrait of the house." Elizabeth appears to have taken a particular fancy for Theobalds—probably from its proximity to the Chase at Enfield and to Waltham Forest, where she could enjoy the pleasures of hunting—for her visits were pretty frequent. Nor did her Majesty come alone. In 1583 she was attended by a large retinue, and stayed four days; the Earls of Leicester and Warwick, the Lord Admiral (Lord Howard), Lord Hunsdon, Sir Christopher Hatton, and Sir Francis Walsingham, were there with her. In the "Life of Lord Burleigh," "The Compleat Statesman," commonly known as "The Diary of a Domestic," it is written, " Her Majestie sometimes had strangers and ambassadors come to see her at Theobalds : where she hath byn sene in as great royalty, and served as bountifully and magnificently as at any other time or place, all at his lordship's chardg : with rich shows, pleasant devices, and all manner of sports could be devised, to the great delight of her Majestie and her whole traine."

Early in the summer of 1592, during one of her "progresses," the queen paid a visit to this place. It is thus mentioned in a letter from one of his friends to Sir Robert Sidney :—" I suppose you have heard of her Majesty's great entertainment at Theobalds ; of her knighting Mr. Robert Cecil, and of the expectation of his being advanced to the Secretaryship. But so it is, as we say in Court, that the knighthood must serve for both." (" Sidney Papers.")

As time went on wealth and honour multiplied upon Cecil. The queen created him Baron Burleigh, and she honoured him with her presence at Theobalds no less than a dozen times. Lord Burleigh entertained her Majesty most sumptuously, each visit, it is said, putting him to the expense of some £2,000 or £3,000. Some idea may be formed of his lordship's style of living from the fact that he had in his train twenty gentlemen, each with £1,000 a year. Indeed, it might truly be said of Theobalds in his day—

"Here he lives in state and bounty,
    Lord of Burleigh, fair and free;
Not a lord in all the county
    Is so great a lord as he."

Lord Burleigh was not a man who thought that greatness consisted in living in a great house ; and although his business was much at Court, still he felt he had duties at Cheshunt, and he fulfilled them heartily: relieving the poor, and maintaining, at a cost of £4,000 a year, a style of living which £40,000 a year certainly could not match at the present time. The usual expense of his house-keeping at Theobalds was £80 per week ; his stables cost him a thousand marks (£666 13s. 4d.) per annum. The sum of £10 per week was allotted to setting the poor to work in his garden ; and 20s. a week was distributed by the vicar of Cheshunt as his almoner.

In the " Diary of a Domestic" it is said in respect of Theobalds that the gardens, fountains, and walks were perfected most costly, beautifully, and pleasantly, where one might walk two miles in the walks before coming to the end. " The house at first," says the "Domestic," "he meant for a little pile, as I heard him say ; but after he came to entertain the queen so often there, he was forced to enlarge it, rather for the queen and her great train, and to give work to the poor, than for pomp and glory, for he ever said it would be too big for the small living he could leave his son." Lord Burleigh's character is summed up by his biographer as follows :—" His nature, though cold, was not mean or sordid, nor his heart narrow or selfish ; neither, with all his firmness (which some might call sternness), was his temper unkind, or his manners harsh, but the contrary ; in thirty years together he was seldom seen angry. He had his children, grandchildren, and great-grandchildren ordinarily at his table. If he might ride privately in his garden on his little mule, or lie for a day or two in his little lodge at Theobalds, secluded from business or too much company, he thought this his greatest and only happiness." At length a heavy loss befel him, and his second wife, Mildred, with whom he had lived on affectionate terms for forty-three years, passed away. He felt lonely and desolate in the midst of shows and tournaments; and his depression of spirits, coupled with the infirmities of old age, brought him to his end in 1598, and in his seventy-eighth year.

At his death Theobalds and the neighbouring estates passed into the possession of his youngest son, Sir Robert Cecil, who became Earl of Salisbury soon after the accession of James I. He not

The king had dined early in the day with Sir Henry Cocks at Broxbourne, and was accompanied by Sir Edward Denny, High Sheriff of Essex, and many of the Scottish and English nobility. An eye-witness of the reception, John Savile, thus describes the scene :—"As his Highness was espied coming towards Theobalds, the concourse of people was so frequent, every one desiring a sight of him, that it were incredible to tell of. And it was wonderful to see the infinite number of horse-

OLD THEOBALDS PALACE.
(From an Engraving in the "Gentleman's Magazine," 1836. See page 384.)

only succeeded to his father's country seat, but, like him, held the highest offices of state. He became Prime Minister to Queen Elizabeth, and was confirmed in that office by King James. Although the talents of Sir Robert were not equal to those of his father, yet he was the ablest statesman of his time. In three successive years he was made Baron of Essenden, Viscount Cranbourne, and Earl of Salisbury. In order to conciliate the favour of the new sovereign, Sir Robert embraced the earliest opportunity of honouring him. Accordingly, when his Majesty came from Scotland to take possession of the throne of England, in May, 1603, Sir Robert Cecil gave him a noble reception and princely entertainment at Theobalds.

men and footmen that went from the city of London that day thitherwards, and likewise from the counties of Kent, Surrey, Essex, and Middlesex, besides other counties. . . . When we were come to Theobalds, we understood his Majesty to be within the compass of three-quarters of a mile from the house. At which tidings we divided ourselves into three parts, each one taking a place of special note, to see what memorable accidents might happen within his compass : one standing at the upper end of the Walk, the second at the upper end of the first court, and the third (myself) at the second court's door ; and we made choice of a gentleman of good sort to stand in the court that leads into the hall, to take notice what was said or done by his Highness to the nobility of our land, or said or done by them to his Majesty, and to let us understand of it. All which accidents, as they happened in their several places, you shall hear in as few words as may be.

"Thus, then, for his Majesty's coming up the Walk. There came before him some of the nobility, some Barons, Knights, Esquires, Gentlemen, and others—amongst whom was the Sheriff of Essex and most of his men, the trumpets sounding next before his Highness, sometimes one,

answer that 'he should be heard, and have justice.'

"At the entrance to that court stood many noblemen, among whom was Sir Robert Cecil, who there meeting his Majesty, conducted him into his house; all which was practised with as great applause of the people as could be—hearty prayers and throwing up of hats.

"His Majesty had not stayed above an hour in his chamber, but hearing the multitude thronging so fast into the uppermost court to see his Highness, as his Grace was informed, he showed himself

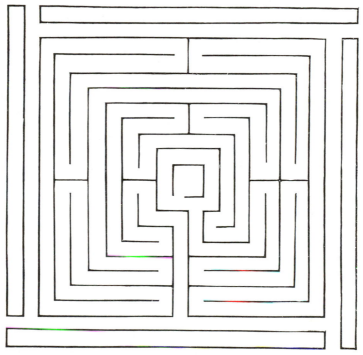

THE MAZE AT THEOBALDS. (*See page* 382.)

sometimes another; his Majesty not riding continually betwixt the same two noblemen, but sometimes with one and sometimes with another, as seemed best to his Highness; the whole nobility of our land and Scotland round about him, observing no place of superiority, but all bareheaded; all of whom alighted from their horses at their entrance to the first court, save only his Majesty, who alone rode along still, with four noblemen laying their hands upon his steed, two before and two behind. In this manner he came till he come to the court's door, where I myself stood, where he alighted from his horse, from which he had not gone ten princely paces but there was delivered to him a petition by a young gentleman; his Majesty returning his gracious

openly out of his chamber window by the space of half an hour together. After which time, he went into the labyrinth-like gardens to walk, where he recreated himself in the meanders, compact of bays, rosemary, and the like overshadowing his walk, to defend him from the heat of the sun, till supper time. At which there was such plenty of provision for all sorts of men in their due place as struck me with admiration.

"And first, to begin with, the ragged regiment, and such as were debarred the privilege of any court, these were so sufficiently rewarded with beef, veal, mutton, bread, and beer, that they sang 'Holy day' every day, and kept a continual feast. As for the poor maimed and distressed soldiers, which repaired thither for maintenance, the wine, money, and meat which they had in very bounteous sort, hath been a sufficient spur to cause them to blaze it abroad since their coming to London : whose thankfulness is not altogether unknown to myself, some of whom, hearing that I was about to publish this small 'Remembrance,' made means to me to give me true information of such princely exhibition as they daily received during the time of his Majesty's abode at Theobalds."

The king appears to have won golden opinions during his stay at Theobalds by publishing a proclamation ordering that the price of victuals, such as meat, bread, butter, and cheese, should not be raised to exorbitant prices within the verge of his court. He arrived on Tuesday, the 3rd of May, and proceeded on to London, by way of Stamford Hill, on Saturday, the 7th ; and it is on record that he spent the intervening Wednesday in a visit to Enfield Chase.

In 1606 the earl gave a second entertainment to his sovereign, and to Christopher IV., King of Denmark, who stayed with him four days. The king was so delighted with Theobalds, and its convenient situation for his favourite amusement of hunting, that he desired to become possessed of this noble mansion, and make it his principal place of abode. He therefore gave in exchange for it the more valuable mansion of Hatfield, and shortly after commenced the work of improving and embellishing Theobalds by enlarging the park, apportioning, as we have already seen, a good slice of Enfield Chase,* with parts of Northaw and Cheshunt Common. The king at that time enclosed Theobalds with a brick wall ten miles in circumference, part of which wall still remains in the grounds of Albury House, and other parts at Bury Green and Cuffley.

The scene which presented itself at Theobalds during the feastings and masks in honour of the visit of Christian IV. has been described by one of the guests in the following terms :—"After dinner the representation of Solomon and his Temple, and the coming of the Queen of Sheba, was made, or (as I may say better) was meant to have been made. The lady who did play the queen's part did carry most precious gifts to both their Majesties, but forgetting the steps arising to the canopy, overset her caskets into his Danish Majesty's lap, and fell at his feet, though I rather think it was in his face. Much was the hurry and confusion ; cloths and napkins were at hand to make all clean. His Majesty then got up, and

would dance with the Queen of Sheba ; but he fell down, and was carried to an inner chamber. The entertainment and show went forward, and most of the presenters went backward or fell down : wind did so occupy their upper chambers. Now did appear, in rich dresses, Faith, Hope, and Charity. Hope did essay to speak, but wine did render her endeavours so feeble that she withdrew. Faith was then all alone, for I am certain she was not joined with good works, and left the court in a staggering condition. Charity came to the king's feet ; she then returned to Hope and Faith, who were both sick in the lower hall."

Theobalds was exchanged for Hatfield House, with Robert, first Earl of Salisbury, by James I., in 1607, and in 1614 his Majesty received a second visit from the King of Denmark, and entertained him for fifteen days with an uninterrupted succession of feasting and diversions. Fond as the king was of hunting—so fond that the people used to say, " God's peace be with you, as King James said to his hounds "—he was a bad rider, and often thrown. Thus, " when staying at Theobalds in the depth of winter, he rode out one day after dinner, and his horse stumbling, he was cast into the New River. The ice broke, and in plunged his august Majesty head foremost, while nothing but his boots remained visible. It would have gone ill with him that day had not Sir Richard Young alighted, and ran to the rescue. His attendants had to empty him, like an inverted cask, of the river water he had drunk so freely against his will ; and a warm bed at Theobalds soon restored him to his pleasures and follies."*

From Ellis's " Letters " we learn that James did many wicked, cracked-brained things at Theobalds, for he had " fools, fiddlers, and master-fools ; " and Jesse tells us how some called him " Old wife," and his minions addressed him as " Your sowship ; " that the ladies of his court rolled about intoxicated, and he himself was carried off to bed, after having proposed five-and-thirty healths ; how oaths were never off his lips, nor cowardice and hypocrisy ever out of his heart ; and how, as the counterpart of all his vice and foolery, he translated the Psalms, wrote books of piety, and welcomed bishops to his presence as warmly as if they had been buffoons. One of these was Joseph Hall, Bishop of Norwich. He had previously been curate of Waltham Abbey, and he preached several times before James and his court at Theobalds. Laud notes in his " Diary," September 17th, 1609:

---

* Ellis's Letters, "Joseph Meade to Sir Martin Stuteville, January 11th, 1622."

" My first sermon before King James at Theobalds."

James died at Theobalds on the 27th of March, 1625, and the blood was hardly cold in his veins when a knight-marshal was seen issuing from the palace to proclaim his successor. His name was Sir Edward Zouch, and when he reached the court-gate, and silence had been secured by the heralds, he solemnly proclaimed James's son Charles as king, but by an unfortunate and, as many thought, ominous slip of the tongue, instead of styling the new sovereign " the rightful and *indubitable* heir," he used the words " rightful and *dubitable* heir," and was corrected in his error by the secretary.

March 27th, 1625.—Laud tells us in his " Diary" that whilst preaching at Whitehall this day he heard the news of the death of James I. " The king died at Theobalds about three-quarters of an hour after eleven in the forenoon. He breathed forth his soul most religiously, and with great constancy of faith and courage. That day, about five o'clock, Prince Charles was solemnly proclaimed king. God grant to him," adds Laud, " a prosperous and happy reign !" Prayers and pious wishes, it would seem, are not always fulfilled. At Theobalds Laud did homage to Charles I. on being made Bishop of Bath and Wells.

On the day following the death of King James, Charles took coach at Theobalds with Buckingham, and went to London, and was proclaimed at Whitehall and Cheapside. The usual route by which the king went from London to Theobalds may still be traced by the names of streets on the north side of Holborn: namely, Kingsgate Street, King Street, King's Road, and Theobalds Road.

Theobalds continued a royal residence till the commencement of the Civil War, and to this place Charles retired when he found himself no longer safe at Westminster. From here, in July, 1635, he wrote to the Earl of Salisbury to obtain a supply of food for his Majesty's deer in the park from the adjoining parishes, for, owing to great drought, Cheshunt could not furnish a sufficient quantity of hay and oats. Here the king received the petition from both houses of Parliament in 1645, and from hence he, a short time afterwards, set out for the north, and raised aloft his standard at Nottingham. During the contest between the king's forces and the Parliamentarians, the palace was plundered and very much defaced, and the manor appears to have been parcelled out among the officers of the Parliamentary army.

Norden, in his account of Hertfordshire in the reign of Elizabeth, states that he found the palace of " Thibauldes, or Theobalde," so vast a subject that he despaired of being able to do it justice. " To speake," he says, " of the state and beuty thereof at large as it deserveth, for curious buildinges, delightfull walkes, and pleasant conceites, within and without, and other thinges very glorious and ellegant to be seene, would challenge a great portion of this little treatise ; and therefore, leaste I should come shorte of that due commendation that it deserveth, I leave it, as indeed it is, a princely seat."

In a survey of the house, taken in 1650, when it was being pulled down, it was stated to consist of two principal quadrangles, besides the Dial Court, the Buttery Court, and the Dove-house Court, in which the offices were situated. The Fountain Court, so called from a fountain of black and white marble in the centre, was a quadrangle, eighty-six feet square, on the east side of which was a cloister eight feet wide, with seven arches. On the ground-floor of this quadrangle was a spacious hall paved with Purbeck marble, and the roof arched with carved timber of curious workmanship. On the same floor were the Lord Holland's, the Marquis of Hamilton's, and the Lord Salisbury's lodging-rooms (for the last-mentioned nobleman was made keeper of Theobalds House by King James in 1619), the council chamber, and the chamber for the king's waiters. On the second floor was the Presence Chamber, " wainscoted with carved oak, painted of a liver colour, and richly gilded, with antique pictures over the same ; the ceiling full of gilded pendants, setting forth the room with great splendour ; there were large windows, and several coats-of-arms set in the same." These windows opened south on the walks in the great garden leading to the gate going into the park, where was an avenue of trees a mile long. There was also the Privy Chamber, the Withdrawing Room, the King's Bedchamber, and a gallery 123 feet long by twenty-one feet broad, " wainscoted with oak, and paintings over the same of divers cities, rarely painted, and set forth with a frett seelinge, with divers pendants, roses, and fleurs-de-lys, painted and gilded with gold, also divers large stagges' heads sett round the same, and fastened to the sayd roome, which are an excellent ornament to the same." The windows of this gallery looked " north into the park, and so to Cheshunt." On an upper floor were the Lord Chamberlain's lodgings, my lord's withdrawing chamber, and several other apartments.

Near the Chamberlain's lodgings, on the east, was a leaded walk, 62 feet in length and 11 in breadth, with an arch of freestone over it ; " which sayd arch and walk," says the Survey, " looking eastward into the Middle Court, and into the highway leading from London to Ware, standeth high, and may easily be discerned by passengers and travellers, to their delight." On the west of the Lord Chamberlain's lodgings was another walk of the same dimensions, looking westward into the Fountain Court. At the corners of these walks stood "fower high, fair, and large towers, covered with blue slate, with a lyon and vaines on the top of each, and in the walk over the hall, in the midst of the fowre corners, one faire and large turrett, in the fashion of a lanthorne, made with timber of excellent workmanship, curiouslie wrought, standinge a great height, with divers pinacles at each corner, wherein hangeth twelve bells for chiminge, and a clocke with chimes of sundrie worke." The walk from the lower gate up to the middle of the Fountain Court is described as leading "through the severall courtes, so that the figure of Cupid and Venus (which stood between the pillars of the fountain) maye easily be seene from the highway when the gates are open." This walk, continues the Survey, "is so delightful and pleasant, facing the middle of the house, and the severall towers, turretts, windowes, chimneyes, walkes, and balconies, that the like walke, for length, pleasantness, and delight, is rare to be seene in England."

The Middle Court was a quadrangle 110 feet square, having on the south side the Queen's Chapel (with windows of stained glass), her presence chamber, privy chamber, bed chamber, and coffer chamber. The prince's lodgings were on the north side; on the east side was a cloister, over which was a green gallery, over 100 feet in length by 12 in breadth, "excellently well painted round with the severall shires in England, and the armes of the noblemen and gentlemen in the same." Over this gallery was a leaded walk (looking eastward towards the Dial Court and the highway), on which were two "loftie arches of bricke, of no small ornament to the house, and rendering it comely and pleasant to all that passed by." On the west of the quadrangle was another cloister of five arches, over which were the duke's lodgings, and over them the Queen's Gallery, 109 feet by fourteen feet.

On the south side of the house stood "a large open cloister, built upon severall large faire pillars of stone arched over with seven arches, with a faire raill and balisters, well painted with the Kinges and Queenes of England, and the pedigree of the old Lord Burleigh and divers other ancient families, with paintings of many castles and battailes, with divers superscriptions on the walls." This cloister was standing in 1765, and the mutilated remnants of the "pedigrees," as they then existed, were engraved for Nichols's "Progresses of Queen Elizabeth." The whole house was built, as the Survey states, of excellent brick, with coins, jambs, and cornices of stone. "The basement of the house," observes Mr. John C. Earle, in an account of the palace published in 1869, "was faced with fine ashlared limestone, and the cornice, of which a small portion remains, was of the Doric order. The upper storeys were of fine red brick, divided from one another by stone cornices. From what remains of these cornices, it appears that the upper portion of the edifice was of the Ionic or Corinthian order; and it is highly probable that the three classical orders—Doric, Ionic, and Corinthian—were used one above the other, as in many buildings of the same period—Burleigh House, for example, the schools at Oxford, and the second quadrangle of Merton College."

Paul Hentzner, a German traveller, has left us the following description of the gardens of Theobalds, as they appeared in 1598, just after the death of Lord Burleigh :—" Here are great variety of trees and plants; labyrinths made with a great deal of labour; a *jet d'eau*, with its basin of white marble; and columns and pyramids of wood and other materials up and down the garden. After seeing these, we are led by the gardener into the summer-house, in the lower part of which, built semi-circularly, are the twelve Roman emperors in white marble, and a table of touchstone; the upper part of it is set round with cisterns of lead, into which the water is conveyed through pipes, so that fish may be kept in them, and in summer time they are very convenient for bathing; in another room for entertainment very near this, and joined to it by a little bridge, was an oval table of red marble."

In addition to the great gardens were the priory gardens, with other enclosures for pheasants, aviaries, and menageries, for James was very fond of wild beasts, and had a collection of them worthy of a Zoological Garden. In one of his letters to Buckingham, when the latter was at Madrid, we find him inquiring about the "elephants, camels, wild asses," &c. He had always a large camel-house at Theobalds, whilst the tennis-court, stables, kennels, and falconry, were on a scale of magnitude proportionate to the palace.

In the gardens of Theobalds was one of those curious contrivances called mazes, or labyrinths, such as we have seen at Hampton Court.* "In the reigns of Henry VIII. and Elizabeth," observes a writer in the *Archæological Journal* (Vol. xv.,

---

* See *ante*, p. 171.

p. 228), "mazes were much in vogue, and there must then have been a frequent demand for fabricators of verdant subtilties, a maze formed by neatly-clipped hedges being an usual adjunct to the royal residences, and probably also to those of the nobility." Although these mazes have been for the most part destroyed, their past existence is indicated by the retention of the name of Maze in the vicinity of the spots they had once occupied, such as Maze Lane and Maze Pond,* in South-wark, marking the site of the Princess Mary Tudor's residence, alluded to by Miss Strickland in her "Lives of the Queens of England," and called the Manor of "Le Maze" in the reign of Henry VI. ; also by the name of Maze Hill at Greenwich,† which was once supplied with a similar means of amusing the royal inmates of the adjoining palace.

Of Theobalds itself nothing remains but the park, and a few of the walls of the royal gardens and outhouses. Three or four large mansions have been erected on the site of these gardens and terraces, and the noble cedars, poplars, and evergreens, attest the former splendour of the place. The garden walks still remain as of old, though no longer trodden by the feet of brave cavaliers and fair ladies of the court. In one portion of the walls which remain are a number of small niches, which look as if they had been intended for saints, though they were not built till long after the saints were banished from our churches. Their use is a mystery. In one corner of the garden was an alcove in the wall, where Dr. Watts used to sit whilst a visitor here ; and tradition says that he wrote here some of his hymns and poems, including possibly "The Little Busy Bee."

Though Theobalds was demolished by order of Parliament during the Commonwealth, and the money arising from the sale of the materials was divided among the army, self-interest or shame restrained in some degree the violence of the destroyers. The commissioners who were appointed by Parliament in 1650 to make a survey of the palace reported that "it was an excellent building, in very good repair, by no means fit to be demolished, and that it was worth £2,000 per annum, exclusive of the park ; yet, lest the Parliament should think proper to have it taken down, they had estimated the materials, and found them to be worth £8,275 11s." Notwithstanding this report, the greater part of the palace was taken down, and the materials sold ; the royal park was converted into farms, and several "pleasant residences" have been erected where royalty once

delighted to assemble and enjoy the beauties of a rural retreat. An almshouse adjoining the stables, built probably by Lord Burleigh, continued to be a refuge for the aged poor. It is mentioned in a "Life of the Earl of Salisbury," printed in 1612, that it was occupied by "aged and over-worne captaines, gentlemen by birth and calling." This building, which had the arms of Cecil in front, and was furnished with a hall and chapel, was standing till about the year 1812.

The park contained 2,500 acres, and was valued, together with six lodges, at £1,545 15s. 4d. per annum. The deer was valued at £1,000, the rabbits at £15, and the timber at £7,259 13s. 2d., exclusive of 15,608 trees marked for the use of the navy, and others already cut down for that purpose. The materials of the barn and walls were valued at £1,570 16s. 3d.

Among the few parts of the palace that were left standing after the dismantlement, about 1650, was one of the chapels, which continued to be used by the Presbyterians till the year 1689, when the site of the palace and the park were granted by William III. to the Earl of Portland. Charles II. had previously made a grant of the park and manor to the man who had seated him on the throne of his father. This was George Monk, Duke of Albemarle. After the death of Monk, in 1607, his son Christopher enjoyed it ; but on his death without issue it reverted to the Crown, where it remained until granted to the Earl of Portland, as above mentioned. Somehow, however, the manor of Theobalds did not go with the park and house ; but after frequently changing hands, it became, towards the close of the last century, the inheritance of Oliver Cromwell, Esq., the last male descendant of Henry, the Protector's son. From the Earl of Portland the property passed to his son, whom George I. created a duke ; and about the middle of the last century the property was sold to one of the Prescott family, who afterwards became possessed of the manor. The last remains of the palace were eventually destroyed, and on their site were erected the houses which now form Theobalds Square, in the village of Cheshunt. About the same time a new park of 200 acres was enclosed by Sir G. Prescott, who also built a handsome brick mansion, on rising ground, about a mile north-west from the site of the palace, and at a short distance from the New River, which runs through the grounds. The new house is somewhat similar in plan to that of St. James's Palace. A considerable improvement and addition was made to it by the late Sir Henry Meux, who held it under Sir George Prescott some years since.

* See "Old and New London," Vol. VI., p. 104.
† *Ibid*, Vol. VI., p. 230.

Mr. S. Beazley, the architect, dramatist, and man of letters, designed a new staircase here for the Meuxes, who affected to drop the "x" in pronouncing their names, and to sound the name as if it were "Muse" or "Mews;" and when done, he styled it in jest a "Gradus ad Parnassum," the latter being the fabled seal of the Heavenly Nine. Lord William Lennox wrote the following *jeu d'esprit* on the name : —

"There's *Meux* entire—called Mews the swells among,
　Though *Mieux* is better in a foreign tongue;
　Tant Mieux, why change the sounds? nay, 'tis no myth,
　Tayleur was Taylor once, and Smythe was Smith."

The property, which is now called Theobalds Park, was bought by Sir Henry Meux in 1882. It is one of the most compact estates for its size of any within the same distance of London. There are several roads through it, but no right of carriage-way to any but the owner, although the public have the privilege of passing through it on foot.

Sir Thomas Abney had a house at Theobalds, and here Dr. Watts lived with him for some time before his removal to Stoke Newington.* In a summer-house in the garden, as stated above, he is said to have composed many of his hymns.

In the *Gentleman's Magazine* for February, 1836, there is an engraving of "the Royal Palace of Theobalds," derived from a drawing in the Fitzwilliam Museum at Cambridge. It had been previously known only from a vignette in Pickering's edition of Izaak Walton's "Complete Angler." The embattled gatehouse, with its oriel window above the archway, and the clock-tower and other buildings beyond, recalls to mind to a certain extent the appearance of Wolsey's Gateway and the older portions of Hampton Court Palace. The central tower, with its turrets and cupola, was doubtless a conspicuous object from many parts of the surrounding country; at all events, it would appear to have been visible to Izaak Walton's worthy anglers, Auceps and Piscator, in their walk along the banks of the Lea; for the former remarks, "I shall by your favour bear you company as far as Theobalds," and the latter shortly after says, "I must in manners break off, for I see Theobalds House."

CHAPTER XL.

CHESHUNT.

"There the most daintie paradise on ground,
　Itselfe doth offer to the sober eye,
　In which all pleasures plenteously abownd,
　And none does others happiness envye.
　The painted flowers, the trees upshooting hye;
　The dales for shade; the christall running by,
　And that which all fair works doth most aggrace,
　The art which all that wrought appeared in no place."—EDMUND SPENSER.

Situation and General Appearance of the Parish—Its Etymology—Supposed Site of a Roman Station or Camp –Discovery of Roman Coins, &c.—The Mound at Bury Green—A Curious Manorial Custom—Census Returns—The River Lee—A Disputed Landmark—Early History and Descent of the Manor of Cheshunt—The Manor of Moteland, or St. Andrew's le Mote—The Great House—The Parish Church—The Cemetery, &c.—Cheshunt College—Pengelly House—Cheshunt Park—The Cromwell Family—Other Notable Residents and Seats—Waltham Cross—"The Four Swans" Inn—The Spital Houses—Holy Trinity Church—The Benedictine Convent—Goff's Oak—St. James's Church.

CHESHUNT, which will now form the subject of our remarks, is both extensive and pleasingly diversified with agricultural and park-like scenery. It is, in fact, undulating, well-wooded, and well-watered, and irregular in plan. The most populous part of the village, called Cheshunt Street, is built on either side of the great North Road, a continuation of the road from London through Enfield Highway, by Waltham Cross—which, by the way, is really part of Cheshunt—and so on to Ware; so that the inhabitants, if they had happened to have been at their windows on that eventful day, would have witnessed John Gilpin's involuntary ride to that place, and also his return journey, though the fact is not commemorated by Cowper in his inimitable ballad. The older part of the parish, however, is grouped round the church, and is called Church Street, or Church Gate. Here were some old mansions, including Pengelly House, and two or three with projecting upper storeys. The parish is intersected from north to south by water. The Lea bounds it on the east, and the New River cuts it through nearer the western limit; the Great Eastern Railway has two stations in the parish—one at Waltham Cross and the other at Cheshunt.

The name of the parish is a curious admixture

---

* See "Old and New London," Vol. V., p. 539.

of the Roman and the Saxon element, if it be true, as generally stated, that it is derived from "Ceastre," "Castrum," and "Hunt," implying that it had been a Roman encampment in a forest, or weald. Salmon, in his "History of Hertfordshire," states that here was a Roman station or fortified camp connected with the military road called Ermine Street, of which we have spoken in a previous chapter,* and which road was intersected by another leading

Salmon to place here the *Durolitum* of Antoninus; and this opinion has been thought to receive support from the fact of Roman coins of the Emperors Hadrian, Claudius Gothicus, and Constantine, having been discovered here. These were exhibited at a meeting of the Society of Antiquaries in 1724. In Gough's "Camden," however, it is questioned whether *Durolitum* should not rather be placed at Durnford, vulgarly called Turn-

CHESHUNT CHURCH.

to the camp, which was situated at Kilsmore, near Cheshunt Street. Be this as it may, however, the subject has been one of dispute among antiquarians, some asserting that the supposed vallum and fosse in Kilsmore field were nothing more than a cut originally intended for the New River, but laid aside as less convenient than the present channel. This fosse, at all events, has been entirely effaced by a large reservoir, formed by the New River Company; but the farm close by still bears the name of Kilsmore.

This supposed fosse and military way induced

ford, a little village at the north end of Cheshunt, by Cheshunt Wash. The notion of Cheshunt having been the site of a Roman settlement may seem to be further strengthened by an urn, said to be Roman, having been found here; it is to be seen embedded in the front of an inn called "The Roman Urn," in Crossbrook Street. The urn was found on the spot many years ago, whilst some excavations were being made; but its date is far from certain.

Salmon also makes mention of an old tumulus, or Druidical mound, near Bury Green, with ascending paths corresponding to the four cardinal points; this is also disputed, some topographers

* See *ante*, p. 368.

supposing it to be a hillock on which, in days long gone by, stood a windmill; whilst Clutterbuck thinks it more likely to be the site of an old manor house.

It is supposed that the boundary of the kingdom of the East Saxons passed through Theobalds and across Goff's Lane, to Beaumont Green, and so on to the ancient city of Verulam (St. Albans). It was marked by a bank, but no trace now remains.

One peculiarity of the manors in Cheshunt is recorded by Mr. Thorne, who writes:—"An irregular line, known as the Bank's line, runs north and south through the parish; east of it, or *below bank*, by far the larger and more valuable portion, the land and tenements are subject to borough-English, *i.e.*, descend to the youngest son, while west of the line, or *above bank*, the eldest son succeeds." This custom, observes Salmon, could not have been introduced except by different laws of different governments.

Cheshunt was originally divided into eight villages, or hamlets, namely : Waltham Cross, Carbuncle Street, Turner's Hill, Cheshunt Street, Hamon (now Hammond) Street, Appleby Street, Wood Green, and Cockerams. The parish is divided into three wards, known as Waltham Cross, Cheshunt Street, and Woodside Cross Wards; and, inclusive of the ecclesiastical districts of Waltham Cross and Goff's Oak, it contains nearly 8,500 acres, and is estimated at thirty miles in circumference, with a population, in 1881, of 7,700, being an increase of rather more than 1,000 during the preceding ten years.

The parish is separated from that of Waltham Abbey by the River Lea, which, forming two channels at that part, has given rise to much litigation and contention between the inhabitants of the two parishes, each party claiming the piece of valuable marsh-land between the streams, and each asserting that to be the original stream which affords the greatest extent of territory. This undecided dominion has sometimes been attacked and defended by the weapons of the law, and at others by personal prowess. These disputes first began between the Abbot of Waltham Abbey and the townsmen of Waltham about the year 1245. The abbot and his convent having possession of the marsh, which they had enjoyed for many years, the townsmen killed some of their cattle and drove out the rest. Disturbances arose; the subject was brought before the King's Bench; but the townsmen acknowledging their error, the quarrel came to an end. A fiercer and greater strife, however, soon after broke out with reference to this piece of land between the Abbot of Waltham and the

Lord of the Manor of Cheshunt, but the question does not appear to have been satisfactorily settled, for in 1601, on the men of Cheshunt "beating the bounds," they are considered to have over-stepped the mark, as the following entry in the parish records of Waltham testify:—"The curate of Cheshunt and some of the churchwardens . . . . did come in their perambulation to our high bridge, and for so doing, and coming out of their own liberty, they were for their pains thrust into a ditch, called Hook's Ditch." The situation of the place where this disaster occurred appears to be not far from the disputed piece of marsh-land. The rich and fertile marshes of which those in dispute form a part were laid under water in the time of King Alfred (897), and were then navigable, so that the Danes sailed up the river to Hertford, where they built two forts for the security of their ships; but in order to secure them from returning, Alfred, with pioneers, divided the principal stream of the Lea with several rivulets, so that their ships were left on dry land, which so terrified them that they abandoned their forts, and being hotly pursued, were compelled to flee the country. These marshes were formally called the King's Meads, many being drained and capable of bearing grass, and the king gave them for "common" to the several adjacent parishes.

Cheshunt contains several subordinate manors. The principal manor, from which some of the others have branched off since the time of the Domesday Survey, was given by the Conqueror to his nephew, Earl Alan, surnamed the "Red," who commanded the rear of his army at the battle of Hastings, and was rewarded with the earldom of Richmond, in Yorkshire, the manor of Cheshunt being assigned to him in order to support his newly-acquired dignity.

Earl Alan was a son of Eudes, Earl of Brittany, by a sister of William the Conqueror. The following is the entry relating to this parish in "Domesday Book":—"Earl Alan himself holds Cestrehunt. It was rated at twenty hides. Arable land thirty-three carucates. In demesne are ten hides, and there are four carucates, and two may yet be made. Forty-one villanes, with a priest and twelve bordars, have seventeen carucates there. Ten merchants pay ten shillings for custom there. There are eight cottagers and six bondmen, and one mill worth ten shillings. From a stream sixteen-pence. Meadow, twenty-three carucates, and fodder for the lord's horses. Pasture for cattle. Pannage for one thousand two hundred hogs, and forty pence." On the death of Earl Alan, without issue, in 1089, the manor passed to his half-brother, surnamed

Niger, who also died without issue, and was succeeded by his brother Stephen, and with his descendants it remained till the beginning of the thirteenth century, when it was granted by the Crown to William, Bishop of Carlisle. In 1241 Henry III. gave the manor to Peter de Savoy, uncle of Eleanor, his queen, and in the following year granted him the right of holding an annual fair of two days' duration within this manor. Another fair, to last four days, was subsequently granted to Peter de Savoy, but both have died out. Cheshunt Fair, which had from time immemorial been held in Cheshunt Street on the 24th of August, was abolished by the local magistrates in 1859.

The manor, after the death of Peter de Savoy, saw several successive changes of ownership. In 1525 it was granted by Henry VIII. to his illegitimate son, Henry Fitzroy, who was created Duke of Richmond and Somerset, but on his death, at the age of seventeen, it again reverted to the Crown. Edward VI. granted it to Sir John Gates, on whose attainder for high treason in supporting the claims of Lady Jane Grey to the throne, his estates were forfeited, and once more this manor came to the Crown. Queen Mary granted it to Sir John Huddlestone, who shortly after conveyed it to the family of Cock of Broxbourne. It was afterwards owned by Lord Monson, who in 1782 sold it to the Prescotts, Sir George R. Prescott, Bart., being the present owner.

The old manor house of the chief manor has disappeared, and even its site is uncertain. But on the north of Goff's Lane, a short distance northwest of the church, stands a curious old-fashioned house of red brick, among some trees in a meadow. It seems as if it had been surrounded by a moat, and is called St. Andrew's le Mote, though locally known as the " Great House," or the " Moated House," or the " Haunted House." It must be owned that its appearance would give such an impression. It is now a solid square, but evidently has formed part of a larger structure. It must have been built as far back as the fifteenth century at least, and some arches in the cellars (said to be a portion of a crypt or chapel) are probably older still. The great hall, which reaches to the roof, is certainly of a date anterior to Henry VII.; but the story is that it was built by Cardinal Wolsey. For this, however, there is no proof, nor even that he ever lived here, though the Manor of Moteland here was given to him by the tyrant. The building is said originally to have contained more than thirty rooms, and to have been quadrangular in plan. What at present remains consists of the hall above

mentioned, with apartments towards the north, and a vaulted crypt underneath, which is said to have been the chapel, and to have been paved with embossed tiles. The dimensions of the hall are twenty-seven feet by twenty-one, and it is thirty-six feet high. It has an arched roof supported by timber-worked ribs of chestnut, in the Gothic style; the sides are wainscoted, and the floor is paved with black and white marble, so that altogether it remains in much the same state as when the Tudors and Stuarts occupied the throne, except that the minstrels' gallery and the buttery-hatch at the lower end are gone, and that the daïs has also disappeared. The hall is hung with portraits of very doubtful authenticity, and first on the list is one of Wolsey—probably a copy. There are altogether about a hundred portraits of kings, statesmen, court ladies, judges, &c., mostly of the fifteenth, sixteenth, and seventeenth centuries, though some are even more recent. Near the fireplace hangs the portrait of Wolsey, and above this a family piece of the Shaws, who formerly owned the manor, painted by Sir Peter Lely, in which is depicted Sir John Shaw, his wife, and nine children; among the other portraits are Queen Elizabeth, Charles I., and Charles II., ascribed to Vandyck, William III. and Queen Mary, Sir Hugh Myddelton, James II., Richard Cromwell, Archbishops Laud and Juxon, Lord Falkland, Thomas Lord Fairfax, and several members of the Mayo family. The apartment also contains several suits of chain and other armour, many banners, escutcheons, and weapons of war, besides a curious old-fashioned chair and a few other bits of furniture, which, to keep up the tradition of the place, are said to have belonged to Cardinal Wolsey. Nearly all the pictures are in a sad condition of decay, being left to the care of a labourer's family, who live in the back part of the house, and show the place to visitors. In an upper chamber, called the haunted room, and said to have been the scene of a barbarous murder, are an arm-chair and a mutilated rocking-horse, both said to have belonged to Charles I., who, as a child, must often have been at Theobalds. In the vaults below the house is a chopping-block, which the guardians of the place tell the credulous visitor was used by Cromwell in the execution of his captives. Some years ago two skeletons, with a pitcher and a lantern, were discovered enclosed in a cavity in the wall, in a corner of the crypt.

After the time of Wolsey we find the manor in the hands of the families of Dennis and Dacre, whose monuments are to be seen in the church.

From them it passed to the Shaws, one of whom repaired it in the middle of the last century, modernising it in the most tasteless manner; and early in the present century a subsequent owner, the Rev. Charles Mayo, completed the task of mutilation, destroying half of it in order to provide materials for the repair of the rest, and at the same time filling up the moat which surrounded it.

The parish church, dedicated to St. Mary the Virgin, stands about a quarter of a mile south of the "Great House," and half a mile west of the high road. It is a fine handsome Early Perpendicular structure, very much of the same type with those of Bishop Stortford, Thaxted, Dunmow, Saffron Walden, and other neighbouring towns. It consists of nave, chancel, and side aisles, and a handsome embattled tower, with good western doorway, adorned with shields; there are niches for saints in the angles of the west window, but their occupants are gone. The tower is built of flint and stone, and has an octagonal cupola containing six bells, dating from 1636 to 1760. Early in the present century the body of the church was thoroughly repaired and galleries were erected, and in 1855 it was "re-pewed" and re-arranged. In 1872 the church was considerably enlarged and restored, not over-judiciously, by Mr. Joseph Clarke. The galleries were taken down, the plaster was removed from the walls, and the pillars, which are of Purbeck marble, were divested of the paint with which they had been covered; but the south aisle was enlarged at the east end in such a manner as to spoil the symmetry of the building. At the north-east angle of the church was an ancient vestry, with a small room over it. Between the nave and chancel on either side is a curious ornamental recess, like a window, pierced through the solid wall. Its object and design is uncertain. On the south side is an opening, through which access was gained to the rood-loft. The new chancel is handsome and spacious, but painfully new. The font is probably that of the original church, long previous to the fifteenth century. Several of the windows are filled with stained glass, as memorials of local worthies.

As might be supposed from the former presence of the Court at Theobalds, the church contains several fine Jacobean monuments. On the north side of the chancel is a Gothic altar tomb to Sir Robert Dacres, a member of the Privy Council of Henry VIII., on the top of which is placed a Jacobean monument to one of King James's physicians. Others, of various types of merit, are to be seen on the walls.

At the west end of the north aisle there is a fine piece of sculpture, a marble statue and tomb of one David Dodson, who died in 1761, and who seems to have had little scruple in blocking up a fine window with his effigy. The statue, however, is evidently by a master-hand, and has not been properly appreciated.

There is a brass under the communion table to Nicholas Dixon, Vicar of Cheshunt, the builder of the present edifice (on the site of a former church). He died in 1448, having held several offices at Court which sound rather secular to our ears— "Clerk of the Pipe Office, Under Treasurer, and Baron of the Exchequer."[*]

At the north-west corner of the churchyard is a large square heavy tomb, under which rest the bodies of several members of the Cromwell family, and of their successors, the Russells. Richard Cromwell, however, though he died here, lies at Hursley, near Winchester. There are also monuments to various members of the Meux, Prescott, and Daking families, and one to the only son of Lord Chancellor Eldon, with an inscription from the pen of his uncle, Lord Stowell.

Near the vicarage gate is an old stone coffin, without a lid, probably of Anglo-Saxon date. This was discovered, bottom upwards, a few feet from the chancel door, in 1872, on digging the foundations for the extension of the south aisle.

The cemetery, in Bury Green Road, to the south-west of the church, was formed in 1855, on land given by the late General Osborn. It is about five acres in extent, and in the centre is a building with a square tower and spire, and comprising two mortuary chapels.

Two of the houses at the corner of Church Street, on the opposite side of the way, are said to be the originals of the Great and Small House in Mr. Anthony Trollope's novel of "The Small House at Allington," being sketched from the life by the author during a stay in the village.

Nearly opposite the church is Cheshunt College, which was founded in 1768 by Lady Huntingdon at Trevecca, in South Wales, but transferred here after her death, in 1792. The institution, which has since been affiliated to the University of London, is for the training of young men for the Noncon-formist ministry. The college was originally a gentleman's mansion, and is of the Queen Anne type. Of this house a part remains, now used as a lecture-room. Other buildings of a commonplace character were erected in 1863; these included a chapel and library. In 1872 a new structure, of Decorated Gothic, with some foreign details, was

---

* Chauncy's "History of Herts," Vol. I.

opened. It contains lecture-rooms and dwelling-rooms for about forty students. Its tall campanile, or spire, is visible for miles round on every side. The library is octagonal. The hall contains some fine portraits and engravings of John and Charles Wesley, Lady Huntingdon, and other members of the Ferrers family—for she was by birth a Shirley—and also of several of the presidents of the college. The grounds, some fifteen acres in extent, are bounded by the New River, which runs at their foot.

On the bank of the water is a summer-house, of the square type so common along the course of the New River. It is called "Dr. Watts' Wig," from some tradition—possibly baseless—that it was haunted by that worthy in his lifetime. Near the college is a narrow thoroughfare, called Dr. Watts' Lane, "from a questionable tradition," writes Mr. Thorne, in his " Environs of London," " that it was the favourite stroll of the great Nonconformist divine during his visits to Richard Cromwell."

Besides the above institution Cheshunt is well supplied with schools, the oldest in point of foundation being Dewhurst's, at Church Gate, which

RICHARD CROMWELL.

dates from the middle of the seventeenth century. This school was enlarged and considerably improved in 1847.

Pengelly House, near the church, occupies the site of the residence of Richard Cromwell, the deposed Protector, who, after his return from the Continent about the year 1680, assumed the name of Clarke, in order to secure himself from the intrusions of his father's friends, and lived here in retirement as a private gentleman during the remainder of his life. Here also he died, in July, 1712, in the arms of the gardener of Baron Pengelly. To all except his nearest friends Richard Cromwell always avoided speaking of his former greatness. Dr. Watts, who was one of his most frequent visitors, used to say that he never heard Richard allude to his former station except now and then in a very distant manner. In Noble's

" Memoirs of the Cromwell Family " appears the following singular anecdote concerning Richard, which was related to the Rev. George North, Vicar of Codicote, near Welwyn, by two persons who conversed with him in the last years of his life at Cheshunt :—" When Richard left Whitehall he was very careful to preserve the *Addresses* which had been sent to him from every part of the kingdom, expressing ' that the salvation of the nation depended upon his safety, and his acceptance of the sovereignty,' and many of them proffering him the lives and fortunes of the addressers. In his retirement at Cheshunt no one was admitted to visit him without strong recommendations of being of agreeable conversation and strict honour. One of the two persons above alluded to, named Windus who lived at Ware, was introduced to him as such, with an admonition to conform to his peculiarities, without asking any questions or seeming to make any observations. After an hour or two spent in ' conversation and drinking, Richard started up, took the candle, and the rest of the company, who all knew, except the last admitted man, what was going forward, took up the bottle and the glasses, and followed the quondam Protector up to a dirty garret, in which was nothing but a little round hair trunk. Mr. Cromwell pulled it out to the middle of the room, and calling for a bumper of wine, drank " Prosperity to Old England." All the company did the same. When the new man, Mr. Windus, was called to do so, sitting astride, as they had done, upon the trunk, Cromwell desired him to take care, and sit light, for he had no less than the lives and fortunes of all the good people of England under him. The trunk was then opened, and the original addresses showed him, with great mirth and laughter. This was his method of initiating a new acquaintance.' "

Richard Cromwell was buried at Hursley, in Hampshire, the manor of Hursley having descended to him in right of his wife, though he was obliged to contest the possession of it with his daughters in a court of law. Serjeant Pengelly, who was retained by him on this occasion as counsel, and was afterwards Chief Baron of the Exchequer, is supposed to have been a natural son of his employer, a supposition which Mr. Noble, in his work above quoted, admits to be rendered probable by Richard's gallantry. Richard Cromwell appeared personally in the court at Westminster to contest the action against his daughters, and when he appeared in Westminster Hall, the judge, Sir John Holt, Lord Chief Justice of England, struck with the sad reverse of fortune and the unfeeling behaviour of his daughters, and on account of his old age, conducted him into a private apartment; refreshments were provided for him, and it was ordered that he should be accommodated with a seat in court. The old man gained the cause, and had the painful satisfaction of hearing his daughters severely censured; Queen Anne had the good feeling to applaud the judge for

being marked out with roads for building purposes in the most utilitarian fashion.

About a mile north of the church is another property which has for generations been connected with the Cromwells, and their heirs, the Russells: namely, Cheshunt Park. The estate was originally a subordinate manor of Cheshunt, and known as Crossbrook, and also as Cullings. It is not a little singular that, having at one time formed part of the royal manor of Theobalds, which was granted

by Charles II. to George Monk, Duke of Albemarle, for restoring the monarchy, it should eventually have come into the possession of the last male descendant of Oliver Cromwell. On the death of Christopher, the second Duke of Albemarle, without issue, the property reverted to the Crown. It appears, however, to have been granted anew to Ralph, Duke of Montagu, who had married the widow of the Duke of Albemarle, as his descendant, John, Duke of Montagu, sold it in 1736 to a Mrs. Letitia Thornhill, from whom it passed to the Cromwells, through the marriage of Richard Cromwell, grandson of Henry Cromwell, Lord Lieutenant of Ireland, with Sarah, daughter of Ebenezer Gatton, and niece and one of the co-heiresses of Sir Robert Thornhill, the father of the above-mentioned Letitia. The estate subsequently became vested in Oliver Cromwell, the great-grandson of Henry Cromwell, son of the Protector. This gentleman practised as a solicitor in London, and became the biographer of his illustrious namesake. He built on his estate here a seat, to which he gave the name of Brantingfay, but which has now become changed to Cheshunt Park. The house contained several ancient and curious pictures and portraits,

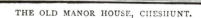

THE OLD MANOR HOUSE, CHESHUNT.

the attention he had shown to one who had once held sovereign power. As Richard was leaving Westminster Hall his curiosity led him to the House of Lords. He was asked when he was there last. "Never," he said, pointing, with a smile, to the throne, "since I sat in that chair."

Pengelly House, during the last ten or twelve years, has been completely transformed and much spoilt in its appearance; but the summer-house in the garden, in which Richard Cromwell used to smoke his pipe, still remains. The house was for some time the residence of Hugh Stracey Osborne, an East India civilian, and more recently of Mr. Benjamin Attwood, a millionaire, but is now (May, 1883) in the market to be sold, the estate which ranged from the Protector's parents down to the above-mentioned Oliver. After his death in 1821, at the age of seventy-one, the property descended to his only surviving child, Oliveria, who had married Mr. Thomas A. Russell. Sir Robert Heron, in his "Notes," relates that the last Oliver Cromwell was very desirous of leaving his name to his son-in-law, and "applied several times for the royal license that Mr. Russell should assume it; but the old king, George III., positively refused, always saying, 'No, no; no more Oliver

his unambitious son, Richard. Many other relics of the Protector are in the Rev. J. D. Williams's Cromwellian Museum at Paragon Road, Hackney.

In College Road is a building called St. Mary's Hall, erected in 1868, and used for the purposes of lectures and other entertainments. Here the Petty Sessions and Sessions under the Criminal Justice Act are held. The magisterial business for this division of the county was formerly conducted at the "Green Dragon" inn, at Church Gate.

WALTHAM CROSS.

Cromwells!'" George IV., when Prince Regent, appears also to have thought that the country had had enough of the Cromwells, for he, too, is said to have refused his royal leave and license to a repetition of the request. Mrs. Russell was the last person who bore at birth the name of Cromwell through direct male descent. She died in 1858, and her husband followed her to the grave a few years later. Their eldest son, Cromwell Russell, married the daughter of the Rev. W. A. Armstrong, of Pengelly House, and they left an only child, a daughter, who married the Rev. Paul Bush, Rector of Duloe, Cornwall, and who still owns a variety of Cromwellian relics, including several of the great Protector's autograph letters, and the great seal of

Cheshunt and its immediate neighbourhood abounds in beautiful walks, and in many parts extensive views of the surrounding country are obtained. Many parts of the land are cultivated as market gardens. The soil is particularly suited to the growth of roses, and the old-established nurseries of Messrs. Paul, in Cheshunt Street, form quite a show in the summer months.

Salmon, writing in 1728, observes of Cheshunt that "it changes its inhabitants so often that there are not two gentlemen in the parish who were born in it;" and nearly the same may be said of it at the present day. There are, nevertheless, some good seats and residences in the parish, besides those already mentioned, notably the Cedars; Theobalds, long the residence of Lady Prescott; Wood Green Park, where lived the Hon. John Scott, son of the first Lord Eldon, and who was so pleased with the neighbourhood that, as we have seen above, he desired to be buried in Cheshunt churchyard; Claremont, a good house in a pleasant park a little to the north-east of Church Gate; and Aldbury House, half a mile to the south. Some remarkable men, too, have held property in this parish, among whom may be mentioned Charles, Lord Howard of Effingham, Lord High Admiral of England in 1588, the hero of the Spanish Armada. He was the owner of a farm house in Cheshunt Street, now called Effingham Place, which he gave to one of his captains, named Bellamy, with whose descendants it has since continued. General Whitelock, whose name became notorious at the beginning of the present century for his conduct while in command of the forces in South America, and whose action at Buenos Ayres led to his trial by court-martial and dismissal from the service, afterwards lived here for some time, and was often compelled to hear that

> " Grey hairs are honourable,
> But Whitelocks are abominable."

Here, too, also lived in retirement, after dismissal from the public service, another individual whose name figures in English history, namely, Lord Somers; and Lord Grey de Wilton, who was a Knight of the Garter in the time of Queen Elizabeth, died here in 1562. William Herbert, the editor of "Ames's Typographical Antiquities," died here in 1795; and James Ward, R.A., who gained some celebrity as an animal painter, lived for the last thirty years of his life at Round Croft's Cottage, and died there in 1859.

The hamlet of Waltham Cross, near the entrance to this parish on the London road, derives its name from one of those elegant stone crosses which the pious affection of Edward I. caused to be erected to the memory of his wife, Eleanor of Castile, in the places where her body was rested for the night on its journey from Hareby, in Lincolnshire, to the place of its interment in Westminster Abbey. Of the several crosses which were in this manner erected—namely, at Lincoln, Grantham, Stamford, Geddington, Northampton, Stony-Stratford, Dunstable, St. Albans, Waltham, and Charing—only three remain, namely, those at Geddington, Northampton, and Waltham. Like those at Geddington and Northampton, that at Waltham was originally surrounded by a flight of steps, but these have long been removed, and its base covered in with brickwork. The upper parts of the cross are also greatly mutilated, much of the

foliage being defaced, and the pinnacles and other ornamentation broken. The form of the cross is hexagonal, and it is divided into three storeys, of which the centre one is open, and contains statues of the queen in whose honour it was erected. Each side of the lower storey is divided into two compartments beneath an angular coping, charged with shields pendent from different kinds of foliage, and exhibiting the arms of England, of Castile, Leon, and Ponthieu. The cornice over this storey consists of foliage and lions' heads, surmounted by battlements pierced with quatrefoils. The second storey consists of twelve open tabernacles in pairs, but so divided that the pillar intersects the middle of the statue behind it. These terminate in ornamental pediments, with a bouquet on the top, and with a cornice and battlement, and support the third storey, which is of solid masonry, ornamented with single compartments in relief resembling those below, and supporting the broken shaft of a plain cross. The statues of the queen are crowned; she holds a cordon in her left hand and a sceptre in her right. This cross stands close to the "Falcon" Inn, which has been built up against it, in the angle formed by the high road and another road which branches off eastward towards Waltham Abbey.

The following lines, "suggested by a sight of this cross," appear in the *Mirror* for 1831:—

> "Time-mouldering crosses, gemm'd with imagery
> Of costliest work and Gothic tracery,
> Point still the spots, to hallow'd memory dear,
> Where rested on its solemn way the bier
> That bore the bones of Edward's Elinor,
> To mix with royal dust at Westminster.
> Far different rites did thee to dust consign,
> Brunswick's fair daughter, Princess Caroline !
> A hurrying funeral and a banished grave,
> High-minded wife ! were all that thou couldst have.
> Grieve not, great ghost ! nor count in death thy losses,
> Thou in thy lifetime hadst thy share of crosses."

The cross was completed in 1294, the work having been executed by Alexander of Abingdon, Domenic de Leger of Rheims, and Roger de Crundale. The stone was brought from Caen, in Normandy, and the total cost is stated to have been £95.

In a volume entitled "Memorials of Queen Eleanor," it is remarked that "the Waltham Cross has suffered grievously from neglect and wilful injury, and not a little, we are compelled to say, from modern restoration." The members of the Society of Antiquaries have twice interested themselves in preserving it from decay : once in 1721, and again in 1757, when Lord Monson, the then Lord of the Manor of Cheshunt, at the request of the Society, surrounded the base with brickwork, as the whole of the steps, ten in number, had been taken away. At that time it was discovered that the roof of a neighbouring house, which still disfigures the view of the cross, leaned against one of the statues of the queen. In 1796 the cross was again found in a very neglected condition. Mr. Gough, in the "Velusta Monumenta," observes that the cross probably stood isolated from the town, like that near Nottingham, or at least that the only building near it was "Ye Olde Foure Swannes Hostelrie." At one time there was attached to the cross a board, pointing the direction of the adjacent roads. At the beginning of the present century an attempt was made to remove the entire structure into Theobalds Park; but fortunately the materials were found to be so decayed that the idea was abandoned, and it became an almost shapeless mass of stone, and a few years more would have left nothing remaining of Waltham Cross. About 1830 the attention of the neighbouring gentry and others, however, was called to it, while there was yet time to save something of its pristine form, and while it afforded indications by which much that was deficient might be restored, and a subscription was at once set on foot for the purpose of raising the necessary funds for repairing the monument. In 1833 the work was commenced, under the direction of Mr. W. B. Clarke. The result was the restoration of the cross as it now appears. Her Majesty the Queen and the Prince Consort stopped to inspect this relic of antiquity on their way from Cambridge to London in October, 1843.

The "Four Swans" inn, mentioned above, and which stands on the opposite side of the road, is undoubtedly an old building; but it is questionable whether it can properly lay claim to the antiquity that is locally assigned to it, for in it, according to tradition, "the body of Queen Eleanor remained for the night preceding its solemn entry into London." Salmon considers this inn to have been the original manor-house of the honour of Richmond; and Gough, in the work above referred to, says that "it bears marks of great antiquity in the forms of its chimneys, and the quantity of chestnut timber employed about it." A large signboard, supported on tall posts placed on the opposite sides of the way, swings across the road, having on the inscription, "Ye Olde Foure Swannes Hostelrie, 1260."

In the parish register of Waltham Holy Cross (or Waltham Abbey) there is the following entry:—"Julii, 1612, Margaret, the daughter of Edward Skarlett, of Cestrehunt, was buried 26 daye, dwel

ling at the signe of Ye Old Swanne in Waltham Cross." In days gone by this inn was a well-known posting-house, and more recently it numbered Charles Lamb among its patrons.

This village being the resort of travellers, and a general halting-place for the stage-coaches on the Great North Road to or from London, rendered another inn upon the spot necessary, and accordingly one was erected at the corner of the road to Waltham Abbey. The cross itself, as shown above, is almost taken into the end of it, whereby much of its beauty is concealed, and many of its ornaments disfigured. It has been suggested that a roadside chapel at one time stood on the site of this inn, which was formerly called "The Falcon," but which is now known as the "Great Eastern."

The hamlet of Waltham Cross was made into a separate parish for ecclesiastical purposes in 1855. The church, dedicated to the Holy Trinity, is a plain brick building, of Gothic architecture. It was built in 1832, and altered and improved in 1872. In 1870 this district was endowed as a vicarage.

There are almshouses for four poor persons at Waltham Cross, called the Spital Houses, the income of which, together with others for ten widows at Turner's Hill, amounts, in the gross, to £550 yearly. The Spital Houses are stated by the Parliamentary Commission survey in 1650 to have been used "time out of mind" for the "entertainment of lame, impotent, and decayed persons." They were rebuilt in 1830.

Here was, before the Dissolution, a small convent of Benedictine nuns, whose name is still kept in memory by the Nunnery Farm, towards the north-east of the village, not far from the banks of the River Lea. But little is known of the history of this convent. It appears to have been founded in the reign of Stephen, by Peter de Belingey, in honour of the Blessed Virgin, for nuns of the Sempringham order. It was afterwards possessed by the canons of that order, but Henry III. placed in it nuns of the order of St. Benedict, and made them independent. After the Dissolution the convent was granted to Sir Anthony Denny, and it has since passed through the hands of several different owners. At the beginning of the present century the remains of the convent formed the domestic parts of a large mansion.

About a mile to the north-west of Cheshunt Church is a small hamlet, called Goff's Oak, from an old survivor of the forest, an oak, now on its last legs, which stands on the south side of the common, in front of a small roadside inn. The traditional history of this celebrated tree is inscribed as follows under a rude drawing of the tree, which is to be seen at the above-mentioned house :—" It was planted in the year 1066 by Sir Theodore Godfrey, or Goffe, who came over with William the Conqueror, and it is not at all improbable but that some neighbouring land, called Cuffley, belonged to this person at that time. The dimensions of the tree are very large, as it is twenty feet in girth three feet from the ground. The trunk is hollow, and several persons can stand in the cavity which time has made. This cavity is now boarded in, but a door admits visitors into

the interior ; and few persons will regret the time spent in examining it. A respectable inn is within a few yards of the tree, and bears the name of the tree for its sign ; its predecessor was burnt down in 1814, and was called the Green Man."

The hamlet of Goff's Oak was formed into an ecclesiastical parish in 1871. The church, dedicated to St. James, had been built some years previously, having been consecrated as far back as 1862. It is a small brick edifice, in the Gothic style, but deserves no especial mention in these pages.

CHAPTER XLI.

NORTHAW.

Etymology of Northaw—Condition of the District at the time of the Conquest—Disputed Ownership—Nynn House, and Manor—The Hook—Northaw Place—Acreage and Population—The Village and Parish Church—A Chalybeate Spring.

THIS parish, the name of which in old documents is sometimes written Northall and Northolt, lies on a hill to the east of the Great North Road some three miles north-east from Potter's Bar Station on the Great Northern Railway. Its etymology is, doubtless, the same as that of Northolt,* in Middlesex, the north *haw*, or *holt*, which signifies a wood.

At the time of the Conquest all this district probably formed a continuation of the extensive woodland afterwards known as Enfield Chase, or it may have been merely waste ground, producing no revenue to the Crown, as it is not mentioned in the " Domesday Survey." Towards the end of the eleventh century, however, it appears to have belonged to St. Albans abbey, for it was at that time held under a lease from the Abbot Paul by Peter de Valoines, or Valence, and his son Roger. After the death of the abbot, Valoines continued to retain possession by consent of the monastery ; but on the latter making a request, at some later date, for possession to be given up, Robert de Valoines, who then held it, refused, and appealed to the king, Henry II., who was then in France. The decision of the king was in favour of Valoines, or, in other words, he commanded the abbot to " give up the wood."

Armed with the king's authority, de Valoines returned to England, and " having obtained the possession, during the short time he enjoyed it (as one who unjustly possest it) often wasted the same, causing it to be cut beyond measure. When the abbot heard these things, he sent officers to

view the waste, who found that the damage committed there could not be repaired. Then he hastened to Robert, Earl of Leicester, then Chief Justice of England, and obtained his letters that he would restrain the injurious acts of Robert de Valoines ; but he, slighting the commands of the earl, did *twice the damage* he did before, which the abbot hearing, did address himself to Queen Eleanor. . . whose admonitions Robert obeyed for a time, but soon after committed *double damage again*. Then the abbot complained of these wrongs to the Pope, who sent his letters to Theobald, Archbishop of Canterbury, and Hillary, Bishop of Chichester, that they cause the said Robert within thirty days to restore the possession of the wood to the abbot, and upon his contempt to declare sentence of excommunication against him."

The abbot's right to the wood, however, was eventually confirmed by Henry II., and Northaw continued in the possession of the priory of St. Albans until the dissolution of religious houses, when it came to the Crown. In 1539 it was granted by Henry VIII., under the title of the manor of " Northawe, Nynne, and Cufley," to Sir William Cavendish, Gentleman Usher to Cardinal Wolsey, and the author of his " Life ; "* but it was alienated early in the reign of Elizabeth to the Earl of Warwick, in exchange for other property. The earl built here a mansion, called " Nyn House," on the site of the present manor-house. It was a spacious structure of brick, occupying three sides of a quadrangle, with a courtyard in

---

* See *ante*, p. 218.

* See *ante*, p. 147.

the centre, and graced with "delightful gardens and walks, and sundry other pleasant and necessary devices.* Sir Samuel Pennant, who was Sheriff of London in 1745, died at Nynn House in 1750, during the year of his mayoralty. In 1774 a Mr. John Granger, who assumed the name of Leman on coming into possession of the manor, pulled down the old house, and destroyed the gardens. The materials of the building were used in the erection of the present Northaw House, which stands about half a mile distant from the site of the old mansion.

The manor, on the death of the Countess of Warwick, in 1603—4, passed by deed of settlement to her brother, Lord William Russell, and it was a few years later sold to the Lemans, with whose family it remained for several generations, down to the middle of the last century, when it was bequeathed to the above-mentioned John Granger. About 1822 the property passed into the hands of the Rev. Dr. Trenchard, on whose death it was inherited by his son, Mr. Ashfordby-Trenchard. This family held the manor till 1876, when it was sold to Mr. John P. Kidston, the present owner. This gentleman has greatly improved and enlarged the house. The grounds are extensive, beautifully laid out, and contain an ornamental lake about five acres in extent.

There are a few other good houses in the parish, notably "The Hook," a substantial mansion of the old-fashioned type, on the south side of the village ; and Northaw Place, which stands a little to the west of the church, built towards the end of the seventeenth century.

The parish itself, although of considerable extent, embracing no less than 3,000 acres, contains only about 600 inhabitants, showing but a slight increase since the census of 1871. The parish is wholly agricultural.

The village green occupies a central position in the parish. It stands on a hill some three miles north-east from Potter's Bar Station on the Great Northern Railway. On one side of the green stands the parish church, a new building, of Early English architecture. It is built of stone, and consists of chancel, nave, south aisle, transepts, and a square tower at the south-west corner. The church, dedicated to St. Thomas à Becket, was erected in 1882, in the place of one destroyed by fire in the previous year. The predecessor of the present building—a pseudo-Perpendicular structure —was a comparatively modern edifice, dating from the beginning of the present century. It was built in the place of an older church, probably Late Norman or Early English. It was a commonplace cruciform building, covered with a coating of cement.

At Lower Cuffley, a valley lying about midway between the villages of Northaw and Cheshunt, is a chalybeate spring, which, at the time when the royal court was held at the neighbouring Palace of Theobalds, was much resorted to ; but it shared the fate of the spring at Barnet * and other similar places, and its medicinal qualities seem to have lost their virtue as soon as the spring ceased to be fashionable. Mr. Cussans, in his "History of Hertfordshire," says that "the water contained a large quantity of iron, and a favourite diversion of the inhabitants was to induce strangers to make tea with it. Though perfectly colourless, as soon as the boiling water was poured on the tea, the iron combined with the tannin, and formed ink— as much to the astonishment of the tea-makers as to the delight of the practical jokers."

CHAPTER XLII.

ENFIELD SMALL-ARMS FACTORY AND WALTHAM POWDER-MILLS.

"Fire answers fire."—SHAKESPEARE : *King Henry V*, Act IV.

The History of the Rifle—Situation of the Royal Small-arms Factory—Particulars of its Establishment—Extent of the Buildings, &c.—Perfection of the Machinery and Plant—The Government Powder Mills—Situation of the Buildings—Description of the Works—The Composition of Gunpowder—Quantities produced.

BEFORE we leave Hertfordshire and Middlesex for the towers of Waltham Abbey and the green glades of Enfield Forest, we must pause, and devote a chapter to two public manufactories lying close together on the banks of the Lea, the one known as the Enfield Small-arms Factory, and the other as the Royal Gunpowder Factory, Waltham. Practically they belong to no parish or county, but are national to the fullest extent of the term, so we make them a connecting link between the district that we have visited and the county of Essex, on which we are about to enter.

The Royal Small-arms Factory is the establishment through which all the small-arms of every

---

description have been supplied—at all events, since the Crimean War—to the regular army, the militia, yeomanry, and volunteers. Its long ranges of buildings and tall chimneys are conspicuous objects from whatever side they are viewed.

With reference to the special manufacture carried on here, a short account of the rifle itself may not be judged out of place.

"As early as 1498," observes a writer in *Chambers's Cyclopædia*, "the citizens of Leipzig possessed the germ of the future rifle, for their arms had a grooved bore, but the grooves were

vidual skill of the marksman. The spiral groove gives to the bullet, if it fits into the grooves, a rotation rapid in proportion to the force of the explosion and the sharpness of the twist in the spiral. This revolution of the bullet on its own

ENFIELD SMALL-ARMS FACTORY.

axis keeps that axis, gravity excepted, in the line in which it leaves the piece. In 1628 Arnold Rotsiphen patented a new way of 'makeing gounes,' which, from a subsequent patent granted him in 1635, appears to have consisted, among other improvements, in rifling the barrels. It would be tedious to enumerate the various principles of rifling which were tried during the two centuries following Rotsiphen; suffice it to say, that scarcely a form of rifling now prevails but had its prototype among the old inventions. The difficulty of mechanical appliances making the rifling true deferred, however, their general introduction, and the cost of rifled arms limited their use to the purposes of the chase. The revolutionary government of France had rifles issued to portions of their troops, but they met with so indifferent a success that Napoleon recalled them soon after he came to power. In the Peninsula, however, picked companies of sharpshooters practised with rifles with deadly effect on both the English and

straight. Not many years after, in 1520, Augustin Kutter (or Koster), of Nürnberg, was celebrated for his rose or star-grooved barrels, in which the grooves had a spiral form. It took its name from the rose-like shape of the bore at the muzzle; and, setting aside superiority of workmanship subsequently developed, Kutter's arm was the veritable rifle, and to him, therefore, so far as history shows, is due the invention of this terrible weapon, which reduces the flight of the projectile to a question of the indi-

French sides. During the American War—1812–14 —the Americans demonstrated incontestably the value of rifles in warfare, but many years were yet to elapse before they were definitively placed in the hands of soldiers, many of those of every nation in the Crimea having fought with the ineffective and almost ridiculous 'Brown Bess.' Soon after the French invaded Algeria they had armed the Chasseurs d'Orleans with rifles, to counteract the superior range of the Arab guns. The inutility of the old musket was shown in a

right, however, to state that this contrivance is claimed for Mr. Greener as early as 1836.) Notwithstanding the many advantages of the Minié system, it was found defective in practice. Experiments were set on foot in all directions, and resulted in 1853 in the production of the 'Enfield rifle,' which had three grooves, taking one complete turn in seventy-eight inches, and fired a bullet resembling the Minié, except that a wooden cup was substituted for one of iron. From 1853 to 1865 this was the weapon of the British army.

THE POWDER MILLS, WALTHAM.

battle during the Kaffir War, where our men discharged 80,000 cartridges, and the damage to the enemy was twenty-five men struck. After experiments with the old musket, it was found that its aim had no certainty whatever beyond 100 yards. It was soon discovered that a spherical ball was not the best missile, one in which the longer axis coincided with the axis of the gun flying truer—the relative length of the axis and the shape of the head being matters of dispute. In England no improvement took place until 1851, when 28,000 rifled muskets to fire the Minié bullet were ordered to be issued. The Minié bullet, being made smaller than the bore of the piece, could be almost dropped into the barrel. (It is

In 1865 the adoption of breech-loading arms caused the Enfield to be converted into a breech-loader by fitting the 'Snider' breech mechanism to the Enfield barrel. This arrangement was, however, only temporary; and after a most exhaustive series of trials before a special committee on breech-loading rifles, the Henry barrel was in 1871 adopted, in conjunction with the Martini breech, for the new small-bore rifle for the British army, now known as the Martini-Henry rifle. No fewer than 104 different kinds of breech-loading small-arms were submitted to this committee, who decided that the Henry ·45-inch bore barrel 'was the best adapted for the requirements of the service,' on account of its 'superiority in point of

accuracy, trajectory, allowance for wind, and pene-
tration,' and also on account of its great durability.
The Henry system of rifling is the invention of
Mr. Alexander Henry, gunmaker, Edinburgh, and
its essential peculiarity consists in the form of the
rifled bore. . . . The length of the Henry
barrel is $32\frac{1}{2}$ inches. The mean diameter of the
bore is ·450 of an inch, and the rifling takes one
complete turn in 22 inches. Its bullet is solid,
with a slight cavity in the rear, and weighs 480
grains, the charge of powder being 85 grains."

The Royal Small-arms Factory, at Enfield Lock,
on the narrow strip of land between the River Lea
and the water-way known as the "Lea and Stort
Navigation," about a mile and a quarter from
Enfield Wash, dates its erection from 1855–6. It
is true that a small ordnance factory was established
here by the Government early in the present
century, where a few thousand muskets were
laboriously forged by hand each year; but when
the sudden introduction of the rifle and the demands of the Russian War called for a supply of
arms, which the trade, not only of Birmingham,
but of all Europe and America, was unable to
meet, the Government determined to erect machinery for the fabrication of arms on its own account.
For this purpose the factory at Enfield was entirely
re-modelled, but the successive adoption of the
Snider and Martini-Henry rifles, as above shown,
has been the means of producing a great change
in the plant.

The manufactory on its present footing originated
in the dissatisfaction for some time felt by the
Board of Ordnance at being almost wholly dependent on private manufacturers for so important
a part of the *matériel* of war, and in the recommendation, based on that feeling, of a Committee of
the House of Commons on small arms, which sat
in the session of 1854. The following interesting
particulars of the establishment of this factory we
quote from Tuff's "Enfield":—"Before 1804,
when the manufactory in its original form was
established at Enfield, the Government depended
on the private trade for their small arms, and when
that failed to provide a sufficient supply, recourse
was had to the foreign market. At one time,
indeed, the art of making muskets became extinct
in this country. This occurred in 1802; and Lord
Chatham, then Master General of the Ordnance,
stated the circumstance publicly. Mr. John
Colgate, who held an appointment in the Ordnance
Department, was sent to Liège in 1779 to superintend the setting up of 40,000 stand of arms for
the service of the British Government. Major
General Miller was despatched to Liège on a

similar service in 1794, to Hamburg in 1795, and
again to Hamburg in 1800, the store of arms in
the Tower being at that time entirely expended.
Again, in 1823, the names of not less than twenty
English artificers had been ascertained who were
in full employment in the national armoury establishments of Russia and the United States, and no
doubt many more might have been discovered.
This was attributable to the encouragement and
inducements to emigrate held out to our skilled
artificers in that branch of trade by foreign nations,
backed by the want of employment in their
vocation at home; and it was apprehended at that
time by men conversant with the subject that,
unless the fostering care of the Government was
continued in support of its armoury institution, the
art must again be lost, or so far reduced that the
country would a second time be left to depend
on the casual supplies furnished by individual
manufacturers. It has always been contended by
men who have advocated the formation of Government armouries that the views of tradesmen were
confined to individual profit. When they entered
upon a contract, their only object was to bring
their workmanship to such a state as to pass the
official examination; they had no motive, it was
said, to improve, or inducement to perpetuate, the
art. When the call for arms by the Government
ceased with a war, they turned their industry to
other occupations, and their workmen were driven
to seek employment in foreign countries, or left to
neglect the art at home. It was also alleged that
a national establishment offered the most perfect
means of making experiments for the improvement
of the service, and caused the saving of money in
time of war as well as of peace, by operating as a
check upon the prices of private manufacturers.
But its principal object was to keep up among us
the art of making military guns.

"It was considerations such as these and others
that induced the Government, upon the recommendation of the committee of 1854—the year of
the Crimean War—to establish a manufactory of
small arms to a limited extent, under the direction
of the Board of Ordnance."

While the Parliamentary committee was sitting,
a deputation of practical men, previously sent out
by the Board of Ordnance to make inquiries in
the United States of America as to the mode of
manufacturing small-arms there, and having extensive powers to purchase machinery to be applied
to their fabrication in this country, was pursuing
its mission; and on the report of the committee,
the House of Commons voted a sum not exceeding
£150,000 towards the experiment. It should be

mentioned here that down to this date most of the small-arms used by our soldiers were manufactured at Birmingham and in other parts of the kingdom, and purchased by the Government.

Since the above period extensive ranges of buildings have been constructed here. They occupy three sides of a square, are built of brick, in a good substantial manner, but quite devoid of ornamentation. About forty acres of ground describes the extent of the factory premises, including the land used as butts for testing each piece that is turned out. Machinery for the manufacture of rifles was imported from America, and was placed under the supervision of Mr. Perkins, as manager. The factory was subsequently taken in hand entirely by the Government, the first superintendent being Colonel Manley Dixon, R.A., who had charge of the works till 1872, when he was succeeded by Colonel Fraser. The factory at the present time is carried on under the superintendence of Colonel H. T. Arbuthnot, R.A., with a staff of military and civil officers, the whole being under the direction of the War Department. The machinery here is probably the most perfect of any gun-making establishment, whether private or Government, at home or abroad; and as the manufacture proceeds it produces the various parts which are ultimately brought together to produce the gun with such accuracy of finish, that if a number of such guns were taken to pieces, and each part thrown together in a heap, the parts could be taken up indiscriminately, and be fitted together to make up guns without the slightest alteration or re-adjustment of either. This great nicety of finish is of immense importance, with regard to both convenience and economy, for if any part of a rifle becomes damaged or rendered unserviceable, the regimental armourer has merely to remove the injured portion, take the corresponding piece from his repository, and at once fit it into its place, without trouble or loss of time.

The mechanism of the "Martini-Henry" is much more simple than either of its predecessors above mentioned, for whilst the old "Enfield rifle" was composed of no less than fifty pieces, and the "Snider" of thirty-nine, the "Martini-Henry" consists of only twenty-seven pieces. Taking the average for the last four years, the number of weapons turned out at the factory in the course of a year is as follows :—Rifles (various), say 40,000 ; pistols, 5,000 ; and swords for rifles, 8,000. The plant and general facilities of the factory are in such condition that under great pressure 150,000 arms could be manufactured annually. The motive power is mainly steam, but one water-wheel is still

used in certain work. The number of hands employed here is generally about 1,500.

The interior of the factory consists of a series of large work-rooms. The first usually entered by visitors is called the "action shop," from the fact that here everything relating to the action (or breech-loading and lock apparatus) being finished in it. The room is 200 feet in length, and contains nearly a thousand different machines. The turning-lathes, or machines for forming the butt or stock, are of the most ingenious character, and finish the work in such a delicate manner that the "action" can be instantly fitted to it without the slightest trouble or difficulty. The fitting the lock into the stock was a work involving much time and labour when performed by hand. By this machine a lock can be completely let into the stock in three minutes; indeed, the whole process of making and perfecting the stock does not occupy more than half an hour, and the only hand labour employed upon it is that which causes the friction of a little sand-paper along its surface after its removal from the last machine. Besides the work-rooms, several buildings are occupied as stores of stocks, barrels, &c., which are kept constantly in readiness for use as may be required.

The factory is open to visitors, even without previous application, on Mondays and Thursdays ; but the proof-house, immediately to the south of the factory, is not usually shown. Every "piece" manufactured here is *tested* in the meadows close by.

The Powder-mills stand on the left hand as you enter Waltham Abbey, between two branches of the River Lea, which, as already stated, here is divided into several channels. They are screened from sight by groves of poplars and willows, mostly planted in long rows diagonally, after the fashion described by Virgil, in his "Georgics," under the name of a "quincunx."* This shelter is useful to keep away all grit and dust, and also, as already noticed, in order to counteract the violence of an explosion. These are the only powder-mills belonging to the Government, those at Faversham, Dartford, and Hounslow, being in private hands. They employ about 250 hands, and they cover a long strip of land about 200 acres in extent, which runs along the banks of the river from south to north.

It is almost needless to add that these powder-mills are very closely guarded, and are shown only to such strangers as have a genuine object in view in inspecting them. There is no special day set apart for their inspection.

---

* Virgil, Georg. II., 277, &c.

The appointment of superintendent of the powder-mills is made by the War Office, and is always held by an officer of the Royal Artillery. It is held generally for five years. The present superintendent is Colonel C. B. Brackenbury.

The visitor who wishes to inspect the works on entering the grounds passes along a very beautiful avenue of poplars, and finds himself at the gates of the superintendent's office. He is here warned that he must not carry lucifer-matches or other explosive articles about him, and that whenever he is required to put on leather-soled boots he will do so, as a single particle of grit from the high road, if it were to be driven into some parts of the mills, would cause an explosion.

The wood used for making charcoal is to a great extent grown on the estate. It is either alder, willow, or dog-wood; the latter comes chiefly from Germany, and each kind of wood is used in the composition of different sorts of powder, and is treated differently.

The wood is stacked about the grounds in every available corner, awaiting the time when it will be wanted, in order to be manufactured into that deadly combustible which renders the hearths and homes of soldiers desolate, and the necessity for which is a scandal to the Christian name. However, we must accept the actual state of things.

All the "hands" employed are bound to be steady and sober; no smoking is allowed on the premises; and each man on coming to work puts on a suit of greyish-black. Many of the "hands" are the sons of parents who were employed here before them; and the fact that they carry their lives constantly in their hands, and work with death ever before their eyes, has a sobering effect on them, and even (so I was informed) on their families at home.

The authorised visitor to the works, having been duly challenged at the gates by the police, and passed to the office of the superintendent, is placed in the care of an experienced guide, and thence conducted to the various "houses" where the several operations of gunpowder-making are carried on. These houses are separated by considerable spaces thickly planted with willow and alder wood. Thus if an explosion were to take place in one house the force would be broken by a screen of trees, and the other houses would not be likely to be affected by it.

The three ingredients of which gunpowder is composed are saltpetre, sulphur, and charcoal. For ordinary English gunpowder the proportions by weight are—saltpetre 75, sulphur 10, and charcoal 15 per cent. The processes required for the manufacture of one of the newest kinds of powder, called prismatic, are as follows:—1, refining the saltpetre; 2, refining the sulphur; 3, burning wood to produce charcoal; 4, mixing the ingredients for the "green" charge; 5, incorporating the "green" charge; 6, breaking down the mill-cake; 7, pressing the powder; 8, granulating; 9, dusting and glazing; 10, prismatic pressing; 11, stowing, to dry the powder; 12, blending prismatic powder.

1. The saltpetre arrives in bags from India, and is refined by boiling in a large quantity of water, and filtering the solution, which then runs into shallow receptacles, where it cools down, being kept in a state of agitation by wooden rakes. The saltpetre crystallises out in a form which closely resembles snow. It is then shovelled into vats, where it receives several washings.

2. The sulphur is next refined by being placed in a retort, and heated until it first melts and then commences to sublime, that is, to pass into a state of vapour. The vapour is led through a pipe kept cool by water outside it, and condenses into a treacle-like fluid, which passes into a receiver, and is then ladled out into tubs, where it sets into the beautiful yellow material which is known as refined sulphur. The impurities are, at the same time, left behind in the retort. Before being used for gunpowder, the sulphur has to be ground into a fine powder.

3. The woods used for gunpowder charcoal are three, as mentioned above. The larger descriptions of powder are made of willow and alder, the willow giving a rather stronger powder than the alder; while the fine-grained powders for use in small-arms are made of dog-wood, which is more expensive, and has not hitherto been grown largely on English soil. The woods are packed in iron cylinders, called slips, and introduced into furnaces also lined with iron. The flame from the fuel plays round the outside of the iron furnace-lining, heating it and the slip within. The various juices of the wood begin to distil, and the gases so produced pass through two holes in the far end of the slip and corresponding holes in the back of the furnace, whence they are carried down into the fire and contribute to the fuel, so that after the process has once been established the wood helps to burn itself. When the work of burning is completed, the slip, with its heated charcoal within, is taken out of the furnace, and placed in an iron cooler for twenty-four hours, after which it is emptied out, but not used for several days, in order to avoid the possibility of any heat existing in it. The charcoal is then ground in an apparatus like a coffee-mill.

4. The next process is that of mixing the ingredients. Hitherto the visitor has entered the houses without any other precaution than the leaving behind of any dangerous material; but henceforth a new danger has to be provided against. The dust from powder flies about the houses, blackening the floor, and filling every cranny with explosive material, in spite of constant sweeping and washing. It is therefore most important that not a single particle of sand or grit should be introduced, lest the motion of a foot on the floor or any friction in the processes themselves should create heat enough to ignite the smallest atom of powder. All persons who enter the powder-houses are therefore obliged to have their feet encased in special leather boots, which never touch the ground outside. A small threshold board, about a foot high, marks the division between the black powder-house, which is called " clean " in the parlance of the factory, and the beautiful outside world, with its waving trees and glittering streams, which are all classed under the one word " foul." If by inadvertence a visitor plants his outside feet within the charmed precincts, he is instantly obliged to withdraw them, and the spot which he touched is carefully purified with wet mops.

In the mixing-houses the air is full of dust, and we literally breathe powder. Fifty pounds of the thin ingredients are placed in a drum, which revolves with great rapidity in one direction, while an orb armed with forks revolves within it in an opposite direction. In about five minutes the process of mixing is complete, and from that moment the three ingredients begin to be highly dangerous.

5. Though the " green " charge is explosive, it is not yet enough intimately mixed to make good gunpowder. It is accordingly next carried in bags to the incorporating mills, which are heavy iron or stone rollers, travelling round in pairs, each roller following its fellow in monotonous round upon its powder-bed, fenced from the rest of the incorporating house by the inclined sides of a sort of basin. The crushing and grinding motion thus produced brings each particle of the three ingredients into mutual contact, and produces, after a certain number of hours (which differ according to the powder to be produced), a soft cake, which is called the mill-cake. Before the runners are set in motion, the green charge placed upon the bed is sprinkled with distilled water, the quantity of which varies, according to the nature of powder sought and the condition of the atmosphere.

6. The mill-cake is then taken to the breaking-down house, where it is made to pass, carried on a canvas band, between a series of grooved rollers, which crush it into dust much more powerfully explosive than the " green " charge of the mixing-house.

7. The " meal," as it is now called, is next carried to the press-house. The press is a very strong box, containing a number of copper or gun-metal plates, so arranged that the meal can be filled in vertically between them, while they are kept separate by means of grooved plates. When the box is full, the grooved plates are withdrawn, and the spaces left by them filled up with meal, so that nothing now prevents the copper plates from coming together except the meal between them. The side of the box which has hitherto been open is now closed, and the box itself turned over, so that the copper-plates become horizontal. What is now the top of the box is then opened, and the whole placed on an hydraulic press. A ram rising from beneath thrusts the layers of copper plates and powder against a square block of wood above, which just fits into the box. The pressure is continued until the meal has become " press-cake " of the density required for the particular powder which is being made. The time is notified by the release of a spring when the box has risen high enough; this spring rings a bell in a smaller room, where the powder-men are now ensconced; for there are always some 800 pounds of powder in the press-box, and any atom of grit might possibly cause an explosion. A huge traverse of masonry stands between the press-house and the room where the men remain during the process. In addition to the lower growth of the willow and groves of alders, walnut and ash trees surround these terrible press-houses, which are thus mysteriously hidden, not only from the outer world, but even from the rest of the works. The dusky shade and the dark reflection of the green trees in the water, and the black powder-houses themselves, lend an air of mystery to these temples of the art of destruction.

8. The press-cake is carried by water, in black roofed boats, not unlike gondolas, to the granulating-house, where it enters a machine not unlike the breaking-down machine already described, but larger, and with toothed instead of grooved rollers. The cake is here cut by the rollers into " grain " of various sizes, and sorted by sieves kept in perpetual agitation under the stream of grain.

9. The dusting and glazing operations are carried on in long cylindrical reels and wooden barrels, of which different sorts are used, according to the work required. For some powders a little black-lead is introduced, to give them a glossy facing.

10. We now come to the prismatic press-house. The grain suitable for making prismatic powder is carried also in boats to the prismatic press-house, where stands an elaborate machine, consisting mainly of a huge iron circular block, which contains thirty holes. In each hole is put a cylindrical plug of phosphor-bronze, the interior of which is cut exactly to the shape of the prism required. A so-called "charger," with thirty funnels corresponding with the thirty holes in the block, moves backwards and forwards on rails. It is filled with the

a considerable amount of moisture; this is now to be expelled by means of heat. For this purpose the powder is placed on trays in drying-chambers, which are gradually raised to a heat differing according to the character of the powder required. For some powder it is as much as 125 degrees Fahrenheit.

12. But in spite of all the care taken, and though a series of scientific experiments follow the powder through all its stages, there always exists a certain amount of difference between quantities of powder,

THE CATTLE MARKET, WALTHAM.

grain outside the machine, then pushed directly over the block; two motions of a handle then cut off exactly the quantity of grain required, and allow it to fall from the funnels into the phosphor-bronze moulds below. The charge is then withdrawn, the top of the machine brought down to seal the tops of the holes, and then, by hydraulic pressure, thirty plungers, one for each hole, rise up and compress the charges of grain, so as to form them into prisms of the size and shape required. The top is then raised, and the pressed prisms are thrust out of their moulds by pressure from below. The skill required in powder-making may be estimated from the fact that the time necessary to press prismatic powder which will produce certain definite effects varies greatly, according to the state of the atmosphere. The variation at Waltham Abbey has been found to be as much as between twenty-five and sixty-five seconds.

11. All powders hitherto made here have in them

which are called "lots," made at different times and under different atmospheric conditions. It is, therefore, very important to bring the material to a certain average, so that the accurate shooting of artillery or of small-arms may be counted upon. For this purpose every "lot" of powder is proved by actually firing a charge of it. The lots which give the higher results are then mixed in strict proportion with lower lots, so that it is impossible, in making up a cartridge, to take an undue quantity of either the higher or the lower lot. This process is called "blending," and after it is gone through, a charge is again taken and fired, to secure the fitness of the powder for its destined use.

All sorts of strange stories are told about the experiences and hairbreadth escapes of employés in these interesting works. Thus, on one occasion a lucifer-match was found to have passed between the rollers of the granulating machine; and on another occasion a key was discovered in the same condition. It seems little less than a miracle that such a thing could have happened without causing an explosion.

The works here can turn out about 30,000 barrels of powder in a year, or about 700 barrels weekly. It may be of interest to add that, including the sidings and canals, there are about

allowed to dig in them, these grounds are virgin soil, and accordingly they nourish a profusion of wild flowers which are scarcely known outside. Hence they are a favourite haunt of botanists who can procure admission to them; but the favour is sparingly accorded.

The introduction of gunpowder into England is connected with the honoured name of Evelyn, as that family are said to have brought from Holland the secret of its manufacture. Mr. George Evelyn,

ON THE LEA.

cluding the sidings and canals, there are about ten miles of water on the estate, of which three and three-quarter miles are navigable. In addition to the screens of trees, the more dangerous portions of the works are isolated by solid traverses of earth or brick, to minimise the effects of explosion.

The "works" which I have described can boast of almost a venerable antiquity. In the "Anglorum Speculum, or the Worthies of England" (1684), it it is stated that there were gunpowder mills "on the River Ley, between Waltham and London." In 1735 Farmer speaks of them, in his "History of Waltham," as being the property of a Mr. John Walter; and in the same book there is a delightful description of gunpowder. As nobody is

grandfather of the author of "Sylva," received, about 1590, a licence to set up powder mills at Long Ditton and at Godstone, Surrey.

"The works at Faversham, afterwards for so many years the Government gunpowder factory, date from Elizabeth's reign; but they were then secondary in importance to those at Godstone. There seems reason, however, to suppose that powder-mills existed at Waltham Abbey as far back as 1561, for in that year we find John Thomworth, of Waltham, in treaty, on behalf of Elizabeth, for the purchase of saltpetre, sulphur, and staves for barrels. Fuller also refers, in his "Worthies," to the powder mills of Waltham Abbey, of which he was appointed vicar in 1641. In 1787 these mills were sold to the Crown by John Walton, and reorganised under the superintendence of the famous Sir William Congreve. The old royal factory at Faversham was given up after the Peace of 1815, being let, and afterwards sold, to the well-known firm of John Hall & Co. . . . The Waltham Abbey works have been greatly enlarged in recent years, and no expense has been spared to render them, by the introduction of new and improved machinery, the most complete, as well as the safest, in the world." *

Henceforth our travels will be in Essex.

CHAPTER XLIII.

WALTHAM ABBEY.

Situation of the Town—Its Etymology—Foundation of the Abbey by Jovi—Its Re-foundation by Harold—The Legend of the Holy Cross—Gifts bestowed on the Abbey—Harold's Tomb—The Church despoiled by William the Conqueror—Its Recovery under subsequent Sovereigns—Disputes between the Abbot and Townspeople—Henry III. and the Abbot's Dinner—An Incident touching the Reformation—Income of the Abbey at the Dissolution—Fuller, the Historian—The Conventual Estate passes into Secular Hands—Description of the Abbey Church —Sale of the Church Bells—Present Condition of the Remains of the Abbey—Rome-Land—The Abbey Gateway and Bridge.

WALTHAM ABBEY, or Waltham Holy Cross, as it was once called, must be carefully distinguished from its neighbour in Hertfordshire, which is described in a previous chapter.* It is a large, irregular town, and evidently one of considerable antiquity, as is shown by the variety of projecting gables, and the quaint carved figures which still stand in bold relief at the corner of more than one of its streets, like those with which one meets at Ipswich, Saffron-Walden, and many other towns of the eastern counties. The town is situated on low ground near the river Lea, which here forms a number of small islands, and is skirted by fruit-ful meadows, that have long been famous for the succulent and nourishing qualities of the grass. The spot was originally part of the Forest of Essex, and it derived the name of Waltham from the Saxon words *weald-ham*, the dwelling or hamlet on the weald, or open forest.

The town is twelve miles north-east from London, and about three-quarters of a mile eastward from Waltham Station on the Cambridge line of the Great Eastern railway. The road thither from the railway station, however, is by no means attractive: it is straight as an arrow, and is little more than a raised causeway between low-lying green meadows, with a deep ditch on either side. The river Lea, which we cross—the Lea of quaint old Izaak Walton—here separates into a variety of streams, and we pass no less than four bridges before we find ourselves at the end of a narrow street, with gabled tenements on either side, and close under the shadow of the tower which has been our beacon.

Waltham appears to have been a place of note long before the Norman Conquest. It is first mentioned in a document dated as far back as the time of Canute the Great, at which period its then owner, Tovi, or Tovius, standard-bearer to that monarch, founded on the outskirts of the forest here a church and a village, placing in the former two priests, and erecting in the latter some tene-ments for his "villains," and placing in them "threescore-and-six dwellers." After his death, Athelstan, his son and heir, a prodigal young man, squandered his inheritance, and Waltham appears by some means or other to have reverted to the Crown. The religious establishment of Tovi, however, continued, and probably with some aug-mentation, till the reign of Edward the Confessor, who bestowed certain lands here on his brother-in-law, Earl Harold, son of Godwin, Earl of Kent; but the grant was made upon the condition that Harold should build a monastery in the place, "where *was a little convent*, subject to the canons and their rules." The "little convent" mentioned in the Confessor's charter, evidently alludes to Tovi's foundation, which might have been aug-mented by casual donations previous to this men-tion of it.

In 1062, the year in which the grant was dated, Harold refounded or enlarged the original estab-lishment of Tovi, endowing it as a convent, doubling the number of its canons, settling on them ample estates, and founding hard by a school of religious and useful learning.† Farmer, in his "History of Waltham," says that each of the canons had one manor appropriated for his sup-port, and that the dean had six; making in all seventeen. From the charter of confirmation granted by Edward the Confessor, it appears that

---

* See *ante*, p. 392.

* Encyclopædia Britannica.
† "Dugdale's Monasticon," Vol. VI., pt. I. p. 56.

Harold endowed his new foundation with the manors of Passefeld, Welda or Walde, Upminster, Wahlfara or Wallifare, Tippedene, Alwartune, Wudeforde, Lambehyth, Nasingam, Brekendune, Melnho, Alrichsey, Wormelei, Nethleswelle or Neteswell, Hicche, Lukintone, and Westwaltham. "All these manors the king granted them with sac, soc, tol, and team, &c., free from all gelds and payments, in the most full and ample manner, as appears by the charter among the records of the tower."

The parish derived its second name of "Holy Cross" from a cross, bearing on it a figure of the Saviour, which was said to have been found at Montacute, in Somerset, and to have been brought miraculously by oxen, undriven, to this place. The cross itself is said to have shown very miraculous powers; and among the wonders told of it is that Harold was cured of the palsy in consequence of a pilgrimage to it.

The following is a translation of the legend of Waltham Abbey, by the late Mr. W. Burges, from the *De inventione Stæ Crucis*," probably written some time at the end of the twelfth century:— "Once upon a time, when Canute reigned over England, there lived at a place in Somersetshire, named Montacute (but called Lutegaresberi by the common people), a smith who was adorned with all the Christian virtues. Thus he was 'vir magnæ simplicitatis et bonæ indolis, sine malicia timens Deum, &c. Indeed, so much was he respected, that the parish priest committed to his care the water, fire, and lighting of the church. One night, when this worthy man was in a deep sleep, he saw in a vision 'venerandi decoris effigiem,' who told him when he went to his duties at the church next morning, to request the priest to assemble the whole of his parishioners, and after prayer, exhortation, and fasting, to lead them in procession to the top of the hill, and there to dig until he found the treasure hid for ages, viz., the cross, the sign of the passion of our Lord. The smith took no notice of this communication, and accordingly the vision appeared again the night following, but with a severe countenance. The smith, by the advice of his wife, this time also neglected the admonitions of the vision, and thus gave the latter the occasion to make a third visit, thereby completing the usual number. At last the smith did tell the priest, and the latter, with not only his own parishioners, but also with many people from the surrounding country, set off in procession, singing litanies, the smith leading the way: and when they had attained the top of the hill with 'uberrima lacrimarum effusione,' proceeded to

dig, and after going to the depth of forty cubits, were rewarded by the discovery of a stone of wonderful size, with a great fissure through the middle. The next thing was to remove part of the stone, which was done 'non minus fletuum ubertate quam manuum impulsione,' and then appeared the wonderful crucifix of black marble (silex), which was destined to work so many miracles, and eventually be the war-cry of the English upon the field of Senlac. Another but smaller crucifix was also found placed under the right arm, and under the left a bell of ancient workmanship, such as are seen round the necks of cattle. The discovery was completed by a book of the gospels.

"Not knowing exactly what to do, a tent was placed over the excavation until the lord of the place could be sent for. The lord was 'Tovi le prude,' a very great man indeed, being described as 'totius Angliæ post regem primus.' He, when he came, 'vidit et gavisus est.' After which it was determined to remove the objects to the atrium of the parish church. The next morning, Tovi and sundry church dignitaries, both episcopal and abbatial, being present, the smaller crucifix was given up to the parish church, but the other objects being placed upon a wagon, 'cum ornamentorum decora varietate,' were to be deposited wherever the twelve red oxen and twelve cows who were attached to the wagon might carry it. Tovi then mentioning the names of his various residences, devoutly prayed that the car and oxen might proceed to one of them, promising, moreover, in that case, that he would endow the servants of the Holy Cross with the revenues of the town where the cross should be deposited; the wagon, however, stood still, nor could all the efforts either of the bystanders or of the oxen get it to move. At last Tovi remembered the poor hunting-lodge he had begun to build at a place called Waltham, when, 'mirabile dictu, fide mirabilius,' the oxen began to move at such a rate that it seemed more as if the wagon impelled the oxen than that the latter drew the wagon. On the day appointed for the exaltation, when the workmen attempted to drive a nail into the right arm, for the purpose of fastening on the jewelled ornaments given by Tovi, immediately, says the chronicler, blood issued from the stone in the same manner as in former time water issued from the rock. The blood was of course preserved, and formed another of the very many relics which enriched the consecrated house at Waltham.

Glitha, the wife of Tovi, presented a splendid golden and jewelled crown, besides the circlet, which she wore in common with all noblewomen, which was fixed round the thigh of the image, while her bracelets and other jewels were fashioned into a subpedaneum, into which was inserted a wondrous stone, whose property was to emit rays during the night, and thus afford light to travellers. Tovi appears to have made a foundation for two priests and other clergy, besides enriching the church with various gifts of gold and silver. . . . After the erection of the new church the crucifix still continued its miracles, the most famous of which took place when Harold was on his way to fight the Normans : he went to Waltham to pay his devotions, and to pray for victory. When he had prostrated himself to the ground in the form of a cross, the image which before looked upwards, now bowed down its head, 'a bad sign indeed, and significant of the future :' and the chronicler adds that he had this fact from Turkil, the sacrist, who was at the altar at the time. . . In 1192 the cross was covered anew with silver, but the ornaments on the figure itself were left untouched, probably in consequence of what had happened a few years before, when the crucifix being under repair, Robert, the goldsmith of St. Alban's, took off the circlet round the thigh (probably that given by the wife of Tovi), and all those present were struck blind for a considerable time."

It was to the "Holy Cross" that Harold dedicated his new foundation, which he enriched with a vast number of relics and costly vessels. We learn from the Harleian Manuscripts that "among other rich gifts bestowed by Harold on his new college were the following:—Seven little caskets or boxes (*scrinia*) for precious things, three of gold, and four of silver gilded, enriched with gems and full of relics. Four great thuribles (*censers*) of gold and silver. Six great candlesticks, two of gold and four of silver. Three large vessels or pitchers of Greek workmanship, silver and richly gilded. Four crosses of gold and silver studded with gems. Another cross of silver of the weight of fifty marks. Five suits for the priests, ornamented with gold and precious gems. Five other vestments ornamented with gold and gems, one extremely rich and weighty. Two copes covered with gold and gems. Five chalices, two of gold and three of silver. Four altars with relics, one of gold, and three of silver gilded. A silver horn, and various other articles. The relics were still more valuable and numerous, and many (if we may credit the legends) were the miracles wrought by them." [*]

It is the received account that Harold was killed at the battle of Hastings, and that his corpse was carried from the field and buried at Waltham

Abbey. His tomb was shown for many centuries as marking the resting-place of the last of our Saxon kings, though Giraldus Cambrensis among old historians, and Sir Francis Palgrave among modern writers, doubt the fact, and relate a tradition that Harold escaped alive from the field of Hastings, and lived in religious seclusion at Chester, where he ended his days as a monk or lay brother. The latter author considers that the tomb at Waltham was nothing more than a cenotaph, though it bore on it the inscription, " Hic jacet Harold infelix," words which certainly would seem to assert a positive fact ; and Fuller, in his " Church History," gives a circumstantial account of the opening of the monument towards the end of Elizabeth's reign, when a skeleton was discovered inside it. Farmer's history, quoted above, contains a copper-plate engraving of a mask sculptured in grey marble, which, he says, was one of the ornaments of the tomb, and was then in his own possession. The burial of Harold here is accepted as probably true by no less an authority than Dr. Freeman, though disputed by Mr. John H. Parker.

Be this, however, as it may, whether Harold found here his last resting-place or no, it may easily be supposed that William the Conqueror owed little kindness and showed little favour to the religious house which owned his vanquished rival for its founder. He accordingly laid heavy hands upon the church of Holy Cross, robbing it of vestments, plate, and jewels, though, somehow or other, he left the monks in possession of their manors and other estates ; and in subsequent reigns their properties in the neighbourhood appear to have increased, for Matilda, the first wife of Henry I., bestowed on the convent the abbey mill, which still stands close to the gateway shown in our illustration, and was, at that time, a valuable gift ; while the same king's second wife, Adeliza of Lorraine, bestowed on it all the tithes of Waltham, including not only those of her tenants, but of her own demesne land. Stephen appears to have done little more than confirm the charters of his predecessors.

Mr. Freeman, in an article in the "Transactions of the Essex Archæological Society," is inclined to fix the date of the consecration of the new church as 1059 or 1060, and he has at the same time endeavoured to reconcile the various accounts concerning the burial of Harold. He supposes that he was in the first instance interred under a heap of stones upon the sea-coast of Sussex, and afterwards re-buried at Waltham. The new foundation here, as may be easily imagined, suffered greatly under the two first Norman kings ; but as the

---

two queens of Henry I. were both connected with the place, it began to recover in his reign, and in that of his successor, Stephen.

Henry II. did not find that the monks of Waltham turned to good account the gifts so generously bestowed on them; and, therefore, as we find recorded in his charter, he dissolved the foundation, and scattered the dean and eleven canons to the wind. The last dean was Guido Rufus, who, having previously been suspended by the Archbishop of Canterbury, resigned his deanery in 1177 to the king. The story is thus told by a local antiquary:—"This preliminary proceeding having taken place, the king visited Waltham on the eve of Pentecost, when Walter, Bishop of Rochester, on the part of the Archbisop of Canterbury, Gilbert Bishop of London, John Bishop of Norwich, and Hugh Bishop of Durham, assembling by precept from the King and mandate of the Pope (Alexander III.), the said archbishop consenting, sixteen regular canons of the Order of St. Augustine, namely, six of Cirencester, six of Oseney, and four of Chich, were inducted into the church, and Walter de Gaunt, a canon of Oseney, was constituted the first abbot of the new foundation. The church was at the same time declared exempt from episcopal jurisdiction; and Pope Lucius III. subsequently by his bull confirmed to this monastery the exemption from all episcopal jurisdiction. The church thus settled was dedicated first to the Holy Cross, and afterwards to St. Lawrence." At the same time, anno 1191, the use of the *pontificals*, namely, the mitre, crosier, ring, &c., was granted to the abbot. The charter of Henry II. thus defines the ancient liberties of Waltham Church:— "Semper fuit regalis capella ex primitiva sui fundatione nulli Archiepiscopo vel Episcopo, sed tantum ecclesiæ Romanæ et Regiæ dispositioni subjecta." It may be remarked that Waltham is still exempt from the Archdeacon's visitation.

Henry not only confirmed to the newly-founded canons the lands which they had held by gift from Harold, but added to them other possessions in the neighbourhood, including the manors of Epping and Siwardston, or Sewardstone; adding to his charter, by way of preamble, the remarkable expression that it was "fit that Christ his spouse should have a new dowry." The convent was further enriched by a charter from Richard I., confirming all former grants, and also bestowing on the canons the entire manner of Waltham, with "the great wood and park called 'Harold's Park,'" the market of Waltham, and most of the village of Nasing—460 acres in all—on the easy terms of the monks paying £60 into his royal exchequer in lieu

of all services. Richard also, by another charter, confirmed all the former grants, and made further gifts to the monastery, among which was the stately mansion called Copped Hall, but appointed the latter to be held in fee, and hereditarily, of the church of Waltham, *Sancte Crucis*, by Robert Fitz-Aucher. Other pious persons, in the course of the same reign, gave broad lands to the monks "*pro salute animarum suarum;*" and Henry III., who frequently took up his residence at the abbey, requited the hospitality of the canons by giving to them the right of holding a fair annually for seven days. He also augmented their revenues with many rich and costly gifts, and from his date the abbey gradually became so distinguished by royal and noble benefactors as to rank with the most wealthy institutions in the kingdom.

Henry's favours to the monastery were not entirely disinterested; for he resided here, it is said, in order to save the expenses of keeping a court; and he occasionally sought and found in the abbot sympathy and help in his distresses.

In 1242, according to Matthew Paris, the church was re-dedicated, though he does not enlighten us as to the occasion on which this ceremony was performed. Most probably it was on the occasion of the addition of new buildings on the south side of the old Norman church, including what now is called "our Lady's Chapel."

"When Simon de Seham was abbot, in the 30th Henry III. (1245), a dispute arose between the abbot and the townsmen of Waltham about the common lands. 'The men of Waltham,' says Farmer, 'came into the marsh, which the abbot and his convent formerly enjoyed as several to themselves, and killed four mares, worth forty shillings sterling at least, and drove away all the rest: the abbot was politicly pleased for the present not to take notice thereof. Next year the same men of Waltham went to the abbot the Tuesday before Easter, in the name of the whole village, and demanded of him to remove his mares and colts out of the marsh. This the abbot refused to do, adding, that if his bailiffs had placed his cattle otherwise than they ought, they might do well to have it amended, and yet so as to defer the matter till the Tuesday after Easter. On that Tuesday, Richard, brother to the king, Duke of Cornwall, came to Waltham, at which time both the men and the women of the town repaired to the gate of the abbey to receive the abbot's final answer.'

"He put them off with the information that he was preparing for a journey into Lincolnshire, to meet the justices itinerant, and said that he would settle the affair at his return. Not satisfied, they went into the pasture, and in driving out the abbot's mares and colts, drowned three worth twenty shillings, spoiled ten more to the value of ten marks, and beat the keepers, who resisted them, even to the shedding of blood. Fearing, however, that they should be prosecuted, on the return of the abbot, they desired a 'love day,' and

amerced twenty marks, which the abbot remitted; and, on their submission, he *assoyled* them from the excommunication."*

Not long after the above incident the same abbot was engaged with Peter, Duke of Savoy, the king's uncle and lord of the manor of Cheshunt, in a law-suit about boundaries, each asserting his right to some meadow-land lying between two branches of the river Lea, on the west side of the town. Of the altercations that arose in

WALTHAM ABBEY—INTERIOR.

offered to pay damages for the injury committed; but, instead of doing so, they went to London and accused the abbot to the king of having wrongfully taken away their common land, and bringing up new customs, adding that he would 'eat them up to the bone.' The abbot then excommunicated the men of Waltham; and they impleaded him at common law for appropriating their common land to himself. They were unsuccessful, and after a long suit in the King's Bench, were glad to confess that they had done wrong, and they were

consequence of this disagreement we have spoken in a previous chapter.† This dispute about the debatable land was often revived afterwards, and was undecided when the last abbot resigned the convent to Henry VIII.

In 1258, the Parliament having refused money to Henry III., the king prevailed upon the Pope to send a messenger, named Mansuetus, to Eng-

---

* "History of Waltham," pp. 71--2.   † See *ante*, p. 386.

land, asking a supply from the abbeys and churches. The abbot of Waltham was among the first to be applied to on this occasion ; and, partly by threats and partly by entreaties, he was induced to issue a security for 200 marks. A similar application was made at another time to the abbots of Waltham, St. Albans, and Reading, for the sum of 5,000 marks, which the king had promised to the young Earl of Gloucester, as a marriage portion with his niece, the daughter of Guy, Earl of Angoulême.

can hardly digest the breast of a chicken.' The king pledged him in return, and having dined heartily, and thanked him for his good cheer, he departed. A few days after, the abbot was sent for to London, and lodged in the Tower, where he was kept a close prisoner, and, for some time, fed upon bread and water. At length, a sirloin of beef was set before him, on which he fed as heartily as one of his own ploughmen. In the midst of his meal, the king burst into the room from a private

GATEWAY AND BRIDGE, WALTHAM ABBEY. (*See page* 415).

But this was not successful ; the three abbots declaring that they were unable to raise such a sum, nor could they justify such an act, even if they were able.

Farmer relates the following pleasant anecdote of Henry III. ; but the abbot who enjoyed the benefit of his prescribed regimen is not named :— " Having disguised himself in the dress of one of his guards, he contrived to visit, about dinner time, the Abbey of Waltham, where he was immediately invited to the abbot's table ; a sirloin of beef being set before him, he played so good a part, that the abbot exclaimed, 'Well fare thy heart, and here's a cup of sack to the health of thy master ; I would give a hundred pounds could I feed so heartily on beef as thou dost, but my poor queasy stomach

closet, and demanded his hundred pounds, which the abbot gave with no small pleasure, and on being released returned to his monastery with a heart and pocket much lighter than when he left it a few days before."

Such stories have been told also of other English kings, from the early Norman days down to those of Henry VIII.

Stow, in an account of Wat Tyler's rebellion, says that King Richard II. was " now at London, now at Waltham," so that it is clear that more than one king made the abbey a place of residence.

We read but little more of Waltham Abbey until we come to the reign of Henry VIII., when it accidentally became the scene of a conversation, the results of which have ultimately changed the whole course of ecclesiastical affairs in England, by bringing about an event on which the Reformation mainly hinged. It was here that Thomas Cranmer, then a plain Fellow of Jesus College, Cambridge, happened to be resident, on account of the plague, as tutor to the sons of Mr. Cressy, whose wife was the future archbishop's relation, when he was accidentally introduced to Fox and Gardiner, just at the time when the propriety of King Henry's divorce was being canvassed in privileged and "well-informed circles." We allude to the occasion when, in reply to Fox and Gardiner, he said that, instead of waiting month after month and year after year, to learn the Pope's will, it would be better to have the moot-point about a man's marriage with his brother's widow referred to the universities and learned divines of this and other nations. When Fox reported this speech to the king, the latter said, with an oath, that the Cambridge fellow "had the sow by the right ear." And so it proved in the end.

But this service did not save the abbey from the king's greedy commissioners. In 1539, its gross income, according to Speed, was £1,079 12s. 1d., while the clear income is reckoned by Dugdale at £900. And so the fiat went forth. The canons were forced to quit their comfortable nests, and their broad acres and manors were seized by the king and his ministers. The last of a long line of two-and-thirty abbots was Robert Fuller. He was afterwards chosen prior of St. Bartholomew's, in Smithfield, which he held *in commendam*, and which he was also obliged to surrender to the king in 1540. Abbot Fuller may fairly be reckoned among the literati of his monastery; and from his " History," written in a folio volume 460 pages, his namesake Fuller, who was curate of Waltham in the time of the Commonwealth, compiled almost all the particulars of the account of Waltham Abbey, which he appended as a supplement to his " Church History of Britain," published in 1656.

By Edward VI. the conventual estate was granted to Sir Anthony Denny, whose grandson, Sir Edward Denny, the second owner, was raised by Charles I. to the earldom of Norwich. From him it passed, by the marriage of his daughter and heir, to the celebrated James Hay, Earl of Carlisle; and from the Hays it came into the possession of the Wakes, whose head, Sir Herewald Wake, is now lord of the manor. His grandfather, Sir Charles Wake, was an extensive contributor to the funds raised about thirty years ago for beautifying and restoring the noble church, and the east window of painted glass was his donation.

"Originally the abbey church was a very magnificent building, and its curious remains must be regarded as the earliest undoubted specimen of the Norman style of architecture now existing in England. Though erected by Earl Harold, in the Anglo-Saxon period, it cannot be justly referred to any other style than that which the Normans permanently introduced after the Conquest. The great intercourse between the two great countries, which King Edward the Confessor so particularly encouraged previously to that era, and the preference which he gave to Norman customs and Norman artificers, will readily account for this church being constructed from Norman designs. Edward himself caused the abbey church of Westminster to be rebuilt on similar principles; and in respect to the monastery at Waltham, that monarch, as appears from his charter, dated in 1062, may be almost regarded as its coeval founder with Earl Harold."

Sufficient is known of this structure to state that its original form was that of a cross, and that a square tower, which 'contained a ring of five great tuneable bells,' arose from the intersection of the nave and transept; the two great western supporters of which are connected with and partly wrought into the present east end. Some part of the old central tower fell from mere decay; the remainder was purposely destroyed, as we gather from the following entry in the churchwardens' accounts:—" Anno 1556. *Imprimis*. For coles to undermine a piece of the steeple which stood after the first fall, 2s." It was the opinion of the late Sir Gilbert Scott that the central tower of St. Albans abbey was designed to be destroyed in the same way, but that it was saved by an accident.

The interior of the church is certainly striking for its massiveness rather than its beauty. Passing under the western tower we enter the church through a very handsome Pointed arch, adorned with floriated, crocketed, and finialed work, and through a porch or vestibule with a handsome groined roof, both probably of the reign of Henry III.

The first two and most westerly arches of the nave are pointed; but they probably were made to supersede the semicircular Norman originals, six in number, which divide the main body of the church from its side aisles. The columns vary from each other both in diameter and in ornamentation. They are thus described:—"Spiral grooves (deeply cut), proceeding from the base to the capital, diversify two of these columns; and two others are surrounded by indented zig-zags, in successive rows; thus assuming a strict similarity of character with the great columns of the nave in Durham Cathedral. Another tier of large arches, springing from very short columns and pilasters, surmounts the former arches, on each side; except at the west end, where, as before stated, two of the lower ones have been altered into the high-pointed form, and carried up to the string-course of the *triforium*, or clerestory, which contains the principal windows that give light to the nave. These are each fronted by a central and two smaller arches, between which and the windows there is a narrow passage extending along the sides. Most of the mouldings are of the zig-zag form, but there are some distinct variations of character. The length of the church is 106 feet; its breadth, including the aisles, is about 53 feet. A ground plan, a perspective view, and a longitudinal section, of the interior of Waltham church as it was half a century ago, may be seen in Britton's "Architectural Antiquities," Vol. iii.

We have already said that Harold's tomb stood several yards beyond the east end of the present church, and that its site is bare, and that his bones, if they be there, now lie *sub Jove frigido*. But besides the founder Harold, many eminent persons, in the good old palmy days of its glories, found their last resting-place within these monastic walls. "Hugh Nevil, Protho-forester of England, who died 'full of years,' A.D. 1222, according to Matthew Paris, was buried here 'under a noble engraven marble sepulchre;' not the least remnant of which is now known to exist. His son also, John Nevil, the successor to his revenues and offices; and Robert Passelew, archdeacon of Lewes, a despised and discarded minion of Henry III., who died at his house at Waltham, in the year 1252, were also among the number of those interred here. Near the altar rails is a defaced grey slab, which is indented with a mitred figure; this, with two or three brass plates of Queen Elizabeth's time, are the oldest memorials which now remain.

On the south side of the communion rails is the Jacobean tomb of a person of quality, presenting an amusing contrast to another handsome monument on the north to a wealthy and respectable gentleman of plebeian and commercial antecedents.

As may be easily imagined, the Dennies did not hold the fair abbey lands and monastic buildings of Waltham without leaving their dust behind them in its aisles. Thus, if we search the parish registers, we find that "Edward Denny, first and only Earl of Norwich" (of that creation), was buried in this church in December, 1630. And near the east end of the south aisle is a mural monument in memory of Sir Edward Denny,

Knt.,—"'Sonn of ye Right Honourable Sr Anthony Denny, Counsellor of Estate and Executor to King Henry 8, and of Joane Champernon, his wife,'—and his Lady who was the daughter of Pierce Edgecombe, Esq., of Mount Edgecombe, and 'svmtime Maide of Honor to Qveene Elizabeth,—and who, 'ovt of meane Fortvnes bvt no meane affection, prodvced this Monvment.' Sir Edward was one of the Counsel of Munster, in Ireland, and governor of Kerry and Desmond. He died on the 12th of February, 1599, aged 52 years, and is represented in plate armour, lying on his side: his head is partly supported by his helmet, and partly by his left hand, the elbow resting upon a cushion; his right hand being brought across the body, rests upon his sword. His Lady has a ruff and close boddice; and kneeling in front are their ten children, *viz.*, four boys and six girls. The inscription states, that 'this worthy Knight, cvt off like a pleasavnt frvite before perfect ripeness,'—was 'religiovs, wise, jvst, right valiant, most active, learnings frinde, prides foe, kindly lovinge, and mvtch beloved;' and that 'he was honored wth ye dignitie of knighthood, by dve deserte, in ye Field.' Over the tomb are the family arms (with quarterings), *viz.*, Gu. a saltire Arg. between Crosses pattée, Or."

About 1864 a partial restoration of the old abbey church was commenced, and the cost of the work done since that time has amounted to upwards of £8,000. The church is now no longer the dreary and dilapidated building that it was less than a quarter of a century ago, although the edifice has not been thoroughly restored, but merely saved from that utter decay and ruin by which it was at one time threatened. The Lady Chapel, on the south side of the chancel, and the most ruinous part of the old structure, has been repaired at a cost of £1,000, defrayed by Sir T. Fowell Buxton, Bart., and has been thrown open into the body of the church; the hideous old deal pens, called "pews," have been replaced by oaken benches all looking eastward, and all the galleries have been removed. The ceiling—the dark colours of which for years only served to add a sense of weight and oppression where all should be light and graceful—has been replaced by one of wood, painted in bright colours, and far more suited to Norman architecture, though perfectly flat and horizontal. Instead of the large square holes in the walls, filled with glass, that had long served as windows, new windows set in a framework of the Norman style have been inserted throughout: and almost all the windows have been filled with painted glass as memorials of departed friends.   The chancel was repaired at the expense of the late Sir Charles Wake, Bart., the lord of the manor of Waltham.   The new reredos was the gift of Mr. Edenborough, of Thrift Hall, in the neighbourhood of the town ; whilst the remainder of the work has been carried out at the cost of the parishioners and their friends.

The Lady Chapel, which is probably of Henry III.'s time, is supported by graduated buttresses, ornamented with elegantly-formed niches.   Beneath it is a crypt, " the fairest," says Fuller, " that ever I saw," the roof of which is sustained by groined arches.   The superstructure was modernised, so that scarcely a vestige of its ancient character remained.   The crypt was used as a place of worship, and it had its regular priest and other attendants ; the reading-desk was covered with plates of silver.   In the Churchwardens' Accounts, mention is made of six annual *Obits*, to defray the expenses of which various lands were bequeathed, and a stock of eighteen cows was let out to farm for 18s.   The sum allotted for each *Obit* was thus expended :—To the parish priest, 4d. ; to our Ladye's priest, 3d. ; to the charnel priest, 3d. ; to the two clerks, 4d. ; to the children (choristers), 3d. ; to the sexton, 2d. ; to the bellman, 2d. ; for two tapers, 2d. ; for oblation, 2d. ; &c.

In the burial-ground, close to the south entrance, is a very fine wide-spreading elm, the trunk of which, at several feet above the earth, is nearly twenty feet in circumference.   The present tower stands at the west end of what is now the parish church, but was formerly the nave.   It is a heavy and uninteresting structure, and is a poor substitute for its predecessor, though good for its time ; it was built by the parishioners in the reign of Queen Mary, out of "their stock in the church box."   This "stock" was an aggregate from various sources, as the sale of stone, lead, and timber from the monastic buildings ; but it was chiefly obtained by the sale of the goods of a *brotherhood* belonging to this church, consisting of three priests, three choristers, and two sextons, which was not dissolved until Edward the Sixth's reign.   Two hundred and seventy-one ounces of plate, the property of this fraternity (which had been saved from confiscation on account of the avowed intention of the parish to erect the above tower), were sold for £67 14s. 9d.   At the same time many rich dresses were disposed of, including a cape of cloth of gold to Sir Edward Denny for £3 6s. 8d., and two altar-cloths of velvet and silk, value £2.   It is not improbable but that the brotherhood thus despoiled was that of an *hospital*, which had been originally founded within the precincts of the monastery by

the abbot and convent of Waltham, about the year 1218.

It appears from Fuller that the bells out of the old tower were hung for some years in a temporary frame of timber which stood at the south-east corner of the churchyard, and remained there till the tower was finished, when, the funds falling short, the good people of Waltham resolved to sell their bells to raise money—like some " Vandals " of more recent times at Sandwich—so that Waltham, " which formerly had steeple-less bells, had now a bell-less steeple."   It would be unfair to suppress the fact that in the very dark days which mark the beginning of the present century the inhabitants of Waltham did their best to atone for the faults of their forefathers by hanging a new peal of bells in the tower.

Some idea of the former extent of this church may be conceived from stating that the ancient tomb considered to be King Harold's, though situated about forty yards from the present termination of the building, stood in the eastern part of the original choir.   This tomb is described as " plain " in form, but of " a rich grey marble " ; having sculptured on it " a sort of cross fleury, much descanted on by art."   Fuller says that it was supported by " pillarets," one pedestal of which was " in his own possession."   In Queen Elizabeth's reign, a gardener in the service of Sir Edward Denny discovered, in digging, a large stone coffin, inclosing a corpse, supposed to be that of King Harold ; but the remains, on touching, mouldered into dust.   Near the same spot, about ninety years ago, a second coffin was found, containing an entire skeleton inclosed in lead.

" Waltham Holy Cross," writes the author of " Professional Excursions," in 1843, " as the favourite foundation and the grave of Harold, must not be overlooked, though dilapidated, neglected, and hurrying to decay.   Within its cloisters Cranmer, Fox, and Gardiner unintentionally met together, little dreaming of the various positions they were afterwards destined to hold in our ecclesiastical history.   The church," he adds, " is a massive deformity, but contains within some curious specimens of Norman architecture, which the dirty lanes and shabby streets must not prevent us from seeking to examine."

With reference to the present aspect of the remains of the monastery, Mr. Burges, in his " Legends of Waltham Abbey, and History of the Church " (1860), quoted above, remarks :—" We know this from the chroniclers, that the church was very magnificent, that it was made of stone, that it had a roof covered with lead, and that in some parts (perhaps in the apse, or in the baldachin over the great altar) there was a great deal of gilding and bronze plates. Now the eastern end of Harold's church has long ago disappeared— most probably it did not last above seventy or eighty years; but the nave and aisles perfectly correspond with the description, of course omitting the gilding and bronze plates, which would naturally be restricted to the east end. Thus the height of the nave walls is fifty-two feet. The aisles have originally been vaulted, the arches are elaborately decorated with chevrons and billet moulds; there are no mouldings to speak of, and every part could be done with an axe—in fact, it is exactly such a building as would be erected without regard to expense in a rude age. . . It was in all probability about the time of Stephen that the apse of Harold's church was taken down, and a new central tower and choir added. This choir was, no doubt, rather a large one . . . sufficiently extensive to afterwards accommodate the new foundation of Henry II., who turned out the seculars, and substituted a much larger number of monks in their place. We know that he did build sundry domestic buildings, which were absolutely necessary for a monastic establishment, and were not so for a body of secular priests, who probably lived in the town; and we are also informed that he did intend to rebuild the church, but upon consideration the monks were inducted into the old building. Most probably the increased accommodation was got by bringing the choir down into the central tower; and perhaps we may assign the northern clerestory of the nave to the first works begun by this monarch, as the style is very advanced and rich Norman, while the building now called the 'potatoe house,' as well as the cloisters (the springing of the groining of which was discovered in the late repairs), must be referred to the end of his reign, or to those of either of his sons, for the mouldings are by no means Romanesque. . . Some time in the reign of Edward II. it was found that the vaulting of the aisles had pushed out the side walls, so the said vaulting was forthwith destroyed. The bays at the west end had also got a lurch towards the west, probably in consequence of want of care in the foundations, or perhaps from the incomplete state of the western towers. The result was that the architect for the time did not make a restoration of the westernmost arches, but boldly got rid of the nave arch, and turned a new-pointed one at the triforium level, thus making a composition of two bays instead of three. It is needless to say that the effect is by no means improved. But the fourteenth century architect was

a man of genius, and when he proceeded to give us a new west front, he really produced a most striking and original composition; and although the great west window has been irrevocably destroyed by the tower in Philip and Mary's time, the beautiful west door and the charming windows and side turrets still remain to call forth our warmest admiration. It is by no means improbable that the same architect erected the 'lady chapel,' but in his later years, for although what remains of the tracery of the western window is very good, yet the mouldings are small, poor, and sub-divided, and utterly unworthy of the architect of the western front. . . A small three-light window is the only trace of Perpendicular work in the building as it at present remains. At the Reformation the east end, as reverting to the Crown, was destroyed, but the nave, belonging to the parishioners, was preserved intact. The tower, which appears to have been a sort of debatable ground, saved all further trouble by falling down in the time of Philip and Mary, and the townsmen, who had bought the bells, then set to work and built up a new tower at the west end of the church out of the old materials of the choir, which they bought or exchanged with Mr. Henry Denny.

"Fuller, who was presented to the curacy in 1648, has given us, in his 'History of Waltham Abbey,' several very interesting extracts from the parish books relative to the sale or purchase of articles required by the church during the various changes in religion which took place in the sixteenth century. An attempt was made to execute repairs in Charles the First's time, but owing to Archbishop Laud not having been consulted, it fell to the ground. Some repairs, however, were undertaken during the reign of Charles II. Among them was the re-facing of the second pillar from the east on the south side, for a coin of that king was found in the foundation. In the eighteenth and the early part of the present century, all sorts of the greatest barbarities were inflicted upon the unfortunate church. The roof was lowered, and a plaster ceiling put underneath; more of the windows of the north side were destroyed; two galleries were erected at the west end, and another in the south aisle, whereby great holes were cut in the pillars, to their no small detriment; and lastly, the whole area filled with very high pews. The roof, being in good repair, although by no means of the original pitch, has been retained, but the plaster ceiling has, of course, been removed, and its place supplied by boarding painted in imitation of the only contemporary ceiling remaining, namely, that at Peterborough. The centres, however, represent the signs of the zodiac, the labours of the year, and the elements."

In 1859 the work of restoring the interior was undertaken by Mr. W. Burges. Nothing, however, was done to the exterior, beyond making necessary repairs. The east end of the church is, except the main walls, entirely new, and in a style much later than the body of the church: namely, that of the first half of the thirteenth century. Within the great arch which spans the eastern wall are three lancet

thrown into the church; some ruinous walls; a small bridge and gateway, near the Abbey Mills; and a dark vaulted structure of two divisions connected with the convent garden, and which adjoined the Abbey House, inhabited by the Dennys. Not any remains exist of the Abbey House (which is reported to have been a very extensive building), except, perhaps, the vaulted structure mentioned above; and of a large mansion which was erected upon its site, nothing is left but a plastered wall.

COPPED HALL, NEAR EPPING. (*See page* 417.)

windows immediately above the altar, and a rose window of early French character. In the process of restoration the greatest care seems to have been taken in the matter of decoration. Thus the altar-piece and the three lancet windows are occupied with subjects representing the human nature of our Saviour, the rose window above illustrating His Divine nature.

Though the buildings of Waltham Abbey were once so extensive as to include a space of many acres, scarcely any part remains but the nave of the abbey church, which, as shown above, is now the parochial church, an attached chapel on the south side, called the Lady Chapel, long used as a school-room and vestry, but now utilised for service, being

In the convent garden, which is now tenanted by a market-gardener, is an aged *tulip-tree*, reported to be the largest in England.

To the north of the abbey church is a farm-house, constructed out of the abbot's stables and faced with fine bricks. The gardens are still partly surrounded by the abbey walls, and a small chapel, or oratory, in the grounds, arched with a groined ceiling of fine Early English work, is now used as a room to grow mushrooms. Beyond the farm-house is a quaint old bridge, said to be Norman, and often called after Harold; three out of its five ribs still remain. In a meadow beyond are the abbey fish-ponds, now dry, in which doubtless fine carp and tench were preserved for the brethren on fasting days. They now grow abundance of wild flowers.

Near the Abbey Mill, which is still occupied for grinding corn, is a wide space of ground, surrounded by small dwellings, called the Bramblings, but formerly Rome-land (as at St. Albans and at Norwich), which is conjectured to have been so called from its rents being in former times appropriated to the use of the Holy See. The weekly market is held here on Tuesdays; on one side of

rest on corbels, formed by two demi-angels supporting shields, on which were engraved the royal arms of the time of Edward III.: viz., France and England, quarterly.

The various streams of the Lea in this neighbourhood are said by tradition to flow in the very same channels which were cut by the great Alfred when he turned aside the course of the river, and left the Danish fleet aground.

"Fragments of sculpture, figured tiles, metal

AMBRESBURY BANKS. (*See page* 418.)

the spot still stands a stack of chimneys, which formed a portion of King Henry's hunting-box. It was probably here that the conversation (related above) was held which affected so deeply the course of the Reformation in this country. If so, this chimney-stack is an historic landmark.

The gateway and bridge shown in the illustration on page 409 stand a little to the north of the abbey, close above the Abbey Mill. The gateway is of stone; but it has been repaired from time to time with bricks of various sizes and hues, which lend it a great variety of colour, and render it a great favourite for the water-colour painter. It consists of two Pointed arches, one larger than the other. The outer mouldings of the larger arch

work, &c.," writes Mr. Thorne, in his "Environs of London," "are occasionally exhumed on the site or in the neighbourhood of the abbey. Considerable quantities of pilgrims' jettons, or groats, have been found in the town. The 'Holy Cross' itself doubtless attracted numerous pilgrims to Waltham. A few years ago a stone mould was dug up in Coleman Street, London, from which metal casts were taken, to be worn by Waltham pilgrims as the badge or insignia of their pilgrimage. The mould was cruciform, with a figure of a cross in the centre, surrounded by the legend, 'Signum Sancte Crucis de Waltham.'"

Among the worthies connected with this place whose names we have not already mentioned was

John of Waltham, Master of the Rolls, Keeper of the Privy Seal, Lord High Treasurer, and Bishop of Salisbury, who was excommunicated by Courtenay Archbishop of Canterbury; he was buried in Westminster Abbey. Another celebrity was Roger de Waltham, Canon of St. Paul's, and the author of several books, under Henry III.

The history of Waltham town is so nearly identified with that of the abbey that the completion of the latter leaves but little to record with respect to the former. Henry III., as we have shown above, was not only a great benefactor to the abbey, but granted to the abbot the right of holding a weekly market and an annual fair of seven days' duration. The demands of the abbot for "stallage" at the fair led to frequent disputes with the citizens of London, and quiet was obtained only after the Londoners had refused to resort to Waltham Fair for some three years or more, when, in 1256, the abbot agreed to refund all distresses, and granted to the Londoners "acquittance of all such stallage for ever." The market is still held weekly on Tuesdays, and the fairs take place in May, June, and September. The old market-house, a building of the Elizabethan era, was pulled down about 1850. In it were preserved for many years a pair of stocks, bearing the date 1598. They are still standing—not, however, in their original place or position, but set up on one end of the roadside, near the church.

William Vallens, in his "Tale of Two Swannes," written in 1590, thus quaintly describes this place as it was under the latter years of Elizabeth :—

" Down all along through Waltham Street they passe,
  And wonder at the ruines of the Abbay
  Late supprest, the walles, the walkes, the monumentes,
  And everything that there is to be seene."

He proceeds to describe at considerable length, and with great minuteness, the "locke" on the river, with its "double doores of wood," and a "cesterne all of planke," both then novelties to the eyes of travellers in the infancy of canal navigation.

The town still in many parts wears an antiquated appearance, and the venerable abbey and gateway give a character of the "olden time" to the scene; but still the place is not behind-hand in the march of progress, for it has its weekly newspaper, its local board of health, its burial and school boards, its literary institute and reading-rooms, two or three cricket-clubs, and a "fishery." The Lea in this locality is much resorted to by the disciples of Izaak Walton—barbel, bream, trout, jack, chub, and roach, abounding in plenty. Free fishing is also afforded on the Lea Navigation. Hofland, in treating of Waltham Abbey in his "Angler's Manual," writes :—" Often have I fished here in May, and, under the gentle influence of the season and the spot, recalled to mind the beautiful lines of the highly-gifted, but unfortunate, Lord Surrey :

' The sovte season that bud and bloome forth bringes,
  With grene hath cladde the hyll and eke the vale;
  The nightingall with fethers new she singes,
  The turtle to her mate hath told her tale;
  Somer is come, for every spraye now springes,
  The fishes flete with new repayred scale,
  The adder, all her slough away she flynges,
  The busy bee her honey now she mynges.' "

There are in the town and its immediate neighbourhood malt-kilns, a brewery, flour-mills, a manufactory of percussion caps, &c. The cemetery, which was opened in 1857, covers about four acres, and contains two mortuary chapels. The County Court, which was built in 1849, stands on the site of some old silk-printing works. The "Tulip Tree," a celebrated inn here, is, of course, named after the famous tree mentioned above as growing in the abbey precincts.

As was usual in other places, so here the brethren of the abbey supplied the religious wants of the neighbourhood on all sides, and accordingly the region which they served was very large. Hence the parish of Waltham extends over Sewardstone, and High Beech has only recently been cut off, and made into a separate incumbency.

CHAPTER XLIV.

WALTHAM (continued) AND EPPING.

" Sweet sylvan Epping rears its rural head."

Extent of Waltham Abbey Parish—Census Returns—Rural Appearance of the Locality—Principal Seats and Mansions—Warlies—Copped Hall—Ambresbury Banks—The Story of Queen Boadicea's Conflict with the Romans—Obelisks in the Neighbourhood—Highwaymen and Footpads—The Village of Epping—Epping Church.

WALTHAM HOLY CROSS is a very extensive parish, consisting not only of the township of Waltham Abbey, but of a large portion of the country east, north, and south, containing altogether nearly 12,000 acres. Inclusive of Sewardstone and other subordinate districts, it stretches away northward for some three miles to the parish of Nasing, eastward for about three miles to the boundaries of Epping, and southward to the village of Chingford, whilst on the south-east it embraces High Beech, which lies about three miles from the town. Sewardstone and High Beech are situated on the borders of Epping Forest, and will be dealt with in a subsequent chapter. Holyfield in the north and Upshire in the east are two little scattered agricultural hamlets, containing in the aggregate some 7,000 acres. In 1871 the population of Waltham parish, exclusive of the ecclesiastical district of High Beech, amounted to about 4,500, a number which had increased during the next decade to 5,300. According to the census for 1881, the number of inhabitants in Waltham Abbey township alone was close upon 3,000.

The whole of the district comprised within the jurisdiction of the metropolitan police, and lying to the north-east of Waltham town, is exceedingly rural, being mostly meadow-land, used for grazing purposes, intersected by the Cobbin Brook, a tolerable rivulet, which winds and gurgles in a sinuous course by Epping Upland, or Old Epping, and skirting the south-east side of Waltham, unites its waters with that of the river Lea about half a mile south of the town. The country round about is pleasingly diversified with hills and vales, and in parts well wooded, but possesses no history. Warlies Hall and Copped Hall are the chief seats in this district; but there are a few others, with moderate estates attached to them, such as Thrift Hall and Monkham, besides several farms and hamlets, one of which latter bears the name of Harold's Park, and may mark the site of the "great wood and park called Harold's Park," mentioned in the preceding chapter as having been bestowed by Richard I. on the canons of Waltham Abbey.*

A short distance to the west of Harold's Park are Galley Hill and Galley Wood. Thomas Fuller, who lived at Waltham for many years, wrote in 1640:—"On the one side of the town itself are large and fruitful meadows . . . . On the other side a spacious forest spreads itself, where fourteen years since one might have seen whole herds of red and fallow deer." What is left of Epping Forest, originally known as the Forest of Essex, and later on as Waltham Forest, in the immediate neighbourhood of the town, crowns the high ground away to the east and south-east.

Some two or three miles to the east of Waltham Abbey, in a sheltered valley on the road to Copped Hall, lies Warlies, the seat of Sir Thomas Buxton. The property, consisting of about 1,000 acres, was purchased by the late Sir Edmund Buxton, M.P., the son and successor to the honoured name of the first Sir Thomas Fowell Buxton, many years M.P. for Weymouth, and the associate of Wilberforce in his philanthropic efforts to abolish African and West Indian slavery.

Copped Hall—so named from the Saxon "cop," the top of a hill—lies a mile or so eastward, nearer to Epping. It is one of the finest modern seats in the county. It was built about the middle of the last century, near the site of an older structure raised by the monks of Waltham Abbey in the good old days when they had possession of the manor. The park, upwards of 4,000 acres in extent, is situated partly in the parish of Waltham and partly in that of Epping.

Mr. Weldon, in his "Guide to Epping Forest," says:—" In the proceedings of the Privy Council, in the reign of King Edward VI., there is an account of the Princess Mary, afterwards Queen, living at Copped Hall, and three of her principal servants being summoned before the Privy Council, and commanded to inform their mistress that her chaplains were prohibited from celebrating mass, or using any of the ceremonies of the Roman Catholic religion. On their return she ordered them not to speak to her chaplains, but sent them back with a letter addressed to King Edward, dated from her 'poore howse at Copped Hall, 19th August, 1551,' and, on their refusal to acquaint her with the further charge given by the Council, the Lord Chancellor Riche, Sir Wm. Petre one of the principal secretaries of state, and Sir Anthony Wingfield comptroller of the household, were deputed to wait on her with a letter from the King, and to enforce the orders of the Privy Council. The Princess seems to have received them anything but graciously, saying they ought to 'shewe more favore to me for my father's sake, who made the more parte of you almoste of nothing.' She delivered to the Lord Chancellor 'a ringe, for the king, upon her knees; most humbly, with very humble recommendaciones, saienge she would die his true subjecte & sister, & obaye his commandements in all things excepte in theis matters of religeon, towchinge the masse, & the newe service.' Among the same extracts from the proceedings of the Privy Council, three years afterwards, in the first year of the reign of Queen Mary, is a letter, dated March 17, 1554, directed to 'Lord Oxforde, & the above Lord Riche, to be presente at the burninge of such obstinat persones as presently are sent doune to be burned in diverse partes of the county of Essex, & to be aydinge to the Sherife of the said shiere therein.'"

See *ante*, p. 407.

The old hall itself, built in the place of a yet earlier structure, was a large quadrangular red-brick mansion, and it stood to the south of the present hall, on lower ground. It was built in the reign of Elizabeth, from the designs of Thorpe, for Sir Thomas Heneage, the Treasurer of the Royal Chamber and Vice-Chamberlain of the Queen's Household, to whom the estate had been granted by the Crown. The chief feature of the hall in Sir Thomas Heneage's time was the great gallery, fifty-six yards in length.

The author of "Anglorum Speculum, or The Worthies of England," thus writes in 1684 :— "Copt Hall, or Coppice Hall, seated on a hill in the midst of a park, was built by the Abbot of Waltham, and enlarged by Sir Th. Heneage : in which there is the most proportionable gallery in England." He adds :—"An. 1639, a Hericano forced the stones of the great east window, like pellets, quite through this gallery, in length 56 Yards. Dr. Jackson about the same time observed the like wind as Ominous and presaging our Civil Dissentions."

Thorne, in his "Environs of London," says :— "Charles Sackville, the witty Earl of Dorset, and the patron of wits and poets, lived at Copped Hall, and here Shadwell wrote part of his 'Squire of Alsatia.' Charles II. dined with the Earl of Middlesex at Old Copped Hall in June, 1660; and William III., when on his way to Newmarket, dined and stayed the night here, April 4, 1698."

Later on Copped Hall was held successively by the Earls of Winchelsea and the Lords Grey. Between 1753 and 1757 it was rebuilt by its then owner, Mr. John Conyers, who at that time resided at Epping Place, and whose descendants remained seated here for upwards of a century. The family of Conyers appears to have been of very ancient standing in Yorkshire. Tristram Conyers, or Coniers, a gentleman possessed of an ample fortune, settled at Walthamstow early in the seventeenth century, and this branch became naturalised as an Essex family. Several of its members occupied prominent positions in that century. Gerard Conyers was an alderman of London, and received the honour of knighthood; and Edward, who then represented in Parliament the borough of East Grinstead, became the owner of the manor of Epping and Copped Hall, by purchase from Lord North, about the year 1728. In 1753 Mr. John Conyers found the old hall in such a dilapidated condition, that he determined upon pulling it down, and rebuilding the house on a different site. Time had loosened the foundation of the grand old Elizabethan mansion, and a hurricane had long previously blown down its

great gallery; and the beautiful painted glass window of its ancient chapel, which is believed to have been originally painted for Henry VIII.'s chapel at New Hall, near Chelmsford, in this county, whence it was obtained, eventually found its way to St. Margaret's Church, Westminster.*

The present mansion of Copped Hall is a spacious building, almost square, consisting of a centre, with pediment and two wings, and, standing on high ground, is visible for miles round. It is constructed of white brick of a superior make, and since its erection it has been much improved and enlarged by James Wyatt. The late Mr. H. J. Conyers was a first-rate sportsman and master of hounds. "Copt Hall," writes the author of "Professional Excursions in 1843," "is remarkable for the smooth and nicely jointed brick-work of the exterior, and the *brusque* manner of its owner ; but he is the spirit of the chase, and Nimrod's hounds apologise for Nimrod's manner." After paying a tribute to Mr. Conyers as a master and landlord, he adds :—"The mansion looks cold and solitary at a distance, perched upon a knoll unbroken by intervening foliage ; but a spirit of improvement prevails over the asperities of Nature, and the neighbouring forest is a theatre of endless amusement and delightful recreation." It now belongs to the family of Mr. Wythes, who was a railway contractor, "raised from the ranks" by his own energy and enterprise.

The traveller, in passing along the narrow roadway which skirts the forest between Waltham and Epping, sees the mansion on a bold eminence away to the left, the land falling from the spot on which he stands to a deep valley, and rising again by easy gradations in groves and plantations, like a succession of wooded terraces, to the park and green lawn on which the hall-door opens. The little river Cobbin steals quietly along on the north side of the park, whilst just on the outskirts of the park, about thirty or forty yards to the south-east, are the remains of an extensive earth-work, probably British, called the Ambresbury Banks, supposed by antiquarians to be a military camp, and the scene of Boadicea's battle and final defeat. The earth-work, which is about half a mile in circuit, is tolerably perfect, and is so largely overgrown with beeches, oaks, hornbeams, and hazels, as to form a favourite spot for picnics in the summer.

With reference to these earth-works, we find in Gough's "Camden" (Vol. II., p. 49) the following remarks, communicated to the author by Mr. Smart Letheuillier :—"This entrenchment is now

---

* See "Old and New London," Vol. III., p. 568.

entirely overgrown with old oaks and hornbeams. It was formerly in the very heart of the forest, and no road near it, till the present turnpike road from London to Epping was made, almost within the memory of man, which now runs within a hundred yards of it, but the entrenchment cannot be thence perceived, by reason of the wood that covers it. Its figure is irregular, rather longest from east to west, and on a gentle declivity to the south-east. It contains nearly twelve acres, and is surrounded by a ditch and high bank, much worn down by time, though where there are angles they are still very bold and high. There are no regular openings, like gateways or entrances, only in two places, where the bank has been cut through, and the ditch filled up very lately, in order to make a straight road from Debden Green to Epping Market. The boundaries between the parishes of Waltham and Epping run exactly through the middle of this entrenchment . . . As I can find no reason to attribute this entrenchment either to the Romans, Saxons, or Danes, I cannot help concluding it to have been a British *oppidum*, and perhaps had some relation to other remains of that people which are discoverable in our forest." Mr. W. Winters, in a letter in *Notes and Queries* (4th Series, Vol. X., p. 395), remarks :—" Gough seems to raise a doubt about the exact position of the combatants being Amesbury (or Ambresbury), simply on the ground of what Mr. Letheuillier had stated. He also affirms that ' the want of barrows is an argument that a great slaughter could hardly have happened here.' Philip Morant, the Essex historian, not willing to give up the point so easily, states that ' by comparing all accounts and circumstances, he is persuaded that the field of battle was between Waltham and Epping, or thereabouts, not far from London.' "

Another writer in *Notes and Queries* (5th Series, Vol. V., p. 396) suggests that these works are really not a camp, but " part of a series of beacon hills ;" but be that as it may, their form and general appearance bear a strong resemblance to other works of a similar character which are undoubtedly known to have been used for military purposes. Old soldiers who have served in India and South Africa have been known to have remarked on seeing these earth-works that they must have been a camp, used by Oliver Cromwell or some such officer !

The City arms, on an iron post at the roadside, in front of the works, denote that here is the limit of the jurisdiction of the Lord Mayor of London.

The story of the great conflict between the Britons and Romans, which is said to have taken place here, is graphically told by Coller, in his " History of Essex," as follows :—" The king of the Iceni, the people who inhabited Suffolk and Norfolk, and part of Cambridgeshire, appears to have retained his kingdom under the protection of the conquerors ; and when he died he left half his territory and treasures to the Romans, under the impression that the other half would be secured for his family. The Romans, however, seized the whole. Boadicea, the widow, remonstrated. The extortioners endeavoured to silence her by insult ; she was publicly scourged like a common slave, and her daughters were given over to dishonour by the soldiery. This outrage aroused all the spirit of the ancient Briton. The wretched queen, instead of sinking under her miseries, boldly raised the standard of revolt and vengeance, and fearfully were the Romans made to pay for their breach of faith and want of honesty. Suetonius, the propraetor, was at this period (A.D. 61) engaged in an expedition against the sacred Isle of Mona, or Anglesea, the last home and refuge of the Druids, and this part of the country lay comparatively unprotected. There was, indeed, a garrison of Roman veterans at Colchester, but they appear to have been paralysed as the storm of war came swelling up from Suffolk. Conscience—for then, as now, such was the effect of crime—' made cowards of them all ; ' and superstition gave birth to all sorts of hideous portents and omens to unman them. Tacitus, in his ' Annals,' says that the statue of the goddess of Victory at Camelodunum fell down and turned, as if yielding to the enemy ; howlings were heard in the theatre, and strange noises in the council-house ; a fearful apparition was seen in the estuary of the Thames, towards Mersea Island, which had become a pleasant resort of the Romans ; and enthusiastic women foretold the coming destruction—which, considering the force that was advancing and the panic of the defenders, required no great prophetic powers. When, therefore, the Britons in overwhelming numbers appeared upon the wooded hills around Colchester, and were joined by the men of Essex, who flocked in thousands to the standard of the queen, they met with only a feeble resistance. The ninth legion, which had hastened to the rescue, was defeated, and the whole of its infantry slain : and the exasperated Britons swept into the capital of the colony, slaughtering all, even the women and children, and mercilessly destroying every object of art and emblem of the Roman sway. The soldiers threw themselves into the temple of Claudius, which they defended for two days, but at length perished by fire. Excited by their success, and enriched by plunder, the victors then appear to have turned their backs upon Colchester, leaving it a scene of utter desolation. Boadicea, at the head of her troops, directed her march along the Roman way by Coggeshall, Rayne, and Dunmow, to St. Albans, which also fell a like prey to her fury. Every station that could be reached was devastated; and the number of the Romans and their allies who were thus slain is stated to have been 70,000. The sounds of this calamity at length reached Suetonius, who hurried back with his army. The Britons mustered in arms at least 100,000—some historians state their force at 250,000—far outnumbering the Romans, who had, however, on their side the advantage of experience and skill in the art of war; and Boadicea, retiring at their approach, established herself in an entrenched camp in the forest, where, a short distance from Epping, near Copped Hall, and now known as Ambresbury Banks, the remains of her stronghold may still be traced. Here she decided on awaiting the Roman foe. Some writers have assumed that the last struggle was at Islington, others at Messing; but Morant and others, whose authority is decisive, say—'The famous battle between Suetonius and Boadicea was fought somewhere between Epping and Waltham, near which a fine camp remains.' Here, then, the opposing forces were drawn up. The Britons, like the Russians at the Alma, had brought the ladies to see the fight and witness their triumph. Their wives and children were taken in wagons to the field, and ranged in a line along the rear of the battle—to become its victims, and to swell the slaughter of those they loved. The skilful Romans had chosen ground accessible at only one point, with a forest at the back. Having provoked the enemy to the assault, here they remained till the Britons had exhausted themselves, and expended their darts in the attempt to force the narrow pass; then assuming the form of a wedge, their infantry bore down upon them like an avalanche, while their horsemen with their spears swept the field. The Britons were routed; and hemmed in by the rows of wagons behind, the warriors, their wives and children, fell in one indiscriminate slaughter. The Romans lost only 400, but 80,000 of the Britons were left upon the forest turf; and Boadicea escaped, only to die soon after either of grief or poison. Truly has it been said that 'we dwell amidst the ruins of successive races, and heed them not.' How little does the quiet traveller from Epping to Waltham or Loughton think that a scene of blood like this has passed upon the very spot he is crossing! When, too, the members of the summer pic-nic party gather round the gipsy feast

spread upon the table of turf, and within the shade of the brushwood and clumps of hornbeams with which the site of the camp is now overgrown, how little do they reflect that the bones of 80,000 lie beneath the surface, and with them are buried the wreck and remnants of the rule of that people who first possessed power in the land—for this was the last expiring effort of the Britons; and though partial revolts took place, we do not find that they again, as a people, raised the arm against the Romans in battle."

There is an obelisk on some rising ground at Chingford, some five miles to the south-west of Ambresbury Banks, set up some years ago by the Ordnance Survey, and maintained at the instance of the Astronomer-Royal. That obelisk gave rise to a discussion in the pages of *Notes and Queries* in 1882, it having been asserted by one writer that it marked the site of Queen Boadicea's death. Be that as it may, another correspondent writes:—"There still remains the old belief that the great battle between the Romans under Suetonius and the Britons under Boadicea, the widow of Prasutagus, king of the Iceni, was fought a few miles from Chingford; and the story that a stone or obelisk was set up to mark the presumed spot where, after the slaughter of her army, the queen, who had sworn not to survive a defeat, took poison and died, is a popular belief. The description of the field of battle, as given by Tacitus, is very vague. It has, I think, been usually imagined that it was near the old British camp called Ambers' Banks, or Ambresbury Banks. . . . If any memorial stone exists, it might be looked for in that part of the county. In Chapman and André's fine map of Essex, published in 1777, there is an obelisk marked as then standing on Copped Hall Green, and a second obelisk situated about a mile more westward."

The two obelisks here referred to are still standing in the neighbourhood of Warlies Park, which lies about a mile to the north-west of the entrenchment. "If there is any history attached to these obelisks," writes another correspondent of *Notes and Queries*,* "it is not to be found in accessible sources. No inscription appears on either; they are of brick, one being stuccoed; and they cannot be older than the eighteenth century. But if any value is to be placed on tradition, it is not dealing unfairly with the tradition that clings to this part of the county of Essex to admit the possibility of the historic site being placed here. The point has not been thoroughly sifted. Morant says, speaking of Ambresbury Banks, 'hereabouts appears to have been fought,' &c., which is only tantamount to a recital of the ancient tradition. . . . It is by no means an improbability that the site was 'hereabouts.' Ambresbury Banks was not a temporary camp; there must have been a British village or settlement here. It stands on the highest ground, as British villages would do. Closely adjacent, a bye-road defiles down the hill through the forest, itself the site of an ancient trackway, into the river plain. The higher part of Copped Hall Green is broken up into irregular lumps of earth-work, which may be modern or may be of high antiquity. Obelisk No. 1 stands in a meadow just northward of this waste spot, and gives name to the adjoining farm. The narrow defile through the forest and the open plain below are fully characteristic of the battle-field familiar to us in the chronicles. Some such track was occupied by the forces of Suetonius, down which he issued, cleaving as with a wedge the host of the British; and it was across such a plain that the defeated thousands would disperse. Obelisk No. 2 stands in a meadow on the other side of Cobbin's Brook, and gives name to an adjoining wood. Here, it may well be believed, the unfortunate Boadicea retired, in order to crown with her own death the disasters of the day."

This locality possesses not only the earth-work known as Ambresbury Banks, but also another camp some two miles distant, at Loughton, so that there is really a choice of sites whereon to fix the scene of Boadicea's famous battle. It is a commonly received opinion that the Romans had their camp at Ambresbury Banks, while the British queen drew up her forces at Loughton. "These two camps," observes General Pitt-Rivers, in his report on the excavation of Ambresbury Banks, "owe their preservation to the fact of this region having been always forest, and not cultivated ground; and this is a point worth noting on the part of those who are inclined to lay stress on the value of tradition as evidence of time and place. It is certain that neither Cæsar nor Boadicea, nor any of the heroes and heroines of olden times, to whom these things are ascribed, had any special eye for locating themselves in places which might not in after years be destroyed by the plough; yet tradition concerning these people hangs naturally about such places as remain to us from ancient times rather than about those innumerable spots in our long and highly cultivated country in which ancient monuments have been destroyed by agriculture."

No doubt the existence of the Ambresbury Banks, as the camp is locally called, has tended to keep

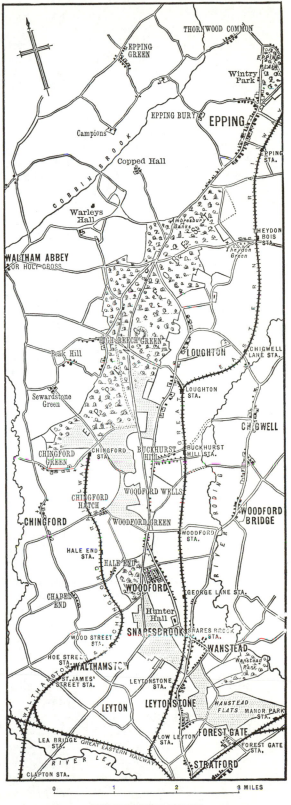

MAP OF EPPING FOREST.

up in these parts the memory, or rather the tra- dition, of Boadicea's defeat, which without such a *memoria technica* would probably have died out.

"If we are to find a clue to the date of Ambres- bury Bank in its name," writes Mr. Frederic John- son in Weldon's "Guide to Epping Forest," "we cannot make the work more modern than about A.D. 500. The word Ambresbury is commonly said to be much the same as Ambrose-bury, from a patriotic chieftain named Ambrosius Aurelius, who died soon after A.D. 500. This place, like one in Wiltshire, is called Ambresbury and Amesbury, and we must explain the name in each case alike. The story of Ambrosius is connected with the times and legends of King Arthur and the Knights of the Round Table, and it is even said that Ambrose, or Ambrosius, was the true name of the magician Merlin."

In the pages of Morant's "History of Essex" the camp is said to be the fortress of Boadicea, and other writers have followed in his wake. But with the present information it would seem hardly safe to state positively that Ambresbury Camp was actually the work of the Romans. At the same time, it is within the bounds of possibility that Boadicea made here her last stand against the Romans under Suetonius. General Pitt-Rivers, who carefully examined the "Banks" in 1881, wrote upon them a paper which was read at a meeting of the Essex Naturalists' Field Club, and also at the York meeting of the British Asso- ciation in that year. In it he shows that on the east side a ravine approaches the camp from the valley below, and divides into two forks as it nears the camp, and that the rampart at this place is drawn across the points of these forks, so as to sweep down them. On the south side also ad- vantage is taken of another ravine to strengthen the fortifications on that side. "These are points," adds General Pitt-Rivers, "which, although in- fluencing the principles of defence which have prevailed at all times, are more especially British, as distinct from Roman. The Romans, caring more for their internal discipline and the position of their cohorts than for external defence, arranged their camps on geometrically constructed lines, and often disregarded natural features altogether. It is true that at the northern corner of Ambresbury Camp the rampart turns at an abrupt angle, but this is owing to the fact that at that particular spot there are no natural features to guide camp- builders : the ground is a dead flat, and as the turn had to be made somewhere, it was made abruptly, as so often occurs in British camps."

The camp is an irregular square, and to some

slight extent follows the conformation of the ground which surrounds it. This fact would seem to justify a doubt as to its being of Roman origin ; and such a negative inference is corroborated by the fact that no Roman pottery or vessels or coins were discovered *in situ* when some explorations were made. There is in the camp a well which feeds a pond of water with a dam across it.

Probably the exposure of these banks to the action of the weather for so many centuries may have rubbed off the angles, and made the square less perfect than once it was. The diagrams appended to General Pitt-Rivers's paper in the "Transactions" of the Essex Field Club show how much the weather has altered the sectional aspect of the camp, lowering the summits, and filling up the trenches to such an extent that it has been uncertain till lately whether the bottom of it was flat or pointed.

The plan given in that paper, drawn by Mr. D'Oyley, the surveyor of the forest, shows six gates or entrances, whereas the Romans, as we know, were usually content with four. Here, how- ever, also, time and exposure may have altered the configuration of the site.

"In choosing their sites, the constructors of both camps seem to have been careful to secure a water supply. The interior of the enclosure is well wooded, and on the south the thicket is so dense as to hide the bank and be almost impene- trable. In modern times the timber has been much diminished, and the diggers for sand and other materials have done much mischief, in some places having destroyed portions of the bank itself. Happily, this is now stopped, and although the camp lies in two parishes, it will be safe from further depredations. It must be borne in mind that the search after antiquities in Epping Forest is a new thing. People have been content to look after butterflies and blackberries, and various other productions of Nature ; and they have not gone to look for the work of men's hands. However, a beginning has been made, and already most valu- able results have been achieved."[*]

Epping lies about a mile and a half north-east- ward from Ambresbury Banks, and is just beyond our limits ; as, however, the manor belonged in early times to Harold, and was given by the Con- queror to Waltham Abbey, we may be pardoned for making some little mention of it here. The town, called Epping Street, is situated on the road to Newmarket, on the ridge of hills that run north and south through the forest. In the old "coaching

---

[*] Weldon's "Guide to Epping Forest."

days" the place carried on a flourishing trade in sausages, poultry, and butter, which usually commanded high prices at the London market; and for its size, it also contained a very large number of inns and public-houses, many of which, since the Great Eastern Railway diverted the traffic from the high road, have been converted to other uses. At the time when the neighbourhood was the haunt of highwaymen, some of the forest taverns served as harbours for those "knights of the road," among whom might be reckoned the famous Dick Turpin. As far back as the close of the seventeenth century this locality appears to have been as bad as Hounslow Heath, in respect to its dangers from footpads and highwaymen. Macaulay tells us that on the Peace of 1698, a large number of the discharged soldiers turned footpads and marauders, and that "a fraternity of plunderers—thirty in number, according to the lowest estimate—squatted under the shades of Epping Forest, near Waltham Cross, from which they sallied forth with sword and pistol to bid passengers stand. . . It was necessary that during some time cavalry should patrol every evening on the roads near the boundary between Middlesex and Essex." It sounds almost incredible, but as lately as the year 1775 the guard of the Norwich stage-coach was killed in this forest, after he had himself shot dead three highwaymen out of seven that assailed him.*

The following scrap of information, taken from an old newspaper, shows that the roads hereabouts had their terrors down to even a later date :—"On Tuesday, January 22nd, 1793, a Mr. Alderman Plomer was taking an airing in his carriage in Epping Forest; he was stopped near the eight-mile stone by a single highwayman, who presented a pistol, and robbed him of a watch and about fourteen guineas."

The parish of Epping, which is between thirty and forty miles in circumference, is divided into three parts—the Town, the Upland, and Ryehill Hamlet. Its weekly market is still kept up on Fridays, when the main street of the town wears a somewhat busier appearance than usual. The Town Hall is used occasionally for concerts and lectures.

Near the western end of the street stands the Church of St. John the Baptist, a modern Gothic structure, built a few years ago, in the place of a chapel which the monks of Waltham had set up in days of old to serve as a chapel-of-ease to the mother church. At that time the whole, or nearly the whole, of this parish belonged to the Abbey of Waltham; and the houses of the town or village appear to have been clustered round the church, which lies some two miles away to the north-west, on Epping Upland, the present street being of comparatively modern date. The tall brick tower of the parish church, standing as it does on high ground, is a conspicuous landmark for the country round; the rest of the building is of little or no interest.

CHAPTER XLV.

EPPING FOREST

" 'Midst those trees the wild deer bounded
Ages long ere we were born,
And our great-grandfathers sounded
Many a jovial hunting-horn."—T. CAMPBELL.

Primeval Condition of the Forest, as the Great Forest of Essex—Gradual Diminution of the Forest—Forest Charters of King John and Henry III.—Laws for the Regulation of the Forest—A Quaint Oath—Lord Warden, Steward, and other Officers of the Forest—The Swainmote Court and Court of Justice Seat—Extent of the Forest in the Middle Ages—Present Form of the Forest—Disposal of the Crown Rights in the Forest—Encroachments by Lords of Manors—The Battle of the Commoners with the Lords of Manors—Parliamentary Scheme for the Preservation of the Forest—The Matter taken up by the Corporation of London—The Case Settled by Arbitration—Dedication of Epping Forest to the "Free Use" of the People—The Science of Forestry—The Deer of the Forest—The Present Condition and General Appearance of the Forest.

"THIS is the forest primeval," writes Longfellow of the Forest of Acadie; and he might have applied the epithet to that of Epping, much of which still happily remains in its "primeval" wildness. It was called of old "the forest of Essex," as being the only forest within the county. Afterwards it was known as "Waltham Forest," and it is only within the last two or three centuries that its present name of Epping Forest has prevailed. It covers most of the district lying between the Lea and the Roding. Roughly speaking, the forest is divided into two main portions, lying respectively west and east of the latter river. The west is more properly Waltham Forest, whilst the eastern portion is known as the Forest of Hainault.

Epping and Hainault Forests are comprehended

---

* *Annual Register*, 1775, pp. 97 and 182.

in the Chase of Waltham; and, according to Evelyn, the first onslaught was made upon them by King Henry VIII., when he suppressed the monasteries, converting the property to his own use, and disposing of the oak timber. Previous to that time but little oak was used in building, the commonest woods sufficing for ordinary habitations, until the general clearance brought about a greater demand for material of a better class.

In its primitive condition, the great "waste" covered the larger part of the county, stretching from the Forest of Middlesex at Waltham, in the west, to Colchester in the east, and hence it was properly called the "Great Forest of Essex." With reference to the forests of Essex and the forest laws, Mr. Coller, in his history of that county, writes:—" The forests were fearful sources of feuds and oppression; and Essex, being covered extensively by one of these royal nuisances, was frequently excited by the occurrences and conflicts to which it gave rise. The wild woodlands which at one period stretched over so large a portion of the county became vested in the Crown, and long after the Conquest these tracts of wilderness were found in the heart of Essex. Here the sovereigns and the gallants of the Courts hawked and hunted during their sojourn at Havering-atte-bower, or the Palace of Chigwell—which appears to have been erected solely for a royal hunting-lodge—or in their visits to the Palaces of New Hall and Writtle. . . In this forest the stag was chased, and the wild boar, an important part of the game of these woods, brought to bay—for the fox appears to have been looked upon with contempt by the Nimrods of those days. Here, in later times, the outlaw, like him of Sherwood, composed of about equal portions of the poacher, the bandit, and the hero, found ready shelter. And here, too, at a period bordering on our own days, the burglar and the highwayman shaped their caves and concealed their plunder. The forest regulations were terrifically severe, though often set at nought. The killing of a stag in these hunting-grounds of the king was regarded as more heinous than murder. The slaughter of a man could be expiated by a pecuniary fine; but one of the game laws of the Conqueror enacted that the killing of a deer, boar, or hare in these forests should be punished with the loss of the offender's eyes. This law was renewed by Richard I., with the addition of further disgusting mutilation. Civilisation, with its multiplying people, increasing the necessity for larger supplies of food, and thus raising the value of the land, has laid so steady a siege to the forest

of Essex that no idea can be formed of its extent from the remnants of it which are left, under the names of Hainault, Waltham, and Epping. It stretched at one period along the whole of the northern boundary, from nearly Bow to Cambridgeshire, filling up the whole of the vast space between Hertfordshire and the line of road from Brentwood and Romford in that direction—even extending beyond it—and running from Bishops Stortford to Colchester. This latter portion was stripped of its forestal character by King John. Stephen had previously disafforested Tendring Hundred, and given it over to the husbandman, who has long since converted it into a fertile and flourishing district. . . Gradually these open woodlands have disappeared. The popular feeling —in no age very strong in favour of game preserving—was aided in this case, when hunting formed so important a part of the pastimes of the nobility, by the barons and the landowners—the predecessors of those who are now the greatest sticklers for upholding the laws of the chase, and the sworn opponents and punishers of poachers of all descriptions. The rights of the Crown, as they were called, trenched seriously upon the privileges of the local lords, land which had long been granted out and grubbed up being still considered as forest. This led continually to the institution of vexatious suits, and the exaction of heavy fines from the king's tenants and the freemen. At length it produced open conflicts with the Crown; and the united barons, by an act of compulsion, wrung from King John the Charter of Forests—'a bar,' says the historian, 'to oppression, and a happy instrument of improving our agriculture.' 'Every article of this charter,' adds Rapin, 'is a clear evidence how the subject was oppressed under the pretence of preserving the royal forest.' The spirit of that charter was jealously guarded. In the conditions exacted from Henry III., an additional charter of forests was included, by which capital punishment for these offences was abolished, and they were made punishable by fine and imprisonment. Further, the proprietors of the land recovered the right of cutting and using their own wood with pleasure. The Commons gave Edward I. the bribe of a fifteenth of all the goods of the kingdom to have its provisions carried out. From this period the Forest of Essex rapidly disappeared, as shown by the perambulations made in the reigns of four succeeding monarchs."

In past ages this vast wilderness, given up to wild beasts and the pleasures of the chase, was governed by certain laws and customs which were unknown outside—a carefully constructed legal organisation, fragments of which have survived until modern times. The laws for the regulation of the forest, and of those who dwelt within its borders, in the olden time were both various and singular. Among them were the following, which we glean from the "People's History of Essex":— "A toll was exacted from a man if he required a passage through the forest, on account of the disquiet it gave to the wild beasts. It was a fine for any one to keep a mastiff there without having three claws of one of its fore-feet struck off; and every inhabitant of the forest, on reaching the mature age of twenty-one, was compelled to take an oath in the following quaint old lines, which certainly were not likely to awe the mind by their dignity, or exorcise evil thoughts by their sweetness; but they were supposed to have a restraining influence in the solitary sylvan ramble when a hare crossed the path, or a stag came within reach of the cross-bow :—

> " 'You shall true liege man be
> Unto the king's majesty ;
> Unto the birds of the forest you shall no hurt do,
> Nor to anything that doth belong thereunto ;
> The offences of others you shall not conceal,
> But to the utmost of your power you shall them reveal
> Unto the officers of the forest,
> Or to them who may see them redrest.
> All these things you shall see done,
> So help your God at his holy doom.' "

The office of Lord Warden of the forest was formerly a post of great importance and profit. It was for many years held by the late Earl of Mornington, through the marriage of his father, the Hon. Mr. Long-Pole-Wellesley, with Miss Tilney, the great heiress of Wanstead House. The warden had the same duty in the forest as the sheriff had in the county. The right belonged for centuries to the De Veres, Earls of Oxford, the lords of Hedingham Castle. They succeeded the Clares, who were stewards from the reign of Henry III. to that of Edward III. They had considerable rights within its boundaries, and were always keepers of the palace at Havering-atte-Bower. They ranked among the most powerful barons of England, and played a distinguished part in the history of the country from the Conquest to the beginning of the seventeenth century. The office of King's Forester was long held by the Archers of Copped Hall. The steward appointed a lieutenant, a riding forester, and three yeomen foresters ; and the perquisites of the warden and steward are thus stated :—"They had all the deer-browsing wood, all wayfs and strays within the limits of the forest ; likewise all the amerciaments in the swain-motes and wood comptes, agreeably

to the assize of the forest (the amerciaments for venison and the bodies of oaks only excepted). Upon the sale of every wood they were entitled to the second best oak contained therein ; and the buyer and seller thereof were obliged to present them with one bow and one broad arrow, paying at the same time each of them one penny out of every shilling. They likewise received from the sale of every covert or hedge-row, of every shilling one penny." There was also a chief forester, generally a member of some noble family, one of the Fitz-Archers of Copt Hall holding it in the reign of Edward I. ; but with the decay and diminution of the forest the office appears to have become extinct. There were also in bygone times four verderers, elected by the freeholders of the county at large. Anciently important duties attached to all these officers. There were three courts in which they exercised their power. The Verderers,' or Forty-day Court, as it was called, from being held every forty days, was the first that took cognisance of offences. The verderers, as judicial officers, appointed to observe and keep the assizes and laws of the forest, were sworn " to view, receive, and enrol the attachments and presentments of all manner of trespasses of vert (that is, anything growing in the forest that would afford cover for the deer) and venison, and to do equal justice as well to the poor as to the rich." They punished trifling offences, but sent other presentments to the Swainmote Court, where the matters were decided upon by a jury, and then returned to the Court of Justice Seat—the highest forest court. This was held by the Lord Chief Justice in Eyre, under the king's commission, and, though limited to forest offences, it seems to have been similar to a Court of Assize. Formerly these courts were held at Chelmsford ; but as the forest was driven by the agricultural pioneer to the south-western borders, they were removed to Chigwell.

For the following particulars we are indebted to Weldon's " Guide to Epping Forest."

"Richard Montfitchet, who was reinstated as Forester in 1217, appears to have had his time fully occupied with the duties of his office, the power and privileges connected with which must have been eminently congenial to the sporting tastes of an Anglo-Norman. What these powers were is shown in the close rolls, as well as the care and jealousy with which the ancient forest laws were maintained. It was the duty of the Forester to preserve the boundaries of the forest intact, and to permit no encroachments within them. Should a neighbouring landowner desire to free his woods from the view of the Foresters and Regarders, to cultivate a portion of them, or to enclose a park, and kill the game on his own manors, he had to obtain the royal permission, and an official writ was addressed to the Forester on the subject. Such a writ, on behalf of the Abbey of St. Edmund's-Bury, was despatched from Oxford to Sir Richard de Montfitchet on the 20th of July, 1216. By it he was informed that a charter had been given to the abbot and monks there serving God, granting that their woods at Harlow, Stapleford, and Werketon should be for ever free from regard, waste, and view of the Foresters and Regarders, and that the abbot and monks should have the use of the same woods at their own will, except always driving forth the game. And on the same day, under another writ to de Montfitchet, free warren was granted for ever to the Bishop of London and his successors in his manor of Clackington, and that of Walton-cum-Thorpe, which is the manor of the Chapter of St. Paul's, London. Also that the said bishop and his successors for ever had full liberty to take stags and hinds, and all sorts of wild animals within the limits of the said manors. The Forester was also commanded to make two deer leaps in his great park at Ongar, as he had right and custom to have. And also about the same time Montfitchet received the following mandate :—' We command you to allow the Abbess of Barking her reasonable estovers* in her wood at Hainault for her firing, her cooking, and her brewing, if she has been accustomed so to do, in the time of our Lord King John our father ; also to permit the same abbess to have her dogs to chase hares and foxes within the bailiwick if she was accustomed to have them in the time of our aforesaid father.' The king made numerous gifts of timber and firewood out of the forest, for which writs were issued to the Forester of Essex. For instance, he was ordered to give Rose de Sculiz, a nun of Barking, an oak out of the forest of Essex, to repair her chamber in the said abbey, taken where it would least injure the said forest."

By a charter of King John, dated March 25, in the fifth year of his reign, and confirmed by Edward IV., all that part of the forest which lay to the north of the road from Stortford through Dunmow to Colchester, was ordered to be disafforested. Its extent was further diminished by a perambulation made in 29 Edward I., in pursuance of the Charta de Foresta ; but its boundaries were finally determined by an inquisition and perambulation taken in September, 1640, by a commission under the great seal of England, in pursuance of an Act of Parliament for settling the bounds of the forests in general. The boundaries as thus fixed include the whole of Wanstead, Leyton, Walthamstow, Woodford, Loughton, Chigwell, Lamborne, Stapleford Abbots, Waltham Holy Cross, Epping, and Nazing, and parts of Chingford, Stratford, East and West Ham, Little and Great Ilford, Barking, Dagenham, Theydon Bois, and Navestock. The extent of the forest was estimated at 60,000 acres, of which 48,000 were enclosed and private property, the remaining 12,000 being unenclosed wastes and woods. What is called Henhault, or Hainault, Forest is a part of this district.

From the earliest times then, as we have seen, this extensive tract of woodland had been a royal forest—one of those districts quaintly described by Manwood as " a certain territory of woody grounds and fruitful pastures, privileged for wild beasts and fowls of forest chase and warren, to rest and abide there in the safe protection of the king, for his delight and pleasure." " Queen Elizabeth, in one of her visits to the lodge bearing her name, is reported to have granted to the poor of several adjoining parishes the privilege of lopping wood. The custom still exists—or did until lately—for the possessors of that privilege to assemble on the eleventh of November in each year, in order to strike an axe into the boughs of the trees at the hour of midnight. This right is also exercised upon parts of the forest which have been for many years enclosed, and extends in full operation till the twenty-third of April in the following year." *

The ancient bounds of the forest have been a matter of controversy from time to time, but from the days of the Long Parliament down to the year 1851, as stated above, it consisted of two parts—the Forest of Hainault and Epping Forest, the former comprising the high ground lying to the east of the Roding, and north of the high road to Romford, and the latter lying between the Roding and the Lea, and stretching northward from Stratford to Epping. Hainault Forest, in which the Crown had a more clearly-defined interest than in Epping, possessing not only rights of forest, but the soil of several large woods acquired at the dissolution of monasteries, was disafforested by Act of Parliament in 1851, and was subsequently enclosed.

The enormous tract of land which was settled under the statute of Charles I., in 1640, as the limits of Waltham Forest, doubtless included very extensive private estates, subject to rights of forest and chase ; the greater part of the residue had been granted or sold by Henry VIII. and succeeding

VIEWS IN EPPING FOREST.

1. Connaught Water, Chingford. 2. A Glade at Theydon Bois. 3. On the way to Copped Hall from Loughton. 4. High Beech.

sovereigns. In its present form the principal portion of Epping Forest commences at Chingford Station, and proceeds northward beyond Theydon Bois to the outskirts of Epping itself. But southward from Chingford Station there is a somewhat broken stretch of forest and waste, reaching down to Wanstead Flats and the City of London Cemetery at Aldersbrook. To that cemetery London is largely indebted for the preservation of Epping Forest as a place of recreation for the people. Extra-mural interment has thus contributed to extra-mural enjoyment; for, if this parcel of land had not been acquired by the Corporation for a burying-place, they could scarcely have maintained the right which served to break down the usurpations of the encroaching "land-grabbers." But on this subject we shall have more to say hereafter.

In Epping Forest an enclosure had never been recommended in the interests of the Crown; but a most complicated system of ownership prevailed. The soil of the open waste belonged to the lords of about seventeen different manors, each owning the part situate within his own bounds. Certain rights of pasturage existed over the whole tract, and certain rights of woodcutting in particular parts; and over all the Crown had the right to preserve deer and to keep the forest *in statu quo* for the sake of the deer, the ancient rights of "vert" and "venison." To these ancient rights the public had, from the time when the forest became of any use for recreation, looked to preserve their playground intact, but their hopes had been somewhat cruelly disappointed. An economic air prevailing at the Treasury and the Office of Woods, it was resolved, soon after the disafforestation of Hainault, to sell the Crown rights in Epping to the lord of the manor, and a pitiful sum of about £18,000 was thus realised for the national exchequer. The consequence of this action was not only to remove the safeguard of the Crown's rights, but to give a false impression that the effect of their acquisition by a lord was to enable him to enclose against all comers.

In 1851, when Hainault Forest was disafforested, the area of the open forest was little short of 6,000 acres, but this in 1871 had dwindled to just under 3,000. In 1882, when Epping Forest was handed over by Her Majesty for "the free use and enjoyment of the people for ever," it extended to about 5,600 acres, nearly the whole of which had been purchased by the Corporation of London, while some 400 acres remained enclosed, partly under such conditions as prevented building, thus tending to enhance the value of the forest as an "open space."

Between the years 1851 and 1863, when the "Open Spaces Committee" was appointed, rapid strides had been made by the encroaching fences in Epping Forest, particularly in the manor of Loughton, where an enclosure of enormous extent had startled the public into a watchful attention from which it never subsequently relapsed. That enclosure comprised in the whole about 1,300 acres—land covered with wood, and situate in the heart of the wildest and most beautiful tract of the forest. It was not carried out without some regard to supposed rights. Having bought the interest of the Crown, the lord of the manor assumed that he had only the commoners in his own manor to deal with. These he compensated by the distribution among them of between 300 and 400 acres of the forest, and, having thus obtained their consent, he put a fence on his own account round the remaining 900 or 1,000 acres. The lord of the manor, however, seems to have forgotten to take into consideration that keen instinct of resistance to enclosure which is seldom wanting among the poor agricultural classes, when their real or presumed "rights" are being entrenched upon. The inhabitants of Loughton, high and low, had been accustomed to get their winter supply of fuel by lopping the trees in the forest. To the poor this practice had been a double benefit, not only furnishing their own hearths, but giving them constant employment during the winter months in lopping for their richer neighbours. They asserted that the right had come down to them from the time of Elizabeth, and was the right of the inhabitants at large, and not to be got rid of by allotments of land to a favoured few.

In the preceding chapter we have spoken of the highwaymen who infested these parts in former times; here we have had to deal with modern thieves and plunderers, in the shape of "land grabbers." Well and wittily wrote Samuel Butler in "Hudibras":—

> "The fault is great in man or woman
> Who steals a goose from off a common:
> But who shall plead that man's excuse,
> Who steals the common from the goose?"

It was all very well for the queen to bestow a baronetcy on the Lord Mayor of London, Alderman Ellis, and the honour of knighthood on the two sheriffs, Mr. Reginald Hanson and Mr. William Anderson Ogg; but the real men who fought and won the battle on behalf of the toiling masses were Mr. John T. Bedford, a common councilman, Mr. George Burney, an old member of the Commons Preservation Society, Mr. Frederick Young, the Chairman, and Mr. W. G. S. Smith, the

Honorary Secretary of the " Forest Fund." To these names must be added that of an old forester named Thomas Willingale, whose rude forefathers for generations had lived by the irregular products of that forest. This last-named individual was the " Village Hampden " who organised the bands who pulled down the enclosures—an overt act, which served as a declaration of war. Burney, who was also a commoner in the forest, took down from London three omnibus-loads of navvies, and in the course of a morning's work levelled the fences round the obnoxious enclosures which the commissioners wished to legalise.

It was really, if the full truth must be stated, a sort of triangular duel between the Crown, the lords of the manor, and the people. The Crown sold its rights for mere nominal sums, and then the landowners and the landless multitude were the only combatants, and the former thought that they would be able to drive the latter to surrender their rights on their own terms. But they found, when too late, that they had " reckoned without their host." The lords of several of the manors sold their " waste," as the open lands were called by them, and allowed it in every direction to be enclosed and built upon.

In the end, after long litigation, and after several lawless encounters, the question was brought formally under the notice of the House of Commons, and an Act passed appointing a commission to inquire into the contending rights, and to report to Parliament a scheme for the preservation and management of the forest in the interests of the public.

A few days before this Act received the royal assent, another champion took up the gage on the part of the public. The Corporation of London had an ancient traditionary connection with the forest. It was reputed that certain rights of hunting there had been granted to them by royal charter, and though the existence of the grant could never be established, there were not wanting curious entries in the Corporation records bearing upon the claim. Fortunately, however, a connection of a very different character had recently arisen, which, though it could not furnish the motive for interference, supplied a most powerful weapon of attack. The Commissioners of Sewers had purchased for the purposes of a cemetery the demesne lands of the ancient manor of Aldersbrook. In the time of Charles I. the lord of this manor claimed for himself and his tenants rights of common of pasture for their beasts throughout the length and breadth of the forest waste. Upon this claim (one of many of a similar character) the Corporation, when they had resolved to help the public, founded a Chancery suit, which, commenced on the 14th of August, 1871, was terminated by the memorable judgment of Sir George Jessel, in November, 1874. All the lords of manors were defendants to this suit, and no expense was spared on either side to gain the victory. In the result the case of the Corporation was established at all points, the right they claimed was declared to exist, and all enclosures made within twenty years before the filing of the Bill—that is, since the 14th of August, 1851 —were pronounced illegal.

So far, a decisive victory was gained; but still much remained to be done in order to secure its fruits, and to this end the vast resources of the Corporation were devoted. The lords of the manors who had enclosed had sold large tracts of the forest, amounting in all to about 1,000 acres. It was impossible to make all the purchasers parties to the suit, and recourse was of necessity had to the Epping Forest Commission to enforce the judgment against these persons, subject to such modifications as might be found just and expedient. Portions of the land sold had been built over, and it was obviously impossible to pull down streets of villas ; but larger portions remained in their natural condition or had been merely broken up for agriculture, and these portions the Corporation and the Commons Preservation Society thought should be restored to the public. Unfortunately, the commissioners took a different view, and thus prolonged the struggle for some years.

On the 23rd February, 1877, the final report of the Epping Forest Commissioners was presented to Parliament. Their recommendations, as summed up briefly by the author of Weldon's " Guide " already quoted, were : " The forest to be disafforested, the Crown rights to cease, the forest to be managed by the Corporation of London as conservators, who are from time to time to appoint a committee, not exceeding twelve in number, to act for the conservators ; and Colonel Palmer, Sir Thomas White, and Sir Antonio Brady, the surviving verderers, and one other verderer to be elected, to be members of that committee. In future, two of the verderers to be elected by the parliamentary voters of the northern part of the forest, and two by those of the southern. Rights of common, pasture, lopping, pannage, and so forth, to continue, subject to the scheme. The conservators to keep the forest unenclosed as an open space for the recreation and enjoyment of the public at all times ; they shall preserve its natural aspect, protect the timber and other growths, and prevent the digging of gravel or other strata. The conservators to purchase the right of any lord of the manor or other person who owned the soil of any land within the forest at a specified rate; but where such land had been built on before 21st August, 1871, the occupiers were to pay a rent-charge; enclosures on which there was no building to be thrown open within twelve months after the scheme coming into operation. Enclosures made since 1851, the soil of which did not belong to the lord of the manor, should be permitted to be retained by the owners of the soil, and remain enclosed, upon payment of a perpetual annual rent-charge. An exception to those rules was made in the case of churches, chapels, and charitable institutions, as long as they are used for such purposes. The conservators were to cause certain unlawfully enclosed lands to be thrown open; might make bye-laws for the regulation of persons using the forest, both for recreation and under common rights, and generally for preventing its improper use or disfigurement. The Corporation to have power to apply the duty raised by the metage on grain to afford the necessary funds. They were to appoint from time to time, as reeves and assistant reeves, persons who were recommended by the vestries of such parishes, the reeves to be the officers of the conservators, who could reject unqualified persons."

In the end further difficulties arose, and fresh litigation ensued; but towards the close of the Session of 1878 an Act was passed appointing Sir Arthur Hobhouse sole arbitrator, to determine all the nice questions arising between the purchases from the lords and the public, subject to an instruction that nothing was to remain enclosed save what was necessary to render the villas and manors habitable and marketable by their owners. This task—no light one—Sir Arthur Hobhouse completed in July, 1882, to the satisfaction of all concerned. The result was the rescue of some 500 or 600 additional acres, and that without, it is confidently believed, the infliction of any real hardship upon a single individual.

The Act effectually preserves the forest as an open space for the use and enjoyment of the public. It provides for a Ranger of the Forest, appointed by the Crown, and constitutes the Corporation of London conservators, stipulating that in this capacity the Corporation are to keep the forest unenclosed, and to preserve, as far as possible, its natural aspect; especially to protect and preserve the ancient earthworks called Ambresbury Banks, the Purlieu Bank, and other forest marks and boundaries. The conservators are further to protect the timber and other trees, pollard, shrubs, underwood, gorse, turf, and herbage, and to prevent the lopping, cutting, and injuring the same, and the digging of the soil. The ancient house known as Queen Elizabeth's Lodge is vested, by assent of the Queen, in the conservators, for preservation and maintenance as an object of antiquarian interest. The lands held by grantees are to be thrown open, the arbitrator to decide what sum shall be paid in respect of them, and also as to the mode and conditions of quieting in title, of lands not thrown open, with buildings erected thereon. There are to be four verderers elected by the commoners. The verderers are to be members of the Epping Forest Committee, a body consisting of twelve members of the Common Council, in addition to the verderers. Power is given to this body to make bye-laws for various purposes: amongst other things for excluding gipsies, hawkers, beggars, rogues and vagabonds, and for preventing bird-catching, and regulating the killing, taking, injuring, shooting, chasing, or disturbing of deer, game, or other animals, or fishing in the waters.

Two months previously—namely, on the 6th of May—when the queen formally opened this delightful pleasure-ground in its present form, and pronounced it "free to the public for ever," the difficulties which had attended the achievement of the above object became very generally known. His Royal Highness the Duke of Connaught was appointed ranger, and at the above-mentioned date the queen paid a visit to the forest for the purpose of declaring it freely open to the public, her Majesty at the same time planting an oak in commemoration of the event, and signifying her wish that the wood at High Beech, in the neighbourhood of Chingford, hitherto known as Beech Wood, should henceforth be known as "Queen Victoria's Wood."

An article in *The Times*, in July, 1882, on the occasion of the termination of the inquiry into the complicated interests connected with Epping Forest, contained the following interesting remarks:—"The whole science of forestry, with its deep mysteries as to vert and venison, is clean dead and gone. So little remains of the knowledge of the real history of these forests that, by a strange mistake, they are sometimes supposed to have been as beautiful and admirable features of feudal as of modern England. It is the fate of Epping as a forest to pass from the domain of the Crown to that of the people; to the ragged-schools and Bands of Hope who picnic under its trees has fallen one of the most important of the *jura regalia*. Only a king might make a forest. No subject, as such, however potent he might be, might have a forest, inasmuch as sovereign prerogatives were incident to it. A subject might own a chase, which possessed no particular laws and where the common law was in force, where there were no verderers, regarders, or agisters, no Court of Attachments, no Swainmote, no Justice Seat. If the king granted a forest to a subject, it fell to the rank of a chase. Precise and important distinctions were drawn between the two. The beasts of the forest were the hart, the hind, the hare, the boar, and the wolf—that is, 'beasts that do haunt the woods more than the plains.' The beasts of the chase were five also—the buck, the doe, the fox, the marten, and the roe. Each forest included also a warren, and the beasts and fowls of warren were the hare, the cony, the pheasant, and the partridge. Venery was then a science with a precise nomenclature, and hunters were as much pedants as feudal lawyers. The hart in its second year must be called a broker, and a boar of the fourth year a sanglier. Good woodmen spoke of a bevy of roes and a rout of wolves, and they referred to the footmarks of the hart as the slot, and to traces of the fallow deer as its 'view.' One cannot study the old forest laws without seeing that our forefathers loved the forests as much as their sons do. Every twig and every cony were sacred in their eyes. It was the duty of the good woodman to preserve with care venison and vert—that is, the beasts of the chase, and the trees and cover which sheltered them. No man might without licence cut down the trees within the forest, even if they grew in his own freehold. Still more heinous was the offence of ploughing up the thickets and covers, or erecting houses, or making inclosures. In every forest a fence month was strictly observed, and for fifteen days before Midsummer, and for as many after, no one was permitted to wander about or drive his flocks in the forest, so that it might be, in the words of one old writer, 'a sanctuary of peace for the wild beasts.' Hawking and hunting within the forest domains, being pastimes for kings and princes, could not, of course, be enjoyed by common people; and to slay a deer, so long as the forest laws were in force, was a crime blacker than murder or arson. The most striking peculiarity of these wastes was the fact that the common law did not extend to them. There, in theory at least, only the judgments and determinations of the king were binding. The word of his vicar, the Lord Chief Justice of the Forest, was supreme. In the Court of Attachments or Woodmote, which sat every forty days, in the Swainmote, which sat thrice a year, and in the Justice Seat, which was held at intervals of three years, were administered laws wholly repugnant in spirit to those which were put in operation at Westminster. All the ordinary rights of property, all the common ideas of law, were set at nought; and history is full of complaints and murmurs respecting the hardships caused by the servile system administered in these 'oases of despotism.'

"Almost all traces of this state of things have long passed away from Epping. The rights of the Crown were in some cases sold, and even before they were extinguished the sharp distinctions of the forest laws had fallen into disuse. The commoners turned their cattle into the forest to feed, subject to the supervision of the reeves and forest courts. From time to time a lord of the manor enclosed a tempting piece of land to round off his property, or a cottager stole a morsel to make a garden. For a long time the forest was almost ungoverned, or was subject only to imperfect usages, indifferently observed and little understood. Thanks to the labours of the Corporation, this is altered. Rights are defined, and a code of management as precise as the old forest laws themselves has been established. One thing we may learn from those old laws the memory of which is disappearing: they were framed by men who prized the greenwood, who regarded every tree as precious, who would not have a bird or a hare disturbed, who viewed with suspicion improvements which affected the forest domains. It was this jealous spirit which preserved them in the past, and its continuance will be the best preservation in the future. Another thing, also, may be gathered from the same sources. The avowed justification of these exceptional domains in the past was that the king's labour 'doth maintain and defend every man's rest and peace;' that 'his diligence doth preserve and defend every man's private pleasure and delight;' and that it was for the advantage of the realm that he should have his fit place of recreation and pastime. All that is the sentiment of a past age, and modern sovereigns need no such means of entertainment. But we shall be keeping up this spirit of zeal for the welfare of the realm by permitting the common people to take their pleasure where sovereigns once found theirs."

Lysons, in his "Magna Britannia," describes the forest as "of large extent, full of game, and well stocked with deer, the fattest and largest in the kingdom." Notwithstanding that the Crown had long ago parted with the ownership of the soil, it still retained the right of "vert" and "venison," that is, the right to keep an unlimited number of deer, with their "herbage, vert, and browse," which is held to include a right over "all the beasts of the forest, the trees, and underwood, and whatever grows within it ; and the power of granting licenses to hunt and shoot within its boundaries."

The result of the purchase of the several manorial rights, and of the supervision of the forest by the Lord Mayor and Corporation, is to be seen in the gradual growth of the trees, and in the number of

bourhood about the "knights of the highway" and other less romantic transgressors.

The forest, it appears, was stocked with both red and fallow deer down to the end of the last century, for in the report of the Commission of 1793, Sir James Tylney Long, at that time warden, although he was "not able to ascertain what number of bucks and does are kept, or abide in the forest in general," stated that "about five brace of bucks and three brace of does have

ROYAL FOREST HOTEL, CHINGFORD.

the deer which browse in its remoter glades. These are supposed to have increased from about eighty to one hundred. They are thought by many naturalists to be of a different breed from those in any park in the kingdom, and to represent with perfect identity the wild denizens of the forest in Anglo-Saxon times. They are but slightly spotted or marked, and when first born they are not spotted at all. Although they are shy and wild, and seldom come near the haunts of men, they fight terribly among themselves, especially at the rutting season, in autumn. The deer, as might naturally be supposed, were terribly thinned by the highwaymen and poachers of the last century, and many strange stories are still told in the neigh-

been, one year with another, killed in the forest, by warrants of authority from his Majesty ; and about fourteen brace of bucks and seven brace of does for individuals who claim a right to have venison in the forest. My claim to red and fallow deer in the said forest is without stint." By 1863 the deer appear to have fallen off in number very considerably. Mr. Howard, in that year, told the committee of the House of Commons that "there are no longer any deer in Epping Forest ; practically they do not exist ;" he added, however, "there may be a dozen, perhaps." But this was probably untrue ; they never were really reduced so low.

Of the Epping Hunt, which was for so many

years associated with the forest, we shall speak more fully in dealing with Buckhurst Hill; and of Queen Elizabeth's fondness of frequenting its sylvan glades for the purposes of the chase, on reaching Chingford.

Fisher, in his "Companion to the History of England," states that "Henry VIII. went out with his hounds, and breakfasted under a great tree in Epping Forest the very day that his once-lov'd wife (Anne Boleyn) was to perish in the Tower."

still a text-book for botanists. Indeed, nearly every part of the forest is profuse in mosses, wild flowers, grasses, and fresh-water algæ.

In the less frequented parts, and especially in the damp and boggy places, many interesting, and, indeed, uncommon plants occur. Let us hope that the wholesale drainage will not be continued so as to utterly destroy the plants peculiar to naturally damp situations. One of the smallest and most lovely of these Epping Forest plants is the blue Ivy-leaved Bell-flower (*Campanula hederacea*) seen at the bottom of our illustration; another, the rose-coloured Bog Pimpernel (*Anagallis tenella*) seen on the right, and below it the Round-leaved Sun-dew (*Drosera rotundifolia*), an insectivorous plant studied and described by Charles Darwin. Another bog

FLOWERS FROM EPPING FOREST.

But the site of this tree is not known, and the story may not be true.

Of the geology of this district there is little at present to be said; and for the best of all reasons: because the Essex Field Club has only just taken the subject seriously in hand. It may be said, however, generally, that the surface of the district is mainly composed of London clay, which overlies the primitive stratum of chalk, and which here and there is capped with patches of gravel and Bagshot sand.

Epping Forest is intersected by railways, with stations at short intervals, so as to furnish points of approach in all directions. It has all the charms of hill and dale, open plain and pleasant avenue, with deep umbrageous recesses here and there, comprising altogether every variety of forest scenery, fringed with far-spreading landscapes, reaching into half-a-dozen counties. As a rule, the oaks and other trees are of somewhat stunted growth, but there are, of course, exceptions. Of the famous Fairlop Oak we shall speak in dealing with Hainault Forest. The neighbourhood of Woodford is particularly rich in its flora, and the "Plantæ Woodfordiensis" of Richard Warner is

plant is illustrated on the top right of our illustration in the lovely drooping Marsh Thistle (*Carduus palustris*). A decidedly uncommon orchid is common not far from High Beech, viz.: the Smaller Butterfly Orchis (*Habenaria bifolia*), illustrated at the top left; many other orchids may be found, notably the Helleborine and Marsh Helleborine *Epipactis latifolia* and *E. palustris*). The Grass of Parnassus (*Parnassia palustris*), also grows in wet places, a most beautiful, interesting, and curious plant. The Butcher's Broom (*Ruscus aculeatus*) may also be found in many damp spots, together with its near ally the Lily of the Valley (*Convallaria majalis*). The Wood Sorrel (*Oxalis acetosella*)— probably the true Shamrock—is very frequent; so are many diverse species of St. John's Wort

(*Hypericum*), together with both the British species of Golden Saxifrage (*Chrysosplenium*). This brief list does not give one-hundredth part of the many beautiful plants of the forest either prized for their beauty, rarity, or, may-be, their botanical interest.

Amongst the ferns of the forest one of the most interesting is the Adder's-tongue (*Ophioglossum vulgatum*), illustrated at the top right, the Hart's-tongue (*Scolopendrium vulgare*), the Scaly Spleenwort (*Ceterach officinarum*), the Toothed Bladder Fern (*Cystopteris dentata*), the Prickly Shield Fern (*Polystichum aculeatum*), the Male Fern (*Lastrea filix-mas*), Common Polypody (*Polypodium vulgare*), very frequent about old stumps, and illustrated at the foot of our engraving, Wall Rue (*Asplenium ruta-muraria*), upon crumbly old walls, and the Common Brake (*Pteris aquilina*) grows profusely all over the forest.

Many edible species of fungi may be found in the forest, and most of these have been painted by Mr. Worthington G. Smith, the originals being at all times accessible to the public in the New Natural History Museum at South Kensington. The true Mushroom (*Agaricus campestris*) grows in open grassy places, together with the Fairy Ring Champignon (*Marasmus oreades*). The Parasol Mushroom (*Agaricus procerus*) is frequent in partially open places, the Red-fleshed Mushroom (*Agaricus rubescens*) is very common in the woody parts, together with the delicious Edible Boletus (*Boletus edulis*) and the Edible Chantarelle (*Cantharellus cibarius*). The Vegetable Beef-steak—so named by Dr. Bull—is very frequent on the old oaks, and sometimes on old beeches and other trees. The Giant Puff-ball (*Lycoperdon giganteum*) is common in the open grassy places; various truffles have also been found, and many poisonous species, and species of great botanical interest. Many other edible species occur besides the above mentioned, and numerous highly-poisonous plants, as the Scarlet Fly Mushroom (*Agaricus muscarius*) under the birches. Before venturing to eat edible fungi, all beginners should carefully examine Mr. Smith's paintings at the British Museum.

The forest has, however, its insect plagues. A correspondent of the *Times* has remarked that the greatest delinquent among the insects that spoil the foliage of our oak-trees is the larvæ of *Tortrix viridana*, which may be found in abundance during May, rolled in a leaf or between two adjacent leaves connected by a slight silken web. The moth itself appears at the end of June, and is frequently a perfect pest on account of its numbers. " In walking through Epping Forest," he adds, " I noticed that every tap on an oak branch caused a cloud of these insects to fly out. The moth when expanded is something under one inch across the wings, the upper pair of which are of a pure green colour."

Epping Forest is a rare hunting-ground, not only for the botanist and the entomologist, but also for the ornithologist; song-birds of almost all the known species are, at one time or another during each succeeding year, to be met with here. In Mr. Jefferies' book, " Nature near London," many interesting details respecting the feathered visitants of our suburban forests may be found.

The inns and hostelries of the neighbourhood are all reminders of the rural character of the place. Besides the " Royal Forest Hotel," we have the " Foresters," the " Roebuck," the "Warren House," the " Bald-faced Stag," the " Horse and Well," the " Robin Hood," the " King's Oak," and the " Owl." Most of these are still frequented during the summer months by ruralising parties from London, who make the shady bowers and sylvan retreats of the forest in their vicinity resound with their noisy mirth.

The hearthstones of many of the forest cottages were, and some are still, removable; and as they served in Romney Marsh, and in many sea-coast towns, as places for storing kegs of illicit brandy, so about Epping and Loughton and Chingford they supplied the parents and grandparents of many of the present race of cottagers with storehouses for haunches of venison which were not altogether honestly obtained.

The story of the preservation of the forest has been told in pamphlet form by Mr. J. T. Bedford, who, from his position of Chairman of the Epping Forest Committee, was in a position to observe and to recount the various steps which led to the final event—its dedication to the use and enjoyment of the people " for ever." From this pamphlet it appears that the forest now consists of about 6,000 acres, rather more than 5,500 of which have been purchased by the Corporation, and in acquiring which about 1,200 claims had to be considered. The costs incurred in the prolonged struggle to secure this vast tract of land from further encroachment were, no doubt, heavy : the aggregate of the purchase money, compensation for rights of lopping, the price of Wanstead Park, and legal expenses, amounting to some £256,275. But in exchange for this outlay a domain of rare beauty has been secured to ever-growing London, and generations yet unborn are likely to be grateful for the boon that has been conferred upon them; so that the almost romantic story of its rescue ought not readily to be forgotten by those who enjoy its cool shades and sylvan recesses.

CHAPTER XLVI.

EPPING FOREST (*continued*)—SEWARDSTONE, HIGH BEECH, AND CHINGFORD.

> " A mound of even-sloping side,
> Whereon a hundred stately beeches grew,
> And here and there great hollies under them.
> But for a mile all round was open space,
> And fern and heath."—TENNYSON.

Preliminary Remarks—Situation and Boundaries of Sewardstone—Seats and Mansions—High Beech Green—St. Paul's Church—Fairmead Lodge—Sotheby and Tennyson—Residents at High Beech—Fairmead House—John Clare—High Beech Hill—The " Robin Hood " and " King's Oak "—" Harold's Oak "—Queen Victoria's Wood—Lappitt's Hill—Bury Wood and Hawk Wood—Situation and Etymology of Chingford—Its Extent and Boundaries—The Manor of Chingford St. Paul—The Manor of Chingford Earls—Friday Hill—Buckrills—A Singular Tenure—Census Returns—Chingford Old Church—The Ordnance Survey Obelisk—Queen Elizabeth's Lodge—The Royal Forest Hotel—Connaught Water.

THE topography of the various districts which form integral parts of Epping Forest, and their associations with past history, may perhaps furnish the reader with a few entertaining chapters. Though they lead us far away from literary associations, yet they open up fresh fields for our pilgrim feet. Little importance can, however, be attached to the present celebrity of the once great Forest of Essex, for even the last of historic events connected with it—the Epping Hunt—has become a thing of the past, having lingered among the relics of the ancient sports of London citizens down to a very recent date. The picturesque scenery and historical associations of the forest have, however, more lasting charms, and may tempt the reader hither—not merely in the hurly-burly of the Easter holiday, but on any quiet day when he may enjoy undisturbed the rich beauties of its glades and woody knolls.

The towns, villages, and seats which now stud the district we are about to traverse, and the roads which intersect the sylvan waste, may have been the labours of a few centuries ; inns and lodges would be among the earliest adjuncts to a vast district, peopled, as it were, by hundreds of retainers, whose business it was to defend this " royal chase ; " for the privileges of hunting here were confined to the sovereign and his favourites. Again, the thousands who flocked thither with such privilege would well repay the hospitalities of an inn and " hosteller," even were we to leave out of the reckoning the boon companionship of foresters and the debauched habits of marauders who fattened upon the infringement of the royal privilege, as in wholesale deer-stealing for the London markets. Houses of call of this description, to suit the requirements of the wayfarer, from the humble roadside tavern or ale-house to the spacious " hotel," are to be met with in almost every part of the forest.

With these few remarks we will resume our perambulation. Sewardstone, our first halting-place southwards from Waltham Abbey, is a hamlet belonging to that parish. It lies between two and three miles distant, on the lower road leading to Chingford. The district is situate just on the borders of the forest, on its western side, and it stretches away from High Beech and Sewardstone Wood in the east to Sewardstone Mill on the River Lea in the west, and from Waltham Abbey in the north to Low Street, Chingford, in the south. It includes within its boundary Sewardstone Street, Sewardstone Green, Sewardstone Bury, Sewardstone Wood, and Sewardstone Mills, at which last-named place are some extensive dye-works ; with this exception, the locality is almost wholly agricultural. The land is pleasantly broken up into miniature hills and valleys, and in parts is well wooded. Among the better class of residences here may be mentioned Gilwell Park, near the Green ; Sewardstone Lodge, the grounds of which slope down to the Lea ; the Grange, on the north side of the village ; and Yardley House, nearer to Chingford. Mr. Thorne, in his " Environs of London," says :—" Sewardstone has a tradition that it was once a distinct parish, named after one Seward, a great Saxon thane, and used to show a heap of broken ground as the site of the old church."

From Sewardstone, we pass by a narrow winding lane eastward, for about half a mile, to High Beech Green, another hamlet and ecclesiastical district of Waltham Abbey. The cottages and other houses are somewhat scattered and straggling, and close by is a small brick-built church, St. Paul's, which was erected in 1836. Further eastward, by the side of the Epping road, stands another church, which was built in 1872, to serve as a chapel-of-ease to Loughton parish. It is a handsome structure, in the Early English style, erected from the designs of Mr. A. W. Blomfield. The building is cruciform in plan, with a semi-circular apsidal chancel and a tower and tall spire ; the latter is a conspicuous landmark for miles round, and is a pleasing object in the forest scenery at several points. This church, as we learn from

Weldon's "Guide to Epping Forest," was built at the expense of a neighbouring resident, "whose munificence was such that he erected it on ground in which he had not the sole interest."

High Beech Park, Wallsgrove House, and Alder Grove Lodge, are among the seats in this locality. Fairmead Lodge, which lies about half a mile south of the church, and looks out upon Fairmead Plain, was for many years, at the end of the last and beginning of the present century, the home of William Sotheby, who here wrote his "Orestes," and entered the field against Pope by translating the "Iliad" of Homer into English verse. Tennyson also at one time lived in this neighbourhood, at Beech Hill House, a building which has now disappeared; here he wrote his "Talking Oak" and "Locksley Hall."

To Fairmead House, then a private lunatic asylum, John Clare was taken in 1837, at which time a son of Thomas Campbell, the poet, was also an inmate. The pair soon got upon friendly terms, and became constant companions in their rambles, which, after a time, they were permitted to make into the forest. In one of his poems, written at that time, Clare wrote :—

> "I love the forest and its airy bounds,
> Where friendly Campbell takes his daily rounds."

In the summer of 1841 Clare quitted the pleasant shelter which he had found here, and started off, "without a penny in his pocket," to walk to his native town, Northborough, in Northamptonshire, which he reached in three days. He soon found himself, however, in the County Lunatic Asylum, where he continued till his death, in 1864.

High Beech Hill—now known as "Queen Victoria's Wood," since the visit of Her Majesty to the spot in May, 1882—is the highest plateau of the forest. This is, perhaps, the most favourite resort of the many thousands who take holiday in the forest during the summer and autumn. Here the London clay formation reaches its greatest altitude—759 feet above the sea-level ; and from this elevated spot some beautiful views of the surrounding country are obtained, including a broad sweep of undulating forest. Westward the eye wanders unobstructed over the valley of the Lea, and northward the view extends far into Hertfordshire, whilst to the south-west the vision ranges over a great part of Kent, from Shooter's Hill down to Gravesend.

The scenery here is very beautiful, almost rivalling in effect some parts of the far-famed New Forest, in Hampshire. "Nothing can be more delightful," observes Mr. Weldon in his book above quoted, "than a ramble among the beech woods on a hot summer day. The shadows are so cool and deep ; the belts of golden light that lie across the greensward at every opening among the trees are so bright and sunny ; the far-stretching vistas so mysterious and seductive to the imagination ; and the trunks and branches of the beeches so smooth, round, and well filled, and so covered with heavy masses of beautiful transparent foliage, that you feel as if in an enchanted place. You think longingly of the long-ago times when an English county merited its beautiful poetical name of 'Buckinghamshire'—the home of the beech-trees ; beech being the modern form of the old Teutonic *buck*, or *buch*."

Within the immediate neighbourhood of High Beech Hill are two well-known hostelries, the "Robin Hood" and "King's Oak." Near the latter inn is the stump of an old tree, commonly called "Harold's Oak," from which the latter inn takes its name ; and the green close by of late years served as the "meet" for the counterfeit "Epping Hunt," of which we have spoken above, and of which we shall have more to say on reaching Buckhurst Hill. The "meet" of late years had degenerated into a very disorderly gathering of London roughs, and in 1882 the fiat was issued by which this time-honoured custom—certainly "more honoured in the breach than in the observance" —was brought to an end. It is now no more, and we may be sure will not be revived by the Lord Mayor and Aldermen of London.

On the east side of High Beech Hill, in the thick of the forest, is an excavation, almost hidden from sight by the overhanging trees and brushwood, which has become locally known as "Dick Turpin's Cave," from a tradition that it was one of the lurking-places of that notorious highwayman. This part of the forest, as we have seen in a previous chapter,[*] was anything but safe for wayfarers, unless well armed, down to the end of the last century, deer-stealing being of common occurrence here. In Epping churchyard lies buried a poor fellow whose business it was to convey the venison to the metropolis, but who, in one of his midnight returns, was shot by an unknown hand, the almost headless body being found on the road next morning.

Mr. Thorne, in his "Environs of London," thus paints in glowing colours that portion of the forest lying to the north-east of High Beech Hill, and stretching away to the "Wake Arms" on the

---

* See *ante*, p. 423.

Epping road, about a mile and a half distant. "Here," as he tells us, "you may explore a charming bit of wild forest, guided by a winding forest road, and keeping the high road well to your right. Rough and broken, in parts open, elsewhere thick with pollard oaks and hornbeams, and an ever-varying undergrowth of hollies, thorns, and sloes, rose-bushes, sweet-briars, and brambles, and not wanting many an unlopped beech, oak, or ash, its sunny glades and gentle undulations reveal as you wander on a thousand peeps of sylvan loveliness. Deep moist dells, rich in fungi, or banks of furze, fern, and heaths, foxgloves, and honeysuckles, tempt your admiration at every turn; song-birds are on every spray; the call of the cuckoo is heard the summer through, and not unfrequently you may catch a glimpse of a nimble woodpecker, blue-tit, or wryneck. A mile beyond 'Wake Arms' is the earth-work known as Ambresbury Banks." Of this interesting relic of early days, however, we have spoken at length in a previous chapter.

On the south side of High Beech Hill, is "Queen Victoria's Wood." It is not often that a crowned head has paid a visit to the county of Essex. Queen Elizabeth reviewed her troops at Tilbury Fort, and George III. once or twice reviewed the regiments of the line and militia at the camps of Warley Common and at Colchester; but beyond that, such records are very scant—if, indeed, any will be found—until we come to the memorable 6th of May, when Queen Victoria here declared the forest to be free and open to the use and enjoyment of the people for ever. It was at this favourite spot, on the high ground close by King's Oak, that the pavilion, with its amphitheatre of seats, was erected on the occasion of her Majesty's visit. The spot, perhaps, could not have been better chosen, for not only is it the most elevated part of the forest, and consequently the best point for obtaining an idea of the extent of the surrounding wilderness, but it is also in itself one of the richest "bits" of forest scenery. The trees of Beech Wood perhaps are not so venerable as the famous Burnham beeches, with their enormous girth of trunk, their gnarled and twisted roots, and rugged limbs; but the beeches here* have the advantage of being all unlopped, well grown, and expansive, and many of them gigantic in stature; they are not the stunted and mutilated giants, as at Burnham, but send out their limbs to the full extent of their natural growth and beauty.

"The trunk of the beech," writes Mr. Walker, in his "Saturday Afternoon Rambles round London," "is itself a beautiful and distinguishing character. Not ribbed and furrowed like the bark of the elm, but with a smooth skin of a beautiful light grey, a noble and soaring pillar carries the eye upwards to clustered columns which spread aloft." The Burnham beeches are pollards, having undergone the treatment which Cowper has described in his picture of

"Trees that had once a head,
But now wear crests of oven-wood instead."

"Tradition ascribes the pollarding of the Burnham beeches to Cromwell's soldiers. Probably," adds Mr. Walker, "the only value of the statement is in the testimony it gives to the age of the trees."

It is not, however, merely for the growth of its trees that this part of Epping Forest is famous. Here the naturalist, the entomologist, and the botanist alike, will find full scope for the study of his particular science. Many of the plants here are unmistakably of Northern origin. Ferns in great variety flourish in this neighbourhood, as also do flowering plants and shrubs; whilst birds of almost all kinds seem to abound here more than in any other part of the forest.

Southward from Beech Wood a broad open track winds through the forest towards Queen Elizabeth's Lodge and the new hotel in the neighbourhood of Chingford; whilst a little to the west, by Fairmead Lodge, is another broad green opening, leading on to Lappitt's Hill, whence, near the "Owl" public-house, a good view is obtained across London to the Surrey hills, the "ivy-mantled tower" of Chingford Church being visible away to the left. Other parts of the forest close by, such as Bury Wood and Hawk Wood, are well worth a visit. A large slice of the forest close by Fairmead Plain was some time ago enclosed, and in part built upon; the trees were grubbed up and the forest ways stopped; but where the land had not been utilised for building purposes the greater part has been reclaimed.

Chingford lies on the edge of the forest, and derives its name from the King's Ford,* the ford across the Lea by which the Court crossed to hunt in the royal forests of Epping and Hainault. One of the meadows between the old church and the river Lea still bears the name of the "King's Mead." It is not uncommon to find the aspirate interpolated in words derived from "king." Thus,

---

* The case is far different in other parts of Epping Forest, where the annual lopping process has kept them in the condition of stunted pollards.

* Kelly, in his "Post Office Directory of Essex" says that the name comes "from a ford over the Ching, on the east bank of which rivulet it is situated."

Chigwell, as we shall presently see, is in early records written Cingwell, probably King's Well. The name of the parish, in early records, is written in a variety of ways—Chilgelford, Cingeford, Cingheford, Eehingelsford, Schingelford, Shymgylford ; but one and all apparently mean the same—a royal ford over the river, as mentioned above.

The parish of Chingford is seven miles in circumference, and it forms the south-western angle of the half-hundred of Waltham. The Lea divides

In the Domesday Survey the manor of Chingford St. Paul is described as comprising six hides, and containing " 50 acres of meadow, pannage for 500 hogs, two fisheries, nine beasts, two sumpter-horses, 27 hogs, and 100 sheep ; " and it is also added that there were "always four slaves." The extent of the manorial rights were encroached upon both by Peter de Valoines and Geoffrey de Magnaville ; and in a survey of the manor taken in 1245, we find it reduced to five hides. Lysons.

CHINGFORD CHURCH.

it from Edmonton on the west; whilst the land round about, swelling up into eminences, affords fine views across the country into Kent on the one side, and of various places in Hertfordshire on the other. A part of the parish is still open forest and woodland ; and most of the habitations of the villagers are somewhat isolated from each other. Several good mansions and residences of the better class, however, dot the landscape.

There are in Chingford two manors : one called Chingford St. Paul, as having belonged to St Paul's Cathedral until the dissolution, and the other called Chingford Earls (originally Chingford Comitis), from having in far distant times belonged to the Bourchiers, Earls of Essex.

in his "Environs of London," mentions some curious customs appertaining to this manor in former times. Among them it is stated that "the tenants were obliged to till the lord's land with a good plough, six horses, and two oxen, and to find a horse for harrowing ; " and that "Gilbert de Ecclesia was obliged, by the tenure of his lands, to find a man to gather nuts for the lord of the manor." One of the early records of the manor, about the year 1220, is an agreement between the Abbot of Waltham and the Dean and Chapter of St. Paul's, by which the latter are exempted from several payments and services before due to the hundred of Waltham : among these were "wardpeny" (money paid for watch and ward) and

" borchal-peny." This manor, which enjoyed an exemption from the forest laws, and sundry privileges granted to the Dean and Chapter of St. Paul's, was " surrendered " to Henry VIII. in 1544, and has since been in private hands. Edward VI. granted it to Sir Thomas Darcy, but it was shortly afterwards again surrendered to the Crown, and was given by Queen Mary to one of the ladies of her bedchamber, Susan Tongue, the widow of Thomas Tongue, Clarencieux King-at-Arms. The property

Thomas Boothby, from whose family it descended by marriage to the Heathcotes, by whom it is still owned. The old hall stands near the banks of the Lea, and is now a farm. Friday Hill, a house about a mile to the east of the church, and the seat of the Heathcotes, has long been used as the manor-house of Chingford. A view of Friday Hill House is given in the *European Magazine* for June, 1798.

Lysons identifies the old manor-house of

QUEEN ELIZABETH'S LODGE.

afterwards passed to the Leighs, and later on to the Snells of Brill, in Buckinghamshire. The manor of Chingford St. Paul is now owned by Miss Hodgson.

The manor of Chingford Earls, at the time of the Conquest, was held by " Orgar the Thane, under Robert Gernon." It was at one time in the possession of the Earls of Athol, and subsequently of Lord Roos. In the fifteenth century it was granted to the Bourchiers, Earls of Essex, but was soon after restored to the Roos family, with whom it continued till 1542, when it was given by Thomas, Earl of Rutland, to Henry VIII., in exchange for other lands. In or about 1666 the manor-house, called Chingford Hall, was purchased by a Mr.

Chingford Earls with the building known as Queen Elizabeth's Lodge, of which we are coming to speak.

Another manor here, called Buckrills, is mentioned by Kelly, in his " Directory of Essex," as owned by Mr. James D. Waters; but little or nothing is known about its history.

In this parish is, or was, an estate called Brindwoods, which was formerly held under the rector of the parish by a singular tenure, thus described by Morant, in his " History of Essex:"—" Upon every alienation the owner of the estate, with his wife, man-servant, and maid-servant, each single upon a horse, come to the parsonage, where the owner does his homage and pays his relief in the following manner. He blows three blasts with his horn, and carries a hawk on his fist ; his servant has a greyhound in a slip, both for the use of the rector that day. He receives a chicken for his hawk, a peck of oats for his horse, and a loaf of bread for his greyhound. They all dine ; after which the master blows three blasts with his horn, and so they depart." According, however, to Lyson's " Environs," by the end of the last century all memory of the custom had clean died out, so far as the rector and the parishioners were concerned. It is strange to find a parish so little conservative of ancient tenures.

Chingford is a very scattered parish, and apparently the chief population has drifted away from its former centre, as the old church stands far away from the abodes of man, except one old farmhouse and the vicarage. Its site is high, for Essex at least. In 1871 the number of the inhabitants was about 1,250, but during the next decade it had increased to nearly 1,400. This increase may be partly accounted for by the fact that since 1874 Chingford has been in direct railway communication with London, the forest branch of the Great Eastern Railway having been in that year opened, with its terminus near the new church at Chingford Green. Here are located the largest number of houses forming the village ; others are at Forest Side, about half a mile eastward, and others again form the hamlet of Chingford Hatch, about a mile to the south-east.

The old church, dedicated to All Saints, still stands, though disused for these many years, except for funerals ; it is rich in colour, and very picturesque, being almost covered with ivy, the growth of several centuries. It consists of a nave, south aisle, and chancel, with a tower at the west end and a south porch of red brick. The walls are of late Early English or of the Decorated period, but the windows are Perpendicular, inserted at a later date. The south porch has Tudor details. The glass has been taken out from all the windows except those in the chancel, so the wind whistles through the desolate nave, into which the ivy also has crept.

In the chancel are three fine mural monuments of the Jacobean period, and others of a later date on the floor, in memory of Sir J. Sylvester, Recorder of London, and members of the Boothby and Heathcote families. The brasses have been carried off from all. The font was removed into the new church (St. Peter and St. Paul), which stands on Chingford Green, and proclaims as loudly as its style can do that it was built early in the reign of Victoria, before the principles of Gothic architecture were well known. It is, in fact, a nondescript Gothic structure of white bricks, interlaced with squares of dark flints : a poor imitation of Dunstable and Luton churches. It has a stone spire, and looks pretty, but meaningless.

About half a mile to the north-west of this church is an obelisk, built by the directors of the Ordnance Survey, and kept up at the desire of the Astronomer-Royal, as marking the exact meridian of Greenwich. It is occasionally used for the purpose of testing and verifying calculations. In the *Illustrated London News* it is said— but without the least proof—that this obelisk marks the place of the death of Queen Boadicea, and was erected to her memory ! Thus, indeed, history is too often written.

The roadway running north-eastward from Chingford Green, by the railway-station, opens directly upon the forest at one of its most frequented points, by the front of Queen Elizabeth's Lodge and the new Royal Forest Hotel, near which is the broad green track to the left that winds away through the forest to High Beech, mentioned above, and also a most charming glade, that of Fairmead, which stretches away towards the north-west.

The old Lodge is a tall, irregular square structure of the Tudor era, consisting of three storeys, with gable ends and high pitched roof. It is built of brick and timber, somewhat rudely plastered, and its exterior is very picturesque, resembling the houses in the West of England. At its door were two fine elms, but both were blown down in 1881--2. The basement is used as a kitchen and parlour, with capacious fire-places and antique fire-dogs. The staircase, which projects into the hall, is wide and large, and composed of strong timbers, which will last till " the crack of doom ;" its width is about six feet, and it is divided by six landings, with four stairs between each, and each stair or step consists of a solid oak sill.

The principal room on the first floor has its walls hung with tapestry, in good preservation, and a chimney-piece opening with a flattened arch. The height of the basement and first floor has been sacrificed to the storey above, as they occupy about half of the whole elevation.

The top floor is not cut up into chambers, as usual, but consists of one large room—or hall, if such a term can be applied to an upper room— with an arched timber roof, and not unlike a chapel in its general appearance. Its walls are said to have been hung with tapestry when the manor courts were held in it. It is now used for trade feasts and other gatherings. It is entered from the staircase by a low wide doorway. It is about twenty-five feet in width by about forty feet in length; it is open to the roof, the tiles being merely hidden by plaster-work, and the sides consist of massive timbers filled in with plaster. It was originally lit by four windows. The roof, it should be added, is supported by timbers springing into two pointed arches, which render it probable that the original roof was of a different form, as well as material, to the present. The timbers of the staircase sides and roof are massive, and spring into arched forms, so as to impress the beholder with their strength and durability; and it is observable that all the doorways in the building consist of flattened arches. The local tradition reports that Queen Elizabeth was accustomed to ride up the stairs on horseback, and alight at the door of the large room upon a raised place, which was of old called the *horse-block*. Marvellous as the story may seem, the width and solidity and the many landings of the staircase are in its favour; and in order to test its feasibility, it is stated that early in the present century a wager of ten pounds was won by a sporting celebrity riding an untrained pony up the assigned route of the chivalrous queen. It is well known that Queen Elizabeth was ex-

tremely fond of the pleasures of the chase, and that she hunted at the age of fifty-seven is an established fact, so that her freak of riding up-stairs would be but a trifle to her Majesty.

It is satisfactory to know that by the Act of Parliament of 1878, under which the forest was made over to "the people," the Corporation of London are bound to keep Queen Elizabeth's Lodge in repair, as "an object of antiquarian interest."

The Royal Forest Hotel, which adjoins Queen Elizabeth's Lodge, is the constant resort of London excursionists and holiday-makers. Throughout the summer, and especially at Eastertide, Whitsuntide, and on Bank Holidays, the glassy glades in front of it are crowded with picnic parties.

Near the Lodge, on the road to High Beech, is a large piece of water, still retaining all its rural picturesqueness, frequented by wild fowl, and a great resort for insects, and full of aquatic plants. Hence it is constantly visited by microscopical and naturalist and field clubs. It is now called Connaught Water, after the new royal ranger of the forest. The fine oaks which surround it speak as plainly as in words that "this is the forest primeval."

CHAPTER XLVII.

EPPING FOREST (*continued*)—BUCKHURST HILL, LOUGHTON, AND THEYDON BOIS.

"In this lone open glade I lie,
Screened by deep boughs on either hand,
Where ends the glade—to stay the eye,
Those black-crowned, red-boled pine-trees stand."—MATTHEW ARNOLD.

Recent Improvements in Epping Forest—Connaught Water and other Lakes—Buckhurst Hill—Its Etymology—Census Returns—The Railway Station—St. John's Church—Congregational Church—Langford Place—The Essex Naturalists' and Field Club—The Epping Hunt—The "Bald-faced Stag"—The "Roebuck"—Situation of Loughton—Census Returns—Descent of the Manor—The Hall—The Old Parish Church—A Memorial Church—St. John's Church—General Appearance of the Village—Staple Hill—The "Lopping" Process—Loughton Camp—Debden Hall—Theydon Bois.

IT has been remarked by one of our best writers on landscape that "the forest, like other beautiful scenes, pleases the eye, but its great effect is to arouse the imagination." Mr. William Paul, Fellow of the Linnean Society, in a lecture on "The Future of Epping Forest," delivered in 1880 before the Society of Arts, spoke as follows:—"The scenery of Epping Forest, as a whole, is hardly of a character that can be correctly spoken of as sublime or beautiful, although beautiful spots may occasionally be met with, and it possesses the elements of both picturesqueness and grandeur. But there are no mountains or torrents, no frowning precipices, no furious eddies, no foaming cascades. It would, perhaps, be correctly described

as a tract of woodland and pasture, the surface broken into hill and dale, interspersed with a few fine trees and groves; the old trees possessing a rare and glorious beauty, but not being numerous or prominent enough to impart dignity to a forest of 6,000 acres. It is picturesque from its natural ruggedness; it is grand from its extent. These two forms or expressions of beauty—picturesqueness and grandeur, which are inherent—should never be lost sight of, or suffer diminution at the hands of the improver."

Since the forest has been taken in hand by the Corporation of London, alterations have been effected in different parts, which, if they may not be called "improvements" so far as the mere natural appearance of the forest is concerned, may at any rate be put down as works of great utility and convenience, and also as enhancing the enjoyment of visitors in the future. One of these is the Ranger's Road, a new thoroughfare from Chingford to Loughton, made in 1880, and formally opened by the Duke of Connaught as Ranger of Epping Forest; and another is the large sheet of water mentioned at the end of the preceding chapter, which, from being the dismal swamp that it formerly was, when known as the Forest Pool, has been converted into an ornamental lake, some seven acres in extent, and renamed Connaught Water. This lake, which contains two islands, and is used for boating, &c., is fed by the little Ching rivulet. Another lake has also been formed at Staple Hill, near Loughton. As the forest is now well drained, and as many new paths and roadways have been formed through it—one of the latter extending its whole length, from Woodford to Epping—the danger of losing one's way is reduced to a minimum.

A broad roadway, called the Green Ride, skirts the Connaught Lake on the west side, and then passes on through the forest, crossing another roadway called Earl's Path, and so on in a north-easterly direction, by Monk Wood, to Ambresbury Banks and Epping; whilst on the south side of the lake the Ranger's Road leads towards the north-east in the direction of Loughton.

We now pass on eastward from Queen Elizabeth's Lodge across an open part of the forest, keeping in view the tall square tower of the waterworks on the top of Buckhurst Hill.

Buckhurst Hill, it has been suggested, may have been so named from Sackville, Lord Buckhurst, the accomplished poet, and favoured flower of Queen Elizabeth's court; but more probably it comes from the Anglo-Saxon *Boc-hyrst*, a beech-forest. Thorne, in his "Environs of London," says that perhaps the name may be derived from "Book-forest: *i.e.*, a portion of the forest set apart, or severed, by royal charter from the neighbouring open forest." The vulgar name of the place is, or was, formerly Buckett's Hill: hence John Clare, in one of his sonnets on Epping Forest, writes—

> "There's Buckett's Hill, a place of furze and clouds,
>   Which evening in a golden blaze enshrouds."

Poor Clare, when he wrote these not very original lines, it must be remembered, was an inmate of Fairmead Asylum, not very far off.

This locality was formed into an ecclesiastical district out of the parish of Chigwell in 1838, since which time the number of its inhabitants has very largely increased. In 1871 it amounted to 2,500, being nearly three times as many as it was ten years previously, whilst according to the census returns for 1881 it has now reached about 4,000. At the foot of the hill, further eastward, is a railway-station on the Epping and Ongar branch of the Great Eastern Railway, around which are clustered several small cottages and "villa residences." From the top of the hill some beautiful views are obtained over the surrounding country, including the high ground on the opposite side of the valley of the Roding; whilst a pleasant and picturesque piece of the forest ground lies along the old Cambridge road to the left, between Woodford Wells and Loughton.

The church, dedicated to St. John the Baptist, was built in 1837, and occupies a commanding site at the top of the hill. It is in the Early English style. It has been enlarged at different periods, and now consists of a chancel, nave, aisles, and a tower with spire. A Congregational church is a handsome stone building of Gothic architecture, of the Early Decorated style. The pinnacled tower at its western end is about 100 feet in height, and, like the spire of St. John's Church, is a conspicuous object for miles around.

At the lower end of Palmerston Road, opposite the Congregational church, and on the ground now occupied by a private house called Langford Place, stood the hunting seat or palace of Henry VIII., known as Poteles, or Langford Place. It remained with the Crown till the reign of Elizabeth, when it passed into private hands. Mr. James Jones, in his "Directory of Woodford," &c., says:—"There is no traceable account when the old building was pulled down. In the year 1773 a farm-house occupied the spot, known as King's Place Farm; this was, a few years ago, converted into a beautiful villa residence, and retains the royal name of 'Langford Place.' The Congregational chapel is called King's Place Congregational Church, and the carriage-way commencing near the 'Three Colts' Tavern, Prince's Road, and which crosses the Queen's Road to the entrance of Roebuck Lane, is named King's Place. Some fields to the north-east of the palace site, by the river Roding, are known as the King's Meadow."

The Essex Naturalists' and Field Club has its head-quarters at Buckhurst Hill. This society has of late years done much towards throwing additional light on the antiquarian objects in the neighbourhood.

Here are two wayside inns of celebrity, both of which, in their turn, have been the scene of the

"Epping Hunt," namely, the "Bald-faced Stag" and the "Roebuck." This assembly took place annually on Easter Monday at the former inn, down to about 1853, when the landlord grew tired, or ashamed, of the company that it brought down from London, and handed over the arrangements to his neighbour, mine host of the "Roebuck." Subsequently, as stated in the preceding chapter, the "hunt" was transferred to High Beech, where a publican kept it going till 1882 ; but as in that year and the previous year it had become a scene of riot and a public nuisance, it was suppressed by the aid of the police, and it is now a thing of the past.

The custom is said to have begun in 1226, when King Henry III. granted the liberty of hunting over this country to the citizens of London. Mr. Rounding, who was the landlord of the "Horse and Well," was the last huntsman, and for some years it was not an uncommon sight to see him with as many as 500 mounted followers. The "meet" formerly took place on the ridge near Buckhurst Hill, overlooking Fairmead. It is asserted that the Lord Mayor and Aldermen of London, as the recognised heads and leaders of the citizens, used to attend the hunt in state ; but this is probably untrue.

From Hone's "Every-day Book," Vol. II. (March, 1827), page 459, we extract the following interesting particulars concerning the Epping Hunt :— "In 1226 King Henry III. confirmed to the citizens of London *free warren*, or liberty to hunt a circuit about their city, in the warren of Staines, &c. ; and in ancient times the lord mayor, aldermen, and corporation, attended by a due number of their constituents, availed themselves of this right of chase 'in solemn guise.' From newspaper reports, it appears that the office of 'common hunt,' attached to the mayoralty, is in danger of disuetude. The Epping Hunt seems to have lost the lord mayor and his brethren in their corporate capacity, and the annual sport to have become a farcical show.

"A description of the Epping Hunt of Easter Monday, 1826, by one 'Simon Youngbuck,' in the *Morning Herald*, is the latest report, if it be not the truest ; but of that the editor of the 'Every-day Book' cannot judge, for he was not there to see : he contents himself with picking out the points ; should any one be dissatisfied with the 'hunting of that day' as it will be here presented, he has only to sit down in good earnest to a plain matter-of-fact detail of all the circumstances from his own knowledge, accompanied by such citations as will show the origin and former state of the usage, and such a detail, so accompanied, will be inserted—

'For want of a better, *this* must do.'

On the authority aforesaid, and that without the introduction of any term not in the *Herald*, be it known, then, that before and at the commencement of the hunt aforesaid, it was a cold, dry, and dusty morning, and that the huntsmen of the east were all abroad by nine o'clock, trotting, fair and softly, down the road, on great nine-hand sky-scrapers, nimble daisy-cutting nags, flowing-tailed chargers, and ponies no bigger than the learned one at Astley's ; some were in job-coaches, at two guineas a-day ; some in three-bodied nondescripts, some in gigs, some in cabs, some in drags, some in short stages, and some in long stages ; while some, on no stages at all, footed the road, smothered by dust driven by a black, bleak north-easter full in the teeth. Every gentleman was arrayed after his own peculiar taste, in blue, brown, or black—in dress coats, long coats, short coats, frock coats, great coats, and no coats ; in drab slacks and slippers; in grey tights and black-spurred Wellingtons ; in nankeen bomb-balloons ; in city-white cotton-cord unmentionables, with jockey toppers, and in Russian-drill down-belows, as a *memento* of the late Czar. The ladies all wore a *goose-skin* under-dress, in compliment to the north-easter.

"At that far-famed spot, the brow above Fairmead Bottom, by twelve o'clock, there were not less than three thousand merry lieges then and there assembled. It was a beautiful set-out. Fair dames, 'in purple and in pall,' reposed in vehicles of all sorts, sizes, and conditions, whilst seven or eight hundred mounted members of the hunt wound in and out 'in restless ecstasy,' chatting and laughing with the fair, sometimes rising in their stirrups to look out for the long-coming cart of the stag, 'whilst with off-heel assiduously aside' they 'provoked the caper which they seemed to hide.' The green-sward was covered with ever-moving crowds on foot, and the pollard oaks which skirt the Bottom on either side were filled with men and boys.

"But where is the stag all this while? One o'clock, and no stag ! Two o'clock, and no stag !—a circumstance easily accounted for by those who are in the secret, and the secret is this : there are buttocks of boiled beef and fat hams, and beer and brandy in abundance, at the 'Roe-buck' public-house, low down in the forest ; and ditto at the 'Bald-faced Stag,' on the top of the hill ; and ditto at the 'Coach and Horses' at Woodford Wells ; and ditto at the 'Castle,' at

Woodford; and ditto at the 'Eagle,' at Snaresbrook; and if the stag had been brought out before the beef, beer, bacon, and brandy were eaten and drank, where would have been the use of providing so many good things? So they carted the stag from public-house to public-house, and showed him at threepence a-head to those ladies and gentlemen who never saw such a thing before; and the showing and carting induced a consumption of eatables and drinkables—an achievement which was helped by a band of music in every house, playing

THE "ROEBUCK."

hungry tunes to help the appetite; and then, when the eatables and drinkables were gone and paid for, they turned out the stag.

"Precisely at half-past two o'clock the stag-cart was seen coming over the hill from the 'Bald-faced Stag,' and hundreds of horsemen and gigmen rushed gallantly forward to meet and escort it to the top of Fairmead Bottom, amidst such whooping and hallooing as made all the forest echo again, and would have done Carl Maria Von Weber's heart good to hear. And then, when the cart stopped and was turned tail about, the horsemen drew up in long lines, forming an avenue wide enough for the stag to run down. For a moment all was deep, silent, breathless anxiety; and the doors of the cart were thrown open, and out popped a strapping four-year-old red buck, fat as a porker, with a chaplet of flowers round his neck, a girth of divers-coloured ribbons, and a long blue and pink streamer depending from the summit of his branching horns. He was received, on his alighting, with a shout that seemed to shake heaven's concave, and took it very graciously,

looking round him with great dignity as he stalked slowly and delicately forward down the avenue prepared for him; and occasionally shrinking from side to side, as some super-valorous cockney made a cut at him with his whip. Presently he caught a glimpse of the hounds and the huntsmen, waiting for him at the bottom, and in an instant off he bounded, sideways, through the rank, knocking down and trampling all who crowded the path he chose to take; and dashing at once into the cover, he was out of sight before a man could say 'Jack Robinson!' Then might be seen gentlemen running about without their horses, and horses galloping about without their gentlemen; and hats out of number brushed off their owners' heads by the rude branches of the trees; and everybody asking which way the stag was gone, and nobody knowing

THE "BALD-FACED STAG."

anything about him; and ladies beseeching gentlemen not to be too venturesome, and gentlemen gasping for breath at the thoughts of what they were determined to venture; and myriads of people on foot running hither and thither in search of little eminences to look from; and yet nothing at all to be seen, though more than enough to be heard; for every man and every woman, too, made as loud a noise as possible. Meanwhile the stag, followed by the keepers and about six couple of hounds, took away through the covers towards Woodford. Finding himself too near the haunts of his enemy, man, he there turned back, sweeping down the Bottom for a mile or two, and away up the enclosures towards Chingford, where he was caught nobody knows how, for everybody returned to town, except those who stopped to regale afresh, and recount the glorious perils of the day. Thus ended the *Easter Hunt* of 1826."

The above humorous and clever sketch may be regarded as a fair sample of the Epping "Hunt" as it was known to the parents of the present generation—at all events down to a date long subsequent to the accession of Queen Victoria.

sports; and some surprise existed in the House of Commons when, in 1863, the Epping Forest Prevention Bill being before the Committee, Mr. Alderman Copeland, M.P., in response to an inquiry as to whether the City of London did not claim the privilege of hunting, answered, 'Not that I am aware of.'" The real or supposed connection of the civic authorities with the Epping Hunt has been seized upon by other satirists than D'Urfey. It was made the subject of a poem by Tom Hood, to which George Cruickshank added illustrations. In this poem the author gives the following

THEYDON BOIS.

A correspondent of *Notes and Queries** in 1872, however, states that, being about to publish a guide to Epping Forest, he has made inquiries, but without success, in order to find out whether the Lord Mayor and Aldermen ever attended Epping Hunt in state. He adds:—"I have since come across some lines, printed in Strutt's 'Sports and Pastimes,' which relate—

"'Once a year into Essex a hunting they go,' &c.

Three stanzas are given, taken from an old ballad, called the 'London Customs,' printed in D'Urfey's collection. From time to time these lines revived the assertion, but it is doubtful with what truth. It is, nevertheless, the fact that the Lord Mayor and Aldermen in times gone by took part in these

ludicrous account of the adventures of a Mr. John Huggins at the Epping Hunt :—

"With Monday's sun John Huggins rose,
　　And slapped his leather thigh,
　And sang the burden of the song,
　　'This day a stag must die.'

"Alas! there was no warning voice
　　To whisper in his ear,
　'Thou art a fool for leaving *Chepe*,
　　To go and hunt the *deer*.'

"Then slowly on through Leytonstone,
　　Past many a Quaker's box—
　No friends to hunters after deer,
　　Though followers of a *Fox*.

"And many a score behind—before—
　　The self-same rout inclined;
　And, minded all to march one way,
　　Made one great march of mind.

*   *   *   *   *

" Now Huggins from his saddle rose,
　And in his stirrups stood ;
And lo ! a little cart that came
　Hard by a little wood,

" In shape like half a hearse—though not
　For corpses in the least ;
For this contained the *deer alive*,
　And not the *dear deceased* !

" Now Huggins, standing far aloof,
　Had never seen the deer,
Till all at once he saw the beast
　Come charging in his rear.

" Away he went, and many a score
　Of riders did the same,
On horse and ass—like High and Low
　And Jack pursuing Game.

" A score were sprawling on the grass,
　And beavers fell in showers ;
There was another *Floorer* there,
　Beside the Queen of Flowers.

*   *   *   *

" Away, away he scudded, like
　A ship before the gale ;
Now flew to ' *h*ills we know not of,"
　Now, nun-like, took the vale.

" ' Hold hard ! hold hard ! you'll lame the dogs,'
　Quoth Huggins. ' So I do ;
I've got the saddle well in hand,
　And hold as hard as you !'

" But soon the horse was well avenged
　For cruel smart of spurs,
For riding through a moor, he pitched
　His master in the furze !

" Now seeing Huggins' nag adrift,
　A farmer, shrewd and sage,
Resolved, by changing horses here,
　To hunt another stage.

" So up on Huggins' horse he got,
　And swiftly rode away ;
While Huggins mounted on a mare,
　Done brown upon a bay.

" And off they set in double chase,
　For such was fortune's whim,
The farmer rode to hunt the stag,
　And Huggins hunted him !

" And lo ! the dim and distant hunt
　Diminished in a trice ;
The steeds, like Cinderella's team,
　Seemed dwindling into mice.

*   *   *   *

" Now many a sign at Woodford town,
　Its Inn-–vitation tells:
But Huggins, full of ills, of course
　Betook him to the Wells.

" When thus forlorn a merry horn
　Struck up without the door—
The mounted mob were all returned ;
　The Epping hunt was o'er !

" And many a horse was taken out
　Of saddle and of shaft ;
And men, by dint of drink, became
　The only ' *beasts of draught*.'

" For now begun a harder run
　On wine, and gin, and beer ;
And overtaken men discussed
　The overtaken deer—

" And how the hunters stood aloof,
　Regardful of their lives,
And shunned a beast whose very horns
　They knew could *handle* knives.

" And one how he had found a horse
　Adrift—a goodly gray !
And kindly rode the nag, for fear
　The nag should go astray.

" Now Huggins, when he heard the tale,
　Jumped up with sudden glee ;
' A goodly gray ! why, then, I say,
　That gray belongs to me !'

" And let the chase again take place
　For many a long, long year—
John Huggins will not ride again
　To hunt the Epping deer !

MORAL.

" Thus pleasure oft eludes our grasp
　Just when we think to grip her ;
And hunting after happiness,
　We only hunt a slipper."

The anecdotes of " hair-breadth escapes " of some of the gallant sportsmen, and of other incidents connected with the Epping Hunt, as may be supposed, are "plentiful as blackberries" among the older inhabitants of these parts. Among anecdotes of another kind, the following is perhaps worth recording :—Lord Brougham, when staying in the neighbourhood, went on one occasion to witness the hunt, about which he was " very facetious," and asked many questions. He said to a man, " I suppose you are waiting for the Lord Mayor and Aldermen ? If you will show me them when they arrive, I will give you a crown." The man said, " I do not think I should know them for certain ; but if you will give me half-a-crown, I will show you Lord Brougham alive." This so disconcerted his lordship, that he went home immediately.

The " Bald-faced Stag," which stands by the roadside, at a short distance south of St. John's Church, is one of the oldest houses in the neighbourhood ; it is a large, square, white-washed building, with a high-pitched tiled roof, and is a favourite resort for Londoners during the summer. It contains some curious carving, and a fine portrait of Queen Anne. It was formerly a manor-house. The old coach road, at the beginning of the present century, ran in a straight line northward of the "Roebuck," traversing in its course the ground now covered by St. John's Terrace. At that time the whole locality was covered by forest, but later on the course of the road has been carried in a more direct line.

If it be true that "the finest scenery in the world is improved by a good inn in the fore-ground," the saying is certainly true of the spot which we have now reached. The "Roebuck" is on the main road from London, and between Buckhurst Hill and Loughton; it stands on high ground, within a few minutes' walk of Buckhurst Hill Station of the Great Eastern line, and close to some of the loveliest parts of the forest. Over-looking as it does one of the finest panoramas in the suburbs of London, no more charming des-tination could be found for excursions, picnic parties, bean-feasts, trade dinners, school outings, and bicycling club runs. The banquet hall, ad-joining the inn, will accommodate from 300 to 500 guests, and is available for balls, meetings, concerts, dramatic performances, &c. The "Hunt" room and the "Elizabeth" room will each seat seventy guests at dinner. The pleasaunce, in the rear of the inn, includes twenty-three acres of meadow land, lawns, and fruit garden.

Loughton, which lies about a mile distant from the "Roebuck," is long and straggling, extending for nearly two miles along the Epping road. It is about twelve miles from London, and six miles south-east from Waltham Abbey. The parish is all within the bounds of Epping Forest, and, according to the census returns of 1881, contains a population of 2,851, being an increase of about 400 during the preceding decade. On the east side of the main road is the Loughton Station of the Great Eastern Railway. The views in and around the village are very picturesque, and the ground of a remarkably undulating character, the views from Golding's Hill and other elevated parts extending to the Thames and the Kentish hills in one direction, to Hampstead and Highgate in another, and eastward across the valley of the Roden to the vicinity of Navestock, some twelve miles distant.

This parish formed a portion of the endowments which were bestowed by Harold on Waltham Abbey, and it continued a part of the abbey lands until the dissolution of that monastery. It was granted by Edward VI. to Sir Thomas Darcy; but his possession was of short duration, for in the reign of Queen Mary it again reverted to the Crown, by whom it was attached to the Duchy of Lancaster. In the reign of Elizabeth it became the property of the Stonards, from whom it was carried by the marriage of an heiress to Sir Robert Wrothe, of Durants, in Enfield.* The manor continued in the possession of this family for more than a century, when it passed by bequest to the Nassaus, Earls of Rochford. About the middle of the last century it was sold to Mr. William Whitaker, a merchant of London, from whom it descended to the present owner, the Rev. John Whitaker Maitland, the families of Whitaker and Maitland having become united by marriage.

The Hall, which stood about a mile distant eastward of the high road, was burnt down in 1836. It was a large building in the Elizabethan style, and it is said to have received many dis-tinguished visitors. In 1561 Queen Elizabeth honoured the Stonards with a visit here. James I. is reported to have been here on more than one occasion; and the Princess of Denmark (after-wards Queen Anne) is stated, in the "Beauties of England," to have retired hither from the court of her father, James II., "when she saw him pursuing the arbitrary measures which terminated in his expulsion from the throne." Mr. Thorne, in his "Environs of London," however, considers that it was most likely only for a night or so that the princess was here, "when on her way to Notting-ham, under the escort of Compton, the military Bishop of London."

The present Hall, now a farm-house, was con-structed partly out of the materials of the ancient building. The great gates of the old Hall still remain, and are elaborate specimens of hand-wrought iron-work.

The old parish church of Loughton, dedicated to St. Nicholas, stood near the Hall; but being in a sadly dilapidated condition, and at an inconvenient distance from the village, was pulled down in 1847, with the exception of the chancel, which has been retained for use as a mortuary chapel. In 1877 a new "memorial church" was built on part of the site of the demolished structure. It was erected by Mrs. Whitaker Maitland, in memory of her husband, her sons, and all those members of the family who lie buried in the churchyard. The brasses from the old church have been placed here: among them are three with effigies of John Stonard and his wives, Joan and Catharine, and dated 1541; another to William Nodes, gentle-man, and his six sons, dated 1594, has the effigy of a man in the costume of the period, with a ruff round his neck; and some to the Wrothe family, dating back to 1673.

---

* See *ante*, p. 373.

St. John's Church stands on an eminence at the north-east corner of the village, and is much more conveniently situated for the parishioners than the old parish church. It was erected in 1846, and is a brick-built cruciform structure, in the Norman style, with a low square central tower, containing eight fine-toned bells. Some of the windows are filled with stained glass. The church was enlarged and partly re-seated in 1877.

In the village are six almshouses, founded in 1827 by Mrs. Whitaker, besides which the wants of the necessitous poor are ameliorated by local charities. A pretty drinking-fountain stands at the corner of the roadway leading to the railway-station, and altogether the village wears a "sober, sylvan look."

Nearly opposite the railway-station a road winds to the north-west through the forest by High Beech, and so on to Waltham Abbey. To the right of this road, immediately on entering the forest, is Staple Hill, a spot which has become of historic interest as that where the "lopping" process used to be carried out by the natives of these parts, and of which we have spoken in a previous chapter.* Mr. Coller, in his "People's History of Essex" (1861), writes of Loughton :—"There seems to be a want of energy, and an unwillingness to move from their native place, which greatly characterise the inhabitants, not only of this village, but of this part of the county generally, and which certainly impedes their advancement in the social scale. The proximity of the forest, and the pretext of procuring firewood by means of the loppings of the trees, which the inhabitants claim a right to cut during the winter months, encourage habits of idleness and dislike of settled labour, and in some cases give occasion for poaching, all of which are injurious to the poor."

The forest, indeed, has been so constantly "lopped" that most of its trees are pollards with old and hoary stems, which, having been debarred from their natural growth, have twisted their stems and roots into all sorts of fantastic forms. It is probable that many of these trees, small as they may look, are as old as our Plantagenet kings, if not older still. Among them the beech, the holly, and the hornbeam, are remarkable for their abundance.

The walks in or near the forest at this point are of such a character as to prove a great attraction for visitors ; and consequently Loughton is largely patronised by excursionists and others during the summer months. At the top of Staple Hill a

"shelter" has been erected for the convenience of visitors, and at the foot of the hill a moderate-sized lake has been formed.

Proceeding for about half a mile along the new grass-covered forest roadway which skirts the base of Staple Hill, and striking off into the wood on the left on reaching the top of the next hill, the rambler, by a little diligent searching, may explore the remains of an ancient earth-work, which was discovered in 1872 by Mr. B. H. Cowper. This camp covers about the same amount of ground as Ambresbury Banks—some twelve acres ; but it is more irregular in shape, though, being surrounded by trees on every side, it has stood the ravages of time and the effects of rain and storms far better, though in parts the earth-works and trenches have been partially levelled. It has, however, lain for centuries unnoticed in the shade, and apparently its existence was unknown to Morant, the indefatigable historian of Essex. It follows the configuration of the hill which it crowns, and must have been chosen and fashioned with great military skill, as it commands a spur and ravine by which alone it could have been approached. Mr. Cowper is sanguine enough to believe that he has discovered at the north-west corner the place where Boadicea must have led on her attack, and where, being defeated, her soldiers must have been driven down, the sides of the camp itself being partly demolished and carried down into the valley.

In order to carry out the systematic examination of these two entrenchments—the Loughton Camp and Ambresbury Banks—which had not been cut into before the examination made by the Essex Field Club in 1881, it was resolved to commence upon the Loughton Camp as early as possible in 1882 ; and permission having been granted by the Epping Forest Committee of the Corporation of London, the work was carried out in the months of May and June of that year. The mode of working was similar to that employed at Ambresbury Banks, and consisted in cutting sections through the rampart and ditch, in order to expose the old surface line. With a view to facilitate the carrying on of the necessarily tedious work of watching the removal of the earth, a sub-committee of the Essex Field Club was appointed to co-operate with those engaged in the work. The first section was twelve feet in width, and its cutting involved the removal of one hundred and fifty cubic yards of earth. But few objects were found in this cutting. On the old surface, nearly under the centre of the rampart, two or three fragments of pottery, several flint "flakes," and pieces of charcoal, were turned up. The pottery is extremely rude, and consists of

* See ante, p. 428.

badly-burnt rough clay, containing quartz grains, and showing no traces of lathe turning. The great amount of denudation which this earth-work has experienced, owing to its exposed situation and the light character of the soil, has caused the complete silting up of the ditch in most parts, and it was found in this first section that the silting was so very similar in appearance to the undisturbed earth, that the form of the ditch could not be satisfactorily made out. This last circumstance, combined with the paucity of the evidence obtained, determined the extension of the investigation, and another cutting seven feet wide was therefore commenced. In this second section no pottery was found, but numbers of flint flakes and a partially-finished flint celt, all on the old surface line, and buried well beneath the rampart. Further evidence of human occupation in the way of charcoal and burnt clay, marking the sites of fireplaces, were also found on the original surface. The evidence thus far obtained did not appear to those who had undertaken the work of excavation sufficiently complete to enable them to form any conclusive opinion as to the age of the earth-works, although the relics thus far found, conjoined with the absence of all Roman remains, point to a very early, and most probably pre-Roman, period. Inside the encampment can still be traced the well, and the ditch along which the water used to trickle into a pond, the dam at the bottom of which is almost perfect. The little stream still flows in the winter months.

At a short distance further northward, and a little to the right of the high road, in the midst of some charming scenery, stands Debden Hall, a picturesque and well-built mansion, in a park of some 150 acres, adorned by grand old forest trees, with wooded dells, stream and waterfall, &c.

About half a mile eastward from Debden Hall is Theydon Bois, which lies on the very confines of our survey, at the north-east angle of Epping Forest. It is a pretty village, and with its triangular green fringed with an avenue of oak-trees, has almost a foreign appearance. It is called Bois after a family who in early ages possessed the manor, and who, in their turn, doubtless bore that name from dwelling in the wood, which in Norman and French was "*le Bois*."

The church here has been transplanted, the original structure, which stood to the south on the high ground, having been pulled down, and its materials worked into the new structure—a tasteful little building, with a tall and tapering spire. One or two monuments and graves, with their contents, were transferred, among them some members of the Hall-Dare family, the squires and patrons of the living.

The old manor-house, called Theydon Hall, long the residence of the Hall-Dares, is situated on rising ground a short distance to the west of the church and the common; it is now a farm-house.

In the church is a well-preserved painting of the royal arms, and the initials "J. R.," clearly denoting "Jacobus Rex," our first English James. Below the escutcheon is a portrait of the king—an unmistakable Stuart, but more like Charles I. than his father. It was probably owing to the remote position of the church in "the woods" that this royal heraldry escaped the hands of the Parliamentary Roundheads of Cromwell's time. The old churchyard is still enclosed, and its tombs are carefully kept.

Theydon has no literary history; but it has had one celebrated character as a resident within its bounds. John Elwes,* the miser, lived here, and from this place he used to ride up to London with his bacon and eggs.

CHAPTER XLVIII.

CHIGWELL.

" Far as the eye may distant views command,
Here—there—vast oaks in pride of foliage stand."—LORD LEIGH's *Walks in the Country.*

General Appearance of the Village of Chigwell—Its Etymology—Census Returns—Descent of the Manor—Rolls Park—Woolstons—Lexborough—The Warren—Belmont—The Parish Church—Archbishop Harsnett—Local Charities—Club-room—The Grammar School—The " King's Head " Tavern—Charles Dickens's " Maypole " Inn—Chigwell Row—Woodlands—Bowls—Gainsborough's Picture of " The Woodman "—The Mineral Waters.

AT Chigwell we come once more face to face with Charles Dickens, who has laid in this neighbourhood many of the most striking scenes in his " Barnaby Rudge." It is a very rural and retired village, with a " decent church "—as yet happily unrestored—" topping the neighbouring hill," and with one of the pleasantest and most attractive of old roadside inns directly opposite. Indeed, Chigwell is generally regarded as one of the prettiest villages in Essex. Although much of the beautiful woodland scenery with which it was formerly surrounded has been given over to the builder, or converted to agricultural purposes, much still remains. Down to within the last quarter of a century or so portions of Epping Forest extended well into the parish on its western and northern sides, whilst eastward and southward lay Hainault Forest; but

ings are afar off, and Chigwell does not partake in their character.

The name of the parish is variously written in ancient documents as Cinghewella, Cingnehella, Chiwellia, Chickwell, and Cykewell. In Anglo-Saxon times it was written Cingwella (*cing* signifying king), *i.e.*, the king's well; the name is supposed to be taken from a well in Chigwell Row.

According to a survey taken in the reign of James I., the number of acres in the parish at that time was 4,027, which included 1,500 acres of

CHIGWELL GRAMMAR SCHOOL.

WILLIAM PENN.

since the latter has been disafforested and the former has been curtailed by enclosures, many characteristics of the Chigwell of former days have been obliterated.

Chigwell is about ten miles from London, on the road to Ongar and the "Rodings," or "Roothings"—a district of Essex remarkable for the stiffness of its clay, the poorness of its soil, and locally for the dulness of its inhabitants. In a word, if Essex be the Bœotia of England, the Rodings are the Bœotia of Essex. But the Rooth-

Epping and Hainault Forests. The present area of the parish, including Buckhurst Hill, is a little over 4,500 acres. The population a quarter of a century ago was 2,600. In 1871 this number had nearly doubled itself; and according to the census returns for 1881 it has now reached 5,400. A fair is held here annually in September. The parish is thickly studded with good mansions, mostly the residences of City merchants; and there are also several fine old halls and manor-houses, where in bygone times dwelt the lords of the soil.

The principal manor-house of Chigwell, called Chigwell Hall, lies a little to the north-west of the church, by the side of the roadway leading to Buckhurst Hill and Loughton. It was once part of the possessions of Earl Harold, but at the time of the Norman Survey it was held by Ralph de

Limeses, Baron of Ulverlie, in Warwickshire, with whose descendants it remained for several generations. The manor was subsequently owned by the Fitzwalters, and in the sixteenth century it was conveyed to Sir Thomas Audley, Lord Chancellor of England, for Brian Tuke, Treasurer of the King's Chamber, and others, for the king's use. Edward VI. granted the manor, together with West Hatch, which lies about a mile south-west from Chigwell Church, to Sir Thomas Roth, with whose family it continued till

tensive hamlet, with a church or chapel of its own. Since the Conquest, however, it has been united to Chigwell. In old records the name of this estate is variously written Ulfelmstun, Wolfamston, Woolvermeston, Walston, and Woolston. In the time of Edward the Confessor, like the rest of the neighbourhood, it belonged to Earl Harold; but after the Conquest it formed part of the royal demesnes, and was farmed by a "sheriff." The estate was given by Henry II. to the De Sandfords, "to be holden by the 'grand sergeantry' of finding a damsel to wait in the queen's chamber on the day of her coronation."

Lexborough—the name of which alone survives in Lexborough Lane—is said to have been a mansion which in the last century was inferior to few in the county. It has long since been pulled down, and is now forgotten.

CHIGWELL CHURCH.

the middle of the seventeenth century, when it was sold to Sir William Hicks of Ruckholts, whose son, Sir Harry, in 1720, built the plain brick residence nearly opposite to West Hatch, called Bowling Green. Chigwell Hall was sold by Sir Harry Hicks to Mr. William Davy, Treasurer of St. Luke's Hospital; but the Hicks family still retained the manor, with which was included more than a thousand acres of the forest.

Rolls Park—or Barringtons, as it was formerly called—about half a mile north-east of the church, by the side of the high road to Abridge and Ongar, comprises a well-built mansion, an estate of some 100 acres, and was for two centuries or more in the possession of the family of the late Admiral Sir Eliab Harvey.

On the opposite side of the road, but nearer to Abridge, is another fine estate, called Woolstons, or Wolverston, which appears at one time to have been a distinct parish, or at all events a very ex-

The Warren, the "great house," the old red brick house that stood in its own grounds within a mile or so of the "Maypole," the seat of the Haredales, is probably in part a creation of Charles Dickens's fertile brain; but it is popularly identified in the neighbourhood with a house between Woodford and Chigwell Row, which has been of late burnt down and rebuilt. The Warren, according to Charles Dickens, was attacked by the rioters because its owners were Catholics, and burnt to the ground. It will be remembered how Mr. Haredale found the mysterious murderer lurking among the ruins, and, with the help of the sexton, conducted his prisoner to Chigwell, and thence to London.

At the west end of the lane, by the church, stood at one time an old moated mansion, but faint traces are visible. Across the meadows to the left of this lane, adjoining the estate of Belmont, is a large modern mansion of red brick, which stands out pleasantly from amidst the surrounding trees.

The church is remarkable for its noble south Norman door, and for a fine brass of very late date (1631) to Archbishop Harsnett of York, who founded the grammar-school in this parish. The church, which is dedicated to St. Mary, is approached on the south side by two avenues of clipped yews, whose interlacing branches have imparted to them a close resemblance to the fan-traceried roof of the late Perpendicular period. One of these avenues leads up to the entrance of the chancel, and the other to the wooden south porch. The edifice consists of a nave and chancel, with north aisle, and a tower and spire at the western end. The chancel is modern, and several of the windows are filled with painted glass. The Norman doorway mentioned above is enriched with a plain zig-zag moulding, and the windows are mostly of the Perpendicular style. A gallery extends across the western end of the nave, and in the centre of the aisle is a private gallery, containing the sittings of the lord of one of the neighbouring manors. This gallery is approached by a wooden staircase built on the outside of the north wall, which does not add to the beauty of the building.

Among the monuments in the church is one to Thomas Coleshill, who died in 1595, having been " servant to Edward VI., Queen Mary, and Queen Elizabeth;" it bears the kneeling effigies of himself and his wife. The brass to Archbishop Harsnett is of the highest interest to antiquarians, seeing that it is the latest known example of an ecclesiastic of the Church of England, figured as habited in stole, alb, dalmatic, and cope. The figure of the archbishop is full-length, with mitre and crozier. The inscription on the brass, which is said to have been written by the archbishop himself, is in Latin, of which the following is a translation :—" Here lieth Samuel Harsnett, formerly vicar of this church. First the unworthy Bishop of Chichester, then the more unworthy Bishop of Norwich, at last the very unworthy Archbishop of York, who died on the 25th day of May, in the year of our Lord 1631. Which very epitaph that most reverend prelate, out of his excessive humility, ordered by his will to be inscribed to his memory." This brass was formerly on the east wall, but is now on the floor of the chancel.

" Samuel Harsnett," writes the author of " England's Worthies," " born at Colchester, was Bishop of Chichester, then of Norwich, and at last Archbishop of York, and Privy Councillor to King Charles. He founded and endowed a fair grammar-school at Chigwell. He bequeathed his library to Colchester, provided they (his books) were kept in a decent room, for the use of the clergy of that town. He dyed A.D. 1631."

" Dr. Harsnett," observes Mr. Coller, in his " History of Essex," " was the son of a baker in St. Botolph Street, Colchester; and probably at an early age the eloquent preacher and the future prelate might be seen dealing out from his father's counter the bread which perisheth, his humble parents little imagining he was destined to wield the bishop's crozier instead of the baker's peel. He was born in 1561, and having acquired some learning, was sent to Cambridge, where he made great progress. In 1586 he was elected master of the free school at Colchester, which, after a year, he resigned, and in 1597 became vicar of this parish of Chigwell, for which locality, being perhaps his first ministerial charge, he ever after felt a peculiar interest. Afterwards he became Archdeacon of Essex; and having had charge of various other parishes in the county, in 1609 he was made Bishop of Chichester. On being translated to the see of Norwich, in 1619, he was fiercely assailed by the Puritans, and was accused by the Commons of various misdemeanours. He triumphed over all, however, and in 1628 became Archbishop of York."

Archdeacon Paley was for a short time, about 1770, vicar of Chigwell.

The living of Chigwell is somewhat peculiar, being both a rectory, which is a sinecure, and a vicarage, to which the rector presents. From the year 1329 down to 1408, as we learn from Mr. Jones's local Directory already quoted, the rectory was in the hands of lay patrons, being held by the families of Goldingham, Bourchin, and Doreward. In 1432 John Doreward gave the advowson of this parish church and rectory to the priory and brethren of St. Botolph, Colchester, and they procured a licence to appropriate it to themselves and their successors, by virtue of which they presented twice to the vicarage; but in the reigns of Henry VI. (1451) and Edward IV. (1466) the rectors regained their right, soon after which Thomas Kemp, Bishop of London, founded a chantry in St. Paul's Cathedral, and endowed it with the advowson of Chigwell, and with lands here and at Great Clacton, united it to the office of confessor in that cathedral.

There are several local charities for the relief of the poor, and also three almshouses, called " Coulson's," founded in 1557, and rebuilt by public subscription in 1858; each occupant receives a small sum of money quarterly.

A club-room for working-men was built here in 1876, and is used for reading and recreation.

Near the eastern end of the churchyard is the grammar-school founded by Archbishop Harsnett in 1629. It had long been neglected, and its pupils had dwindled to a very small number. But it is now a spacious brick building, with good playground and class-rooms, and has been very greatly enlarged and improved under the provisions of a new scheme lately given by the Educational Commissioners and the Court of Chancery. Amongst the numerous ordinances made by the founder for the good management of the schools is the following :— " I constitute and appoint that the Latin school-master be a graduate of one of the universities, not under seven-and-twenty years of age, a man skilful in the Greek and Latin tongues, a good poet, of a sound religion, neither papist nor puritan, of a grave behaviour, of a sober and honest conversation, no tippler nor haunter of public-houses, no puffer of tobacco, and above all that he be apt to teach and strict in his government ; and all election or elections otherwise made I declare to be void, *ipso facto*, as if he were dead." The master was also directed to teach Lilly's Latin and Cleonard's Greek grammars ; for phrase and style he was to infuse into his scholars no other than Tully and Terence ; for poets, his pupils were to read the ancient Greek and Latin ; " no novelties nor conceited modern writers." The qualifications required for the other master were :—" That he write fair secretary and Roman hands ; that he be skilful in cyphering and casting of accounts ; and that he teach his scholars the same faculty."

William Penn, the founder of Pennsylvania, was educated at Chigwell, most probably at Archbishop Harsnett's school.

But the chief interest of Chigwell is centred in the " King's Head " tavern, opposite the church : a long plaster-fronted inn, with projecting storeys, fanciful gables, and small diamond-paned lattice windows—a building evidently dating from the Stuart era. " The King's Head " bears on its swinging signboard a portrait of Charles I., painted some years ago by Miss Herring, though the portrait is stupidly supposed by some to represent his father and predecessor, James I.

As we look on the pleasant front of this old inn we fancy that we can recognise most of the features of the old " Maypole " as described by Charles Dickens : through the red curtains of the " common room," by the light of the warm fire glowing within, we can almost see John Willett, the " sturdy " landlord, the " parish clerk and bell-ringer of Chigwell," with his rusty black breeches and coat,

and the rest of the convivial company who congregated here in the winter evenings, among whom, of course, were " Tom Cobb, the general chandler," and " Phil Parkes, the ranger." The large room on the first floor is still popularly known as John Chester's Chamber, in allusion, of course, to " Barnaby Rudge." In this room the Verderers' or Forest Courts were held till their abolition in 1855.

Everything about Chigwell is particularised in the most minute manner by Charles Dickens. Even down to " the clock of Chigwell Church, hard by the ' Maypole,' striking two at night," and poor brutish Hugh lazily loitering outside the " Maypole " door : in fact, the village and the whole neighbourhood figures largely in Dickens's historical romance of " Barnaby Rudge," which was originally published in " Master Humphrey's Clock."

Dickens was very fond of the village, and frequently visited it. " Chigwell," he writes to John Forster, " Chigwell, my dear fellow, is the greatest place in the world. Name your day for going. Such a delicious old inn opposite the churchyard, such a lovely ride (drive ?), such beautiful forest scenery, such an out-of-the-way rural place ; such a sexton ! I say again, name your day." The day was named at once, and the whitest of stones marks it in now sorrowful memory. " His promise was exceeded by our enjoyment ; and his delight in the double recognition of himself and of *Barnaby* by the landlord of the nice old inn, far exceeded any pride he would have taken in what the world thinks the highest sort of honour."*

The quaint old kitchen of the " Maypole " is the scene with which the story opens in " Barnaby Rudge ;" but the " Maypole " does not, and did not, really exist at Chigwell, though there is a " Maypole " at Chigwell Row, a mile and a half distant. Under Dickens's description of the " Maypole," the " King's Head " is really sketched in such a masterly style as to render its recognition unmistakable :—

" In the year 1775 there stood upon the borders of Epping Forest, at a distance of about twelve miles from London—measuring from the 'Standard' in Cornhill, or rather, from the spot on or near to which the 'Standard' used to be in days of yore—a house of public entertainment called the 'Maypole ;' which fact was demonstrated to all such travellers as could neither read nor write (and at that time a vast number, both of travellers and stay-at-homes, were in this condition) by the emblem

* Forster's " Life of Dickens."

reared on the roadside over against the house, which, if not of those goodly proportions that maypoles were wont to present in olden times, was a fair young ash, thirty feet in height, and straight as any arrow that ever English yeoman drew.

"The 'Maypole'—by which term from henceforth is meant the house, and not its sign—the 'Maypole' was an old building, with more gable ends than a lazy man would care to count on a sunny day ; huge zig-zag chimneys, out of which it seemed as though even smoke could not choose but come in more than naturally fantastic shapes, imparted to it in its tortuous progress ; and vast stables, gloomy, ruinous, and empty. The place was said to have been built in the days of King Henry VIII. ; and there was a legend not only that Queen Elizabeth had slept there one night while upon a hunting excursion, to wit, in a certain oak-panelled room with a deep bay-window, but that next morning, while standing on a mounting-block before the door with one foot in the stirrup, the virgin monarch had then and there boxed and cuffed an unlucky page for some neglect of duty. The matter-of-fact and doubtful folks, of whom there were a few among the 'Maypole' customers— as, unluckily, there always are in every little community—were inclined to look upon this tradition as rather apocryphal ; but whenever the landlord of that ancient hostelry appealed to the mounting-block itself as evidence, and triumphantly pointed out that there it stood in the same place to that very day, the doubters never failed to be put down by a large majority, and all true believers exulted as in a victory.

"Whether these, and many other stories of the like nature, were true or untrue, the 'Maypole' was really an old house, a very old house, perhaps as old as it claimed to be, and perhaps older, which will sometimes happen with houses of an uncertain, as with ladies of a certain, age. Its windows were old diamond-pane lattices, its floors were sunken and uneven, its ceilings blackened by the hand of time and heavy with massive beams. Over the doorway was an ancient porch, quaintly and grotesquely carved ; and here on summer evenings the more favoured customers smoked and drank—ay, and sang many a good song too, sometimes — reposing on two grim-looking high-backed settles, which, like the twin dragons of some fairy tale, guarded the entrance to the mansion.

"In the chimneys of the disused rooms swallows had built their nests for many a long year, and from earliest spring to latest autumn whole colonies of sparrows chirped and twittered in the eaves. There were more pigeons about the dreary stable-yard and out-buildings than anybody but the landlord could reckon up. The wheeling and circling flights of runts, fantails, tumblers, and pouters, were perhaps not quite consistent with the grave and sober character of the building, but the monotonous cooing, which never ceased to be raised by some among them all day long, suited it exactly, and seemed to lull it to rest. With its overhanging storeys, drowsy little panes of glass, and front bulging out and projecting over the pathway, the old house looked as if it were nodding in its sleep. Indeed, it needed no very great stretch of fancy to detect in it other resemblances to humanity. The bricks of which it was built had originally been a deep dark red, but had grown yellow and discoloured, like an old man's skin ; the sturdy timbers had decayed like teeth ; and here and there the ivy, like a warm garment to comfort it in its age, wrapped its green leaves closely round the time-worn walls."

The chimney corner at the "Maypole" was, of course, the head-quarter of village gossip—

"And news much older than the ale went round."

That the worthy host, John Willet, considered the "Maypole" the very perfection of what an inn should be may be inferred from the following dialogue which occurred between himself and a traveller whom he encountered as the latter was making his way towards the village :—

"'Pray,' said the gentleman, 'are there any inns hereabouts ?'

"At the word 'inns,' John plucked up his spirit in a surprising manner; his fears rolled off like smoke; all the landlord stirred within him.

"'There are no inns,' rejoined Mr. Willet, with a strong emphasis on the plural number; 'but there's a Inn—one Inn—the "Maypole" Inn. That's a Inn indeed. You won't see the like of that Inn often.'

"'You keep it, perhaps?' said the horseman, smiling.

"'I do, sir,' replied John, greatly wondering how he had found this out.

"'And how far is the "Maypole" from here?'

"'About a mile'—John was going to add that it was the easiest mile in all the world, when the third rider, who had hitherto kept a little in the rear, suddenly interposed :

"'And have you one excellent bed, landlord? Hem ! A bed that you can recommend—a bed that you are sure is well aired—a bed that has been slept in by some perfectly respectable and unexceptionable person ?'

" ' We don't take in no tagrag and bobtail at our house, sir,' answered John. 'And as to the bed itself——' "

In what follows the reader gets a glimpse of the interior of the "Maypole," painted in Dickens's own masterly style.

"Having, in the absence of any more words, put a sudden climax to what he had faintly intended should be a long explanation of the whole life and character of his man, the oracular John Willet led the gentleman up his wide dismantled staircase into the 'Maypole's' best apartment.

"It was spacious enough, in all conscience, occupying the whole depth of the house, and having at either end a great bay window as large as many modern rooms, in which some few panes of stained glass, emblazoned with fragments of armorial bearings, though cracked and patched and shattered, yet remained, attesting, by their presence, that the former owner had made the very light subservient to his state, and pressed the sun itself into his list of flatterers, bidding it, when it shone into his chamber, reflect the badges of his ancient family, and take new hues and colours from their pride.

"But those were old days, and now every little ray came and went as it would, telling the plain, bare, searching truth. Although the best room of the inn, it had the melancholy aspect of grandeur in decay, and was much too vast for comfort.

"No effort had been made to furnish this chilly waste, but before the broad chimney a colony of chairs and tables had been planted on a square of carpet, flanked by a ghostly screen, enriched with figures grinning and grotesque. After lighting with his own hands the faggots which were heaped upon the hearth, old John withdrew to hold grave counsel with his cook touching the stranger's entertainment; while the guest himself, seeing small comfort in the yet unkindled wood, opened a lattice in the distant window, and basked in a sickly gleam of cold March sun."

It would seem as if Dickens could never exhaust his pen in describing the comforts of this grand and quaint old inn. "Cheerily," he tells us, "though there were none abroad to see it, shone the 'Maypole' light that evening. Blessings on the red—deep, ruby glowing red—old curtain of the window, blending into one rich stream of brightness fire and candle, meat, drink, and company, and gleaming like a jovial eye upon the bleak waste out of doors! Within, what carpet like its crunching sand, what music merry as its crackling logs, what perfume like its kitchen's dainty breath, what weather genial as its hearty warmth! Blessings on the old house, how sturdily it stood! How did the vexed wind chafe and roar about its stalwart roof; how did it pant and strive with its wide chimneys, which still poured forth from their hospitable throats great clouds of smoke, and puffed defiance in its face; how, above all, did it drive and rattle at the casement, emulous to extinguish that cheerful glow, which would not be put down, and seemed the brighter for the conflict.

"The profusion, too, the rich and lavish bounty, of that goodly tavern! It was not enough that one fire roared and sparkled on its spacious hearth; in the tiles which paved and compassed it five hundred flickering fires burnt brightly also. It was not enough that one red curtain shut the wild night out, and shed its cheerful influence on the room. In every saucepan-lid and candlestick, and vessel of copper, brass, or tin, that hung upon the walls, were countless ruddy hangings, flashing and gleaming with every motion of the blaze, and offering, let the eye wander where it might, interminable vistas of the same rich colour. The old oak wainscoting, the beams, the chairs, the seats, reflected it in a deep dull glimmer. There were fires and red curtains in the very eyes of the drinkers, in their buttons, in their liquor, in the pipes they smoked."

Lord George Gordon, according to the narrative of the "Gordon Riots," as detailed in "Barnaby Rudge," was one of the visitors of the "Maypole" in March, 1780, a few weeks before he set London in a blaze. The stirring events of that eventful period form, indeed, the chief historical element in the above-mentioned novel. Thus Dickens writes: —"The 'Maypole' cronies, little dreaming of the change so soon to come upon their favourite haunt, struck through the forest path upon their way to London, and avoiding the main road, which was hot and dusty, kept to the bye-paths and the fields. As they drew nearer to their destination they began to make inquiries of the people whom they passed concerning the riots, and the truth or falsehood of the stories they had heard. The answers went far beyond any intelligence that had spread to quiet Chigwell. One man told them that that afternoon the Guards, conveying to Newgate some rioters who had been re-examined, had been set upon by the mob, and compelled to retreat; another, that the houses of two witnesses near Clare Market were about to be pulled down when he came away; another, that Sir George Saville's house in Leicester Fields was to be burned that night, and that it would go hard with Sir George if he fell into the people's hands, as it was he who had brought in the Catholic Bill."

To the readers of "Barnaby Rudge," the assertion that a century ago highwaymen and footpads were to be met with on the road between Chigwell and Whitechapel will be no news at all. This road too, probably about Stratford, must have been in Dickens's eye when he drew the following picture of the meeting of Barnaby Rudge and Gabriel Varden :—"And now he approached the great city, which lay outstretched before him like

bark of dogs, the hum of traffic in the streets; then outlines might be traced—tall steeples looming in the air, and piles of unequal roofs oppressed by chimneys; then the noise swelled into a louder sound, and forms grew more distinct and numerous still, and London—visible in the darkness by its own faint light, and not by that of Heaven—was at hand."

The following lines show us the same road under a different aspect :—"Everything was fresh and gay, as though the world were but that

THE "KING'S HEAD," CHIGWELL.

a dark shadow on the ground, reddening the sluggish air with a deep dull light, that told of labyrinths of public ways and shops, and swarms of busy people. Approaching nearer and nearer yet, this halo began to fade, and the causes which produced it slowly to develop themselves. Long lines of poorly-lighted streets might be faintly traced, with here and there a lighter spot, where lamps were clustered round a square or market, or round some great building; after a time these grew more distinct, and the lamps themselves were visible—slight yellow specks, that seemed to be rapidly snuffed out, one by one, as intervening obstacles hid them from the sight. Then sounds arose—the striking of church clocks, the distant

morning made, when Mr. Chester rode at a tranquil pace along the forest road. . . . In the course of time, the 'Maypole's' massive chimneys rose upon his view; but he quickened not his pace one jot, and with the same cool gravity rode up to the tavern porch. John Willet, who was toasting his red face before a great fire in the bar, and who, with surpassing foresight and quickness of apprehension, had been thinking, as he looked at the blue sky, that if that state of things lasted much longer it might ultimately become necessary to leave off fires and throw the windows open, issued forth to hold his stirrup; called lustily for Hugh."

     *   *   *   *   *

CHIGWELL ROW.

"It was a long time before there was such a country inn as the 'Maypole' in all England: indeed, it is a great question whether there has ever been such another to this hour, or ever will be. It was a long time, too—for Never, as the proverb says, is a long day—before they forgot to have an interest in wounded soldiers at the 'Maypole,' or before Joe omitted to refresh them, for the sake of his old campaign; or before the sergeant left off looking in there now and then; or before they fatigued themselves, or each other, by talking on these occasions of battles and sieges, and hard weather, and hard service, and a thousand things belonging to a soldier's life. As to the great silver snuff-box which the king sent Joe Willet with his own hand, because of his conduct in the Riots, what guest ever went to the 'Maypole' without putting finger and thumb into that box, and taking a great pinch, though he had never taken a pinch of snuff before, and almost sneezed himself into convulsions even then? As to the purple-faced vintner, where is the man who lived in those days and never saw *him* at the 'Maypole,' to all appearance as much at home in the best room as if he lived there? And as to the feastings, and christenings, and revellings at Christmas, and celebrations of birthdays, wedding-days, and all manner of days, both at the 'Maypole' and the 'Golden Key'—if they are not notorious, what facts are?

"Mr. Willet the elder, having been by some extraordinary means possessed with the idea that Joe wanted to be married, and that it would be well for him, his father, to retire into private life, and enable him to live in comfort, took up his abode in a small cottage at Chigwell, where they widened and enlarged the fire-place for him, hung up the boiler, and furthermore planted in the little garden outside the front-door a fictitious maypole; so that he was quite at home directly. To this, his new habitation, Tom Cobb, Phil Parkes, and Solomon Daisy, went regularly every night, and in the chimney-corner, they all four quaffed, and smoked, and prosed, and dozed, as they had done of old. It being accidentally discovered after a short time that Mr. Willet still appeared to consider himself a landlord by profession, Joe provided him with a slate, upon which the old man regularly scored up vast accounts for meat, drink, and tobacco. As he grew older this passion increased upon him; and it became his delight to chalk against the name of each of his cronies a sum of enormous magnitude, and impossible to be paid; and such was his secret joy in these entries, that he would be perpetually seen going behind the door to look at them, and coming forth again, suffused with the liveliest satisfaction.

* * * * *

"It was remarkable that although he had that dim sense of the past, he sought out Hugh's dog, and took him under his care; and that he never could be tempted into London. When the Riots were many years old, and Edward and his wife came back to England, with a family almost as numerous as Dolly's, and one day appeared at the 'Maypole' porch, he knew them instantly, and wept and leaped for joy. But neither to visit them, nor on any other pretence, no matter how full of promise and enjoyment, could he be persuaded to set foot in the street; nor did he ever conquer his repugnance or look upon the town again."

About a mile and a half to the south-east of the church is Chigwell Row, or, as it really ought to be called, Chigwell Rough,* a hamlet running along the high ridge which extends eastward towards Lamborne and Romford. Half a century ago one would have naturally described it as lying on the borders of Hainault Forest; but, thanks to the lax administration of the Woods and Forests, and the greed of the lords of the surrounding manors and other landowners, those pleasant glades have long since been disafforested and enclosed, and the beauty of the district is gone. It may have come to be called the "Row" because a series of villas and mansions were built along the north side of it, the south side being left open. It commands a fine view of the Thames from London to Gravesend, and over Kent from Shooter's Hill to the Knockholt Beeches near Sevenoaks. At its easternmost end is a "Maypole" Inn, but not the veritable "Maypole" of Charles Dickens's novel. One of the villas on the north side was occupied for some years by Mr. Thomas Faed, R.A., the celebrated Scottish artist; Woodlands, the only large house on the south, was the residence of the late Mr. Joseph Walford, Q.C., a man whose name will be long remembered in these parts, not only as a lawyer, but as a Toxophilite, and the life and soul of the Epping and Harlow Archery Balls.

Chigwell Row has lately been made a separate ecclesiastical district, and a church has been erected for its wants on some waste land, which abutted on the forest.

At the corner of Chigwell Row stands Bowls, the seat of the Stuart family. It probably derived its name from an old inn where bowls were played which once covered its site.

---

* Indeed, it is generally supposed that the word "row" is only a corruption of "rough."

The celebrated picture of "The Woodman," by Gainsborough, from which many prints and drawings have been made, was done from a hale woodcutter who worked for Dr. Webster, of Chigwell Row. Near Chigwell Row was a spring of mineral waters, of a purgative character. It was discovered about the reign of James II. or William III., and written up by Dr. Frewen, a native of Chigwell, but it never attained any great celebrity or popularity.

CHAPTER XLIX.

WOODFORD AND WALTHAMSTOW.

" A noble horde,
A brotherhood of venerable trees."—WORDSWORTH.

Boundaries of Woodford—Its Etymology—Its Subdivision—Descent of the Manor—The Manorial Custom of "Borough English"—Woodford Hall—Census Returns—Woodford Bridge—The Church—Claybury Hall—Ray House—Church End, Woodford—The Parish Church—Woodford Hall—Mrs. Gladstone's Convalescent Home—A Pauper's Legacy—Woodford Green—Congregational Church—The Union Church —Art and Industrial Society, and Social Institutions—Harts—Monkhams—The Firs—Prospect Hall—Woodford Wells—" The Horse and Well "—Knighton House—The Manor House—Noted Residents—Walthamstow—Its Area and General Appearance—Walthamstow Slip— Census Returns—Etymology of Walthamstow—Descent of the Manor—Highams—Salisbury Hall—Chapel End—Bellevue House—The Parish Church—Almshouses—Walthamstow House—Benjamin Disraeli's School-days—Noted Residents of Walthamstow—The Town Hall, and other Public Institutions—Hoe Street—Hale End—Marsh Street—St. James's—The Reservoirs of the East London Waterworks Company —Geological Discoveries—An Old Bridge—St. Stephen's Church—Whip's Cross—St. Peter's Church, Forest Side—Forest Grammar School.

ONCE more, as may be inferred from the lines which we have chosen as a motto for this chapter, we have found ourselves back amidst the dingles and shady groves of Epping Forest, of which there is still a considerable slice remaining within the boundary of the parish of Woodford. This is a very large and scattered parish, extending from Walthamstow in the west to Chigwell in the east, and from Chingford and Buckhurst Hill in the north to Snaresbrook and Wanstead in the south. The parish derives its name from the "ford" over the river Roding, where now is Woodford Bridge, on the road to Chigwell, but which once, doubtless, was in the midst of a "wood" of oaks and hornbeams. The river Roding, it may be added, was at that time of more importance than now, and is said to have been navigable for light barges as high above Woodford as Abridge.

Woodford includes the four districts of Old Woodford (or Church End, as it is popularly called), Woodford Green, Woodford Wells, and Woodford Bridge. Of these, the three first lie, in the order above named, along the high road from London to Epping. They are all remarkable for the broad belts or tracts of open woodland which skirt the road on either side, compelling the houses for the most part to retreat gracefully from the dusty highway.

The parish forms part of the Hundred of Becontree—the last hundred in the county Londonward. This hundred, with the privilege of baronial authority, anciently belonged to the monastery of Barking, but after the dissolution it passed to the Crown. "Woodford," writes Mr. James Jones in his local Directory, "was one of the seventeen lordships given by Earl Harold to the Abbey of Waltham, and was confirmed to that house by the Charter of Edward the Confessor in 1062. The canons of Waltham held it at the time of the survey; and when Henry II. converted the secular canons there into regulars, in 1177, he confirmed to them this manor, as did also Richard I. by his charter of 1198. Among other liberties belonging to this Abbey, they were permitted to assart their lands in Woodford and many other places, and enclose them with a ditch and a low hedge, that they might take of their woods at their pleasure; to have the forfeitures and assarts of their own men, to hunt the fox, hare, and cat, in the forest; that their dogs should not be repudiated." The manor and church of this parish continued in the possession of the abbots and monks of Waltham Holy Cross down to their dissolution, in 1540, when it passed to the Crown. In 1545 John Lyson had the property which, being exchanged with Edward VI., was given by the king to Edward Fynes, Lord Clinton and Tey, from whom it was shortly afterwards conveyed to Robert Whetstone, whose son, Sir Bernard Whetstone, succeeded him in the manor. In 1624 the property was conveyed to the Rowes, by whom it was sold in 1675 to Sir Benjamin Thorowgood, who was Lord Mayor of London in 1685, and whose son conveyed it early in the last century to Richard, Earl Tilney, from whom it descended (through the Tilneys and Longs) to the late Lord Mornington. The manor-house had been in the meantime disposed of, but the manor was devised by Lord Mornington to the present owner, Earl Cowley.

"The custom of the manor here," remarks Mr. Frederic Johnson, in Weldon's "Guide to Epping Forest," "is what is called 'Borough-English,' under which the youngest son inherits. Though the origin of this is not clear, it certainly prevailed greatly in the kingdom of the East Saxons. By its name, it has been observed to have been chiefly used in boroughs, as it is still at Maldon, in this county, and elsewhere; and the term English which stands near the church, was sold by Lord Tilney to Mr. Christopher Crow, by whom it was disposed of, in 1727, to the Hunts, from whom, again, it was purchased by the Maitlands. A few years ago the estate was bought by the British Land Company, who, after making various roads through it, sold it in plots for building purposes, and it is now known as the Woodford Hall Estate, the Hall itself being purchased by the

CHURCHES AT WOODFORD.

denotes its derivation from our Saxon ancestors. According to Littleton's 'Tenures,' it is very improperly called Borough-English. His words are: 'Some boroughs have a custom that if a man have issue many sons, and dieth, the youngest shall inherit all the tenements which were his father's within the said borough as heir unto his father, by force of the custom which is called Borough-English.' Upon which Sir Edward Coke makes this remark: 'Neither in an uplande towne can there be a custom of Borough-English, or gavelkinde; but these are customs which may in cities or boroughs.' "

The manor-house of Woodford, called the Hall, trustees of Mrs. Gladstone's Convalescent Home, and most happily utilised in aid of suffering humanity, mostly in the person of Londoners.

The parish of Woodford contains within its bounds some 2,150 acres. In 1821 the population was 2,700, which number had increased in 1871 to 4,600, and this again during the next ten years to upwards of 7,100. Woodford has two stations on the Epping and Ongar branch of the Great Eastern Railway, about a mile apart: one at George Lane, for Church End; and the other further eastward, in Snake's Lane, for Woodford Green and Woodford Bridge.

The hamlet of Woodford Bridge, as stated

above, is so called because it stands near a bridge across the Roding, which here is quite a pretty rural stream, making its way between green meadows and pollard willows, and looking as if it was the haunt of kingfishers and other aquatic birds.

A triangular village green, planted with tall elms, stands on the rising ground by the roadside, near Claybury Hill. Here a new church was erected in 1854. It is built in the Early English style, and forms an ornament. It is sad to record the fact that the beauty of this spot has been sadly spoilt by speculative builders, who have contrived to disfigure the green with most hideous and abnormal structures.

"The road over the bridge, leading to the pretty village of Chigwell," writes a local historian, "is one of the ancient Essex roads into Suffolk and Norfolk. Along this road probably the monks travelled when conveying from London the remains of King Edward the Martyr for re-interment at Bury St. Edmunds in 1013, and which, on their way there, were deposited for one night by the monks in a wooden chapel, or shrine, now the little ancient church of Greenstreet, or Greensted, near Chipping Ongar, Essex."

The following brief notice of this place appeared in the *Ambulator*, published in 1793 :—" Woodford Bridge, a village in the parish of Woodford, nine miles from London, on the road to Ongar, situated on a fine eminence, forming a very picturesque appearance. Near the bridge is a neat pump of excellent water, brought hither in 1776 at a great expense by the proprietor of the estate for the accommodation of the poor inhabitants ; and not far from this is a manufactory of artificial stone. Near the village is Ray House, the seat of Sir James Wright, Bart. (the proprietor of the artificial stone manufactory), and a pretty villa built by Cæsar Corsellis, Esq., on the site of a house that had been the residence of Mrs. Eleanor Gwynne, mother of Charles first Duke of St. Albans." But the abode of Nell Gwynne in this locality, it is to be feared, is not a very trustworthy tradition.

Claybury Hall stands on high ground southward of Woodford Bridge, near the green, and at one time commanded some extensive views of forest scenery. Towards the end of the last century the estate was enlarged by the then owner, Mr. James Hatch, who had purchased the mansion and grounds of Luxborough House, mentioned in the preceding chapter, the former of which he pulled down, and the latter, with some others, he added to his own demesne.

Ray House is still standing, in Snake's Lane, a little to the west of Woodford Bridge. It was formerly the seat of the Clevelands and Hannots, and was purchased in 1770 by the above-mentioned Sir James Wright, who was some time Governor of Virginia, and afterwards minister at Venice. The manufactory which he established here was for the production of artificial slates, " by a process he had learned at Venice." Lysons, in his " Environs of London " (1796), in speaking of this manufactory, says :—" This slate is used for covering roofs and fronts of houses ; for making pendent frames for hay-ricks and stacks of corn, and safe guards to preserve them from vermin ; it is also used for water-pipes and gutters. The buildings where the manufacture is carried on are of this slate, and were erected about thirty years ago."

The western end of Snake's Lane opens into the main road through Woodford to Epping. The principal part of Woodford, or Church End, lies a little to the south. It is a village of scattered mansions, nearly all standing in their own grounds. It comprises no regular High Street, and scarcely a row of shops.

The church, dedicated to St. Margaret, is, with the exception of the tower, a commonplace specimen of the Gothic style of architecture which was in vogue at the time of its erection, in 1817, when it was built on the site of a previous structure, ruthlessly demolished in the previous year.

There is a print of the old church as it was before it was pulled down in 1816, but it is very scarce. It was an irregular nondescript edifice, covered over with plaster, so as to conceal any distinctive features. The tower was surmounted by a cupola, and had small pinnacles at the corners, instead of being battlemented, as now. The present church, which is built of brick, coated with stucco, consists of a nave, aisles, chancel, and south porch, with the tower above mentioned, which has been left standing. The nave is separated from the aisles by six pointed arches, carried up to the roof, which is of open wood-work, supported by eight pillars, and surmounted in the centre by an octagonal lantern. The east window is filled with painted glass, containing figures of our Saviour, the four Evangelists, and St. Peter and St. Paul.

A monument in the north-east corner of the church commemorates Elizabeth Lee, Countess of Lichfield ; and there is a brass on the south wall to a Mr. Wynche, dated 1590. Near it is a tablet to the memory of Mr. Errington, who died in 1595. On the east wall is a tablet to the memory of a daughter of Sir Josiah Child, brought from Wanstead. A curious monument close by records a lady, Mrs. Anne Thelwall; and on the north wall is the monument to Mrs. Selwyn, grandmother of Bishop Selwyn.

At the south-west corner of the churchyard is a tall Corinthian column of veined yellow marble, surmounted by an urn. On the pedestal is a long inscription, setting forth that it commemorates "the ancient and knightly family of Godfrey, which flourished many years in the county of Kent," one of whom was Sir Edmund Bury Godfrey, whose murder excited much agitation in the reign of Charles II.* This monument, which was raised particularly to the honour and glorification of Mr. Peter Godfrey, sometime M.P. for London, who died in 1742, was designed by Sir Robert Taylor, and was erected at a cost of £1,500. The pillar has lately been restored and re-painted.

In the north-west corner of the churchyard is a mausoleum of the Raikes and Pelby families. Among other tombs and monuments to local worthies is one to Sir Thomas George, Garter King-at-Arms, who died in 1703.

On the south side of the church is a yew-tree of enormous growth; the trunk, at three feet from the ground, is over fourteen feet in girth, whilst its boughs form a circle of nearly two hundred feet. The local tradition is that this tree is as old as the church, but it probably is older even than the fabric which was pulled down in 1816.

On the north side of the churchyard stands Woodford Hall, a large and substantial brick mansion, surrounded by pleasant grounds. The house was formerly the seat of the Hickmans and Maitlands, but, as stated above, is now converted into a convalescent home for the poor of London. The Home was established by Mrs. Gladstone, whose name it bears, in 1866, at Clapton, during the cholera epidemic at the east end of London. In the following year it was incorporated with that of Mrs. Charlesworth at Snaresbrook, and was finally transferred to Woodford Hall in 1869. The institution will accommodate about eighty inmates, from either the hospital or sick-room, who may have been suffering from any form of disease not contagious. They are admitted free of charge. It may be added that this charity depends largely for its support upon voluntary contributions, and that the offices of the Home are at 30, Clarges Street, Piccadilly.

Connected with this parish are several other charities; those in money alone reach to about £80 a year, and some of them had a curious origin.

For instance, a pauper lunatic, one Sarah Ginn—a somewhat suggestive name for a pauper lunatic—having had a legacy bequeathed to her, which realised £59, it was assigned to the parish in consideration of her maintenance, together with an annuity to her husband. The said legacy, which was ultimately to revert to the poor of the parish, was invested in parish trustees, where it remains, and the amount of dividends is included in the distribution of bread to the poor at Christmas. Full details of the various charities in this parish, and also extracts from the old vestry-books, are given in Mr. Jones's "Directory of Woodford," from which we cull the following singular entry:—

"Walter Hickman, who died at Woodford Hall in 1540, bequeathed to Clement, his son, four of his best ambling mares, his best gown lined with fitches, and his russit gown lined with fox; to the church of Woodford he left ten pounds to redeem paschal money at Easter, so that everybody in the parish, when they came to God's board, might say a paternoster and an ave for his soul and all Christian souls."

In Weldon's "Guide to Epping Forest" it is stated that in one of the registers is an account of all the collections for charitable purposes (in the nature of briefs) made at Woodford during a great part of the seventeenth century, commencing in 1643. "One of the most remarkable," adds the writer, "is that for the benefit of King Charles's chaplains and domestic servants, collected about twelve months after he was beheaded. Their petition states that they, the late King's Majesty's domestic servants, to the number of forty, being in present distress, by reason that their sole dependence was upon the late King's Majesty, and that their means from the revenue of his late Majesty were still detained, upon some reason known to the committee, and could not be paid, they were therefore so necessitated that they could no wise subsist for the maintenance of themselves, their wives, and families; and they prayed the charity of all good Christians."

Woodford Green, around which are clustered the principal portion of the shops, hotels, and private houses, as well as one or two large and imposing chapels, lies about half a mile northward from the parish church.

The Congregational church, an ecclesiastical-looking edifice in the Gothic style, was built in 1873, and consists of an apsidal nave, aisles, transept, and a lofty tower and spire. The building will seat about 800 persons, and there are schools adjoining. "The history of the Congregational Church in Woodford," writes the

---

* See "Old and New London," Vol. V., p.p. 289-90.

author of the local Directory above quoted, "dates back to the latter end of the eighteenth century, when Christian men came from London, and preached the Gospel under a fine old tree which stood on the village green. This led to hiring a room for Divine service in Horn Lane, and in 1798 the first chapel was built, under the direction of two of the trustees of Cheshunt College, in which for a considerable time the students of the college

The village is well supplied with water by the East London Water Company.

Woodford has its Art and Industrial Society, which was formed in 1879, for the purpose of encouraging art and industry, especially amongst the poor. Numerous prizes are competed for each year, and the exhibitions are held annually, in Easter week, in the lecture hall at the rear of the Congregational Church.

MONKHAMS. (See page 463).

preached. This chapel is now used as the Mission Room, and is commonly known as the Old British School." In 1837 a new and much larger chapel was erected; but though it was again enlarged in 1862, and otherwise improved, it was taken down in 1873, to give place to the present structure.

The Union Church, so called from its members being composed of "Congregationalists" and "Free Methodists," was erected in 1869, on the site of a former chapel for the Independent Methodists. A conspicuous feature of the building is a tall clock-tower. The Wesleyans have a chapel in Derby Road: it was built in 1876. There are schools in connection with it.

Among other institutions which have been established at Woodford for the social improvement of the working-classes are the Musical and Horticultural Societies, the Becontree Philanthropic and Debating Club, and a "Young Men's Mutual Improvement Society." The "Temperance cause" is well supported here, for besides the Woodford Temperance Society and the George Lane Institute, which have been established for the purpose of affording the working-men of the district the means of social intercourse, mental improvement, pleasant recreation, and non-intoxicating refreshments, there is on the Green, near Higham Hall, a very large and conspicuous Temperance Hotel, or "coffee tavern," named after Sir Wilfrid Lawson, who opened it in May, 1883. It was erected under the auspices of Mr. Andrew Johnston, late M.P. for South-Essex. This latest addition to the public institutions of Woodford has given rise to the following epigram :—

> " All hops abandon ye who enter here:
>   The wicked Wilfrid haunts this watery cavern ;
> No wine, no whiskey, not e'en bitter beer
>   Flows through the channels of the Coffee Tavern.
> The steaming coffee and the fragrant tea
>   Are ready where each eye can plainly see 'em.
> ' Tea-total ' then let each incomer be,
>   And while ' Te Total' let him sing ' *Te Deum*.' "

Several good mansions standing within their widow of Mr. John Warner, a London banker, who left it to her son, Mr. Richard Warner, the naturalist, who here planted a botanical garden, and very successfully cultivated rare exotics. Mr. Warner was the author of "Planta Woodfordiensis," a work of great value to the botanist, though now a little out of date, as he follows Ray's system of classification and nomenclature ; and as several of the ferns which he describes more or less minutely are now extinct, the work is very much super-

THE " HORSE AND WELL," WOODFORD WELLS. (*See page* 464)

own grounds are still scattered round about in the neighbourhood of Woodford Green. The oldest of these, perhaps, is " Harts," which stands to the north-east. It was built early in the seventeenth century by Sir Richard Handforth, Master of the Wardrobe to James I., who is said to have been frequently entertained here when hunting in Epping Forest. The house was afterwards the seat of the Onslow family, to whom it was conveyed by marriage ; and here Mr. Arthur Onslow, sometime Speaker of the House of Commons in the reign of George II., was born. On the removal of the Onslows into Surrey, this estate was sold to a Mr. Sherman, a draper, of Cheapside. His daughter and heiress disposed of it to Mrs. Warner, the seded by the " Flora of Essex," by Mr. G. S. Gibson of Saffron Walden. " Warner," writes Mr. Thorne, in his " Environs of London," " was also distinguished as a book-collector, for his critical knowledge of Shakspere, and by translations from Plautus ; and did what he could to advance and perpetuate after his death the tastes he cultivated in life by bequeathing his fine library to Wadham College, Oxford, and a sum of money for founding a botanical lectureship."

Monkhams, the seat of Mr. Henry Ford Barclay, fronts the eastern side of the Green, which extends from his gates northwards as far as the new church of All Saints, the tall spire and fine proportions of which form a charming picture, from whatever side you view them. The church is modern, having been erected by subscription in 1874 ; it is of stone, and in the Early English and Decorated style. It was built from the designs of Mr. F. E. C. Streatfeild, and consists of a nave, aisles, chancel, north transept (used as a vestry), and tower surmounted by a shingled spire. The north aisle was added in 1876. The reredos, given by one of the churchwardens, is constructed of stone and marble, and is carved with a representation of the Crucifixion of our Lord. The east window, of stained glass, was the gift of Mr. Henry F. Barclay ; the organ was presented by Mrs. Barclay, and the font by Mrs. Buxton.

The Firs, on the west side of the Green, opposite Monkhams, is the residence of Mr. Andrew Johnston, who was the colleague of Mr. Wingfield-Baker in the representation of South Essex in Parliament from 1868 to 1874. Mr. Johnston served as High Sheriff of the county in 1881, and in the same year was chosen Chairman of the Essex Quarter Sessions.

Prospect Hall, by the side of the high road at the north end of the Green, is considered one of the finest brick-built mansions in the parish. It dates its erection from the middle of the last century, and was for many years the seat of Mr. Robert Moxon, by whom it was built. It was subsequently occupied as a school, at which time the south wing was added, but was subsequently converted into two private houses.

Woodford Wells, about half a mile farther north-ward, on the road towards Epping, and lying at the foot of Buckhurst Hill, is connected with Wood-ford Green by rows of humble roadside cottages, and a few villa residences of a better kind. The hamlet—which has a cheerful rural appearance, situated as it is just on the borders of Epping Forest—received its designation of Woodford Wells from a medicinal spring which appears to have been in repute about the middle of the last century. History is silent as to when or how it was discovered. The "Wells," however, have never reached the popularity attained by those of Hampstead, or Epsom, or Tunbridge, nor, so far as I have been able to learn, is their memory enshrined in any popular novel or comedy. In an "Itinerary of Twenty-five Miles Round London," published towards the end of the last century, the writer thus describes this locality :—"A mineral spring, which rises in the forest at a little distance from the 'Horse and Groom' [now known as the "Horse and Well"], was formerly in good repute, and much company resorted to drink the waters at a house of public entertainment called

'Woodford Wells ;' but the waters have long lost their reputation."

The house of public entertainment above referred to had been at that time converted into a private dwelling-house ; but the memory of the "wells" is perpetuated by an ornamental drink-ing-fountain, covered by a tall roof of enamelled slate, which has been erected over a well in front of some wooden cottages opposite the "Horse and Well" Inn.

Among the more important mansions at Wood-ford Wells are Knighton House, the seat of Mr. Edward North Buxton, one of the Verderers of Epping Forest ; and the Manor House, which was formerly used as the parish workhouse, but has been again converted into a private residence. This old house is said to have been once occupied by Robert Devereux, the celebrated Earl of Essex. Mr. James Thorne, in his "Environs of London," states that tradition has fixed upon Grove House, which stood west of Woodford Church, as having been a hunting lodge of the Earl of Essex, and adds, "but there is no authority for the assertion." Mr. Thorne gives the following particulars of Grove House :—"It was spacious, and some of the rooms were large and curiously fitted. One, known as the ball-room, had on the walls twelve paintings in tempera of landscapes and subjects of rural life ; the 'water-work' for the walls Falstaff recommends to Mrs. Quickly as a substitute for her tapestry. The house was taken down in 1832, and the site and grounds built over."

A few names of note occur among the residents at Woodford. The pious George Herbert, author of "The Temple," lived here for some time with his brother, Sir Henry Herbert, having removed hither for the benefit of the air when suffering from an attack of ague.

Woodford was the birthplace of Sydney Smith, the witty canon of St. Paul's, of the late eminent ecclesiastical architect, Mr. George Edward Street, and also of Sir Thomas White, who was Lord Mayor of London in 1877.

Sir James Campbell, who in 1649 founded a free school at Great Ilford, was a resident at Wood-ford, as also was Nicholas Lockyer, some time Provost of Eton, but ejected for nonconformity at the Restoration ; he died here in 1685. The Rev. Thomas Maurice, the author of a work on "In-dian Antiquities," and an assistant librarian at the British Museum, was for many years curate of Woodford.

Walthamstow, which adjoins Woodford on the west, is a very extensive parish, as may be inferred when it is stated in Kelly's "Post Office Directory of Essex" that it contains over fifty miles of road-way. It is bounded on the north by Chingford, and on the south by Leyton, and has a broad tract of marsh land towards the Lea, by which river it is separated from Middlesex. Altogether, the area of the parish is some 4,500 acres, some considerable portion of which is covered by the delightful wood-land scenery of Epping Forest. Its surface is pleasantly undulated; on the forest side are to be found many spots of sylvan beauty, particularly in the neighbourhood of the "Rising Sun," on the new road made through the forest from Whip's Cross to Woodford, on either side of which are banks and hollows, well overgrown or partially hidden among pollard oak, horn beam, and the luxuriant holly, evergreen in the winter.

Down to about a century ago this district was almost covered by the forest, which extended in parts almost close up to the river Lea; but in 1777 this was disafforested, and has since then been largely cultivated as pasture-land, which is now in turn being rapidly swallowed up for building pur-poses. A considerable portion of the parish, however, on the north side, around Chapel End and Hale End, two outlying hamlets, stretching away to the river Lea, are still broad belts of meadow land, through the centre of which winds the old road to Chingford and Waltham Abbey.

Previous to the embankment of the Thames near the outlet of the river Lea, the marshes here-abouts were frequently overflown, the water extend-ing at times to a mile in width. Even now, in very wet weather or uncommonly high tides, the marshes in the neighbourhood of Lea Bridge, at the south-western extremity of the parish, are sub-merged.

Running parallel with the entire southern boun-dary of the main portion of the parish, and divid-ing the adjoining parish of Leyton into two parts, is a long strip of land, concerning which there is a tradition that it was acquired by Walthamstow in a very singular manner. In a "History of Waltham-stow," published in 1861, the author observes:—"Tradition says that a dead body was found in the river Lea at this point, and that the parishioners of Leyton would not pay the expenses of burial; that in those days it was customary in such cases for the parish who buried the body to claim as much of the land from the other parish as those persons who carried the body could reach, stretching out their hands in a line, and walking together. They were allowed to walk from the point where the body was found to the greatest extremity of the parish, and claim the land; if so, they certainly availed themselves of the privilege, for they walked through Leyton to the Eagle Point at Snares-brook."

Walthamstow can scarcely be called a town, or even a village, but is rather a collection of distinct hamlets and clusters of houses, called "streets," or "ends," each of which is known by some par-ticular name—as St. James's Street, Hoe Street, Wood Street, Clay Street, Marsh Street, Hale End, Church End, Chapel End, Shernhall Street, Whip's Cross, Higham End, and Woodford Side. The principal part of the parish lies on the roads lead-ing to Waltham Abbey and to Woodford; it is about six miles from the churches of Shoreditch and Whitechapel, and there are four railway-sta-tions on the Chingford branch of the Great Eastern Railway in its transit through the parish, namely, at St. James's Street, Hoe Street, Wood Street, and Hale End. In 1871 the number of the inhabitants was a little more than 11,000, which almost doubled itself within the next ten years.

The more thriving parts of the parish lie on a pleasant slope, well sheltered from the east and north winds; and that its climate is mild may be gathered from the fact that two centuries ago, as we shall see, the vine flourished here sufficiently to produce good wine. It has already been mentioned that the eastern suburbs afford a curious contrast to those of the west and south-west of London, and Walthamstow is an instance in point. It has really next to no literary history; at all events, it figures scarcely at all in the biographical or historical anecdotes of the last two centuries. It has reared few poets, painters, historians, or men whose names have become famous: in fact, its annals are almost a blank; and possibly on that very account it may have been, and may be, all the happier.

The name of Walthamstow does not claim an entry in the Diary of worthy John Evelyn. Horace Walpole lived at its very Antipodes, as far south-west of Charing Cross as Walthamstow lies north-east; and probably, surrounded by his fair Lepels and Waldegraves, he would have disdained the vulgar city whose houses rose on the slopes on the east of the Lea. Besides, though everybody knew the Thames at Teddington and Twickenham, who had ever heard of the Lea, except in connection possibly with Izaak Walton, whom, doubtless, he regarded as having been a sort of myth, and quite out of society? In fact, though he was an occa-sional visitor at Wanstead House, Walpole pro-bably would scarcely have been sure whether Walthamstow was in Essex or in Hertfordshire.

The derivation of the name of the village is simple enough; for Stow, or Stowe, in the Anglo-Saxon, denotes a place, or, according to Halliwell's

Archaic Dictionary, "a place for putting things in," a word which still survives as a verb to "stow-away," and also as a substantive in "stowage." The term is common both as a suffix and a prefix; thus we have Longstow and Bristow (now Bristol), as also Stowmarket and Stow-on-the-Wold.

In the reign of Edward the Confessor the great part of this parish belonged to Waltheof, son of Seward, Earl of Northumberland, other portions being in the possession of Peter de Valoines, Ralph de Toni, and one Halden, "a freeman." Waltheof, it is recorded, defended himself bravely against the Normans; but having submitted to the rule of the Conqueror, was restored to his paternal estates. His bravery and eminent qualities appear to have stood him in good stead with William, for he not only received back his confiscated broad acres, but received in marriage Judith, the king's niece, and had conferred upon him the Earldoms of Northumberland, Northampton, and Huntingdon. Waltheof, however, in the end became drawn into a conspiracy to bring about the king's deposition, the secret of which he unwittingly confided to his wife, who, as the story goes, "having placed her affections upon another, betrayed him, and gladly communicated the intelligence of the plot to her uncle." The result was that Waltheof was condemned and executed. In the Domesday Survey this manor is entered as belonging to Waltheof's widow, the Countess Judith. Waltheof left two daughters, one of whom conveyed this estate by marriage to the above-mentioned Ralph de Toni, who was a son of Toni, standard-bearer to the Conqueror; hence the designation of Walthamstow Toni, which the chief manor bears to this day. It continued with this family till the death of the last heir-male, Robert de Toni, early in the fourteenth century, when it passed, by the marriage of his sister, who had inherited the estate, to Guy de Beauchamp, Earl of Warwick. The manor remained in the Warwick family till the fifteenth century, when it was conveyed by marriage to Thomas, Lord Roos. In the seventeenth century the manor was owned by Sir George Rodney, who sold it to Lord Maynard, with whose descendants it has since continued.

Besides the principal manor of Walthamstow Toni, there are four other manors in the parish, named respectively Low Hall, Higham Bensted, Salisbury Hall, and the Rectory Manor.

The manor of Higham Bensted, or Highams, belonged in the reign of Edward the Confessor to the above mentioned Halden the freeman. It would be not only tedious, but needless, to name its successive owners since that time; suffice it to

say that among them have been the knightly families of the Lovels and Herons.

Higham House, a large square brick mansion with wings, occupying a commanding situation on the north side of the parish, on the borders of Woodford, was built in the last century by Anthony Bacon, from whom it was bought by Governor Hornby. It is now the property of the Warner family.

The manor of Walthamstow Sarum, or Salisbury Hall, is situated at Chapel End, on the western side of the parish. It took the name of Salisbury from the unfortunate Margaret Plantagenet, Countess of Salisbury, under whom the manor was held by the Tyrwhit family. In the middle of the sixteenth century it was granted to Sir Thomas White.

Chapel End is so called from having had in former times a chapel there, dedicated to Edward the Confessor. The present church of this district, dedicated to St. John, is a plain, uninteresting structure, of "mixed"—*i.e.*, nondescript—architecture, and was built in 1829.

Bellevue House, a modern erection, is pleasantly situated near the borders of the forest. It is built of brick, with stone dressings, and has a semicircular portico supported by Ionic columns. The park and pleasure-grounds are extensive; they are beautifully wooded, and contain a fine lake. The house stands on an eminence which commands the vale of Lea, the forest, and a large tract of Essex, with glimpses of the scenery in Herts, Middlesex, Kent, and Surrey.

The parish church, dedicated to St. Mary the Virgin, stands in the district called Church End, about midway between the stations of Hoe Street and Wood Street. The church is built of brick, thickly coated over with cement, and is as devoid of architectural interest as could be wished by the most austere of Puritans. It comprises a nave, aisle, chancel, and an embattled tower at the western end, containing six bells. The building, which stands on the site of an earlier structure, was erected in the early part of the sixteenth century. Sir George Monoux appears to have defrayed the expense of the tower and north aisle, and to have built the chapel at the east end of it, in which he and Lady Monoux are interred; the south aisle was built by Robert Thorne, a merchant of London and Bristol, and the founder of the grammar-school at Bristol. The following inscription was formerly to be seen at the eastern end of the south aisle:—" Christian people, pray for the soul of Robert Thorne, with whose goods this syde of the church was new edyfied and finished in 1535."

In 1817 the church was enlarged, repaired, and "beautified," at a cost of upwards of £3,000; in 1843 £1,000 more were expended in remodelling the nave and in enriching the east window with stained glass; and in 1876 further alterations were made in the interior by reducing the hitherto unsightly galleries to about half their original proportions, converting the old-fashioned pews in the body of the church into open benches, and replacing the ceiling with a roof of stained wood.

The monuments in the church are interesting. Among them is one in the north aisle to Lady Lucy Stanley, daughter and co-heiress of Thomas, Earl of Northumberland, and wife of Sir Edward Stanley; it comprises a life-size kneeling effigy under an arch. On the east wall of the chancel is an elaborate monument to Elizabeth, Lady Merry, wife of Sir Thomas Merry, dated 1632. This monument, which was executed by Nicholas Stone, contains busts of Sir Thomas and Lady Merry, and also of their four children. On the east wall of the north aisle are brasses, with effigies of Sir George Monoux, the founder of this part of the church, and of Ann, Lady Monoux. Sir George, who filled the office of Lord Mayor of London, died in 1543; his wife died in 1500. The brass is also engraved with the arms of the Drapers' Company. At the west end of the south aisle is a large white marble monument, with statues of the deceased, life-size, to Sigismond Trafford, of Dunton Hall, Lincolnshire, who died in 1723, and his wife Susannah, who died in 1689. Dr. William Pierce, Bishop of Bath and Wells, lies buried in the chancel. A small tablet on one of the pillars commemorates Sir James Vallentin, sheriff of London, who died in 1870. There are also monuments to the Bonnells, Maynards, Coles, Lowthers, &c. The churchyard, at the north entrance to which is a fine elm-tree, contains a large number of tombs and monuments, one of which, to Thomas Turner, dated 1714, has a yew-tree growing at each corner.

In the Book of Chantries in Essex, under date of 1547, occurs the following entry:—"Lands and tenements put in feoffment by George Monoux, Gent., to the mayntenance of a priest to sing masse in the church there, and also to teach a few scholars there, during the term of twenty years; and one Sir John Hughson, clerk, of the age of forty years, and of good conversation, literate, and teaches a school there, ys now incumbent thereof. The said incumbent celebrateth in the church of Walthamstow; £7 yerely valew of the same doth amount to the sum of £6 13s. 4d.—rent resolute none—goods and chattles none."

In 1650 the commission appointed to inquire into the state of ecclesiastical benefices estimated the annual value of Walthamstow vicarage at £40, including tithes and glebe. The commission reports further that John Wood was their vicar; but that "he is questioned for his abilities, and is disliked by the greater part of the inhabitants, who will not come to church to hear him, whereby there is great distraction in the parish."

In "The Complete English Traveller," published in 1771, the author writes:—"From the architecture of the church at Walthamstow, it appears to have been first built soon after the monastery of the Holy Trinity in 1112, and probably by the same foundress, who was Matilda, the wife of Henry I. However, if it was not built at that time, it was at least soon after; but it has had so many additional repairs since that time, that little remains of the ancient edifice are to be seen." The author speaks of a gallery being at that time at the west end of the church, and adds, "but there are none in the side aisles."

Thomas Cartwright, afterwards Bishop of Chester, was vicar of this parish in the middle of the seventeenth century; and Edward Chishull, a learned antiquary and divine, was instituted to the living in 1708.

In Lyson's "Environs of London" it is stated that among the Cartæ Antiquæ in the muniment-room at St. Paul's cathedral, there is an order for the more solemn observation of processions at Walthamstow, bearing date 1328.

Close by the churchyard stands a picturesque row of red brick almshouses for thirteen pensioners, and also the Grammar School, founded and endowed by Sir George Monoux, whose monument we have seen in the church. Walthamstow is altogether well off for almshouses and charitable institutions, for besides those just mentioned, a Mrs. Mary Squires founded in 1795 almshouses for six poor widows, each of whom receives a certain yearly stipend; and in 1810 Mrs. Jane Collard founded ten almshouses for ten married couples, each couple receiving 4s. weekly. The charities in this parish amount altogether to rather more than £1,150 annually. St. John's Industrial Home, in Shernhall Street, at a short distance eastward from the church, was founded under the auspices of the Roman Catholic body in 1873, and affords a comfortable home and training in various useful pursuits for 150 boys. Shern Hall is a large and ancient brick building, standing in extensive grounds, and was for several years the residence of Cardinal Wiseman.

Walthamstow House, close by, is another large brick mansion, standing within its own grounds. It was built and occupied by Sir Robert Wigram, the second baronet, but has since been occupied as a school, and is now St. Mary's Orphanage.

It may interest many of our readers to know that Benjamin Disraeli, the future Prime Minister of England, was partly educated at a private school kept by a Unitarian minister, Mr. Cogan, at Higham Hill, in this parish.

The writer may be pardoned for quoting from his own "Life of Lord Beaconsfield" the following particulars of his lordship's schoolboy days :— "One of his schoolfellows still living tells me that

"He is said to have had Mr. Milner Gibson among his schoolfellows at the suburban academy at Walthamstow. He never went to either of our great Universities, and the knowledge which he picked up at school was fragmentary and out of the beaten path, though naturally it was subsequently enriched by Continental travel.

"It is remarkable that with both of his early novels he interwove a school-fight, in which an oppressed boy rises against his oppressor, and gains his revenge. Is it possible—or rather, is it not pro-

GRAMMAR SCHOOLS AND ALMSHOUSES, WALTHAMSTOW CHURCHYARD.

as a boy young Disraeli was not remarkable for his attention to his lessons, or for his fondness for classical or mathematical studies ; but that he was a great dandy, and also a devourer of curious and out-of-the-way literature, old romances, plays, and histories ; and that he would often keep the other boys awake at night by telling them all sorts of stories, which he would invent as he went along. 'The child,' in his case, 'was the father of the man.' He was shy and reserved, and would wander by himself in the glades of the forest hard by, his only companions being a book and his master's favourite dog. His holidays were doubt- less divided between his father's house in Blooms- bury and his grandfather's villa at Enfield.

bable—that this sketch was so far autobiographical, and that he fought his way among the boys at Walthamstow, having found the finger of scorn pointed at him on account of his Jewish origin?"

Besides the houses already mentioned, there are still several others to be met with in different parts, which, from their spaciousness, and the fact of their standing apart in their own grounds—to shun, as it were, the obtrusiveness of their humbler neigh- bours—clearly show that they were in former times the abodes of the flourishing and opulent citizen. Sir Charles Pope, Bart., had a villa here ; as also had Gwillim, the herald, as appears by his account of Queen Elizabeth's funeral, printed in the "Monumenta Vetusta." George Gascoigne, a celebrated poet of the reign of Queen Elizabeth, is, according to Lysons, supposed to have been a native of Walthamstow. Here, at all events, he lived late in life. The dedication of his "Complaynt of Philomeal" is dated from his " pore house at Walthamstow, the sixteenth of April, 1575."

Here lived Sir William Batten and his wife, Elizabeth, Lady Batten, who is frequently mentioned in Pepys' "Diary" as a gossiping friend of his wife, and as occasionally visited by the ill-matched

&c. He read all, and his sermon very simple. Back to dinner at Sir William Batten's ; and then, after a walk in the fine gardens, we went to Mrs. Browne's, where Sir William Pen and I were godfathers, and Mrs. Jordan and Shipman godmothers to her boy. And there, both before and after the christening, we were with the woman above in her chamber: but whether we carried ourselves well or ill, I know not, but I was directed by young Mrs. Batten. One passage of a lady that eate

FOREST GRAMMAR SCHOOL.

couple here. Lady Batten married for her second husband a foreigner with a title, possibly a Baron or Count Leyenberg, for as Lady Leyenberg she lies buried here. Her husband was a frequent companion of Pepys in his travels about London and its suburbs. The following entry in the Diary of the latter occurs under date May 29, 1661 :—

"King's birthday: rose early, and put six spoons and a poringer of silver in my pocket, to give away to-day. Sir W. Pen and I took coach, and (the weather and the way being foule) went to Walthamstowe ; and being come there, heard Mr. Radcliffe, my former schoolfellow at St. Paul's (who is yet a merry boy), preach upon 'Nay, let him take all, since my lord the king is returned,'

wafers with her dog did a little displease me. I did give the midwife ten shillings, and the nurse five shillings, and the maid of the house two shillings. But forasmuch as I expected to give my name to the childe, but did not, it being called John, I forebore to give them my plate."

It appears from Pepys' "Diary," July, 1667, that good wine was produced from a vineyard adjoining Sir William Batten's house here. "He did give the company that were there a bottle or two of his own last year's wine, grown at Walthamstow, than which the whole company said they never drank better foreign wine in their lives."

Pepys notes in the October following the death of his friend, Sir William Batten, recording also the gratifying fact that his body was carried from London "with a hundred or two of coaches" to its final resting-place at Walthamstow.

The Town Hall, in the Orford Road, a short distance southward of the church, was built in 1876; it is constructed of brick and stone in the "modern French" style, and contains offices for the Vestry and Local and Burial Boards. The building occupies the site of, and is in part incorporated with, an old hall which had been for many years used for meetings and public entertainments. The parish can also boast of its Working Men's Club and Institute, and a Social Club. A cemetery was formed here in 1872. It covers about eleven acres, and contains the usual mortuary chapels.

Besides the mother church of Walthamstow, the parish possesses four or five district churches, besides chapels for Roman Catholics and for the various denominations of Dissenters, among which the Congregationalists largely preponderate.

Hoe Street, or High Street, which crosses the parish from the Lea Bridge Road in the south to Clay Street in the north, was once the chief thoroughfare leading from Walthamstow to Stratford Langthorne Abbey, and thence over Bow Bridge to London. A large number of houses have been of late years erected close by Hoe Street Station, and there are also several good shops.

Hale End, the most northerly hamlet of Walthamstow, bordering upon Chingford Hatch, is for the most part open meadow-land; but a great part of it is laid out in plots for building. This district is said to have been named Hale End from one Thomas Hale, who was the owner of a large house there in the early part of the seventeenth century.

Marsh Street is one of the principal thoroughfares, east and west, through the parish; it runs parallel with the railway on its northern side, by the district known as St. James's Street, and so on towards the Lea and Tottenham. Many of the old-fashioned houses and shops in Marsh Street are giving place to new and more fashionable buildings. The Congregational Church in this street, erected in 1870, is a large stone building of Gothic design, with a tall tower and spire.

The St. James's Street district comprises a large collection of humble cottages, built mostly of wood, and a few houses and shops lining the roadway near the railway-station, a large brewery, &c.

St. James's Church, built in 1840, is a brick building with semi-circular headed windows, &c., but of no interest. St. Saviour's Church, in Markhouse Road, about half a mile to the south from St. James's, was erected in 1874, from the designs of Mr. T. F. Dolman, the cost being defrayed by Mr. Richard Foster and Mr. John Knowles. It is built of Kentish rag, in the Early Decorated style.

To the south-west of St. James's Street, and covering a large space of ground between the railway and river Lea, some 150 acres, are the reservoirs of the East London Waterworks Company, the construction of which was commenced in 1869. These reservoirs, which have the appearance of a miniature lake ornamented with tree-covered islands, are capable of holding 500,000,000 gallons of water. The formation of these reservoirs led to important geological discoveries, the subsoil being found to be very rich in remains of the pre-historical period, extending back to the time when the whole district hereabouts was fen and forest. The area, as we have already shown, formed a portion of the great forest of Essex, which, under the name of Walthamstow Forest, was disafforested in 1777. If history may be relied upon, wolves were met with there so late as the end of the fifteenth century, and early in the twelfth century it abounded in wolves, wild boars, stags, and wild bulls. From an account of the discoveries which were made during the formation of the reservoirs, and which appeared in a monthly magazine in 1869, we quote the following interesting particulars :—

"First underneath the turf is about two feet of clayey loam, a deposit from occasional floods; below this is an irregular bed of peat, usually about three feet thick, abounding in oak and alder timber, and hazel-nuts, now the colour of ebony; next comes a most interesting line of varying thickness, formed of white marly matter, being, in fact, the small shells and calcareous mud of the pools that once dotted the surface. The shell beds may be traced in winding courses, as the bottoms and sides of former shallow pools. The shells are in myriads, with both valves, and in their natural position, as on the banks of the Lea now. Besides the fresh-water shells, there are land shells, blown or drifted into the stream or pools. A pretty collection may readily be made of six kinds of snail-shell, five Limneas, three kinds of Planorbis, two of the Unio, and others : twenty-six species in all.

"But the shells were not the only creatures which resorted to the ponds of the old forest-marsh. In the marl, and a bed of clay and peat below it, there have been and are being found the following :—A few bones of fishes; a few bones of birds; the present ox; the ancient ox (*Primigenius*); the elk, determined by Professor Owen (see *Geological Magazine*, September, 1869; *Times*, September 17th, 1869); reindeer, fallow-deer, abundant; hog, horse, beaver, wolf, dog, goat; and lastly, the traces of man. We may mention two bronze spear-heads, one bronze arrow-head, one bronze knife, one iron sword, late Celtic, part of the bronze sheath of a late Celtic dagger, part of an armlet turned out of Kimmeridge coal, a pierced axe-head of stag's horn, a bone knife, a stag's horn club, various antique pottery, flint scraper, &c. Most of these objects have been sent to the British Museum, and determined by Mr. Franks. Cæsar records the existence both of the elk and the reindeer in the forests of Germany in his time. The remains above mentioned cover the whole historic period, but do not go further back." We shall have more to say with reference to the geological discoveries which have been made in what is called the London Clay when we reach Ilford.

Close by this spot there were formerly some extensive copper mills. These were bought by the Waterworks Company, and a canal made therefrom to convey the water from the former mill-stream to the filter beds. It is stated that in the formation of this canal the remains of anchors and boats were found in the marshes by the workmen. A large number of persons were previously employed at the copper mills. A coin was made there, having on it the figure of a lion, and the inscription, "British Copper Company Rolling Mills, Walthamstow—ONE PENNY."

Many years ago, in consequence of the frequent overflowing of the river Lea, a wooden bridge was constructed from about the foot of Syborne's Hill nearly to Lea Bridge, by which the inhabitants of Walthamstow used to pass on their way towards Hackney and London. In the place of that wooden bridge, which is stated to have been erected by Sir George Monoux, a large bridge of brick and stone, about a quarter of a mile in length, consisting of thirty-four arches, was built about a century ago.

St. Stephen's Church, in the Grove Road, is a large building of yellow brick, of Early English design, and was consecrated in 1878: it consists of chancel, nave, aisles, transepts, baptistery, and a small bell-turret. The "consolidated chapelry" of St. Stephen was formed in 1880 from the parishes of

St. Mary, Walthamstow, and St. Mary, Leyton, to meet the requirements of the district lying between the Orford and Beulah Roads on the north and the Lea Bridge on the south; the latter thoroughfare, which communicates with the forest at Whip's Cross, lies almost wholly within the boundary of Leyton. Here within the last few years building has been actively carried on, streets and terraces having sprung into existence with remarkable rapidity; and tramcars ply on the road between Lea Bridge and Whip's Cross.

Whip's Cross is at the extreme southern angle of the parish, and forms the entrance to the forest at the point where the roadway crosses through to the "Eagle" at Snaresbrook. It is supposed that Whip's Cross was so named from having been in former times the starting-point from which persons who were found stealing wood or deer from the forest were whipped at the cart-tail through Wood Street to Stoker's Corner. No doubt this whipping process was of frequent occurrence in former times: that is, if the thieves did not escape with their booty scot free. Among the Remembrancia of the City of London is a letter from Sir E. Phellips, dated in 1614, desiring the arrest of one Harte, as "the greatest destroyer of Deere in Waltham Forest," probably about this neighbourhood.

The church of St. Peter, at Forest Side, is a brick building of no architectural pretensions: one of those, in fact, which may be commended more for their usefulness than their beauty.

The Forest Grammar-school is pleasantly situated in an open part of Epping Forest, near Snaresbrook, but in Walthamstow parish, and forms a large and handsome range of brick buildings, with boarding-houses, spacious school-rooms, &c. This school, which is in connection with King's College, London, was founded in 1834 by a number of the resident gentry of the neighbourhood. There are about 130 pupils, and in each year two scholarships of £35 and £45 respectively are given. The chapel, which is of Gothic design, was built by subscription in 1856, and enlarged in 1874.

CHAPTER L.

SNARESBROOK AND WANSTEAD.

" Everywhere
Nature is lovely : on the mountain height,
Or where the embosom'd mountain glen displays
Secure sublimity, or where around
The undulated surface gently slopes
With mingled hill and valley—everywhere
Nature is lovely ; even in scenes like these,
Where not a hillock breaks the unvaried plain,
The eye may find new charms that seeks delight."

General Appearance of the Locality—Snaresbrook—The "Rights" of Commoners—The "Eagle" at Snaresbrook and the Eagle Pond—
The Infant Orphan Asylum—Merchant Seamen's Orphan Asylum—Christ Church—Almshouses of the Weavers' Company—Area and
Population of Wanstead—Its Boundaries, &c.—Etymology—Traces of Roman Occupation—Descent of the Manor—The Earl of
Leicester and Queen Elizabeth—A "Spa" at Wanstead—Pepys' Opinion of Wanstead House—Visit of John Evelyn—Wanstead
House Rebuilt by Sir Richard Child, afterwards Earl Tylney—Description of the House and Grounds—The Great Telescope—The
Maypole from the Strand—Death of Lord Tylney—Subsequent History of Wanstead House—Its Demolition—Wanstead Park secured
for the People by the Corporation of London—The Park, Gardens, and Grotto—Lake House, the Residence of Thomas Hood—Cann
Hall—The Parish Church—The Village of Wanstead—The George Inn—An Expensive Pie—Park Gate—Wanstead Flats—The Princess
Louise Home and National Society for the Protection of Young Girls—Dr. James Pound—The Maypole from the Strand—James Bradley,
the Astronomer—Admiral Sir William Penn—William Penn, the Founder of Pennsylvania.

NOTWITHSTANDING that the district through which we are about to travel is singularly flat, and that scarcely a "hillock breaks the unvaried plain," lying as it does on the southern margin of Epping Forest, it contains many charming spots of forest woodland, even if the scenery is too tame to be styled beautiful. The Roding meanders through broad green meadows, and in one part in its progress through Wanstead Park opens out into a fine expanse of water, dotted over with little islands. Hence Snaresbrook and Wanstead have long attracted crowds of pleasure-seekers from the metropolis during the summer months, and no doubt in many cases sent them back to the busy world of London with agreeable memories of the charms of country life.

Snaresbrook is really but a hamlet belonging to the parish of Wanstead, but we have taken it first, seeing that it lies nearest to Whip's Cross, the spot with which we concluded the preceding chapter. The forest at this point opens out in the form of a fan, crossed by two good roads, that to the right leading to Leytonstone and Wanstead "Flats," and the other direct on to the "Eagle" at Snaresbrook, on the Woodford Road. If, before the preservation of the forest was taken in hand by the Corporation of London, the "rights" of the commoners extended to gravel and sand-digging, they seem to have exercised those rights to the utmost extent in this part of the forest, causing the destruction of a large number of fine trees, principally oaks, and the formation of numerous cavities, which become ponds in rainy seasons.

The three principal features of Snaresbrook are the "Eagle" Inn, the Infant Orphan Asylum, and the large lake, known as the Eagle Pond, that fronts both of them—a sheet of water some eight acres in extent, which has been secured for public enjoyment, in the shape of angling and boating in summer, and for skating in winter. As late as the beginning of the present century herds of deer roved freely about the forest glades in this locality, whilst the large pond was a favourite haunt for waders and other species of wild fowl. But with the gradual encroachment which has been made on the forest in the way of "enclosures," Snaresbrook has become almost severed from it, whilst rows of "genteel" cottages and smart villas have of late years sprung up, forming a strong contrast to the few old-fashioned houses of the wealthy citizen of which the hamlet at one time mainly consisted.

The "Eagle" Inn, which stands by the side of the roadway at the eastern end of the great lake, has long been a well-known hostelry in this neighbourhood, and, with its large gardens and pleasure-grounds, has become a favourite resort of East End holiday-makers.

As to the "Eagle" itself, let it be noted here that birds have never been plentiful as signs of inns in this country, and of them, the "Cock" and the "Swan" are decidedly the most popular. The "Eagle" is of rarer occurrence, and when it does occur, it is generally in combination, as the "Eagle and Child," the "Eagle and Ball," or the "Eagle and Serpent." It is probably of heraldic origin, though here on the borders of the forest it may have been suggested as a sign from some local occurrence, in which that prince of birds played a prominent part. Mr. Larbord, however, in his "History of Sign-boards," omits all mention of the "Eagle" at Snaresbrook. Tom Coryatt, who travelled over a large part of Europe in the reign of James I., and wrote an amusing account of his travels, gives, in his "Crudities,"* a curious instance of signs representing birds in the neighbourhood of Paris, while in his account of the bridges which span the Seine he mentions one of them as being called the "Bridge of Birdes," instead of the Miller's Bridge, as formerly. He adds that the reason why it is called the Bridge of Birdes is "because all the signes belonging unto shops on each side of the street, are signs of birdes."

On the south side of the lake, with its grounds extending to it, stands the Infant Orphan Asylum, an institution which was founded by Dr. Andrew Reed, for the maintenance and education of the orphans of persons who in former times had "seen better days."

This charity was instituted at Hackney in 1827, and incorporated in 1843, after the completion of the present asylum, of which the foundation-stone was laid by Prince Albert in 1841. It was formally opened by the queen's uncle, Leopold, King of the Belgians, in 1843. The building presents a long front, with projecting wings, in the Elizabethan or late Tudor style. It is built of fine brick, pointed with stone, of which material also are the dressings throughout. The object of this institution is to "board, clothe, nurse, and educate (in accordance with the principles of the Church of England) poor orphan children, or the children of confirmed lunatics." It is designed more especially for such as are "respectably" descended, and many orphans of clergymen, of officers in the Army and Navy, of members of the medical and other professions, and of merchants once in affluent circumstances, have found refuge within its walls; none, however, are excluded whose parents have maintained themselves by their own honest industry, independently of parochial aid. The children are received from their earliest infancy, and can remain in the asylum till they reach the age of fourteen or fifteen years. Elections to fill up vacancies take place in May and November, and the average number admitted annually is about sixty. The number of orphans received into the asylum from its foundation till the year 1880 was 3,000. Nearly the whole of the yearly income is dependent upon voluntary contributions; it may, therefore, not be out of place to state that the head offices of the institution are at No. 100, Fleet Street.

Another very useful charity at Snaresbrook is the Merchant Seamen's Orphan Asylum, situated to the right of the Chigwell Road, a short distance beyond Snaresbrook railway-station. It was established in 1817 at St. George's-in-the-East, in the neighbourhood of Wapping, whence it migrated to the Borough Road. The present building was erected in 1861, from the designs of Mr. G. C. Clarke, and has been twice since enlarged. The buildings are in the Gothic style, of red brick, relieved by bands of black brick, and with white stone dressings. A tall tower and spire forms a conspicuous feature of the building.

The objects of this institution, which is under the patronage of the Queen, and the head offices of which are in Leadenhall Street, London, are the "boarding, education, and maintenance of the children of British Merchant Seamen deceased from all parts of the world." The income of the institution is about £8,000 yearly, and up to 1880 more than 1,400 children had enjoyed its benefits. The number of inmates at the end of 1882 was 270; the premises are available for 300 children. The addition of a chapel to the building in 1882 brought the Prince and Princess of Wales from London to inaugurate it.

By the side of Sprathall Green, which separates the hamlet of Snaresbrook from that of New Wanstead, stands Christ Church, a building of Gothic design, which was erected in 1861, as a chapel-of-ease to Wanstead parish. It has since been enlarged, and a tower and spire added. Some of the windows are filled with stained glass.

A little further to the south are the almshouses of the Weavers' Company, for twelve poor freemen and twelve widows. They were transferred hither about 1860 from the densely-crowded neighbourhood of Potter's Fields and Old Street Road, London, where the charity had existed from the time of its foundation, in 1725.

The parish of Wanstead, including the hamlet of Snaresbrook, covers an area of some 2,000 acres, and contains a population of about 9,500, having doubled itself since 1871. This number, however, includes the inmates of the Infant Orphan Asylum. The village lies to the right of the Chigwell Road, between it and the river Roding. It is about half a mile south-eastward from Snaresbrook station on the Ongar branch of the Great Eastern Railway, and seven miles from Whitechapel or Shoreditch churches. Wanstead Park stretches away on the east: the long level waste known as Wanstead Flats, some 800 acres in extent, lies beyond the village on the south, and Leytonstone bounds it on the west.

The name of Wanstead seems to be derived, according to Lysons, "from the Saxon words *wan* and *stede*, signifying the white place, or mansion."

---

* Coryatt's "Crudities," Vol. I., p. 29.

More recent authorities, however, observes Mr. James Thorne, in his "Environs of London," suppose it to be a corruption of "*Woden's stede*, or place," implying the existence here of "a mound, or other erection, dedicated to the widespread worship of Woden." Traces of Roman occupation have been found in the southern parts of the parish, in the neighbourhood of Aldersbrook, in the shape of a tesselated pavement, coins, ruined foundations, urns, pateræ, calcined bones, and other relics.

time of the Domesday Survey. After many subsequent changes of ownership, it devolved upon the knightly family of the Herons. Sir Giles Heron, a son-in-law of the great and good Sir Thomas More, held it at the time of the Reformation, and in consequence of his refusal to acknowledge the king's supremacy, he was attainted, and his estates confiscated. The manor of Wanstead remained in the hands of the Crown until Edward VI. granted it to Lord Rich, who made it his "country resi-

THE "EAGLE," SNARESBROOK.

These objects were discovered early in the last century, during the planting of an avenue in Wanstead Park. The piece of Roman pavement which was laid bare measured about twenty feet by sixteen feet, and was formed of small square coloured tesseræ, the centre of which was the figure of a man mounted on a horse, and surrounding it was a scroll pattern border. A small brass coin of the Emperor Valens, and also a silver coin, were among the objects discovered.

The manor of Wanstead was given in Saxon times to the Abbey of St. Peter's, Westminster, and the grant was confirmed to the monks by Edward the Confessor. Soon after, however, it passed— probably by exchange—to the Bishop of London, under whom it was held by Ralph Fitz-Brien at the

dence," and is supposed to have rebuilt the manor-house, then called "Naked Hall Hawe."

Here Queen Mary arrived on August 1st, 1553, on her way from Norwich to London to assume the crown; here she received the congratulations, more or less sincere, of her sister Elizabeth; and from hence she made her formal entrance into London on the 3rd of the same month.

The estate was sold in 1577 to Robert Dudley, Earl of Leicester, who enlarged and greatly improved the mansion, and who, in May, 1578, here feasted his royal mistress, Queen Elizabeth, for several days during the time that he was basking in her favour. For the entertainment of her Majesty on this occasion, Philip Sidney condescended to task a genius worthy of better things with the composition of a masque in celebration of her beauties and royal virtues, entitled "The Queen of May." "In defence of this public act of adulation," writes Miss Aikin, "the young poet had probably the particular request of his uncle and patron to plead, as well as the common practice of the age ; but it must still be mortifying, under any circumstances, to record the abasement of such a spirit to a level with the vulgar herd of Court flatterers."

From Wanstead the virgin queen continued her

not particularised, were valued at £11 13s. 4d. The library, consisting of only an old Bible, the Acts and Monuments, "old and torn," seven Psalters, and a Service Book, was estimated at 13s. 8d. The horses, however, were more numerous, or of good breed, for they were valued at £316 0s. 8d.

On the death of the earl, in 1558, Wanstead, with other lands in the adjoining parishes, became the property of the countess, his widow, who afterwards married Sir Christopher Blount ; but by some family arrangement this manor became vested

WANSTEAD HOUSE. *(From an Old View.)*

"progress" through Essex and Suffolk to Norwich, where she was received with great enthusiasm. At Wanstead, in September of the same year, Leicester publicly married Lettice, Lady Essex, a private marriage having previously been performed at Kenilworth.

At the time of his death, in 1588, the earl was much involved in debt, and in consequence an inventory and estimate was taken of all his property, real and personal. From this it would appear that Wanstead House was not very elegantly furnished, for the entire contents of the mansion, including library, pictures, and furniture, and also the horses, &c., were valued at only £1,119 6s. 6d. The pictures, among which were three portraits of Henry VIII., the Queens Mary and Elizabeth, Lady Rich, and thirty-six others

in Charles Blount, Earl of Devonshire, on whose death, in 1606, it appears to have escheated to the Crown. In the autumn of 1607 James I. spent some time here, after his return from a western progress. The manor of Wanstead afterwards became the property of George, Marquis of Buckingham, from whom, in 1619, it was purchased by Sir Henry Mildmay, Master of the Jewel Office. Sir John Chamberlain, a courtier of the reign of James I., under date London, August 23, 1619, writes to Sir Dudley Carleton at the Hague :— "We have great noise here of a new spa or spring of this nature found lately about Wanstead, in Essex, and much running there is to it daily by both lords and ladies and other great company, so that they have almost drawn it dry already ; and if it should hold on, it would put down the waters of Tunbridge, which for these three or four years have been much frequented, insomuch that they who have seen both say it is not inferior to the spa for good company, numbers of people, and other appurtenances." The spring, however, would seem to have passed out of fashion, and so out of memory also.

The estate subsequently became forfeited to the Crown, but was granted by Charles II. to his brother James, Duke of York, and he transferred it to Sir Robert Brookes, who was here visited by Samuel Pepys. The genial gossiper writes in his "Diary," under date of May 14, 1665 :—"To church, it being Whit Sunday ; my wife very fine in a new yellow bird's-eye hood, as the fashion is now. I took a coach, and to Wanstead, the house where Sir H. Mildmay died, and now Sir Robert Brookes lives, having bought it of the Duke of York, it being forfeited to him : a fine seat, but an old-fashioned house, and being not full of people, looks flatly."

Sir Robert Brookes, who was for some time M.P. for Aldborough, in Suffolk, held this manor from 1662 to 1667. He afterwards retired to France, and died there in bad circumstances. From a letter among the Pepys MSS., Sir Robert appears to have been drowned in the river at Lyons. As we learn from Pepys' "Diary" (April 17, 1667), there appears to have been some talk of Admiral Sir William Penn, the father of the founder of Pennsylvania, becoming the purchaser of Wanstead House. Under date of May 1, Pepys writes :— "Sir W. Pen did give me an account this afternoon of his design of buying Sir Robert Brookes's fine house at Wanstead : which I so wondered at, and did give him reasons against it, which he allowed of, and told me that he did intend to pull down the house, and build a less, and that he should get £1,500 by the old house, and I know not what fooleries. But I will never believe he ever intended to buy it, for my part, though he troubled Mr. Ganden to go and look upon it, and advise him in it."

From the Mildmays, Wanstead passed by sale to Sir Josiah Child, who spent a large portion of his fortune in improving the grounds, by planting fresh trees and forming canals and a lake. Under date of March 16, 1683, John Evelyn writes in his " Diary":—"I went to see Sir Josiah Child's prodigious cost in planting walnut-trees about his seate, and making fish-ponds, many miles in circuit in Epping Forest, in a barren spot, as oftentimes these suddenly monied men for the most part seate themselves. He, from a merchant's apprentice and management of the East India Company's Stock, being ariv'd to an estate ('tis said) of £200,000, and lately married his daughter to the eldest sonn of the Duke of Beaufort, late Marquis of Worcester, with £50,000 portional present and various expectations." And again, under the same date :—" I din'd at Mr. Houblon's, a rich and gentile French merchant, who was building a house in the Forest, neare Sir J. Child's, in a place where the late Earle of Norwich dwelt some time, and which came from his lady, the widow of Mr. Baker. It will be a pretty villa, about 5 miles from White-chapell."

Sir Josiah Child was an alderman and goldsmith of London, and the founder of Child's Bank, at Temple Bar.* He died in 1699, and was buried in the old church at Wanstead. His son and successor, Sir Richard Child, was successively created Baron Newton and Viscount Castlemaine and Earl Tylney. He pulled down the old house, and built a new mansion near its site, called Wanstead House. This building, according to the "Complete English Traveller" (1771), was regarded a century ago as "one of the most elegant houses in England, both for the building and the gardens." In fact, it was a palace nearly equal to Canons in its palmy days, if not superior to it. The writer describes it thus in detail :—" It is constructed according to the best rules in the Corinthian order, and the front entirely of Portland stone. The portico in the centre is supported by pillars of the Corinthian order, and under it is the landing place that leads to the great hall, where there are a vast variety of ornaments and paintings by the best masters in Italy. The dining-room is on the left of the hall, being twenty-four feet square, and adjoining to it is the drawing-room, of the same size. On the right of the hall is another dining-room, twenty-five feet square, and a drawing-room thirty by twenty-five. On the chimney-piece of the drawing-room is the representation of an eagle taking up a snake, elegantly cut in white marble ; and from this room is an entrance to the bed-chamber, from which is a passage into the ball-room, which is seventy-five by twenty-seven feet, and connects the whole front line of apartments.

" The spacious gardens were laid out before the house was begun, and are extremely elegant.

" Mr. Campbell, the author of 'Vitruvius Britannicus,' was the architect employed in contriving this noble house, or rather, palace ; and although in particular parts it has beauties exceeding many of the best houses in the kingdom, yet when all the parts are taken together, it seems to want some of that proportion necessary to set off the whole."

---

* See "Old and New London," Vol. I., p. 36.

The author adds that the present lord has resided many years in Italy, without any prospect of returning to England, and much regrets the fact that so magnificent a palace should be uninhabited, and left to the care of a handful of servants. As Lord Tylney had no heirs, he augurs that ere long the estate will pass into the hands of some other family, who will prefer English freedom to Italian slavery. He was not far out in his guess; for a few years afterwards Wanstead passed to Sir James Long, who took the name of Tylney.

I have said that Wanstead House was a palace; and in order to justify my words, I add some details of the building. The principal front of the house was 260 feet in length, and in the tympanum of the grand portico in the centre were the arms of the Tylney family, finely sculptured. The building itself consisted of two storeys, the uppermost containing the ball-room, state bed-chambers, and other principal apartments. The great hall was lavishly decorated. The ceiling, by Kent, was gilt, and enriched with paintings of Morning, Noon, Evening, and Night. The walls were ornamented with paintings from Roman history, by Cassali, representing Coriolanus and his mother Porsenna, and Pompey's last interview with his family. Here also were two large statues, brought from the ruins of Herculaneum—one of Domitian, and the other of Livia, the wife of Agrippa. The ball-room was magnificently fitted up, according to the taste of the last century, the furniture being richly embossed and gilt, and the walls hung with tapestry. The latter represented the story of Telemachus and the battles of Alexander. Over the chimney was a fine painting of Portia, the wife of Brutus, by Schalken. In the saloon were several statues, and also a picture of Pandora, by Nollekens, the father of the sculptor of that name. The remaining rooms contained a large number of paintings by the best masters, including Guido, Titian, and Lely.

Lord Tylney, though he lived so much abroad, appears to have been very proud of his new mansion; at all events, Horace Walpole writes thus of him and the place in a letter to Richard Bentley, dated 17th July, 1755:—" I dined yesterday at Wanstead; many years have passed since I saw it. The disposition of the house and prospect are better than I expected, and very fine. The garden—which, they tell you, cost as much as the house, that is, £100,000—is wretched; the furniture fine, but without taste. The present earl is the most generous creature in the world; in the first chamber I entered he offered me four marble tables that lay in cases about the room. I compounded, after forty refusals of everything I commended, to bring away only a haunch of venison. I believe he has not had so cheap a visit a good while. I commend myself as I ought; for, to be sure, there were twenty ebony chairs, and a couch, and a table, and a glass, that would have tried the virtue of a philosopher of double my size."

On the death of the earl, without issue, in 1784, this manor, with other large estates, devolved upon his nephew, Sir James Tylney-Long, Bart., of Draycot, Wiltshire, whose only son, James, a minor, succeeded to the baronetcy and estates in the year 1794. He died shortly after, when Wanstead became the property of his sister, Miss Tylney-Long, also a minor, who thus became one of the richest heiresses in England. During her minority Wanstead House was taken as the residence of the Prince de Condé. Louis XVIII. and other members of the exiled Bourbon family also occasionally lived here during that time.

There were many suitors for the hand of the young heiress, and the prize was eventually won by the Hon. William Pole-Wellesley, elder son of Lord Maryborough, afterwards Earl of Mornington. They were married amid great ceremony at St. James's Church, Piccadilly, on the 14th of March, 1812, when he assumed the additional names of Tylney and Long. The following details of the dresses worn by the bride and bridegroom, and other particulars of the wedding, culled from the newspapers of the time, may interest some of our readers. The dress of the bride, we are told, consisted of a robe of real Brussels point lace, placed over white satin; the bonnet was made of Brussels lace, ornamented with two ostrich feathers; she likewise wore a deep lace veil and a white satin pelisse trimmed with swansdown. The dress cost 700 guineas, the bonnet 150, and the veil 200. Mr. Pole-Wellesley wore a plain blue coat with yellow buttons, a white waistcoat, buff breeches, and white silk stockings. The lady's jewels consisted principally of a brilliant necklace and earrings; the former cost 25,000 guineas. Every domestic in the family of Lady Catherine Long, the bride's mother, was liberally provided for. The fortune remaining to Mrs. Tylney-Long-Pole-Wellesley, after allowing for considerable sums given as an additional portion to each of the Miss Longs, and an annuity to Lady Catherine, was £80,000 per annum.

At the time of the marriage Mr. Wellesley is said to have been deeply in debt, and matters seemed to have gone from bad to worse afterwards, for in the course of a few years, by reckless expenditure, he contrived to get through the whole of his recently acquired fortune, and had so encumbered the estates, that in June, 1822, the whole of the contents of Wanstead House were swept away under the hammer of the celebrated auctioneer, George Robbins, of King Street, Covent Garden. The sale produced as much excitement as the dispersal of the contents of Strawberry Hill by the same auctioneer, just twenty years later; it lasted thirty-two days, and realised the sum of £41,000. No purchaser could be found for the house as it stood, so it was accordingly taken down, the materials being sold in separate lots. Among the objects of antiquarian interest disposed of were the celebrated ebony chairs and sofa, once the boasted *gems* of Queen Elizabeth, and which are so particularly mentioned by Horace Walpole in one of his letters for their singular beauty and antique character. After experiencing various transfers and vicissitudes of fortune, these articles came into the possession of Lord Tylney. They were purchased at the sale here by Graham, of Waterloo Place, by whom they were afterwards sold to Lord Macdonald.

At the sale of the contents of the mansion the family portraits were reserved; but even these subsequently shared a similar fate, for they, too, were sold in 1851, at the auction-rooms of Messrs. Christie and Manson, "in consequence of the non-payment of expenses for warehousing-room." Their dispersion was the last event in the history of Wanstead House, which once had vied with Canons in its glories, and now came to share the same fate.

On the death of his uncle, in 1842, and the consequent accession of his father to the earldom of Mornington, Mr. Pole-Tylney-Long-Wellesley became Viscount Wellesley; and three years later, on the death of his father, he succeeded to the title of Earl of Mornington, and became head of the noble house of Wellesley. His marriage with the rich heiress of Wanstead turned out to be altogether an ill-assorted union. He not only treated her shamefully, but spent all her princely fortune, and she died, it is said, of a broken heart three years after the sale of her goods and the destruction of her house.

Mr. Wellesley, notwithstanding all his reverses, did not long remain a widower; for, perhaps with the view of retrieving his shattered fortunes, in 1828 he married, as his second wife, a daughter of Colonel Thomas Paterson. The death of this lady in 1869 was thus commented on in the *Athenæum* at the time:—"The Countess of Mornington, widow of the notorious William Pole-Tylney-Long-Wellesley, Earl of Mornington, who died recently, in her seventy-sixth year, adds an incident to the romance of the Peerage. After the ruin into which the reckless earl's affairs fell, some

forty years ago, this lady was for a brief time an inmate of St. George's Workhouse, and more than once had to apply at police-courts for temporary relief. Yet she might have called monarchs her *cousins*. She was descended from the grandest and greatest of all the Plantagenets. Her mother (wife of Colonel Paterson), Ann Porterfield of that ilk, came, through the houses of Boyd, Cunningham, Glencairn, and Hamilton, from Mary Stuart, daughter of King James II. of Scotland, and seventh in descent from Edward I. of England. The earldom of Mornington, extinct in the elder line of the Wellesleys, has lapsed to the Duke of Wellington." The manor of Wanstead, with some adjacent lands, became the property of another Wellesley, Lord Cowley.

"In the latter part of the eighteenth century," writes the author of "Provincial Excursions" in 1843, "Wanstead House still displayed all the splendour which the Childs, the Tylneys, and the Longs, had lavished upon a palace fit for the abode of gentle and royal blood. Little did I dream that in one quarter of a century I should see its proud columns prostrate in the dust, its decorations annihilated, its pictures and sculptures dispersed by the magic of the hammer; at one period simply a deserted mansion, at another a refuge for exiled princes; then for a brief space polluted by riot and profligacy; and ultimately its lawns and gardens swept away, its stately groves and avenues remorselessly destroyed, and myself present at the sad catastrophe. Such, however, were its short and painful annals; and, except the grotto, not one stone now remains upon another. The palace, destined to stand for ages, and on which time had made no inroads, was removed, with the approbation of the Lord Chancellor, when little more than a hundred winters had passed over it: when its features were just mellowed, its woods and plantations in full luxuriance, and all around it smiling in perfection. Wanstead House was the most attractive object (of its kind) near London, and a national ornament." And the writer goes on to lament that the Government did not purchase it for some national institution, scientific or educational, adding his belief that it would not have been allowed to perish if its walls had been covered with ivy, and the fabric been in the last stage of decay. "I was familiar," he adds, "with every little bower and secluded avenue; I knew where its blossoms were fairest and the fruits choicest; could thread the mazes of its delightful foliage and exotic gardens, its limpid waters, and its verdant lawns, all which I have visited at dawn and at sunset, in midday and at night."

Mr. Rush, the American Minister, in his "Diary from 1817 to 1825," writes thus of Wanstead House:—"With our boys we visited Wanstead House, in Essex, the superb dwelling of Wellesley Pole, before it was stripped of its furniture and the whole pulled down; the bare mention of which house makes me remind you of what * * * * told us the rich proprietor once told him: that no wonder he was brought to the hammer, when every one knew that to keep it up with its accustomed hospitality, adding the carriages and servants necessary for the London season, when Parliament was sitting, required at least seventy thousand sterling a year, when all that he had was but sixty thousand."

The park and gardens are thus described by Mr. William Tegg, in his "Sketch of Wanstead Park" (1882):—"In the avenue which led from the grand front of the house to Leytonstone, but which has since had a road cut through it, is a circular piece of water, which seemed equal to the length of the front. On each side of the approach to the house was a marble statue: on the one side Hercules, and on the other side Omphale. To compensate, as it were, for the defect of wings, obelisks and vases extended alternately to the house. The garden front had no portico, but a pediment enriched with a bas-relief, and supported by six three-quarter columns. From this front was an easy descent to the river Roding, which was formed into canals; and beyond it the walks and wildernesses rose up the hill, as they sloped downwards before. A grotto, consisting of shells, pebbles, fossils, and rare stones, looking glasses, and a fine painted window, &c., with domed roof, built at an immense expense by the late Countess of Mornington, is now the only remaining monument of this finely-situated estate."

The outlying portions of what once was the estate of Lord Tylney, after lying waste for years, were purchased from Lord Cowley by the Corporation of London, and conveyed to the Epping Forest Committee, in trust for the public. They have been laid out as a "park" for the people, and were publicly inaugurated as such in August, 1882.

The park includes two or three lakes, with islands, on which the moor-hens and other aquatic birds build their nests, and at the end furthest from the high road a heronry. Near this is the grotto mentioned above: it is much larger than Pope's grotto, which we described at Twickenham.* It is often said that the cost of erecting it was no less than £40,000: but it is to be hoped that this is an exaggeration. In the "Beauties of England" it is stated that the cost of the construction of this grotto was £2,000, independently of its costly materials.

The main feature of the park is its wild and rustic appearance, the wood being thick and picturesque. Nearly all the ponds are plentifully stocked with fish, and especially perch, and their surface abounds with water-lilies. The Corporation secured this park of 184 acres by an exchange of fifty acres of land scattered about and a payment of £8,000 to Lord Cowley, the latter putting up fences to shut them off from the rest of his estate, and making a road a mile long to give access to them at either end, to Forest Gate Station on one side, and Leytonstone on the other.

At a short distance to the south-west of the site of Wanstead House stood a building called Lake House, which was the last appendage of the mansion, for which it was originally built as a banqueting-hall or summer-house. In it, from 1832 to 1835, Thomas Hood, the author, resided. The house was more generally called the Russian Farm. In a description of the building given by Thomas Hood, junior, in a memoir of his father, the author writes:—"The fact was, it had formerly been a sort of banqueting-hall to Wanstead Park, and the rest of the house was sacrificed to one great room, which extended all along the back. There was a beautiful chimney-piece, carved in fruit and flowers by Grinling Gibbons, and the ceiling bore traces of painting. Several quaint Watteau-like pictures of the Seasons were panelled on the walls. But it was all in a shocking state of repair, and in the twilight the rats used to come and peep out of the holes in the wainscot. There were two or three windows on each side, while a door in the middle opened on a flight of steps leading into a pleasant wilderness of a garden, infested by hundreds of rabbits from the warren close by. From the windows you could catch lovely glimpses of forest scenery, especially one fine aspen avenue. In the midst of the garden lay the little lake from which the house took its name, surrounded by high masses of rhododendrons." Here Hood wrote the novel of "Tylney Hall," much of the descriptive scenery being taken from Wanstead and its neighbourhood; and here he also wrote a little volume containing the poem entitled the "Epping Hunt," from which we have quoted largely in a previous chapter.*

The estate and manor of Canons Hall, now known as Cann Hall, which lies to the south of the

---

site of the Lake House, and is intersected by Cann Hall Lane, connecting Leytonstone Road with Wanstead Flats, was in former times held by the prior and canons of the Holy Trinity in London, from whom it passed successively to the Strelley, Boothby, and Colegrave families.

The parish church of Wanstead, dedicated to the Virgin Mary, stands within the park. It was built in 1790, at the expense of Sir James Tylney-Long,

crowned Ionic turret at the western end. The interior is extremely plain, but well finished: it consists of a chancel, nave, and two aisles, separated by Corinthian columns. The east window is of stained glass. In the chancel is a superb marble monument to Sir Josiah Child, who died in 1699. This monument, which was preserved from the old church, consists of a recumbent life-size effigy of the baronet, with semi-recumbent effigies of his son,

MONUMENT TO SIR J. CHILD, WANSTEAD CHURCH.

in the place of an earlier structure, which had become dilapidated and inconveniently small. The old church is described by the author of the "English Traveller" in 1771 as having been lately "repaired, and fitted up in the neatest manner for Divine service." But only twenty years afterwards the edifice was ruthlessly pulled down, to make room for a bran-new Italian edifice which looks as if it had been put there to match the stables at the other end of the mansion. The new church, built from the designs of Thomas Hardwick, is constructed of brick, cased with Portland stone, and has a Doric portico, and a small cupola-

Sir Richard Child, and his wife.* In the church-yard was buried, in 1647, John Saltmarsh, a noted Puritan and divine.

The long, straggling village of Wanstead is pleasantly situated at the southern extremity of Epping Forest, and on the western side of the park. It contains a few picturesque old houses, not the least interesting, perhaps, being the "George" Inn. Let into the side wall of this hostelry is a stone bearing the date 1752, and commemorating a somewhat ludicrous event which then happened.

* Another member of the Child family is buried at Woodford. See *ante*, p. 460.

The inscription, which was restored in 1858, runs as follows :—

"In memory of yᵉ Cherry Pye
As cost ½ a Guinea yᵉ 17th of July.
That day we had good cheer,
And hope to so do many a year.
R. C. 1752. Dadᵈ Terrey."

The story is that during some alterations which were being made in the house at the above date, while the labourers were at work a pie was sent from the Rectory to the baker's shop, next door to

To the south-west of Wanstead Park are several avenues, belts of trees, and broad strips of greensward, which have long been the resort of holiday-makers and school parties in the summer-time. The principal avenue, composed of very fine trees, is nearly a mile long ; and between it and the park is a pretty residence, called Park Gate, the seat of Alderman T. Quested Finnis.

Wanstead Flats—which stretch away southward from the park towards Forest Gate Station on the

PARK GATE.

the " George." The men awaited its return, doubtless in gleeful expectation of a cheap, but delicious, feast. As the pie was being borne home, and as the baker was passing the "George," the men leaned over the scaffold, and took it off the baker's tray. For this little freak they were summoned before the local magistrate, and fined half-a-guinea, which, I presume, was duly paid, for after leaving the court the men decided on placing a stone in the wall to commemorate the joke—if such they considered it—each contributing a small sum towards its expense.

In the village there are chapels for Congregationalists, Wesleyans, and Primitive Methodists, and also a Friends' meeting-house.

Great Eastern Railway, and the Manor Park and the City of London Cemeteries—are about 400 acres in extent, and their area was formerly overgrown with furze, heath, and a few scattered trees ; but of late years its appearance has been considerably changed by the formation of brick-fields, &c. Early in the present century George III. held a review of 10,000 troops on Wanstead Flats, and in 1874 the open portion was secured by the Government for the purposes of military drill and exercise. For very many years this locality was a familiar haunt of the gipsy tribe, and of others who follow the wandering life of that fraternity, their caravans and tents being scarcely ever absent from the borders of the Flats.

At Wood House, on Wanstead Flats, is "The Princess Louise Home and National Society for the Protection of Young Girls." This institution, the objects of which are sufficiently indicated by its title, was founded in the year 1835, since which time it has been the means of rescuing upwards of twelve hundred young girls between the age of eleven and fifteen, who, from various circumstances, had stood in danger of ruin. With such an object and with such results, it need scarcely be added that the institution is one which must recommend itself to the hearty sympathy and support of all.

Dr. James Pound, a distinguished naturalist and astronomer, was rector of this parish from 1707 till his death, in 1724. Pound, who was a friend of Sir Isaac Newton, wrote several papers on astronomy, which were printed in the "Philosophical Transactions." He also taught the science of astronomy to his nephew, James Bradley, who lived with him for some time as a curate, and who later on, succeeded Halley in the post of Astronomer-Royal.

When the maypole which "once o'erlooked the Strand"* was taken down, about the year 1717, it was bought from the parishioners by Sir Isaac Newton, who sent it hither as a present to Dr. Pound, who had obtained leave from his squire, Lord Castlemaine, to erect it in Wanstead Park for the support of what was then the largest telescope in Europe, being 125 feet in length. The maypole, it should be stated, measured 100 feet. It had not long stood in the park, when one morning some amusing verses were found affixed to it, alluding to its change of position and employment. They are given by Pennant as follows :—

> "Once I adorned the Strand,
>   But now have found
>   My way to pound
> On Baron Newton's land,
> Where my aspiring head aloft is reared,
> T' observe the motions of th' ethereal lord.
> Here, sometimes raised, a machine by my side,
> Through which is seen the sparkling milky tide ;
> Here oft I'm scented with a balmy dew,
> A pleasant blessing which the Strand ne'er knew.
> There stood I only to receive abuse,
> But here converted to a nobler use ;
> So that with me all passengers will say,
> 'I'm better far than when the Pole of May.'"

Bradley was born in 1692, and after taking his degree at Oxford, in 1714, resided principally with his uncle at Wanstead. Dr. Pound had fitted up here an observatory, furnished, amongst other in-struments, with a transit-instrument, some time before its introduction at the Royal Observatory by Halley, and under him Bradley acquired that accuracy and care in observing for which he afterwards became famous. On the death of Dr. Keill, in 1721, Bradley was elected Savilian Professor of Astronomy at Oxford, and in 1727 he commenced a series of observations, which resulted in the discoveries of aberration and nutation. Mr. Bradley had begun his observations at Kew in 1726 with a zenith-sector belonging to Mr. Molyneux, whose telescope was rather more than twenty-four feet in length ; but in 1727 a sector of twelve feet radius was made for him by Graham, and set up at Wanstead. This famous instrument was afterwards transferred to the Royal Observatory at Greenwich, and, on a grant being made in the year 1749 for new instruments, was purchased by the Government.

Another distinguished resident at Wanstead was Admiral Sir William Penn, the father of the founder of Pennsylvania. Born in the year 1664, young Penn spent much of his boyhood at Wanstead, whither his parents had removed soon after his birth ; and here, "playing by the pools or rambling in the leafy shades of the widely-spreading woods of Epping Forest, the lad commenced his active life." Penn's father was one of the greatest sea-captains of his age, and his mother was the daughter of a rich merchant of Rotterdam. "Thus," observes a writer in *Sunday at Home*, "the union of British energy and Dutch shrewdness which surrounded Penn's childhood contributed some appropriate elements towards the formation of that broad statesman-like mind which distinguished the founder of Pennsylvania."

At Chigwell, in the picturesque ivy-covered grammar-school founded by Archbishop Harsnett, as we have already seen,* young Penn's school-days began ; and at the early age of eleven years, we are told, he became the subject of serious religious impressions, which, together with the training which he received there, were the determining causes of his future piety. "His father and mother, though by no means destitute of estimable qualities, were emphatically 'people of the world'—fond of the theatre and dance, the wine and the gaming party." It was well for Penn that his stay at home, after leaving Chigwell, was not long ; but that, at the age of fifteen, he was sent to study at Oxford University. During his stay at Oxford Penn formed the acquaintance of a disciple of Fox,

---

* See "Old and New London," Vol III., p. 88.

* See *ante*, p. 453.

named Thomas Loe, by whose preaching and teaching he became converted to Quakerism. His enthusiasm for his new faith took such a pugnacious form, that he not only absented himself from the services in the college chapel, or refused to wear the surplice of a student, but, along with some companions who had become Quakers, he attacked some of his fellow students, and tore the obnoxious robe off their backs : a proceeding which led to his expulsion from the University. He was soon after sent to pursue his studies on the Continent, and during his residence abroad formed a close friendship with Algernon Sydney. In 1668 Penn found himself an inmate of the Tower, on account of a publication which he had written, entitled "The Sandy Foundation Shaken," and while imprisoned in the Tower he wrote his most famous work, "No Cross no Crown." In 1670 his father died, leaving him an estate worth £1,500 a year, together with claims upon Government for £16,000 ; and in the following year he was again committed to the Tower for preaching, and as he would not take an oath at his trial, he was sent to Newgate for six months. Here, among other works, he wrote a treatise, entitled "The Great Cause of Liberty of Conscience." After regaining his liberty, he visited Holland and Germany in company with Fox and Barclay, for the advancement of the cause of Quakerism. On his return, in 1672, he married a daughter of Sir William Springett, having purchased an estate near Chalfont St. Giles, in Buckinghamshire, at which village also resided for a while John Milton and his secretary, Thomas Ellwood. About ten years later he turned his attention to the New World, obtaining from the Crown, in lieu of his monetary claim upon it, a grant of the territory now forming the State of Pennsylvania. "His great desire," observes the writer of his biography in *Chambers's Encyclopædia*, "was to establish a home for his co-religionists in the far West, where they might preach and practise their convictions in unmolested peace." Penn, with several friends, was well received by the settlers, and shortly afterwards he founded the city of Philadelphia. Towards the end of the reign of Charles II. he returned to England, to exert himself on behalf of his persecuted brethren at home. In 1699 he paid a second visit to the New World, and found Pennsylvania in a flourishing condition. He returned to England two years afterwards, leaving the management of his affairs in the hands of a Quaker agent, named Ford, who for years cheated Penn in every possible way. On Ford's death, his wife and son sent demands on him for £14,000, and these claims were so ruthlessly pressed, that Penn allowed himself to be thrown into the Fleet Prison to avoid extortion. Through the exertions of his friends, however, he was ultimately released, but not until his constitution was fatally shattered, and he lingered on at his residence at Ruscombe, in Berkshire, till July, 1718, when he died. He was buried at Jordans, near Chalfont.

Lord Macaulay wrote thus in praise of William Penn :—"Rival nations and hostile sects have agreed in canonising him. England is proud of his name. A great commonwealth beyond the Atlantic regards him with a reverence similar to that which the Athenians felt for Theseus and the Romans for Quirinus. The respectable society of which he was a member honours him as an apostle. His name has become throughout all civilised countries a synonym for probity and philanthropy."

CHAPTER LI.

LEYTON AND LEYTONSTONE.

Extent and Boundaries of Leyton Parish—Walthamstow Slip—Census Returns—Discovery of Roman Remains and other Antiquities—Ancient Earthworks—General Appearance of the Village of Leyton—Railway Stations—Park House—Ruckholt House—The Manor House—Leyton House—Etloe House—The Parish Church—John Strype—The Vicarage—All Saints' Church—Schools and Charitable Institutions—Lea Bridge, and the East London Waterworks—Temple Mills—Eminent Residents of Leyton—Leytonstone—Census Returns—The Church of St. John the Baptist—Holy Trinity Church—Congregational Church—Union Workhouse—Children's Home.

THE parish of Leyton, which includes the rapidly-increasing hamlet of Leytonstone, extends from Walthamstow on the north side to Stratford on the south ; it is bounded on the east by Snaresbrook and Wanstead, whilst on the west the river Lea separates it from the county of Middlesex, Lea Bridge being its extreme western limit ; and it is from its proximity to the Lea that it is supposed to be derived—Ley, or Lea Town : the Town on the Lea. The village of Leyton, from its situation, is called Low Leyton; whilst the upper part of it by a sort of reduplication, has gradually come to be called Leytonstone, that is, Leyton's Town. The entire parish covers a large area of ground, and the whole district is fast losing its rural character; the sylvan scenery which it once possessed in those parts where it abutted upon the forest, or in the more open parts about Wanstead, being rapidly encroached upon for building purposes.

A portion of land within the bounds of this parish, hardly more than a hundred yards in width, but running from the eastern to the western boundary, or, in other words, from near Wanstead Orphanage to the river Lea, and embracing parts of the Green, Capworth Street, and Beaumont Road, is known as the "Walthamstow Slip." Its singular acquisition by that parish has been already referred to in a previous chapter.* Though lying in the heart of Leyton, this slip of land belongs, for ecclesiastical purposes, to the parish of Walthamstow. For a long time the vicars of the two parishes of Walthamstow and Leyton sought to rid their respective parishes of this anomaly; a scheme was matured, and with a view to the transference of the above-mentioned slip from the parish of Walthamstow to that of Leyton, that portion of the latter parish which lies to the north of Lea Bridge Road, from its junction with Chestnut Walk, near Whip's Cross, to Copeland's Corner, and to the east of Hoe Street from Copeland's Corner to Boundary Road, has been transferred, by an order of her Majesty in Council, to the new parish of St. Stephen, Walthamstow.†

Some idea of the progress made in building here may be formed from the fact that in 1861 the parish, exclusive of the ecclesiastical district of Leytonstone, contained a population of only 4,700, which in 1871 had increased to 10,300, whilst, according to the census returns for 1881, it now numbers nearly 23,000.

It is, or was, generally accepted that Leyton is the same as the ancient Roman station called Durolitum, though some antiquarians fix that at Romford. The discovery of coins, bricks, and pottery of Roman work here would seem to show that it was a place of some importance during the period of the Roman occupation. Indeed, various antiquities have been at different times found in this parish; but the evidence of its having been the site of a Roman station, though supported by Camden and others, does not appear to be sufficiently strong to warrant it being positively asserted. Camden himself speaks with hesitation; and

though willing to suppose it the *Durolitum* of Antoninus, from its name Leyton, or the Town on the Ley, retaining some traces of the former appellation, which "in British signifies *Water of Ley*," acknowledges that, to justify this opinion, the distance of Durolitum from London (fifteen miles) must be regarded as inaccurate. "It is most probable," remarks the author of the "Beauties of England," "that the remains discovered at Leyton and in its neighbourhood belonged only to some Roman villas. That the arguments for the site of Durolitum being in this parish are not incontestable is evidenced by the contrariety of opinions respecting that station: Baxter places it at Waltham, Salmon at Cheshunt, and Stukeley at Romford."

The following particulars of antiquities discovered here are given by Gough, in his "Britannia" (Vol. II., p. 50), from a letter communicated by Mr. Lethieullier:—"In the year 1718, Mr. Gansell (then owner of the manor-house) having occasion to enlarge his gardens, on digging up about two acres of ground, found under the whole very large and strong foundations: in one place all stone, with considerable arches, an arched doorway with steps down to it, but filled up with gravel. In many of the foundations were a great quantity of Roman tiles and bricks, mixed with more modern materials, and several rough and broken pieces of hard stone, some part of which, when polished, proved to be Egyptian granite; two large, deep wells, covered over with stone; and in digging a pond, after the workmen had sunk through a bed of clay about ten feet, they met with a great quantity of oak timber, mortised together like a floor, grown very hard and black, but uncertain how far it reached. Several Roman brass and silver coins, both Consular and Imperial, to the time of Julius Cæsar, were scattered about, as well as some silver coins with Saxon characters. The ground where these discoveries were made adjoins the churchyard, where, some time before, a large urn of coarse red earth was found."

At a place called Ruckholts, about a mile to the south of the church, are the remains of some old entrenchments with a square double embankment, and fortified by what once was a moat. They are about 100 feet across, and are supposed to date from the Roman or Early British times. These remains are situated on a small eminence rising from the banks of the Lea, and trees have been planted over the chief part of the area.

Before the Conquest the monks monopolised the greater part of the lordships and lands of this parish. Part of the lands were given by Harold as

* See *ante*, p. 465.　　† See *ante*, p. 471.

an endowment to the Abbey of Waltham; the manor of Leyton belonged to the Abbey of Stratford Langthorne; whilst the Priory of St. Helen's, in Bishopsgate, owned the estate of Marks.

It is less, however, for its antiquarian interest than for its fine old houses, half concealed amid "ancestral" trees, the prim suburban villas scattered about, the views over meadow and marsh land, and the glimpses of forest scenery, that our attention is arrested as we pass the twin villages of Leyton and Leytonstone.

In spite of the efforts of the modern bricklayer and builder, who has lined every roadway with villas of the suburban type, Leyton still retains a few old cottages, with timbered fronts and sides and red-tiled roofs, which tell of the times when the Stuarts sat on the throne. A few also of the limes and chestnuts which once graced these roadways remain in front of the houses to which they served as screens; but these are growing fewer year by year, while

> " Trade's unfeeling train
> Usurp the land and dispossess the swain."

The market-gardens, too, and the farm-houses which gave the village a rural aspect at the accession of her present Majesty, have nearly all been swallowed up in like manner by the building societies, who have parcelled out the land into unsightly plots. The village is between five and six miles from London, and has a station on the Great Eastern Railway. There is also a station at Leytonstone.

Like Chigwell and Walthamstow, and other suburban villages eastward of the metropolis which we have visited, Leyton was in former times the abode of a large number of City merchants and other wealthy personages; these, however, have mostly migrated westward, but many of their fine old houses still remain.

At Knott's Green, a hamlet on the road from Snaresbrook to Low Leyton, is the seat of Mr. G. Gurney Barclay, surrounded by gardens and grounds which have attained a local celebrity, and which has become famous for its observatory.

Park House was another fine mansion; but this has been enlarged, and converted to educational purposes, and is now known as St. Agnes' Roman Catholic Poor School.

Ruckholt House, a good-sized modern building, near the railway-station, occupies the site, or at all events has been built in the place of the old manor-house of that name, which was taken down about the middle of the last century. The old house, which was originally the seat of the Hickes family, seems to have degenerated towards its latter years,

for in 1742 it was taken by one William Barton, who opened it as a place of public amusement for breakfasts and afternoon concerts, after the fashion of Belsize at Hampstead,* and Kendal House at Isleworth.† The concerts were held weekly during the summer, oratorios being occasionally performed. In some of the advertisements announcing the performances here, the old mansion is stated to have been one of Queen Elizabeth's palaces, but there does not appear to have been any foundation for the assertion.

The seats of most pretension now standing are the Manor House, belonging to the Pardoes; Leyton House, a large mansion, standing in its own extensive grounds, some time the residence of Mr. Alderman Sidney; and Etloe House, a large white-fronted building, about a quarter of a mile north-west of the church. This last-named house was erected rather more than a century ago, and was for some years the residence of Cardinal Wiseman.

The parish church of Low Leyton, dedicated to St. Mary, is constructed of brick, in part plastered over, and is altogether poor and ugly. It consists of a nave, chancel, and north aisle, and a tower at the western end.

The church is neatly modernised; not a single trace of antiquity remains. The tower was pulled down and rebuilt in the seventeenth century, the nave and chancel underwent the same process in the eighteenth century; and all that remains to show what once has been is a really fine collection of Jacobean monuments. On the walls are one or two modern specimens of the skill of Flaxman and Chantrey. Near the vestry door, at the south-east corner, is a rather boldly-sculptured mural tablet to Sir Robert Beachcroft, Alderman and Lord Mayor of London, with the date of 1721. Below are the insignia of his office: the Lord Mayor's fur cap, sword, and mace.

At the north-west angle is a mural monument with a Latin inscription to William Bowyer, the printer, and friend of Dr. Johnson, who succeeded Edward Cave as proprietor of the *Gentleman's Magazine*. It was apparently erected by his son-in-law, John Nichols, whose name is added below.

The monuments have nearly all been displaced and replaced in the various beautifying processes which the church has undergone of late. Two large and stately memorials of the Hickes family, which formerly stood on the north and south of the communion table in the chancel, are now

---

* See "Old and New London," Vol. V., p. 495.
† See *ante*, p. 59.

under the tower at the west end, where they are lost to view. These are described by Lysons in his "Environs of London." One of them, formerly on the south side of the chancel, commemorates Sir Michael Hickes, whose effigy in armour, life-size, is represented in alabaster; the monument also comprises the effigy of his wife, in a mourning habit, holding a book. Sir Michael Hickes died in 1612. The other monument commemorates Sir William Hickes, who died in 1680; another Sir William Hickes, his son (1702), and Martha Agnes, Lady

of either, stands erect, but helpless, at the other end. The sculptor, however, has thrown great spirit into his figures, though at the present day they will appear to most people utterly unsuited to a sacred edifice.

On the walls are two or three brasses, of different dates and styles; one of the time of Henry VII. commemorates a maiden lady, Ursula Gasprey, her father's only child, who utters a prayer in Latin verse—

"Ursula Virgineis me pia junge choris;"

MONUMENTS IN LEYTON CHURCH.

Hickes, wife of Sir William Hickes the younger (1723). On the first-mentioned monument the knight and his lady are lying with their feet together and their heads apart, as if they had just had a conjugal "row." This idea, however, is negatived by the language of regret at parting, and of hope to meet in another and better world which are ascribed to them in Latin verses of doubtful correctness and elegance. On the other monument Sir William Hickes is dressed in a court suit, wig, and ruffles, reclining in a semi-defiant attitude, with his bâton as Warden of Waltham Forest in his right hand. At one end of the tomb stands his son, also in a court suit, and in a military attitude; whilst his lady, who for her age might be the wife

another, apparently of the reign of James I. or Charles I., exhibits a London tradesman in the habit of the day, with his wife and a bevy of children, also suitably attired.

The third brass has a quaint English inscription in rhyme—I cannot say in poetry. It records the death of a Lady Mary Kingestone in 1557:—

" If you wyll the truythe have,
    Here lyethe in thys grave,
    Dyrectly under thys stone,
    Good Lady Mary Kyngestone ;
    Who departyd thys world, the truth to say,
    In the month of August, the XV day ;
    And, as I do well remember,
    Was buryed honorably 4 day of September,
    The yere of our Lorde, rekynyd truly,

MVc fourty and eyght varely ;
Whos yerly obyte and anniversary
Ys determined to be kept surely,
At the costs of hyr sone, Sᵣ Henry Jernynghame
   truely ;
Who was at thys makyng,
Of the Quenes gard cheffe capteyn. "

Lady Kingestone—or Kingston—was the wife of Sir William Kingston, and daughter of Richard, Lord Scroope. She had been first married to Edward Jerningham.

Among other monuments in the church may be mentioned those of Charles Goring, Earl of Norwich,

part of the last century. John Strype, the celebrated historian and antiquarian, lies buried in the chancel, but his gravestone has been covered and concealed by the new flooring. He was duly licensed by the Bishop of London, and though never actually inducted, held this vicarage during the long period of sixty-eight years. He died at the residence of his grand-daughter, at Hackney, in December, 1737, at the age of ninety-four.

Strype is said to have been of German descent, but to have been born at Stepney in 1643. He graduated at Cambridge, and on being admitted to

LEYTON VICARAGE.

PORTRAIT OF STRYPE.

who died in 1670, and of Sir Richard Hawkins, dated 1735. Not the least interesting memorial, however, is a tablet to the memory of William Bowyer, the eminent printer, and author of "Critical Conjectures on the Greek Testament," who died in 1777, and whose " Life," as written by Mr. John Nichols, " his apprentice, partner, and successor," and at whose expense the tablet was erected, contains many interesting particulars of the state of literature and of literary characters through a great

holy orders, was presented to the incumbency of Theydon Bois, but resigned a few months afterwards, on being appointed minister of this parish. He was for some years "lecturer" of Hackney, until his resignation of that post in 1724, and he held also with his Essex living the sinecure of Tarring, in Sussex, to which he was presented by Archbishop Tenison. The history of Strype's long life, in so far as it is of any public interest, consists merely of the list of his successive publications, among the more important of which may be mentioned " Memorials of Archbishop Cranmer," " Life of Sir Thomas Smith, Principal Secretary of State to Edward VI. and Elizabeth," " Historical Collections relating to the Life and Acts of Bishop Aylmer," " Annals of the Reformation," Lives of Archbishops Grindal, Parker, and Whitgift, and

"Ecclesiastical Memorials of the Church of England under Henry VIII., Edward VI., and Queen Mary." In 1720 he produced an edition of Stow's "Survey of London." Strype probably spent the first fifty years of his life in collecting the materials of the voluminous works which he gave to the world in the succeeding forty.

The churchyard is full of handsome tombs, showing that the dead who lie here occupied highly "respectable" positions in life. Amongst others who are so recorded are Sir John Strange, Master of the Rolls, and author of some legal reports; and Pope's friend, David Lewis, author of the forgotten tragedy of "Philip of Macedon." A gravestone to the memory of Mrs. Elizabeth Wood bears upon it the following punning inscription:—

" Wail not, my wood, thy trees untymely fall,
　They weare butt leaves that autumn's blast could spoyle;
　The bark bound up, and some fayre fruit withal,
　Transplanted only, she exchanged her soyle.
　She is not dead, she did but fall to rise,
　And leave the woods, to live in Paradise."

The Vicarage, which stands at the fork of two roads in the high street, was built by Strype, and has some nice carvings of the Stuart era on the lintel and posts. The following extract from one of the old parish registers, probably written by Strype himself, may interest our readers:—

"*An Account of yᵉ Building of yᵉ Vicar's House of this Parish.*"—"The Vicarage House of this Parish of Low Leyton, having been of a long time very ruinous, and being at its best state but mean and unfit to receive a Minister with his family, yᵉ present Incumbent, John Strype, M.A., having lived seven years and upwards in yᵉ said Parish, and officiated there as their Minister, thought fit at yᵉ general Vestry at Easter, Anno 1677, to acquaint yᵉ Parishoners with a promise they had made him, at his first coming among yᵐ: wᶜʰ was, to repair, or rather if need were, to rebuild yᵉ said Vicarage House. Upon wᶜʰ Motion, yᵉ Vestry appointed Matthias Goodfellow and Robert Harvey, Merchants, to take a view of yᵉ old Vicarage House, and to consider and report yᵉ charge of rebuilding it. Wᶜʰ was done wᵗʰⁱⁿ a short time after by yᵉ former of them, having taken a surveyor and workmen along with him. And a report thereof was accordingly returned at yᵉ next Vestry, wᵗʰ a Model drawn by Mʳ· Richard Sadleir, an Inhabitant of this Parish, for yᵉ intended new House, Containing 30 Foot in Front and 26 Foot in Rear. Hereupon a Voluntary Subscription was made by divers of yᵉ wel-affected Parishoners, towards yᵉ charge of yᵉ work . . . . Upon this encouragemt yᵉ said Incumbent undertook yᵉ Building thereof himself,

and entered into articles wᵗʰ John Mount of Walthamstow, Bricklayer, to build and finish yᵉ House wᵗʰ al manner of Workmanship and Materials necessary thereunto. And so yᵉ Foundation of this House was begun to be laid in yᵉ Month of August, Anno 1677, And al finished in yᵉ Month of September yᵉ year following. And yᵉ above-named John Strype came into it, to dwel and reside there (by yᵉ Favour of God), yᵉ 26th day of September, in yᵉ year 1678."

During the time of the Civil War a captain of a troop of horse, under the Parliament, named Kem, was foisted on the parish as vicar or parson. He preached, as Laud tells us, one Sunday in August, 1641, in the chapel of the Tower of London, before the illustrious prisoner, "in a buff coat and a scarf, but with a gown on. He told the people they were all blessed that died in this (Parliamentary) cause, with much other such stuff."

In consequence of the great increase in the population of Leyton of late years a new church (All Saints') was built in 1864. It is constructed of brick and stone, cruciform in plan, with south and west porches. The architecture is of the Decorated style, and the east window, of five lights, and also two others in the chancel, are filled with stained glass.

The National Schools, built in 1847, are in the Elizabethan style, and were raised by subscription, at a cost of £1,200, on the site of the old free school founded at the end of the seventeenth century by Robert Osler, who endowed it with a rent-charge of £12, for seven boys of Leyton and seven of Walthamstow.

There are several charities in the parish, chiefly gifts in money and bread to the poorest inhabitants. The parochial almshouses, by the churchyard, a low range of eight single-roomed tenements, were founded by one John Smith, a merchant of London, in 1656. In the Lea Bridge Road are the Almshouses of the Master Bakers' Pension Society.

Lea Bridge and the road thence to Woodford were made in 1756-7. The bridge itself is partly in the parish of Hackney. It consists of a single arch, built of iron; the approaches to it being of brick with stone dressings and facings. Close by the bridge are the reservoirs of the East London Water Company, the engine-houses, with their tall brick shafts being conspicuous objects by the roadside. Near the bridge is a station on the Great Eastern Railway. The Lea at this point divides itself into two or three different channels in its course through Hackney Marshes. On one of these branches, about a mile southward from Lea Bridge, were the old Temple Mills, said to have anciently belonged to the Knights Templars, and afterwards to the Knights of St. John of Jerusalem.* In 1720 these mills were used for brass works; but at the beginning of the present century they were appropriated to the manufacture of sheet lead, and subsequently used as flock mills. The building, which was principally of wood, was pulled down many years ago; and the stream which worked the mill is now under the control of the East London Water Company, above mentioned. The mill spanned the stream, and adjoined the "White Hart" public-house, an hostelry well-known to anglers in these parts.

Among the natives of Leyton was Sir Thomas Rowe, or Roe, Ambassador for James I. to the Great Mogul and to the Sultan of Turkey, and author of a narrative of his travels in that capacity. On his return from the East, Sir Thomas was made Chancellor of the Order of the Garter, and also sworn a Privy Councillor. The celebrated Alexandrian Manuscript of the Greek Testament, of which a *fac-simile* was published by Dr. Woide towards the end of the last century, was brought to this country by Sir Thomas. He died in 1644.

Thomas Lodge, the dramatic poet and actor, known also as a translator of the works of Josephus and Seneca, &c., lived at Low Leyton, as he dates from that place one of his plays, "The Wit's Miserie," which was printed in 1596.

The hamlet of Leytonstone lies to the east of Low Leyton, and stretches for about a mile along the Epping Road in its course from Stratford, from which place it is about two miles north as the crow flies. The main street runs parallel with the Epping and Ongar branch of the Great Eastern Railway, the railway-station being close to the church. The district was formed into a separate ecclesiastical parish in 1845. In 1861 the population of Leytonstone was about 2,400. This number had doubled itself in the course of the next ten years, since which time there has been a proportionate increase, streets and rows of "villas" having rapidly sprung up in all directions, particularly eastward, towards the districts once covered by Hainault Forest.

The church of St. John the Baptist was built in 1843; it is constructed of white brick, with stone dressings, and consists of a chancel and nave, with a pinnacled tower at the western end, containing a clock and six bells. The east window, a triple lancet, is filled with stained glass.

In 1879 another ecclesiastical district was formed at Harrow Green, at the north-western extremity of the parish, abutting upon Ruckholts. This new district has been made up of portions of the several parishes of Leytonstone, Leyton, Wanstead, West Ham, and St. Paul's, Stratford New Town. The church, dedicated to the Holy Trinity, was built in 1878.

The Congregational Church, built in 1877–78, is a large edifice of Lombardo-Gothic design. There are also chapels for other denominations of Dissenters. The Union Workhouse for the parish of West Ham, the inmates of which generally number between 700 and 800, is situated at Leytonstone, as also is the Bethnal Green Industrial School, which was erected in 1868, and provides a home for some 400 children. Another useful philanthropic institution here is the Children's Home, in Forest Place, established in 1865.

Much of the land in the parish which has not been already swallowed up by the greedy builder is cultivated either as market-gardens or as nursery-grounds for choice flowers and ornamental trees.

CHAPTER LII.

HAINAULT FOREST AND ALDBOROUGH HATCH.

"To Hainault Forest Queen Anne she did ride,
And beheld the beautiful Oak by her side;
And after viewing it from the bottom to top
She said to her Court, 'It is a Fair-lop!'"— OLD SONG.

Situation, Boundaries, and Extent of Hainault Forest—Its Etymology—Its Ownership by the Abbey of Barking—It passes to the Crown—Subsequent Disposal–Is Disafforested—The Hamlet of Barking Side—Census Returns—The Church—Dr. Barnardo's Homes for Friendless Children—The "Maypole" Public-house—Fairlop Oak and Fairlop Fair—Aldborough Hatch.

HAINAULT FOREST, as we have stated in a previous chapter,† was that portion of the Forest of Waltham which *lay* (alas! I can no longer write "which *lies*")

to the south and east of the River Roding. In former times, as already stated, it extended northward as far as Theydon Bois, embracing Chigwell and Woodford Bridge, its southern entrance being at Aldborough Hatch. The word Hatch, as my readers are probably aware, was the old Saxon term for a wicket-gate, and it still survives in the buttery-hatch of our colleges and old manor-houses. From constant enclosures, however, the area of the forest had been so far diminished, that since the commencement of the present century Chigwell Row and Forest Gate may be said to have formed its northern boundary, whilst it extended from Woodford and Leytonstone in the west nearly to Havering-atte-Bower in the east. According to the survey of the Commissioners of Land Revenue, made in 1793, and the estimate of the Commissioners of Woods and Forests, the entire area of Hainault Forest at that time was about 17,000 acres; but by 1851, when it was resolved to "disafforest" and enclose it, these acres had dwindled down to about 4,000, of which nearly 3,000 were comprised in the "King's Woods," or royal forest. Almost the only part which has remained unenclosed since 1853, when the work of reclamation began, is Crabtree Wood, which lies a short distance eastward of Chigwell Row. There are a few other patches adjoining Claybury, and at Hog's Hall, near Barking Side.

Hainault Forest is supposed by some writers to have been named from Hainhault, in Germany, "on account of its having been stocked with deer from that place," and by others that it was so called out of compliment to Philippa of Hainhault, the consort of Edward III. Mr. James Thorne, in his " Environs of London," however, says :—" The name, formerly *Hen holt*, has been derived from the Anglo-Saxon *hean*, poor, of little value (having reference to the character of the land, as in Hendon, Henley, &c.), and *holt*, a wood. Dr. Morris has suggested that it may come from *hayn*, a cleared and enclosed space, and *holt*.[*] It is not unlikely, however," adds Mr. Thorne, " looking at the character of the district, that it was originally *héan holt*, the high wood."

Down to the present century this district was wild and uncultivated, in a great measure covered over with forest trees—chiefly pollard oak and hornbeam—and underwood, and with here and there broad sweeps of turf dotted with golden furze, and purple with broom and heather, affording safe retreats for the gipsy tribes who located themselves in these quarters.

The portion of Hainault Forest lying within the manors of Barking and Dagenham belonged to the Abbey of Barking, and at the Dissolution it passed to the Crown. From the time of Charles I., however, different portions of the forest have been

sold, and the manor of Barking alienated, but what was called the " soil of the King's Woods," together with the timber growing thereon," was reserved, as well as the right of "vert and venison." In 1851 an Act of Parliament was passed empowering the Government, after giving full compensation to the lords of manors, freeholders, and others, in respect to their several rights in the forest, to " destroy or remove the deer, cut down the timber, enclose and appropriate the land, make roads," &c.; and in 1853, as stated above, the work of clearance and reclamation was begun in earnest, Messrs. Charles Gore and Thomas F. Kennedy being then the Commissioners of Woods and Forests. The trees, over 100,000 in number, were laid low by the woodman's axe, and produced nearly £21,000, which went a great way towards paying the preliminary expenses of the proceedings. The Crown had obtained, either by allotment or purchase, some 2,000 acres and the whole of the timber; and the remainder was appropriated to the several parishes and lords of manors. The Crown lands were thoroughly drained and fenced, and now form a compact property, known as the Crown Farm. What was once Hainault Forest has thus become—from a wild and desolate, but beautiful, waste—a broad expanse of productive, fertile land, the property being cut up and divided by roads, and for the most part put under cultivation as farms. But the rights of the British public were ignored, no village Hampden having up here, as at Loughton, come forward to assert and vindicate them.

On the south-west side of this district, which now figures on the map simply as Hainault—or Henhault—is the straggling hamlet of Barking Side. The village consists of a few small houses and labourers' cottages by the roadside, a church, a public-house or two, and a charitable institution. It lies some two miles south from Chigwell Row, and three miles north from Ilford station on the Great Eastern Railway, and it was formed into an ecclesiastical district in 1841, out of Great Ilford and the civil parish of Barking. Its area is some 2,500 acres; whilst its inhabitants, principally employed in agricultural pursuits, number nearly 3,000, or about double of those enumerated in the census of 1871.

The name of Barking Side would seem at first very inappropriate to a place which lies in the opposite direction of Barking from Ilford; but it must be remembered that the name was given with reference, not to that place, though it may have been the Eald Ford, but to the Forest, which was older still.

---

[*] " Etymology of Local Names," p. 55.

The church, dedicated to the Holy Trinity, is a small building in the Norman style, erected in 1840: it consists of a chancel and nave, with a bell-turret.

Dr. Barnardo's Village Home for Orphan and Destitute Girls is the principal feature in this village. This institution, called the East End Juvenile Mission, and one out of eighteen depôts established in the eastern districts of London, was founded in 1866, for the purpose of "reclaiming, educating, and benefiting, spiritually and physically, adults and children of the poorest classes."

The Homes surround a space of about four acres, which is laid out as a sort of college quadrangle, the houses being grouped around it on all sides. Each of these is fitted for the reception of twenty girls, who are mostly between four and fourteen years of age, though some remain till seventeen, and some are infants only a few weeks old. The total of the houses is at present thirty; but ground has been secured for the erection of ten or twelve more as soon as donors are forthcoming. Many of those already in working order were opened by the Princess Mary of Teck, as recorded on stones let into their fronts; others were given or opened by Lord and Lady Cairns, Lord and Lady Aberdeen, the Duchess Dowager of Manchester, and other titled persons; whilst not a few commemorate a parent or a child. The inscriptions on their fronts are quite touching.

The girls are all brought up for domestic service, and are taught reading, writing, arithmetic, and needlework; and all take their turns at laundry and house work. The steam laundry alone, when in full operation, is a sight worth a visit; and the size of it may be inferred from the fact that often 10,000 articles are washed in it in a single week. The washing, not only of all the thirty "Homes," but that of all the boys at the Home at Stepney Causeway—a kindred institution—is done here. The girls are allowed, in some cases, to remain till seventeen, when they are drafted off into service. Some hundreds of them have been despatched to Canada, for service there; and they cannot be sent too young for the wants of the colonists. Some who are delicate have been sent for a winter sojourn on the north coast of Africa. Two adjoining mansions, with grounds and gardens, have been absorbed into the institution; the one serving as an infirmary, whilst the other is appropriated as school-rooms for the various classes. The whole of the school staff is under Government inspection, and has a resident master and mistress, who have a separate house assigned to them.

The children have their meals and, for the most part, sit and play in their respective Homes, though they meet on equal terms in the common ground. In the centre of the quadrangle is a dovecot or pigeon-house, and little gardens are attached to every cottage. Nothing can be prettier or neater than the general appearance of these Homes; and the bright happy faces of the children tell more plainly than words can do that they are well cared for and well treated. In fact, after a month or two in the Home, the faces of even the dullest and stupidest-looking children show a marked improvement. It is said that the demand for servants from the Homes average a thousand in a year, while the supply can never reach a hundred. The average death-rate of all the children in the several Homes is under one per cent.

The whole of the large sum collected annually by Dr. Barnardo is expended on the children, their clothing, education, and maintenance; and some of the ladies in charge of the Homes give their services gratuitously from love of the work. All the Homes have been erected by private donors, individually or collectively. It is said that the sums collected amount to over £40,000 yearly.

Prizes are distributed annually to a large number of former occupants of these Homes who, by their industry and good conduct, may have retained their situations with credit, after leaving the institution, for a number of years. At a meeting held at Exeter Hall for the above purpose in June, 1883, presided over by Earl Cairns, it was stated that during the preceding year 4,100 boys and girls had enjoyed the advantages of the Homes and institutions connected with them. A new Home, the "Leopold," had been opened during the year, and a Servants' Free Registry added. A scheme had been elaborated for sending 100 boys and 100 girls to the Colonies — emigration being the best possible mode of completing the rescue of many of those who have been trained in the Homes. One of the supporters of the Homes, having purchased 1,000 acres of land in one of the Midland counties, had offered to take 100 boys to train as agriculturists. The income of the year, it was announced, had been £45,136, a considerable increase over the most prosperous of previous years.

The old "Maypole" public-house here has been popular in its time with East London holiday-makers, on account of its proximity to the spot whereon formerly grew the famous Fairlop Oak; but it is open to question whether the worthy host was justified in placing in his bar the following couplet:—

"My liquor's good, my measure's just:
Excuse me, sirs, I cannot trust."

The Fairlop Oak stood about a mile to the east of the "Maypole," on ground which now forms part of the Crown Farm. It has been noticed as not a little singular that the survey of the Board of Agriculture makes no mention of this oak in its list of particular trees in the county.

Mr. Coller, writing of the forest in his "History of Essex" (1861), observes :—"The parts of it about Leyton and Woodford are pleasant airing-grounds for the inhabitants of eastern London on holidays, to whom it is a luxury to breathe the fresh air of a real forest. Doubtless it is a special delight for the fair labourers in the factories of fashion to escape from their prison-houses, and, as a wag has sung—

oak, and of the scenes enacted beneath its spreading branches :—

> " Deep in the forest's dreary tracts,
>   Where ranged at large fierce Waltham blacks ;
>   Where passengers with wild affright,
>   Shrunk from the terrors of the night,

there stood that pride of Hainault Forest, the Fairlop Oak, which for so many years over-shadowed with its verdant foliage the thousands who

DR. BARNARDO'S HOMES.

> " ' Like Robin Hood, to feel themselves the free,
>   And draw their *beaux* beneath the greenwood tree.'

Even in this respect, however, the popularity of the forest has fallen off since excursion trains have stood at all the outlets of London, ready to whirl the parties further countryward, though the rabble rout that burlesques the grandeur of the old royal hunting party is still to be heard in the forest on Easter Monday. Fair and bright, too, have been the days of forest life under the Fairlop oak, which stood near Great Ilford." Not only, however, as we have already shown,* has the Epping Hunt become a thing of the past, but both the Fairlop Oak and the saturnalia which for a century or so were known as Fairlop Fair have now altogether disappeared.

A writer in the *Literary Chronicle* for 1823 gives us the following particulars of this celebrated

crowded under it, and the antiquity of which the tradition of the country traces half-way up to the Christian era. This vegetable wonder, which was rough and fluted, measured at three feet from the ground about thirty-six feet in girth, and the shade of its branches was proportionally large.

" Under this oak a fair was long annually held on the first Friday in July, which was founded by one Daniel Day, a block and pump maker, of Wapping, commonly called *Good* Day, who died on the 19th of July, 1767, aged 84. Mr. Day was the proprietor of a small estate in Essex, at a short distance from Fairlop Oak. To this venerable tree he used, on the first Friday in July, to repair, having previously invited a party of his neighbours to accompany him, and here, under the shade of its thickest branches and leaves, the party dined on beans and bacon. For many years Mr. Day continued annually to visit this favourite tree ; and attracting public curiosity to the spot, a sort of

* See *ante*, p. 443.

fair was established, which caused a great circulation of money, and introduced that kind of civilisation which is the sure concomitant of commerce in a part of the country which had for ages been wild, dangerous, and almost unexplored. In addition to the entertainment given to his friends, Mr. Day never failed, on the day of the fair, to provide several sacks of beans, with a proportionate quantity of bacon, which he distributed from the trunk of the tree to the persons there assembled.

was applied to the extremities of its decaying branches, to one of which was affixed a board with this inscription :—' All good foresters are requested not to hurt this old tree, a plaster having lately been applied to its wounds.'

"But these precautions were insufficient to protect it from thoughtless visitors, who would make a fire within the cavities to cook their provisions ; and in the month of June, 1805, the tree was thus set on fire, and continued burning until the

FAIRLOP OAK, 1800.

"For several years before the death of the benevolent, though eccentric, founder of this fair and public bean-feast, the pump and block makers of Wapping, to the number of thirty or forty, went annually to the fair in a boat made, like an Indian canoe, of one piece of timber. The amphibious vehicle was covered with an awning, mounted on a carriage, and drawn by six post-horses, the whole being adorned with ribands, flags, and streamers, and furnished with a band of musicians.

"The oak, so long the great object of attraction, after having endured the fury of the whirlwind and the tempests of ages, at length fell, subdued by Time; for ' what will not Time subdue?' About twenty years ago the tree was fenced round with a close paling, and Mr. Forsyth's composition

following day, by which the trunk was considerably injured, and some of the principal branches wholly destroyed ; but though thus mutilated, ' the stately ruin yet still wonder gained,' and might then have been apostrophised in the language of the poet :—

" ' Thou wert a bauble once, a cup and ball,
    Which babes might play with ; and the thievish jay,
    Seeking her food, with ease might have purloin'd
    The auburn net that held thee, swallowing down
    Thy yet close-folded latitude of boughs.
    Time was when, sitting on thy leaf, a fly
    Could shake thee to thy roots, and time has been
    When tempests could not.
    Time made thee what thou wert—king of the woods ;
    And time hath made thee what thou art—a cave
    For fowls to roost in.'

"The high winds of February, 1820, however,

stretched its massy trunk and limbs on that turf which it had for so many ages overshadowed with its verdant foliage ; and thus it exhibited a melancholy memento of the irresistible power of time to bring to an end not only the flower of a season, but the towering growth of many ages.

"But, although the oak is gone, and the only remains of it, we believe, are to be found in the neighbouring church of Wanstead, where the pulpit has been made of a part of it, yet the fair is still held regularly, and is a place of great resort to the inhabitants of London, who flock in crowds, and, forming gipsy parties, spend the day.   But the poet Gay must describe the scene :—

> " ' Here pedlars' stalls with glitt'ring toys are laid,
> And various fairings of the country maid.
> Long silken laces hang upon the twine,
> And rows of pins and amber bracelets shine.
> Here the tight bass-knives, combs, and scissors spies,
> And looks on thimbles with designing eyes.
> The mountebank now treads the stage, and sells
> His pills, his balsams, and his ague-spells ;
> Now o'er and o'er the nimble tumbler springs,
> And on the rope the vent'rous maiden swings.
> Jack Pudding, in his party-coloured jacket,
> Tosses the glove, and jokes at ev'ry packet ;
> Here raree shows are seen and Punch's feats,
> And pockets pick'd in crowds, and various cheats.' "

The pulpit of St. Pancras Church, in the Euston Road, it may be added, was also made from the wood of this famous oak.*

The author of a *brochure*, entitled "Fairlop and its Founder," printed in 1847, varies the account of the origin of the fair with a few additional details. He writes :—"When entire, the oak is said to have had a girth of thirty-six feet, and to have had seventeen branches, each as large as an ordinary tree of its species. . . . . Far back in the last century, there lived an estimable block and pump maker in Wapping, Daniel Day by name, but generally known by the quaint appellative of *Good Day*. Haunting a small rural retreat which he had acquired in Essex, not far from Fairlop, Mr. Day became deeply interested in the grand old tree above described, and began a practice of resorting to it on the first Friday in July, in order to eat a rustic dinner with a few friends under its branches. His dinner was composed of the good old English fare, beans and bacon, which he never changed, and which no guest ever complained of. Indeed, beans and bacon became identified with the festival, and it would have been an interference with many hallowed associations to make any change, or even

addition. By-and-bye, the neighbours caught Mr. Day's spirit, and came in multitudes to join in his festivities. As a necessary consequence, trafficking people came to sell refreshments on the spot : afterwards commerce in hard and soft wares found its way thither ; shows and tumbling followed : in short, a regular fair was at last concentrated around Fairlop Oak . . . . . Mr. Day had thus the satisfaction of introducing the appearances of civilisation in a district which had heretofore been chiefly noted as a haunt of banditti.

"Fun of this kind, like fame, naturally gathers force as it goes along. We learn that for some years before the death of Mr. Day, which took place in 1767, the pump and block makers of Wapping, to the amount of thirty or forty, used to come each first Friday in July to the Fairlop beans-and-bacon feast, seated in a boat formed of a single piece of wood, and mounted upon wheels, covered with an awning, and drawn by six horses. As they went, accompanied by a band of musicians, it may be readily supposed how the country-people would flock round, attend, and stare at their anomalous vehicle, as it hurled madly along the way to the forest. A local poet, who had been one of the company, gives us just a faint hint of the feelings connected with this journey :—

> " ' O'er land our vessel bent its course,
> Guarded by troops of foot and horse ;
> Our anchors they were all a-peak,
> Our crew were baling from each leak.
> On Stratford Bridge it made me quiver,
> Lest they should spill us in the river.

"The founder of the Fairlop feast was remarkable for benevolence and a few innocent eccentricities. He was never married, but bestowed as much kindness upon the children of a sister as he could have spent upon his own. He had a female servant, a widow, who had been eight-and-twenty years with him. As she had in life loved two things especially, her wedding-ring and her tea, he caused her to be buried with the former on her finger, and a pound of tea in each hand—the latter circumstance being the more remarkable as he himself disliked tea, and made no use of it. He had a number of little aversions, but no resentments. It changed the usual composed and amiable expression of his countenance to hear of any one going to law. He literally every day relieved the poor at his gate. He often lent sums of money to deserving persons without any charge for interest. When he had attained a considerable age, the Fairlop oak lost one of its branches. Accepting the fact as an omen of his own approaching end, he caused the detached limb of the tree to be fashioned

---

* See "Old and New London," Vol. V., p. 353.

into a coffin for himself, and this convenience he took care to *try*, lest it should prove too short. By his request his body was borne in its coffin to Barking Churchyard by water in a boat."

Gilpin, in his "Remarks on Forest Scenery," written in the last century, describes the branches of Fairlop oak as "overspreading an area nearly 300 feet in circumference. About a yard from the ground," he adds, "where its rough fluted stem is thirty-six feet in circumference, it divides into eleven vast arms; yet not in the horizontal manner of an oak, but rather in that of a beech." In his day it had "suffered greatly from the depredations of time." In 1805, as stated above, it lost some of its greater branches, and was otherwise considerably injured by a gipsy party, who had kindled a fire in too close proximity to its aged trunk; and although considerable care was afterwards taken to preserve it, the work of decay went on gradually, until, in the month of February, 1820, the "grand old oak" was blown down in a violent gale. The fall of the tree, however, did not put a stop to the "fair," notwithstanding that it was popularly supposed to have been held "by charter, under the shadow of the great oak." Even when the power of holding it was supposed to have been taken away by the Disafforesting Act in 1852, so firm a hold had the idea of celebrating Fairlop Fair taken on the minds of the East Londoners, that they still hovered round its site for their annual "outing" for some three or four years, until the ground was actually enclosed. Mr. Thorne, in his "Environs of London," says that "even now (1876), on the 'first Friday in July,' the block-makers of Wapping visit Barking Side in their ships, drawn by six horses, and after skirting the scenes of their old revels, dine at the 'Maypole,' or one of the neighbouring inns. A sort of fair continues to be held on the unenclosed waste, but it is a fragmentary, disreputable mockery . . .
It may be noticed," he adds, "as illustrating the tenacity with which the memory of Fairlop is held, that the London Foresters named the lifeboat which they presented to the Lifeboat Society in 1865 'The Fairlop.'" Indeed, down to within the last few years Fairlop Fair, on the first Friday in July, was a favourite Cockney holiday-making, and almost as celebrated at the east end of London as the Epping Hunt used to be at Eastertide. The open space of ground whereon the old tree once flourished was on this one particular day in the year crowded by company of every description.
"Lord, what a group the motley scene discloses!
 False wits, false wives, false virgins, and false spouses."

Aldborough (or Aldbury) Hatch is a small hamlet and ecclesiastical district of Barking. It lies about two miles north-east of Ilford, and is a straggling little place, with a population of about 500. The church, a small Gothic structure, was opened about the year 1863. Here, on the verge of the old forest (as implied by the name), is a dreary level district, lately disafforested, and largely built over with straight roads and middle-class dwellings. It is a woodland district simply spoiled.

Morant, in his "History of Essex," says that the place was called Aldbury Hatch, as "denoting an old seat near a hatch, or low gate, belonging to the forest." According to Lysons, a mansion stood here at the beginning of the present century. There are other places in this neighbourhood bearing the same affix to the name, as Pilgrims' Hatch, Howe Hatch, &c., all of which mark the entrances at former times to the once great Forest of Waltham, just as Colney Hatch* has reference to a side entrance to the Royal Chase of Enfield.

CHAPTER LIII.

ILFORD.

"There rolls the deep where grew the tree.
O Earth! what changes hast thou seen!
There, where the long street roars hath been
The stillness of the central sea."—TENNYSON.

Chadwell Heath—Chadwell Street—The Old Coach Road—Will Kemp's Dance from London to Norwich—Great Ilford—Census Returns—Etymology—The River Roding—Ilford Church—Public Reading-Room and Library, &c.—Ilford Hospital—Cranbrook House—Valentines—Discovery of an Ancient Stone Coffin—Elephants in Essex.

MAKING our way southward, by a winding country lane, past Hatch Farm, towards the main road which runs east and west through the heart of the county of Essex from Colchester, Chelmsford, and Romford, through Ilford and Stratford to London, we leave on our left the uninteresting locality of Chadwell, and the outlying hamlets of Padnall and Great and Little Newberies. Chadwell Heath is in-

See *ante*, p. 342.

tersected by the London road, about two miles west of Romford. In the last century it was perhaps as dangerous for the solitary wayfarer as Hounslow Heath or Finchley Common, being in those days much infested by highwaymen. The road across the heath is now dotted with a few commonplace cottages and a roadside inn, whilst a windmill or two, at a short distance off from the main road, imparts a picturesque variety to what might otherwise be a very dull and monotonous scene. There is also a station here on the Great Eastern Railway. By the side of the high road, at the eastern end of the heath, stands Whalebone House, so called from two large whalebones which grace the entrance to its grounds. These bones have long been objects of curiosity to passers-by, being fixed in a conspicuous position by the road-side. They are said to have belonged to a whale caught in the Thames, and placed here in memory of Oliver Cromwell, it having been taken the same year in which he died. Their original length was twenty-eight feet.

A little to the west of the heath is another cluster of houses, of a similar character to those which we have just left, and known as Chadwell Street. The inhabitants of both these hamlets depend chiefly upon agriculture for their means of livelihood. One row by the roadside has been occupied for generations by a colony of poor Irish. Chadwell Heath is a hamlet of the parish of Dagenham, whilst Chadwell Street forms part of Barking. In the fields round about here, and also in the neighbourhood of Ilford, Stratford, and other suburban parts in this locality, oxen were largely used till lately by the farmers for draught and for ploughing, instead of horses, as in most other counties.

The road from Chadwell Street to Ilford runs almost in a straight line westward, passing between broad stretches of meadow and tillage lands, which have not been obliterated by the "demon of bricks and mortar." The coaches and waggons on this road in the good old days before railways were invented were quite a sight just before Christmas and New Year's Day. A wag writes to Sir Harry Bunbury :—

> " Can you, dear sir, a man of taste,
> Revive old whimsies gone and past ?
> And fie ! for shame, without reproach,
> Stuff as you do the Bury coach.
> With strange old kindness send me presents
> Of partridges and dainty pheasants ?"

Along this road the Earl of Oxford and Lord Robert Dudley conducted the Duke of Finland in state from Colchester to London when he came as a suitor for the hand of Queen Elizabeth, soon after her accession.

Along this road, too, Will Kemp danced his frolic dance for a bet, from London to Norwich, in 1600. He writes :—"Many good fellows being there (at Stratford and Langton) met, and knowing how well I loved the sport, had prepared a bear-baiting ; but so unreasonable were the multitudes of people that I could only hear the bear roar and the dogs howl ; therefore, forward I went with my hey-de-gaies to Ilford, when I again rested, and was by the people of the town and country thereabout very well welcomed, being offered carouses in the great spoon, one whole draught being able at that time to have drawn my little wit dry ; but being afraid of the old proverb, 'He hath need of a long spoon that sups with the devil,' I soberly gave my boon companions the slip."*

The "great spoon" at Ilford would appear, from a marginal note in the original narrative, to have been no spoon at all, but a jug holding above a quart.

Ilford, or rather, Great Ilford—for there is a distinct village known as Little Ilford, some three-quarters of a mile off to the south-west—is situated between six and seven miles from Whitechapel Church, and has a station close to the town, on the Colchester line of the Great Eastern Railway. It forms a "ward" of Barking parish, and is described in the "British Traveller," in 1791, as "a small village, where there are some agreeable houses." Since that time, however, the little village has grown into a town almost equalling in population that of the mother parish, from which, for ecclesiastical purposes, it has become separated, and constituted a district parish. The population of Great Ilford, according to the census of 1871, was close upon 3,700, a number which, during the next decennial period had swelled up to 4,400.

In the Domesday Survey the name of the place is entered as *Ilefort*. As the River Roding here crosses the road close by the western end of the village, there can be little doubt that the name of Ilford was derived from that circumstance ; but it is doubtful whether the ford was of such a dangerous character as to be called an "*ill* ford," as Morant suggests ; it is far more possible, as Lysons supposes, that in the Saxon times it was known as the " eald (old) ford."

The Roding, or Roden, rises near Easton Park, not far from Dunmow, and flows in a southerly direction past Chipping Ongar, Kelvedon Hatch, Navestock, Loughton, and Chigwell, to Woodford Bridge, and so, past Ilford and Barking, into the Thames. After passing Ongar, its banks are low

---

* See Kemp's "Nine Days' Wonder," performed in a dance from London to Norwich. (Camden Society.)

and rather marshy, and from Ilford and Barking its course is protected by artificial embankments. Under the name of Barking Creek, it is navigable up to Ilford, and doubtless in former days it was in this part of its course a "creek" rather than a river. Its entire course is a little over thirty-five miles.

The district through which this river winds its course north of Ongar is collectively styled "the Rothings," or "Roodings," and its inhabitants are thought by the rest of the county to be very dull. Hence they say of a stupid fellow, all over Essex, that he "comes from the Roothings." The stream takes its rise a little to the south of the village of Great Camfield, whence it passes through the green meadows of several villages, which derive their names from their position on or near the river. These are : High Rothing, Aythorp Rothing, Leaden Rothing, White Rothing (West), Margaret Rothing (East), Abbot's Rothing, and Rothing Beauchamp. Rothing Berners and Rothing Morrell are also named from this river. We have already made the acquaintance of the Roding at Woodford.* There are large corn-mills and wharves by the side of the river at Ilford, and some extensive lime-works and brick-fields not far distant ; but the High Street is a dull and unthrifty-looking place, with a mouldering air about it.

The "Red Lion" and "Angel" were great posting-houses in former times, but their "occupation is gone ;" notwithstanding that the town has a quieter appearance than it had in the old coaching-days, before the formation of the railway, much of its prosperity is doubtless derived from the navigation of the Roding up to this point from its junction with the Thames.

In 1830, Great Ilford, Barking Side, Aldborough Hatch, Chadwell Street, and a portion of Hainault Forest, were formed into a separate parish by the Ecclesiastical Commissioners, the combined district being now known as the Vicarage of Great Ilford ; but this is for ecclesiastical purposes only. As we have already shown, a sub-division was made in 1841 on the north side of Ilford, the ecclesiastical district of Barking Side being formed, which was followed in 1863 by that of Aldborough Hatch.

The church of Great Ilford, dedicated to St. Mary, was built in 1830, and enlarged in 1866. It is constructed of brick, a poor specimen of the Early English style, and consists of an apsidal chancel, nave, aisles, western porch, and a tower and spire. The last named portion, which contains a clock and six bells, as we learn from Kelly's "Directory of Essex," was erected in 1866,

to the memory of Mr. J. Davis, of Cranbrook Park, and his wife, by their children. The pulpit, of carved stone, also a memorial of Mr. Davis, was erected by subscriptions. The chancel windows are stained, and were inserted in memory of Mr. Davis by the magistrates of the Petty Sessions, of which that gentleman had been chairman for many years. Five other windows are also filled with painted glass, in memory of some members of the family of Thompson, of this parish.

A reading-room and lecture-hall for the benefit of the working-classes, and also a drill-hall for the use of the volunteers, were erected by the late Miss E. Thompson. The reading-room has a library attached to it.

On the south side of the road stands Ilford Hospital, dedicated to St. Mary and St. Thomas the Martyr, an institution founded by Adeliza, Abbess of Barking in the reign of Stephen, for a prior, chaplain, and thirteen poor brethren, or lepers. It was endowed with the tithes of part of Barking parish, and strict statutes for its *régime* were drawn up by Stratford, Bishop of London, in 1346. At the Reformation its revenues were valued at £16 annually. Queen Elizabeth granted these tithes and the site to the Fanshawes, by whom it was converted into an almshouse for six poor men, with a chaplain to perform Divine service in the chapel. Each inmate receives the sum of £2 11s. annually, and the salary of the chaplain was fixed at £14 a year. The estate is now vested in the Marquis of Salisbury, who is the master of this semi-ecclesiastical establishment, and who pays the yearly stipends. The hospital occupies three sides of a small quadrangle ; the apartments of the pensioners are situated on the east and west sides, the chapel being between them, on the south. The chapel appears to date from the fifteenth century ; it is a long and narrow structure, 100 feet by 20 feet, and was the only place of worship for the inhabitants of Great Ilford before the erection of the new church. In the garden court is an ancient well.

About half a mile northward from the village is Cranbrook Park, a large old-fashioned mansion, but in parts modernised and improved, in accordance with the tastes of the present day. It was the seat of Sir Charles Montague, who died in 1625, and whose monument we shall see on reaching Barking Church. It contains a noble suite of rooms overlooking the garden front.

Valentines,* which adjoins the above estate on the north, was built towards the end of the seven-

---

* See *ante*, p. 458.

* Valentines is the Essex mode of writing Valentine House, as it was usually called a century ago. Thus we have Rochetts as an abbreviation for Rochett House, and Dagnams for Dagnam Hall.

teenth or beginning of the eighteenth century by Mr. James Chadwick, son-in-law of Archbishop Tillotson, and is now the seat of Dr. C. M. Ingleby, whose name is so well known as a Shaksperian scholar. In the house is some fine carving by Grinling Gibbons. The mansion was enlarged and the grounds improved by Mr. Robert Surman, who purchased the estate from the family of the Raymonds, baronets. Gilpin, in his "Forest Scenery," speaks of a remarkable grape-vine here, which would seem and about eight feet high. A walk in the grounds, between two rows of yew-trees that seem to have long seen their best days, and which form an avenue like those in the gardens of Trinity College, Oxford, is known as Bishop's Walk : it was doubtless so called in honour of Tillotson. Having been in early days curate of Cheshunt, and afterwards the occupant of a country house at Edmonton, Tillotson must have been familiar with the forest lands of the north-east of London, and

VALENTINES, NEAR ILFORD.

almost to have rivalled the famous vine at Hampton Court,* of which, indeed, it is often said to be the parent stem. It was of the Hamburg sort, and was planted in a hot-house in the garden in 1758, and produced from three hundredweight to four hundred and a quarter of fruit annually. The profits on the grapes in some years have been supposed to amount to £300. It has, however, been dead for many years past, and looks like a withered gate-post, but it has thrown out from the root a strong rod which still bears fine grapes. Mention is also made of a fine tulip-tree planted here, which was upwards of four feet and a quarter in girth, doubtless was a frequent visitor at his son-in-law's quiet home, after his warm debates with Papists and Calvinists. This estate has long been celebrated for its trees and gardens, the latter being rich in evergreens. The grounds include a lake about nine acres in extent, formed by damming up a brook that trickles down from what once was the forest.

Lysons states that "in a field behind Valentines a stone coffin, containing a human skeleton, was found in the year 1724 ;" and that "in the same field was discovered, in 1746, an urn of coarse earth, filled with burnt bones." These remains were, no doubt, Roman, but they do not seem to have been preserved.

The great Roman encampment at Uphall, now a

* See *ante*, p. 170.

farm, is in the Ilford ward ; but as it lies nearer to the town of Barking, we shall deal with it under that heading.

A large quantity of remains of elephants, and of other animals belonging to a Pleistocene epoch, have from time to time been dug up here and in the neighbourhood. The Ilford brick-fields, by the London road, and also at Uphall, have become classic ground with geologists, in consequence of the large number of these remains which have been gether from various parts of the county. "In this collection," observes Mr. Clarke, in his "History of Walthamstow," "there are fossil bones of the hyæna, hippopotamus, and other large animals, and many tusks and teeth of the mammoth—an animal of the size of which we may form some idea when we consider that the head alone has been found to weigh 400 lbs. There have also been found embedded in the London clay, which extends to, and forms part of the soil of, Walthamstow, organic re-

ILFORD HOSPITAL.

found in them. They occur chiefly in the lower brick-earth, underlying what is called the Thames Valley gravels, and comprise not merely elephants, but several other species of mammalia, among them being the rhinoceros, the bear, tiger, wolf, bison, great stag, ox, horse, and beaver. Mr. Phillips, in his "Geology of the Valley of the Thames," says that the place of these deposits in time is probably "somewhere between that of the late pre-glacial and early post-glacial ages, when the levels of the country were different from what they are at present."

Mr. J. Brown, F.G.S., of Stanway, a well-known geologist of Essex, formed a very extensive collection of fossils and organic remains, brought to-mains of the crocodile and turtle, together with various specimens of vegetable remains, and among them some tropical plants . . . At Ilford, in 1812, while digging for brick-earth, the bones and teeth of huge elephants, differing from those of Asia and Africa, identical with the Siberian mammoth, were found ; and the teeth and tusks of the hippopotamus, and bones of the rhinoceros and of large oxen, have also been found there. The remnants of these giants of ancient days have enriched various geological museums." The magnificent collection of Pleistocene mammalia formed by Sir Antonio Brady, and which found its way into the British Museum, was formed almost exclusively from the Ilford pits.

Mr. Manley Hopkins, in an interesting article on this subject in *Once a Week* (1860, Vol. III., p. 53), writes :—" To ' those who understand their epoch,' it is a result of exceeding interest to have witnessed a great science grow in their own life of forty years, from stammering childhood to adolescence : to have seen almost the first uncertain beams of geology struggling in the morning sky, and then, from hour to hour, pouring in a flood of accumulating facts, and classifying them into a marvellous system. Persons born since the commencement of the present century remember geology in its pre-scientific condition, and will recall with a thoughtful smile the detached fact, the isolated mineral specimen, or remarkable local formation which first drew their attention to the subject.

" The long, grey, old church of West Ham, which stands half a mile river-ward of Stratford, contained in years past some objects likely to attract the wandering eyes of a child during a sermon. The great silken colours of the West Ham Volunteers hung dustily and discoloured below the tall chancel arch. Below them, an elaborate lion and unicorn, the size of cubs, smiled ferociously on the preacher as he passed between them to his elevated pulpit ; and at the east of the church, leaning against an altar-tomb, two immense bones rested— one being a shoulder-blade, three feet in length, and the other a rib—concerning which relics the inquirer was shortly answered that they were *mammoth bones.* The spark of interest thus kindled in our own breast towards osteology might have easily died out again, had it not been followed, some two-and-thirty years ago, by a neighbour presenting to our youthful collection of curiosities a few pieces of fossilated ivory, exhumed at Ilford, in a spot where the ground had been opened for brick-making. Many persons visited the *diggings* daily ; but until lately, when an enlightened curiosity has been established, the discoveries ceased to command attention ; and doubtless great numbers of mammoth relics have been found, and then lost for ever. During the last two years, however, greater care has been taken. The proprietor of the brick-field gave to a gentleman in the neighbourhood, much devoted to geology, full powers over all the animal remains discovered, and—what was of the highest importance—left orders that his workmen should notify to Mr. Brady their having come across any bones. Thus he was enabled to examine them *in situ,* and to prevent in a great measure their injury or destruction. In this one field (and there are two other brick-fields near it) the remains of at least eight elephants have been brought to light. A short account of their discovery was read by Mr.

Brady at a meeting of the British Association at Aberdeen, in September, 1859. The bones of the elephant (*Elephas primigenius*) are found associated with those of the rhinoceros, the Irish elk, the horse, and the ox. An immense tusk was discovered fourteen feet below the level of the soil, to see which, before it was disturbed, Sir Charles Lyell and other eminent geologists were invited. The tusk was deficient of both extremities, but the portion rescued was nine feet long, and of great thickness. Since that time a bone of enormous thickness, belonging to a whale, has been extracted.

" The geological position of these relics is the Pleistocene, or latest tertiary formation. The vein in which they occur varies from five to six feet in thickness, and consists of sandy gravel. It underlies the band of brick-earth already mentioned, into which some of the bones intrude, and thus attract the notice of the brick-makers. Above the brick-earth is the extensive and valuable bed of scarlet gravel for which this part of Essex is celebrated. This bed, with the vegetable mould which covers it in, is from four to six feet in depth at Ilford. In other spots the gravel has been worked as deep as twenty feet. Beneath all is the great deposit of the London clay.

" Though the excavations at Ilford have been singularly productive in the discovery of animal remains, it is not to be understood that they exist in that site only. In other parts of Essex, and also in Middlesex, coming within the basin of the Thames, similar bones have been brought to light. Remains of the elephant have been met with at Grays, at Harwich, at Erith, at Brentford, at Kingsland, and, within a few months past, at Charing Cross. At Erith the lion and hyæna, and at Grays the bear, add the carnivora order to the list of animals given above.

" A view of the circumstances leads to the plausible conjecture that, in its main features, the configuration of land and water was the same when these herds of strangely-associated animals lived as it is now. The estuary of the Thames probably ran up farther inland, and the waters of the river, before they had cut themselves deep channels, and before the hand of man was at work to confine them within useful limits, spread widely in marsh and morass, till they touched the feet of the hills in Kent and Essex . . . It must always be remembered, in the case of the Essex deposits we have described, that they are in the *drift*—a name at once suggestive of the washing together, or other transportation of rocks and organisms, which may previously have been scattered, and distant from each other. Indeed, where carnivora abound, the weaker kinds among the other orders must necessarily disappear. To meet with traces of their association in one place would indicate a disturbance either of the surface on which they dwelt or of their very natures. We can hardly conceive of 'a happy and united family' upon so grand a scale, and without the restraints of a cage or a keeper."

It is remarkable that along with these traces of the elephant and the mammoth there are no vestiges whatever of man or of his works; so that, in all probability these huge beasts lived here in a wide and lonely forest, which in a comparatively recent age was submerged, and became in course of time, first an arm of the sea, and ultimately a riverside plain, as we see it now.

CHAPTER LIV.

LITTLE ILFORD, WEST HAM, ETC.

"Miratur portas strepitumque et strata viarum."—VIRG. Æn. I.

Boundaries and Extent of Little Ilford—Census Returns—The Parish Church— Mr. Lethieullier's House at Aldersbrook—Ilford Gaol—The "Three Rabbits"—West Ham—Its Division into Wards—Population—Market and Fairs—Chemical Works and Factories—The Parish Church—A Curious Fresco—Upton Park—Forest Gate—Taverns and "Tea-Gardens"—Emmanuel Church- St. James's Church—Extent and Population of Forest Gate—Pawnbrokers' Almshouses—Legg's Almshouses—Former Condition of Stratford—The Abbey of Stratford-Langthorne—Pumping Station of the Metropolitan Drainage Works—St. John's Church—Christ Church—St. Paul's—St. Francis of Assisi—Congregational Church—Town Hall—Stratford New Town—Vegetable Market—Old Ford—Bow Bridge—Roman Roads.

LITTLE ILFORD, which nearly adjoins its great sister south-west, is a quiet, out-of-the-way village. The River Roding, winding its way through fields and market-gardens, forms its boundary on the east, separating it from the parish of Barking. On the south and west lie East Ham and Stratford, whilst to the north the parish stretches away to Wanstead, and includes within its boundary in that direction the City of London and Manor Park Cemeteries, the former covering upwards of 250 acres, and the latter about 45 acres. They are both neatly laid out, and planted with trees and evergreens of the ordinary type.

In 1871 Little Ilford had a population of 675, which during the next decade had become nearly 1,000.

The church, which hides itself in a grove of elms and chestnuts, and is dedicated to the Virgin Mary, is poor and uninteresting. It is built of brick, and consists of chancel, nave, north chapel, and bell-turret. From the frequent coats of plaster it is impossible to make out the date of its erection, but two of the windows at the west end of the nave are as early as the Norman era, and may, indeed, be Anglo-Saxon. Among the monuments preserved from the old church is one on the north wall of the chancel to William Waldegrave, who died in 1610, and his wife, who died in 1595; it comprises coloured effigies of the deceased, with kneeling figures of their three sons and four daughters. There is a brass to Thomas, son of Sir John Heron, private secretary to Henry VIII. He died at Aldersbrook, in this parish, in 1517. Another brass

records Anne, only daughter of Barnard Hyde, of London, who died in 1630, and her brother William, who died in 1614. One of these brasses represents a lady in a ruff of the Jacobean type, and also includes a baby in swaddling clothes. Two more brasses, long buried under the floor, were discovered in 1883, by the Vicar, the Rev. Arthur Shadwell, a son of the late Vice-Chancellor Sir Lancelot Shadwell. There are also monuments to the Fry family, formerly residents, and well known for their philanthropy; also to the Lethieulliers, a family whose name occupied a high position in Essex in the last century. One of these latter monuments—to be seen in a sort of chapel on the north side of the nave—commemorates the learned antiquarian whose writings we have had occasion to quote in describing this neighbourhood. The inscription runs as follows:—"In memory of Smart Lethieullier, Esq., a gentleman of polite literature and elegant taste, an encourager of art and ingenious artists, a studious promoter of literary inquiries, a companion and a friend of learned men; industriously versed in the science of antiquity, and richly possessed of the curious productions of nature, but who modestly desired no other inscription on his tomb than what he had made the rule of his life—to do justly, to love mercy, and to walk humbly with his God. He was born Nov. 3rd, 1701, and died without issue Aug. 27th, 1760."

This Mr. Lethieullier lived for some years at Aldersbrook, a manor-house in this parish. He is said to have much improved the grounds, in which he built a small "hermitage," as a shrine for many of the antiquities that he had collected in his travels. This structure, however, was pulled down, together with the manor-house, by Sir James Tylney Long, who purchased the property a few years after the death of Mr. Lethieullier, and built a farm-house on the site of the old mansion.

Ilford Gaol, or House of Detention for the county of Essex, a large brick building, was erected on the north side of the London and Romford road, about fifty years ago. It has lately been pulled down, and its site covered with cottages, the only prison in the county being at Springfield Hill, near Chelmsford, and the prisoners from this district being conveyed to the metropolitan prison.

Lysons, in his " Environs of London," says that in the parishes of Ilford, East Ham, West Ham, Leyton, and Wanstead, on the level part of Epping Forest—that is, on Wanstead Flats—"a great mart for cattle brought from Wales, Scotland, and the north of England, is held annually, from the latter end of February till the beginning of May. The business between the dealers," he adds, " is princi-pally transacted at the sign of the ' Rabbits,' on the high road, in Little Ilford parish." This " mart," whatever it may have been towards the end of the last century, when Lysons wrote, has long been done away. The " Three Rabbits," however, is still a favourite "house of call " for graziers and cattle-dealers of Essex on their way to and from London.

West Ham is a very extensive parish, stretching from Wanstead and Leyton in the north to the Thames in the south, and from Little Ilford and East Ham in the east to the river Lea in the west. It is divided into three " wards," namely, Church Street, Stratford, and Plaistow. This division has reference chiefly to secular matters ; for eccle-siastical purposes it is divided into several districts. The population of the entire parish in 1871 was 62,900, and that of Church Street, or West Ham proper, 7,900 ; but such has been the rapid ex-tension of building in the parish since then that these numbers have more than doubled. In the middle of the last century West Ham and the low-lying district surrounding it was largely inhabited by merchants and wealthy citizens of London ; but the mansions which they occupied have mostly disappeared, or been so altered to convert them to other purposes that they are scarcely distinguish-able. In an official return made in 1762, the number of houses in West Ham parish was stated to be 700, of which by far the larger proportion were entered as " mansions." In Morant's " History of Essex," written about six years later, this place is de-scribed as " the residence of several considerable

merchants, dealers, and industrious artists." Even at the beginning of the present century the number of the inhabitants of the parish did not amount to 6,500, the number of houses being about 1,100.

West Ham formerly had a market, the charter for which was procured, in the middle of the thirteenth century, by Richard de Montfichet, whose ancestor, William de Montfichet, founded an abbey at Stratford-Langthorne, in this parish, en-dowing it with the manor of West Ham and other estates. An annual fair of four days' duration was granted at the same time, but both have fallen into desuetude for many years. Much of the prosperity of West Ham and its adjoining townships is due to the formation of the Victoria and Albert Docks at Plaistow, the construction of the railway-works at Stratford, and the establishment within the bounds of the parish of extensive chemical works, flour-mills, smelting and copper works, shipbuilding establishments, and other large works and factories, where employment is given to thousands of hands.

The parish church of West Ham, dedicated to All Saints, occupies a central position in what would formerly have been called the village, and about half-way between the main road at Stratford and Plaistow. It is a large building of brick and stone, partly ancient and partly modern, and principally of Perpendicular architecture. It consists of a chancel, with north and south aisles, nave and aisles, and an embattled tower at the western end. The church contains the monu-ments of several eminent persons who have been buried here, including Sir Thomas Foote, Bart., Lord Mayor of London in 1650, who died in 1688 ; Henry Ketelby, who held a law office under the Crown in the reign of Henry VIII., and other members of his family are also commemorated. Robert Rook, who died in 1485, has an altar-tomb in the north chapel, with figures of himself and family. Sir James Smyth, sometime Lord Mayor of London, who died in 1706, has an elaborate monument.

In 1844 a large mural painting was discovered in this church, but after a brief exposure, was again covered with lime-wash. An anonymous pamphlet was published at the time, purporting to give a description of the picture ; but, as Mr. H. W. King observed at a meeting of the Archæological Institute in November, 1865, the writer evidently did not understand the subject, and was unac-quainted with Christian iconography, therefore his account was inaccurate and of no archæological value. " The renovation of the interior of the church in September, 1865," remarked Mr King, "afforded a favourable opportunity for endeavouring to disclose the picture anew, and under the superintendence of the Rev. R. N. Clutterbuck, of Plaistow, it was successfully developed, though apparently in a less perfect condition than when exposed in 1844. Its situation was upon the eastern part of the wall of the north clerestory, and it extended as far as the second pendant of the roof, measuring eight feet in width by five in height. It does not appear that more than this was visible when previously exposed; but, from some heads which were found on the south side of the chancel arch, it seems clear that this is only one wing of the subject, which probably extended over the east wall of the nave, and to an equal distance on the north and south sides. The whole subject undoubtedly represented the 'Final Doom of Mankind.' Upon the east wall was doubtless depicted our Lord as Judge. The right wing, which remained, represented the 'Reward of the Righteous,' and the left the 'Condemnation of the Wicked,' but not a trace of the latter could be discovered. Was this a forecast of the theology of to-day?

The picture upon the north wall, representing the 'Resurrection of the Just,' was executed not in distemper, but in oil colours, on very rough plastering, and covered also part of the stones of the arch; in one place, where a beam of the aisle-roof comes through the wall, it was continued upon the surface afforded by its section. It appears to be the work of the latter part of the fifteenth century, and was of inferior, though somewhat elaborate, execution. The upper part of the painting, extending as high as the wall-plate, and forming a background to the whole, was richly grouped, though rudely executed, tabernacle work, chiefly white shaded with grey, the windows and crochets strongly outlined in black; and some of the windows were coloured red. From the general treatment, it seems clear that this tabernacle work is a conventional representation of the Heavenly Jerusalem. In the niches were several celestials, each wearing a circlet, with a small cross over the forehead, and among them two of the heavenly choir playing upon gitterns. At the lower part of the painting, below the basement of the canopy, were two angels raising the righteous by the hand. They seem to have issued through the portcullised gates behind them. There are two of these gates at the lower part of the picture, besides that in the upper part of the canopy, into which one of the blessed is entering. From one of them the angels who are assisting the risen seem themselves to have issued, and to be leading the righteous into the other. The risen saints were grouped along

the line of the arch in that crowded manner usual, as Mr. Clutterbuck remarks, with mediæval limners. They are singularly irregular in size, the largest being placed just over the crown of the arch, and diminishing as they approached the caps of the columns. All were nude, with their hands either joined in prayer or extended as if in admiration. Among the group were two ecclesiastics with red mitres, and a cardinal with a red hat.

The writer of the pamphlet above referred to also noted a figure with a beard, which is supposed to represent a 'monk, friar, or priest,' and a royal personage wearing a crown of gold. The two angels mentioned as raising the blessed were larger than the other figures, and in pretty good preservation: their faces painted with care, and not without dignity. They were vested in white albs, without cincture or apparels. Close to the angle of the wall, where the painting was much mutilated, three demons were visible; one seemed to be falling headlong, as if to denote the abortive malice of the evil spirits unable to hurt the redeemed, now placed beyond their power. It appeared to the author of the pamphlet that the lower one had a person in his arms, as if bearing him away, with an expression of malicious pleasure in his countenance. The writer also conceived that he saw in this part of the picture the representation of flames in which others were tormented, which he supposed to be 'the suburbs of Hell.' If such existed, it might possibly have represented Purgatory, but it was not apparent either to Mr. Clutterbuck or myself. 'The Doom of the Lost' was no doubt depicted upon the opposite wall, upon the left hand of the Judge, and there was but the least possible space upon the north side for the introduction of any other portion of the Judgment scene. Since I offered a brief unpremeditated description of this painting at the meeting of the Institute, the Rev. R. N. Clutterbuck has kindly placed in my hands the memoir which he has prepared for the Journal of the Essex Archæological Society; and in the present report I have, with his permission, availed myself of his more detailed observations. As the picture was very imperfect, and wholly unintelligible except to those who could read it by a scaffold, Mr. Clutterbuck observes that he could not suggest any sufficient reason for its preservation, all the rest of the plastering having, moreover, to be removed, for the purpose of pointing the inner masonry. There were indications that the whole interior of the church had been freely polychromed in distemper, but only one small portion of diapered pattern of late date could be copied. We are indebted solely to the exertions of Mr. Clutterbuck for the development of this interesting example of mural decoration."*

In the churchyard lies buried a distinguished naturalist, Mr. George Edwards, F.R.S., who was born at Stratford in 1693, and died at Plaistow in 1773. He became celebrated for his knowledge of natural history, more especially with regard to birds; and besides various papers in the " Philosophical Transactions," he published seven large quarto

Richard Jebb, who was some time physician-in-ordinary to George III., who conferred upon him a baronetcy.*

West Ham is well off for charitable institutions. Near the church are almshouses for twenty poor women, each of whom receive a small sum of money weekly. Roger Harris's Almshouses, in Gift Lane, provide homes for six others; and there are also numerous bequests to the poor of the parish, amounting in the aggregate to about £450 per annum, left from time to time by various

WEST HAM CHURCH.

volumes on subjects in natural history, upwards of 600 of which, it is said, had never before been described. Here, too, is the tomb of James Anderson, LL.D., the editor of " The Bee," and author of several papers on agricultural and industrial subjects.

Dr. George Gregory, author of the " Economy of Nature," a " Dictionary of Arts and Sciences," and a translation of Bishop Lowth's " Lectures on the Sacred Poetry of the Hebrews," was vicar here from 1804 till his death, in 1808.

Dr. Samuel Jebb, a noted physician in his day, author of several professional works, and editor of the works of Aristotle and Bacon, was baptised in West Ham Church, in 1729, and lived in the parish for many years. He was the father of Dr.

benefactors, whose gifts are distributed by a local charity board. In West Ham Lane is the West Ham, Stratford, and South Essex Dispensary, erected in 1878, on a site given by Mrs. Curtis.

The Congregationalists, Unitarians, Wesleyans, and other Nonconformist bodies, have chapels here, and there are several schools.

The hamlet of Upton lies about a mile to the north-east of West Ham Church, its northern extremity bordering on the London road. Here are one or two interesting old houses, notably the " Cedars," formerly known as Upton Lane House. It was for many years the residence of Mrs. Elizabeth Fry, the prison reformer, sister of the late Mr. Samuel Gurney, the equally well-known philanthropist, who lived at Upton Park, close by. His residence, called Ham House, was taken down a few years after his death, which occurred in 1856. The park, comprising about eighty acres, lies between Ham Lane and Upton Lane, and formerly belonged to Dr. Fothergill, by whom the gardens were laid out; it still contains many trees which he first introduced to this country in the early part of the last century. Shortly after the house was demolished an offer was made to purchase the park for building purposes; but, fortunately, this gardens is entirely defrayed by the Corporation of London.

Forest Gate, a rising and populous hamlet of West Ham, lies to the north of the London road, and stretches away to Wanstead Flats. It has a station on the Colchester line of the Great Eastern Railway, near the entrances to the Manor Park and Ilford Cemeteries. Near the railway-station is the "Eagle and Child" tavern, and not far distant is the "Spotted Dog"; each has "tea-gardens" and

WEST HAM PARK.

proposal was met by another to secure it as a public park and recreation-ground for the poor of this rapidly-increasing locality. Mr. John Gurney, the grandson of Mr. Samuel Gurney, accepted the latter proposition, and offered it for that purpose for the same sum that had been named by the building society, namely, £25,000, the Gurney family at once contributing £10,000 towards that amount. The Corporation of London also voted £10,000, and the remainder having been made up by local subscriptions, the park—under the new name of West Ham Park—was formally opened by the Lord Mayor on the 20th July, 1874, and has since proved an inestimable boon to the neighbourhood. The cost of maintaining the park and

pleasure-grounds attached, and both are well-known resorts for East-end holiday-folk.

A district, embracing parts of Upton and East Ham, was formed into a separate parish for ecclesiastical purposes in 1852. The principal church of the district, dedicated to Emmanuel, stands at the corner of Upton Lane, in the main road. It was built by Sir Gilbert Scott, but has since been enlarged; it is of Gothic design, and consists of chancel, nave, aisles, and central bell-turret. St. James's Church, built in 1881, is a pseudo-Gothic structure of the most simple kind. The district contains two or three temporary iron churches, besides several chapels for different denominations of Dissenters. The Jews' Cemetery, and also the West Ham Cemetery, are in this district.

The area covered by the district of Forest Gate, although only 800 acres in extent, comprises a population of more than 20,000, or nearly treble of what it was ten years ago.

In Woodgrange Road are the Pawnbrokers' Almshouses, which were founded in 1849 by the Pawnbrokers' Charitable Institution—they provide homes for seven couples ; whilst Legg's Alms-houses, in Forest Lane, founded in 1858 by one Jabez Legg, of Stratford, afford homes to six poor women.

West Ham, although third in point of size of the nine parishes comprised in the Hundred of Becontree, is by far the most densely populated. "West Ham," writes Mr. Coller in 1861, in his "History of Essex," "from its traffic, trade, and importance the capital of the Hundred, is the most thickly-peopled parish in Essex, more than dou-bling the whole population of some of the smaller Hundreds in the county. It has, in fact, become a busy suburb of the metropolis, which has rubbed off its once rural character. Its little hamlets have grown into large towns. Fields over which the plough passed a quarter of a century ago are covered with workshops and teeming factories. On its river bank have risen up the largest ship-build-ing works in the world. Its quiet creek and marsh land have been converted into mighty docks, furnishing a haven and a home for commerce from all countries of the earth. Its pleasant spots, on the edge of business, but just beyond reach of the sound of the hammer and wheel, and the wearying hum of the London hive, are studded over with handsome residences."

We touched so lightly upon Stratford in OLD AND NEW LONDON,* that there is ample oppor-tunity for a further description. This place is described in the "British Traveller," 1771, as "for-merly a small village, but now greatly increased by a vast number of additional buildings. It stands," he adds, "in the parish of West Ham, and is only parted from Bow in Middlesex by the river Lea, over which there is a bridge." This is the celebrated Bow Bridge, said to have been the first stone bridge built in England. †

It is amusing to read in the work above quoted:— "Many of the rich citizens of London have fine houses in Stratford and its neighbourhood, it being particularly convenient for such as live eastward of the Royal Exchange. Almost all the lands in the neighbourhood are either let out to gardeners or improved in the culture of potatoes. Vast quanti-ties of all kinds of roots, herbs, and greens, are daily sent hence to the London markets ; and upon the whole the place is in a very thriving condition, having many good inns, with other places of public entertainment. If the new buildings from Mile End to Bow, and from thence to Stratford, are con-tinued, both these places will be, as it were, joined to London." What would the writer have said if he could have looked forward a century, to see a population of 30,000 covering the market gardens, and the place "joined to London" literally by railways, tramcars, and omnibuses.

The Abbey of Stratford-Langthorne stood on the marshes, a little to the west of West Ham. The pumping-station of the northern system of the Metropolitan Main Drainage Works at Abbey Mills occupies part of the site, whilst a few fragments of the old monastery may with difficulty be traced in the walls of the "Adam and Eve " public-house, close by. The abbey itself was founded about the year 1135 by William de Montfitchett for brethren of the Cistercian order, and was dedicated to the Virgin Mary and All Saints. It was richly endowed by its founder, who gave it all his lord-ship here. In the days of its splendour it possessed 1,500 acres of land in this parish, with the manors of West Ham, Wood-Grange, East Ham, and Plaiz (now Plaistow); thirteen manors in other parts of the county, besides lands in other counties. The abbey grounds and gardens covered sixteen acres, and were enclosed by a moat ; but at that time no scientific improvements had been made in the way of drainage, and the consequence was that the waters of the Lea occasionally invaded the sacred precincts of the monks. On one occasion they were actually driven away by the floods, and were compelled to seek refuge on their property at Billericay, some miles off.

The story is thus told by Leland :—

" This house, first sett amonge the lowe marshes, was after with sore fludes defacyd, and removed to a celle or graunge longinge to it called Burges-tide, in Essex, a mile from Billirica. These monks remained in Burgestide untyll entrete was made that they might have sum helpe otherwyse. Then one of Richards, kings of Englande, tooke the ground and abbey of Strateforde into his protection, and recdifienge it, brought the foresayd monks agayne to Strateforde, where among the marshes they re-inhabytyd."

Thus re-established, the abbey seems to have gone on prosperously, and to have taken a leading position among the religious houses in the kingdom, many high personages resorting to it. In 1307 the abbot was summoned to Parliament; in 1335, John de Bohun, Earl of Hereford and Essex, High Constable of England, was buried within its precincts; and the Countess of Salisbury, whom the remorseless Henry VIII. caused to be beheaded in her old age on a charge of high treason, appears to have resided in the abbey about the time of its dissolution, at which period its revenues were valued at £652 3s. 1¼d. Its possessions were subsequently granted to Sir Peter Mewtis, or Meautis, who had been Ambassador to the Court of France. The building itself, like many of these religious edifices, was allowed to fall into decay when the monks had been expelled. Early in the seventeenth century a descendant of Sir Peter alienated "the site of the abbey, with the abbey mills and 240 acres of land," to Sir John Nulls, and since that period the property has passed through many different hands.

In the "Beauties of England," published in 1803, Mr. Britton writes :—"The chief remains of the monastic buildings now standing are a brick gateway, which was formerly the entrance to the conventual precincts, and an ornamental arch, which appears to have been the entrance to the chapel." Lysons, writing a few years previously, observes :—"The foundations of the convent were dug up and removed by the present proprietor, in doing which, no antiquities worthy of note were found, except a small onyx seal, with the impress of a griffin, set in silver, on which is the following legend : ' *Nuncio vobis gaudium et salutem,*' perhaps the priory seal of one of the abbots." The "brick gateway" and the "ornamented arch" have now disappeared from the scene. Indeed, the obliteration of the abbey has been so complete that we cannot even record of it, in the words of the poet, that—

> " The sacred tapers' lights are gone,
> Grey moss has clad the altar stone,
> The holy image is o'erthrown,
>   The bell has ceased to toll ;
>
> The long-ribbed aisles are burst and shrunk,
> The holy shrine to ruin sunk,
> Departed is the pious monk :
>   God's blessing on his soul."

With the exception of a few that may have been worked into the walls of some of the neighbouring houses, it would be difficult for the most diligent searcher to discover a stone of the once important abbey of Stratford-Langthorne.

The pumping-station in connection with the northern sewer of metropolitan main drainage at Abbey Mills covers about seven acres of the ground once covered by Stratford Abbey. The sewer itself enters the parish at Old Ford, and crosses the West Ham Marshes by a grass-covered embankment. It afterwards traverses Plaistow, and then passes eastward in a straight line through East Ham, on its way to the outlet into the Thames, at the mouth of the Roding at Barking Reach. The works at Abbey Mills are of great capacity, comprising sixteen pumps, worked by steam-engines of immense power, their combined force being capable of lifting some 15,000 cubic feet of sewage per minute from the low-level sewer, and forcing it through large iron cylinders into the outfall sewer. The buildings, which are mostly of brick, are of an ornamental character, two octagonal chimney-shafts, each more than 200 feet high, being conspicuous for miles round.

The ecclesiastical parish of St. John was formed in 1844 from the mother parish of West Ham. The church, a handsome building in the Early English style, had been built about ten years previously. It stands in the middle of the town, at the point where the main road from the east of London diverges towards Romford and Leytonstone.

Christ Church was formed into an ecclesiastical parish in 1852 out of the parish of West Ham. The church, which stands in the High Street, close by the Main Drainage Works, is built of stone in the Decorated style, and is conspicuous by its tall spire.

St. Paul's Church, in the Maryland Road, Stratford New Town, dates its erection from 1865, when the district was carved out of the mother parish, and converted into a separate ecclesiastical parish.

The Roman Catholic Church of St. Francis of Assisi, in Grove Crescent Road, was built in 1868, and is in the Italian style of architecture. Near it is a Congregational Church, also of Italian design, but erected in a much larger and more costly manner.

The Town Hall, in the Broadway, at the corner of West Ham Lane, is a large and handsome building, of Italian design, opened in 1869. The façade towards the Broadway consists of a portico of two stages, formed with columns of polished red granite. To the right of the main front is a tower 100 feet high; the building itself is surmounted with statues of Science, Art, Commerce, Britannia, St. George, &c. Stratford is included in the Local Board district of West Ham.

Stratford New Town may be said to owe its existence to the Great Eastern Railway, the two main branches of which, leading respectively to Cambridge and Colchester, diverge at this point.

Here, about the year 1847, the company established its chief depôt for carriages, engines, and rolling stock, and yards for their repairs. Employment is here given to about 3,000 hands.

A market for the sale of vegetables, fruit, &c., has been established, adjoining Stratford Bridge Station, by the Great Eastern Railway Company, warehouses and sidings being constructed for the development of the trade.

In the olden days, when a pilgrimage to the image of "Our Ladye of Berkynge" was thought conducive to the health of the soul, a procession of courtly equipages was no unfrequent sight on the dull road leading through Whitechapel into Essex and the other eastern counties, though now almost wholly abandoned to farmers, graziers, and butchers. For example, the Princess Maud, after she had become the consort of King Henry I., would often strive to keep alive the flame of that piety which, as a child, she had imbibed in the convent of Romsey, by going on this pilgrimage at Eastertide or Whitsuntide.

At this period the river Lea was crossed by the pilgrims and other travellers at the Old Ford, as the place is still called, but the inconvenience and danger of wading through so considerable a river induced the royal devotee to turn the road to a more convenient part of the stream, where she erected Bow Bridge, which is said to have been the finest example of pontine architecture then in the kingdom, and of which, as well as of its successor, an account will be found in OLD AND NEW LONDON.*

The name of Stratford evidently points to the existence near this spot of a ford, which doubtless connected London with the old Roman street or road (*stratum*) to Camelodunum, whether that was at Maldon or, as is more probable, at Colchester. At Old Ford have been found several sarcophagi of a plain description, with flat covers. They are fully described, and some of them are engraved, in the third volume of the "Transactions of the London and Middlesex Archæological Society;" whilst in a lane at Stratford, called Blind Lane, between Old Ford and Leyton, were dug up about the middle of the last century a large Roman urn and fragments of pottery, confirming the derivation of Stratford from the Latin *stratum*.

The line of communication anterior to the erection of Bow Bridge was, in the opinion of Dr. Stukeley, who wrote very largely—and sometimes very fancifully—upon the Roman remains in this country, by a road extending from Chichester

to Dunwich, in Suffolk, which, having crossed the Watling Street at Tyburn, passed along Old Street, north of the city, continued forward to Colchester, following as nearly as possible the course of the high Essex road of the present day. The same author also informs us that "when the Romans enlarged the city, and enclosed it by a new wall, they also made a branch from St. Giles's, which is now called Holborn, built a gate at Newgate, and continued the road to Cheapside." This line of communication was continued east of the city; and Maitland, in his "History of London," describes it to be the "Roman vicinal way through Aldgate by Bethnal Green, to the trajectus or ferry at Old Ferry," where it, no doubt, joined the *Via Icenaia* described by Dr. Stukeley. From this it would appear that the great Roman road into Essex crossed the river Lea by means of a ferry at Old Ford, in which direction it continued for many centuries after the Romans left this island, or, in fact, until the erection of a bridge at Bow.

Morant, in his "History of Essex," has particularly noticed these roads, as also the circumstances which led to the erection of the bridge. "The ancient road from this county to London was by Old Ford, that is, through the ford there without a bridge; but that passage being difficult and dangerous, and many persons losing their lives or being thoroughly wetted, which happened to be the case of Maud, Queen Consort of King Henry I., she turned the road from Old Ford to the place where it now is, between Stratford, Bow, and West Ham, and caused also the bridges and causeway to be built and made at her own charge."

In the Itinerary of Antoninus, two of the great Roman roads are stated to have passed through Essex. One of these followed very nearly the track of the present highway through Stratford and Ilford, and some remnants of what appear to have been parts of its banks are, or were till recently, visible at West Ham, and again near Ingatestone, this conclusion being strengthened by the fact that this road was made long prior to the fixing of boundaries of the ancient forest on that side.

The native Britons, as readers of ancient history know, suffered severely under their Roman masters, large bodies of them being forced to work in making causeways across marsh lands, cutting down woods, draining morasses, and embanking the Thames with river walls. Campbell writes thus of the Roman roads in England, Vol. II., p. 250 :— "The commodious communication between the several parts of a country by means of roads, causeways where necessary, and bridges over intervening rivers, is of general convenience to the inhabitants, a constant source of opulence, and a signal proof of sound policy. The Romans were distinguished by their attention to the straightness, solidity, and admirable disposition of their larger and their lesser roads, which, though used for other purposes, were chiefly intended for military ways; and this wise economy of theirs was carried through all the provinces of their extensive empire. It is, however, remarkable that scarce in any of the countries they possessed there are still remaining more authentic monuments of these useful and stupendous works than in Great Britain, which, with indefatigable pains and most extensive learning, have been studiously traced, accurately described, and the stations on them, with as much certainty as might be pointed out by our industrious and laborious antiquaries.

"The Roman roads, while yet in a great measure entire, appeared of such amazing grandeur and solidity, manifested such a wonderful sagacity in the design, and such prodigious labour and expense in the execution, that it is no wonder, in the barbarous ages succeeding to the ruin of that empire, we find these noble and stately works confidently ascribed to giants and art magic. The intention of these military ways was worthy of the genius, and expressive of the policy, of that wise and potent people. They were so many links or lines uniting the provinces to the seat of empire.

"They extended, therefore, from Rome to the limits (however remote) of her dominions. To form some idea of them, the shortest and surest method is to consult the Pentingerian Tables. It is evident from hence that they were very numerous, and the certainty of this is confirmed by the remains which are still to be seen in many countries. In our own, as Camden observes, they are most visible, or, in other words, best preserved, and the manner of their construction (by which they have lasted more than twelve centuries) most apparent in wild heaths, over which they were carried, because near towns and villages they were pulled to pieces for the materials. In the 'Itinerary' ascribed to Antoninus there are fifteen roads, with the stations marked upon them, and the distances between them in miles, which, taken all together, make a total of two thousand five hundred and seventy-nine miles, the construction of which must have necessarily consumed much time, required much toil, and demanded immense treasures."

The Saxons, on becoming masters of the south of England, showed their appreciation of the use and value of the roads bequeathed to them by their predecessors, the Romans. The Danes, however, wreaked their vengeance on them as well as on the churches, and after the Norman Conquest, when trade and commerce were at a low ebb, they fell into disrepute, and were allowed to be gradually destroyed, especially in the neighbourhood of towns, where their materials were made of use for building purposes.

CHAPTER LV.

PLAISTOW AND EAST HAM.

"Upon a fertile spot of land
Does Plaistow, thriving Plaistow, stand."

Flat and unattractive Appearance of Plaistow—Its Sedate Aspect in Former Times—Its Sources of Wealth—The Destitute Children's Home—The Metropolitan Main Drainage Works—Census Returns—Silver Town, Canning Town, and Hall Ville—Plaistow Church—St. Andrew's Church—Congregational Church—East London Cemetery—Poplar Small-pox and Fever Hospital—Chemical Works and other Manufactories—The Royal Victoria and Albert Docks—North Woolwich—St. Mark's Church—St. John's Church—North Woolwich Gardens—Distinguished Residents at Plaistow—Descent of the Manor of East Ham—St. Nicholas's Roman Catholic School—A Curious Manorial Custom—Situation and Extent of the Parish—The Parish Church—Emmanuel Church—St. John the Baptist—Plashet House—Greenstreet House—Anne Boleyn's Tower—St. Edward's Reformatory—The High Level Sewer—Beckton Gas and Coke Works.

THOUGH level and dull, this locality has inspired the poets; at all events, there is extant a poem of eight pages, "In Praise of Plaistow"—from which the motto of this chapter is extracted—printed anonymously, without the author's name, place, or date, about the middle of the last century. At that time the land hereabouts was to a great extent unencumbered by houses, and no doubt highly productive, from an agricultural point of view. Potatoes would seem to have been the chief product of the soil, whilst the grass-land in the marshes served for the fattening of sheep.

"Potatoes now are Plaistow's pride,
Whole markets now are hence supplied;
Nor finer mutton can you spend
Than what our fattening marshes send." *

Plaistow, as shown in the preceding chapter, is a "ward" of the parish of West Ham, and the place is passed over in the "British Traveller"

* White's "Eastern Counties," Vol. II., p. 299.

(1771) with the curt remark that it "contains several genteel houses." These houses were occupied mostly by wealthy citizens and merchants of London, among whom were the Howards, the Gurneys, and the Sturges. Altogether, the village in those days must have worn a very sedate appearance. There was no church in the hamlet, but there was a Friends' meeting house and a Congregational chapel. The former now serves the purposes of a School Board school, and the latter has been adapted to business purposes.

The huge sewer of the Metropolitan Main Drainage Works passes through the village, and is then carried over the level market-gardens and meadow-land south-east to its outfall at Barking Creek. From a little, straggling, obscure village of "genteel houses," Plaistow has grown to be the larger ward of West Ham parish; and the population, which a century ago amounted to but a few hundreds, may now be reckoned by thousands, the combined districts of Plaistow (proper), Canning Town, and Silver Town, containing rather more

The Victoria Docks, and the large manufactories and centres of industry of Canning Town, Silver Town, and Hall Ville—all of which places lie southward of the village of Plaistow—have absorbed the greater part of the marsh-land and market-gardens between it and the Thames. Since the introduction of these works into the neighbourhood, the whole aspect of the locality has changed. Most of the old mansions have been either pulled down, cut up into tenements, or converted to other uses than those for which they were built. One antiquated building in the Broadway, formerly known as the "great house," or Broadway House, is now a "Destitute Children's Home;" it was established in 1872, is supported by voluntary contributions, and provides a home for sixty outcasts.

than 67,000 inhabitants, or more than double the number when the census was taken in 1871. Silver Town is the name given to the district that has sprung up around Mr. Silver's India-rubber Clothing Works at North Woolwich; and Canning Town and Hall Ville are also named after the principal employers of labour in their respective districts. The most thickly-populated parts are in the neighbourhood of the docks. The London and Tilbury Railway Company have two stations here, and the North Woolwich branch of the Great Eastern line has a station in the Barking Road, Canning Town.

Plaistow was constituted an ecclesiastical parish, formed out of the mother parish of West Ham, in 1844. The church, which was erected a few years previously, is a small brick building of Gothic design, consisting of chancel, nave, and aisles, and containing a monument to the late Sir John Henry Pelly. The first Sir John Pelly, a friend of Sir Robert Peel, who died in 1852, was the owner of the manor of East Ham Burnels. He was also a Governor of the Hudson's Bay Company, and for some time Governor of the Bank of England. Pelly Road, in this parish, is, of course, named after him.

The works and manufactories which have added so largely to the growth of this neighbourhood of late years cover an immense space of marsh-land, which had been used principally for grazing purposes. These various branches of industry comprise chemical, creosoting, artificial manure, and other works ; but the most important sources of employment in this district are the docks and the various places of business adjoining connected with the shipping.

ANNE BOLEYN'S CASTLE. (*See page* 515.)

St Andrew's Church, in St. Andrew's Road, was built in 1870, and is a spacious and lofty edifice in the Early English style.

The various bodies of Nonconformists are well supplied with chapels, one of the most imposing being the Congregational Church in Balaam Street. There are several schools in the district; and on the west side of the village, covering between forty and fifty acres of ground, is the East London Cemetery, which was opened in 1871.

The Poplar Small-pox and Fever Hospital, in the Southern Road, is among the most recent additions to the public institutions of Plaistow. It was erected in 1880, and consists of three large blocks of brick buildings, with accommodation for about one hundred patients.

The Victoria Docks, which cover an area of about 200 acres, are situated at a short distance eastward of Bow Creek, or the entrance of the river Lee. These docks were formed in 1855 ; they contain upwards of a mile of wharfage and quay frontage, and are under the management of the London and St. Katharine's Dock Company. They are fitted with all the most recently invented appliances for loading and unloading vessels, whilst its basins are capable of accommodating the largest-sized vessels that come into the port of London. The entrance-lock is 320 feet long and 80 feet wide, and has a depth on the sill of 28 feet at high water. The hydraulic lift dock, which has long been worked here, is an ingenious contrivance for the dry-docking of vessels. It is thus described in the *Globe Encyclopædia* :—" On two parallel sides of a channel, 300 feet long and 60 feet broad, sixteen upright cast-iron columns, in a row, are sunk in the ground. At the base of each column there is a hydraulic press, and the top of each piston or ram carries a cross-head, from the ends of which two iron girders are suspended by iron bars. These girders extend across the excavation to the cross-head of the corresponding column on the opposite side. There are thus thirty-two girders, forming a kind of platform capable of being raised or lowered. On this platform rests a wrought-iron pontoon, open at the top, having sufficient buoyancy to support a vessel. To apply the apparatus, the girders and pontoon, weighted with water, are sunk to the bottom of the lift, and the vessel to be raised is drawn in directly over the centre of the pontoon. The rams are then slowly raised by hydraulic power, the vessel being at the same time secured by wedges and blocks. When out of the water, the pontoon is emptied by valves, which are afterwards closed. The girders being again lowered, the pontoon, with the vessel upon it, remains afloat, and may be towed to a convenient spot. As many vessels as there are pontoons can be docked in a similar manner."

In cutting through a peat bog in the formation of the Victoria Docks there were found a large quantity of hazel, yew, oak, nuts, and other vegetable remains, more or less fossilised. The late Sir Antonio Brady, by whom this discovery was noticed at the meeting of the British Association in 1859, afterwards came into possession of the huge bones of a large whale, which had been dug out of this peat bog at a depth of fourteen feet below the surface of the soil, together with a very perfect millstone, about twenty-two inches in diameter, and a brass dish, " clearly indicating," as Sir Antonio observed, " that the marsh, wherein now dwell thousands of human beings, had been formed in the historic period."

In 1880 an extension of the Victoria Docks eastward was opened, the combined docks being named the Royal Victoria and Albert Docks. By this addition the quays of London have been brought three miles and a half lower down the river than they had hitherto extended, and great ocean steamships have been enabled to avoid the dangerous and expensive towage to Blackwall. The Albert Docks help to separate the heavy goods traffic from the lighter trade of the Thames ; they are not merely a luggage siding, but afford a direct route for reaching the Victoria Docks. A line of railway extends the whole length of the

docks. There are three stations: so that from Fenchurch Street and Liverpool Street, as termini, and from several junctions, travellers can be conveyed to the river gates of the docks. The quays are intersected and connected everywhere by railways for moving coal, iron, and other merchandise. The land for the docks was bought in 1864. It was at first intended to form merely a canal, to avoid Woolwich Reach ; but instead of a mere channel, a basin was cut nearly 500 feet wide, more than a mile long, and flanked by large sheds for receiving and warehousing goods. The combined docks are two miles and three-quarters long, with a water area of 175 acres, and about seven miles of quays. The entrance for vessels is at the point where the river, at the mouth of Galleon's Reach, widens into a lake, and affords ample room for the larger ships to manœuvre in.

The entrance lock is 500 feet long, by 80 feet wide, and has four pairs of wrought-iron gates. The depth of water at the sills is thirty feet at Trinity high water. Beyond the lock is a porch, or entrance basin, of about twelve acres, where passenger ships take their living freights on board. A passage 300 feet long and 80 feet wide, spanned by a swing-bridge, leads thence into the main dock, which is about a mile and a quarter long, and has a uniform width of 490 feet. The walls of the dock are about forty feet high, five feet thick at the top, and nineteen feet at the base. The sheds for the reception of goods are respectively 360 feet long by 120 feet broad. The sides and roof are constructed of corrugated iron. On the north side alone these sheds are sixteen in number. The hydraulic cranes, for loading and unloading vessels, travel by wheels along the quays. The great main basin of the Albert Dock is connected with the Victoria Dock by a passage 80 feet wide.

The total cost of construction of the Albert Docks was a little more than £1,000,000. A considerable saving in expense in their formation was effected by the use of large blocks of concrete, made chiefly of material dug on the spot, mixed with Portland cement, instead of using bricks, for the walls of the basins. Each leaf of the dock gates weighs 80 tons, making 160 tons for the gates ; but they are adjusted to such a nicety that four men at the windlass can move them, and when they are closed a penknife could not pass between the gate and the sill.

The Albert Dock, like the Victoria, was sunk through peat soil, enriched with the remains of successive growths of forest trees, marshy with water which everywhere showed traces of iron, and containing a few horns of deer and a few relics of pre-historic man. A canoe twenty-seven feet long, found during the excavations, was deposited in the British Museum.

The effect of the construction of the Albert Dock is that the part of the north shore of the Thames which contains North Woolwich and Silvertown is now completely cut through by a straight line of water. The Victoria Dock previously extended nearly half across the isthmus of this peninsula.

An army of 12,000 labourers ply their calling daily in this and the other docks (the St. Katharine, the London, and the Victoria), under the control of the London and St. Katharine's Dock Company. The Victoria and Albert Dock is lighted throughout by electricity, by which means ships can be loaded or unloaded at night in cases of necessity.

North Woolwich, which lies between the Victoria and Albert Docks and the river, and forms the extreme southern point of the peninsula above referred to, belongs really to the county of Kent, although it is surrounded by, and locally within, the county of Essex. The place was formerly included in the ecclesiastical district of St. Mark, Victoria Docks, but in 1877 it was separated into a distinct parish. The church, dedicated to St. John the Evangelist, was built in 1872. Here is a terminus of a branch of the Great Eastern Railway; and close by, skirting the river-side, are North Woolwich Gardens and Royal Hotel. The gardens form a popular resort for holiday-folks from London during the summer. They extend for some distance along the north bank of the Thames, beyond the steamboat pier and railway-station, and at the entrance to the gardens is the large hotel with which they are connected. One of the chief attractions of this place of amusement is its "monster platform" for open-air dancing, with such occasional extra attractions as "barmaid contests," "baby shows," and the like; the gardens, however, have never acquired the celebrity of those of Vauxhall or Cremorne, which to a certain extent they have been designed to imitate.

Besides the personages already mentioned as living at Plaistow, the parish has numbered among its inhabitants one or two other distinguished residents. Here, for instance, lived Aaron Hill, a dramatic writer of some note in the early part of the last century, and here he wrote several of his poems. Here Edmund Burke, who was fond of the country, resided for a short time before buying Gregories, his favourite seat at Beaconsfield, in 1767. Prior, in his "Life of Burke," writes:— "About this time (1759) he occasionally resided at Plaistow, in Essex. A lady, then about fourteen years old, and residing in the neighbourhood, informs me that she perfectly remembers him there. His brother Richard, who found employment in the City, was with him frequently, and both were much noticed in the neighbourhood for their agreeable and sociable qualities. Among their visitors calculated to attract notice in the country are several known as popular authors, and a few as men of rank." Luke Howard, a distinguished Fellow of the Royal Society, and author of an important work on the "Climate of London," lived for many years in a large house in Balaam Street. The house, however, has been much altered since Howard's time.

It may be added that there is another Plaistow, near Bromley, in Kent, about which we shall have to write in another volume.

East Ham, whither we now direct our steps, is —or was till recently—a dreary, outlandish place, of very little or no interest, except, perhaps, to market-gardeners. At a very early period, before the Conquest, East and West Ham formed one parish, and this part of it, which then belonged to the Crown, was given to the Abbey of Westminster—a grant which was confirmed by Edward the Confessor. In the reign of Henry III. the property belonged to the Montfitchets, and early in the fourteenth century it was divided, the easternmost manor—since known by the name of East Ham—being given by John de Lancaster to the abbot and convent of Stratford, in whose hands it remained till the dissolution of monasteries. The Manor House, near the church, was many years ago converted into a farm-house; it now serves the purposes of St. Nicholas's Roman Catholic School.

The parish comprises several hamlets and manors, as Wall End, Plashet, Manor Park, Green Street, and East Ham Burnels. Mr. Coller, in his "History of Essex," tells us that there used to be a tradition current amongst the "homagers" of the different manors to the effect that "the tenants of the manor of East Ham are obliged to treat and entertain the tenants of the other manors of West Ham, West Ham Burnels, and Plaiz, the origin of which custom is said to be this: that when the lord of these manors was taken prisoner in France, and sent to his tenants for relief, the tenants of all the other manors complied, and those of East Ham refused; so that, to punish them for their disobedience, he laid the burthen upon them."

East Ham was originally a long, straggling village, built for the most part along the sides of the cross-road which runs from Little Ilford, in the north, to the Thames, opposite Woolwich, in the south, and intersected by the road to Barking. It is between five and six miles from Whitechapel Church, with which it has a direct communication by the lower road through Poplar, leading to Barking and Grays. There is a station of the Tilbury and Southend Railway on the north side of the village, and the church stands at the south side, nearly two miles distant. East Ham is described in the "British Traveller," in 1771, as "a small, but pleasant, village, situated on an eminence, from which there is a view of the Kentish coast, the whole being extremely rural." For the "eminence" and "the view of the coast" it is feared the writer must have drawn largely upon a lively imagination. The extent of the parish, according to Kelly's "Directory of Essex," is about 2,500 acres; whilst the population, which in 1871 was a little over 4,300, now amounts to upwards of 9,300.

The church, dedicated to St. Mary Magdalen, is built of flint and stone, very ancient, and in a dilapidated condition. In the "Transactions of the St. Paul's Ecclesiastical Society" for 1882 will be found a detailed account of this little church, certainly a Norman structure. It stands near to what was once the high road; but it now seems as if the village had deserted it, leaving it as an outlying bulwark against the marshes, which stretch away southwards towards the Thames at Barking. It consists of nave and chancel, without side aisles, and its eastern end is apsidal. In the chancel is a Norman arcade of intersecting arches, carried round continuously, but sadly spoiled and mutilated by pews of the worst type. On the walls are the remains of some good Early English fresco paintings. It is sarcastically remarked that the condition of the entire fabric is such as would delight the Society for the Preservation of Ancient Buildings with its "extreme simplicity, high pews, modern windows, and obstructive gallery—a typical unrestored church!" The tower is low and massive, with double buttresses at the angles, the lower part being of Norman workmanship and the upper part modern. Most of the windows are modern and uninteresting, but there are traces of Early English windows, now built up. The apsidal sanctuary is lighted by three narrow lancets. In the south wall is a piscina, with a double drain, divided by a column forming two plain pointed arches, between which is a bracket for a lamp. Behind the communion-table is a sumptuous monument of black and white marble to Edmond Nevill, Lord Latimer, and (reputed) seventh Earl of Westmoreland, of that family. The monument comprises life-size effigies of Lord and Lady Lati-

mer, with their seven children, in devotional attitudes. At the back, over some eulogistic verses, is the following inscription :—"In memory of the Right Honorable Edmond Nevill, Lord Lattimer, Earle of Westmerland, and Dame Jane, his wife, with the Memoralls of their 7 children, which Edmond was lineally descended from the honorable blood of Kings and Princes, and the 7th Earle of Westmerland of the name of Nevills." Close by is the following epitaph to a daughter :—

"Upon the Death of the right Vertuous faire Noble Ladie Katherin Nevell, first daughter of Edmond, Earle of Westmerland, and Jane, his wife, who died a Vergine, the fifth of December, 1618, being of the Age of xx3 years.

> "Surviving Marble, choysly keep
>   This noble Virgine Ladye to sleep.
> A Branch, untimely Fal'n away
>   From Nevelles Royallized Tree ;
> Great Westmerland, too deere a Pray
>   For Death, if she could ransomd bee.
>
> "Hir Name was Katherine, not in faine
>   Hir nature held referance,
> Hir Beutie and hir parts againe,
>   Were all compos'd of Excellence.
>
> "Blud, Beuty, Vertue, did contend—
>   All Thies avanc'd in Eminence—
> Which of them could her most commend,
>   When Death, Enamord, tooke her hence.
>
> "Yet Marble tell the time to come,
>   What Erst she was when I am Dumbe."

Edmond Nevill's claim to the earldom of Westmoreland, which terminated in 1570 with the attainder of Charles Nevill, the sixth earl, was expressly disallowed by the Lords Commissioners in 1605. There are two seventeenth century brasses in this church, and in the churchyard lies buried the celebrated antiquary, Dr. Stukeley ; he was interred here in 1765, "in a spot which he had long before fixed on, when on a visit to the Rev. Mr. Sims, the vicar." His grave is not marked by any monument, and the turf, agreeably to Stukeley's own request, was laid smoothly over it.

In 1863 a new church, called Emmanuel, was built near the Barking Road. It is in the Early Decorated style, and was erected from the designs of Mr. A. W. Blomfield. It is constructed of Kentish rag, and is cruciform in plan, with a central square tower, surmounted by a dwarf spire. The church of St. John the Baptist, built in 1866, is also cruciform.

There have been several charitable bequests to the poor of East Ham ; and there are also in the parish almshouses, founded, with property left for the purpose, by Giles Bream, in 1621.

Plashet, a quiet little hamlet of East Ham, is chiefly noticeable for its manor-house—called Plashet House—which, from the early part of the present century, was for many years the residence of Mrs. Fry, the prison philanthropist, whom we have already mentioned in our account of West Ham.* Here she was visited by the King of Prussia and other distinguished personages.

Green Street, about half a mile southward of Plashet, and lying between Ilford Lane and Plaistow, is another hamlet of East Ham. Greenstreet House—commonly called "Anne Boleyn's Castle"—is a large, old red-brick mansion, supposed to occupy the site of the seat of the Nevills, whose tomb we have seen in the East Ham Church. The most conspicuous feature of the building is a tall tower, locally called Anne Boleyn's Tower, from a tradition that that unhappy lady was confined in it. Indeed, there are many legends connected with Anne Boleyn lingering about this fine old house. One is that "the tower was built for her by her royal lover in the days of his courtship; and that here the beautiful Anne sat listening to the wooing of a king, with the parting sigh of the cast-off Catherine still fresh in his ears. The tale, as told by an old writer, is that—'Anne Boleyn was betrothed to a young nobleman, who died. About ten months after his death the king demanded her hand; she, as was the custom, requested to be allowed to complete the twelvemonth of mourning for her lover, to which Henry agreed, and for her amusement built the tower in question, from which she had a fine view of the Thames from Greenwich to below Gravesend.' Further, it is asserted that when the fickle passion of the king—and as fatal as fickle—had been quelled, and the axe was sharpening for the beautiful neck which he had here embraced, the fair victim was confined for a time in this building, whence she was taken to Greenwich, and so on to the Tower. These traditions have been questioned; and the sceptic has pointed to marks about the building evidently of later date than the eighth Henry. These, however, have been accounted for as modern reparations; and it is not improbable that upon these old window-sills Anne Boleyn rested her fair arm while meditating, first upon the sunrise, and then upon the clouded setting, of her greatness. Certainly some of the apartments were at one period fitted up with royal magnificence."† It is stated that a room in the tower was hung with leather richly embossed with gold, but that an avaricious owner of the property rent this down and burnt it, in order to collect the precious metal.

From the Nevills this property passed to the Holcrofts, and still later to the Garrards. In 1869 the house, together with fourteen acres of land adjoining, was purchased, and converted into St. Edward's Catholic Reformatory School. The house, which has been enlarged, now affords a home for some 200 boys, who are taught agriculture and various useful trades and occupations.

The Metropolitan Northern High Level Sewer crosses the broad expanse of East Ham Level about midway between the church and Beckton Road. The sewer itself, which is of brick in three channels, each nine feet in diameter, is covered in by a high turf-covered embankment. During the excavations for ballast to form this embankment in 1863, about 900 yards west of the church, the workmen came upon what appears to have been a rather extensive Roman cemetery. The remains discovered consisted of leaden coffins, with a sarcophagus of stone, which were disinterred on the high ground abutting on the marshes. Cinerary urns, with other Roman *fictilia*, were found near the coffins, showing that the spot had been used as a place of sepulture by a Roman colony.

East Ham Level was a portion of the estuary of the Thames until the construction of the river wall. Mr. Ynyr Burges, in describing before the Archælogical Institute the Roman vestiges which had been discovered here, remarked that the Anglo-Saxons could scarcely have had the ability to carry out so gigantic an operation as the drainage of the marsh, and added that we may reasonably conclude that the undertaking had been achieved by the Romans, who were, as Mr. Burges observed, skilled alike in the arts of peace as in those of war—the Roman general, as a rule, *Idem pacis erat meduisque belli*. A public roadway crosses East Ham Level from the church to North Woolwich, where there is a steam ferry to Woolwich.

A large portion of East Ham Level, between he entrance to the Albert Dock and the River Roding, is occupied by the Beckton Gas Works. These works, which were established in 1869, and cover some 150 acres, have a river frontage of about 1,000 feet, protected by a substantial wall of brick and stone, from which extends an iron pier. The gas is conveyed from these works to the City and West End of London through several miles of tubes. These works, and the buildings to which they have given rise in their immediate neighbourhood, have converted the once dreary waste of East Ham Level into a thriving, if not altogether picturesque and charming, colony.

---

* See *ante*, p. 504.　　† Coller's "History of Essex."

ANCIENT BELL TOWER, BARKING ABBEY.

CHAPTER LVI.

BARKING.

"It hath a very ancient and fish-like smell."—The Tempest, Act II., Sc. 2.

Situation and Extent of the Parish—Census Returns—Etymology—Early History and Foundation of Barking Abbey—The Abbey Burnt by the Danes—Rebuilt by King Edgar—William the Conqueror takes up his Abode there—The Importance of the Abbey in Saxon Times—The Convent Damaged by an Overflow of the Thames—Curious Entries of the Revenues of the Abbey - Dissolution of the Abbey—The Abbey Gateway—Extent of the Original Buildings—Noted Abbesses—Manorial Estates of the Abbey—The Parish Church—The Rural Deanery of Barking—The Manor of Barking—The Story of Osborne's Leap—The Manor of Clayhall—Malmains—Bifrons—Eastbury House—The Road to Tilbury—Barking Town—Barking Creek—The Outfall of the Main Drainage Works—Powder Magazine, &c.—The Roman Entrenchment at Uphall.

LITTLE or no romance now attaches to the parish of Barking, though once it was holy ground. It lies at a short distance eastward of the district which we have just explored, on the opposite side of the Roding, which, below the town, before falling into the Thames, widens out into Barking Creek, a great place for small coasters. But more practical interests have superseded the halo of sanctity which once hung around it. Barking is by no means the little fishing village which it was at one time reputed to be, but a town which has been of late years much improved, with good houses and shops, and a population of 8,000, the number of its inhabitants having nearly doubled in the course of the last quarter of a century.

Its name, possibly, is derived from the Anglo-Saxon *beroc*, or *beorce*, "a birch-tree," and *ing*, "a meadow," denoting a meadow of birch-trees; but more probably a corruption of *Burgh-ing*, "the meadow fortification." This latter presumption seems to be borne out by the fact that an "encampment" is still to be traced of the most extensive dimensions—being more than forty-eight acres in extent—on the north side of the town, and which we shall visit in due course. It may be remarked that the syllable *—ing*, generally as a termination, is very frequent throughout Essex: as Margarett*ing*, *Ing*rave, Mountness*ing*, &c.

As was usually the case with parishes in which large monastic houses stood, Barking was very extensive, being nearly thirty miles round, reaching up to the borders of Hainault Forest, on the north of the Chelmsford Road, and including the hamlets of Ilford, Chadwell, Aldborough Hatch, and Barking Side.* But most of these have been cut off, and erected into separate ecclesiatical districts. The advowson belongs to All Souls College, Oxford, to which it was given by William Pownsett, of Loxford, who had been steward to the last abbess.

It was proposed as far back as 1650 that the parish should be divided into three. The entire parish contains upwards of 12,300 acres, and, according to the census returns for 1881, the population of the whole amounts to nearly 17,000.

London (the founder also of Chertsey), who died here in A.D. 685, and was buried in St. Paul's, where his shrine was one of the chief attractions.*

The abbey was dedicated to the Blessed Virgin, and was of the Benedictine Order. St. Ethelburgha, sister to Erkenwald, was abbess of the convent, where she led an austere life, and where she died in the odour of sanctity in 676. She was succeeded by her sister, Hildelha, who died in 700. Edilburga, wife of Ina, King of the West Saxons, having lived during her widowhood as a nun here,

BARKING CREEK.

Barking is believed to have formed part of the demesne lands of the East Saxon kings; but little or nothing is known of its early history until the foundation of the abbey, about the year 670, in the reigns of Sebbi and Sighere, kings of the East Saxons; the founder was a grandson of Uffa, the first Saxon king of the East Angles, and the first bishop who sat in the see of London after the erection of St. Paul's by Ethelbert. This was one of the earliest, as well as largest, of conventual houses near London, and its site must have been chosen, not for its beauty, but its solitude. It owed its foundation to St. Erkenwald, Bishop of

was canonised after her death, as also were two of her successors.

The history of the abbey is briefly told. It was burnt by the Danes, A.D. 870, and, after having lain desolate for a century, was rebuilt by King Edgar, as an offering in satisfaction for an insult offered by him at Wilton to a holy recluse, the same who became Abbess of Barking, and was canonised as St. Wulphilda. Under its Saxon abbesses Barking became one of the sacred spots of England, and Bede gives us, in his "Ecclesiastical History," a long list of the miracles worked within its walls.†

* See *ante*, pp. 490, 495.

* See "Old and New London," Vol. I., p. 236.
† See Chapters VII.—XI.

At the Conquest it was a place of note, and the Conqueror is said to have visited the place on his way to take up his abode at the Tower of London. Here, under the shadow of the venerable abbey church, and within a few miles of the reputed tomb of his rival Harold, William withdrew after his ill-omened coronation; and here he established a Court, which gradually attracted many, if not most, of the nobility of the south of England, thus making it for a time the head-quarters of "rank and fashion"—a strange contrast to the present appearance of the place.

From the gate of Barking Abbey also William is said by historians to have set out on his first royal progress through his newly-conquered kingdom.

Richard of Barking became Abbot of Westminster, Councillor to Henry III., Chief Baron of the Exchequer, and Lord Treasurer of England. He died A.D. 1246, and was buried in his abbey church.

The convent, under Algifa, Queen Maude, Adeliza, and other great Norman ladies, became one of the chief places of education of the daughters of noble families; here was also a school for youths, and amongst the children here brought up were the two sons of Catharine, widow of Henry V. Eleanor, Duchess of Gloucester, after her husband's murder, found a refuge in the Abbey of Barking, and died here A.D. 1399. "On her brass in Westminster Abbey," observes Mr. Thorne, "she is represented as a nun of Barking." In right of their large temporal estates the Abbesses of Barking held a seat in the great council of the kingdom.

It has often been asked whether women ever sat and voted in the Upper House of Parliament. As a step towards the solution of the question, attention may be drawn to the fact that in the Saxon times four abbesses—those of Barking, Wilton, Shaftesbury, and St. Mary's, Winchester—held seats in the Witenagemot, or great council of the kingdom. But whether they voted is not satisfactorily known. It appears that the Abbess of Barking enjoyed precedence above her other sisters.

It would seem that the first blow to the prosperity of the abbey was caused by a breach of the river banks at Dagenham, which flooded its low-lying lands, and caused a "public appeal" for assistance. The "Harleian Manuscripts" tell us that King Richard III. issued a license to the Prior and Convent of the Holy Trinity, in London, to grant the Abbess of Barking an annuity of twenty pounds—which was a large sum in

those days—"probably," suggests Mr. Thorne, "to assist her in her efforts to reclaim the drowned lands."

It may show the importance which was attached to this abbey in former times when it is stated that the Church of All Saints, or Allhallows, in Tower Street, had the distinguishing title appended thereto by the Abbess and Convent of Barking, to whom the vicarage originally belonged. King Richard I. added a chapel to the Church of Allhallows–Barking; and Edward I. presented a statue of "Our Lady of Barking" to the treasures of the church.

The abbess possessed thirteen knights' fees and a half, and she held her lands of the king as a barony; and though her sex prevented her from attending the king in the wars, yet she always furnished her quota of men, and had precedence over the abbesses. In her convent she always lived in great state; her household consisted of "chaplains, an esquire, gentlemen, gentlewomen, yeomen, grooms, a clerk, a yeoman cook, a groom cook, a pudding-wife, &c."

The following curious entries from the records of this house, extracted from the Harleian MS., 433, are worth the notice of the antiquarian readers :—

"Maistr. William Talbot hath the psonage of Alhalowes Berking, of London."

"Elizabeth abbess of Berking hath annuyte of xv li. graunted by Docto. Talbot pson of Berking in London, and the same graunt to hir and hir successors is confirmed by the king."

"A licence given to M. Chaderton dean of Berking, and to the chanons there to graunt to Elizabeth abbesse of Berking an annuyte of xv li. to them graunted by yre."

"The pryor and convent of the Holy Trinitie in London have a licence to graunt for ever unto th' abbess of Berking an annuyte of xx li. of al yre lands in London."

The amount of the rents received from several of the above places, as well as the kind of household anciently kept up in this monastery, appears from the following statement preserved among the Cottonian manuscripts and in the *Monasticon*, and which, for its curiosity, we are induced to give at length.

"This is the charthe longynge to the office of the celeresse of the monasterye of Barkinge as hereafter followethe :—

"First she must luke whanne she commethe into here office, what is owynge to the said office, by diverse fermours and rent gedererers, and see that it be paid as soone as she may."

She was then to receive "yerly of the collectore of Werley" at the two feasts of St. Michael and Easter, each 1. s. And of the collectors of the following places the following sums. Bulfanne yearly v l. Mockinge iiii. l. and of the "fermes ther" lx. s. Of the collector of Hockley at the two feasts of Easter and Michælmass x. l. Tollesbury, * * * Wigberewe x. l. Gynge at Stone, xlviii. s. Slapton viii. l. Of the fermour of Lytlyngton xv. l. Uphall "by yere" vi. l. xiii. s. iv. d. Dunneshall lvi. s. viii. d. Wanynges iv. l. x. s. Of the collector of Barkinge "of the rentis and fermes of Barkinge and Dagenham, to the longing to the sayd office, by the yere, xij. l. xviii. s." "Of the chanons of Seynt Powles," a rent of xxii. s. "Of the prior and convent of Seynt Bartholmewes in London," xvij. s. And of John Goldington for a yearly rent of divers tenements at "Seynt Mary Schorehogge," xxii pence. For a tenement in Friday Street yearly xxiii. s. and iiii. d. "but it is not knowen wher it stonds," and "she shuld receive yerly xxx. s. of the rent of Tybourne, but it is not paid."

Then follow the various particulars the cellaress was to provide for the convent.

The Issues of the Larder.—"And also she must be charged with all the orskeyns that she selleth; and of all the inwardes of the oxen; and with all the tallowe that she selleth, coming of hyr oxen: also of every messe of the beyofe that she selleth: and all these be called the yssues of the larder.

The foryn Receyte.—"And also yf she sell oney hey at ony ferme longynge to her office, she must charge her selfe therwith, and it is called a foryn receyte.

"Some totalis of all the said charthe . . . .

Beyinge of Greynys.—"Wher of what parte of the said some sche must purvey yerly for three quarters malte, for the tounes of St. Alburgh, and Cristmasse, eche them xij. bushell, and than must sche pay to the brewer of each toune xx. d. And then must sche purvy for a quarter and seven bushells of whete fore pitaunce of William Dune, Dame Mawte Loveland, Dame Alys Merton, Dame Mawte the kynges daughter: and for russeaulx in Lenton and to bake with elys on Schere Thursday. And then must sche pay to the baker for bakinge of every pitaunce vi. d. And also sche must purvey for one bushell of greyne beanes for the covent ayenst missomer.

Beying of Store.—"And sche must purvy for xxii. gud oxen by the yere fore covent.

Providence for Advent and Lentten.—"Also sche must purvy for two cadys of heryngs that be rede for the covent in Advent: and for vii cadys of red heryng for the covent in Lenton: and also for three berell of white heringe for the covent in Lentyn: and also sche must purvey for xii. c. lib. almondes for the covents in Lentyn, and for xviii salt fish for the covent in Lentyn; and for xiv. or ellys xv. salt salmones for the said covent in Lentyn: and for three peces and xxiv. l. fyggis: and one pece reysenez for the covent in Lenton. And also for xxviiil. l. ryse for the covent in Lenton; and for viii galons mustard for the covent.

Ruscheaw Sylver.—"And also sche must pay to every lady of the covent, and also to the priorisse, to two celeresse and kechener, for ther doubls, for ther rushew sylver, by xvi. times payable in the yere to every lady, and doubill at eche time ob. but it is paid nowe but at two times that is to say, at Ester and Michelmes: also sche must paye to every lady

of the covent, and to the said foure doubles, to eche lady and double ij. d. for their cripsis and crumkakes alway payd at Shroftyd.

Anniversaryes.—"And also sche must pay for v anniversaries, that is to say, Sir William Vicar, Dame Alys Merton, Dame Mawte the kynge's daughter, Dame Mawte Loveland, and William Dun: and also to purvey for xii gallon good ale for the pittance of William at the day of anniversary.

Offeringes and Wages, and Gyftes of the Selleris.—"And also sche must pay in offryng to two celleresses by yere xii. d. and then shall sche pay to the steward of howshold, what tyme he brynght home money from the courtis, at eche tyme xx. d. and then schall sche gyve to the steward of howshold at Cristymes xx. d. and to my lady's gentylwoman xx. d. and to every gentilman xvi. d. and to every yoman as it pleaseth her to doo, and gromes in like case: and then must sche bye a suger looffe for my lady at Cristmas: and also sche must pay to hyr clerk for his wages thirteen shillings fourpence; to hyr yoman cooke twenty-six shillings eightpence: and sche shall pay for a gown to her grome coke and her poding wief by the yere ii. s.

Fitance of the Covent.—"And also sche must purvy for iii. casse of multon for the covent, for the pitaunce of Sir William Vicar: also sche must purvey for a pece of whete, and iii. gallons melke for firmete on Seynt *Alburgh's* daye: also she must purvey iiii bacon hojis for the covent, for pitance of Dame Alys Merton, and Dame Mawte the kinge's daughter, at ii times in wynter; and sche must bye vi grecys, vi sowcys for the covent, and also vi inwardys, c. egges to make white podinges: also bred, peper, saferon for the same podinjes: also to purvey iii galons gude ale for besons. And also to purvey marybones to make white wortys for the covent: and then must sche purvey at Seynt *Andrewestyd* a pitance of fysche for my lady and the covent: and then must sche pay at Shroftyde to every lady of the covent, and to iiii doubles, for their cripcis, and for the crumkakes to every lady and doubill ii. d. and thanne must sche purvey for my lady abbess against Shroftyd, viij. chekenes: also bonnes for the covent at Shroftyd. Also iiii galons melke fur the covent the same tyme: and yen must sche purvey for every Sonday in Lenton pituance fysche for the covent: and also to be sure of xii stubbe elles and lx. schafte eles to bake for the covent on Schere Thursday: and also one potel tyre for my ladye abbess the same day, and two galons of rede wyne for the covent the same day: and also to purvey three galons of good ale for the covent every weke in Lenton, and to have one galone red wyne for the covent on Ester evyn: and also to purvey for three casse of multon for the covent, for the pitaunce of William Dune: and also to purvey for every lady of the covent, and v double to every lady, and double di. gose delivered at the fest of the Assumption of our Lady.

Eysylver.—"And also sche must pay to xxxvii ladyes of the covent for their *eysylver* fro Michelmes tyll Allhallowday, to every lady by the weke i. d. ob. and then to every lady by the weke fro Allhallowe-day tyll Advent i. d. ob. q. and then to every lady be the weke fro advent Sonday till Childermas day i. d. q. and then to every lady for the same eysylver be the weke fro Cheldermesday unto Aschwednesday i. d. ob. q. and then fro Ester unto Michelmasse to every lady be the weke i. d. ob. and then must sche paye to eche lady for ye eysylver for eche vigill fallyng within the yere ob. and then must sche pay to the priorie eche weke in the yere, except Lenten xxxii. egges, or elles ii. d. ob. q. in money for them every weke, except iiii weke in Advent, in the wheche sche shall not pay but xvi. egges be the weke : and also sche must pay to the said priorie for every vigill fallynge within the yere viij. egges, or elles ob. dim. q. and iiii. part of q in money for the same.

Beyinge of Butter.—" And then must sche purvey for fest butter of Seynt Alburgh for xxxvii lades and iiij. doubles, that is to say, the prioresse, ij. celleressys, and the kechener, to every lady and double i. cobet, every disch conteynyng iii cobettes : and then must sche pay to the sayd ladys and doubles for the storying butter by v tymes in the yere, that is to wite, in Advent, and three tymes after Cristmas, to eche lady and double at every ob. and also sche must purvey for the said lades and doubles for the fest butter at Ester and Whitsontide, lyk as sche dyd at Seynt Alburgh's tyde : also sche must purvey for the sayd lades of the covent, and the said iiii doubles, and the priory for ther fourtnyght butter fro Trinitie Sonday unto Holy Rounde daye, that is to seyd, to every lady double, and priory, at eche fourtnyght betweene the sayd two festes i cobette butter, iii cobetts makyng a disch : and also sche must purvey to the said ladys with ther doubles to the fest butter of Assumption of our Lady, to every lady and double i. cobett butter.

Hyreing of Pastur.—" And then must sche be sure of pasture for her oxen in tym of yere, as her servants can enfourme her.

Mowyng and making of Heye.—" And also to see hyr heye be mowe, and made in time of ye yere, as yeryng requeryth.

Costys of Reparations.—" And thanne must sche see that all manner of howses within her office be sufficiently re-payred as well withought at hyr fyrmes, manners, as within the monastery.

This ys the Forme of brening of the Celeresse Beofe ; foist the Clerke shall enter into her Boke as followeth.—" The Satyrday the xx daye of September she answereth of iiii or v messes remaynyng in store of the last weke before, and of lxiii messes of beofe comyng of an oxe slayn that same weke : and also sche must answere of iiii. xx messes of beofe be byr boughte of the covente, of that they lefte behynd of ther lyvere paying for every messe i. d. ob. las in all by i. d. ob. *summa* cxlvii. messe, thereof delyvered to eche lady of the covent for iii dayes in the weke iii messe of beofe, that is sonday, tewesday, and thursday : and thanne schall sche pay to the priory for the seid iii dayes vi messes of beof, for eche day ij messe ; and yff there fall no vigill in the sayd iii dayes, and where there falleth a vigill in ony of the iii. and the next settyrday sche must loke what beof every houshold will have, and thereafter must sche purvey her beofe in the market ; for she shall stey but every fortnyght, and yff sche be a good huswyff.

The Levery of Red Herynge in Advent.—" First sche schall delyvere to eche lady of the covent every weke in Advent for monday and wednysday, for eche day to every lady iii heryngs : and to the priory every weke in Advent for the sayd ij days viii heryngs.

The Levery of Almonds, Rysse, Fyggs, and Reyssons in Lenton.—" First to my lady abbesse in almondes for Advent and Lenttyn iiii. l. and to every lady of the covent for Advent and Lentten ii. l. almondis, and to the prioresse ii celarisses and kechenere for ther doubill to eche doubell ii. l.

Rysse.—" And eche lady of the covent for all the Lentten D. l. ryse, and eche of the said iiii double to eche double for all the Lentten D. l. rysse.

Fyges and Reysons.—" And eche lady of the covent every weke in Lenton i. l. fyges and reyssons, and eche of the sayd iiii doubles every weke in Lentton i. l. fyges and reysons, and to the priori every weke i. l. fygs and reysons.

Levery of Herynge.—" And to every lady of the covent for every day in the weke in Lentton iiii heryngs red and white, that is, every lady xxviii heryngs be the weke, and to the priori be v dayes, that is, monday, tewsday, wedynesday, thursday, and sattyrday ; and the sonday they recevy fische, and for the friday fygs and reysons.

Levery of Fische.—" And to every lady of the covent in Lent-ton eche oder weke, one messe salt fysch, and to the prioresse ii celleresses and kechener for the doubles eche other weke in Lentten, to eche double i messe salt fysch ; and to the priory eche other weke in Lentton ii messe salt fysch, every salt fysch conteynyng vii messe.

Levery of Salt Salmon.—" And to every lady of the covent in Lentton eche other weke i messe of salt salmon ; and like-wyse to eche of the sayd iiii doubles i messe of salmon ; and in lykewyse each other weke to the priorye ii. messe of salt salmon yeldyng ix messe.

The Levery of Sowse—" Be it remembered that the celeresse must se that every lady of the covent have hyr levery of sowse fro my lady abbesse kychen at Martynmese tyme ; and every lady to have three thynges ; that is to say, the cheke, the ere, and the fote, is a levery ; the groyne and two fete ys anodyr levery ; soe a hoole hoggs sowsse, shall serve three ladyes. And thanne must sche have for three doubles in lyke wyse, to every double three thyngs ; and the three doubles be the prioresse, the high celeresse and the kychener ; the under celeresse schall not have of double : and then must gyff to every lady and double beforesaid of sowce of hyre owne provisione two thyngs to every lady ; so that a hoole hogg sowse do serve four ladyes.

Pitaunce Pork.—" And sche must remember to aske for the covent at my lady abbesse kychen allwey at Martynmesse pittaunce porke for every lady one messe, and for foure doubles, that is to sey, the priorisse, two celliresses, and the kychener, to every double one messe : and then must sche purvey pittaunce porke for the covent, wheche longeth to hyr owne office, for to doo at two tymes in wynter, and that is, ones for Dame Alys Merton and another for Dame Mawte the king's daughter, at eche tyme to every lady one messe, and eche double one messe ; and every hogge shall yield xx messe.

Pittaunce Mutton.—" And also sche must aske for the covent at my lady abbesse kychen pittaunce mutton three tymes in the yere, betweene the Assumption of our Lady and Michelmasse, at eche tyme to every lady one messe, and to the priorisse the high celleresse, and to the kychener for three doubles, for every double one messe, and every mutton shall yelde xii messe. And then must sche purvey for pittaunce mutton for the covent wheche longeth to hyr owne office to doo at two tymes in the yere, that is, once for Syr William Vicar, and another tyme for William Dune ; to every lady and doubell beforesaid, one messe mutton at eche tym, every mutton yeldynge xii messe.

Soper Eggs.—" And the under celeresse must rememder at eche principal fest, that my lady sytteth in the fraytour ; that is to wyt, five tymes in the yere, at eche tyme shall aske the clerke of the kychen soper eggs for the covent, and that is Estir, Wytsontyd, the Assumption of our Lady, Seynt Alburgh, and Cristynmasse, at eche tyme to every lady two eggs, and eche double two eggs, that is the priorisse, the celeresse, and the kycheper.

Rusheaulx in Lenton.—" Also sche must remembir rusheaulx in Lenton, that my lady abbesse have viii of the . . . .

Leveray of Geese and Hennes —"Also to remembir to ask of the kychyn at Seynt Alburgh's tyme, for every lady of the covent halfe a goose, and for six double, for every double *dim.* goose, that is, the priorisse, two celeresse, the kychener, and two chaunteresse. Also to eche at the said fest of Seynt Alburgh of the said clerke, for every lady of the covent one henne, or elles a coke, and for ix doubles, to eche double a henne, or elles a coke, and the be iii priorisses, the chaunteresses, ij cellerysses, the kychener, and the two freytouresses.

Leveray Bacon.—"Also to remember to aske the levery bacon for the covent alwey before Cristmasse, at my lady abbesse kychyner, for every lady of the covent iiii messe, and that is, to the priorisse the cellerysse, the kychener ; and sche shall understond that a flytch of bacon conteynigh x messe.

Levery Ottmeale.—"Also to remember to deliver every lady of the covent every moneth in the yere, at eche tyme iiii dyshes of otemelle, delivered to the covent coke for rushefals, for Palme Sundaye, xxi pounder fyggys. *Item* delyveryd to the seyd coke, on Sherthursday viii pounde ryse. *Item* delyveryd to the said coke for Sherethursday xviii pounde almans *Memorandum* that a barrell off herring should contene a thousand herrings, and a cade off herryng six hundereth, six score to the hundreth."

At the dissolution of monasteries, Barking had, according to Speed, an income of £1,085, and was surrendered to the greedy king by its last abbess, Dorothy Barley, who "retired on a pension." The king leased the abbey and its adjoining lands to one of his courtiers, Sir Thomas Denny. It was granted under Edward VI. to Lord Clinton, who sold it forthwith to Sir Richard Sackville, and it has since changed owners repeatedly, like most of such properties. The Manor of Barking, which once was an appendage to the abbey, was seized by Henry VIII., has passed from royal into private hands, and now belongs to Sir E. Hulse.

Of all the once magnificent buildings of the abbey nothing now is left, except a solitary embattled gateway, once known as the "Chapel of the Holy Rood Loft atte Gate," but now commonly called the "Fire-bell Gate," from a tradition that it contained the bell rung for curfew and for alarm of fires. The gateway is substantially in good condition, though the mullions and tracery of its windows have been sadly mutilated. The gateway still guards the entry into the churchyard and church ; in the room over the entrance is still to be seen a relievo of the Crucifixion, much defaced by "pious" iconoclasts. It is needless to say that the fire-bell is no longer there ; nor are there any traces of its position. Another gateway leading into the precincts of the abbey was needlessly taken down in 1881.

A few yards north of the church stood the abbey itself, but of the conventual buildings scarcely a stone remains, except a few fragments of the walls, which now serve as the walls of a market-garden that covers the sacred spot. Bones and other remains have often been dug up here. Lysons, in his "Environs of London," gives a ground plan of the abbey church, "taken from the ruins of its foundation in 1724." But Mr. Thorne sees reasons for doubting the accuracy of its details. According to this plan, it was a hundred and seventy feet long, and cruciform in shape, the width of the transepts being a hundred and fifty feet. This was erected in the middle of the thirteenth century, in the place of an older and smaller structure.

No print or painting of the church remains, the work of the "Reformers" being complete here ; but it was doubtless a noble building in its time. According to the plan in Lysons it consisted of nave, chancel, and transepts, the two former with side aisles, and the Lady Chapel east of the chancel. Besides the high altar, there were in it altars of Our Lady, of the Resurrection, and of St. Peter and St. Paul, and the shrines of St. Hildelitha and St. Ethelburgha. In the year 1876 the foundations of the Lady Chapel and the skeletons of two ladies, probably abbesses, buried in front of the altar, were discovered in the grounds belonging to the national school, a part of the site which does not appear to have been excavated previously.

"As for Barking Abbey" (writes the author of "Professional Excursions" in 1843), " where canonisation descended as an heirloom, and miracles grew like mushrooms, the owl has forsaken it and the bat disdains it. The curfew has fallen from the belfry, and the *pudding-wife's* occupation is gone."

Mr. Thorne tells us that "the library of Magdalen College, Oxford, possesses a relic of the abbey in the shape of a beautiful French manuscript, containing the Lamentations of St. Bernard, the Meditations of St. Augustine, and a Life of St. Louis, presented to the convent by the Countess of Oxford—the wife of the twelfth earl of the old line of De Vere."

Many charters and privileges, as might be expected, were bestowed on the convent by our Norman kings.

Among the names of the ladies who sat in the abbess's chair are to be noticed those of De la Pole, Montacute, Merton, De Vere, and à Becket—the last named being a sister of the martyred archbishop.

Among the possessions of the abbey long before the Conquest, and possibly from its first foundation, was the manor of Barking ; this was seized by the greedy tyrant, Henry VIII., and remained vested in the Crown until sold by Charles I. to the Fanshawes, from whom it passed, through some intermediate hands, to the Lethuilliers, and from them again to the Hulses, its present owners.

The abbess had not only a host of dependants and retainers, but also a prison in which to detain offenders; and if any of her servants married his daughter beyond the limits of the manor, he had to pay a fine to the abbey.

There were in Barking several subordinate

traces of Early English and Perpendicular work. It contains some fine monuments: the best and finest is in memory of Sir Charles Montagu, of Cranbrook, Essex (brother of the first Earl of Manchester), who is represented as dying on the field of battle, a page holding his horse at the door of a tent. There are three good brasses on the chancel floor; and other mural tablets deserve attention, especially one to Sir Orlando Humfreys. One or two curious aumbries still remain in the north side of the chancel.

EASTBURY HOUSE.   (*After Lysons.*)

manors, as those of Wangay, Fulks, Loxford, Malmains, Cranbrook, Westbury, Eastbury, &c.

The parish church, dedicated to St. Margaret, is large; it comprises nave, chancel, and north and south aisles, with a tower at the west end. It must once have been fairly handsome, but it has been terribly "beautified" and modernised, its once open timber roofs having been replaced by ornamental plaster ceilings of the Stuart period. It was built chiefly in the fourteenth century, but its date is not at all clearly shown by its architecture, the tracery of its windows having been superseded by modern insertions. One portion of the church, including the piers between the nave and north aisle, near the western end, is Norman, and there are

In the church were three chantries: one at the altar of the Resurrection, in the north transept, and others at the altar of King Edward and the shrine of St. Ethelburgha.

It appears that the vicars of Barking were considered as part of the household of the lady abbess, and had a seat and a knife and fork (if forks were then invented) at the chaplain's table, their servants sitting "below the salt," with the domestics of the convent; but this right, being found troublesome, was commuted for a money payment.

Barking is a rural deanery, in the diocese of St. Albans; and the Bishop of St. Albans Fund, which was established a few years ago, is, in point of fact, a home mission and church extension society for the metropolitan portion of the diocese situated in this deanery. Its sphere includes thirty ecclesiastical parishes, embracing the town districts of Stratford, Canning Town, Victoria Docks, and North Woolwich, and suburban places like Barking, Leyton, Leytonstone, Walthamstow, Wanstead, and Woodford. These districts now contain a population of about 224,000, being nearly double the population of 1871. Many parts of the deanery are inhabited by clerks and workmen who have been forced out of London by the

has been already told by us in OLD AND NEW LONDON.*

The manor of Clayhall, in this parish, was held under the abbess and convent of Barking by the following singular services: namely, that every tenant should come in person to the abbey church on the vigil of St. Ethelburgha the Virgin, and there attend and guard the high altar from the first hours of vespers till nine the next morning; and that he should be ready at all times, with a horse and a man, to attend the abbess and her steward when going upon the business of the con-

MARKET HOUSE, BARKING.

reduction of cheap house accommodation; and the publicans are often almost the only people in the parish who keep a domestic servant. At the commencement of 1883 there were 88 Dissenting and seven Roman Catholic chapels in the deanery, with a total of 32,100 sittings, while the total provision made in churches, with mission-rooms, &c., was 28,600.

After the Dissolution, the manor of Barking, which was paramount over the Hundred of Becontree, remained with the Crown till the time of James I., when it was sold to the Fanshawes. In the reign of Queen Elizabeth the property was in the hands of Sir William Hewitt, Lord Mayor of London. The story, as given by Strype, of the manner in which it passed into the possession of Mr. Osborne, the ancestor of the Dukes of Leeds,

vent anywhere within the four seas. And, lastly, that the abbess should have, by way of heriot, upon the death of every tenant, his best horse and accoutrements; these services, however, did not exempt them from the quit rents. Besides the above tenure, there were other "vexatious contingencies," namely, one Robert Gerard was, among other services, "to gather a full measure of nuts, called a pybot, four of which should make a bushel; to go a long journey on foot once a year to Colchester, Chelmsford, Ely, or the like distances, on the business of the convent, carrying a pack, and other shorter distances, such as Brentford, &c., and maintaining himself upon the road. He was to pay a fine upon the marriage of his daughter, if she married beyond the limits of

* See Vol. I., p. 401.

the manor. If his daughter had an illegitimate child, he was to make the best terms he could with the abbess for the fine called Kyldwyte. It appears, also, that he could not even sell his ox, fed by himself, without the abbess's permission."

In former times there were several manor-houses in the parish, but they have mostly disappeared, or been altered to suit other purposes.

Malmains, which stood about a mile and a half north-east from the church, was the residence of Sir William Hewitt, mentioned above. Bifrons, on the road between Barking and Eastbury House, was in the last century the seat of Bamber Gascoigne, M.P., a maternal ancestor of the Marquis of Salisbury. It was so fancifully named because of its double front.

Eastbury House, on the road to Dagenham and Rainham, about a mile from Barking, is a large, dreary, tumble-down mansion, square in plan, of an almost collegiate type, built of red brick, with tall gables, square mullioned windows, and stacks of graceful chimneys, which still retain their original freshness. The rooms inside were panelled, and some of them were painted in fresco; but the interior of the house has been modernised.

A representation of the house, in Lysons' "Environs of London," shows two tall towers, which rise above the top of the house; but now there is only one: the other was destroyed by lightning some years ago. It is said, but erroneously, that Lord Monteagle was staying here when he received the letter which, being submitted to James I., led to the discovery of the Gunpowder Plot.

"Eastbury House," writes the author of "Professional Excursions," "has some pretensions to be immortalised as the reputed residence of Lord Monteagle, who was so singularly instrumental in discovering the Gunpowder Plot, which still annoys us with its barbarous ceremonies on the 5th of November. It is a wretched, neglected building, fit only for 'treason, stratagems, and spoils,' and has only a few whimsical shafts to recompense the trouble of leaving the highway and encountering an ague." The old mansion is called by the natives "Gunpowder House," from a tradition that Guy Fawkes and his fellow conspirators used it as a rendezvous; but there is no historical evidence of this, and even the tradition is confused and contradictory.

It is religiously believed by the natives that preparations had been made by those connected with the "Gunpowder Plot" to witness the catastrophe from the top of the great tower, which commands a view over London. We have, however, shown in a previous chapter that the conspirators hired a house for that purpose at White Webbs, Enfield,* in which they also held their secret meetings. The house belongs to the Sherry family, and entrance to it is most churlishly refused to visitors.

The road by Eastbury House leads on by Grays to Tilbury and Southend. It must have been by this road that Queen Elizabeth rode down to her camp at Tilbury to inspect her troops on that historical occasion just when the panic of the great Spanish Armada had reached our shores, and when she addressed to her gallant soldiers those words which are recorded in every English History:—"My loving people," said the queen, "we have been persuaded by some that are careful of our safety to take heed how we commit ourselves to armed multitudes, for fear of treachery; but I assure you I do not desire to live to distrust my faithful and loving people. Let tyrants fear; I have always so behaved myself that, under God, I have placed my chiefest strength and safeguard in the loyal hearts and good-will of my subjects; and, therefore, I am come amongst you at this time, not as for my recreation and sport, but being resolved in the midst and heat of the battle to live or die amongst you all, to lay down for my God, for my kingdom, and for my people, my honour and my blood even in the dust. I know that I have but the body of a weak and feeble woman; but I have the heart of a king, and of a King of England too, and think foul scorn that Parma, or Spain, or any prince of Europe, should dare to invade the borders of my realms."

The town of Barking is mainly agricultural; it is straggling and irregular in plan, and is joined to London by a double line of railway: the one to Fenchurch Street, and the other by way of Stratford to Bishopsgate. It is on the route to Southend.

In the High Street is an old market-house (said by Lysons to have been built by Queen Elizabeth), around which a market is still held on Saturday. The streets are poor, narrow, squalid, and badly drained. By the wharf at the end of the town is a corn-mill, standing on the site of the old Abbey Mill. From this wharf, Pepys tells us in his "Diary," under date August 18th, 1662, the timber cut down for the navy in the royal forests of Hainault and Epping was shipped for Woolwich. The chief traffic now consists of fish, coals, and corn.

At Uphall, a farm a little to the north of the

---

* See ante, p. 369.

town, near the Roding, are the remains of a square
fortification nearly forty acres in extent.   They are
certainly Roman, and are supposed to mark a
fortification, or else the site of a town or military
station, probably the first of a series on the road
between Augusta (London) and Camelodunum,
Maldon, or Colchester.   The banks and trenches
minutely described by Lysons have been partially
effaced by the plough, but near the north-western
angle is still to be seen a "very fine spring of
water, which was guarded by an inner work and a
high keep, or mound of earth."   The mound is
still there, and the spring still bubbles up as it
did in the days of Julius Cæsar.   Probably the
stones of the encampment were utilised in building
the abbey at Barking which the Danes destroyed.

The men of Barking would seem to have been
bold and adventurous.   One of them, David Ingram, gives an account of his voyage to North
America, along with "Master" Hawkins, and his
travels in Mexico and in other parts of that
continent in 1582.   His curious narrative is to be
seen in the first edition of "Hakluyt's Voyages,"
though omitted from later issues.   It was probably
thought too wonderful to be true.

From the town wharf down to its junction with
the Thames, the banks of Barking Creek are
artificially raised by strong walls, along which there
is a public path.   But the walk is not attractive.
Nor, perhaps, are its attractions increased by the
fact that just above it, on its western side, is the
outfall into the Thames of the main drainage works
of London, which were carried out under Lord
Palmerston's premiership by Sir Joseph Bazal-
gette.*

Mr. Thorne, in his "Environs of London," states
that here 10,000,000 cubic feet of sewage are
brought daily down from London in a concrete
sewer which crosses the marshes, and deposited in a
reservoir, which is discharged into the Thames at
high water.

The reservoir, or main outfall, is constructed on
lands in Barking parish.   It is built on the marsh-
land on the west side of the mouth of Barking
Creek, and covers an area of nearly ten acres.   It
is divided into four compartments, and will hold
39,000,000 gallons of sewage.   The walls are of
brick, the floor of stone, and the concrete foundations are carried down to a depth of about twenty
feet.   At Lodge Farm, Barking, some of the sewage
is scientifically applied to agricultural purposes, and
with great success ; and it seems a very great
pity, to say the least, that all the London sewage

is not applied in like manner towards reclaiming
and fertilising all the waste lands on the Essex
borders.

"Primarily the duties of the Metropolitan
Board of Works," observes the *St. James's Magazine,*
"are constructional in character, and all the other
details of its finance and government are merely
subordinate to this original object.   This fact has
endowed the body with more than ordinary
importance, for its main functions are spending
ones, and resulting in the realisation of great
structural works, designed for the benefit of the
inhabitants of the metropolis.   Instituted almost
solely for remedying the defects and dangers of an
undrained, or at least imperfectly drained, city, its
first task was a solution of the vexed and unsatisfactory problem of 'London drainage.'   The
polluted character of the river Thames at the
period of the Board's inauguration was a notorious
fact, and, aided by the designs of many eminent
engineers, it set about its work with well-meant and
disinterested energy.   With almost unlimited funds
at its command, no obstacle prevented the carrying
out a scheme of efficient drainage, which it was
fondly hoped would set at rest for all time the
dangers associated with congested sewers, and their
intermittent efflux into a tidal river.   The final
scheme as now carried out was the construction of
a series of main drains parallel to the Thames,
whose functions were to intercept everything
seweral in character from the houses within the
superficial boundary of the Board's jurisdiction ;
in short, collecting, or rather directing, the overflow
of London's sewage (so as to prevent its mingling
with the river through the City and suburbs) to a
more distant point of disemboguement . . . .   Let
us now, after a few years' interval, examine in all
seriousness the *gain* derived from so large an
expenditure.   There was undoubtedly a fundamental error in deciding to concentrate the daily
discharge of seven or eight hundred thousand tons
of sewage into the river Thames, at points abutting
on the eastern boundaries of the metropolis itself.
It was assumed by the engineers of the Board
that pumping out this large and fluctuating volume
of semi-liquid sewage could be beneficially effected
at the top of the tide, resulting in the final dispersion of the corrupt mass by tidal and river influences.
In the early days of this great engineering feat,
adverse criticism from any quarter met with scant
courtesy.   Even those experienced chemists and
agriculturists who besought the Board to consider
the value of that which was thus ruthlessly consigned
to what they regarded as annihilation, and beyond
the reach of being a danger to the metropolis, at

See "Old and New London," Vol. V., pp. 41, 42.

least were snubbed. The loss of £4,000,000 (besides the cost of its dispersion) was as nothing, for was the Thames not purified between the bridges, so much so as to enable steamboat passengers to enjoy a sail in warm weather without the disgusting dangers of noisome smells from a malodorous stream? The first serious challenge of dissent offered to this assumed happy condition of things, and which somewhat disturbed the equanimity of the Board and its engineers, proceeded from the River Thames Conservancy, which, from a carefully prepared river chart and innumerable soundings, showed that mud-banks of an abnormal character were being formed, and that these were attributable to deposits from the Crossness and Barking sewer discharges. Notwithstanding the apparent accuracy of these asseverations, proceeding from an important body, the whole affair was speedily settled by the Board proving, from its own and independent engineering evidence, that the very idea of such a state of things was absolutely preposterous. The River Thames Conservators did not need to be apprehensive of stoppage to navigation, for the millions of tons of sewage matter pumped into the river Thames in the course of the year was sent away, by a happy condition of natural influences, to seaward, where its baneful and dangerous character would be utterly destroyed. The contentions of the Metropolitan Board have been unavoidably persistent as well as consistent, for it is invariably argued, and with much plausible appearance of reason, that all the filth of London, through its agency, is rendered harmless and innocuous, and that neither water, air, land, or sea can be injuriously interfered with, in consequence of its system of drainage. A body of undoubted importance, entrusted with an onerous task, was naturally treated with much forbearance in the past; for during the early years of its existence much allowance had to be made for the novelty of dealing in so comprehensive a manner with a leviathan undertaking such as the disposal of London's sewage. Germs of disease deposited on the river sides and at the bottom of the stream are simply storehouses for future supplies of forces charged with danger and death, the natural result of the collection of London's sewage into vast longitudinal sewers, which at intervals may be dammed back to meet tidal or other exigencies, and which, when so retarded must push back with force the gases produced from the accumulation and churning of such varied qualities of filth. Sewer gas, as it is now called, under such circumstances, readily escapes from the sources of its generation, and with its deadly influences and surroundings permeates the dwellings with which the system of London drainage so effectually entangles the homes of the ratepayers. New types of disease, frequently baffling the skill of the most accomplished physicians, are the result of such baneful contamination from a source which is difficult to control. The main drainage system of London (and by its example and teachings provincial cities and towns as well) has created new professions, in whose ranks special experts have risen up to grapple with dangers and inconveniences before unknown."

The drainage system of London, on the north side of the Thames, comprises the High Level, the Middle Level, the Low Level, and the Western District Sewers, together with the Outfall at Barking Creek. The High Level drains Hampstead, Highgate, Kentish Town, Highbury, Stoke Newington, Hackney, and passes under Victoria Park to Old Ford; its length is about nine miles. The Middle Level runs by way of Kensal Green, Kensington Park, Notting Hill, Bayswater, Oxford Street, and so under a number of minor streets, to Old Ford, being about twelve miles long. The Low Level commences near Pimlico, and will pass along under the Thames Embankment to Blackfriars, and thence through the City and Whitechapel to West Ham. The Western District Sewers drain Acton, Hammersmith, Fulham, Chelsea, &c., on a plan different from that of the main drainage in other localities. The Outfall, an immense work, six miles long, continues the Upper and Middle Level Sewers from Old Ford to West Ham, and all the three sewers thence to Barking Creek, where we now leave it.

At the mouth of the creek, on the east side, are a powder-magazine, a coastguard station, and some large factories.

It is mentioned as a notorious fact by Campbell, in his "Political Survey of Great Britain," that the drainage and reclaiming of the fens and marshes along our rivers was principally the work of the clergy, who in the Saxon times were the most learned and the most wealthy order in the country. And there is no part of England where such qualifications were more in demand than along the banks of the Lea and the Thames, in the neighbourhood of London.

CHAPTER LVII.

DAGENHAM.

" Rivus multâ mole docendus aprico parcere prato."—HORACE.

Ripple Side, Barking—Ripple Castle—Extent and Boundaries of Dagenham—Census Returns—The Village—Church—Parsiowes—Valence—
Dagenham Breach—Discovery of a " Moorlog"—The River Walls of the Thames—Dagenham Lake—Its Proposed Conversion into a
Dock—Failure of the Scheme—Origin of the Ministerial Fish Dinner.

BEYOND Barking Level the land immediately abutting upon the Thames is mostly a dreary marsh, crossed and intersected by straight dykes and sluggish pools, but further inland are broad stretches of pasture-land, serving as an admirable grazing-ground for cattle. The roadway running eastward from Barking towards Rainham, for the first mile or two, till past the high ground whereon stands Eastbury House, is called Ripple Side. A square brick-built house by the roadside, near the commencement of Dagenham parish, erected about a century ago, is somewhat pretentiously named Ripple Castle, doubtless on account of the taste of the builder having led him to ornament its parapet with battlements, and to flank the front of the house with circular towers pierced with narrow loopholes, but it is a poor imitation of a castellated structure, at best.

Dagenham, which is the next parish in succession eastward of Barking, extends from the banks of the Thames far northward, by Chadwell Heath, into what used to be Hainault Forest, a distance of some seven miles inland, the northern border being fully five miles off from the straggling village. The eastern boundary of the parish is the Beam rivulet, which unites with the Rom. The village lies away about a mile northward of the high road from Barking to Rainham, two miles north-west from Rainham Station, on the Tilbury and Southend line of the Great Eastern Railway, and twelve miles from Whitechapel Church. The area of the parish is 6,600 acres, and the population in 1881 was 3,400, being an increase of about 600 during the preceding decade. This number is inclusive of the inhabitants of Becontree Heath, which gives its name to the Hundred, and lies away towards the north, in the vicinity of Chadwell Heath.

Dagenham is not mentioned in "Domesday Book," being included under the general heading of Barking, it having originally formed part of the abbey demesnes. In Hodelerd's grant to the convent it is called Dechenham. There are four manors, or reputed manors, in this parish, namely, the manor of Dagenham proper, and also those of Cockermouth, Parslowes (or Parsloes), and Valence.

The village is surrounded on all sides by corn-fields and market-gardens. It is a long, straggling village, made up of rows of small cottages, and one or two houses of a better class, with the ordinary admixture of general shops, &c. The church, which stands near the eastern end of the street, is dedicated to St. Peter and St. Paul, and consists of chancel, with north aisle, nave, and an embattled tower at the western end, surmounted by a slated spire, and containing a peal of six bells, put up in the early part of the reign of George the Third. The stone-work of the tower is ancient, but has been partly encased with brick and otherwise altered, whilst on an arch above the doorway is carved the inscription : " Wm. Mason, architect, 1800." The chancel and aisle date from the thirteenth century. The nave was rebuilt, and the remainder of the church in part "restored" by a brief in 1800. But the restoration was not satisfactory; at all events, the building was again thoroughly "restored" in 1878, the walls of the chancel being refaced, the floor of the church lowered, open benches substituted for the old-fashioned "pews," the north gallery taken down, and the ceilings throughout fresh plastered, and painted with a flowing leaf pattern. During these repairs and alterations, the original altar-slab, bearing the five marks symbolical of the wounds of Our Saviour, was discovered ; it has been replaced on the present table. The remains of an ancient piscina, which had been bricked up and obscured by plastering, was also brought to light, and has been repaired.

In 1878 a stained glass window was inserted in the chancel in memory of Mr. T. L. Fanshawe, of Parslowes, in this parish. Among the memorials in the church is a tomb, with brasses, to Sir Thomas Urswyk, a former Recorder of London, dated 1470 : it bears the effigies of himself, his wife, four sons, and nine daughters. A monument of white and grey marble, comprising the effigy of a judge in his robes, and also one of his lady in a mourning attitude, bears the following inscription :—" Here lyes interr'd the body of Sir Richard Alibon, Knt., a person of extraordinary, both natural and acquired, parts, eminent in ye knowledge and practice of the law, of the honourable Society of Gray's Inn, recommended by his merits to the favour of King James the Second, to whom he was a council learned in yᵉ laws, and advanced to be one of the Justices of the Court of King's Bench, being the first of yᵉ Roman faith these 150 years who had bin called to a place of so high a rank." He died August 22nd, 1688, aged fifty-three. This monument was erected by his widow, "Dame Barbara Alibon, who was daughter to John Blakestone, Esq., and granddaughter to Sir Wm. Blakestone, Knt., of Gibside, in the county of Durham." Two helmets and some fragments of gauntlets of ancient date, belonging to the knightly

under the Abbess of Barking. The house is a good old modernised mansion, surrounded by a moat. The lawn and pleasure-grounds slope down to the edge of the moat, and contain some fine cedars.

A turning out of the main road, by the side of the "Chequers" Inn, leads to the river-side at Dagenham Reach, about a mile distant. To the left of the road thither is a large sheet of water, an inlet from the Thames, nearly two miles in length, and covering an area of upwards of forty acres.

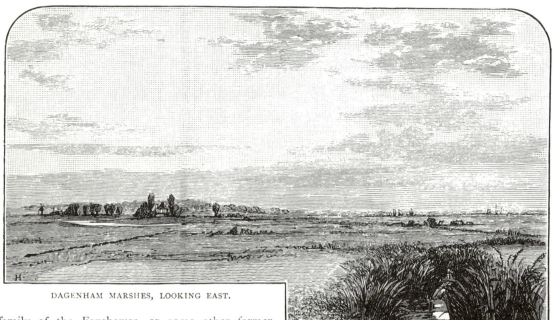

DAGENHAM MARSHES, LOOKING EAST.

family of the Fanshawes, or some other former lords of the soil in these parts, are preserved in the church. In the churchyard is a memorial to George Clark, a police constable, who was murdered at Eastbrook End, in this parish, in 1846. It was "erected by the inhabitants and his brother officers of the K division."

Langhorne, the poet, was for some time curate of Dagenham.

Parslowes, the seat of the Fanshawes for the last two centuries, stands on the west side of the parish, a little to the north of the Rainham Road. It is a spacious brick building, with an embattled pediment and turrets, but dating, however, only from the beginning of the present century, when the house was new fronted. The gardens and pleasure-grounds alone surrounding the mansion are about seven acres in extent; the estate altogether, however, extends to about 600 acres.

The estate of Valence, which lies a short distance further to the north, is so named from having been held by the Valences, Earls of Pembroke,

This sheet of water is a lasting mark of the inundation known as Dagenham Breach, which early in the last century laid desolate this part of the parish.

Morant, in his "History of Essex," gives the following detailed account of the breach:—"It happened 17th of December, 1707, at an extraordinary high tide, accompanied with a violent wind, and was occasioned by the blowing up of a sluice, or trunk, made for the drain of the land-waters in the wall and banks of the Thames. If proper and immediate help had been applied, it could have been easily stopped, with a small charge, the ditch, or drain, of the marsh grounds, which led to such sluice, being, at the first blowing up of the sluice, not above fourteen or sixteen feet broad, and might in a day or two have been easily stopped by the bringing on a small dam, in form of a semicircle, to the Thames wall, if many hands had been employed; but, through the neglect thereof, the constant force of the water setting in and out of the levels soon made the gap wider, so that a large channel was torn up, and a passage made for the water, of one hundred yards wide, and twenty feet deep in some places. By which unhappy accident, about 1,000 acres of rich land in the levels of Dagenham and Havering, worth about

of Havering and Dagenham. By which Act, for ten years, from 10th of July, 1714, the master of every ship or vessel coming into the port of London was obliged to pay threepence per ton, coasters three shillings each voyage, and colliers one penny per chalder, except fishing-vessels, ships in ballast only, and coasters, particularly Harwich boats. Colchester packet-boats to be charged with the duty of three shillings a voyage only four times in the year."

The work of repairing the breach was then

THE WALLS OF THE THAMES.

£3 an acre, were overflowed, and a sand-bank was raised in the Thames, at the mouth of the breach, which reached half across the river, and near a mile in length, likely to prove a great obstruction to, and even utterly to destroy, the navigation. The expense of repairing this breach was, at first, laid upon the proprietors of the lands, but after many wearied and unsuccessful attempts of theirs for about seven years, until they had expended more than the value of the land, it was given wholly over as impracticable. However, being deemed a public concern, upon application to Parliament an Act was obtained for the speedy and effectual preserving the navigation of the River Thames by stopping the breach in the levels

undertaken by one William Boswell, who, for the sum of £16,500, agreed to stop up the gap in the river-wall, and remove the shelf that had been thrown out into the Thames, but after the trial of various schemes he found himself unable to complete the undertaking, and the work was abandoned. In 1715 an engagement was entered into with Captain John Perry, who had been employed by the Czar Peter in building the city of Veronitz, upon the River Don. Captain Perry undertook the work for £25,000, and a promise that if that sum was not sufficient he should be recommended to Parliament for a further grant. By the time he commenced his work the breach had been worn into several large branches, like the natural arms of a river, by the force of the reflux water from the marshes on every turn of the tide. The longest of these branches extended upwards of a mile and a half, and was in some places between 400 and 500 feet broad, and from twenty to forty feet deep. By extraordinary exertions, by driving dove-tail pieces in a peculiar manner, and by various other expedients, Captain Perry at length, after about five years' labour, succeeded in stopping the breach, but not before the works had been *three* times nearly destroyed and washed away by the strength and rapidity of the tides. The expense of this important undertaking amounted to £40,472, only £25,000 of which was allowed by the original contract; but £15 000 was afterwards voted by Parliament to Captain Perry, who was, nevertheless, after all, a loser of several thousands of pounds by his successful work.

But this is not the only occasion on which the river has proved wantonly destructive to the low-lying districts on its north side. In 1376, we are told, the tide made a breach at Dagenham, which drowned so many acres of land belonging to the abbey at Barking* as seriously to affect the wealth and prosperity of that institution, and to drive some of the "religieuses" to take refuge on the high ground at Billericay. We do not learn how the misfortune was repaired.

During the progress of the work carried out by Captain Perry, the workmen cut into a "moorlog," or vein of buried wood, which appears to run for miles along the side of the river, and they thought that a buried "forest primeval" lay revealed beneath their feet. It was discovered three or four feet under the surface of the marsh, and was found to be about ten feet in depth. It contained yew-trees from fourteen to sixteen inches in diameter, and perfectly sound; willows more than two feet in girth, but like touchwood; and mingled with it was small brushwood, and even hazel-nuts, which appeared sound to the eye, but crumbled to the touch. Several stags' horns were also met with lying about the moorlog. Coller, in his "History of Essex," says:—"Some have indulged learned surmises that these are the remains of the devastation of the Deluge; others that they are the remnants of the old forest beaten down and buried by storms and inundations at a later age; but the most practical conclusion is that they were purposely laid there by some of the rude engineers of olden times, as foundations for works to shut out the troublesome flow of the Thames on to the neighbouring lands."

Mr. Smiles, in his work on "Engineers," informs us that the Thames is kept in its bed by 300 miles of embankment between London Bridge and the Nore. How the River Thames came to be reduced to reasonable dimensions and confined to its present channel, how it is kept within it, and how the thousands of acres of low land lying between both banks and the higher grounds are kept protected from overflow at every tide, at full and new moon, or during particularly wet seasons, are questions of no common interest, and on which a very general ignorance prevails. The average rise of the tide in the Thames is, at London Bridge, eighteen feet, at Deptford, twenty, at Purfleet, seventeen, at Holy Haven, fifteen, and at the Nore, fourteen.

"From Fulham to the Nore," observes a writer in *Once a Week*,* "every high tide would lay a very large proportion of the neighbouring country under water, and at spring tides would restore the appearance of the basin of the Thames to what it must have presented to Cæsar's eyes if he chanced to sight it first at flood tide, were it not for the system of embankments which line both sides of the river, as well as of its tributaries.

"Conjecture has ever been busy among local and general historians as to the origin of these embankments, and the credit of their construction has been very generally given to the Romans. Indeed, this mighty nation of fighting and paving men share the honour of many of the most stupendous works which are scattered over the face of Europe pretty equally with a certain personage, who, if he have rightly earned the titles of the 'first Whig' and the 'first gentleman,' might seem equally deserving—to judge from the works ascribed to him—of that of the 'first engineer' as well. . . . What public works, however, of enormous dimensions and immense difficulty cannot be clearly traced to the Great Enemy and his gang are generally fathered next upon the Romans—and with far more solid grounds for the conjecture. Old Rome's public works stand to this day the noblest memorial of her greatness, and are still food for wonder to an engineering and scientific age. A very curt enumeration of the baths, sewers, aqueducts, amphitheatres, temples, and other public buildings, which are due to Roman enterprise, would fill a volume; whilst the long lines of hard, durable road which to this day intersect the countries they conquered are solid and striking memorials of their large perception of what are the tangible appliances of a centralised government, as well as of their skill as paviors. Roman soldiers, we know, were 'navvies' as well as fighting-men, and could handle the spade and basket as well as 'the sword and the buckler.'

"No wonder that in the days of our youth, when we were of that inquiring turn of mind which prompts children to ask disagreeable questions of their elders and betters, the sight of Romney

---

* See *ante*, p. 506.

* See Vol. V., p. 665.

Marsh, with its four-and-twenty thousand acres rescued from the tides, should have prompted the question, 'Who did it?' and as little wonder that the prompt reply should have been, 'The Romans, my lad!' As little wonder that, travelling on the long, dreary, monotonous roads that traverse the huge flats of Cambridgeshire and Lincolnshire, we should have asked the same question about the banked-out rivers there, and have met with the same reply; or, again, that, peering over the side of that primitive Ramsgate steamer, the old *City of London*, in her tedious dawdle down the Thames, the miles after miles of river embankment which protected the low ground on each side from inundation should have caught our observant eye, and elicited the same question, with the same result; or that thereupon our young, active imagination should have fallen to work at once to conjure the well-bleached stakes which, in tier above tier, support the bank into the thigh-bones of the old Roman soldiers of whom we had read so much at school—not without much suppressed execration of them and their historians—and should have forthwith much commended this original mode of utilising the remains of ancient heroes. It was not, however, until years and years after those inquiring days, when we had travelled between these Thames embankments scores of times, in all sorts of craft and at all periods of the tides, had taken long walks along their summits, examined their construction, and lost ourselves in the prairie wilderness and among the network of drains that lie in their rear, that we began to be conscious that they constitute a national work, which, if hardly deserving the higher title of 'stupendous,' may fairly lay claim to that of 'enormous,' both in regard to their extent and their utility. . . . The marsh-lands on each side are intersected by tributary streams and creeks, and a moment's consideration will elicit the reflection that every one of these must be banked on each side throughout the whole of its course through the flat country, and until land of a higher elevation than the highest spring tides is attained, or of course the water would, as the tide rose, steal round the back of the principal embankment by the channel of these creeks and tributaries, and render them simply useless. Indeed, nothing will tend more to a due conception of the importance of every yard of these enormous works than the reflection that the failure of the smallest portion of any part of them tends instantly to the destruction of the object of the whole; it is like the springing of a leak in a ship, or the snapping of one imperfectly welded link in a chain-cable. The failure itself may be trifling, but its consequences are almost illimitable. . . . The uplands on each side of the River Thames below London, and with these the swamps which fringed them, were in large measure bestowed on ecclesiastical bodies in very early times. The Abbey of Stratford, for instance, was founded and endowed in 1135, and that of Lesnes, near Abbey Wood, in Kent, 1178. On the one shore were this Stratford Abbey, the famous nunnery at Barking, the cell at Grays Thurrock, St. Osyth, and others; and on the south shore Lesnes, Dartford, Ingress, &c. The monks and nuns, finding themselves not unfrequently flooded out of their dwellings, and obliged to seek refuge in the higher lands, very early set on foot a process of what was called then, and for many centuries, 'inning' their marsh-lands, that is, enclosing them with embankments; and as early as Henry II.'s time this process began to be deemed a matter of national importance. It is remarkable, by the way, that to the same monarch—as Count of Anjou—the French historians ascribe the consolidation of the great Loire embankment. But that from the time of Edward II. downwards the 'inning' process continued to be considered a national affair is evidenced by the perpetually recurring commissions to view, take order for the repair of the banks, ditches, &c., and for the safeguard of the marshes from the overflowing of the tide, as well as by the continued assessments or taxes on the neighbourhood granted for defraying the expenses of the works. According to the rule of these more advanced days, however, there is also to be detected a constantly recurring difficulty in collecting the taxes. . . . The works remained uncompleted, the low lands were constantly overflowed, and at length private enterprise stepped in to supply public torpor—and not without making a good bargain for itself out of the transaction. Thus, in Queen Elizabeth's days 'one Jacobus Aconcius, an Italian,' undertook to 'in,' or reclaim, about 2,000 acres of drowned land in Plumstead and Erith Marshes, on condition of getting one-half of his recovery in fee-simple for his pains. In 1622, one Jonas Croppenburg, a Dutchman, made a similar bargain about Canvey Island, only, more modest than Jacobus, he restricted his demand to one-third of the land recovered; and about the same time one Cornelius Vermuyden, a German, undertook the recovery of Dagenham and Havering Marshes on similar conditions. The same Vermuyden, some thirty years later, when he is described as a Colonel of Horse under Cromwell, superintended the rescue of something between four and five hundred thousand acres of similar land in the counties of Lincoln, Cambridge, and Hunts, and must have been a genius and a man well ahead of his age.

"By some such process, then, as these, it seems most probable that the Thames embankments gradually crawled into existence during the centuries which intervened between the days of the Henry Second and those of the Protector, comparatively small detached portions of embankment being pushed forward, like military outworks, from the higher lands first of all, and by degrees being extended and united, until the work resolved itself into what at first sight might appear to be one uniform settled plan, acted on at once and from the beginning—an idea consistent only with the exploded theory of Roman construction. That the vestiges of the old approaches have been gradually swept away in order to make the most of the space, and in proportion as their utility was superseded by the more advanced works, has, no doubt, favoured the Roman theory. It is, however, impossible not to regret that so much of them, at any rate, as might provide for accidents was not allowed by common prudence to remain, in spite of the levelling and economising mania. A fracture of even a small portion of the system is a disaster the extent of which there is no foreseeing. This has been already alluded to in the way of illustration. A few facts will help out the theory. A breach of the embankment, in 1324, laid 100 acres of the valuable land between what is now St. Katharine's Docks and Shadwell under water for a year. In 1376 the whole of the lands about Dagenham, and those belonging to the nunnery at Barking, were inundated. Some 1,000 acres at Stepney were flooded in 1448. The whole of Plumstead Marshes were drowned in 1527, and not completely recovered until 1590. The entire country from Purfleet to Grays was laid under water in 1690. And even cockney anglers can tell something about the great inbreak of 1707, which swept away 400 feet of the river wall at Dagenham, overflowed 1,000 acres, and was only repaired after years of labour by Captain Perry, at an expense of £40,472, leaving behind its mark in the shape of that little winding lake in which bream and eels so plenteously swarm."

The "Dagenham Lake Subscription Water"—for such is the name by which this unreclaimed portion of the drowned land has long been known to London anglers—is well stocked with pike, carp, roach, and eels. It is somewhat irregular in shape, particularly on the north side; on the east side it unites with the Beam, and thence, flowing on southward to the Thames, forms an island nearly a mile square. In the "Memoirs of Eliza-beth Fry," it is stated that that lady used for some years (1826 onwards) to spend her summers in a cottage by Dagenham Lake, "surrounded by trees, mostly willows, on an open space of lawn, with beds of reeds behind them, and on either side covering the river bank." This, in all probability, was the cottage still standing on the west side of the island : it is a picturesque old building, with a thatched roof, and an external wooden gallery communicating with the upper storey. On the south side of the island, in former times, stood a building known as the Breach House—or, as it was sometimes called, the Beach House ; but this has long ago disappeared, and has given place to a large factory.

About twenty years ago a company was started, and an Act of Parliament obtained for the purpose of purchasing Dagenham Lake, and converting it into a dock. Sir John Rennie and Mr. J. Murray were appointed engineers, and some progress was made with the works ; but at the end of about a twelvemonth they were stopped, owing to the monetary difficulties at that time, and have not since been resumed. According to the original prospectus, this dock was to have been "one of the largest in the Port of London, and be capable of receiving the largest ships afloat." All that is now visible in connection with the undertaking is included in some half-dozen wooden sheds, standing by what was doubtless intended as the entrance to the great tidal basin, and another wooden structure by the side of the lake ; an elevated tramway running from the river-wall, or embankment, some half a mile inland, for the carriage of material ; a large brick building, that was for many years afterwards used as an ice-house ; and, finally, a large board, placed conspicuously by the river-side, bearing the inscription, "Dagenham Docks to be Sold."

It would not be supposed à priori that there would be any more intimate connection between Dagenham Breach and the Ministerial Whitebait Dinner than there was between Tenterden Steeple and the Goodwin Sands. But the contrary is the case. The annual whitebait dinner was originally a private feast, given by Sir Robert Preston to his friends, who went down the river annually to inspect the sea-walls at Dagenham Breach, and it gradually grew to the importance of a State entertainment. The story of the origin of this annual festivity is thus told by Mr. John Timbs, in his "Club Life of London" :—"On the banks of Dagenham Lake or Breach, in Essex, many years since, there stood a cottage, occupied by a princely merchant, named Preston, a baronet of Scotland and Nova Scotia, and some time M.P. for Dover.

He called it his 'fishing cottage,' and often in the spring he went thither with a friend or two, as a relief to the toils of his parliamentary and mercantile duties. His most frequent guest was the Right Hon. George Rose, Secretary of the Treasury and an Elder Brother of the Trinity House. Many a day did these two worthies enjoy at Dagenham Reach; and Mr. Rose once intimated to Sir Robert that Mr. Pitt, of whose friendship they were both justly proud, would, no doubt, delight in the comfort of such a retreat. A day was named, and the Premier was invited; and he was so well pleased with his reception at the 'fishing cottage'—they were all two- if not three-bottle men—that, on taking leave, Mr. Pitt readily accepted an invitation for the following year.

"For a few years the Premier continued a visitor to Dagenham, and was always accompanied by Mr. George Rose. But the distance was considerable; the going and coming were somewhat inconvenient for the First Minister of the Crown. Sir Robert Preston, however, had his remedy, and he proposed that they should in future dine nearer London. Greenwich was suggested; we do not hear of whitebait in the Dagenham dinners, and its introduction probably dates from the removal to Greenwich. The party of three was now increased to four, Mr. Pitt being permitted to bring Lord Camden. Soon after a fifth guest was invited— Mr. Charles Long, afterwards Lord Farnborough. All were still the guests of Sir Robert Preston;

and one by one other notables were invited—all Tories; and at last Lord Camden considerately remarked that, as they were all dining at a tavern, it was but fair that Sir Robert Preston should be relieved from the expense. It was then arranged that the dinner should be given as usual by Sir Robert Preston—that is to say, at his invitation— and he insisted on still contributing a buck and champagne; the rest of the charges were thenceforth defrayed by the several guests, and on this plan the meeting continued to take place annually till the death of Mr. Pitt.

"Sir Robert was requested, next year, to summon the several guests, the list of whom, by this time, included most of the Cabinet Ministers. The time for meeting was usually after Trinity Monday —a short period before the end of the session. By degrees the meeting, which was originally purely gastronomic, appears to have assumed, in consequence of the long reign of the Tories, a political or semi-political character. Sir Robert Preston died; but Mr. Long (now Lord Farnborough) undertook to summon the several guests, the list of whom was furnished by Sir Robert Preston's private secretary. Hitherto, the invitations had been sent privately; now they were dispatched in Cabinet boxes, and the party was, certainly for some time, limited to members of the Cabinet. A dinner lubricates ministerial as well as other business; so the 'Ministerial Fish Dinner' may contribute to the grandeur and prosperity of our beloved country."

CHAPTER LVIII.

MILLWALL, LIMEHOUSE, AND POPLAR.

"Where could I wish myself now?
In the Isle of Dogs."—BEAUMONT AND FLETCHER.

Situation and Boundaries of Millwall—Origin of the Name of the Isle of Dogs—The Chapel House—Blackwall—Millwall—Acreage of the Isle of Dogs—Fertility of the Soil—Geology—A Submerged Forest—The Manor of Pomfret—Inundations of the Marsh—How Samuel Pepys attended a Wedding Party—Ferries, and the Ferry House—Condition of the Isle of Dogs in the Last Century—Manufactories and Ship-building Yards—Roman Cement and Terra Cotta—The *Great Eastern* Steam Ship—Cubitt Town—St. Luke's Church—Limehouse—Poplar.

IN the preceding chapter we have reached the utmost limits of our perambulation in an easterly direction, but there still remains a district north of the Thames as yet unexplored by us in our pilgrimage, and to which we will now direct our attention, as it is unrecorded in OLD AND NEW LONDON. Down to the end of the last or beginning of the present century, the region in question was almost uninhabited, but of late years it has become one of the busiest and most thriving

localities in the suburbs of London. Millwall— or, as it is commonly called, the Isle of Dogs— forms part of the parish of All Saints, Poplar. It is in the parliamentary division of the Tower Hamlets, and it belongs to the Hundred of Ossulston, in the county of Middlesex. It was formerly included in the parish of Stepney, and in ancient times it was known by the name of Stepney Marsh. The district is bounded on the north by the London and Blackwall Railway, on the east by Blackwall and the River Thames, on the west by Limehouse and the Thames, and on the south by the Thames opposite Greenwich. Its formation is that of a horseshoe, the curve being described by the River Thames between Limehouse and Blackwall, a distance of about four miles.

There are various conjectures as to the origin of the name of the Isle of Dogs. In Strype's edition of Stow's "Survey," we read :—"The fertile soil of the marsh here is much admired, usually known

Lysons similarly questions the tradition. "On the common tradition of the origin of the name Isle of Dogs," he remarks in a foot-note, "I much doubt the fact, as it would have been much more convenient to have their dog kennels on the other side of the water." In Fearnsides Tombleson's "Thames" appears the following version of the story :—"The name of the Isle of Dogs is traditionally derived from the circumstance of King Edward III., when the court resided at Greenwich,

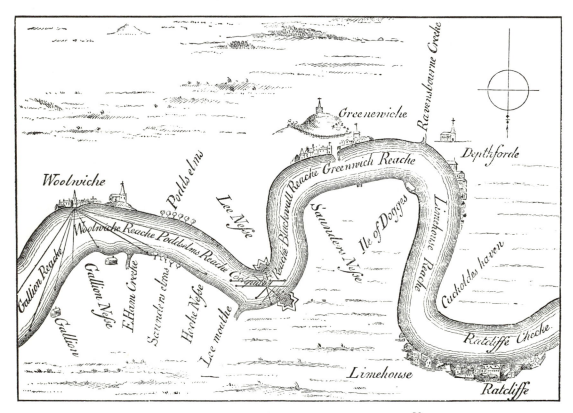

THE THAMES, FROM RATCLIFFE TO WOOLWICH, IN 1588.

by the name of the Isle of Dogs, so called because when our former princes made Greenwich their country seat, if for hunting (they say), the kennels for their dogs were kept on this marsh, which, usually making a great noise, the seamen and others thereupon called the place the Isle of Dogs: though it is not an isle, indeed scarce a peninsula, the neck being about a mile in length." Mr. Brewer, in the "Beauties of England and Wales," implies a doubt as to the above tradition. He writes :—"The origin of this term is not known. A futile tradition says that the place derives its name from the king's hounds having been kept there when the royal family resided formerly at Greenwich Palace, to which it lies opposite."

having kept there his hounds ;" whilst in the "Encyclopædia Londinium" the details are slightly varied, thus :—"Although it is now converted to commercial purposes, the Isle of Dogs derived its name from being the depôt of the spaniels and greyhounds of Edward III., and this spot was chosen because it lay contiguous to his sports of woodcock shooting and coursing the red deer in Waltham and the other royal forests in Essex, for the more convenient enjoyment of which he generally resided in the sporting season at Greenwich." Mr. B. H. Cowper, in his "Historical Account of Millwall," questions this derivation, and observes :— "This same tradition has named Henry VIII., Charles II., and other monarchs as having kept their dogs here. But surely if it had been so there would be some historical proof; in this case no one has pretended to adduce it. Therefore, this tradition must be for the present regarded as uncanonical and apocryphal. There is, however," he adds, "another story, which is thus given by Strype and Seymour:—'The next place to be noted on the Thames,' says the latter, 'is the Isle of Dogs, a low marshy ground, so called, as it is reputed, from a waterman's murdering a man in this place who had a dog with him, which would

reign of Elizabeth." Among other instances, he adduces the following :—

"In 1656, on the trial of James Naylor, the celebrated Quaker, for blasphemy, mention is made of the Isle of Dogs. The case of the prisoner was debated by the Parliament. 'The debate turned on the questions of slitting the tongue or boring it ; of cutting off his hair ; of whipping ; of sending him to Bristol, the Isle of Scilly, Jamaica, *the Isle of Dogs*, the Marshalsea.' (See 'Footsteps of our Forefathers,' by J. G. Miall, p. 281, London, 1851.)

DAGENHAM.   (*See page* 527.)

not leave his master till constrained by hunger to swim over to Greenwich, and doing this frequently, it was observed by the watermen plying there, who, following the dog, by that means discovered the body of the murdered man. Soon after the dog, swimming over to Greenwich, snarled at a waterman who sat there, and would not be beaten off, which the other watermen perceiving, and knowing of the murder, they apprehended this strange waterman, who confessed the fact, and was condemned and executed for it.'"

Mr. Cowper, to whom we are mainly indebted for the material for this notice of the Isle of Dogs, writes :—"I have not met with any reference to or use of this name earlier than the close of the

"In Beaumont and Fletcher's *Thierry and Theodoret*, Act II., sc. 2 (Dyce's Edition, Vol. I., p. 154), this passage occurs :—

"*Theodoret :* 'There's something for thy labour.'

"*Bawdber :* 'Where could I wish myself now? In the *Isle of Dogs*, so I might 'scape scratching, for I see by her cat's eyes I shall be clawed wonderfully.'

"Middleton and Dekker, in the *Roaring Girl*, have this passage :—

"*Moll Cutpurse :* 'O, sir, he hath been brought up in the *Isle of Dogs*, and can both fawn like a spaniel and bite like a mastiff, as he finds occasion.'

"I am indebted to Cunningham's 'Murray's

Handbook of London' for the two last references, as well as for the next one.

"'Thomas Nash wrote a play called the *Isle of Dogs,* for which, in 1598, he was imprisoned in the Fleet. Mr. Dyce is of opinion that it was a place where persons took refuge from their creditors and the officers of justice (Middleton's Works, Vol. II., p 535). But this I doubt.'

"Norden, in his Map of Middlesex, 1593, designates this locality 'Isle of Doges Ferme,' and indicates the existence of some building about where Chapel House now stands. The sign used denotes 'Howses of Knightes, Gent., &c.' In this place a stream is represented as running from Limehouse to Blackwall, as well as others which do not exist now. There is no further reference to the Isle of Dogs in this work, but under Blackwall we read: 'neere which is a harbor in the Thamis for shipping. The place taketh name of the blackenes or darkenes of the water bankes or wall at that place.'"

In a map entitled "Thamesis Descriptio," dated 1588, and of which a copy, drawn by Joseph Ames, was published in 1738, two islets are shown between the bed of the river and the embankment which there curves inward, at the point now occupied by the "mast pond." The larger of these islands is termed the "Ile of Dogges."

With reference to the Chapel House mentioned above, which at the commencement of the present century was used as a farm-house, Maitland writes: —"The Chapel House, in the Isle of Dogs, or Poplar Marsh, is the ruins of a stone chapel, but when or by whom built is unknown." In Strype's "Stow" the following particulars are given:— "There is in this marsh, just opposite to Greenwich, a house called the Chapel House, where are the remains of a chapel built of stone. And near this are foundations of houses found, and sometimes hooks of a great size, as though if some great gate taken up, which maketh it probable that hereabouts were inhabitants formerly, perhaps fishermen, or such as had their livelihood from the water. And that, by some inundation, or the unhealthiness of the situation, they left those parts for some more safe and commodious settlement." Mr. Brewer, in his "Beauties of England and Wales" (1816), observes:—"The cold and swampy character of this tract of land would appear repulsive to all thoughts of human habitation; but piety, which in its obsolete modifications sometimes sought strange recesses, induced an unknown devotee to found a chapel in the midst of the marsh, which is believed to have been dedicated to St. Mary. The site of this small religious structure is now occupied by a disconsolate dwelling, termed Chapel House Farm.

This building exhibits no marks of antiquity, excepting the lower part of the walls, which are composed of small stones and flints, but a Pointed window was destroyed some few years back." Again, the account of this place given by Lysons in 1795 is as follows:—"In the Isle of Dogs stood an ancient chapel, called the Chapel of St. Mary, in Stepney Marsh. It is mentioned by that name in a will of the fifteenth century.* The object of its foundation does not appear. It is not likely that the marsh should ever have had many inhabitants. Perhaps it was a hermitage, founded by some devout person for the purpose of saying masses for the souls of mariners. This chapel has been converted into a neat farm-house, which stands upon the same foundation, and is the only dwelling-place upon the marsh. It exhibits no remains of antiquity, except in the lower part of the walls, which are full of small stones and flints. A Gothic window was removed about three years ago."

For the above string of quotations we are indebted to Mr. Cowper's "History of Millwall," wherein the author observes:—"In all probability Lysons derived his principal fact—that of the designation of the chapel—from Strype. His theory is confessedly a mere supposition. My own view of the original design of this place is that it was a chapel connected with and dependent upon the monastery of St. Mary of Graces, near the Tower of London. This hypothesis is borne out in part by facts, and is, in the whole, more probable than any of the many I have heard. It is matter of regret that our information is so exceedingly scanty, that during its existence this chapel has not been observed to be mentioned more than once. . . . I think it was connected with the monastery in question, which we know held possessions in the marsh; and we cannot say this of any other. St. Thomas of Acons and St. Katharine's do not appear to have had any possessions here at the dissolution of the monasteries; in fact, after the estate of St. Mary of Graces fell into the hands of the Bishop of London, he appears to have been sole proprietor for some years. Another fact worthy of consideration is that the chapel was

---

* "Strype, writing in 1720 (Appendix to Survey, i., p. 120), says, In the Bishop of London's Register of Wills are mentioned these places in this (*i.e.,* Stepney) parish, above 300 years ago.
"*Capella Beatæ Mariæ in Marischo in parochia de Stepney* (*i.e.,* the Chapel of St Mary in the Marsh, in the parish of Stepney).
"Lymeostes, otherwise Lymehouse, in Stepney.
"*Roger Potter de Potiler in parochia de Stebunheath* (*i.e.,* Roger Potter, of Poplar, in the parish of Stepney). These references must relate to about the year 400.
"I may observe, in passing, that an ancient ferry in the Isle of Dogs is known as Potter's Ferry. The coincidence is noticeable, but no proof of the ferry being named after such an individual."

also dedicated to St. Mary. A third fact worth notice is that the lands in this marsh must have been owned by the monastery prior to any mention made of the chapel. My impression is that its situation and its distance from the monastery on Tower Hill rendered this appropriate as a retreat for spiritual exercises, or as a species of penal colony, to which refractory and erring brethren (for such there were sometimes) were commanded to retire for salutary discipline and penance."

Thirty years ago the condition of Chapel House was much the same as it was when Lysons wrote his description. Two or three additional tenements had been erected on the west side of it, but they were mean and inconvenient, and the trees had been nearly all removed. The ground near Chapel House in every direction showed traces of having been at some remote period occupied with buildings, &c., but more especially to the south-west, from the Chapel House to the river. On the formation of the Millwall Dock, in 1867-8, all traces of the Chapel House were swept away, its site being absorbed in the new docks.

Mr. Cowper, in his work already quoted, inclines to the opinion that the term "Isle of Dogs" was not originally applied to the whole of the district of which we are treating, but to the larger of two islets indicated in Adam's Map of the Thames (1588), above referred to. This map Mr. Cowper regards as "teaching us the important and satisfactory truth that what is now known as such is not the Isle of Dogs proper. The Isle of Dogs," he continues, "is the little spot or island which lies within the curve of the river wall, at the place indicated. Unfortunately for us, this part has been very much altered, and hence we should scarcely expect to find many or any of its original features. However, there is an almost island which answers pretty well to the position of that laid down in the map. This is in the mast pond at the establishment of Messrs. Ferguson. It is a small spot on the south side of the pond, adjoining Tindall's Dock and the mast house (which pond is an indentation of the river bank, and called Drunken Dock), and appears to remain as the last vestige of the primary Isle of Dogs. There is no difficulty in saying how the name became applied to the entire marsh, it being natural to suppose that this was gradually accomplished. Norden's Map is confirmatory to some extent, and explanatory, inasmuch as he calls the portion of the marsh adjacent to Chapel House 'Isle of Dogs Farm.' It seems reasonable, then, to suppose that the term was applied first to the islet in question; secondly,

to the farm nearest to it, and to which it perhaps belonged; and afterwards to the entire marsh. Such is the conclusion to which I have come; and I have called it satisfactory because it shows that there was nothing in the place itself which should make it deserve such a cynical and uninviting name as this. The existence of the original Isle of Dogs has not been noticed by any previous writer on the subject, so far as I am aware.

"The question, however, still remains unanswered—how was the name Isle of Dogs originated? Those who have passed along Millwall (i.e., the western embankment) may have observed, what renders it very probable, that the vast majority of dogs, &c., which find a grave in the river are thrown up and left here by the tide. Indeed, some portions of the embankment, where it slopes toward the river, are a perfect charnel-house of the canine race. Probably it has long been so, and the original Isle of Dogs would stand as a net to the stream, by which such substances or objects would be arrested in their course, and left high and dry at low water. Hence, I suspect, the elegant appellation under consideration. I should have been more diffident in reference to this delicate theory, had I not (since it first occurred to my own mind) heard it propounded by others, and stated to actually exist in print."

The Isle of Dogs—or, as it was called, Stepney Marsh—was included in the parish of Stepney probably as far back as the time when England was first divided into parishes; but it now forms part of the parish of Poplar, which, with Limehouse and Blackwall, is of more recent origin than Stepney. Blackwall is the name given to the eastern side of the district under notice. The earliest mention of the locality under that name, observes Mr. Cowper, on the authority of Dugdale, occurs in a deed dated 1377, wherein John Bampton, William Rykhill, Thomas Aspale, and Thomas Mylende, were appointed commissioners for viewing and repairing the banks of the Thames between "Blakewale" and the Hospital of St. Katherine. "In 1480 (20th Edward IV.), Thomas, Bishop of London, Edmund, Abbot of Graces, William Wursley, Dean of Paul's, Sir J. Ebryngton and Sir Thomas Frowyk, Knts., and others, had the like assignation for those embankments, &c., betwixt the town of Lymeostez and the wall called Black Wall." The reference here made to "the wall called Black Wall" justifies the theory propounded in 1592 by Norden, who wrote:—"Black Wall, neere which is a great harbor for shipping in ye Thames, known also by ye name of Black Wall, so called of ye blacke banke or wall of the Thamise." This quotation, remarks Mr. Cowper, is literal as it stands in the MS. ; probably the first Black Wall should be *Bleak* Wall, or Blake Wall. Stow, in his "Survey" (1603), calls it Blake Wall.

The name of Millwall originated from the circumstance of a number of windmills standing along the river wall on the west side of the marsh. These mills were seven in number, and occupied the marsh wall, overlooking Deptford. In a view of London, taken from One Tree Hill, in Greenwich Park, and published in the middle of the last century, these seven mills are represented upon the river bank, opposite Deptford, together with the same number of smaller buildings, one beside each of the mills. Chapel House is also shown in this view. Another view, dated 1754, in the *Gentleman's Magazine*, is similar in all respects.

Mr. Cowper, in his "History of Millwall" (1853), says that the foundations of two or three of the mills may yet be traced, and adds that "one of them without its sails still exists on the premises of Mr. Weston." The premises here referred to, which have long been known as Weston's Roman Cement Works, are now partly occupied as a rosin-oil distillery. The basement of the old mill stands in this part of the premises, now called Barrell's Wharf, and down to very recently it was in use as a flour-mill, but worked by steam power instead of as a windmill. The remains of the mill form an octagonal brick building of three floors, and it still contains some of the internal fittings which were used in the grinding of corn. These works adjoin the old "Windmill" public-house, close by Millwall pier.

The whole aspect of the Isle of Dogs is altogether changed from what it was previous to the end of the last century. By a survey taken in 1740 it was estimated that there were 836 acres of land in marsh. This was reduced to 500 by the formation of the West India Dock at the beginning of the present century, and more recently further reductions have been made in the marsh-land by the construction of Millwall Dock. The island is now traversed from north to south by the North Greenwich and Cubitt Town branch of the Blackwall Railway, whilst the various dock basins and warehouses, &c., have usurped the greater part of the land, which at one time was famous for its fertility, and consequently for its value for grazing purposes. In Strype's edition of "Stow" we read :—"Such is the fertility of this marsh, that it produceth sheep and oxen of the largest size, and very fat. They are brought out of other countries, and fed here. I have been assured by a grazier of good report

(saith the Rev. Dr. Woodward) that he knew eight oxen sold out of this marsh for £34 each. And all our neighbourhood knew that a butcher undertook to furnish the Club at Blackwall with a leg of mutton every Saturday throughout the year that should weigh twenty-eight pounds, the sheep being fed in this marsh, or he would have nothing for them, and he did perform it." Again, in the same strain, Maitland writes :—"The Isle of Dogs, or Poplar Marsh, is a spot of ground of such fertility and excellence of grass, that it not only raises the largest cattle, but it is likewise the great restorative of all distempered beasts." Middleton says :—"It is, perhaps, the richest grass in the country, but if it were the most barren in the kingdom, it might be enriched by the easiest of all possible means : namely, by only opening the sluices to admit the tide, and thereby lay the land under water ; and after the water had remained long enough for the rich substances which are constantly floating in the river, so near the metropolis, to have subsided, permitting the water to drain off by the same sluices into the Thames again. This operation repeated a few times would not fail to improve the land in a very high degree."

"The surface soil of the marsh," observes Mr. Cowper, "is dark, and underlaid in general by a bed of clay or mud, belonging to the *Pleistocene* formation. In some places beneath the soil a bed of pebbles is met with near the surface ; in other places, however, beneath the surface soil and clay, and above the gravel or pebbles which overlie the great clay deposit of the London basin, a stratum, consisting of mud and vegetable matter, is met with." Brewer says :—"Small quantities of peat have been found in this marshy district." In Weale's "Survey of London" we find :—"Subterranean forests exist at Purfleet, Grays, Dagenham Marsh, and Tilbury Fort. In the Isle of Dogs a forest of this description was found at eight feet from the grass, consisting of elm, oak, and fir trees, some of the former of which were three feet four inches in diameter, accompanied by human bones and recent shells, but no metals or traces of civilisation. The trees in this forest were all laid from south-east to north-west, as if the inundation which had overthrown them came from that quarter." "In making the excavations for the Docks," observes a writer in the "Encyclopædia Londinensis," "a wonderful phenomenon of nature was discovered. Eight feet beneath the surface appeared a forest, concealed for unnumbered centuries from every human eye. It presented a mass of decayed twigs, leaves, and branches, encompassing huge trunks rotted through, yet perfect in every fibre; the bark was uninjured, and the whole evidently torn up by the roots. A great deal of this timber was dried and burnt by the inhabitants of Poplar. Some violent convulsion of nature, perhaps an earthquake, must have overturned the forest, and buried it many feet below the present high-water mark; but when or how it happened is beyond the tradition of the most remote ages."

The extent of this deposit appears to have been considerable. When the City Canal was in course of formation, large quantities of submerged wood, with bones, &c., were brought to light; and Lysons tells us that during the construction of the Brunswick Dock (now the export basin of the East India Dock), in 1789, "a great quantity of fossil nuts and wood were found." As far back as the middle of the seventeenth century these discoveries appear to have been going on, as the following entry in Pepys's "Diary" will show. Under date of September 22, 1665, he writes:—"At Blackwall. Here is observable what Johnson* tells us that in digging the late dock, they did, twelve feet under ground, find perfect trees overcovered with earth. Nut-trees, with the branches and the very nuts upon them; some of these nuts he showed us, the shells black with age, and their kernal upon opening decayed, but their shell perfectly hard as ever. And a yew-tree, upon which the very ivy was taken up whole about it, which, upon cutting with an addes (adze), was found to be rather harder than the living tree usually is. The armes, they say, were taken up at first whole about the body, which is very strange." Pepys's description of the nuts, &c., found at Blackwall two hundred years ago would answer exactly for similar discoveries which have been made during excavations which have been carried on within the last twenty or thirty years. "The extent and character of these relics," remarks Mr. Cowper, "justify the opinion that they are found where they grew, and that they were submerged either by the elevation of the bed of the river, or, as I consider the more probable view, by the subsidence of the entire district in which they are found. . . . The subterranean forest which is thus from time to time disturbed is, it would appear, of considerable extent. It is traced from the river-side opposite the dockyard at Deptford, across to the East India Docks, and reappears in Essex. The species of wood which have been

identified appear to be chiefly these:—elm, oak, fir, yew, and hazel; besides which there are ivy, rushes or reeds, land and fresh-water shells, and traces of man, the elephant, and the deer. . . . As it respects the human and elephantine remains, there may be some mistake; it is, however, asserted that such have been found here."

With reference to the early history of the Isle of Dogs, we cannot do better than quote from Mr. Cowper's very interesting work:—"By many it is conjectured that this tract of land was reclaimed under the Romans, who, it is well known, executed many important works in all parts of the kingdom. They possibly commenced this work by raising mounds and banks to define the course of the river, for the guidance and safety of the vessels which navigated it, and they may have actually reclaimed it. There may be said, however, to be nothing certain known. Whether the land was recovered in successive portions or by one effort, history says not. When such enclosures were made by private individuals or the lord of the manor, records could scarcely be expected at so early a period as that to which we must refer part at least of those in the Isle of Dogs. . . . The date of its recovery must have been considerably earlier than the reign of Edward the Confessor.

"In endeavouring to arrive at a fair conclusion respecting the period of our embankments, a careful consideration of data is necessary. It has been stated that our history does not reach back to the period of their construction, and yet we have more than vague conjectures in support of the opinion which would assign them to the time of the Roman occupation of Britain."

It is somewhat singular that the number of "mills" enumerated in "Domesday Book" as belonging to Stibenhede (Stepney) is seven, the precise number which we have seen occupied Millwall at the commencement of the century.

In the "Testa de Nevill," which relates to times of Henry III. and Edward I., William de Vere is described as holding of the Bishop of London a fourth part of his estate in "Stubeneth." Mention is also made of Ricardus de Pontefract, or Pomfret, who held a third part of his estate in Stebeneth. "It is not stated," remarks Mr. Cowper, "in what part of the parish the estate of De Vere lay. It seems to have been parted with in 1396, when the reversion of the manor of Poplar was granted by the celebrated William de Wickham (of Wykeham), Bishop of Winchester, Sir Aubrey de Vere, and others, to the Abbey of St. Mary de Graces." The estate of the Pontefracts, or Pomfrets, was in Stepney Marsh. The manor

---

* Johnson appears to have been the originator of Blackwall Dock during the Commonwealth. He was a friend of Samuel Pepys.

of Pomfret consisted of eighty acres of land, a windmill, &c. Maitland, speaking of the old chapel in this marsh, supposes it may have "belonged to the manor of Pountfret, which anciently lay in this parish, the capital mansion whereof, by the discovery of large foundations and gate hooks, may not only be presumed to have stood here, but likewise diverse other houses, which probably were inhabited till the great inundation toward the close of the fifteenth century, occasioned by a breach in

the Blessed Virgin, in the 26th year of Henry VI., a breach made in the said bank of the before specified John Harpour for the length of twenty rods, unto the land of John Fyloll, insomuch as a thousand acres of land lying within the said Marsh were drowned. And that he, the said John, and all those whose estates he then had, were obliged, in respect of their land adjoining to the said bank, to take care of its amendment."

The portion of the embankment thrown down on

MILLWALL DOCKS.

the bank of the River Thames near the great ship-yard at Limehouse Hole."

In the fourteenth and fifteenth centuries considerable repairs seem to have been rendered necessary to the river wall and embankments, in consequence of the damage caused by inundations. Upon an inquisition taken in 1449, the jurors presented, "that by the violence of the tides upon the banks of Stebenhithe Marsh, a great part of the banks adjoining to that Marsh was then ruinous and broken, through the neglect of the landholders there. And that through the default of one John Harpour, gentleman, in not repairing his banks opposite to Deptford Strond, there was, on the Monday, being the Feast of the Annunciation of

the above occasion has preserved to modern times the name of the "Breach," in the same manner as Dagenham Breach, already described.* From this breach it has been considered probable that what was called "Poplar Gut" derived its existence. About the middle of the seventeenth century the river again broke in at the same place, which, it would appear, had never been properly repaired. This breach is referred to by Pepys in his "Diary," under date of 23rd March, 1660, which was probably within a few days of the occurrence :—" In our way we saw the great breach which the late high water had made, to the loss of many thousand

---

* See *ante*, p. 528.

pounds to the people about Limehouse." In a survey of the parish by Gascoyne, taken in 1703, this part of the river wall is called "Old Breach, the Forland, now a place to lay timber;" and the long strip of water known as Poplar Gut, till its removal on the construction of the West India Docks and City Canal, was designated the Breach. Among the plans and designs published by order of Parliament, in reference to the docks projected in the Isle of Dogs, &c., at the close of the last century, there is one in which this part of the

buttons, and gold broad lace round my hands, very rich and fine. By water to the Ferry, where when we come, no coach there; and tide of ebb, so far spent as the horse boat could not get off on the other side the river to bring away the coach. So we were fain to stay there, in the unlucky Isle of Doggs, in a chill place, the morning cool and wind fresh, above two, if not three hours, to our great discontent. Yet, being upon a pleasant errand, and seeing that it could not be helped, we did bear it very patiently; and it was worth my

MILLWALL, FROM THE RIVER.

embankment is named the Breach. Even down to the present day the spot is remembered by this name by the older inhabitants, and also as a place where timber was laid.

There have been ferries across the Thames from Greenwich and Deptford to the Isle of Dogs from a very early period, and two of the principal thoroughfares in the island are the "West Ferry" and "East Ferry" Roads. Our old friend Pepys favours us with one or two amusing entries in his "Diary" respecting these ferries, and the condition of the locality in his time. Under date 31st July, 1665, he writes:—"Up and very betimes by six o'clock at Deptford, and there I find Sir George Carteret and my Lady ready to go; I being in my new coloured silk suit, and coat trimmed with gold

observing to see how upon these two scores, Sir George Carteret, the most passionate man in the world, and that was in great haste to be gone, did bear with it, and very pleasant all the while; at least, not troubled much so as to fret and storm at it. Anon the coach comes; in the mean time, there coming a news thither with his horse to go over, that told us he did come from Islington this morning, and that Proctor, the vintner of the Miter, in Wood Street, and his son are dead this morning there of the plague; he having laid out abundance of money there, and was the greatest vintner for some time in London for great entertainments. We, fearing the canonical hour would be past before we got thither, did, with a great deal of unwillingness, send away the licence and wedding ring. So that when we come, though we drove hard with six horses, yet we found them gone from home; and going towards the church, met them coming from church, which troubled us."

The troubles of the genial secretary, however, notwithstanding that he was too late to witness the wedding ceremony, soon wore off, for on the conclusion of the day's festivities, and the retirement of the bridal party for the night, he had the satisfaction of kissing the bride in bed. But it will be best perhaps to record the fact in Pepys's own words :—" I kissed the bride in bed, and so the curtaines drawn with the greatest gravity that could be, and so good night. But the modesty and gravity of this business was so decent, that it was to me indeed ten times more delightful than if it had been twenty times more merry and jovial."

From the above quotation it would appear that there was a communication between the Deptford Ferry and the old ferry opposite Greenwich; it was probably a footway, by what is mentioned by Peter Cunningham in his "Handbook of London" as a "Half-penny Hatch." Norden, writing in 1592, mentions the Ferry House in the Isle of Dogs, and adds that there are "horse ferreyes at Greenwich." Mr. B. H. Cowper considers it probable that the one referred to was "the old Willow Bridge Ferry, or not far from thence." He adds: "no doubt this ferry was the means of communication between Greenwich, Chapel House, and Blackwall." The "news," or postman, alluded to by Mr. Pepys took this route on his way from Islington to Greenwich. Later on, we find Pepys again in the Isle of Dogs. He had evidently been enjoying himself with some friends, probably at Hackney. In his record of the event he writes :— " We set out so late that it grew dark, so as we doubted the losing of our way; and a long time it was, or seemed to be, before we could get to the water side, and that about eleven at night, where, when we came, all merry, we found no ferry boat was there, nor no oares to convey us to Deptford. However, afterwards "oares" was called from the other side at Greenwich; but when it come, a frolick, being mighty merry, took us, and there we would sleep all night in the coach, in the Isle of Dogs. So we did, there being now with us my Lady Scott; and with great pleasure drew up the glasses and slept till daylight; and then, some victuals and wine being brought us, we ate a bit, and so up and took boat, merry as might be, to Sir George Carteret's : there all to bed." Again, he writes under date of 17th December, 1665 :—

" Word brought me that Cutler's coach is, by appointment, come to the Isle of Dogs for me, and so I over the water, and in his coach to Hackney; a very fine, clear, cold, frosty day."

Beyond the seven mills on the west side of the island, of which we have already spoken, there appears to have been but few, if any, buildings standing near the river-side down to the beginning of the last century. In "An Actual Survey of the Parish of St. Dunstan, Stepney, *alias* Stebunheath," taken in 1703 by Joel Gascoyne, the circuit of the Isle of Dogs is thus laid down. Starting from north-west corner, we first come to " Fowler's yard," and then to the " Star," a public-house lying a little off from the river-side. The " Old Breach," of which we have already made mention, is next indicated; after which come the " seven mills." Then follows the " Drunken Dock," near the mast house, and further on is a building called " Starch House," which stood close to the ferry. Proceeding along the river-side, the next places marked are—" Roult's Yard," occupying the site of the present Canal Dock; " Cold Harbour," " Globe Stairs," and " Sir H. Johnson's upper dock." " In the body of the map," observes Mr. Cowper, to whom we are indebted for this description, " the ' Chappell ' is the only building indicated. The old road is laid down, and its direction very exactly indicated. The other road, which crossed over the east end of the Breach (Poplar Gut), is also given; it appears to have been at this time a field-way, and to have gone south no further than Chapel House, with which, however, it does not appear to have been connected. The ditches seem to be all marked, and the number and form of the fields well defined."

In a survey of the Marsh, taken in 1740 by Dr. Scattiff and T. Willson, the mills are represented as eleven in number, and extend from the Breach to the inlet called the mast-pond. A little to the south of the Canal Dock yard is " the Folly," or " Folly House," which stands upon the river wall : this house is not marked in the survey of 1740, but in 1790 it is mentioned by Pennant, who writes :— " We finished our walk, and dined at a small house, called the Folly, on the water's edge, almost opposite to the splendid hospital at Greenwich, where we sat for some hours, enjoying the delicious view of the river, and the moving picture of a succession of shipping perpetually passing and re-passing."

On the 2nd of February 1791, there was a very high tide; the Thames again overflowed its banks; and the Isle of Dogs was once more inundated.

As we have shown in the preceding chapter, the basin of the Thames, between London and the Nore, consists of a long and very irregularly-shaped flat, lying between high grounds, which sometimes, as at Purfleet, Greenhithe, and Northfleet, come quite down to the river itself, and sometimes recede for miles up into the country, as at Pitsea, where the basin is seven miles in width. The river, as we have seen, is prevented from periodically or occasionally covering the whole of the floor of this basin by a system of embankments, which extend, with occasional interruptions by high lands or houses, from Fulham and Putney above bridge down to the sea, a distance of upwards of fifty miles. A great extent of the river-side streets and houses form, in effect, part of the system of embankment of the river in its course through London—most of Southwark, Lambeth, Deptford, and Greenwich on the one side, and of Shadwell and Limehouse on the other, lying below the level of high water spring tides, and being, in fact, all afloat whenever the tide flows higher than usual. The long straggling street at Millwall presents a good specimen of this sort of embankment; for in walking down it it is impossible not to be aware that it is constructed on artificially raised ground, from which one looks down on the Thames on one side and the flat Isle of Dogs on the other; indeed, the very name of the place, or rather, its termination, is suggestive, the title of "wall" being—both in Kent and Essex—universally applied to the embankments; and the names "Millwall," "Blackwall," "Rotherhithe-wall," "Narrow-wall," "Broadwall," all denote either places built upon the embankment, or streets which owe their existence to its protection.

Since the commencement of the present century there has been a constant growth of factories and establishments of various kinds in the Isle of Dogs, and consequently a corresponding increase in its population and the number of its houses. The East and West India Docks, and the Millwall Docks, which occupy what may be called the central part of the island, we shall describe in the next chapter.

With reference to the progress of factories here, Lysons, in 1811, makes the following remarks in the supplement to his "Environs of London":— "Some very extensive iron-works have been lately established at Millwall, near the Canal and West India Docks, by Jorkes, Coulson, & Co. In their forge and rolling-mills, which are worked by two powerful steam-engines, one of sixty, the other of twenty-horse power, are manufactured from scrap iron bar and bolt iron, for the use of ship-builders

and coachmakers, and iron-hoops, sheet and rod iron for home consumption and exportation. Various other articles are made at the manufactory, such as anchors and mooring-chains of any size; and all kinds of heavy forged iron-work for the navy and land service, for various purposes of machinery, &c. Near the same spot Sir Charles Price & Co. have a mill for crushing rapeseed and linseed, a turpentine distillery, and a manufactory of rosin."

At the present time there is almost a complete belt of docks, factories, and engineering establishments extending along the bank of the Thames from Limehouse to Blackwall; these include, besides the above-mentioned works, a large number of others, mostly connected with ship-building and mercantile interests. Among the largest establishments are armour-plate rolling-mills, chemical works, rope manufactories, constructive iron and bridge works, timber wharves, and works for the manufacture of anchors, chains, buoys, &c. Among the oldest establishments on the island are the extensive premises of Messrs. Ferguson, mast and block manufacturers, which have been in existence here upwards of a century.

Messrs. Blashfields' cement and terra-cotta works, which were established here early in the present century, have acquired celebrity for the manufacture of Roman cement, plaster of Paris, Portland cement, and useful and decorative objects in terra-cotta. The following account of these works, communicated by Mr. J. M. Blashfield, appears in Mr. Cowper's "History of Millwall":— "The cement commonly known as Roman cement was first discovered by Parker in 1796, and was then made from nodules of indurated clay, or septaria, found upon the beach of the Isle of Sheppy. Since the expiration of Parker's patent, it has been chiefly made from similar material found off the coast of Harwich. Nearly two-thirds of the brick-work of the Thames Tunnel is united with a cement formed by a combination of the Harwich and Sheppey stones, and was made at these works. Here was also made the cement for the Nelson Pillar, the Royal Exchange, the foundation walls of the new Houses of Parliament, the Lyceum Theatre, the St. James's Theatre, many of the great railway tunnels, and other important works.

"The largest manufactory for plaster of Paris in England is at these works. The raw material is procured partly from Rouen, in Normandy, and partly from Newark, in Nottinghamshire; the latter is most celebrated for its whiteness of colour, but is not so hard as that made from French stones. The cement invented by Mr. Aspdin, of Wakefield, and known as Portland cement, is now made here, and is composed of clay and limestones, washed together in given proportions, then dried, burnt, and ground to powder ready for use.

"Terra-cotta of a light colour is made by combining the clays of Dorset and Devon with silica and other fusible bodies, and mixing them to the consistence of painters' putty or bakers' dough. It is then wrought by an artist into the required shape by hand, somewhat similar to the mode adopted for modelling a statue which is intended to be carved in marble or cast in bronze. The work, when finished, is slowly dried, and when quite dry removed into a reverberatory kiln, and burnt to a white heat in the same mode as burning china. If a number of articles are required of similar design, a plaster mould is made from the clay model, into which the prepared clay is pressed ; and after about an hour's time the mould is removed, and the pressed model worked, finished, and dried. By this latter mode, architectural works which are to be repeated may be made with great economy.

"The red terra-cotta made at these works is from a marble obtained in the township of Bedford, near Bolton, and is, when burnt, equal in hardness and colour to the best ancient specimens of pottery. Etruscan and Greek vases are made of this, and it is of this material the roof of the Alhambra courts of the Crystal Palace at Sydenham is made. The roof of the Pompeian House at Sydenham was also made here, and is, in part, of this red marble.

"Statues of heroic size, and the largest pieces of pottery ever fired, have lately been wrought at this place, in the Dorset and Devon clays. The great statue of Australia, modelled by Mr. Bell for the terrace of the Crystal Palace, was made here in this way. So also was the Venus de Medici and the colossal Triton for the fountains of the same place. Capitals of columns, busts, vases, consoles, balustrades, chimneys, flower-pots, and a variety of other articles, are constantly being fabricated here, and artists of the first eminence are employed upon the models."

On the portion of Millwall immediately opposite Deptford are some extensive iron-works and ship-building yards. The premises known as Millwall Iron-works were filled out in 1836, by Mr. (afterwards Sir) William Fairbairn, the celebrated engineer, of Manchester, and were planned on a very elaborate scale, comprising engineers' fitting and erecting shops, joiners' and pattern-makers' shops, iron and brass foundries, smithies, &c., besides

every appurtenance in the yard for constructing vessels of the largest class, both in wood and iron. Here were built several vessels of war for the navy, including the *Grappler*, *Megæra*, &c. These iron-works were for many years held by the eminent ship-building firm of Messrs. Scott Russell & Co., and were partly destroyed by fire in 1853, when the damage done was estimated at £60,000. Mr. Scott Russell became well known in the engineering and mercantile world for his researches and experiments, which resulted in the practical application of the "wave-line" theory in connection with ship-building, and he also acted as the secretary of the Great Exhibition of 1851, of which he was one of the original promoters.

These premises possess a river frontage of great extent, and are an object of great attraction to the steamboat traveller, from the interest naturally excited in witnessing so many vessels constantly in course of construction.

Here was built the largest vessel that ever floated in the Thames, or, indeed, anywhere else : namely, the *Great Eastern*. This huge steamship, whose subsequent career perhaps has hardly been on a par with the interest which was evinced during her construction, occupied about six years in building, having been commenced in 1853, and equipped ready for sailing by January, 1860. It was built for the Eastern Steam Navigation Company, and was intended for the Indian and Australian route by the Cape of Good Hope. During the construction of the vessel, the proportions of the ship were seen to great advantage as she lay with her broadside to the river, her form being to a great extent free from the forest of poles which usually serve as the stages used in ordinary ship-building.

The hull of the vessel is built entirely of iron, and is 680 feet in length, 80 feet in breadth, and 58 feet in height from keel to deck. The ship is divided transversely into ten separate compartments of 60 feet each, rendered perfectly watertight by bulkheads, having no openings whatever lower than the second deck, whilst two longitudinal walls of iron, 36 feet apart, traverse 350 feet of the length of the ship.

Some idea of the magnitude of these dimensions may be formed when it is stated that the *Great Eastern* is six times the size of the *Duke of Wellington* line-of-battle ship ; that her length is more than three times that of the height of the Monument on Fish Street Hill, while her breadth is equal to the width of Pall Mall ; and that a promenade round the deck affords a walk of more than a quarter of a mile. She was designed by Mr. Isambard Kingdom Brunel, F.R.S., the "father of Transatlantic steam navigation." The hull of the ship, together with the paddle-engines, were built by Messrs. Scott Russell and Co., whilst the screw-engines were manufactured by Messrs. Watts and Co., of Birmingham. Mr. Scott Russell, to whom the entire merits of the ship as a piece of naval architecture belong, wrote during its construction :—" It is to the company's engineer, Mr. J. K. Brunel, that the original conception is due of building a steamship large enough to carry coals sufficient for full steaming on the longest voyage. He, at the outset, and long before it had assumed a mercantile form, communicated his views to me, and I have participated in the contrivance of the best means to carry them into practical effect. I think, further, that the idea of using two sets of engines and two propellers is original, and was his invention. It was his idea also to introduce a cellular construction, like that at the top and bottom of the Britannia Bridge, into the construction of the great ship. These are the main characteristics which distinguish this from other ships, and these are Mr. Brunel's. Her lines and her structure in other respects are identical with those of any other ships which are constructed like this on a principle of my own, which I have systematically carried out during the last twenty years, and which is commonly called the 'wave' principle. In other respects, also, her materials are put together in the manner usual in any other ships."

The bottom of the ship is almost flat. Up to the water-mark the hull is constructed with an inner and outer skin, nearly three feet apart, and each composed of three-quarter inch plates. Between these, at intervals of six feet, run horizontal webs of iron plates, which materially increase the power of resistance both of the inner and the outer skin. About 10,000 tons of iron plates were used in the construction of the hull. These plates are 30,000 in number, and are each secured by 100 iron rivets.

The distinguishing feature of the *Great Eastern*, in addition to her vast size, is the combined application of steam-power through the paddle-wheel and the screw. The engines are considerably larger than any hitherto made for marine purposes. The vessel has ten boilers and five funnels, and the boilers are placed longitudinally along the centre of the ship, and are entirely independent of each other. Each paddle-boiler has ten furnaces, and each screw-boiler twelve furnaces, thus giving to the whole the large number of one hundred and twelve furnaces. Independent of her steam-power, her means of propulsion is aided by six masts, no

less than 6,500 square yards of canvas being used in the construction of her sails. The paddle-wheels are fifty-eight feet in diameter, and the weight of each wheel is computed at ninety tons, whilst the screw propeller is twenty-four feet in diameter, and the engine shaft 160 feet in length. The ship was designed to accommodate 4,000 passengers—800 first class, 2,000 second class, and 1,200 third class —independently of the ship's complement of about 400 hands. Her registered tonnage is 23,000.

The first attempt to float this monster vessel was made in November, 1857, but unsuccessfully. On Sunday, January 31st, 1858, however, in the presence of a vast concourse of spectators, she yielded to the hydraulic pressure that was brought to bear upon her, and glided slowly, but gracefully, into the Thames, where she lay at rest, while being fitted for sea, till September, 1859, when she was towed down the river to Gravesend. In the following June the *Great Eastern* made her first sea trip. It may be of interest to record that when first floated the vessel registered sixteen and a half feet aft, and fourteen feet eleven inches forward, or within six inches of the amount calculated.

In a work entitled "A Floating City," by Jules Verne, some interesting particulars of the great ship and its subsequent career are given. From it we learn that "after twenty passages from England to America, one of which was marked by very serious disasters, the use of the *Great Eastern* was temporarily abandoned, and this immense ship, arranged to accommodate passengers, seemed no longer good for anything. When the first attempt to lay the Atlantic cable had failed—partly because the number of ships which carried it was insufficient—engineers thought of the *Great Eastern*. She alone could store on board the 2,100 miles of metallic wire, weighing 4,500 tons. She alone, thanks to her perfect indifference to the sea, could unroll and immerse this immense cable. But special arrangements were necessary for storing away the cable in the ship's hold. Two out of six boilers were removed, and one funnel out of three belonging to the screw-engine ; in their places large tanks were placed for the cable, which was immersed in water to preserve it from the effects of variation of the atmosphere ; the wire thus passed from these tanks of water into the sea without suffering the least contact with the air. The laying of the cable having been successfully accomplished, and the object in view attained, the *Great Eastern* was once more left in her costly idleness."

The vessel was afterwards taken in hand by a French company, which was floated with a capital of 2,000,000 francs, with the intention of again conveying passengers across the Atlantic, and the immense ship was accordingly re-arranged for that purpose. The interior of the ship was fitted with every convenience, and even luxury, to suit the requirements of passengers. The ladies' saloon and the grand saloon were ornamented with lustres, swinging lamps, and pictures, and the magnificent rooms lighted by side skylights, supported on

Since the launch of the *Great Eastern* the Millwall Iron Works have been in the hands of Messrs. Mare & Co.; and more recently the premises known as the Northumberland Works have been utilised for the manufacture of the machinery and other necessaries used in the supply of the electric light. The *Northumberland* armour-plated ship was launched from these premises in 1866.

Immediately beyond Potter's Ferry, which lies

LAUNCH OF THE GREAT EASTERN.

gilded pillars, and communicating with the upper deck by wide staircases with metallic steps and mahogany balusters. The laundries and the crew's berth are shut off at the fore part; on deck are arranged four rows of cabins separated by a passage, and at the stern three immense dining-rooms run in the same direction as the cabins; a passage leads from the saloons at the stern to those at the bows round the paddle-engine, between its sheet-iron partition and the ship's offices.

The ill-fated vessel, however, never seems to have prospered; and more than once she was nearly lost in the Atlantic, through failing to answer her helm, or through some other accident. Now it appears that she is likely to be used for conveying coals from Newcastle to the port of London.

directly opposite Greenwich Hospital, is Cubitt Town, so called from the fact of a large portion of the land here having been some years ago taken by Messrs. Cubitt & Co., builders, for the construction of works in the manufacture of all kinds of ceramic ware used in building, &c. Rows of streets and houses were built in the neighbourhood of the works, and in 1853, Mr. William Cubitt, M.P., erected a church here for the use of the inhabitants. This edifice, built of brick, with stone dressings, and in the Early English style, stands at the south-eastern extremity of the island, its tower and spire being a conspicuous object from the river.

St. Luke's Church, in Stratford Street, Millwall, consecrated in 1870, is a stone building of modern Gothic design, with a heavy-looking tower and spire.

Limehouse is situated on the north-western side of the canal which separates the Isle of Dogs from the mainland. It is so called from a lime-kiln, generally known as the lime-house, which stood here. Pepys, under date of October 9th, 1661, writes, in his "Diary":—"By coach to Captain Marshe's at Limehouse—to a house that hath been their ancestors' for this 250 years, close by the lime-house, which gives the name to the place."

Norden, writing in 1592, adopts the derivation of Limehouse from the lime-kiln, which, according to Mr. Cowper's statement in his work above quoted, exists to this day; but Stow gives the derivation as a corrupt spelling for Lime-host, or Lime-hurst, the latter of which denotes a plantation, or

designs of Nicholas Hawksmoor, a pupil of Sir Christopher Wren, and was consecrated in 1730. The original drawings and plans for the building are preserved in the British Museum. The steeple of the church is conspicuous from the river, but is not remarkable for its beauty; indeed, this church, like others of which Hawksmoor was the architect, exhibits a style remarkable for its solidity of ap-

LIMEHOUSE CHURCH.

a place of lime-trees. It may be remembered that Shakespeare introduces the name in the play of *Henry VIII.* (Act v., sc. 3), where Porter says:—"These are the youths that thunder at a playhouse, and fight for bitten apples: that no audience but the Tribulation of Tower-hill or the limbs of Limehouse, their dear brothers, are able to endure."

The district was originally a hamlet of Stepney, but was made into a distinct parish in the reign of Queen Anne. The church is one of the fifty which were authorised to be erected by an Act of Parliament passed in the ninth year of that reign. It is dedicated to St. Anne, and was built from the

pearance and singularity of design, which may be described as Romanesque. The edifice is constructed of Portland stone, and was built at a cost of about £38,000. The principal entrance, approached by a flight of stone steps, is formed in front of the segmental vestibule, which is finished with square pilasters, with enriched capitals, supporting an entablature and semi-dome roof. The third storey of the tower forms in the plan a curious outline, and in its elevation is equally unsightly with the part rising immediately above it. The walls forming the vestry-room at the north-east angle of the church, and those corresponding on the opposite side, are carried up several feet above the large cornice, and form two curiously ornamented towers. In the interior of the church there is nothing remarkable as to the general arrangement. The Roman style is preserved throughout. Stone columns, of the composite order, standing upon square pedestals, support an enriched cornice, continued only over part of the side aisles. Small Ionic columns of wood are placed as supports under either gallery, the entrances to which are equally crude in design with many other portions of this edifice. The east window, of painted glass, from a design by West, was executed by Mr. Buckler, the painter of the window in the " Barons' Hall " at Arundel Castle. The pulpit is an elaborate specimen of carved work, and is stated to have occupied two years and a half in its execution.

The "fine and beautiful" Commercial Road, as Baron Dupin calls it in his " Commercial Power of Great Britain," constructed under the direction of Mr. Walker, an eminent engineer in his day, runs directly through the parish. It is seventy feet in width, and forms a direct communication between Whitechapel and the West India Docks.

The Lea Cut and the Regent's Canal both enter the Thames at Limehouse. The former was executed in 1772 for the purpose of obtaining a more direct communication between the Pool and the River Lea, which it joins at Bromley. The Regent's Canal is of more recent formation. Its route is traced through nine parishes; it is eight miles in length, and its mean width thirty-seven feet. It rises eighty-four feet by means of twelve locks, is crossed by about forty bridges, passes by means of a tunnel (upwards of half a mile in length) under the New River and part of Islington, and by another tunnel (a quarter of a mile in length) at Paddington, and communicates with the Grand Junction Canal.

Poplar, which adjoins Limehouse on the east, was likewise originally a hamlet of Stepney, from which parish it was separated in 1817. The district embraces the Isle of Dogs. Dr. Woodward, in " Strype " (Circuit Walk, p. 102), writing in 1720, observes :—" Popler, or Poplar, is so called from the multitude of poplar-trees (which love a moist soil) growing there in former times. And there be yet remaining, in that part of the hamlet which bordereth upon Limehouse, many old bodies of large poplars, standing as testimonials of the truth of that etymology."

The parish church, dedicated to All Saints, was consecrated in 1823. It is a large building, with a handsome steeple, which contrasts favourably with that of Limehouse Church. Poplar Chapel, called

also the East India Company's Chapel, was built during the Commonwealth, and contains two or three monuments to distinguished men, among them being one to Robert Ainsworth, the Latin lexicographer, who died in 1743, and whose epitaph was his own composition ; and another to George Steevens, the Shaksperian critic and editor, who died at Hampstead in 1800, and was buried here. This latter monument was executed by Flaxman.

The old manor-house of Poplar, an ancient wooden building, was situated on the south side of the present East India Dock Road, but was partially pulled down early in the present century. The old house was formerly owned by Sir Gilbert and Sir William Dethick, who held successively the appointment of Garter King-at-Arms in the reign of Queen Elizabeth. The Town Hall and the offices of the Local Board of Works for Poplar are handsome and commodious buildings, the latter being of recent erection.

" To Poplar adjoineth Blackwall "—so wrote Dr. Woodward in " Strype's Appendix " ; and added that it is " a notable harbour for ships, so called because it is a *wall* of the Thames, and distinguished by the additional term Black from the black shrubs which grow on it, as on Blackheath, which is opposite to it, on the other side of the river. '

In the reign of Edward III. Sir John de Pulteney possessed the manor of Poplar. His London house was at Cold Harbour, in Upper Thames Street. Mr. Cowper conjectures that if he ever resided in this neighbourhood, it was at Blackwall, where there is a place called Cold Harbour. " Near the ancient ferry, called Globe Stairs, opposite the ' Artichoke' Tavern," he observes, " there stands an ancient house, which tradition says was successively occupied by Sebastian Cabot and Sir Walter Raleigh. Whatever value may attach to the tradition, the house in question is both curious and interesting. Its framework is of wood, and still likely to last for years. Some grotesque heads and other carvings adorn the outside. The floor of the house is considerably below the present level of the street, and the principal entrance is blocked up. Though now in a narrow and confined situation, originally its windows looked out upon the rising sun, and commanded an extensive view up and down the river, as well as across into Kent. By the gradual encroachments of buildings all around, it has been hemmed in as we now find it."

The Brunswick Wharf, at Blackwall, was opened for the reception of steam-packets in 1840. Lovegrove's Tavern, the " Brunswick," was for many years famous for its fish, and particularly for whitebait dinners.

CHAPTER LIX.

THE EAST AND WEST INDIA AND MILLWALL DOCKS.

" Where has commerce such a mart,
So rich, so thronged, so drained, and so supplied,
As London—opulent, enlarged, and still-
Increasing London?"—Cowper.

The Vastness of Trade and Commerce—Arrival of Coal-ships and other Vessels in the Port of London—Number of Barges and other Craft required for Traffic in 1792—Plunder carried on in the Lighters on the River—Institution of the Thames Police—Proposals for the Establishment of Docks—Foundation of the West India Docks—The Opening Ceremony—Description of the Docks—A Curious Museum—ew Dry Docks—The Wood Wharf—The Rum Quay—The South West India Dock—The Wool Warehouses—The East India Docks—Millwall Dock—Insecurity of Merchandise before the Establishment of Docks or Institution of the Thames Police.

THE docks of London show at once to the most casual observer the great enterprise and prosperity of the metropolis. It will readily be conceived that a population of more than 3,000,000 souls must necessarily, to a great extent, be supported by its trade and commerce, its proceeds in money value far exceeding in amount that of any other community in the world. The merchant is the dealer with the trading universe, the tidal Thames bringing with its flow the treasures of near and distant nations ; and, with the aid of steam, persons of all nations come to us with objects of business and mutual interchange.

Charles Knight, in his " London," says :—" The stranger, especially from an inland county, who takes a passage by one of the steamers which leave London Bridge every half-hour for Greenwich, will be astonished at the apparently interminable forests of masts which extend on both sides of the channel, where a width of three hundred feet *should* be kept for the purposes of safe navigation, but which the crowd of ships from all quarters of the globe, of colliers, coasters, steamboats, and river craft, renders it difficult for the harbour-masters to maintain. If the tide be running upward, laden coal-barges are thronging the channel, proceeding to the wharves in the upper part of the river, and colliers at their moorings are at all times discharging their cargoes into barges alongside. By the regulations of the coal trade, only a certain number of coal-ships are allowed to unload at the same time, the others remaining lower down the river until their turn arrives ; and the coal-meters, who are appointed by the City, are also limited in number. But for these restrictions the river would present a still more crowded appearance, as it has happened that above three hundred colliers have arrived in the lower pool in one day, and even now a very large portion of the river is occupied by this one branch of commerce. Seventy years ago, not only coal-ships, but vessels of every other kind, discharged their cargoes into lighters while at anchor in the stream ; but such a practice would now be impossible, so great has been the increase of commerce. East Indiamen in general came only as far as Blackwall, where they discharged their cargo into decked lighters of from fifty to one hundred tons, and, the hatchways being secured under lock and key, they proceeded to the wharves. West India ships discharged in the river, and the cargoes also, were conveyed in lighters to the legal quays. All other vessels, except they were of small size, were in like manner compelled to use lighters in discharging their cargoes. At the present time the majority of the barges and river craft are solely employed in transporting the cargoes of coal, corn, and timber ships : comparatively speaking, only a small proportion being required for the conveyance of all other commodities, the chief of which are of a bulky kind, and do not offer any great temptation to pilferers."

In 1792 the number of barges and craft required for the traffic between the ships in the river and the quays was 500 for timber and 1,180 for coal, each averaging 33 tons ; 402 lighters of 39 tons ; 338 punts of 20 tons ; 57 lugger boats of 24 tons ; 6 sloops of 27 tons ; 10 cutters of 71 tons ; and 10 hoys of 58 tons : making a total of 3,503 craft. Property of the most costly and valuable description, and every kind of merchandise, was daily exposed to plunder in these open boats, for only the lighters of the East India Company were decked, and it was considered that even they afforded a very insufficient protection. The temptation to pilfering was almost irresistible, those who were honestly disposed taking their share, under the plea that waste and leakage were perquisites. So many persons were engaged in the work of depredation on the river that it was carried on in the most daring and open manner, lightermen, watermen, labourers, the crews of ships, the mates and officers in some instances, and to a great extent the officers of the revenue, being combined in this nefarious system, while on each side of the river there were hosts of receivers, some of them persons of opulence, who carried on an extensive business in stolen property. In 1798, the Thames Police, called then the Marine Police, was instituted for the repression of these offences, but the source of the evil was still untouched, the temptation remaining undiminished so long as the exposure of property was rendered unavoidable by the absence of sufficient accommodation in quays and warehouses.

During the last century scarcely an effort had been made for the accommodation of the vastly increased trade of London, and the mercantile interests experienced, in consequence, impediments and losses, which it is wonderful did not arouse them earlier to provide a remedy. About the year 1793 the complaints of the merchants began to attract more attention than they had hitherto received, and they held meetings, at which various remedies were proposed, but for a time no substantial improvement resulted therefrom. Many plans were brought forward, among them being the following, each of which embraced the Isle of Dogs in their scheme :—

The City plan, of which the chief feature was a dock of 102 acres in the Isle of Dogs, to contain above 400 ships, and another at Rotherhithe, of the same extent, for colliers. Another plan, drawn up by a Mr. Walker, was to excavate fifty-five acres for docks, thirty-five acres additional being intended for quays, wharves, and warehouses. One of the entrances was to be by a canal intersecting the Isle of Dogs, at a point near the southern shore. The cost was estimated at £880,000.

The last of these plans was designed by Mr. Reaveley ; it displayed considerable ingenuity, and its chief features were :—(1) To form a new channel for the river in a straight line from Limehouse to Blackwall, the Long Reach round the Isle of Dogs thus constituting a dock, with flood-gates at each entrance. (2) To continue the new channel below Blackwall towards Woolwich Reach, so as to convert another bend of the old channel into a dock. (3) To make a new channel from Wapping, and to form three docks out of the three bends, to be called Ratcliffe Dock, Blackwall Dock, and Greenwich Dock.

In 1799 an Act of Parliament was passed for rendering more commodious and for better regulating the Port of London ; and in that same year another Bill was also passed for the formation of the West India Docks. These docks, which occupy the whole length of what may be called the "neck" of the Isle of Dogs, from Limehouse to Blackwall, are said to be the largest in the world. They are nearly three times as extensive as the London Docks, and are almost 300 acres in extent.

The West India Docks were the first public wet-docks constructed on the north bank of the Thames in the port of London. There had, however, been for many years a wet-dock at Blackwall, at the ancient ship-yards there ; besides which, a Mr. Perry, in 1789, had constructed the Brunswick Dock, which, as we shall presently see, was afterwards enlarged to form the export basin of the East India Docks.

The Act empowering the formation of these docks includes the City Canal, or South Dock ; and the preliminaries having been duly arranged, the works were commenced in February, 1800, and the "first stone" was laid in July of the same year. Inscriptions setting forth the objects for which the docks were made, written on two rolls of vellum, one in English and the other in Latin, together with several coins of different values, were enclosed in glass bottles, which were deposited in the first stone, at the south-east corner of warehouse No. 8.

The docks were formed from the designs of Mr. Jesson, and were formally opened on the 27th August, 1802, the opening ceremony being performed by Mr. William Pitt, the then Prime Minister, in the presence of a vast concourse of spectators. The first ship to enter the new docks was the *Henry Addington*, a vessel newly built, and one of the finest in the West India trade. For twenty-one years after the opening of the docks all vessels in the West India trade frequenting the port of London were compelled to use them.

The principal, or western, entrance to the docks is near the West India Dock Station of the Blackwall Railway, a little to the east of Limehouse Church. It is surmounted by the model of a sailing-vessel, and over the entrance is inscribed :— "The West India Import Dock—begun 12th July, 1800 ; opened for business 1st September, 1802."

At the principal entrance is a bronze statue, erected to perpetuate the memory of Robert Milligan, "a merchant of London, to whose genius, perseverance, and guardian care, the surrounding great work principally owes its design, accomplishment, and regulation." This statue, which was executed by Sir R. Westmacott, is of life-size, placed on a granite pedestal, and enclosed by an iron railing. Close by are two guard-houses, which were erected for the accommodation of small detachments of troops, detailed by the Government when first the docks were constructed for the more efficient protection of the company's property. These troops supplied a cordon of night sentries round the docks, each sentry having in his sentry-box a bell, which he sounded at regular intervals.

There were originally only two docks, one for imports and the other for exports. The original plan was not filled up by the completion of the docks before 1805. Since that period many additions and alterations have been made.

The whole system of West India Docks now comprises three parallel docks, with warehouses, quay sheds, and sheds for export goods, covering an area of 264 acres, of which 160 acres are land, and 104 acres water. The storage capacity of the warehouses in the West India Dock system is 166,700 tons of goods. The area of the Western and South Dock quays is 1,566,500 square feet, and of the warehouses 1,141,000 square feet. The Dock Company employ on their permanent staff about 2,500 persons. In addition to these a very large number of persons are employed as the exigencies of the work may require. The staff employed at the West India Docks alone is as follows :—

	WEEKLY COST.	ANNUAL COST.
Major or controlling Staff ... ... (184)	£400	£21,000
Minor Staff ... ... (454)	525	27,000
Porter and Labour Staff and extra Labourers } averages (1717)	2,336	120,000

Visitors usually commence their inspection at the northernmost or Import Dock. This dock contains in water space thirty superficial acres; it is 2,600 feet long, and 500 feet wide, with warehouses half a mile in extent. Ships from all parts of the world discharge here, and their cargoes are housed in the adjoining warehouses, which contain canes, horns, camphor, tea, pepper, pimento, rice, tin, copper, ginger, sugar, molasses, coir, coffee, plumbago, oils, &c.

At No. 11 warehouse, which was partially destroyed by fire on the 28th December, 1873, is a small museum, containing specimens of the various kinds of goods housed at the docks. As a sample of the interest attaching to this museum, it may be mentioned that cochineal, one of the products here exhibited, is the dried carcase of an insect, and produces a brilliant crimson dye. About 70,000 of the insects are required to weigh one pound. They are of two kinds : the black, females which have produced young ; and the grey or white, which have arrived at maturity and have not bred. As the finest dye is in the skin, the black insects are the most profitable, being apparently all skin, and being hollow are known as "shelly cochineal." The insects are suffocated and dried in ovens.

In this warehouse can be seen a machine worked by hydraulic pressure for sampling tin. One ingot of tin in each ten is "sampled" for the market, and, the sample being sent to the brokers in the City,

the sale is effected and the value of the ten ingots is fixed by the evidence of the sample cut from one. The value of the metals, tin and copper, lying at this warehouse is nearly £30,000, and the weight is 350 tons. The weight of an ingot of tin is from ninety to a hundred pounds, and the value about £3 10s.

The vessels from China, which arrive early in July laden with the new season's teas, are generally discharged here ; and when, as is now usual, pressure is put upon the company, it is not uncommon for a ship bringing 50,000 packages of tea to be discharged within twenty working hours.

On the north quay of the Import Dock many cargoes are to be seen. In the warehouses along the quay the article chiefly housed is sugar; the floors and quay are stained with sugar drainage, and in some parts saturated with molasses from the lower-class sugars. Sugar is imported of many different qualities, and in various kinds of packages, the large hogsheads being the most unwieldy. Mauritius sugar comes in mats formed of leaves, and East India sugar in bags woven from jute. Jaggery is a very low quality sugar from the Madras coast, and the bags in which it is imported become so thoroughly soaked with sugar that after being emptied of their contents they are sold to itinerant dealers, who boil them to extract the sugar, and sell the bags to the paper-makers. All the bags are raised from the hold of the ship by cranes, worked like the majority of cranes in the docks, by hydraulic pressure.

The coffee imports are concentrated at No. 10 warehouse, and about one-sixth of the imports of coffee into London comes to this warehouse. The warehouse is supplied with machinery for the bulking, re-filling, and beating of casks of coffee by hydraulic power, superseding manual labour. All coffee of one mark and of the same quality or description, frequently from fifty or more packages, has to be mixed together on the floor of the warehouse, to ascertain the net weight for Customs duty and for trade purposes, and also to ensure the quality being of one average. In former years this mixing was done by hand, and as the company's housings of coffee are about 20,000 casks in a year, in addition to about 70,000 bags, it follows that much labour was required. It is now the practice, after turning out the contents of the casks, to scoop the berries into iron hoppers, whence they run into the casks on the floor below. In order to make the coffee lie close, so that the actual quantity turned out might be re-filled into the package, it was the practice for a gang of five men to beat the casks with wooden mallets, and even then the whole of the contents could frequently not be returned to the packages, and bags, named by the trade "overtakers," were used to take the surplus; but the mechanical beaters of this patent machinery perform in one minute the work which occupied five men six minutes; moreover, the whole of the coffee can now be easily returned to the original packages. There are eleven of these machines in use.

In passing to the West Wood Wharf, a siding or line of railway will be observed at the south end of No. 10 Warehouse, in which trucks are placed with goods from the steamers, which discharge at Southampton. The trucks are loaded alongside the vessels at Southampton, and run direct to this siding, whence the goods are raised by the crane to the loophole, and manipulated as if coming from vessels discharging alongside the quay in these docks.

The swing bridges carrying the railway over the adjoining locks weigh 300 tons each, and are moved by hydraulic machines, requiring only one man to set them in motion.

Blackwall Basin, which is on the east side of the northern bridge, is the tidal basin for the reception of ships entering the West India Dock; and on the south side of the basin is a dry dock for repairing and painting ships, which was opened on the 6th March, 1878, and was constructed at a cost of from £60,000 to £80,000. Its dimensions are: length 480 feet, breadth of bottom 80 feet, and entrance 64 feet, depth on gill 23 feet.

At the Wood Wharf, large quantities of mahogany, furniture wood, and teak, amounting to about 50,000 tons per annum, are stored, and the heavy logs are carried with comparative ease by travelling machinery. Quantities of lignum vitæ from Jamaica are seen; this is used chiefly for blocks, pulleys, rulers, &c. Satinwood and ebony, in considerable quantity, are also to be seen here, as also logwood, sapan wood, red sanders wood, and other woods used for dyeing purposes.

The largest log of mahogany ever known to have been imported arrived on the 30th of October, 1879, by the *Grizzehaum* from Tabasco. It was more than 60 feet long, and nearly 12 tons in weight.

The Rum Quay is the depôt for all wines and spirits in the Company's charge, and is capable of storing 40,000 puncheons. The average quantity of the rum in the vaults and warehouses is 35,000 puncheons, containing about $3\frac{1}{2}$ million gallons, and of the value of £700,000, the Customs duty, at 10s. 2d. per proof gallon, being in addition about £1,800,000. The vaults are good specimens of groined brickwork, the arches being elliptical, and springing from octagonal stone piers. Notwithstanding the forest of casks (which, however, do not intrude themselves in the prevailing darkness, though the odour of rum does), the visitor might easily suppose he was in the crypt of some immense cathedral. The only light obtained is from side windows, outside which are fixed concave reflectors; and as the vaults are 154 feet wide, the centre, without the aid of the reflectors, would be, in winter time, totally dark.

Each puncheon is marked in white paint with the "rotation" number and year of bonding, and the contents and "ullage," and a reflector formed of a piece of tin, nailed on a stick, is used to throw the borrowed light on these marks by the cooper whose duty it is to sound each cask daily, to ascertain that it remains in good condition. By the sound which the blow of the hammer produces, he is able to tell within half a gallon the vacuity of each cask, and should it appear to increase he marks the cask to watch it, and have it removed for examination should any flaw develop itself.

The plan of using reflectors is adopted on the score of safety from fire, no candle or lamp being allowed to be taken on the Rum Quay. Balmain's luminous paint has been used in the vaults with success.

On the vatting floor of this department are vats varying in capacity from 320 to 15,000 gallons, their aggregate capacity being 59,210 gallons. In these vats merchants are allowed to mix rum intended for exportation.

The centre dock is the Export Dock, covering 24 acres of water, 2,600 feet long by 400 feet in width, in which ships of light draught are accommodated to load.

The South West India Dock, commenced in 1866, and opened on 5th March, 1870, contains upwards of 26 acres of water, is 2,650 feet in length, and 450 feet in width, with a uniform depth of 29 feet. Some of the largest ships carrying colonial and East Indian cargoes which arrive in the Port of London discharge and load in this dock. The Import ships discharge usually on the south side, and the Export ships load chiefly on the north side; two berths, however, at the eastern and western ends of the south side are reserved for loading.

In the basin at the east end of the dock are loaded the fine vessels of the Glen Line, trading between London and China.

The extensive wool warehouses, situated on the south quay of this dock, were erected in 1873, for the storage and showing of wool, and have show room for 15,000 bales at one time. 113,000

J R Well

WEST INDIA DOCKS.

bales were housed and shown here in 1879, and 133,000 in 1880.

Other objects of interest to visitors are the steam fire engines, the cooperage, chain-testing house, and sawmills, together with the various workshops, where at times 400 mechanics and labourers are employed, in connection with the maintenance and repair of the docks, warehouses, and machinery of the company.

The East India Import and Export Docks and basin, at Blackwall, contain a water space of 32 acres; they were formerly the property of the East India Dock Company, and were constructed chiefly for the accommodation of East India shipping. The then capital or joint stock of the company was £463,876, and with, or out of, this capital were constructed the above-mentioned docks, including necessary warehouses, quays, roads, &c.

As far back as 1592 Blackwall was noted for its "great harbour of shipping," which harbour in all probability gave rise to the idea and subsequent formation of docks. Before the East India Docks existed, there was a wet dock constructed in 1789 by a Mr. Perry, called the "Brunswick Dock," which was afterwards enlarged to form an export dock to the East India Dock. In excavating for this dock a great quantity of fossil nuts and wood were found.

Pepys, in his "Diary," dated September 22nd, 1665, writes:—"At Blackwall, in digging the late docke, they did, twelve feet under ground, find perfect trees over-covered with earth. Nut-trees, with the branches, and the very nuts upon them; some of these nuts he [Johnson] showed us. Their shells black with age, and their kernel, upon opening, decayed, but their shell perfectly hard as ever."

The following inscription is placed under the clock tower of the principal entrance to the dock in the East India Road:—

"Under auspices of our most Gracious Sovereign George III., the sanction of his Majesty's Government and the patronage of the East India Company, these Wet Docks appropriated to the commerce of India and ships in that employ, were accomplished in those eventful years 1804, 1805, and 1806, the first stone being laid March 14th, 1804. They were opened by the introduction of five ships from 1,200 to 800 tons, with valuable cargoes, on August 4th, 1806. The grand undertaking originated in the laudable endeavours of the managing owners of ships in the Company's service, and the important national objects of increased security to property and revenue, combined with improved accommodation, economy, and dispatch, were thus early realised through the liberal subscriptions of the proprietors, and the unremitting attentions of the Directors of the East India Dock Company.—Joseph Cotton, Chairman; John Woolmore, Deputy Chairman; John Rennie, Ralph Walker, Engineers."

In May, 1838, the East India Dock Company was amalgamated with the West India Dock Company, and the name of the Company was changed to the "East and West India Dock Company."

The East India Dock Basin was originally five acres in extent, but in 1874, in consequence of the increase in the size and draught of ships using the port of London, it was deepened and enlarged, and a new river entrance lock was constructed to the eastward of the old entrance. These works, from the peculiar situation of the basin between the rivers Thames and Lea, involved considerable engineering difficulties; but they were all successfully surmounted, and the basin, in its present form, was opened for business by the admission of one of the large steamers of the Orient Steam Navigation Company, in August, 1879.

The basin now has a depth of thirty-three feet of water at ordinary spring tides, with thirty-one feet of water on the sills of the new entrance lock. It thus provides, even at the worst neap tides, sufficient water to admit the largest vessels using the port of London, and is superior in depth and consequent accommodation for deep-draughted vessels to any other dock on the Thames.

On the north and east quays of the basin extensive warehouses have been erected, the ground floors being constructed for the reception of export, and the upper floors for import goods. A novel feature in the construction of these warehouses and quays is the overhead gallery, or crane-road, at the first floor level, on which travelling hydraulics for discharging cargoes into the loopholes of first and upper floors are worked without interference with the lower quay, and the railway lines thereon provided for the accommodation of export business. Numerous loopholes opening into reception and delivery yards at the rear or sides of the warehouses are also provided to enable the extensive land carriage business to be conducted without interference with the quay-side work. Contiguous to the East Quay berth are the extensive premises of Messrs. Donald Currie and Co.

In July, 1879, nearly the whole of the south quay of the Eastern Import Dock subsided suddenly, owing to the disturbance of a treacherous vein of quicksand on which the walls were founded. The accommodation at this quay was formerly insufficient for the rapid discharge of the large vessels using the docks, and advantage was taken of the accident to reconstruct it in the present form, increasing the width of quay space considerably, and providing sufficient quay shed accommodation to enable the Company to at once land any cargoes under cover.

A special feature in this quay is the adoption of the plan of having two-storey quay sheds, which was first introduced in the South West India Dock of this Company.

Owing to the great variation in the length of the ships using these docks, it was found convenient, and for the greater facility of the Company's business, to substitute movable for fixed cranes. The Dock Company, therefore, in reconstructing the quay, converted all the existing fixed hydraulics into travelling cranes, by which means any number

The whole of these extensive works, involving an outlay of nearly £60,000, were completed in the very short period of sixteen months from the date of commencement.

Millwall Dock is situated in the centre of the Isle of Dogs, to the south of the West India Docks, and has entrances in both Limehouse Reach and Blackwall Reach. This dock, and the adjoining land belonging to the Company, cover altogether an area of nearly 200 acres. The dry dock, inside the wet dock, is 430 feet in length, and 65 feet

VAULTS AT THE DOCKS.

required can be concentrated at one ship, and the goods, as discharged, can be placed direct from the ship's holds on to the ground or first floor of the quay sheds.

The new quay was constructed without interfering with the business of the dock, or using any cofferdam, the system adopted being a close timber-piled quay, strongly secured by land ties at the rear of the old wall, the dock bottom behind the timber piling being dredged down to the London clay, and a massive concrete wall built *in situ*. Special means were adopted for mixing and putting the concrete into position, without the large percentage of loss of cement which frequently occurs in the construction of concrete work under water.

wide at the bottom. Millwall Dock, which was opened in 1868, has a trade with all parts of the world, but is especially the dock for grain import. Not only was the last vestige of the old Chapel House swept away on the formation of this dock, as mentioned in the preceding chapter, but the work saw also the removal of the last of the old metropolitan turnpike gates.

Some idea of the immense advantage to merchants and others obtained by the formation of the docks of London may be gained when we state that the number of ships entering the East and West India Docks alone is upwards of 2,000 annually. Even the entries in the port of London during a single week are enormous, as will be seen from the following return for the week ending June 30th, 1883 :—Number of vessels entered in, 238 ; number of steamers entered in, 154. Number of vessels entered out, 133 ; number of steamers entered out, 93. Number of cargo vessels cleared out, 123 ; number of cargo steamers cleared out, 92. Tonnage of vessels entered in, 149,593 ; tonnage of steamers entered in, 109,252. Tonnage of vessels entered out, 81,949 ; tonnage of steamers entered out, 59,568. Tonnage of vessels cleared out, 78,092 ; tonnage of steamers cleared out, 60,523. Total number of British vessels cleared out, 96 ; British tonnage cleared out, 64,372. Number of British steamers cleared out, 75 ; tonnage of British steamers cleared out, 50,304. Number of British sailers cleared out, 21 ; tonnage of British sailers cleared out, 14,068.

To form a proper conception of all the benefits to society, and to the mercantile world in particular, from the establishment of the India Docks, would require a mind of no common powers, and no small share of acuteness. What has been saved by these docks, and by the adoption of a general warehousing system, assisted by the river police, can be appreciated only by a recapitulation of what had been lost, previous to the introduction of the measures connected with these valuable improvements.

Mr. Colquhoun, in his work on "The Commerce and Police of the River Thames," written as long ago as the beginning of the present century, says :— "Let the mind only contemplate the commerce of a single river, unparalleled in point of extent and magnitude in the whole world, where 13,444 ships and vessels discharge and receive in the course of a year above 3,000,000 packages, many of which contain very valuable articles of merchandise, greatly exposed to depredations, not only from the criminal habits of many of the aquatic labourers and others who are employed, but from the temptations to plunder, arising from the confusion unavoidable in a crowded port, and the facilities afforded in the disposal of stolen property. "It will then be easily conceived that the plunder must have been excessive, especially where, from its analogy to smuggling, according to the false conceptions of those who are implicated, and from its gradual increase, the culprits were seldom restrained by a sense of moral turpitude, and this at a time too when, for want of a marine police, no means existed whereby offenders could be detected on the river. The fact is, that the system of river depredations grew and ramified as the commerce of the port of London advanced, until at length it assumed a variety of shapes and forms,

each having as many heads as a hydra. The first of these were *River Pirates*.

"This class was mostly composed of the most desperate and depraved characters ; and their attention was principally directed to ships, vessels, and craft in the night, which seemed to be unprotected. Among many other nefarious exploits performed by these miscreants, the following was not the least remarkable :—"An American vessel lying at East Lane Tier was boarded in the night, while the captain and crew were asleep, by a gang of pirates, who actually weighed the ship's anchor and hoisted it into their boat, with a complete new cable, with which they got clean off. The captain, hearing a noise, came upon deck at the moment the villains had secured their booty, with which they actually rowed away in his presence, impudently telling him they had taken away his anchor and cable, and bidding him good-night."

Much about the same time the bower anchor of a vessel from Guernsey was weighed and carried off with the cable. "Previous to the establishment of the docks, ships being very much lumbered were considered as the harvest of the river pirates, with whom it was a general practice to cut away bags of cotton, cordage, spars, oars, and other articles from the quarter-deck, and to get clear off even in the day-time. And as all classes of labourers, lumpers, &c., were in a manner guilty, they naturally connived at each other's delinquency, so that few or none were detected. It was frequently the practice of river pirates to go armed, and in sufficient force to resist. Their depredations were extensive among craft wherever valuable goods were to be found ; but they diminished in number after the commencement of the war ; and now, since the establishment of the docks and the marine police, a solitary instance of robbery is scarcely ever heard of. . . . . What were called *Night Plunderers* were composed of watermen, associated in gangs of four or five in number, and their practice was likewise to get connected with watchmen employed to guard lighters and other vessels while cargoes were on board, and to convey away in lugboats every portable article of merchandise they could lay their hands upon.

"These corrupt watchmen did not always permit the lighters under their own charge to be pillaged ; but their practice was to point out others which lay near their own, perhaps without a guard, and which on this account might be easily plundered. An hour was fixed upon for effecting this object ; and the receiver, a man generally of some property, was applied to to be in readiness at a certain hour before daylight to warehouse the goods. A lugboat was seized on for the purpose, and the articles removed into it out of the lighter, conveyed to a landing place nearest the warehouse of deposit. The watchmen in the streets leading to the scene of villainy were generally bribed to connive at it, under the pretence that it was a smuggling transaction, and thus the object was effected. Several cargoes of hemp obtained in this manner were conveyed up the river, and afterwards carted in the day-time, till, by the vigilance of the police-boats, a detection took place, and the whole scene of mischief was laid open. In many instances where goods could not be plundered through the connivance of the watchmen, it was no uncommon thing to cut lighters adrift, and to follow them to a situation calculated to elude discovery. In this way, whole lighter loads, even of coals, have been discharged at obscure landing-places on the river, and carted away during the night. Even the article of tallow, from Russia, which, from the unwieldiness of the packages, appears little liable to be an object of plunder, has not escaped the fangs of these offenders. The class called *Light-Horsemen*, or nightly plunderers of West India ships, are said to have originated in a connection between some mates of West India ships, and some criminal receivers residing near the river, who used to apply to them to purchase what is called *sweepings*, or rather, the spillings or drainings of sugar remaining in the hold, and between decks, after the cargo was discharged, and which were generally claimed as perquisites. In getting these articles on shore, it was necessary the revenue officers should connive, which they did, and the quantity of spillings was, of course, gradually increased year after year. In fact, to such a pitch of infamy was the business carried that, an agreement being entered into with those concerned on board, and a gang of plunderers on shore, composed of receivers, coopers, watermen, and labourers, they were permitted, on payment of from thirty to fifty guineas, to come on board in the night; to open as many hogsheads of sugar as were accessible, and to plunder without control. For this purpose, a certain number of bags, dyed *black*, and which went under the appellation of *Black Strap*, were provided. The receivers, coopers, watermen, and lumpers, all went on board at the appointed time. The hogsheads of sugar, packages of *coffee*, &c., were opened, the *black bags* filled with the utmost expedition, carried to the receivers, and again returned to be re-filled, till daylight, or the approach of it, checked the pillage for a few hours. On the succeeding night the depredations were renewed, and thus, on many occasions, from fifteen to twenty

hogsheads of sugar, a large quantity of coffee, and in many instances rum (which was removed by a small pump called a jigger, and filled into bladders with nozzles), was plundered in a single ship, in addition to the excessive pillage committed in the same ship by the lumpers, or labourers employed during the day in the discharge of the cargo. And, previous to the establishment of the docks, it has been estimated, upon credible authority, that above one-fifth of the vessels on the Thames suffered by nightly plunder. The ships subject to this species of robbery, generally known from the character of the mates or revenue officers on board, were denominated *Game Ships*. On board some of these, the labourers, called lumpers, would frequently solicit to work without wages, trusting to the liberty of plundering. Another class called *Heavy Horsemen*, made up of lumpers, &c., were exceedingly depraved. They generally went on board ships furnished with habiliments made on purpose to conceal sugar, coffee, cocoa, pimento, ginger, and other articles, which they generally conveyed on shore by means of an under-waistcoat, containing pockets all round, and denominated a *Jemmie ;* and also by providing long bags, pouches, and socks, which were tied to their waists under their trowsers. These miscreants have been known to divide from three to four guineas apiece every night, from the produce of their plunder, during the discharge of what they called a Game Ship, besides the hush-money paid to officers and others for conniving at their nefarious practices; *Game Watermen* were so denominated from their having been known to hang upon ships under discharge for the whole of the day, in readiness to seize and instantly convey on shore bags of sugar, coffee, and other articles, pillaged by the lumpers. By such connections as these, mates, boatswains, carpenters, seamen, and shipboys have been seduced, and even taught to become plunderers and thieves, who would otherwise have remained honest and faithful to the trust reposed in them. Many of these watermen lived in ease and affluence.

"*Game Lightermen* were those who used to be in the habit of concealing in the lockers of their lighters sugar, coffee, pimento, ginger, &c., which they received from mates and others on board of West Indiamen. The lockers in these lighters were generally secured by a padlock, and these were seldom taken out till after the lighter had been supposed to have been completely unloaded. It was then the practice to remove to the road where empty craft used to be abreast of the Custom House quay, and then carry away the stolen or smuggled articles. And it has not seldom happened that many of these *Game Lightermen* have, under pretence of watching their own lighters, actually plundered the goods under their charge to a very considerable amount, without detection. The artful and insidious conduct of these lightermen was also exhibited in a very glaring point of view in the case of a Canada merchant, who had been accustomed to ship quantities of oil annually to the London market. Finding a constant and uniform deficiency in the quantity landed greatly exceeding what could arise from common leakage, the effect of design, he began now to discover one of the causes at least of his great losses. He therefore attended the discharge of the lighter until the whole of the casks were removed, when he perceived a great quantity of oil leaked out, which the lightermen had the effrontery to insist was their perquisite. The proprietor then ordered casks to be brought, and filled no less than nine of them with the oil that had thus leaked out. He next ordered the ceiling of the lighter to be pulled up, and found between her timbers as much as filled five casks

ENTRANCE TO THE EAST INDIA DOCKS.

which his correspondents were unable to explain, and having occasion to visit London, he was resolved to see his cargo landed with his own eyes, so as, if possible, to develop a mystery heretofore inexplicable, and by which he had regularly lost a considerable sum for several years. Determined, therefore, to look sharp after his property, he was in attendance at the wharf in anxious expectation of a lighter which had been laden with his oil on a preceding day, and which, for reasons that he could not comprehend, did not get up for many hours after the usual time. On her arrival at the wharf, the proprietor was confounded to find the whole of his casks stowed in the lighter with the bungs downwards; and convinced that this was

more. And thus, but for his own attendance fourteen casks of oil would have been appropriated to the use of the lightermen who, after attempting to rob him of so much property, complained bitterly of his ill-usage in taking it from them.

"*Mud-Larks* were those who played a smaller game, being accustomed to prowl about at low water under the quarters of West India ships, with pretence of grubbing in the mud for old ropes, iron, coals, &c., but whose object in reality was to receive and conceal small bags of sugar, coffee, pimento, and sometimes bladders containing rum. These auxiliaries were considered as the lowest cast of thieves. As for the revenue officers, many of them found means not only to promote pillage in West India ships, but also in ships from the East Indies, and in every ship and vessel arriving and departing from the River Thames. This class of officers generally made a point of being punctual upon duty, and, never being found absent by their superiors, they obtained preference to those particular ships which afforded the best harvest, either from being under the care of mates or others with whom they were connected ; or from the cargo being of a nature calculated to afford a resource for plunder. They were also generally acquainted with the *copemen*, or receivers ; and at those seasons of the year when the crowded state of the port rendered it necessary to have *extra* and *glut* officers, the general distress of this class of men rendered them very easy to seduce, and to become the willing instruments of plunder.

"*Scuffle-Hunters* were so called from their resorting in numbers to the quays and wharves where goods were discharging under pretence of finding employment as labourers, &c., and then taking advantage of the circumstance of disputes and scuffles arising about who should secure most plunder from broken packages, &c. These men were reckoned the very scum of society. But with the establishment of the docks, these and every other pest

of the community already mentioned have sunk into that obscurity and nothingness best befitting the present improved state of commerce and morals." Still, as a memento of the dangerous depravity to which we are no longer subjected, a few more instances, as quoted by Mr. Colquhoun, may not be without their effect :—" The receivers, or *copemen*, he observed, who formed the junto of wholesale dealers, and were accustomed to visit ships on their arrival, carried on their negotiations in a language whose terms were peculiar to themselves. They also procured bladders with wooden nozzles for the purpose of containing rum, brandy, and other liquors, and furnished boats to convey the plunder from the ships during the night. Some of these receivers, to tempt and seduce those who would permit them to plunder the cargo, would advance them considerable sums, which, however, rarely amounted to a moiety of the value of the goods obtained, and frequently not one-fourth part. Other classes of receivers being generally engaged in business as small grocers, or chandlers, and old iron and junk sellers, they were accustomed to protect the plunder in its transit from one criminal dealer to another by means of small bills of parcels."

CHAPTER LX.

THE RIVER LEA.

"This Prince in many a fight their forces still defyd,
The goodly River Lee he likewise did divide ;
By which the Danes had then their full fraught naivès tew'd,
The greatnesse of whose streame besiegèd Harford rew'd."—DRAYTON'S *Polyolbion.*

Etymology of the River Lea—Its Source—Luton—Brocket Hall—Hertford—Ware –Amwell and its Quaker Poet-- Haileybury College—The Rye House—Stanstead Abbots—Hoddesdon—Broxbourne—Cook's Ferry—Bleak Hall—The East London Waterworks—Lea Bridge—Fishing on the Lea—-Hackney Marshes and Temple Mills—The Navigation of the Lea—Conservancy of the River.

DURING our perambulations, since we first reached the banks of the Lea, in the neighbourhood of Enfield Highway and Waltham Abbey,* we have occasionally touched slightly upon this very "fishful" stream. The Lea, however, is so essentially the Londoner's favourite river, next to, if not equally with, the Thames, that we may well be excused if we dwell a little longer upon its charms before we take our leave of the north suburban district once and for all.

The name of the river, which is of Saxon origin, has been variously written, but the most common spelling in the present day is *Lea*. The Conservancy, however, still adhere to the old form *Lee*.

By some of the older historians it was spelled *Luy*. In Shakespeare's *Henry VI.* it is written *Ley*. Drayton, in his "Polyolbion," spells it both *Lea* and *Lee ;* and Sir John Hawkins, in his "Life of Walton," spells it *Lea*.

The Lea, however, belongs really more to Hertfordshire than to Essex or Middlesex, as it bounds the latter counties on the west and east for only the last ten or twelve miles nearest London. It meets the Essex border at the point where it receives the Stort,* at Roydon, and flows nearly

---

* See *ante*, pp. 375 and 404.

* The Stort, which gives its name to (Bishop) Stortford, rises in Hertfordshire, but soon enters Essex, along the western border of which it flows till it meets the Lea at Roydon. Its whole course is not above twenty-four miles, the last ten of which are navigable. The Stort and Lea, in spite of modern railways, are still largely used to convey corn malt, wood, and agricultural produce to London.

due south near Broxbourne, Hoddesdon, and Cheshunt in Herts, and Waltham Abbey, Chingford, Leyton, and Stratford in Essex, in its course to the Thames, a distance of about twenty miles. Its banks are low and marshy, and greatly overspread by floods in the winter. The marshes are from half a mile to a mile in width. The stream is frequently divided into several channels, so that it is difficult of navigation. In some places also cuts have been made to shorten or improve its course. Some of the Acts of Parliament relating to this navigation are 400 years old.

The source of the river, according to Drayton, is to be found in some springs at Lea Grave, about a mile north of Luton, of which he sings as—

> "The head,
> Whence Lee doth spring, not farre from Kempton * towne."

A quaint account of the course of this river, wonderfully exact and accurate upon the whole, may be seen in Vallen's "Tale of Two Swannes" (1590), from which I have taken some few of the mottoes for my chapters, and which is reprinted *in extenso* at the beginning of Mr. J. E. Cussans' "History of Hertfordshire."

Lambarde, however, describes its course in a more prosaic manner. He writes:—"It begynnethe near Whitchurche, and from thence passinge by Hertforde, Ware, and Waltham, openethe into the Thames at Ham, in Essex, whence this place is at this day called Lea-mouth. It hath of long tyme borne vessels from London twenty myles towards the head, for in the tyme of King Alfrede the Danes entered Ley-mouth, whence King Alfrede espied that the channell of the ryver might be in such sorte weakened that they should want water to returne. He caused, therefore, the water to be abated by two greate trenches, and setting the Londonners upon them, he made their batteil, wherein they lost four of their capitaines. Not long after they were so pressed that they forsoke all, and left their shippes as a prey to the Londonners, which breakyne some and burninge other, conveyed the rest to London."

The actual source of the Lea, however, is in a field at Houghton Regis, about a mile from Dunstable, and, like that of most other rivers, it soon spreads out in the form of a pond. Although there may be nothing particularly attractive in the spring or its immediate surroundings, the village of Houghton Regis, with its clusters of thatched-roofed cottages and its fine old church, is one which may be admired for its picturesque rural scenery. For

some distance from its source the Lea is little more than a ditch in appearance, and it is not until it reaches Luton—a place of note for its straw-hat factories—that it becomes anything like a respectable stream. Luton Church, a large building of Perpendicular architecture, contains many interesting features, but has suffered much from the hands of would-be restorers. The river next passes through Luton Park, the seat of Mrs. Gerard Leigh, in its course supplying two large lakes in the grounds, said to contain, the one fourteen, and the other forty acres. The mansion, called Luton Hoo, was visited by Dr. Johnson and his friend Boswell when it was the seat of Lord Bute. It was almost wholly burnt down in 1843, but has since been rebuilt. Having passed the little town of Whethamsted, the river flows on for about two miles to Brocket Hall, once the seat of Lord Melbourne and of Lord Palmerston. The house is a large brick structure, and the Lea spreads out before it in the form of a spacious lake. After leaving Brocket Hall, the Lea flows on through a fertile country—somewhat level, perhaps, but pleasant withal—and, leaving the town of Hatfield on the right, winds its way through a corner of Hatfield Park, the seat of Lord Salisbury. The mansion, called Hatfield House, is a large and stately building of brick with stone dressings, in the Tudor style, and it contains the finest collection of ancient manuscripts of any mansion in the kingdom. Elizabeth was for some time a prisoner here before her accession to the throne, and an old oak at a corner of an avenue on the northern side of the park is called the "Queen's Oak," from a tradition that it formed the boundary of her daily walk.

On reaching Hertford the Lea is joined by another stream, and is visibly increased in volume. Although the town of Hertford is one of great historic interest, a portion of the castle is almost the only antiquarian object existing; this consists of two or three brick towers with a few chambers attached, and some portions of the outer walls. The first lock on the River Lea is about midway between Hertford and Ware. This latter place is supposed to have derived both its origin and its name from a "weare" or dam constructed by the Danes in the reign of King Alfred (A.D. 896), for the purpose of protecting a large fort which they had erected at the spot whereon the town of Ware now stands. By the concurrent testimony of old writers, the Lea was once navigable for ships as far as Hertford, up to which the Danes came by water. Alfred blocked them up in the fortress which they had built, and deprived them of their

---

* Kempston.

ships. The injury done to the river was not repaired till the seventeenth century, and the navigation restored. On the banks of the Lea, a short distance from Ware Church, and just beyond Ware lock, are slight remains of a Benedictine priory, which was founded here in the reign of Henry III.

A little to the south of Ware, nearly opposite Ware Park, and at a point where the Lea trends southward towards Essex and Middlesex, lie Chadwell Springs, which form the source of the New River, by means of which so large a portion of London is supplied with water. The site of the principal spring is marked by a stone erected by the New River Company, and bearing an inscription which sets forth that it was opened in 1608, and that the water is conveyed forty miles.

As we leave Ware a vision of Alfred rises up as we think of his memorable exploit of diverting the channel of the Lea, leaving the Danish ships high and dry behind their *weir*. Following the course of our river, we soon reach Amwell—the Emmewell of the Domesday Book—perhaps the prettiest village on the banks of the Lea. This spot, which is well wooded, is invested with an interest of its own, as having been the residence of the Quaker poet, John Scott, on whom a pleasant and chatty paper from the pen of Charles Knight appears in the first volume of *Once a Week*. The house which Scott formerly occupied still stands. It is an old-fashioned, comfortable, red-brick building of no great pretensions. Its gardens and grounds, which once covered upwards of twenty acres, were sold in 1864 for building purposes; but his curious grotto, inlaid with spar, shells, and fossils—once regarded as a rival to that of Pope at Twickenham, and visited by "the quality" from London, and by such learned philosophers as Dr. Samuel Johnson—forms now the central attraction in some tea-gardens, and visitors are admitted to it on payment of 6d. a head. The grotto is curiously cut out in the chalky soil on which the village stands, and comprises six or seven chambers.

Amwell can boast of having numbered among its residents one other poet at least in the person of William Warner, an "attorney of the Common Pleas," who held fair rank as a poet in the reign of Queen Elizabeth, and was the author of "Albion's England" and other poems. Warner is said to have been a Warwickshire man, and to have been educated at Magdalen Hall, Oxford. He died here in 1608—9.

On Amwell Hill are traces of ancient fortifications or earthworks, and others are visible between Ware and Hertford. These are supposed to be the remains of those thrown up by the Danes and King Alfred.

On a stone upon an eyot, or ait, at the source of the New River at Amwell, are the following lines, from the pen of Archdeacon Nares :—

"Amwell! perpetual be thy spring,
    Nor e'er thy source be less,
Which thousands drink who little dream
    Whence flows the boon they bless.

"Too often thus ungrateful man
    Blind and unconscious lives ;
Enjoys kind Heaven's indulgent plan,
    Nor thinks of Him who gives."

Nowhere in its entire course does the Lea run clearer or purer than about Amwell, where the soil is chalky. It must have been about here that was caught "that great trout, near an ell in length, which had his picture drawne, and now to be seen at mine hoste Rickabie's at the 'George,' in Ware," as honest Izaak Walton writes in chapter iv. of his delightful "Angler." Amwell was one of the favourite meets of Walton and his friend "Venator," as all readers of his "Complete Angler" are aware ; and it was probably about here that "Piscator" conducted his friend to "an honest alehouse," where is to be found "a cleanly room, lavender in the windows, and twenty ballads stuck about the wall."

Scott has paid his tribute to Izaak Walton, who, he writes :—

"Oft our fair haunts explored ; upon Lea's shore
    Beneath some green turf oft his angle laid,
    His sport suspending to admire their charms."

On a woody knoll, just above the New River, and in the midst of the village, stands Amwell Church, an exceedingly picturesque old edifice. Its situation has been beautifully described by John Scott in the following lines :—

"The pleased eye, which o'er the prospect wide
Has wandered round, and various objects marked
On Amwell rests at last, its favourite scene.
How picturesque the view ! where up the side
Of that steep bank her roofs of russet thatch
Rise, mixed with trees, above whose swelling tops
Ascends the tall church tower, and loftier still
The hill's extended ridge."

Scott's style throughout is strictly pastoral, as his description of the view from Amwell Hill will show :—

"How beautiful,
How various is yon view ! Delicious hills
Bounding smooth vales, smooth vales by winding streams
Divided, that here glide through grassy banks
In open sun, there wander under shade

> Of aspen tall, or ancient elm, whose boughs
> O'erhang grey castles, and romantic farms,
> And humble cots of happy shepherd swains.
>
>   *   *   *   *   *
>
> Far towards the west, close under shelt'ring hills,
> In verdant meads by Lea's cerulean stream,
> Hertford's grey towers ascend ; the rude remains
> Of high antiquity, from waste escaped
> Of envious time and violence of war."

Amwell Church displays the architecture of the fourteenth century ; its very perfect apse peeps from behind the richest foliage ; and, altogether, the place would be interesting without its associations. Besides William Warner, mentioned above, and whom John Scott calls "the gentle bard, by fame forgotten," here lie at rest among the "rude forefathers of the hamlet" Robert Mylne, the engineer of old Blackfriars Bridge, and the Rev. Richard Jones, some time Professor of History and Political Economy at Haileybury College. Scott himself lies buried in the Quakers' burial place at Ware.

Within the limits of the parish of Amwell, though nearly two miles from that village and church, stands Haileybury College, once the chief place of training for cadets destined to enter the old East India Company's Civil Service, as Addiscombe was for its Military Service. The buildings are very extensive, and surround a quadrangle larger than that of Christ Church, Oxford, and equal to Trinity College, Cambridge. They are in the classical style, and heavy and dull to the last degree ; they were designed by W. Wilkins, R.A. In this college Sir James Mackintosh, Malthus, Empson, and other well-known men, were professors ; and Lord Brougham and other leaders of the old Whig party were frequent visitors within its walls. In 1862, the buildings having been closed since the abolition of the great Company whose nursery it was, a public school was founded here by a proprietary connected with Hertfordshire. Fresh buildings, and a handsome new chapel, from the designs of Mr. Blomfield, have been added. The result is a public school of 500 boys, mostly destined for a university career, and holding its own in the competition for Oxford and Cambridge scholarships, and in the cricket-field and at football, with the rest of our public schools. Its first master under the new *régime* was the Rev. Arthur Butler, who was succeeded by Dr. E. H. Bradby.

But we must leave Amwell and follow as closely as we may the windings of the Lea as it meanders in "silver thread" through the green pastures of Hertfordshire to the old Rye House—that favourite retreat of the thoroughbred cockney, where he may find "art, science, history, romance, boating, fishing, horticulture, a lovely English landscape, and jolly English cheer, all in one short holiday." We can scarcely wander through the valley of the Lea as honest Izaak wandered ; for the river has been made navigable by long formal cuts, and the old stream is in most places strictly preserved ; so we are compelled to pursue our way in part along by the less picturesque New River.

The celebrated Rye House, so well known as a place of entertainment to Londoners, especially those from the northern and eastern parts, is situated in the parish of Stanstead Abbots. It is so called from being within the manor of Rye, formerly belonging to the Abbey of Waltham. It was alienated about 1440 to Sir Andrew Ogard, who erected on it a small castle, which is described by William of Worcester in the minutest detail, with the exact measurement of each court, the moat, the granary, &c. The purchase-money, he tells us, was £1,130, a large sum in those days.

The Rye House was noted for the "plot" laid there in 1683 against the lives of Charles II. and his brother James. The place, which lay on the then road to Newmarket, was in the occupation of a maltster named Rumbold, one of the conspirators, and the place was hit upon as the most convenient to intercept the royal party on their return from the races ; but the scheme failed, owing to the king's return taking place some days sooner than was anticipated.

The story of the "Rye House Plot," for alleged complicity in which the noble Sidney and Lord William Russell were brought to the scaffold, is told in every History of England, but nowhere better than in Mr. A. C. Ewald's "Life and Times of Algernon Sidney." Russell, Sidney, and Hampden, with three other Whig statesmen, had formed themselves into a "Council of Six," and were concerting measures to exclude James, Duke of York, from the throne. "Whilst the Council of Six were meditating their plans, whatever they might be, an inferior order of conspirators were holding meetings and organising an insurrection perfectly unknown to the Council. The chief of these conspirators were West, an active man, who was supposed to be an Atheist ; Colonel Rumsey, an officer who had served under Cromwell, and afterwards in Portugal ; Ferguson, an active agent of the late Lord Shaftesbury ; Goodenough, who had been Under-Sheriff of London ; Lieutenant-Colonel Walcot, a Republican officer ; and several lawyers and tradesmen. The aim of these men seems to have been desperate and criminal in the extreme. They talked openly about murdering the King and his brother, and even went so far as to organise a scheme for that purpose. Among this band was one Rumbold, a maltster, who owned a farm called the Rye House, situated on the road to Newmarket, which sporting town Charles was accustomed to visit annually for the races. Rumbold laid before the conspirators a plan of this farm, and showed how easy it would be to intercept the King and his brother on their way home, fire upon them through the hedges, and then, when the deed of assassination was committed, escape by the by-lanes and across the fields. The murderous scheme of the maltster was, however, frustrated by Charles having been obliged to leave Newmarket eight days earlier than he had intended, owing to his house having taken fire. Treachery now put a stop to any further proceedings of the conspirators."

False witnesses, however, were found to connect the honoured names of Russell and Sidney with this villainous scheme, and the result was that orders were given for the arrest of the members of the Council of Six. The sequel is but too well known.*

"The Rye House," writes Mr. Cussans in his noble "History of Hertfordshire," "has become celebrated in history for its having been tenanted by Rumbold, a maltster, one of the persons engaged in the alleged conspiracy to assassinate Charles II. and his brother the Duke of York, on their journey from Newmarket to London; but the scheme failed, in consequence of the royal party returning sooner than was anticipated. Lord William Russell and Algernon Sidney were said to have been inculpated in the plot; and after a trial in which their connection with this scheme was by no means satisfactorily proved, however much they may have been concerned in other treasonable designs, they were publicly executed."

Mr. Cussans adds that for many years, till the passing of the new Poor Law Act, the Rye House was used as a workhouse for the parish of Stanstead. "Little of the old building," he writes, "remains. A tavern has been built in the ancient forecourt, upon the banks of the Lee, and is much frequented by the lower classes from London. The moat, at one time an important part of the fortification of the castle, is now used as a bed for water-cresses. Mr. Teale, the present tenant, purchased the property in 1867."

The remains of an embattled gate-house of brick, with a stone doorway and vaulted chambers, are shown to visitors as part of the original structure built in the reign of Henry VI. The place now forms one of the attractions of a modern hostelry,

and the grounds are pleasantly laid out, with the extra advantages of a maze, bowling-green, &c. Among the curiosities preserved here is the "great bed of Ware." Little if anything is satisfactorily known of the origin of this curious piece of furniture, which is said to be sufficiently capacious to accommodate six couples. At the head is carved the date, 1435, and it is referred to in Shakespeare's "Twelfth Night":—

Sir Anthony Aguecheek:—"Will either of you bear me a challenge to him?"

Sir Toby Belch:—"Go write it in a martial hand; be curt and brief; it is no matter how witty, so it be eloquent and full of invention. Taunt him with the licence of ink; if thou *thou'st* him some thrice, it shall not be amiss; and so many lies as will lie in thy sheet of paper, although the sheet were big enough for the bed of Ware in England."

Charles Knight, in the article in *Once a Week* above referred to, thus sums up the attractions of the Rye House:—"Hither come for their annual festivals clubs of Odd Fellows and of Jolly Fellows —the skilled artisans of great London establishments, such as printers and pianoforte makers. They dine in a vast saloon, formed out of an extension of the old offices of Rumbold the maltster, who dwelt in the Rye House. Up the old turret they climb, and look out upon the green fields through which the Lea flows amidst osiered banks. They crowd into punts, and aspire to angle where Walton angled. They speed over the meadows, and try their unaccustomed hands at trap-ball and quoits. The provident host of the Rye House is justly proud of the patronage of these great associations of ingenious workmen, who dine economically, and care more for ale than champagne. His dining-room is radiant with bright gilt frames, holding pleasant certificates of their excellent fare from the representatives of the merry and contented hundreds who have thus forgot their accustomed lot for the summer holiday long to be remembered. The form of enjoyment is changed: the conveniences for enjoyment have multiplied since Walton described his holidays— 'stretching our legs up Tottenham Hill;' 'taking our morning draught at the Thatched House at Hodsden;' 'leading our mates to an honest alehouse, where we shall find a cleanly room, lavender in the windows, and twenty ballads stuck about the wall;' listening to the song of 'a handsome milkmaid, that had not yet attained so much age and wisdom as to load her mind with any fears of many things that will never be.' We have no time in our days for such lingering delights; we have no taste

---

* See "Old and New London," Vol. III., p. 45.

for such simple luxuries. We ourselves rejoice to find as good a dinner at the Rye House as at the Bedford, instead of bringing out of our fish bags 'a piece of powdered beef and a radish or two.' We sit contentedly sipping our sherry and water and puffing our cigar under alcoves festooned with roses, instead of indulging in such rare gratification as that with which happy Isaak finished his three days' sport—'a bottle of sack, milk, oranges, and sugar, which all put together make a drink like nectar—indeed, too good for anybody but anglers.'

No milkmaid's mother sings 'an answer to it, which was made by Sir Walter Raleigh in his younger days.' The forms of our pleasures and their accompaniments in other respects incessantly change, but their natural backgrounds are eternally fresh and perennially welcome."

Stanstead Abbots is so called because it formerly belonged to the Abbey of Waltham. Of the church there is little to say, except that it contains some fine monuments, and dates from the latter half of the 14th century. In this parish is an old

COOK'S FERRY. (*See page* 566.)

The habitual economy of those times enabled the industrious tradesman to be occasionally expensive in his tastes. The cheapness and rapidity of modern conveyance permits the London artisan to have a full day's relaxation with that best of economies, the economy of his time. Our holiday enjoyments are perhaps not quite so poetical as when the cheerful old Piscator went out with a determined purpose to be happy. On the banks of the Lea no milkmaid now charms us with 'that smooth song which was made by Kit Marlow,' of

'Come live with me and be my love,
And we will all the pleasures prove
That valleys, groves, or hills, or field,
Or woods and steepy mountains yield.'

endowed school and almshouses, founded in 1636 by Sir Edward Baish, a gallant Royalist, who spent nearly all his fortune in the cause of the King. Close by is Easney, more properly Isenye, a seat of the Buxton family, erected by Waterhouse in 1868--70. At Stanstead Bury are the remains of a Roman fortress, in which was a small chapel.

Once more resuming our pilgrimage along the banks of the Lea, we soon pass under the railway-bridge of the Cambridge branch of the Great Eastern Railway, and shortly after arrive at the junction of the Stort with the Lea, at which point Essex begins. Close by is a fishing cottage, which stands on the most northerly detached portion of Epping Forest, whence a footpath across a couple of fields leads to Nether Hall; little is left of the old moated building, however, beyond the ruined gateway, which is of brick, consisting of two floors, with a half hexagon tower on each side of the entrance.

Our river now flows on a little to the east of Hoddesdon, or, as it was formerly written, Hodsdon. The village possesses no interesting features to detain us on our way; but it is worthy of note from its association with the River Lea through the pens of Izaak Walton and Matthew Prior. The "Rambles by Rivers," says that a cottage at the northern extremity of the village has been pointed out as the original "Thatcht House" where Venator proposed to "drink his morning's draught;" but, he adds, it is very doubtful if it be so. The river about this part has long been a favourite resort of the London angler; trout, chub, pike, perch, barbel, gudgeon, dace, and roach, are enumerated in almost every chapter of Walton's "Angler" as found about Amwell, Hodsdon, and Waltham Abbey; indeed, the first-named fish

AT LEA BRIDGE.

latter, in his ballad of "Down Hall," makes mention of the "Bull" Inn here as the place where he stopped on his way to take possession of his residence of that name :—

> "Into an old inn did their equipage roll
> At a town they call Hodsdon, the sign of the Bull,
> Near a nymph with an urn that divides the highway,
> And into a puddle throws mother of tea;
> *   *   *   *   *   *
> She roasted red veal, and she powdered red beef;
> Full well she knew how to cook up a fine dish,
> For tough were her pullets and tender her fish,
>   Down, down, derry down."

The "nymph with an urn," it may be added, has long ago disappeared, and the "Bull" has been rebuilt since Prior's time. Mr. Thorne, in his gave its name to Trout Hall, which is so constantly mentioned by Walton, though its exact site is disputed, and near which the pretty milkmaid sang to the "brethren of the angle" Kit Marlow's well-known lines, above quoted. The scene must be laid somewhere near Hodsdon, for Peter says, "My friend Coridon and I will go up the river towards Ware;" to which Piscator replies, "And my scholar and I will go down towards Waltham." The "fresh sheets" at the inn "smell of fresh lavender," and the discourse on the way to the river-side and back is on the nature of the trout. The spreading birches and sycamore trees, of which honest Izaak Walton talks so much, should surely help to identify the spot.

"Coridon and I," observes Piscator later on, "have not had an unpleasant day, and yet I have caught but five trouts; for, indeed, we went to a good, honest alehouse, and there we plaid at shovel-board half the day. All the time that it rain'd we were there, and as merry as they that fished."

Sir John Hawkins, in his notes on the "Complete Angler," relates the following story:—"A lover of angling told me he was fishing in the river Lea, at the ferry called Jeremy's, and had hooked a large fish at the time when some Londoners, with their horses, were passing: they congratulated him on his success, and got out of the ferry-boat; but, finding the fish not likely to yield, mounted their horses, and rode off. The fact was, that angling for small fish, his bait had been taken by a barbel, too large for the fisher to manage. Not caring to risk his tackle by attempting to raise him, he hoped to tire him; and, for that purpose, suffered himself to be led (to use his own expression) as a blind man is by a dog, several yards up and as many down, the bank of the river; in short, for so many hours that the horsemen above-mentioned, who had been at Walthamstow, and dined, were returned, who, seeing him thus occupied, cried out—'*What, master, another large fish!*'—'No' (says the Piscator), '*the very same.*'—'Nay' (says one of them), '*that can never be; for it is five hours since we crossed the river!*' and, not believing him, they rode on their way. At length our angler determined to do that which a less patient one would have done long before: he made one vigorous effort to land the fish, broke his tackle, and lost him."

After passing Dobbs' Weir and the lock, the Lea forms a decided curve westward to Broxbourne, the next place of interest at which we arrive. The church and parsonage, standing on rising ground above an old water-mill, look highly picturesque, as seen from the river. The church dates from the time of Henry II.; it is of considerable size, and the tower is surmounted by a plain spire and beacon turret. On the north side of the chancel is a chapel, built by Sir William Say, and containing an altar-tomb in memory of the founder, who died in 1559. This church contains many other monuments and brasses, which will be regarded with interest, as illustrating the costumes of the Tudor period.

The parish of Nazing borders the Lea for some distance on the opposite, or Essex, side of the stream. Nazing Church is visible away on a distant hill, whilst Holyfield Hall,* with its contiguous farm-buildings, surrounded by venerable elms, occupies the rising ground nearer the river, which now flows onward in almost a direct line due south.

Wormley Church, a little farther on—on the Hertfordshire side of the river—is a small building, partly of Norman workmanship, and containing several ancient brasses. The remains of Cheshunt Nunnery lie near the river-side, just beyond Wormley; and, farther on, we pass Cheshunt Mill Lock and Waltham Common Lock, above which a private canal runs across the Gunpowder Wharves. Our river about here is divided into several different channels, narrow and tortuous; the Navigation Cut, however, affords an almost direct route for the next half-dozen miles. Enfield and Waltham Abbey, with the Small Arms Factory and Powder Mills, which we now pass, have each and all been fully described in these pages.*

At Cook's Ferry, which is now occupied by a bridge, and forms the communication between Edmonton and Chingford, stands or stood a small building called "Bleak Hall," the house to which, by tradition, Piscator is said to have taken his "scholar," and which was then, according to Izaak Walton, "an honest alehouse, where might be found a cleanly room, lavender in the windows, and twenty ballads stuck about the walls; with a hostess both cleanly, and handsome, and civil." This house is generally called Bleak Hall, and is pointed out and engraved in Sir H. Nicolas's Notes to the "Complete Angler" and elsewhere as the original Bleak Hall of Izaak; but, unless he made a slip of the pen, it cannot be so, for in the conversation on the night spent there (Chap. v.), as quoted above, Piscator speaks of going with his scholar "down *towards* Waltham," whereas this is some miles *below* Waltham.

Stonebridge and Tottenham locks come next in order as we follow the course of the Lea, and then we arrive at the reservoirs belonging to the East London Waterworks Company, at the point where the old copper-mills of Walthamstow formerly stood.† A canal as straight as an arrow, formed by raised embankments, connects the Walthamstow reservoirs with those by Lea Bridge, of which we have already spoken. The East London Waterworks Company draws largely on the Lea for its supply. This company is the largest purveyor of any of the metropolitan water companies; the quantity of water sold by it in the course of a year amounts to upwards of 11,000 million gallons, against 10,000 million gallons supplied by the New

---

* See *ante*, p. 417.

* See *ante*, pp. 376, 393, and 404. † See *ante*, p. 470.

River Company, the next largest; but while the working expenses of the latter during the same period absorbed nearly £146,600, those of the former amount only to about £89,800.

"In the year 1828," writes Mr. F. Johnson, in "Weldon's Guide to the Lea," "objections were made to the source from whence the East London Company obtained their water, it having been asserted that, as the tide of the Thames affected the water of the Lea in that part where the Company raised their water, the water 'partook of the nature of Thames water.' To remove all doubt on the point, the Company obtained Parliamentary powers, in the year 1849, to change the source of supply; they constructed the reservoirs and canal at Lea Bridge, for the purpose of bringing water from a part of the river which was far above tidal influence. They had already purchased out the Hackney Common, which had been established here about 1750, whose water-wheels drove machinery to grind corn and raise water for the supply of the neighbourhood."

Lea Bridge was built in 1821, at a cost of £4,500. Close by it, and extending some distance along the banks of the river, are places for the hire of boats for rowing on the Lea; here are also the head-quarters of several rowing-clubs. Both fishing and boating are carried on in the neighbourhood of Lea Bridge to a very great extent; indeed, the incipient cockney fisherman and aquatic sportsman generally seem to regard the several streams and channels into which the Lea is divided in its course between Walthamstow and Bow as the chosen and highly-favoured scene of their diversions. Bathing also is here largely indulged in during the summer months, notwithstanding the very dangerous condition of the stream for that purpose, being full of weeds and deep holes. The result is that, with the reckless boating exploits of inexperienced young men and women from the eastern quarters of London, and the frequent fatalities resulting therefrom, as well as from bathing, the deaths by drowning in the River Lea add considerably to the death-roll of the metropolitan area. During each of the five years ending December 31, 1881, the number of bodies found in the Lea were respectively 47, 49, 55, 39, and 46; making a total of 236.

One of the most noted houses resorted to by anglers in the neighbourhood of Lea Bridge was the "Horse and Groom," but it was swept away on the extension of the waterworks. The fishery along the Lea is carefully preserved, with the exception of two or three intervening spots from Ware to Temple Mills, and let out for the most part to the persons who rent the several public-houses on its banks. From these the angler obtains permission to ply his cunning on payment of a yearly subscription, or the occasional angler may pay by the day.

At the old "White House," on the banks of the river, about the middle of Hackney Marshes, are the head-quarters of a fishery extending to Temple Mills. This house is traditionally said to have been the residence of the noted highwayman, Dick Turpin, before he took up his abode in the recess in Epping Forest now called Turpin's Cave.

The "Navigation Cut" crosses the marshes between high embankments a little to the west of the old river, which forms picturesque bends and meanderings, through the level meadows of which Hackney Marshes are composed. At Hackney Wick Bridge the old turnpike-road—following the course of the Roman road spoken of in a previous chapter [*]—after passing through Homerton, enters Essex. It crosses the Navigation Cut by a high, narrow bridge, and thence continues over the marsh to the "White Hart," at Temple Mills. The ford which was in use when this road was the ancient way into Essex has continued as a ford to this day, but a bridge is now (July, 1883) in course of erection on the spot, so that the ford will be no longer necessary. It is not quite clear whether Mr. J. T. Smith wrote only in fun or seriously, in his "Book for a Rainy Day," about crossing "the Lea" with "the lowing herd;" but, at all events, the fording of cattle at this point is a frequent occurrence, the meadows affording excellent pasturage.

Of Old Ford, Bow, and Stratford, and other places through which the Lea passes in its course to join the Thames, we have already spoken.

It is stated by Campbell, in his "Political Survey of Great Britain," that the Lea was the first river distinguished by the care of the Legislature in rendering it navigable. [†]

The first instance of a Parliamentary provision for the navigation of the Lea, however, was made as far back as the reign of Henry IV. (1424). The Act passed in the thirteenth year of Elizabeth (1570) was for making the navigation more perfect by the formation of a new cut from London to the town of Ware, and ten years later the river was cleansed and widened as far as that town, and made navigable by an Order in Council. It was ultimately determined by the Star Chamber that the river should be made free for barges and boats, and several Acts of Parliament dealing with the

---

* See *ante*, p. 508.
† See Statute 13 Eliz., cap. 18.

matter were subsequently passed. Towards the end of the last century, it having been shown after a careful survey that great improvements could be made in the navigation by the formation of new cuts or canals out of, or into, the channel of the river between Hertford and Bromley, a sum of money was granted by Parliament for that purpose, and the formation of what is now known as the " Navigation Cut" was carried out. In 1868 an Act of Parliament was passed constituting a Board of Conservancy for the management of the River Lea,

instead of trustees, as of old. Of this Board five members are appointed by the landowners on the banks of the river and its tributaries, one by the barge-owners, one by the heads of the local authorities of towns on the river, two by the New River Company, two by the East London Water-works Company, one represents the Lord Mayor, Aldermen, and Common Council of London, and one the Metropolitan Board of Works. The funds arising from tolls are laid out in the improvement and maintenance of the navigation.

CHAPTER LXI.

THE RIVER THAMES.

" Oh, could I flow like thee, and make thy stream
My great example, as it is my theme !
Though deep, yet clear ; th ugh gentle, yet not dull
Strong without rage ; without o'erflowing full."—SIR JOHN DENHAM.

The Thames as a Political Boundary, and as a Boundary of Counties—Tributary Rivers—Breadth of the River—Its General Aspect and Character of Scenery—The Embankments—Shoals and Floods—Tides—The Thames as the Common Highway of London—Anecdote of Cardinal Wolsey—Sir Walter Raleigh and Queen Elizabeth—Abdication of James II.—Funeral of Lord Nelson—Water Traffic in the Time of Richard II.—The Conservancy of the Thames—Boating on the Thames.

IN the pages of OLD AND NEW LONDON mention has been made, at some length, of the river Thames as the "silent highway" of London * ; but as only the part "above bridge" was there dealt with, our discourse here will be of the Pool and the lower reaches in the course of the river to its confluence with the German Ocean.

"At a very early period of English history," writes the author of Bohn's "London and its Vicinity," "the Thames appears to have been considered as a political boundary of great importance. The division of the country into shires is supposed to have been established on its present basis by King Alfred ; and we therein find that the Thames was taken as the boundary of many of these districts. . . . . Long before the time of Alfred the river was adopted as the political limit of the Roman provinces of Britannia Prima on the south, and of Flavia Cæsariensis on the north. In the seventh century, also, it formed one of the boundaries of the Saxon kingdoms of Mercia and West Seaxe, in the middle of England ; and of those of East Seaxe, South Seaxe, and Cantium on the eastern coast."

The Thames, we may remark in passing, rises in the south-eastern slopes of the Cotswold Hills, near Tetbury, and near Cheltenham. For about twenty miles it belongs wholly to Gloucestershire,

when, for a short distance it divides that county from Wiltshire. It then separates Berkshire first from Oxfordshire, and then from Buckinghamshire. Next it serves as the boundary line between the counties of Surrey and Middlesex ; and afterwards, to its mouth, between those of Kent and Essex. It falls into the sea at the Nore, which is about 110 miles nearly due east from the source of the river, and about twice that distance measured along its windings. The Thames is navigable for sea-going vessels as far as London Bridge, forty-five miles from the Nore, or nearly a fourth of its entire length, and for large barges, for nearly 130 miles above London Bridge, whilst the area of the basin drained by the river is estimated at above 6,500 miles.

In that portion of its course with which we have now to deal the Thames is joined by some half-dozen rivers of minor importance. The Lea, as we have seen, unites with it a little below Blackwall, on the northern shore ; whilst a little higher up, on the opposite side, the Deptford Creek forms the mouth of the Ravensbourne, which rises among the Surrey hills, in the neighbourhood of Hayes Common and Addiscombe. This river winds its course through Lewisham, and is navigable for a very short distance inland, when it dwindles down to a very insignificant mill-stream.

The next affluent of importance, on the Essex shore, is the Roding, which flows into the Thames

* See Vol. III., pp. 287-322.

at Barking Creek,* and is navigable as far as that very ancient town. A rivulet, called the Beam, springing from the hills round Havering-atte-Bower, falls in at Dagenham Reach; and at Rainham Creek the Ingerburn, or Bourne brook—a stream which has a rather long course, but is of little size or importance—discharges itself. Further down, at Purfleet, another small stream from Childerditch Common is swallowed up in our mighty river. Passing again to the south side, we find that the Darent and the Cray, from the Kentish hills, join in the marshes of Dartford, shortly before falling into the Thames. In the last twenty miles of its course the Thames does not receive any affluent worth notice; for the Medway does not join it till the Nore is reached.

In its passage through the metropolis the Thames varies in breadth from 260 to 500 yards. At London Bridge, the river at high tide is 290 yards across; at Blackwall Wharf it is 380; at Gravesend it is 800; at Coal-house Point, where the Lower Hope Reach commences, it is 1,290 yards—being an increase of some 1,000 yards in about 29 miles; about ten miles lower down, at the London Stone, by Yanlet Creek, where the jurisdiction of the Corporation of London ends, the river is nearly four miles and a half across; whilst, as it approaches the Nore, it expands to seven miles broad.

"Though there are none of the wilder features of nature observable at the estuary of the Thames," writes Mr. James Thorne, in his "Rambles by Rivers," "the prospect is at least one of mingled amenity and grandeur. The broad calm river passes imperceptibly into the majestic sea. Along the entrance of the united Thames and Medway ride some of those magnificent ships whose thunders have made the prowess of the British navy memorable in the annals of the world. In continual passage are vessels of every class and of every nation, bringing hither the fruits of every clime, or bearing to every shore the products of British skill. One who has followed the Thames from its parent rock, through so many beautiful and fertile districts; past so many places dignified by the memory of great events and illustrious men, of British worth and British genius; by so many trophies which mark the peaceful triumphs of British wealth and commerce, now that he contemplates this parting scene, may well regard with pride and admiration the noble river which so greatly contributes to the grandeur and the glory of his country and his countrymen. And as he looks forth on the ocean sprinkled over with the shipping of the world, it will almost seem that the language is verified in which one of our older poets addressed his native land:

" 'Now all the riches of the globe beside,
    Flow into thee with every tide;
    And all that Nature doth thy soul deny
    The growth is of thy fruitful industry;
    And all the proud and dreadful sea,
    And all his tributary streams,
    A constant tribute pays to thee,
    And all the liquid world is one extended Thames.' "
                                                    COWLEY.

" It will require no very great stretch of imagination," writes Mr. S. C. Hall in the "Book of the Thames," "to pass from the little streamlet in Trewsbury Mead to the 'Pool' below the Tower. The river, born in a sequestered nook, grows and gathers strength until it bears on its bosom 'a forest of masts;' enriches the greatest and most populous city of any age; ministers to the wants and luxuries of nearly three millions of people—there alone; becomes the mainstay of commerce, and the missionary of civilisation to mankind, carrying innumerable blessings throughout the Old World and the New; yet ever the active auxiliary, and never the dangerous ally—keeping from its birth to its close the character so happily conveyed by the famous lines of the poet:

'Though deep, yet clear; though gentle, yet not dull;
Strong without rage; without o'erflowing, full.'

Few, therefore, are the poets of England who have no word for 'Old Father Thames!' Even its minor enjoyments have been fertile themes for the muse; and numerous are they who laud the 'gentle craft' of the angler, whose 'idle time is never idly spent' beside the river, which, above all others, invites to contemplation, and promotes familiar intercourse with Nature. Here, too, the botanist and the entomologist gather a rich harvest of instruction; while to the landscape painter, wander where he will, it is ever an open volume of natural beauties, which are the only veritable teachers of art."

The general character of the scenery of the Thames is that of a calm and tranquil beauty, rather than of bold and romantic grandeur. The scenery on either side, and particularly on the Essex shore, is somewhat flat and dull, rising, however, into little hillocks away in the distance; but this dulness is compensated for by the broad expansive reaches that occur all along its course. The banks, or river walls, along the Essex shore, as we have shown in a previous chapter,* are

THE THAMES—BARKING REACH.

mostly artificial, the meadows being, in places, below the level of the river at high water. The general construction of these embankments is what is technically called the "earthen mound." It consists of a heap of earth, the section of which forms a scalene triangle, with the side towards the river inclined at an angle of about 20°, and that towards the land at one of about 45°. They are fortified chiefly by tiers of stakes, driven into the river face of the wall, and the intervals filled in with lumps of chalk or stone, rammed in to a level with the heads of the stakes or "stalks," as they are more generally called. Since the river steamer has added its "churning" power to the influence of tide and wind, however, the wall has been faced with a granite pavement.

"The banks of the lower part of the Thames," observes the author of Bohn's "Pictorial Handbook of London," "are marked by the same want of a definite plan which renders the upper part of the stream less useful than it might be made. The period at which they were first formed is very remote, being by some supposed to date as far back as the time of the Romans. This, indeed, seems very probable, for the manner in which the banks are executed, though eminently successful, is marked by all the clumsiness of a first essay. The marshes they protect from the river are sometimes (as at Woolwich) not less than four feet three inches below the level of the high water in spring tides. Those of the Isle of Dogs are now (1854) being enclosed by an embankment upon piles, with a superstructure of brickwork, executed in conformity with a plan prepared by Mr. Walker, under the direction of the Navigation Committee; thus indicating that the attention of that body has been fairly called to the necessity of co-ordinating all encroachments upon the channel of the river to one general system. The result of the several works upon the bed of the Thames, and the demolition of the old bridge, has been hitherto to lower the bed, and to compromise the safety of several of the bridges in the stream, and of some of the buildings on the shore. . . . . Moreover, in the lower Thames, that is to say, in those parts of its course below London Bridge, numerous shoals exist, which are highly prejudicial to the safety of the navigation, whilst at the same time, there is no reason why they might not be carried further out towards the embouchure if the course of the river were regularised, and the dredging operations made to conform to the necessities of the port. The shoals exist in the parts of the Thames in which the deep sea navigation terminates, where, in fact, from the more energetic action of the tides, the floods from the upper country begin to deposit the matter they hold in solution."

The occasional floods which occur in the valleys of the Thames and the Lea arise entirely from the surface waters, hardly ever from the melting of snow in the higher lands near their sources. Indeed, the climate of this part of England, and the feeble elevation of its hills, does not admit of the fall of snow in quantities sufficient to affect the sources of the river supply. Under these circumstances the floods are found to occur in the rainy seasons—in November and December, in

of the London Dock on the north, and the St. Saviour's Dock on the south; a similar shoal was formed opposite to the Lime Kiln Dock; another in a wide reach a little above the Greenland Docks; a fourth near Deptford Creek. Opposite Saunders Ness, shoals have been formed on each side of the river, owing to the check given to its velocity by the abrupt bend which it here assumes; whilst a small shoal in the middle of the stream, a little lower down than these side ones, appears to have owed its origin to the interference which it produces in the direction of the currents. Another small

THE THAMES—WOOLWICH REACH.

April and May, without, however, being in any manner peculiarly confined to those months. The flood waters brought down to the rivers are highly charged with earthy matter, and the germs of organised life; they, in fact, materially influence the formation of the alluvial deposits of the rivers. The volume of water brought down by the Thames not being sufficient to form a delta, the particles which the stream holds in solution are gradually deposited on the mudbanks, and form shifting shoals, which extend from about Woolwich to the Nore, and even beyond.

Numerous shoals have existed in the bed of the river near the entrance to the Pool, but in most instances these have been reduced by dredging. For instance, a shoal existed on the north shore, opposite to the recesses formed by the east entrance

shoal has been produced in the still water opposite the entrance of the West India Docks.

Below the above-mentioned points of the river it is very difficult, from the nature of the currents, to define with certainty the exact position of the shoals; still less would it be possible to effectually remove them, or to stop their formation. A writer on the physical geography of the Thames, observes, "At Woolwich the water becomes brackish at spring tides, and the greater specific gravity it thence attains modifies the conditions of the deposition of the matter it holds in suspension. The difference between the lengths of time during which the flood and the ebb tides prevail also diminishes as the river approaches the sea. Moreover, the action of the current upon the shores of the embouchure at the same time that it removes the land on both sides, and thus changes the form of the outfall, so also does it carry into those portions of the estuary where still water is to be met with the materials resulting from the degradation of the shores. The variations of the tides from the neap to the spring, the changes in the force and direction of the deep-sea current—possibly from the effects of storms in very different and distant latitudes—the irregularities of the volume of fresh water brought down from the upper regions of the Thames, combine to render its *régime* in the lower and wider portions of its course very irregular and capricious. The sands of the Nore vary often in their outline, and their distance from the surface of the water; the erosive force of the current upon the banks also varies in intensity, according to the action of the causes shortly enumerated above.

"The tide in the Thames ascends about fifteen miles above London Bridge to Teddington, below which place the river is exposed to the action of the tides from a peculiar combination of causes. The tide-wave from the Atlantic divides at Land's End into two streams, one of which runs up the British Channel, and enters the Thames round the North Foreland; the other passes along the west coast of England and Scotland, and returns southward by the eastern shore and enters the Thames also, after passing the Yarmouth Roads. The tide in the river is then composed of two tidal waves, distant twelve hours from each other, so that the day and night tides are equal; the tides meet between the Foreland and the Kentish Knock. The velocity of the wave from the North Foreland to London is very great, being about fifty miles per hour; above the bridges, from the resistances it meets, the velocity is so much diminished that the wave is not propagated more rapidly than twelve miles an hour on the average. The difference of time of high water between London Bridge and Richmond is one hour eighteen minutes . . . Professor Airy observed that the rise of the water in the Thames, at a given interval from low water—in half an hour, for instance—is considerably more than its descent in the same interval before low water. There exists, in fact, the rudiment of a bore. The duration of slack water, or the interval between the change of direction of the stream, is forty minutes during the spring tides and thirty-seven minutes during the neaps, at Deptford. The vulgar establishment is the interval by which the time of high water follows the moon's transit on the day of new and full moon. What Sir John Lubbock calls the corrected establishment, or the lunar hour of high water, freed from the semi-menstrual irregularity, is found to

be, at the London Docks, one hour twenty-six minutes. The interval of the high tide and moon's transit is, however, affected by a considerable inequality, which goes through its period twice in a month, depending on the moon's distance from the sun in right ascension, or on the solar time of the moon's transit. Its value is two hours. The direction of the winds has a great influence on the tides of the Thames, not only as to the height they attain, but also as to their duration. Thus, with north-westerly gales, they do not rise so high, nor does the flood run so long as with the wind in any other quarter. With south-westerly gales, however, and with those from the east, the tides often rise as much as four feet above their usual levels."

In the old chronicles and memoirs that have been rescued from oblivion will be found many a graphic description of the use made of the river as the common highway of London. "These old writers," observes Charles Knight, in his "London," "were noble hands at scene-painting. What a picture Hall gives us of the populousness of the Thames !—a perfect contrast to Wordsworth's—

' The river glideth at his own sweet will '—

in the story which he tells us of the Archbishop of York, after leaving the widow of Edward IV. in the sanctuary of Westminster, sitting 'alone below on the rushes, all desolate and dismayed,' returning home to York Place in the dawning of the day; 'and when he opened his windows and looked on the Thames, he might see the river full of boats of the Duke of Gloucester, his servants watching that no person should go to the sanctuary, nor none should pass unsearched.'" Cavendish, in his "Life of Wolsey," furnishes as graphic a description of the great cardinal hurrying to and fro on the highway of the Thames between his imperious master and the injured Katharine, when Henry had become impatient of the tedious conferences of the Court at Blackfriars, sitting on the question of his divorce, and desired to throw down with the strong hand the barriers that kept him from the Lady Anne :—"Thus the court passed from session to session, and day to day, in so much that a certain day the king sent for my lord at the breaking up one day of the court to come to him into Bridewell. And, to accomplish his commandment, he went unto him, and being there with him in communication in his grace's privy chamber from eleven till twelve of the clock and past at noon, my lord came out and departed from the king, and took his barge at the Black Friars, and so went to his house at Westminster. The Bishop of Carlisle, being with him in his barge, said unto him (wiping the sweat from his face), 'Sir,' quoth he, 'it is a very hot day.' 'Yea,' quoth my lord cardinal, 'if ye had been as well chafed as I have been within this hour, ye would say it were very hot.'"

But it is rather with "below bridge" than "above bridge" that we have to deal here. Not only between Westminster and Blackfriars, nor even the Tower, but also between the Tower and Greenwich, was the Thames especially the royal road. When Henry VII. willed the coronation of his queen, Elizabeth, she came from Greenwich, attended by "barges freshly furnished with banners and streamers of silk." When Henry VIII. avowed his marriage with Anne Boleyn, she was brought by "all the crafts of London" from Greenwich to the Tower, "trumpets, shawms, and other divers instruments all the way playing and making great melody." The river was not only the festival highway, but the more convenient one, for kings as well as subjects. Hall tells us in his "Chronicles" : "This year (1536), in December, was the Thames of London all frozen over, *wherefore* the king's majesty, with his beautiful spouse, Queen Jane, rode throughout the City of London to Greenwich." The " Privy Purse Expenses of Henry VIII." contain several items of sums paid to watermen for waiting with barge and boat. The barge was evidently always in attendance upon the king, and the great boat was used for the conveyance of household stuffs and servants from Westminster to Greenwich or to Richmond. On one occasion, in 1531, we find a record of payment " to John, the king's bargeman, for coming twice from Greenwich to York Place with a great boat with books for the king." Later on we see the " great Eliza" on the Thames in all her pomp, as Raleigh saw her out of his prison window in the Tower, in 1592, as described in a letter from Arthur Gorges to Cecil :—" Upon a report of her majesty's being at Sir George Carew's, Sir W. Raleigh having gazed and sighed a long time at his study window, from whence he might discern the barges and boats about the Blackfriars stairs ; suddenly he brake out into a great distemper, and sware that his enemies had on purpose brought her majesty thither to break his gall in sunder with Tantalus' torment, that when she went away he might see death before his eyes ; with many suchlike conceits. And, as a man transported with passion, he swore to Sir George Carew that he would disguise himself, and get into a pair of oars to ease his mind with but a sight of the queen."

James II., on his abdication, availed himself of the river transit as far as Gravesend, in his journey to France. The provisional government and the Prince of Orange had come to the conclusion that James would turn his face towards France, his majesty having had the choice of either returning to London or retiring to the Continent, as he should think fit. James accordingly returned to London, and invited his son in-law, the Prince of Orange, to meet him at Whitehall, that they might " amicably settle the distractions of the nation." What William and his party wanted, however, was the immediate expatriation of the king, which could be converted into a virtual abdication ; and to this end they drove, being assisted by some whom James still considered his personal friends. The king was waited upon at the palace by his ex-minister, Halifax, and told that he must go to Ham House, near Richmond, as the Prince of Orange intended entering London on the following morning. James, we are told, merely said that Ham was cold and damp, and that he should prefer going to Rochester. " As this was a step towards France," writes the author of the " Comprehensive History of England," " he was soon informed that his son-in-law agreed ; and about noon on the following day James embarked in the royal barge for Gravesend. He was attended by the Lords Arran, Dumbarton, Lichfield, Aylesford, and Dundee, and followed and watched by a number of Dutch troops in other boats. . . . That night he slept at Gravesend, and on the morrow he proceeded to Rochester." Thence, as readers of English history know, the king was rowed down the Medway in a small boat, and then, embarking on board a fishing-smack, which had been hired for the voyage, passed over in safety to the coast of France.

Among the "processions" on the Thames in more recent times, was that which conveyed the remains of Lord Nelson, after lying in state in the Painted Hall of Greenwich Hospital, to Whitehall, on the 8th of January, 1806, preparatory to their interment in St. Paul's Cathedral.

From the time of Fitz-Stephen, at the beginning of the thirteenth century, to that of " the moral Gower," as Chaucer calls him, it may be easily imagined that the water-communication between one part of London and another, and between London and Westminster, was constantly upon the increase. A portion of London Bridge was movable, and this enabled vessels of burden to pass up the river to unload at Queenhithe and other wharves. " Stairs (called bridges) and water-gates," writes Charles Knight, " studded the shores on both sides. Palaces arose, such as the Savoy, where the powerful nobles kept almost regal state. The courts of law were fixed at Westminster, and thither the citizens and strangers from the country daily resorted, preferring the easy highway of the Thames to the almost impassable road that led from Westminster to the village of Charing, and thence onward to London. John Lydgate, who wrote in the time of Henry V., has left us a very curious poem, entitled 'London Lyckpeny.' He gives us a picture of his coming to London to obtain legal redress of some grievance, but without money to pursue his suit. Upon quitting Westminster Hall, he says—

> 'Then to Westminster *Gate* I presently went.'

This is undoubtedly the Water-gate ; and without describing anything beyond the cooks, whom he found busy with their bread and beef at the gate, 'when the sun was at high prime,' he adds,

> 'Then unto *London* I did me hie.'

By water he no doubt went, for through Charing he would have made almost a day's journey. Wanting money, he has no choice but to return to the country, and having to go 'into Kent,' he applies to the watermen at Billingsgate :

> 'Then hied I me to Billingsgate,
>   And one cried *hoo!*—go we hence ?
> I pray'd a bargeman, for God's sake,
>   That he would spare me my expense ;
> "Thou 'scap'st not here," quoth he, "under two pence."'

"We have a corroboration of the accuracy of this picture in Lambarde's 'Perambulation of Kent.' The old topographer informs us that in the time of Richard II. the inhabitants of Milton and Gravesend agreed to carry in their boats, from London to Gravesend, a passenger, with his truss and farthell, for twopence. The poor Kentish suitor, without twopence in his pocket to pay the Gravesend bargemen, takes his solitary way on foot homeward. The *gate* where he was welcomed with the cry of *hoo*—ho, ahoy!—was the great landing-place of the coasting vessels ; and the king here anciently took his toll upon imports and exports."

"In the beginning of the seventeenth century," writes Charles Knight, "the river was at the height of its glory as the great thoroughfare of London. Howell maintains that 'the river of Thames hath not her fellow, if regard be had to those forests of masts which are perpetually upon her ; the variety of smaller wooden bottoms plying up and down ; the stately palaces that are built upon both sides of her banks so thick ; which made divers foreign ambassadors affirm that the most glorious sight in the world, take water and land together, was to come upon a high tide from Gravesend and shoot the bridge at Westminster.' Of the 'smaller wooden bottoms,' Stow computes that there were

in his time as many as two thousand ; and he makes the very extraordinary statement that there were forty thousand watermen upon the rolls of the company, and that they could furnish twenty thousand men for the fleet. The private watermen of the court and of the nobility were doubtless included in this large number."

The Conservancy of the Thames by the Corporation of London, as shown in a previous chapter,* extends from Staines in the west to Yantlet Creek in the east, a distance of about eighty miles, the Lord Mayor acting as bailiff over the waters, in preserving its fisheries and channels, and as meter of marketable commodities—fruit, vegetables, salt, oysters, corn, and coal. The rules and bye-laws for the regulation of the watermen and lightermen, and also for the regulation of the steamboat and other traffic on the river, are drawn up by the court of mayor and aldermen in their capacity as Conservators of the Thames. By the Thames Conservancy Acts and the Thames Navigation Acts, passed between the years 1857 and 1878, special bye-laws have been framed for regulating the traffic on the river during boat-races. One of these bye-laws is to the effect that "any vessel being on the river Thames between Cricklade, in the county of Wilts, and Yantlet Creek in the county of Kent, on the occasion of any boat-race, regatta, public procession, or launch of any vessel, or any other occasion when large crowds assemble thereon, shall not pass thereon so as to obstruct, impede, or interfere with the boat-race, regatta, procession, or launch, or endanger the safety of persons assembling on the river, or prevent the maintenance of order thereon ; and the master of every such vessel, on any such occasion as aforesaid, shall observe the directions of the officer of the Conservators engaged in superintending the execution of this bye-law ; and if any such master fails in any respect to comply with the requirements of this bye-law, or does anything in contravention thereof, he shall be deemed guilty of an offence against this bye-law, and shall for every such offence be liable to a penalty of not exceeding £5."

Boating has always been a favourite pastime with Londoners, who still largely indulge in it ; and it is but right, therefore, that stringent rules should be laid down to guard against accidents.

The loss of life upon the Thames, by collision of vessels and other accidents, is of frightful amount ; as many as 500 persons are, on an average, annually drowned in the river, and one-

---

* See *ante*, p. 187.

third of that number in the Pool. The most disastrous catastrophe that has taken place on the river of late years occurred at Gallion's Reach, near Blackwall, on the evening of the 3rd of September, 1878, when upwards of 500 persons lost their lives through a collision between an outward-bound vessel called the *Bywell Castle*, and a river steamboat named the *Princess Alice*, which was returning from a pleasure-trip heavily laden with passengers.

"From steeple-chasing," writes Lord William Lennox in " Drafts on my Memory," "I turn to boating, a delightful pastime before the introduction of river steamers played such havoc with it in the more frequented parts of the river.

'Some o'er the Thamis rowed the ribboned fair,

writes Byron in 'Childe Harold'; and unquestionably, however agreeable it might have been in the days of the noble poet to have found oneself like Dibdin's ' Jolly Young Watermen, never in want of a *fair*,' we should scarcely like in these days to trust any lovely daughter of Eve in a frail wherry subject to the tender mercies of the steamboat captains. The Thames, like the roads of England, have been completely sacrificed to steam ; and a morning sail or an evening pull on the water is now only to be ranked among the pleasures of memory. Some seventeen years ago boating was a great amusement, both to the higher and the humbler classes ; and in those days there were some splendid six, eight, and ten-oared boats, manned by the flower of the English nobility. Now the steamboats have entirely monopolised Father Thames ; and since the time these fire-flies have taken possession of the no longer ' silent highway,' oars and sculls are at a sad discount. Who now would venture his life in a wherry, when, owing to the modern invention of ' steam for the million,' boats are whizzing up and down the river from sunrise to sunset, dodging in and out, dashing and slashing very much after the principle of the cutting-in, panel-breaking coachman of the Fourth George's time ? What would the water poet, that renowned king of scullers of 1630, John Taylor, have said, had he lived during the present period ; he that was wont to boast that he often ferried the immortal Shakespeare from Whitehall to Paris Garden, or his contemporary Ben Jonson from the Bankside to the Rose and Hope playhouses? With his tirade against coaches, then but lately introduced, what would he have said to the modern importation of cabs, 'buses, and other vehicles, from the well-appointed four-in-hand ' team,' to a Whitechapel cart ? The poor water poet must have drowned himself in his own element : for mark

what a picture he drew even then of the fearful calamity that assailed his vocation :—" I do not inveigh,' says honest John, 'against any conveyances that belong to persons of worth or quality, but only against the caterpillar swarm of hirelings. *They have undone my poor trade* whereof I am a member ; and though I look for no reformation, yet I expect the benefit of an old proverb, ' Give the losers leave to speak.' This infernal swarm of trade-spillers (coaches) have so overrun the land that we can get no living upon the water ; for I dare truly affirm that every day in any term, especially if the court be at Whitehall, they do rob us of our living, and carry five hundred and sixty fares daily from us. I pray you look into the streets, and the chambers or lodgings in Fleet Street or the Strand, how they are pestered with them, especially after a masque or play at the Court, when even the very earth quakes and trembles, the casements chatter, patter, and clatter, and such a confused noise is made, so that a man can neither sleep, speak, hear, write, nor eat his dinner or supper quiet for them.' "

In 1815 a sporting event came off on the Thames, namely, a grand rowing match for two hundred sovereigns, between " Squire " Osbaldeston, with Mitchell, of Strand Lane, and Captain Bentinck, of the Guards, with Cobb, of Whitehall ; the terms being to row a pair of oars from Vauxhall to Kew Bridge. The details of this race, and of one or two others shortly after, are thus given in Lord W. Lennox's " Drafts on my Memory " :—" At the word ' off' Mr. Osbaldeston's boat shot half a length ahead, and the boats remained in this position until within a few yards of Battersea Bridge, when the Captain laid out, and the boats were about even. Soon after the church had been passed the opponents changed places, and from this point the gallant Guardsman continued to gain, winning the match at length by four minutes and a half. A wonderful feat took place in September of the same year, when Messrs. Bishop and Horneman accomplished the task of rowing with a pair of oars from London Bridge to Gravesend, up to Richmond Bridge, and back to Westminster (a distance of nearly a hundred miles) in the short space of thirteen hours and thirty-five minutes—an hour and twenty-five minutes within the time of the wager. What made this exploit so wonderful was, that from Gravesend to Erith Reach, they had a heavy sea and a dead ' noser,' as I can vouch for, for it nearly water-logged their boat, and capsized mine.

" In 1830 I was present at a most extraordinary match against time, made by a distinguished amateur, F. Cresswell, Esq., for fifty sovereigns, that he and William Lewis, a waterman of Old Swan Stairs, would row in a Thames wherry from Billingsgate down to Gravesend, up through Richmond Bridge, and back to the Old Swan, in thirteen hours and a half. At starting the odds were two to one in favour of time. The day was calm, although it rained heavily for some time, and the tide in their favour almost the whole of the way to Gravesend. They turned without landing, so as to avail themselves of the flowing tide, and on their return, the tide above Sion House being favourable, they reached the Swan Stairs at 5. 20, winning their match by an hour and forty minutes."

Having thus far laid before the reader a general view of the chief features of Old Father Thames, we will, in the opening chapter of our next volume deal with the Pool and its commercial activity, and then ask the reader to accompany us in an imaginary trip as far as the most easterly limits of the Thames Conservancy, and jurisdiction of the Lord Mayor.

GENERAL INDEX.

N.B.—*A separate Index to the Illustrations is appended to each Volume.*

Abbey Mill, Waltham, I. 415
Abbey Mills Main Drainage Works, I. 507
Abbey Wood, Kent, II. 43 (*see* Lesnes Abbey), 48, 49
Abbot, Archbishop, II. 164, 165
Abbs Court, Hampton Wick, residence of Edward Wortley Montagu, I. 142 (*see* Apps Court)
Abercorn family, The, I. 262, 299, 301
Aberdeen, Earl of, I. 225, 262, 268, 298
Abernethy, Dr., I. 348, 357
Abershaw, Jerry, the highwayman, II. 316, 490, 492
Abney, Sir Thomas, at Theobalds, I. 384
Acton, the old "oak-town," I. 8, 20; early history of, 8, 9; later account of; a part of the see of London; the church; donors to, 9; its rectors, 9, 10; a Puritan stronghold, 9, 10, 11; Cromwell at, 10; Baxter and Sir Matthew Hale, residents, 11; Baxter and Hale's house, 12; distinguished residents, 13, 14; old mansions near; the High Street; the pump; the parish church, 14; the parish registers; rectors of Acton, 15; once a fashionable resort, 16
Acton Green, I. 7, 8, 16; skirmish in 1642, 16
Ada, Lord Byron's daughter, I. 23
Addington, Surrey; its boundaries and etymology; Castle Hill; singular tenure of the manor; descent of the manor; privileges of the lord, II. 130; St. Mary's parish church; its monuments, 131; burial-place of Archbishop Tait; a cluster of tumuli; Addington Park, 132; its purchase as a seat for the Archbishops of Canterbury; the mansion; the grounds and park, 133; the Archbishops who have lived here, 134, 135
Addiscombe; its early history, II. 136; the house rebuilt by Evelyn's son-in-law; its successive owners; now a military college, 137, 138, 139
Addison, Joseph, I. 92, 96, 100, 107, 142
Adelaide, Queen, I. 298, 301, 302, II. 300
Aidon, Mr. W., gardener to George III. at Kew, II. 411
Aikin, Miss Lucy, I. 151, II. 233, 335, 338, 410, 478
Ailsa, Marquis of, I. 59, 83
Ainsworth, Mr. Harrison, I. 224
Akenside, the poet, I. 191, 280, II. 365
Albany, Duke of, II. 285, 296
Albemarle House, academy, Hounslow Heath, I. 66
Aldborough Hatch, Hainault Forest, I. 489, 495, 517; the church, 495
Aldenham House, Bushey, I. 303, 315; the manor of Aldenham; Kemp Row; descent of the manor, 308; the present owner; the parish church; monuments, 309
Aldersbrook, Ilford, I. 501
Ambresbury Banks, Epping Forest, I. 418, 437, 442; Boadicea's battle with the Romans, and defeat, 418—420; the obelisks, 420, 421; the earth-works, 418, 421; General Pitt-Rivers on the, 421, 422, 430, 448

Amelia, Princess, I. 17, 18, 20, II. 352, 353, 356
Amhurst, Nicholas, the author, I.
Anderson, Mr. J. Corbet, the historian of Croydon, II. 149, 152, 169, 172, 179
Andrewes, Bishop, II. 227
"Anglers," The, tavern, Teddington, I. 124
Anglesey, Marquis of, I. 203, 206, 228
Ankerwyke and Magna Charta, I. 191
"Anna Boleyn's Castle;" its present uses, I. 515
Anne Boleyn's Walk, Wickham House, II. 127
Anne Boleyn's Well, Carshalton, II. 201
Anne of Cleves, II. 317, 324, 335
Anne, Queen, at Hampton Court, I. 155, 156
Anne, Queen, style of houses, Turnham Green, I. 7, 8
Anselm, Archbishop, II. 163
Antraigues, Count and Countess d', Murder of, II. 455
Apps Court, II. 284; its former owners, 285
Apsley, Lord, II. 95
Arabin, General; his old mansion of Burroughs, I. 207
Arbuthnot, the poet, I. 97, 100
Archbishops buried at Croydon, II. 154
Archdeacon, Curious duties of the, in the eleventh century, II. 163
Archdeacon's Well, The, Keston, II. 116
Archer, Lady, II. 455
Archery, The practice of, at Harrow School, I., 263—266; shooting for the silver arrow, 263—265
Argyll, Duke of, I. 21, 69, 90
Argyll and Greenwich, Duke of, II. 322, 357
Arlington, Earl of, II. 321; error in his title, I. 201
Armada, News of the destruction of the, I. 154
Armstrong, Sir W., Woolwich guns constructed on the plan of, II. 23, 24
Arnold, Dr. Thomas, I. 183, 184
Arno's Grove, Southgate, I. 346
Arras tapestry in Hampton Court Palace, I. 163
Arrow, Shooting for the silver, at Harrow School, I. 263—265
Arundel, Archbishop, I. 273, II. 159, 161, 163
Arundel, Henry, Earl of, and Nonsuch Palace, II. 231, 232, 234, 235
Asgill House, Richmond, II. 340, 341
Ashby family of Brakespeare, Harefield, Middlesex, I. 247, 248
Ashford, Middlesex, I. 29, 184; the village; descent of the manor; military reviews by George III.; population; St. Matthew's parish church; the original edifice; tombs; the parish registers; curious entries in the church books; charitable institutions, 185
Ashford Common, Middlesex; reviews formerly held here, I. 185
Ashley, Sir Anthony, created Earl of Shaftesbury, II. 321, 322
Ashmole, Elias, the antiquary, I. 332
Assheton, Rev. Dr., II. 106
Asylum for Fatherless Children, Reedham, II. 147

Asylum for Female Orphans, Beddington, Surrey, II. 185, 191
Atterbury, Bishop, I. 100, II. 92, 93, 344
At-Hall family, The, Hall Place, Bexley, II. 51, 56
Athelstan, Coronation of, II. 298
Aubrey, the historian of Surrey, II. 156, 165, 173, 203, 221, 259, 273, 288, 429, 480
Auckland, Lord, II. 100, 101, 105
Aumale, Duc d', a resident at Orleans House, Twickenham, I. 88
Aungier's "History of Isleworth," I. 46, 51, 55
Awsiter family, The, I. 215, 217
Aylesford, Countess of, I. 298
Ayloffe, Sir Joseph, I. 279

B

Babbage, Charles, mathematician, I. 348, 362
Baker, the chronicler, II. 333, 334
"Bald-faced Stag," Kingston, II. 316
"Bald-faced Stag" inn, Buckhurst Hill, I. 434, 443, 444, 446
Bampfylde, Sir Charles Warwick, I. 86
Bancroft, Archbishop, II. 164
Bandinelli, the sculptor, I. 165
Bankes, Lady, the gallant defender of Corfe Castle, I. 242
Banks, Sir Joseph, I. 44
Banks, the sculptor, I. 238
Banstead, Surrey; situation and general appearance; view from the Downs; the Downs famous for sheep-farming; geology of the Downs; Roman coins, &c., found here, II. 214; Pepys' notice of Banstead Downs, 214, 215; races held here formerly; attractions of the Downs two centuries ago, 215; descent of the manor, 215, 216; Banstead House; Cold Blow Cottage; Nork House; the village of Banstead; the parish church, 217; monuments; Walton-on-the-Hill; Walton Place; the church; discovery of a Roman villa; Woodmansterne; the church; "The Oaks," 218; General Burgoyne; a *fête champêtre*, 219; Lord Derby a resident here, 219, 220; Coulsdon; the common; the church; descent of the manor, 221
Banstead Downs, II. 199, 207, 231, 248, 249, 263, 264
Barclays, The, of Woodford, I. 464
Barking Creek, I. 497, 510, 516, 525
Barking; its situation and extent; population; etymology, I. 516; Barking Abbey; its history, 517; the abbey at the time of the Conquest; its importance in Saxon times; the convent damaged by an overflow of the Thames; curious entries of the revenues of the abbey, 517—520; dissolution of the abbey; the abbey gateway; extent of the original buildings; noted abbesses, 521; manorial estates of the abbey; St. Margaret's parish church; the rural deanery of Barking, 522; the manor of Barking; Clayhall Manor, 523; Malmains; Bi-

frons; Eastbury House; the road to Tilbury; Barking town; railway stations; the Roman entrenchment at Uphall, 524; Barking Creek; the outfall of the main drainage works, 525, 526

Barking Side, I. 490, 497, 517

"Barnaby Rudge," Scene from Chigwell in, I. 449, 453, 455, 456

Barnard, Sir John, II. 428

Barnard, Lady Anne, the authoress, II. 485

Barn Elms, II. 458, 459, 460, 461, 462, 463

Barnardo, Dr., his Homes for Friendless Children, I. 491

Barnes; situation, extent, and boundaries of the parish; etymology, II. 450; history of the manor; its several lessees; the parish church; its brasses, 452; donors to the parish; its rectors, 453, 454; extracts from the parish registers; the yews in the churchyard, 454; Barnes Terrace; murder of the Count and Countess d'Antraigues; Barnes Common, 455; Theodore Hook's impertinent hoax, 455, 456; noted residents, 456; Castlenau; the Hammersmith Suspension Bridge, 457; cultivation of cedar-trees carried on at Barnes; Barn Elms, 458; Jacob Tonson and the Kit-Cat Club, 458, 459; Sir Francis Walsingham and Queen Elizabeth; anecdote of Heidegger, 459; Cowley, the poet; Pepys' visits to Barn Elms, 460; duel between the Duke of Buckingham and the Earl of Shrewsbury; madder grown at Barn Elms, 461; Indian corn cultivated here by Cobbett; Sir Richard Hoare at Barn Elms, 462; Sir John and Lady Kennedy, 462, 463; Sir Lancelot Shadwell, the Vice-Chancellor, 463

Barnet, Middlesex, I. 277, 316

Barnwell, George, the apprentice, II. 309

Barrington, Hon. Daines, the antiquary, I. 180

Barry, Sir Charles, architect, I. 309

Barry, Mrs., the actress, I. 13, 15

Bartlett, Rev. W. A., the historian of Wimbledon, II. 470, 471, 473, 479, 485, 487, 497

Bartolozzi, the painter, II. 400

Barton, Elizabeth, the "Holy Maid of Kent," I. 213

Barton Booth, the actor, I. 226

Bassano, the painter, I. 359

Baston, or Boston House, Hayes, Kent, II. 110, 111

Bath, Earl of, his panegyric on Strawberry Hill, I. 117

Bauer, Francis, the microscopist, II. 400, 408

Baxter, Richard, I. 11, 12, 13, 333

Baxter, William, a distinguished Harrovian and antiquarian, I. 267, 484

Beaconsfield, Lord; his sister Sarah, I. 93

Beam rivulet, The, I. 527

Bear-baitings of Brentford; allusions in Butler's "Hudibras" to, I. 37

Beard, the singer; his wives, I. 134

Beauclerk, Lord Vere, I. 70; Lady Diana, II. 368, 374

Beauclerk Closet, The, Strawberry Hill, I. 116

Beaumont Green, Cheshunt, I. 386

"Beauty Room," Hampton Court Palace; the fair Miss Gunnings and the, I. 166

Beckenham, Kent, II. 89, 96, 97; its situation; population; railway stations; Beckenham Place, the principal street, 100; early history; St. George's Church; monuments and tablets, 101; the parish register; a curious bequest, 102; other churches and chapels, 103; principal seats, 103, 104; Clay Hill; Shortlands; Langley Park; Lord Auckland; Eden Farm, 105; Kelsey Park; Foxgrove Manor, 106

Beddington, Surrey, II. 183; its etymology; early history of the manor; evi-

dences of Roman occupation; the manor of Home-Beddington; the village, 184; population; railway stations; the Female Orphan Asylum; St. Mary's Hospital, 185; Beddington House and the Carew family, 185—190; the house sold to the Corporation of the Asylum for Female Orphans; the parish church, 191; monuments, 191, 192; discovery of frescoes, 193; Beddington Cave, 194

Bedfont, Middlesex; East and West Bedfont; its Norman church; its peacock-shaped yew-trees; Hood's lines; Pope's satire on gardening, I. 195; fresco paintings in the church; Roman remains near; Bedfont Manor; the Spelthorne Sanitorium; the "Black Dog" inn; population, I. 196

Bedford Park, Chiswick; Earls of Bedford, I. 8

Bedford, Mr. J. T., Chairman of the Epping Forest Committee, I. 428, 434

Beeby, the antiquarian of Bromley, Kent, II. 84, 86, 87

Beech Hill House; the poet Tennyson, I. 436

Beech Hill Park, Enfield, I. 351, 368

Beech Wood, High Beech, now Queen Victoria's Wood, I. 430, 437

Beechey, Sir W., the painter, I. 165, II. 295

"Beer, A yard of," Bexley, Kent, II. 53

Beggars and vagabonds, Precautions against in Twickenham, I. 78, 79

"Beggar's Opera," The, I. 65, 67, 100

Bell, Ancient, at Brentford, I. 35

Bellevue House, Walthamstow, I. 466

Belmont, Chigwell, I. 451

Belmont Hill, Great Stanmore, I. 299

Belmont House, Sidcup, II. 54

Belucci, the painter, I. 296

Belvedere, Kent, II. 41, 45; owners of the mansion near; now the Royal Alfred Institution for Aged Merchant Seamen, 46; the church, 47

Benhilton parish, Sutton, II. 210

Ben Jonson, the dramatist, I. 34, II. 464

Bennets of Dawley, ancestors of the Earls of Tankerville, I. 201

Benson, Archbishop, II. 135

Bentley Priory, Middlesex, I. 270, 297, 305; its history; the Marquis of Abercorn, 300; distinguished residents; Queen Adelaide's country-seat; Sir John Kelk, 301

Bentley, Richard, Horace Walpole's friend, I. 114, 128

Beresford Street and Square, Woolwich, II. 17, 20

Berkeley family, Cranford one of the occasional residences of the, I. 197

Berkeley, Henry, M.P. for Bristol, and advocate of the ballot, I. 197

Berkeley, Hon. Grantley, and Cranford House, I. 197

Bernays Memorial Institute, Great Stanmore, I. 298

Berry, Agnes and Mary, Horace Walpole's correspondence with, I. 118, 122, II. 323, 326, 327, 374; Lord Jeffery's letters to, I. 121; their death, 123

Berrymead Priory, Acton, I. 9

Berry Wood, Bushey, I. 308

Bessborough, Lords, II. 466

Betham, Rev. E., rector of Greenford, I. 219, 220

Bethell, Alderman Slingsby, Lord Mayor, I. 21

Bettenson family, The, II. 71, 81

Beveridge, Bishop, I. 20

Beverley Brook, Wimbledon, II. 479

Bexley, Kent; its situation; etymology of name; early history; St. Runwald; Lord Bexley; population of the entire parish, II. 50; general description; the parish church; its restoration, 51; brasses and monuments; St. John's Church; the

old manor house; Bexley Heath; the church; vegetable produce, 52; a "yard of beer," 53

Bexley Heath, Kent, II. 50, 51, 52, 53; churches and chapels, 52

Bexley, Lord, II. 50, 54, 63, 101

Bickley, Kent, I. 70; the church; Bickley Hall, 83

Biden, Mr., the historian of Kingston, II. 302

Bingham, Lord, I. 183

Bishop, A, said to be playing the part of a highwayman, I. 67

Bishops consecrated at Croydon, II. 156

Blackboy Lane, Staines, I. 189

"Black Dog" inn, and its landlord, Bedfont, I. 196

Blackstone, Sir William, I. 285

Blackwall, I. 537, 538, 542, 548, 554

Blackwater, The river, I. 226

Blair, the poet, II. 454

Blakeney, Field Marshal Sir Edward, I. 76

Blendon, Kent, II. 50; the hall, 52, 55

Blount family, The, Tittenhanger, Middlesex, I. 315, 316

Blount, Martha, the alleged wife of Pope, I. 96, II. 327; Dr. Johnson's account of the poet's last illness, 105

Bloxam, the antiquary, I. 275, 328

"Blue Riband of the Turf," Origin of the phrase, II. 262

Blunt, Rev. H. J., Account of Sion House by, I. 45, 47, 48

Boadicea, Queen; her battle with the Romans and final defeat, I. 418—420

Bohn, Mr. H. G., the publisher, I. 86

Bolingbroke, Lord, of Dawley Court, Middlesex, I. 99, 100, 104, 105, 201; poetical allusion to; Lady Luxborough's mention of his house; Pope and Voltaire's visits to Dawley; Pope's letter to Dean Swift; Disraeli's account of Bolingbroke, 202

Bolton, William, last prior of St. Bartholomew's; his flight to Harrow, I. 257, 258

Bonar, Mr. and Mrs., Murder of, II. 73, 76

Boniface, Archbishop, II. 163

Boreham Wood Station, I. 303

Borough-English, Custom of, I. 57, 459, II. 477

Borstall, or Bostal, Plumstead, II. 35; Bostall Wood, 50

Boston House, Brentford, I. 39

Boston Manor, Brentford; its other names, I. 39

Boston, Thomas, vicar of Hillingdon; parish records by, I. 229

Botwell Manor, Hayes, Middlesex, I. 210

Bourchier, Archbishop, II. 163

Bourne Place, Bexley, Kent, II. 56

Bourne rivulet, The, II. 173, 221

Bovill, Sir W., Lord Chief Justice, II. 310

Bow Bridge, Essex, I. 506, 508; Bow Creek, 511

Bowater, Gen. Sir Edward, II. 356

Bowes Park, Southgate; St. Michael's Church, I. 346

Bowling Green, Chigwell, I. 451

Bowling Green, Great Stanmore, I. 302

Bowling Green House, Enfield, I. 350, 369

Bowls, Chigwell, I. 457

Bowyer, William, the printer, I. 22, 485, 487

Boydell, Josiah, antiquarian, I. 178, 179

Boyle Farm, Thames Ditton; its various residents, II. 274, 275—277

Boyle, Robert, the philosopher, I. 93

Brackenbury Chapel, Harefield Church, I. 247, 248

Bradley, the astronomer, I. 482, II. 395, 397

Bradshaw, the regicide, II. 131

Brady, Sir Antonio, I. 499

Brady, Nicholas, the hymnist, II. 388

"Brakespeare Arms," Harefield, Middlesex, I. 248

Bramblebury House, Plumstead, II. 37

Brass Foundry, The, Woolwich, II. 18, 21

Brent, The river, I. 20, 24, 29, 44, 218, 220, 222, 223, 274, 278, 279, 320

Brentford, I. 29; traffic through; origin of the name, 29, 31; the Priory of the Holy Angels, 29; George II.'s fondness for Brentford; danger from highwaymen, 30; Cæsar's crossing of the Thames near, 31; the "Brentford Eyot"; geology of Brentford; its history in Saxon times, 32; battles fought during the Commonwealth era; Cromwell at; Samuel Pepys at; the plague at; Cosmo, Grand Duke of Tuscany, at; the "Two Kings of Brentford," 33; Cowper and Prior's allusions to; the dirt of; Gay and Thomson's allusions to; Goldsmith's mention of; Charles Dickens and Brentford; the High Street and the Duke of Wellington; the hostelries; the "Wagon and Horses" and Samuel Pepys, 34; the "Tumble-down Dick," 35; ballad allusions to Richard Cromwell; a brutal murder at; Old Brentford Church; New Brentford Church; ancient bell, 35; St. Paul's Church, Old Brentford; various works; chimney of the Grand Junction waterworks, 36; drinking fountain; the bearbaitings of; the market-place; election contests of former periods, 37; Wilkes and Colonel Luttrell; Lord North's letter; popularity of Wilkes, 38; a Middlesex election; an "elector" of Middlesex; Boston House; Sion House Academy; Wyke Farm, 39; Mrs. Trimmer; sports and diversions; curious entries in the account-books, 40
Brent Street, Hendon, churches and chapels at, I. 280
Brereton, Sir William, Parliamentary general, II. 149, 161
Bridgend, Kent, II. 50, 52
Bridgman, Sir Orlando, I. 126, 128
Bristol House, Putney Heath; its owners, II. 486
Britton, the topographer, I. 270, 507, II. 124
Broadway House, Plaistow; its present uses, I. 510
Broadway railway station, Ealing, I. 20, 21
Brockley Hill, Edgware; a supposed Roman station, I. 285, 297, 302, 304
Bromefield Park, Southgate, I. 346
Bromley, Kent; origin of name; the town, II. 83; Dr. Hawkesworth; the grave of Dr. Johnson's wife; the Town Hall, 84; New Bromley; the parish church, 85; some account of the first church, 86; Dr. Johnson's wife's grave, 87; Latin inscription on the tomb; the south door of the church; parish registers; a veritable centenarian, 88; the vicarage; curious archæological discovery; St. John's Church; the Bishop of Rochester's former palace, 89; Bromley College; Simpson's Moat; Bromley Hill, 93; Lord Farnborough; Plaistow; Sundridge Park, 94; geological formations; Grove Park; Mottingham hamlet; Catford, 95; Catford Bridge, 96
Bromley Palace, Kent; the Bishop of Rochester's residence; the laurel-tree, II. 89; the "Bishop's Well," 90; lines on "St. Blaise's Well"; historical incidents connected with the palace, 91, 92
Brondesbury, Willesden, I. 225
Broome, the poet, I. 97
Brougham, Lord, I. 446, II. 355, 485
Brown, "Capability," architect, II. 55, 292, 294, 476
Browne, Lyde, Mr.; his house at Wimbledon; other residents, II. 487
Browning, Robert, the poet, I. 304
Bruce, James, the Scotch traveller, I. 267
Brydges, James, afterwards Duke of Chandos (q.v.), I. 287, 289, 290, 298, 332; Smollett's account of his defalcations, 290
Buccleuch, Duke of; his house at Richmond, II. 375, 376

Buckhurst Hill, I. 436; its etymology; the railway station; St. John's Church; the Congregational Church; Langford Place; the Essex Naturalists' and Field Club, 442; the Epping Hunt; the "Baldfaced Stag" and "Roebuck" inns; the "Horse and Well" inn, 443; the Epping Hunt of 1826, 443—445
Buckingham, Execution of Stafford, Duke of, I. 364
Buckingham, Duke of, How Charles I. received the news of his death, II. 49
Buckingham, Duke of, Duel between the Earl of Shrewsbury and, II. 461
Buckstone, Mr. J. B., comedian, II. 98
Budd, Mr. Henry, curious condition of his will, I. 94
Bulkeley, Sir Richard, II. 242
Bull Lands, Twickenham, I. 78
Bull's Cross, Enfield, I. 349, 350, 373, 376
Bullsmore Lane, Enfield, I. 371
Bulwer Lytton, Sir Edward, I. 14; battle of Barnet, 325—327
Bunsen, Baron, I. 283, 334
Burdett, Sir Francis, I. 21, 39, II. 380, 486, 493
Burdett-Coutts, Lady, II. 314, 486
Burges, Mr. W., the historian, 405, 412, 414
Burgoyne, General; his marriage to Lord Derby's daughter, II. 219, 264; his defeat at Saratoga, 219
Burnham Beeches, Epping Forest, I. 437
Burrage Town, Plumstead, II. 35
Burrell family, The, II. 101, 104, 106
Burroughs, West Drayton, General Arabin's former residence; early history of the place, I. 207
Burrows, Prof., Sketch of Sion House by, I. 46
Burton, the antiquary, II. 311
Bury Green, Cheshunt, I. 385
Bushey, Middlesex, I. 270, 272, 302; Bushey Heath; description of the scenery; Bushey manor; the parish church, 305; monuments, 306; St. Peter's Church; Bushey Hall; Hartsbourne Manor House; census returns; Oxhey; Watford; the Salters' Almshouses, 307; Aldenham; acreage and population; descent of the manor; Kemp Row, 308; Tibhurst manor; Kendall manor; Pickets or Newberry; Aldenham House; Penn's Place; St. John's parish church, 309; the Grammar School; discovery of Roman remains, 310
Bushey Park; its extent; the Diana water; William IV.'s residence; Lord North's residence; the great chestnut-trees; various divisions of the park, I. 131; Oliver Cromwell's encroachments on the park; Bennet, the village shoemaker, and the right of way, 132
Bushey Grove, I. 308
Bushey Hall hydropathic establishment, I. 307
Busk, Captain Hans, and the volunteer movement, II. 501, 502
Butler, author of "Hudibras," II. 312
Butler, Dr. G., head master of Harrow School, I. 261, 267, 268
Butler, Dr. H. Montagu, head master of Harrow School, I. 261, 267
Butts, the polling-place for Middlesex at Brentford, I. 38
"Butts," The, Harrow School, I. 263, 264
Buxton family, The, Waltham, I. 411, 417
Byng, Admiral, I. 318, 319
Byron, Admiral, of the Wager, I. 76
Byron, Lord, a distinguished Harrovian, I. 261, 262, 268, 274, II. 361; his tomb, Harrow Churchyard, 256
Byron, the late Lady, I. 23

C

"Cabal," The, II. 319, 320

Cæsar, Sir Julius, II. 528
Cæsaromagus, near Brentwood, place of Cæsar's crossing the Thames, I. 32
Cæsar's Camp, near Shepperton, I. 179
Cæsar's Camp, Wimbledon Common, II. 479, 494; opinions of antiquaries thereon, 494—497
Cæsar's crossing the Thames; antiquarian doubts of the locality, I. 179—181, II. 297, 299
Cæsar's Well, Keston Common, source of the Ravensbourne, II. 97
Caldecott Hill, Bushey Heath, I. 305
Caledon, Countess of, I. 315
Cambridge, Archdeacon, Schools of, I. 76
Cambridge Cottage, Kew Green, II. 408
Cambridge House, Twickenham; its successive owners, I. 82, 83
Cambridge, Duke of, II. 315, 316, 353, 399
Cambridge Park, Twickenham, I. 75
Cambridge, Richard Owen, I. 76, 82; some account of, 82, 83
Camden, Charles Pratt, Baron, II. 75, 76
Camden Place, Chislehurst, II. 70, 73, 74; last residence of Napoleon III., 74
Camlet Moat, Enfield, I. 349, 352, 367, 369
Canaletti, the painter, I. 165, 359
Cann Hall, Wanstead, I. 479
Canning, Elizabeth, Story of, I. 375
Canning Town, Plaistow, I. 510
Cannizaro House, Wimbledon; its residents, II. 487, 488
Cannon Row, Woolwich, II. 10, 17
Cannon's Bridge, Ruislip, I. 243
Canons, near Edgware, I. 284, 285, 286, 287 (see Chandos)
Capel family, The, II. 395
Capels, Enfield, I. 373, 376
Capper family, The, Bushey, I. 306
Capworth Street, Leyton, I. 484
Caracci, the painter, I. 359
Cardigan, Earl of, Duel between Capt. Tuckett and the, II. 494
Carew family, The, and Beddington House, II. 180, 183, 184, 185—191, 195, 198, 201, 208, 216, 221, 243, 251
Carey, Henry, Queen Elizabeth and, I. 150, II. 336
Carnarvon, John, Marquis of, I. 293
Caroline, Queen, wife of George II.; her gardens and grotto at Richmond, II. 345, 346; Merlin's Cave, 346, 347; Stephen Duck, her librarian, 346, 348; her residence, 357; Kew Palace leased by, 395
Carpenders Park, Bushey, I. 307
Carriage Department, Woolwich Arsenal, II. 26
Carshalton, Surrey, II. 183; its situation and boundaries; derivation of the name, 197; the "Domesday" notice; history of the manor, 198; a weekly market once held here; market gardens and fish culture; Fuller's remarks on the productions of the parish, 199; a "poetic" description of the village; the taverns "poetically" described, 200; the river Wandle, 200, 201; the pond; Anne Boleyn's Well; All Saints' Church; monuments and epitaphs; the parish registers, 202; the railway station; Stone Court; its historical associations; Carshalton House and Dr. Radcliffe, 203; anecdotes of Dr. Radcliffe, 204, 205; Carshalton Park, 205, 206; Culvers; Leicester House, once the Metropolitan Convalescent Asylum; May-Day customs at Carshalton, 206
Carshalton House, II. 201, 203
Carshalton Park, II. 201, 203, 205, 206
Cartridge Case Factory, Woolwich Arsenal, II. 27
Cartwright, Major, political reformer, I. 339, 362
Cass, Rev. F. C., on the battle of Barnet, I. 322, 325, 327
Cassiobury, Herts, Earl of Essex's seat, I. 307
Castlebar Hill, Ealing, I. 20, 22

Castle Hill, Ealing, I. 20, 21, 205

Castlemaine, Lady, created Duchess of Cleveland, II. 237, 238, 248, 249

Castlereagh, Lord, Duel between Canning and, II. 493

Caterham Valley, Surrey, II. 145, 147; descent of the manor, 148

Caterham, Surrey; its church and residents, II. 148, 221; the Metropolitan District Imbecile Asylum, 148

Catford, Kent, II. 95, 97; Catford Bridge; the " Ravensbourne " inn, 96

Cathcart, Lady, The unfortunate, I. 363

Cat's Hill, East Barnet; signs of the " Cat," I. 331

Cave, Dr., the author, I. 58

Cave-Brown Rev. J. II. 158, 160

Cawarden, Sir Thomas, the steward of Nonsuch estate, II. 233, 234

Cecil family, The, II. 473, 476, 482

Cecil, Sir William, afterwards Lord Burleigh, I. 376, 377; his son, Sir Robert Cecil, Earl of Salisbury, 364, 365, 378, 379, 380

Cedar House, Cowley, Middlesex; its history; the cedar; Mr. Samuel Reynardson, I. 227, 229

Centenarians, I. 15, 35, II. 88, 156, 206

Chadwell Heath, I. 495, 496, 527; railway station, 496

Chadwell Street, I. 496

Challice, Mrs., the authoress, I. 216

Chambers, Sir W., II. 347, 400, 466

Chandos, Duke of; he appropriates the public money, I. 287; builds a magnificent mansion at Canons; its situation; its cost; brief description, 288; thickness of the walls; the park and gardens; some account of the duke and his family, 289; his third wife; Mrs. Pendarves' description; pomp of the duke when at church, 290; his liberality; Pope's reference to the duke, 291; the duke's library; his style of living; the garden, terraces, hall, and library; Hogarth and the duke, 292; the duke's speculations in the South Sea scheme; the downfall of Canons; sale of the property, 293; the new purchaser; Whitworth Church, 296; the duke's residence at Arno's Grove, Southgate, 346

"Chandos Arms," Edgware, I. 284, 286

Chantrey, the sculptor, I. 485, II. 43, 73, 251, 304, 515

Chapel, The, Hampton Court Palace, I. 164, 165

Chapel End, Walthamstow, I. 465, 466

Chapman's " Hand-book of Kingston," II. 297

Chapone, Mrs. Hester, I. 329

Charcoal - burners, Colliers, or, II. 171; references to, by the early poets, 172

Charles I., his residence at Hampton Court, I. 153

Charles II., I. 33, 154, 155, II. 248, 265, 320, 321; portraits of his " beauties," 165

Charlotte, The Princess; her marriage and death, II. 293; souvenirs of, 294, 295; her mausoleum, 296

Charlotte, Queen, State bed of, Hampton Court Palace, I. 165; death of, II. 395

Charlton, Kent, II. 8, 10

Charlton, Sunbury, Middlesex, I. 176

Chase Park, Enfield, I. 358

Chase Side, Enfield, I. 349, 351, 362; the house, 358; eminent residents, 362, 363

Chatham, Lord, II. 107—110

Chatterton's verses to Horace Walpole, I. 118

Chauncy, the historian, I. 309, 310, 313, 315, 320, 321

Cheam, Surrey, II. 208, 214; healthy character of the parish; its boundaries and extent, 222; Lynce's Corner; the village and population; the modern Nonsuch Park; descent of the manor, 223; East and West Cheam; customary services of tenants under the feudal system, 224; the Lumley family, 224, 225; Lower Cheam Park; the parish church, 225; monuments and brasses, 226; noted rectors of Cheam, 227; St. Philip's Church; National and Sunday Schools; Cheam School, 228; eminent persons educated here; an old manor-house; White Hall, 229; "Bobus" Smith; Cheam Park; Lower Cheam Park, 230

Cheeseman family, The, I. 215, 216

Chenevix, Mrs., the toy-shop keeper of Regent Street; Horace Walpole purchases the leasehold of her property to erect Strawberry Hill, I. 111

" Chequers " inn, Uxbridge, I. 233

" Cherry Tree " inn, Southgate, I. 345, 346

Chertsey; the bridge over the Thames; the church; the Roman encampment near, I. 184

Cheshunt, I. 350; situation and general appearance of the parish, 384; its etymology; supposed site of a Roman station or camp; discovery of Roman coins, &c.; the mound at Bury Green, 385; a curious manorial custom; census returns; the River Lea; a disputed landmark; early history and descent of the manor of Cheshunt; subordinate manors, 386; manor of Moteland, or St. Andrew's le Mote; the great house, 387; St. Mary's Church; brasses and monuments; the cemetery; Cheshunt College, 388; Pengelly House; Richard Cromwell, 389; Cheshunt Park; the Cromwell family, 390; relics of the Protector, 391; other notable residents and seats; Waltham Cross, 392; the " Four Swans " inn; Holy Trinity Church; the Spital Houses; the Benedictine convent; Goff's Oak, 393, 394

Cheshunt Street, I. 384, 385, 386, 392

Cheshunt Wash, I. 385

Chess, The river, I. 233

Chessington, Surrey; its situation, II. 271; boundaries; the church; charitable bequests; Castle Hill; descent of the manor, 272; Hook; Barwell Court, 273

"Chestnuts," The, Ickenham, Middlesex; its distinguished residents, I. 238

Chestnut-trees, Great avenue of, Bushey Park, I. 131

Chicheley, Archbishop, II. 156, 163

Chigwell, I. 424; the " King's Well," 438; general appearance of the village, 449; its etymology; census returns; the manor-house, 450; descent of the manor; Rolls Park; Woolstons; Lexborough; the Warren; Belmont, 451; St. Mary's Church; monuments and brasses; Archbishop Harsnett, its rectors; local charities, 452; the grammar school; the " King's Head " tavern; the " Maypole " inn; Charles Dickens's love of the village; his descriptions of Chigwell, 453—457; Chigwell Row; Woodlands; Bowls, 457; Gainsborough's picture of " The Woodman "; the mineral waters, 458

Chigwell Hall, the manor-house, I. 450; descent of the manor, 451

Chigwell Row, I. 450, 451, 457, 490

Child, Sir Francis, the banker, and Osterley Park, I. 43

Child, Sir Josiah, I. 476, 480; his son, Earl Tylney, 476

Children's Convalescent Institution, Kingston, II. 315

Chiltern View, Uxbridge, I. 233

Chingford, I. 417, 420, 435; its etymology; the " King's Ford," 437; extent of the parish; the manor of Chingford St. Paul, 438, 439; the manor of Chingford Earls, 438, 439; Chingford Hall; Friday Hill; Buckrills' Manor; Brindwoods estate; curious tenure, 439; extent of the parish; population; All Saints' Church; monu-

ments and brasses; St. Peter and St. Paul's Church; the railway station, 440

Chipping Barnet, Middlesex, I. 312, 319, 320, 323, 330

Chislehurst, Kent; situation of the parish, and derivation of its name; its population; Camden Place, II. 70; history of the manor; the old manor-house; an ancient cock-pit; granite cross to the memory of the Prince Imperial, 71; St. Nicholas' Church, 72; brasses and monuments; the Roman Catholic Chapel; remains of the Emperor Napoleon III., 73; remains of the Prince Imperial; Christ Church; Church of the Annunciation; St. Mary's Hall; St. Michael's Orphanage; Governesses' Benevolent Institution; Camden Place, 74; Camden, the antiquary; Charles Pratt, Lord Camden, 75; the murder of Mr. and Mrs. Bonar; the ex-Imperial family take up their abode at Camden Place, 76; some account of Napoleon III.; his death, 77; his funeral, 78, 79; death of his son; removal of the Empress; noted residents of Chislehurst; the manor of Scadbury; descent of the manor, 80; the Walsingham family; the family of the Bettensons, 81; Sir Nicholas Bacon, Lord Keeper; Frognal; the Farrington family, 82

Chiswick; the horticultural fêtes of former days; its distinguished residents; the church, I. 5; the ferry, II. 455

Chiswick House, Entertainments given in, I. 5

Cholmondeley, Marquis of, I. 86, II. 312

Chopped-straw Hall, I. 111

Christians and Jews, Difference made between, in travelling, I. 29

Chudleigh, Miss, I. 156, 157

Church, the topographer of Sutton, II. 207, 213

Church End, Finchley, I. 338, 340; the cemetery, 340

Church End, Hendon, I. 279

Church End, Walthamstow, I. 465

Church End, Willesden, I. 224

Cibber, Colley, the player, I. 111

Cignani, the painter, I. 164

City of London Cemetery, Ilford, I. 501

Clare, John, poet, I. 436, 442

Claremont, Surrey; Sir John Vanbrugh's residence; Holles, Earl of Clare and Duke of Newcastle, II. 292; Lord Clive and subsequent owners, 292, 293; the estate becomes the residence of Prince Leopold and the Princess Charlotte; death of the princess, 293; recollections of Princess Charlotte, 294; the grounds of Claremont; the Queen and Prince Albert's residence here in their earlier years, 295; other royal visitors; the Duke of Albany's brief residence here, and death, 296

Clarence, Duke of (William IV.), II. 323, 329, 350, 351, 363, 374, 383, 396

Clarence House, Richmond Park, II. 350

Clarendon, Lord, and the Great Rebellion, I. 232

Clarke, the historian of Walthamstow, I. 499

Clarke, Dr., physician, II. 101, 250

Clarkes, The family of the, Swakeleys, Middlesex, I. 238, 239, 243

Clattern Bridge, Kingston, II. 303; Clattern House, 309

Clay Hall, Enfield, I. 359

Clay Hill, Beckenham, II. 104

Clay Hill, Enfield, I. 369

Clay, Sir W., Fulwell Lodge, Hanworth, I. 76

Clay Street, Walthamstow, I. 465, 470

Claybury Hill, Woodford; the church, I. 460

Claygate, Thames Ditton, II. 279

Cleiver, Dr. William, vicar of Croydon, II. 153, 157

Clerk of the parish, A female, I. 332

Cleveland, Duchess of (see Castlemaine)

Clive, Lord, II. 285, 292, 293, 295

Clive, Mrs. Catherine, actress, I. 76, 78, 122, 139

Clocks, Remarkable, in Hampton Court Palace, I. 160, 161, 165

Clock-tower Court, Hampton Court Palace, I. 160, 161

Close, Rev. F., Dean of Carlisle, I. 224

Coaches, Number of, formerly passing through Hounslow, I. 62

Cobbett, the historian of the Reformation, I. 242

Cobbett, Rev. R. S., the historian of Twickenham, I. 74, 81, 83, 93, 97, 98, 111; on the illness and death of Pope, 104

Cobbin Brook, Waltham, I. 417, 418, 421

Cobden Hill, Radlett, I. 310

Cobham, the actor, II. 361

Cock Fosters, Middlesex, I. 328, 351, 365, 368; its etymology, 368

Coghills, The family of the, I. 309

Cold Harbour, Hayes, Middlesex, I. 210

Coleridge, Lord, II. 218

Colham Garden, Hillingdon, I. 207

Colham Green, Middlesex, I. 228

Colham Manor, Middlesex; history and descent of the manor, I. 227, 228

Coller, the historian of Essex, I. 419, 424, 448, 506, 513, 530

Collier's Water, Croydon, II. 178, 229

Collier's Wood, Merton, II. 181

Collins, Anthony, deistical writer, I. 44

Collins, the poet, II. 374

Colman, the dramatist, I. 196, II. 362, 363

Colnbrook, Middlesex, I. 205, 228

Colne, The river, I. 44, 186, 195, 203, 205, 226, 230, 233, 237, 244, 248, 250, 304, 307, 315; Cowper's translation of Milton's lines on the, 237

Colney Hatch, Middlesex; the County Lunatic Asylum; its situation and etymology, I. 342; its erection, 343; some description of the building; St. Paul's Church; the New River pumping-works; Wood Green and the Alexandra Palace; Nightingale Hall, 344; the Printers' Almshouses; Clock and Watch Makers' Asylum; the Great Northern cemetery, 345

Colston, Edward, the Bristol philanthropist, II. 429

Colton, Rev. Caleb, the gamester, II. 325, 406, 407

Commercial Travellers' Schools, Pinner, I. 249, 250, 251; liberality of Mr. James Hughes and Mr. George Moore, 251.

Comte de Paris, I. 90, 91

Coney Hall Hill, Hayes Common, Kent, II. 127, 129

Conference between the Royalists and Roundheads, Uxbridge, I. 232

Congreve, the dramatist, I. 96, 100

Connaught, Duke of, Ranger of Epping Forest, I. 430, 442

Connaught Water, Epping Forest, I. 441, 442

Conolly, Dr., and Hanwell Lunatic Asylum, I. 27, 28

Constable, the painter, II. 106, 139

Convalescent Homes: Hampton, I. 134; Snaresbrook, I. 461; Woodford, I. 459, 461

Conway, Field-Marshal, Walpole's cousin, I. 89, 111, 112, 117, 120

Conyers family, The, Walthamstow, I. 418

Cook, Miss Eliza, II. 488

Cooke's "Topography," Quotations from, I. 61, II. 98, 111

Coombe Hill, Archæological discoveries at, II. 300

Coombe House, Kingston; its residents, II. 315

Coombe Springs, Kingston, II. 316

Coombe Warren, Kingston; its distinguished residents; view from, II. 316

Coombe Wood, Kingston; its springs, I.

170, II. 297; the Duke of Cambridge, II. 315; duel fought here, 493

Cooper's Hill, Egham, I. 191

Copley, the painter, father of Lord Lyndhurst, II. 154

Copped Hall, Epping, I. 407, 417, 424; history of the old hall; its owners, 418

Copped Hall, Totteridge; eminent residents, I. 334

Copse Hill, Wimbledon, II. 488

Copt Hall, Hendon, residence of the Nicoll family, I. 280

Corbett, Bishop, the wit, I. 86

Corney, Bolton, antiquarian critic, II. 455

Corney House, Chiswick, I. 5; Corney Reach, II. 455

Cornwallis, Archbishop, II. 165

Coronation-stone, The, Kingston, II. 297, 307; list of monarchs crowned here, 308

Costard, Rev. Geo., vicar of Twickenham, I. 76, 93.

Cosway, the artist, I. 285

Cotman's Town, Hayes, Middlesex, I. 210

Cottenham, Lord, Lord Chancellor, I. 269, 333, 488; his house now a convalescent hospital, 488

Coulsdon, Surrey, II. 208, 220; descent of the manor, II. 220

Countryman in London, Anecdote of a, I. 30

Courtenay, Archbishop, II. 163

Court of Conservancy of the Thames, The, I. 187

Cotesworth, Dr. Caleb, physician, Large fortune left by, I. 57

Coventry, Lady, I. 93, 166

Coway Stakes, Shepperton, I. 31, 179, 275; opinions of antiquarians on their origin, 180, 181

Cowley, the poet, II. 460

Cowley, I. 208; its situation and boundaries; Cowley Peachey; the parish church; population; Cowley Grove, 226; Cedar House and its associations, 227

Cowley Brook, Middlesex, I. 226

Cowley House, Middlesex, I. 226

Cowley Grove, and General Van Cortlandt, Middlesex, I. 226

Cowper, the poet, I. 34, 437, II. 267

Cowper, Mr. B. H., I. 448; discovery of an ancient earthwork by, 447; on the Isle of Dogs, 534—539, 542; on the history of Millwall, 536—547, 538, 548

Cox, Mr. Serjeant, Recorder of Portsmouth, I. 284

Coxe, Rev. A. C., on Hampton Court Palace, I. 158

Crab, Robert, the English hermit, I. 240

Crack-nut Sunday, II. 305

Cran, or Crane, The river, I. 44, 195, 196, 197

Cranbrook Park, Ilford, I. 497

Crane, Sir Francis, II. 436, 437

Cranford, Middlesex; the bridge; the manor-house and the Berkeley family; population, I. 196; descent of the manor; Cranford House; the parish church; monuments and tablets; famous rectors, 197

Cranmer, Archbishop, II. 164; his alleged descendants, 526, 527

Cranstoun, Lord, II. 191

Cranworth, Lord, II. 112, 116

Crawford, Charles, the poet, II. 375

Cray, The river, II. 50, 51, 56, 63, 65

Crays, The, Kent, II. 51; origin of the name, 56; Hughson's reference to Crayford; great battle between Saxons and Britons, 57; Roman remains, 57; descent of Earde manor; Howbury; Sir Cloudesley Shovel; manufactories, 58; population; Church of St. Paulinus; tombstones; North Cray, 59; Vale Mascal; the Marquis of Londonderry, 60, 61; St. James's parish church; the parish registers; Ruxley; Foot's Cray; Hughson's account of, 62; St. Paul's Cray; St. Mary Cray; the church; the railway

station, 63; restoration of the church; Orpington, 64; its early history; the parish church; the hop gardens, 67; hop picking, 68; a group of hop pickers, 69, 70

Crewe, Sir Clipesby, I. 60

Cricklewood, Middlesex, II. 225

Crisp, an historian of Richmond, II. 364, 369, 378

Crispe, Sir Nicholas, II. 461

Crofton Hamlet, Orpington, Kent, II. 66

Croker, Right Hon. J. W., II. 282

Cromwell, Oliver, I. 14, 33, 153, 154, 388, 389, 390, 391, II. 471, 472, 473; his supposed residence at Burroughs, West Drayton, I. 207

Cross House, Ealing, I. 22

Crossness Point, II. 35, 39, 40; the main drainage outfall, 40

Crowley, Sir Ambrose, alderman, II. 527

"Crown" inn, Uxbridge, I. 232

Croydon, Surrey; its situation; extent of the parish; history of the manor, II. 149; etymology of name, 151; discovery of coins, 151, 152; historical associations, 152; the old and new churches of St. John the Baptist; destruction and rebuilding, 153; monuments and epitaphs, 154, 155; mural painting in the church, 155; the parish registers, 156; storms; Dr. Cleiver and the highwayman, 157; present condition of the Archbishop's palace; "standing houses" of the Archbishops of Canterbury in former times, 158; early history of Croydon Palace; its situation and extent; fish-ponds, &c.; the great hall, 159, 160; the guard-chamber, 160, 161; the chapel, 161; biographical sketches of successive Archbishops of Canterbury who resided at Croydon, 161, 163–165; Whitgift's Hospital, 165; its foundation in Elizabeth's reign; curious discovery on the site; sum expended in building the hospital, 166; Whitgift's instructions concerning the charity; description of the building, 167; biographical sketch of Whitgift, 168, 169; present administration of the charity, 169, 170; Whitgift's schools; the "Swan" and "Crown" Hotels; Davy's almshouses; Smith's, or the "little" almshouses; Royal Masonic Benevolent Institution; Croydon General Hospital, 170; charitable bequests to the poor; colliers, or charcoal-burners, 171; the "saucy collier of Croydon and the devil"; references to the colliers of Croydon by early playwrights; description of Croydon in the reign of Elizabeth; its present appearance; an ancient mill, 172; the Bourne brook; the town becomes incorporated; markets and fairs; census returns, 173; railway communication; the first iron tramway, 174, 175; sanitary condition of Croydon, 175, 176; the Town Hall; the market-house; public hall, &c.; breweries and manufactories; Croydon Union; the barracks; churches and chapels, 176; the cemetery; schools; coursing meetings; a souvenir of the old coaching times, 177; inns; noted residents; subordinate manors of Croydon, 178, 179, 180

Croydon Palace; its present condition and early history, II. 158—161; Archbishops of Canterbury who lived there, 161—165

Crystal Palace, The, II. 98

Cucking-stool, Use of the, II. 300, 302

Cuddington, Cheam; Nonsuch Palace erected here, II. 230, 511

Cumberland, Duke of, the "butcher," I. 170

Cumberland, Duke of, son of George III.; attempt to assassinate him, II. 407, 408; his son, the blind king, 408

Cumberland, the actor ; his son Richard, I. 134

Curtis, Alderman Sir William, I. 346

Cussans, Mr., the historian, I. 308, 309, 310, 312, 395, 560, 563

D

Dagenham, Essex, I. 496 ; its extent and boundaries ; population ; the village ; the parish church ; monuments and brasses, 527 ; Parslowes ; Valence ; the "Chequers" inn ; Dagenham Breach, 528 ; repair of the breach, 527 ; discovery of a "moorlog," 530 ; the river walls of the Thames, 530, 531 ; Dagenham Lake ; proposed conversion into a dock ; failure of the scheme, 532 ; origin of the Ministerial whitebait dinner, 532, 533 ; remains of submerged trees, II. 39

Dalhousie, Lord, I. 262, 269

Damer, Hon. Mrs., the sculptress, I. 89, 90, 114 ; Strawberry Hill her abode for several years ; list of her sculptures, 120

Dance, James, the actor, II. 360

Dancer, Daniel, the miser of Harrow Weald, I. 271, 272 ; some account of, 272, 273

Dancer's Hill, South Mimms, I. 317

Danes, Defeat of the, at Brentford, by Edmund Ironside, I. 32

Daniel, the poet, I. 86

Danson Park, Welling, Kent , Hughson's description, II. 53

Dartford Heath, Kent, ii. 51

Darwin, Charles, the philosopher, II. 113, 119.—121

Dawley Court, Harlington, Middlesex ; its successive owners ; Lord Bolingbroke's ownership, I. 201, 227 ; Voltaire and Pope's visits here ; Disraeli's account of Bolingbroke, 202 ; the place now a brick-field, 203, 227

Dawley village, Middlesex ; its other names, I. 199

Day, Daniel, and the Fairlop Oak, I. 492 —495

"Dead Man's Bottom," Hadley, Middlesex, I. 328

"Dead Men's Graves," Brentford, I. 33

Deaf, Colleges for teaching the, Ealing, I. 22

Deanery, A layman holding a, I. 58

Debden Hall, Loughton, I. 449

De Bohuns, The family of the, I. 351, 352, 364

Decker, Sir Matthew, II. 364

Dee, Dr., the astrologer, I. 118, II. 336, 428, 433—436

De Foe, Daniel, I. 292, II. 529, 536, 537

Delaval, Sir James, how he obtained precedency before the Duke of Somerset, I. 80

Demainbray, Dr. Stephen, astronomer, I. 218

Denham, near Uxbridge, I. 237, 244, 247

Denham, Sir John, the poet, I. 191, II. 332, 373, 375 ; his father and Pope, 191

Dennies, The, of Waltham, I. 410, 411, 412, 413, 414

Denton, Sir Alexander, the judge, I. 22

Depôt Barracks, Woolwich, II. 30

De Quincey on highwaymen, I. 67, 68

Derby, Present Earl of, II. 113 ; General Burgoyne's marriage to the daughter of a former earl, 218, 219 ; Lord Derby acquires the fee-simple of "The Oaks"; Charles Greville's description of the Earl, 220

Derby, Countess Dowager of, temp. Elizabeth, I. 244, 245

Derby, Countess of, Milton's friend, I. 248

Derby Stakes, Institution of the, II. 264, 265

Derby, Winning horses of the, II. 265 ; anecdotes of the Derby, 265—267

Desmond, Earl of, and Osterley Park, I.

Devonshire, Christian, Countess of, II. 464, 465

Devonshire Cottage, Richmond ; its residents, II. 374

Devonshire, Duke of, I. 5, 7

Dial Square, Woolwich Arsenal, II. 22

Diamond, Dr. Hugh, I. 93

Diana's Dyke, Ewell, II. 238, 242

Dibdin, Charles, the sea-poet, I. 21, 138

Dickens, Charles, I. 34, 56, 93, 94, 176, 322, 328, 449, 451, 453—457, II. 260, 329, 332

Disraeli, Benjamin, I. 468, II. 282

Disraeli, Isaac, I. 348, 362

Ditton Marsh, Esher, II. 285

Docks, The ; river pirates on the Thames, I. 556—559 ; number of vessels entering the port of London in a week in 1883, 556

Dodd, Dr., I. 22

Doddridge, Judge, I. 191

Dodsley, the bookseller, I. 71, 82, 108

Doggett's coat and badge, Race for, II. 445

Dogs, Isle of ; origin of the name of, I. 534 ; Mr. Cowper on the, 535—538 ; acreage of the Isle of Dogs, 538 ; geology of, 538, 539 ; early history of, 539 ; ferries across the Thames to the Isle of Dogs, 541, 542 ; Pepys' difficulty, 541

Dogs, Pope's fondness for, I. 101, 102

Dollis Hill House, Willesden, I. 225

Donne, Dr., the poet, I. 93, II. 528

Dorman's or Domer's Well, Southall, I. 218

Downe, Kent, II. 118 ; Darwin, the naturalist, 119—121 ; Downe Hall, his residence ; manor of Downe Court, 121 ; Sir John Lubbock, 122 ; Cudham, or Coodham ; the church ; the route from Keston, 123

Drake, Sir Francis, II. 287

Draper, William, son-in-law of John Evelyn ; Addiscombe House rebuilt by, II. 136,137

Drayton Green, Ealing, I. 205

Drayton, Michael, author of the "Polyolbion," I. 86, 363, 559, 560, II. 280

Drinking-fountain at Brentford, I. 37

Drummond, The family of, I. 299

Drury, Rev. Dr., head master of Harrow School, I. 263, 267, 268

Dryden, the poet, I. 94, 104, II. 528

Du Cane, Sir Edmund, II. 316

Ducarel, Dr., the historian of Croydon, II. 151, 158, 159, 163, 170

Ducie, Lady, Menagerie of, at Osterley Park, I. 43

Duck, Rev. Stephen, librarian to Queen Caroline, II. 346, 348, 350, 405, 406

Dudding Hill railway station, Middlesex, I. 223

Dudley, Earl of Leicester, and Queen Elizabeth, I. 474, 475

Dudley, Sir Robert, II. 383

"Duke of Northumberland's River," Bedfont, Middlesex, I. 195

"Dunciad," Publication of the, I. 97, 98

Duncroft House, Staines, I. 191, 216

Duneira Cottage, Wimbledon, II. 488

Dunton House, Isleworth, I. 59

Duppa, Bishop ; his almshouses, II. 370,388

Duppas Hill, Croydon, II. 169, 182

Durants manor-house, Enfield ; its history, I. 373, 374

Durdans, Epsom, II. 243, 248, 249, 252, 257 ; its successive owners, 259

Durham, Earl of, II. 488

Duval, Claud, the highwayman, I. 67

Dyer, the poet, II. 182, 214

Dyrham Park, South Mimms ; its owners, I. 317

Dysart, Elizabeth, Countess of, II. 317 (see Duchess of Lauderdale)

Dysart family, The, II. 320, 323, 329

Dyson, Jeremiah, clerk to the House of Commons, I. 280

E

"Eagle" inn, Snaresbrook, I. 444, 472

Eagle Pond, Snaresbrook, I. 472, 473

Ealing ; its various spellings ; early history of the manor ; the parish church ; its vicars, 20 ; distinguished persons buried in it ; other churches and chapels, 21 ; distinguished residents in the parish, 21, 22 ; the Great School, 22 ; Ealing Common ; Fordhook House ; its celebrated residents ; the "Old Hat" tavern, 23

Ealing Dean, I. 20, 21

Ealing Great School ; celebrated persons educated there, I. 22

Ealing House ; its successive owners, I. 21

Ealing Grove, I. 21

East Barnet, Middlesex, I. 320, 329 ; Lyonsdown ; population ; St. Mary's Church, 330 ; the Boys' Farm Home, 331 ; the Clock House ; Cat's Hill, 331 ; Oak Hill Park ; Belmont, 332

East Bedfont, Middlesex, I. 195

Eastbury House, Barking, I. 524, 527

Eastcote, or Ascot, Ruislip, Middlesex, I. 243

East End, Finchley, I. 338, 339

Easter sepulchres, I. 200, 224

East Ham, Essex ; descent of the manor ; a curious custom, I. 513 ; railway stations ; extent and population ; St. Mary Magdalen's Church ; monuments ; other churches ; charitable bequests, 514 ; Plashet House ; Green-street House, or "Anne Boleyn's Castle" ; its present uses ; the Metropolitan Northern High Level Sewer ; East Ham Level ; the Beckton gas-works, 515

East India Docks, The, I. 554, 555 ; their amalgamation with the West India Docks, 554

East Laboratory, Woolwich Arsenal, II. 27

East Lodge, Enfield ; its owners ; Lord Chatham and the miller, I. 368

East London Cemetery, I. 511

East London Waterworks Company, I. 470, 566 ; quantity supplied annually, 566

East Molesey, Surrey ; its population ; the parish church ; its monumental tablets, II. 281 ; descent of the manor, 282 ; the "Spa"; Kemp's Eyot, or Ait, 283

East Wickham, Kent ; descent of the manor ; the church ; a curious fresco painting, II. 40

"Eclipse," The race-horse, I. 294,295, II. 264

Economic Museum, Twickenham ; destroyed by fire, I. 77

Eden Farm, Beckenham ; Lord Auckland, II. 105

Eden, Mr. William, afterwards Lord Auckland ; some account of, II. 105

Eden Park, Beckenham, II. 124

Edgware, I. 277, 297 ; situation and boundaries ; general appearance ; the "Chandos Arms," 284 ; etymology of Edgware ; descent of the manor ; the market ; curious local customs ; the parish church, 285 ; monuments and brasses ; almshouses ; railway station ; population ; Edgware races ; Little Stanmore, or Whitchurch ; acreage and population ; early history of the manor ; Canons, 286 ; the family of the Lakes ; James Brydges, afterwards Duke of Chandos (see Canons, Chandos) ; the race-horse "Eclipse," 295 ; Whitchurch parish church ; tomb of the "Harmonious Blacksmith"; almshouses, 296

Edgware Bois, manor of, I. 285

Edmonton, Middlesex ; Johnny Gilpin's ride, I. 347

Edward VI. at Enfield, I. 353 ; at Hampton Court, II. 149, 164

Edwards, the actor, II. 361

Eel-pie Island, Twickenham ; the Eel-pie House, I. 75

Egerton, Lord Keeper, I. 244, 245, 247

Egham, Cooper's Hill ; Sir John Denham, the poet ; the Indian Civil Engineering College, I. 191

Egmont, Earl of, II. 217

Eldridge, Henry, the painter, I. 306

Elections for Middlesex, I. 37, 38, 39

"Elector" of Middlesex, An, I. 39

Electric telegraph, Early days of the, I. 28

Elephantine remains at Ilford, I. 499—501

Elgin, Lord, the ambassador, I. 269

Elizabeth, Queen, and Sir Thomas Gresham, I. 41; her dislike of Lady Mary Grey, 42; her visits to Hanworth Park, 69, 70; her promise to Henry Carey, 150; her residence at Hampton Court; her Maids of Honour; her style of living at Hampton, 152; portrait of, 167; supposed verses by, 168; her visits to Harefield, 244, 245; her visits to Enfield, 351, 353, 354; her palace at Enfield, 353, 354, 358, 360; her love of hunting, 364; at Theobalds, 377; at Epping, 433; at Scadbury, II. 81, 82; at Croydon, 149, 160, 164, 183, 236; her visits to the Carews at Beddington, 189, 190, 197, 236; at Nonsuch, 229, 234, 235, 236, 237, 238, 298; at Richmond, 335; her residence there, 336; her closing days; her death, 337; Essex's ring, 338; her habits at Richmond, 338, 339; her burial; discovery of some of her dresses, 339; the queen and Dr. Dee, 435; at Barn Elms, 459; at Wimbledon, 473; at Mitcham, 528

Ellenborough, Earl of, II. 465

Ellis, Alderman, Lord Mayor of London, I. 428

Ellis, Dr., superintendent of Hanwell Lunatic Asylum, I. 27

Ellis, Hon. Mrs., monument to, II. 287

Ellis, Welbore (afterwards Lord Mendip), I. 109

Elm Grove, Ealing, I. 23

Elmer's End, Beckenham, II. 100

Elstree, Middlesex, I. 284, 286, 297, 302, 303, 312; situation of the village, 302; etymology of Elstree; the manor and manor-house of Elstree Hall; St. Nicholas' parish church; burial-places of Martha Ray and William Weare; the Female Orphans' Home, 303; Elstree Hill House; Elstree reservoir; watercourses; pudding-stone, 304

Elsynge Hall, Enfield, I. 352, 359; its early history, 359, 360, 361

Elsynge manor, Enfield, I. 375

Eltham, Kent, II. 7, 8, 32, 34, 51

Elwes, John, the famous miser, I. 271, 449

Emfield Lodge, Southall, I. 216

Enfield, Middlesex; general description of the parish, I. 347, 348; situation and boundaries, 348; parochial divisions, 349; the town and principal streets; Enfield Court; the New River; Enfield Highway; Enfield Wash, 350; railway stations; census returns; historical reminiscences; the barony of Enfield; etymology; descent of the manor, 351; fairs and markets; site of the old manor-house; Camlet Moat; Oldbury, 352; Edward VI. at Enfield; the palace, 353, 354; Dr. Uvedale; the market-place, 355; St. Andrew's Church; its monuments, 356; brasses and epitaphs; the vicarage; the Free Grammar School; Schools of Industry; John Keats' schooldays; charitable institutions, 357; Old Park; Chase Park; Chase Side House; Enfield Green; Little Park; Beycullah Park; Enfield races; churches and chapels, 358; other churches; the cemetery; Forty Hall; Elsynge Hall, 359; Sir Walter Raleigh and Queen Elizabeth, 360; Anne, Countess of Pembroke; Myddelton House, 361; Gough Park; distinguished residents; beautiful women of Enfield, 363

Enfield Chase, I. 328, 347, 349; general description of a chase, 363; form and extent of Enfield Chase, 363, 364; its

early history; the last of the Staffords, Dukes of Buckingham; description of Enfield Chase in 1779; the Princess Elizabeth as a hunter; James I. at Enfield Chase, 364; a portion of the Chase added to Theobalds; seizure of the Chase by the Commonwealth; sale of portions of it; Macaulay's account of Enfield Chase; Evelyn's visit; the Chase re-stocked with deer by Charles II.; the Chase used as a sheep-walk, 365; punishment for cutting down and destroying trees in the Chase; its final enclosure, 366; officers belonging to the Chase; Camlet Moat, the supposed seat of the Chief Forester's Lodge; Trent Park, 367; Beech Hill Park; the East Lodge; Chase Lodge, Hill Lodge, and Claysmore; the Roman road; Cock Fosters, 368; dangers of the roads in former times; White Webbs House; the Gunpowder Plot, 369; the "King and the Tinker," 370, 371

Enfield Court; Colonel Somerset, I. 350

Enfield Green, I. 358

Enfield Highway, I. 349, 350, 351; position and extent; population; the Lower North Road, 371; Mr. Spencer and his bride; Matthew Prior and John Morley; St. James's Church; Ponder's End; St. Matthew's Church; Lincoln House, 372; Durants; Sir Thomas Wrothe, 373; the Manor of Suffolks; Enfield Wash, 374; the story of Elizabeth Canning, "Mother Wells," and the gipsy Squires; Roselands; Elsynge Manor; the River Lea, 375; Bull's Cross; Capels, 376

Enfield House, I. 353

Enfield Small-arms Factory, I. 351, 371; history of the rifle, 395; situation of the Small-arms Factory, 396; particulars of its establishment, 397, 398; extent of the buildings; perfection of the machinery, 399

Enfield Wash, I. 349, 350, 351, 359, 374

Epitaphs, Curious, I. 76, 248, 280, 357, II. 59, 107, 154, 155, 192, 202, 226, 251, 304, 404

Epping, Parish and town of, I. 422, 423

Epping Forest, I. 349; primeval condition of the forest, as the Great Forest of Essex, 423, 424; gradual diminution of the forest; forest charters of King John and Henry III., 424; laws for the regulation of the forest; a quaint oath; Lord Warden, Steward, and other officers of the forest; the Swainmote Court and Court of Justice Seat, 425; extent of the forest in the Middle Ages, 426; present form of the forest; disposal of the Crown rights in the forest; encroachments by lords of manors; the popular forest champions, 428; battle of the commoners with the lords of manors; Parliamentary scheme for the preservation of the forest; the matter taken up by the Corporation of London, 429; the case settled by arbitration; dedication of Epping Forest to the "free use" of the people, 430; the science of forestry; the deer of the forest, 431, 432; present condition and general appearance of the forest, 433, 434; situation and boundaries of Sewardstone; High Beech Green; St. Paul's Church, 435; Fairmead Lodge; Sotheby and Tennyson; residents at High Beech; Fairmead House; John Clare, the poet; High Beech Hill; the "Robin Hood" and "King's Oak"; "Harold's Oak," 436; Queen Victoria's Wood; Lappitt's Hill; Bury Wood and Hawk Wood; Chingford, 437; its etymology; extent and boundaries; manor of Chingford St. Paul, 438; manor of Chingford Earls; Friday Hill; Buckrills; a singular tenure, 439; census returns;

Chingford old church; the Ordnance Survey obelisk; Queen Elizabeth's lodge, 440; the "Royal Forest Hotel"; Connaught Water; recent improvements in the forest, 441; Connaught Water and other lakes; Buckhurst Hill; its etymology; census returns; the railway station; St. John's Church; the Congregational church; Langford Place; Essex Naturalists' and Field Club, 442; the Epping Hunt, 443—446; the "Bald-faced Stag," 446; the "Roebuck"; Loughton; its situation; census returns; descent of the manor; the Hall; St. Nicholas' Church; brasses, 447; St. John's Church; Staple Hill; the "lopping" process; discovery of an ancient earthwork; Loughton Camp, 448; Debden Hall; Theydon Bois, 449

Epping Hunt, The, I. 432, 435, 436, 495; account of the hunt of 1826, 443—445; adventures of a Mr. Huggins, 445, 446

Epsom, Surrey; situation of the town; railway communication; etymology of its name; Ebba, a Saxon queen, II. 242; mention of the parish in "Domesday Book"; descent of the manor; the manors of Horton and Bretgrave; the medicinal spring of Epsom; Epsom salts; the town becomes a fashionable resort; postal communication in the seventeenth century, 243; improvement at the Wells; public breakfasts and amusements, 244; Epsom society at the beginning of the last century, 244, 245; watering-places in and near London in the seventeenth century, 246; discovery of the mineral waters at Epsom; the properties of the waters; the rise of Epsom from an obscure village to a fashionable watering-place, 247; Epsom in the time of Charles II.; a royal visit; Lady Castlemaine, 248; Epsom in the reign of Queen Anne; decline of Epsom's popularity; the saline waters, 249; Mrs. Mapp, the bone-setter; description of the town of Epsom, 250; the inns and hotels; the court-house and other public buildings; the assembly rooms; the parish church; its monuments, 251; other churches and chapels; almshouses; Royal Medical Benevolent College, 252; Pit Place, 253; Lord Lyttelton's ghost, 253—255; Horton Place, 255, 256; Woodcote House, 256; Woodcote Park; Ashtead, 257; Durdans, 257, 259

Epsom races; the popularity of the "Derby"; a description of Mr. Frith's picture of "Derby Day," 260; the Grand Stand; the company on the Downs; the race, 261; scenes and humours of the course and the road between London and Epsom, 261, 262; origin of the term "Blue Riband" of the turf, 262; early history of horse-racing; introduction of racing on Banstead Downs, 263; popularity of racing, 264; institution of the "Derby" and "Oaks" stakes, 264, 265; the races patronised by royalty; list of winning horses since 1830; Derby anecdotes, 265, 266; Count La Grange and Gladiateur; Bend Or; Eclipse; Charles Greville's character of Epsom races, 266; silence of English poets with respect to horse-racing, 267; retrospective view of the Derby, 267, 268; plunging; the races and electric telegraphy, 268; successful jockeys, 269; Martin F. Tupper on Epsom Downs, 270, 271

Epsom salts, II. 243, 246, 247

Erith, Kent; its situation, and derivation of its name; descent of the manor; a Saxon law-suit, II. 41; St. John's Church; its monuments, 42, 43; the town, 43; census returns; chapels and schools ; Erith formerly a maritime port ; historical incidents ; the pier and public gardens, 44 ; discoveries of geological remains ; Erith marshes ; powder magazines ; explosion of a magazine ; Belvedere, 45 ; owners of the mansion ; the Royal Alfred Institution for Aged Merchant Seamen ; the village of Belvedere, 46 ; All Saints' Church ; Abbey Wood ; Lesnes Abbey, 47 ; some account of the abbey, 48, 49 ; Bostall Heath, 50

Erith Marshes, II. 45

Ermine Street, Roman road, Enfield, I. 368, 371, 385, II. 152

Esher, Surrey ; its situation and etymology ; the railway station, II. 285 ; the manor of Sandon, now called Sandown ; Sandon Hospital or Priory ; Sandown racecourse ; the " Travellers' Rest" ; Anna Maria and Jane Porter, 286 ; the old parish church ; Christ Church ; Esher Place ; Wolsey's Tower, 287 ; its historical associations, 288 ; the fall of Wolsey, 289, 290 ; descent of the manor of Esher ; the Right Hon. Henry Pelham ; demolition of the mansion and its re-erection, 291

Esher Place, Surrey, II. 287, 288, 291, 292

Essex, Earl of, II. 236, 237, 321, 452

Essex Field and Naturalists' Club, I. 442, 448

Etloe House, Leyton, I. 485

Evans, Dr., an historian of Richmond, II. 363, 376, 380, 384

Ewell, Surrey ; situation and boundaries of the parish ; the " Spring " inn ; the Hog's-Mill, or Ewell River ; the road from Cheam to Ewell ; description of the village ; sheep fair, II. 239 ; railway stations ; population ; manufactories ; roads in the neighbourhood ; Roman remains ; descent of the manor, 240 ; the parish church ; monuments and brasses, 241 ; extract from the parish register ; Ewell Castle ; Diana's Dyke ; eminent residents, 242

Exe, The river, I. 177, 185

F

Fairfax, General, robbed by a highwaywoman, I. 65

Fairfax House, Chiswick ; relics of Hogarth, I. 5

Fairfield, Kingston, II. 312, 314

Fairlop Fair, I. 492, 494, 495

Fairlop Oak, The, I. 433, 492—495 ; Daniel Day, 492—494 ; objects made from it, 494 ; its size, 495.

Fairmead Plain, Epping Forest ; William Sotheby, poet ; Fairmead House ; John Clare, poet, I. 436, 437, 442

Fairy Hill, Mottingham, Kent ; singular incident, II. 95

Farley, or Farleigh, Surrey ; its etymology, II. 146 ; the manor ; the church ; Farley Court, 147

Farmer, the historian, I. 404, 406, 407

Farnaby family, The, II. 124, 125

Farnborough, Kent ; its situation, II. 116 ; etymology ; vegetable productions ; the " Woodman " tavern ; early history ; Farnborough Hall ; Tubbendens, 118 ; descent of the property ; St. Giles' Church ; tablets ; population ; Greenstreet Green and Knockholt Beeches, 118

Farnborough, Lord, II. 88, 93, 94, 117

Fellowes, Sir John, II. 202, 203.

Feltham ; population of the parish ; the early manor ; the parish church, I. 172 ; Ryland, the engraver ; Miss Kelly, the actress ; the Middlesex Industrial School or Reformatory ; the convalescent home ; the nunnery, 173

Fenton, the poet, I. 97

Ferrers, Earl, I. 93 ; his coach, 14

Field, George, art critic, I. 60

Fielding, Beau, II. 237

Fielding, Henry, the novelist, reminiscence of, I. 23, 139, 140, his Twickenham residence ; spelling of his name, 93

Finchley, Middlesex, I. 280 ; situation and extent ; descent of the manor ; the old manor-house ; noted residents ; Church End ; population, I. 338 ; races ; St. Mary's Church ; monuments and brasses ; rectors ; Major Cartwright, political reformer ; Christ's College ; East End hamlet ; churches and chapels, 339 ; the " Old White Lion" public-house or " Dirt House" ; Marylebone, St. Pancras, and Islington cemeteries ; churches and chapels ; Finchley Common ; its extent ; encampments and reviews, 340 ; highwaymen ; "Turpin's Oak" ; the " Green Man " tavern ; capture of Jack Sheppard ; the life of a highwayman, 341

Firs, The, Woodford, I. 464

Fitzhardinge-Berkeley, Hon. Thos. Moreton, I. 197

Fitzwilliam House, Richmond, II. 363 ; Sir Matthew Decker ; Lord Fitzwilliam, 364

Flambards manor-house, Harrow, Middlesex, I. 254

Flaxman, the sculptor, I. 279, 485, II. 154, 251, 287

Flora of Epping Forest, I. 431, 432

Flower, Alderman Sir Charles, I. 281

Flowerpot Gate, Hampton Court Palace, I. 168

Foley, the sculptor, I. 358

Football, Playing of, on Shrove Tuesday, at Twickenham, I. 79

Foote, the comedian, I. 139, 141

Foot's Cray, Kent, II. 54, 55, 56, 82, 101 ; All Saints' Church ; brasses and monuments ; Foot's Cray Place ; the Vansittart family, 62 ; origin of the name, 63

Ford Hall, Ealing, I. 21

Ford, Mr., the historian of Enfield, I. 346, 349, 351, 352, 353, 358, 360, 362, 363, 365, 369, 370, 372

Fordhook House, Ealing, I. 23

Forest Gate ; taverns and tea-gardens ; churches, I. 505

Forest of Surrey, Former great, II. 153

Forrest, Mr., designer of garden improvements at Sion House and Frogmore, I. 55, 56

Fortescue House, Twickenham, I. 77, 80

Forty Hall, Enfield ; the manor-house of Worcesters, I. 349, 359, 360, 361

Forty Hill, Enfield, I. 349, 350, 351, 359, 361

Fountain Court, The, Hampton Court Palace, I. 164

" Four Swans Inn," The, Waltham Cross, I. 393

Fox, Charles James, I. 184, II. 488

Fox Grove, Beckenham, II. 101, 106

Fox Hall, Enfield, I. 350

Frayswater, The River, I. 233

Freake, Sir Charles, I. 77

Free Grammar School, Kingston ; early history of St. Mary's Chapel, II. 310, 311 ; eminent persons educated here, 311, 312

Freeman, the historian, II. 149

Frere, John Hookham, II. 215

Frere, Sir Bartle, II. 489

Friar's (or Prior's) Place Farm, Acton, I. 9, 14, 16

Friern Barnet, Middlesex, I. 329, 330, 335, 337, 342 ; the manor ; its descent, 336 ; St. James's Church, 337 ; almshouses ; the new church, 338

Frith, the artist, II. 260

Frognal Manor, Chislehurst, II. 80, 81, 82

Frowkyes, The family of the, I. 317, 338

Fuller, Dr. Thomas, the historian, I. 197, 329, 373, 403, 406, 410, 412, 413, II. 152, 168, 178, 199, 245, 246, 334, 335, 430, 478

Fust, Sir Herbert Jenner, II. 80

Fynes-Clinton, Mr. H., story of his greatgreat-grandfather, I. 237

G

Gade, The river, I. 233

Gainsborough, the painter, I. 458, II. 400—404

Gale, the antiquarian, I. 275, II. 152, 495

Galley Hill, Waltham, I. 417

Galley Wood, Waltham, I. 417

Gardens, The, Hampton Court Palace, I. 168 ; the vine, 170

Garrick, David, actor, I. 36, 137, 278, II. 360, 361, 363 ; his early career and marriage, I. 137 ; the jubilee of Shakespeare ; his death, 138 ; anecdotes of, 138—140 ; his widow, 137, 138, 140 ; lines by Garrick, 137—139 ; his nephew, 134

Garrick's Villa, Hampton, I. 136 ; its preservation intact, 140, 141

Garrow, Dr., the historian of Surrey, II. 153, 178

Garth, the physician, I. 96, 97, II. 292

Garth family, The, II. 513, 514

Gay, the poet, I. 34, 97, 100, II. 267, 302, 317, 323, 373, 383, 384

Gay's Summer-house, Ham ; Dr. Charles Mackay on, II. 327, 328

Gaynesford family, The, II. 202, 203

George I., I. 156, 168

George II., I. 14, 156 ; his fondness for Kew and Brentford, 32 ; anecdotes of, II. 344, 345, 390, 391

George III., Anecdotes of, I. 17, 39, 135, 168, II. 341, 393, 394, 400, 404, 405 ; his early seclusion, II. 391 ; death of his grandfather, 392 ; his long residence at Kew, 392 ; his insanity, 393

George IV., Education of, II. 398

" George " inn, Wanstead, I. 480 ; the cherry pie, 481

" George " inn, Uxbridge, I. 232

George Lane, Woodford, I. 459

Geraldine, "The fair," I. 149, 150, 162, 167

Gibbets, The, on Hounslow Heath, I. 65, 66

Gibbon, the historian, II. 105, 312

Gibbons, Grinling, the sculptor, I. 479, 498, II. 257

Gibbs, Sir Vicary, II. 107, 110

Gibbs, Mr., of Aldenham House, Middlesex, I. 303, 309, 310

Gibbons, Sir John, I. 194

Gifford, William, the editor, II. 437

Gifford, Lord, II. 467

Gill's Hill, Radlett, I. 303, 311

Gilpin, the author of " Forest Scenery," I. 495, 498, II. 229, 433

Gilpin's (John) ride, I. 347, 384

Gilray, the caricaturist, II. 498

Gipsies, Queen of the, II. 101

Girtin, the artist, II. 9, 10

Gladsmore Heath, I. 325 ; the battle of Barnet, 328

Glyn, The family of, I. 299

Godolphin, Mrs. Margaret, I. 93

Goff's Lane, Cheshunt, I. 386

Goff's Oak, I. 386, 393, 394 ; the " Green Man " inn, 394

Golder's Green, Hendon, Middlesex ; the " White Swan," I. 280

Golding's Hill, Loughton, I. 447

Goldsmid, Mr. Abraham, financier, II. 514

Goldsmith, the poet, I. 34, II. 245, 276, 305, 358, 383

Golf, the game of, II. 482, 483

Goodenough House, Ealing, I. 22

Gordon House, Isleworth, II. 60

Gothic House, Wimbledon ; its residents, II. 485

Gough, the antiquarian, I. 288, 300, 348, 356, 361, 362, 372, 385, 393, 418, 484, II. 75, 470,

Gough Park, Enfield, I. 362

Graham, Sir Robert, Exchequer Baron, II. 306
Grammar School, Barnet; its history, I. 321, 322; Charles Dickens on, 322
Grammont, Count de, II. 461
Grand Junction Canal, I. 24, 29, 36, 206, 208, 215, 217, 230, 233, 243, 244, 248
Grand Stand, Epsom, II. 260, 261
Gray, the poet, II. 250
Grays, The family of the, Wembley, Middlesex, I. 274
"Great Eastern" steam-ship, The, I. 544—546
Great Eastern Railway, I. 351, 371, 384, 404, 442, 447, 459, 485, 488, 507, 508
Great Hall, Hampton Court Palace, I. 154, 161—164; theatrical entertainments held in, 163, 164
Great Ilford, I. 496
Great Northern Cemetery, I. 345
Great Northern Railway, I. 286, 316, 320, 329, 335, 346, 351, 358, 394, 395
Great Stanmore, Middlesex; Brockley Hill, the supposed Roman Sulloniacæ; discovery of Roman antiquities; the great forest of Middlesex; "Domesday" notices of Stanmore, I. 297; descent of the manor; the village; Stanmore Hill; population; the Bernays Memorial Institute; St. John the Evangelist's Church, 298; tablets and memorials; Stanmore Park; its different owners; Bentley Priory, 299; its subsequent history, 300; Lord Abercorn owns the priory; then the property of the Marquis of Abercorn; then leased by Queen Adelaide; then purchased by Sir John Kelk, 301; Stanmore Hall and other residences; the Bowling Green, 302
Green, Matthew, the poet, II. 350
Greenfield Common, Laleham; supposed Roman camp near, I. 182
Greenford, Middlesex; various names given to the place, I. 218; its etymology; the old manor; the parish church; the chancel, 219; monuments and inscriptions; its rectors; Greenford Green, 220
Greenford Magna, I. 218, 219, 220
Greenford Parva, I. 218, 220, 221
Greenhill, Middlesex, I. 271
Gresham, Sir Thomas, and Osterley Park, I. 41
Grey, Lady Mary, sister of Lady Jane, I. 42; her imprisonment in Osterley Park, ib.
Grime's Dyke, Harrow Weald, I. 270
Grindal, Archbishop, II. 154, 165
Grote, the historian of Greece, II. 104
Grottoes, Addison on, I. 107
Grove House, Chiswick, I. 5
Grove House, Woodford, I. 464
Grove Park, Chiswick, I. 7, 16
Guard Chamber, Hampton Court Palace, I. 165
Guido, the painter, I. 477
Guilford, Countess of, II. 485
Gumley House, Isleworth, I. 58
Gumley, the glass manufacturer of Isleworth; marriage of his daughter to the Earl of Bath, I. 58
Gunnersbury, I. 7, 17, 20; its former residents, 17; geological excavations made at, 32
Gunnersbury Park, I. 17; its distinguished residents, 17, 18; pictures in, 18
Gunning, General; the "Gunning beauties," I. 93
Gunnings, The Miss, I. 93, 166
Gunpowder mills, Hounslow; explosions of the, I. 68
Gustavus IV. of Sweden at Hampton Court, I. 157
Gwydir, Lord, II. 100, 101, 104, 106, 181

H

Hacket, Bishop of Lincoln, formerly rector of Cheam, II. 222, 225, 227

Hackman, Rev. James, I. 303
Hadley, Middlesex, I. 320; etymology; descent of the manor, 327; Hadley Green; the village and common; Hadley Wood; Gladsmore Heath, or Monken Mead; Dead Man's Bottom; St. Mary's Church, Hadley, 328; two historic trees; the Priory; almshouses; noted residents; population, 329
Hadley Common, Barnet, I. 349, 366; the Battle of Barnet, 319
Hadley Green, Middlesex, I. 316, 327, 328
Hainault Forest, I. 349, 423, 424, 426, 427, 433, 450, 457; its situation, boundaries, and extent, 489; etymology; its ownership by the Abbey of Barking; it passes to the Crown; its subsequent disposal; disafforested; the hamlet of Barking Side; census returns, 490; Holy Trinity Church; Dr. Barnardo's Homes for Friendless Children; the "Maypole" inn, 491; the Fairlop Oak and Fairlop Fair, 491, 492, 493, 494, 495
Hale End, Walthamstow, I. 465
Hale, Sir Matthew, I. 11, 12, 13, 15
Hales, Dr. Stephen, incumbent of Teddington; Pope's friendship for, I. 128
Halfway Street, Bexley, II. 50, 51, 54
Haling, Croydon, II. 152, 173, 179; distinguished residents at Haling House, 179
Hall, Mr. S. C., the author, II. 286
Hall Place, Bexley, II. 51, 56
Hall, The, Loughton, I. 447
Hall Ville, Plaistow, I. 510
Hallam, Henry, the historian, II. 110
Hallam, Mrs. Anne, actress, II. 528
Hallet, the cabinet-maker, and purchaser of Canons estate, I. 294
Halliday, Sir Andrew, physician, I. 141
Halliford, Middlesex, I. 176
Ham, Surrey; situation, II. 316; boundaries of Ham-with-Hatch; etymology; descent of the manor; Anne of Cleves; John Maitland, Earl of Lauderdale, and Lady Dysart; Ham House; Leigh Hunt's description, 317; the avenue of elms; Tennyson's lines, 318; situation of the house; Sir Thomas Vavasour, its builder, 319; its successive owners; Lady Dysart, afterwards Duchess of Lauderdale; the "Cabal" Ministry, 320; interior of the house, 320, 321; members of the "Cabal," 321; death of the Duchess of Lauderdale; the Duke of Argyll and Greenwich; the gardens and grounds; Horace Walpole's description of a visit, 322; Queen Charlotte's impression of the mansion; Lady Dysart, Bishop Blomfield, and the Duke of Clarence; Ham Walks, 323; the village and church; Ham Common and the National Orphan Home, 324
Ham House, II. 317; the avenue of elms; the red-brick mansion, 318; said to be built for Henry, Prince of Wales, 319; its successive owners, 320; interior of the mansion, 320, 321; Queen Charlotte's impressions of the house, 323
Hamilton, Duchess of, I. 93, 166
Hamilton, Lady, and Lord Nelson, II. 519—524
Hammersmith Suspension Bridge, II. 457
Hammersmith turnpike trust, Value of the, I. 29
Hampton, I. 132; early mention of the place; Cardinal Wolsey's lease of the place for Hampton Court; extent of the manor; the parish church, 133; eminent persons buried here; its parochial charities, 134; its inns and tavern signs, 134, 135; Hampton races; bridge across the Thames; incident of a royal visit; the Thames Angling Preservation Society, 135; the water supply from the Thames, 136; quantity taken from the river daily; New Hampton; its churches; vicars of

Hampton; Garrick's villa; Hampton House, 136; Angelo on Garrick's villa; early days of Garrick, 137; his wife, 138; a Shakespearian jubilee; death of Garrick; epigrams on him, 138; anecdotes of Garrick, 138—140; his widow; present state of Garrick's villa, 140; Sir Christopher Wren; other residents at Hampton; Sir Richard Steele, 141; Hampton Wick; Edward Wortley Montagu, 142
Hampton Court Palace; Cardinal Wolsey's choice of a residence at, I. 142; original copy of his lease, 142, 143; rebuilding the manor-house; little of Wolsey's building now remains, 143; the ancient building; curious items of the wages of the workmen employed; number of persons kept at Hampton by Wolsey, 144; some account of Wolsey, 144, 145; his rapid advancement, 145; his pomp and style of living; Dr. Johnson's character of Wolsey; the young Lord Percy and Anne Boleyn, 146; Anne Boleyn's dislike of Wolsey; Hampton Court "presented" to the king; incident of Wolsey's wealth; Wolsey's occasional residence at Hampton Court, 147; account of his feast here to the French ambassadors, 147—149; Mr. Howitt on Wolsey; Henry VIII.'s residence at Hampton Court for the rest of his life; Edward VI.'s residence here, 149; the "fair Geraldine," 149, 150; Henry Carey and a woman's promise, 150, 151; Mary and Philip reside here; the Princess Elizabeth and the Duke of Savoy, 151; Mary's death, 151, 152; Queen Elizabeth keeps Christmas at Hampton; her "Maids of Honour"; her style of living at Hampton Court, 152; James I. at home here, 153; remarkable events transacted here; Charles I.'s residence here, 153; Oliver Cromwell's behaviour here, 153, 154; Charles II. and Catharine of Braganza, 154, 155; James II. at Hampton Court; William III. and Queen Mary's residence; the king's death, 155; Queen Anne's occupation of the palace; George I. and II. dislike the palace, 156; Miss Chudleigh; Dr. Johnson's request for a residence at Hampton Court; the Prince of Orange's abode here; other residents at the palace, 157; early reminiscences of the palace, 158; description of the building; the principal entrance; Wolsey's courts, 159; the Clock Tower Court, 160; a curious time-piece, 160, 161; the Great Hall, 161—163; the tapestry, 163; theatrical entertainments given in the hall, 163, 164; the Withdrawing room; the Kitchen Court; the Fountain Court, 164; the chapel, 164, 165; the State apartments, 165; the "Beauty" Room; the Tapestry Gallery, 166; the cartoons of Raffaele, 167; the gardens, 168; the vine; the Wilderness and maze; the Home Park; the Royal Stud-house, 170; narrow escape of the palace, 171
Hampton Court and East Moulsey, Bridge connecting; incident of a stag-hunt at, I. 135; the railway station, II. 281
Hampton Green, I. 141
Hampton House, afterwards Garrick's villa, I. 136; its preservation, 140, 141; statue of Shakespeare in the garden, 137, 140
Hampton race-course, I. 135
Hampton Wick, I. 142, 170; the parish church, 142
Handel, the composer, and the "Harmonious Blacksmith," I. 284, 285, 296
Hanger Lane, Ealing, I. 21
Hanger Vale, Ealing, I. 21

Hanging Wood, Woolwich; robberies here in former times, II. 11

Hanway, Jonas, I. 25, 26, II. 310

Hanwell; its situation, I. 20, 23, 24; the parish church, 24; Jonas Hanway's tomb, 25; the charitable institutions, 26; lunatic asylum, 26, 27, 28; the electric telegraph in its infancy, 28

Hanworth, I. 69; the church, 70

Hanworth Park; Katharine Parr a resident here; episode of the Princess Elizabeth here, I. 69; Queen Elizabeth visits and hunts here; its change of owners; the present mansion; the books and MSS. of Mr. Henry Perkins; its present owner, 70

Hardinge, Mr. Justice, I. 87

Hardwicke, Lord Chancellor, II. 203, 514

Harefield, Middlesex; its situation and extent; its early history; descent of the manor; Queen Elizabeth's visit, I. 244; Lord Keeper Egerton and the Countess of Derby; the house burnt down; Sir Charles Sedley; the Newdigate family, 245; Milton's mention of Harefield, 246; Moor Hall; the parish church, 247; monuments and epitaphs; the neighbourhood of Harefield, 248

Harefield Place, Middlesex, I. 245, 246, 248

Harlesden, Middlesex; All Souls' Church; Harlesden House, I. 225

Harlington, Middlesex; its situation and population; ancient spelling of the name, I. 198; descent of the manor; the parish church, 199; its rectors; tombs and monuments; the Easter sepulchre; the old yew-tree and its clippings, 200; charities of the parish; Dawley Court and its successive owners; Lord Bolingbroke, 201; some poetical glimpses of the place; some account of Bolingbroke, 202; changes at Dawley; the building pulled down; "The Moats" grange, 203

Harlow, the sign-painter, II. 251

Harmondsworth, Middlesex; situation and nature of the soil; old religious houses here; descent of the manor; the old barn, I. 203; the parish church; the village and its population; the supposed Roman encampment; Sipson or Shepiston hamlet; Longford hamlet, 204

"Harold's Oak," Harrow, High Beech Hill, I. 436

Harold's Park, Waltham, I. 407, 417

Harrington, Earls of, II. 325, 329

Harris, Mr. Thomas, of Covent Garden Theatre, I. 236

Harris, the historian of Kent, II. 8

Harris, Rev. Dr., II. 252

Harrow, Middlesex; its situation, and nature of the soil; Norden's account of the parish, I. 249; the manor-house unknown, 252; early history of Harrow; the present manor-house of "Heggeton," or Headstone; etymology of Harrow, 253; origin and descent of the manor; Lord Northwick; extent of the old parish of Harrow; Charles Lamb's visits to Harrow, 254; the parish church; Archbishop Lanfranc's building, 255; view from the church tower; Byron's tomb; restoration of the church, 256; tombs and monumental inscriptions; old rectors of Harrow; Prior Bolton takes refuge in the church, 257; town and public institutions of Harrow, 258; the principal street, 259; founding of the school by John Lyon; extract from the founder's will; orders, statutes, and rules for the government of the school; forms and divisions; numbers educated at the school, 260; cost of board and education; prizes and scholarships; description of the school buildings, 261; athletic sports and recreations; lines in honour of Lyon, the founder, 262; the practice of archery, 263; shooting for the silver arrow, 264—266; head

masters and distinguished Harrovians, 266—269

Harrow, Church of; some account of, 255; view from the spire; Byron's tomb; restoration of the church, 256; tombs, monuments, and brasses in; old rectors of the parish, 257; burial of Dancer, the miser, 272

Harrow Hill, Middlesex, I. 269

Harrow Park, Middlesex, I. 254

Harrow Weald, I. 254, 270, 271, 272; the great forest of Middlesex; Grime's Dyke, 270; Daniel Dancer, the miser, 271, 272

Harsnett, Archbishop, of York, I. 452; his schools at Chigwell, 452, 453

Hart, the tragedian, I. 299

Harts, Woodford; its various owners, I. 463

Hartsbourne Manor-house, Bushey, I. 307

Hasted, the Kentish topographer, II. 7, 49, 54, 58, 75, 107, 111, 117

"Hat," the hatter's sign, I. 23

Hatton, Middlesex, I. 196

Hawkins, Sir John, I. 92, 93, 559, 56

Hawk Wood, Epping Forest, I. 437

Hawkesworth, Dr., of Bromley, II. 84

Hawksmoor, Nicholas, architect, I. 313, 314, 537

Hawtrey family, The, Ruislip, Middlesex, I. 242, 243, II. 141

Hayes, Middlesex; population and history; early mention of the place; its probable Saxon etymology; extent of the manor in "Domesday," I. 208; early mention of the church; descent of the manor; old mansions formerly in the parish, 209; old manors in the neighbourhood of Hayes, 210; the parish church, 210, 211; its walls, doorways, nave, pulpit, muniment chest, and chancel, 211; monuments; the parish registers; the rectory house and gardens; former rectors, 213; educational arrangements of the parish; the Tithe Commutation Act; the Hayes registers, 214

Hayes End, Middlesex, I. 210

Hayes, Kent, II. 89, 97; its situation and rural appearance; etymology, 106; the parish church; brasses and monuments; curious epitaph; discovery of Roman remains; charitable bequests; the "George" inn; Hayes Place, 107; Lord Chatham, 107—110; Hayes Common; Sir Vicary Gibbs; Baston House, 110

Hayes Common, Kent; old mansion of Baston, 110, 111

Hayes Place, Kent; Lord Chatham's residence, II. 107, 108; its historical associations, 109, 110; other owners, 109

Hayley, the poet, II. 312

Hayter, the painter, II. 294

Head, Sir Francis, II. 141, 178, 181

Head masters of Harrow School, Celebrated, I. 261

Headstone, or "Heggetone," Pinner, I. 251

Hearne, Thomas, antiquarian, I. 306

Heath, Dr., head master of Harrow School, I. 263, 266, 267

Heathfield, Lord, I. 5, 22

Heath Lane Lodge, Twickenham, I. 93

Heath Row, Harmondsworth, I. 203, 204

Heidegger, John James, Master of the Revels, II. 365, 368, 459, 460

Helps, Sir Arthur, II. 178, 407

Hendon, Middlesex, I. 29, 274, 284; extent and boundaries of the parish, 277, 278; the river Brent and Silk stream; etymology of Hendon; descent of the manor; immunity from tolls, 278; the manor-house; Hendon Place; the parish church; tombs and monuments, 279; curious epitaph; the churchyard; the vicarage; almshouses; Brent Street; Golder's Green; Page Street; Copt Hall, 280; the Nonconformist Gram-

mar School; Roman Catholic institutions at Mill-Hill, 281; St. Paul's Church; Littleberries, 282; account of, 282, 283; Highwood Hill; distinguished residents, 283, 284

Henri Grace de Dieu, The, II. 15, 44

Henry III., I. 14

Henry VIII., Extravagance of, in building palaces, II. 233

Henry VIII. and Hampton Court Palace, I. 143, 164; Wolsey's "present" of the palace to the king, 147; the king's residence here; his wives, 149

Henry, Prince, son of James I., II. 339

Hentzner, Paul, the German traveller, I. 164, 165, 382, II. 231, 232, 338

Herbert, George, I. 464

Herbert, Lord, I. 262, 269

Herbert Hospital, Woolwich Common, II. 33

Herbert family, Monuments to the, I. 279

Herring, Archbishop, II. 154, 156, 160, 164

Hervey (Earl of Bristol), Mr., I. 157

Hervey, Lady Lepel, I. 96, 152, II. 388

Heston, Middlesex, I. 23, 41; the parish church, 43; early history of the parish; eminent residents of, 44

Hetherington, Rev. William, donor to the blind, II. 59

Heywood, the poet, II. 263

Hickes family, The, I. 485, 486

Hickes-on-the-Heath, Ealing, I. 23

High Barnet, Middlesex, I. 39; its extent; etymology; the manor; general appearance of the town; population; the market and fair; St. John the Baptist's Church, 320; the Grammar School; some account of the school, 321; the old "Crown" inn; Jesus Hospital; almshouses and charitable institutions, 322; the Town Hall; barracks; chapels and meeting-houses; Ravenscroft Park; the "Physic Well"; historical associations, 323; inns and taverns, 324; the battle of Barnet, 325, 326; the obelisk, 327

High Beech, I. 417; High Beech Green; St. Paul's Church, 435

High Beech Hill, now called "Queen Victoria's Wood"; the "Robin Hood" and "King's Oak" inns, I. 436

High Beech Park; Walsgrove House; Alder Grove Lodge, I. 436

High Bridge, The, Uxbridge, I. 233

High Canons, Middlesex, I. 314

High Grove, Ruislip, Middlesex, I. 243

Higham End, Walthamstow, I. 465, 470

Highams, Walthamstow, I. 466

Highwaymen, Danger from, I. 30, 65, 66, 123, 423, II. 34; some celebrated highwaymen, I. 67, 68, 341, II. 316, 490

Highwood Hill, Hendon, I. 278, 280, 283, 332; eminent residents here, 283; Baroness Bunsen's account of, 283, 284

Hillingdon, I. 207, 208, 210, 226; its etymology; Hillingdon Heath; Dawley Court; the manor of Colham, 227; the church; its monuments, 228; tomb of Rich, the actor; the parish registers; Thomas Boston, the vicar; burial of Bishop Juxon; a curious engraving, 229; doles of beef given away; situation and population of the village; the "Red Lion" inn; flight of Charles I. from Oxford; Hillingdon End, 230

Hillingdon End, Middlesex, I. 230, 233

Hillingdon House, Uxbridge, I. 236

Hind, Mr. J. R., the astronomer, I. 83

Hinton, Rev. Edward, II. 513

Hither Green, Kent, II. 95; Hither Green Lane, 97

Hoare, Mr. Henry, II. 528

Hoare family, The, II. 452, 462

Hoe Street, Walthamstow, I. 465, 470, 484

Hofland, Mrs., authoress, II. 368

Hogarth, I. 5, 292, 340

Hog's-Mill, or Ewell River, II. 239, 272, 509

Holbein, the painter, I. 167, II. 71, 190, 231, 237
Holdernesse, Earl of, I. 60, 287
Holinshed, the chronicler, II. 343, 359, 472
Holland, the actor, I. 141
Hollar, the artist, II. 340
Holles, Thomas Pelham, Earl of Clare and Duke of Newcastle, and Esher Place, the builder of Claremont, II. 291
Hollond, Mr. R., the aëronaut, I. 299
Holwell, Mr. John Zephaniah, of Pinner, I. 251
Holwood Hill, Keston, Kent, Roman entrenchment near, II. 111
Holwood House, Keston, II. 112, 113, 114; its owners and historical associations, 112, 113
Home Park, Hampton Court Palace, I. 168, 170
Hone, Quotations from, II. 111, 113, 136, 209, 218, 226, 239, 263, 390
Hood, Thomas, the poet, I. 185, 195, 479
Hook, Theodore, I. 243, 268, II. 278, 407, 455; his assurance, I. 245, II. 455
Hooker, Sir W. J., II. 423
Hooker, Sir J. D., II. 424
Hooker, Sir William, botanist, II. 399, 411, 416, 424
Hop gardens of Kent, Description of the, II. 66—68; a hop-picker's excursion, 69, 70
Hopkins, John, the usurer; "Vulture Hopkins," II. 482, 485
Horne, Bishop, the commentator, I. 238
"Horse and Well" inn, Woodford, I. 434, 464, 567
Horse-racing, Establishment of, II. 263
Horseshoe Pond, Gunnersbury House, I. 20
Horsington Hill and Wood, Middlesex, I. 220
Horticultural Society, Chiswick, I. 5; nursery of, 23
Horton Place, Epsom, II. 255; its successive owners, 256
Hostelries of Brentford, The, I. 34, 35
Houfnagle, View of Nonsuch Palace by, II. 232
Hounslow, I. 61, 62; other spellings; Holy Trinity Priory; martyrdom of Archbishop Scrope; weekly market, 61; remains of the conventual buildings; St. Mary's Church; traffic through the town in the old days; town hall and churches; Hounslow Heath, 62 (see Hounslow Heath); horse-racing on the heath; the gunpowder mills, 68; Wilkes' poetical productions, 68, 69; Whitton Park; Hanworth; episode in the life of Elizabeth, 69; the Duke of St. Albans owner of the property; Old and New Hanworth House; Hatton, 70
Hounslow Heath; extent of, I. 62, 63; Cobbett's opinion of its soil; military camps held here, 63; Charles II. and James II. encamped here, 63, 64; reviews of troops held here, 64; popularity of the camp, 65; the heath the highwaymen's ground, 65—68; the gibbets, 65, 66; Wilkes' poem of "Hounslow Heath," 197
Howard, Miss, Charitable bequest of, I. 250
Howard, John, the philanthropist, I. 362
Howbury, Crayford, Kent, II. 58
Howe, Baroness, her demolition of Pope's house, I. 110
Howitt, William and Mary, I. 149, 159, 167, 286, II. 275
Howley, Archbishop, II. 131, 132, 133, 134, 135
Hughson, the topographer, II. 55, 56, 57, 62
Hume, David, philosopher, I. 89
Hunt, Leigh, II. 217, 385, 490
Huntingdon, Lady, I. 388, 389
Hutton, Archbishop, II. 164
Hyde, The, Kingsbury, I. 274; Goldsmith's residence, 276

I

Ickenham; "The Chestnuts"; population of the village; the village green and pump; the parish church; descent of the manor, I. 238; Swakeleys; history of the estate; Pepys' visit; sale of the property, 239; a curious baptismal register; Crab, the English hermit, 240
Ilford, Essex; Chadwell Heath, I. 495; Chadwell Street; the old coach road; Great Ilford; census returns; etymology; the River Roding, 496; the "Rothings" or "Roodings"; the "Red Lion" and "Angel" inns; St. Mary's Church, Great Ilford; Ilford Hospital; Cranbrook Park; Valentines, 497; remarkable vine here; discovery of an ancient stone coffin, 498; elephants in Essex, 499, 500
Imber Court, Thames Ditton, II. 279, 280, 281, 286
Indian Civil Engineering College, Egham, I. 191
Infant Orphan Asylum, Snaresbrook, I. 472, 473
Inns at Hampton, I. 134, 135
Ireland, the historian of Kent, II. 38, 41, 54, 57, 66, 95, 100, 116, 117, 146
Ironside, Mr. Edward, the historian of Twickenham, I. 76, 82, 87
Isleworth, I. 29, 44; its various spellings; derivation of, 44; historical reminiscences; position of Isleworth; public house always open at, 56; history of the manor, 56, 57; the parish church; its monuments and brasses, 57; extracts from the parish register, 57, 58; its vicars; charitable bequests; residents of Isleworth; Gumley House; Shrewsbury Place, 58; Kendal House, 58, 59; Lucy House, 59
Isleworth House, Richmond Road, I. 60

J

Jacket's Court, North Cray, II. 60
Jack Sheppard, I. 224, 341
James I., his residence at Hampton Court, I. 152, 153; his entry into London, 351; at Enfield Chase, 364; at Theobalds, 365, 378, 379; he exchanges it with Hatfield, 380; his death at Theobalds, 381; his visit to Nonsuch, II. 237; at Wimbledon, 473
James II. I. 155, II. 340
Janssen, Sir Theodore, II. 476
Jebb, Sir Richard, George III.'s physician, I. 368
Jeffreys, Judge, I. 14
Jenkins, Rev. H., antiquarian, I. 31
Jerdan, Mr. William, I. 307
Jerrold, Douglas, II. 455
Jersey, Earl of, I. 43, 215
Jesse, Mr., I. 144, 166, II. 196, 201, 353, 377, 430
Jessel, Sir George, Master of the Rolls, II. 409
Jesus Hospital, Barnet, I. 321, 322
Jewish cemetery, Willesden Lane, I. 225
John, King, and Magna Charta, I. 191
Johnson, Dr., I. 22, 34, 105, 107, 137, 140, 329, II. 84, 128, 177, 310, 386, 462, 525, 528; his opinion of Pope, 103; his character of Cardinal Wolsey, 146; his application for apartments in Hampton Court, 157; grave of his wife, II. 84, 87, 88
Johnston, Sir Alexander, husband of Hon. Mrs. Damer, the sculptress, I. 90
Johnstone, Secretary, I. 81; Pope's attack on, 75, 87; vine cultivation by, 87
Jones, Sir William, linguist, I. 261, 267
Jones, Inigo, I. 20, 53, 92, 189, 315, 347, 359
Jordan, Mrs., II. 350, 360, 383
Juxon, Archbishop, I. 229, II. 149, 157, 159, 161, 164, 350

K

Kean, Edmund, the actor, II. 360—363, 368; his last performance, 362; his parentage, 361, 362
Keats, the poet, I. 357
Kelk, Sir John, of Bentley Priory, I. 298
Kelly, Miss, the actress, I. 173
Kelsey Park, Beckenham, II. 106
Kemp, Will; his dance from London to Norwich, I. 496
Kempe, the antiquary, II. 116
Kempton Park, Feltham; the race-course, I. 175
Kempton House, Feltham, I. 175
Kendal House, Isleworth; story of the Duchess of Kendal, I. 58; a breakfast announcement; popularity of the place; perspective view of the house in the British Museum, 59
Kennedy, Sir John, II. 462, 463
Kent, Duke of, I. 22, 170
Kent, Duchess of, II. 293, 295
Kent, the painter, II. 477
Kent, the gardener, II. 287, 291, 292
Kenton, Middlesex, I. 277
Keston, Kent; the source of the Ravensbourne, a curious legend; Roman entrenchments on Holwood Hill; Keston Common, II. 111; the "Keston mark"; Holwood, Pitt's residence, 112; the "Wilberforce Oak"; Holwood House; some account of Holwood House, 113; Keston Church, 115; monuments; the Archdeacon's Well; Warbank; etymology of Keston; descent of the manor; Roman remains, 116
Keston Common, Kent, II. 111, 112
Kew; its situation and soil; etymology; the village; railway accommodation; population; Suffolk Place, II. 389; early days of George III. at Kew, 391; his seclusion in his youth; death of George II.; Lord Bute selected for Prime Minister; quiet life of George III. at Kew, 392; Gresse, the artist, and the king; Queen Charlotte's Christmas-tree; the king's insanity, 393; Goupy, the artist; royal disregard of grammar; demolition of Kew Palace; account of the old building, 394; the Capel family its first owners; Samuel Molyneux; the house leased from the Capels; death of Queen Charlotte, 395; marriage of the Dukes of Clarence and Kent, in 1818; the king at church, 396; Bradley's great telescope; the Kew Observatory, 397; some additional details, 398; St. Anne's Chapel, Kew Green; scheme for its enlargement, 399; eminent persons buried here, 400; Gainsborough, the painter, 400—404; anecdotes of George III.; the Rev. R. B. Byam, Vicar of Kew and Petersham; the National Orphan Home; Stephen Duck, 405; the eccentric Caleb Colton, 406, 407; the Duke of Cumberland, 407; attempt to assassinate him; Cambridge Cottage; Bauer, the microscopist, 408; discovery of photography; Sir Joseph Puckering, 409; Kew Bridge, 410
Kew Bridge, I. 29, 32, II. 410
Kew Gardens; Sir Henry Capel's garden in the seventeenth century, II. 410; the pleasure gardens and Kew House begun by the Prince of Wales; improvement under Sir Joseph Banks; the gardens taken in charge by the Commissioners of Woods and Forests; appointment of Sir W. Hooker as director; transformation of the Botanic Gardens; formation of the Museum of Practical or Economical Botany; extent and condition of the gardens in 1840, 411; general description of Kew Gardens, 412; the entrance gateways; the old orangery, now Museum No. 3; the Temple of the Sun; the

herbaceous grounds, 413; Museum No. 2; the Temple of Æolus; the Tropical Aquarium; the Victoria Regia; the Orchid House; the Succulent House, 414; the Tropical Fern House, 416; the great Palm House, 417; Museum No. 1; the old Arboretum; the Pleasure Grounds; the Chinese Pagoda, 418; the Ruin; the Temple of Victory; the flagstaff; the Pagoda; the Temperate House, or Winter Garden, 419; Miss North's collection of paintings, 420, 421; the Queen's Cottage; Mr. William Aiton, 422; William Cobbett; Sir W. J. Hooker, 423; Sir Joseph D. Hooker; the Herbarium; the Jodrell Laboratory, 424

Kew Observatory, The, II. 397, 398
Kilmorey, Earl of, I. 60, 82, 87, 88
Kilwardby, Archbishop, II. 149, 163, 173
King, Dr. William, I. 21
"King and the Tinker" inn, Enfield, I. 370, 371
King Charles's Swing, Hampton Court Palace, I. 170
King, Edward, antiquary, II. 102, 104
Kings of Brentford, The two, I. 33, 34
Kingsbury, Middlesex; rural character of the village; the old field-paths; boundaries; old names; the Kingsbury reservoir; the "Welsh Harp"; the races; the parish church; supposed Roman encampment, 275; monuments in the church; Kingsbury Green; The Hyde; High House farm and Oliver Goldsmith, 276; the Passionist Convent; John Lyon, the founder of Harrow School, 277
Kingsbury Lake, or reservoir, I. 274
Kingsbury races, I. 275
"King's Head" inn, The, Enfield, I. 355
"King's Head" tavern, Chigwell, I. 453
"King's Head" tavern, Teddington, I. 124
Kingsley, Rev. Charles, Quotation from, II. 336
"King's Mead," The, Chingford, I. 437
"King's Oak" inn, High Beech Hill, I. 434, 436, 437
King's Wood, Beckenham, II. 104
King William IV.'s Naval Asylum, II. 100
Kingston, Duke of, I. 9, 13
Kingston-on-Thames, Surrey; its situation, II. 296; boundaries; nature of the soil, and health qualities of the district; water-supply; Seething Wells hot springs; acreage and population of the town; its early history; discovery of Roman antiquities; origin of the name of Kingston, 297; coronation of Athelstan; early charters and privileges granted to the townsmen; curious entries in the chamberlains' and churchwardens' accounts; loyalty of the inhabitants, 298; death of Lord Francis Villiers in the Civil War; frequent discovery of ancient warlike weapons at Kingston; the castle; supposed evidences of a Roman ford here, 299; archæological discoveries; Kingston Bridge; the old bridge; historical reminiscences; tolls, &c., 300; the ducking, or cucking stool, 300, 302; Clattern Bridge; an ancient mill; the parish church, 303; monumental inscriptions, 304; Crack-nut Sunday; curious entries in the churchwardens' and chamberlains' accounts, 305; noted residents; other churches and chapels, 306; the coronation stone, 307; monarchs crowned here; the town hall; the corporation; the civic regalia, 308; the market-place and its historical reminiscences, 308, 309; the assize court; old houses in the town; House of Correction; the drill-hall and barracks; public free library and literary institution, 309; Cleave's almshouses; healthy situation of the town; railway communication; New Kingston; modern improvements; the cemetery; St. Mary's Chapel, 311;

its historical associations; the Free Grammar School, 311; eminent persons educated in the old school; fairs, 312; amusements of the townspeople, 313; the Fairfield; Thames angling; Surbiton; St. Mark's Church, 314; other churches; Norbiton; the church; charitable institutions; Coombe House, Lord Liverpool's residence; Coombe Wood, 315; Coombe and New Malden; Coombe Warren; the "Bald-faced Stag" and Jerry Abershaw, the highwayman, 316
Kingston Bridge, I. 142, II. 300
Kit-Cat Club, The, I. 94, II. 456, 458, 459
Kitchen Court, Hampton Court Palace, I. 164
Kneller Hall, Twickenham, I. 94, 95; present state of the house, 95
Kneller, Sir Godfrey, I. 69, 75, 76, 94, 165, 166, 299, 458; anecdotes of, 95
Knight, Charles, I. 22, 65, 156, 563, 573, 574, II. 33, 516
Knight-Bruce, Sir James L., II. 467, 468
Knighton House, Woodford, I. 464
Knott's Green, Leyton; Mr. Gurney Barclay's house and observatory, I. 485
"Kyngham," Game of the, Kingston, II. 313

L

Laboratory pattern room and museum, Woolwich Arsenal, II. 22
Labouchere, Mr., I. 111
Lacy House, Isleworth; its different owners, I. 59
Lade, Sir John, once coachman to George IV., I. 189
La Guerre, the painter, I. 94, 292, 296
Lake House, Wanstead; Thomas Hood's residence, I. 479
Lake, Sir James Winter, I. 347
Lakes, The family of the, Edgware, I. 285, 287, 290, 296, 298
Laleham, Middlesex; remains of a Roman castrametation on Greenfield Common; descent of the manor; the Lowther family, I. 182; the parish church; the Earl of Lucan; house of Dr. Arnold; Dean Stanley's account of Dr. Arnold, 183; his life at Laleham; the Thames at Laleham; St. Anne's Hill, the residence of Charles James Fox, 184
Laleham Burway, Middlesex, I. 184
Laleham House, Middlesex, I. 183
Lamb, Charles, I. 254, 348, 362
Lambarde, the Kentish topographer, I. 560, 574, II. 41, 44, 56, 57, 517
Lambert, Sir Daniel, II. 218
Lamorby, Kent; its various names, II. 52, 53, 54, 56
Lanfranc, Archbishop, II. 149, 159, 161, 163
Langdale, Lord, II. 467
Langley Park, Beckenham, II. 64, 102, 104, 128; the Burrell family, 104
Langton, Archbishop, II. 163
Lappitt's Hill, Epping Forest, I. 437
Larwood, Mr., the sign-board chronicler, I. 23, 330, 341, 345, 371, 473, II. 99, 100, 170, 178, 212
Lass of Richmond Hill, The, II. 376, 377
Latimer's Elm, Hadley, I. 329
Laud, Archbishop, I. 380, 381, 412, 488, II. 91, 159, 164, 167, 351, 464, 466
Lauderdale, Duke of, I. 317, 320, 322, 325, 327; his duchess, 317, 318, 320, 321, 322, 327
Lawn Cottage, or Ragman's Castle, Twickenham, I. 86
Lawrence, Sir William, surgeon, I. 21
Lawrence, Sir Thomas, painter, II. 295
Lawrence, Mrs., Gardens of, Ealing Park, I. 23
Layman, A, holding a deanery, I. 58
Lea, The River, I. 348, 351, 375, 384, 395, 398, 404, 408, 415, 416, 437, 439, 465,

466, 484, 488, 502, 506, 508, 511; its etymology, 559; its source; Luton; Brocket Hall; Hertford, 560; Ware; Chadwell Springs; Amwell and its Quaker poet, 561; Haileybury College; the Rye House, 562; the Rye House plot; the "great bed of Ware," 563; Stanstead Abbotts, 564; Hoddesdon, 565; Broxbourne; Cook's Ferry; Bleak Hall; the East London Waterworks, 566; Lea Bridge; fishing on the Lea; Hackney Marshes and Temple Mills; the navigation of the Lea, 567; conservancy of the river, 568
Lea and Stort navigation, I. 351, 376, 398, 566, 567, 568
Lea Bridge Road, I. 484; Lea Bridge, 567
Le Brun, the painter, I. 166
Leeds, Duke of, II. 475
Leicester House, Carshalton; once the Royal Hospital for Incurables, II. 206
Leland, the antiquarian, I. 29, 228, 233, 506, II. 300, 307, 389, 425; his death, 231
Lely, Sir Peter, painter, I. 166, 167, 299, 477, II. 368
Lennard, Sir John Farnaby, II. 116, 124
Lennard family, The, II. 124, 125
Leopold of Saxe-Coburg, King of the Belgians, II. 287, 293, 294, 296, 375, 380
Lesnes Abbey, Erith, II. 8, 39, 41, 51; description of, 47; history, 48, 49
Lesnes Heath, Erith, II. 47, 50; the "Leather Bottle" inn, 47
Letchmoor Heath, Middlesex, I. 309
Letheuillier, Mr. Smart, the antiquarian, I. 418, 419, 484, 501; seat of the family, II. 104
Lewis, the Richmond brewer, and the right of way through Richmond Park, II. 352, 469
Lewis, the topographer, I. 176, 221, II. 125
Lewisham, Kent, II. 97, 98
Lexborough, Chigwell, I. 451, 460
Leyton, Essex; extent and boundaries of the parish, I. 483; Walthamstow Slip; census returns; Roman remains and other antiquities; ancient earthworks at Ruckholts, 484; general appearance of the village; railway stations; Knott's Green; Park House; Ruckholt House; the Manor House; Leyton House; Etloe House; St. Mary's Church; monuments, 485; brasses, 486; other monuments; Strype, the historian, 487; the churchyard; the vicarage; All Saints' Church; schools and charitable institutions; Lea Bridge and the East London Waterworks, 488; the "White Hart" inn; eminent residents of Leyton; Lodge, the dramatic poet, 489
Leytonstone, Essex, I. 484, 485; census returns; St. John's Church; Holy Trinity Church; Congregational church; the Union Workhouse; Children's Home, I. 483
Lichfield House, Richmond; Miss Braddon, novelist, II. 388
Lightfoot, Hannah, the Quakeress, II. 399
Lightfoot, Rev. John, botanist and naturalist, I. 226, 235
Lilly, the quack, II. 313
Lincoln House, Enfield, I. 373
Lind, Jenny, the "Swedish nightingale," II. 488, 489
Lindley, Dr., botanist, I. 8, II. 411, 412
Lindsay, Mr. W. S., I. 177
Littleberries, Hendon; Mr. Scharf's account of, I. 282, 283
Little Ealing, I. 21, 29
Little Ilford, I. 496; its boundaries and extent; population; St. Mary's parish church; brasses and monuments; Mr. Lethieullier's house at Aldersbrook, 501; Ilford Gaol; the "Rabbits" sign, 502

Little Park, or New Park, Enfield, I. 358, 361

Little Stanmore, I. 274, 284, 286, 302; early history of the manor, 286, 287

Little Strawberry Hill, I. 119, 122

Littleton, Staines, I. 177; old mansion at, 181

Liverpool, Lord Charles Jenkinson; his residence at Addiscombe, II. 137

Liverpool, Earl of, II. 300

Lodge, Thomas, dramatic poet, I. 489

Londesborough, Lord, II. 316

London and North Western Railway, I. 222, 223, 249, 270, 299, 308

London Colney, Middlesex, I. 312, 314; Colney House; cost of erection; the village; St. Peter's Church; Tittenhanger; its successive owners; Colney Heath; St. Mark's Church, 315

Londonderry, Marquis of, II. 60, 61; duel between Henry Grattan and, II. 493, 494

London International College, Spring Grove, I. 60

London Orphan Asylum, Watford, I. 305, 307

Long Ditton, Surrey, II. 272; population; the old church; the present edifice, 273; descent of the manor, 274

Longevity, Extraordinary, II. 305

Long, Sir James Tylney, Warden of Epping Forest, I. 432, 502

Longfellow, the poet, I. 423

Longford hamlet, Harmondsworth, Middlesex, I. 204, 228

Longley, Dr., head master of Harrow School, I. 261, 266, 267; Archbishop, II. 132, 135

Long-Pole-Wellesley, Mr., marriage of, I. 425

Lonsdale, Lord, II. 359, 455

Lord Mayor of London stopped by a highwayman, I. 30

Losse family, The, Edgware, I. 286

Loughton, Essex, I. 421, 428, 442; population; the railway station; descent of the manor; the Hall; St. Nicholas' parish church, 447; St. John's Church; Staple Hill; Coller's description of the village; ancient earth-works, 448.

Louis Philippe, King, I. 87, 88, II. 296, 380

Louise, Princess, and Marquis of Lorne, II. 296

Lovelace, Earl of, I. 23.

Lovelace, the Cavalier poet, II. 13, 14

Lower Cuffley, Cheshunt, I. 395

Lower Halliford, I. 177, 179

Lower North Road, Enfield, I. 371

Lower Sydenham; its church; eminent residents here, II. 98.

Lubbock, Sir John, II. 113, 118, 122

Lucan, Earl of, I. 183

Lumley family, The, II. 224, 225, 226, 232, 235, 240, 241, 511

Lunatic Asylum, The, Hanwell, I. 26; some account of, 27, 28

Lyndhurst, Lord, II. 487

Lyne-Stephens, Mrs. (Mademoiselle Duvernay), II. 465, 466

Lyon, John, the founder of Harrow; extract from his will; orders, statutes, and rules for the government of the school, I. 260, 277; lines in honour of him, 262

Lyttelton, Lord, II. 128, 129; and the ghost, II. 253—255

Lytton, Lord, I. 151, 326, 328, 329, 334

Lytton, Sir E. Bulwer, I. 334, II. 317

M

Macaulay, Lord, I. 365, 423, 483, II. 87, 92, 109, 243, 322, 323, 460, 461

Macfarlane, the historian of George III.'s time, I. 39

Mackay, Dr. Charles, II. 344, 364, 395, 433

Macready, the player, I. 304

Magna Charta, and the place where it was signed, I. 191, II. 41

Maid of Honour Row, Richmond, II. 365; Maids of Honour, 382

"Maids of Honour," Queen Elizabeth and her, I. 152

Maitland, the historian, I. 536, 540

Malden, Surrey; its etymology; its situation and boundaries; population; improvement in the roads; descent of the manor, II. 509; the original House of Scholars founded by Bishop Merton, 510; Merton College, 510, 511; Worcester Park; the parish church, 511; its renovation; mural tablets; Bishop Ravis, 512

Mallet, David, the poet, I. 16, 105, II. 367, 385

Mann, Sir Horace, I. 17, 29, 70, 109

Manners-Sutton, Archbishop, II. 132, 133, 134, 135, 165; George III.'s desire for his appointment, 134

Manning, Cardinal, I. 176, 207, 269, 281, 334; his father, 334

Manor House, Leyton, I. 485

Manor House, The, Twickenham; its owners, I. 74

Manor Park, I. 513

Manor Park cemetery, Ilford, I. 501

Mapp, Mrs., the bone-setter, II. 250

Marble Hill, Twickenham, I. 83; the Countess of Suffolk at, 83, 85, 86; description of the countess, 85, 86; Mrs. Fitzherbert and others residents there, 86

Marchmont, Lord, I. 105

Marden Park, Caterham Valley, II. 148, 221

Marine Society, Establishment of the, I. 25, 26

Market-house, Uxbridge, I. 234

Market-place, The, Brentford, I. 37

Marlborough, Duke of, I. 21, 60; Sarah, Duchess of, II. 476, 477, 479

Marlow, William, F.S.A., I. 75

Marryatt, Captain, I. 348, 362, II. 485

Marryatt, Mr. Joseph; his son, Captain Marryatt, II. 485

Marsh, Dr. William; his daughter, II. 101

Marsh Street, Walthamstow, I. 465, 470

"Martinus Scriblerus," The, I. 97

Mary, Queen, and Philip of Spain, at Hampton Court, I. 151, 164

Mary, Queen of William III., I. 155; portraits of the ladies of her court, 166

Mathews, Charles, the actor, II. 360, 456; his son, 525

Matthew Paris, the chronicler, I. 297

Maurice, the poet, I. 117, II. 372, 375, 376

May Place, Crayford, II. 58

Mayfield Place, Little Orpington, Kent, II. 66

Mayhew, Mr. Augustus, I. 94

Maynard family, The, II. 533, 534

"Maypole" inn, Fairlop, Hainault Forest, I. 491, 492, 495

"Maypole" tavern, Chigwell; Charles Dickens's creation of, I. 453, 454—457

Mazes, or labyrinths, I. 171, 382, 383

Meadhurst Park, Feltham, I. 173

Meadowbank, Twickenham, Mr. Bishop's observatory at, I. 83

Meereditch, or Mardyke, branch of the river Lea, I. 348

Melvill, Canon, II. 453

Melville, Lords, II. 487, 488

Mendez, Moses, the poet, II. 529

Merchant Seamen's Orphan Asylum, Snaresbrook, I. 473

Merlin's Cave, Richmond Park, II. 345, 346, 347, 405

Merton; situation and boundaries; the village and its surroundings; paper-mills and factories; railway stations; population; how the poor are robbed, II. 516; early historical events; descent of the manor, 517; Merton Abbey; the statutes of Merton; Thomas à Becket

and Walter de Merton; dissolution of the abbey, 518; remains of the monastic buildings; Merton Church; Merton Place; recollections of Lord Nelson's residence here, 520; Sir William and Lady Hamilton and Lord Nelson, 521—523; the fate of Lady Hamilton, 524

Merton Abbey, II. 518, 519

Merton College, II. 510, 511

Metropolitan Convalescent Institution, Burrows, Hendon, I. 280

Metropolitan District Railway, I. 7, 20, 62

Metropolitan Main Drainage Works, I. 510, 525, 526

Metropolitan Workhouse School, Southall, I. 217

Meux, Sir Henry, the present possessor of Theobalds, I. 383, 384

Middlesex, Great ancient forest of, I. 270, 274, 297

Middlesex Industrial School, Feltham, I. 173

Military Store Department, Woolwich Arsenal, II. 23

Mill Hill, Hendon, I. 278, 280, 281, 284, 334; Mill Hill College; the Nonconformists' Grammar School; eminent persons educated here; Roman Catholic institutions at Mill Hill, 281

Mill Hill, South Acton, I. 16

Millais, the artist, II. 107, 129

Miller, Jo, the wit, I. 16

Miller, Mr. T., II. 9, 10

Mills, Sir Charles, of Hillingdon, I. 209, 215, 227, 236

Mills, Mr., the historian of Hayes, Middlesex, I. 209, 210, 214

Milton, the poet, I. 244, 245, 246, 247, 248, 274, II. 281

Minchenden House, Southgate, I. 346

Ministerial whitebait dinner, Origin of the, I. 532, 533

Minstrels' Gallery, Hampton Court Palace, I. 163

Millwall; its situation and boundaries, I. 533; origin of the name of the Isle of Dogs, 534—536; the Chapel House, 536, 537, 538; Blackwall; acreage of the Isle of Dogs; its fertility; geology, 538; a submerged forest; the manor of Pomfret, 539; inundations in the marsh, 540; how Pepys attended a wedding party, 540—542; ferries and the Ferry House; condition of the Isle of Dogs in the last century, 542; manufactories and shipbuilding yards, 543; Roman cement and terra cotta, 543, 544; the "Great Eastern" steamship, 544—546; Cubitt Town; St. Luke's Church, 546; Limehouse, 547; Poplar, 548; the Millwall Docks, 555

Misbourne, The river, I. 233

Mitcham; its etymology; situation and boundaries of the parish; general description of the village; the river Wandle, II. 524; mills and factories; the cultivation of flowers and medicinal plants; Mitcham Common, 525; the Green; Mitcham famous for cricketing; railway communication; the "King's Head" inn; a "Mitcham whisper"; history of the manor; Hall Place, 526; Rumball's Farm; the Cranmer family; the parish church; monuments, 527; the registers; other churches and chapels; almshouses; Queen Elizabeth's visit to Sir Julius Cæsar; Sir Walter Raleigh; Dr. Donne; Mitcham Grove; its various residents, 528, 529

Moat Mount, Hendon, I. 284

Mole, The river, II. 280, 281, 282, 285, 287; the poets on, 280; its course, 281

Molesey Grove; Sir Robert Walpole and J. W. Croker residents here, II. 284

Molesey Hurst, Surrey; prize fights in former times; cricket matches, II. 283

Molesey Park, II. 282

Moll Cutpurse, the highway woman, I. 65

Molyneux, Samuel, astronomer, II. 395, 397

Monken Hadley, Middlesex, I. 316, 320, 323, 325, 327

Monken Mead ; obelisk to commemorate the battle of Barnet, I. 328

Monkhams, Woodford, I. 463

Monk Wood, Epping Forest, I. 442

Monk's Orchard, Shirley, II. 136

Monro, Dr. John, physician, I. 329

Montagu, Basil ; his mother, I. 303

Montagu, Edward Wortley, seat of, I. 142

Montagu, Lady Mary, I. 92 ; Pope once the friend of, 99, 100

Montpelier Row, Twickenham, I. 94

Moore, Archbishop, II. 165

Moore, Edward, poet, II. 291

Moore Hall, Harefield, Middlesex, I. 244, 247

Morant, the historian of Essex, I. 420, 422, 439, 447, 495, 502, 508, 528

Morden ; its situation and boundaries ; description of the village ; census returns ; history of the manor ; the Garth family, II. 513 ; Morden Hall ; Mr. Abraham Goldsmid ; Morden Park ; the parish church, 514 ; its brasses and monuments ; the schools, 515

More, Mrs. Hannah, I. 136, II. 528

More, Sir Thomas, I. 167

More Hall, South Mimms, the residence of Sir Thomas More, I. 316, 327

Morgan, Lady, II. 284

Morland, George, the painter, I. 190, 335

Mornington, Earl of, I. 458 ; marriage of his father, 425

Mortlake ; situation and boundaries ; population ; its etymology ; descent of the manor, II. 425 ; the parish church, 426, 427 ; eminent persons buried here ; Sir John Barnard, 428 ; other churches and chapels ; Boot and Shoemakers' Benevolent Institution ; Oliver Cromwell's house, 429 ; Sir Henry Taylor ; East Sheen ; Mr. Edward Jesse, 430 ; Amy Robsart ; Sir Robert Dudley ; Sir William Temple, 431, 432 ; Dr. Pinckney's School ; Lords Castlereagh and Gray ; Sir Archibald Macdonald ; Mr. W. S. Gilpin, the gardener, 433 ; Dr. Dee, the astrologer, 433—436 ; Mortlake tapestry works, 436, 437 ; potteries, 437 ; the boat-race winning-post, 438

Mottingham, Kent ; the manor-house, II. 95

Mount Mascal estate, North Cray, II. 60

Mulberry-trees, Cultivation of, II. 525

Munro, Dr., the physician, I. 306

Murray, Lady Augusta, wife of the Duke of Sussex, I. 94

Murray, Gen. the Hon. Sir Henry, II. 486

Murray, the publisher, II. 487

Museum of the Royal Artillery, Woolwich, II. 26, 27

Myddelton House, Enfield, I. 350, 361, 369, 370

Myddelton, Sir Hugh, and the New River, I. 347, 361

N

"Nag's Head" inn, Enfield, I. 351

Napoleon III. ; his last resting-place, II. 73 ; his short residence at Chislehurst, 77 ; his funeral, 78, 79 ; his will, 79, 80

Napoleon, Louis, Duel between Count Léon and, II. 494

Nasmyth steam-hammers, Woolwich Arsenal, II. 25, 26

National Orphan Home, Ham Common, II. 324, 405

Neasdon, Middlesex, I. 223, 225

Nell Gwynne, I. 33, II. 251

Nelson, Lord, and Sir W. and Lady Hamilton, II. 519, 520, 521, 522, 523 ; recollections of Nelson, 520, 521

Nevill family, The, East Ham, I. 514, 515

New Barnet, I. 320

New Hampton, I. 136

New Malden, Kingston ; the church, II. 316

New Organ Hall, Shenley, Middlesex, I. 312

New River, The, I. 349, 350, 358, 362, 384, 389

New Southgate (see Colney Hatch)

New Terrace, The, Richmond Park, II. 353

New Wimbledon, II. 479

Newberries Manor, Radlett, I. 309, 312 ; the Phillimore family, 312

Newcastle, Duke of, II. 292, 295

Newdigate family, The, and Harefield, I. 244, 245, 248

Newell, Kent, II. 65

Nicholas, Dr., the schoolmaster, I. 22

Nichols, John, the historian, I. 22, 244, 485, 487, II. 75

Nichols, John Bowyer, editor of the Gentleman's Magazine, I. 22, 105

Nicoll family, The, Hendon, I. 280, 281, 282, 285, 346

Nonconformists, The, at Uxbridge, I. 236

Nonsuch Palace, Surrey, II. 201, 206, 511 ; its situation, 230 ; early history ; Hentzner's description, 231 ; Horace Walpole's account ; Houfnagle's view of the palace ; Evelyn's description, 232 ; the Parliamentary survey of Nonsuch ; Miss Aikin's account ; its care entrusted to Sir Thomas Cawarden, 233 ; the palace purchased by the Earl of Arundel ; Queen Elizabeth entertained here five days, 234 ; the Queen acquires the property, 235 ; her last visit to Nonsuch ; the Earl of Essex's disgrace and execution, 236 ; the Stuart sovereigns its next owners ; its fate at the Commonwealth ; Pepys' visits to Nonsuch ; the Duchess of Cleveland acquires the estate, 237 ; the mansion, together with Worcester Park, pulled down in her lifetime ; "Diana's Dyke" ; the present mansion built in the Regency days ; size of the trees in the park ; Archbishop Whately, 238

Norbiton, Kingston, II. 310, 315 ; its churches, 315

Norbury, Thornton Heath, Surrey, II. 178, 180

North, Sir Edward (afterwards Lord), I. 131, 251, 254, I. 485, 487

Northampton, Earl of, I. 279

Northaw, Middlesex, I. 323, 348 ; etymology ; condition of the district at the time of the Conquest ; disputed ownership ; Nynn House and manor, 394 ; the Hook ; Northaw Place ; acreage and population ; St. Thomas's Church ; a chalybeate spring, 395

Northaw House, I. 395

Northcourt, The, I. 218

North Cray, Kent, II. 56, 59 ; neighbouring estates, 60 ; some account of the Marquis of Londonderry, 60, 61 ; North Cray Place ; St. James's Church ; the parish registers ; Ruxley, 62

Northolt, or Northall ; general description of the locality ; the parish church ; its brasses and tablets, I. 218

Northwick, Lord, I. 254

Northwood, Ruislip, Middlesex ; Northwood Hall ; Theodore Hook's assurance, I. 243

North Woolwich ; church ; the gardens, I. 513, II. 44 ; steamboat ferry, II. 6, 9

Northumberland Heath, Crayford, II. 41, 56

Norwood, Middlesex, I. 23, 26, 210 ; the "north wood" ; situation of the "precinct " of Norwood ; population ; early history of the manor ; the village ; the parish church, 215 ; monuments ; the yew-tree ; charitable bequests, 216

Norwood Common, Middlesex, I. 59

Norwood, the "north wood," Croydon, II. 153, 207

Noy, the lawyer, temp. Charles I., I. 36

Nye, Rev. Philip, Puritan rector of Acton, I. 10, 11.

Nynn House, Northaw, Middlesex, I. 394

O

Oakleigh Park, Barnet, I. 335

Oaks stakes, Institution of the, II. 264, 265

"Oaks, The," Banstead, Surrey ; General Burgoyne's marriage, II. 218, 219 ; the Earl of Derby's ownership, 219, 220

Oatlands, Surrey, I. 178, II. 296

O'Kelly, Captain Denis, I. 294, 295

Old Brentford, I. 31 ; the church, ib.

Oldbury, Enfield ; Humphrey de Bohun's castle, I. 352

Old Ford, I. 508

"Old Gang Aboot," George III. and, I. 39

Oldham, Nathaniel, I. 21

"Old Hat" tavern, near Hanwell, I. 23

Oldmixon, John, political writer, I. 21

Old Oak Common, I. 8, 16

Old Organ Hall, now Newberries, Middlesex, I. 313

Old Park, Enfield ; its various owners, I. 358

Onslow, Lord, and the highwaymen, II. 491

Ordnance Factory, I. 351

Orford, Lord, II. 352

Orleans Club, Twickenham, I. 88, 89

Orleans House, Twickenham ; its first resident, Secretary Johnstone ; afterwards the property of Lord Brownlow Bertie ; then purchased by Sir George Pococke ; Louis Philippe resident here in 1800, I. 87 ; anecdotes of Louis Philippe ; then becomes the property of the Duc d'Aumale ; then sold to the Orleans Club ; description of the house, 88

Ormond, Duke of, II. 344

Orpington, Kent, II. 56, 64 ; population ; early history of the place ; the parish church ; the priory, 65

Osborne, Thomas, Earl of Danby, II. 475, 485

Ossulston, Hundred of, I. 208, 221, 335, 533

Osterley Park, I. 36, 39, 41, 60, 215 ; Sir Thomas Gresham's erection of ; Queen Elizabeth at ; Sir Thomas Gresham, 41 ; Lady Mary Grey, sister of Lady Jane, an inmate of ; Queen Elizabeth's jealousy of Lady Mary's marriage ; Lord Desmond, 42 ; Sir William Waller its owner ; then the property of Child, the banker ; then the property of the Earl of Jersey ; the house ; its pictures and books ; damaged by fire, 43

Overgrown metropolis, Dread of, in former times, I. 3

Owen, Dr. John, the Puritan ; his costume, I. 21

Owen, Sir Richard, II. 354, 358

"Owl" inn, Epping Forest, I. 437

Oxhey, Bushey, I. 307

P

Paddington Canal, The, I. 217, 218

Page Street, Hendon, I. 280

Paget family, The, I. 203, 204, 206

Pagoda House, Richmond ; the Selwyn family, II. 387, 388

Paley, Archdeacon, I. 452

Palmerston, Lord, I. 262, 268

Paris, Comte de, I. 89, 90, 91

Park House, Leyton, I. 485

Parker, Archbishop, II. 53, 149, 164

Parkhurst, the Hebrew lexicographer, II. 251, 259

Parr, Queen Katharine, I. 69, 74

Parr, Dr., assistant master at Harrow, I. 263, 266, 268, 298

Parslowes, Dagenham, I. 527, 528

Paulet, Sir Amias, I. 145

Paull, Mr., Duel between Sir Francis Burdett and, II. 486, 493

Peacocks, Yew-trees in the shape of, Bedfont, I. 195

Peckham, Archbishop, II. 149, 159, 163

Peek, Sir Henry W., II. 308, 485

Peel, Sir Robert, a distinguished Harrovian, I. 268

Pelham, Mr. Henry, brother of Duke of Newcastle, II. 286, 287, 291; Latin inscription to, 292

Pembroke Lodge, Richmond Park, II. 353, 354, 355

Penge, Kent; population, II. 98; the "Crooked Billet" inn; railway stations; the Croydon Canal; churches; the Waterman's and Lighterman's Asylum, 99; King William IV.'s Naval Asylum, 100

Pengelly House, Cheshunt, I. 384, 389, 390

Pennant, Sir Samuel, I. 395, II. 225

Penn's Place, Manor of, Middlesex, I. 309

Penn, William, the Quaker, I. 129, 453, 482, 483, II. 15, 16; his father, 482

Pennywell, Middlesex, I. 297

Pepys, Samuel, I. 33, 38, 322, 323, 345, 469, 476, 534, 535, 536, 539, 542, II. 9, 15, 20, 44, 214, 215, 237, 244, 247, 248, 251, 259, 263, 264, 460, 461

Pepys family, Tomb of the, I. 333

Perceval, Right Hon. Spencer, I. 269; House of, Ealing, 23

Percy, Algernon, Sion House repaired and renovated by, I. 53

Percy family, Some account of the fortunes of the, I. 53

Perivale, Middlesex; situation of the village, I. 220; early history of the parish; the parish church; its brasses and monuments, 221

Perkins, Mr. Henry, I. 70

Perrott, Sir George, I. 183

Perry, the editor, II. 487

Perryn House, Twickenham, afterwards the Economic Museum, I. 77

Petersham, Surrey; its situation; the manor, II. 324; the church; its monuments, 325; distinguished persons buried here, 326; the Misses Berry and Horace Walpole, 326, 327; Gay's Summerhouse, 327, 328; Petersham Lodge and Catherine Hyde, Duchess of Queensberry, 328; anecdotes of the duchess; other owners of the property; Sudbrooke; Bute House; Douglas House; Charles Dickens, 329

Petersham, Lord; his coat, II. 325

Petersham Lodge; its residents, II. 328; the Duchess of Queensberry, 328, 329

Petersham Park, II. 353

Peto, Sir Samuel Morton, I. 243

Philipott, the Kentish historian, II. 60, 64, 95

Phillips, Prof., on the geology of Brentford, I. 32

Phillips, Sir Richard, II. 458, 459

Phillips, the painter, II. 486

"Physic Well," The, Barnet; Samuel Pepys, I. 323

Pie Powder, Court of, I. 352

Pin, The river, I. 250

Pinner, Middlesex; the village; population, I. 249; Miss Howard's charity; market and fairs; the parish church; memorials, 250; centenarians; a barbarous custom; schools and cemetery; Pinner Hill; Pinner Wood House; Pinner Place; Pinner Grove; Pinner Park; Pinner Green and Wood Hall; Woodring; Mrs. Horatia Ward; the Commercial Travellers' Society's schools, 251; Headstone, or the Manor Farm, 252

Pinner Place, I. 251

Pinner Wood House, I. 251

Piombi, Sebastian del, the painter, I. 165

Piozzi, Mrs., II. 525

"Piper's Green," Edgware, I. 285

Pit Place, Epsom, and Lord Lyttelton's ghost, II. 253—255

Pitt diamond, The, I. 39, 40

Pitt, George Morton, a resident at Orleans House, Twickenham, I. 87

Pitt, Thomas, Governor of Madras, I. 39; the Pitt Diamond, 39, 40

Pitt, William, Earl of Chatham, II. 392

Pitt, William, I. 533, II. 105, 107, 108, 357, 484; his residence, Keston, 112, 113, 114, 487, 488; his duel with George Tierney, 490, 492, 493; at Wimbledon, 484

Place House, Little Ealing, I. 21

Plague, Visitation of the, I. 33, 35

Plaistow, Essex; its flat and unattractive appearance, I. 509; its sources of wealth; the Metropolitan main drainage works; population, 510; railway stations; churches and chapels; hospitals; works and manufactories; the Victoria Docks, 511; vegetable fossil remains; the Royal Victoria and Albert Docks; railway stations, 512; North Woolwich; the gardens; St. John's Church; eminent residents, 513

Plaistow, Kent, II. 83, 94

Plashet House, East Ham; Mrs. Fry, I. 515

Platten, Mr., I. 32

Plumer, Sir Thomas, Vice-chancellor, I. 295

Plum Lane, Plumstead, II. 34

Plumstead, Kent, II. 8; its situation and extent; census returns, 34; "Domesday" records; descent of the manor; Burrage Town; Borstall, or Bostal; Suffolk Place Farm, 35; soil and climate; Plumstead Common, 36; the old Artillery practice-butt; the Slade; Bramble Briers, or Bramblebury House; brick-kilns and sand-pits; the cemetery, 37; the old parish church, 38; extracts from the parish registers; St. Margaret's new parish church; other churches and chapels; Brookhill School; Woolwich Union; the railway station; geological formation of the district; Plumstead Marshes; the Main Drainage Works at Crossness Point, 39

Plumstead Common, II. 36, 37, 38

Podger, the gate-keeper of Bushey Park, I. 131; his death, 134

Pollock, Chief Baron, I. 70

Ponder's End, I. 349, 350, 351, 367

Pope, I. 5, 21, 39, 40, 85, 86, 93, 95, 195, 201, 202, 291, 292, 293; 316, II. 322, 323, 350, 373, 383, 384, 388, 397; anecdotes of him, 87; his poetical description of the Duke of Wharton, 91; his parentage and early life, 95, 96; his early translations; Miss Martha Blount; his translation of the "Iliad," 96; the "Odyssey"; an almost fatal accident, 97; publication of the "Miscellanies," "Martinus Scriblerus," "Dunciad," and other works, 97, 98; his death and burial; his skull; his character and temperament, 98; his love of solitude; his personal appearance; lampooned in verse; his alleged horse-whipping, 99; his friendship at one time with Lady Mary Montagu; his friends; Swift's activity in promoting the subscription for the "Iliad"; his popularity; Voltaire's visit, 100; his reply to Frederick, Prince of Wales; Warburton's acquaintance with Pope; Spence's anecdotes of Pope, 101; Pope's fondness for animals, 101, 102; his love of economy; Swift's apostrophe to Pope, 102; his rank as a poet; Dr. Johnson's opinion of his merits, 103; Thackeray's opinion, 103, 104; Rev. T. Thomson on Pope, 104; his last illness and death, 104, 105; his lines about himself; his will, 105; his

villa at Twickenham, 105, 106; his garden; the willow-tree in his garden, 106; his grotto, 106, 107; the poet's description of his grotto, 107, 108; his apostrophe to the pilgrim visitor; his love of his "Tusculum"; "the cave of Pope," 108; sale of the mansion to Sir William Stanhope; the property passes to Right Hon. Welbore Ellis (afterwards Lord Mendip), 109; its successive owners, 110; Pope's villa razed to the ground, and a new mansion erected by Baroness Howe; description of the spot by a foreigner, 110; subsequent history of the property, 110, 111

Poplar, I. 548

Porter, Misses Jane and Anna Maria, II. 286, 287

Porter, Sir R. Ker, painter, II. 287

Porter, Mrs., the actress, I. 284

Porters Estate, Middlesex, I. 312, 313

Portland, Earl of, Marriage of, II. 464

Portland, Duchess of, I. 235

Potter, Archbishop, II. 154, 156

Potter's Bar, Middlesex, 310, 368, 394, 395; St. John's Church; Dyrham Park, 317; Wrotham Park; its destruction by fire, 318; Hadley Common; Christ Church, 319

Pound, the astronomer; his long telescope, and Pennant's lines thereon; his nephew Bradley, I. 482

Poussin, Nicholas, the painter, I. 165

Powder-mills, The Government, Waltham, I. 399; the manufacture of gunpowder, 400—403

Powell, William, the "Harmonious Blacksmith," and Handel, I. 284, 296

Poyle Park, Colnbrook, Middlesex, I. 195

Prescott family, The, I. 383, 387

Prince Imperial, The, II. 71, 72, 74, 80

Prince Rupert's Tower, Woolwich, II. 16

Princess Frederica's Convalescent Home, Hampton, I. 134, 164

Princess Helena College, Ealing, I. 22

Prior, the poet, I. 34, 94, 372, 565, II. 205, 215, 384

Pritchard, Mrs., actress, I. 83, 86

Prizes and scholarships at Harrow School, I. 261

Probert, the murderer, I. 303, 311

Proby, Rev. Charles, vicar of Twickenham, I. 76, 98

Proctor, Dr., rector of Hadley, I. 328, 329

Prolific families, II. 305

Proof butts, Woolwich Arsenal, II. 27, 28

Prospect Hall, Woodford, I. 464

Pudding-stone, where found, I. 304

Pugets, the family of the, I. 333, 334

Puritan rectors of Acton, I. 10

Purley, Surrey; its history; Purley House; the "Diversions of Purley," II. 141; John Horne Tooke; a remarkable libel case, 142; the eligibility of the clergy, 143, 144; Horne Tooke's epitaph, 145

Purley House, John Horne Tooke's residence, II. 141, 145

Puttenham, the poet, II. 526

Q

Quaggy, The stream of the, II. 97

Quakers, The, at Uxbridge, I. 236

Quare, Daniel, the horologist, I. 165

Queen Elizabeth's Dairy, Barn Elms, II. 458

Queen Elizabeth's Lodge, Epping Forest, I. 430, 437, 439, 440, 441, 442

Queen Elizabeth's Tree, Nonsuch Park, II. 238, 239

Queen Elizabeth's Walk, Waddon, II. 183

Queen Henrietta Maria, II. 474, 475

Queen Victoria, II. 285, 295

Queen Victoria's Wood, High Beech, I. 430, 436, 437

Queen's Gallery, or Tapestry Gallery,

Hampton Court Palace, pictures in the, I. 166

"Queen's Head," Pinner, I. 249

"Queen's River," Bedfont, Middlesex, I. 195

Queen's Staircase, Hampton Court Palace, I. 168

Queen's Town, Willesden, I. 224

Queensberry, Duke of, II. 384; Duchess of, II. 317, 323, 328, 329, 383

Quick, the actor, II. 360

Quin, the actor, II. 367, 385, 386

R

Radcliffe, Dr., II. 203, 204, 205, 244

Radlett, Middlesex, I. 308, 312; Christ Church, 310; Gill's Hill; the murder of William Weare; Medburn; Newberries Park, 311

Raffaelle's cartoons, Hampton Court Palace, I. 166, 167, II. 436

Raffles, Sir Stamford, I. 283

Ragman's Castle, Twickenham, I. 86; its successive owners, 86, 87

Raikes, Mr., Anecdotes by, II. 284

Raleigh, Sir Walter, I., 14, 348, 360, II. 189, 190, 197, 528

Ramohun Roy, the Oriental philosopher, I. 90

Rangers of Richmond Park, II. 351, 352, 353, 357

Ravenscroft Park, Barnet, I. 323

Ravenscroft, Thomas, benefactor of Barnet, I. 321, 322

Ravensbourne, The river, II. 83, 89, 93, 95, 96, 97, 98, 100, 105, 108, 111; sketch of its course, 97

Ravis, Bishop, II. 512

Rawlinson, Sir William; tomb of, in Hendon Church, I. 279, 280

Ray House, Woodford, I. 460

Ray, Miss; tomb of, I. 303

Raynton, Sir Nicholas, Lord Mayor, I. 355, 357, 359

"Red Lion" inn-yard, Brentford; murder of Edmund Ironside at, I. 32

"Red Lion" inn, Hillingdon; Charles I. resting there, I. 230

Redding, Cyrus, I. 30, 65, 66, II. 406, 407, 490; his recollections of Pitt, 484

Reed, Rev. Dr. Andrew, II. 147, 206

Reedham Asylum, Surrey, II. 147

Registrar-General, Returns of the, I. 2

"Rehearsal," The Duke of Buckingham's play of the, I. 33, 34

Rembrandt, the painter, II. 340

Rendall, Matthew, curate of Teddington, suspended in 1635 for preaching long sermons, I. 129

Rendlesham, Lord, I. 308, 309

Reynardson, Mr., of Cedar House, Cowley, Middlesex, II. 227, 229

Reynolds, Archbishop, II. 163, 173

Reynolds, Sir Joshua, I. 99, 116, 138, II. 110, 320, 381, 400, 401, 403, 404

Rich, the actor, II. 227, 229

Richardson, Sir John, the lawyer, II. 487

Richmond, Surrey, II. 330; its former name, Shene or Sheen; its situation; its boundaries and extent; beauty of its scenery, 331; opinions of the Vicomte d'Arlington, Charles Dickens, and another writer, 331, 332; Thomson, the poet's descriptive lines, 332; Richmond Hill; the manor of Shene; the death of Edward III., and first mention of the palace, 333; Edward IV.'s interview with the Earl of Warwick here, 333, 334; Camden's account of the palace; its vicissitudes; a royal hoard discovered here on King Henry's death, 334; visit of the Emperor Charles V.; Anne of Cleves at Richmond; the Princess Elizabeth entertained here by Queen Mary, 335; Queen Elizabeth at Richmond, 336; her death, 337, 338; her

habits, 338, 339; her burial at Westminster; Prince Henry a resident at Richmond; Queen Henrietta Maria, 339; survey of the palace by order of Parliament; Hollar's etchings of the palace; its demolition; fragments of the palace; Asgill House, 340; anecdote of George III. and the gamekeeper; the monastery of Sheen, 341; the head of James IV. of Scotland; the convent of Observant Friars, 343; earliest record of a park at Richmond; the Lodge in the Little Park; it becomes a royal residence; leased to the Duke of Ormonde, but soon forfeited; then sold to the Prince of Wales; how the Prince of Wales received the news of his father's death, 344; Queen Caroline's fondness for Richmond; George II.'s partiality for punch; the king and the gardener; the Lodge settled on Queen Charlotte; the gardens and ornamental buildings, 345; descriptions of Merlin's Cave, 346; the character of Merlin, 347; Stephen Duck appointed keeper of the grotto and library, 348; the Hermitage; Clarence House, 350; the New or Great Park; its size; its enclosure in 1637; the park seized by the Commoners and given to the citizens of London, 351; given to the Hyde family at the Restoration; a lawsuit on the right of way through the park; the Rangership, 352; extent and general appearance of the park, 353; its natural history, 353, 354; Pembroke Lodge, 354; Lord John Russell, 355, 356; Thatched House Lodge, 356; White Lodge, 357; Sir Richard Owen, 358; railway accommodation; population; the Green; the Free Public Library, 359; number of readers, 360; the theatre, 360—363; eminent tragedians at the Richmond theatre, 360—62; remains of the old palace, 363; Fitzwilliam House, 363, 364; Sir Matthew Dekker, 364; John James Heidegger; Abbotsdene, 365; the parish church; monuments, 366; Thomson's monument, 367; eminent persons buried at Richmond Church, 368; extracts from the parish register; other churches and chapels, 369; the cemetery; the Wesleyan Theological Institution, 369, 370; almshouses; the Hospital; societies and public institutions, 370; drainage and water supply; Richmond Bridge, 371—373; regattas, 373; hotels; Devonshire Cottage; the Vineyards, 374; Richmond Hill; the Terrace; the Wick; the Duke of Buccleuch's House, 375; the Lass of Richmond Hill, 376, 377; the "Star and Garter," 377—380; hostelries; Sir Joshua Reynolds's retreat; George III. and the card-maker; Duppa's almshouses; Ancaster House; Cardigan House; the delicacy, "Maids of Honour," 381; institution of maids of honour, 382; eminent residents; Sir Robert Dudley; the Duke of Clarence; the Duchess of Queensberry; Gay, the poet, 383; the Duke of Queensberry, 384; James Thomson, the poet, 384—387; Rosedale House; Pagoda House, 387; the Selwyn family; the Herveys; Bishop Duppa's almshouses; other residents, 388

Richmond, the painter, II. 357

Richmond Wells, Richmond; performances here, II. 363

Rickmansworth, Herts, I. 237, 243, 244, 249, 308

Riddles Down, Surrey, II. 147, 197

Ridge, Middlesex, I. 312; St. Margaret's parish church; monuments, 316

Ridgeway, Enfield, I. 358

Rifle, History of the, I. 396; various improvements in the condition of the, 397;

the Government Small-arms Factory, 398, 399 (see Volunteer)

Rifle Ordnance Factory, Woolwich, II. 25

Rights of way through Bushey Park, I. 132; through Richmond Park, II. 352, 356

Ripon, Lord, I. 262, 268

Ripple Side, Barking, I. 527

"Rising Sun," Walthamstow, I. 465

Rivers, Lord, Anecdote of, II. 476

Robertson, Canon, II. 71, 75, 80, 81

"Robin Hood" inn, High Beech Hill, I. 434

Robinson, Dr., the historian of Enfield, I. 353, 355, 360, 374, 375

Robinson, H. Crabb, I. 66, 345, 351, 358

Robinson, John, anecdote of George III. and, I. 39

Rochester, Bishops of, Former palace of, Bromley, II. 83, 89

Rockingham, Lord, II. 466, 487, 488

Roding or Roden, The river, I. 423, 442, 458, 472, 473, 489, 496, 497, 501, 507, 516

"Rodings" or "Roothings," The, I. 497

"Roebuck" inn, Loughton, I. 434, 443, 447

Roehampton; situation and general appearance of the parish; population; Putney or Mortlake Park; the Earl of Portland, Lord Treasurer, II. 464; Christian, Countess of Devonshire, 464, 465; Roehampton Grove; Mrs. Lyne-Stephens (née Mademoiselle Duvernay); the Roman Catholic convent; Lord Ellenborough, 465; the parish church; Roehampton House; Parkstead; the Earl of Bessborough; Manresa House; a Jesuit Community; Lord Rockingham, 466; Lord Gifford; Lord Langdale, 467; Sir James Knight-Bruce, 467, 468; Royal School for Daughters of Military Officers; Mount Clare, 468; Downshire House; Dover House; Roehampton Gate, 469

Roehampton Gate, II. 356, 467, 469

Roehampton House, II. 466

Rolls Park, Chigwell, I. 451

Roman remains near Woolwich, II. 8

Romano, Giulio, the painter, I. 165

Roots, Dr., antiquarian, II. 299, 313, 316, 495

Rosebery, Lord, II. 259

Rotch, Benjamin, M.P., II. 259

Rothschild family, I. 18, 225

Rotunda, The, Woolwich; curiosities in, II. 31, 32

Rous, Provost, a resident at Acton in Commonwealth times, I. 11, 15

Rowlandson, the caricaturist, II. 497, 498

Roxeth, Harrow, Middlesex, I. 254, 273

Royal Alfred Institution for Aged Merchant Seaman, Belvedere, Kent, II. 46

Royal Arsenal, Woolwich; its early history, II. 14—16; convict labour, 16, 17; establishment of a foundry here, 17; evidences of an earlier antiquity, 17—21; removal of the laboratory thither, 19; growth of the Arsenal, 19, 20; description of the several buildings, 21—28

Royal Artillery Institution, Woolwich, II. 31

Royal Cambridge Asylum for Soldiers' Widows, Norbiton, II. 315

"Royal Forest Hotel," Chingford, I. 434, 440, 441

Royal Gun Factories, Woolwich Arsenal, II. 23

Royal Gunpowder Factory, Waltham, I. 395

Royal Military Academy, Woolwich, I. 10, 32, 33

Royal Military Repository, Woolwich, II. 11, 31

Royal Naval School, St. Margaret's, I. 59, 77

"Royal Oak" tavern, Teddington, I. 124

Royal Small Arms Factory, I. 351

Rubens, the painter, I. 165, 167, 359, II. 237, 436
Ruckholt House, Leyton, I. 485
Ruckholts, Leyton, I. 484, 489
Ruislip; boundaries and population, I. 240; outlying hamlets; agricultural produce, &c.; extract from the "Domesday" survey; Ruislip priory, 241; the manor; the vicarage; the parish church; monuments; the parish records, 242; primitive condition of the inhabitants; Ruislip Common; Ruislip Park; Eastcote; High Grove House, 243
Runnymede, and the signing of Magna Charta, I. 191
Rushey Green, Kent, II. 95
Ruskin, John, Abode of, II. 66, 372
Russell, Earl, II. 355, 356
Russell, Lady Rachel, I. 284, 333
Russell, Major-General Richard, grandson of Oliver Cromwell, I. 229
Russell, Mr. Scott, engineer, II. 98
Ruxley, Kent, II. 59; Ruxley Heath, 60; the old church, 62
Ruxley Lodge, Thames Ditton, II. 279
Ruysdael, the painter, II. 340
Rysbach, the sculptor, I. 279, II. 202
Ryves, Dr. Bruno, vicar of Acton and Stanwell, I. 10, 15, 195

S

Sancroft, Archbishop, II. 164
Sala, Geo. A., II. 490
Salis, Count de, I. 227
Salisbury Hall, Walthamstow, I. 466
Salisbury, Marquis of, holder of an advowson, I. 332
Salmon, the antiquary, I. 385, 386, 391, 484, II. 197, 313
Salter, Mr., the angler, II. 278
Salters' Company almshouses, Watford, I. 307
Sambrooke Park, Southgate, I. 347
Sanatorium, Harrow School, I. 262
Sanderstead, Surrey; its situation and position, II. 139; the manor; All Saints Church; its monuments; Sanderstead Court and Queen Elizabeth, 140
Sandon Farm, Esher, II. 285
Sandown, Esher, Surrey, I. 175
Sandown races, II. 286
Sandwich, Lord, I. 135, 141
Savage, the poet, I. 104
Savery's Weir, Roman coins found near Staines, I. 186
Saville House, Twickenham, residence of Lady Mary Wortley Montagu, I. 92
Saville, Sir George, Richardson's "Sir Charles Grandison," I. 92
Scadbury, Kent, 70, 71; its early history; descent of the manor, 80, 81; the manorhouse, 82
Scawen, Sir William, II. 198, 202, 203
Schalch, Andrew, of the Arsenal, Woolwich, II. 11, 17, 21
Scharf, Mr. George; his account of Littleberries, Hendon, I. 282, 283
Schomberg, Duke of, I. 33
Scott, Sir Gilbert, architect, I. 21, 228, 235, 236, 242, 256, 262, 273, 305, 345, 346, 410, 505, II. 107, 154, 315, 481
Scott, Sir Walter, I. 311, 352, 367
Scott, the Quaker poet, I. 561, 562
"Scribleriad," Cambridge's poem of the, I. 82
Scrope, Archbishop, Martyrdom of, I. 61
Seaford, Lord, II. 293
Sedley, Sir Charles, I. 245, II. 247, 251
Seething Wells, Kingston, 297, 303
Selwyn family, The, II. 387, 388
Severndroog Castle, Shooter's Hill, II. 33
Sewage, Utilisation of, I. 5
Sewardstone, Epping Forest, I. 423; its situation and boundaries, 435
Shadwell, Sir Lancelot, I. 218, II. 443, 463

Shakespeare, I. 244, 245, II. 285, 380
Sheen or Shene manor, I. 44, 45, II. 317, 333; death of Edward III., 333; the palace, 334; the monastery of Sheen, 341, 343
Sheldon, Archbishop, II. 154, 156, 164
Shelley, the poet, I. 39, II. 410
Shenley, Middlesex; extent and population, I. 312; descent of the manor; Shenley Hall, or Salisbury; Newberries; Old Organ Hall; Porters; Holmes, otherwise High Canons, 313; the village of Shenley; the chapel-of-ease; St. Botolph's parish church; an old parish clerk, 314
Shenstone, the poet, I. 34, II. 367
Shepperton, Middlesex; its situation; Cæsar's crossing-place; population; the manor and its history; the parish church, I. 177; its rectors; angling in the Thames; Shepperton Green; antiquarian discoveries at Shepperton, 178; antiquarian remains of the locality; the Wall Closes; the Coway stakes, 179; opinions of antiquarians thereon, 180, 181
Sherbrooke, Lord, II. 148, 181
Sheridan, Richard Brinsley, I. 59, 261, 268
Shernhall Street, Walthamstow, I. 465, 467
Sherrick Green, I. 225
Shirley, Surrey; general characteristics of the village; broom-making industry; the parish church; Shirley House, II. 136
Shirley Common, II. 124
Shooter's Hill, Woolwich, II. 8, 10, 32, 33, 34, 35, 36, 39, 41, 53, 58, 83
Shortlands, Kent; Grote, the historian of Greece, II. 104
Shovel, Sir Cloudesley, II. 58, 59
Shower, Sir Bartholomew, of Pinner Hill, I. 250, 251
Shrewsbury, Earl of, killed in a duel by the Duke of Buckingham, II. 461
Shrewsbury Place, Isleworth, I. 58
Sidcup, Kent; its situation and population; St. John's Church, II. 54; Ursula Lodge; Blendon Hall; Hall Place, 55; the family of At-Hall; Bourne Place, 56
Siddons, Mrs., actress, II. 360
Sidmouth, Lord, II. 353, 357, 428
Silk stream, The, Kingsbury, I. 274, 278
Silver Hall, Isleworth, I. 59
Silver Town, Plaistow, I. 510
Sion House, seat of the Duke of Northumberland, I. 44; the original religious house, and Shakespeare's allusion to it; dimensions of the premises; foundation of the monastery; its income at the dissolution of the monasteries; its foundation customary at the period; number of persons in the monastery, 45; rule of St. Bridget the rule of the monastery; sketch of Sion House; early history of the house, 46; duties of the abbess, chamberess, &c.; wardrobes of the "daughters of Sion," 47; duties of the cellaress, 48; the sisters' meals, 48, 50; the monastery the property of the sovereign at the Dissolution; subsequent history of Sion House, 50; relics in the monastery, 51; visitation under Lord Cromwell, 51, 52; granted to the Protector Somerset; afterwards reverted to the Duke of Northumberland; the house of Percy condemned for supposed complicity in the gunpowder plot to pay a fine of £30,000, 52; the fine liquidated by the king's acceptance of Sion House; renovation of the building; Charles II. at Sion House; temporary residence of Queen Anne; royal visits since, 53; description of the building, 53, 54; pictures; the lion from Northumberland House, 54; the gardens, 55; the late Dowager Duchess of Northumberland a distinguished botanist, 56
Sion House Academy, Brentford, I. 39

Sipson hamlet, Harmondsworth, Middlesex, I. 204
Skelton, the poet, II. 212
Skippon, Major-General, I. 11, 15
Slade, The, Plumstead, II. 37
Sladen family, The, Bushey, I. 307
Smallbury Green, Heston, Middlesex, I. 44
Smee, Mr., his account of Beddington Park gardens, II. 185, 188; his experimental garden, 195, 196, 221
Smiles, Dr., Quotation from, I. 25, 530
Smith, Mr. J. T., I. 38, 155, 167, 347, 361, 567, II. 484
Smith, Sydney, I. 464
Snaresbrook; general appearance of the locality; the rights of commoners; the "Eagle" inn, I. 472; the Eagle pond; the Infant Orphan Asylum; the Merchant Seaman's Orphan Asylum; Christ Church; the Weavers' Almshouses, 473
Somerville, Mrs., Quotation from, II. 76
South Acton; its church, I. 15
Southall, Middlesex, I. 23, 215; the church; the manor-house, 216; the "southern holt," or wood; its grounds; the manor; the Metropolitan Workhouse School, 217; the former weekly market, 218
Southall Park, I. 218
Southall Green, I. 216
Southam, Middlesex, I. 320
South End, Bromley, II. 96, 97; "Jack Cade's Island," 96
South-Eastern Railway, The, II. 51, 54, 70, 82, 83, 136
Southey, the poet, II. 350
Southgate, Middlesex; the "Cherry Tree" inn; the church; Arnold's Court, the seat of the Welds, I. 345; Arno's Grove; Minchenden House; Bromefield Park; Bowes Manor; Bowes Park; Culland's Grove; Palmer's Green; Winchmore Hill; St. Paul's Church, 346; Bush Hill Park; Sir Hugh Myddelton and the New River; Edmonton; the Firs, 347
South Mimms, Middlesex; census returns; general appearance of the village; the old North road, I. 316; the manor of South Mimms; St. Giles's Church; tombs and brasses; the almshouses, 317
Spa, The mineral, South Acton, I. 16
Speech-room, The new, Harrow School, I. 261, 262
Speed, the historian, I. 191, 410, 521
Spelman, the antiquary, II. 343
Spelthorne Sanatorium, The, Bedfont, I. 196
Spencer, Earl, of the Reform Bill era, I. 269
Spencer, Viscount, lord of the manor of Wimbledon, II. 476, 477
Spenser, the poet, II. 328
Sports and diversions of Brentford; curious entries of the account-books, I. 40
Spottiswoode, Mr. William, I. 269
Spring Grove, Isleworth; Honnor's Home, I. 60
Spring Park, Shirley, II. 136
St. Albans, Duke of, his house at Hansworth, I. 70, 299
St. Anne's Hill, Chertsey, I. 182, 184
St. James's Street, Walthamstow, I. 465, 470
St. Leonards, Lord, II. 275—277
St. Margaret's, Isleworth, I. 59; the Royal Naval School, 59, 77
St. Mary Cray, Kent, II. 56, 70; the church; the railway station, 63; the manor; the market house, 64
St. Paul's Cray, Kent, II. 56, 63, 70; the church, 63, 64
Stafford, Archbishop, II., 159, 160, 163
Staines; situation of the town; the river Colne; Roman coins found here, I. 186; Roman origin of Staines; the City boundary stone; the Court of Conservancy of the Thames, 187; Domesday survey of Staines; its early history; its

distance from London by water; the parish church and its precursors, 188; tombs; curious entries in the church books; the town and its streets; the Society of Friends; the railway station, 189; the market; population; its inns; royal passages through the town; the "Vine" Inn; curious anecdote; its water supply; the Thames at Staines; Staines bridge, 190

Staines Moor, Middlesex, I. 191, 195

Staines, Sir William, Lord Mayor of London, Anecdote of, I. 237

Stamford Brook Green, Turnham Green, I. 7

Stanhope, Sir William, the purchaser of Pope's house, I. 106, 109

"Standing houses," Use of, by former Archbishops of Canterbury, II. 158,159

Stanmore, I. 270, 297

Stanmore Common, I. 299, 305

Stanmore Heath, I. 304, 307

Stanmore Park, I. 299

Stanwell, Middlesex; its situation; early history, I. 192; descent of Stanwell manor, Lord Windsor, 193, 194; situation of the village; population; St. Mary's parish church; the "Easter Sepulchre," its former monumental brasses, 194; Dr. Bruno Ryves, its vicar, 195

Stanwell Moor, Middlesex, I. 195

Stanwell Place, Middlesex, I. 194

Staple Hill, Loughton; the lake, I. 442, 448

"Star and Garter" Hotel, Richmond, II. 359, 374, 377—380, 381; eminent personages who have resided here, 380

Star Chamber, an apartment in Strawberry Hill, I. 114

State apartments, Hampton Court Palace, I. 165, 166; the portraits, 165

Steele, Sir Richard, I. 141, 163, 171

Steinman, the Croydon historian, II. 153, 155, 157, 170

Stephenson, Sir William, I. 238

Stepney Marsh, I. 537

Stevens, G. A., lecturer, II. 312

Steyne, The, Acton, I. 13, 15

Stillingfleet, Bishop, I. 93

Stockmar, Baron, II. 293

Stone, Andrew, preceptor to George III., I. 93

Stone Causeway, Harrow Weald Common, I. 272

Stone, Nicholas, sculptor, I. 298, 299, 329, 357, 467

Stonebridge Park, Middlesex, I. 223, 225

Stow, the chronicler, I. 29, 81, 409, 538, II. 9, 15, 152, 163, 166, 290, 359, 459, 473

Strafford, Earl of, I. 318, 351

Strand-on-the-Green, Acton, I. 7, 16, 17, 35, II. 410

Stratford, Essex; its former condition; the Abbey of Stratford-Langthorne, I. 506; pumping-station of the Metropolitan Drainage Works; St. John's, Christ Church, and St. Paul's Churches; the Town Hall; Stratford New Town, 507; the vegetable market; Old Ford; Bow Bridge, 508; Roman roads, 508, 509

Strawberry Hill, Twickenham, I. 71, 78; Horace Walpole's description of the property at the time of his purchase (1746), 111, 112; he enlarges the building, 112; description of the building, 112; its principal contents, 113—116; catalogue of its contents; the building shown to few persons, 116; the chapel in the garden, 116, 117; Maurice's eulogium of the whole; the Earl of Bath's panegyric; the building suffers from the Hounslow powder-mills explosion, 117; some account of Horace Walpole, 117, 118; his contributions to literature; his love of letter-writing; the poet Chatter-

ton; his select circle of friends, 118; his gallantry, and what nearly came of it; becomes Earl of Orford; he dislikes his new honours, 119; bequest of Strawberry Hill; Mrs. Damer becomes the owner; list of her works in sculpture; resigns the property to the Waldegrave family; sold by auction; Eliot Warburton's remarks on the fate of Strawberry Hill, 120; Lord Jeffery's account of the sale; Lady Waldegrave's *réunions* at Strawberry Hill, 121; death of Lady Waldegrave; the property unsold in 1882, 122

Strawberry Hill Shot, I. 111

Strawberry Vale, Twickenham, I. 75

Street, Mr. G. E., architect, I. 317, 328, 464

Strong, the mason, I. 288

Strype, the historian and antiquary, I. 487, 488, 534, 536, 538, 548, II. 165, 169, 340

Stud-house, The, Hampton Court Palace, I. 170

Stukeley, the antiquarian, I. 7, 179, 181, 182, 187, 275, 297, 484, 508, 514, II. 496

Successful jockeys, Anecdotes of, II. 269, 270

Sudbrooke, Petersham; its various owners; now a hydropathic establishment, II. 329, 353

Sudbury, Harrow; the common; St. John the Baptist's Church; Sudbury Hall, I. 273

Sudbury, Archbishop de, II. 163

Sudbury Hall, Middlesex, I. 273

Sudden accession to fortune, I. 57

Suffolk Place Farm, Plumstead, II. 35

Suffolks, the manor of, Enfield, I. 374

Sumner, Archbishop, II. 132, 135

Sumner, Dr., head-master of Harrow School, I. 266

Sunbury, Middlesex; its various names; history of the manor; the manor-house; the old manor of Chenetone, and its history, I. 173, 174; Kempton Park; Kempton House, 175; the parish church; other chapels and churches; Sunbury Place; Sunbury Deeps; Dickens's reminiscences, 176

Sunbury Common, I. 175

Sundridge Park, Bromley, Kent, II. 94, 95

Surbiton, Kingston, II. 303, 310, 314; its churches, 314, 315

Surbiton Common, II. 299

"Surplice," The race-horse, II. 262, 265

Surrey, the "South Rie" of our forefathers, I. 2, 125, II. 130, 509

Sutton, Surrey; its situation and boundaries; shepherds' crowns; chalk pits; irregular growth of the town; Sutton Common; Bonnell Common; census returns, I. 207; descent of the manor, 208; local improvements; the parish church; monuments, 209; rectors, 210; Benhilton, 210, 211; the "Cock" and "Greyhound" inns, 211, 212; Jackson, the pugilist; Mr. Solly's residence; the South Metropolitan District Schools, 212; Middlesex County Lunatic Asylum; "Little Hell," 212; rise of the Wandle river, 479

Sutton Court, Chiswick, I. 7

Sutton Lane, Chiswick, I. 7

Swakeleys, Middlesex; history of the descent of the estate; Sir Robert Viner; Pepys' visit here; the house passes into the Clarke family, 239

Swanley, Kent, I. 64

"Swan and Bottle" inn, Uxbridge, I. 233

Swannery, A, I. 131

"Swan-upping," I. 130

Swift, I. 83, 86, 97, 100, 102, 106, 197, 202, 287, 290, 292, II. 284, 323, 350, 432

Sydenham, II. 89

Sydenham waters, The, II. 98

Sydney, Lord, II. 72, 80, 82

Syon Hill, Isleworth, I. 60

Syon vista, Kew Gardens, I. 60

T

"Tabard" inn, The, Turnham Green, I. 8

Tabley, Lord de, Family of, I. 200

Tait, Archbishop, II. 132, 135, 161, 466

Talfourd, Judge, I. 281

Talworth, Surrey, II. 272; the church; Talworth Court, 273

Tankerville, Earls of, I. 200

Tanner, Bishop, antiquarian, I. 29, 203, 254

Tapestry Gallery, The, Hampton Court Palace, I. 166

Tattenham Corner, Epsom, II. 261

Taylor, Sir Robert, architect, II. 53, 340

Tea, Use of, in Queen Anne's time, I. 156

Teck, Duke of, II. 353, 357, 380, 405

Teddington; growth of the village, I. 123; its situation; angling in the Thames; the Queen's barge; derivation of "Teddington;" uncertain nature of its foundation, 124; Teddington a "tithing" in the Hundred of Spelthorne, 124, 125; descent of the manor, 125, 126; the last court-leet; "Queen Elizabeth's Hunting Box," 126; St. Mary's Church, 127; its monuments, 128, 129; its incumbents; church of St. Peter and Paul; rapid growth of Teddington; eminent inhabitants of Teddington, 129; the lady and the groom; Teddington Lock; the "intake" of the London water companies; swan-upping, 130

Teddington Lock, The "intake" of the London water companies at, I. 130

Temple, Sir William, I. 197, II. 431, 432

Temple, Dr., now Bishop of Exeter, I. 95

Tenison's, Archbishop, chapel, Hounslow, I. 64; Archbishop Tenison, II. 164, 177

Tennis Court Lane, Hampton Court Palace, I. 164

Tennyson, the poet, II. 302, 303, 317, 318, 338, 353, 376, 389, 410, 413, 519

Tenterden, Lord Chief Justice, I. 279

Terrick, Bishop, I. 76

Thackeray, the novelist; his grandfather, I. 329

Thames, The river; the Thames as a political boundary, and as a boundary of counties, I. 568; tributary rivers, 567, 568; breadth of the river; its general aspect and character of scenery, 569; the embankments, 570; shoals and floods, 570, 571; tides, 571, 572; the Thames as the common highway of London; anecdote of Cardinal Wolsey, 572; Sir Walter Raleigh and Queen Elizabeth; abdication of James II.; funeral of Lord Nelson; water traffic in the time of Richard II., 573, 574; the conservancy of the Thames, 574; boating on the Thames, 574—576; the Pool, II. 1; the commerce of London, 2; Execution Dock; the Thames gibbets; the *Warspite*, *Arethusa*, and *Chichester*, training ships; the *Dreadnought;* a floating small-pox hospital; Bugsby's Reach; Woolwich Reach, and Gallion's Reach; Plumstead and Erith Marshes; sewage outfall of the Metropolitan Main Drainage Works; Dagenham; Erith; the Darent and the Cray; Long Reach; Purfleet; powder magazines; the *Cornwall* reformatory ship; Greenhithe and Northfleet; Stone Church; Ingress Abbey, 3; the training ship *Worcester;* West Thurrock, Gray's Thurrock, and Little Thurrock; Belmont Castle; South Hope Reach; discovery of fossils and remains of animals; "Cunobelin's Gold Mines," or "Dane-Holes"; Gravesend; Tilbury Fort, 4; West Tilbury; Tilbury docks; Hope Reach; East Tilbury; Thames Haven; Canvey Island; Had-leigh Castle; Leigh; Yanlet Creek; the boundary marks of the Thames Conservancy; Southend, 5

Thames Angling Preservation Society, I. 135, 176, II. 278, 314

Thames Conservancy, The, II. 314

Thames Ditton, Surrey, II. 273, 274; its situation and boundaries; railway communication; population; the parish church; its brasses, 274; prolific offsprings; monuments; William and Mary Howitt; ancient weapons found here; its occupants, 275; the Dandies' Fête, 276; Lord St. Leonards, 276, 277; Ditton House, 277; the "Swan" tavern; Thames Angling Preservation Society; a famous angler; lines composed by Theodore Hook in a punt off Thames Ditton, 278; early history of the manor of Thames Ditton; Claygate, 279; Imber Court; the river Mole; the poets on this river, 280; its course, 281

Thames Street, Hampton, I. 136

Thames Valley Railway, I. 175, 178

Thatched House Lodge, Richmond Park; its residents, II. 356

Theatre, The, Richmond, II. 360—363

Thelusson family, The, I. 308, II. 94

Theobalds, Middlesex, I. 347, 348, 351, 353, 358; James I. at, 364, 365; its situation, and history of the manor; the estate purchased by Sir William Cecil, afterwards Lord Burleigh, 376; Queen Elizabeth's visits to Theobalds; Lord Burleigh at Theobalds, 377; Sir Robert Cecil, Earl of Salisbury; King James's reception, 378, 379; the King desires to exchange Theobalds with Hatfield; James entertains Christian IV. of Denmark here; the King's narrow escape; behaviour of King James, 380; his death, 381; description of the palace and gardens, 381, 382; demolition of the palace; present condition of the estate, 383, 384

Thetford, Viscount, and Earl of Arlington, I. 201

Theydon Bois, the old manor-house, I. 449

Thomson, the poet, I. 34, 71, 82, 323, II. 291, 323, 332, 354, 367, 370, 373, 375, 384—387, 407; opinions of Thomson's character, 385, 386; his house now a hospital, 387

Thornhill, Sir James, the painter, I. 288, 346, II. 136, 137, 466

Thorneycroft, Messrs., manufactory of, Chiswick, I. 5

Thorney Broad and its trout-fishing, West Drayton, I. 208

Thornton Heath, Surrey, II. 180, 181

Thorpe, the Kentish antiquary, II. 51, 52, 107

Thrale, the brewer, II. 177

Thurtell, the murderer, I. 303, 311

Tibhurst Manor, Aldenham, Middlesex, I. 309

Tickell, Richard, the poet's grandson, I. 134; suicide of, ib.

Tierney, George, Duel between Mr. Pitt and, II. 490, 492, 493

Tillotson, Archbishop, I. 498, II. 164

Tite, Sir William, architect, I. 281

Titian, the painter, I. 477

Tittenhanger, I. 315, 316

Tobacco, Sir Walter Raleigh and the use of, I. 14

Toland, Dr., on Epsom, II. 244, 245, 249, 261

Tollemache, General, II. 321

Tollemache, Sir Lionel; his wife, afterwards Duchess of Lauderdale, II. 320

Tollemaches, The, the Earls of Dysart

Tonson, Jacob, the bookseller, II. 458, 459

Tooke, John Horne, I. 20, 35; the "Diversions of Purley," II. 141, 142; his prosecution for libel, and the eligi-

bility of a clergyman for a seat in Parliament, 142—145; his epitaph, 145; his life at Wimbledon, 484

Tooting; its etymology; the river Graveny, II. 530; doubtful parish boundary lines; Tooting-Bec Common; early history of the manor, 531, 532; encroachments on the manor; the Maynard family; Sir Paul Wichcote; Sir James Bateman; the parish church; the new church, 533; sepulchral monuments, 534; the village of Tooting; the Jewish Convalescent Home, 536; Daniel Defoe, 536, 537; Summer's Town; St. Mary Magdalene's Church; Tooting Common, 538

Totteridge, Middlesex, I. 320, 335; its etymology; descent of the manor; census returns; condition of the roads; St. Audrey's Church, 332; tombs; yew-trees in the churchyard; the Priory; Pointer's Grove, 333; Copped Hall; Totteridge Park; Wykeham Rise; Baron Bunsen a resident, 334

"Toy" inn, Hampton, I. 135

Tramway, The first iron, II. 174, 175

Trapp, Dr. Joseph, rector of Harlington; lines on his monument, I. 200

Trent Park, or Cock Fosters, I. 351, 352, 366, 367; its various owners, 368

Trevor, Thomas, ancestor of the Viscounts Hampden, I. 358

Trimmer, Mrs., I. 40

Trinder, Rev. D., on Teddington, I. 124, 125

Trollope, Anthony, I. 329, 388

Trollope, Mrs., novelist, I. 329

Trumbell, Sir William, I. 23, 96, 102

Trumpeters' House, Richmond Palace, II. 340

Truro, Lord Chancellor, I. 346

Tubbendens, Farnborough, II. 117

"Tumble-down Dick" hostelry, Brentford, I. 35; songs and ballads on, ib.

Tumbling Bay, Hampton, I. 136

Tupper, Mr. M. F., II. 213, 214, 217, 220, 221, 239, 245, 270, 271, 274, 275, 283, 287, 294, 297, 394, 418, 515, 517, 520

Turner, the painter, II. 372

Turnham Green, I. 7, 32; former condition of, 7

Turpin, Dick, the highwayman, I. 336, 341, 369, 567, II. 33; his "Cave," High Beech Hill, 436

Tweeddale, Marchioness of, I. 93

Twickenham, I. 30, 70; its situation, 70, 71; Hofman's description of the locality; various spellings of the name, 71; poems descriptive of Twickenham by Walpole, Pope, Dodsley, Thomson, and others, 71, 72; situation of the town; extent; climate, 72; the original manor, 72, 74; Eel-pie Island; Pope's description of the river-side approaches; the parish church, 74, 75; the new church; Sir Godfrey Kneller, 75; Pope's monument to his parents and himself; other tombs and monuments, 76; churches and charitable institutions, 76, 77; the town hall; Perryn House, afterwards the Economic Museum; its destruction by fire, 77; extracts from the parish registers, 78; curious entries, 78, 79; anecdote of Sir James Delaval and the Duke of Somerset; residents at Twickenham, 80; various accounts of Twickenham, 81; Twickenham Park and its history, 81, 82; Cambridge House, 82; literary tastes of its owner; Meadowbank, Mr. Bishop's residence, 83; Marble Hill, 83, 85, 86; the witty Bishop Corbett, 86; Ragman's Castle, 86, 87; Orleans House and its several owners, 87, 88; the Orleans Club, 88; York House and its owners, 89, 90; the Grove and the Duke of Wharton, 91;

92; Lady Mary Montagu; Twickenham House, 92; Lord Ferrers' house; Fielding, 93; a few noted residents, 93, 94; Kneller Hall and Sir Godfrey Kneller, 94, 95; Alexander Pope (q.v.); Strawberry Hill (q.v.)

Twickenham Park; its earlier history, I. 81; more recent particulars; its different owners, 82

Twickenham Common, I. 93

Twickenham House, residence of Sir John Hawkins, I. 92, 93

Twyford, or West Twyford, Middlesex; population of the small parish; Twyford Abbey; the manor, I. 221; descent of the manor; the chapel, 222

Tylney, Earl (see Wanstead Manor House)

Tyrconnell, Earl of, II. 293

U

Umbrella, Invention of the, I. 26

University Boat-race, The; the crowds of spectators brought together to witness the race; the "blue" fever, II. 429; interest to Londoners occasioned by the University boat-race, 430; scenes on the river; the "Press" boat and the umpire's steamer; by rail to the scene of the race, 442; Putney and Mortlake on boat-race day; description of the race; past history of rowing as an old English amusement, 443; the race for Doggett's coat and badge, 444; a London regatta, 445; the first students' race upon the Thames; the earliest race between the Universities of Oxford and Cambridge, 446; accounts of subsequent races, 447—450; table showing the results of the race from its institution, 450

Unwin's suburban guides, Quotations from, II. 94, 104, 116, 117, 123, 124, 183, 186, 197, 207, 223, 239, 455

Uphall, Essex; Roman encampment here, I. 498, 524, 525

Upper Halliford, Middlesex, I. 177

Upton Park, Essex, I. 504; the Gurney family, 504, 505

Ursula Lodge, Sidcup, II. 55

Uvedale, Dr. Robert, I. 355

Uxbridge, Middlesex, II. 208, 226; its etymology, 230; its antiquity; meeting of the Royalists and Roundheads, 231, 232; public reception of the treaty; the Treaty House; inns of the town, 232; the High Bridge; the "Swan and Bottle" inn; early fortifications; Roman roads; population; the "Chequers" inn; the corn and flour trade; fairs, 233; the market-house; the great Oxford road; the parish church, 234; nave, oak roof, and chancel; the curfew; the parish registers; the Rev. John Lightfoot; anecdote of the Duchess of Portland, 235; new churches; the Nonconformists; Hillingdon House; Uxbridge Common; Mr. Harris, of Covent Garden Theatre, 236; burnings at Uxbridge; some anecdotes; Sir William Staines, Lord Mayor; the river Colne; fisheries near Uxbridge; Denham village, 237

Uxbridge Moor, I. 236, 237

V

Vale Mascal, North Cray, Kent, II. 60

Valence estate, Dagenham, I. 527, 528

Valentines, Ilford, I. 497

Valley of the Thames, I. 208, 236

Vanbrugh, Sir John, architect, II. 21, 22, 136, 137, 292

Vancouver, the navigator, II. 326, 375, 380

Van den Wyngaerde, the artist, II. 365

Van Mildert, Bishop, II. 487

Van Orlay, the artist, I. 163

Vansittart family, The, II. 50, 63, 137

Vansittart, Right Hon. Nicholas (Lord Bexley), II. 63, 105

Vaughan, Dr., head master of Harrow School, I. 261, 262, 267

Vaughan Library, Harrow School, I. 262

Vavasour, Sir Thomas, builder of Ham House, II. 318

Velasquez, the painter, I. 165

Verelot, the painter, I. 165

Verrio, the artist, I. 165, II. 257, 321

Verum, The river, I. 233

Vicars, Captain Hedley, II. 101

Vicomte d'Arlingcourt on Richmond Park, II. 331, 333

Victoria and Albert Docks, I. 502, 512, 513

Victoria Docks, I. 502, 510, 511, 512; fossilised peat bogs, 512

Villiers, Lord Francis, Death of, II. 299

Vincent, Mr., the historian of Woolwich Arsenal, II. 10, 12, 15, 17, 20, 24, 25, 27, 28, 29, 33, 35

Vines, Remarkable, I. 170, 498

Vineyards, The, Richmond, II. 369, 374

Voltaire, I. 201, 202

Volunteer encampment at Wimbledon, II. 497—509

Vulliamy, the clockmaker, I. 161

W

Waddon, Surrey; its etymology, II. 182; Waddon Lane; the Wandle; Waddon Mill; "Queen Elizabeth's Walk," 183

"Wagon and Horses" inn, Brentford, I. 34

Wake, Archbishop, II. 154, 156, 158

"Wake Arms" inn, Epping Road, I. 436, 437

Wakefield, Priscilla, the authoress, II. 458, 464, 476, 490

Waldegrave, Frances, Lady, her career at Strawberry Hill, I. 121; her second husband, Mr. Chichester Fortescue (now Lord Carlingford), 122

Waldegrave, Lord, the Strawberry Hill property inherited by, I. 120

Walker, William, astronomical lecturer, I. 213

Waller, Sir William, and Osterley Park, I. 43

Waller, the poet, I. 155

Wallington, Surrey; traces of Roman occupation; its early history; descent of the manor, II. 104; railway communication; "Jerusalem," or Carshalton-on-the-Hill; Mr. Smee's experimental garden; the Wandle; Wallington House; A Labourers' Friendly Society, 196; the parish church; Beddington Corner; Wallington Green; geology of the district, 197

Walpole, Robert, Lord, II. 352

Walpole, Sir Robert, II. 345, 348, 351, 358, 428

Walpole, Horace, I. 17, 18, 69, 70, 71, 81, 83, 85, 91, 92, 93, 95, 109, 111, 127, 164, 189, II. 359, 363, 383, 392, 477, 478, 185, 190, 206, 231, 248, 275; his mansion at Strawberry Hill, 111—116; some account of Walpole, 117, 118; his narrow escape of his life; becomes Earl of Orford; his death, 119; his personal appearance; Lord Macaulay's estimate of his character; Dr. Aikin's estimate of him; Crabbe's mock-heroic lines on Walpole; bequest of Strawberry Hill, 120; Walpole's visit to Ham House, II. 322; his friendship with and letters to the Misses Berry, 326, 327

Walsingham, Sir Francis, II. 459

Walsingham family, The, II. 71, 80, 81, 452

Walter, John, founder of the Times, monument in Teddington church to, I. 128

Waltham Abbey, I. 386, 393, 395, 398,

399, 403; situation of the town; its etymology; foundation of the abbey; its re-foundation by Harold, 404; legend of the Holy Cross, 405; gifts bestowed on the abbey; Harold's tomb; the church despoiled by William the Conqueror, 406; its recovery under subsequent sovereigns, 407; disputes between the abbot and townspeople, 408; Henry III. and the abbot's dinner, 409; an incident touching the Reformation; income of the abbey at the dissolution; Fuller, the historian; the conventual estate passes into other hands; description of the abbey church, 410; restoration of the abbey, 411; sale of the church bells; present condition of the remains of the abbey, 412; Rome-land; the abbey gateway and bridge, 415; worthies connected with the abbey; history of Waltham town, 416; extent of Waltham Abbey Parish, 416, 417; census returns; rural appearance of the locality; principal seats and mansions; Warlies; Copped Hall, 417; some account of the place; Ambresbury Banks, 418; Queen Boadicea's conflict with the Romans, 419, 420; obelisks in the neighbourhood, 421, 422; highwaymen and footpads; the village of Epping; St. John's Church, 423

Waltham Cross, I. 392, 393; Queen Victoria's visit; the "Four Swans" inn; Holy Trinity Church; the Spital Houses, 393

Waltham Cross, I. 384, 386, II. 251

Waltham Forest, I. 423, 424

Waltham Government Powder Mills; situation of the buildings, I. 399; description of the works, 400

Walthamstow, I. 464; its area and general appearance; Walthamstow. slip; census returns; the railway-stations; its etymology, 465; descent of the manor; Highams; Salisbury Hall; Chapel End; Bellevue House; St. Mary's Church, 466; its renovation; monuments; almshouses; the grammar school; Walthamstow House, 467; Benjamin Disraeli, 468; noted residents of Walthamstow, 469; the Town Hall and other public institutions; Hoe Street; Hale End; Marsh Street; St. James's Street; St. James's and St. Saviour's Churches; East London Waterworks reservoirs; geological discoveries, 470; an old bridge; St. Stephen's Church; Whip's Cross; St. Peter's Church, Forest Side; the Forest Grammar School, 471

Walthamstow Slip, I. 465, 484

Walton, Izaak, I. 93, 178, 190, 208, 237, 384, 416, 465, 561, 563, 565, 566, II. 183, 278, 303

Walton-on-Thames, I. 177, 181; II. 296

Wandle, The river, II. 152, 173, 176, 182, 183, 184, 185, 187, 200, 201, 221, 469, 479, 483, 513; description of, 195, 196; the "beaver's" haunt, 479, 516, 524, 525, 528

Wandletown, unabridged form of Waddon, II. 182

Wanstead; area and population; its boundaries; etymology, I. 473; traces of Roman occupation; descent of the manor; the Earl of Leicester and Queen Elizabeth, 474; a "spa" at Wanstead, 475; Pepys' opinion of Wanstead House; visit of John Evelyn; Wanstead House rebuilt by Sir Richard Child, afterwards Lord Tylney; description of the house and grounds, 476, 477; death of Lord Tylney; Miss Tylney-Long, the heiress; her marriage, 477; the estate sold by auction; Mr. Pole-Tylney-Long becomes Earl of Mornington; death of the Countess of Mornington; death of the second Countess; demoli-

tion of the house, 478; the house and grounds described; the property secured to the people by the Corporation of London; the park, gardens, and grotto; Lake House; Cann Hall, 479; St. Mary's Church, Wanstead; monuments; the village of Wanstead; the "George" inn, 480; an expensive pie; Park Gate; Wanstead Flats; the Princess Louise Home; Dr. Pound, astronomer; his nephew, Bradley; his instruments; Admiral Sir William Penn; William Penn, 482; some account of Penn, 483

Wanstead Flats, I. 473, 481, 482, 502

Wanstead Manor House; Robert Dudley, Earl of Leicester; Queen Elizabeth; descent of the property, I. 474, 475, 476; Pepys visits the place; John Evelyn's visit; Sir John Child becomes the owner; his son, created Lord Tylney; description of the house and gardens, 476; palatial style of the building; Horace Walpole's account of a visit; death of Lord Tylney; the estate becomes the property of his sister, Miss Tylney-Long; her marriage to William Pole-Wellesley, afterwards Earl of Mornington; cost of the bride's dress, 477; sale of the mansion; Mr. Pole-Tylney-Long-Wellesley becomes Earl of Mornington; death of his wife; he marries again; death of the Countess of Mornington; the estate becomes the property of Lord Cowley; description of the house in 1843, 478; Rush's description; sketch of the park; purchased by the Corporation of London for the public use; the park, gardens, and grotto, 479

Wanstead Park, I. 472, 473, 474

Warbank, Keston, II. 116

Warburton, Bishop, II. 101, 105

Warburton, Eliot, I. 112, 120

Ward, Mrs. Horatia Nelson, Nelson's adopted daughter, II. 251

Warham, Archbishop, II. 163, 164, 178

Warlies Hall, Waltham, I. 417

Warlingham, Surrey; its situation, II. 145, 147; population; early history; "whipping the apple trees"; the church; ancient encampments, 146

Warner, the Woodford naturalist, I. 461

Warren, The, Chigwell, I. 451

Warren, The, Woolwich; now the Arsenal, II. 8, 10, 17, 19, 21

Warwick, Earl of, the king-maker, I. 324—327, II. 333

Water-supplies from the Thames, I. 136

Water companies near Hampton, I. 136

Waterland, Dr., I. 93

Watford, I. 305, 307, 315

Watling Street, Hendon; supposed Roman remains near, I. 278, 284, 297, 303

Watling Street, Kent, II. 8, 57, 152

Watts, Dr., I. 383, 384, II. 252; Dr. Watts' Wig and Lane, I. 389

Watts, Alaric A., the poet, II. 331

Weald Park, Harrow, I. 270

Weare, William; tomb of, I. 303; murder of, 310, 311

Webb, Mrs. Anne, Curious bequests of, I. 185

Weever, the author of "Funeral Monuments," I. 189, 329, II. 47

Wegg, Silas, the doggrel poet, II. 200

Weldon, Mr., the topographer, I. 417, 425, 436, 459, 461, 567

Wellesley House, Twickenham; now the City of London Police Orphanage, I. 77

Welling, Kent; its situation and etymology; Danson Park, II. 53

Welsh Charity School, Ashford, Middlesex, I. 185, 186

Welsh Harp railway station, I. 274, 275

Wembley, I. 223, 254; the manor, 273; the manor-house; Wembley Park; Wembley Hill; the "Green Man"

Tavern; gentlemen's seats; Wembley Green, 274

Wesley, I. 79, 213

Wesleyan Theological Institution, Richmond, II. 369, 370

West Bedfont, I. 195

West Drayton, Middlesex, I. 205; its vegetable productions; the manor and its descent, 206; remains of the manorhouse, 206, 207; Burroughs, formerly General Arabin's seat; the parish church; the parochial cemetery; the railway station; population; St. Catharine's Roman Catholic Church, 207; Thorney Broad and trout-fishing; the racecourse; Yiewsley, 208

West Ham, Essex; its division into wards; population; markets and fairs; All Saints' parish church; monuments; a curious fresco, 502, 503; eminent persons buried in the churchyard; charitable institutions; chapels; Upton Park, 504; the Gurney family; West Ham Park; Forest Gate; taverns and tea-gardens; Emmanuel and St. James's Churches, 505; population of Forest Gate; almshouses, 506

West Ham cemetery, I. 506

West India Docks; vastness of trade and commerce; arrival of coal-ships and other vessels in the port of London; number of barges and other craft assigned for traffic in 1792; plunder carried on in the lighters in the river, I. 549; the Thames police; proposals for the establishment of docks; foundation of the West India Docks; the opening ceremony, 550; description of the docks; a curious museum, 551; new dry docks; the Wood Wharf; the Rum Quay; the South West India Dock; the wool warehouses, 552

West London District Schools, Ashford, Middlesex, I. 186

West Middlesex Waterworks Company, II. 457

West Molesey, Surrey; the church; cemetery; Sir R. W. Carden, II. 283; Robert Baddeley, the actor, 283, 284

West, Temple, of West Wickham, II. 128, 129

West Wickham; annals of the parish, II. 124; Wickham Court; history of the mansion; the gallery of portraits, 125; fortifications of the house, 126; its internal fittings; the lawn, 127; the church; monuments and brasses; the parish registers, 128; Temple West's residence; Glover, the poet; discovery of palæolithic weapons and implements; a group of remarkable trees, 129

Westmacott, the sculptor, II. 527

Wey, The river, II. 281

Weybridge, II. 296

Whalebone House, Ilford, I. 496

Wharton, Duke of, I. 91, 92; account of, 92; his unfinished poem on Mary Queen of Scots, 92

Whately, Archbishop, II. 238

Whetstone, Middlesex, I. 332, 333; its situation; St. John's Church; census returns; George Morland, the artist, 335; general appearance of the village, 336

Whip's Cross, Walthamstow, I. 465, 472, 484; why so named, 471

Whitaker and Maitland, The families of, I. 447

Whitchurch, Edgware, I. 284, 285, 286, 297; the parish church, 292, 296; its monuments, 296

White, Sir Thomas, I. 464

White Gate, Woolwich, II. 10

Whitehead, Paul, politician and satirist, I. 93, 128

Whitehead, the poet, II. 179

Whitelock, the historian, I. 7, 33

White Lodge, The, Richmond Park; Queen Caroline's residence, II. 357; the Bog Lodge; Spanker's Hill, 358

White Webb's House, Enfield, I. 366, 369; the Gunpowder Plot, 369

Whitgift, Archbishop, II. 149, 154, 156, 161, 164, 165, 166, 167, 168, 169, 179, 183

Whitgift's Hospital, Croydon, II. 165; its foundation; its cost, 166; instructions concerning the charity; description of the building, 167; character of Whitgift, 168, 169; the school-house, 170

Whitgift's Grammar School, Croydon, II. 177

Whitton, Hounslow Heath, Sir Godfrey Kneller's house, I. 69

Whitton Park, Hounslow Heath, I. 69

"Widow's Struggle," The, inn, Hampton, I. 135

Wilberforce, William, philanthropist, I. 238, 282, 283, 334, II. 105, 112, 137, 486, 487, 488

Wilberforce, Bishop, II. 113, 193

"Wilberforce Oak," The, II. 113

Wilderness, The, Hampton Court Palace, I. 170

Wilkes, John, the demagogue; his popularity; Hogarth's portrait, I. 38; his personal appearance, 39; his residences at Teddington and Mill Hill, 129, 281

Wilkes, Rev. Wetenhall, the poet, I. 68, 69, 197

Willesden, Middlesex; the railway station, I. 222; extent and population; the railway junctions; the River Brent; old name of Willesden; the parish church, 223; enlargement and restoration; monumental brasses; old customs of the parish; old curates; supposed exploits of Jack Sheppard at Willesden; Church End; Queen's Town, 224; Willesden Green; Brondesbury; the Jewish cemetery; Harlesden; Cricklewood; Neasdon; railway depôts; Sherrick Green; Dollis Green; Stonebridge Park, 225

Willesden Green, I. 224, 225; its inns, 225

William III. and Queen Mary at Hampton Court; his delft-ware; his death, I. 155

William, Prince of Orange, the Stadtholder, at Hampton Court, I. 157

Wimbledon; situation and boundaries of the parish, II. 469; its etymology; early history of the manor, 470; Burstow Park, 471; the Cromwell family, 471—473; the Cecils; Queen Elizabeth at Wimbledon; James IV.'s visit to the Earl of Exeter; Queen Victoria at the manor house; Viscount Wimbledon, 473; Queen Henrietta purchases the manor, 474; Thomas Osborne, Earl of Danby, afterwards Duke of Leeds, 475; it finally comes to Lord Spencer; the present manor house, 476; the Artesian well; description of the original manor house, 477, 478; the old village; the parish church, 480, 481; the old parsonage; other churches and chapels; the cemetery; public institutions of the parish; Wimbledon Green, 482; the London Scottish Golf Club, 482, 483; the Wimbledon Sewage Works, 483; eminent residents; Pitt; Horne Tooke, 484; Wimbledon House; Joseph Marryatt; Gothic House; Captain Marryatt; the Countess of Guilford; Lord North, 485; General Sir Henry Murray; Sir Francis Burdett, 486; William Wilberforce, 486, 487; Mr. Lyde Browne, 487; Lord Melville; the Marquis of Rockingham; Lord Cottenham; Eliza Cook, 488; Jenny Lind, 488, 489; Sir Bartle Frere, 489; extent and boundaries of the Common; its scenery; the windmill and the Roman well; the gibbets, 490; highwaymen, 490; celebrated duels fought on the Common, 491—494; Cæsar's Camp, 494; opinions of antiquarians thereon, 494—497; the first volunteer movement;

first volunteer review at Wimbledon, 497; numerical strength of the volunteers of old; enthusiasm of the country in 1803, 498; patriotic songs; a defence of the volunteer system, 500; revival of the volunteer movement in 1859; formation of the force, 501; Captain Hans Busk; the first volunteer review by Queen Victoria, 502; inauguration of the National Rifle Association at Wimbledon, 502; camp life at Wimbledon, 507; prizes, &c.; the Elcho Challenge Shield; the Ashburton Shield; the butts; concluding remarks, 508

Wimbledon Common, II. 479, 489

Wimbledon House, II. 476; description of, 477, 478; the second house, 479; the modern mansion; its various owners, 485

Wimbledon Lodge, II. 486

Wimbledon Sewage Works, II. 483

Winchmore Hill, Southgate; St. Paul's Church, I. 346

Windmill Hill, Enfield, I. 349, 351, 358, 366, 368, II. 350, 351, 364

Windmill Lane, Brentford, I. 40; Mrs. Trimmer's residence, ib.

Windsor Street, or the Lynch, Uxbridge, I. 233, 237

Withdrawing-room, The, Hampton Court Palace; its tapestry, I. 164

Woffington, Peg, the celebrated actress, I. 128, 137; monument to, in Teddington Church, 129

Wolsey, Cardinal, I. 133, 142, 143, 144, 279; lease of the Manor of Hampton Court, 142, 143; some account of Wolsey, 144—146; his style of living at Hampton Court; Dr. Johnson's character of Wolsey, 146; Anne Boleyn and Wolsey's fall, 146, 147; wealth of Wolsey; he "presents" Hampton Court to the king, 147; Wolsey's entertainment to the French Ambassador while at Hampton Court, 147—149; fall of Wolsey, II. 289, 290; Wolsey as a messenger, II. 359; Thomas Cromwell and, 472, 473

Wolsey's Court, Hampton Court Palace, I. 159

Wolsey's Hall, Hampton Court Palace, I. 162

Wolsey's red hat, I. 114

Wolsey's Tower, Esher, II. 287, 288, 291

Wolsey's Well, Esher, II. 286

Wood, Alderman Matthew, I. 122

Wood, Anthony, A', I. 15, 21, 58, 82, 220, II. 341, 383

Woodcote House, Epsom; the mansion and its owners, II. 256

Woodcote Park, Epsom, II. 243, 244, 252, 256, 257

Wood End Green, Hayes, Middlesex, I. 210, 214

Woodford, Essex; its boundaries; its subdivision; descent of the manor, I. 458; manorial custom of "Borough-English;" Woodford Hall; census returns; the railway station; Woodford Bridge, 459; Claybury Hall; Ray House; Church End; St. Margaret's Church; monuments, 460; Sir Edmund Bury Godfrey; Woodford Hall; Mrs. Gladstone's Convalescent Home; a pauper's legacy; Woodford Green; the Congregational Church, 461; Union Church; social institutions, 462; Harts; Monkhams, 463; All Saints' Church; the Firs; Prospect Hall; Woodford Wells; the "Horse and Well"; Knighton House; the manor-house; noted residents, 464

Woodford Bridge, I. 458, 459, 460

Woodford Hall, I. 459, 461

Woodford Side, Walthamstow, I. 465

Wood Hall, Pinner, Middlesex, I. 251

Woodlands, Chigwell, I. 457

Woodmansterne, Surrey, II. 218; its healthy condition, 220

Woodriding hamlet, Pinner, Middlesex, I. 251

Woodside, Surrey; the Croydon races, II. 136

Wood Street, Walthamstow, I. 465

Woolstons, Chigwell; its various names, I. 451

Woolwich; situation and extent of the town, II. 6; its etymology; "Domesday" record of Woolwich; descent of the manor, 7; a curious tradition respecting North Woolwich; Roman occupation of Woolwich; a market established here; acreage of the parish, and census returns; description of the town, 8; steamboat piers, and railway stations; early naval importance of the town; Pepys' official visits to the dockyard; dangers of the neighbourhood; Woolwich a century ago, 9; omnibuses and steampackets established, 10; Hanging Wood; Woolwich as a fishing village; St. Mary's parish church, 11; other churches and chapels; the Goldsmiths' Almshouses; parochial almshouses, 12; Lovelace, the Cavalier poet; Grimaldi, the clown; situation and extent of the dockyard; its early history, 14, 15; enlargement of the dockyard; the docks re-modelled under Sir John Rennie; the docks "disestablished"; subsequent use of the dockyard; convicts and the hulks, 16; situation and extent of the Royal Arsenal; Beresford Street and Beresford Square; condition of the locality a century ago; an explosion at the gun foundry at Moorfields; Andrew Schalch, 17; early history of the ordnance armoury at Woolwich; "Greenwich Barne"; extracts from Ordnance records, 18; the laboratory establishment removed hither from Greenwich; Woolwich Warren, 19; general view of the Arsenal; mutiny among the Woolwich rope-makers; establishment of the brass foundry here, 20; number of men employed here; "watering time"; description of the Arsenal building; the entrance, 21; Dial square; the old brass gun foundry; the laboratory workshop; the patternroom and museum, 22; the Military Store Department; the gun factories, 23; "Woolwich infants," 24; the great Nasmyth hammer, 25, 26; the Carriage Department; regulations for the admission of the public; Museum of the Royal Artillery, 26; the East Laboratory; the Sale Yard; the "proof butts," 27; the convicts' graves, 28; barracks for sappers and miners; depôt for field-train artillery; the "ordnance hospital," barracks for the Royal Horse and Foot Artillery, 28; the Bhurtpore trophy; the Crimean memorial, 29; the Royal Engineer Barracks; the Army Service Corps; the Depôt Barracks, 30; the Riding School; the Royal Artillery Institution; the Royal Military Repository, 31; the Rotunda, 31, 32; the Royal Military Academy, 32; memorial of the Prince Imperial; a mineral well; Shooters' Hill; the "Bull" inn, 33; Plum Lane, 34

Woolwich Cemetery, Plumstead Common, II. 12, 37; the *Princess Alice* catastrophe, 38

Woolwich Common, II. 8, 10, 11, 28, 33

Woolwich Dockyard; its history, II. 14, 15, 16; convict labour in, 16, 17 (*see* Royal Arsenal)

Woolwich guns, Manufacture of, II. 23, 24

Worcester Park, II. 230, 511, 513

Worcesters manor-house, Enfield, I. 359, 369

Wordsworth, Dr., head master of Harrow School, I. 261, 262, 266

Wordsworth, the poet, II. 354, 374, 455

Worton House, Isleworth, I. 60

Wraxall, Sir N. W., II. 104, 105, 137, 157, 254, 255, 392, 485

Wren, Sir Christopher, I. 57, 141, 155, 161, 164, 170, 314, II. 8, 356

Wrotham Park, South Mimms, I. 318, 319

Wrothes, The family of the, Enfield, I. 373, 374, 447

Wyatville, Sir J., II. 32, 238, 399, 419

Wycherley, the dramatist, I. 96

Wyke Farm, Brentford, I. 39

Wynford, Lord, II. 63, 80

Y

Yates, Mrs., actress, II. 368

Yeading or Yealding manor, Hayes, Middlesex, I. 210

Yeoveney, Staines, I. 191

Yew-trees, Old, I. 195, 200, 216, 229, 238, 314, 332, 356, 461, II. 65, 119, 131, 454

Yiewsley, West Drayton, I. 208, 226

York, Duke of, Duel between Colonel Lennox and the, II. 491

York House, Twickenham, I. 89; historical associations of the place, 89, 90; its subsequent owners, 90; description of the house, 91

Young, Thomas, and "Pope's Villa," I. 110

Z

Zoffany, the painter, I. 5, 16, 17, 35, II. 400, 404

Zucchero, the painter, I. 167